THE ROUTLEDGE COMPANION TO THE CHRISTIAN CHURCH

The nature and history of the Christian church is of immense importance to students and scholars of theology and its related disciplines. *The Routledge Companion to the Christian Church* is the definitive handbook to the study of the Christian church. It introduces students to the fundamental historical, systematic, moral and ecclesiological aspects of the study of the church, as well as serving as a resource for scholars engaging in ecclesiological debates on a wide variety of issues.

Divided into six parts, the book gives a comprehensive overview of the Christian church, including:

- the church in its historical context
- denominational traditions
- global perspectives
- methods and debates in ecclesiology
- key concepts and themes
- ecclesiology and other disciplines: the social sciences and philosophy.

Written by a team of leading international scholars from a wide variety of denominational and disciplinary backgrounds, *The Routledge Companion to the Christian Church* addresses the contemporary challenges to the Christian church, as well as providing an accessible and lively resource to this changing and developing field. It is an indispensable guide to the Christian church for students of theology and beyond.

Gerard Mannion is Chair of the Ecclesiological Investigations International Research Network. A Roman Catholic layperson and Irish citizen, he studied at Cambridge and Oxford Universities. He has lectured at Church-linked colleges of the universities of Oxford and Leeds and was previously Associate Professor of Ecclesiology and Ethics at Liverpool Hope. Director of the Centre for the Study of Contemporary Ecclesiology, he has published widely in the fields of ecclesiology and ethics, as well as in other aspects of systematics and philosophy.

Lewis S. Mudge is Robert Leighton Stuart Professor of Theology, Emeritus, at San Francisco Theological Seminary and the Graduate Theological Union, Berkeley, USA. He is the author of *One Church: Catholic and Reformed* (1963), *The Crumbling Walls* (1970), *The Sense of a People* (1992), *The Church as Moral Community* (1998), *Rethinking the Beloved Community* (2001), and *The Gift of Responsibility* (2008).

THE ROUTLEDGE COMPANION TO THE CHRISTIAN CHURCH

Edited by
Gerard Mannion and Lewis S. Mudge

NEW YORK AND LONDON

First published 2008
by Routledge
270 Madison Ave, New York, NY 10016

Simultaneously published in the UK
by Routledge
2 Park Square, Milton Park, Abingdon, Oxon OX14 4RN

Routledge is an imprint of the Taylor & Francis Group, an informa business

© 2008 Editorial material and selection by Gerard Mannion and Lewis S. Mudge

© 2008 Individual contributors their contributions

Typeset in Goudy Oldstyle by
Book Now Ltd, London
Printed and bound in Great Britain by
MPG Books Ltd, Bodmin

British Library Cataloguing in Publication Data
A catalogue record for this book is available from the British Library

Library of Congress Cataloging in Publication Data
The Routledge companion to the Christian church/edited by
Gerard Mannion and Lewis S. Mudge.
p.cm.
Includes bibliographical references and index.
1. Church history. I. Mannion, Gerard, 1970– II. Mudge, Lewis Seymour.
BR145.3.R68 2008
262–dc22   2007021222

ISBN 10: 0–415–37420–0 (hbk)
ISBN 10: 0–203–93607–8 (ebk)

ISBN 13: 978–0–415–37420–0 (hbk)
ISBN 13: 978–0–203–93607–8 (ebk)

Dedicated to you,

Dear Reader:

May this book increase your knowledge and love of the Christian church,
whoever you are, wherever you come from and whatever your own story.

May it serve, in some small way, in furthering the ecumenical endeavour of greater
understanding, dialogue, unity and harmony amongst the one human family.

CONTENTS

CONTRIBUTORS

Paul Avis is an Anglican priest and General Secretary of the Council for Christian Unity of the Church of England. He is a research fellow in the Department of Theology, University of Exeter, and Director of the Centre for the Study of the Christian Church. His recent publications include *Anglicanism and the Christian Church* (2nd edn, 2002); *A Church Drawing Near: Spirituality and Mission in a Post-Christian Culture* (2003); *A Ministry Shaped by Mission* (2005); *Beyond the Reformation: Authority, Primacy and Unity in the Conciliar Tradition* (2006); and *The Identity of Anglicanism: Essentials of Anglican Ecclesiology* (2008). He is the convening editor of the journal *Ecclesiology*.

Gregory Baum was born in Berlin, Germany in 1923 and emigrated to Canada from England in 1940. Following a BA in Mathematics and Physics, McMaster University, Hamilton, Ontario, 1946 and an MA in Mathematics, Ohio State University, Columbus, Ohio, 1947, he achieved the DTh (doctor of theology) at the University of Fribourg, Switzerland, in 1956, followed by studies in sociology at the New School for Social Research, New York City, 1969–71. From 1959–86 he was Professor of Theology and Religious Studies at St Michael's College in the University of Toronto and from 1986–95, professor at McGill University's faculty of religious studies where he is presently Professor Emeritus. The editor of *The Ecumenist*, 1962–2003, his books since 1988 include *Solidarity and Compassion* (1988); *The Church in Quebec* (1992); *Essays in Critical Theology* (1994); *The Church for Others: Protestant Theology in Communist East Germany* (1996); *Nationalism, Religion and Ethics* (2001); and *Amazing Church* (2005). He has been honoured as an Officer of the Order of Canada.

Thomas F. Best (Revd Dr), a pastor of the Christian Church (Disciples of Christ), is Director of Faith and Order, World Council of Churches. After studies at Harvard, Oxford and in New Testament at the Graduate Theological Union, Berkeley, Dr Best taught in the Religious Studies Department, Butler University, Indianapolis. In 1980–1 he served as Director of the Institut zur Erforschung des Urchristentums in Tübingen before joining the staff of Faith and Order in 1984, and was named Director of Faith and Order in 2005. Dr Best is the author of numerous articles on ecclesiology in the ecumenical context (including entries on Church Union in *The Oxford Dictionary of the Christian Church*, 3rd edition, and in *Religion in Geschichte und Gegenwart*, 4th edition) and on worship (including articles in *The New SCM Dictionary of Worship and Spirituality* and *Studia Liturgica*).

Eddy van der Borght, ordained a minister of the United Protestant Church in Belgium (1989) and PhD Leiden (2000), is Assistant Professor in Systematic Theology, Vrije

Universiteit Amsterdam. He has published on the theology of ministry, ecumenical theology and issues related to faith and ethnicity. He is editor-in-chief of the *Journal of Reformed Theology* and of the series *Studies in Reformed Theology*.

John J. Burkhard is a Conventual Franciscan and Professor of Systematic Theology at the Washington Theological Union where he has taught since 1991. Before that he taught for 18 years at his community's theologate of St Anthony-on-Hudson, in Rensselaer, New York. He has also taught at the Catholic University of America, St Peter's Regional Seminary in Cape Coast, Ghana, and St John's University, Collegeville, Minnesota. Dr Burkhard's writings have been primarily on the Church and ministry. In 2004, Liturgical Press published his book *Apostolicity Then and Now: An Ecumenical Church in a Postmodern World*, and his translation of Ghislain Lafont's *A Theological Journey: Theology in History and for Our Time* was published later in 2007. Dr Burkhard is currently working on a book on the Church as the Body of Christ that is tentatively entitled *The Body of Christ: An Exegetical, Historical, Ecumenical, and Systematic Study*. He regularly teaches courses on the Church, christology, fundamental theology, and the priesthood.

Mark Chapman is Vice-Principal of Ripon and Cuddesdon College, Oxford and a member of the Faculty of Theology at Oxford University. He teaches modern church history and Anglicanism and has published widely in many different areas of theology, ethics, and church history. His most recent books are *Blair's Britain: A Christian Critique* (2005), *Anglicanism: A Very Short Introduction* (2006) and *Bishops, Saints and Politics: Anglican Studies* (2007). He is also a Church of England priest.

Sophie Chirongoma, from Zimbabwe, is a doctoral student in the School of Religion and Theology at the University of KwaZulu-Natal, South Africa and an active member of the Circle of Concerned African Women Theologians. She teaches African history, religion and culture in the Access Programme at UKZN, and has published in the field of women, religion and health in Africa.

Paul M. Collins (Revd Dr) is Reader in Theology at the University of Chichester, UK. A priest of the Church of England, he has worked in theological education for 20 years at Chichester Theological College, then at The Queen's Foundation, Birmingham and presently at the University of Chichester. His research interests include the doctrines of the Trinity, *Theosis*, and the Church and inculturation, especially in South India. His major publications include *Trinitarian Theology West and East* (2001), *Context, Culture and Worship: The Quest for Indian-ness* (2006) and *Christian Inculturation in India* (2007). The outcome of his research project in India has also recently been made available as a database on the internet: http://inculturation.chi.ac.uk/index.cfm. He is currently a member of the Faith and Order Advisory Group of the Church of England.

Eamonn Conway is a priest of the Tuam diocese and Head of Theology and Religious Studies at Mary Immaculate College, University of Limerick, where he also co-directs the Centre for Culture, Technology and Values. He is author of *The Anonymous Christian – A Relativised Christianity? An evaluation of Hans Urs von Balthasar's criticisms of Karl Rahner's theory of the anonymous Christian* (1993), and has edited five other books, most recently *The Courage to Risk Everything, Essays Marking the Centenary of Karl Rahner's Birth* (2004). He currently leads a pan-European research project on 'Culture, Technology and Religion' funded by the Metanexus Institute. He has had several publications in international journals, and has lectured in Europe, Australia and the USA. Until recently he served on the Irish Government's Information Society Commission, and was elected to the Board of Directors of *Concilium: International Review for Theology* in 2006.

G.R. Evans is Emeritus Professor of Medieval Theology and Intellectual History in the University of Cambridge and author of studies on a number of patristic and medieval authors and on ecumenical and ecclesiological problems. Her many books (to date 25) include *Problems of Authority in the Reformation Debates* (1992), *The Church and the Churches* (1994), *Communion et réunion: Mélanges J.M.R. Tillard* (with M. Gourgues), BETL, CXXI (1995), *Method in Ecumenical Theology* (1996), *The Reception of the Faith* (1997), *Calling Academia to Account* (1998) and *Academics and the Real World* (2002).

Michael A. Fahey, S.J. is Professor of Theology at Boston College (USA). He previously taught at St Michael's College, Toronto, and at Marquette University, Milwaukee. He studied philosophy in Leuven in the 1950s and in the late 1960s did doctoral studies in theology at the University of Tübingen under Professors Hans Küng and Joseph Ratzinger. He holds dual citizenship (Canada and USA). In 2005 he received an honorary doctorate from St Michael's College in the University of Toronto. From 1996 to 2005 he served as editor of the journal *Theological Studies*. Recently he was the recipient of a *Festschrift* entitled *In God's Hands: Essays on the Church and Ecumenism* (2006). His publications focus particularly on ecclesiology and ecumenism. He has served as president of the Catholic Theological Society of America as well as the American Theological Society.

Alison Forrestal is Lecturer in Early Modern Continental History at the National University of Ireland, Galway. A specialist in early modern Catholic cultural history, she has published *Catholic Synods in Ireland, 1600–1690* and *Fathers, Pastors and Kings: Visions of Episcopacy in Seventeenth Century France*. She is currently writing *Vincent de Paul: An Icon in the Making* and co-editing *After the League: Politics and Religion in Early Bourbon France*.

Kondothra M. George (Revd Dr) is Principal and Professor of Systematic Theology at the Orthodox Theological Seminary, Kottayam, India, affiliated to the Serampore University. A member of the Joint Working Group between the Roman Catholic Church and the World Council of Churches, Fr George also served as Moderator of the Programme Committee and the Executive Committee of the WCC for a seven-year term. Presently he is also co-chairperson of the Federated Faculty for Religion and Culture in Kerala, India. A graduate in chemistry, he did his initial theological studies in India, his Master's degree at Louvain University and doctoral work – in Greek Patristics – at the Catholic Faculty in Paris and the Sorbonne. From 1989–94 he was Professor and Associate Director at the Bossey Ecumenical Institute near Geneva and also served as a member of the Faith and Order Commission of the WCC. A fraternal delegate to the Asian and Middle Eastern Catholic Bishops Synod at the Vatican in 1998, Fr George was deeply involved in the Roman Catholic–Oriental Orthodox Theological Dialogue sponsored by the Pro Oriente Foundation in Vienna, as well as in the Eastern Orthodox–Oriental Orthodox Theological Commission appointed by the Orthodox Churches. His special areas of interest and publication include ecclesiology, cultural hermeneutics, eco-theology and spirituality, theological aesthetics and literature.

James R. Ginther received his PhD in Medieval Studies from the University of Toronto in 1995. He lectured in medieval theology in the Department of Theology and Religious Studies at Leeds University until 2002 when he moved to Saint Louis University. He is now Associate Professor of Medieval Theology. He is the author of numerous articles on thirteenth-century theology, and a monograph entitled *Master of the Sacred Page: A Study of the Theology of Robert Grosseteste (1229/30–1235)* (2004). He also co-edited a collection of essays in memory of Walter H. Principe CSB in 2005. He has forthcoming *A Handbook of Medieval Theology* for Westminster/John Knox Press. Dr Ginther is also the Co-Director of the Institute of Digital Theology, a research institute that develops multimedia projects to support teaching and research in theological studies. He lives in St Louis with his wife, Diana, and two children.

Paula Gooder studied theology at Oxford University where she also completed her doctorate on Heavenly Ascent traditions and the writings of Paul. From there she went on to teach first at Ripon and Cuddesdon College, Oxford and then at the Queen's Foundation for Ecumenical Theological Education, Birmingham. She now works freelance as a writer and lecturer in biblical studies. Her current research interests are the mysticism of Paul the Apostle, the history of interpretation of 2 Corinthians and the development of ministry and Christian community in the New Testament period.

Steve de Gruchy is Professor of Theology and Development in the School of Religion and Theology at the University of KwaZulu-Natal, South Africa and editor of the *Journal of Theology for Southern Africa*. He is an ordained minister in the United Congregational Church of Southern Africa (UCCSA) and has served that church in various capacities, including being Director of the Moffat Mission Trust in Kuruman. He has been on working groups with the World Council of Churches, the South African Council of Churches and the Council for World Mission. His research and teaching focus on the historical and contemporary engagement of Christianity with social life in Africa. He has published widely on the South African Church struggle against apartheid and on the contemporary challenges of the Church in Africa in the post-colonial period.

Roger Haight, S.J. is a Jesuit presently teaching at Union Theological Seminary in New York City. He earned his doctorate in theology at the Divinity School of the University of Chicago in 1973. Thereafter he taught in Jesuit faculties of theology in Manila, Chicago, Toronto and Boston. He specializes in historical and systematic theology, particularly the areas of faith and revelation, christology and ecclesiology. He has recently completed *Ecclesial Existence*, a constructive representation of the Church from an interdenominational perspective, and the third volume of his trilogy, *Christian Community in History*.

Nicholas M. Healy, a Roman Catholic, was educated in England and Canada and has his PhD from Yale University (1992). Besides articles on Rahner, Barth and other topics, he has written a book on ecclesiology – *Church, World and the Christian Life* (2000) – and one on Thomas Aquinas (2003). He is presently working on a book entitled *Stanley Hauerwas: A Very Critical Introduction* (Eerdmans). Longer term, he hopes to write a systematic theology of the Church. After 15 years teaching at St John's University in New York, Healy is now Dean of the College of Arts and Sciences at the University of San Diego, USA.

Adam Hood MA, BD, DPhil (Oxon) is Vice-Principal and Director of Research of the Queen's Foundation for Ecumenical Theological Education, Birmingham, UK. Amongst his publications are *Baillie, Oman and Macmurray: Experience and Religious Belief* (2003). Interests include the philosophical theology of John Oman and the relationship between the philosophy of mind, as found in the analytic tradition, and Christian theology. He is married with two children and includes reading and golf amongst his hobbies.

Paul Lakeland is the Aloysius P. Kelley, S.J. Professor of Catholic Studies at Fairfield University in Connecticut. His most recent books are *Postmodernity: Christian Identity in a Fragmented Age* (1997), *The Liberation of the Laity: In Search of an Accountable Church* (2003), which received the 2004 US Catholic Press Association Award for the best book in theology, and *Catholicism at the Crossroads: How the Laity Can Save the Church* (2007). He is a member of the American Academy of Religion, where he recently completed a six-year term as Chair of the Theology and Religious Reflection Section, and the Catholic Theological Society of America. He is Chair of the Editorial Board of *Religious Studies Review* and co-convener of the independent ecumenical association of systematic and constructive theologians, the Workgroup for Constructive Theology, based in Nashville, Tennessee. He is currently at work on an edition of the selected writings of Yves Congar.

Richard Lennan is currently Associate Professor of Systematic Theology at Weston Jesuit School of Theology in Cambridge, Massachusetts. From 1992–2007, he taught at the Catholic Institute of Sydney and served, from 2005–7, as President of the Australian Catholic Theological Association. His most recent book is *Risking the Church: The Challenges of Catholic Faith* (2004).

Gerard Mannion is Director of the Centre for the Study of Contemporary Ecclesiology, chairs the Ecclesiological Investigations International Research Network and is editor of the publication series of the same name. Educated at the Universities of Cambridge and Oxford, he previously taught at church colleges in the Universities of Oxford and Leeds and as Associate Professor of Ecclesiology and Ethics and Co-Director of the Applied Ethics Initiative at Liverpool Hope University. A 2004 Coolidge Fellow at Union Theological Seminary, New York, with Michael Fahey he serves as founding co-chair of the ecclesiology group of the American Academy of Religion. His numerous publications include *Schopenhauer, Religion and Morality* (2003), *Readings in Church Authority – Gifts and Challenges for Contemporary Catholicism* (co-editor) (2003) and *Ecclesiology and Postmodernity – Questions for the Church in our Times* (2007). He is editor of the forthcoming *John Paul II: An Assessment of His Life, Thought and Influence* (forthcoming 2008) and also co-editor (with Philomena Cullen and Bernard Hoose) of *Catholic Social Justice: Theological and Practical Explorations* (2007) and *The Ratzinger Reader* (with Lieven Boeve, forthcoming 2008). A Roman Catholic layperson and Irish citizen, his other passions include rugby union, running and social justice.

Peter De Mey PhD, teaches ecclesiology and ecumenism at the Faculty of Theology of the Katholieke Universiteit Leuven. He is the Director of the Centre for Ecumenical Research of the same university. He is currently the secretary of the Societas Oecumenica (European Association for Ecumenical Research) and a member of the steering committee of the Ecclesiological Investigations Group of the American Academy of Religion.

Michael H. Montgomery has been Director of Congregational Studies and Church Relations at Chicago Theological Seminary since June 2006. He has received a BA from Coe College, 1977, an MBA from the University of Chicago, 1980 and an MDiv, 1983 and a PhD, 2003 from Chicago Theological Seminary. Montgomery also served United Church of Christ congregations in Nebraska, Iowa and Illinois before returning to CTS to study the theology and sociology of religious communities in America. Montgomery's academic interests include the study of congregations, liberal church renewal, sociology of religion and practical theology. His research languages are ethnography and statistics and he has presented academic papers on liberal church renewal and American civil religion at the Association for the Sociology of Religion. He has consulted with congregations interested in revitalization and the United Church of Christ's major gifts solicitation ministry. Montgomery is married to the Revd Peggy McClanahan, senior minister at Pilgrim Faith United Church of Christ in Oak Lawn, Illinois. They have two college-aged sons.

Lewis S. Mudge is Robert Leighton Stuart Professor of Theology, Emeritus, at San Francisco Theological Seminary and the Graduate Theological Union, Berkeley, USA. He holds BA, MA and PhD degrees in religious studies from Princeton University, and the BA and MA in theology from Oxford University, where he was a Rhodes Scholar. He served as Secretary for Theological Studies of the World Alliance of Reformed Churches (1957–62), Professor of Religion and Philosophy at Amherst College (1962–76), and Dean of the Faculty and Professor of Theology at McCormick Theological Seminary, Chicago (1976–87) and San Francisco Theological Seminary (1987–95). He has served on the Faith and Order Commission of the National Council of Churches, USA and as a consultant to the Commission on Faith and Order of the World Council of Churches. He has been Chair of the Theology Commission of the US Consultation on Church Union. He was co-moderator (with Fr Bernard Sesboue) of the International Reformed–Roman Catholic Dialogue Commission, second series. He took part in the WCC study on ecclesiology and ethics, serving as principal drafter of the 1996 Johannesburg statement 'Costly Obedience'. He is the author of *One Church: Catholic and Reformed* (1963); *The Crumbling Walls* (1970); *The Sense of a People* (1992); *The Church as Moral Community* (1998); and *Rethinking the Beloved Community* (2001). He is co-editor (with James Poling) of *Formation and Reflection* (1987) and (with Thomas Wieser) of *Democratic Contracts for Sustainable and Caring Societies* (2001). His forthcoming book, *The Gift of Responsibility*, will appear in 2008.

Christopher Ocker is Professor of History at the San Francisco Theological Seminary and the Graduate Theological Union at Berkeley. His publications include *Johannes Klenkok: A Friar's Life*, c. *1310–1374* (1993); *Biblical Poetics before Humanism and Reformation* (2002); and *Church Robbers and Reformers in Germany, 1525–1547* (2006).

Neil Ormerod is Professor of Theology and Director of the Institute for Theology, Philosophy and Religious Education at Australian Catholic University. He has published widely, including a series of articles for *Theological Studies* on the topic of systematic ecclesiology. He has also published in the areas of the Trinity and Christian anthropology. Most recently he has published *Creation Grace and Redemption* (Orbis) and is collaborating on a work on globalization and the mission of the Church.

David Pascoe (Revd Dr) is a diocesan priest of the Roman Catholic Archdiocese of Brisbane, Australia. At present he holds the position of President of St Paul's Theological College, Brisbane, a member school of the Brisbane College of Theology, an ecumenical theological consortium. After completion of doctoral studies at Weston Jesuit School of Theology, Cambridge, MA, he has lectured in systematic theology, primarily ecclesiology and sacramental theology. He is also a member of the Uniting Church in Australia–Roman Catholic National Dialogue.

Peter C. Phan, a Vietnamese-American theologian, currently holds the Ignacio Ellacuría Chair in Catholic Social Thought at Georgetown University, Washington, DC. He has earned three doctorates (STD from the Universitas Pontificia Salesiana, and PhD and DD from the University of London). He has written and edited over 20 books and 300 essays. He is the general editor of the *Theology in Global Perspective* series for Orbis Books, which promotes an ecumenical, intercultural and interreligious approach to theology.

Anthony G. Reddie was born and brought up in Bradford, West Yorkshire. He holds a BA in (Church) History and a PhD in Education and Contextual and Practical Theology – both degrees conferred by the University of Birmingham. He is presently Research Fellow and Consultant in Black Theological Studies for the Queen's Foundation for Ecumenical Theological Education and the Methodist Church. He is also an honorary lecturer in both the theology and education departments of the University of Birmingham, where he supervises postgraduate students and is an internal marker of postgraduate dissertations and theses. He is the author and editor of several texts, including *Growing into Hope* (1998); *Legacy* (editor, 2000); *Faith, Stories and the Experience of Black Elders* (2001); *Nobodies to Somebodies* (2003); *Acting in Solidarity* (2005); *Dramatizing Theologies* (2006); and *Black Theology in Transatlantic Dialogue* (2006). Dr Reddie has been the editor of *Black Theology: An International Journal* since 2001.

Henk de Roest was born in 1959 and studied philosophy of religion and practical theology at Leiden University. He was ordained minister in the Dutch Reformed Church in 1987, serving two parishes just north of Amsterdam. In 1998 he obtained his doctorate with distinction at Leiden University with a thesis called 'Communicative Identity – Habermas' Perspectives of Discourse as a Support for Practical Theology'. From 1999–2001 he was Lecturer in Practical Ecclesiology at Utrecht University. From September 2001 he held the Chair of Practical Theology at Leiden University and from January 2007 he has held the same Chair at the Protestant Theological University, Leiden. Keywords in his research are: ecclesiogenesis, community formation, homiletics, missional communication of the Christian faith, inclusive church, church closings, leadership, group dynamics and the future of the churches. Henk de Roest is Chairman of the Eastern Europe Committee of the Dutch Theological Faculties and Institutions.

Risto Saarinen, born in 1959, is Professor of Ecumenics at the University of Helsinki. He has doctorates in theology (1988) and philosophy (1994) from Helsinki. From 1994–9 he served as Research Professor at the Institute for Ecumenical Research, Strasbourg, and continues to act as visiting professor there. Saarinen has been a member of the Lutheran–Orthodox Joint Commission since 1995 (Vice-Chair since 2004), and adviser to the Council of the Lutheran World Federation since 2003. He is a member and ordained pastor of the Evangelical Lutheran Church of Finland. Saarinen's publications include *Gottes Wirken auf uns* (1989); *Weakness of the Will in Medieval Thought* (1994); *Faith and*

Holiness: Lutheran–Orthodox Dialogue 1959–1994 (1997, Russian edition 2002, updated website of the dialogues at www.helsinki.fi/~risaarin); *God and the Gift: An Ecumenical Theology of Giving* (2005); and *North European Churches from the Cold War to Globalisation* (with Hugh McLeod, 2006).

Steven Shakespeare is the Anglican Chaplain and Associate Director of the Centre for the Study of Contemporary Ecclesiology at Liverpool Hope University, UK where he also teaches and researches in the Theology and Religious Studies Department. His publications include *Kierkegaard, Language and the Reality of God* (2001); *The Inclusive God. Reclaiming Theology for an Inclusive Church* (co-authored with Hugh Rayment-Pickard, 2006); and *Radical Orthodoxy: A Critical Introduction* (2007). He is currently writing a book on the relationship between Derrida and theology.

Gemma Simmonds, C.J. is a sister of the Congregation of Jesus lecturing in ecclesiology and spirituality at Heythrop College, University of London. She has an MA from Newnham College, Cambridge (modern languages), an MTh from Heythrop (systematic theology) and a PhD (St Edmund's College, Cambridge), supervised by Professors David Ford and Peter Bayley, which offers a contemporary rereading of the Jansenist crisis in conversation with Henri de Lubac and the Ressourcement Movement. Her current research is on women in the Church, issues in contextualized spirituality, Henri de Lubac, Marie-Dominique Chenu and *ressourcement*, and Mary Ward. Her publications include a translation of Henri de Lubac, *Corpus Mysticum* (2006); 'Women in University Chaplaincy', in John Sullivan and Peter McGrail (eds), *Dancing on the Edge: Church, Chaplaincy and Higher Education* (2006); 'Women Jesuits?' in Thomas Worcester (ed.), *The Cambridge Companion to the Jesuits* (2007), and various articles in scholarly journals and textbooks, including several in *The New SCM Dictionary of Spirituality* (ed. Philip Sheldrake, 2005).

Simone Sinn (Revd) is a pastor of the Evangelical Church in Württemberg, Germany. She studied at the Irish School of Ecumenics, Dublin from 1999 to 2000. Her MPhil thesis, *The Church as Participatory Community: On the Interrelationship of Hermeneutics, Ecclesiology and Ethics*, was published by Columba Press in 2002. She received a certificate in diaconal studies at the Institute for Diaconal Studies in Heidelberg in 2002 and earned her theological degree at the University of Tübingen in 2003. Currently, she serves as a theological assistant at the Department for Theology and Studies in the Lutheran World Federation, Geneva.

David Tombs is a political theologian. Originally from London, he is currently working on the Belfast-based reconciliation studies programme of the Irish School of Ecumenics, Trinity College Dublin. He has degrees in theology and philosophy from Oxford, Union Theological Seminary (New York) and London. His publications include *Latin American Liberation Theology* (2002); *Explorations in Reconciliation: New Directions for Theology* (edited with Joseph Liechty, 2006); and *Truth and Memory: The Church and Human Rights in El Salvador and Guatemala* (edited with Michael A. Hayes, 2001).

Hans Waldenfels, S.J. was born in 1931 in Essen, Germany and entered the Society of Jesus in 1951. He undertook philosophical studies at Pullach near Munich (Lic. phil.), theological studies in Tokyo (Lic. theol.) and studies in the philosophy of religion under Professors Takeuchi and Nishitani in Kyoto. His Dr theol. was from the Gregorium

University in Rome and his habilitation (Dr theol. habil.) from Würzburg, Germany. He was Professor of Fundamental Theology at the University of Bonn from 1977–97, serving twice as a dean and as speaker for the postgraduate programme for religious studies. He has been a visiting professor of universities in Moscow, Warsaw, Bamberg, Vienna, Rome, Prague and Milwaukee (Wade Chair) and was awarded a Dr theol. h.c. by the University of Warsaw. His numerous publications have been translated into many languages and include *Absolutes Nichts* (1976, also in English); *Kontextuelle Fundamental-theologie* (1985); and the *Lexikon der Religionen* (1987). He is also editor of the Bonn series *Begegnung – Kontextuelldialogische Studien zur Theologie der Kulturen und Religionen*, of which 14 volumes have been published to date.

Natalie K. Watson (Dr) is a theologian, writer, editor and publisher based in Peterborough, UK. She studied theology at the universities of Tuebingen, Germany and Durham, UK. She has taught theology and church history at Ripon College Cuddesdon and has more recently been Head of Publishing at the Methodist Publishing House in Peterborough. She is the author of several books and articles on feminist theology and related subjects, including *Introducing Feminist Ecclesiology* (2002) and *Feminist Theology* (2003).

ACKNOWLEDGMENTS

First of all, our very deep gratitude to all of our contributors for their efforts on behalf of what we hope readers will enjoy as a truly enthralling collection and enduringly valuable resource. An enormous thank you, also, for their belief in and ongoing support of such a huge project to Lesley Riddle, Gemma Dunn and Amy Laurens at Routledge. And an especially heartfelt expression of our appreciation to Maureen Allen and Kate Hughes at BookNow for their efficiency and meticulous work during the production processes of the final volume, as well as to Jonathan Burd for compiling the index.

INTRODUCTION

Ecclesiology – the nature, story and study of the Church

Gerard Mannion and Lewis S. Mudge

The nature, story and study of the Christian church have become very popular areas of inquiry across various religious communities, in courses of theology and religious studies and in the field of scholarly debate. The very fact that you have this volume in your hands is itself proof that, in recent decades, ecclesiology has become of great topical interest once again. This also means, as a perusal of the chapters will quickly indicate, that the amount of literature in and on ecclesiology itself has grown to enormous proportions. If one looks at the content of academic journals in recent years from a wide variety of sub-disciplines – historical, ethical, systematic, practical, missiological, sociological and philosophical – one finds an increasing number of papers where the central focus is particularly upon the church itself and ecclesiological questions and concepts. There have even been a number of journals established in recent years which are devoted solely to questions of an ecclesiological nature, and many publishers have commissioned series of ecclesiological relevance. The number of conferences devoted to ecclesiological themes across the international scholarly community is legion.

In short, ecclesiology is very much a branch of study which is becoming more and more popular. This *Routledge Companion to the Christian Church* is thus a single-volume work that can serve as a core textbook to introduce students and general readers alike to the fundamental historical, systematic, moral and – of course – ecclesiological aspects of the study of the Church, as well as serving as a resource for scholars engaging in ecclesiological debates on a wide variety of issues.

This Companion offers a wealth of information on the Church both past and present. It deals with numerous circumstances and relationships in which churches have been and are involved. It does so from perspectives that represent the best in contemporary scholarship. The editors and writers offer this volume to the world of browsers and readers, believers or otherwise, who sense the importance of this subject in a day of intra- and inter-religious conflict, and yet also perhaps of religious potential for bringing healing to the human race. Thus this volume is designed to rectify a yawning 'gap' in the literature and provide a true 'companion' to ecclesiology – a work of reference which will be invaluable to all engaged with and interested in the story and nature of, as well as the future prospects for, the Christian church.

The first part of the volume explores ecclesiology in its historical context, before turning in Part II to explore differing denominational 'traditions' in ecclesiology. Part III examines 'global perspectives' of ecclesiology from across the different continents, whilst Part IV is concerned with different methodologies in ecclesiology and contemporary debates (such as liberation ecclesiology, feminist ecclesiology and ecumenical ecclesiology). Part V covers a range of concepts and themes in ecclesiology which are the subject of debate across historical and contemporary discussions alike, such as authority, magisterium, laity, ministry and the inter-relationship between ecclesiology and other areas of theological scholarship such as doctrine, hermeneutics and ethics. The final part explores ecclesiology in a transdisciplinary context, namely how ecclesiology and ecclesiological themes are explored in the social sciences and philosophy.

Our contributors, by and large, have also listed a selection of 'Further reading' to guide readers whose appetites have been whetted towards further engagement with relevant sources, texts and themes. We have assembled a group of contributors who are leading experts in their field, both emerging and newer ecclesiological voices of insight and internationally renowned figures. We have tried to involve as diverse a group of contributors as we possibly could, in terms of ecclesial background and geographical location, although naturally one could always hope for greater diversity still. Some ecclesial traditions have supplied more contributors than others, but in the main this reflects those churches where ecclesiological inquiry has been traditionally strong and vibrant.

Although many of the chapters are divided into historical periods, their primary focus is not simply *history* as such, but more the *ecclesiological* practices, events, debates and ideas prevalent in such eras. Indeed, the 'historical' parts really are different creatures to the other sections and, indeed, lay much of the groundwork for the later theoretical, thematic and discursive chapters. So, for example, the account of Lutheran ecclesiology will assume much of the historical material given in the chapter on the sixteenth-century controversies in ecclesiology. In other words, the part on ecclesiological 'traditions' will be more focused upon particular issues, methods and debates – attending to details and themes that a historical overview does not cover (for example, the Lutheran perspective on Roman Catholic and Lutheran dialogues in recent years). Whilst certain key themes, people and events will feature in more than one chapter, we have striven for complementarity rather than overlap.

Of course, no chapter can hope to be *the* definitive, comprehensive and fully exhaustive account of any particular topic. Rather, they offer representative overviews, touching upon certain key themes and people. They seek to be reflective and, where appropriate, both stimulating and even provocative.

Ecclesiological preliminaries

The word 'ecclesiology' needs some explanation. The term, for some, has connotations of institutionalism and prelacy, and perhaps also of precious self-concern.[1] Many people will think of competing claims by religious bodies to be the 'true church,' or of the 'marks' which are said to make a communion or congregation authentic. Others will think of conceptions of church governance, or of the relationships between the church and the civil order, or of the strategic and programmatic considerations which occupy church leaders. Some will even think of the claim that the church is a body 'outside of which there is no salvation.' The classical categories for speaking of the church – visibility and invisibility, validity and efficacity, 'right' preaching and celebration, apostolicity as episcopal succession or faithfulness to teaching, and so on – were formulated to address questions arising at different times and places. We dare not fail to learn the lessons they teach.

In this volume, the word 'church' refers to the visible community in which Christians come together for worship, prayer, communal sharing, instruction, reflection and mission. Most Christian bodies, but not all, see this visible community as imperfectly representing on earth an invisible communion of saints called together by God in Jesus Christ. The church can thus be viewed as one social institution among many, but also as a shared form of life shaped by profound theological self-understandings. Seen institutionally, the church has subsisted in a variety of communal forms and structures of governance throughout a long and very complex history. Understood theologically, the church has been the object of many varying images, descriptions, terminologies, and conceptualities interwoven with the circumstances of that history. The systematic study of the church in all these interacting dimensions constitutes the field of ecclesiology. This realm of inquiry relates constructively to most of the other principal themes of Christian thought: among them the doctrine of God, christology, soteriology, theological anthropology, and theological ethics.

The nature of 'church' has become, in recent years, a question of great importance to Christian thought and action. This is not only because ecclesiological questions lie at the heart of continuing church divisions after years of Faith and Order debate. It is also because we know today that Christian thought and action inevitably reflect the character of the historical 'footprint,' at any time or place, produced by acted-out interpretation of the significance of Jesus. That historical-sociological-institutional footprint has helped to shape understandings of the gospel down the ages. Constructive theology has always functioned to produce versions of the faith suitable to the kind of social reality the church has become at any time or place.

Authentic ecclesiology asks what the coming of Jesus Christ means as expressed 'in the form of a community' (Bonhoeffer). Ecclesiology looks at the churches' forms of governance, liturgical life and corporate witness as primary instruments by which the gospel is lived and communicated. Ecclesiology becomes the normative study of communities which make social and symbolic space in the world for the workings of grace. In such a perspective, ecclesiology becomes far more than an afterthought added at the end of the book. It becomes far more than an institutional setting for the protection and promulgation of truths reached in other ways. It becomes fundamental to Christian theological reflection as such. Seen as 'fundamental theology',[2] ecclesiology concerns the nature of the social space which makes language about God, and therefore faith itself, possible.

What sort of community can sponsor and sustain a kind of discourse which employs, but transcends the limits of, that space's characteristic imagery, concepts, language, and action patterns toward some sort of signification of the absolute? If theology itself, by definition, is discourse which regulates the language and activity of a religious community (George Lindbeck), then there must be some quality of the social space concerned that permits us to understand this discourse as pointing beyond itself. Theology does not become 'language about God' on the basis of its contents or argumentative strategies alone, as if human discourse could lift itself to God by its own bootstraps. It becomes language about God because it is the language of a certain kind of witnessing, serving, community. Hence theology's root question is whether, in the light of what we know today about the relativity of cultures and about language's limited ability to access reality, a community in and through which the God of Jesus Christ becomes present within history's contingencies can be conceived. Only then can we ask if such communities are possible under the conditions of postmodernity, and, if so, whether such a community actually exists.

We need to ask how far, in what way, and in what terms the institutional church has been aware of its own social reality, aware of the social conditions that shape doctrinal construction. Seen from the perspective sketched above, little can be more important for understanding of the faith. Ecclesiology has to do with our understanding of the community in relation to which virtually all theology is produced, the community whose nature shapes what is thought and hence shapes the way the faith itself is understood. In ecclesiological inquiry, therefore, theology is exploring the historical conditions of its own existence. Seen in those terms, ecclesiology becomes the primordial theological discipline. First, it formulates the social conditions of faith-articulation as such. Then it explores the character of the self-understandings that arise within these communal–institutional gatherings.

The articles in this volume, individually and together, demonstrate the many ways in which churches have taken form and come to certain self understandings, in relation to many different social-cultural-historical circumstances. These articles are written differently from how they might have been written a century ago. They presuppose new developments in historiography, new use of social science methods, new forms of understanding derived from ecumenical contacts, and the like. All these elements and more flow into the ecclesiological self-consciousness of today.

Today we ask what sort of articulate communal expressions of faith will play the most significant roles in the complex human commonwealth now emerging on this planet. We cannot see the future clearly enough to be sure. But faith's persistence in recognizable forms will surely depend in no small part on the evolution of its communal embodiments. The social forms and relationships of religious communities will decisively influence the way faith itself is construed and understood. Without communities and traditions of some sort to express and live out coherent religious traditions, people will not be able to put words to ultimate concern or primordial trust, let alone follow the life paths to which such experiences in the past have led. Shared symbolizations of faith will be needed, in short, if faith itself is to remain consciously alive in the world. The theologies of the future will be grounded in the self-understanding and practical reasoning of believing communities, and at the same time will help make such communities possible. Christian churches need now to consider the forms of life in which their insights can best be pursued in the new human situation we see coming into being. It is important to humanity – to believers, agnostics, atheists, and even to those increasing numbers who do not care one way or another – that religious traditions should learn how to live with depth and integrity as parts of this human scene, yet share the task of representing, in their many ways, the people of earth as a spiritual community.

Many features of the world in which our children and grandchildren will live are already apparent. Humanity today has reached an unprecedented and multidimensional degree of interdependence. And yet our worldwide networks of information exchange and interlocking economic relationships have virtually no spiritual dimension. This combination of material interdependence with spiritual fragmentation will likely become more marked as the twenty-first century unfolds. In this situation religious bodies have an enormous opportunity to serve human well-being and thereby their own. In particular, religious traditions and the communities that sustain and are sustained by them can articulate with coherence and staying power depth concerns for the many. There is, in fact, a widespread impulse today to revisit ancient traditions in search of symbols capable of binding communities together and sustaining a moral vision of the universe. In a world whose communication networks are allergic to spiritual substance, faith communities can become the social spaces in which questions that are impossible for secular human beings even to formulate on their own can continue to be asked. If religious communities do not keep ultimate questions alive as issues for human beings, there will be no one to listen to the answers they have to offer.

But there are dangers that go with this opportunity. The impulse to recover tradition may lead only to new and fractious fundamentalisms. What comes out may be unimaginative parochialism or religiously tinged ethnic awareness, functioning largely for self-protection and self-esteem. If ancient traditions are to be recovered, they must come to be understood in new ways. Historic faith traditions can no longer represent themselves as one-possibility interpretations of the world, standpoints which make their adherents superior to others or give them special access to truth. It is plain, even for many of those seeking to repristinate the old ways of life, that no such way is the sole valid possibility for human beings. The closer one is to the life of actual people, the clearer this is. Christians live on the same city blocks with Christians of quite different traditions, practices and confessional positions, not to mention with Moslems, Jews, Hindus, Buddhists, 'new age' cultists, secular humanists and a host of others. This fact confronts us anew with the need to live our own particular tradition of faith with full respect for those who live other traditions or no apparent tradition at all.

Our responses to these challenges, whatever forms they may take, need to press towards a new, post-Enlightenment conception of human universality, one that does not depend on the notion that all educated human beings will believe and think in the same way. We must now think in terms of an unending conversation between divergent yet interacting symbolizations of human depth and destiny. The human world, not merely the world of religious communities, needs to think of itself as a dialogical communion of many spiritual cultures. Final truth can only be a truth about this dialogue itself, not a fixed conception of reality sustained by some one culture which holds symbolic and technological hegemony over all the others.

As we address such challenges, it is essential not merely to innovate, not merely to react to immediate circumstances. We must bring to our struggles a deep knowledge of roads travelled before. This 'Companion' to the Christian church is designed to help readers journey along the way of trying to understand from whence they have come, in order to grasp in conversation with many contemporary companions the directions in which they will now choose to go.

These are not only challenging times, they are also exciting times for the church around the globe. We hope that the synoptic and comparative picture of the church that you have in your hands will both reflect and further fuel that excitement towards the practical ends of dialogue, understanding and greater human community to which the Gospel calls us.

Feast of Pentecost 2007

Notes

1 *The Compact Oxford English Dictionary* (Oxford: Clarendon Press, 1971) affirms that ecclesiology concerns the nature of the church, but tells us that this term 'now, usually' means 'the science of church building and decoration'. Obviously, the possibility of misunderstanding lies close at hand.
2 Here the term 'fundamental theology' is employed in the sense given it by David Tracy in *Blessed*

Rage for Order (New York: Seabury, 1975) and *The Analogical Imagination* (New York: Crossroad, 1981), but drawing somewhat different conclusions. For Tracy, the defining characteristic of fundamental (not 'fundamenta*list*') theologies of every kind is 'a reasoned insistence on employing the approach and methods of some established academic discipline to explicate and adjudicate the truth-claims of the interpreted religious tradition and the truth-claims of the contemporary situation' (*Analogical Imagination*, 62). As Tracy says, the discipline employed is usually philosophy of some kind or the philosophical dimension of some other discipline. As utilized in this introduction the discipline is a philosophical approach to human science or critical social theory. The feature of the human world on which philosophical attention is focused is thus the existence of traditioned communities which are experienced by their members as making transcendent reality present in shared forms of life.

Part I

HISTORICAL ECCLESIOLOGY

1

IN SEARCH OF
THE EARLY 'CHURCH'

The New Testament and the development
of Christian communities

Paula Gooder

Introduction

When did 'the Church' begin? People often assert that Pentecost sees the birth of the church, and on one level this is true. The coming of the Holy Spirit at Pentecost transformed the disciples from a frightened group of people into a band of confident, articulate missionaries. Pentecost is a vastly significant moment in the development of the church but to say, as some do, that it is the birth-*day* of the church is to give both too late and too early a date to the birth of the church: too late a date because it focuses the church solely around the action of the Holy Spirit and not around the presence of the person of Jesus; and too early a date because it is only towards the end of the first century, at the very earliest, that the Christian community began to have the kind of structure that many would recognize as 'church'. The church did not so much have a birth-*day* as a birth-*century*.

A reading of the New Testament also indicates that it is not possible to chart with certainty the beginning of *the* church. Instead what we observe from its pages is the growth of a number of Christian communities alongside each other: some of them live together in harmony, while others compete and have conflicts with each other. Some of these communities have strong allegiances to Judaism, while others are more markedly Gentile. The growth of the earliest Christian communities was neither linear nor monochrome. They grew haphazardly, chaotically and without discernible structure – at least at first. It is the aim of this study to sketch out the complexity of the development *into* church that marks the first century CE.

One of the challenges for those attempting to recover the details of how the earliest Christian communities grew is to find ways of piecing together the information that we possess. The methodological challenges that arise here are common to much New Testament scholarship. For many years one of the favourite methods of approach was through word study. The most influential of such approaches is Kittel's famous *Theological Dictionary of the New Testament*, which is based upon the attempt to understand and reconstruct early theological ideas using the theologically significant (Greek) words found in the New Testament.[1] In 1965, however, James Barr pointed out the severe shortcomings of this approach.[2] One of his major criticisms was that the work of the dictionary is in the realm of

9

'concept history' and yet it deals solely with words. The word *ekklēsia* illustrates the problem he identifies. Although the word *ekklēsia* is vital for understanding how the early church developed, to look only at this word and no other would deliver an impoverished picture of what the early church comprised. Furthermore, it is not possible to explain the development of Christian community with primary recourse to this word as its usage is sporadic and inconsistent.

It is important, however, not to allow the pendulum to swing back too far. Barr's critiques of Kittel are apposite and persuasive but they do not give grounds for discarding word studies entirely. The value of word studies, although limited, remains. Word studies provide a useful foundation which can be built on in further study. Problems lie not in word studies themselves but in assuming that they can provide an entire answer to any given question.

This chapter seeks to illustrate the ways in which New Testament scholarship has attempted to trace the development of the early church and the challenges raised by such attempts. It cannot reconstruct the history of the early church itself – this would require at least three volumes by itself; instead, it looks at some of the ways in which scholars have attempted to undertake the task. This survey is limited and far from exhaustive – for example I have not even attempted to present the vast amount of scholarship on the development of 'ministry' in the early church;[3] instead, I have sought to present major themes and indicative methodologies of current New Testament scholarship on the subject.

As a result, this chapter falls into two main sections. The first section is an examination of terminology and comprises a word study of the Greek term *ekklēsia* as well as an exploration of other words and phrases used to describe the earliest Christian communities in the various books of the New Testament. This then provides a foundation for the second section, which will seek to illustrate some of the most important areas in the study of early Christian communities in the New Testament period.

Terminology

The use of the word ekklēsia

It is popular to make a lot of the etymology of the word *ekklēsia*. The word is derived from the Greek *ek* = out and *kaleo* = called; thus great emphasis is placed, in some circles, on the 'church' being the 'called out people of God'. There is no evidence in the New Testament, however, that *ekklēsia* is used to mean 'called out'. This illustrates amply the dangers of using etymology as a way of investing a word with meaning.[4] The origins of a word do not tell you what it means now. We can only discover this by observing how it is used in context. The word *ekklēsia* has a rich usage in both Greek and Jewish literature but this has no direct link with being 'called out'.

The word was used commonly in Greek circles to refer to the meeting of all male citizens in Greek cities who gathered together to make decisions about the legislative and judicial welfare of the city.[5] Luke uses it in this way in Acts to refer both to the lawful gathering of citizens (19.39) and to an unlawful gathering which 'did not know why they had come together' (19.32). This indicates that in Acts 'gathering' is a primary meaning of the word – not what is done once the gathering has taken place. *Ekklēsia* is also used in Greek translations of Jewish texts to translate the Hebrew word *qahal* and within the Septuagint (LXX) seems to have developed a meaning almost synonymous with *sunagōgē*. As in Greek its primary meaning is assembly.

However, we cannot leave it here. The background of the word indicates that it was often used to describe an activity – assembly – but common New Testament usage indicates that it began to describe not so much an activity as a reality.[6] In other words, *ekklēsia* could have a meaning whether or not the Christians were actually assembled; thus Paul could talk of the *ekklēsia* of God (e.g. 1 Cor 10.32) as an entity, though at other times it was used to describe an actual gathering of Christians (e.g. Rom 16.5). The most common use of the word is in describing local gatherings but even in this period it was used occasionally in a range of texts to point towards a more abstract reality (see Mt 16.18; Acts 9.31; and Rom 16.23).

But why pick on *ekklēsia* at all? Why not choose an entirely different word? J.T. Burtchaell argues that the words *sunagōgē* and *ekklēsia* began as virtual synonyms, and that the early Christian community adopted *ekklēsia* because *sunagōgē* was already being used by their Jewish compatriots.[7] Giles takes the argument a little further and demonstrates that the word *sunagōgē* developed in meaning during this period, from meaning 'all Israel as God's covenant community'[8] to referring to the communities of Jews living outside Palestine and meeting together on a regular basis, and from there to the building in which these communities met. *Ekklēsia* developed in a similar way through Christian history, so that in the post-New Testament era it could be used of the building in which Christians met, as well as the community and the actual act of meeting. The first century CE marks the period of its development and it was only later that its meaning became more fixed. We can see evidence of continuing fluidity in the epistle of James, since 2.2 uses the word *sunagōgē* of what is presumed to be a gathering of Christians. This indicates that the words were not entirely fixed in their use at this point, though it is unusual enough to be surprising.

The problem of the word *ekklēsia* is that it was used in some parts of the New Testament but not in others. It appears in Matthew and Acts but not in Mark, Luke or John; in Paul but not in 1 and 2 Peter, and only occurs once in Hebrews. This indicates that many New Testament writers not only could but did describe the Christian communities known to them using words other than *ekklēsia*. The author of 1 and 2 Peter used many descriptions of the community to which he wrote (1 Pet 2.5–10); even Paul, who did use the word, used other words as well, such as offspring of Abraham (Gal 3.29). Thus *ekklēsia* was used alongside many other words and phrases in the first century to denote Christian communities and, although it was more commonly used than any other description, it was far from being the only one used in this period.

A final issue concerning the word *ekklēsia* is that of translating it into English. It is the custom in modern English translations of the New Testament to render the word *ekklēsia* as church. The problem with this, as Meeks notes, is that is an 'anachronism, which cannot fail to mislead'.[9] Although, in many instances, Christians had 'begun using the term in a peculiar way that must have been puzzling to any ordinary Greek'[10] it had not yet, in this period, fully developed to the extent that the formal word 'church' can accurately be used for it. Giles notes that the two alternative options for translation are community (followed by Luther and Barth using the German *Gemeinde*) and congregation (followed by Tyndale and the 39 Articles);[11] but, as 'congregation' has lost its universal meaning in common parlance, community best renders the meaning of *ekklēsia* today.

This study of the word *ekklēsia* demonstrates the value and the limits of word studies. While a study of the word *ekklēsia* in the New Testament provides us with a helpful way-in to understanding the development *into* church that took place in the first century CE, it can do no more than point us in the right direction. Over-concentration on words can assume

11

too monochrome and 'technical' a meaning, which as we have demonstrated does not exist for *ekklēsia* in the New Testament era. It can also miss important aspects of a concept. In other words, there is much more to an understanding of the early church than just the word *ekklēsia*; in order to gain a clearer picture it is important to explore images of Christian community in the different New Testament texts.

Other descriptions of Christian communities in the first century

As we have seen, *ekklēsia* is not the only word or phrase used to designate Christian communities in this early period. The use of other images was widespread: Minear estimates that there are more than eighty different images used for the church in the New Testament texts.[12] In what follows, therefore, we shall explore the most important, either in terms of number of times used or in terms of influence.

The gospels

The gospels contain few examples as their prime concern is the life and ministry of Jesus. The communities into which the gospel writers were writing stand as shadowy groups behind the text. It is clear that such communities exist. For example, Kee in his influential book on the *Community of the New Age* noted that all the images used to signify Christian existence in Mark were corporate,[13] something that indicates that Mark was really talking to a community. However, while these communities exist they are given no titles – other than in Matthew's gospel where the community is twice addressed as *ekklēsia* – and their existence must be identified and interpreted through a careful reading of the text.[14]

Acts of the Apostles

Outside the gospels many more descriptions and/or titles of the early Christian communities can be found. Acts has the most widely differing appellations, from 'those who believe' and 'those who call on the name' to brothers and sisters (*adelphoi*), saints (*hagioi*), disciples (*mathētai*), Christians (*christianoi*) and 'the way' (*ho hodos*), as well as *ekklēsia*.[15] The phrases in English beginning with 'those who . . . ' all translate participles in Greek and are used to describe the action of the people referred to (having believed, having been saved, having turned to God). These are not so much 'titles' as descriptions. The other words are more interesting as they may indicate the way in which the early communities referred to themselves in this period.

Acts is not alone in referring to the early Christians as brothers and sisters.[16] It is widely used in Paul, Hebrews, James, 1 and 2 Peter, the Johannine epistles and Revelation. In all of these contexts *adelphoi* is used to refer to fellow believers. If we are seeking an internal title for the early Christians then we need look no further. The sense of community among the earliest Christians was so great that they addressed each other using familial terms. This tradition goes back to Jesus himself who calls his disciples *adelphoi* (Mt 28.10; Jn 20.17) and encourages the disciples to do the same (see for example Lk 22.32). However, this was a common form of address among communities in the first century: Josephus asserts that it was used by the Essene community (*Jewish War* 2:122) and Plato uses it for his compatriots (*Menexenus* 239a). The widespread use of the terms tells us of the close bonds of the early

Christian communities but does not differentiate them in any way from other communities of the period.

Hagioi, normally translated saints, is also widely used in the New Testament and can be found in Acts, Paul, Hebrews, 2 Peter and Revelation. As the term is rare in Attic Greek, this seems to draw upon a Hebrew bible heritage and refers, generally speaking, to those things or people that are set apart for God. In Acts there are times when it appears to be used as a 'category of social and religious identity'.[17] Thus when Ananias is asked by God to take care of Paul (Acts 9.13) he responds that he has heard 'how much evil he has done to your saints [*hagiois*] in Jerusalem'. Revelation also uses the word in this way; the word and its cognates occurs twenty-two times to refer to the 'Holy Ones' who will wait in heaven alongside the Prophets and Apostles. As with *adelphos*, the word is used as an internal title to be used and recognized by those within the Christian community. Another word used in Acts as a term for Christians almost from the start is disciples (*mathētai*). In the gospels the word is used to refer to all those – not just the twelve – who followed Jesus during his ministry (Lk 6.13). It is natural, therefore, that in Acts this word should be used to refer to those who continued to follow Jesus after his ascension into heaven.

Acts is also one of the two books in the New Testament that call the early community 'Christians' (*Christianoi*). This word appears both in Acts (11.26; 26.28) and in 1 Peter (4.16). It is not at all clear where the term came from. The ending *-ianus* is Latin and can be found in other forms such as Galbiani, Augustiani and even Herodiani (rendered in English Herodians). It is used in two different ways. The word Augustiani comes from the time of Nero and is the title given to those 'who attended his [Nero's] athletic and histrionic performances and manifested [whether or not they felt] wild enthusiasm for the great – divine – man'.[18] If the term *Christianoi* is connected to Augustiani then it is almost certainly given from outside and used as a means of describing a group of adherents to this 'Christ'. Alternatively, the word Herodiani refers to the household slaves of the Herodians. Given that Paul regularly describes himself as a 'slave' of Christ, it is also possible that it was first used by the Christians themselves to denote that they are a member of the household of Christ.[19]

The word Nazarenes is used once in Acts in the mouth of Tertullus, the advocate who accused Paul before Felix in Acts 24. In verse 5, Tertullus maintains that he is a 'ringleader of the faction of *Nazōraioi*'. Much has been made of the etymology of this word, with little success and it is most likely the word comes from Jesus' place of origin – Nazareth – and that it became used by some for those who followed him.[20] Possibly the most intriguing phrase used by the author of Acts is 'The Way'. This designation occurs in various places in Acts (though nowhere else in the New Testament).[21] As with many of these terms the origin of the phrase is disputed. Barrett argues that the writings from Qumran contain the closest parallels and that here it refers to strict observance of the Mosaic law.[22] It is unlikely that this is the meaning in the book of Acts but it does, perhaps, indicate that the earliest Christians were not alone in regarding their community as a way of life or a journey along a road.

The Pauline and deutero-Pauline Epistles

One of Paul's major images for the church is the body of Christ. The language of being a body was relatively common in the Greek-speaking world. For example, a stoic parable used the image of a body to argue that all members of a city were dependent upon each other, so that the idle nobility were as essential to the working labourers as the stomach is to the legs and arms.[23] What makes Paul's image unusual, however, is that the body in his writings belongs to someone – Christ. In the Greek imagery the body was an abstract, unnamed body but in Paul the body is the body of Christ, who as the human Jesus was known to many. It is important to recognize, however, that Paul uses this image fluidly. As Minear points out, the 'variety of usage should warn us against seeking to produce a single inclusive definition of the image, and against importing into each occurrence of the analogy the range of meanings which it bears in other passages'.[24] The image is and should remain a metaphor, and, like all metaphors, its meaning is not clear, never fixed and certainly not easy to identify.

The author of the epistle to the Ephesians talks about the community in terms of citizenship. In Ephesians 2.12 and 19, the author sets up the imagery of belonging. The recipients of the letter were once strangers (*apēllotriōmenoi*), foreigners (*xenoi*, 2.12) and exiles (*paroikoi*) but now they are citizens (*sumpolitai*), part of the household (*oikeioi*, 2.19) and built on a foundation stone (2.20). The language the author uses here slips between national, local and domestic identity, and even includes references to building. Again, as with *adelphoi*, the imagery bears a strong sense of belonging. Ephesians goes on in this same passage to add yet another image to the three already in place: the citizens, members of the household, are built on the foundation stone of the apostle and prophets with Christ as the cornerstone, so that they can grow into the temple (2.21). Best points out that although the shift in imagery may seem unexpected, the connection is straightforward, since the Jerusalem temple was often called the house of God.[25]

1 Peter

The author of 1 Peter picks up this imagery, though in a slightly different way. 1 Peter, like Ephesians, identifies the Christian community as the house of God (4.17) and in doing so makes the link with them being God's temple. In 4.17 the phrase *oikou tou theou* refers to God's judgement coming first on the house of God, a concept that in the Hebrew bible almost invariably refers to the temple (see for example Ezek 9.6).[26] This link is even more obvious in 2.5–10, where it is clear that the building being built from the living stones is the temple. In 1 Peter 2.9 the author also introduces the concept of national identity, not this time through the Greek imagery of citizenship but through the Hebrew notion of being 'a chosen race, a royal priesthood, a holy nation, God's own people'. The language of this verse depends strongly on both Exodus 19.6 ('you shall be for me a priestly kingdom and a holy nation') and Isaiah 43.20 ('to give drink to my chosen people'). The language of race (*genos*), priesthood (*hierateuma*), nation (*ethnos*) and people (*laos*) makes it clear that the people of God are now to be found in the followers of Christ. A similar language of belonging can be found in the book of James which addresses its recipients as 'the twelve tribes in the Dispersion'.

This belonging is juxtaposed in 1 Peter with exile. The people are not citizens, as in Ephesians, but aliens (*paroikoi*) and exiles (*parepidēmoi*) (1.1 and 2.11). In 1.1 'exiles' is used alongside the word elect (*elektos*) and dispersion (*diaspora*), stressing that belonging to God means that the Christian community will be treated like exiles.[27] Thus in 1 Peter, Christian community involves both belonging and exile.

Revelation

The image of the Bride of Christ is often cited as an influential depiction of the church in the book of Revelation.[28] A careful examination of the passage, however, indicates that this is a misreading of the text. The image of the bride begins in 19.7–8 when we are called upon to rejoice because the marriage of the Lamb has come. Here it is clear that the righteous deeds of the saints are the garments worn by the Bride and that those who are invited to the feast are 'blessed' (19.9). The image is picked up again in Revelation 21.1–4 which describes the descent of the Holy City, the New Jerusalem, dressed as a bride for her husband, in v. 27 those who are clean are described as entering it. This image, therefore, cannot be the church itself and is probably, as Smalley argues, the New Covenant.[29]

This is yet one more instance of the importance of taking each text on its own merit. The connection between Revelation 21 and the church almost certainly came through other New Testament passages. For example, in 2 Corinthians 11.2 Paul states that he promised the Corinthians 'in marriage to one husband, to present you as a chaste virgin to Christ' and in Ephesians 5.22–25 the analogy that the wife is to her husband as the church is to Christ again suggests the metaphor of marriage. This connection has prompted people to pick up the same connection in Revelation 21 though this time with less support from the text.

Conclusions on terminology

The overall impression of early Christian communities gained from our exploration so far is one of fluidity. Although the word *ekklēsia* is widely used in the New Testament texts, it is not used in every part of the New Testament nor is it used in the same way in the places where it is used. In fact, the New Testament seems to bear witness that the word is changing in meaning during the first century itself. It was probably first used as an alternative to synagogue to differentiate what the early Christians did when they met together from what their Jewish neighbours did when they met together. Most of the times when the word is used it refers to a specific local community, though from time to time it is used to refer to a more universal phenomenon, the 'church of God'. Nowhere in the New Testament does the word *ekklēsia* mean the building in which the assembly met (not least because there is no evidence that such buildings existed in the first century), in contrast to the word synagogue in the first century which does seem to be used to refer to the building of the synagogue (see for example Mt 12.9, 'He left that place and entered their synagogue'). The word *ekklēsia* does develop to mean this later in the Christian era but has not done so in the first century.

Alongside the word *ekklēsia* a whole range of words exist to describe Christian communities. Some of these appear to be titular but many of them are metaphorical and/or descriptive. Acts contains the greatest number of possible 'titles' for the earliest communities, whereas the epistles use more metaphors. One of the striking features of the metaphors is that they too seem fluid in this period and either change in their usage (as with the body of Christ) or slip from one metaphor to another (as with the citizen, household, temple image of Ephesians). It appears, therefore, that the early Christians were fumbling to find words and images to describe themselves both internally and externally. Some of the words used survived and became dominant in the tradition; others did not.

This exploration of terminology has provided an initial sketch of the development into church that took place in the first century CE. This sketch now needs to be filled in a little more through a historical exploration of what might have happened to move the earliest disciples from disparate followers of Jesus to more coherent and structured communities towards the end of the first century CE.

Tracing the history of the earliest Christian communities

Methodological difficulties

The task of tracing the history of the earliest Christian communities is a little like trying to describe, in a single narrative, the path of twenty rubber balls thrown into the air and left to bounce wherever they come down. Even to attempt to describe the 'development' of early Christian community presupposes a greater degree of uniformity than is probably true. It is simply not the case that the 'church' developed in a linear manner from the moment of Pentecost to present-day worshipping communities. We have seen already that 'Pentecost' cannot be claimed to be the birthday of the 'church' anymore than 'church' can properly be used as a title for Christian communities in this era. The task of the next part of the study is to explore what we can know historically about Christian communities in this period and to attempt to map some sort of development 'into' church.

The difficulties of this task are rooted in the perennial problems which beset New Testament scholarship in all areas of first-century reconstruction, and are related to the fragmentary nature of the evidence we have available.[30] The New Testament provides us with numerous snapshots of life in early Christian communities but what is unclear is what, if anything, connects these snapshots. So, for example, we know from Acts 19 that there was a community in Ephesus. We also know that a letter in the Pauline tradition (whether or not it was by Paul is disputed by scholars) was written to the community at Ephesus. In addition, certain scholars believe that the Johannine literature – or a least parts of it – originated from a community based in Ephesus. What we do not know, however, is whether the community baptized into Jesus by Paul and addressed in the epistle to the Ephesians was the same community as the Johannine community or a rival to it. There is no evidence at all to guide us in making a decision about this. Just as we do not know anything about historical, developmental connections between communities, we also know nothing about the uniform (or otherwise) adoption of practices. For example, in 1 Corinthians 11 Paul makes what has become an influential statement about the celebration of the Lord's Supper which many people today cite as evidence of New Testament practice; but we do not know whether the guidelines laid down by Paul were ever followed either by the Corinthians, the rest of the Pauline communities or by non-Pauline communities. It is quite possible that Paul has a more normative influence on the church in the twenty-first century than he ever did on the first-century communities.

A further methodological problem lies in the fact that, inevitably, we bring to the task of tracing the development of the church biases derived from church traditions and expectations. This has recently been well illustrated by Burtchaell. In his book, Burtchaell surveys the way in which church hierarchy has been interpreted throughout the Christian centuries. He concludes that writers on the subject discuss the structure of the church in conformity with their own views about the Reformation, and goes on to say,

> Some because they acknowledge apostolic succession and ordained office as essential to authentic Christianity, have claimed to see enough hints and harbingers of office in the New Testament to verify a radical continuity between the two periods

(and indeed between the polity then and the polity in their present church). Scholars of a contrary loyalty and interpretation have seen a radical discontinuity and have taken the earlier 'unofficered' church as the inspired norm.[31]

Any attempt at historical reconstruction must tread a careful line between these two approaches, recognizing that later Christian tradition does develop out of the seeds found in the first century but that practices, usage of words and so on change radically as Christianity develops.

From Jesus to Pentecost

In recent years, there have been numerous attempts to demonstrate that Paul, not Jesus, was the founder of Christianity.[32] The case breaks down, however, in the face of the variety of the New Testament material. Paul may have been hugely influential in the crafting of theological ideas still held by Christians today, but his is not the only voice in the New Testament. The sheer variety and competing claims of earliest Christianity militate against believing that there is a single 'founder' at all. The truth of the claims made by scholars such as B. Mack lies in the fact that Jesus made no obvious attempt to 'found' anything. He was a radical preacher seeking to transform the lives of first-century Jews in Galilee and Judea. The 'founders' of Christianity were those who gathered around the earthly and risen Jesus Christ and sought to communicate what they learnt to all they met. Paul was one of these disciples but not the only one.

Nevertheless the origins of Christianity must be traced back to the person of Jesus. The factor that holds the earliest Christians together is an encounter with Jesus – whether earthly, or risen and ascended. The earliest disciples are characterized by the fact that they gathered around Jesus and took part in what M. Hengel calls the 'messianic task', which is to share the good news of Jesus.[33] As R. Haight puts it, 'Jesus remembered was the object of their experience; and the preaching they took up was Jesus' preaching'.[34] Jesus lies at the heart of earliest Christianity; he may not have been its founder, but its foundations are rooted in his person. The major factor that contemporary churches can be said to share with the earliest Christians is the desire to gather around the person and teachings of Jesus Christ.

From Galilee to Antioch

The earliest 'Jesus communities' were made up of Jesus' disciples, both the twelve and the wider group who followed him around during his ministry, and were essentially rural in nature. They largely originated in Galilee and its environs and returned there between Jesus' death and the feast of Pentecost (Mt 28.7, 19, 16; Jn 21.2). The Acts of the Apostles has been understood to imply that from Pentecost onwards there was a single Christian community based in Jerusalem which developed, in a clear manner, outwards from Jerusalem to the ends of the earth. New Testament scholarship increasingly recognizes this perception to be untrue. As Cameron and Miller say it 'is no longer possible to posit a monolinear trajectory of development, true to a single, original impulse from which these many different groups must be thought of as divergent'.[35] Instead, scholars posit numerous different groups, some of which gave rise to New Testament texts, others of which did not. Of course the problem is evidence – or the lack of it. It is difficult to reconstruct anything of this multiplicity given that Acts appears to tell a story of a single expanding community.[36]

17

Logic demands that there were members of the wider band of disciples, who followed Jesus in Galilee, who remained in their home towns and believed in Jesus. The problem is that the canon has preserved texts which are predominantly, possibly even exclusively, non-Palestinian in origin.[37] Theissen has attempted to explain this by arguing that as 'a renewal movement within Judaism, the Jesus movement was a failure' and that it succeeded as a result of the more conducive atmosphere of the Hellenistic world.[38] This may be true but does not account for the success of the Jesus movement during Jesus' lifetime in precisely the same environment that Theissen considers was not conducive only 20 or so years later. Attempts have been made to identify Galilee as the social setting for the provenance of the hypothetical document 'Q'[39] and from this to understand something of the nature of the earliest rural Christian communities.[40] The problem with this, of course, is that 'Q' is a hypothetical source whose existence is far from universally accepted;[41] it is a fascinating theory but cannot be proved. We do not know whether rural, Galilean Christianity survived or not, but we do know that a number of early communities rapidly became urban, finding roots in Jerusalem, Antioch and many of the cities around the Roman Empire.[42]

Hellenists and Hebrews

It has been common in New Testament studies to maintain that the single Jerusalem church split into two groups, the Hellenists and the Hebrews, very soon after Pentecost. This view can be traced to F.C. Baur, who described the presence of two opposing parties:[43] 'Palestinian Jewish Christians' who were conservative and backward looking and the 'Hellenistic Gentile Christians' who were liberal and forward looking, as Dunn puts it: 'the one holding fast to tradition, the other sitting loose to it in the light of changing circumstances'.[44] The argument continues that the Hellenistic Christians were members of separate Greek-speaking synagogues and consequently worshipped there, rather than in the Aramaic-speaking synagogues of their Hebraic neighbours. Hengel maintains that it is the Greek language that contributes to the Hellenist distinctiveness and that 'the spirit inspired inter-pretation of *the message of Jesus in the new medium of the Greek language*'[45] was the thing that prompted a widespread purge within the Hellenistic synagogue communities but left the Aramaic-speaking community relatively unscathed. This purge, he believed, caused the Hellenistic Christians to leave Jerusalem for Antioch and in the process transform Christianity into 'an active and successful city religion'. The Hellenistic Christians then initiated a movement, of which Paul was the major protagonist, in which law-free salvation was offered to all and was opposed by the traditional Jewish Christians, of which Peter was the major protagonist, causing a schism at the heart of early Christianity.[46]

C. C. Hill's book, *Hellenists and Hebrews*, effectively demonstrates the flaws in this theory.[47] As Hill demonstrates, this case is built on very few verses in Acts: the divisions in the early Christian community are derived from Acts 6.1ff and the persecution of the Hellenists, but not the Hebrews, on Acts 8.1–4. Acts 6.1ff offers a single example of tension along the vague lines of 'Hellenists' and 'Hebrews' and while Hengel may well be right that this indicates that they worshipped in different synagogues on the grounds of language there is no further evidence to support the theory that differing language gave rise to a systemic schism in the early Christian communities. Nor is there anything in Acts 8.1–4 to indicate that the selectiveness of persecution was attributable to differing ideologies among the early Christians.

The Jerusalem Council and the 'Schism' of the church

What then was the cause of the dispute which is recorded in Galatians 2 and Acts 15? To begin with we must acknowledge the complexity of unpicking the relevant texts; these two do not fit easily together and establishing a chronology that works with both texts is almost impossible.[48] Hill proposes that it is possible to discern three separate but interrelated incidents here. The first, the Jerusalem council, circles around circumcision and whether Gentile Christians ought to be circumcised in order to gain access to Christ. The answer given is clear: Gentiles should not be required to be circumcised (Gal 2.7–9). This may not have been the radical decision that it sounded. It seems possible that there was a variety of practice about circumcision even among Jewish communities at this stage. An interesting example is Timothy who, though having a Jewish mother, had not been circumcised at birth. The next event recorded in Galatians 2.11–14 but not in Acts concerns table fellowship. It is all very well to say that Gentiles do not need to be circumcised but what then happens about eating together? When it became clear, therefore, that Jews and Gentiles were eating together, further instructions seem to have been sent from Jerusalem which were then adopted by Peter, Barnabas and the other Jews in Antioch. The only person in disagreement about this seems to have been Paul, who was outraged by what he saw to be Peter's duplicity. Hill, following Haenchen and a number of other scholars, sees Acts 15.20 and 29 as another episode in the dispute in which a compromise position, the Apostolic or Jerusalem decree, was reached between the Jewish and Gentile communities.[49]

Hill argues, in my view persuasively, that it does not represent a split between 'conservative Jewish Christianity' and 'liberal Gentile Christianity'. Instead, it was an attempt to work out in practice what it means to be a follower of Jesus. If Hill is correct, what happened was that persecution caused all but the apostles to flee Jerusalem and as a result the message of Jesus became more widely available to Gentiles, especially once Paul began his mission. As Gentiles began to become followers of Christ the first question was whether they should be circumcised. The second question was, if they are not circumcised, what happens about table fellowship. What is unclear is what the outcome of this was. If Haenchen and others are correct and the Apostolic or Jerusalem decree (Acts 15.20, 29) did follow the Antioch incident, then a compromise position was reached – at least temporarily, because it becomes an issue again in Corinth (1 Cor 8.1ff). If not, we are left with a resounding silence from Peter who though upbraided by Paul in Galatians 2 is not recorded as having responded to him. Nevertheless, it is too simplistic to assume an unhealed schism that took place after these incidents. 1 Corinthians 16.1 indicates that Paul had requested both the Galatians and the Corinthians to collect money for the church in Jerusalem, which he proposes to send on to them in due course. This is not the action of someone 'in schism' from the Jerusalem church, rather one who despite differences is determined to maintain a link with other Christian communities at the time.

There is not, therefore, a split between liberal and conservative early Christians, but a range of opinion worked out in the face of practical problems. We see at least three, if not more, positions held. There is the church in Jerusalem who, after discussion, were willing to give up the demand that Christians be circumcised but wanted to insist on the restriction of table fellowship; the Jewish Christians in Antioch who at first adapted to change by eating with the Gentiles but were then swayed by the Jerusalem delegation; and Paul who was passionate about the inclusion of Gentiles but maintained other aspects of Jewish law such as laws about sex and idolatry.[50] All maintained the importance of Jewish law. The question was not whether it should be maintained but in what form. The conflicts we observe taking place in these communities were about how one adapts to change and whether one should hold fast more to principle or to inclusion. We should remind ourselves that this dispute included only three voices – the Jerusalem Christians, the Antiochene Christians and Paul. We have no idea what other Christian communities thought of this dispute – nor even if they were aware of it.

Community

The above discussion has highlighted the importance for the early church of eating together and brings us to the concept of community in the early church. A common portrayal of the early Christian communities has been that Christianity began among the poor and dispossessed. For example, A. Deissmann says that the 'New Testament was not a product of the colourless refinement of an upper class. . . . On the contrary, it was, humanly speaking, a product of the force that came, unimpaired and strengthened by the Divine Presence, from the lower class'.[51] From there the early Christians developed the radical economic community represented in Acts 2–5 in which they sold all they possessed and shared their profits equally. Only at a later date did the wealthy gain any particular role in early Christianity.[52]

This, again, is too monochrome a portrayal of the earliest communities. It is quite clear from the gospels that some of the earliest followers of Jesus had sufficient financial security for them to support Jesus and his followers (Lk 8.2–3). Furthermore, the Acts account of the radical economic community adopted by the disciples in Jerusalem demonstrates how difficult this was to maintain: Ananias famously struggled to declare all he had (Acts 5.1–5); in Acts 6, we discover that the Hellenists feel that their widows are being neglected in the distribution; and in Acts 12.12 a report of Peter going 'to the house of Mary, the mother of John' implies that this house had not been sold and shared as others had been. Economic community was not without its problems even then. These problems do not undermine the importance of this strand of early Christianity, as the concept of radical poverty can still be found as an ideal in the *Didache*.[53] The reality may have been difficult to maintain but the ideal persisted nonetheless.

While one strand of early Christianity was probably rooted among the poor and dispossessed, another was rooted across the boundaries of class and wealth. In recent years, considerable work has been done on the social context of Corinth as a model for understanding the sociology of early Hellenistic Christianity.[54] A new consensus is now emerging among scholars that suggests that although the lower classes played an important part in the early Christian communities, it is much more likely that these communities represent a cross-section of society and that the tensions we see in the Corinthian communities stemmed from the inequality of power that arose in such a mixed community.[55] R. Stark backs this up from an entirely different perspective. His statistical exploration of persecution in the first century indicates that, although terrible when it happened, it was not widespread enough to be systematic. This he attributes to the wealthy and powerful members of the earliest communities whose influence would have 'mitigated repression and persecution'.[56]

Table fellowship and baptism

In Corinth one of the places in which tensions in community emerged was during the sharing of table fellowship (1 Cor 11.17–34). It seems that the sharing of table fellowship lies at the very centre of the earliest communities. Table fellowship, however, was more broadly conceived in the early church than it is in the church today and encompassed the early Christian habit of sharing a common meal, as well as a symbolic remembrance of Jesus' last supper with his disciples and his practice of breaking bread and giving thanks. Burtchaell's reconstruction of the development of worship in early Christianity suggests that table fellowship is *the* central moment of gathering among the earliest Christians. Burtchaell proposes that, to start with, the earliest Christians took a full part in the worship of temple and synagogue. But, he argues,

> during those earliest days of community stress, the only worship situation where they might arrange to find themselves exclusively in sympathetic company was at the domestic Sabbath suppers. It was inevitable that those suppers would become the treasured occasions for worship among the Jesus people. They would and did also serve as the most appropriate occasions to evoke the Lord's death and his suppers with the disciples before and afterwards.[57]

This seems to be born out by Acts 2.46 ('Day by day, as they spent much time together in the temple, they broke bread at home and ate their food with glad and generous hearts'). It is in this context, then, that we can begin to understand more about the stresses and strains to the earliest communities brought about by the Jerusalem council and the Antioch incident. The decision that Gentiles did not have to be circumcised in order to be a part of the new covenant solved some problems but raised many more. If the primary moment of meeting together involved food, how then would Jews meet with fellow followers of Christ who were not Jewish? The question of table fellowship would in this context run right through the middle of early Christian communities. If the central act of the remembering of Christ became impossible then the communities would face profound levels of division.

Although this does not seem to be an issue in Corinth, another has become important there (1 Cor 11.17–34). Here the table fellowship had become more concerned with table than fellowship. Theissen's reconstruction of the problem is compelling. He argues that the rich were enjoying food of better quality and quantity than the poorer members of the community.[58] Whatever the initial problem, Paul's response suggests a development/change in the significance of table fellowship. In 1 Corinthians 11.22 he suggests that they should eat and drink at home and in 11.34 that if they are hungry they should eat first. Thus the community meal becomes more about fellowship than it does about eating; it is the meeting together to remember Jesus that is the most important. Nevertheless there is no evidence at all that, as R. Jewitt somewhat provocatively puts it, the 'purely symbolic meal of modern Christianity, restricted to a bite of bread and sip of wine or juice' had any place at all in the first-century gatherings of Jesus' followers.[59]

Alongside table fellowship, another important act of the earliest communities was baptism: a practice which, like table fellowship, found its roots in the life and ministry of Jesus. There is ample evidence that baptism was practised within the early communities in most strands of early Christianity (see Mt 28.19; Jn 3.22–26; Acts 2.38–41; 1 Cor 1.14). Just as gathering together, sharing food and breaking bread can be traced back to the disciples' life together with Christ, so also baptism can be traced back to the time of Jesus. These symbolic actions are as vivid a link to the historical Jesus as the stories of the teaching and life of Jesus were, if not more so. Theissen maintains that both baptism and Lord's Supper had a stage of development that took place in the first century. At first they were simply symbolic recollections of the actions of John and Jesus but later, in the theology of Paul, became associated with the death of Jesus.[60]

Households and synagogues

One of the contrasts between the Jerusalem and Antioch churches, and those of Paul, may lie in the way in which they were constituted. Burtchaell believes that the predominantly Jewish communities developed alongside synagogues as a particular expression of Jewish faith and worship, whereas Meeks identifies the household as the primary formative influence. It may well be that in all the diversity of the first century both are correct.

Burtchaell's theory is that the early Christian communities developed alongside their Jewish counterparts until this was simply no longer possible. He notes that Meyers and Strange could find no physical archaeological identifiers of Christianity until the fourth or fifth century. Thus 'a study of the earliest Christian remains in Palestine means studying Jewish remains'.[61] The implication of this is that Christian self-definition was not sufficient in this period to leave behind archaeological remains that were clearly Christian, as opposed to Jewish. Burtchaell goes on to argue that in large cities such as Jerusalem and Alexandria there were enough synagogues to allow groups (e.g. Pharisees, Sadducees, Essenes) each to have their own synagogues, but in small towns and cities of the Diaspora there would have had to be only one synagogue.

In this setting the early Christians would have been viewed as yet one more 'group' and would have vigorously argued their case about the true interpretation of scripture with their fellow Jews until common existence became no longer possible. Burtchaell's theory is that then they would have taken the structures and patterns of worship from the synagogue into their own exclusively Christian situations of worship. Hence his theory about table fellowship, explored above: they would have begun meeting together to eat, share stories about Jesus' life and read out letters from influential people such as Paul, but would have worshipped at the synagogue; only when they could no longer go to the synagogue would they have brought the synagogue practices into their own Christian setting.[62]

Meeks argues that the primary point of contact (and therefore of mission) was not the synagogue but the household: '[o]ur sources give us good reason to think that it [the household] was the basic unit in the establishment of Christianity in the city, as it was, indeed, the basic unit of the city itself'.[63] If Meeks is right, then at least in the Pauline communities there was a double network of relationships: a vertical one between the *paterfamilias* (head of the household) and the rest of the members of the household, and a horizontal one linking households together across the city. This structure would have formed community relationships and given missionary opportunities. Although Meeks acknowledges that synagogues, voluntary associations and philosophic or rhetorical schools all had influence in the forming of Christian community, he believes that it was the household that was most formative.

The positions of Burtchaell and Meeks may both be right. When the early Christians gathered together, even at the earliest stage, to share table fellowship apart from the synagogue, it would have been in a household. The rate at which they wore out their welcome at their local synagogue would have varied, probably in direct proportion to how many Gentile Christians there were in the community. So in some communities, like Jerusalem, where separate synagogues were possible, the synagogue model of '*ekklēsia*' may well have had a greater influence than in places where Christians stopped going to the synagogue at a relatively early date.

This moment of 'eviction' from synagogue seems to have had greater impact on some early communities than on others. Scholars see behind the writing of Matthew and John the scars of communities struggling to come to terms with the parting of the ways between the 'Jewish' and 'Christian' communities.[64] This 'parting of the ways' is long, drawn out and ill defined. Some groups within Christianity may have withdrawn or been evicted from the synagogue relatively early on in the first century, but others continued as Jews for a long time. In fact recent research suggests that even in the second century there is evidence of interdependency between Judaism and Christianity. This raises the question of whether the terms 'Judaism' 'Christianity' and 'parting of the ways' can be accurately used at all in this period.[65] As with the word 'church' they point to a reality that came into existence well after our period. Here, as with many other themes that we have explored, the answer varies from community to community, but our evidence remains so scant that it is very difficult to produce a reliable reconstruction of how it happened.

Christian self-definition does not seem to have been achieved in many Christian communities in the first century CE. The lack of boundaries between the early Jesus movement and their Jewish neighbours does not mean that boundaries did not exist. Both Paul, in 1 Corinthians 5.1–13, and Matthew 18.17 speak of the exclusion of members from the community. In Paul this was on the grounds of incest and in Matthew on the grounds of ignoring the community. This indicates that even fairly early on in the first century attempts were made to draw some boundaries around the communities, even if they are not where we might expect them to be.

Conclusions on tracing the history of early communities

The traditional scholarly view, that a single Christian community based in Jerusalem spread outwards first to Antioch and then to other Roman cities as a result of the persecution of Hellenistic Christians, seems no longer sustainable. Although we are hampered by lack of sources, the development of early Christian communities seems much more varied and less systematic than has been traditionally assumed. Some rural Palestinian communities drop silently out of view, but not necessarily out of existence. Other Hellenistic communities struggled with the practical issues of the mission to the Gentiles, while the communities with a higher proportion of Jewish Christians struggled to come to terms with the choices the Hellenistic communities made. There is little evidence for absolute schism and more evidence for conflict, compromise and debate. It is likely that both the synagogue and the household influenced the development of Christian community but in different measure depending on the particular community. While some communities withdrew or were evicted from the Jewish synagogue, others did not and continued their allegiance into the second century CE and beyond. The search for the 'church' of the New Testament can feel a little like the search for the Holy Grail: romantic, desirable, but ultimately impossible. We can tell a little of individual communities and certain points in the first century but how – indeed if – they all relate to each other globally and chronologically remains unclear.

Overall conclusions

The aim of this chapter has not been to recover the development of 'the early church' as such but rather to point to the major trends of scholarship in the area. There are three main ways of exploring early ecclesiology: through word studies, through looking at Christian community in each New Testament book, and through attempting to recover the history of Christianity in the first century. I have attempted to represent each of these strands, however briefly. Each strand contributes something to the task. Word studies allow one to focus closely on a single area but can exclude important information; a book by book approach gives broad coverage but no indication of connections between communities; and a historical/sociological approach gives connections but has insufficient data available to provide a full picture. Furthermore the ideal, particularly of Acts, of presenting a linear development from the Ascension of Christ to Paul's arrival at Rome obscures much of the diversity of the period.

Our search so far has delivered certain key features. Although the major New Testament texts present a picture of uniformity, beneath these lie indications of diversity. There were numerous ways of describing early communities and numerous experiences of developing within and alongside Judaism. What we can tell of one community is not necessarily true of all communities. Nevertheless there were intimations in this period that communities were not regarded entirely in isolation and that there was an abstract reality which could be termed – by some at least – the *ekklēsia* of God. The word study, book by book exploration of descriptions, and historical/sociological exploration all show a diverse church which in this period is growing towards, but does not reach, a sense of self-definition and which certainly does not have a monochrome sense of what this might be.

Challenges for the future are many. More work is needed on the best methodologies to employ to help us 'recover' an understanding of early Christian community; and we need further exploration of how we tell a story of such diversity in any kind of coherent way. Add into this the need for an understanding of how second order issues such as ministry, liturgy, etc. varied from community to community, and the challenges to future scholarship become vast. A further challenge to ecclesiologists also emerges from this work. Most ecclesiologies begin with an exploration of the early church as a model for reflection on the historical or current church; this study has raised the question of how possible this is. If the early Christian communities were diverse in their expression of faith and identity what does that do to attempts to locate ideas and practices in the 'early church'? What it means is that those who hope to find order and hierarchy in the early church are able to do so and those who hope to find fluidity and equality can also do so. This should alert us to the fact that the church in the first Christian century was as varied as it is today and that discerning models of order in the first century may not be as definitive as we might think.

Notes

1 G. Kittel *et al.*, *Theological Dictionary of the New Testament*, Grand Rapids, MI: Eerdmans, 1965.
2 J. Barr, *The Semantics of Biblical Language*, Oxford: Oxford University Press, 1961.
3 The development of ministry in the early church is a second order issue and one so large it is impossible to do it justice here. See Chapter 31 of this volume for a more detailed treatment of ministry in general.
4 The point that James Barr famously made in Barr, *Semantics*.
5 See discussion in E. Ferguson, *The Church of Christ: A Biblical Ecclesiology for Today*, Grand Rapids, MI: Eerdmans, 1996, p. 130; W.A. Meeks, *The First Urban Christians: The Social World of the Apostle Paul*, 2nd edn., New Haven, CT: Yale University Press, 2003, p. 108; K.L. Schmidt, 'Ekklesia', in *Theological Dictionary of the New Testament*, ed. G. Kittel *et al.*, Grand Rapids, MI: Eerdmans, 1965, pp. 501–36, at pp. 513–17.
6 See K. Giles, *What on Earth is the Church? An Exploration in New Testament Theology*, Downers Grove, IL: IVP, 1995, p. 240.

7 James Tunstead Burtchaell, *From Synagogue to Church: Public Services and Offices in the Earliest Christian Communities*, Cambridge: Cambridge University Press, 1992, esp. p. 345.

8 Giles, *What on Earth is the Church?*, p. 240.

9 Meeks, *First Urban Christians*, p. 108.

10 Meeks, *First Urban Christians*, p. 108.

11 See Giles, *What on Earth is the Church?*, pp. 241–3.

12 P.S. Minear, *Images of the Church in the New Testament*, London: Lutterworth Press, 1960, p. 28.

13 H.C. Kee, *Community of the New Age: Studies in Mark's Gospel*, New Testament Library, London: SCM, 1977, p. 107.

14 The reconstruction of gospel communities is one of the most important strands of current New Testament scholarship, though this consensus is beginning to be challenged; see Richard Bauckham, *The Gospels for All Christians: Rethinking the Gospel Audiences*, Grand Rapids, MI: Eerdmans, 1998.

15 Cadbury suggested that there were nineteen different words and phrases used for the Christian community in Acts (H.J. Cadbury, 'Names for Christians and Christianity in Acts', in *The Beginnings of Christianity*, ed. K. Lake *et al.*, London: Macmillan, 1933).

16 It is clear that the author of Acts intends this term to be inclusive: in Acts 16:40 Paul and Silas went to Lydia's house and encouraged 'the brothers' there and it is hard to believe that Lydia would be excluded by this term.

17 R. Hodgson, 'Holiness', in *The Anchor Bible Dictionary*, ed. D.N. Freedman, New York: Doubleday, 1992, pp. 249–54, at p. 251.

18 C.K. Barrett, *The Acts of the Apostles*, The International Critical Commentary, Edinburgh: T&T Clark, 1998, p. 556.

19 This would be supported by Bickerman's argument that *chrēmatizō* (were called) is better translated as 'assume the name' or 'styled themselves' (E.J. Bickerman, 'The Name of Christians', *Harvard Theological Review* 42 (1949), 109–24).

20 See discussion in Barrett, *The Acts of the Apostles*, p. 1098.

21 See 9:2; 19:9, 23; 22:4; 24:14, 22.

22 Barrett, *The Acts of the Apostles*, p. 448.

23 See Titus Livius, *Ab Urbe Condita* 2.32.

24 Minear, *Images of the Church*, p. 174.

25 E. Best, *Ephesians*, International Critical Commentary, Edinburgh: T&T Clark, 1998, 287–88.

26 See discussion in P.J. Achtemeier, *1 Peter*. Minneapolis: Fortress Press, 1996, pp. 315–16.

27 For the definitive discussion of the use of term alien in 1 Peter see J.H. Elliott, *A Home for the Homeless: A Sociological Exegesis of 1 Peter, Its Situation and Strategy*, Philadelphia: Fortress, 1981.

28 See for example Minear, *Images of the Church*, p. 55.

29 S. Smalley, *The Revelation to John*, London: SPCK, 2005, p. 536.

30 'The basic problem in writing a history of early Christianity lies in the fragmentariness of the sources and the haphazard way in which they have survived', M. Hengel, *Acts and the History of Earliest Christianity*, London: SCM, 1979, p. 3.

31 Burtchaell, *From Synagogue to Church*, p. 274.

32 See for example M. Casey, *From Jewish Prophet to Gentile God*, Cambridge: Clarke, 1991; B. Mack, *The Lost Gospel: The Book of Q and Christian Origins*, New York: HarperCollins, 1993; G. Vermes, *The Religion of Jesus the Jew*, London: SCM, 1993.

33 M. Hengel, 'The Origins of Christian Mission', in *Between Jesus and Paul: Studies in the Earliest History of Christianity*, ed. M. Hengel, London: SCM, 1983, p. 62.

34 R. Haight, *Christian Community in History*, 2 vols, vol. 1, New York and London: Continuum, 2004, p. 72.

35 R. Cameron and M.P. Miller, 'Introduction: Ancient Myths and Modern Theories of Christian Origins', in *Redescribing Christian Origins*, eds R. Cameron and M.P. Miller, Atlanta, GA: SBL, 2004, p. 20.

36 Scholars such as D.E. Smith have gone so far as to argue that the first-century church in Jerusalem is a Lukan fiction.

37 A possible exception to this is the epistle of James, which if written by James the brother of Jesus could have found its origin in Jerusalem.

38 G. Theissen, *The First Followers of Jesus, A Sociological Analysis of the Earliest Christianity*, London: SCM, 1978, p. 112.

39 'Q' is the explanation that many scholars give for the remarkable overlap that exists between Matthew, Mark and Luke. They propose that the three gospel writers had a common source which they used in the creation of their gospels; this they call 'Q'.

40 See J.S. Kloppenborg Verbin, *Excavating Q: The History and Setting of the Sayings Gospel*, Edinburgh: T&T Clark International, 2000.

41 See M. Goodacre, *The Case against Q*, Harrisburg, PA: Trinity Press International, 2002.

42 Important here is the work of Meeks, *First Urban Christians*.

43 See discussion in C.C. Hill, *Hellenists and Hebrews, Reappraising Division within the Earliest Church*, Minneapolis: Fortress, 1991, pp. 5–9.

44 J.D.G. Dunn, *Unity and Diversity in the New Testament: An Inquiry into the Character of Earliest Christianity*, London: SCM, 1977, p. 275.

45 Original italics, M. Hengel, *Between Jesus and Paul. Studies in the Earliest History of Christianity*, London: SCM, 1983, p. 24.

46 Though Hengel points out that Peter was not Paul's real opponent but acted as a mediator between Judaists and Gentile Christians (Hengel, *Acts and the History of Earliest Christianity*, p. 92).

47 Hill, *Hellenists and Hebrews*.

48 See the extensive discussion in Hill, *Hellenists and Hebrews*, pp. 103–47, for a full treatment of the issues.

49 Hill, *Hellenists and Hebrews*, pp. 143–6.

50 For a full discussion of the place of Jewish law in the early church see M. Bockmuehl, *Jewish Law in Gentile Churches: Halakhah and the Beginning of Christian Public Ethics*, Edinburgh: T&T Clark International, 2000.

51 A. Deissmann, *Light from the Ancient near East*, London: 1927, p. 144, cited in G. Theissen, *The Social Setting of Pauline Christianity, Essays on Corinth*, trans. J.H. Schutz, Edinburgh: T&T Clark International, 1982, p. 69.

52 For a discussion of some of the motivations that lie behind this position see A. Malherbe, *Social Aspects of Early Christianity*, Philadelphia, 1983, pp. 4–13.

53 See particularly 11 and 13.

54 The most influential arguments can be found in Meeks, *First Urban Christians*; Theissen, *Social Setting*; and David G. Horrell, *The Social Ethos of the Corinthian Correspondence: Interests and Ideology from 1 Corinthians to 1 Clement*, Edinburgh: T&T Clark, 1996.

55 For a full discussion of the issues see Horrell, *Social Ethos*, pp. 63–125.

56 R. Stark, *The Rise of Christianity: A Sociologist Reconsiders History*, Princeton, NJ: Princeton University Press, 1996, p. 46.

57 Burtchaell, *From Synagogue to Church*, p. 285.

58 Theissen, *Social Setting*, pp. 147–62.

59 R. Jewitt, 'Tenement Churches and Pauline Love Feasts', *Quarterly Review* 14 (1993), 42–58, at 44.

60 G. Theissen, *The Religion of the Earliest Churches: Creating a Symbolic World*, Minneapolis: Fortress, 1999, p. 124.

61 E.M. Meyers and J.F. Strange, *Archaeology, the Rabbis, & Early Christianity*, Nashville: Abingdon, 1981, p. 169 (cited in Burtchaell, *From Synagogue to Church*, p. 275).

62 Burtchaell, *From Synagogue to Church*, pp. 272–338.

63 Meeks, *First Urban Christians*, p. 29.

64 See discussions in R.E. Brown, *The Community of the Beloved Disciple*, London: Geoffrey Chapman, 1979 and G. Stanton, 'The Communities of Matthew', in *Gospel Interpretation: Narrative-Critical & Social-Scientific Approaches*, ed. J. D. Kingsbury, Harrisburg, PA: Trinity Press International, 1997, pp. 49–64.

65 For a full discussion of the issues see A.H. Becker and A.Y. Reed, *The Ways That Never Parted: Jews and Christians in Late Antiquity and the Early Middle Ages*, Texts and Studies in Ancient Judaism 95, Tübingen: Mohr Siebeck, 2003.

Further reading

Adam H. Becker and Annette Yoshiko Reed. *The Ways That Never Parted: Jews and Christians in Late Antiquity and the Early Middle Ages.* Texts and Studies in Ancient Judaism 95; Tübingen: Mohr Siebeck, 2003.

James Tunstead Burtchaell, *From Synagogue to Church: Public Services and Offices in the Earliest Christian Communities.* Cambridge: Cambridge University Press, 1992.

R. Cameron and M.P. Miller (eds), *Redescribing Christian Origins.* Atlanta, GA: SBL, 2004.

Everett Ferguson, *The Church of Christ: A Biblical Ecclesiology for Today.* Grand Rapids, MI: Eerdmans, 1996.

Kevin Giles, *What on Earth Is the Church?: An Exploration in New Testament Theology.* Downers Grove, IL: InterVarsity Press, 1995.

R. Haight, *Christian Community in History.* 2 vols. Vol. 1. London: Continuum, 2004.

M. Hengel, *Between Jesus and Paul. Studies in the Earliest History of Christianity.* London: SCM, 1983.

Wayne A. Meeks, *The First Urban Christians: The Social World of the Apostle Paul.* 2nd edn. New Haven, CT: Yale University Press, 2003.

P.S. Minear, *Images of the Church in the New Testament.* London: Lutterworth Press, 1960.

R. Stark, *The Rise of Christianity. A Sociologist Reconsiders History.* Princeton, NJ: Princeton University Press, 1996.

G. Theissen, *The Social Setting of Pauline Christianity. Essays on Corinth.* Edinburgh: T&T Clark International, 1982.

2

THE CHURCH IN THE EARLY CHRISTIAN CENTURIES

Ecclesiological consolidation

G.R. Evans

It is recorded that believers in Jesus Christ were first called Christians at Antioch (Acts 11.26). These first 'Christians' saw themselves as followers of a person, Jesus Christ. Jesus' ministry had been spent in the company of a group of disciples who had followed him, but it was a very different matter for that group to 'constitute' itself after his death. The transition of thinking which taught them to regard themselves as a community and to begin to define the nature and purpose of that community and work out how it should conduct its affairs is not fully mapped in the New Testament, What happened in the next few centuries to clarify matters revealed a series of tugs and strains in the fabric. Not the least of these was the gradual divergence of ways of thinking in the Eastern and Western halves of the ageing Roman Empire as the two language communities of Greek and Latin speakers pulled apart, eventually to diverge so completely that for a thousand years after the Empire fell very few writers would be able to command both languages, let alone understand the subtle cultural differences they expressed.

The church lived its first centuries in chronological order, of course, but it did not crystallize its thinking generation by generation in an orderly way. Topics presented themselves episodically, because someone asked an awkward question or the political situation in the late Roman world shifted, so that it is likely to be easier to understand the emergence of the key ideas by taking them thematically.

In what follows the first group of questions considered are those which had to do with deciding who made up the church, what constituted membership and whether it could ever be possible to know for sure who God himself considered to belong. The following sections look at the meaning of baptism as an entry qualification and what the church did about those who were baptized and then lapsed from the faith, but later wanted to return to the church. It concludes with the challenges presented by the Pelagians, who questioned the need for baptism as a means of cleansing the individual of original sin and as a consequence threw baptismal theology into a new crisis.

The second section of this chapter deals with the emerging arrangements by which the church came to run itself as an institution. It continued to believe itself to be a vehicle and instrument of God's free-acting grace but it found it needed to think about organization. We look first at the idea of holding councils, which began as early as New Testament times. Then comes the relationship of church and state; the relationship between the local and the universal churches; the development of a recognized structures for ministries and a system of ordination; the place of sacramental and pastoral duties in the theology of ministry; provinces and primacy; the maintenance of the faith, with the role of creeds and the ministry of the Word. The chapter ends with a consideration of the relationship between faith and order in the theology of the church, and the problems caused by heresy and schism.

Theology and practice

Throughout this early formative period there was both a 'daily life' of the community to be arranged and a developing sense that the church was something higher and deeper. One of the most important ecclesiological ideas, which only really crystallized in the second half of the twentieth century under the stimulus of the ecumenical movement, is that the church is first and foremost a 'communion' (*koinonia*). In the Western tradition 'communion' is 'fellowship', in the sense of friendly sharing of a common life with mutual support. This sort of 'fellowship' language in Latin is exemplified in Hilary of Poitiers' (*c*. 315–67/8) talk of the *fidelium coetus* (In Ps. 131.23, CSEL, 22, p. 680). Communion is also seen in the West as a mystical union of Christians with one another and with Christ. For example, the ninth article of the Apostle's Creed, a Western document, speaks of the *communio sanctorum*. But the conception of a mystical communion was to become far more refined and sophisticated in the Greek tradition because the heritage of late Platonic mysticism remained alive and growing there. The 'spiritual' approach continued to be central in the Eastern half of the Roman Empire after the Council of Nicaea had put its mind to some ecclesiological matters. Cyril of Jerusalem explained for the benefit of catechumens that the church is a spiritual society (Cat. 18.22–28). It is a safe sheepfold for all kinds of people. That is why it is called 'catholic' (universal). Cyril was not discussing the complex problems about the institutional structure of the church which had been debated in the Latin-speaking West in the previous century, especially in Africa in the time of Cyprian (Cyprian died a martyr in a period of persecution in 258). Cyril's outline ideas are far from superficial, but their profundity is in the area of 'mystery' and they do not lend themselves to rational analysis. Cyril's line was followed by subsequent Eastern writers, such as John Chrysostom (*c*. 347–407). Cyril of Alexandria (d. 444) emphasized the importance of unity of faith as the marker of the 'oneness' of the church (*In Psalmo* 44.10, PG 69.1042). Gregory of Nazianzus (329/30–89/90) describes this mystical making one with Christ not only of the individual believer but of the community of believers, as a 'new mystery'.

Alongside this 'spiritual' notion of the nature of the church its daily realities had to be lived. There are plentiful indications from the New Testament onwards that the 'fellowship' of the common life was frequently disrupted by disagreements, particularly over details of practice, but also about the shared beliefs of the community. The mystical union was threatened by arguments about who was 'in' and who was 'out of' the community, and whether those who had left could be admitted back in and on what terms. The church was engaged in trying to explain itself to itself through these debates. From the distance of two thousand years it is possible to observe the interaction of theory and the urgencies of the problem-solving needed to keep the community together. It is important to remember how much harder it was for those living through these events to take this kind of sage overview.

The disputes about membership

Charism and the invisible church

Was the Christian's relationship with Christ going to be first and foremost a matter for the solitary individual within his or her own soul, a personal relationship, or was it to involve membership of a community with others? Jesus had summed up the Ten Commandments in terms of the dual expectation that the believer should love God wholeheartedly and love his neighbour as himself (Mk 12.33). When Jesus sent out his disciples two by two (Mk 6.7) and promised his disciples that the prayer on which two agreed to ask for some particular thing, would be answered (Mt 18.19), he was later taken to be laying down norms. The individual's love of God was to have a context in the relations within the community and his or her activities were to be subject to its expectations. John the Baptist had been a lone and somewhat wild figure, but he was seen as having a divinely-appointed place in the providential plan. It is stated that Philip's baptism of the eunuch he found reading the book of Isaiah in his chariot (Acts 8.26–39) was directly prompted by the Holy Spirit. This baptism took place by the roadside and not in church, but it was not the act of a breakaway rebel. Indeed Philip was one of the seven men of honest reputation who were given special responsibility for making sure that the practical requirements of the widows and needy were not neglected by the community of believers (Acts 6.5).

That did not mean that 'individualists' did not exist and sometimes cause problems, when they believed themselves to be directly guided by the Holy Spirit and did not consult fellow-Christians. There were some who seem to have felt free to develop their teaching independently, without reference to the community as a whole. 'Charismatics' who believed the Holy Spirit spoke to them directly and were not willing to submit their views to revision or correction by the community could be dangerous to the continuing unity of the church, for forming consensus was not their way.

Such individuals prompted the crisis which is recorded in Acts 15.1. They came down from Judaea and were teaching Christians in other places that they would have to be circumcised as Moses had instructed or they could not be saved. This challenge was addressed (Acts 15.2–27) by holding a meeting of the community, which was later construed as a primitive 'council', with the various opinions being put to the whole community until agreement was reached. The 'ruling' or 'decree' was to be disseminated by chosen and trusted individuals and it was to carry the authority of the apostles and elders at Jerusalem 'with the whole church'.

This early emergence of an 'orderly' means of making decisions in matters of faith and maintaining and preaching the faith was going to be of central importance. From it would develop the whole complex structure of the institutional church designed to protect 'unity of faith' within an 'order' and eventually a structure. In this episode are to be glimpsed hints of the emergence of important principles: that decisions should be taken by consensus, and involve the whole community; that the community needed leaders and that it was going to be important that they should be properly authorized and their role and authority made clear; that not only this question of continuing with circumcision but many other things were going to need to be considered for acceptance or rejection as essential to the Christian life; and that it was also going to be necessary to decide what could and could not be a legitimate variation of practice from place to place.

All this pointed to the need to be clear who was 'inside' the church and who was not. It turned out that this was not at all easy to answer.

If God wished to speak to individuals in the person of the Holy Spirit he must be free to choose how and when and to whom he did so. Grace is essentially a free gift. God could 'accept' an individual if he chose (Rom 1.5, Rom 12.6–8). Divine grace could not be impotent to work directly to achieve the effects of baptism, forgiving sins. And, conversely, even if someone was baptized, even if someone was in a position of leadership in the church, it could not be taken for granted that such a person was accepted by God. Although the Holy Spirit was believed to 'work' at the moment of baptism to free the person baptized of sin and its consequences, he could not be constrained or obliged to do so. Nor could it be taken for granted, it was quickly realized, that those appointed to be elders or ministers would always be worthy. The Holy Spirit was believed to act in ordinations through the laying on of hands (cf. Acts 13.3). Under persecution many thus ordained fled from their pastoral duties or apostatized.

Someone with genuine 'gifts of the Spirit' must surely be thought to enjoy some form of 'membership' of the church, even if the individual thus favoured had not been baptized. Tertullian took some first steps towards defining grace and its operations, but the subject was first fully explored by Augustine, partly as a consequence of his dispute with the Pelagians, which we shall come to in a moment. This 'Western' context helped to ensure that the vocabulary and concepts were more refined in the Latin half of the Roman Empire than in the half that did its theology in Greek and whose theology and spiritual life were already beginning to take on a different style and flavour as a consequence.

Augustine's position on all this was in some respects paradoxical. He held that the Holy Spirit cannot be received outside the church (Sermon 267.4 and 268.2) and that there was no salvation outside it (*nulla salus extra ecclesiam*). Yet in *The City of God*, Augustine insisted that the church is invisible, because only God knows who are his own. And they are his own because he has freely chosen them before the world began and before they were created (Rom 8.29). They have no say in his choice and he will never change his preferences. Augustine asserted that the visible church, the community of the baptized and worshipping, is a mixed community in which the wheat and the weeds grow together until the harvest (cf. Mt 13.28–30). Only at the Last Judgement (Mt 25.32) will it be revealed who belongs to the church and who is a member of the other 'city' of the damned.

Baptized but still a sinner

There were several reasons for the early practice of delaying baptism until late maturity. One was educational. The would-be Christian first had to become a catechumen and take instruction. The catechumenate was taken seriously. A catechumen who 'lapsed' and then decided he wanted to return would have to go back to the beginning and spend three more years with the 'hearers' before being allowed to pray with the catechumens, says Canon 14 of the Council of Nicaea.[1] Catechumens went to church but sat apart, and left before the celebration of the eucharist began. As each Easter approached those who were to be baptized formed a special group for their final instruction. So they were conceived as part of the local church community but not yet really as members, and the preparation for baptism was recognized to be a preparation for the full membership of the church.

Cyril of Jerusalem (*c.* 315–87, bishop of Jerusalem from *c.* 349) is the author of the *Catechetical Discourses*. These were the instructions given to candidates for baptism in fourth-century Palestine in the period before Easter, evincing strong confidence in the efficacy of baptism and the elements of anointing, renunciation of sin, washing away of sins and the use of the laying on of hands. The Latin commentary on the Apostles' Creed of Rufinus (c. 345–411) is partly dependent on Cyril of Jerusalem's *Catechetical Discourses*, so the picture it gives does not merely reflect Eastern attitudes. Ambrose in *De officiis ministrorum* gave his remarks on Christian ethics Ciceronian foundations, in a series of explanations on faith and sacraments for candidates for baptism.[2] Augustine's *De catechizandis rudibus* gives a vivid picture of the sophistication of some of those who came for instruction and the difficulties of teaching adults in the North Africa of his day. Adults could also, as Augustine discovered in his own version of the 'faith and works' question, be reluctant to begin on amendment of life until they had completed their classes and perhaps even until they had actually been baptized.

The baptism which ultimately took place at Easter was seen as an act of the church within which each individual was purged of sin by the action of the Holy Spirit in the presence of the community. Theodore of Mopsuestia (c. 350–428) describes the union of believers through baptism and by the action of the Holy Spirit as 'constituting' the body of Christ. It is the faith of the believer which 'attracts' the Holy Spirit, not the use of the water in itself, he stresses.[3] The Holy Spirit will not rest on someone without faith. But the Spirit will not descend except through baptism (cf. I Timothy 3.2 and 6).[4]

The development of the penitential system and restoration to the church

Baptism was held to purge the individual of both original and actual sin, completely. But it was unrepeatable. He who put his hand to the plough must not look back (Lk 9.62). The move to infant baptism in the West at the end of the fourth century, although it reflected the emergence of a stronger doctrine of baptism which made people afraid to risk that their children might go to hell if they died unbaptized, inevitably meant that more individuals would commit sins after baptism than could be hoped for if people delayed baptism until an advanced age. It was not until after the patristic period that the penitential system seems to have developed to accommodate the need for a mechanism to deal with the minor sins of a population baptized as babies. The emphasis of the first centuries was upon the major sins of murder, adultery and apostasy. These were treated as matters of concern to the whole local community. Such sinners were to be excommunicated, cut off from normal participation in the life of the community and the celebration of the eucharist. Canon 5 of the Council of Nicaea decreed that this was to extend throughout the church. Other bishops were to recognize it so that sinners did not simply decamp to other places and carry on regardless.[5]

The period of penance could be very lengthy. Canon 11 of the Council of Nicaea deals with those who have apostatized even though they have not been in danger or threatened at a time of persecution. They should be shown mercy and readmitted to the community, but only after three years among the hearers (*audientes*) and six years among the prostrators and two more years when they are allowed to join the community in the eucharistic prayers but not in the 'offering' itself.[6] After an appropriate period of demonstrating the seriousness of their repentance they might be publicly restored by the bishop's absolution in the presence of the whole congregation. This was a very public penance and it ended with an ecclesial act. Even so, the sinner was not quite in the position he had been before. In many communities a reconciled penitent who had formerly been a priest was no longer allowed to exercise his ministry.

A crisis of rigorism

Cyprian, bishop of Carthage from 248 (d. 258), became a Christian convert only in 246, in mature life. Soon after he was elevated to the episcopate a period of persecution of Christians began (the Decian persecution) and he went into exile. He continued to carry out the duties of his office as best he could by correspondence. When it was safe to return, in 251, he came back to find a scene familiar in the period of the persecutions. A number of his flock had abandoned the faith in fright. Others had procured certificates for their own protection, which declared that they had sacrificed to idols as the persecutors required, although in fact many of them had not really done so. Those who hid behind these certificates were known as the *libellatici*.

This situation, it seemed to Cyprian, presented him with important issues of principle. Should these apostates be allowed to return to the church as though nothing had happened? Local 'confessors', Christians who had courageously refused to compromise their faith, were allowing the lapsed to come back and maintaining that any penitential payment which might have been appropriate to 'make up for' what they had done was satisfactorily allowed for by calling in aid the surplus 'virtue' or 'merits' of those who had died as martyrs for their faith. Cyprian disagreed and two Councils were held at Carthage in 251 and 252. The first of these concluded that there must be at least an appropriate period of penance to ensure that the community was seen to take the matter seriously.

The second of these Carthage Councils (252) was concerned with Novatian, a priest in Rome who had led a secession which had become a schism, in disapproval of the failure to take sufficiently seriously the implications of apostasy under persecution. The Novatianists favoured a rigorist approach which refused completely to readmit those who repented of their lapse.[7]

One of the most important questions this period of controversy brought to prominence was whether baptism by those excluded from the communion of the catholic church (heretics or schismatics) was valid and efficacious, and if it was not both these things, whether a repentant person who now wished to be admitted could or should be baptized, on the principle that he or she had not really been baptized at all so this was not really a rebaptism. For a sacrament to be 'valid' meant that it had been done 'properly', that is, in a way complying with the formal conditions for that particular sacrament. For it to be 'efficacious' meant that it was regarded as 'a true vehicle of grace'. It was never a problem that the alleged baptism might have been carried out by someone who was not ordained. Anyone could baptize. So this did not raise directly the question whether an 'unworthy minister' could invalidate a sacrament by his bad behaviour. (Augustine of Hippo was to help consolidate the church's emerging view that the minister of the sacrament is really God so an unworthy minister does not get in the way of the sacrament's validity.) The practical solution was that someone who had been baptized, in any context and by anyone, even heretics, was usually admitted to the church by imposition of hands, at least in the West.

But that did not satisfy everyone. The extreme rigorists denied both the validity and the efficacy of heretical baptisms. Cyprian found himself embroiled in a vigorous dispute with the Bishop of Rome when he and the African bishops at two more councils of 255 and 256 tried to insist that schismatics should be (re)baptized. Their argument was that a sacrament could not be administered validly except within the true church. (Here Augustine was to refine the principle adumbrated by Cyprian, that sacraments do not have automatic effects.)

A sensible solution was agreed in the early fourth century. From the time of the pronounce-ment of the Council of Arles in 314, responding to the Donatist reluctance to accept those baptized outside their own communion, it became accepted that the basic requirement was that the baptism should be carried out in the name of the Trinity and with water.

Pelagianism

The 'ecclesial' contextualization of baptismal theology was challenged in a further way from the end of the fourth century by the Pelagian controversy and its aftermath. Pelagius, a society preacher probably of British origin, made a name for himself in Rome by teaching his congregations that they could be good if they tried. This teaching can be retrieved now only in part, and our picture of it is heavily coloured by Augustine's hostile rewriting of what Pelagius was saying. His main idea seems to have been that the Christian life was merely a life of imitation of the best models, and the best model of all was Christ. God's good opinion could be won by the living of a virtuous life. Pelagius probably did not exclude the help of God's grace, or undervalue the work of Christ, or forget the effects of human weakness to the extent Augustine alleged.

Augustine, seeking to counter what he considered to be Pelagius' bad influence, placed more and more emphasis on the helplessness of the human individual; as he saw it, Pelagius did not sufficiently recognize the immense generosity of the divine gift. Everyone since Adam is a sinner. Everyone was contaminated by Adam's original sin and everyone but a newborn infant was guilty of particular actual sins as well. It was an act of incomprehensible mercy on God's part to discount all this in the case of the people he chose to be in his 'city'. To preach that one could earn a place there by one's own efforts was to insult God and treat his generosity as something cheap. Pelagians, as Augustine observed, were not above playing safe and bringing their infant to be baptized just in case.

The debates about organization and institutional structure

The traditional 'marks' or 'notes' of the church (describing it as 'one, holy, catholic and apostolic') were first formally pronounced by the Council of Nicaea in 325. They have a settled air. Yet this was not the calm pronouncement of a church confident in its own iden-tity and merely stating the obvious. In reality the Council of Nicaea was an emergency meeting, summoned by Constantine who had recently become the Roman Empire's first Christian Emperor.[8]

It was urgently needed to deal with the fundamental challenge posed by the followers of Arius to the way Christians understood the divinity and humanity of Christ. This was a theme not far removed from ecclesiological concerns as they then stood. Athanasius, Arius' chief adversary, took the idea of the mystical body very seriously. Those who are 'in Christ' are made sons of God by adoption, by an incorporation which enables them to participate in his death and resurrection and also in his immortality.

The Council produced the Nicene Creed, a brief official statement of the orthodox faith which (in the slightly revised form put out by the Council of Constantinople in 381), has remained fundamental throughout almost all of Christendom ever since. The World Council of Churches made a special study of it in the last decades of the twentieth century precisely because it was the document most likely to be 'owned' by the majority of the divided ecclesial communities attempting ecumenical rapprochement.

In time this came to be regarded as the first 'Ecumenical Council', that is, a formal gathering of the whole ('universal') church in the persons of the leaders of the churches all over the world, in the presence of the Holy Spirit, capable of defining the essentials of the faith in a way which would be authoritative for all Christians everywhere and for all time. That first list of 'marks' of the church appears almost as a 'throw-away line', a natural starting-point with which everyone can be expected to agree. Its appearance as a bold statement tells us a good deal about the emergence of the key threads in the formation of the idea of the church up to that point.

The church, in the account the early writers give of it, resembles an organic growth in response to practical problems and questions of principle arising, rather than an imposed plan. When it came to the theory, the minds of the New Testament writers ran to metaphor rather than to philosophical or theological concepts. Clusters of passages containing attempts to express aspects of the idea of the church occur in the New Testament texts, revealing that some of these images and analogies established themselves early. These principally concerned the relationship of Christ and the church. Christ loves the church; Christ is head of the church and the church is subject to Christ (Eph 5). Christ is the 'head' of the 'body' which is the church (Col 1.18). Christians could even been seen as forming 'one Christ' through their union with Christ. (una quaedam persona, as Augustine (354–430), Bishop of Hippo, puts it).[9] Concomitant with this sense of the church's intimate association with Christ are the frequent insistences on the divine 'ownership' of the church, and a budding sense of the activity within it of the individual Persons of the Trinity – for example in the emphasis on the church as the church of God in which the Holy Spirit appoints ministers (Acts 20.28). The Holy Spirit also appears as a directing influence in the New Testament account of the early church in the form of a 'witness' (Acts 20.23). The taste for imagery and analogies was persistent. Hermas, a freed Christian slave of the second century, wrote The Shepherd, a series of visions. In one of the visions the church appears to him in the form of a tower. Two centuries later, Augustine, preaching a long series of sermons on the Psalms, looked at the heavens for a comparison. Just as the moon and stars are established in the heavens, so is the universal church (luna et stellae in caelis sunt fundata, quia et universalis ecclesia). The universal church is like the moon and the individual local churches are like the stars.[10]

Church and state

The highly political complexion of the way the Council of Nicaea was held is a reminder that the young church was not emerging in a vacuum. A consciousness of the political and social context was apparent from the first, when Jesus, asked whether his followers must pay the taxes the state imposed, replied that they should render to Caesar what was Caesar's (Mt 22.21; Mk 12.17). It was also of a piece with Paul's teaching that slaves should obey their masters (Col 3.22).

Christianity did not set out to be revolutionary in the ways feared by the civil authorities of Jesus' day. He was not a Messiah who was going to lead a rabble through the streets or start an uprising. He had made that plain by riding into Jerusalem not in triumph but on an ass (Mt 21.2). But the Christians rapidly turned out to be a collective thorn in the flesh of politicians in a rather different way. As the Roman Empire grew, it perforce took in adherents of many different religions in the lands it conquered. Its usual practice was to encourage syncretism. In many cases, lists of equivalent deities were easy enough to draw up. The

Romans called the king of the gods Jupiter and the queen of the gods Juno and the Greeks called them Zeus and Hera respectively. Polytheists were not unduly disturbed by the addition of more gods to the pantheon, though there were some discomforts when it came to the inclusion of the mystery religions of Asia Minor, such as Mithraism.[11] It was not a long step to the expectation that citizens would be willing to worship their emperor if required, and regard him too as a god. This became a useful instrument of state control in the Roman Empire. Augustine speaks of this 'civic religion' in Book VI.7–12 of his *The City of God*.

Jews and Christians would not accept this approach. They were determined monotheists and that led to a series of persecutions in the early church. At first these were not initiated by the state and seem to have been prompted by hostility to Christians because they were 'different', did not 'join in', and alarmist myths circulated about them. Imperial authority stepped in during the reign of the Emperor Decius, who in 249 ordered all his subjects to sacrifice to the pagan gods. Decius died in 251 but the Emperor Valerian began further persecutions in 257–8, imposing the death penalty on Christian clergy who would not sacrifice to the gods. Diocletian began a new period of persecution in 303, ordering church buildings to be burned and copies of the Christian scriptures seized. Christians were not to meet for worship and they were to enjoy the privileges of citizenship only if they agreed to sacrifice to the pagan gods. This sort of thing went on in the East longer than in the West, where Constantine became Emperor in 306. Frightened Christians, even their leaders, were sometimes terrorized into apostasy, even handing over their copies of the scriptures to the state bullies, making them *traditores*, 'handers-over' (the literal meaning of 'traitors').

The ecclesial implications of the conversion of the Emperor Constantine were therefore very considerable. Christian expectations were transformed and placed on a secure basis socially and politically. The missionary activities of Christians had, from the first, been influenced by the existence of the Empire, with its trade and travelling routes and its organizational unity. The letters to the young churches which were eventually included in the New Testament testify to that. Something of a consolidation was now possible.

But the same new security could prompt a backlash. A century later, when the Empire was under serious threat from barbarian invaders and Rome itself fell in 410, wealthy educated pagans began to flee from Italy to the fringes of empire in North Africa. Augustine wrote *The City of God* partly to answer their indignant questions when they arrived in his congregations at Hippo. They were asking him why, since the Empire had become officially Christian, it had begun to go downhill politically and economically. His answer was that one must take a large view of the providential purposes of God. He had his plan. Within that plan the fall of the Roman Empire was a minor matter. It was not to be taken to suggest that the God of the Christians was less than omnipotent.

The end of empire proceeded, and the church's continuing administrative role became important in maintaining some continuity of civilization and practical provision of the necessities of secular life. The correspondence of Gregory the Great (c. 540–604), who became Pope from 590 after a lengthy career in the secular and ecclesiastical civil service, is concerned with the distribution of grain as well as questions of theology and spiritual jurisdiction.

Local and universal

One of the ecclesiological fundamentals already to be found in the New Testament is the acceptance that local communities are in some sense 'churches', although there is only one church. The New Testament texts are not at all tidy in their indications here, except insofar as they see a 'church' as having a geographical location and a territorial identity. There cannot be two churches in one place. Paul writes to some of these 'local' churches as 'the church of God that is in Corinth' (1 Cor 1.2, RSV) or 'the church of God that is in Corinth including all the saints throughout Achaia' (2 Cor 1.1, RSV). But he also addresses himself to the local church as though it is a self-contained entity: 'the church of the Thessalonians' (1 Thess 1.1), or simply to the community, 'the saints and faithful brothers and sisters' (Col 1.2).

The letters to the churches which are preserved in the New Testament, mostly written by Paul, make it plain that these local communities were full of independent life, engaged in debate, sometimes on matters of considerable importance to the future unity of Christian faith, and also subject to unedifying quarrels, for which Paul reprimands them in terms which were later seen to have clear ecclesiological implications. For example, he writes to the church at Corinth (1 Cor 1.10) begging the Christians there to ensure that they do not allow divisions to persist among them but strive to be united in the same mind and the same purpose. So these multiple local churches were from the first not mere local church buildings or places of worship. They were communities or fellowships, and it was evident that there would have to be clarification of the ways in which they were related to one another and to the one church.

One possibility, later strongest in the West, was to view the local churches as parts of the whole. This way of thinking encouraged Ambrose of Milan (c. 339–97), for example, to see schism and heresy in terms of a fragmentation of Christ's body into broken pieces.[12] This went naturally with the view that those present at a meeting of the churches or 'council' represented the relevant local churches and only those churches could subsequently be bound by what had been agreed. That became the normative assumption when 'councils' were held at which representatives of the churches of a particular geographical area came together at intervals to discuss matters of common concern. A group of local churches might set out disciplinary rules or decisions about the choice of liturgical rites, on the understanding that these would apply in the places where the participating churches held territorial sway.

But there was also a conception of a relationship more like that of microcosm to macrocosm, flowing naturally from the way Paul expressed himself in writing to the church of his day at Corinth. Theodoret (c. 393–c. 460) saw the many geographically distinct churches as one church spiritually (In Cant. Cant., 3.6.1–4, PG 81.166). This was the way of looking at it which tended to be preferred in the East; in the Anglican–Orthodox ecumenical dialogues of the late twentieth century it remained natural to the Orthodox to see the local church as the whole church in microcosm, rather than as a geographically distinct section of it.[13]

The leader of the 'local church'?

Whichever model or image is to be preferred, a number of practical questions had to be addressed. How was the local church 'unit' to be defined and its boundaries settled, and how was it to be decided what it was allowed to do for itself?

The answer which emerged is that each church has a separate leader, its 'bishop'.

Augustine also had important things to say about the mode of episcopal leadership. The bishop was to be 'with and among' his people, their servant, not lording himself over them, though Gregory the Great inclined rather more to the view that a bishop is an overseer, and a *rector* or ruler. But they agreed that the bishop in some sense held the local diocesan church together in his person.

This made him the natural representative of his people, the right person to go on their behalf to any meetings of the churches in councils or synods and to speak for them. 'The bishops assembled at Nicaea, . . . constitute the great and holy synod.'[14] The representative function was understood to allow him to act 'in the person' of the community. This personal role made the bishop a point of intersection in the wider and longer life of the church. He and his fellow-bishops met in councils and synods and that was one plane of the church's life. The church had a historical continuity, which formed another plane, and here too the bishops were important, because they carried the apostolic succession in their persons. The local community was the third plane. Three planes intersect at a point, and by analogy the three 'planes' of the church's life were seen to intersect in the 'person' of a bishop.

These are in themselves purely ecclesiological developments, but it should not be forgotten how important the social implications of a bishop's standing could be. Ambrose (c. 339–97) was bishop of Milan from 373/4. At the time when the local people clamoured for him to be made their bishop he was not yet baptized, although he had been brought up in a Christian family; he remained a mere catechumen at the time. In 1 Timothy 3.6–7 Paul had expressed the concern that the rapid promotion of a recent convert was likely to expose him to temptation. The Apostolic Canons (80) laid down the rule that no one should be made a priest or a bishop as soon as he had been baptized. Canon 2 of the Council of Nicaea 325 reinforces this rule, noting that 'a catechumen needs time and further probation after baptism'.[15]

'Diocesan bishops are not to intrude in churches beyond their own boundaries', says the Council of Constantinople 381, Canon 2.[16] An *ecclesia* (Greek *ekklēsia*) was from an early stage a geographical area in which a single leader or *episcopus* (Greek *episkopos*) had pastoral care of the people.

Within his diocese he allowed priests to minister in a fashion which made them his 'vicars', exercising on his behalf a ministry which remained the bishop's. Thus when a priest wished to travel to another diocese his bishop would write a letter for him to take with him, introducing him to his new bishop, testifying to the fact that he was genuinely a priest and a priest in good standing. Canons 15 and 16 of the Council of Nicaea emphasize the importance of clergy remaining in the diocese, that is, the local church where they were ordained, with provision for them to be sent back there smartly if they try to move elsewhere without permission.[17]

Initially the diocese was normally in a major city. There was the bishop's *cathedra* or throne, and from there he taught the people. The principal church building of the diocese derived its title of 'cathedral' from the cathedra's presence. The unitary character of a diocese as a local church was put under some stress as the typical diocese ceased to be a church centred on a city and moved out to include rural areas. And the vocabulary used to describe the diocese has never become wholly consistent. What is now generally called a 'diocese' in the West and a 'paroikia' in the East could be described in either way in Africa, though 'diocese' was usual there by the fourth century. *Diocesis* is used in the *Gesta* of the Council of Carthage 411 (Chapter 162.28., CCSL 149A pp. 3–257). Nevertheless, the bishop's role as leader of the community was not compromised by this blurring of the original notion of a local church with its pastor.

There is already a recognition of the privileged position of the apostles and of Paul, the 'last' of the apostles in the New Testament, This seems to have involved an element of local leadership, for which the heirs of the apostles had particular responsibility. Acts 20.17 speaks of the elders of the church. In Acts 20.28 Paul's farewell to the elders at Ephesus includes the assertion that the Holy Spirit has made them overseers of the flock there. Clement of Rome before the end of the first century emphasizes the importance of the line of succession of ministry from the apostles and of the apostles from Christ.

This expectation of continuity of succession in the original commission to the apostles created fresh difficulties as the local churches grew. One pastoral leader could not always cope with the work, and the notion of assistant bishops or priests became established. These additional ministers tended to be seen as exercising the bishop's ministry and not their own.

The emergence of different ministries

One of the decisions recorded in the Acts of the Apostles (Acts 6.5) was that the role of those who were to look after the practical needs of the community, and ensure that widows and orphans did not go hungry and unprotected, should be formally separated from that of the leaders. The word *diaconos* is not used in this passage, but it appears elsewhere (Phil 1.1 and 1 Tim 3.8), where deacons seem to be envisaged as aides or assistants to bishops, a role not incompatible with their having complementary functions such as those hinted at in Acts 6.

Clement of Rome (fl. *c.* 96), one of the earliest successors to Peter as leader of the church in Rome, mentions deacons in his Epistle to the Corinthians. Nevertheless, his first category of specialist ministry, that of the deacons, did not long remain distinct in the way Acts 6 indicates. By the time Ignatius of Antioch (*c.* 35–107) was writing his letters, the diaconate had begun to become the first stepping-stone on a ladder to be climbed by those in search of the highest ecclesiastical office, with the diaconate occupying a third place below bishops and priests, though practice still varied from place to place and there was a good deal of continuing fluidity.

It was part of this emerging pattern that although deacons had a role in worship in the ministry of the Word, reading the Gospel as well as the Epistle and leading the prayers of the congregation, they did not consecrate the bread and wine. Canon 18 of the Council of Nicaea notes that deacons do not have authority to 'offer' at the eucharist.[18] Canon 18 of Nicaea also condemns any breach of hierarchical discipline, as when deacons presume to give the body of Christ to priests who are their seniors even though they themselves do not have the authority to consecrate the elements.[19] (Deaconesses, says Canon 19 of the Council of Nicaea, do not receive imposition of hands and are to be regarded as laity.)[20]

A debate about terminology and function extended through the early centuries and beyond. Were the 'elders' of the New Testament (for example, Acts 14.23; Tit 1.5; Jas 5.14), *presbyteroi* or e*piskopoi* and what was the difference at that time, if any?

One of their roles was to preside at the eucharist, saying, *in persona Christi*, the words of Jesus which consecrated the bread and the wine (Lk 22.17–19). *Sacerdos* was not one of the terms about whose application to the roles and functions of ordained ministers there was active dispute in the first centuries. The word *sacerdos* was not particularly controversial in this connection. It is an Old Testament term in the Vulgate and was already discussed by Tertullian and Ambrose in that context. Cyprian is interested in the way Christ is identified as a priest in the order of Melchisedech (Heb 5.10), but there is no hint in the early church of the kind of argument which split the church in the Reformation of the sixteenth century, in which one side claimed that to call a minister a priest is to allow him to usurp a ministry unique to Christ. The East in particular did not work out a sacramental theology in any systematic way in the early centuries.

Another role of the bishop, and of the priest acting on behalf of his bishop, was that of pastor or shepherd of the local flock, a self-evidently ecclesial responsibility. The terms *sacerdos et pastor* are linked by the Council of Tours 567 (CCSL 148A pp. 176–99). Isidore of Seville (*c.* 560–636) comments in his *Sententiae* that 'just as the shepherd stays awake to guard his sheep against attack [by wolves], so the priest of God is careful to ensure that Christ's flock is not laid waste by the Enemy' (PL 83.714).

Of the remaining roles of the senior ordained ministry, the declaring of absolution to repentant sinners began by being restricted to the bishop. It passed to priests when the public penance of the early period became the routine private penance which everyone would need to make from time to time. The penitent confessed to his priest and was absolved. There was no longer an expectation that such absolution could be granted only by a bishop.[21]

It remained true throughout our period that only a bishop could ordain priests or, by joining with other bishops, participate in the ordination of a bishop. That authority to ordain never moved to priests themselves.

Provinces

Clusters of dioceses formed themselves into geographical groups, roughly following the secular organization of the Roman Empire. A metropolitan city would have its metropolitan bishop, who was recognized as leader by the bishops of lesser cities on the strength of the secular importance of the city where he had his see. Sometimes in African provinces the senior bishop was simply the one who had been consecrated earliest. The Council of Nicaea of 325 first rationalized and gave an authoritative stamp to this practice and it was the first council to use the term 'metropolitan' for such senior bishops, with, as a rule, the bishop of the diocese which was the local capital city at their head. Canons 4, 6 and 7 deal with problems which had arisen in the local application of what ought to be consistent principles. There are a number of fine points concerning the respective claims of ancient custom about metropolitan jurisdictions and exactly which senior bishops may use the title.

The working relationship of the senior bishop of the province to the other bishops gave rise to a number of practical considerations with ecclesiological implications. For example, were the lowlier bishops his suffragans? What say should he have in the replacement of bishops in the sees of his province? Should local councils and synods be summoned by the metropolitan? (The terms are largely interchangeable, derivatives respectively of the Latin and Greek for much the same thing.) On such points there was variation of understanding and practice, but on one matter there seems to have been unanimity. The metropolitan bishop did not hold a higher order. He remained still a mere bishop.

By the sixth century the aggregation of local sees into groups extending over larger geographical areas had enlarged itself still further. The great patriarchates of the ancient world were identified at the Council of Nicaea in 325 as Antioch, Alexandria and Rome; Constantinople was added in 381, for Constantinople was the 'new Rome' founded by Constantine the first Christian Emperor. The first Council of Constantinople in 381 (canon 3) expressly decreed that 'because it is new Rome, the bishop of Constantinople is to enjoy the privilege of honour after the bishop of Rome'.[22] Jerusalem was added to complete the five at the Council of Chalcedon in 451. The Patriarchs exercised authority over the metropolitans, both in terms of the authority to ordain metropolitans and the judicial authority to hear disciplinary accusations against them and to act as a court of appeal from judgements of the metropolitans in their own courts. Primacy did not constitute a higher order, however, nor did being a metropolitan. A retired primate or metropolitan was a bishop. A retired bishop would remain a bishop.

Primacy

Beyond this change lay the shadow of another, very far-reaching development. The Patriarch was primate of a large and significant area. But which primate was primate of all? Rome, claimed Gregory the Great, on the authority of Jesus' words to Peter, first Bishop of Rome, when he told him that he was the rock on which the church was to be built (Mt 16.18).

The emergence of an ecclesiology of primacy also threw up new challenges about the role of councils and synods. The essence of a council was that it brought together all the 'local' bishops who would then confer and reach decisions which were sent out as 'decrees'. Unanimity was a requirement strongly emphasized by the early councils. Not only the creeds and canons of councils were considered 'authoritative' but also a good proportion of any additional material which happened to survive, such as letters sent from the Council to those who had not been present.[23]

Would a primate have authority to overrule a council? The Eastern patriarchates had more or less accepted the primacy of Rome during the first centuries, at least as a primacy of honour. But a primacy of jurisdiction was another matter, as was any notion that Rome had a primacy which would allow it to determine disputed matters of faith or order on behalf of the whole church. Ambrose had a great respect for Roman primacy and went so far as to say that he thought significant questions of faith and order, including problems arising in the relations of churches, ought to be referred to the Bishop of Rome for determination (Letter 56.7 and 13.7). Optatus of Milevis and Augustine were of much the same view.

The popes themselves were not slow to foster this kind of thinking, notably Damasus (366–84), Siricius (384–99) and Innocent (402–17), popes of Augustine's lifetime. Leo I (440–61) wrote to Anastasius the Bishop of Thessalonica in 446 to set out a comprehensive view (Letter 14.11. PL54.7577). Jesus gave Peter supreme authority in the church. Peter was the first Bishop of Rome and, Leo claims, he handed on that authority to his successors. Gregory the Great took this further, refusing to acknowledge the claim of the Patriarch of Constantinople to the title of 'Ecumenical Patriarch'.

The maintenance of the faith

It was decided in the period recorded in Acts 6 that one of the responsibilities of leadership was to teach the faith. It was also accepted very early that there must only ever be one faith. One of the most necessary tasks of the first centuries was to work out how this was to be done within the church in a way which would protect the integrity of this faith.

A defining moment is described in Acts 15, when a division of teaching threatened the unity of the community. Some of its leaders thought that the requirements of Old Testament practice, such as circumcision, ought to apply to Jesus' followers too. Others favoured a new beginning, in keeping with the freedoms Jesus had promised. This was no small question and the community at Jerusalem dealt with it by behaving like a council and seeking consensus through debate. They also appointed missionary leaders to convey their consensus to other communities.

The conception of the unity of the faith became linked with the notion that the church could not ultimately lose it or go seriously wrong so long as it kept together and spoke with one voice. Cyril of Jerusalem wrote (*Catechetical Lectures*, 18.16 and 19) that Jesus' words to Peter when he described him as the Rock on which the church would be built (Mt 16.18) amounted to a promise that the church would be indefectible. This confidence was spelt out by Vincent of Lérins in his *Commonitorium*. The church is to hold what has been held 'everywhere, always and by everyone', he says. This is what it is for the church to be truly *catholica* and *universalis*. The traditions of the universal church which the catholic and apostolic church follow must share the unanimous consensus of old.[24] Augustine spoke in similar language about the 'consensus' of the faithful in his *De peccatorum meritis et remissione et de baptismo parvulorum* (III.ii.2, CSEL 60, p. 130). At this point in the church's history there was no real anxiety that there might be any conflict between consensus and authoritative top-down teaching, or between a monarchical primacy and a collegial conciliarity.

The affirmation of faith in the church: the creeds

The 'Apostles' Creed' was used only in the West. Unlike the Nicene Creed its origins are liturgical and it is essentially an expression of the faith of the church as a body. The Apostles' Creed encapsulates the notion of 'one faith, one baptism'. It seems to derive from the creed used in the early Roman church, and it has the characteristic three sections relating to the three questions asked of those who offered themselves for baptism, concerning faith in God the Father, Christ and the Holy Spirit respectively. Ambrose of Milan mentions it in Letter 42.5, about 390, describing it as the composition of the apostles, for by that date the story of the apostles meeting to compose it by providing a clause each was well established.

The ministry of the Word

Among the surviving texts of the first centuries in the West are exegetical sermons preached by bishops. Ambrose of Milan, Augustine of Hippo, Gregory the Great were all fond of preaching lengthy series in which they worked their way through books of the Bible. Each sermon was substantial in itself and would require the congregation's attention for an hour or more. Such preaching was done from the cathedra, or bishop's seat in the cathedral, and formed part of a liturgy. This solemn instruction in the way the text of scripture was to be understood went far beyond the preaching of a sermon on a 'set text' or reading. It reflected a respect for the Word and a seriousness about ensuring that the people were familiar with it and could think about it intelligently (at a period when Latin was the vernacular and they would have no difficulty in understanding what was read to them).

Yet clarity about what was and what was not to be regarded as scripture was slow to emerge and the process underlines at every point the importance of the church as the vehicle of transmission and approval and acceptance of the Christian writings from which the 'canon' of scripture was ultimately agreed upon. The *Didache* (first to second century) was considered to be part of scripture by Clement of Alexandria (*c.* 150–*c.* 215). Eusebius of Caesarea (*c.* 260–*c.* 340) knew of it and also Athanasius, the contemporary of Arius. It contains details of the church life of the earliest Christians, their preference for baptism by immersion, their fasting on Wednesdays and Fridays, the forms of their eucharistic prayers. The *Didascalia Apostolorum*, probably written in Syria in the early third century by a converted Jew, gives guidance to Christians on a number of practical points of the Christian life. It was worked into the *Apostolic Constitutions*. The *Apostolic Constitutions* themselves, also probably deriving from the Syrian churches, were a fourth-century product of an authorship coloured by more than a hint of Arianism. The Apostolic Canons form the last chapter of the *Apostolic Constitutions* and date from about 350–80. They are of interest for the way they list the books of scripture in the last of the canons, including among them these canons themselves.

Jerome (c. 345–420), who was encouraged by Pope Damasus to prepare a new, definitive Latin translation of the Bible at a period when Augustine was preaching on the Bible as the established Word of God, was still discussing exactly which books were scripture and which were not. The 'canon' was probably defined only about 382. The emergence of an agreement about what was to be included was itself an act of the church.

Maintaining the faith and matters of 'order'

Where does the boundary lie between a matter of faith (on which the church must preserve 'one mind) and a matter of order? It was accepted from an early stage that local worshipping communities did not have to use exactly the same liturgies. Hippolytus, probable author of the *Apostolic Tradition* (the original Greek text is now incomplete but Latin translation survives), describes various rites, including baptism, eucharist and ordination. This may represent the way things were done in Rome in the early third century, but it did not constitute a fixed point of reference for other places. Yet in all variations of rites is embedded a theology which must reflect the expectation that Christians shared one faith and that faith will never change. Paul says that women should learn in silence in church (1 Tim 2.11). Is this a matter of faith (which cannot change) or of order (which may)?

The idea that baptism can happen only once and that it irrevocably changes the relationship of the person baptized not only to God but to the church is hinted at in Ephesians 1.13, and Clement of Alexandria spoke of baptism as a 'sealing'. Is ordination too a once-and-for-all and irrevocable act? The terminology of 'character' seems to have been a medieval and Western invention, but the underlying questions were arising much earlier. If something subsequently happens to bring into question his acceptability for ordination, can someone once ordained have its effect removed, or can he only be suspended from the exercise of a perpetual ministry? For instance, does the presumption that priests must be 'entire' males affect the answer to this question? The Council of Nicaea 325, Canon 1, sets out the rules for priests who become eunuchs in the expectation that they will embody the general principles appropriate to the decrees of a 'universal' council. Someone who has been castrated for medical reasons or 'by barbarians' may remain a priest, but if someone voluntarily castrates himself he is to be suspended.[25] Would it be appropriate for fundamental questions of this sort to be answered differently in different places?

Keeping the church together: heresy and schism

Schism is division of the church; heresy is obstinate persistence in a belief which the church has 'decided' is not part of the faith. But like 'faith and order', 'schism' and 'heresy' overlap. Augustine considered that schism was a heresy because he regarded the doctrine of the unity of the church as itself a point of faith. The lists given earlier of categories of outsider who could and could not be admitted to the catholic communion illustrate the complexity of the question when wrong faith became church-dividing. Lucifer Calaritanus, Bishop of Cagliari (d. 370/71) was passionately of the view that there must be no associating with heretics, in particular with the Arians (*De non conveniendo cum haereticis*).

A person with uncertainties about what to believe is not a heretic. Nor is someone with doubts. The heretic is someone who wilfully goes against the consensus of the community about the content of the faith. But how is that consensus formed and expressed and how does it become clear when it has reached a defining moment? It is all very well to say that *haeresis* involves the making of a deliberate choice to keep to a wrong or false belief, but who is to declare that it is 'wrong'? Where does authority lie in the church to determine the matter?

The early church had to make its collective mind up on such points at the same time as it was dealing with a series of very difficult questions about some of the most central points of the faith. It had to determine the locus of its own authority while exercising that authority. One possibility was to lodge decision-making authority with the bishops as leaders of the community. Tertullian insisted that the true church is to be identified in a visible episcopal succession through history, to which is entrusted the stewardship of the tradition which began with Christ's commissioning of his disciples to be the apostles; only this church can be trusted to interpret the scriptures faithfully and so it also has a duty to maintain and communicate the faith. But the bishops made their decisions collectively, in council, and with a conscious reference to the importance of preserving unanimity down the ages to which Vincent of Lérins made implicit reference in his *Commonitorium*.

The Donatist schism

In about 311 Caecilian was consecrated as Bishop of Carthage by Felix of Aptunga. He had handed over the scriptures during the persecution initiated under the Emperor Diocletian and had consequently become a *traditor*. The bishops of Numidia objected that this consecration could not be valid and consecrated a rival. A schism began, directly reflecting the problematic character of the question of the overlap of faith and order. Attempts to resolve the matter by the Synod of Arles in 314, and then two years later by the Emperor, failed, for the Donatists had coalesced into something of a local interest group. They claimed that they had the authority of Cyprian for their position. The rigorist tradition had a strong appeal to them because they wanted to hold that they were protecting the purity of the church. Donatists saw it as a mark of the true church that it should be without spot or wrinkle, an ecclesiology arguably incompatible with a doctrine of the mixed church as propounded by Augustine, which was itself a challenge to the doctrine of the holiness of the church which was so important in the East. The Donatists' idea was that those who communicate with anyone who countenanced what they regarded as a contaminated non-church were themselves contaminated. The continuing modern topicality of all this has become apparent with the controversies about the use of 'flying bishops' to accommodate those who cannot accept the ordination of women or practising homosexuals.[26]

Gangs of wandering trouble-makers calling themselves Donatists began to constitute a social nuisance and government attempts were made to suppress these *circumcelliones* in the mid-340s. Not all the Donatists were mere bandits. Tyconius the Donatist wrote a treatise on the interpretation of scripture containing an exegetical theory which commanded the respect of Augustine and which he himself utilized. Their position had become newly topical with further government intervention from 405, culminating in a conference at Carthage in 411, at which the Emperor's emissary issued a final condemnation of the Donatist position.

The chief intellectual protagonist against the Donatists was Augustine of Hippo. Augustine was prompted by the debates about Donatism to give serious thought to the question of how far schism was itself to be regarded as a heresy.

The Easter controversy

Of great importance ecclesially was the dispute about the way the date of Easter should be calculated. The Council of Nicaea wrote a letter to the Egyptians in which it announced (prematurely) that the disagreement about the date of Easter had been resolved: 'All the brethren in the East who have hitherto followed the Jewish practice will henceforth observe the customs of the Romans and of yourselves and of all of us who from ancient times have kept Easter together with you.'[27] Hilary of Poitiers describes the celebration of the eucharist as an expression of the unity of the church (*De Trinitate*, 8.15ff). The debate about the date of Easter, which was still going on in the seventh century, drew much of its energy from the sense on both sides that the unity of the church was manifested in the celebration of Easter in a eucharist held on the same day everywhere, so that the difficulty of agreeing which day this should be in any given year was actually dividing the church.

Conclusion

To get a sense of where these matters lay at the end of the sixth century, particularly in the West, we need only look at the situation in England at the time of the mission of the Augustine who became Bishop of Canterbury. As bishop he sent Pope Gregory the Great a series of mainly ecclesiological questions which are reported by Bede, together with Gregory's replies.[28] One question concerns the legitimacy of variation of rites. Gregory's advice to Augustine is that he should make a selection of practices, drawing upon those with which he is familiar from his own early life in Rome and those he knows from his contacts with Gaul, and create a set of rites which will be appropriate for the use of the new church in England. Another question is about the consecration of bishops. Although a single bishop could ordain priests, it was well-established (Canon 4 of the Council of Nicaea) that in normal circumstances all the bishops of a province should come together to ordain a new bishop. If the distances are too great or there are special circumstances, the number may be reduced but at the very least, it took three bishops to ordain a bishop. Augustine asks whether even this can be relaxed in emergency, for example, where distance makes it a practical impossibility to gather a sufficient number of bishops together. Gregory accepts that Augustine can hardly expect bishops to come over from Gaul to help him ordain the bishops he needs for the new English church. But he instructs him to ordain the bishops he will need in the first instance in such a way that they will be within reach and the emergency will not need to occur in future. Another question concerns territorial jurisdiction and questions of seniority among bishops. Augustine cannot be given authority over the bishops of Gaul because earlier popes gave the *pallium* (the stole of office) to the Bishop of Arles. So if he finds anything reprehensible going on he must treat the local bishops as equals and discuss with them tactfully how they may put matters right in their own dioceses, says Gregory. So on many of these points of technical but ecclesiologically significant detail, answers could now be furnished with some confidence.

The church had a written history now. Eusebius of Caesarea (*c.* 260–*c.*340, Bishop of Caesarea from at least 315) had the idea of writing a history of the church, mainly in the East and mainly in the form of a compilation of extracts from the writings of others; others took up the idea, however, and began to create a historiographical tradition.

And the church had a prophetic as well as a temporal future. The *Didache* discusses the second coming and includes prophecy about Antichrist (16), but as the generations went on, theories about the place of the church in the world to come developed with the ecclesiology.

Notes

1 *Decrees of the Ecumenical Councils*, ed. G. Alberigo *et al.*, and ed. and tr. N.Tanner, Washington DC: Georgetown University Press, 1990, 2 vols, Vol. I, p. 13.
2 Ambrose, *De officiis ministrorum*, ed. G. Krabinger, Tübingen, 1857.
3 Theodore of Mopsuestia, *On the Minor Epistles of St. Paul*, ed. H.B. Sweet, Cambridge, 1880, 2 vols, II, pp. 99–108.
4 Theodore of Mopsuestia, *On the Minor Epistles of St. Paul*, II, pp. 111–14.
5 *Decrees of the Ecumenical Councils*, I, p. 8.
6 *Decrees of the Ecumenical Councils*, I, p. 11.
7 This was in line with the teaching of Tertullian (*c.* 160–*c.* 225), for whom rigorism went with asceticism and a kind of early Puritanism.
8 The convention developed that a secular ruler was permitted to call such a council but not participate in the decision-making.
9 *Enn in Ps.* 30(2) I.4, CCSL 38, p. 193.
10 *In Ps.* 8.ix, CCSL 38, p. 53.
11 F. Cumont, *Les réligions orientales dans la paganisme romaine*, Paris: Chicago UP, 1906.
12 *De poen.* 2.iv.24, CSEL, 73, p. 173.
13 See Chapter 22, 'Ecclesiology and Ecumenism'.
14 *Decrees of the Ecumenical Councils*, I, p. 16.
15 *Decrees of the Ecumenical Councils*, I, p. 6.
16 *Decrees of the Ecumenical Councils*, I, p. 31.
17 *Decrees of the Ecumenical Councils*, I, pp. 13–14.
18 *Decrees of the Ecumenical Councils*, I, p. 14.
19 *Decrees of the Ecumenical Councils*, I, p. 14.
20 *Decrees of the Ecumenical Councils*, I, p. 15.
21 B. Poschmann, *Penance and the Anointing of the Sick* (Freiburg: Herder, 1964), remains a definitive discussion of the history of these transitions.
22 *Decrees of the Ecumenical Councils*, I, p. 32.
23 *Decrees of the Ecumenical Councils*, I, p. xi.
24 'In ipsa item catholica ecclesia magnopere curandum est, ut id teneamus quod ubique, quod semper, quod ab omnibus creditum est', Vincent of Lérins, *Commonitorium*, 2.5, ed. R. Demeulenaere, CCSL 64 (1985), p. 149. 'Universalis ecclesiae traditiones. . . . in qua item catholica et apostolica ecclesia sequantur necesse est universitatem antiquitatem consensionem', ibid., p. 186.
25 *Decrees of the Ecumenical Councils*, I, p. 6 ff.
26 See the discussion of the emergence of neo-exclusivism in Chapters 7 and 13.
27 *Decrees of the Ecumenical Councils*, I, p. 19.
28 Bede, *Ecclesiastical History*, ed. Bertram Colgrave and R.A.B. Mynors, Oxford: Clarendon Press, 1969, pp. 78–102.

Further reading

Augustine, *The City of God* (Penguin Classics, 2003), introduction by G.R. Evans.

Allan Brent, *Hippolytus and the Roman Church in the Third Century* (Brill, Leiden, 1995).

James Tunstead Burtchaell, *From Synagogue to Church* (Cambridge University Press, 1992).

Henry Chadwick, *The Early Church* (Penguin Books, 1967), a classic which has appeared in several later editions.

Stuart G. Hall, 'The early idea of the Church', in *The First Christian Theologians*, ed. G.R. Evans (Blackwell, 2004).

J.N.D. Kelly, *Early Christian Creeds* (Longman, 1950), a classic which has appeared in several later editions.

——*Early Christian Doctrines* (Adam and Charles Black, 1958), a classic which has appeared in several later editions.

David Rankin, *Tertullian and the Church* (Cambridge University Press, 1995).

Norman Tanner (ed. and tr.), *Decrees of the Ecumenical Councils*, ed. G. Alberigo *et al.*, (Georgeton, 1990), 2 vols.

3

THE CHURCH IN MEDIEVAL THEOLOGY

James R. Ginther

Medieval Ecclesiology as a category of thought is a combination of historical fact and theological fiction. There is no doubting the existence of a social and institutional entity bearing the name *ecclesia* during the medieval period, and indeed it would be difficult to study any aspect of medieval Europe and not discover some role or influence of a church.[1] Moreover, ecclesial functions and structures did not remain static over the period's thousand years and there is clear documentary evidence that on occasion Christians did take time to reflect upon what church means in order either to evoke or explain change. This in itself surely must be indelible evidence of an extant ecclesiology.

The historical fact has been enhanced, however, by theological fiction. Such a phrase is hardly pejorative and it does not imply that medieval ecclesiology was lacking any truth values. Rather, ecclesiology as a theological fiction points to two essential features. First, since the Church was a major medieval institution, its leaders and defenders exploited all available resources to protect and enhance it, including Roman civil law. Canon lawyers drew out the notion of discussing an institution as a person with its own standing before a court – the *persona fictiva*. The Church as a whole claimed the status of 'person' in law, a legal fiction that reinforced its corporate identity but never undermined the truth value of any legal or theological claim.[2] Second – and in keeping with the Latin verbal root of 'fiction' (*fingere*, to create or shape) – the phrase reminds us that this part of medieval theology has often been constructed (*fictus*) according to modern and post-modern theological agendas. Ecclesiology is the 'wax nose' of medieval theology: it can be shaped and re-shaped because, despite being grounded in historical fact, ecclesiology of the Middle Ages remained undeveloped. The doctrine of God, salvation, Incarnation, the life of virtue and penance, the sacraments – all these were recognizable categories of theological discourse and theologians continually addressed them throughout the Middle Ages. The same cannot be said for ecclesiology and attempts to identify an ecclesiological textual tradition have often yielded more frustration than fruit. Perhaps the greatest student of medieval ecclesiology, Yves-Marie Congar, concluded after the first twenty years of his research into pre-modern ecclesiology that the Middle Ages did not enjoy a 'proper' ecclesiology until the last quarter of the thirteenth century.[3] Congar was not alone in this opinion, as Artur Landgraf had come to a similar conclusion in his careful study of twelfth-century theology.[4] There are moments, indeed centuries, when the ecclesiological sources apparently fell silent.

That silence easily allowed for modern theological assumptions to overpower the narrative. Congar's claim to a 'proper ecclesiology' emerging only in the late thirteenth century is based as much upon the documentary evidence as his own ecclesiological commitments that were riveted to the twentieth century.[5] Even Landgraf's more moderate conclusion was based upon the assumption that treatments of the papacy were the definitive factor of any ecclesiology. In other words, the disparate data relevant to constructing a doctrine of *ecclesia* in the Middle Ages has been organized around themes that may have greater contemporary force than medieval fact. For example, can medieval ecclesiology be condensed into a juris-dictional tension between community (conciliarism) and leadership (papacy)? This is often presented as a fundamental issue, one sparked obviously by the Reform movements of the fifteenth and sixteenth centuries (but with some antecedents that stretch back into the core of the medieval period). This tension was clearly extant in both recent Vatican Councils and it remains a touchstone even as Catholic ecclesiology has begun to speak more about 'communion' than jurisdiction and leadership. The tension also enjoyed a serious revival in the middle of the twentieth century for medieval historians, thanks in large part to scholars such as Walter Ullmann, Brian Tierney and Francis Oakley.[6] But was this tension really at the core of all theological reflection on the nature, function and structure of the Church?

The silence of ecclesiological discourse is more apparent than real. I argue that the present model used to explore the theology of Church in the Middle Ages does not fully capture all the data and sources available to the historical theologian and that a new meth-odology needs to be adopted. By including additional sets of texts in their analysis, historical theologians can better capture the multivalent vision that medieval thinkers had of Church. Study of medieval ecclesiology must include an account of both ecclesial events and texts. To make this case, I first discuss whether the issue hinges on only one point of departure – in this case whether a bottom-up approach is better than a top-down one. Then I will outline the standard account of medieval ecclesiology, which will be followed by a suggestion on how it may first be amended. Finally, I want to introduce a set of textual resources rarely employed in the scholarship of medieval ecclesiology, namely expositions of the Psalms and commentaries on the Dionysian corpus.

Points of departure

If we find the current account of medieval ecclesiology deficient, the first solution might be to address its *point of departure*. Until recently those who studied the medieval understanding of Church had adopted a 'top-down' approach, or what Nicholas Healy has called *blueprint* ecclesiology: scholars consider the nature and function of the Church in ideal and abstract terms, so much so that they find it difficult to relate to the events on the ground as it were, and so are reduced to describing how 'real' churches only fail to live up to the ideal stan-dards.[7] This informs historical study in the sense that ecclesiological principles function a-historically and so, many assume, they can easily be applied to any given period. The alter-native is to adopt a 'bottom-up' approach which, according to Roger Haight, begins with the actual experience of being 'in church' and subsequently becomes the basis for under-standing how general principles may be abstracted from the concrete.[8] Haight in fact has adopted what Healy theorizes for contemporary ecclesiology, namely an approach to Church that focuses more on the drama of ecclesial experience than on the 'epic' narrative its expo-nents create.[9]

For any study of medieval ecclesiology, however, historical theologians must seek both points of departure – and for two important reasons. First, medieval thought gravitated to an essentialist analysis of all reality because the phenomena of everyday experience were considered to be illusory and misleading.[10] That approach was certainly echoed within the theological reflection on Church, and if so it would be difficult to avoid this aspect of medieval ecclesiology and still remain an honest exponent of the sources. Second, the contrast of these two points of departure can imply that they are almost incompatible, or at least leads to the conclusion that each provides a different etiology for medieval ecclesiology. To argue that somehow the abstract account of ecclesiology had no bearing on the events on the ground assumes an almost Durkheimian view of the development of ecclesial community. There were certainly moments of 'collective effervescence' that advanced the medieval view of Church, but the shaping of real-time ecclesial experience was itself shaped or ordered by the abstract and essentialist musing of Christian leaders. It would seem necessary, therefore, to consider the ecclesial experience and theological reflection about it in tandem when creating a narrative for medieval ecclesiology.

Such a broader and more coherent account of medieval ecclesiology necessitates fresh consideration, if we are to come to a better understanding of how medieval Christians identified themselves as part of a believing and worshipping community. This is no easy matter. Despite his demand for a new reading of medieval ecclesiology, Haight relies heavily upon those scholars who worked in a manner completely opposite to his own bottom-up approach.[11] How can he determine that he really has begun at the bottom, at the very locus where Christians engaged one another in community? Indeed, Haight's method requires a careful interplay between the practice of micro-history and the 'grand narrative' in order to establish what the 'in church' experience really was for the Middle Ages.[12]

How then do historical theologians keep their bearings as they wade deeply into the daily life of medieval Christians while simultaneously rising up to catch a view of the ideals that medieval theologians embraced in ecclesiological thought? The answer, I want to argue here, lies in providing a more coherent account of the resources they ought to utilize. If anything, historical theologians need to exploit in their research sets of texts that hitherto have not been (or at least rarely) attached to the study of medieval ecclesiology. I want to suggest that a richer set of texts comprises two general categories. Together they can be a helpful heuristic device for future study of the medieval theology of church.

Events as ecclesiological texts

In order to demonstrate why it is essential to expand the resources for medieval ecclesiology, let us focus now on its standard account.[13] Many scholars have described medieval ecclesiology as juridical in nature and papal in orientation.[14] It was juridical in nature because it was mainly concerned about institutional structures and how those structures operate within the context of Church–State relations. Granted, the Church–State dichotomy does not accurately represent the medieval experience, since most medieval thinkers would have found it bewildering to conceive of the 'State' as something outside of the Church. Nevertheless, most medieval ideas of the Church addressed the problem of where temporal authority fits into the Church, be it at the local, provincial or universal level.[15] This complex relationship has often been reduced to the tension between 'kingdom' (*regnum*) and 'priesthood' (*sacerdotium*). On a theoretical level secular rulers and church leaders alike were quick to identify their own and the other's jurisdiction and provide sophisticated reasons why a certain activity or social relationship fell under the authority of one or the other. More pragmatically speaking, political programmes could not but impinge on ecclesial territory and almost every religious practice had political implications. The result was an intertwining of 'Church and State' if only because the political leaders were Christian and any community of Christians was practically part of social structures.[16]

Medieval ecclesiology was papal in orientation because the papacy was at the apex of the ecclesiastical hierarchy. Nearly every medieval discussion of the idea of the Church addressed in some form or another the role and authority of the papacy, either in terms of the Church's relationship with temporal authority, or in terms of the pope's relationship with other members of the hierarchy. No matter what the point of departure was for any medieval text that historians have identified as ecclesiological, the papacy has always played a definitive role.[17]

The source for this general definition has been careful and scholarly historical observation, based on a wide reading of the sources. Scholars have examined the general narratives of the medieval church so as to extrapolate the implicit ecclesiology that motivated changes in structure, undergirded development of ministerial programmes and methods, and shaped relations amongst the various powers in Europe and the Mediterranean. While there have been some textual markers along the way – such as explicit statements in conciliar pronouncements, epistolary exchanges and theological tractates – for the most part the general contours of medieval ecclesiology are found in analysing the historical reality of Christian communities of the Middle Ages. In other words, one can describe this kind of ecclesiology as being centred in the event.

Event-centred ecclesiology is wholly sensible, as it begins with the assumption that the Church is first and foremost an historical entity. Even if one accepts ahistorical first principles in ecclesiology, one uncovers their meaning in how those principles were instantiated in a world of competing and complying social groups, all of which are made up of imperfect human beings. To accept the historicity of ecclesiology is also to recognize the incarnational nature of Christian communities. The communion of believers, the mystical body of Christ, extends the Christian axiom, the 'Word made flesh'. Equally importantly, event-centred ecclesiology puts greater hermeneutical pressure upon the historical theologian, who cannot simply conclude that any text containing ecclesiological content simply means what it says, but must rather interpret those textual resources within the broader context of the historical development or implementation of those principles, not to mention the presuppositions and historical experience of that text's author and initial readers.

Indeed, texts do matter in event-centred ecclesiology. In the late thirteenth century a *reflexive ecclesiology* began to make an appearance in texts. By 'reflexive' I mean that ecclesiology becomes more explicit in its formulation, a formulation that resulted from reflection on both ecclesial events and texts such as the *Politics* of Aristotle. This is what Congar meant by a 'proper ecclesiology' (*une ecclésiologie proprement dite*) appearing for the first time in the late thirteenth century.[18] This shift towards a more formal treatment of ecclesiology was still centred on an event, however, because it was the conflict between Pope Boniface VIII (r. 1294–1303) and Philip IV of France (r. 1285–1314) that engendered many of the treatises and polemical tractates. What had begun initially as a dispute over taxation exploded into a struggle over who had ultimate authority over the French church. Supporters of the royal side went so far as to question the legitimacy of Boniface's election, since his predecessor had resigned. This in turn launched a polemical debate about the process of papal resignation.[19] The struggle also led to one of the clearest claims of papal supremacy over temporal authority: the famous bull, *Unam Sanctam* (1302). As absolute as Boniface VIII's claim was for being the source of both spiritual and temporal power, it was a hollow one because the French crown ran roughshod over all papal prerogatives and eventually gained immense influence over the papacy for the remainder of the fourteenth century.[20]

Nonetheless, the most obvious change was the appearance of works with the title *tractatus de ecclesia*.[21] A complete census of such texts has yet to be achieved. A quick survey of the *In principio* database of medieval manuscripts (Brepols Publishers) reveals about thirty-nine works with the title *de ecclesia* (excluding hymns and works about a specific church), many of which have yet to be edited and studied. It is useful to note that at least three of these works were written prior to 1250: the *De mysteriis ecclesie* attributed to Hugh of St-Victor (PL 177.335–80), and two disputed questions, *de ecclesia bonorum* and *de ecclesia malorum* of Alexander of Hales. Another unexplored textual source for medieval ecclesiology is the liturgical guides to the dedication of a church.[22] Regardless of these neglected sources, medieval ecclesiology has normally been divided into two phases: a 'pre-history' from circa 400 to circa 1260, and the history of medieval ecclesiology, fully developed, from about 1260 to the end of the Middle Ages.[23]

Critiquing event-centred ecclesiology

The most obvious criticism of this account is the narrow understanding of 'event'. It assumes that the salient events that shaped or drove ecclesiological thought were found in the development of competing power structures in medieval Europe. In this context, historical theologians have accepted two significant watershed moments for medieval ecclesiology. The first was the transformation of the papacy during the Carolingian period from a religious centre of power constantly under threat in the Italian peninsula to an ultramontane authority that now enhanced (or shared, according to some proponents) the imperial power of Charlemagne's court and his successors.[24] The second is the so-called Gregorian reform of the eleventh century, when the papacy was finally released from secular influence and began its slow but assured rise to primacy in Latin Christendom.[25] These two watershed moments then become the focal points for tracing how Christians perceived the Church in terms of the political machinery of each period, demonstrating that ecclesiological thought must account for the origins of these momentous changes, and then how they subsequently played out in the following centuries.[26] In some instances these rarefied events of power struggles did have a broad impact, such as the eleventh-century reforms of papal elections which eventually became the model for the elections of all bishops in the Latin West. It begs the question, however, as to whether the significance of any ecclesial reform is determined by its relation to the events of the great men of the period. In this respect, medieval ecclesiology has yet to exorcise the demons of a traditional historiography, as other parts of medieval studies have already done in a perfunctory manner.

Nonetheless, it is unnecessary to cast the herd of swine over the cliff in order to envisage medieval ecclesiology afresh. Instead, to these events of the great men we ought to add two significant event-centred sources that can broaden our understanding of the 'in church' experience that is so necessary for an ecclesiology from below. The first is the physical locus of the Christian community itself: the buildings. If the assumption is that historical theologians can infer an ecclesiological mindset from the recorded events of medieval communities, then surely the same type of inferential reading is equally possible for ecclesial architecture and its adornment. Such a strategy, ironically, would take historical theologians back to the original meaning of 'ecclesiology', namely a study of church architecture.[27] Reading church architecture as a theological text would require careful attention to how medieval Christians themselves invested meaning into sacred space.[28] For example, perhaps the most common perception of the gothic church is the introduction of the altar screen as a replacement of the rood beam of earlier centuries. By enclosing the chancel or quire, it has appeared to the modern reader that this was one way to reinforce the division between the laity and a far more hierarchically minded clergy. True worship focused on the celebration of the eucharist, found only at the high altar, and the altar screen appears to have been a physical way of excluding the laity from that experience. For those who have studied religious experience from the twelfth to the fifteenth centuries, such an observation seemed incongruous with the increasing emphasis on the pastoral responsibilities of the clergy during the same period. Pastoral care required the priest to have greater and more meaningful contact with his parish by means of regular confession, preaching and the beginnings of catechetical instruction.[29] Moreover, in the midst of this supposed exclusion of the laity from the eucharist by means of architecture, there is the well-documented event of the laity demanding the elevation of the host during Mass.[30] This demand only makes sense if architecturally they were still able to see the altar. More recent scholarship has therefore presented a very different view of the meaning of that architectural plan of the gothic church: the altar screen was not a means of excluding anyone, but rather it was a physical reminder that the tasks assigned to both clergy and laity were not the same. The former was to celebrate the eucharist vicariously while the latter fulfilled their responsibility of prayer and meditation.[31]

Reading accurately and correctly the ecclesiological inferences of a church building demands a second set of event-centred texts: the liturgy.[32] No other textual loci reveal a more bottom-up 'in-church' experience than the missals, pontificals, graduals, lectionaries, psalters and ordinals. This assertion may appear to be completely incompatible with a bottom-up methodology, since liturgy is often presented as a principal example of imposing structures upon a community from above. However, the liturgy was hardly a monolithic or universal experience in the Middle Ages. There were certainly attempts to foster a universal liturgy, based in particular on the liturgy in Rome; but the repeated attempts only demonstrate how local cultic practices stubbornly resisted the universalizing tendencies of certain prelates and popes. Beginning in the eighth century, for example, the papacy attempted to reshape the worship experience of all Frankish kingdoms and had the full support of the new Carolingian court. The main obstacle was the Gallican rite in the Frankish territories: to impose a papal sanctioned liturgy required that rite to be eliminated altogether. The strategy only enjoyed partial success, for even with its adoption the Roman liturgy was soon 'contaminated' with the remnants of its Gallican competitor.[33] Such events indicate that formal imposition from above was often subverted by local concerns from below.

What does liturgy tell us about medieval ecclesiology? The obvious and already well-digested factor is the sacramental nature of ecclesial experience. The often touted ecclesiological problematic of church-and-world dialectic is found in liturgical life in as much as the Church was to transform the world. Indeed, the Christian encounter with the immanent occurred in the transformation of worldly elements of worship: water, bread, wine, oil, etc. The eucharistic focus of medieval ecclesiology is also a well-trodden path, broken first by the innovative scholarship of Henri de Lubac.[34] What remains, however, is to discover how specific communities – defined in terms of parish, diocese, province, or even by the notional term 'nation' – etched out their own specific vision of Church with the liturgical stylus. For example, was a community's self-perception unveiled in the celebration of specific feasts days (as opposed to the many they ignored)? The study of the *use* of saints' lives (and not just their composition) can be another point of access to the 'in church' experience during the Middle Ages. Such a strategy challenges the modern reader of medieval hagiography to consider the manner in which these texts were implemented within a specific liturgy, how that liturgy framed the reading of the saint's life, and then how that reading shaped – and was shaped by – the communal life of the local church.[35]

Other questions to pose are: Do specific customaries or local rites reflect a unique form of community of one part of medieval Christianity? How does the liturgy transform a sacred space, which then contributes to the ecclesial experience of the community as a whole? Is there a unique ecclesiological outlook that differentiates (or at least coincides with) the functionality of a monastic church from that of a parish church or a cathedral? And finally, how did the liturgical experience make an impact upon those whose task was to reflect upon the sacred page, formulate the abstract (and sometimes obtuse) theological problems and subsequently shape the future pastors and prelates?

Texts as ecclesiological events

Historical theologians gain access to events through the textual artifacts of medieval culture and in these we may discover each event's ecclesiological import. It has become a common-place in Medieval Studies that medieval culture was highly textual even though the number of literate persons accounted for a tiny minority. Medieval Christians considered texts to be the mirror in which they observed themselves as individuals and as members of a society, republic or body of believers. They advanced in learning by means of texts, for in the monastic cloister or the university classroom the main pedagogical tool was an authoritative text. Even for the illiterate texts mattered, for they gained access to their content through the voices of their literate leaders and in doing so formed communities that were woven together (*textus*) in the authority of a text.[36] In this respect, texts are events in themselves.[37]

Text as an ecclesiological event is already evident in the onset of what I have called the reflexive ecclesiology of the later Middle Ages. My concern here is to expand this category to include a genre of texts that rarely emerges in any discussion of medieval ecclesiology. I want to suggest that, at the very least, historical theologians ought to consider two additional types of texts: commentaries on the Psalms and expositions of the Dionysian corpus.

Interpreting the Psalms

An anonymous letter penned around 1130 advised its readers on a bible reading programme. After listing the order of reading the Old Testament books, the author notes: 'Finally, the Psalter, Job and the Song of Songs are to be read; because there is nothing in them useful to be understood literally, they should be read immediately concerning Christ and his Church.'[38] It would seem that the medieval scholastic was disposed to reading the sapiential books, and the Psalms in particular, ecclesiologically.[39]

That suggestion gains confirmation when we examine commentaries composed by the medieval theologians. Many took their initial exegetical cues from the *Ordinary Gloss* (*glossa ordinaria*), an exegetical tool that physically surrounded the biblical text in its manuscript copies. The bulk of this commentary was comprised of extracts from the church Fathers, although the *Gloss*'s compilers did not hesitate to add their own observations. The aim of a glossed Bible was to provide some means of making biblical interpretation a little more uniform and so avoiding wild differences in how a biblical text was understood.[40] The opening comment on the Psalter reads: 'the subject of this book is the whole Christ, bride-groom and bride'.[41] Now the term 'whole Christ' (*Christus integer*) might lead us to believe that only christology is at the heart of Psalms exegesis; however, the prefatory comments of scholastic theologians reveal the Psalter to be a point where christology and ecclesiology simply intersected. Peter Lombard, in his own great gloss, provides a three-fold explanation of how the Psalter speaks of the Church: 'the text concerns the Church in three modes: in terms of perfected members, other times in terms of the imperfect, and now and then in terms of evil men and women, who are in the Church in body but not in mind; in the Church by name, but not by divine will'.[42] Two decades later, Peter the Chanter confirms this three-fold approach to an ecclesiological reading of the Psalms, but describes the perfected members as either the martyrs or the penitents.[43] And a generation later, Hugh of St-Cher provides an even more explicit list of members that includes apostles, martyrs, confessors, virgins, hermits, prelates, the chaste, and the married.[44] Exposition of the Psalter appears to have been an ideal place to construct a theological perception of the Church.

This kind of ecclesiology was a reflection upon the Church's intentions, structures and ministries, but it was formulation shaped by a central text, the Psalter in this instance. Now this does not mean that we have finally found the *real* or more genuine ecclesiology of the Middle Ages, since it is apparently untainted by power and politics. To centre on a text could not mean a total and complete detachment from the reader's context. That may have been the ultimate trajectory, but as all expositors knew full well, that aim lay well beyond the text itself. Theologians may have yearned for liberation from their corrupted bodies so that one's soul could flee into God, but in reality the soul remained imprisoned in a material world where they had to continually engage in the social, institutional and political context. Reading a text was a historical event in and of itself.

The Psalter was a text that traversed a large swathe of medieval Christianity and for that reason became a way of examining the varieties of religious experience.[45] No matter where one turned, whether it be to the liturgy of the Mass, monastic life, individual spiritual expression, or vernacular literature, one encountered in some form or other the influence of this collection of ancient Hebrew poetry, brought to life in its Latin and vernacular transla-tions. When clerics learned to read, they commonly used the Psalter as their textbook. One could easily obtain a Psalter from the cathedral church to which one's school was attached; furthermore, future priests would be required to know it intimately as a liturgical book. Since the Psalter was the main 'reader' for teaching Latin, a cleric was often called *psalter-atus*.[46] As more laypeople became literate throughout the twelfth and thirteenth centuries, they also employed the Psalter as a primer. Even if one did not learn Latin itself, the Psalter provided for the reader the opportunity to practise letter-recognition, as well as pronunci-ation.[47] Indeed, one anonymous twelfth-century commentary opens the exposition with the question: 'Why do both men and women first learn the Psalter?'[48]

The answer was that the Psalms were the voice of the Church. It was the only part of scripture that was chanted or spoken by the community as a whole, or at least by the *schola cantorum* representing the community.[49] These many voices sung in unison the Antiphon, a portion of a Psalm sung during the procession. They sang responsively the Gradual, a Psalm chosen to be sung in between the scriptural readings. They also chanted the 'Alleluia', the preface to the reading of the Gospel, which was also drawn from the Psalms (Ps 85.7), and the offertory chant which was composed of two verses from Psalm 44. On special days, the choir chanted the community prayers such as Psalm 84 on the first Sunday in Advent or

Psalm 7 on Epiphany, to name but two of many examples.[50] All this was in addition to the daily recital of the Psalms in the Divine Office.[51]

The Psalter could therefore bridge the ordinary experience of being 'in church' and the more rarefied idealistic constructions of the theologian in the schools. It could provide a means of exploring the affective realities of community, as exemplified in the classic work of Augustine's *Enarrationes in Psalmos*. There Augustine spoke to the collective response of the ecclesial community to desire to be united with God. That was often connected to the unity of believers who were bound together in the mystical body of Christ.[52] The Psalms could also be a locus to explore the mimetic relationship between individual spirituality and corporate reading, as in the exposition of Gerhoh of Reichersberg. Gerhoh argued that a full meditative reading of the Psalms centred on becoming David, the author, in the process of reading – reading that could only be accomplished within a communal context.[53] The Psalms also became a place where the Church's features were married to pastoral theology, including preaching.[54] There remains so much more that the study of the Psalms could yield for medieval ecclesiology, but it will require a careful understanding of the intellectual, material and theological contexts of those commentaries.[55]

The Dionysian corpus

The second set of texts that needs to be added to the toolbox of the historical theologian is commentaries on the Dionysian corpus. For medieval thinkers, the patristic writer with the name of Dionysius the Areopagite was the Greek philosopher who converted to Christianity under the sway of St Paul (Acts 17). In the Latin West, his narrative was sometimes conflated with Saint Denis, the supposed first Bishop of Paris and later the patron saint of France – and so his true origins were not recovered until the fifteenth century. The writings of Pseudo-Dionysius were first translated into Latin in the ninth century, and then at least three other times in the twelfth and thirteenth centuries. Those writings are often considered a commonplace *par excellence* for essentialist ecclesiology. Grounded in the neo-Platonism of sixth-century Syriac Christianity (and not first-century Athens), these texts embraced the principal of emanation, in that Christians encounter the ineffability of God through two descending hierarchies, the angelic and the ecclesiastical.[56] Moreover, the manner in which this corpus came into play in medieval ecclesiology was an attempt to clarify actual practices in terms of the essentialist notion of hierarchy. In particular, the angelic hierarchy became a model by which theologians began to re-investigate the nature and ordering of ecclesial leadership.[57] Its final imprint upon medieval theology was to give greater theological and philosophical support to the claims of papal monarchy which emerged initially in the late twelfth century but really became part of the ecclesiological discourse in the fourteenth and fifteenth centuries.[58]

Our understanding of the influence of Pseudo-Dionysius in medieval thought, particularly in terms of angelic and ecclesiastical hierarchies, has been hampered by the lack of critical editions of the medieval commentators. That is slowly being corrected and it is laborious, if not thankless, work. There is no denying the essentialist outlook that these texts both inhabit and encourage within their readers, and indeed they are certainly a significant means of recovering just what kind of ideals medieval thinkers considered in this type of 'blueprint' ecclesiology. At the same time, the *Ecclesiastical Hierarchy* may be more grounded in reality than has been first supposed. This specific hierarchy is grounded in the ecclesial experience of sixth-century Syria, where specific liturgical acts are described and classes of religious orders delineated. How is it that Western, Latin theologians embraced this text? The answer lies in the fact that it demanded some serious mental gymnastics on their part, especially when it came to presenting the bishop as the true hierarch – something about which the monastic Pseudo-Dionysius was hardly explicit. Robert Grosseteste provides a good example of the challenge raised by this text. Grosseteste was a thirteenth-century philosopher turned theologian who eventually became Bishop of Lincoln (1235–53).[59] He took great pains in his own commentary to demonstrate that the ecclesiastical hierarch must be the bishop and not the monk – a point he carefully reiterated in a sermon preached during his episcopate as part of a monastic visitation.[60] The result, in fact, is a blending of speculative theology within a neo-platonic context (re-shaped in the fourteenth century by Aristotelian political thought) and a practical consideration of the liturgical and administrative structures of the Western, Latin church. The 'in church' experience was a fundamental context for interpreting this text and future study of these texts may reveal a more comprehensive (or perhaps more complex) account of the role the Dionysian corpus plays in medieval ecclesiology.

Conclusion

Text and event are the natural correlates for ecclesiological thought in historical Christianity. As a people of a book, Christianity has continually shaped its self-understanding by reflecting upon scripture. How Christians constructed community in the Middle Ages could be no different. Moreover, how that community unfolded in relation to political and cultural movements has also shaped the way in which the sacred page has been read. Most historical theologians accept these two axioms, but for medieval ecclesiology their implications have not been fully examined. What I have suggested here is a major programme of research, one that demands an interdisciplinary approach to the period. This programme also requires a larger set of resources that can reconstruct the intricate relationship between the hard realities of ecclesial community and the pristine ideals of a community in full union with God. Both elements tugged at that medieval conception of Church: Christians understood that to be part of the world meant full and complete political and social engagement, but it was with an existence that was transitory and often illusory. Ecclesiology may very well need to begin at the bottom, but for the medieval theologian that was not the place to remain.

The rediscovery of medieval ecclesiology does not demand a full rejection of the traditional account. It has served both historians and theologians well, and it is clearly based on rigorous research and good scholarly analysis. I have argued that the standard account is simply incomplete; it can now act as a sure foundation as historical theologians attempt to establish a fuller account of the medieval idea and practice of Church.

Notes

1 In the light of the multivalency of the word 'church', I have capitalized it when referring to it as a theological construct, as opposed to a geographical location, specific Christian community or a physical building.
2 On the role of the *persona fictiva* in medieval law, see Alexander Philipsborn, 'Der Begriff der juristischen Person in römischen Recht', *Zeitschrit der Savigny-Stiftung für Rechtsgeschichte* 71 (1954), 41–70. The first, sustained use of this construct in canon law emerged during the pontificate of Innocent IV (r. 1243–54): see M.J. Rodriquez, 'Innocent IV and the Element of Fiction in Juristic

Personalities', *The Jurist* 22 (1962), 287–313. For a broader summary, see Brian Tierney, *The Foundations of Conciliar Theory* (Cambridge: Cambridge University Press, 1955), pp. 98–103.

3 Yves Congar, 'Ecclesia ab Abel', in *Abhandlung über Theologie und Kirche. Festschrift für Karl Adam*, ed. M. Reding, pp. 79–108 (Dusseldorf: Patmos, 1952), p. 93; reprinted in Yves Congar, *Études d'ecclésiologie médiévale* (London: Variorum Reprints, 1983), II; idem, *L'Église de Saint Augustin à l'époque moderne* (Paris: Cerf, 1970), pp. 217–18.

4 Artur Landgraf, 'Scattered Remarks on the Development of Dogma and on Papal Infallibility in the Early Scholastic Writings', *Theological Studies* 7 (1946), 577–82; translated and printed in Artur Landgraf, *Dogmengeschichte der Frühscholastik*, 4 vols (Regensburg: Pusset, 1952–6), 1.1.30–36. Cf. Brian Tierney, *Origins of Papal Infallibility, 1150–1350*, Studies in the History of Christian Thought 6 (Leiden: Brill, 1972), p. 13.

5 Joseph Famarée, *L'ecclésiologie d'Yves Congar avant Vatican II: histoire et église, analyse et reprise critique*, Bibliotheca Ephemeridum theologicarum Lovaniensium 107 (Leuven: University of Leuven Press, 1992), esp. pp. 20–25. See also Timothy MacDonald, *The Ecclesiology of Yves Congar: Foundational Themes* (Landham: University Press of America, 1984), pp. 41–52.

6 See for example, Walter Ullmann, *The Growth of Papal Government in the Middle Ages: A Study in the Ideological Relation of Clerical to Lay Power* (New York: Barnes and Noble, 1953); Francis Oakely, *The Western Church in the Later Middle Ages* (Ithaca: Cornell University Press, 1979); Tierney, *Foundations of the Conciliar Theory*; and idem, *Origins of Papal Infallibility*.

7 Nicholas Healey, *Church, World and the Christian Life: Practical-Prophetic Ecclesiology* (Cambridge: Cambridge University Press, 2000), pp. 25–51.

8 See Roger Haight, *Christian Community in History*, 2 vols (New York: Continuum, 2004–5), esp. pp. 4–6, 26–7. Haight's methodology is the result of over twenty years of reflection upon ecclesiological thought. See his ground-breaking article: 'Historical Ecclesiology: an Essay on Method in the Study of the Church', *Science et Esprit* 39 (1987), 27–46, 345–74.

9 Healey, *Church, World and the Christian Life*, pp. 52–4.

10 Thomas F. O'Meara, 'Philosophical Models in Ecclesiology', *Theological Studies* 39 (1978), 3–21, explores this in some detail in relation to ecclesiological thought.

11 Haight, *Christian Community in History*, 1.267–423. In fairness, Haight's aim is a general narrative and cannot be expected to provide the intricate details of church life of over one thousand years in the span of less than two hundred pages. And yet this very mandate makes the narrative all the more telling, for general accounts force the writer to privilege clearly certain events as summative of the whole period.

12 For a brief account of the theory and practice of micro-history, see Elizabeth A. Clark, *History, Theory and Text: Historians and the Linguistic Turn* (Cambridge MA: Harvard University Press, 2004), pp. 75–9. For a cautionary tale about the use of micro-history (and its historiogaphical lineage) for the Middle Ages, see Leonard E. Boyle, 'Montaillou Revisited: *mentalité* and methodology', in *Pathways to Medieval Peasants*, ed. J.A. Raftis, Papers in Medieval Studies 2 (Toronto: PIMS, 1981), pp. 119–40.

13 I first criticized this account in my doctoral thesis: James R. Ginther, 'The *Super Psalterium* of Robert Grosseteste: A Scholastic Psalms Commentary as a Source for Medieval Ecclesiology', unpubl. PhD diss. (University of Toronto, 1995), pp. 4–11. I have more recently examined it in the context of my study of the theology of Robert Grosseteste: *Master of the Sacred Page: A Study of the Theology of Robert Grosseteste, ca. 1229/30–1235* (Aldershot: Ashgate, 2004), Ch. 7.

14 Yves Congar, *L'Eglise de Saint Augustin à l'époque moderne* (Paris: Cerf, 1970), pp. 12–268 (Chs 1–8); Edward J. Gratsch, *Where Peter Is: A Survey of Ecclesiology* (New York: Alba House, 1975), pp. 53–107; Eric Jay, *The Church: Its Changing Image Through Twenty Centuries*, 2 vols (Atlanta: Knox Press, 1978), 1.97–141; and most recently, Benard P. Prusak, *The Church Unfinished: Ecclesiology Through the Centuries* (New York: Paulist Press, 2004), pp. 176–228.

15 See for example, Ernst H. Kantorowicz, *The King's Two Bodies. A Study in Mediaeval Political Theology* (Princeton: Princeton University Press, 1957); Karl F. Morrison, *The Two Kingdoms: Ecclesiology in Carolingian Political Thought* (Princeton: Princeton University Press, 1964).

16 See Stephen Kuttner, 'Methodological Problems Concerning the History of Canon Law', *Speculum* 30 (1955), 539–49, at 542.

17 See the seminal study of Ullmann, *The Growth of Papal Government in the Middle Ages*. A more recent study is Bernhard Schimmelpfennig, *The Papacy*, trans. James Sievert (New York: Columbia

University Press, 1992), which was originally published in German with a more descriptive title: *Das Pappsttum von der Antike bis zur Renaissance*, second edition (Darmstadt: Wissenschaftliche Buchgesellschat, 1988). See also Michael Wilks, *The Problem of Sovereignty in the Later Middle Ages. The Papal Monarchy with Augustinus Triumphus and the Publicists* (Cambridge: Cambridge University Press, 1963), esp. pp. 15–64.

18 See above n. 3.

19 John R. Eastman, *Papal Abdication in the Later Middle Ages*, Texts and Studies in Religion 42 (Lewiston: Mellon Press, 1990); and Giles of Rome, *De renunciatione pape*, ed. J.R. Eastman, Texts and Studies in Religion 51 (Lewiston: Mellon Press, 1992). See also Wilks, *Problem of Sovereignty*, *passim*.

20 See Joseph R. Strayer, *The Reign of Philip the Fair* (Princeton: Princeton University Press, 1980); Jeffrey H. Denton, *Philip the Fair and the Ecclesiastical Assemblies of 1294–1295*, Transactions of the American Philosophical Society 81, pt. 1 (Philadelphia: American Philosophical Society, 1994), esp. 27.

21 Oakley, *The Western Church in the Later Middle Ages*, pp. 157–74; Scott H. Hendrix, 'In Quest of the *Vera Ecclesia*: the Crisis of Late Medieval Ecclesiology', *Viator* 7 (1976), 347–78, at 347–8.

22 For an example of this available in English translation, see James of Voragine, *The Golden Legend*, trans. W.G. Ryan, 2 vols (Princeton: Princeton University Press, 1993), 2.385–95.

23 The year 1260 as the dividing line is still a matter of debate. Henri Acquillière argued that the first treatise on ecclesiology proper was James of Viterbo's *De regimine christiano* (c. 1301–2): Henri X. Arquillière, *Le plus ancien traité de l'église: Jacques de Vitèrbe, De regimine Christiano (1301–1302). Etude des sources et édition critique* (Paris: Beauchesne, 1926). Yves Congar, 'Aspects écclési-ologiques de la querelle entre mendiants et seculiers dans la seconde motié du XIIIe siècle et le debut de XIVe', *Archives d'histoire doctrinale et littéraire du moyen age* 28 (1961) 35–151, at 99–104, argued that the advent of a developed ecclesiology was precipitated by three events: the secular–mendicant controversy at the University of Paris, the arrival of Aristotle's *Politics* in 1260, and the conflict between Philip IV of France (r. 1285–1314) and Pope Boniface VIII (r. 1294–1303). By 1260, the first two events were making their impact on the theological literature, and so it would appear appropriate to use 1260 as the dividing line. R. James Long, 'The Question "Whether the Church Could Better Be Ruled by a Good Canonist than by a Theologian" and the Origins of Ecclesiology', *Proceedings of the PMR Conference* 10 (1985) 99–112, has argued that Godfrey of Fontaine's Quodlibetal question of 1293 was the first formally and exclusively ecclesiological trea-tise of the Middle Ages. This discrepancy perhaps points to the fact that the years 1260 to 1293 were a period of transition, as the events of the day and the new sources slowly made their impact on the texts *de ecclesia*.

24 Haight, *Christian Community in History*, 1.271–2. The classic account for this first watershed moment is Morrison, *Two Kingdoms*; but see also Rosamund McKitterick, *The Frankish Church and the Carolingian Reforms, 789–895* (London: Royal Historical Society, 1977).

25 Haight, *Christian Community in History*, 1.274–80; Congar, *L'Eglise*, pp. 95–107; Gerd Tellenbach, *Church and State and Christian Society at the Time of the Investiture Contest*, trans. R.F. Bennett (Oxford: Blackwell, 1940, repr. University of Toronto Press, 1982); Ullmann, *Growth of Papal Government*, pp. 262–343.

26 An excellent example of this is Stanley Chodorow's *Christian Political Theory and Church Politics in the Mid-twelfth Century: The Ecclesiology of Gratian* (Berkeley: University of California Press, 1972). See also Colin Morris, *The Papal Monarchy: The Western Church from 1050 to 1250* (Oxford: Clarendon Press, 1989).

27 *Oxford English Dictionary*, second edition, ed. J.A. Simpson and E.S.C. Weiner, 20 vols (Oxford: Clarendon Press, 1989), 5.51.

28 Richard Kieckhefer, *Theology in Stone: Church Architecture from Byzantium to Berkeley* (Oxford: Oxford University Press, 2004).

29 Joseph Goering, 'The Changing Face of the Village Parish II: the Thirteenth Century', in *Pathways to Medieval Peasants*, ed. Raftis, pp. 323–34; Leonard E. Boyle, 'The Fourth Lateran Council and Manuals of Popular Theology', in *Popular Literature of Medieval England*, ed. T.J. Heffernan, Tennessee Studies in Literature 28 (Knoxville: University of Tennessee Press,1985), pp. 30–43.

30 Miri Rubin, *Corpus Christi: the Eucharist in Late Medieval Culture* (Cambridge: Cambridge University Press, 1991), esp. pp. 164–212.

31 Eamon Duffy, *The Stripping of the Altars: Traditional Religion in England,* c. *1400 –* c. *1580* (New Haven: Yale University Press, 1992), pp. 91–130; Kieckhefer, *Theology in Stone,* pp. 31–2. See also Philip G. Lindley, 'The Great Screen and its Context', in *Alban and St Albans: Roman and Medieval Architecture, Art and Archeology,* ed. M. Henig and P.G. Lindley, Transactions of the British Archeological Society 25 (Leeds: Maney Publishing, 2001), pp. 256–70.

32 See the example of how the liturgy can transform the reading of a building in Andreas Speer, 'Is there a Theology of the Gothic Cathedral? A Re-reading of Abbot Suger's Writings on the Abbey Church of St-Denis', in *The Mind's Eye: Art and Theological Argument in the Middle Ages,* ed. J. Hamburger and A.-M. Bouché (Princeton: Department of Art and Archeology, 2006), pp. 65–83.

33 Cyril Vogel, *Medieval Liturgy: an Introduction to the Sources,* trans. W.G. Storey and N.K. Rasmussen (Washington DC: Pastoral Press, 1986), esp. pp. 85–92; Kenneth Levy, 'Toledo, Rome and the Legacy of Gaul', *Early Music History* 4 (1984), 49–99, at 49–51.

34 Henri de Lubac, *Corpus mysticum: L'eucharistie et l'Eglise au moyen age* (Paris: Aubier, 1949, English trans. by Gemma Simmonds, London, SCM, 2006). See also Artur Landgraf, 'Die Lehre von geheimnisvollen Leib Christi in dem fruhen Paulinenkommentaren und in der Frühscholastik', *Divus Thomas* 24 (1946), 217–48, 393–428; 25 (1947), 365–94; 26 (1948), 160–80, 291–323, 395–434; partially reprinted in Landgraf, *Dogmengeschichte,* 4.2.48–99; Walter H. Principe, 'Quaestiones Concerning Christ from the First Half of the Thirteenth Century: IV. Quaestiones from Douai 434: Christ as Head of the Church: The Unity of the Mystical Body', *Mediaeval Studies* 44 (1982), 1–82; and, Emile Mersch, *Le Corps mystique du Christ,* 2 vols, Museum Lessianum – Section théologique 28–29 (Louvain: Museum Lessianum, 1933), esp. 2.157–60. For a good summary of the modern context for this research, see Edward P. Hahnenberg, 'The Mystical Body of Christ and Communion Ecclesiology: Historical Parallels', *Irish Theological Quarterly* 70 (2005), 3–30.

35 For a general approach to this strategy, see Andre Vauchez, *Sainthood in the Later Middle Ages,* trans. J. Birrell (Cambridge: Cambridge University Press, 1997), esp. pp. 145–246.

36 See Brian Stock, *Listening for the Text: On the Uses of the Past* (Baltimore: John Hopkins University Press, 1990); Gabrielle M. Spiegel, *The Past as Text: The Theory and Practice of Medieval Historiography* (Baltimore: John Hopkins University Press, 1997). See also the comments of Karl F. Morrison, 'Sounding Hermeneutics: Two Recent Works', *Speculum* 73 (1998), 787–98.

37 See Chapter 33, 'Hermeneutics and Ecclesiology' for a discussion of the wider ecclesiological significance and importance of 'texts' and of their interpretation.

38 Beryl Smalley, *The Study of the Bible in the Middle Ages,* third edition (Oxford: Blackwell, 1983), pp. 88–9. The letter is printed in *Thesaurus novus anecdotorum,* ed. E. Martène and U. Durand, 5 vols (Paris: Delaulne, 1717), 1.486–90, at 489: 'Ad ultimum Psalterium, et Job, et Cantica Canticorum: in quibus, quia nullus intellectus ad litteram utilis est, de Christo et Ecclesia statim primo legantur.'

39 I have taken my initial cue from Scott H. Hendrix, *Ecclesia in Via: Ecclesiological Developments in the Medieval Psalms and the Dictata Super Psalterium (1513–1515) of Martin Luther,* Studies in Medieval and Reformation Thought 10 (Leiden: E.J. Brill, 1974); although Hendrix gives very short shrift to medieval commentaries.

40 G.R. Evans, *The Language and Logic of the Bible: the Earlier Middle Ages* (Cambridge: Cambridge University Press, 1984), pp. 37–47. See also Jenny Swanson, 'The *Glossa Ordinaria*', in *The Medieval Theologians,* ed. G.R. Evans (Oxford: Blackwell, 2001), pp. 156–66.

41 *Biblia latina cum glossa ordinaria,* 4 vols (Strassbourg: Rusch, 1480–81; repr. Turnhout: Brepols), 1992, 2.458: 'Materia est integer Christus, sponsus et sponsa.'

42 Peter Lombard, *Glossa super Psalterium,* PL 191.59: 'Item de ecclesia, tribus modis: aliquando secundum perfectos, aliquando secundum imperfectos, interdum secundum malos qui sunt in Ecclesia corpore, non mente; nomine, non numine.'

43 Peter the Chanter, *Glossa super Psalmos* (London, Lambeth Palace MS 71, fol. 1rb): 'Quandoque de Christo per transumptionem in uoce membrorum . . . quandoque de membris Christi, id est de ecclesia et tripliciter de eis: aliquando de ipsis ut de imperfectis, aliquando de perfectis – aliquando de penitentibus, aliquando de martiribus, aliquando de malis propter bonos.'

44 Hugh of St-Cher, *Postilla in Psalterium,* in *Cardinalis Hugonis de St.-Caro opera omnia,* 8 vols (Venice: Pezzana, 1732), prol. (2.2v).

45 The traditional, four-fold exegesis of Scripture was particularly applicable to the Psalter in light of the prophetic status medieval theologians gave to David himself as the principal author. Moreover, to many expositors any allegorical reading was a *de ecclesia* reading of the text. A short didactic verse on the four-fold sense of Scripture written in the margins of a glossed Psalter captures this view succinctly: 'Dicitur: historicus sensus narrans uelud est res/ Moralis sensus datus est exponere mores/ Militat ecclesia que continet allegoriam/ Sensus anagogicus templum tenet ille triumphans' (Oxford, Bodelian Library MS e Museo 15, fol. 1rb, my emphasis).

46 Pierre Riché, *Ecoles et enseignement dans le haut moyen âge* (Paris: Picard, 1979), p. 223.

47 Nicholas Orme, *English Schools in the Middle Ages* (London: Methuen, 1973), pp. 46–7, 60–64; Malcom B. Parkes, 'The Literacy of the Laity', in *Literature and Western Civilization: The Medieval World*, ed. D. Daiches and A.K. Thorlby (London: Aldus Books, 1973), pp. 555–76; reprinted in, *Scribes, Scripts and Readers. Studies in the Communication, Presentation and Dissemination of Medieval Texts* (London: Hambledon Press, 1991), pp. 275–97. See also, Paul Saenger, 'Books of Hours and the Reading Habits of the Later Middle Ages', *Scrittura e civiltà* 9 (1985), 240–69.

48 Cited in Friedrich Stegmüller, *Repertorium biblicum medii aevi*, 11 vols (Barcelona: Matriti, 1950–80), 2.214 (n. 1794): 'Quare psalterium primo discatur a mulieribus et a viris: Dicendum est imprimis, cur Psalterium ab omnibus primitus discatur.'

49 See John A. Lamb, *The Psalms in Christian Worship* (London: Faith Press, 1962), pp. 80–99.

50 S.J.P. Van Dijk, 'The Bible in Liturgical Use', in *The Cambridge History of the Bible*, ed. G.W.H. Lange, 3 vols (Cambridge: Cambridge University Press, 1969), 2.220–52, at 239–40.

51 On the origin and history of the Divine Office, see Lamb, *Psalms in Christian Worship*, pp. 54–69, 99–120; S.J.P. Van Dijk and J. Hazeldon Walker, *The Origins of the Modern Roman Liturgy* (London: Darton, Longman & Todd, 1960); Andrew Hughes, *Medieval Manuscripts for Mass and Office: a Guide to their Organization and Terminology* (Toronto: University of Toronto Press, 1982), pp. 50–80, 160–244; Eric Palazzo, *Histoires des livres liturgiques. Le Moyen âge des origines au XIIIe siècle* (Paris: Beauchesne, 1993), pp. 131–58.

52 For Augustine see Michael C. McCarthy, 'An Ecclesiology of Groaning: Augustine, the Psalms, and the Making of the Church', *Theological Studies* 66 (2005), 23–48. See also Stanislaus J. Grabowski, *The Church: An Introduction to the Theology of Augustine* (St. Louis: Herder, 1957).

53 Karl F. Morrison, 'The Church as Play: Gerhoch of Reicherberg's Call for Reform', in *Popes, Teachers and Canon Law in the Middle Ages*, ed. J.R. Sweeney and S. Chodorow (Ithaca: Cornell University Press, 1989), pp. 114–44. For the general context, see Wolfgang Beinert, *Die Kirche, Gottes Heil in der Welt; die Lehre von der Kirche nach den Schriften des Rupert von Deutz, Honorius Augustodunensis und Gerhoch von Reichersberg; ein Beitrag zur Ekklesiologie des 12. Jahrhunderts*, Beiträge zur Geschichte der Philosophie und Theologie des Mittelalters, n.s., 13 (Münster: Aschendorff, 1973).

54 See my own two studies: James R. Ginther, 'A Scholastic Idea of the Church: Robert Grosseteste's Exposition of Psalm 86', *Archives d'histoire doctrinale et littéraire du moyen âge* 66 (1999), 49–72; and 'The Scholastic Psalms Commentary as a Textbook for Theology: the Case of Thomas Aquinas', in *Omnia Disce: Medieval Studies in Memory of Leonard E. Boyle, OP*, ed. A.J. Duggan, J. Greatrex and B. Bolton (Aldershot: Ashgate, 2005), pp. 211–29.

55 The literature on the medieval psalter and its cultural and religious role is vast, but see the exemplary essays in *The Place of the Psalms in the Intellectual Culture of the Middle Ages*, ed. N. Van Deusen (Albany: State University of New York Press, 1999).

56 Haight, *Christian Community in History*, 1.301–5. The two best general introductions to the Dionysian corpus are Paul Rorem, *Pseudo-Dionysius: A Commentary on the Texts and an Introduction to their Influence* (New York: Oxford University Press, 1993); and René Roques, *L'univers dionysien: structure hiérarchique du monde selon le Pseudo-Denys* (Paris: Aubier, 1940). Andrew Louth, *Denys the Areopagite* (London: Chapman, 1989) is also of some use.

57 Walter H. Principe, 'The School Theologian's View of the Papacy, 1150–1250', in *The Religious Roles of the Papacy: Ideals and Realities, 1150–1300*, ed. C. Ryan, Papers in Mediaeval Studies 8 (Toronto: Pontifical Institute of Mediaeval Studies, 1989), pp. 45–116.

58 For example, see G.H.M. Posthumus Meyjes, *Jean Gerson, Apostle of Unity. His Church Politics and Ecclesiology*, trans. J.C. Grayson, Studies in the History of Christian Thought 94 (Leiden: Brill, 1999).

59 On the life and works of Grosseteste, see R.W. Southern, *Robert Grosseteste: the Growth of an English Mind in Medieval Europe* (Oxford: Clarendon Press, 1987); and James McEvoy, *Robert Grosseteste* (Oxford: Oxford University Press, 2000).
60 James R. Ginther, 'Monastic Ideals and Episcopal Visitations: the *Sermo ad religiosos* of Robert Grosseteste, Bishop of Lincoln (1235–53)', in *Medieval Monastic Preaching*, ed. C.A. Meussig (Leiden: Brill, 1998), pp. 231–53. A working edition can be found in Candice Taylor Hogan, 'Robert Grosseteste, Pseudo-Dionysius and Hierarchy: A Medieval Trinity. Including an Edition of Grosseteste's Translation of, and Commentary on, *De ecclesiastica hierarchia*', unpublished PhD diss., 2 vols (Cornell University, Ithaca NY, 1991).

4

ECCLESIOLOGY AND THE RELIGIOUS CONTROVERSY OF THE SIXTEENTH CENTURY

Christopher Ocker

Ecclesiologies of the sixteenth century have two main intellectual contexts. One is the religious controversy over the papacy commonly known as the Reformation. The other is the social imaginary presupposed by parties to the debate.[1] What distinguishes the early Protestants from the most important previous critics – John Wyclif, who argued against the papacy, church property, religious orders, and transubstantiation; the English dissenters accused of his heresy; and Jan Hus and his followers in Bohemia – was their geographical breadth and their long-term success.[2] Yet their success also poses a problem to the student of the history of religion and theology. Rigid divisions between later confessional churches can easily overshadow one's view of the early Protestant movements. A great quantity of scholarship from the last thirty years has corrected this problem. This chapter summarizes the religious controversy, then examines Protestant views of the church, Catholic views, and finally a common presupposition about the human community in the light of the unresolved conflict over Martin Luther.

The religious controversy

Although the controversy over Luther may seem bi-polar (it started as a conflict between supporters and opponents of Martin Luther, who was condemned for heresy in 1520 and 1521), it quickly spawned a variety of movements that defy easy categorization.[3] Some people defended Luther and opposed the traditional church. Many became broadly anti-clerical, which helped inflame the unrest that culminated in the Peasants' War of 1524/5 and lingered as periodic iconoclastic riots, or threats of riots, in German and Swiss towns over the next fifteen years.[4] Others defended papal government, the priesthood, seven sacraments, and church traditions, often embracing, at the same time, the reform of religious life, monasticism, the bishop's office, or papal government. Although sermons, pamphlets, and theological treatises drew religious landscapes in stark Catholic–Protestant contrasts,[5] the convoluted progress of Protestantism in Germany paints a mottled picture.[6] The lineaments of ecclesiological debate were described by the polarizing literature, but the debate's historical meaning must be coloured in transient shades.[7]

In the thirty years after Luther's condemnations, a main party of 'Protestants' took shape in Germany around the League of Schmalkalden, a defensive alliance formed at the end of

1530 by the estates who in 1529 protested attempts in the imperial Diet to revive Luther's sentence and hinder evangelical reforms.[8] The League became the nucleus of early Protestantism, with the university at Wittenberg and the charismatic Luther remaining the international magnet of religiously discontented intellectuals that they had become in the 1520s. Wittenberg's status was further elevated by Philip Melanchthon's continental reputation as a humanist. In the 1530s and early 1540s the Elector Johann Friedrich's aggressive leadership in the League amplified the opinion of Wittenberg scholars in public debate, with Melanchthon prominent among them. Yet the League's aims were not entirely clear. It was more repulsed by anti-clerical extremists, such as Anabaptists or the followers of the 'spiritualist' Caspar Schwenckfeld, than by Catholics. The members of the League seem to have hoped, at different times and to varying degrees, merely to expand and maintain a political block within the community of imperial estates, *or* rebel against the emperor, *or* accomplish the nationalization of the imperial church and free it of foreign (Habsburg and papal) interference, *or* merely promote evangelical reform.[9] One or another of these ambitions at one time or another were also, at least partly, embraced by some Catholic princes and theologians.[10] There were Catholic theologians who tried to undermine Luther's attraction by means of Catholic, evangelical reform, for example at the court of Matthew Lang, cardinal and Bishop of Salzburg, as early as 1523; in the reform convention sponsored by Archduke Ferdinand of Austria and the papal legate Lorenzo Campeggi at Nürnberg in 1524; and in later conciliatory gestures by Catholic reformists before and after the famous imperial religious colloquies of 1540 and 1541.[11] The controversy remained undecided during Luther's lifetime. The parties to it promoted confessional boundaries within a religious landscape that seemed to lose its natural barriers when Luther survived his excommunication. It remained uncertain exactly what the old church and the new would become.

The eventual outcome of the controversy in Germany was legal tolerance of Protestant churches (but not toleration of the Protestant faith as such), achieved gradually through the course of the 1530s and 1540s in an unpredictable and piecemeal fashion typical of political life in the empire. Tolerance was finally ratified in the Treaty of Passau of 1552, contracted between Protestant estates and Ferdinand of Austria, since 1531 'king of the Romans', on the emperor's behalf, and by the Imperial Diet of Augsburg of 1555. The outcome could seem bi-polar enough, and eventually tri-polar. There were two unevenly distributed churches, Catholic and Protestant, with the north mostly Protestant, the south mostly Catholic, principalities of either confession in the west, and some monasteries, cities, small lordships, and principalities, either Catholic or Protestant, scattered throughout.[12] This geographical, confessional complexity within Germany was further confused by on-going debates over church property, the rise of international Calvinism and theological controversies among Protestants, the inevitable twists of imperial coalition-building, the disasters of the Thirty Years War, and whatever feelings peasants and townsfolk (that is, people who did not make policy and whose patronage of churches was small) may have had in these bewildering circumstances: which is to say that although there can be little doubt by 1555 how confessions were defined, or how ecclesiological debate would be pursued, the religious landscape of central Europe for the next century remained in flux.[13] Yet the religious controversy in Germany had established parameters of debate over the nature and organization of the Church throughout Europe.

It was testimony more to the force of conflict than to the power of conversion. The religious controversy swept across northern Europe. By 1555, parties advocating rebellion against the papacy and traditional church practices also dominated the Swiss cities of

Zürich, Basel, Bern, Geneva, St. Gall, and their dependencies. Clergy in papal rebellion contributed to the nationalization of the Swedish church; helped to orchestrate the dissolution of monasteries in England and aided the crown's control of English bishops; aided the Danish crown's confiscation of monasteries and its nationalization of bishops; and would soon help organize a national church in Scotland, give shape to a rebellion against the Habsburgs in the Netherlands, and help drive France into civil war. Yet the Protestant church never built an international organization to compete with papal government in early modern Europe, and in many places, especially in its eastern European enclaves in the later sixteenth century, its theological complexion could seem doubtfully reformed or even dubiously Christian, to Protestants and Catholics alike. There had arisen a spectrum of views of the Church ranging from the hyper-papalism of Albert Pighe on the right (as we will see) to a new, latter-century wave of Anabaptists on the left, namely those inspired by the anti-Trinitarian biblicism of the physician and refugee from Pavia to Lesser Poland Giorgio Blandrata, the Transylvanian Protestant bishop Francis David, and eventually the Sienese émigré to Poland and Transylvania Fausto Paolo Sozzini, more commonly known as Faustus Socinus.

Although Lutherans, Calvinists, and Anabaptists denounced each other, a standard list of Lutheran complaints united these movements within and outside Germany against the traditional church. The complaints originated with Luther, and his vernacular writings spread them wide in the early 1520s.[14] Their ecclesiological element included well-known rejections: of the authority of the pope, the mass as a meritorious sacrifice, the invocation and adoration of the saints, intercession for the dead, perpetual monastic vows, and the status of confirmation, marriage, holy anointing, ordination and, usually, penance as sacraments. Protestants denounced because they confronted Catholic resilience. Catholic feeling, and often Catholic ministry, could still be found in one way or another in or very near to most of Protestant Europe at mid-century. To take the most successfully de-Catholicized cities and territories, such as Denmark or Geneva, as the century's norm is simply wrong. During the religious controversy, the actual distance between Catholic and Protestant churches was passable.[15] In very many places, a Catholic presence was near at hand, and conversion could and often did take place in both directions.

We should therefore approach debates over the nature of the Church against the backdrop of the controversy's uncertain fluctuations; and since the controversy took shape in Germany, it is reasonable to pay special attention to central Europe. Arguments can be grouped along the rigid lines of theological polemic, but one must not assume that polemic demarcated separate societies. Sixteenth-century religious movements remained plaited together, bound both by their disagreements and their common presuppositions.[16]

Protestants in a Catholic church

In the summer of 1530, the general meeting of German imperial estates, the Imperial Diet, took place at Augsburg. Anxious for broad German participation in the defence of eastern Europe from the Ottoman Turks, the Habsburg emperor, Charles V, who was also king of Spain, and his brother Ferdinand, the archduke of Austria, agreed that theological commissions representing Martin Luther's supporters and opponents would debate their doctrinal differences. For the debate, Philip Melanchthon wrote the Protestant position-piece known as the Augsburg Confession. It was the basis of a predictably acrimonious dialogue at the Diet.[17] After the dialogue collapsed, intransigence grew.[18] But with the formation of the

League of Schmalkalden at the end of that year, the Confession also became an authoritative standard of evangelical doctrine and was repeatedly used by Protestants as the basis of theological dialogue in the empire.[19] Although contrasts are often drawn between Lutheran and the distinctly Swiss-Zwinglian views of the eucharist, temporal authority and society in south German cities, Swiss influence declined with the defeat of Zürich at the battle of Kappel in 1531, and it was soon eclipsed, until mid-century, by the mediating theology of Martin Bucer; Bucer also informed the most influential French reformer, John Calvin.[20] Melanchthon's 1530 text was therefore a monumental expression of an emerging, transregional Protestant identity.

Melanchthon represented the Protestant view of the church like this:

> there should be one holy church forever. The church is the congregation of the saints, in which the gospel is purely taught and the sacraments are correctly administered. And for the true unity of the church it is enough to agree on the teaching of the gospel and the administration of the sacraments. Nor is it necessary that there be similar human traditions and rites or ceremonies instituted by human beings; as Paul said, 'one faith, one baptism, one God and father of all'. Although the church may properly be the congregation of the saints and of those who truly believe, nevertheless, since in this life many hypocrites and evil people are mixed in with it, it is permitted that sacraments be used that are administered by evil men. . . . Both the sacraments and the word are effective on account of the command of Christ, even though produced by evil men. Donatists and those like them are damned . . .[21]

This articulated an evangelical mainstream and, Melanchthon said, mere Catholic truth: 'Since our churches do not dissent from the Catholic church in any article of faith, but rather eliminate some few abuses that are new and against the intention of the canons accepted by the vice of the times, we ask that the imperial majesty hear mercifully what might be at variance and what are its causes, so that the people not be forced to observe those abuses against conscience.'[22] The Confession then recounts the practices corrected: receipt of the eucharist in both kinds by the laity, marriage of priests, the restoration of the mass to its evangelical form, a broadened understanding of absolution in the practice of confession, the liberation of human conscience from human traditions, the restoration of monasteries to their original tasks of charity and Christian acculturation, and opposition to the abuse of episcopal power.[23] Protestants did not think these issues needed to be weighed the same. The lay reception of the cup in the sacrament of the Lord's Supper, clerical marriage, the non-sacrificial character of the eucharist, and the wording of the canon (the central liturgical portion) of the mass were non-negotiable, together with faith, good works and Christian freedom. But the new theologians allowed for compromise on questions of ceremonies, episcopal government, feast days, and fasts. The emperor could decide what should happen to cloister and church property.[24]

The elimination of abuses was to be the mere consequence of Christ's direct rule of the Church when a ministry had been reformed. Luther and Melanchthon taught that 'Christ rules the church by no power but the word,' and that the community of the faithful comprises an invisible society of saints.[25] The church's tangible, earthly form is apparent where preaching, evangelical sacraments, faith, confession and, Melanchthon added, obedience to gospel ministers were found.[26] A consensus of new theologians agreed that the true

Church was primarily an invisible, spiritual community of saints, but externally evident by, or bearing the 'marks' of, its faith, gospel preaching and the correct administration of the two New Testament sacraments of baptism and the eucharist; they sometimes added the correct exercise of discipline as further visible evidence of a true church.[27] These external evidences complemented the traditional 'marks' of the Church – sanctity, unity, universality and apostolicity, which Protestants emphatically accepted – without that very tangible universal government seated in Rome.[28] But the basic distinction between the Church as an invisible, spiritual community and as the more ambivalent worldly conglomeration of saints and sinners was hardly a novel idea. Its origin was Augustine.[29] Neither was the solution to ambivalence novel: *tactile* certainty over the trueness of a church had long involved definitions of sacraments and true Christian ministry.[30] Nor was the emphasis on the particular sacraments of baptism and the eucharist novel. Both had already been emphasized as the means by which people are integrated into the mystical body of Christ.[31] But the Church's external form did not, in the Protestant view, rest on legally constructed powers – on popes, bishops, or their courts. Rather, the bishop's office had to be restored to its purely pastoral dimensions and distinguished from temporal rule, even if most early Protestant theologians could allow the on-going position of bishops in the diets of the Holy Roman Empire, Denmark and Sweden, and in English parliament.[32] A bishop, said Melanchthon, is different from a priest only by human authority. Human authority is valid, but not as a measure of religious truth, which must rest on the gospel. Whatever a bishop may be temporally was irrelevant to faith. Melanchthon had said in his defence of the Augsburg Confession, 'The adversaries make a great deal of noise about the freedoms and privileges of the clergy. . . . in our Confession nothing is said against the freedoms of churches or the privileges of priests which they have been given by temporal authority, emperors, kings, and princes. For, we really teach that one should respect temporal order and law.'[33] Nor did the 'priesthood of all believers' extinguish the sacramental role of the clergy. Lutheran and Reformed catechisms variously insisted on the minister's unique function in the congregation's experience of Christ, vis-à-vis preaching, the evangelical sacraments of baptism and the eucharist, and the execution of church discipline, which as a public act variously included communal or princely participation.[34]

It has been said that Luther, possibly abetted by an Ockhamistic fideism, lost a concept of the Church as an organic unity concretely experienced in the sacraments, 'One sometimes gets the impression that Luther speaks little of the mystical body.'[35] This misrepresents William Ockham and overstates the case for Luther and the majority of early Protestant teachers, as becomes clear when we consider the internal Protestant controversy over the sacrament of the eucharist.[36] The controversy is perhaps most famous for Luther's confrontation with Zürich's Huldrich Zwingli and the Basel reformer Johannes Oecolampadius at Marburg in 1529, in conjunction with the Landgrave of Hesse's attempt to build a Protestant coalition that included major cities of the south, where sympathy for Zwingli's views ran strong. Since the Peasants War, Luther had been linking Zwingli and Oecolampadius' 'sacramentarian' doctrine to the views of Anabaptists and rebels. Although sometimes described as a third Protestant tradition alongside Calvinists and Lutherans – a 'radical Reformation', in the famous phrase of George Hunston Williams – their number were, from the beginning, diverse and tragic, scarcely forming a group.[37] They included Balthasar Hubmaier, persecuted by Zwingli before he was executed by burning at Vienna in 1528; the Thuringian revolutionary Thomas Müntzer, who was executed outside the city of Mühlhausen near the end of the Peasants War in May, 1525; and the Wittenberg professor,

Andreas Bodenstein von Karlstadt, who, in a difficult nine-year period after the war, abjured his views at least twice and moved his residence some eight times. Having finally abandoned his earlier extremes on baptism, he became a professor of Hebrew at Basel in 1534.[38] Hubmaier's blunt reasoning may stand for most early Anabaptists, when he argued that the Church is built on our faith; our faith rests on preaching the Word of God; and the Word of God says (Mk 16.16), 'the one who believes and is baptized will be saved, but the one who does not believe will be condemned'.[39] Infants are not yet capable of believing and therefore must not be baptized until they reach maturity, ran the argument. Again, 'Where there is no [believer's] baptism by immersion, there is no church, no ministers, neither brothers nor sisters, no fraternal correction, bann or restoration.'[40] Bodenstein's account of the sacraments sounded especially similar to Zwingli's concept of a symbolic memorial of Christ's passion and death and, more importantly, Luther had been saying that such 'sacramentarians' and Anabaptists stood for the same distortions of doctrine. Thanks in part to the inspiration of their criticisms of Luther and the influence of mysticism, Anabaptists have been linked to the irenic and esoteric traditions of early modern 'Christians without a church'.[41]

Anabaptists lived among the refugees at Strasbourg in the late 1520s and early 1530s. Controversy over their promoters helped Martin Bucer develop his own view of spiritual presence in the eucharist, which was accepted by theologians in most of the south German cities that had earlier preferred 'sacramentarian' views. The controversy also helped Bucer and Wolfgang Capito, the most influential Strasbourg ministers in the early 1530s, to clarify for south German cities the role of magistrates in the administration of public religion; Philip Melanchthon, Johannes Brenz, and probably Wencelas Linck and Andreas Osiander were also provoked by the Anabaptist threat to sharpen their views on the relation of temporal authority to the Church.[42] The debate over Anabaptists had, in other words, ecclesiological consequences at both conceptual and practical levels. It helped firm-up an ecclesial Protestantism that saw the external church as society.

For, two of the Strasbourg refugees prominently argued against a church of such external forms.[43] Sebastian Franck claimed that outward signs were given to the Church only to accommodate its immaturity,[44] and these sacraments quickly degenerated after the death of the apostles. The only true church that remains is spiritual, he said, 'Therefore the unitary Spirit alone baptizes with fire and the Spirit all the faithful and all who are obedient to the inner Word in whatever part of the world they be.'[45] Caspar Schwenckfeld had long emphasized the internal word of Christ as essential to a true experience of the eucharist.[46] When admonished to join a parish in Strasbourg in 1529, he demurred that Christ was sufficiently within him and required no external supports.[47] To the Augsburg Confession's article on the Church he simply said, 'this article on the universal Christian church is abbreviated, obscure, and not understandable, doesn't talk about the church of Christ distinctly, nor in the way that Holy Scripture speaks about it', which he rectified by explaining at some length the nature of the Church as a purely spiritual and, one could say, subjective phenomenon.[48] Both Franck and Schwenckfeld have been called, awkwardly, 'conventicular spiritualizers'.[49] They thought Christians should meet in small groups without regard for physical sacraments, formal organization and external structures, which they believed were irrelevant to the true spiritual communion of the Church. They represent, at a formative moment, a Protestant extreme which continued to find its adherents, posing an on-going threat to the more churchly reformed.[50]

Given Protestant emphasis on a concept of the Church as an invisible society ruled directly by Christ, it does not surprise that among themselves they should argue over the character of external forms. Self-differentiation from Anabaptists helped the adherents of the Augsburg Confession, that is, the main Protestant force during the religious controversy, insist that the Church remained a visible, sacramental fellowship which babies enter by baptism and in which believers are nurtured by Jesus Christ himself.[51] Luther, his friend Nikolaus Amsdorf (an important north German reformer in his own right) and others may have distrusted Martin Bucer, who developed the concept of spiritual communion in the sacrament of the Lord's Supper that is often associated with John Calvin.[52] But, excepting theologians of Zürich, Bern, Basel and Constance, there grew a functioning consensus among Protestants on sacramental doctrine and, with it, views of the Church, and the consensus remained largely intact until the aftermath of the War of Schmalkalden in 1547, when the eucharistic debate was rekindled within Germany and beyond in disputes over Calvin and Melanchthon.[53]

In short, controversy with Anabaptists helped Protestants perceive themselves as advocates of a universally valid (i.e. Catholic) evangelical tradition. Pope Pius III (1534–49) helped them distinguish this position from the current of institutional reform – not just papal reform but conciliar reform, too. Pius admitted that churches were corrupt. Cardinal Gasparo Contarini's reform commission produced a damning inventory of abuses in the same year in which the Pope called a general council to convene at the city of Mantua (1537): bad priests, benefice marketeering, the accumulation of bishoprics by cardinals, absentee cardinals and bishops, ineffective ecclesiastical courts, indiscipline in religious orders, the superstitious preaching of pardoners, mendicant purveyors of cheap absolutions, and the tolerance of celebrity prostitutes by bishops in Italian cities.[54] Although the intended council did not open until 1545 at Trent, the League of Schmalkalden and its theologians reacted to the summons with alarm. Through the rest of the 1530s, the Protestant estates of the League emphasized the continuity of their church with the past, a crucial tactic in the effort to retain confiscated church properties, while their theologians insisted that human traditions carried the church away from an evangelical mainstream of truth.[55] This required a discriminating view of the past and the assertion of an evangelical continuum passing through the fathers of the church to present times, which could also be discerned, when useful, in canon law.[56] When a general council was summoned by Pius III, Protestants reacted with a pronounced scepticism over conciliar authority as such.[57] They countered, saying that attendance could not be compulsory, and the council's decisions were only authoritative insofar as they agreed with scripture. The first four ecumenical councils, they believed, measured well. But in their view, to compel attendance and enforce decrees against the gospel and evangelical ministry was to cancel the validity of the Council of Trent.[58]

Catholic ecclesiology

Luther, Melanchthon, Bucer and their associates in the League of Schmalkalden perceived themselves as Catholic reformers who apply conclusions drawn from the gospel. Adapting a point from Lucien Febvre, on the surprising comparison of François Rabelais and John Calvin, one could view them as promoters of an evangelism distinct from that of those Catholics inspired by Erasmus who did not rebel against the papacy but were deeply critical of church government and everyday religious life – a kind of left wing of Catholic evangelism.[59] Yet however similar Protestants were to Catholics, the rejection of the council always distinguished them from their neighbours in the 'old faith', as it came to be called. Rejection of the council reinforced the main issue dividing Protestant from Catholic conceptualizations of the Church in the sixteenth century, namely, the papal office.

Among Catholic theologians, there was wide agreement that the bishop of Rome enjoyed judicial pre-eminence but disagreement over the limits of papal jurisdiction and how its basis might be conceived. The early sixteenth-century conciliarists Jacques Almain and Jean Major, together with the Gallicans who vexed the twenty-third session of the Council of Trent, and Pierre d'Ailly and Jean Gerson before them, thought councils exceeded popes only in emergencies.[60] No consensus had emerged around Marsiglio of Padua, whose *Defender of the Peace* denied popes any essential supremacy or coercive authority over anyone, yet granted that 'the best arrangement for church ritual and the observance of the faith is attained by the appointment of such a mortal head' as the bishop of Rome, by choice of believers.[61] Even the advocates of the schismatic Council of Basel,[62] whose conciliar legacy Pope Pius II described in 1460 as 'pestiferous muck', intended not to destroy papal plenitude of power but to establish a kind of constitutional monarchy in the church that placed popes under ecumenical councils but did not eliminate popes.[63] Protestants universally agreed with Luther that the papacy had become a tyrannical institution, that is, antichrist.[64] The position was summarized in a document written by Melanchthon and subscribed by thirty-two theologians at the diet of the League of Schmalkalden in February and early March 1537. It includes a restatement of the Augsburg Confession's view of the bishop's pastoral office.[65] The Protestants could allow bishops, even prince-bishops with temporal jurisdictions in the Holy Roman Empire, if a prince-bishop's pastoral responsibilities were separated from his temporal ones, preferably to be divided between distinct people. In addition, there was, to them, no distinction between the sacramental status of bishop and priest.[66] The arrangement was a matter of convenience, not divine law. The problem, they said, was the indiscriminate way men were admitted to the priesthood.[67] Temporal power came to dominate the bishop's office. This required re-establishing the bishop's religious role, as John Hooper insisted in 1549, a concern shared by Catholic reformers.[68] There was room for bishops. There was no Protestant room for popes. But the goals of Protestant ecclesiology were not revolutionary. 'There should be one holy church forever', said Melanchthon in the Augsburg Confession. They were correcting 'just a few abuses'. [21, 22]

However much Protestants and Catholics stood on opposite sides of the papacy, it would misrepresent theologians of the old faith to say that in reaction their opponents drove them to papal absolutism. Conciliar ideas had an intricate afterlife in tractates 'on the Church' produced by Catholic theologians during the religious controversy. 'What, in the tractates, might awaken the impression that they're only about scholastic subtleties became the object of extended and embittered controversy at Vatican I', Ulrich Horst recently noted.[69] The themes are familiar from the conciliar movement: the problem of heretical and putative popes (the legend of Pope Joan),[70] infallibility, the relation of episcopal to papal power, and the source of plenitude of power in the church. These issues framed a Catholic theologian's opinion of the church as a social body.

Let us consider one extreme. Albert Pighe was a Dutch theologian and mathematician who studied at Louvain and Paris and became provost of the cathedral chapter at Utrecht. He participated in the imperial colloquies of Worms and Regensburg in 1540 and 1541, where Protestants resented his views.[71] His *Hierarchiae ecclesiasticae assertio* (1538) was famous for arguing that no one could judge a pope as guilty of heresy, because it was unimaginable that Christ would allow the church to be imperilled in this way: 'that an instance of heresy can have no place in [the pope], Christ mercifully and necessarily provided to his church'.[72] Pighe meant to associate the mystical body of Christ with both its hierarchical structure and the economy of grace, its worldly form and its spiritual nature as a fellowship with Christ and the saints.[73] This concentrated the infallibility of the Church in the holder of papal office. It was a narrow assertion of the Church's survivability.

The problem of survival had been made famous 250 years earlier in the *Rationale divinorum* of Guillaume Durand, when he explained why the Blessed Virgin receives special liturgical honours on the seventh day of the week. The reason, he said, was Mary's faith. Between the death and resurrection of Christ, she alone remained true to the Son of God, while the apostles fled.[74] The papal defender during the crisis of the Council of Basel, Juan de Torquemada (d. 1468), repeated the idea that the Church survived for a time in Mary alone; the point had also been adapted in more speculative terms by William Ockham, who noted that the Church could survive in a woman, such as Mary, or a mere baptized infant (an unconscious survival of the Church, without the exercise of faith).[75] Should the individual who guarantees the survival be the pope? The Dominican Tommaso de Vio Cajetan, one of the most important theologians and biblical scholars of the sixteenth century (and Luther's interrogator at Augsburg in 1518), had argued at the time of the Fifth Lateran Council (1512–17) that the church is preserved from error by virtue of its link to the apostles, with Peter at their head, while Peter's successor receives a personal gift of grace that assists his definitions of the faith – a divine guarantee of infallibility.[76] The point was to establish an organic relationship. It extended far beyond Christ and the bishop of Rome, while underscoring their privileged positions as head and vicar. It was still possible for some to spread infallibility through the Church at large, just as Marsiglio of Padua and the conciliarists, in their distinct ways, had spread the source of power through the body of the faithful.[77] But papalists argued over the nature of the personal locus of ecclesiastical power and certainty. The Franciscan Alfonso de Castro argued in 1543 for a distinction between pope and office. The apostolic see consists of pope and cardinals together and never erred, he said, in spite of fallible popes.[78] Similarly, the Salamanca Dominican, Domingo Báñez, countered that the church is a community of the faithful and stands under the successor of Peter de facto, regardless of who may occupy the office.[79] The church is subjected to the office, whoever may hold it. The church is infallible with the pope, argued the Louvain theologian Jean Driedo, such that a pope could personally err, but the Roman church could not.[80] But in spite of these equivocations on the pope's personal authority, Pighe had stated strongly a certainty to which others aspired. His thesis on infallibility was *probably* true, said the Dominican Juan de la Peña, the Jesuit Francisco Suarez and the Jesuit Roberto Bellarmino late in the century.[81]

Theologians traced ecclesiastical power to sources that ranged from dispersed among the faithful (it resided in the Church as a whole prior to its localization in Peter's successor, according to the Dominican Francisco de Vitoria), to a power concentrated in the pontifical office, to one concentrated as an endowment in the pope's soul. Yet all agreed that the church in the world could not fall away from God. Such fallibility would contradict God's purpose to save human beings within it. Protestants, too, argued that the Church must in some ultimate way be infallible. Protestant theologians, in general, also considered their church to exist objectively in the world, but as a dispersed and oppressed evangelical minority through much of the past and certainly in the present, identifiable by faith and now compelled by the correct preaching of the gospel to abandon papal tyranny and corruption. Protestants were their own kind of 'infallibilists': the gospel cannot lead one astray and faith in it is a gift of the Holy Spirit. To believe is to experience the agency of a flawless God. Moreover, this experience depended on true preaching and the correct administration of the sacraments, that is, a human ministry which *could* be experienced outside Protestant congregations. Although the faithful should withdraw from papal obedience, an authentic Catholic church, to Protestant theologians, still extended beyond their called-out churches.[82] For their part, Catholics could also approach Protestant views of institutional decline, for example, by accepting the historical claim that the church had fallen into corruption at some point in the past, as was debated at the colloquy of Martin Bucer, Philip Melanchthon and the Catholic Georg Witzel, together with the counsellor of the Catholic Duke of Saxony and the chancellor of the Protestant Landgrave of Hesse, in Leipzig in early 1539.[83] Any excursion into Catholic ecclesiology beyond the religious controversy brings one eventually into the theological Pure Land of Christology.[84] Both sides of the religious controversy tried to describe, in terms concrete and certain, the reliability of a society that was by definition mystical.[85] As a body, baptized people were supposed to throb with the Church's divine being, either because God's dispostion of acceptance and goodwill was confirmed by evangelical preaching and sacraments, or because rivers of grace flowed through the priesthood. Where Protestants relied on a concept of inspired Bible hearing (it guaranteed that the gospel would be found in scriptural sermons), Catholic theologians argued (and all Protestants denied) that to the strangely numinous community of the Church there corresponded a legislative power.

If the 'neuralgic' subject for Protestants was the papacy, for Catholics it became, during the religious controversy, the conditions on which an infallibly reliable papal definition depends, discussion over which carried on all the way to Vatican I.[86] The force of conciliarism was felt here. Torquemada had said that an infallible papal decree required consultation with the well instructed, such as occurred in a general church council. Moreover, if a matter of faith were decided unanimously by the council and only contradicted by the pope, the council should prevail, because a pope can err in faith, although his judicial power cannot be exceeded.[87] In the early sixteenth century, the influential Dominican theologian of Salamanca, Francisco de Vitoria, insisted that a binding definition of faith required popes to exercise due diligence, 'to do what was in them' (*facere quod est in se*), while councils had an authority entirely analogous to the pope's.[88] The point was quickly modified by Dominicans of the Salamanca school. The council gives aid and the pope must seek counsel, but he makes the decision, explained Vitoria's student the Dominican Melchior Cano about the time of the first session of the Council of Trent.[89] Cooperation was the normal precondition for grace as commonly understood by Dominican theologians. Any malevolent consequence of cooperation was eventually restricted to the pope as an individual, when acknowledged at all. He sins if he fails to exercise due diligence in doctrinal definition, said Juan de la Peña in his lectures on Aquinas' *Summa Theologica* of 1559/1560; Gregorio de Valencia (d. 1603) agreed that such a pope was morally compromised but the infallibility of his decision remains.[90] Late in the century Bellarmine expressed a consensus of sixteenth-century papalists, who had been shaped largely by Torquemada and Cajetan, when he said that an infallible papal authority, regardless of the inhabitant of the throne, was morally certain to be a matter of the faith, because God guarantees the infallible outcome of papal definitions.[91] Although early in the century Cajetan, Sylvester Prierias and Vitoria, for example, had argued that it was possible to resist a pope without falling into rebellion, by appealing to a church council against the pope's wishes,[92] the century's trend was to isolate a pope's private potential to err from the infalliblity of his office, while closing any gap that might separate popes and councils. This antidote to both Protestant and conciliar chal-lenges to papal authority shaped all papalist ecclesiologies in the sixteenth century. To write against early Protestants was to defend the papal office, as Luther's most famous opponents all did.[93]

But it is nevertheless striking that a Catholic consensus on absolute papal authority faltered. Cajetan had argued that total power in the church resides in the pope, and all other powers merely participated in his, just as Christ established the Roman see over all other churches, making it the head to the body that he rules.[94] The alternative was to see sacra-mental power dispersed among bishops, which had strong precedents in patristic and early scholastic theology.[95] Debate over episcopal authority dominated the twenty-third session of the Council of Trent, which in 1562–3 discussed the obligation of bishops to reside in their dioceses. Was a bishop's residency required by divine law? Only after intense negotia-tion did the Council reach its insipid decision on episcopal residency (an absence of more than five months must ordinarily be approved by the pope or metropolitan), but more importantly it concentrated the sacramental powers of priests in the bishop's office.[96] 'The *sacerdotium* was now presented as *hierarchia ordinis* and was as such oriented to the bishop, not the priest. . . . The bishop belongs to the sacramental hierarchy by divine ordination and forms the first and highest rank of this hierarchy.'[97] The alternatives were either a sacra-mental power spread among bishops and priests to form a distributed source of primacy (pope as *centrum unitatis* over individual churches) or one flowing as a kind of sacramental and juridical circuit through a papal switch to form a collective primacy (the Church is a whole with the pope at its head).[98] But the pope's juridical primacy remained secure.

In either case, God's historical incarnation inaugurated a legislative power. Protestants generally restricted such legal authority to the human realm, to be arranged by custom, convenience, or replaced by New Testament forms. This is not to say they denied a legis-lative aspect to church affairs, or that most of them simply consigned the external church to temporal government, as Luther suggested in the early 1520s, as Thomas Cranmer advo-cated in 1540, and as Thomas Erastus would insist for the Palatinate in the 1570s.[99] Rather, their argument was designed to force the question of spiritual renewal in a way that the routine government of the church had, they concluded, fatally compromised. 'If anyone should rightly ponder and scrutinize this whole form of ecclesiastical government which is today under the papacy, he won't find [anywhere] a robber's nest more licentious and lawless, in which bandits lurk more unbridled without law or limit.'[100] By eliminating foun-dations of church power in divine law, or by restricting divine law to religious purposes, Protestants believed they restored the universal rule of Christ, just as their opponents believed the unity of Christ's body was preserved through the legislative powers of bishops and popes, the remedy to the disruption of Luther's rebellion.[101] Beneath this great differ-ence lay the agreements they took for granted. To Protestants and Catholics alike, the Church was a spiritual communion, must take a visible form that involved sacraments and correct doctrine, and was subject to management by ordained specialists. We need not contrast 'inward' Protestants with 'outward' Catholics. They agreed on the Church's inward being and disagreed on how it should be externally defined.

A common social imaginary

Theologians also generally agreed that the Church was coterminous with society and, to one extent or another, self-governing.[102] This question is often approached as a problem of ideologies: which Protestant theologians worked for temporal supremacy in the church? Hardly any. Although the religious controversy involved state interests, insofar as rulers wanted better religion and better access to church property, early Protestant theologians avoided the questions of political philosophy that were known from fourteenth-century and later conciliar debates. Instead, they presented their rulers and themselves as mere defenders of religion, just as Catholic rulers were obliged to be.[103] It has often been said that Protestant confessions held distinct positions on state power, but in fact a theologian's political circumstances more reliably shaped his views: there was no necessary connection between Reformed churches and proto-republican thought or Lutheran churches and absolute power.[104] Among Catholic theologians, the problem of state power appeared most obviously in conjunction with the rule of non-Christians. Did a pope possess authority over the world as Christ's vicar, such that he could distribute things the way Pope Alexander VI divided the New World between Spain and Portugal in 1493?[105] Or was conquest conditioned by pagan title to property, the terms of war, the presence or absence of heresy, the availability and comprehensibility of missionary preaching, and the will of native people, issues first debated by the Parisian conciliarist Jean Major and his student Francisco de Vitoria even before the *conquista* of the isles of the west?[106] The debate was made famous by the mid-century exchange between the Dominicans Juan Ginés de Sepúlveda and Bartolomé de las Casas.[107] But this had nothing to do with the religious controversy, and the rise of Protestantism had no particular impact on Catholic *political* thinking. Henry VIII claimed to be head of the English church as a Catholic. He and his chancellor Cardinal Thomas Wolsey represented a practical fusion of temporal and spiritual office; any number of Catholic rulers or even the papacy might have envied the accomplishment.[108] Protestants were well aware that successful rulers dominated churches, among whom the Emperor Charles V was an eloquent example in both Spain and the Netherlands.[109] The fact gave ballast to the Protestant charge that their opponents were church robbers. They themselves merely restored churches to their true purpose in the world, said the two leaders of the League of Schmalkalden to the emperor when they responded to his invitation to an imperial dialogue on the religious controversy in the spring of 1540.[110] On the Continent, Protestants could criticize the kings of England and Denmark as the destroyers of churches.[111] The difference between Catholics and Protestants was the legislative authority of church courts, of which the papacy was the acknowledged summit. Catholic rulers tried to reform (or use) churches through them. Protestant rulers tried to preserve (or use) churches without them.

Protestant and Catholic reformers agreed that the crucial sphere of religious society was locally organized as the parish. The size and number of parishes in urban and rural communities varied greatly throughout Europe.[112] But size and parts regardless, it was the geographical space of a clergyman's domain. Catholic reformers frequently tried to protect the parish priest from the interference of foreign clergy and fraternal bodies, confirming the spiritual lordship of the parish priest as the Fourth Lateran Council (1215) once did.[113] 'The council of Trent really canonized the parish', but confraternities and sodalities continued to grow as vehicles of religious acculturation.[114] The council positioned the bishop as the governor of religious reform and good order.[115] But the parish priest was the spiritual guide through life's passages, from baptism through marriage to extreme unction. This was where the stakes of ecclesiological debate were highest.

Apart from Anabaptism, Protestants presupposed the geographical organization of local churches as parishes and contended for their control. They famously disagreed over the relationship between temporal authority and clergy in the struggle, but the difference should not be overdrawn. The contrast is often made between Protestant principalities of the Holy Roman Empire and German-speaking Swiss cantons, with Strasbourg leading south German cities from the Swiss toward a Lutheran or semi-Lutheran position during and after its controversy over Anabaptism in the early 1530s. Zürich and Bern represented a complete integration of church and civil authority. Geneva represented their strict separation. The Germans tended to presuppose the integration of church structures under temporal government, but in practice, 'the laity intervened very little, outside a few free cities like Strasbourg and Ulm'.[116] A century after the religious controversy, Lutheran jurists were still debating the extent of rulers' rights in the church, in spite of the integration of clerical management structures into territorial administrations.[117] The autonomy of church ministry had not been lost even where Calvinists might have thought it was most imperilled. All theologians agreed that Christian magistrates and clergy must work together for godly ends, which of course was exactly what clergy would have wanted to take for granted.

All sides to the religious controversy were actually trying to reform the same beast, which was the human self as a morally and spiritually degraded being. It is perhaps not surprising that, in spite of the difference between married and unmarried clergy, Protestants and Catholics promoted parallel agendas of family, sexuality and social regulation.[118] But given the universal demand for conversion, why didn't they all encourage a degree of ecclesiastical diversification to improve the penetration of religion into private and public life?

The reason was heaven. The primary identity of the Church was as a spiritual communion in which the majority lived invisibly and indivisibly perfect lives in the immediate presence of God, united to God's resurrected body. The rest on earth were, ordinarily, joined to them by the Church's ministry, while the earthly community of all the baptized had, one way or another, to facilitate, propagate and reflect the mystical body. It is, by current standards, a strange way to view the world. Its valuation of the present in terms of another world, an imagined future, feels utopian. But to all well-instructed clergy, whose numbers were growing, the godly dead were no mere archetype of a common life. The living approached the tranquillity of glorified saints when they experienced union with Christ in church. Their sense of the importance of salvation, their longing for social paradise, could only intensify their debate. Because ultimately Protestant and Catholic theologians aspired to the same end.

Notes

1 'There is no question here of expounding on its own terms and in the manner of successive monographs the ecclesiology of the reformers', Yves Congar observed at the beginning of his compact treatment of Protestant ecclesiology. Yves Congar, *L'Eglise de saint Augustin à l'époque moderne*, Paris: Les Éditions du Cerf, 1970, p. 352. The same is certainly true for me. I offer a synoptic interpretation of sixteenth-century argument between Catholics and Protestants over the Church, emphasizing debates during the first generation of Protestants. The origin of two issues to become extremely important in seventeenth-century Protestant ecclesiology must be passed over, namely covenantal conception of the Church and the ecclesiology of disestablished churches in England. For the former, see David A. Weir, *The Origins of the Federal Theology in Sixteenth-Century Reformed Thought*, New York: Oxford University Press, 1990. For the latter, see Stephen Brachlow, *The Communion of Saints: Radical Puritan and Separatist Ecclesiology, 1570–1625*, Oxford University Press, 1988, and see, also, the following chapter in this present volume. I must also pass over the debate on the exact meaning and force of Luther's doctrine of two kingdoms. For that, see James

Estes, *Peace, Order and the Glory of God: Secular Authority and the Church in the Thought of Luther and Melanchthon, 1518–1559*, Leiden: E.J. Brill, 2005 and cf. also Chapter 9 of this volume.

2 For Wyclif and his influence, consider the essays gathered in *Lollards and their Influence in Late Medieval England*, ed. by Fiona Somerset, Jill C. Havens, Derrick G. Pitard, Woodridge: Boydell, 2003. For the Hussite revolt, the standard work in English remains Howard Kaminsky, *A History of the Hussite Revolution*, Berkeley: University of California, 1967, but consider also Thomas A. Fudge, *Magnificent Ride: the First Reformation in Hussite Bohemia*, Aldershot: Ashgate, 1998.

3 Hans-Jürgen Goertz, *Pfaffenhaß und groß Geschrei. Die reformatorischen Bewegungen in Deutschland, 1517–1529*, Munich: C.H. Beck, 1987, pp. 244–50 and passim. Dorothea Wendebourg argued that the Protestant movements were only united in the minds of Catholic opponents, 'Die Einheit der Reformation als historisches Problem', B. Hamm, B. Moeller, D. Wendebourg, *Reformations-Theorien. Ein kirchenhistorischer Disput über Einheit und Vielfalt der Reformation*, Göttingen: Vandenhoeck und Ruprecht, 1995, pp. 31–51. Christopher Haigh distinguished several English Reformations, *English Reformations: Religion, Politics and Society under the Tudors*, New York: Oxford University Press, 1993. For a general introduction to the Reformation movements, the following are especially useful: Euan Cameron, *The European Reformation*, Oxford University Press, 1991, pp. 199–291; Diarmaid MacCulloch, *The Reformation: A History*, New York: Viking, 2003; Jean Delumeau, Theirry Wanegffelen, *Naissance et Affirmation de la Réforme*, Paris: Presses Universitaires de France, 1997, pp. 29–173; and Marc Venard et al., *Le temps des confessions (1530–1620/30)*, volume 8 of *Le temps des confessions des origines à nos jours*, edited by Jean-Marie Mayeur, Charles Pietri, André Vauchez, Marc Venard, Paris: Desclée, 1992, pp. 15–279, 353–67, 475–87.

4 Sergiusz Michalski, 'Die Ausbreitung der reformatorischen Bildersturms, 1521–37', *Bildersturm. Wahnsinn oder Gottes Wille?* edited by Cécile Dupeux, Peter Jezler, Jean Wirth, Munich: Wilhelm Fink, 2000, pp. 46–56.

5 Georg Kuhaupt, *Veröffentlichte Kirchenpolitik. Kirche im publizistischen Streit zur Zeit der Religionsgespräche (1538–1541)*, Göttingen: Vandenhoeck und Ruprecht, 1998, passim.

6 Compare France's uncommitted clergy and intellectuals (Calvin's despised 'Nicodemites' and their mobility between reformed and Catholic groups during and after the religious wars, and surviving Catholic aristocratic networks in Protestant England. Thierry Wanegffelen, *Ni Rome ni Genève*, Paris: Honoré Champion, 1997; Michael Questier, *Catholicism and Community in Early Modern England: Politics, Aristocratic Patronage, and Religion, c. 1550–1640*, Cambridge University Press, 2006.

7 Or one could say, the debate belonged to a society shaped by the synergy of conflictual relationships and harmonizing energies, as the early conflict sociologist Georg Simmel once argued societies to be. Georg Simmel, *Soziologie*, 5th edn, Berlin: Duncker und Humblot, 1968, p. 191.

8 On the protests of the Diet of Speyer after which Protestants were named, see now Armin Kohnle, *Reichstag und Reformation*, Gütersloh: Gütersloher Verlagshaus, 2001, pp. 369, 374.

9 Thomas A. Brady, *Protestant Politics: Jacob Sturm (1489–1553) and the German Reformation*, Atlantic Highlands, NJ: Humanities Press, 1995, pp. 142–283; Christopher Ocker, *Church Robbers and Reformers in Germany, 1525–1547: Confiscations and Religious Purpose in the Holy Roman Empire*, Leiden: E.J. Brill, 2006, pp. 50–131, 258–78.

10 Albrecht Pius Luttenberger, *Glaubenseinheit und Reichsfriede. Konzeptionen und Wege konfessionsneutraler Reichspolitik 1530–1552. Kurpfalz, Jülich, Kurbrandenburg*, Göttingen: Vandenhoeck und Ruprecht, 1982, passim.

11 Franz Posset, *The Front-Runner of the Catholic Reformation: the Life and Works of Johann von Staupitz*, Aldershot: Ashgate, 2003, pp. 319–25; *Acta Reformationis Catholicae Ecclesiam Germaniae Concernentia Saeculi XVI*, vol. 1, *1520 bis 1532*, edited by Georg Pfeilschifter, Regensburg: Friedrich Pustet, 1959, pp. 107, 204; Thomas Fuchs, *Konfession und Gespräch. Typologie und Funktion der Religionsgespräche in der Reformationszeit*, Cologne: Böhlau, 1995, passim; Heribert Smolinsky, Peter Walter, eds, *Katholische Theologen der Reformationszeit*, volume 6, and volume 64 of *Katholisches Leben und Kirchenreform im Zeitalter der Glaubensspaltung*, Münster: Aschendorff, 2004, especially the contributions on Julius Pflug, Claude d'Espence, Georg Cassander, Johannes Wild and Jacob Schipper. Consider also the *Gutachten* Gropper produced for Charles V at the Second Regensburg Colloquy in 1546, Julius Pflug's draft of reform proposals, and Pflug and Helding's draft of an agreement. *Acta Reformationis Catholicae Ecclesiam Germaniae Concernentia*, 6 vols, Regensburg: Friedrich Pustet, 1959–74, 6:156–255 nr.13–15, esp. pp. 168–9, 239–40, 253–4.

12 Venard *et al*. *Le temps des Confessions (1530–1620/30)*, pp. 368–70.

13 Jacques Toussaert once estimated that there existed a moral Christianity among 80 per cent of the people, a dogmatic one among 15 per cent, and a sacramental one among 5 per cent. *Le sentiment religieux en Flandre*, Paris: Plon, 1963, p. 67 and cited by Delumeau and Wanegffelen, *Naissance et affirmation*, p. 372. For the problem of religious uncertainty, ibid., pp. 372–92.

14 His anti-papal themes had already appeared prominent in his Latin writings of 1518 and 1519. Mark U. Edwards, *Printing, Propaganda, and Martin Luther*, Berkeley: University of California Press, 1994, pp. 165–9.

15 Delumeau, Wanegffelen, *Naissance et affirmation*, pp. 371, 373.

16 Delumeau and Wenegffelen note a common civilization; parallel campaigns against theatre, drunkenness, vagrancy, bad priests and the threat of an increasingly credit-based economy; a parallel response to the growing importance of the laity; a desire to restore theology; controversy over predestination and Augustinianism; the same problems of the relations of Church and State; and sometimes the same musicians. Ibid., pp. 374–92.

17 Fuchs, *Konfession und Gespräch*, pp. 369–79.

18 Fuchs, *Konfession und Gespräch*, pp. 381–8. Kohnle, *Reichstag und Reformation*, pp. 381–94.

19 Fuchs, *Konfession und Gespräch*, pp. 429–56 and passim. Four Protestant cities (Strasbourg, Constance, Lindau and Memmingen refused to subscribe to the confession, on account of its Lutheran doctrine of the Eucharist, and subscribed to the alternative 'Tetrapolitan Confession', which played little role in imperial politics. Strasbourg soon subscribed to the Augsburg Confession, too, and joined the new League in 1531, then helped draw other south German cities into the League, including Constance, Lindau, and Memmingen. Gabriele Haug-Moritz, *Der Schmalkaldische Bund, 1530–1541/42*, Leinfelden-Echterdingen: Verlag Weinbrenner, 2002, pp. 43–53 for the early formation of the League and pp. 98–121 for the role of confession in it.

20 Willem Van 't Spijker, 'Calvin's Friendship with Martin Bucer: Did It Make Calvin a Calvinist?', *Calvin Studies Society Papers 1995*, 1996, edited by D. Foxgrover, Grand Rapids, MI: Calvin Studies Society, 1998, pp. 169–86. Zurich's international role, and its influence in debates over the Eucharist, a theology of covenant and the singularity of temporal and spiritual government, was restored by Heinrich Bullinger at mid-century. Bruce Gordon, 'Switzerland', *The Early Reformation in Europe*, ed. A. Pettegree, Cambridge University Press, 1992, pp. 85–6, and the contributions of W. Janse, D. Shaw, J.A. Löwe, J.W. Baker, Janusz Małłek, Erich Bryner, and Lorenz Hein in *Die Zürcher Reformation: Ausstrahlungen und Rückwirkungen*, ed. by A. Schindler, H. Stickelberger, Bern: Peter Lang, 2001, pp. 203–20, 303–49, 405–31.

21 *Confessio Augustana*, articles 7–8, translating the Latin version. *Die Bekenntnisschriften der evangelisch-lutherischen Kirche*, sixth edition, Göttingen: Vandenhoeck und Ruprecht, 1967, pp. 61–62. My translation differs slightly from *Creeds and Confession of Faith in the Christian Tradition*, edited by J. Pelikan, V. Hotchkiss, 4 vols, New Haven: Yale University Press, 2003, 2:62.

22 *Confessio Augustana*, preamble before article 22, *Bekenntnisschriften*, p. 84. *Creeds and Confessions* 2:77 for another translation. Consider also Melanchthon's explanation of the preamble in the *Apologia Confessionis Augustanae*, articles 7–8, *Bekenntnisschriften*, pp. 233–46. The Tetrapolitan Confession, although at greater length, also described the Church as the community of those who have faith in Christ, among whom sinners are intermixed, and visible in the fruit of faith, namely true confession, evident where the gospel is preached and the evangelical sacraments are administered. *Die Bekenntnisschriften der reformierten Kirche*, ed. E.F.K. Müller, Leipzig: A. Deichert, 1903, pp. 70–1. *Creeds and Confessions* 2:235–36.

23 *Confessio Augustana.*, articles 22–8, *Bekenntnisschriften*, pp. 85–135. *Creeds and Confessions*, 2:77–116.

24 Melanchthon and Georg Spalatin's advice to the Protestant estates before the dialogue occurred. *Corpus Reformatorum* 2:280; Fuchs, *Konfession und Gespräch*, pp. 369–70.

25 Luther's 1518/9 gloss on Hebrews 1.8 and the phrase 'throne of God', which he says refers to the people of God not by outward appearance (they are exiles, impoverished, etc.). WA 57/3:107–8; Melanchthon, *De ecclesia et auctoritate verbi Dei* (1560) CR 23:598–99. See also Yves Congar, *Die Lehre von der Kirche vom Abendländischen Schisma bis zur Gegenwart*, vol. 3, fascicle 3d of the *Handbuch der Dogmengeschichte*, Freiburg: Herder, 1971, p. 45.

26 Luther, *Eine kurze Form der zehn Gebote* (1520), iii. WA 7:218–20; Melanchthon, *Loci theologici* (1559), xii, CR 21:825–47; idem, *Examen ordinandorum*, 'de ecclesia', CR 23:37–40; Congar, *Die*

Lehre von der Kirche, p. 44 with n. 86. Almost all Lutheran catechisms ommitted discipline from the marks of the Church, but in the next two generations after Luther numerous included Melanchthon's demand for obedience to ministers. Jacob Haitsma, *De Leer aangaande de Kerk in de Reformatorische Catechismi uit het Duitse en Nederlandse Taalgebied van 1530–1600*, Woerden: Zuijderduijn, 1968, p. 290. For the variety of Protestant treatments of the visible and invisible Church, Wilhelm Locher, *Sign of the Advent: A Study in Protestant Ecclesiology*, Fribourg: Academic Press, 2004, pp. 23–135.

27 For Luther, *Schmalkald Articles* xii, *Bekenntnisschriften*, pp. 460–1; *Creeds and Confessions* 2:146; *Shorter Catechism*, on the third article of the Apostles Creed, *Bekenntnisschriften*, pp. 511–12; but compare the *Longer Catechism* on the third article of the Apostles Creed, which emphasizes the forgiveness of sins, the sacraments and absolution, *Bekenntnisschriften* pp. 657–8; *The Large Catechism of Martin Luther*, trans. R.H. Fischer, Philadelphia: Fortress, 1959, p. 61. The definition of external marks was emphasized in reformed confessions. *Confessio Tetrapolitana* (1531 xv; *Conclusiones Lausannae disputandae* (1536); *Confession de la Foy laquelle tous bourgeois et habitans de Genève* (1536), xviii; *Confessio gallicana* (1559) xxvii–xxviii; *Confessio Helvetica posterior* (1562), xvii.11, The Forty-Two and the Thirty-Nine Articles of the Anglican Church (1552, 1563), xx (1552), xix (1563); *Professio fidei Catholicae . . . in Ecclesia Peregrinorum Francofordiae* (1554), iv; *Summa Capita Articulorum Fidei* (The Erlau [or Eger] Valley Confession, 1562), under the heading 'Signa verae Ecclesiae', *Bekenntnisschriften der reformierten Kirche*, pp. 70–1, 110, 115, 198, 228, 290, 512, 664; *Creeds and Confessions* 2:235–6, 317, 382–3, 494, 533; John Calvin, *Christianae religionis Institutio* (1536), ii, *Calvini opera selecta*, ed. P. Barth, 5 vols, Munich: C. Kaiser, 1926–62, 1:86–92, esp. 91, and for the appearance of visible signs of the church in subsequent editions, 5:15 and *Calvin's Institutes*, ed. J.T. McNeill, Louisville: Westminster/John Knox, 1960, pp. 1023–4 (*Institutes* IV.i.9–10 with the apparatus. Discipline was considered a mark of the Church by *Confessio Helvetica prior* (1536), xiv; *Confessio Belgica* (1561), xxix; *Scots Confession* (1560), xviii; *Compendium doctrinae christiane quam omnes Pastores et ministri ecclesiarum Dei in tota Ungaria et Transsylvania . . . decent ac profitentur* (1562), vii. *Bekenntnisschriften* pp. 104, 244, 257, 429. Balthasar Hubmaier described the Church as built from its confession of faith in Christ and governed by the discipline of fraternal admonition. Consider also the Schleitheim Confession (article 2), *Creeds and Confessions* 2:682, 697; Balthasar Hubmaier, *Schriften*, G. Westin, T. Bergsten, Gütersloh: Gerd Mohn, 1962, pp. 218–19. Sebastian Castellio, against Calvin's church regimen in Geneva, countered that 'the true church will be known by love which proceeds from faith. . . . These and similar matters are certain, however dubious may be the obscure questions about the Trinity, predestination, election, and the rest on account of which men are regarded as heretic', *Reply to Calvin* (1567), ed. and trans. R. Bainton, *Concerning Heretics*, New York: Columbia University Press, 1935, p. 267. For the marks of the Church in Lutheran and Reformed catechisms, Haitsma, *De Leer aangaande de Kerk*, pp. 63–5, 84–5.

28 A. Kolping, 'Notae ecclesiae', *Lexikon für Theologie und Kirche*, 2nd edn, 10 vols, Freiburg: Herder, 1957–67, 7:1044–8; E. Dublauchy, 'Église', *Dictionnaire de Theologie Catholique*, 15 vols, Paris: Letouzey et Ané, 1908–72, 4/2:2129; Ulrich Horst, *Die Lehrautorität des Papstes und die Dominikaner-Theologen der Schule von Salamanca*, Berlin: Akademie Verlag, 2003, p. 133. For the traditional marks in Lutheran and Reformed catechisms, Haitsma, *De Leer aangaande de Kerk*, pp. 65–7, 85–6.

29 See Chapters 2 and 36 of this volume.

30 Congar, *L'Eglise*, pp. 70–71, 160–76, 355–57; Paul Althaus, *The Theology of Martin Luther*, trans. R. Schulz, Minneapolis: Fortress, 1966, pp. 296–303. For the polemical context of the development of Luther's 'spiritualizing' emphasis, Werner Elert, *The Structure of Lutheranism*, trans. W.A. Hansen, St Louis: Concordia, 1962, pp. 257–74. See also Karl Holl, 'Die Entstehung von Luthers Kirchenbegriff', idem, *Gesammelte Aufsätze zur Kirchengeschichte*, 3 vols, Tübingen: J.C.B. Mohr, 1928–32, 1:288–325.

31 Emphasized in early scholastic theology. Josef Finkenzeller, 'Kirche IV', *Theologische Realenzyklopedie* 36+ vols, Berlin: De Gruyter, 1977-, 18:231; Hugh of St-Victor, *On the Sacraments of the Christian Faith*, II.ii.1, trans. R.J. Deferrari, Cambridge, MA: Mediaeval Academy of America, 1951, p. 254.

32 *Confessio Augustana* xxviii with *Apologia* xvii, *Bekenntnisschriften*, pp. 120–33, 396–403. Consider also the recommendation of Wolfgang Musculus and Bonifacius Wolfhart to the Schmalkald diet

in 1538, Bucer's recommendation to the same diet, an anonymous recommendation published by the League's diet in 1539, the diet's answer to the imperial invitation to a religious colloquy in 1540, and Bucer's advice to the archbishop of Cologne Hermann Wied and King Edward VI. Ocker, *Church Robbers*, pp. 186, 192–3, 197–8, 207–10, 232–4; Gottfried Hammann, *Martin Bucer, 1491–1551 zwischen Volkskirche und Bekenntnisgemeinschaft*, Stuttgart: Franz Steiner, 1989, pp. 235–37; Eike Wolgast, *Hochstift und Reformation*, pp. 91–9; Thomas A. Brady, *Protestant Politics*, pp. 258–60; Andreas Gäumann, *Reich Christi und Obrigkeit. Eine Studie zum reformatorischen Denken und Handeln Martin Bucers*, Bern: Peter Lang, 2001, pp. 232–5; Hammann, *Martin Bucer*, pp. 251–73; Martin Bucer, *De regno Christi* (1550), trans. W. Pauck, *Melanchthon and Bucer*, Philadelphia: Westminster, 1969, pp. 283–95. Consider also Calvin, *Institutes*, IV.xi.1–8; *Opera selecta* 5:195–204, McNeill, Battles trans., pp. 1211–29.

33 Translating the German, *Bekenntnisschriften*, pp. 396–7. The Latin text reads: 'The adversaries make a great deal of noise about the privileges and immunities of the clerical estate. . . . but we are arguing about other things. . . . For we have often declared that we do not challenge civil ordinances or donations of princes or privileges.' Cf. *Sources and Contexts of the Book of Concord*, ed. R. Kolb, J.A. Nestingen, Minneapolis: Fortress, 2001, 137–9.

34 Conveniently seen in their catechisms. Haitsma, *De Leer aangaande de Kerk*, pp. 170, 180–1, 208–10, 229–31.

35 Yves Congar's conclusion about Luther, *L'Eglise*, pp. 353–4.

36 Marilyn McCord Adams, *William Occam*, 2 vols, Notre Dame: University of Notre Dame Press, 1987, 1:551–629. Ockham juxtaposed hierarchical and organic conceptions of the Church. William of Ockham, *On the Power of Emperors and Popes*, trans. A.S. Brett, University of Durham Press, 1998, pp. 28–9 and passim. See also Jürgen Miethke, *De potestate papae: die päpstliche Amtskompetenz im Widerstreit der politischen Theorie von Thomas von Aquin bis Wilhelm von Ockham*, Tübingen: Mohr Siebeck, 2000, pp. 286–7.

37 George Hunston Williams, *The Radical Reformation*, 3rd edn, Kirksville, MI: Sixteenth Century Journal Publishers, 1992.

38 Friedrich Wilhelm Bautz, 'Bodenstein, Andreas', *Biographisch-Bibliographisches Kirchenlexikon*, 25 vols, Hamm, Herzberg, Nordhausen: Bautz, 1990–2005, 1: 652–5.

39 Balthasar Hubmaier, *Der Uralten und gar neüen Leeren Urtail, das man die jungen kindlen nit tauffen soll, biß sy jm glauben underricht sind* (1526). Hubmaier, *Schriften*, p. 242. For Karlstadt and Hoffman, Calvin Augustine Pater, *Karlstadt as the Father of the Baptist Movements*, Toronto: University of Toronto Press, 1984, pp. 47–91.

40 Hubmaier, *Grund und Ursach, das einn yedlicher mensch, der gleich in seiner Khindthait getaufft ist, schuldig sey, sich recht nach der Ordnung Christi, ze tauffen lassen* (1527), Hubmaier, *Schriften*, p. 333. See also Eddie Mabry, *Balthasar Hubmaier's Doctrine of the Church*, New York: University Press of America, 1994, pp. 69–100.

41 Leszek Kolakowski, *Chrétiens sans Église. La conscience religieuse et le lien confessionnel au xviie siècle*, Paris: Gallimard, 1969, pp. 140–1, with 53–68 for similarities and dissimilarities with other Anabaptists.

42 Brady, *Protestant Politics*, pp. 104–31; Estes, *Peace, Order and the Glory of God*, pp. 111–28; Andreas Gäumann, *Reich Christi und Obrigkeit*, pp. 257–63, 315–57.

43 Gäumann, *Reich Christi und Obrigkeit*, pp. 326–57, esp. 355–7 for the continuation of a dissident minority in Strasbourg; and Elsie Anne McKee, *Katharina Schütz Zell*, 2 vols, Leiden: E.J. Brill, 1999, 1:77–82, 91–101, 109–15.

44 Estes, *Peace, Order and the Glory of God*, pp. 93–133. John Calvin similarly argued that sacraments were necessary to accommodate human dullness. *Instruction et confession de foy dont on use en l'Eglise de Genève* (1537), ed. A. Zillenbiller, *Ioannis Calvini scripta ecclesiastica*, vol. 2, Geneva: Droz, 2002, p. 95; *Institutio religionis Christianae* (1536), iv, *Opera selecta*, 1:118.

45 *Spiritual and Anabaptist Writers*, ed. G.H. Williams, Philadelphia: Westminster, 1957, pp. 152–3; Williams, *The Radical Reformation*, pp. 695–6.

46 Caspar Schwenckfeld, *De cursu verbi Dei* (1527), *Corpus Schwenckfeldiorum*, 19 vols, Leipzig: Breitkopf und Hertl, 1907–61, 2:590–9.

47 Williams, *Radical Reformation*, pp. 385–6.

48 *Judicium uber die Augsburgische Confession* (1530), *Corpus Schwenckfeldiorum* 3:901–24.

49 Williams, *Radical Reformation*, p. 1299.

50 Schwenckfeld lived and taught until 1561. Michael Servetus promoted another form of divine immanentism, and adult baptism, in his *Christianismi restitutio* (1553). Roland H. Bainton, *Michel Servet: Hérétique et Martyr, 1553–1953*, Geneva: Droz, 1953, pp. 77–88; Williams, *Radical Reformation*, p. 456. Faustus Socinus considered the sacraments relatively unimportant, ibid., pp. 1170–72. For English baptists, Brachlow, *The Communion of Saints*, pp. 150–202.

51 Either under the signs of bread and wine, which were given by Christ to accommodate human 'stupidity', or as a corporeal presence with the bread and wine. For the former, John Calvin, *Traicte de la sainte cene de nostre seigneur et seul saveur Jesu Christ* (1541) CR 33:435 and passim; idem, *Opera selecta*, 1:505 and passim; Martin Bucer, *Axiomata apologetica* and *Formula Concordiae* (1536), *Martin Bucers Deutsche Schriften*, ed. R. Stupperich, 17+ vols, Gütersloh: Gerd Mohn, 1960+, 6/1:83–93, 121–29. Martin Luther, *Vom Abendmahl Christi*, WA26:261–509.

52 Martin Brecht, *Martin Luther*, 3 vols, trans. J.L. Schaaf, Minneapolis: Fortress, 1993, 3:39–59.

53 John Calvin, participant in the colloquies of 1540 and 1541, emphasized the evangelical consensus, in his *De la cene, Opera Selecta* 1:526–30; Brian A. Gerrish, *Grace and Gratitude: The Eucharistic Theology of John Calvin*, Minneapolis: Fortress, 1993, pp. 139–45; Brecht, *Martin Luther*, 3:314, on Luther's objections to the Cologne Reformation proposal of 1544, and an early sign of the new eucharistic controversy; Oliver K. Olsen, *Matthias Flacius and the Survival of Luther's Reform*, Wiesbaden: Horrosowitz, 2002, pp. 101–31; Elert, *Structure of Lutheranism*, pp. 300–21; Jill Raitt, *The Colloquy of Montbéliard: Religion and Politics in the Sixteenth Century*, Oxford University Press, 1993, pp. 73–109; Ernst Bizer, *Studien zur Geschichte des Abendmahlsstreits im 16. Jahrhunderts*, Darmstadt: Wissenschaftliche Buchgesellschaft, 1962, pp. 65–364.

54 Elisabeth Gleason, *Gasparo Contarini. Venice, Rome, and Reform*, Berkeley: University of California Press, 1993, pp. 129–76; *Concilium Tridentinum*, 13 vols, Freiburg im Briesgau: Herder, 1901–38, 12:134–45; Elizabeth Gleason, ed. *Reform Thought in Sixteenth-Century Italy*, Chico: Scholars Press, 1981, pp. 85–100; and John C. Olin, *Catholic Reform from Cardinal Ximenes to the Council of Trent, 1495–1563*, New York: Fordham, 1990, pp. 65–79 for English translations.

55 Georg Kuhaupt noted the subsumation of theological to political concerns in polemical literature, 1538 to 1541, Kuhaupt, *Veröffentlichte Kirchenpolitik*, pp. 317–18. For property, Ocker, *Church Robbers*, pp. 104–31.

56 See the contributions by M. Schulz, I. Backus, J. van Oort, E. Norelli, and E.P. Meijering in *The Reception of the Church Fathers in the West: From the Carolingians to the Maurists*, 2 vols, edited by Irene Backus, Leiden: E.J. Brill, 1997, pp. 573–700, 745–74, 839–87. For Martin Bucer's use of canon law, consider Gottfried Seebaß, 'Martin Bucers Beitrag zu den Diskussionen über die Verwendung der Kirchengüter', *Martin Bucer und das Recht. Beiträge zum internationalem Symposium vom 1. bis 3. März 2001 in der Johannes a Lasco Bibliothek Emden*, ed. by Christoph Strohm, Geneva: Librairie Droz, 2002, pp. 167–83; Ocker, *Church Robbers*, pp. 183–212. Caspar Schwenckfeld also surveyed the canon law for its agreements with Scripture (1530), as did Nürnberg's Lazarus Spengler at the request of the Margrave of Brandenburg (1529); it was published at Wittenberg with a preface by Martin Luther. Schwenckfeld, *Eyn kurtzer außzug auß dem bäbstlichen Rechten*, *Corpus Schwenckfeldiorum*, 3:754–5 for Spengler and 753–809 for Schwenckfeld's treatise.

57 Martin Luther, *Die Lügend von St. Johannes Chrysostomo* (1537), WA 50:52–54 (but in 1537, Luther briefly supported a council, believing he was calling his opponents' bluff, Brecht, *Martin Luther*, 3:182; Antonius Corvinus, *Von der Concilien Gewalt und Autoritet*, n.pl.: n. publ., 1537, Geisendorf, *Bibliotheca Corviniana*, Nieuwkoop: De Graaf, 1964, pp. 166–67 nr. 106; Philip Melanchthon, *Causae quare synodum indictam a Romano Pontifice Paulo III recusarent princeps, status, et civitates Imperii*, Wittenberg: Georg Rau, 1537, B4 and passim; Philip Melanchthon, *De ecclesia et de auctoritate verbi Dei* (1539, CR 23:595–642; John Calvin, *Supplex exhortatio ad Carolum Quintum* (1543), CR 34:523–27; John Calvin, *Acta synodi Tridentinae cum antidoto* (1545), CR 35:370–506; Philip Melanchthon, *Ursach, warumb die Stende, so der Augspurgischen Confession anhangen, christliche lehr erstlich angenommen, und endlich dabey zu verharren gedenken: Auch: Warumb des verminte Trientische Concilium weder zu besuchen, noch darein zu willigen sey*, Nürnberg: Vom Berg, 1546; Heinrich Bullinger, *De conciliis* i.6–12, 21–5, ii.11–13, Zürich: Christopher Froschauer, 1561, ff. 20r-50v, 86r-110v, 163v-180v. But in 1537 Luther briefly supported a council, believing he was calling his opponents' bluff. Brecht, *Martin Luther*, 3:182.

58 Emperor Charles V saw the new council as a kind of 'international conference composed of procurators of the diverse national churches of Christendom'. Charles-Joseph Hefele, J. Hergenroether, H. Leclercq, *Histoire des Conciles*, 11 vols, Paris: Letouzey et Ané, 1907–52, 9:242.

59 Lucien Febvre, *The Problem of Unbelief in the Sixteenth Century: the Religion of Rabelais*, trans. Beatrice Gottlieb, Cambridge, MA: Harvard University Press, 1982, pp. 275–333 and passim.

60 Francis Oakley, 'Almain and Major: Conciliar Theory on the Eve of the Reformation', 'Conciliarism at the Fifth Lateran Council', and 'Conciliarism in the Sixteenth Century: Jacques Almain Again', in Francis Oakley, *Natural Law, Conciliarism and Consent in the Late Middle Ages*, London: Variorum, 1974, nr. 10–12. James K. Farge, *Orthodoxy and Reform in Early Reformation France: The Faculty of Theology in Paris, 1500–1543*, Leiden: E.J. Brill, 1985, pp. 27 n. 93, 222–45.

61 *Marsilius of Padua: Defender of the Peace*, xvi.1–19, xxviii.25, trans. A. Gewirth, 2 vols, New York: Columbia University Press, 1956, 1964, 2:241–53, 401–4, here 403.

62 It became schismatic in 1439, when the papal party withdrew from the council convened at Basel in 1433 and moved to Florence, until 1448.

63 Pius II, 'Exsecrabilis', Heinrich Denzinger, Adolf Schönmetzer, *Enchiridion symbolorum definitionum et declarationum de rebus fidei et morum*, 36th edn, Freiburg: Herder, 1976, nr. 1375, p. 245; Antony Black, *Council and Commune: The Conciliar Movement and the Council of Basle*, London: Burns and Oates, 1979, pp. 210–15 and passim; Klaus Ganzer, 'Gesamtkirche und Ortskirche auf dem Konzil von Trient', *Römische Quartalschrift* 95 (2000),167–78, here 170–1.

64 Martin Luther, *On the Papacy in Rome* WA 6:285–324, LW 39:49–104. For the development of Luther's view of the pope, see Brecht, *Martin Luther*, 1:307–9, 372–3.

65 *Bekenntnisschriften*, pp. 471–98. *Creeds and Confessions* 2:150–65.

66 Contrast the Council of Trent, from the controversial Twenty-Third Session, Chapter 4, which argues that bishops possess a superior ordination to priests: Denzinger, Schönmetzer, *Enchiridion*, nr. 1767; *Canons and Decrees of the Council of Trent*, ed. and trans. H.J. Schroeder, St Louis: Herder, 1941, pp. 433–4, 161–2 (English).

67 Melanchthon, *Apologia* xxviii. *Bekenntnisschriften*, pp. 397–400.

68 Kenneth Carleton, *Bishops and Reform in the English Church, 1520–1559*, Rochester: Boydell, 2001, p. 26; Albrecht Pius Luttenberger, *Glaubenseinheit und Reichsfriede. Konzeptionen und Wege konfessionsneutraler Reichspolitik 1530–1552 (Kurpfalz, Jülich, Kurbrandenburg*, Göttingen: Vandenhoeck und Ruprecht, 1982, p. 140, for the large number of ecclesiastical estates who avoided the religious controversy, other bishops who both avoided confessional confrontation and promoted reconciliation (Moritz of Eichstätt, Johann of Weeze Bishop of Constance, Wolfgang of Passau, and Archbishop Johann III of Trier), and still other prelates who promoted Catholic reform (Abbot Philip of Fulda, Bishop Erasmus of Strasbourg, the Archbishop Herman of Wied, Bishop Johann of Meißen, Bishop Franz of Münster, Minden and Osnabrück).

69 Ulrich Horst, *Die Lehrautorität des Papstes und die Dominikanertheologen der Schule von Salamanca*, Berlin: Akademie Verlag, 2003, p. 193.

70 Elisabeth Gössmann, *Mulier Papa: der Skandal eines weiblichen Papstes. Zur Rezeptionsgeschichte der Gestalt der Päpstin Johanna*, Munich: Iudicium, 1994, pp. 60–1, 110–48; Craig M. Rustici, *The Afterlife of Pope Joan: Deploying the Popess Legend in Early Modern England*, Ann Arbor: University of Michigan Press, 2006, pp.106–25; Horst, *Lehrtätigkeit*, p. 144.

71 Pighe participated in discussions of human nature there, as John Calvin recalled in his 1543 rebuttal of Pighe's views of free will. CR 34:230–404. He had also, like Calvin, appeared at the earlier meeting in Hagenau. *Akten der deutschen Reichsreligionsgespräche im 16. Jahrhundert*, 2 vols+, edited by Klaus Ganzer and Karl-Heinz zur Mühlen, Göttingen: Vandenhoeck und Ruprecht, 2000+, 1/2:1225 (Doctor Albertus Pius Traiectensis). CR 39:64–67 nr. 228.

72 Albertus Pighius, *Hierarchiae ecclesiasticae assertio*, vi.8, 16 (Cologne, 1538), quoted by Horst, *Lehrautorität*, p. 138 n. 87.

73 Congar, *L'Eglise*, p. 362.

74 Guillelmus Durandus, *Rationale divinorum officiorum*, IV.i.32, VI.lxxii.25, Turnhout: Brepols, 1995, 1998, pp. 252, 343; Horst, *Lehrauthorität*, p. 128 with note 41.

75 Juan de Torquemada, *Summa de ecclesia*, i.30 ad nonum (Venice: Michaelis Tranezinus), 1561, ff. 32–35, esp. 35, arguing that once the Faith began it could not cease, and citing Anselm's *Cur Deus homo*, Alexander of Hales, and Guillaume Durand. But consider also Torquemada, *Oratio synodalis de primatu*, ed. E. Candal, Rome: Pontificium Institutum Orientalium Studiorum, 1954, pp. 54–5 (although the Blessed Virgin possesses greater dignity than all the apostles on account of her fullness of grace and immovable faith, she did not receive the power of the keys. For Ockham, John Kilcullen, 'Ockham and Infallibility', *The Journal of Religious History*, 16 (1991), pp. 387–409; and William Ockham, *Dialogus*, I.v22., translated by John Scott, www.britac.ac.uk/pubs/dialogus/

t1d54.html. The problem was also discussed by Domingo Bañez in his 1584 commentary on Aquinas' *Summa theologica*: Horst, *Lehrauthorität*, p. 128 with notes 41–3.

76   Tommaso de Vio, *Auctoritas pape et concilii sive ecclesie comparata*, Rome: Marcellus Silber, 1511, no pagination, ix, especially at ¶ Ad aliam, ¶ Et scito, where he argues that assisted by divine providence, neither church, synod, nor pope can err. Congar, *L'Eglise*, p. 351; Anton Bodem, *Das Wesen der Kirche nach Kardinal Cajetan. Ein Beitrag zur Ekklesiologie im Zeitalter der Reformation*, Trier: Paulinus-Verlag, 1971, p. 89 for apostolicity; pp. 122–35 document Cajetan's emphasis on the presence of Christ and the distribution of grace throughout the church in his biblical commentaries and works on Aquinas.

77   Riccardo Battochi, *Ecclesiologia e politica in Marsilio da Padova*, Padua: Istituto per la storia ecclesiastical padovana, 2005; Black, *Council and Commune*, pp. 74 (Heimerich van der Velde), 213–14 (later Parisian conciliarists) and Febronius.

78   Alfonso de Castro, *Adversus omnes haereses*, viii (Cologne, 1543), ff. 14v-15r and cited by Horst, *Lehrauthorität*, p. 142 n. 100.

79   Horst, *Lehrautorität*, p. 147.

80   John L. Murphy, *The Notion of Tradition in John Dreido*, Milwaukee: Seraphic Press, 1959, pp. 194–211; Congar, *L'Eglise*, p. 362 n. 81. For recent literature on Dreido, Ronny Beier, 'Driedo(ens), Johannes', *Biographisch-Bibliographisches Kirchenlexikon*, 12:280–4.

81   Horst, *Lehrauthorität*, pp. 190–1.

82   Martin Luther, *Von der Konziliis und Kirchen*, WA 50:563, commenting on St Peter's speech at the Council of Jerusalem (Acts 15), where Peter argues that he teaches no new doctrine but that of the patriarchs: 'holy people have always existed who became holy through the grace of Christ alone and not through law, just as the text and faith of the gospel, baptism, sacraments, the keys, and the name of Jesus Christ, etc., have remained under the devil of the papacy, even though the pope with his cursed lies opposed them and dangerously seduced the world'. John Calvin, *Institutio* IV.ii.11–12, in passages added in 1539 at Strasbourg and in 1543 in Geneva: *Opera selecta* 5:40–42, McNeill, Battles, pp. 1051–53; Elert, *Structure of Lutheranism*, pp. 274–7. It was the demand for reform of the church that led Protestants, for example John Knox, to expand their concept of church from the small group to society at large. Pierre Janton, *Concept et sentiment de l'Église chez John Knox*, Paris: Presses universitaires de France, 1972, pp. 129–55.

83   They agreed that the early church should be the standard, and agreed on doctrines of justification, the Eucharist, monasticism, the adoration of the saints, feast days, the sacrament of holy anointing, fasts, and the place of temporal government. They disagreed over the exact time the church fell into corruption, around the year 600 (von Karlowitz's position) or before. Fuchs, *Confession und Gespräch*, pp. 401–2; Barbara Henze, *Aus Liebe zur Kirche Reform: Die Bemühungen Georg Witzels (1501–1573) um die Kircheneinheit*, Münster: Aschendorff, 1995, pp. 152–208.

84   For example, in Cajetan, Canesius, and Bellarmine. Bodem, *Das Wesen der Kirche*, pp. 101–75; Diez, *Christus und seine Kirche*, pp. 179–248; Thomas Dietrich, *Die Theologie der Kirche bei Robert Bellarmin (1542–1621)*, Paderborn: Bonifatius Verlag, 1999, pp. 191–231.

85   Horst, *Lehrauthorität*, pp. 149, 165–6, 170–1 for the problem of certainty in Catholic theology.

86   Horst, *Lehrauthorität*, p. 193; Richard Costigan, *The Consensus of the Church and Papal Infallibility: A Study in the Background of Vatican I*, Washington, DC: Catholic University of America, 2005, pp. 200–4 and passim for papalist and Gallican ecclesiology from Bossuet to Vatican I.

87   Torquemada, *Summa de ecclesia* ii.112 AD 6, iii.64, ff. 257v-258r, 352v-354r (if pope and council diverge on a matter of faith previously defined by the apostolic see, the pope prevails; if not yet defined and taken up by the council and the pope dissent the council prevails); Congar, *L'Eglise*, p. 343. Consider also the fifteenth-century Franciscan Anthony of Florence, the thirteenth-century commentator on canon law Johannes Teutonicus, and Alanus Anglicus: ibid., pp. 347–9 with n. 30.

88   Horst, *Lehrauthorität*, pp. 38–40, 106, 189, 191.

89   His *Loci theologici* were written at Salamanca between 1542 and 1551. Horst, *Lehrauthorität*, pp. 99, 100–1; Cano, *Loci theologici*, v.5 q. 2; *Opera*, ed. Hyacinth Serry, Patavia: Typis Seminarii, 1734, pp. 158–60.

90   Horst, *Lehrauthorität*, pp. 191–2.

91   Horst, *Lehrauthorität*, pp. 167, 175, 179, 192. The Franciscan general Francisco de Sosa, consulted by the supreme council of the inquisition, alleged a continuity of opinions on moral certainty

over the authority of any particular inhabitant of the papal office, which included the agreement of Torquemada, Cajetan, Cano, Bellarmino, Bañez and others. Ibid., p. 179. One may add the Louvain faculty of theology in 1544. Congar, *L'Eglise*, p. 387. Pope Paul IV in 1559, in response to the Peace of Augsburg, carefully observed that a person duly appointed to a high church office, from bishop to archbishop, to patriarch, to cardinal, to the Roman pontifex, rendered his promotion null and void if *before* his promotion or assumption he deviated from the Catholic faith. Carl Mirbt, *Quellen zur Geschichte des Papsttums und des römischen Katholizismus*, 2nd edn, Tübingen: J.C.B. Mohr, 1901, p. 201 nr. 288. Consider also Peter Canisius: Diez, *Christus und seine Kirche*, pp. 342–62.

92 Horst, *Lehrauthorität*, p. 70.

93 For example, Congar's list: Sylvester Prierias, Johann Eck and Cristoforo Marcello, *L'Eglise*, 361.

94 Cajetan, *Auctoritas papae et concilii sive ecclesii comparata*, ix, ¶Ad declarationem, ¶Ad aliam, ¶Ad rationem. For debate whether the papacy was at Rome by divine law, Horst, *Lehrauthorität*, pp. 102, 163, 165, 169–70.

95 Karlfried Froehlich, 'Saint Peter, Papal Primacy, and the Exegetical Tradition, 1150–1300', *The Religious Roles of the Papacy: Ideals and Realities, 1150–1300*, ed. C. Ryan, Toronto: Pontifical Institute of Mediaeval Studies, 1989, pp. 3–44; Ganzer, 'Gesamtkirche und Ortskirche', pp. 168–9; Carleton, *Bishops and Reform*, pp. 30–1; Hefele, Hergenroether, Leclercq, *Histoire des Conciles*, 9:235–6, 347–52, 624–31, 802–81, 892–909; Horst, *Lehrauthorität*, pp. 85–7; Black, *Council and Commune*, pp. 211–14; Thierry Wanegffelen, *Une difficile fidélité. Catholiques malgré le concile en France xvie-xviie siècles*, Paris: Presses universitaires de France, 1999, pp. 80–8.

96 *Canons and Decrees of the Council of Trent*, session 23, de reformatione i, pp. 164–6, 436–8.

97 Ganzer, summarizing the conclusions of Josef Freitag. Ganzer, 'Gesamtkirche und Ortskirche', pp. 173–75; Josef Freitag, *Sacramentum Ordinis auf dem Konzil von Trient. Ausgeblendeter Dissens und erreichter Konsens*, Vienna: Tyrolia-Verlag, 1991.

98 Ganzer, 'Gesamtkirche und Ortskirche', pp. 173–5. Klaus Ganzer, 'Gallikanische und römische Primatsauffassung im Widerstreit. Zu den ekklesiologischen Auseinandersetzungen auf dem Konzil von Trient', *Historisches Jahrbuch* 109(1989):109–63, here 162.

99 Estes, *Peace, Order and the Glory of God*, pp. 7–41; Carleton, *Bishops and Reform*, pp. 18–23; Ruth Wesel-Roth, *Thomas Erastus: Ein Beitrag zur Geschichte der reformierten Kirche und zur Lehre von der Staatssouveränität*, Lahr: Moritz Schauenburg, 1954, pp. 43–82.

100 John Calvin, *Institutio* IV.v.13, *Opera selecta* 5:84, in a passage added in 1543, as was his appeal to Bernard of Clairvaux, *De moribus et officio episcoporum*, ii, in the paragraph immediately preceding it.

101 Consider Josse Clichthove's *Antilutherus*, Paris: Simon Colinaeus, 1524, which answers Luther's concept of Christian liberty with a defense of legislative authority in the church, of the mass, and of monastic vows; Cajetan's and Peter Canisius' stress on the consequences of the incarnation, Anton Bodem, *Wesen der Kirche*, pp. 99–175; Diez, *Christus und seine Kirche*, pp. 272–7.

102 Excepting Anabaptists, who believed the Church was a distinct community within society: *Le temps des confessions*, pp. 929–32. Gerald Biesecker-Mast, *Separation and the Sword in Anabaptist Persuasion: Radical Confessional Rhetoric from Schleitheim to Dordrecht*, Telford, Pennsylvania: Cascadia Publishing House, 2006, passim.

103 Ocker, *Church Robbers*, passim.

104 'The political and social impact of a confession was ambivalent and depended on historical circumstances', Heinz Schilling, *Civic Calvinism in Northwestern Germany and the Netherlands, Sixteenth to Nineteenth Centuries*, Kirksville, MI: Sixteenth Century Journal Publishers, 1991, pp. 5–6, 69–104. See also James Tracy, 'Luther and the Modern State: Introduction to a Neuralgic Theme', *Luther and the Modern State in Germany*, ed. James D. Tracy, Kirksville, MI: Sixteenth Century Publishers, 1986, pp. 9–19, esp. 17.

105 Alexander VI, *Inter caetera divinae*. Mirbt, *Quellen*, pp. 174–76 nr. 267.

106 Pedro Leturia, 'Maior y Vitoria ante la conquista de América', *Estudios ecclesiasticos* 11(1932):44–82, with the relevant question from Major's *Commentarii in II. Sententiarum*, d. 44 q. 3 (published in 1510) at pp. 79–82; Horst, *Lehrauthorität*, p. 36.

107 Angel Losada, 'Ponencia sobre Fray Bartolomé de las Casas', *Las Casas et la politique des droits de l'homme*, Gardanne: Esmenjaud, 1976, pp. 22–44; Bartolomé de Las Casas, *In Defense of the Indians*, trans. S. Poole, De Kalb: Northern Illinois University Press, 1992.

108 Carleton, *Bishops and Reform*, p. 9 and, for the English reading of Marsiglio of Padua and the idea of royal supremacy, 10.

109 Joseph F. O'Callaghan, *A History of Medieval Spain*, Ithaca: Cornell, 1975, pp. 661–2; Ocker, *Church Robbers*, pp. 205–6; H.E. Rawlings, 'The Secularisation of Castilian Episcopal Office under the Habsburgs, *c.* 1516–1700', *Journal of Ecclesiastical History* 38(1987):53–79; Jochen A. Führer, *Die Kirchen-und die antireformatorische Religionspolitik Kaiser Karls V. In den siebzehn Provinzen der Niederlande, 1515–1555*, Leiden: E.J. Brill, 2004, pp. 89–165.

110 Ocker, *Church Robbers*, pp. 232–5.

111 For example, in the recommendation on church property published by the League of Schmalkalden's diet at Frankfurt in 1539. Ocker, *Church Robbers*, p. 203.

112 *Le temps des confessions*, pp. 923–4 for a summary of sizes and structures.

113 'Omnis utriusque sexus', *Decretales Gregorii IX* V.xxxviii.12, *Corpus iuris canonicis*, 2 vols ed. Emil Friedburg, Graz: Akademische Druck-und Verlagsanstalt, 1955, 2:887; *Enchiridion Symbolorum, Definitionum et Declarationum*, p. 264 nr. 812; *Canons and Decrees of the Council of Trent*, session 24, Chapter 13, pp. 203–4, 472–73.

114 *Le temps des confessions*, p. 925 for the quotation. For the role of fraternities and religious orders, Louis Châtellier, *The Europe of the Devout: the Catholic Reformation and the Formation of a New Society*, trans. Jean Birell, Cambridge University Press, 1989, pp. 1–109.

115 *Canons and Decrees of the Council of Trent*, session 22, Chapters 2, 5, 8; session 24, Chapters 1–11, 18, pp. 153–7, 190–200, 207–10.

116 *Le temps des confessions*, p. 928.

117 Jörn Sieglerschmidt, *Territorialstaat und Kirchenregiment*, Cologne: Böhlau, 1987, p. 268. When the Protestant jurists Matthias Stephan, Sigismundus Finckelthaus, and Zacharias Hermann addressed the question of episcopal authority in the absence of bishops, they entertained three possibilities. It could pass to a prince, to his clerical superintendent, or to both in different capacities, since German bishops had exercised both temporal and spiritual authority, which were now divided between different personnel. In Sieglerschmidt, *Territorialstaat*, pp. 255–75.

118 MacCulloch, *Reformation*, pp. 572–640.

Further reading

J.H. Burns and Thomas M. Izbicki, eds, *Conciliarism and Papalism*. Cambridge University Press, 1997.

Yves Congar, *L'Eglise de saint Augustin à l'époque moderne*. Paris: Les Éditions du Cerf, 1970.

James Estes, *Peace, Order and the Glory of God: Secular Authority and the Church in the Thought of Luther and Melanchthon, 1518–1559*. Leiden: E.J. Brill, 2005.

Richard C. Gamble, ed., *Calvin's Ecclesiology: Sacraments and Deacons*. New York: Garland, 1992.

Ulrich Horst, *Die Lehrautorität des Papstes und die Dominikanertheologen der Schule von Salamanca*. Berlin: Akademie Verlag, 2003.

——, *Papst, Konzil, Unfehlbarkeit. Die Ekklesiologie der Summenkommentare von Cajetan bis Billuart*. Mainz: Matthias-Grünewald-Verlag, 1978.

Gottfried Wilhelm Locher, *Sign of the Advent: A Study in Protestant Ecclesiology*. Fribourg: Academic Press, 2004.

Eddie Louis Mabry, *Balthasar Hubmaier's Doctrine of the Church*. Lanham: University Press of America, 1994.

John C. Olin, *Catholic Reform from Cardinal Ximenes to the Council of Trent, 1495–1563*. New York: Fordham, 1990.

5

THE CHURCH IN THE TRIDENTINE AND EARLY MODERN ERAS

Alison Forrestal

Introduction: the roots of reform in the sixteenth century

The early modern period stands out as one of the most creative in the history of the Christian church. While the Reformation proved viciously divisive, it also engendered theological and devotional initiatives that, over time and despite resistance, ultimately transformed the conventions of ecclesiology, ministry, apostolate, worship and piety. Simultaneously, the Catholic church, in particular, underwent profound shifts in devotion and theological thought that were only partially the product of the shock induced by the Reformation and at best only indirectly influenced by pressure from Protestant Reformers. Yet despite the pre-1517 antecedents of *reformatio*, and the reforming objectives of the Catholic Council of Trent (1545–7, 1551–2, 1562–3), the concept of church reform was effectively appropriated by Protestants from the sixteenth century onwards. Protestant churchmen claimed with assurance that they and the Reformation that they instigated sought the church's 'reform in faith and practice, in head and members'. They stood by this assertion even when their reforms moved outside the official Catholic canonical framework within which they might be instigated.[1] Some went further still: 'Radical' Reformers deliberately sought to 're-form' the church by a drastic break from the existing institution and theology in order to re-construct primitive Christianity.

By implication, therefore, and the point was often explicitly made by Protestant churchmen, the Catholic church remained profane and unreformed, the church of the Anti-Christ. In grasping the labels of 'true' and 'reformed' so tenaciously, Protestant churches placed the Catholic church on the defensive. An important element underpinning the decrees of the Council of Trent, consequently, was emphatically to signal the Catholic church's purity and authority as the church of Christ and the Apostles, and to mark out its commitment to eradicating any misconceptions in doctrine and abuses in worship or morality that crept into its religious beliefs and practice; in this era, the 'catholicity' of doctrine, that is, its uniformity and accuracy, became a central theological concern for the increasingly assertive Catholic church and for its critics.

From the eighteenth century, theologians and historians argued the merits and validity of their denominations within the dualistic framework of Protestant Reformation/Catholic Counter-Reformation.[2] This balance shifted in the twentieth century when Jedin[3] argued for the organic Reformation of the Catholic church prior to and independent of the Protestant Reformation. Importantly, he based his explanation of Catholic renewal and resurgence in the early modern era on the pillars of the papacy, the Society of Jesus (Jesuits) formally initiated in 1533 by Ignatius of Loyola (1491–1556) and the Council of Trent. Jedin's triangular analysis of the achievements of the early modern church was a highly influential example of institutional history, in which a Reformation, Counter-Reformation and modernizing church was analysed from an institutional, clerical and 'top-down' perspective.

Partly in reaction to this narrowly conceived approach, other scholars chose to concentrate principally on non-institutional or non-official forms of catholicism and protestantism. This paradigmic shift encouraged them to look beyond trinities of pope, council and religious order and Luther (1483–1546), Calvin (1509–64) and Cranmer (1489–1556) to the ordinary faithful's lived experience of the church as community, guardian, authority or disciplinarian. Just as importantly, it questioned traditional assumptions that church meant institution and clergy, that the Protestant and Catholic 'lay' faithful were passive recipients of doctrine and discipline and that confessional identity referred principally to attendance at service.[4] In doing so, it alerts us to the importance of broadening our investigative focus beyond the ecclesiology evident within papal and conciliar decisions and within the writings of a limited number of prominent theologians, to include the ecclesiology expressed through the eclectic thought and lives of the less renowned. Moreover, it encourages us to be aware of the burden of tradition within the disciplines of historical theology and church history: it points out that assessments of church, ecclesiology, ministry and vocation in the early modern era may depend substantially on how they are defined, and on whether it is assumed that the term church describes solid institutional and authoritative structures, a fluid, ever-changing and ever-diverse coalition of the baptized, or an amalgam of these definitions. Equally, however, inspecting a church mainly through the study of the 'sentiments and acts' of popular religion can tend to write the institutional out of history or neglect the lively reciprocity of the relations between social and ecclesiastical groups.

Sensitivity to the limitations of research and interpretative approaches is particularly important in charting the path of 'reform' taken by the early modern church. No denomination of the Christian church can legitimately claim to be the only representative of 'Reform' or of 'Reformation' during this period. The Protestant and Catholic churches may each lay claim to them in their ecclesiological self-understanding. The growing evidence of organic advancements in piety and spirituality before 1517 demonstrates that the Protestant churches were not, as often assumed, the sole heirs to Christian Humanism or to those frequently categorized as early Protestants in all but name, such as the irenic Cardinal Jacopo Sadoleto (1477–1547)[5] or Bishop Guillaume Briçonnet (d.1514), who presided over a circle of reform in Meaux. It included Josse Clichtove (1472–1543), the Parisian humanist, discreet theologian of conciliarism, advocate of disciplinary reforms and celebrated publisher of commentaries on the writings of the church fathers.[6] He was a protégé of Briçonnet's vicar, Jacques Lefèvre d'Étaples (c.1455–1536), a charismatic advocate of scriptural scholarship and clerical probity, and editor of the works of, amongst others, Ignatius of Antioch.[7]

The Meaux circle came under some suspicion from the French royal authorities during the 1520s as the impact of Luther's challenge to the Catholic church emerged. Several of its members shared some sympathy with Luther's doctrine of justification by faith and advocacy of vernacular scripture.[8] The diversity of theological views displayed within this catholic and Catholic group reveals the shared heritage of the denominational churches. However, it also complicates the task of identifying specific roots and influences on each church's structural development and theological growth because it is clear that these pious environments sheltered those who remained Catholic and those who subsequently embraced the Protestant cause. For example, one of the most significant influences on Catholic piety and apostolate was the Oratory of Divine Love, a lay dominated confraternity initially established in 1497. It nourished the spiritual formation of several men who were later to assume leading roles in the Catholic hierarchy, such as Paul Carafa (1476–1559), and spawned several religious communities and orders, including the Barnabites (1526), the Ursulines (1535) and the Capuchins (1528).[9] Yet, while Carafa went on to become Pope Paul IV and a notorious foe of heterodoxy, the Capuchins suffered the extreme embarrassment of the defection of their vicar general, Bernardino Ochino (1487–1564), to the Protestant cause in 1542.

The Oratory also germinated several Catholic communities and religious orders characterized by commitment to active service within the world and reluctance to adopt monastic rules of living. All found expression in charitable work amongst the poor, the young or the ill, and the members' ties were further tightened through practices such as common prayer and sacramental participation. A further distinction for some was their origin in and debt to lay confraternities and their longer term interest in treating the lay vocation, for the married or single, as spiritually valid and distinct. The Barnabites, established by Antonio Zaccaria (1502–39), were devoted to *imitatio Christi* through visitations to the sick, poor and imprisoned, catechesis, and the collection of alms for charitable work. The group included a lay oratory, the Married Couples of Saint Paul, as well as clerical Barnabites and female lay Angelics, who lived in community but without vows (this group split into enclosed and lay communities in 1552). Zaccaria insisted that the group's three companies were linked by a common spiritual apostolate, with their male and female members working together in mutual support for their self-transformation and for the transformative good of others. He encouraged the Married Couples to seek perfection in their married state and allowed them to incorporate the spiritual and charitable tasks of *imitatio* into the norms of marriage and family life.

Defining 'church': Ignatius of Loyola and Vincent de Paul (1581–1660)

Recognition of the organic development of a new spirit of piety within the church before the Protestant Reformation invites us to ponder the extent to which those involved considered themselves to be 'reformers'. Zaccaria was never concerned with eradicating constitutional, institutional or doctrinal abuses in the church. Likewise, Ignatius of Loyola displayed virtually no preoccupation with the question of 'reform' in an institutional sense and, until late in his career, he placed scarcely any emphasis on the need to battle against the surge of protestantism.[10] This may have been because, like many of his generation, he took the word 'reform' to refer primarily to the reform of the papacy and curia and neither he nor his companions thought this concerned them directly. So they concentrated their evolving spirituality and activities on missionary work, retreats (where they focused on 'discernment of the spirit', using Loyola's *Spiritual Exercises*)[11] and latterly on teaching.

Loyola's preoccupation with the help and salvation of souls certainly affected his conception of ministry and church. He intended to inject new life into Christian piety, by working within the existing structural framework of the church. The question of counter-reform did become more prominent in Jesuit activity as time passed; Loyola at least tacitly approved the dispatch of Jesuits to Protestant regions from 1550 onwards, and two Jesuits contributed to the decrees issued at Trent.[12] Additionally, however, the Jesuits' fourth vow, to go where sent by the pope, has often been interpreted as a manifestation of their extreme, and ultramontane, loyalty to the pope's authority. It should rather be interpreted as a function of their founder's ethos: drawing on the models of Jesus, the Apostles and Paul, Loyola conceived the Jesuits to be itinerant ministers willing to move quickly to regions within and outside Europe where they were needed.[13]

Loyola's vision of 'christianitas' was central to his concept of the church as a kingdom of souls, needing guidance in spiritual and moral formation. With patristic and medieval roots, it involved shaping the individual in Christian virtues, so that they became both personally and socially equipped to live in the world and to promote the interests of catholicism through patronage, example and divine invocation. The Jesuits proved adept in encouraging the development of confraternities and associations that combined common prayer, sacramental practice, catechesis, formation of conscience and collective works of mercy in order to purge and illuminate souls as they moved towards union with God. This was in direct compliance with Loyola's *Constitutions* for the Jesuits, which stressed the importance of ministering to groups rather than individuals when possible.[14]

A century after Loyola, the highly regarded Vincent de Paul echoed Loyola's reluctance to pin his vision of the church and its future on the defeat of protestantism. Despite his experience of religious war in France (1562–98), de Paul was inspired less by the need to react against protestantism than by his desire to respond to the perennial problem of how to save Catholics from the damnation that resulted from ignorance, wilful or otherwise. Although he accepted the conventional assumption that an effective priesthood should play a primary role in providing sacramental and didactic support he encouraged the laity to assume distinctive and creative responsibility for the preservation of the church's health. This concentration on the needs of the souls that formed the church allowed space for, even demanded, diverse forms of ministry that brought specific apostolic gifts for spiritual welfare.

For Loyola and de Paul, consequently, the term *ecclesia* (church) had two meanings, which were not mutually exclusive: a conglomerate of souls forming the living, breathing body of Christ, and an external structure of hierarchy and authority. De Paul, however, pushed the conceptual breadth of vocation further than Loyola, in his championing of the vocations of women from low social groups. With his collaborator, Louise de Marillac (1581 –1660), he provided a serious vocational opportunity for women in the Daughters of Charity (1633), regardless of their material means, as well as a structure that enabled them to thrive spiritually and to assist the physical and spiritual needs of the laity within their own social groups. Marillac and de Paul's view of *ecclesia* sang loudly of mutual assistance for souls, a principle expressed in Marillac's work in offering retreats and organizing charitable and educational initiatives and de Paul's efforts to train priests, support lay people and establish charitable institutions. Marillac strictly avoided entering the field of priestly training, though some nuns, revered for wisdom inspired by grace rather than theological study, did act as spiritual guides to priests during her lifetime. Within a society that accepted that women were the weaker sex and should be subject to male spiritual guidance, the attribution of engraced wisdom might allow a woman to influence the spirituality of priests, but it did not give her leave to subvert the divine order by stepping into the male domain of ordained ministry.

The church as institution: Tridentine hierarchy and government

Like Loyola, de Paul fully endorsed the place of magisterial hierarchy and paid serious attention to the institutional and theological boundaries of the Catholic church that ruled the
public vocational work of a figure such as Marillac. Although he frequently expressed his
apprehension that the church was in a state of irreparable decline in Europe partly because
of protestantism's victories (and that its hope lay in the virgin lands of the New World),
he really feared that the church was about to implode from within, through the refusal of a
Catholic 'Jansenist' minority to accept the wisdom of the fathers, councils and popes. He
built his orchestrated campaign against the Jansenists in the 1640s on his plea to papal
authority to quash their claim that they were the authentic defenders of Augustine's
doctrine of grace, as well as to condemn their apparent reluctance to approve frequent
sacramental participation and their appeals to the conciliarist doctrine and freedom of
conscience to shield their doctrinal beliefs. Concurrently, however, de Paul continued to
associate with suspected Jansenists, rather than send them to Coventry. He did so partially
to take opportunities to persuade them to renege on their supposed heresies but his links
went further than was necessary for this to happen. He even sent young clerics to reside with
and work for the Jansenist bishop Nicolas Pavillon (1597–1677) in the 1650s. In this affair,
therefore, we see both faces of de Paul's sense of ecclesiology simultaneously: the institutional and the personal; the church as guardian of doctrinal truth and the church as the
inclusive and charitable nurturer of souls.[15]

In these kind of circumstances, however, the limitations of Trent's decrees became
startlingly evident. Theoretically, the Catholic church's reliance on scripture and tradition
responded to theological questions, whether posed by Protestants or Jansenists, and the
Tridentine decrees offered the most recent exposition of key doctrines and the disciplinary
rules that expressed them. Catholic theologians now defined 'catholicity' to ward off not
only the external subversion of Protestant heresies but also to prevent, once more, the fragmentation of the Catholic church from within. But the delegates at Trent had not intended
to offer a composite description of church doctrines. Rather, they responded to specific
doctrinal and disciplinary criticisms made by Protestants, and their decrees were most penetrating in compiling doctrinal and disciplinary rules to ensure regularity of belief, worship
and government.

One key example of this is evident in the consequences of placing bishops at the centre
of the Tridentine reform programme. This was done partially in reaction to dismissal of the
office in some Protestant churches, but Trent also codified teaching and recommendations
that had circulated in the church for centuries when it ordered bishops to instigate disciplinary renewal in their dioceses through annual diocesan synods, the introduction of
seminaries and regular preaching. However, these practical instructions of 'administative
episcopalism' were not accompanied by a complete theology of episcopacy, a fact that is
particularly obvious in the decree on episcopal residence issued in 1646 and that on sacramental order in 1662–3.[16] In these, the Council, despite the warnings of several delegates,
dodged the question of whether bishops held their jurisdiction immediately or directly from
God, or indirectly, by mediation, from the pope. In fact, the papacy and its supporters
(*zelanti*) used the debate to argue strongly for the inclusion of a decree confirming papal
jurisdiction over the entire church, which was utterly contrary to the medieval doctrine of
conciliarism and absolutely unacceptable to most members of the French and Spanish
delegations.

The Council did decree that the priestly orders 'truly and properly' formed one of the seven sacraments, imprinting a unique and ineffaceable character on its recipients which enabled them to consecrate the bread and wine and forgive sins. It further confirmed that bishops belonged to the same sacramental order but were distinguished from priests by their charismatic ability to govern as apostolic successors and their ability to confer the sacraments of confirmation and ordination. Yet ecclesiological dilemmas regarding the source and practice of episcopal jurisdiction remained: did episcopal jurisdiction come directly from God or indirectly via the pope? Precisely what degree of independent jurisdiction could a bishop expect to possess within his diocese? It was not merely papal and episcopal pride or the quotidien authority of an individual bishop that was at stake. The reason that the questions were taken so seriously during and in the centuries after Trent was because, in an institution freshly committing to hierarchical direction, the responses given to them would mould the relationship between members of the church hierarchy and determine the loci of ecclesiastical power and the operation of ecclesiastical government, perhaps permanently.

After Trent, the rigorous administration of Archbishop Charles Borromeo (1538–84) in Milan saw the introduction of regular synods, schools of Christian doctrine for catechesis and ecclesiastical conferences for priests. His firm sense of episcopal leadership, however, brought him into conflict with both the papal and secular authorities; the papacy thoroughly edited the statutes of his 1578 provincial council, even though they accorded with Trent's decrees, and ordered that the council's decrees were to be suspended in Milan until further notice. Only when the furious archbishop personally remonstrated with Pope Gregory XIII were his decrees approved.[17] Equally, however, Borromeo was not averse to using the weight of his status as archbishop to fend off the attempts by Philip II's government to replace the Lombard province of the Holy Office with the Spanish Inquisition; as a result of his robust resistance to Spanish intrusions into ecclesiastical affairs he enjoyed a degree of episcopal independence that was rather unusual in other regions of the empire, and this was later protected by his nephew Federico Borromeo during the 1620s.[18]

This and similar clashes[19] partially reflected Rome's attempts to enhance the pope's authority and coincided with the expansion of the curial congregations responsible for ecclesiastical administration, especially the foundation of the Congregation for the Propagation of Faith in 1622. The trend rested on an absolutist ecclesiology that placed premiums on the doctrines of papal primacy, infallibility and universal jurisdiction. Therefore, although Trent placed bishops at the heart of diocesan affairs and seemed to offer them autonomy in dioceses, the papacy interpreted these principles minimally while bishops frequently tended to interpret them in ways that permitted them substantial, sometimes maximum, liberty of action. For example, Rome refused to approve the decrees of the provincial council of Bordeaux, held by Archbishop Sourdis (1574–1628) in 1624, on the basis that he had neglected to specify that prelates acted as delegates of the apostolic see when performing visitations of convents and monasteries, correcting their abuses or controlling their 'hierarchical' activities of sacramental administration and preaching. This was a daring and deliberate distortion of Trent's legislation, but Sourdis acted, with the enthusiastic approval of the French Assembly of Clergy, in the belief that bishops did not govern dioceses as papal delegates, but by virtue of the jurisdictional power inherent in their office. It was hardly surprising that Rome hawkishly pounced on his decrees, and although used within Bordeaux, they never earned papal approbation.[20]

This episode should also be judged with reference to its place within the serious tensions between bishops and religious orders (regular clergy) through the early modern era.

Although there are countless instances of their co-operation in such activities as missionary work, education or the foundation of monasteries and convents, bishops persistently complained about the unwarranted independence of the regulars, who appeared unwilling to give up the independence that they had won during the medieval period.[21]

At the heart of the issue lay competing conceptions of the church, ecclesiastical government, discipline and hierarchy at local and universal levels. The regulars, the papacy and the bishops all based their conceptions on the traditional notion that the church was a hierarchy of orders, but the regulars and the papacy favoured a broadly conceived system of subdivided hierarchy, whose distinct sections were connected by their common obedience to the pope. This was not a form of presbyterianism, for it accepted the unrestricted authority of the pope as universal bishop of the church while not eliminating bishops' jurisdictional authority altogether. It also relied heavily on the claim that the pope possessed universal jurisdiction and that he granted bishops their diocesan jurisdiction. Therefore, he could quite legitimately exempt members of the religious orders from that jurisdiction when he deemed it necessary.

The 'new world' of the churches: ecclesiological models and boundaries

Mission and settlement

Freedom from episcopal interference was a particularly important right to claim in Catholic missionary environments: the Jesuits and Benedictines refused to accept that the bishop appointed to oversee the English mission in 1624 had any jurisdiction over their activities, prompting a long war of printed propaganda and appeals to Rome.[22] Their opponents, supported by the assertive French episcopate, recognized the pope's primacy as the 'bishop of bishops' and Christ's earthly vicar. They could not agree that the leadership this entailed stretched to papal infallibility or the ability of a pope to intervene in a diocese without the approval of its bishop, whose jurisdiction was received immediately or directly from God. So attentive to this principle were the French that they endeavoured to ensure that it was enshrined as an inalterable episcopal right in the French church and in the ecclesiological structures erected in the new French colonies.[23]

The issue of ecclesial organization and discipline was a primary worry for both the Catholic and Protestant churches in the new colonies established through trade and settlement in the Americas, China, Japan, India and Africa. Catholic missions were often unable to replicate the institutional patterns that operated in Europe because of geographical isolation, insufficient personnel (which was compounded by a contemporary debate over the ordination of natives),[24] tensions between secular and regular clergy and lack of co-operation from secular authorities. Their missionaries had to adapt their usual didactic methods and devotional forms to the languages and cultures of indigenous people and the needs of slaves newly descended from ships.[25] The Jesuits, in particular, came under heavy fire in China from those who considered any engagement or compromise with pagan beliefs to be entirely illegitimate.[26]

The first Protestant mission to the new world took place in 1555, when the Calvinist church in Geneva sent a small cohort of settlers to Brazil.[27] While this mission did not survive, others were longer lived, though with varying degrees of interest in converting natives. Missions to natives were complicated, as the influential minister Cotton Mather

(1663–1728) identified in relation to his own Reformed community in New England, by the fact that the Protestant churches tended to import the denominational debates that characterized protestantism in Europe. To combat this, Mather formulated fourteen classically Protestant doctrinal truths that should form a unified basis of Protestant missionary work in lands that had been divinely granted for the purpose of realizing the perfect Christianity that was impossible in Europe.[28] His view of old Europe bears passing resemblance to that expressed by de Paul,[29] and it was generally matched by other Reformed communities. Roger Williams (1603–83), founder of the Rhode Island colony, considered his Separatist church (that is, independent from the episcopal and monarchically governed Church of England) to be a community of the regenerate, while some Reformed churches claimed that their foundation was the 'new Israel'. They experienced acute anxiety about the certainty of election and established regulations such as proof of repentance for full church membership.[30] These churches wished to segregate themselves from corrupt catholicism, but also from any Protestant influences that might taint their witness to the true faith.

Models of authority: Jansenism and Calvinism

For the Catholic church, the dissension that arose over the rivalry between papal and episcopal jurisdictional power reached new heights during the Jansenist quarrel. Although conflict centred on the interpretation of the Augustinian doctrine of grace proposed by Cornelius Jansen in his 1640 work *Augustinus*, it rapidly expanded to become the scene of a direct competition between papal authority and episcopal jurisdiction and power of judgement. In resisting the papal condemnations (1653, 1656 and 1663) of supposed Jansenist doctrines, the Jansenists were able to play on the sensitivity of French bishops to their hierarchical status and power and their sense of corporate collegiality, as well as on a tradition of gallican independence, in which the bishops opposed any infringements on their jurisdiction by either pope or king. In particular, four bishops chose to represent the cause. They and the Jansenists, led principally by Antoine Arnauld (b. 1612) until his death in 1694, argued eloquently that it was necessary to hold a church council to resolve the question of faith at issue; until the church was seen to concord formally that Jansen's doctrine was heretical, nobody could be forced to act against their conscience. Furthermore, the pope could not proceed against a bishop unless he infringed canonical norms or failed to defend a defined article of faith. Until then, bishops should be permitted to use their episcopal power to judge matters of faith, for which they would answer to God, and to decide whether it was appropriate to take action in their dioceses against Jansenism.[31]

Throughout this war, the Jansenists' opponents accused them of being crypto-Calvinists: disciples of predestination and irresistible grace and enemies of the pope. Stung by this suggestion, the Jansenists fought back but were hampered by the claim made by Pierre Nicole, a leading member of their group, that Peter and Paul had led autonomous communities in Rome, providing a model for popes and bishops to follow ever since. To be fair, the likeness to Calvinist ecclesiology was only superficial; the Jansenists had a well-developed view of episcopacy and certainly did not wish to promote a presbyterian style church without either pope or prelates. Indeed, the Jansenist bishops displayed a keener sense of Cyprianic episcopacy than many other bishops; throughout the affair, the question of jurisdiction did not overtake those of pastoral responsibility and apostolic vocation to become an end in itself. They defended their intransigence by interweaving jurisdictional rights with pastoral needs: they were, as the 'eyes and mouth' of the church and the 'depositories' of faith and discipline, duty bound to ensure the wellbeing, not simply of their own dioceses, but of the entire church.[32]

Calvinist ecclesiology was based on what Calvin considered to be the structure closest to the New Testament pattern and supportive of the ministry of the Word, but this presbyterian form did not prevent him from realizing that a doctrine of ministry and ministerial vocation was vital to a church that claimed to be a divine institution testifying to Christ's grace.[33] While most Calvinist churches conformed to the presbyterian model (with its fourfold ministry of elder, doctor, deacon and pastor) and synodal network,[34] Lutheran churches assumed a variety of ministerial structures, with some retaining the episcopal ministry as historical and scriptural (apostolic). This diversity stemmed from Luther's reluctance to prescribe a uniform structure of ecclesiastical government. However, the variety of organizational models precipitated acute problems for the Erastian Anglican church, for a vocal Reformed element of its membership (commonly known as Puritans), including theologians such as William Perkins (1558–1602), disliked the concept of episcopacy, though some proved willing to accept it in their national church if it was deemed an earthly and politically expedient office, whose members derived their jurisdiction from the monarch. These regarded an episcopate that claimed to hold its jurisdiction by divine right or law as 'popish', so set themselves firmly against the 'innovations' of Laudian protestantism and high Anglicanism that emerged before the Civil War in 1641.[35] Therefore, although Anglican and Catholic apologists argued publicly over the legitimacy of Anglican episcopacy, they shared a similar dilemma after the Reformation: both searched for a mature image of episcopal office but were troubled by the degree of jurisdiction to be offered to its incumbents and whether that jurisdiction was owed directly to God, pope or monarch.

The Anglican debate spilled into the colonies on the eastern seaboard of North America, where Puritan settlers took the opportunity that distance offered to establish experimental forms of ecclesiastical government. Puritan communities (such as the Massachusetts Bay Colony established in 1630 in the wake of more feeble settlements from 1620) founded congregational churches, with federations of parishes run by self-selected councils of parishioners. The belief that their parochially, and therefore congregationally, governed churches had been rightfully distinguished from the corrupt episcopal Church of England was crucial to their identity as new Israels. However, communities which allowed such significant avenues of power to lay people tended to suffer power struggles between ministers and socially prominent laymen; Puritan divines had never agreed on the balance of power that should exist between church elders and the church community in governmental and disciplinary decisions,[36] and the emerging congregations inclined towards egalitarian participation that favoured the laity over ministers. This was a natural result of the Reformation doctrine commonly known as the priesthood of all believers, which confirmed the spiritual equality of all Christians (though not the historical equality, which allowed the Reformers to reject the possibility of female ministers). It was, therefore, also the product of the abandonment of the traditionally distinguishing sacramental element of ministry by Protestant theology. Furthermore, pushed to its extreme conclusion by leading Puritan divines such as Walter Travers (1548–1635), it conceded that a minister was set apart only and crucially by the fact that he had been chosen to serve by the local church fellowship which ordained him.[37]

ALISON FORRESTAL

The sacred and the secular: relations between churches
and sovereigns

In the Catholic church, the Jansenist affair eventually lost momentum after the final papal condemnation in 1713 (*Unigenitus*; even then a special assembly of French prelates deliberately acted 'as judges of faith'),[38] but it badly bruised the papacy and heightened its suspicion of conciliarism and episcopal claims to power. To make this war of practical theology still more complicated, the range of papal power had two aspects: the spiritual and the temporal. While the clergy argued over precedence, status and authority, secular sovereigns watched for signs that the papacy intended to actualize the political theology that claimed that the pope's spiritual and temporal powers were held by divine right or law; as such, the pope could intervene freely in the civil realm, even to the point, if necessary, of deposing an infidel or tyrant king (the hierocratic theory). This assertion was, as Robert Bellarmine (1542–1621) noted, 'odious to the princes of the world'.[39] It was doubly so in an era when the power of sovereigns continued to grow, though not as rapidly as the cult of absolute rule and divine right monarchy (the belief that the king received his royal power directly from God and was answerable only to God).[40]

Amongst other prominent Catholic theologians, Bellarmine faced this challenge, so topical too in the wake of royal assassinations by Catholic subjects,[41] with a powerful justification of the church's, meaning principally the pope's, interest in the exercise of political power. He argued influentially that the spiritual power (founded on divine law) must be considered supreme over the temporal (founded on natural law) because its end was higher and more excellent (equally, Catholic theologians argued that the temporal realm and power were transient and therefore subservient to the persevering 'empire of Christ').[42] The pope was bound to intervene in the temporal realm when secular political action or inaction threatened the faith or the salvation of souls. In these exceptional circumstances, the pope could judge, direct or correct. Bellarmine carefully, however, distinguished between the pope's spiritual and temporal power (his *Controversies* were almost placed on the Index in 1590 as a result), suggesting that the former was immediate or direct while the latter was derived or indirect. For that reason, the pope could never depose a civil sovereign but could, for a spiritual reason, indicate to the faithful that this action was necessary and direct the faithful to ensure that particular civil acts, such as laws protective of the church and the faith, were implemented. In making this case, Bellarmine was tied by the common medieval assumption that the civil and ecclesiastical realms formed the halves of Christian society.[43]

The pope's claims to either direct or indirect power over the civil realm flatly contradicted the vigorous theory of divine right monarchy, espoused not just by the Catholic Louis XIV but also by the Protestant Stuart monarchs. In the state church headed by the latter, Richard Hooker (1554–1600) defended an enduring theory of polity that offered the monarch, supported by parliamentary and convocational consent, spiritual dominion or supreme power in ecclesiastical affairs (but not purely spiritual power). He based this view on a combination of Scripture, tradition and reason, which he also used to criticize the Puritan tendency to construct ahistorical ecclesiastical institutions solely by scriptural rules and models. Because the Church of England's erastian and episcopal configuration was not contrary to Scripture (therefore, it was compatible with Scripture), was consistent with tradition, and fitted contemporary circumstances and requirements, he argued, it was a legitimate and appropriate form of ecclesiastical structure and government.[44]

Although Hooker wrote principally in opposition to Puritans, his argument could be adopted to protect the Anglican church from subversive attacks by Dissenters and Catholics, the former emerging as Separatists within the Anglican church from the 1640s, and the latter a suspected minority within the realm throughout the early modern era. Catholic sovereigns displayed some erastian ambitions too, however. Notably, the French crown intermittently resorted to the threat to form an erastian national Catholic church and was able to overawe papal pretensions to power by bringing bishops over to its thinking, benefiting from the fame and intellectual ability of Jacque-Benigne Bossuet (1627–1704) in particular. He was amongst the bishops who composed and signed the notorious 1682 Gallican Articles, in which the bishops explicitly denied that the king answered to any authority but God's. Furthermore, they took the opportunity to endorse the Council of Constance's conciliarist doctrine, to affirm that the decisions of a church council held precedence over those of a pope, proclaim that papal power was subject to established laws and customs and qualify papal power by confirming that the pope's decisions in matters of faith were not irreformable 'without the consent of the entire church'.[45]

In order to respond to the frequent accusation that Catholics could not maintain their loyalty to a Protestant sovereign because they would always be bound to obey the pope's instructions, Irish Catholic theologians unsuccessfully attempted to translate a version of these doctrines to the difficult situation in Ireland in 1666, where an overwhelmingly Catholic population was ruled by a Protestant sovereign and denied freedom of worship until the repeal of the Penal Laws from the 1770s.[46] This missionary church also encountered tensions within its own ranks; bishops often reported resentment from, and occasionally outright conflict with, regular and secular clergy who refused to submit to their discipline.[47] In France, parish priests (*curés*) endorsed a presbyterian style ecclesiology, in which they functioned as monarchs of their jurisdictions, with no interference from their bishop and a deliberative role in diocesan synods. In addition to adopting the traditional Gersonian belief that they were the direct successors of the seventy-two disciples, they argued that they held the jurisdiction inherent to their office by divine law. Their doctrine placed *curés* and bishops on a parallel jurisdictional footing and neutralized a bishop's influence through most of his see. During the 1650s, *curés* in Paris and other provinces met in assemblies to judge doctrinal issues and issue thinly veiled assertions of autonomy to their bishops.[48] The resilience of their doctrine, and its ability to reanimate, became evident during the later eighteenth century, when the *curés'* festering grievances against what they perceived to be episcopal tyranny drove them to act once again as a corporal, clearly defined, clerical caste and distinguish themselves from the bishops in the Estates General (1789) that ushered in the French Revolution.[49]

Ministries and vocations

Priest and pastor

The identities that French bishops and *curés* proclaimed were both strongly influenced by a dominant contemporary 'school' of theology. At its centre stood Pierre de Bérulle (1575–1629), founder of the French Congregation[50] of the Oratory (1611), although the diffusion of its central tenets probably owed more to Jean-Jacques Olier (1608–57) and Vincent de Paul, founders of the Sulpician Congregation (1645) and the Congregation of the Mission (1625) respectively. By the latter part of the eighteenth century, 60 per cent of French bishops had been trained, generally for three years, in the Sulpicians' Parisian seminary, while the Lazarists managed sixty diocesan seminaries in France. Moreover, the theology and training methods of the French school were adopted in seminaries through the Catholic church until the modern era and its writings became required reading for seminarians.[51]

In addition to its directives to bishops, the Council of Trent had laid down practical instructions for the training of priests in diocesan seminaries and had required that priests reside in their parishes, administer the sacraments and teach their flock through catechesis and preaching. The French school's teaching fleshed out the theology that lay behind or implicitly within these commands and provided the structures and personnel to implement Trent's vision of reinvigoration. In doing so it fostered the confidence of authority, wisdom and prestige amongst bishops and priests.

This unique formulation of priesthood and episcopacy upheld and enhanced the notion that the church was a Pseudo-Dionysian hierarchy of orders. Therefore, bishops were ranked first, or highest, amongst the 'dispensers of the holy things', followed by priests and then deacons. Further down in the hierarchy were, in descending order, the monastic orders, initiates (laity) and catechumens. Within the hierarchy, the priest performed the crucial role of mediating divine grace, so that he drew those below him in rank (that is, principally the laity) towards union with God through administration of the sacraments. As a 'living sacrament', therefore, he continued the salvific work of Christ, the eternal priest, who delegated his authority to him through ordination.[52]

To try to guard against any democratization of ecclesiastical discipline, Bérulle and his associates persistently confirmed that priests should render obedience to their *grands prêtres*, or bishops. They placed the activities of their congregations in dioceses firmly under episcopal obedience, which was both politically advantageous and a reflection of their theological image of episcopacy. Olier summarized this understanding when he identified bishops as fathers, leaders (or heads) and kings in 1651. Innovatively, he recognized a distinct episcopal spirit, held in plenitude, on which priests and laity were dependent for sanctification. In doing so, he echoed Trent's distinction between the episcopal powers of order and jurisdiction. Olier described the operation as a flowing of grace from the bishop to priests; the head of the body animating and therefore perfecting its limbs (priests), by the unique grace that flowed through the veins. This emphasis on a vivifying and nourishing spirit was positive and pastoral, while clearly indicating that the episcopal office was a dynamic and essential element of the church's spiritual wellbeing, its structure and the functioning of the lower clergy.[53] While Olier did not claim that the episcopate was a separate sacrament from the priesthood, he also did not suggest that episcopacy was merely an extension of priesthood. Moreover, unlike, for example, the view offered by certain Anglicans, notably Archbishop Whitgift (c.1530–1604),[54] Olier did not suggest that it was simply a bishop's jurisdictional power that distinguished him from a priest.

Embedded within this theology of priesthood and episcopacy is an endorsement of Trent's emphasis on the cultic role of the priest and his primacy in protecting and developing the church. The Council was thoroughly influenced by the often-voiced assumption that reform of the church would be achieved through reform of those who would go on to lead the laity in true faith and upright Christian virtue. This presumption is related to the increasing emphasis on parochial religious practice during the Tridentine era; in structural terms, parish priests and the bishops above them organized, directed and kept close observation on the religious devotions of the laity. Of course, there were exceptions to this, as the household religion of Catholics in Ireland reveals.[55] However, the plentiful investigations of confraternities have provided evidence of the trend; local, idiosyncratic, confraternities tended to be replaced by those dedicated to universal doctrines such as the Rosary and the Blessed Sacrament and, increasingly, their medieval autonomy was undermined by Trent's order that parish priests and bishops assume control of their accounts and activities.[56] Just as the issues of authority, uniformity and orthodoxy dominated debates over ecclesiological structures, the movement towards uniformity and universality in confraternal and associative devotions reflected the quest for a defined catholicity that characterized the Catholic church after Trent.

Of course, one of the principal reasons for this preoccupation with the sacerdotal role in cultivating holiness was the fact that the Protestant churches undermined it so categorically. As mentioned above, Calvin and Luther both confirmed the need for ordained ministry within their denominations, but the variety that this basic precept permitted meant that Protestantism incorporated episcopally and congregationally governed churches. Significantly, however, the abandonment of a theology of priestly sacramentality and sacrificiality drove the Protestant understanding of ministry towards governmental and didactic, rather than cultic, presentations of the minister's functions. While ordained ministers were, as Calvin had affirmed, specially designated ambassadors of God, this primarily relied on their responsibility to serve their congregation through the pastorate of evangelical preaching, as the Zurich reformer Huldrych Zwingli (1484–1531) noted so trenchantly when he chose to stress ministerial service over dignity or lordship.[57]

Their intense prioritizing of the preached word encouraged Protestant ministers to grasp their mission to act as the 'mouthpieces' of God in honourably proclaiming his Word.[58] It promoted a neo-clericalist ideology that also supported the calls frequently made by churchmen such as the moderate Puritan Lawrence Chaderton (1526–1640) for the laity to obey their ministers' directions in doctrinal, liturgical and moral affairs.[59] Protestant churches deliberately distanced themselves from the Catholic rite of ordination, with its sacramental basis and its positioning of the priest on a higher plane (or hierarchical order) within the church but, despite this, they retained, with just a few exceptions (such as Zwingli's Zurich and Bohemia), the apostolic rite of laying on of hands, and proved conspicuously eager to foster the distinctive position of the minister within the church. Though the 'church's' consent, that is the consent of church members, was theoretically required in all major decisions, this did not prevent ministers from making edifying decisions on its behalf. Clearly, this was an attempt to reconcile clericalism with the vigorous lay leadership that Calvinism, in particular, exhibited. It was a structural and theological problem that the Catholic church tended to shy from confronting institutionally. Yet the search for normative standards in doctrine, worship and government during the early modern period should not be allowed to obscure the fact that it witnessed remarkable development in specific areas of ministry and apostolate.

The female vocation

Traditional histories obscured women's active part in shaping institutions, spirituality and values within Christianity, while modern histories tend to condemn the Catholic church, in particular, for its hostile enclosure of women in convents[60] and its restriction of their activities to childbearing and prayer. In Protestant and Catholic communities, women and men did manage to set influential precedents in forming female apostolic models of ministry; while it is foolish to ignore the fact that gender played an important role in ecclesiastical relations, we must avoid too abruptly demarcating an intransigent male church from its female membership. Men and women were often capable of choosing the teachings most appropriate to their lives and adapting or ignoring conventions and rules as necessary.[61] They were not invariably successful: the Ursuline order did not properly represent the vision of its Italian founder (Angela Merici 1474–1540) of a female confraternity living and working in the world as lay apostles. While some of its Italian communities remained uncloistered, its general development from 1535 was the product of pressure to adapt to conventional conventual structures and expectations of female religious life.[62] But it was achieved by the Daughters of Charity. Though they lived in common, they were adamant in their decision to remain a secular community and confraternity with only simple and annual vows (rather than the solemn vows that represented religious life) because it enabled them to remain uncloistered and free to work routinely with the poor, the sick, the young and the criminal. While circumventing the decree of Trent on enclosure, they ensured that their spiritual motivation and ethos of charity were sustained.

The Daughters, therefore, instigated a new Catholic model of female vocational life, midway between a traditional confraternal association, whose members lived openly in lay society, and an enclosed, cloistered, religious order (non-enclosed 'tertiary' or third orders, which followed the rule of a specific religious order, had previously existed, but these were enclosed by Trent). They also innovated in undertaking a range of responsibilities that cannot all be dismissed as 'feminine' or as alternative expressions of the physical maternity that they had not chosen. To do so is to ignore the positive aspects of the metaphor of motherhood, marian or otherwise: Marillac, their founding superior general, who was the mother of a son, meditated joyfully on the private bond of communication that existed between Mary and the Christ child in her womb and used it as an example of the spiritual strength available to women when Christ became their interiorized guide. Additionally, since the medieval period motherhood had been a metaphor used to describe the person and work of Christ.[63] So the Daughters certainly understood that they were spiritual mothers in their care of the vulnerable; this also partially underpinned their delivery of education, catechesis and retreats. It enabled them to mark out their imitation of Christ in generation, nurture and sacrifice, while using their vocational imperative as a robust justification for working in rough, often male dominated, environments. Their apostolate was active and public, and it was not intent on physically protecting them from the world or their fragile natures, as enclosure was customarily thought to do. By 1789, the Daughters comprised 15 per cent of the 'females in religion' in France and had been established in north Italy, eastern and central Europe. Their experience should not be seen as that of an organization which slipped through the cracks in the implementation of Tridentine rules.

Amongst Catholics, women's participation in apostolic ministry often took place under the umbrella of confraternal organizations, which traditionally borrowed their sense of fraternal and spiritual community from Christ and the Apostles. Confraternities provided important forums for the evolution of collective devotional norms and interior forms of piety, therefore proving crucial to the reinforcement of catholicism after the Reformation. A key example is provided by the Ladies of Charity (1617), whose spirituality was oriented towards charitable sensibility and found social justification in the midst of the growing numbers of poor throughout Europe. In regions of French influence and rule, the wellborn Ladies organized charitable aid to the poor, established schools and raised funds for abandoned children. The work was inspired not simply by compassion or a conventional submission to the duty of almsgiving, but by an apostolic desire to save souls in danger of being lost through lack of training and opportunity. It was simultaneously motivated by the suggestion that Christ stood amongst the poor; service to Christ through them could therefore prove redemptive for those who voluntarily ministered. With the exception of the procurator, the association's officers were female, and the level of entrepreneurial acumen amongst the members for fundraising, budgeting and project management is notable. It was frequently partially the fruit of their experience in managing households and estates while their husbands attended to, for instance, court or professional tasks. They were helped by the fact that French property laws and inheritance customs (like those in German sovereignties) allowed women the freedom to assume these roles when necessary; this may have restricted equivalent activities in Spain and Italy.[64]

Some Ladies assumed responsibility for work that they consciously understood to be an apostolically inspired manifestation of the ministry of teaching. A first-hand record of this is found in a letter written to de Paul by Geneviève Goussault, who presided over the Ladies of Charity of the *Hôtel Dieu* hospital in Paris, describing her travels in western France in 1633. First, it is noteworthy that de Paul did not object to the type of activities that Goussault described. Second, she peppered her letter with scriptural references; she possessed an extremely strong pastoral orientation that she deliberately compared to Christ's care of the vulnerable and underpinned with a recognition that she served Christ the prisoner and the persecuted victim in assisting the people that she met. As the Jesuits did, she may even have seen her travel as a key element to her apostolicity: the missionary sent out by God. She was quite ready, as a result, to lead locals in prayer, to catechize children and adults, to preach to large crowds which included clergy, and to offer herself as an example of the importance of regular sacramental observance and charitable acts. Furthermore, she did not shy from criticizing a local priest or from informing Vincent de Paul that he needed to organize a mission in the region.

The Daughters of Charity restricted the teaching aspect of their ministry to catechesis, provision of retreats and education, though even this could be interpreted as an undermining of the Pauline ban. Yet Goussault ignored Paul's instruction completely; maybe she was able to do so because she had the confidence of noble birth, but that had not protected Protestant noblewomen during the Reformation.[65] It is just as likely that Goussault was so strongly motivated by her call to save souls that she was willing to perform virtually whatever act would achieve this, and to ignore restrictions imposed on her sex by custom or religion.

Perhaps Goussault's high social bearing also contributed to the impression that she made on provincial notables and peasants. Yet, importantly, they told her that they were especially pleased that 'I do not play the role of the reformer, I laugh heartily and I go to my parish church.' She was thought not to patronize her listeners and conversants or irritate them by saccharine piety or condemnations. If we add to this the fact that Goussault had a family of five children, we see that she did not simply transfer the monastery to the world in her apostolate; she thoroughly amalgamated the appropriate elements of both vocations into her family and social life, so that she could pass messages, sometimes seemingly incidentally and without deliberate forethought, on Christian doctrine, virtue and practice through the normal channels of conversation, friendship, visitation and example. Chatting casually to children in the street during a short stop in a town, she recited the Our Father with them as they said their farewells; one impressed individual told her it was evident she loved the poor and was most content when among them, for she 'looked twice as beautiful' while talking to them. According to Goussault, God granted her the courage to speak to large crowds. Clearly, she perceived the inner glow noted by her admirer to be divine grace, to which she owed her fervent wish to follow the powerful example of 'my Saviour'.[66]

There is much in Goussault's activity that coincides with the teaching that François de Sales (1567–1622) presented in his massively popular *Introduction to the Devout Life* (1610), regularly read by the Ladies and Daughters. De Sales endorsed the orthodoxy that spiritual directors should be male, but in practice he did not query the spiritual direction that Jeanne de Chantal (1572–1641), his associate in establishing the Visitation order, and other Visitation nuns offered. He also gave a sense of validity to the lay vocation that often went unrecognized by other Catholic clerical authors, even if many clergy actively supported lay initiatives to establish religious orders and deal with the problems of poverty. In addition to confirming the spiritual equality of men and women, de Sales placed less emphasis on exterior purity, usually made synonymous with virginity, than on interior purity of virtue, thus returning spiritual merit to the widowed and married states.[67]

Still, we should not overestimate the progress made in the development of female apostolic ministry within catholicism during the early modern era. The dominance of the male clerical model of ministry could circumscribe alternatives and complements, as Mary Ward (1585–1645) discovered when she sought to establish an active, unenclosed female equivalent of the Society of Jesus.[68] This model, accompanied by the Tridentine decrees on parochial religious practice and hierarchical supervision of religious practices, was not always flexible enough to allow men and women to develop their lay ministries fully. It often forced women to use an apparently unthreatening rhetoric of obedience and submission to achieve their goals, respond to their spiritual needs and accommodate public expectations of female qualities and behaviour. Male saints were not usually presented as models of humility and obedience, but that was precisely how the Carmelite Teresa of Avila (1515–82) was presented when canonized (1622), despite her clashes with authority, her spiritual leadership and long periods outside the cloister.[69]

Amongst Protestants, the possibilities of female ministry within a 'priesthood of all believers' were felt especially keenly in the Separatist groups that emerged during the social upheaval of the civil war in England. Women were amongst the founding members of the Baptists, Levellers and the Society of Friends (Quakers) and were committed to active roles in the expression and government of their churches.[70] Unlike most churchmen, the Quaker founder, George Fox (1624–91), happily confirmed women's right to preach in meeting houses because he intended to replace the male administered Anglican church and ancient restrictions (which he considered historical rather than scriptural) that inhibited these particular priestly believers from doing so. Female proselytizing was a marked feature of the early Quaker movement (its first major female preacher was Elisabeth Hooton, 1600–72), as was the related collegiality cultivated among its female membership throughout their persecution by the government at home and in the new American colonies. Standing alongside Fox, Margaret Fell (1614–1702) was amongst the Quaker vanguard. In her public ministry, founded on a doctrine of women's spiritual equality with men that she articulated in *Women's Speaking Justified*,[71] she strove to ensure that the movement could expand and consolidate as a Christian denomination. She contributed substantially to the fund established to finance travelling Quaker preachers (Fund for the Service of Truth) and sought tirelessly to overturn the government's intolerance of Quakers by petitioning and negotiating at the highest levels of the administration, even enduring four years of imprisonment (1664–8) when Charles II's government accelerated its campaign to outlaw Dissenters from 1661.[72]

As new religious groups and churches became established throughout the early modern period, their experimental status and intense reflection on appropriate expressions of doctrine and organization produced dissent. The Massachusetts Bay Colony faced several such confrontations. The Quakers were mutilated, executed or banished from it in 1657. Some years earlier, Anne Hutchinson (1591–1643) challenged religious and social stability by calling into question key doctrinal emphases such as proof of repentance and holiness (which she considered the product of a false covenant of works) on the basis of supposed direct revelations from the Holy Spirit. Her church's elders accused her of propagating a form of Antinomianism, meaning that she devalued Christian works in favour of a strict covenant of grace that did not require acts that represented holiness and penance. When she instigated and preached at devotional meetings that seemed to assert her authority independently of the church's, she was banished and joined Roger William's community in Rhode Island (Williams had left Massachusetts after confrontation over doctrines in 1636).[73] It was not merely female proselytizing that raised opposition within churches; all those who undercut a church's conventions of doctrine and worship and unifying truths of faith might expect to meet hostility.

Conclusion

Accurately defining positions of teaching and governmental authority proved as desirable for most Protestant churches as for the Catholic during the Tridentine and early modern eras. In contrast to the former, the Catholic tendency to see the priestly and monastic vocations as the models that all others should aspire to emulate was deep-rooted; when the lay directed Company of the Holy Sacrament in France, for instance, decided to establish pious associations for the religious formation of artisan youths, it was unable to imagine any structure that did not amount to a lay monastic community, where youths lived and worked strictly in common according to the monastic virtues of poverty, chastity and obedience and a structure of prayer, sacramental reception and work.[74] More generally, the laity were not usually comfortably accommodated within the church's official structures of authority; Trent's decisions were taken by theologians, bishops and heads of religious orders, with some influence from the powerful Emperor Charles V, while diocesan synods were also reserved to clergy; because of the principle of subsidiarity, it was normally in the lived experience or actualization of theology that the laity managed to shape their church and develop their ministry within it.

This cautious note should not, however, blind us to identifying key developments within the church. Ecclesiology emerged as a distinct discipline. Institutionally, theologians and controversialists concentrated on the visible or exterior aspects of church, which meant the prerogatives of government and authority, sacramentality and the relationship between church and sovereign. For the Protestant and Catholic churches, these proved profoundly urgent questions, for they sought to justify their claims to apostolicity and salvation through robust declarations of historical continuity of structure, dominion and revelation. Additionally, it was crucial to the churches to cultivate their unity in doctrine and discipline, so that the loci of authority and the power of doctrinal judgment assumed prominent positions in theological polemics and analytical discourses. Institutionally too, the development of secular sovereignties and political theories that bolstered secular power obliged churchmen to celebrate the independence and superiority of the sacred realm while concurrently taking the risk of allying their churches with ambitious political rulers. Each of these issues touched the lives of the faithful within the church, but the ecclesiology displayed in devotion and piety did not always reflect precisely the same concerns and influences as polemical treatises or church councils.

Trent's reliance on clerical leadership and its perpetuation of the superiority of ordained priesthood was partially a defensive response to Protestant subverting of Catholic priest-hood and hierarchy. It encouraged the French school's fruitful reconfiguration of priesthood and episcopacy while giving rise to rivalry within the clerical hierarchy. However, the real innovations in ministry came from those Christians who looked beyond the narrow focus on male clerical supremacy by endeavouring to promote complementary or common ministries for clergy and laity and for men and women. The ecclesiology of souls demonstrated by the associative identity and confraternal strength of Catholic belief, devotion and mission played a fundamental role, though it was not always in harmony with the external ecclesio-logical structure, power and government of the church. Confraternities could bolster both genres of ecclesiology: to homogenize and superintend beliefs and worship under the juris-dictional ascendancy of parish priest, bishop and pope, or to imagine shared spiritual moti-vations and apostolic roles for the faithful of the body of Christ. In this regard, the pattern of development within Roman Catholicism after Trent was similar to that within most Protestant denominations: an initial period of vigorous creativity followed by a period of consolidation and even retraction. This meant that as Protestant denominations solidified their positions, they adopted rules and conventions that obliged women either to retreat from the leadership roles that they had managed to carve out during a formative period, which had necessarily gambled on freedom and resistance to theological and organizational conventionality, or to seek spiritual fulfilment on new and independent terms.

Notes

1 *Decrees of the Ecumenical Councils*, ed. Norman Tanner, 2 vols, London: Sheed and Ward, 1990, ii, Sess. III, p. 407.

2 John W. O'Malley, *Trent and All That. Renaming Catholicism in the Early Modern Era*, Cambridge, MA: Harvard University Press, 2000.

3 Hubert Jedin, *Geschichte des Konzils von Trient*, 4 vols, Freiburg: Herder, 1949–75. The first two volumes are available in English: *A History of the Council of Trent*, trans. Ernest Graf, London: Nelson, 1957–61.

4 Amongst the most influential contributions are: John Bossy, *Christianity in the West, 1400–1700*, Oxford: Oxford University Press, 1985; Jean Delumeau, *Catholicism Between Luther and Voltaire. A New View of the Counter-Reformation*, trans. Jeremy Moiser, London: Burns and Oates, 1977; Heinz Schilling, *Religion, Political Culture and the Emergence of Early Modern Society: Essays in German and Dutch History*, Leiden: Brill, 1992.

5 *Jacopo Sadoleti Cardinalis et Episcopi Carpentoractensis viri disertissimi. Opera quae extant omnia*, 4 vols, Verona: n. p., 1737–8 (including his commentary on Romans, which earned disapproval in Rome for its conciliatory attitude towards Calvinism).

6 Alison Forrestal, *Fathers, Pastors and Kings. Visions of Episcopacy in Seventeenth-Century France*, Manchester: Manchester University Press, 2004, pp. 23–5; Jean-Pierre Massaut, *Josse Clichtove, l'humanisme et la réforme du clergé*, 2 vols, Paris: Les Belles Lettres, 1968; Michel Veissière, 'Guillaume Briçonnet, évêque de Meaux, et la réforme de son clergé', *Revue d'Histoire Ecclésiastique*, 84 (1989), 655–72.

7 Philip Edgcombe Hughes, *Lefèvre: Pioneer of Ecclesiastical Renewal in France*, Grand Rapids, MI: Eerdmans, 1984.

8 Veissière, 'Briçonnet', pp. 669–70.

9 Richard L. DeMolen (ed.), *Religious Orders of the Catholic Reformation. In Honor of John C. Olin on his Seventy-Fifth Birthday*, New York: Fordham University Press, 1994.

10 John W. O' Malley, 'Was Ignatius Loyola a Church Reformer? How to Look at Early Modern Catholicism', in *The Counter-Reformation*, ed. David Luebke, Malden, MA and Oxford: Blackwell, 1999, pp. 65–82.

11 Ignatius of Loyola, *The Spiritual Exercises of St. Ignatius*, trans. George Ganss, St Louis, MO: Institute of Jesuit Sources, 1992.

12 John W. O' Malley, 'Attitudes of the Early Jesuits towards Misbelievers', *The Ways*, 68 (Summer 1990), 62–73.

13 Forrestal, *Fathers*, pp. 74–108; John W. O' Malley, 'The Society of Jesus', in John Patrick Donnelly and Michael W. Maher (eds), *Confraternities and Catholic Reform in Italy, France and Spain*, Kirksville, MO: Thomas Jefferson University Press, 1999, pp. 143–4.

14 *The Constitutions of the Society of Jesus*, ed. George Ganss, St Louis, MO: Institute of Jesuit Sources, 1970; Michael W. Maher, 'How the Jesuits Used Their Congregations to Promote Frequent Communion', in Donnelly and Maher (eds), *Confraternities*, pp. 75–95; idem, 'Confession and Consolation: The Society of Jesus and its Promotion of the General Confession', in Katherine Jackson Lualdi and Anne T. Thayer (eds), *Penitence in the Age of Reformations*, Aldershot and Burlington, VT: Ashgate, 2000, pp. 184–200; John W. O'Malley, *The First Jesuits*, Cambridge, MA: Harvard University Press, 1993, pp. 4–8.

15 *Saint Vincent de Paul. Correspondence. Conferences, Documents*, ed. Jacqueline Kilar, trans. Helen Marie Law *et al.*, 10 vols, New York: New City Press, 1983–, iii, pp. 163–5, de Paul to Jean Dehorgny, March 1647.

16 *Decrees*, ed. Tanner, ii, Sess. VI, pp. 681–2; Sess. XXIII, pp. 742–53.

17 Forrestal, *Fathers*, p. 112.

18 Anthony D. Wright, 'Relations Between Church and State: Catholic Developments in Spanish-Ruled Italy of the Counter-Reformation', *History of European Ideas*, vol. 9, no. 4 (1988), 385–403.

19 See Craig Harline and Eddy Put, *A Bishop's Tale. Mathias Hovius among his Flock in Seventeenth-Century Flanders*, New Haven and London: Yale University Press, 2000, pp. 125–7, for an analysis of Bishop Hovius' battle with Rome in 1607.

20 Forrestal, *Fathers*, pp. 112–13.

21 For example, Alison Forrestal, *Catholic Synods in Ireland, 1600–1690*, Dublin: Four Courts, 1998, pp. 96–9, 163–6.

22 Forrestal, *Fathers*, pp. 87–94.

23 1665: Ibid., p. 119.

24 C. R. Boxer, 'The Problem of the Native Clergy in the Portuguese and Spanish Empires from the Sixteenth to the Eighteenth Centuries', in *Christianity and Missions, 1450–1800*, ed. J. S. Cummins, Aldershot: Ashgate, 1997, pp. 175–95.

25 Maher, 'Confession', pp. 184–200; John Leddy Phelan, 'Pre-Baptismal Instruction and the Administration of Baptism in the Philippines during the Sixteenth Century', in *Christianity*, ed. Cummins, pp. 139–59.

26 For the Jesuit Matteo Ricci's efforts to enter Chinese society through a marriage between Confucian philosophy and Christian faith, see Andrew R. Ross, *A Vision Betrayed. The Jesuits in Japan and China 1542–1742*, Edinburgh: Edinburgh University Press, 1994, pp. 119–54.

27 G. Baez-Camargo, 'The Earliest Protestant Missionary Venture in Latin America', in *Christianity*, ed. Cummins, pp. 303–13.

28 Cotton Mather, *Magnalia Christi Americana*, 7 vols, Edinburgh: Banner of Truth Trust, 1979. See also Ernst Benz, 'Pietist and Puritan Sources of Early Protestant World Missions (Cotton Mather and A. H. Francke)', in *Christianity*, ed. Cummins, pp. 315–42, at 320.

29 See above, p. 89.

30 F. J. Bremer, *Congregational Communion: Clerical Friendship in the Anglo-American Puritan Community, 1610–1692*, Boston: Northeastern University Press, 1994; R. T. Handy, *A History of the Churches in the United States and Canada*, Oxford: Clarendon Press, 1976; A. Zakai, 'The Gospel of Reformation: The Origins of the Great Puritan Migration', *Journal of Ecclesiastical History*, 37 (1986), 584–602. On Williams, see O. E. Winslow, *Master Roger Williams* New York: Macmillan, 1957, and Edmund S. Morgan, *Roger Williams: The Church and the State*, New York: Harcourt, Brace & World, 1967.

31 Forrestal, *Fathers*, pp. 127–33.

32 Ibid., pp. 136–7.

33 John Calvin, *Institutes of the Christian Religion*, trans. Henry Beveridge, Grand Rapids, MI: Eerdmans, 1989, pp. 322–6.

34 Philip Benedict, *The Faith and Fortunes of France's Huguenots, 1600–85*, Aldershot: Ashgate, 2001.

35 W. D. J. Cargill Thompson, 'Sir Francis Knollys' Campaign against the *Jure Divino* Theory of Episcopacy', in C. Robert Cole and Michael E. Moody (eds), *Essays for Leland H. Carlson. The Dissenting Tradition*, Athens, Ohio: Ohio University Press, 1975, pp. 39–77; Patrick Collinson, 'Towards a Broader Understanding of the Early Dissenting Tradition', in ibid., pp. 3–38, at 11.

36 Stephen Brachlow, *The Communion of Saints. Radical Puritan and Separatist Ecclesiology 1570–1625*, Oxford: Oxford University Press, 1988, pp. 157–202.

37 Walter Travers, *A full and plaine declaration of ecclesiastical discipline*, n. p., 1574, p. 75. On Protestant ministry see below, p. 97.

38 Forrestal, *Fathers*, p. 161.

39 Robert Bellarmine, 'Epistola Apologetica Roberti S.R.E. Cardinalis Bellarmini ad Franciscum Card. Sancti Clementis adversus temeritatem et errorest Alexandri Carerii Patavini', in LeBachelet, *Auctarium Bellarminianum*, Paris: n. p., 1913, p. 434.

40 Peter Burke, *The Fabrication of Louis XIV*, New Haven and London: Yale University Press, 1992; Robin Briggs, *Early Modern France, 1560–1715*, Oxford: Oxford University Press, 2nd edition 1998, pp. 73–159.

41 Mark Greengrass, *France in the Age of Henri IV. The Struggle for Stability*, London and New York: Longman, 2nd edition 1995, pp. 60, 251.

42 Charles Plowden, *A short account of the Establishment of the New See of Baltimore in Maryland, and of consecrating the Right Rev. Dr. John Carroll first Bishop thereof*, London: J. P. Coghlan, 1790, pp. 5–6.

43 Robert Bellarmine, *Disputationes de Controversiis . . . Fidei adversus hujus temporis haereticos*, 3 vols, Ingolstadt: n.p., pp. 1586–9; John Courtney Murray, 'St. Robert Bellarmine on the Indirect Power', *Theological Studies*, 9 (1948), 491–535.

44 Richard Hooker, 'Of the Lawes of Ecclesiasticall Politie', VIII, 2–8: *The Folger Library Edition of the Works of Richard Hooker*, ed. W. Speed Hill, 7 vols, various publishers, 1977–88.

45 Forrestal, *Fathers*, pp. 131–2, 158.

46 J. Brennan, 'A Gallican Interlude in Ireland', *The Irish Theological Quarterly*, xxiv (1957), 219–37, 283–309.

47 Forrestal, *Synods*, pp. 132–89.

48 Idem, *Fathers*, pp. 74–108; Richard Golden, *The Godly Rebellion. Parisian Curés and the Religious Fronde 1652–1662*, Chapel Hill, NC: University of North Carolina Press, 1981, pp. 69–75.

49 Nigel Aston, *The End of an Elite: The French Bishops and the Coming of the Revolution, 1786–1790*, Oxford: Clarendon Press, 1992.

50 The term 'congregation' designates a permanent association of secular priests who live in common (and usually with a Rule) but do not form a religious order.

51 Eamon Duffy, 'The English Secular Clergy and the Counter-Reformation', *Journal of Ecclesiastical History*, 34 (1983), 214–20.

52 Jean-Jacques Olier, *Traité des saints ordres*, eds Gilles Chaillot, Paul Cochois and Irénée Noye, Paris: Procure de la Compagnie de Saint Sulpice, 1984, pp. 183–98.

53 Forrestal, *Fathers*, pp. 61–5.

54 Cargill Thompson, 'Campaign', pp. 39–77; Peter Lake, *Anglicans and Puritans? Presbyterianism and English Conformist Thought from Whitgift to Hooker*, London: Unwin Hyman, 1988, pp. 13–70.

55 John Bossy, 'The Counter-Reformation and the People of Catholic Ireland, 1596–1641', *Historical Studies*, viii (1971), 155–69.

56 *Decrees*, ed. Tanner, ii, Sess. XXII, p. 740.

57 *Huldreich Zwinglis Sämtliche Werke*, 14 vols, Berlin: C. A. Schwetschke, 1905, ii, pp. 438–40; W. P. Stephens, *The Theology of Huldrych Zwingli*, Oxford: Clarendon Press, 1986, pp. 260–81.

58 Calvin, *Institutes*, trans. Beveridge, pp. 315–26.

59 Brachlow, *Communion*, p. 161.

60 The Council of Trent universalized the practice of enclosure for female religious in 1563: *Decrees*, ed. Tanner, Sess. XXV, Ch. 5, p. 778.

61 For contrasting views, see Donna Spivey Ellington, *From Sacred Body to Angelic Soul. Understanding Mary in Late Medieval and Early Modern Europe*, Washington DC: Catholic University of America Press, 2001, and Marina Warner, *Alone of All Her Sex*, London: Picador, 1985.

62 Charmarie J. Blaisdell, 'Angela Merici and the Ursulines', in *Religious Orders*, ed. Demolen, pp. 99–136.

63 Caroline Walker Bynun, *Jesus as Mother: Studies in the Spirituality of the High Middle Ages*, Berkeley, CA: University of California Press, 1982.

64 Barbara Diefendorf, *From Penitence to Charity. Pious Women and the Catholic Reformation in Paris*, Oxford: Oxford University Press, 2004, pp. 17–18; Merry E. Wiesner, *Working Women in Renaissance Germany*, New Brunswick, NJ: Rutgers University Press, 1986.

65 Merry E. Wiesner, 'Nuns, Wives and Mothers: Women and the Reformation in Germany', in *Women in Reformation and Counter-Reformation Europe*, ed. Sherrin Marshall, Bloomington, IN: Indiana University Press, 1989, pp. 8–28.

66 *Vincent de Paul*, ed. Kilar, i, pp. 191–6, Goussault to de Paul, 16 April 1633.

67 François de Sales, *Introduction to the Devout Life*, ed. and trans. John Ryan, New York: Image, 1972; Spivey Ellington, *Sacred Body*, p. 170.

68 Henriette Peters, *Mary Ward: A World in Contemplation*, trans. Helen Butterworth, Leominster: Gracewing, 1984.

69 Alison Weber, *Theresa of Avila and the Rhetoric of Femininity*, Princeton: Princeton University Press, 1990.

70 Claire Cross, '"He Goats Before the Flocks". A Note on the Part Played By Women in the Founding of Some Civil War Churches', in G. J. Cuming and D. Bakers (eds), *Popular Belief and Practice: Studies in Church History*, viii (1972), pp. 195–202; D. Ludlow, 'Shaking Patriarchy's Foundations: Sectarian Women in England, 1641–1700', in *Triumph over Silence, Women in Protestant History*, ed. Richard Greaves, Westport, CT and London: Greenwood, 1985, pp. 93–123.

71 Margaret Fell, *Women's Speakng Justified*, London: n. p., 1667.

72 A. Lloyd, *Quaker Social History, 1669–1738*, London: Longman, 1950, pp. 107–19; P. Mack, 'Teaching about Gender and Spirituality in Early English Quakerism', *Women's Studies*, 19 (1991), 223–38.

73 Emery Battis, *Saints and Sectaries: Anne Hutchinson and the Antinomian Controversy in the Massachusetts Bay Colony*, Chapel Hill: University of North Carolina Press, 1962; M. Winship, *Making Heretics: Militant Protestantism and Free Grace in Massachusetts, 1636–1641*, Princeton: Princeton University Press, 2002.

74 Alain Tallon, *La Compagnie du Saint Sacrement, 1629–1667*, Paris: Cerf, 1990, pp. 148–9.

Further reading

Richard L. DeMolen (ed.), *Religious Orders of the Catholic Reformation. In Honor of John C. Olin on his Seventy-Fifth Birthday*, New York: Fordham University Press, 1994.

John Patrick Donnelly and Michael W. Maher (eds), *Confraternities and Catholic Reform in Italy, France and Spain*, Kirksville, MO: Thomas Jefferson University Press, 1999.

Hubert Jedin, *A History of the Council of Trent*, 2 vols, trans. Ernest Graf, London: Nelson, 1957–61.

Carter Lindberg (ed.), *The Reformation Theologians*, Oxford: Blackwell, 2002.

David Luebke (ed.), *The Counter-Reformation*, Malden, MA and Oxford: Blackwell, 1999.

Diarmaid MacCulloch, *Reformation. Europe's House Divided 1490–1700*, London: Penguin, 2003.

John W. O'Malley, *The First Jesuits*, Cambridge, MA: Harvard University Press, 1993.

Jaroslav Pelikan, *The Christian Tradition. A History of the Development of Doctrine*, 5 vols, Chicago: University of Chicago Press, 1983, iv.

Bernard Pujo, *Vincent de Paul. The Trailblazer*, trans. Gertrud Graubart Champe, Notre Dame, IN: University of Notre Dame Press, 2003.

6

THE CHURCH IN
MODERN THEOLOGY

Nicholas M. Healy

For our purposes here, the phrase 'modern theology' refers to that period of theological inquiry which began about the same time as the nineteenth century, and which has only recently and partially been displaced by postmodern issues and methods. The story of the church's self-understanding within this two hundred year period is complex, due not least to the diversity of ways the various Protestant, Anglican, Roman Catholic and Orthodox churches engaged with the modern world. Since this is the story of the church's diverse and developing theological self-understanding, rather than simply the story of the church as such, it is necessary to focus on the work of specific theologians, movements and denominations that illustrate various theological developments, rather than present a straightforward chronological account.

All the churches found it necessary to reconsider their nature and function and their relation to society. While such tasks are hardly novel, they were performed within a new, 'modern' situation in which the churches had greatly diminished control over their social and intellectual environments. Modern societies challenged the church's doctrines and customary practices, its self-understanding – even its very existence. As a consequence, theological inquiry – including ecclesiology – often tended towards apologetics, to constructing, that is, a rational defense of Christianity against its critics. At the least, modern theologians sought to represent Christian doctrine and practice in ways that implicitly addressed modern critiques of religion, theology and the church. Others attempted more explicitly to rebut the challenges of modernity, often by adapting one or other of its philosophies for theological purposes. Yet others, especially within Roman Catholic circles, constructed alternative intellectual systems designed to challenge modernity and force its rejection by believers.

To be sure, apologetics was common enough in the preceding era. However, by the beginning of our period the earlier rationalist apologetics had become ineffective and unconvincing. Summarily: it had sought to prove that God must exist if we are to be able to make sense of the world. But prompted in part by the critical philosophies initiated by Kant, as well as the far-reaching social consequences of the French Revolution and its failure, modern people increasingly came to believe that they could understand the world without speaking about God at all and, further, that they could make sense of God only by first speaking about humanity.[1] If knowledge about God is not necessary or even helpful for rational inquiry about the world and our place within it then, as it seemed to some, it would follow that there is no need for a church that claims to speak the truth about God with authority.

By the beginning of the eighteenth century, many intellectuals, Christian and not, held in common certain beliefs about religion and the church. Religion, they thought, is simple in its essence and knowable through natural reason without revelation. The church's function is to inform its members how to act rightly and motivate them to do so. The rest is up to the individual, for sin is not so corrupting that I cannot respond well if I choose. So, as Kant is often thought to have argued, society needs belief in God in order to overcome our evil propensities and motivate good intentions. But the church's beliefs are rational only insofar as they support moral actions by justifying the hope of eternal reward for the good and fear of punishment for the bad. Further doctrines and practices are relics from a less enlightened time.

The view of the church as moral educator persisted throughout the period and, of course, is held in some form by many people today. It conflicted sharply with the dominant ecclesiology of the Roman Catholic church, already partly established during the seventeenth century, reaffirmed frequently thereafter in response to various challenges, and persisting through to the middle of the twentieth century. It, too, was reductive, describing the church in largely empirical terms as a hierarchical organization, founded by Christ, the function of which is to guard and teach the faith. Christian faith is not only in accordance with reason; the church teaches the faith with an absolute authority guaranteed by the Holy Spirit. Supporting this ecclesiology is a distinctive, 'two-tier' ontology according to which there are two sharply separated forms of reality, nature and supernature, each having its own order and goal and its own form and source of knowledge: natural and supernatural. The church is that body which guards the deposit of supernatural knowledge given it, and only it, at its founding. Therein lies its authority and function, for only through the church can we be ordered beyond nature to our supernatural goal.

One key question posed within Roman Catholicism throughout our period was where to locate supreme authority within the hierarchy. For many, it lay primarily in the pope, who disbursed his personal authority to the bishops. Others argued that the bishops receive their authority directly from their office, as the apostles received theirs directly from Christ rather than through Peter. The latter view was promoted in the seventeenth century by Bossuet and by the Gallican Four Articles (1682) with which he is associated. While the articles accepted the primacy of the pope, the fourth states that papal decrees are not irreformable unless the church has given its consent to them, implying that the church 'is not derived from the pope; it has a reality and vitality of its own'.[2] In the next century, Febronius led a similar effort to reaffirm what was arguably the patristic understanding of the role of the bishops. But though such views were widespread at the start of our period, they were aggressively countered. In 1799, for example, the future Pope Gregory XVI published *Il Trionfo della S. Sede e della Chiesa* ('The Triumph of the Holy See and the Church') in which he argued that the monarchical structure of the church must always have been in place because the authority and infallibility of the church rests upon the infallibility of its head, the Sovereign Pontiff. The institutional and absolutist structure of the church could therefore never change.[3] This tendency within Roman Catholicism to identify the church with its authoritative function and structure would persist, inhibiting more well-rounded theological descriptions.

Attempts to move beyond these two reductive conceptions of the church arose initially with the Romantic reaction to Rationalism that began a decade or two before the turn of the eighteenth century. In brief, the Romantics believed that what can be known through reason alone is surpassed by emotions and intuitions that go beyond words to grasp the depths beneath the surface and the whole beyond the parts. Although this would seem to encourage an individualistic epistemology, and thus an individualistic understanding of religion as a largely personal, inward matter, those influenced by Romanticism were often deeply interested in communal traditions and in the vital role they play in evoking and forming the experiences of the individual.

The first third of the nineteenth century saw an initial attempt to draw upon Romanticism by the '*triumvirate catholique*',[4] Joseph de Maistre, Félicité de Lamennais and Louis de Bonald, who advocated what came to be known as Traditionalism. In spite of political differences, they shared a strong sense of French society as a single whole, rather than the more usual 'two pillars' Catholic view, according to which the state and the church operate in their own spheres of nature and supernature respectively. A key tenet of Traditionalism was the belief that certain truth could not be had by an individual alone. Rather, the general consensus of humanity – society as such – is the sole 'criterion of truth'. Society was set in order at its beginning by an original revelation from God, so society must be properly structured if it is to preserve that revelation intact. The only society able to do this properly is one governed by the Roman Catholic church, because only that church has the pope, and he alone discerns truth with infallible authority. Lamennais (perhaps inconsistently with his advocacy of social democracy) put the argument thus: 'there can be neither public morality nor national character without religion; no European religion without Christianity; no Christianity without Catholicism; no Catholicism without the Pope, and no Pope without the supreme authority which is his alone.'[5] In effect, the Traditionalists' ecclesiology was a social philosophy rather than a theology of the church. De Maistre (a royalist) noted the obvious ideological corollary in his *Du Pape* (1819): 'In civil society a revolution is nothing other than a *political heresy*; and likewise, in Christian society, a heretic is nothing other than a *revolutionary* against the authority of the Church.'[6] Although Lamennais was condemned by Gregory XVI (in 1832), de Maistre's ideas especially became increasingly influential in Rome (see the section below on Roman ecclesiology).

Friedrich Schleiermacher (1768–1834)

The Romantic sensibility informed much more sophisticated work in Germany. Friedrich Schleiermacher, often described as the 'father of modern theology', drew upon both Romanticism and his own Pietistic background, with its strong emphasis upon achieving a personal relationship with Jesus Christ. He taught at the University of Berlin, which had been established at the turn of the century on Enlightenment principles, according to which inquiry is rational only if it proceeds in a properly scientific manner, using critical methods available to all, with no authoritative text. Many believed that theology, based as it was upon the authority of Scripture and the church, did not meet these criteria and should not be taught in a modern university. Schleiermacher's major theological work, *The Christian Faith*,[7] is in part intended to make the case for theology as a modern scientific discipline.[8] A complex yet highly consistent 'system of doctrine' or Christian dogmatics, it opens with a substantial introduction that explicitly avoids drawing upon Christian beliefs. Unlike rationalist and critical philosophies, the introduction is neither a philosophy of God nor a philosophical analysis of the knowing and willing person, but rather a social–philosophical account of religious experience. Schleiermacher considers religion to be essentially 'piety', a form of consciousness deeper than Kant's reason or will, which he defines as a feeling of 'absolute dependence' (p. 12). This feeling is universally available and can be recognized by anyone 'who is capable of a little introspection' (p. 13). Piety is thus a constitutive element of human nature.

But if piety is the religious a priori, it is necessarily social in form, for the pious person seeks fellowship with others who have similar religious feelings (p. 26). It is not the case, however, that the church consists of those who, finding they are religiously like-minded, subsequently come together. Rather, piety is awakened through membership in a religious community. Furthermore, each community has its own particular form of piety – its set of experiences, beliefs and practices – that renders its faith distinctive, even as the expressions of that faith develop as each generation is taught by the previous one and shapes the community in its turn. A religious community therefore

> forms an ever self-renewing circulation of the religious self-consciousness within certain definite limits, and a propagation of the religious emotions arranged and organized with the same limits, so that there can be some kind of definite under-standing as to which individuals belong to it and which do not – this we designate a *Church*.
>
> (p. 29)

Accordingly, the theologian's concern is not with religion-in-general or 'natural religion', since there cannot be a set of experiences, beliefs and practices present in all religions. Piety's forms are always shaped by a particular religious community (p. 30). So theology is the critical analysis and description of 'the totality of the religious affections which form the foundation' of a particular church, as these are set forth by that church's tradition of 'contemplation and reflection' (p. 29). In *The Christian Faith*, Schleiermacher examines the forms of piety found in the Reformed and Lutheran churches with a view to their eventual union.

Schleiermacher's theological method is modern in turning away from directly speaking of the religious 'object' as such, as the earlier Protestant Orthodoxy and Tridentine Catholicism spoke of God by means of doctrinal propositions. Instead, his is something like a phenomenological approach in which the theologian critically analyses the consciousness of a particular religious subject, namely the well-formed member of a particular church. Critically descriptive ecclesiology thus becomes a central concern of theological inquiry as such. Yet doctrine remains vitally important, for Christian-specific beliefs shape the forms of Christian piety.

The Christian church is distinguished above all by love for Jesus Christ, our Saviour. Jesus is the origin and norm of Christian piety. The church's function is to mediate Jesus' experience of God to us. 'The new life of each individual springs from that of the community, while the life of the community springs from no other individual life than that of the Redeemer' (p. 525). The mediating church and the Holy Spirit are almost identical: 'the expression "Holy Spirit" must be understood to mean the vital unity of the Christian fellowship as a moral personality . . . its *common spirit*' (p. 535, emphasis in original). Schleiermacher does not simply identify the church's collective spirit with the Holy Spirit, however. He distinguishes (though does not separate) the visible church, which is divided, confused and sometimes erroneous, from the invisible church. It is only the latter which, through its participation in the Spirit, is infallibly true to Christ (p. 678). As R. Haight puts it, the notion of an invisible church functions for Schleiermacher as a kind of 'code word for the power of God'.[9] One might therefore argue that Schleiermacher's ecclesiology is largely trinitarian.

It is on this trinitarian basis that Schleiermacher can characterize the church as thoroughly historical and always in need of reform. While the norm remains the God-consciousness of Jesus Christ and its expression, and while the Bible certainly expresses that norm (though in a way that requires a subtle hermeneutic), many of the church's forms of piety will and should change. To be sure, there are some forms that are unchanging, such as preaching, the power of the keys, baptism, eucharist, and so on. However, there can be no timeless account of these, nor of any of the church's doctrines and practices. The Christian communities are in process, but they are not necessarily getting closer to the truth and the good. B. Gerrish rightly points out that Schleiermacher's understanding of the church as developing in history differs from that of John Henry Newman and later official Roman Catholicism in that, for him, a particular development may be a mistake rather than an improvement.[10] Nonetheless, because the Holy Spirit works within the collective spirit of the church to conform it to the God-consciousness of Jesus Christ, the church can acknowledge its historicity and its fallibility, yet insist upon its fundamentally secure relation to God.

Möhler and the Tübingen School

Within Roman Catholicism the first major development of the period originated within the University of Tübingen's School of Theology, founded by J. S. von Drey (1777–1853). Drey's own organic ecclesiology, which centred upon the image of the Kingdom of God, was developed in a different direction by another member of the school, Johann Adam Möhler (1796–1838). Möhler's work has two phases, reflected in his two major books. The earlier, *Unity in the Church*,[11] has been especially influential in post-Vatican II ecclesiology, while the later ecclesiology of his *Symbolik* was influential in the Roman school of ecclesiology, as we shall see.

Unity draws in part upon Romanticist themes to describe the church as an organic community informed by love. 'The Church is the external, visible structure of a holy, living power, of love, the body of the spirit of believers forming itself from the interior externally' (p. 209). Each believer comes to be such by 'the influence of the Church community enlivened by the Holy Spirit' (p. 92), which generates a 'new spirit' in the believer, who then possesses a 'new life principle' (p. 98). This inner-to-outer, spirit-to-expression dynamic is characteristic of much of *Unity*. Christ's internal self-consciousness preceded its lived expression in his ministry (p. 96); the Bible is the witness to the expression of the same internal life (p. 97); the visible, social aspects of the church, its hierarchy and practices, are the expression or realization of what is more fundamental, namely the essential aspect of the church, the communion of love and faith united in and through the Spirit.

On this basis, Möhler argues for fundamental unity within diversity. Unity lies in the inner depths. The expressions of that underlying unity grow in both complexity and clarity as the church is guided through its history by the Spirit. On this view, the Protestant Reformation appears largely misconceived because it was overly concerned with externals as such, rather than upon their organic relation to the inner spirit (pp. 201, 264). But equally mistaken were those Catholics who countered the Reformation by appealing to the Middle Ages as if the external condition of the church then was 'necessary for all times'. Both groups missed 'the forming principle, the inner character of the constitution of the Church'

(p. 266). Thus, for example, even though the papal primacy was not in evidence during the first three centuries, one cannot argue from that against the present form of the papacy. Rather, the question is decided by the papacy's consonance with the internal essence. The visible aspects of the church are indeed vital. To think of the church as primarily invisible would be to mistake the nature of Christianity (p. 211). The historical development of the hierarchy represents a genuine insight into the essential aspect of the church, for a 'determined, ordered and continual teaching office' is evidently vital for the continuing tradition (p. 214), while the bishop is a clear 'image' of the organic unity that pertains amongst believers (p. 218).

Roman ecclesiology

Later in his short life Möhler shifted away somewhat from this predominantly pneumatological ecclesiology to one more christologically centred. The *Symbolik* tends to set aside the inner–outer dialectic of *Unity* so that the Spirit now moves 'from above rather than within'. 'Unity in truth' is emphasized to balance the earlier 'unity in love'.[12] Möhler's later ecclesiology contributed to the development of the mix of theological and juridical approaches found in the Jesuit Roman school, organized in 1824. For its members, which included G. Perrone, J-B Franzelin and their pupil, Matthias Scheeben, the church is the mystical Body of Christ (*corpus Christi mysticum*). The Holy Spirit acts in and through the church's hierarchical structures so that the church manifests Christ. In one sense, then, it continues the Incarnation, but only in the sense of revealing Christ, not in being identical with him.[13]

The Roman school stressed the apologetic function of ecclesiology, for example in Perrone's manual, *Praelectiones Theologiae*.[14] Part I of the opening *Tractatus*, 'On The True Religion' addresses the unbeliever (*adversus Incredulos*). It argues for the possibility of divine revelation; that such revelation is necessary, how it is known to be such, and finally, that it exists. Part II then addresses the Protestants (*adversos Heterodoxos*). Revelation, once given, needs to be protected by an infallible authority. Only a church instituted by Christ would have such authority, and such a church would necessarily be one, visible and perpetual. Only the Roman Catholic church is such; therefore it is the one true of Christ and the infallible authority regarding revelation. The Protestant church cannot be a church at all since it does not have this unique authority. There can be 'either no religion, or the catholic religion alone. There is no middle way' (p. 239). In common with many who stressed the church's role as authoritative bearer of truth, Perrone explicitly limits his ecclesiology to the teaching church. 'Here the term church is not meant as the gathering of all the faithful . . . but rather of the universal episcopate. . . . the teaching church' (p. 141).

Newman (1801–90)

In England, the repeal of the Test Act (1828) and Catholic Emancipation (1829) made it possible for members of churches other than the Church of England to take public office, dealing a 'death-blow' to the older idea, found paradigmatically in the ecclesiology of Richard Hooker, that 'church and state in England were one society'.[15] The Oxford Movement arose in part to counter any move by the Whig government to reform the church. Their tracts spoke of the church as a Spirit-informed body of people. Since it is divinely instituted, the church – if it needs reform at all – should reform itself; the state has no such role.

The question of the doctrinal authority of the church was of particular concern to John Henry Newman. He initially argued that the Church of England is the *Via Media*, the middle and best way between the Roman Church and the Protestant sects. But Newman went over to Rome after he came to believe that the English church had abandoned its roots in favour of the liberal, anti-dogmatic and Protestant principle that there should be private judgement in religious matters. In his antipathy to liberalism he was in accord with the Roman school and its focus on the church's teaching authority. In contrast to it, he taught that the church's doctrines and practices develop over its history and will continue to do so. The church's life has been and will be difficult, its visible aspects flawed by confusions and sin. Yet by grace it remains a community of people preserved in truth. In this, and in his affirmation of the laity, Newman anticipated Vatican II. But he had little influence on the course of ecclesiology in his time; his work 'forecast Vatican II rather than actually prepared for it'.[16]

Vatican I (1869–70)

Questions about the church's authority and its relation to modernity were often posed in more general terms as a conflict between liberal Catholics and those who sought to maintain the church in its pre-modern state and who also usually advocated greater powers for Rome. Catholic liberalism was, as Hocedez defines it, 'a tendency . . . to accept in the progress and work of the church the principles which had penetrated all societies under the name of modern liberties.'[17] Liberal Catholicism in France was generally political in nature, while in Germany and England it was more intellectual, represented respectively by such men as J. Döllinger (1799–1890) and Lord Acton (1834–1902).[18]

Things came to a head during the pontificate of Pius IX (reigned 1846–78), whose early liberal sympathies were soon abandoned after his mistreatment by Italian revolutionaries. In December 1864 he issued the encyclical *Quanta cura* and a Syllabus of Errors, in which liberalism was described as rationalistic, anti-hierarchical and set against the legitimate authority of the church. Amongst the errors condemned were the separation of church and state and freedom of worship. In 1869, Pius convened the First Vatican Council. The Franco-Prussian War cut short the proceedings after a year, so only the first part of the proposed dogmatic constitution on the church was presented and voted on. It decreed the doctrine of papal infallibility, namely, that the pope's definitions on faith and morals are irreformable, not because they have been consented to by the church as a whole – whether by a council of bishops or by the whole church in its customs – but of themselves, when the pope speaks ex cathedra, in the 'exercise of his office' by 'virtue of his supreme apostolic authority'.[19]

Neo-scholasticism and Modernism

In his *Unity*, Möhler observed in passing that 'the stiffly medieval group . . . of course in Germany has now hardly any followers'.[20] By the mid-century that was no longer true, largely because of the work of the Jesuit, Joseph Kleutgen (1811–83), who ushered in a new wave of Thomism that would dominate Roman Catholic theology and philosophy for the next eighty years or so.[21] Kleutgen argued that medieval scholasticism provided a far more solid response to modernity than any contemporary effort. Kleutgen and his allies convinced Pope Leo XIII (reigned 1878–1903) to support their cause. In his encyclical, *Aeterni Patris*

(1879), Leo called for a Christian philosophy 'according to the mind of St. Thomas Aquinas'.

Leo himself was generally positive about the relation of church and world. However, the Modernist crisis of the turn of the century ushered in a more defensive era. In 1902, Alfred Loisy (1857–1940), argued (against Adolf von Harnack – see next section) that the church as institution was a development from Jesus' own intentions and that while it preserved Jesus' teaching about the kingdom of God, it is not the kingdom, nor are its hierarchical structures its final form.[22] A similar historical consciousness informs the writings of the other modernists, such as George Tyrell (1861–1909). The Roman school, for whom history was doctrinally irrelevant, countered by arguing that tradition cannot develop, nor could the church's teaching ever need correction. In 1907, Pius X condemned Modernism's use of historical-criticism and its advocacy of doctrinal development. In 1910 an anti-modernist oath was required of all clergy, and the consequent threat of excommunication effectively paralysed intellectual inquiry for decades to come.

Liberal Protestantism in Germany

Significant attempts to grapple more systematically with the issue of Christian identity were proposed in Germany, beginning towards the end of the nineteenth century. The neo-Kantian Albrecht Ritschl (1822–89) rejected Schleiermacher's approach to turn back to morality as the 'essence' of Christianity. Faith, he argued, is a 'value-judgement'; not a mere subjective response but a trust in what has been revealed in the Bible and a judgement about its value for salvation. The church consists of those who have made this value-judgement. They constitute a community of brotherly love that seeks to build up the kingdom of God that Christ founded. The church is thus the locus of this-worldly redemption as it continues the work of Christ, progressively establishing the kingdom within history.

For Adolf von Harnack (1851–1930), the essence of Christianity is discoverable through the historical-critical study of Scripture and the Christian past, which separates the kernel of truth about Jesus from the husk of contingent and irrelevant beliefs. Jesus is thereby revealed not the Incarnate Word of God but as the realization of the Gospel. In his well-known *What is Christianity*, Harnack contends that Jesus' message is one of brotherly love. The true Christian community is one shaped by its effort to foster such love within itself and the world. It is not an institution founded to guard a set of revealed doctrines. The Gospel is thus simple enough, and should not be overlaid with irrelevant practices. Indeed, it is 'so truly human, as to be most certain of being understood when is left entirely free, and also as to produce essentially the same experiences and convictions in individual souls'.[23]

In his *The Social Teaching of the Christian Churches*, published in 1912, Ernst Troeltsch (1865–1923) countered that there is no essence of Christianity or guiding central idea, such as the kingdom of God. Rather, Christianity is 'first and foremost a matter of practice', though not a 'program of social reform'.[24] Its history shows it to be a complex and variegated religion, a product of both its origin and of the cultures in which it took fruit. Troeltsch developed an influential religio-sociological typology. One type is the Church, an institution of grace and salvation that can adjust itself to the world. The second is the Sect, a voluntary society whose members are bound together by their experience of new birth and by their preparation for the awaited Kingdom of God. The third is Mysticism, where religious truth cannot be formulated because it is subject to no criteria except its relation to absolute spiritual truth. Each type is a development from the gospel of Jesus himself.

Salvation is 'always ... inward ethical and spiritual', and Jesus' own message was one of 'free personal piety ... without any tendency toward the organization of a cult, or towards the creation of a religious community'.[25]

Neo-Reformation theology

In the years immediately after the First World War an influential movement began among German-speaking theologians who reacted against the prevailing Cultural Protestantism, with its reduction of theology to reflection upon morality, religious experience or history, and its complete failure to inhibit German militarism prior to the war. They turned away from theological liberalism and back to doctrine, so the loose-knit movement was often called Neo-Orthodoxy, the 'neo-' reflecting its attempt to address critical philosophy. However, it is more appropriate and inclusive to call it the neo-Reformation movement. Among those who developed an ecclesiology is the Swiss theologian, Emil Brunner (1889–1966), whose book, *The Misunderstanding of the Church* displays a common Protestant view. Brunner argues that the *ecclesia*, the true church displayed in the New Testament, is constituted as 'a pure communion of persons entirely without institutional character'.[26] The churches themselves are not signs of this communion. Rather, their function is to serve the *ecclesia* by attempting to create 'true fellowship in Christ'. Their institutional forms are of human origin and should be preserved only insofar as they help this task. Any form of 'sacramentalism' – the idea that the historical church is in some way an incarnation 'in which Jesus Christ is historically manifest', or that some element of the church mediates salvation – is to be firmly rejected.[27]

Far more ecclesiologically innovative is the work of Dietrich Bonhoeffer (1906–45), who followed Karl Barth in rejecting the liberal Protestant assumption that Christianity is a species of the genus 'religion'. Religion is the human quest for saving knowledge of God and as such leads towards individualism. Christianity is not an attempt to know God; it arose as a response to the revelation of God in Jesus Christ. Christ displayed true humanity, which is social in form, for all 'Christian concepts' have a 'social intention', including the concept 'person'.[28] So it is appropriate to present doctrinal theology by starting 'not with the doctrine of God but with the doctrine of the church'.[29] The church community is the new humanity in Christ, the new Adam. Indeed, 'the church is the presence of Christ in the same way that Christ is the presence of God'.[30] The church is the representative of Christ in the world, the place where God's will for humanity becomes visible and concrete. But because the church is the human and social response to revelation, and because it is a concrete rather than ideal community, the doctrine of the church requires a new form of discourse: theological sociology. That is – Bonhoeffer was the very first to propose this – ecclesiology should take the form of a sociology that is materially and structurally governed by God's revelation in Christ.

The ecclesiology of Paul Tillich (1886–1965) has also been influential, though quite different from both Brunner and Bonhoeffer in substance and style. Tillich advocated what he called the 'method of correlation', according to which the church's task is to interpret its doctrines so as to answer the existential questions posed by humanity in its time and place. A highly systematic theologian, Tillich drew upon many sources, including Hegel, Schelling, depth psychology, and the existentialism of Kierkegaard and Heidegger. The norm of theology is the event of 'Jesus the Christ', which is the symbolic manifestation of the Word of God. The event brings us 'the New Being' (p. 174).[31] New Being – reconciliation, recreation, reunion with humanity and God – achieves concreteness in the church, but here Tillich distinguishes between the 'Spiritual Community' and the churches or religious communities as such. The Spiritual Community is the Body of Christ, the invisible church, the truly spiritual reality and source of New Being. The visible churches display the ambiguities and confusions of personal and communal existence. The two are not separate, however. The Spiritual Community is the essence which is realized in the existential churches. The church is therefore paradoxical, a fact reflected in the need for both theological and sociological discourses (pp. 162–5). The marks of the church – unity, holiness, catholicity and apostolicity – are always only 'in spite' of the lives of the actual churches, which are too often in thrall to 'Religion', which is seen here again as 'tragic-demonic self-elevation'. Applied to ecclesiology, Tillich's 'Protestant principle' refers to conquest of religion by the Spiritual Presence, which prevents profanization and demonization from destroying the churches. By itself the principle is not enough, however. It must be complemented by the 'Catholic substance', the 'concrete embodiment' of the Spirit and 'the expression of the victory of the Spirit over religion' (p. 245).

Karl Barth (1886–1968)

The best-known neo-Reformation theologian is, of course, Karl Barth. Barth read Scripture as the Word of God which challenges each individual and the established theology and structures of the church. Barth's theology centres emphatically upon Jesus Christ. So the object of theological inquiry is not God as such, nor is humanity the religious subject. As God-man, Jesus Christ is both subject and object, the one through whom alone God makes himself known to us, and in whom we come to know ourselves, our world and our relation to God. Theology is therefore faith seeking understanding, and as such is a thoroughly ecclesial form of inquiry, leading Barth to title his magnum opus the *Church Dogmatics*. In this multi-volume work, Barth's task is not, as it was for Schleiermacher, to reflect critically upon the church's forms of piety, but to look away from ourselves to Christ in faith to see 'how things look once one is inside the region or culture of the church'.[32]

That the election of Jesus Christ is 'the eternal beginning of all God's ways and works' has substantial implications for Barth's doctrine of the church. The most substantial treatment of the church is in the fourth volume of the *Church Dogmatics*.[33] Here as elsewhere, Barth undercuts any sense of a settled church, secure in itself. The Holy Spirit gathers the church; the church is not constituted by human activity. Its function is to witness to its Lord through its preaching and by its daily life. It is the visible witness to that which is its invisible being and as such is the 'earthly-historical existence form of Jesus Christ',[34] the sign of God's gracious 'Yes' to all people in Jesus Christ.

Although the church is the Body of Christ, Barth does not mean that it is a prolongation of the Incarnation, and denies that it has been given the power to make present that which it signifies. The church is an 'event' rather than an institution. It is *also* an institution, with settled patterns of action including worship, ministry, baptism and the eucharist. But the church's function is not, or not directly, accomplished in performing them. Barth generally does not think sacramentally. The church is a medium through which God may and often does act, but divine action is not bound by human action. The two actions, he seems to suggest at times, especially in writing about baptism, are only contingently related. Yet they are not unrelated, because the human action may genuinely 'correspond' to the divine.[35]

For Barth, then, the church is not some supernatural entity set over against the world. It

115

is very much part of the world and in solidarity with it, even as it differs from it in its knowledge of the way things really are. As the witness to Jesus Christ, the church necessarily turns to the world, showing it the consequences of knowing the truth revealed in the Word. Christ works especially in the church, but he also works elsewhere. Indeed, the church as such is not even necessary for salvation if by that we mean there is something about human beings that would require God to bring them together separate from the world for them to be redeemed.[36] Yet God in fact *has* elected the church gathered by the Spirit in Christ, and has given it the glorious task of joining in Christ's prophetic activity.

Orthodox ecclesiology

During the nineteenth century, Orthodox theology, particularly in Russia, became more open to influences from both Catholicism and Protestantism. In turn, ecclesiological ideas from Orthodoxy have become increasingly prevalent in the West.[37] I.A.S. (Alexei) Khomiakov (1804–60) drew in part upon Möhler to develop a pneumatological ecclesiology based on the concept of *sobornost*, which denotes loving communion oriented around the liturgy. He attacked the individualism of the West, not only in its Protestant forms, but in Roman Catholicism, too, contending that the pope's absolute supremacy makes him that church's sole individual, thereby denying the communion of all. The Spirit conveys truth through neither kind of individualism, only within a communion of love.[38] Khomiakov's pneumatological approach was complemented by Vladimir Soloviev (1850–1900), who argued that the authority of the episcopacy is necessary for genuine unity in communion. Soloviev also drew upon earlier mystical philosophies to propose a sophiological ecclesiology in which divine wisdom is the church, God's 'other' who shares in the triune life. The polymath, Pavel Florensky (1882–1937) systematized this line of thinking, as did Sergei Bulgakov (1871–1944). Bulgakov believed that divine wisdom is realized paradigmatically in the Virgin Mary and collectively in the church, whose members are divinized by the Holy Spirit. In addition, Bulgakov engaged in mystical speculations about the eucharist.[39]

Most of these speculative ideas were generally rejected within Orthodoxy. V. Lossky (1903–58) and others saw them as too infused with idealist philosophy and tending towards pantheism. However, the themes of *sobornost*-communion, the role of the Holy Spirit, and divinization through membership in the church persist. Lossky argues that it is only within the divine life of the church that we can overcome our separation from one another, and achieve unity and true personhood. N. Afanassieff (1893–1966) drew upon contemporary liturgical studies to develop another very influential Orthodox theme, namely that it is in the performance of the eucharist that the church comes into being. The church, he argued, is not the basis for the eucharist but the eucharist the basis for the church. Accordingly, each altar community is truly the church, and together all local churches form a united whole, not as an aggregate making up a complete number, but in that the church is present in all.[40] On this ground, Afanassieff denied the legitimacy of an authoritative hierarchy that has a separate origin than the local churches.[41]

Pre-Vatican II RC ecclesiology

A form of eucharistic and sacramental ecclesiology was developed by one of the outstanding theologian-historians of the couple of decades prior to Vatican II, Henri de Lubac (1986–91).[42] The was related to de Lubac's expansive understanding of catholicism, in which the

Roman Catholic church is inclusive of all that is good in the world, for all that has been touched by the truth and goodness of Christ is in some way embraced by and sacramentally realized within the church. There is therefore a connection at the ontological level between the church and all that lies outside its visible boundaries, both religious and non-religious. Another outstanding theologian of this era who wrote on the church was Y.-M. Congar (1904–96). His historical work, notably on development in the tradition, the laity, and the Holy Spirit, was informed by a desire for a more theological understanding of the church. His ecclesiology was thoroughly trinitarian and, like de Lubac's, focused upon the mystery at the heart of the historical church.

Within the Curia itself, Pius XII's 1943 encyclical, *Mystici Corporis Christi* denied the separation of grace from the juridical aspects of the church. The mystical body is identified with the visible church: 'the Mystical Body of Christ and the Roman Catholic Church are one and the same'.[43] As S. Tromp, the probable author of the encyclical, wrote elsewhere, 'the church is the juridical and ethical continuation of the mission of Christ, in the manner of a true and perfect society, hierarchically constituted, universal and perpetual, equipped with various organs both for providing for its mission and for attaining the end proper to itself'.[44] In the USA, John Courtney Murray ran up against this understanding of the church in working cooperatively with civil and non-Catholic leaders. A believer in the wisdom of the American Constitution's understanding of the relation between church and civil society, Murray sought through legal means to improve those relations in a variety of areas. He argued, on theological grounds, for religious freedom and tolerance.[45] His work was ill-received in Rome at the time, but then with Vatican II became rather more broadly accepted.

Vatican II (1962–5)

Called by Pope John XXIII, the Second Vatican Council has been described as an 'event' as much as 'a set of documents'.[46] It effected reform in a twofold way: by *aggiornamento*, i.e. by positive engagement with the modern world; and by *ressourcement*, by retrieving aspects of the tradition that had become dormant. Its documents display a new style in that they attempt to persuade rather than simply condemn incorrect beliefs. The relation between church and world is treated optimistically and without apologetics for the first time for centuries. And by inviting lay and clerical observers from all the mainline churches, the council officially brought the church into the ecumenical movement.

As a Pastoral Council, Vatican II did not define new dogmas. However, in *Lumen Gentium* (LG), the dogmatic constitution on the church, the bishops set out an authoritative and substantial ecclesiology. The question has been raised as to whether LG presents a single model of the church – 'communion' is often the candidate[47] – underlying the three ecclesiological perspectives of the document's first three chapters, or whether these must remain multiple to capture the complexity of the church without reduction.[48] The first chapter, entitled 'Mystery of the Church', is a thoroughly trinitarian ecclesiology that points to the mystery at the heart of the church's life. Here 'mystery' is not merely something incapable of being fully known. It is that which informs and governs the church's life as it proclaims the coming of the kingdom, rendering the church the sacrament of the kingdom. A plethora of images, most notably 'Body of Christ', develop this vision of the church. An often cited phrase occurs in paragraph 8, where it is stated that the 'church of Christ' 'subsists' in the Roman Catholic church. The word 'subsists' is regarded as a significant modification of the more straightforward identity claim of *Mystici Corporis* cited above. This shift supports the affirmation of the truth and holiness of non-Christian religions in another council document, the *Declaration on the Relation of the Church to Non-Christian Religions* (1965).

In the second chapter LG explicates the model of the 'new People of God' (LG 9). Israel, the chosen people of God, is the figure of the church. In incorporating people of all nations, the church is the 'new people' in Christ, with a 'common priesthood' that shares in Christ's own priestly office (LG 10). At the same time, the document strongly affirms the doctrine of God's universal salvific will. Those who 'through no fault of their own' are not Christians and who are moved by grace to seek God may achieve salvation (LG 16). In a related sense, the pastoral constitution on the church, *Gaudium et Spes* (GS), acknowledges that the 'fault' may sometimes be the church's: 'believers can . . . have more than a little to do with the rise of atheism' (GS 19).

The third chapter then – and only then – addresses the church as a hierarchy, dwelling particularly on the role of the college of bishops, a topic not treated by Vatican I. The subsequent chapter discusses the laity, who have their own apostolate, a point developed by the *Decree on the Apostolate of Lay People* (ALP) (1965). Lay people are a 'leaven in the world' (ALP 2). By their work for the 'evangelization and sanctification' (ALP 6) they participate in the threefold office of Christ as prophet, priest and king (ALP 10). The laity are to take over as far as possible the work of priests (ALP 17) and should be properly trained for their apostolate. The sharp division between clergy and laity displayed in the ecclesiology of the earlier Roman school has largely disappeared.

Two other significant developments bear mention here. The council documents display a greater recognition of the eschatological nature of the church. The Counter-Reformation view of the church as a 'perfected society' now falls away in favour of the 'pilgrim church', the church on its way, not yet complete, and in need of constant purification prior to the eschaton. The second development is the 'Declaration on Religious Liberty' (*Dignitatis humanae*) (1965), which John Courtney Murray helped to write. Here for the first time the Roman Catholic church acknowledged, based on the intrinsic dignity of the person, that freedom from religious coercion is an inviolable right, with the corollary that churches should be independent of civil society.

Ecumenism[49]

A few theologians at the beginning of the modern era sought paths to reunion. Schleiermacher, for example, wrote *The Christian Faith* in part to reunite the Lutheran and Reformed churches in Germany. A decade or two later, some Anglicans worked with Khomiakov to unite their churches. Missionary work in the nineteenth century provided a common purpose that sometimes drew the churches together. Generally, however, these were exceptions to the rule of complacent separateness mixed not infrequently with some degree of disparagement, even hostility.

Little was done in terms of dialogue among authorized delegates of the churches until the early twentieth century, when conferences began to be held on practical and doctrinal issues of contention. This culminated in the formation of the World Council of Churches (WCC) in 1948. Since then, significant agreement has been achieved in both practical and doctrinal areas, though relatively little with regard to the theology of the church. The WCC is not, of course, a church in any sense, but it has certainly helped spur discussions on the theological bases for union. Two decades of dialogue resulted in the publication in 1982 of the document, *Baptism, Eucharist and Ministry* (BEM). Responses to BEM from the churches were mixed but generally positive.

A more fundamental and increasingly popular approach to ecumenical ecclesiology is the aforementioned communion ecclesiology (examples of which are discussed in a section below). Here the church is understood as constituted at its deepest level by its participation in the *koinonia* or communion among the Persons of the Trinity. The unity of the churches lies in its grace-enabled fellowship, particular in its worship together. Each altar community is in communion with every other through its participation in the divine communion. Together they form a communion that includes the communion of the saints. By this means, attention is deflected away from more divisive structures of unity, such as hierarchy and practices, towards union in Christ through the Holy Spirit.

It is too soon to call it a shift in theological culture, but there seems to be an increasing tendency – with many exceptions, to be sure – on the part of theologians to discuss the church in ecumenical terms. That is, while they may not have any particular concern to unite the churches, they assume that the ecclesiologies of churches other than their own have something useful to contribute to their proposal. This approach is fostered by theological conferences in which Christians of all traditions come together, and by those universities in which theological students from various churches work together with professors who represent different Christian traditions.

Rahner (1904–84)

The theology of Karl Rahner has contributed to this shift within Roman Catholicism. Rahner's theology has been very influential in the second half of the twentieth century not least because of his sophisticated appropriation of the dominant philosophical tools of his day – particularly Kant (through Joseph Maréchal) and Heidegger – combined with scholastic formulations. Fundamental to his theology is an ontology in which being is 'of itself symbolic, because it necessarily "expresses" itself.[50] In *The Church and the Sacraments*, Rahner argues that the church is not simply an institution structured by hierarchy and law; it is a symbol, 'the visible outward expression' of God's saving grace.[51] The church's deep structure is therefore similar to that of the Incarnation. The church is a sacrament, the saving presence of Christ visibly embodied within human history.

His argument draws upon his transcendental theology. God's self-offering is present in everything we do; it is 'immediate' and present in all our consciousness, and therefore a 'transcendental' in Kant's sense. The self-offer is freely and graciously given in and through the salvific work of Jesus Christ and the Holy Spirit, and is in addition to all that we are as creatures. It is thus a 'supernatural existential', rather than a natural one (an 'existential' is a characteristic of concrete human existence rather than an essential element of human nature). Thus there is 'holy mystery' at the very heart of everything we are, know and will. And so, too, all we know and will, whether specifically religious or otherwise, is in some sense a grace-enabled response for or against this offer. Thus we are all related to Christ and the Spirit at our very deepest level, whether or not we are Christian or have even heard of Jesus Christ.

This might appear to be a rather individualistic notion of our relation to God, but for Rahner the supernatural existential creates a genuine unity among all humanity, and makes possible full membership for everyone in what he calls, in a novel use of the phrase, 'the

People of God'.[52] Rahner insists that our unity in God's grace is concrete and thoroughly visible, manifested in monogenism, original sin and in 'the one history of the human race'.[53] The People of God is, however, only a preliminary and incomplete manifestation of our acceptance of God's salvific offer, for that is fully realized only in the Christian church, where the offer is known for what it is. Rahner argues that, as a consequence, all non-Christians who have accepted God's offer of grace, whether religious or not, unknowingly direct themselves thereby towards the visible Christian church. They have what Rahner calls (borrowing from sacramental theology) an 'implicit desire' to be full participating members of the historical embodiment of God's salvific offer (*votum Ecclesiae*). This, it would seem, is the case even when they belong to communities that explicitly reject Christianity. Only if they existentially reject the transcendental offer of salvation do they reject their membership in the People of God.

Thus Rahner can propose a thoroughly inclusive ecclesiology, yet one that does not relativize the church's (or Christ's) significance for salvation. Membership in the church remains necessary for salvation, yet salvation is available to all, because all people of goodwill are truly, if often only anonymously, related to Christ in their heart and are therefore included among the true members of his church.[54] The visible church, in consequence, is

> the concrete historical manifestation, in the dimension of a history that has acquired eschatological significance, and in the social dimension, of precisely that salvation which is achieved through the grace of God through the entire length and breadth of humanity.[55]

Preaching and mission retain their importance because the church is more attuned to the reality of God than any other religious body. At the same time, the church can affirm modern society on the basis of the fundamental yet Christ-dependent unity of all humankind. Rahner thereby provided the church with a theological basis to support the call of Vatican II to join with non-Christians of good will everywhere in the humanizing projects of the modern world.[56]

Liberation theology and base communities[57]

Key aspects of Rahner's inclusivist ecclesiology, including its basis in the supernatural existential, are frequently appropriated by liberation theologians, for whom, however, social analysis plays a far more significant role in theological inquiry. The church's 'preferential option for the poor' requires theologians to go beyond philosophical transcendental analysis to consider 'the social relationships of human beings – for example, their class situation, political position, and the like'.[58] Faith and praxis are intimately and necessarily linked, and in a way that goes beyond the 'political theology' of Jürgen Moltmann and J.B. Metz, whose understanding of the political realm is said to be too uncritically empiricist, even 'verging on impressionism',[59] with the result that their conception of faith's bearing upon social and political realities, and those realities upon faith's forms, is too simplistic.

Liberation ecclesiologies are not all the same. One of the more distinctive is that of Leonardo Boff, who argues with Rahner that faith – in the sense of a primordial experience of God – is a reality that is more basic than the church, even as it 'acquires a special density in the church' in its faith in the Triune God.[60] Boff concludes that '[n]o one is outside the church because there is no longer an "outside", because no one is outside the reality of God and the risen Christ'.[61] Boff then contends that the pre-ecclesial experience of God is properly expressed in ecclesial forms only where these forms are not oppressive. The Basic Ecclesial Communities – small, grassroots communities that pray and work for justice together – are the only ecclesial form that is free of oppression. As such, they act as 'a leaven of renewal in the substance of the whole church'.[62] The primary ecclesial virtue, then, is not orthodoxy as expressed in doctrinal unity, which requires an authoritative magisterium, but orthopraxis, expressed ecclesially in authentic community. The larger church's role is not to organize or control social action; it is to strengthen and support popular, grassroots communities and movements for social justice, whether they are specifically Christian or not.[63]

Von Balthasar

Although a contemporary of Rahner, the Swiss theologian, Hans Urs von Balthasar (1905–88) has taken longer to become well known, especially in English-speaking lands. Balthasar's theological approach is steeped in Germanic philosophy and literature, and addresses its attempts to respond to the mechanistic and determinist perspective of philosophical Newtonianism.[64] He was thoroughly versed in Barth's theology and, like Barth, rejected both the Kantian and Schleiermacherian versions of the turn to the subject (and Rahner's version, too) to centre his approach on Christ and the Trinity.

In a seven-volume work, *The Glory of the Lord*,[65] he develops an aesthetic approach to revelation. Jesus Christ is the 'primal phenomenon', for in him formless God has taken on form, permitting the splendour of God to be seen, thereby enrapturing the beholder (p. 20). Through the work of the Spirit, Scripture witnesses to the form or *Gestalt* of Christ, but there is no identity between them. Nor is there between the church and revelation. 'In their power to express Christ, both Sacred Scripture and the holy Church together constitute the work of the Holy Spirit' (p. 602), so that the church is not merely 'an historical effect of Christ' but his 'fullness' and Body. It is, however, weaker yet in its expressiveness than Scripture (p. 603) because it is both sinful in itself, and 'darkened by sinners' within it. Yet still prophecy comes through, for the glory of Christ's life shines within it (p. 604).

In a second multi-volume work, *Theo-Drama*,[66] Balthasar attempts to show that God, church and world can be described using dramatic categories. Christ is 'the matrix of all possible dramas', embodying 'the absolute drama in his own person' (III/62). The Incarnation creates 'an acting area for dramas of theological moment, involving other, created persons' (III/162). Each person has her or his own part, and in playing it and thereby responding to our call, we are individuated and become true persons. In contrast to some communion ecclesiologies, communion with other Christians cannot be a condition for fellowship with God, since 'it is through personal confession of Christ and relationship with him that the individual becomes a member of his Mystical Body' (III/450). Yet the church is not merely the aggregate of its members; in some ways it does precede the individual. One consequence of following Christ in discipleship is solitude, both for the church and the individual. The church 'will have to be "solitary" in an environment that hates her' (III/448). The church lives a tensive existence, caught between the 'already' and the 'not yet', between time and eternity, between its traditions and the need for constant newness, between authority and inspiration (IV/453f.). Consequently the church's history is almost inevitably tragic (IV/455). The struggle for and against God's redemptive activity takes place not only between the world and the church, but within the church itself. Until the eschaton, this cannot be avoided: the church has 'to continue to endure the inner tension between her ideal and her fallen reality' (III/443).

Balthasar develops these broad ideas in various others ways. He uses gender difference to discuss the priesthood and the church's relation to Christ, prompting much negative criticism. More interestingly, perhaps, he evokes Mary, Peter, John and others as motifs to explicate the various aspects and functions of the church.[67]

Pluralist ecclesiologies

The word 'pluralism' in ecclesiology can mean rather too many things. It can mean the view that there are different ways or models for ecclesiology, all of which have something to offer.[68] It can indicate the belief that the plurality of ways of being church historically and in the present is unavoidable and is a resource for ongoing renewal throughout the churches.[69] Or it can indicate a more radical kind of ecclesiological pluralism that differs markedly from the inclusivism of Rahner and others. In the work of John Hick and constructivists like Gordon Kaufmann, Sallie McFague and Paul Knitter, pluralism means that the doctrines of one religion cannot logically be compared with another, and thus they cannot conflict. This is not, or not fundamentally, because they are incommensurate species, like apples and oranges, but because they are all directed towards a reality that is so incomprehensible that truth claims cannot be made about it. Religions, then, are imaginative and mythological constructs by which their adherents seek meaning and organize their lives.

Thus far this more radical kind of pluralism has produced few systematic treatments of the church. One of the more well-rounded is Peter C. Hodgson's *Revisioning The Church: Ecclesial Freedom in the New Paradigm*.[70] Hodgson rejects the inclusivist position because it requires the view that Christianity is superior to other religions. The 'only consistent and intellectually defensible position' nowadays is 'that the great world religions have equally valid claims and that each is culturally relative' (p. 94), so 'what is true for us is not truth for all' (p. 95). Hodgson believes that the church was originally an 'ecclesia of freedom', a 'nonprovincial, nonexclusionary, nonhierarchical, noncultic community' that devoted itself to 'world-transforming praxis' (p. 23f.). Soon, though, the church displayed the contrary characteristics, becoming more like other religious communities. The visible church today is thus a more or less distorted expression of the original ecclesia of freedom formed by a combination of historical factors and the disciples' experience of Jesus (p. 22f.). These essential features make the church 'a unique form of redemptive existence' (p. 27). But it not is necessarily better than others, even ideally, since it is a manifestation of a prior, universal salvific reality, namely the kingdom of God, the 'basileia of freedom' (p. 23), which takes a plurality of 'religiocultural shapes' (p. 106). The church is thus a unique form of the basileia, insofar as it is a manifestation of ecclesia, which is unique. But it is not superior to other forms, since the basileia can be imaged as well in other religious bodies, their 'equally valid claims' (p. 94) arising out of the same source.

Communion ecclesiologies

In the last three decades or so, *koinonia* or communion has become an increasingly popular model of the church. The church is constituted as a communion by its grace-enabled participation in the communion among the divine persons, and is thereby drawn into the life of the Triune God. The ecclesiologies of the Greek Orthodox theologian, John Zizioulas, and the Roman Catholic, Jean-Marie Tillard OP, are outstanding examples of contemporary communion ecclesiology. Both contend that the church is realized most fully in the eucharist, the sacrament of unity. However, it is the bishop, rather than the pope or the priest or the altar community, who is the primary sign of eucharistic unity. Accordingly, the basic form of communion is the 'local church', understood as the diocese. But each such communion is in communion with all others (including the communion of saints), a unity signified by the college of bishops. Ecclesial unity is thus conceived theologically, undermining any tendency towards either fissiparousness or an overemphasis upon the church as institution or hierarchy.

In *Being As Communion*,[71] Zizioulas argues that the church, as *koinonia*, has ontological priority over the individual Christian. Further, as an individual I am not really a person until I have been baptized into the communion of the church. Those who remain outside the church are tragically limited by our 'hypostasis of biological existence' (p. 50); we exist by necessity rather than in freedom; we are deeply separated from others. Entering into the church liberates us from such 'individualism and egocentricity' (p. 64) and transforms us into authentic persons, into beings-in-relation. This transformation saves us, for 'salvation is identified with the realization of personhood in man' (p. 50). When we acquire this 'ecclesial being', we live in the image of the triune God as persons-in-relation.

In his *Church of Churches*,[72] Tillard makes a similar correlation of salvation, communion and the church: 'humanity is truly itself only in *communion*. This is what saves it' (p. 12). Drawing from the fathers, Tillard argues that 'in the first centuries, salvation is called *communion*, for the human being finds his authenticity and affirms his full singularity only in communion'. So it is only in the church that 'the humanity-that-God-wills is recreated' (p. 18). By contrast, the 'drama of our history is precisely that man has become an isolated being', so much so that 'humanity has condemned itself in reality to a state of non-existence' and 'reduced itself to becoming hardly more than a collage of individuals' (p. 17). Yet although Tillard sounds this apologetic note, he acknowledges that communion may well extend beyond the visible *koinonia* of the church into the world (pp. 34f.). This is especially the case for those 'faithful to their religion or to their faith', who 'are spiritually united'. There exists, then, a 'solidarity among believers', so that, 'on a profound plane' a Muslim person at prayer and ourselves 'become one' (p. 35).

The future

The prevalence of communion ecclesiology is now such that for a Roman Catholic theologian to challenge its adequacy is to do more than simply question one theological proposal among others. Before he became Pope Benedict, Cardinal Ratzinger insisted that 'ultimately there is only one basic ecclesiology' (i.e. communion) which must be accepted by any Roman Catholic.[73] Ratzinger's decree is not as restrictive as it appears, however, for he acknowledges there are different forms of the approach. Indeed, communion is such a flexible model that it has been used by advocates of a wide range of perspectives in all the churches.

Yet if the history of ecclesiology is anything to go on, other approaches will be developed in due course, including some that will challenge the emphasis upon communion. New ways of understanding the church arise as much or more by historical and social developments than simply by further ecclesiological reflection. It may be the case already, for example, that individual Christians are so little affected by their church's authorities that whatever the latter decide becomes for them merely another opinion to be accepted or rejected as such if their reasoning or experience or intuition leads to other views. If that is the case, then no amount of theological reasoning, ecumenical or otherwise, is likely to change it. Perhaps a solution would be to locate ecclesial unity in our common faith in Jesus Christ, and rely less upon authorities. That proposal has its own myriad problems, of course, not least that so many Christians know so little about their faith. What unites Schleiermacher and Barth, Rahner and von Balthasar, and many others discussed above, is their view that ecclesiology should rely more heavily upon the Holy Spirit, who brings us to true faith in Christ. Perhaps the future requires us to continue their move in a similar direction.

Notes

1 Here I draw upon Nicholas Lash's wonderfully concise summary of Michael J. Buckley's *At the Origins of Modern Atheism* (New Haven and London: Yale University Press, 1987), in Lash's *Holiness, Speech and Silence: Reflections on the Question of God*, Aldershot, Ashgate, 2004, p. 9.
2 Yves Congar, *L'Eglise: De Saint Augustin à l'époque moderne*, Paris: Cerf, 1970, p. 299.
3 Congar, *L'Eglise*, p. 414.
4 See Edgar Hocedez, *Histoire de la théologie au xixme siècleI*, Paris: Desclée, 1948 (3 vols), vol. 1, pp. 105.
5 Congar, *L'Eglise*, p. 416.
6 Congar, *L'Eglise*, p. 415.
7 Friedrich Schleiermacher, *The Christian Faith*, ed. H.R. Macintosh and J.S. Stewart, Edinburgh: T&T Clark, 1976. Page references in the next five paragraphs are to this edition.
8 Schleiermacher makes the case more directly in earlier works, such as his 1811 *Brief Outline on the Study of Theology*, trans. T. Tice, Richmond, VA: John Knox, 1966.
9 Roger Haight, S.J., *Christian Community in History*: vol. 2, *Comparative Ecclesiology*, New York: Continuum, 2005, p. 333.
10 B.A. Gerrish, *Tradition and the Modern World: Reformed Theology in the Nineteenth Century*, Chicago: University of Chicago Press, 1978, p. 45.
11 J.A. Möhler, *Unity in the Church or the Principle of Catholicism, Presented in the Spirit of the Church Fathers of the First Three Centuries* ed. and trans. Peter C. Erb, Washington, DC: CUA Press, 1996. Page references in parentheses.
12 Peter Erb, 'Introduction' to *Unity*, p. 60.
13 Congar, *L'Eglise*, pp. 428–35.
14 Ioannes Perrone, SJ. *Praelectiones Theologicae*. I translate from the Latin text of an Augustae Taurinorum edition of 1897 (pages number in parentheses); the work was written between 1835–42.
15 Alec R. Vidler, *The Church in an Age of Revolution*, Harmondsworth: Penguin, 1971, p. 45.
16 Congar, *L'Eglise* p. 437.
17 Hocedez, *Histoire*, vol. 2, p. 161.
18 Vidler, *The Church*, p. 150.
19 Vatican I, *Dogmatic Constitution on the Church of Christ*, Chapter 4.
20 Möhler, *Unity*, p. 266.
21 See Gerald A. McCool, *Catholic Theology in the Nineteenth Century: The Quest for a Unitary Method*, New York: Seabury, 1977, esp. pp. 167–215.
22 Alfred Loisy, *The Gospel and the Church*, Philadelphia: Fortress, 1976.
23 Adolf von Harnack, *What Is Christianity?* trans. T. B Saunders, Philadelphia: Fortress, 1957, p. 275.
24 Ernst Troeltsch, *The Social Teaching of the Christian Churches*, New York: Harper, 1960, pp. 19, 60.
25 Troeltsch, *Social Teaching*, pp. 40, 993.
26 Emil Brunner, *The Misunderstanding of the Church*, trans H. Knight, London: Lutterworth, 1952, p. 17.
27 Brunner, *Misunderstanding*, pp. 85–6.

28 Dietrich Bonhoeffer, *Sanctorum Communio: A Theological Study of the Sociology of the Church*, trans. R. Krauss and N. Lukens, Minneapolis: Fortress Press, 1998, p. 21.
29 Bonhoeffer, *Sanctorum*, p. 134.
30 Bonhoeffer, *Sanctorum*, pp. 140–1. In his *Act and Being*, trans H. Martin Rumscheidt, Minneapolis: Fortress Press, 1996, Bonhoeffer attempted a similar theological epistemology.
31 Paul Tillich, *Systematic Theology: III*, Chicago: University of Chicago, 1963. Pages to this volume in parentheses.
32 John Webster, *Barth*, London/New York: Continuum, 2000, p. 51.
33 Barth, *Church Dogmatics 4/3*, Edinburgh: T&T Clark, 1961, p. 484.
34 Barth, *Church Dogmatics 4/1*, Edinburgh: T&T Clark, 1956, 661.
35 The concept of correspondence is treated specifically in *Church Dogmatics 2/2*, Edinburgh: T&T Clark, 1957, pp. 575–83. But as Nigel Biggar notes, the concept is often at work, though often tacitly, in the later volumes. See Biggar, *The Hastening that Waits*, Oxford: Clarendon, 1993, pp. 103–8.
36 Barth *Church Dogmatics 4/3.2*, Edinburgh: T&T Clark, 1962, p. 826.
37 This section deals only with what is distinctive about Orthodox ecclesiology, not the far greater amount it has in common with the West. The selection of theologians follows that of Louis Bouyer, *The Church of God: Body of Christ and Temple of the Spirit*, trans C. Quinn, Chicago: Franciscan Herald, 1982. See Chapter 8 of this volume, 'Ecclesiology in the Orthodox Tradition'.
38 See a summary of his position in I.A.S. Khomiakov, *The Church Is One: Essay on the Unity of the Church*, London: Eastern Orthodox Books, 1988.
39 See Bulgakov's two studies in his *The Holy Grail and the Eucharist*, trans. and ed. B. Jakim, Hudson, NY: Lindisfarne, 1997.
40 See Paul McPartlan, *The Eucharist Makes the Church*, Edinburgh: T&T Clark, 1993, for a very useful comparative study of Orthodox and Roman Catholic Eucharistic ecclesiology.
41 See N. Afanassieff, *L'Eglise du Saint-Esprit*, Paris: Cerf, 1975.
42 See H. de Lubac, *Corpus Mysticum: L'Eucharistie et l'église au moyen âge*, Paris: Aubier, 1944. For a comparison of de Lubac and the contemporary Orthodox theologian, John Zizioulas, see Paul McPartlan, *The Eucharist Makes the Church*.
43 Pius XII, *Humani Generis*, *Acta Apostolicae Sedis*, vol. 42, p. 571.
44 Sebastian Tromp, SJ, *Corpus Christi quod est Ecclesia*, trans. Ann Condit, New York: Vantage Press, 1960, p. 24.
45 See the collection of his essays in John Courtney Murray, *We Hold These Truths: Catholics Reflections on the American Proposition*, London: Sheed and Ward, 1960.
46 Haight, *Christian Community: 2*, p. 387. See John W. O'Malley, SJ, 'Vatican II: Did Anything Happen?' *Theological Studies* 67(2006), 3–33, esp. 4 for the meaning of 'event' here, and generally for an illuminating discussion of just why Vatican II was an event.
47 As Dennis M. Doyle argues in his *Communion Ecclesiology: Visions and Versions*, Maryknoll: Orbis, 2000, pp. 72–8.
48 As T. Howland Sanks concludes in his *Salt, Leaven and Light: The Community Called Church*, New York: Crossroad, 1992, p. 187.
49 See Chapter 22 of this volume, 'Ecclesiology and Ecumenism'.
50 Karl Rahner, *Theological Investigations IV*, trans. K. Smith, New York: Crossroad, 1982, p. 229.
51 Rahner, *The Church and the Sacraments*, trans. W.J. O'Hara, London: Herder, 1963, pp. 23, 34.
52 Rahner, *Theological Investigations II*, trans. K.-H. Kruger, New York: Crossroad, 1990, p. 83.
53 Rahner, *The Church*, p. 12.
54 Rahner, *Theological Investigations X*, trans. D. Bourke, New York: Seabury, 1977, p. 19.
55 Rahner, *Investigations X*, p. 14.
56 The best introduction to Rahner's ecclesiology is Richard Lennan, *The Ecclesiology of Karl Rahner*, Oxford: Clarendon, 1995.
57 See also Chapter 23 of this volume, 'Liberation Ecclesiology'.
58 Clodovis Boff, OSM, *Theology and Praxis: Epistemological Foundations*, trans. R.R. Barr, Maryknoll, NY: Orbis, 1987, p. 11.
59 C. Boff, *Theology*, p. 195.
60 L. Boff, *Ecclesiogenesis: The Base Communities Reinvent the Church*, trans R.R. Barr, Maryknoll: Orbis, 1986, p. 24.

61 L. Boff, *Church Charism and Power*, New York: Crossroad, 1985, p. 152.
62 L. Boff, *Ecclesiogenesis*, p. 33.
63 L. Boff, *Church*, p. 129.
64 Edward T. Oakes, *Pattern of Redemption: The Theology of Hans Urs von Balthasar*, New York: Continuum, 1994, p. 84.
65 *The Glory of the Lord; A Theological Aesthetics*, J. Fessio S.J. and J. Riches, eds, San Francisco: Ignatius, 1982–91. Numbers in parentheses in this paragraph are to volume one.
66 *Theo-Drama: Theological Dramatic Theory*, trans G. Harrison, San Francisco: Ignatius, 1988–98. Volume and page numbers in parentheses.
67 See Balthasar's *Explorations in Theology, II: Spouse of the Word*, San Francisco: Ignatius, 1991.
68 This is the thesis of Cardinal Avery Dulles, SJ, *Models of the Church*, expanded edition, New York: Doubleday, 1974/1987, though he does seem to prefer one over all.
69 This is a theme of R. Haight's *Christian Community*.
70 Peter C. Hodgson, *Revisioning the Church: Ecclesial Freedom in the New Paradigm*, Minneapolis: Fortress, 1988. Page numbers in parentheses. Also discussed in Chapter 7 of this volume, 'Postmodern Ecclesiologies'.
71 Zizioulas, John D. *Being as Communion: Studies in Personhood and the Church*, Crestwood, NY: St Vladimir's Seminary Press, 1985.
72 Tillard, Jean-Marie, OP, *Church of Churches: The Ecclesiology of Communion*, trans. R.C. De Peaux, O.Praem, Collegeville: Glazier/Liturgical Press, 1992. Tillard italicizes every use of 'communion'.
73 Joseph Ratzinger, 'Some Aspects of the Church Understood as a Communion', cited in Doyle, *Communion*, 1, from *L'Osservatore Romano* [English edn], 17 June 1992, p. 1. Doyle's book provides an excellent overview of the various forms of communion ecclesiology.

7

POSTMODERN ECCLESIOLOGIES

Gerard Mannion

Introduction

'What comes after the modern?'

It has often been said that, just as many of the churches had finally begun to come to terms with the 'modern' world, Christians found themselves in a very different era altogether. Nobody could say with certainty precisely what had changed and when – nor why the world had passed on from 'modernity' to something different. Universal agreement could not be found as to whether such changes were good or bad, or what the full implications for Christians actually were. So neither did agreement emerge as to the appropriate response of churches seeking to live out the gospel faithfully in a transformed social, cultural, political and intellectual age.

For the sake of this volume, though, we have somewhat artificially drawn the boundary between the modern era and the postmodern by bracketing under the latter those ecclesiological undertakings which have been explicitly attentive to discourse about 'what comes after the modern', about postmodernity itself. But a mere selection and representative example of such is outlined in what follows.

Postmodernity is, strictly-speaking, only 'post' in a certain sense. In many ways, the era after modernity is still rife with struggles to challenge and even to reject modernity's legacy or to rescue, revise and refine positive aspects of the same.[1] This chapter will not dwell at length upon the task of, in David Tracy's word's, 'naming the present',[2] for numerous studies already exist which do this in greater detail.[3] What this chapter explores are the various ecclesiological *responses* to that present.

But let us nonetheless say a few further words about understanding what we mean by 'postmodern', for some ecclesiological responses have sought to employ the term solely in a pejorative sense, focusing only on *certain* postmodern developments and issues, or theories and theorists. Because, in truth, there are a wide variety of senses in which the term is employed and just as wide a variety of 'postmodern theories' and scholars who would be comfortable with describing their work with relation to the term. Indeed, in many ways *all* ecclesiological work undertaken in the present era can be labelled 'postmodern': ecclesiology *in these times*. It is thus unhelpful to focus exclusively on any particular set of postmodern theories and scholars, although of course no treatment could hope to be exhaustive. Nonetheless it is important to highlight the *variety* of postmodern 'ecclesiologies'.

Although no one definition may entirely suffice, Roger Haight's brief definition, coming from a noted ecclesiologist, will here serve as a good summary of what 'postmodernity' entails, for he sees the word as a loose term that enables the description of a 'culture'. Under its umbrella are gathered a diverse set of experiences, including

> a historical consciousness that is deeper and more radical than that of modernity; an appreciation of pluralism that is suspicious of all absolute or universal claims; a consciousness of the social construction of the self that has completely undermined the transcendental ego of modernity and, ironically, encouraged a grasping individualism; a sense of the size, age, complexity, and mystery of reality that modern science never even suspected.[4]

Note, also, the difference between 'postmodernity' and 'postmodernism' (or–isms) – the former referring to descriptions of our era and its trends, challenges and neuroses, the latter to schools of thought or particular theories in response to the same.[5]

The challenges of this age

Peter Hodgson lists five particular 'crises' of the 'postmodern' era for our world as a whole, namely: the cognitive crisis (in both technical and philosophical rationality); the historical crisis (the end of both religious and secular versions of history working toward some positive end such as salvation, progress, the dictatorship of the proletariat, etc.); the political crisis (shifts in ideologies, in the axes of power in the world, decline of support for the 'social ideals generated by the Enlightenment'); the socio-economic crisis (the dysfunctionalities of free enterprise capitalism and state socialism and the effects of what, in the years after the publication of Hodgson's book, came to be called globalization); and, finally, the religious crisis: Christianity's decline in 'the West' and the attendant emergence of new forms of being religious.[6]

Daniel J. Adams lists four characteristics of postmodernity: firstly 'the decline of the west' (i.e. the demise of the cultural hegemony and the rejection of the predominant worldview that has permeated Europe and North America for so long). Second, 'the legitimation crisis' (the famed 'incredulity towards metanarratives'), which Adams suggests permeates every factor of contemporary life – a plurality of values and value systems emerges. Third, 'the intellectual marketplace' – intellectual and political elites can no longer exercise the universal control over cultural and religious knowledge that they once did. Finally, 'deconstruction', which is linked to the second characteristic and becomes a way of 'delegitimating' accepted interpretations and therefore challenging 'traditional' authority. Objectivity gives way to hermeneutics (the 'science' of meaning and interpretation). Adams himself feels that all four lead towards a near-universal pluralism but that these developments leave us with no way of evaluating such pluralism.[7]

In this chapter, I will work towards challenging such a conclusion and suggesting that ecclesiology's engagement with postmodernity and pluralism itself sheds a critical yet ultimately positive and hopeful light upon both the era and that plurality which is so characteristic of it. Indeed, perhaps plurality (unity in diversity) is a key concept from which to seek to understand the postmodern era in general, and the prospects for ecclesiology and the life and mission of the churches in particular.

Particular postmodern challenges for ecclesiology

The challenges that the church faces are practical as well as cultural and theoretical. The latter are obviously the ecclesiological outworking of those trends detailed above.[8] Ecclesiology in the postmodern era is very much bound up with, and bears the marks of impact from, parallel developments in philosophy, the social sciences, linguistics and cultural theory. In relation to the former practical challenges, the postmodern era is also an era that has seen monumental changes and developments take place in the self-understanding (ecclesiologies) and notion of *mission* in most churches. The impact of drastic changes in church attendance and moral beliefs and practices has had to be endured, assessed and responded to by numerous churches especially in Europe, and increasingly in North America and Oceania.

So, too, the churches in recent decades have witnessed major changes in patterns and forms of ministry, church governance and liturgy; and the numerous intra- and inter-ecclesial implications of the era's various church disputes, schismatic developments and scandals all bear the hallmarks of cultural and social postmodern changes, trends and developments. After almost a century of progress and the generation of enormous hope, the fall of a harsh 'winter' upon the ecumenical quest (now also extended to the 'wider ecumenism' that was concerned with bringing about greater dialogue and community with other faiths and people of no faith alike) has been an especially painful reality to face. The impact of key political, economic and cultural trends upon the churches and ecclesiology is equally marked, e.g. the politicization of the 1960s generation; the threat of nuclear warfare; the Vietnam War; the sexual 'revolution'; the emergence and eventual global 'triumph' of neo-conservatism (somewhat confusingly termed neo-liberalism in some quarters!) in terms of concentration of power and influence; globalization; the collapse of the Soviet Union and Eastern European state totalitarianism; and the ever-worsening situation in the Middle East, with the equally (and of course closely related) ever-worsening relations between 'the West' and Islam, with September 11th and the evidently futile backlash in Afghanistan and Iraq being tragically defining 'moments'. The church, charged with not just proclaiming but with also *living* the gospel, has had to contend with all these and so many more challenges in the postmodern era. Christian social and political ethics in the era have had much to contend with.

In the postmodern era, people have become ever-more 'consumerized' – human being itself, as well as all the main elements of being human, have become 'products' to be bought and sold in an 'open' marketplace. From sexuality to reproduction, from politics to religion itself, all is now seen in terms of consumerist 'choice'. People pick and mix and the church itself has become just as commodified, as people take what they wish and leave what they do not want from Christianity's doctrinal belief system, traditional teaching and liturgical and ecclesial practices and ways of living. The 'consumerist turn' also sees people 'choosing' their ecclesial community both within and across denominations. Nonetheless, those who predicted the final triumph of secularization and eventually of secularism have been proved hopelessly mistaken. Religion has prevailed as a major cultural and existential force in the world (for good or ill, depending on how manipulated and exploited it has been in the hands of states, politicians and ideologues alike).

If Lyotard is correct in briefly defining the postmodern as 'incredulity to metanarratives', then Christianity *in toto* faces a major challenge: the church in general, charged with safeguarding and promoting the Christian metanarrative, and ecclesiology in particular, as a further 'metanarrative' that self-justifies the community called church's place and mission in the world to do so, faces very specific upheavals indeed in such an era.

Postmodernity, theology and the church

Just what constitutes a 'postmodern' as opposed to late modern (or simply anti-modern) response and theory is of course open to much debate. The ecclesiological explorations discussed in this chapter involve a panorama of intellectual influences including, though not exclusively, those schools of thought deemed most 'quintessentially postmodern' (if one dare use such a term of that era!).[9]

The ecclesiological impact of varieties of postmodern theology

It will focus our attention to reiterate various 'typologies' of theology in the postmodern context, for even the genre of 'postmodern theology' itself has multiple forms and tones, the most frequently cited being *reductivistic* (rejecting modern theology and its tenets and pathways), *deconstructionist* postmodern theology (drawing upon the seminal deconstructive theorists to undermine the truth claims and authority of modern theology), *revisionist*, *constructive* or *reconstructionist* (trying to salvage what was fruitful and positive from modern theology and modernity in general) – the latter including 'theologies of communal practice', and, finally, *reactionary* (or conservative or restorationist) postmodern theologies (trying to fight a rearguard action against the perceived threats and evils not simply of modernism but also of the further metamorphosis of such in postmodernity as well, with relativism and nihilism being singled out as especially decadent trends). So, too, there have been various additional recent varieties of feminist theology informed by both postmodern theories and postmodern cultural challenges and themes alike.[10] To their number should be added approaches taken by scholars focusing on the areas of queer theology, animal theology and eco-theology. Of course, many theologies overlap several different subdisciplines at one and the same time, so any attempt to pigeonhole a given work should always be undertaken carefully and be open to the admission that such labelling must remain non-definitive.

Postmodern theologies focus on a range of themes familiar to theology throughout its long story, but they obviously attempt to do so in a novel way, whether critical, reductivistic, constructive, or restorationist.

The trends and attendant challenges of the postmodern era have also been factors in further developing the great ecclesiological potential offered by recent ecclesiological engagements with the social sciences[11] in order to inform ecclesiological thinking. Some scholars, however, vociferously shun such interdisciplinary involvement, as we shall see.

In attempting to survey 'postmodern ecclesiologies', I shall seek to offer a brief sketch of current ecclesiological thought and debate in recent decades by focusing on representative examples of approaches to the study and understanding of the church in the era 'after' modernity.

Prospects for the church in a postmodern world

Much of the work in and around ecclesiology that has been done in recent decades has been in response to, sometimes in reaction to, and sometimes after learning from, the 'signs of the times', i.e. the social, cultural, intellectual, political, economic and, indeed, spiritual and religious developments of the age (just as in each and every one of the other historical epochs you can read about in the earlier chapters of this volume). Whoever does ecclesiology in the postmodern era, from whatever ecclesial and ecclesiological standpoint, cannot deny that our present age is very different from the one that preceded it. Nor would most deny that worrying developments and trends have emerged in this age that pose serious challenges to the church.

As indicated, many have decided that this is such a worrying age that the best response is to 'batten down the hatches', turn inwards, preserve the 'purity' of the church and its message and wait for the postmodern storm to blow over. They are concerned that, in the modern era, theology, the church and the faith itself became too 'infected' by currents of thought and social and cultural trends that actually diluted the gospel and distracted the church from its true mission.

At the opposite extreme, others have decided that this must be the way God wants the world to go. All is now flux and change and this is no bad thing. Embrace postmodernity, its uncertainties and its celebration of difference. Some push this further still: truth *is* relative, all is play, resist all domineering forces, be they political, intellectual, textual or, indeed, ecclesial.

A variety of approaches in-between try to examine what 'went wrong' with the 'project' of modernity (e.g. why so many horrific wars blighted the twentieth century, why the world is richer than ever with greater resources than ever and yet with more people starving to death and living in abject poverty than ever). Yet they also try to salvage what was good, the progressive and laudable things that were achieved in that era, the developments that were forces for good and against evil. So, too, they seek to discern what are negative and worrying developments in the present era and what aspects of postmodernity are, once again, signs of the times that may teach the church and help shape its mission of living out and preaching the gospel in faithfulness *all the better* for those very times.

It is too crude to try to fit the many different ecclesiological approaches in recent decades into binary oppositional 'camps', though (reflecting those forms of theology outlined above) the most frequently mentioned polar opposites include correlationists, revisionists, liberals and pluralists at one end and postliberals, reactionaries, conservatives and neo-exclusivists at the other.

Differing methodologies and differing priorities, along with dependence on differing influences, obviously shape the responses of the various interlocutors in the postmodern ecclesiological arena.

The church and the world

But, in many ways, the key question for ecclesiologists in a postmodern context is their understanding of the relationship of the church to the wider 'world' (and of the church's role and place therein). This also feeds into, as well as presupposes a particular understanding of, the relationship between nature and grace. Ironically, some of those postmodern ecclesiologies that began by making a fuss about the need to appreciate that the 'natural' had been artificially separated from the 'supernatural' in the Middle Ages, end up with a very world-renouncing ecclesiology, which sees the church turning inwards, separated from the taint of the 'secular' and its cultural and intellectual 'vices'.

Thus one of the most pertinent questions for postmodern ecclesiology, which has nonetheless been with the church as a real dilemma and topic of debate from its very beginnings, is the relationship between the church and the world, and the ecclesial attitudes and practices which relate to, shape and reflect this.[12] The World Council of Churches and the Roman Catholic church's Second Vatican Council shifted the balance in ecclesial thinking here towards more openness and engagement with the wider world. However, in recent times, the balance has, in many quarters, swung back in the other direction. Fears of secularization (despite the subsequent realization that this was not as wholeheartedly developed as was once thought), along with a range of reactions to the 'postmodern situation', have caused many theologians, church leaders and, crucially, those engaged with the grass roots movements in various denominations to turn 'inwards' – in other words (in sociological parlance), to perceive of the church as a world-*renouncing* as opposed to a world-*affirming* community. Let us explore the parameters of this debate.

'Postmodern' schools of ecclesiological reflection, reaction and construction: some representative types

Secular and non-realist theologies

A very brief summary of the relevant ecclesiological and historical developments during the 'era' might begin, for some commentators, with the works in Secular Theology (e.g. Thomas Altizer, the earlier Harvey Cox) prominent in the 1960s and its attendant 'religionless' Christianity, the intellectual origins of which can be traced back as far as the work of Dietrich Bonhoeffer in the 1940s. Such movements helped feed into 'Non-realist theology', prominent especially in the 1980s and 90s and concerned with the linguistic, experiential and practical aspects of theology. For such, religious language does not refer to 'realities' in the same way that everyday descriptive language does. So a line of progression might be charted from the existentialist-inspired demythologization of Christian doctrines from the 1930s onwards, on to the 'secular' theologies, and an ever-decreasing belief that the tenets of the faith are to be understood in a literal sense, that they are not 'objectively' true (in the sense that Dublin *is* the capital of Ireland) but are rather *subjectively* true for the personal believer. Thus non-realism (e.g. the work of Don Cupitt). For such, the church serves social and spiritual functions and meets particular positive needs but superioristic, transcendental and, for some, even sacramental claims in any literal, as opposed to figurative or existential, sense must be jettisoned by the church for more humanistic, social and ethical priorities. Attempts to 'secularize' theology and hence to place society over and above the church follow from the work of thinkers such as Thomas Altizer.

'Deconstructing' church

Hence, along the same continuum, one finds the work of scholars such as Mark C. Taylor and Charles Winquist,[13] which put the work of distinctly postmodern theorists such as Jacques Derrida and the notion of deconstructionism, at the service of a very new form of theological discourse – indeed Taylor labels his work a/theology.

Key postmodern theorists emerged from a perhaps unlikely fusion of influential idea developed by thinkers such as Martin Heidegger, Ludwig Wittgenstein, neo-pragmatism (e.g. Richard Rorty) and linguistic structuralism. Enter stage left the product of such a fusion in the form of Jacques Derrida. What Derrida's 'deconstruction' offered to postmodern theology and hence ecclesiology was not simply the completion of Heidegger's supposed 'destruction' of western metaphysics but also the avoidance of any 'one-dimensional' world-views. Instead, Derrida rejected any strategy that leads to monism and a pervasive desire for 'presence' i.e. a self-sufficient, readily available reality, as well as any approach that continued to maintain a dualistic worldview, thereby dichotomizing differences and creating oppositional and adversarial approaches to the world.

Demonstrating that both such views play into one another, Derrida sought to take apart their threads of dependence and the logic of hierarchical opposition he perceived to be at work in language, where the powerful and dominant terms that are treated as 'presence' are actually dependent upon the terms they are opposed to for their very meaning and power. He asserted that no central core of reference actually exists and hence oppositional language can be proved illusory as a positive relativism emerges in the interdependence that consti-tutes language. As such, for example, Derrida demonstrated that texts may frequently be saying things not at first apparent. Indeed they may be saying things completely at odds with the intentions of their authors.

The ecclesiological implications of such an approach are obvious: the special or privi-leged, not to mention the salvific and sacramental role and understanding of the church, are clearly called into question if not dismissed. If relativism emerges as reality, and a positive reality at that, the objective truth claims made by and on behalf of the church become mere 'contenders' in the market. As Terence Tilley *et al.* have stated, 'Taylor's a/theology carries an implied an/ecclesiology – a bypassing or denying the communities called church'.[14]

Deconstructive or eliminative postmodern theology dismisses the need for a worldview by deconstructing the concepts necessary for a worldview such as God, self, purpose, meaning and history. As Stanley Grenz has shown, the deconstructive route obviously further breaks down traditional ontologies, i.e. understandings of existence, of being itself.[15] Yet ecclesiology is founded upon a very particular social ontology – that God, whose essence is a community of co-equal persons, calls humanity to community also: the church is a way of being – a community called into being to be a sign and mediation of the loving being-in-community that is God.

Those attracted by the deconstructive approach argue that it offers a reappropriation of the Christian tradition in an age where ecclesiological discourse has clearly lost its way. The deconstructive approach reflects the reality of our times more closely than attempting to cling on to a long-dead normative ecclesial worldview. Themes such as alterity and the need to always respect 'the other' have become mainstream theological topics for discussion in part thanks to deconstructionism. However, although some might argue that the likes of Taylor offer fresh insights for contemporary ecclesiology – e.g. his assertion that the self must be understood totally in *relational* terms – ultimately, the deconstruction of truth, meaning and history pursued by such, along with the nihilistic collapsing of the categories of good and evil can, at best, serve primarily as useful foils or conversation partners for contemporary ecclesiology. In many ways, the 'secular' and 'post-ecclesiological' or 'post-ecclesiastical' thinking of such writers serves functional as opposed to sacramental ends – purporting to be rooted firmly in a 'this-wordly' ontology and yet, critics say, in practice transcending that very world via a retreat into an obsession with linguistic reflection and analysis. Whilst being attentive to the panoply of postmodern concerns, Robert Scharlemann's work provides an example of those who try to retain, particularly in ecclesio-logical terms, something that critics feel the above thinkers have jettisoned in their meth-odological pursuits, whilst Carl Raschke has openly addressed ecclesiological questions from within such a methodological standpoint.[16]

Postliberalism and 'narrative ecclesiology'

Sharing (somewhat ironically) with the non-realists and deconstructionists the influence of the philosopher Ludwig Wittgenstein, though offering markedly different conclusions, is the movement known as 'postliberalism' (liberal here in the pejorative sense that it is usually employed in the United States) which challenges the secularizing critics of religion in modernity by taking on board aspects of the linguistic and cultural anthropological interpretations of religion and applying them to Christian communities. Christians inhabit a world mediated by their own 'language game' and system of symbols geared towards serving such communities. The truth claims of Christianity are not supposed to be (and will not always make sense if they are) subjected to ordinary scientific and epistemological verification (the latter claim shared by many theologians and ecclesiologists working in the postmodern era).

Although a diverse collection of scholars and theories are bracketed under the term,[17] the distinctive ecclesiological and postmodern thrust of such an approach is captured well by James Foder, who states that postliberal theology (which he conceives as being broader than postliberalism, 'the school', itself), 'emphasizes the particular grammar of Christian faith, concentrating on its scriptural logic and the regulative role of doctrine with a view to sustaining communities of "native speakers" facing diverse pressures (internal and external) that would weaken that competency, threaten the church's identity or otherwise distract it from its central mission as one of communal witness and practice'.[18] Indeed, the pragmatic purpose of even Christianity's *intellectual* content is primarily ordered towards 'the gathering and building up of communities of faith'[19] – the latter obviously being much in accord with George Lindbeck's now definitive account of the 'cultural-linguistic' understanding of the nature of doctrine.[20] Furthermore, it echoes Lindbeck's explication of his method and that of 'narrative theology' in general, whereby the (scriptural) text actually 'absorbs' the surrounding world as opposed to being absorbed by it. This has spawned a variety of influential studies and even further sub-movements and new movements altogether, as the attraction of an approach that does not cower at the perceived rampant secularizing of the postmodern world, but instead reasserts the Christian message as *the* way forward in such times proves obviously seductive. The ecclesiological outworking of such an approach is that the church is seen to be the form of community that can offer the uncertain postmodern world a decisive way forward through the confusion and fragmentation that beset contemporary societies.

Lindbeck's own ecclesiological position has developed significantly from a more sectarian approach in the early 1970s, through the turning point of *The Nature of Doctrine*, and on to what he calls an 'Israelology' whose end is a credible ecumenism for today, an ecclesiology that is descriptive of contemporary ecclesial practice where the theme of the people of God looms large.[21] His critics suggest he merges pre-modern and post-critical hermeneuticals in a fashion that is ultimately at best ambivalent and at worst inconsistent. He is charged with blurring the distinction between the notions of religions and church themselves and with subordinating theological categories (e.g. revelation, the Trinity, Divine salvific activity) to ecclesiology itself. Others point out that his later ecclesiology nonetheless still clearly demarcates between church and the wider world and that he only admits the possibility of a uni-directional positive influence (of church upon world), despite acknowledging the sins and faults of the church. Lindbeck, then, seeks a 're-Christianization' of postmodern society.

But the precise *attraction* of the postliberal approach for its numerous proponents is that it provides continued meaning and identity for Christians and for their communities, offering an intellectually credible bulwark against the anti-religious critiques of modernity and postmodernity itself. For its critics, it is typified by a self-affirming and self-validating 'language game' that looks inwards and changes the 'rules of engagement' with those beyond like-minded communities to suit. The ecclesiologies which emerge are thus exclusivist, sectarian and intellectually disingenuous. The 'church' is idealized in so normative a fashion that it becomes ever more distanced from 'the world' and hence from God's creation, itself. Dan Hardy offers one example of a more world-engaged ecclesiological appropriation of postliberalism, perhaps refracted through his work in various cosmopolitan UK cities.[22] Kathryn Tanner's work, likewise, though she writes from a US and social scientifically informed perspective. Kevin Vanhoozer has also recently offered a most constructive attempt to appropriate Lindbeck's work anew in what he calls a 'canonical-linguistic approach to Christian theology'.[23]

As we shall see below, particularly sharp criticisms have been addressed to other ecclesiologies that have built upon postliberal theory, although developed in somewhat distinct directions such as those offered by Stanley Hauerwas and the recent school of thought which calls itself 'Radical Orthodoxy' (the contributions of which are somewhat ecclesiologically disparate).

'The emerging church'

The 'Emerging Church *Movement*' is characterized by a more amorphous and decentralized ecclesial culture still, and one which seeks to embrace the postmodern world and all of its riches, particularly the internet and multimedia culture that offers previously unparalleled opportunities for debate, discussion and dialogue.

The influence upon such developments of key postmodern theorists such as Michel Foucault (particularly his critique of the repressive structures of societal authority) and Derrida's deconstructionist agenda has led to the increasing development of a distinct strand of ecclesiological studies of such a phenomenon. Initially such studies began from a sociological, ethnographic and anthropological methodology but in recent times more systematic theological contributions have also been forthcoming.

Critics see it as a sell-out to relativistic and liberal postmodernity itself. Others regard it as simply old-style modernist avant-garde faddism. Conservative evangelicals and 'traditionalists' of other denominations see it as a distortion of the gospel itself.

Elsewhere in this volume, such movements, along with the 'megachurch' and 'e-church' emerging ecclesiologies are discussed in a broader context.[24]

A trans-denominational reformation?

Due to the various cultural and intellectual shifts witnessed in the postmodern world, as well as thanks to the many dialogues and ecumenical ventures across the Christian churches, denominational divides have increasingly become less relevant, only to be replaced by ideological, theological, doctrinal and methodological divides both *within* and *across* (as opposed to *between*) denominational barriers. The ecclesiological outcomes of such a development can be seen in both reactionary and constructive pluralistic forms.

Ecclesiology contra postmodernity:
a church 'beyond postmodern criticism'

For many concerned voices, it appears that various theologians and also church officials are increasingly adopting positions which even mirror, in some respects, the postmodern slide towards a form of fundamentalism (i.e. a rigid insistence upon adhering to defined fundamentals), that quest for certitude in a world of flux and change which sociologists have identified as an alternative reaction to the current historical epoch.[25]

Reactionary and conservative postmodern ecclesiologies

Numerous scholars have sought to utilize the insights of postmodern theorists and postmodern epistemological and linguistic categories towards the service of critiquing the age or its 'prevailing' wisdom and trends in themselves. Hence, for example, deconstructionism is also embraced and turned around as a looking glass to show up the ills of modern and now postmodern intellectual and social developments. The Christian 'tradition' is thereby championed anew as *the* antidote to the ills of the age. One finds this approach in very different ways in as diverse a range of thinkers as Jean-Luc Marion, Graham Ward, John Milbank, Stanley Hauerwas and Catherine Pickstock. What unites such approaches is their (somewhat ironic) immersion in postmodern cultural developments in order to offer a riposte and rejection of many of the same cultural forces that fund their 'new' repristinated 'tradition'.

Philosophy and the social sciences, in particular, come under heavy fire from many proponents of such a 'theological' critique which, no less than the work of Barth, whom Hans Küng rightly identifies as a prototype postmodern theologian, avails itself of all the philosophical and social scientific insights and 'tools of the trade' against which it otherwise rebels, in order to construct such a separatist and distinct vision of theology and, a fortiori, of the church. Perhaps Graham Ward's own assessment of Marion (who has frequently been described as a 'postmetaphysical theologian') helps illustrate the position adopted by many such thinkers:

> The postmodernism of such a theology lies both in its ecclesiological conservatism and in its theological exploration of such postmodern themes as the crisis of representation and identity, the other, the unnameable, the aporetic, and the deconstruction of metaphysics. . . . Postmodern critique therefore provides access to or is framed by a Christian faith which is never argued for; it is assumed. . . . Postmodern insights and approaches are employed within the theological discussions concerning ontology and analogy.[26]

The name of Michel de Certeau is frequently bracketed with those listed above and identified with such an approach. But this perhaps does his more constructive, open and indeed genuinely sacramental writings something of a disservice. Indeed, the ecclesiological implications of de Certeau's work are particularly positive and he might be better placed elsewhere in the account of 'postmodern ecclesiologies', being more a representative of an ecclesiology of 'engagement' than of withdrawal[27] (Graham Ward himself can frequently be judged in a similar light). Perhaps, as with numerous Roman Catholic *ressourcement* thinkers, de Certeau's reputation is coloured by the use to which his work is put by some who appropriate his works in the service of very different ecclesiological ends than de Certeau himself may have sought to pursue. Certeau understands the importance of historical consciousness and the notion of ecclesial and doctrinal development (and regression) in a sophisticated way – themes which some postmodern ecclesiological thinkers simply ignore. Certeau offers contemporary ecumenical debates much more fruitful and inspiring suggestions than the writings of those he is frequently bracketed with. His works, as also his life, bear testimony to the absence of certitude and ambiguities that characterize the church in any age.

But those distinctly 'conservative' and reactionary postmodern thinkers are part of that broader trans-denominational development in Christianity that is linked to the aforementioned divisions along the church–world axis. We turn now to explore one very prominent example of such a 'postmodern' ecclesiological shift.

Radical Orthodoxy

Prevalent amongst such movements 'beyond criticism' in recent times has been the (mostly Anglican in its initial stages) 'Radical Orthodoxy' movement which, at least in some of its forms, lends itself to the promotion of a 'neo-exclusivism' and attempts to hark back to some imagined 'golden era' of doctrine and theology 'untainted' by separate philosophical interests and questions of secular relevance. To many of its critics, this movement sets itself up as *the* new authority, defending '*the* tradition' of Christian doctrine. This form of theological thinking has developed in various forms since the publication of the 'classic text' of its founding 'father'.[28]

Such views, along with the other central tenets most representative of Radical Orthodoxy[29] have been widely criticized for breeding a worryingly *insular* ecclesial outlook which often leads to a refusal to enter into genuine dialogue with differing theological and philosophical perspectives, rejecting, in particular, the contributions of the social sciences towards promoting a harmonious communitarian outlook and anthropology. Such a standpoint would also appear to reject many of the claims of other faith traditions.

Although different proponents of Radical Orthodoxy tend to understand and define it in significantly different ways, there is nonetheless a certain amount of continuity and familiar themes and concerns shared by most of the main writers involved. Thus, offering a very sympathetic account, D. Stephen Long states that Radical Orthodoxy,

> is a theologic that mediates politics, ethics, philosophy and aesthetics without becoming correlationist and accommodating the modern spirit. It is postmodern only in that it turns the philosophical advantages toward which postmodernity points, and completes them theologically. It is the return of Christian orthodoxy, but with a historical and linguistic difference that makes possible theological work in politics, economics and ethics. It is a Christian metaphysics that does not begin with transcendentalist assumptions that predicate knowledge of God upon a secure knowledge of ourselves. Instead it assumes that participation in the church makes possible a theological knowledge that must then mediate all other forms of knowledge. . . . It is radical in that it is also capable of calling the church itself back to its roots at the same time that it seeks to bear witness to those roots to all of humanity.[30]

Paul Lakeland offers a more critical analysis of Radical Orthodoxy – bracketing them along-side the likes of George Lindbeck and the postliberalist movement as forms of thinking defined as 'countermodernity'.[31] His critique of Radical Orthodoxy and the work of John Milbank (as its main protagonist), is especially pointed:

> Powerful and enterprising, radical orthodoxy also suffers from a tendency towards Christian exclusivism, if not outright totalitarianism. The pluralism of post-modernity is not construed as a value.[32]

Lakeland's critique cuts to the core issues which those numerous critics have put to the movement. Indeed, such critics also suggest that Radical Orthodoxy has itself shied away from, neglected or at least been inattentive to ecclesiology. However, whilst ecclesiology was certainly a gap in the early writings of its main proponents, and whilst 'tradition' and liturgy seem to preoccupy a great deal more of the movement's debates than ecclesiology (in fact often serving as substitutes for ecclesiological thinking *per se*), more recent writings and newcomers to the movement have sought to address more specifically ecclesiological topics (e.g. essays by Milbank and Graham Ward in the case of the former and the work of D. Stephen Long himself[33] and the US-based 'Ekklesia Project' in the case of the latter).[34] Long is adamant that there exists 'a hierarchical order of social formations that privileges the church above all others'.[35] But for a movement that is essentially *self*-authorizing (with Radical Orthodoxy's growing corpus of literature so often building on the postmodern deconstructivist notion of play at times, whilst elsewhere relying upon bombastic demoli-tions of all opposing voices at others), certain elements of more traditional ecclesiological debate have obviously proved unattractive.

Lakeland's critique helps us to appreciate further the actuality of this 'trans-denominational' reformation currently at large, for we can actually witness parallels with Roman Catholicism at every turn, particularly with his assertion that John Milbank's 'mani-festo is a shameless reassertion of the premodern superiority of Christendom' which is based upon a 'highly idiosyncratic reading of Western civilization'.[36] Furthermore, Lakeland's final analysis of Milbank's vision also draws together the postmodern pitfalls that many commen-tators have sought to highlight within the contemporary Roman Catholic church, as well as in other denominations,

> Much of my unease derives from the shaky marriage between the premodern and the postmodern. The premodern Christian vision was open to the apologetic dimension, and was able through its espousal of a metaphysic to engage, at least in principle, in dialogue with unbelievers. In this it differed little from modern Christian theologies. But the postmodern perspective has abandoned the premodern and modern, and is content with play and the trace of the deconstruc-tionist, the genealogies of the poststructuralist, or the neopragmatist's irony. Milbank wants it both ways: namely to assert the superiority of the Christian meta-narrative, and not to have to justify its claims in the open court of reason.[37]

Perhaps in response to some such criticisms, John Milbank has recently offered his thoughts on ecclesiology and its prospects for the future – i.e. where he thinks the church and Christian theology should be moving towards in this postmodern era. Characteristically eclectic, both historically and intellectually, Milbank wishes to offer less a thesis than to make a point which is, to all intents and purposes, that Radical Orthodoxy, contrary to its critics, not only has an ecclesiology but is the only way forward for ecclesiology in the present age. It is, he claims, actually against sectarian and denominationalism, against what he perceives to be futile and reductivistic ecumenical ventures, against the legacies of the Protestant and Tridentine Reformations and against the various turns in theological and philosophical thought from 1300 onwards.[38]

'Resident aliens': the ecclesiology of Stanley Hauerwas

The work of Stanley Hauerwas obviously represents another of the foremost examples of the advent of this 'trans-denominational' reformation. He declares that 'Modernity and its bastard offspring postmodernity are but reflections of the Christian attempt to make God available without the mediation of the church ... Postmodernism, in short, is the outworking of mistakes in Christian theology correlative to the attempt to make Christianity "true" apart from faithful witness'.[39] In a prolific output of literature, Hauerwas has embraced both narrative theology and Radical Orthodoxy in the service of an ecclesiology that focuses upon the practical imperative for Christians simply 'to be church'. Christians must collectively resist the evils of the liberal postmodern world, particularly those evils which have found their way into church life and theological discourse themselves. Hauerwas's call for the church to be 'a community of character' has inspired a generation of Christian scholars searching for shelter in what they perceive to be the postmodern storm. On the other hand, it is puzzling to his critics that he thinks the more outward-looking discipline of virtue ethics can supply the foundations for such an, in effect, sectarian ecclesiology.[40]

Above all else, Hauerwas wishes to contrast Christianity with postmodernism (which he understands as those who feel we have reached the 'end of history') because Christians have 'a stake' in history' and must 'develop accounts ... that are more powerful than either the modernist or postmodernist can muster'.[41] He has consistently been accused of being a 'sectarian tribalistic fideist', a claim that he just as often denies. Yet if his voluminous output displays any consistency, it is certainly on the church–world question. Thus in his 1983 work, *The Peaceable Kingdom*,[42] he was already pronouncing that 'the world has no way of knowing it is world without the church pointing to the reality of God's kingdom'[43] and furthermore 'it is particularly important to remember that the world consists of those, including ourselves, who have chosen not to make the story of God their story'.[44]

Hauerwas openly bases his metaphysical and so historical judgements on the sweeping metaphysical and quasi historio-metaphysical judgements of Radical Orthodoxy.[45] Indeed, Hauerwas proclaims his indebtedness here to Blond, Pickstock and Milbank,[46] but critics would suggest that Hauerwas fails to see that he and Radical Orthodoxy merely offer another dangerously oppressive grand narrative that seeks to crush all alternatives which 'get in its way'.[47] Hauerwas is frequently taken to task for offering nothing more than an 'ideal' ecclesiology – a vision of a church that never has been, is not, and never will be.[48] Meanwhile, his critics say, Christians have to deal with the real world with all the messiness and sinfulness both within and without the church's confines. Such ecclesiologies as those from Hauerwas and Radical Orthodoxy encourage a renewed 'siege mentality' for Christians who should view themselves and their communities in relation to the world in terms of 'alien citizenship'. The tendency is toward a sectarian mentality, despite whatever aspirational vision for the kingdom is attached to such an ecclesiology.

Indeed, as indicated, from many such ecclesiological voices we hear sentiments that would not seem out of place were they to be uttered by reactionary Roman Catholic thinkers. Radical Orthodoxy and Hauerwas alike affirm the church as the 'true society'. It is not difficult to identify many Roman Catholic 'varieties' of these traits adherent to Radical Orthodoxy and other varieties of 'countermodern' ecclesiological perspectives. And this is so in relation to parallel strategies and arguments and agendas. All this mirrors what Roger Haight has described as a de facto move towards the isolation of Christian theology and the church from culture itself.[49] Let us explore such parallels a little further.

Charting the trans-denominational parallels

Whilst the full range of differing responses to the postmodern era and postmodern theories is also mirrored within the Roman Catholic church, some developments within the 'official' Roman Catholic church in recent decades have been interpreted as an increasing 'reactionary' response to the challenges of postmodernity. This has included a hardening of the stance of that church in relation to those who disagree with its teachings both within and without its walls. Hence, not only has the radical openness to the world which Vatican II proclaimed been transformed into a much more cautious approach, it has also, in recent decades, been supplanted by a more hostile and antagonistic attitude towards the world and those Catholics who believe in greater dialogue than the official paradigm appears to allow for.

David Tracy has also suggested that there are parallels to be drawn between such developments within Roman Catholic theology and those in other denominations. 'Indeed, this new kind of post-Vatican II Catholic theology of Balthasar and Ratzinger is remarkably similar in method to the claim in American Protestant theology proposed by the neo-Barthian anticorrelational theologians',[50] although he qualifies it by going on to state that 'The differences are also, of course, notable: the Protestant theologians, in fidelity to the theology of the Word, emphasize the intertextual developments; the Catholics, in fidelity to the sacramental vision of Catholicism, emphasize the "ecclesial sense" (Ratzinger) or the importance of the incarnational-sacramental "visible form" (Balthasar).'[51] But we can now see still further parallels and perhaps identify a wider range of trends that have emerged throughout many Christian churches since Tracy's article was written.[52]

Normative ecclesiological 'restorationism': Joseph Ratzinger

Ecclesiology is a theme that runs throughout the entire corpus of writings by Joseph Ratzinger the theologian, now Pope Benedict XVI. A synoptic examination of his writings indicates that there is actually much continuity across the decades.[53]

Ratzinger's theological explorations took on an ecclesiological flavour from the very beginning, with his doctoral dissertation exploring the themes of the people and household of God in the writings of Augustine of Hippo. His essential Christian anthropology, along with his understanding of the inter-relation between nature and grace, influence his writings upon the church. So, too, does his Bavarian background, with its strong sense of the role of the church being at the heart of the local community, and the positive sense of ecclesial tradition that accompanies such, also shaping his ongoing understanding of the church. But his theological education and so his initial ecclesiological explorations emerged during a time of upheaval for both the church and wider European society as a whole. Shortly after, of course, the monumental ecclesiological 'revolution' of Vatican II would also have a profound formative and reactive effect upon Ratzinger's ecclesiology.

That doctoral student of Augustine (who also became most familiar with the ecclesiological writings of Martin Luther) maintains a preoccupation with core ideas and themes throughout his ecclesiological writings. Above all else, we see that the fundamental understanding of the relationship of the church to the wider world is the key to understanding his ecclesiology. Related to this is his assessment of the ills and challenges of modernity and later postmodernity vis-à-vis that 'world'. The idea that the church finds itself in a 'situation of Babylonian captivity' in the modern and contemporary world has had a profound effect upon his fundamental ecclesiology.

As a basic synthesis, we might say that, for Ratzinger, the church is the essential and pre-eminent means to salvation for human beings. Thus the church mediates and makes present the grace of God in the world and guides and informs, through its teaching and leadership, the day to day existence of Christians; thus the areas of both faith and morals serve as the remit for the church's concern in a single continuum. Ratzinger's ecclesial writings also contain a preoccupation with *pastoral* matters: he constantly returns to a concern for the 'simple faithful'.

The notion of communion, developed in the Patristic writings and rediscovered anew by Catholic scholars in the 1950s and 1960s, whereby the salvific bonds between Christians in any particular local community are microcosmic reflections of the wider bonds of communion between Christians of all churches within the embrace of the universal church, is another key theme.[54] For Ratzinger, this all has a profound effect upon our understanding of the importance of the ecclesial hierarchy, papal primacy and indeed ecclesial organization in general. His understanding of what criteria must be met in order for a Christian community actually to be considered a 'valid church' centres around the essential prerequisites of valid ministerial orders, including a valid episcopate, and the celebration of a valid eucharist. Communion with Rome is also seen as a prominent defining feature, except for the churches of the Orthodox traditions.

All this also pertains to the understanding of the dynamics of the relationship between the local and the universal church. Although some of his writings around the end of Vatican II suggest otherwise, in the main, and with a renewed emphasis in later years, Ratzinger has steadfastly championed the primacy of the universal church over and against the local: a local community is a church only insofar as it is part of the (authentic) universal church. Following Vatican II and his various deliberations on the ecclesiological debates and documents of the council, including fundamental considerations over the meaning and implications of the council's two ecclesial constitutions, Ratzinger's ecclesiology develops in a direction that some have considered to be conservative and reactionary to developments which Vatican II unleashed in the church. This culminated in his central role in the founding of the journal *Communio* which, as he later said, was much more than a journal: it was an (ecclesiological, indeed ecclesial) *project*.

In turn, his fundamental ecclesiology has led to his very particular understanding of ecumenism, including his negative assessment of some developments towards unity, but also his steadfast commitment to fostering closer ties between the Roman Catholic and Orthodox churches. Just as he perceives there to be a hierarchy of validity amongst the churches and other 'ecclesial communities', so also, in the salvific economy, he maintains the superiority of the church and the Christian faith over and against other faiths as paths towards salvation, even perceiving there to be deficiencies in such faiths.

Another constant theme, increasingly so from the 1990s onwards, is the crucial importance of the role the church has played in the cultural development of the wider societies in which it lives, particularly Europe, and the continuing importance of this role in the future: the church has much to teach the world still, just as it has done so historically. Ratzinger has much to say on what the church can and must offer the postmodern world. His critics argue that he sees only a one-way relationship: the church can teach the world but, seemingly, the 'fallen' world cannot teach the church.

Ratzinger's ecclesiology also informs his understanding of theology and the role of the theologian in particular. He believes Catholic theologians should primarily concern themselves with 'faithfully' explicating the teaching of the church on behalf of the faithful. There is no such thing, for him, as legitimate 'dissent' from official teaching. Thus increasing and renewed centralization of authority upon Rome, and an emphasis upon obedience to church teaching and to church authorities, is a further defining feature of his ecclesiology, especially in the post-conciliar years. He has equally, therefore, served as a rallying figure and champion for many, leading to the foundation of his very own 'fan club', while critics suggest he represents a backward looking and intransigent form of ecclesiology which is exclusivistic and life-denying. Nonetheless, Ratzinger maintains, like Augustine and Luther before him, that the church is a company *always* in need of constant renewal.

What comes after the present? Constructive ecclesiologies in a postmodern context: a few collective and individual examples

Evangelical responses to postmodernity: Stanley Grenz and 'postconservative communitarian ecclesiology'

A wide variety of responses to postmodernity and postmodern thought from within those elements of the church who would describe themselves as 'Evangelical' have led to an explosion in literature which mirrors the full panorama of approaches to the present era that we have noted above with regards to the church in general. As well as a large number of essays and volumes by Anglican evangelical Alister McGrath, one especially indicative collection is that edited by David S. Dockery, *The Challenge of Postmodernism: an Evangelical Engagement*,[55] which gathers together evangelical voices from the entire spectrum of responses to contemporary ecclesial and ecclesiological challenges, including programmatic essays by scholars such as Carl Henry, Thomas Oden and the Canadian theologian Stanley Grenz, who died so unexpectedly and prematurely in March 2005.

Here, as a representative exponent of this ecclesial tradition, we select Grenz, who has been described as evangelicalism's leading theologian (by his collaborator, Roger Olsen), although his enthusiasm for seeing postmodernity as a great opportunity for the church and for entering into constructive dialogue with leading postmodern theories has also earned him the suspicion and disapproval of other evangelicals.

Grenz has consistently outlined a distinctly *positive* evangelical response to the challenges of postmodernity (one which is less apocalyptic in its assessment of the prospects for Protestantism than, say, Graham Ward's). In a large number of works,[56] popular essays, scholarly monographs and edited collections alike, Grenz attempted to develop a positive 'postmodern' ecclesiology and to offer a Christian theology which moves 'beyond foundationalism'.[57] More specifically, Grenz made a plea for evangelicals to occupy the 'centre' in a postmodern world where Christians allow themselves to be polarized between conservatives and liberals and hence for divisions to matter more than communion. Grenz identified himself as a 'postconservative' evangelical and offered his studies as works in the genre of 'constructive theology'.

Grenz wished to move theology beyond divisive debates and stagnant waters towards a vibrant engagement with the contemporary world through a positive celebration of the fundamentals of the evangelical tradition. At the heart of this, for Grenz, was the spirituality fostered through the experience of *conversion*. In a Schleiermachian methodological turn, he asserted that doctrine follows from this as the articulation, the 'second language', of evangelical Christianity.[58] But above all, Grenz understands *community*, hence *ecclesia*, to be the overall fundamental focal point of theology. His ecclesiological thinking thus moved from reflection upon the Trinitarian being of God on to the implications of this for ecclesial and societal living today. His series, *The Matrix of Christian Theology*, remained unfinished at his death, although the second volume, *The Named God and the Question of Being*, has since seen the light of day.

Thus Grenz argued that any authentic postmodern evangelical theology would need to meet certain criteria, including that it be *post-individual* (i.e. an emphasis upon community and so communitarianism's insights can be embraced and appropriated), *post-rational* (rejecting the 'unwarranted' rationalistic thrust of modern theologies in favour of a more 'wholistic' emphasis upon the whole person and community alike as opposed to simply certain features, rejecting Enlightenment dualism and again recentring the person in their social context – we are always beings-in-relation), and focused on *spirituality* (knowledge is worthless on its own aside from the good or otherwise it may help bring about) and hence thoroughly practical and activist in nature. Spirituality fosters our inner resources to work for good.[59] As Grenz states, theology helps shape this inner resource, 'for it seeks to clarify the foundational belief structure which shapes our responses to the situations of life and which structure is reflected in the acts we choose to do'.[60] Applying all this to a specifically ecclesiological application, Grenz states that,

> Although Christian theology has always been 'church dogmatics' . . . , the 'churchly' aspect has become even more crucial in the postmodern context. In a world characterised by the presence of a plurality of communities, each of which gives shape to the identities of its participants, the Christian community takes on a new and potentially profound theological importance as the people who embody a theological vision that sees the divine goal for humankind as that of being the bearers of the image of the God who is triune.[61]

Grenz was not without his critics from both the more conservative and progressive quarters of the church. Thus R. Albert Mohler Jr went as far as to suggest, as other critics did, that Grenz's approach was in danger of essentially departing from the evangelical tradition altogether.[62] For Mohler, 'Given [Grenz's] concessions to postmodernity's scepticism and localizing tendencies, in the end it cannot result in a genuinely evangelical system'.[63] Mohler himself believes that evangelicals should not rush to embrace too much of the agenda of postmodern thinkers. Indeed, he believes the inherent pitfalls of modernity are yet to have disappeared from the contemporary world, 'At this stage of the development of postmodernism, it would appear that the movement is the latest representation of modernity', itself and hence 'nothing less than our fidelity to the Christian faith is at stake'.[64]

More critical voices worried that Grenz offered many suggestions which, in the final analysis, were telling of an inclination towards an *inward* looking ecclesiology, as with those many other contemporary discussions from across the denominational divide. His supporters would argue that Grenz writes from within the context of where many Christians currently locate themselves, with regards to the inter-relation between the church and/or Christianity and ethics today. His conclusion is the emphasis upon community: the church must acknowledge the social understanding of the Christian God and how the commitment to community is what has set it apart through the centuries and should continue to do so in the postmodern era.[65] Community, for Grenz, is 'Theology's integrative motif'.[66]

Communicative practice and revisionism

There are numerous other approaches we simply do not have the space to treat adequately here. Such would include that collection of approaches influenced by 'Critical Theory', and, in particular, the work of Jürgen Habermas, of the 'second wave' of the Frankfurt School, which has left a deep impression upon a number of contemporary approaches to ecclesiology, especially his critique of postmodern theory and his attempts to rescue what good came out of the Enlightenment and modernity in general. His work of most specific reference to ecclesiology, has been the theory of 'communicative action',[67] whereby norms and modes of discourse can be channelled towards ends that seek to radically extend the partially liberating energies of the Enlightenment into every area of human existence and, crucially, *on behalf of* every human person and community alike.[68] The work of scholars such as Bradford Hinze, Mary Ann Hinsdale and Bernd Jochen Hilberath in the field of 'communicative ecclesiology' is a particularly promising example of the ecclesiological appropriation of such insights.

A second major influence upon ecclesiology in postmodern times is revisionism and the 'Blessed Rage' to live with 'Plurality and Ambiguity' personified in the work of David Tracy,[69] which has influenced many of the contemporary ecclesiologies we have discussed here; elsewhere I have explored the value of his hermeneutical approach in particular.[70]

Embracing pluralism anew: liberationist, contextual feminist and interreligious ecclesiological perspectives

Postmodern ecclesiology also embraces and indeed, on some interpretations, also includes, responses to other movements such as liberation, contextual, political, feminist and womanist theologies and their 'new ways' of being church. The various 'theologies of religions' and pluralistic theologies have also offered enormous resources for contemporary ecclesiological reflection, especially insights from experiences of inculturation from churches for whom religious pluralism is a daily lived reality. Contextual and comparative theologies, then, have helped to shape contemporary ecclesiology constructively in so many different ways.

Thanks to such approaches, we have seen the emergence of numerous forms of 'Third World' theologies with their own very different 'inculturated' ecclesiologies and ecclesial and liturgical practices. Suffice to say the ecumenical agenda has been broadened by such approaches to embrace peoples of all faiths and none. Each of these types of ecclesiology which is undertaken in the midst of, and in response to, a postmodern age receive more detailed treatment elsewhere in this volume, hence I shall not duplicate such treatment here.[71]

Particular comparative and hermeneutical forms of ecclesiology

It is instructive perhaps to provide just a few examples of ecclesiologists who have integrated various elements of such constructive approaches into their thinking. The first is Mary McClintock Fulkerson, whose approach we might best term as being 'the Ethnography of Embodied Ecclesial Difference'. She has sought to illustrate that and how 'Postmodernism enters' liberationist feminist theological discourse 'by providing resources designed to advance such liberative ends. The primary litmus for any postmodernism will be its contribution to analyses of the complexities of gender, race, sexual and class oppression. What is "post" about such resources is their refusal of some of the "modern" habits in theology, but only those that inhibit exploration of these conditions of oppression.'[72] Fulkerson has pioneered new directions in feminist theology and ecclesiology alike, embracing critical theory to fruitful ends in both instances.[73]

She has also engaged in numerous ethnographic studies of actual church communities and her insights have helped transform postmodern ecclesiology into a sub-discipline where theory and practice are more closely intertwined. She does not shirk from confronting the most problematic challenges that postmodern life brings to ecclesial living – be it racism, homophobia, prolonged sexism, economic deprivation and the like. She hints here and makes explicit there that perhaps postmodern ecclesiology must fasten on to the fact that embracing the 'other' in a sense of friendship and neighbourliness is the true mark of the church for our times[74]

For Fulkerson, ecclesiology must be pragmatic as well as aspirational. She embraces the postmodern critique of power and culture and turns it to practical constructive effect whereby the church can truly bear witness to the ever-more needed 'good news' amidst the undeniable social travails of these postmodern times. In doing so she offers a critique of prevailing ecclesiological methods as well.[75] Fulkerson demonstrates that cultural-linguistic, neo-exclusivistic and world-renouncing ecclesiologies alike are equally insufficient accounts of what, today, constitutes the church – what the defining 'marks' of ecclesial existence are in the postmodern age.

Our second example is another American Presbyterian, Lewis Mudge, whose approach most recently focuses upon 'Traditioned Cosmopolitans' and the Hermeneutics of Global Ecclesial Existence.[76] He has not only worked tirelessly for both the Faith and Order as well as the Life and Work Commissions of the *World Council of Churches* since the 1950s, but he has also served on numerous inter-church bodies and bi-lateral forums across communions, contributing to a very large number of influential documents (including the WCC's Ethics and Ecclesiology studies). Always bringing a critical eye to such ventures himself, one would expect nothing less from a former student of Paul Ricoeur. Mudge has published a large number of articles and books in the fields of ecclesiology, hermeneutics and their inter-relation. He suggests that a new and non-parochial concept of catholicity can be witnessed in the wider church in recent decades, and he has argued that churches are not just moral communities, but also 'communities of interpretation'. But perhaps his most ambitious project to date is a methodological analysis of the possibility of practising what he terms 'parallel hermeneutics' across differing world faiths and wider communities, so that the global challenges facing all human communities may be better addressed.[77]

Mudge has sought to reflect upon the most challenging issues facing the church in post-modern times, first of all from within the Christian ecumenical context and, more recently, going beyond those confines to explore the hermeneutics and possibilities of shared ethical discourse of a social nature with those in the traditions of Judaism and Islam. His attempts, then, in an ecumenical context, involve a consideration of whether discussions of matters pertaining to faith and order, might not allow some 'ecumenical space' of 'shared resonance' where mutual recognition might take place. Hence he poses the following methodological question,

> Is it possible to think of a sort of ecclesiological hermeneutic of the koinonia we share when we find ourselves united on some moral issue – say the impact of global economic greed on the earth and all its inhabitants? . . . What kind of hermeneutic might this be? . . . The gathering of the People of God in the Spirit is by nature an expressive phenomenon. It can be interpreted as belonging within a household, a space or a cybernetic network of similar expression.[78]

Indeed, it is obvious that much of Mudge's thinking here can be applicable way beyond Christian communities, and even beyond faith communities themselves. Mudge was particularly taken with Robert Schreiter's concept of 'global theological flows'[79] in developing his 'recognition and resonance' model of ecumenical discourse, particularly that of a social-ethical nature.

In the postmodern world, Christianity in general has a problem with its universalizing discourse and Mudge draws out the particular implications of this for contemporary ecclesiology,

> It is ironic that we speak of 'catholicity' but have not generated a global theological flow of discourse about what it means to be church. Perhaps this is because there is no secular flow of discourse corresponding to and helping to sustain the ecclesiological question. Another way to say this is that ecclesiology, the science of the 'space' in which such global theological flows might meet, does not yet constitute a 'global theological flow' in its own right. Nor is any coherent theory of the human or of the human condition emerging here. All of this speaks of the state of affairs in which we find ourselves. *Our theological initiatives and insights come from no central place.*[80]

Hence Mudge wishes to engage in what he calls 'parallel hermeneutics' in order to conceive the inter-faith relationships necessary to confront the forces of globalization.[81] The task is to enable 'parallelism among different interpretive worlds'.[82] Mudge wishes to encourage the formation of a 'covenantal coalition of resisters'.[83] In doing so, his targets are those 'traditioned cosmopolitans' – people who are shaped within a distinctive religious tradition but who are also 'full participants in, adaptable, well-connected citizens of the contemporary world'.[84] For, Mudge believes, despite our differences, 'we all bear hermeneutical responsibilities toward one another: to hear accurately and to reply fairly. We are responsible also for the practical consequences of our interpretive work in the worlds we share'.[85]

Comparative ecclesiology and Roger Haight

Although this method also receives its own chapter, I think it is necessary to single out this approach as perhaps embodying the collective fruits of so many of the constructive approaches outlined above and therefore of offering perhaps the most promising way forward of all for ecclesiology in postmodern times. Both comparative theology (e.g. Keith Ward and Francis Clooney) and comparative ecclesiology (Roger Haight) share the same fundamental starting point of not pretending to be utterly objective and neutral but rather remaining comfortable within their own religious and ecclesial traditions, respectively, yet venturing out into the most thoroughgoing dialogue with other faith traditions, ideologies and churches to learn and be enriched not simply by the riches of other traditions and communities, but also to gain in moving towards a deeper understanding of their own tradition and community. They seek to offer an alternative to the neo-exclusivist 'retreat' from modern religious pluralism and religious studies.

Comparative ecclesiology seeks to contrast the differing approaches and merits of ecclesiology that is carried out from starting points described respectively as being from 'Above' and from 'Below'. Suffice to say here that, for its proponents (including, it must be openly acknowledged, the present author, for this chapter itself is but a modest example of this method), comparative ecclesiology offers a most promising basis for the development of that necessary 'ecumenical intercultural hermeneutic'. The comparisons engaged in can prove fruitful whether across a variety of 'synchronic' or 'diachronic' forms. They can be across history, across communion and denomination or even within denomination or, indeed, between differing ecclesiological methodologies or between the visions of the ecclesial authorities and the local church realities. In his three-volume study, the Jesuit scholar Roger Haight, more than anyone else, has helped demonstrate the great promise of this ecclesiological methodology.[86]

Concluding remarks

The US-based Roman Catholic theologian, Paul Lakeland, believes that 'there are, in the end, two and only two ways in which Christian churches can engage with the postmodern world. They can try to convert it to Christ, or they can not'.[87] Neither 'is wholly right'[88] – liberalism can tend towards relativism and yet can affirm uniqueness without resorting to claims of 'superiority or privileged truth'.[89] Forms of evangelicalism tend to 'equate uniqueness with pre-eminence'.[90] Ultimately, just as Christianity can 'enlighten the postmodern sensibility', so, also, has postmodernity 'a lesson for Christianity' – and, if our postmodern age offers so many different ways of being in the world, Christianity reminds us that it is 'important to choose one' – Lakeland recommends that it stops there and hence allows Christians to be joyful in celebrating who and what they are: 'As Christians we can and should engage the world in all its variety of plumage, and rejoice in its multifarious ways of seeing. We should not try to convert it to what it is not.'[91] For Lakeland, 'otherness and difference' are the keys to developing any postmodern ecclesiology. We have sought to explore a range of ecclesiological perspectives along the way of that postmodern spectrum; we conclude with commending the comparative engagement with the world – an engagement that not only acknowledges the reality of pluralism, but celebrates it as God's own creation.

Notes

1 The classic study on the term and the emergence of the era is Jean-François Lyotard, *The Postmodern Condition – A Report on Knowledge*, tr. Régis Durand, Manchester: Manchester University Press, 1984. See, also the appendix to the same volume, 'Answering the Question: What is Postmodern?', and also *The Postmodern Explained*, Minneapolis: University of Minnesota Press, 1992. On the persistence of modernity see, also, Graham Ward, *The Blackwell Companion to Postmodern Theology*, Oxford: Blackwell, 2001, p. xiii.

2 David Tracy, *On Naming the Present: Reflections on God, Hermeneutics and the Church*, Maryknoll, NY: Orbis, 1994.

3 And I have also discussed various approaches to such a task in Gerard Mannion, *Ecclesiology and Postmodernity*, Collegeville: Liturgical Press, 2007, Chapters 1 and 2, pp. 3–40 (and I draw upon elements of this earlier study here).

4 Roger Haight, *Christian Community in History*, New York: Continuum vol. 1 (2004), *Historical Ecclesiology*, p. 57. One of the best and most readable specific studies of postmodernity is by Paul Lakeland, *Postmodernity: Christian Identity in a Fragmented Age*, Minneapolis: Fortress Press, 1997. See also Hugo A. Meynell, *Postmodernism and the New Enlightenment*, Washington DC: Catholic University of America Press, 2000.

5 Here cf., Daniel J. Adams, 'Towards a Theological Understanding of Postmodernism', *Cross Currents* 47/4 (Winter 1997–8) and Mannion, *Ecclesiology and Postmodernity*, Chapter 1, pp. 3–24.

6 Peter C. Hodgson, *Revisioning the Church: ecclesial freedom in the new paradigm*, Philadelphia: Fortress, 1988, pp. 13–16.

7 Adams, 'Towards a Theological Understanding of Postmodernism'.

8 Again, cf. Mannion, *Ecclesiology and Postmodernity*, pp. 3–40.

9 'Classic' postmodern theorists most frequently discussed include Jacques Derrida, Michel Foucault, Richard Rorty, Jean François Lyotard, Jean Baudrillard, Gilles Deluze and Stanley Fish.

10 Typologies described in both Vanhoozer, ed., *Cambridge Companion to Postmodern Theology* and Ward, ed., *Blackwell Companion to Postmodern Theology*. Cf., also, the very helpful discussion in Lakeland, 'Postmodern Thought and Religion', Chapter 2 of his *Postmodernity*, pp. 39–46. See also Terrence W. Tilley *et al.*, *Postmodern Theologies: the challenge of religious diversity*, Maryknoll, NY: Orbis, 1995; David Ray Griffin, William A. Beardslee and Joe Holland, *Varieties of Postmodern Theology*; and Myron B. Penner (ed.), *Christianity and the Postmodern Turn: Six Views*, Grand Rapids, MI: Brazos Press, 2005.

11 See also Chapter 37 of this volume.

12 Cf. Frank Kirkpatrick, *The Ethics of Community*, Oxford: Blackwell, 2001, p. 103.

13 Cf. Mark C. Taylor, *Deconstructing Theology*, New York: Crossroad, 1982; idem, *Erring: A Postmodern A/theology*, Chicago: University of Chicago Press, 1984; and Charles Winquist, *Desiring Theology*, Chicago: University of Chicago Press, 1995 (cf., especially Chapter 10, 'Desiring Community').

14 Tilley *et al.*, *Postmodern Theologies*, p. 42.

15 See Stanley J. Grenz, *The Named God and the Question of Being: a Trinitarian theo-ontology*, Louisville, KY: Westminster John Knox Press, 2005, pp. 120–30.

16 Cf. Carl Raschke, *The Next Reformation: Why Evangelicals Must Embrace Postmodernity*, Grand Rapid, MI: Baker Academic, 2004 and Robert Scharlemann, *The Reason of Following: Christology and the Ecstatic*, Chicago: University of Chicago Press, 1991.

17 With Hans Frei and George Lindbeck being the two pre-eminent theorists, although Daniel Liechty's *Theology in Postliberal Perspective* (London: SCM, 1990) illustrates such diversity well (see especially, pp. 59–72, 'Church without Dogma').

18 James Foder, 'Postliberal Theology', Chapter 14 of David Ford and Rachel Muers (eds), *The Modern Theologians*, 3d edn, Oxford: Blackwell, 2005, p. 230.

19 Ibid., p. 231.

20 George Lindbeck, *The Nature of Doctrine*. Lindbeck's most explicitly ecclesiological work is a collection of essays, *The Church in a Postliberal Age*, ed. James J. Buckley, London: SCM, 2002.

21 'Confession and Communion: An Israel Like View of the Church', *The Christian Century*, 107, no. 16 (1990). See, also, his 'The Church's Mission to Postmodern Culture' in F. Burnham (ed.), *Postmodern Theology: Christian Faith in a Pluralist World*, New York: Harper and Row, 1989.

22 Cf., Daniel W. Hardy, *Finding the Church: the Dynamic Truth of Anglicanism*, London: SCM, 2001 and his earlier *God's Ways with the World: Thinking and Practising Christian Faith*, Edinburgh: T&T Clark, 1996.

23 Kevin J. Vanhoozer, *The Drama of Doctrine*, Louisville, KY: Westminster John Knox Press, 2005.

24 See Chapter 14.

25 Cf. Zygmunt Bauman, 'Postmodern Religion' in *Religion, Modernity and Postmodernity*, ed. Paul Heelas, Oxford: Blackwells, 1998, pp. 55–78. On 'beyond criticism', cf. George Pattison, *A Short Course in the Philosophy of Religion*, London: SCM, 2001 and Paul Lakeland, *Postmodernity*, pp. 70–1.

26 Ward, 'Postmodern Theology' in Ford, 2nd edn, p. 595. See Jean-Luc Marion, *God Without Being: hors-texte*, trans. Thomas A. Carlson, Chicago: University of Chicago Press, 1991.

27 Cf. Michael de Certeau, 'How is Christianity Thinkable Today?', *Theology Digest* 19 (1971), reprinted in Graham Ward (ed.), *The Postmodern God*, pp. 142–55. See Frederick Christian Bauerschmidt, 'Michel de Certeau (1925–86): Introduction' in the same Ward volume, pp. 135–42 and Graham Ward (ed.), *The Certeau Reader*, Oxford, Blackwells, 2000.

28 Seminal texts pertaining to this 'movement' include, John Milbank, *Theology and Social Theory*, Oxford: Blackwell, 1990; John Milbank, Graham Ward, Catherine Pickstock (eds), *Radical Orthodoxy*, London: Routledge, 1999; John Milbank, *The Word Made Strange*, Oxford: Blackwell, 1997; and idem, *Radical Orthodoxy? – A CatholicEnquiry*, ed. Laurence Paul Hemming, Aldershot: Ashgate, 2000.

29 For an excellent overview, see Fergus Kerr, in Lawrence Hemming (ed.) *Radical Orthodoxy: a Catholic Enquiry*. Cf., also James K. A. Smith, *Introducing Radical Orthodoxy*, Grand Rapids MI: Baker Academic, 2004. For further essays of relevance to Radical Orthodoxy and/or John Milbank, cf., the aforementioned volumes edited by Graham Ward, as well as D. Stephen Long, 'Radical Orthodoxy', Chapter 8 of *The Cambridge Companion to Postmodern Theology*, (ed.) Kevin Vanhoozer, Cambridge: Cambridge University Press, 2003.

30 D. Stephen Long, 'Radical Orthodoxy', p. 144.

31 Paul Lakeland, *Postmodernity*, pp. 64–76. See also his *Liberation of the Laity*, New York: Continuum, 2003: on Lindbeck, pp. 88–9, on radical orthodoxy, 232, 244, 249. Postliberalism is also discussed in William C. Placher, 'Postliberal Theology', Chapter 18 of David Ford (ed.), *The Modern Theologians* (2nd edn), Oxford: Blackwell, 1993.

32 Paul Lakeland, *Liberation of the Laity*, pp. 232–3. See also Christopher Insole, 'Against Radical Orthodoxy: the Dangers of Overcoming Political Liberalism', *Modern Theology*. 20:2 (April 2004), 213–41; and also Paul D. Janz, 'Radical Orthodoxy and the New Culture of Obscurantism', *Modern Theology*. 20:3 (July 2004), 363–405. For a particular *ecclesiological* critique of radical orthodoxy and, indeed of 'movements' and ecclesiological positions of a similar kind, see Steven Shakespeare and Hugh Rayment-Pickard, *The Inclusive God: reclaiming theology for an inclusive church*, London: Canterbury Press, 2006; and Steven Shakespeare, *Radical Orthodoxy: A critical introduction*, London, SPCK, 2007.

33 Cf. D. Stephen Long, *The Goodness of God: Theology, Church and the Social Order*, Grand Rapids, MI: Brazos Press, 2001.

34 See also the work of William T. Cavanaugh, e.g. his overview article, 'Church', in William T. Cavanaugh and Peter Scott (eds), *The Blackwell Companion to Political Theology*, Oxford: Blackwell, 2003, pp. 393–406.

35 Long, *The Goodness of God*, p. 18.

36 Lakeland, *Postmodernity*, p. 68.

37 Ibid., pp. 71–2.

38 John Milbank, 'Ecclesiology: The Last of the Last', Chapter 7 of *Being Reconciled: Ontology and Pardon*, London: Routledge, 2003, pp. 105–37.

39 Stanley Hauerwas, *A Better Hope: Resources for a Church Confronting Capitalism, Democracy and Postmodernity*, Grand Rapids, MI: Brazos Press, 2000, p. 38.

40 Cf. Mannion, *Ecclesiology and Postmodernity*, Chapter 9, pp. 192–222.

41 Stanley Hauerwas, *A Better Hope*, p. 37.

42 Indiana: University of Notre Dame Press.

43 Ibid., p. 100.

44 Ibid., p. 101.

45 Especially Phillip Blond's work here, (ed.), *Post-Secular Philosophy: between philosophy and theology*, London: Routledge, 1998.

46 *A Better Hope*, 224, n.11.

47 A supportive account is John B. Thomson, *The Ecclesiology of Stanley Hauerwas*, Aldershot: Ashgate, 2003.

48 Cf., for example, Robin Gill, *Churchgoing and Christian Ethics*, Cambridge: CUP, esp. Chapter 1, pp. 13–38.

49 Roger Haight, 'The Church as Locus of Theology' in *Why Theology?* (*Concilium* 1994/6), pp. 13–22.

50 David Tracy, 'The Uneasy Alliance Reconceived: Catholic Theological Method, Modernity and Postmodernity', *Theological Studies* 50 (1989), 548–70 at 555.

51 David Tracy, 'The Uneasy Alliance Reconceived', 555, n. 27.

52 Cf. here also Richard Lennan, *Risking the Church: the Challenges of Catholic Faith*, Oxford: OUP, 2005 and Eamonn Conway, 'Speaking a Constant Word in a Changing World. Recognising and Resolving Tensions and Tendencies in a Postmodern Context', *New Blackfriars* 87 (March 2006), 110–20.

53 Cf., for example, *Principles of Catholic Theology: Building Stones for a Fundamental Theology* (San Francisco: Ignatius Press, 1982); *The Ratzinger Report: An Exclusive Interview on the State of the Church*, with Vittorio Messori (San Francisco: Ignatius Press, 1983); *Church, Ecumenism and Politics* (Slough: St. Paul's, 1987); *Called to Communion: Understanding the Church Today* (San Francisco: Ignatius Press, 1996); 'A Response to Walter Kasper: The Local Church and the Universal Church', *America* 185 (19 November 2001); *Truth and Tolerance: Christian Belief and World Religions* (San Francisco: Ignatius Press, 2004). See also John Allen, *Pope Benedict XVI*, London: Continuum, 2005; Miroslav Volf, *After Our Likeness: the church in the image of the Trinity*, Grand Rapids, MI: Eerdmans, 1998, pp. 29–123; and Dennis Doyle, *Communion Ecclesiology: Visions and Versions*, Maryknoll, NY: Orbis, 2000.

54 Cf. also Chapters 6 and 13 of this present volume.

55 David S. Dockery, *The Challenge of Postmodernism: an Evangelical Engagement*, Grand Rapids, MI: Baker Academic, 2nd edn, 2001. For a sample of other evangelical engagements with postmodernity, cf. R. T. France, and A. E. McGrath, *Evangelical Anglicans – their Role and Influence in the Church Today*, 1993; A. E. McGrath, *The Future of Christianity*, Oxford: Blackwell, 2002; Owen C. Thomas, 'The Challenge of Postmodernism' in *Anglican Theological Review*. 72/2, 209–19; David Tomlinson, *The Post-Evangelical*, London, SPCK, 1995.

56 Including his classic, *A Primer on Postmodernism*, Grand Rapids, MI: Eerdmans, 1996.

57 Works of particular relevance here include *Created for Community: Connecting Christian Belief with Christian Living*, 2nd edn, Grand Rapids, MI: Baker Books, 1998; *Theology for the Community of God*, Grand Rapids, MI: Eerdmans, 2000; *Revisioning Evangelical Theology: a Fresh Agenda for the 21st Century*, Illinois: InterVarsity, 1993; *Renewing the Center: Evangelical Theology in a Post-Theological Era*, Grand Rapids, MI: Baker Books, 2000; *Theology for the Community of God*, Grand Rapids, MI: Eerdmans, 2000; and *The Social God and the Relational Self: Trinitarian Theology*, Louisville, KY: Westminster John Knox Press, 2001. Two short representative examples of his work are Stanley Grenz, 'Star Trek and the Next Generation: Postmodernism and the Future of Evangelical Theology', Chapter 5 of David S. Dockery, *The Challenge of Postmodernism*, pp. 75–89; and Stanley Grenz, 'Ecclesiology', Chapter 15 of *The Cambridge Companion to Postmodern Theology*, (ed.) Kevin Vanhoozer, Cambridge: Cambridge University Press, 2003, pp. 252–68.

58 Cf. *Revisioning Evangelical Theology*.

59 Summarized in his 'Star Trek and the Next Generation: Postmodernism and the Future of Evangelical Theology', Chapter 5 of David S. Dockery, *Challenge of Postmodernism*, pp. 84–7.

60 Ibid., p. 87.

61 Stanley Grenz, 'Ecclesiology', Chapter 15 of *Cambridge Companion to Postmodern Theology*, (ed.) Kevin Vanhoozer, p. 252.

62 R. Albert Mohler Jr., 'The Integrity of the Evangelical Tradition and the Challenge of the Postmodern Paradigm', Chapter 4 of Dockery, *The Challenge of Postmodernism*, his critique of Grenz being found at pp. 64–7.

63 Ibid., p. 67.

64 Ibid., p. 70.

65 Grenz, 'Ecclesiology', p. 260.
66 The title of Chapter 7 of Stanley Grenz and John R. Franke, *Beyond Foundationalism: Shaping Theology in a Postmodern Context*, Louisville, KY: Westminster John Knox Press, 2001, pp. 203–38.
67 Developed in his now classic study of that name, published in English in 1981.
68 Cf., e.g., Paul Lakeland, *Theology and Critical Theory: the Discourse of the Church*, Nashville: Abingdon, 1990; and Henk de Roest, *Communicative Identity: Habermas' Perspectives of Discourse as a Support for Practical Theology*, Uitgeverij Kok: Kampen, 1998.
69 Cf. *Blessed Rage for Order: The New Pluralism in Theology*. New York: Crossroad, 1975; *The Analogical Imagination: Christian Theology and the Culture of Pluralism*, New York: Crossroad, 1981; *Dialogue with the Other: the Inter-Religious Dialogue*, Leuven: Peeters, 1990; *On Naming the Present: God, Hermeneutics, and Church*. Maryknoll, NY: Orbis Books, 1994.
70 Mannion, 'Hermeneutical Investigations', Chapter 4 of Kenneth Wilson, Paul M. Collins, Gerard Mannion and Gareth Powell, *Christian Community Now*, London: T&T Clark, 2008.
71 See Chapters 15, 16 and 17 of this volume. Two particularly illuminating examples of how insights from several such methodological approaches can be integrated towards constructive ends are by Peter C. Phan, *Being Religious Interreligiously: Asian Perspectives on Interfaith Dialogue*, Maryknoll, NY: Orbis, 2004; and *Christianity with An Asian Face: Asian American Theology in the Making*, Maryknoll, NY: Orbis, 2003.
72 Mary McClintock Fulkerson, 'Feminist Theology', in Vanhoozer, ed., *Cambridge Companion to Postmodern Theology*, pp. 109–10. Cf. also Serene Jones, 'Companionable Wisdoms: What Insight Might Feminist Theorists Gather from Feminist Theologians?' in Ward, ed., *Blackwell Companion to Postmodern Theology*, pp. 294–308; and also her *Feminist Theory and Christian Theology: Cartographies of Grace*, Minneapolis: Fortress Press, 2000.
73 See her *Changing the Subject: Women's Discourses and Feminist Theology*, Minneapolis: Fortress Press, 1994.
74 Mary McClintock Fulkerson '"They Will Know We Are Christians by Our Regulated Improvisation": Ecclesial Hybridity and the Unity of the Church' in Ward, ed., *Blackwell Companion to Postmodern Theology*, p. 277.
75 Ibid., p. 267.
76 Cf., Lewis Mudge, 'Thinking in the Community of Faith: Toward an Ecclesial hermeneutic', Chapter 6 of Lewis S. Mudge and James N. Poling (eds), *Formation and Reflection: The Promise of Practical Theology*, Philadelphia: Fortress Press, 1987; *The Sense of a People: Toward a Church for the Human Future*, Philadelphia: Trinity Press International, 1992; *The Church as Moral Community: Ecclesiology and Ethics in Ecumenical Debate*, Geneva: WCC Publications, 1998; *Rethinking the Beloved Community: Ecclesiology, Hermeneutics, Social Theory*, Geneva: WCC Publications and University Press of America, 2001; Lewis Mudge, 'Ecclesiology and Ethics in Current Ecumenical Debate', *The Ecumenical Review*, 48 (Jan. 1996), 11–27; and also his 'Towards a Hermeneutic of the Household: "Ecclesiology and Ethics" after Harare', *The Ecumenical Review*, 51 (July 1999), 243–55. See also his forthcoming book on *The Gift of Responsibility: the Promise of Dialogue Among Christians, Jews, and Muslims*, New York: Continuum, 2007.
77 See Gerard Mannion, 'What's In a Name? Hermeneutical Questions on "Globalisation", Catholicity and Ecumenism', *New Blackfriars* (March 2005), 204–15, for a discussion of Mudge's work, alongside other recent treatments of ecclesial hermeneutics, particularly in relation to the challenges posed to the church by globalization. Also of relevance here are the works of Robert J. Schreiter, cf., *The New Catholicity: Theology Between the Global and the Local*, Maryknoll, NY: Orbis, 1997; and *Constructing Local Theologies*, Maryknoll, NY: Orbis, 1985.
78 Lewis Mudge, 'Towards a Hermeneutic of the Household: "Ecclesiology and Ethics" after Harare', *The Ecumenical Review*, 51 (July 1999), 252. His thinking in this paper was developed in his later *Rethinking the Beloved Community*.
79 Ibid.
80 Ibid., 247–48 (my italics).
81 Lewis Mudge, *The Gift of Responsibility*, 'Foreword' (forthcoming).
82 Ibid.
83 Mudge, 'Covenanting for a Renewing of Our Minds: a Way Together for the Abrahamic Faiths', Chapter 8 of Julio De Santa Ana, Robin Gurney and Heidi Hadsell (eds), *Beyond Idealism: a Way Ahead for Ecumenical Social Ethics*, Grand Rapids, MI: Eerdmans, 2006, pp.163–208.

84 Ibid.

85 Ibid.

86 Roger Haight, *Christian Community in History*, New York: Continuum, 2004 and 2007, vol. 1, *Historical Ecclesiology*, vol. 2, *Comparative Ecclesiology*, vol. 3 *Ecclesial Existence*, 2008. See Chapter 21 of the present volume and cf. also Mannion, *Ecclesiology and Postmodernity*, esp. Chapters 2 (pp. 25–40), 6 (pp. 124–50) and 7 (pp. 151–72).

87 Lakeland, *Postmodernity*, p. 112.

88 Ibid., p. 113.

89 Ibid.

90 Ibid. Though we have noted Grenz proposes a very different way forward for Evangelicals.

91 Ibid.

Further reading

Gregory Baum, *Amazing Church: A Catholic Theologian Remembers a Half Century of Change*, Maryknoll, NY: Orbis, 2005.

John Drane, *The MacDonaldsization of the Church*, London: Darton Longman and Todd, 2000.

Paul Lakeland, *Postmodernity: Christian Identity in a Fragmented Age*, Minneapolis: Fortress Press, 1997.

Richard Lennan, *Risking the Church: the Challenges of Catholic Faith*, Oxford: OUP, 2005.

Gerard Mannion, *Ecclesiology and Postmodernity: Questions for the Church in Our Time*, Collegeville: Liturgical Press, 2007.

Mary McClintock Fulkerson, *Changing the Subject: Women's Discourses and Feminist Theology*, Minneapolis: Fortress Press, 1994.

Myron B. Penner (ed.), *Christianity and the Postmodern Turn: Six Views*, Grand Rapids, MI: Brazos Press, 2005.

Carl Raschke, *The Next Reformation: Why Evangelicals Must Embrace Postmodernity*, Grand Rapids, MI: Baker Academic, 2004.

David Tracy, *On Naming the Present: Reflections on God, Hermeneutics and the Church*, Maryknoll, NY: Orbis, 1994.

Miroslav Volf and William H. Katerberg (eds), *The Future of Hope: Christian Tradition amid Modernity and Postmodernity*, Grand Rapids,MI: Eerdmans, 2004.

Part II

ECCLESIOLOGICAL 'TRADITIONS'

8

ECCLESIOLOGY IN THE
ORTHODOX TRADITION

Kondothra M. George

Orthodox theological literature on ecclesiology is not very prolific in comparison with certain other traditions. This is not because *ecclesia* and its study are of minor importance in the Orthodox tradition. In fact, on the contrary, the theme of the Church so pervades all aspects of Orthodox theological reflection and liturgical–spiritual orientation that it is extremely difficult to treat it as an isolated subject. This relative reluctance to deal with ecclesiology as an academic topic is inherited from the Eastern patristic tradition which quietly assumes the living reality of the Church and the ecclesial experience as constituting the very matrix of all theological thinking and spiritual practice. It should also be admitted that there is an element of resistance in traditional Orthodox ethos to the neat academic distinctions and specializations like ecclesiology, christology, pneumatology and so on as detrimental to the holistic and integral character of theology.

In modern times, however, especially within the framework of the twentieth-century ecumenical movement, and the diaspora situation, where the Orthodox churches encountered at close quarters the Western Christian traditions – Roman Catholic, Anglican and Protestant – efforts have been made by Orthodox theologians to articulate their 'ecclesiology' in terms of academic and ecumenical requirements. The involvement of the Orthodox churches in the World Council of Churches (WCC), especially its Faith and Order Commission, created an ecclesiological self-awareness among the Orthodox that led to some substantial Orthodox reflection on the Church, and its nature and mission.

Two families of churches

In the WCC the Orthodox churches are grouped into two families – the Eastern and the Oriental. It was in the twentieth-century ecumenical context that the expressions 'Eastern' and 'Oriental' were routinely used to distinguish these two families.[1] 'Eastern' refers to the family of churches in the Byzantine liturgical tradition in communion with the see of Constantinople (Ecumenical Patriarchate), like the churches of Greece, Russia, Rumania, Bulgaria and so on. These are the Orthodox churches which accept the seven Ecumenical Councils as of fundamental doctrinal and canonical importance. They share the same liturgical texts and practices. Sometimes these churches are referred to by the other family of Oriental Orthodox churches as the Chalcedonian Orthodox since the Council of Chalcedon in 451, the fourth ecumenical council for the Eastern Orthodox, was the point of separation for the Oriental Orthodox.

The other family, namely the Oriental Orthodox, consists of the Armenian, the Coptic, the Ethiopian, the Indian (Malankara) and the Syrian churches. Very recently, in the aftermath of the political division between Ethiopia and Eritrea, a separate church called the Eritrean Orthodox Church, formerly part of the Ethiopian Orthodox Church, was created.

The main conflict was in the area of christology – how the divine and the human natures are united in the person of Jesus Christ. However, strong political, cultural and social factors also played a part. The differences resulted in the breach of communion between these two Eastern families which, in spite of separation, maintain to this day a remarkable unity in theological approach, liturgical–spiritual ethos and general church discipline.[2]

The christological differences between these two families were resolved in a series of unofficial and official dialogues between the two families since 1967. Both families now acknowledge each other as holding the same apostolic faith in spite of the christological misunderstandings in the distant past. What is interesting to us is that these two families, though separated for about 1500 years since Chalcedon, maintained the same ecclesiology. In spite of the christological disputes around the Chalcedonian definition the Oriental Orthodox have accepted the disciplinary canons of Chalcedon that pertained to ecclesiological issues.

As the result of the unofficial dialogue, a consensus emerged. Both sides could affirm together 'the common tradition of the one church in all important matters – liturgy and spirituality, doctrine and canonical practice, in our understanding of the Holy Trinity, of the incarnation, of the person and work of the Holy Spirit, on the nature of the Church as the communion of saints with its ministry and sacraments, and on the life of the world to come when our Lord and Saviour shall come in all his glory' (Geneva, 1970).

The official dialogue confirmed this (Egypt, 1989):

> We have inherited from our fathers in Christ the one apostolic faith and tradition, though as churches we have been separated from each other for centuries. As two families of Orthodox Churches long out of communion with each other, we now pray and trust in God to restore that communion on the basis of the apostolic faith of the undivided Church of the first centuries which we confess in our common creed.

In all matters related to issues with ecclesiological implications in the WCC and the modern ecumenical movement in general, both families maintain the same position. The issue of ecclesiology was behind the creation in 1998 of the Special Commission on Orthodox Participation in the WCC and the changes that resulted from the Commission's work with regard to the self-understating, style and perspective of the WCC.[3]

This became possible largely because of the solidarity of the two families of Orthodox churches and their common ground and shared perspective in ecclesiology as the key issue in ecumenism.

At this point it is useful to distinguish between ecclesiology proper, that is, the theological study of the nature and purpose of the church and the study of canonical–structural issues related to the institution of the church and its historical expansion. There are, of course, points where these two areas intersect or overlap. Still, the distinction is necessary because, on the fundamental biblical-patristic-liturgical theology of the church, there is profound consensual agreement within the whole of the Orthodox tradition, while on questions such as, for example, jurisdiction over the modern diaspora, the relationship between patriarchal sees etc, there can be differences of opinion or even disputes. This latter dimension of ecclesiastical–canonical–institutional matters, which can have ecclesiological implications, arose over the course of centuries, especially in relation to the political–imperial structure of the Byzantine empire.

Sources

The sources of Orthodox ecclesiology are the Holy Scripture, the liturgical texts and practices, the writings of the Fathers of the church and the decisions of the ecumenical councils. In fact, they are one unified source. The biblical texts as interpreted by the teachers and Fathers of the church bring out a vast array of poetic and aesthetic images of the church ranging from Noah's ark in the Book of Genesis to the resplendent bridal image of the church as the new Jerusalem in the Book of Revelation. Instead of going for a prosaic and propositional theology about the church, these images and allusions, evoked by the rich typological, allegorical and metaphorical interpretation of the Fathers, create the contours of a church that easily transcends the structures of an earthly institution. The idea of the church never remains at the level of the abstract intellect, but is celebrated and experienced in the liturgy. The deliberations and decisions of the ecumenical councils are informed by the biblical-liturgical hermeneutic of the eminent teachers of the church. In turn the councils influence the doctrinal–canonical elements of the church. Hence the inter-related sources of Orthodox ecclesiology act as one single source.

Images of the church

Orthodox liturgical texts are teeming with poetic images and figures of speech for the church, all derived directly or indirectly from the Bible. The church is personified as mother of the faithful and bride of Christ, and the third person feminine pronoun 'she', rather than the neuter 'it', is consistently applied to the church in Orthodox theology, hymnology and prayers.

On many an occasion the Holy Virgin Mary stands as a symbol of the church (Rev 12.1). In Orthodox iconography of Pentecost, for instance, the Virgin Mary remains at the centre of the picture surrounded by the Apostles. Obviously she symbolizes the church. The newly baptized are said to be born from the womb of the Mother Church. The maternal image of the church is deep rooted in the liturgical piety of the Orthodox. The Orthodox tradition is averse to a merely sociological understanding of the church as a community of believers.

Among the numerous biblical images for the church in the Old and New Testaments, some are particularly important to Orthodox ecclesiology. Three of them may be mentioned here because they are more frequently used in liturgical texts and hymnology:

The church as the body of Christ

The organic image of a living body symbolizes the body of the believing community in the writings of the Apostle Paul. He takes the human body as the central metaphor (Rom 12.4–5; 1 Cor 12; Eph 4.12; Col 1.24). The one body has many limbs, yet the limbs do not all have the same function. So we, though many, are one body in Christ. We are to relate to each other as limbs of the same body.

In the letters to the Ephesians and Colossians Paul develops the idea of the church as the body of Christ. The organic image implies dynamic growth and interconnectedness within the body. Since Christ is the head, the body constantly grows in the practice of love and truth to the fullness of Christ. (Eph 4.13–16). We are called to be one body and therefore we need to exercise compassion, humility, forgiveness and love to each other, and experience the peace of Christ as one single body (Col 3.12–15). The head and body are interdependent on each other not in a mechanistic way but in a vitally organic way. Christ needs the church as his body, and the church needs Christ as its head (Eph 1.23). The ethical task of the church in the world follows from this body–head relationship. The church acts in history, not simply as a socially committed group of people or a charitable organization determined to do good to fellow human beings, but as the continuation of the incarnation of Christ.

It is the very life of the body that responds to the *love* of Christ its head that is manifested as the church's ethical, pastoral and ultimately salvific concern for the world. The 'church, which is his body, the fullness (*plerōma*) of him who fills all in all' (Eph 1.23) is not simply a means or instrument for Christ to carry out his mission in the world. It is the very presence of the plerōma of Christ.

Paul says that his sufferings for the sake of his fellow Christians are completing in his flesh 'what is lacking in Christ's afflictions for the sake of his body, that is, the church' (Col 1.24).

The church as the living temple

This image is very similar to that of the body in the sense that the temple is conceived as a living organism that pulsates with life, and not a dead material construction in stone and wood. Christ himself is the cornerstone; the apostles and prophets are the foundation; believers are living stones that add to the growth of the building. Foundation and building blocks are all fitted together in a harmonious way, and the whole edifice grows as one body.

This living and ever-growing temple indwelt by the Spirit of God symbolizing the church stands also for the whole created universe. The worship offered in this living temple is the worship of the triune God by the whole creation. On the occasion of the consecration of new church buildings, the Orthodox liturgical texts evoke this connection between the church as the living temple bringing together the whole created order, both earthly and heavenly to worship the Creator God (Eph 2.20–22; 1 Pet 2.4–5).

The church as the bride of Christ

The personified feminine figure of the church is reinforced by the metaphor of the bride. The mystery of deep communion between Christ and his bride is evoked by Paul in relation to the marital bond between husband and wife. Christ's love for his church and the church's loving response to him constitute the basis for the one body. As in the case of the body and the living temple, the bride image is a dynamically organic one and the union of the bride and the bridegroom to the point of making one single body is evocative of the ultimate oneness between Christ and his church without, however, denying their separate existence. The bride is being prepared by Christ for the final presentation at the wedding.

Several points of interest for Orthodox ecclesiology emerge from these metaphors, which are more than simple decorative figures of speech according to the Orthodox perception.

Being rather than doing   Orthodox ecclesiology is less amenable to the instrumentalist language for the church commonly used in the Western Protestant tradition. The church is not Christ's instrument to do things in the world, but his body that carries the very presence of Christ in a visible sacramental way. This does not exclude the church's doing things in the world for Christ and on behalf of Christ. Although here, of course, we are dealing in generalizations somewhat, the Orthodox tradition perceives such instrumentalist language, however useful, to be somewhat cold and detached. An instrument has no organic relationship with its owner-user. My hands, for instance, are useful for the whole body to perform certain functions which other limbs are not able to perform. But the hands are not called instruments of the body; they are the body itself, extended in a particular way, and not a detached mechanical or instrumental device. An underlying and usually unacknowledged aspect of the constant ecclesiological struggle in the fellowship of the World Council of Churches between the Orthodox and the Protestant traditions is precisely this. While the instrumentalist view of the church makes a list of political, economic and ethical things the church should *do*, the organic or 'somatic' view is more inclined to affirm the being of the church, 'her' presence in the world as the living body of Christ witnessing to and worshipping the triune God, and interceding for the world through Christ the mediator. The former view can be sharply critical of the church for not carrying out its function as an instrument of Christ. This is generally perceived as having the advantage of efficiency, moral vigilance, ethical sensitivity and relevance to context, though sometimes it can also lead to moralistic and legalistic positions. The latter view usually refrains from criticizing the church, because she is the 'holy mother church', the body of Christ. It is deeply concerned about the world and its salvation, but not particularly anxious to issue statements on every problem in the world by name, and not very eager to leave its age-old liturgies and spiritual practices for the sake of being 'prophetic' and 'missionary' to the passing phases of society. Here the concepts of mission and salvation are different. It appears to be ethically indifferent and rather anachronistic. None of the three images referred to – body, living temple, bride – can be an instrument in the mechanistic, manipulative and operational sense.

Growth is a process   All three images imply growth or an evolutionary process. The body is growing to the fullness of the head; the living temple never ceases to grow since the believers constantly add to it as new building blocks; the bride is being prepared for the eschatological nuptial moment, to stand before the bridegroom 'without spot or wrinkle'. The process implicit here begins in history, but transcends the space-time limits for eschatological realization. This view contradicts any notion of the church as a merely historical sociological entity that completes its evolutionary growing process in the world itself. The church's growth as the divine–human reality transcends history.

Four marks of the church

For the Orthodox tradition, the Nicene-Constantinopolitan creed formulated by the first two Ecumenical Councils, namely Nicaea in 325 and Constantinople in 381, is a unique summary statement of Christian faith. The patristic consensus, soon after the formulation of the creed and also later, was that no more creeds or confessions of faith were necessary. The Fathers of the church resisted all attempts to add to the minimum credal statement which was drawn up in an extreme situation of serious threat to the fundamental faith of the church.

The Nicene-Constantinopolitan creed attaches four adjectives to the church: one, holy, catholic and apostolic. They have become the principal notes or marks of the undivided church of Christ. All Orthodox ecclesiology can be understood as a commentary on these four marks. These attributes were articulated in the context of doctrinal disputes that threatened to divide the one church. In a situation of division, both sides claim to be the true church. The Donatist controversy in North Africa and the Arian and Eunomian disputes in the fourth century are early examples of such division and parallel claims.

Unity

The visible unity of the body of Christ is upheld by the Orthodox tradition as a fundamental principle of Christian faith. In the Orthodox liturgical texts, the 'seamless tunic' of Christ (Jn 19.23–24) became a key symbol, as used by St Cyprian of Carthage, for the indivisibility of the church. Recognizing the sad divisions that occurred in the one body, the Orthodox church in its liturgical practice prays regularly for the 'unity of all Christians'. More will be said about this later.

Holiness

Holiness of the church belongs to the fundamental ecclesiological understanding of the Orthodox tradition. The church is holy as the body and bride of Christ and as the living temple of the Spirit. As these images show, it is the vital and integral relation of the church with Christ, the Holy One of God, that makes the church holy. The Holy Spirit of God is the animating and sanctifying Spirit of the church; the church constantly calls upon the Spirit – the *epiclesis* or invocation of the Spirit being not simply a liturgical ritual, but vital breathing of the church. The Spirit-filled community is thus rendered holy and becomes the source of sanctifying grace.

The question of the sinfulness of the members of the church is often raised in this connection. In spite of the sins of lay persons or clergy who are members of the church, the Orthodox tradition would never admit that the church is sinful. Members who sin can repent. In fact, it is the mother church, as the liturgical texts indicate, which gathers her children for repentance, individually and collectively. They make their confession to the church also, and it is the church that transmits the forgiveness of Christ to the repentant sinner through her ministers. There may be occasions when the historical community of Christians is found to be sinful, like for example being in alliance with an oppressive dictatorial regime. But here again the onus of repentance and conversion (*metanoia*) falls on those members of the community, and not the church, the Body of Christ.

There is a close connection between unity and holiness of the church.[4] Unity is perfection in classical Greek philosophy. Unalloyed simplicity stands for the indivisibility of an entity; purity or holiness is associated with the simple and incomposite nature of things. However, as we see in Orthodox ecclesiology, diversity or the 'Many' appears simultaneously with the One.

Returning to the question of unity, the Orthodox tradition depends on a number of elements for ensuring and expressing the precious oneness of the body.

The local church The three-fold ministry of *episcopos*, *presbyteros* and *diakonos* underscores the basic ministerial structure of a local church. This order of ministry is *within* the ecclesia, the body of Christ, and is at the service of the ecclesia, the people of God. The ministers are understood to be called by the Holy Spirit, and elected and appointed to their respective offices by the whole worshipping community, i.e. the people of God, through an ordination service in the context of eucharistic celebration. The authority they are entrusted with is the authority of service (cf. Mk 10.43–45) and depends on the totality of the body of Christ. In a given local church the bishop (*episcopos*)[5] is the focus and guardian of unity. He is the sacramental presence of Christ in the midst of the believing community and gathers the community to celebrate the eucharist in one apostolic faith and love. The eucharistic assembly presided over by the bishop together with the clergy and the people in faith, hope and love symbolizes the unity of the church of Christ.

This is essentially the structure of a local church in its simplest form. But the word 'local' can be flexible, from parish level to a nation. In the Orthodox tradition today it may generally mean a *nation* with common ethnic roots, a large cultural grouping with the same linguistic and cultural heritage or a geographically distinct area like an island. Ecclesiologically the expression local church often refers to a regional church. The present autocephalous churches in the Eastern tradition are called local churches. The concept of the local church provides one of the fundamental constitutive elements of Orthodox ecclesiology, Orthodox eucharistic theology requires that all ethnic, socio-cultural, linguistic and gender divisions be overcome in the eucharistic assembly in order to manifest the unity of the one body of Christ.

The Church Catholic In the Orthodox tradition the Church is simultaneously local and universal. The word 'catholic' (from Greek *kata holon* – pertaining to the whole, holistic) is an essential attribute of the Church at least from the early second century onwards (Ignatius of Antioch). Originally it did not have the geographical connotation of a Church that was spread over the whole earth. The early Fathers before Constantine obviously knew the numerical-geographical limits of the church. So the word *catholic* was used more in a qualitative than in a quantitative sense. With Cyril of Jerusalem in the fourth century, we see geographical extension as an element of catholicity. Whenever the Greek word *katholike* is translated as *universalis* in the Latin tradition it seems the emphasis is on the geographical, quantitative dimension because of the self-understanding of the Roman Catholic church as the universal Church ever since the colonial expansion of the West into the rest of the world. The expression *Church Catholic* is used by some Orthodox theologians in order to distinguish it from the (Roman) Catholic church. The Orthodox church also sometimes calls itself the 'Orthodox Catholic Church'.

The question arises as to how the unity of the body of Christ is expressed at the global or universal level. Although the local church expresses the catholicity of the church of Christ at its eucharistic assembly, it also knows that it does so only in communion with other local churches and not exclusively or in separation from others. The traditional Eastern Orthodox answer to the question of universal expression of the unity of the Church Catholic points to the ecumenical synods. Ecumenical synods or universal councils are gatherings of the heads/ representatives of local churches for deliberations and consensual decisions on matters of faith or canonical discipline that affect the whole church. Since they are understood to be convened in the context of the celebration of the one eucharist in the same apostolic faith and love, the ecumenical councils express the unity of the Body of Christ, the Church Catholic. The Orthodox tradition rejects the necessity of any universal administrative/juris-dictional structure or one single universal head for the whole church in order to express the unity and catholicity of the church. It also rejects any idea of independent congregation-alism or the notion of invisible, spiritual unity as adequate.

It may be noted that the ecumenical synods are not regular events or part of the perma-nent structure of the church. As is shown by the past, there are only seven ecumenical coun-cils in the history of the Eastern Orthodox tradition, the last one being held in 787, and only three in the Oriental Orthodox heritage. Eastern Orthodox preparations have been under way since the 1960s for a 'great, and holy council', the proposed 8th ecumenical council in the Eastern Orthodox tradition.

Oriental Orthodox theologians like Paulos Mar Gregorios, who acknowledge the signifi-cance of the ecumenical councils for expressing the unity and conciliarity of the Church Catholic, holds, on the basis of historical experience, that they are not necessary in order to maintain the communion within the Orthodox tradition. He points out that the churches in the Oriental Orthodox family remained in communion with each other despite the fact that some 15 centuries have elapsed since the last ecumenical council in their tradition (namely Ephesus 431), was held. It is the same with the Eastern Orthodox family since the eighth century. In the Western church also, 'ecumenical councils' never happened at regular intervals; sometimes the intervals varied from 16 years to 353 years.[6]

Conciliarity and communion

Conciliarity and communion belong to the core of Orthodox ecclesiology. Both concepts have been placed at the centre of the ecumenical movement as it seeks the unity of divided Christians. For the sake of brevity and clarity we will present some aspects of the views of two prominent and well-respected contemporary Orthodox theologians, one from the Oriental Orthodox family, namely Paulos Mar Gregorios, and the other from the Eastern Orthodox family, namely John (Zizioulas) of Pergamon. Both Metropolitan Paulos Mar Gregorios of New Delhi (Indian Orthodox Church) and Metropolitan John of Pergamon (Greek Orthodox Church) fully agree on the crucial importance of these two themes.

Mar Gregorios traces the origin of the idea of council, from which comes the word concil-iarity, to the Hebrew biblical *sod*, the secret, select assembly with administrative authority or intention to plan an action (Ps 55.14, 83.8). Its Aramaic equivalent is *raz*, a Persian loan word (council, mystery) which was translated in the New Testament as *mysterion* (mystery) and not *sunodos* (synod). In this connection he also considers the New Testament word *Koinonia* or communion. The New Testament speaks about the union between God and humanity in a bold way. This is understood to be the mystery of the union between God and human beings in the Spirit. It is in the mystery of the eucharist that this union is expressed. According to Mar Gregorios, we share in the mystery-council character of the Body of Christ. What we call council (*synod*) in the church is only one expression of this sharing. It does not exhaust the mystery.

Since the church is conciliar by its very nature, conciliarity is not confined to the formal councils of the church. It pervades all aspects of the life of the church. The Russian word *sobornost* used in this connection would mean something like 'council-ness' of the church. Gregorios points out some aspects of conciliarity as understood in the Orthodox ecclesiology:

- Communion in mutual love.
- Communion in the Spirit with God and with each other expressed in the Holy Eucharist.
- A sharing of each other's sufferings, needs and resources.
- A conciliar pattern of leadership such as is envisaged in the college of presbyters presided over by a bishop and assisted by deacons and people.
- Regular conciliar gatherings at various levels. Gregorios thinks that we cannot bring about unity by developing new conciliar structures. What we need to develop is the quality of love and wisdom, humility, faith and true hope within each church and between churches. Conciliarity is love in the truth with faith and hope. The real unity is eschatological, and conciliarity belongs to the eschatological fullness of the church. In the historical realm, this is only partially fulfilled.

As to the question of *communio* between the local churches, it is clear that 'no local church exists except in communion with the one Body of Christ with which other local churches are also in communion'.[7] Gregorios, however, admits that no pattern in existence at present can adequately express the communion between local churches because of divisions in the Church. He points out some of the essential signs of *communio* as follows:

- The eucharist is the primary expression of communio between the local churches. We not only remember each other in the eucharist, but in our communion in the Body of Christ we have communion with all other local churches.
- The communion of the bishops is an expression of the *communio* between the local churches. This can happen in the synods of bishops within and between the local churches. This sign is less essential and indispensable than the eucharist.
- Although the universal councils or ecumenical synods can be useful and beneficial, historically they have never achieved the *communio* of all local churches. They were more imperial than universal. The churches of Georgia, Armenia, Parthia, India, Nubia, and Ethiopia, ancient Christian communities that flourished outside the Roman Empire, do not appear to have participated in the universal councils. It does not appear that universal councils are necessary or essential signs of communion.
- Agreement upon tradition is an essential sign and the basis for *communio* between the local churches. The concord of bishops also depends on this agreement upon tradition.
- The Oriental Orthodox tradition resolutely holds to the view that no one bishop can be the visible principle of unity for the Church Catholic, though it appears that a supreme pontiff with a universal jurisdiction would be a pragmatically desirable and useful sign of *communio* between the local churches.
- Love and trust are above all the essential requirements of *communio* between the local churches.

In line with the general Orthodox understanding, John of Pergamon (Zizioulas) also begins his ecclesiological reflections with the mystery of the church. Even in its institutional dimension, the mystery of the church is inextricably bound to the being of humanity, of the world and the very being of God.[8] In his search for a truly Christian basis for ecclesiology, he examines the ontology of truth or the question of the being of God in ancient Greek philosophy as well as in the Christian patristic tradition.

Patristic thought, says Zizioulas, was highly critical of the classical Greek ontology which was fundamentally monistic. That is to say, the being of God and the being of the world formed an unbreakable unity for the ancient Greeks. The Platonic notion of the creator God presupposed the idea of creation from pre-existing matter. This, according to the Fathers, limited the freedom of God. The patristic thought, therefore, steered clear of both the Greek monism and the unbridgeable 'gulf' between God and the world taught by early Gnostic systems. The ecclesial experience of the Fathers, especially its heart, the eucharistic experience of the church, led them to the conviction that the being of God could be known only through personal relationship and personal love. This notion of the being of God as relational and experienced in life and love leads us to the concept of *communion*. Holy Trinity, or God as communion, is a primordial ontological concept, and not a notion later added to the one 'substance' of God.

The key to *koinonia* or *communio*, central to Zizioulas's ecclesiological reflection, lies in the eucharist that brings together the being of God and the ecclesial being, eschatology and history in their dialectical relationship. All ordinations to the fundamental ministries of the church take place within the eucharistic celebration. The eucharist as the event of communion constantly *constitutes* the church. The usual polarization between institution and event is overcome in the eucharistic community that the Spirit continually constitutes afresh.

Zizioulas, while devoted to eucharistic ecclesiology as central to Orthodox understanding, is critical of the way Nicholas Afanasiev, a modern Orthodox theologian, developed his well-known thesis on 'eucharistic ecclesiology'. Afanasiev's ecclesiology is built on the principle 'wherever the eucharist is, there is the Church'. Zizioulas finds two basic errors in this view: first, even the parish becomes complete in itself as the Church Catholic, since the eucharist is celebrated there. Second, the balance between the local church and the universal church is upset, implying that each local church could, independently of other local churches, be the 'one, holy, catholic and apostolic church'.[9] Zizioulas thinks that a proper understanding of the eucharist itself will guide us in recognizing simultaneously the local and universal dimensions of the mystery of the church. Orthodox ecclesiology, according to Zizioulas, is derived from the very being of the triune God who is *koinonia*, communion of persons. Since the nature of God is communion, it can be applied to the church as *koinonia*. 'There is only one Church as there is one God. But the expression of this one Church is the communion of the many local Churches. Communion and oneness coincide in ecclesiology.'[10]

Zizioulas places a decisive emphasis on a synthesis of pneumatology, christology and ecclesiology. Pneumatology, the study of the person and work of the Holy Spirit, must be made constitutive of the very being of Christ and the church. Eschatology and communion are the two major ingredients of pneumatology. His accent on eschatology is due to the perception that history is never a sufficient justification for the existence of any ecclesial institution. The Holy Spirit points *beyond* history. It is at this border point between history and eschatology that ecclesial institutions become sacramental. They are placed in the dialectic between the already and the not yet, between history and eschatology. Ecclesial institutions thus exist here, not in a self-sufficient way, but *epicletically*, that is on account of the continual calling upon the Spirit (*epiclesis* or invocation of the Holy Spirit in eucharistic liturgy). Since the Holy Spirit constantly constitutes the church in view of its eschatological fulfilment, all pyramidal notions in ecclesiology disappear. The One and the Many co-exist as two aspects of the same being.

The synodal character of the church and the nature of ministry are inter-related. To

Zizioulas, Canon 34 of the so-called *Apostolic Canons* seems to provide the true significance of the synod or council in the Orthodox tradition.[11] There are two principles involved in it:

- That in every province there must be *one* head – an institution of unity. The local bishops and churches can do nothing without the presence of this *one*.
- That the 'one' cannot do anything without the 'many'.

There are several ecclesiological–canonical implications for this indispensable mutuality between the one and the many. For example, both the ordination of the bishop, which requires the community, and the ordination of the laity (baptism) or of any other minister, which requires the presence of the bishop, take place in the context of the eucharist. The eucharist is characterized by its eschatological dimension of the Kingdom of God. The ecclesial institutions, being reflections of the kingdom in the context of the eschatologically oriented eucharist, are *iconic*. That is to say, their being does not lie in themselves, but in God or Christ, and their justification is by reference to something ultimate, and not simply to historical expedience.[12]

The apostolic church

The adjective 'apostolic' has multiple meanings in the Orthodox tradition.

Continuing the witness of the apostles to Jesus Christ crucified and risen is a fundamental characteristic and calling of the apostolic church. The post-ascension scene in Jerusalem where the apostles 'with one accord devoted themselves to prayer, together with the women and Mary the mother of Jesus, and with his brothers' (Acts 1:14), is celebrated in Orthodox iconography and theology as a paradigm of the apostolic church. The event of Pentecost happened in this gathering. This is the worshipping community that gathered in the name of the risen Christ and received the power of the Holy Spirit as promised by Christ to witness to him to the ends of the earth. This is the sharing community which celebrated the eucharist and shared food and other material resources with glad and generous hearts (Acts 2.46–47). The church that is apostolic in all ages and all places is in continuity with this community and participates in the apostolic experience of Christ.

Announcing the gospel of the kingdom to the poor, healing the sick and liberating the oppressed are tasks of the apostolic church. The missionary and social–ethical dimension of apostolicity (from the word *apostolos* = sent out) is not always consistently clear in the history of the Orthodox churches. In modern times the Orthodox communities attempt to revive this essential aspect of the apostolic church.[13]

Apostolic succession is usually understood, especially in the West, as linear succession of the authority and ministry of the apostles passed on individually to the successive generations of bishops. Orthodox theologians in general favour the corporate continuity of eucharistic communities rather than individual handing over as the essence of apostolic succession (Zizioulas, Gregorios) Both models are present in the church due to different patristic perspectives (Ignatius of Antioch, Cyprian of Carthage, Irenaeus of Lyons). In general, Orthodox theology holds to the position that apostles are not simply sent out as individual missionaries, but they constitute the apostolic college around Christ wherever they are. It is not simply a historical mission, it also signifies the eschatological gathering of all in the Kingdom of God (Zizioulas).

The christological image of episcopacy is changed in the individual–missionary model. In the Ignatian model, the bishop stands in the place of Christ or God, surrounded by the college of presbyters and deacons and the people. In the model of Cyprian, Christ is replaced by Peter, and every bishop becomes *alter apostolus* (Peter) occupying the *cathedra Petri* instead of *alter Christus*. This is a deviation from the Orthodox understanding of apostolic succession.[14]

Some present-day concerns

The patriarchates

The thought-world and frame of reference of Orthodox ecclesiology remains attached largely to the time of 'the undivided church' and the political 'oikoumene', that is, the Roman/Byzantine Empire. For example, the inter-patriarchal relations and jurisdictional questions of *Pentarchy*, the concept of the five patriarchates – Rome, Constantinople, Alexandria, Antioch and Jerusalem – ruling over the 'whole church', belong to the imperial structure. They are positions and centres of power once created in an imperial church in order to match the imperial political power structure in the Roman Empire. Hence the expressions Old Rome, New Rome, Third Rome and so on to indicate the shift of ecclesiastical power from Rome, the old capital of the Roman Empire, to Constantinople the new capital, and then, after the fall of Constantinople to the Turks, the claim of the Russian Orthodox Church for Moscow to be the third Rome in terms of power. Many Orthodox themselves would ask if these political considerations of the past have any meaning for the truly Orthodox understanding of the nature and mission of the church. Many would consider it as a political superstructure imposed on the Christian church. The ecclesiastical leadership of the Roman Empire whose borders claimed to be coterminous with 'the whole inhabited earth' (*Oikoumene*) never took seriously the flourishing of the Christian churches outside the imperial borders. One of the issues that fomented the Chalcedonian division in the fifth century between the Byzantine Orthodox (allied then with the Latins) and the Oriental Orthodox was precisely the political-cultural-linguistic insensitivity of the Roman/Byzantine imperial church to the ancient Christian communities outside of its realm of authority and knowledge. Between these two families an official doctrinal agreement was possible in the twentieth century, preparing for eventual eucharistic communion, partly because the imperial structure is no longer there and partly because, and to a very large extent, both families kept 'the same apostolic faith' in spite of the separation for about fifteen centuries. Eucharistic communion is not yet re-established, although theological hurdles are overcome. The reason seems to be partly that the local churches have not put in adequate pastoral efforts to overcome the centuries of hostile teaching, and partly, as some suspect, that the ghost of the empire is still lurking behind traditional ecclesiastical structures.

Eucharistic communion

A persistently thorny question in the ecumenical movement, especially between the Orthodox and the churches of the Reformation in the fellowship of the World Council of Churches, is that of eucharistic communion. Apparently most Protestant partners have never understood why the Orthodox refuse to give communion to non-Orthodox Christians. Here is a fundamental ecclesiological matter that creates unpleasantness in inter-personal and interchurch relations within the contemporary ecumenical setting. The Orthodox concept of the eucharist is that it is the unique sacrament of unity. It is celebrated and partaken of within the one Body of Christ, a truly united church that holds the same apostolic faith in Christ. It is not 'inter-communion' among several different bodies of Christ. It is communion in the one Body of Christ. The ultimate ecclesiological goal of the ecumenical movement for the Orthodox is precisely this communion in one body in one faith in the one Lord. Therefore Orthodox theologians are generally not inclined to expressions like 'partial communion' or 'spiritual communion' which, according to the Orthodox, water down the uniqueness, centrality and visibility of communion in the body and blood of Christ. Eucharistic communion in this interim period cannot be used as a means to reach doctrinal unity in faith or as an interim measure and sign of unity as we wait for the 'full communion'. Orthodox tradition holds that once we have eucharistic communion there is no point in discussions concerning agreement upon the apostolic faith since eucharistic fellowship is the crown of the ecumenical process, and not its starting point or means. Hence Orthodox participation in the ecumenical movement unswervingly focuses its attention on the visible eucharistic communion in the same faith and in the one body as the culmination of the Orthodox search and prayer for the unity of all Christians.

The diaspora

The waves of emigration in modern times, the presence of a strong Orthodox diaspora in traditionally non-Orthodox countries, especially in the West, and to a lesser extent the missionary activities of some Orthodox churches, have raised major ecclesiological-canonical-pastoral questions for the Orthodox tradition. Most 'local churches' or autocephalous national Orthodox churches have now become de facto 'universal' churches primarily because of their diaspora presence on every part of the globe. The local church ecclesiology can be in conflict with this phenomenon of universalization. The lives of Orthodox diaspora communities of different ethnic and linguistic origin overlap in metropolitan areas, most of them still maintaining affiliation to their mother churches, and some, like the Orthodox Church of America, aspiring to create new local churches in the new national cultural contexts. The exercise of jurisdiction of different mother churches over their diaspora in the same place, outside their 'canonical territories', and the tensions this engenders, can create a counter witness to the eucharistic ecclesiology of the Orthodox tradition. The proposed 'great and holy council' of the Eastern Orthodox tradition has put this question as a major agenda item for deliberation and resolution.

Notes

1 Although this arbitrarily distinctive use of the synonyms *eastern* and *oriental* may be of some use in the English language, in most other languages this is not possible.
2 See K.M. George, 'Oriental Orthodox-Orthodox Dialogue' in N. Lossky *et al.* (eds), *Dictionary of the Ecumenical Movement*, Geneva: WCC, 1994.
3 See A.M. Aagaard and P. Bouteneff, *Beyond the East–West Divide*, Geneva: WCC, 2001.
4 See Aagard and Bounteneff, p. 33.
5 Positions like Metropolitan, Archbishop, Patriarch, Pope and Catholicos were later created for administrative and jurisdictional reasons. They are all basically '*episcopos*' or bishop. Sacramentally there is no position higher than *episcopos*. For example, the basic *ecclesiological* title of the Pope of Rome is *Bishop of* Rome. This applies in a similar way to all patriarchal and archiepiscopal posi-

tions, though historically a lot of presumptuous ecclesiastical titles have arisen. A Patriarch or Catholicos is only 'first among equals' (*primus inter pares*) for the smooth governance of the church.

6 The following table may be of interest to support this argument (see Paulos Mar Gregorios, *The Church and Authority: Reflections on the Nature and Life of the Church*, Delhi/Kottayam: ISPCK/ MGF, 2001, p. 27).

1. Nicaea	325	(3 centuries after the birth of Christianity)
2. Constantinople	381	(56 years after Nicaea)
3. Ephesus	431	(50 years)
4. Chalcedon	451	(20 years)
5. Constantinople	553	(102 years)
6. Constantinople III	680–1	(127 years)
7. Nicaea II	787	(107 years)
8. Constantinople IV	869–70	(82 years)
9. Lateran I	112	(353 years)
10. Lateran II	1139	(16 years)
11. Lateran III	1179	(40 years)
12. Lateran IV	1215	(36 years)
13. Lyon I	1245	(30 years)
14. Lyon II	1274	(29 years)
15. Vienne	1311–12	(37 years)
16. Constance	1414–18	(102 years)
17. Ferrara – Florence	1418–39	(20 years)
18. Lateran V	1512–17	(73 years)
19. Trent	1545–63	(28 years)
20. Vatican I	1869–70	(306 years)
21. Vatican II	1962	(92 years)

7 Gregorios, ibid., p. 191.
8 *Being as Communion*, New York: St Vladimir Seminary Press, 1985, p. 15.
9 Zizioulas, ibid., p. 24f.
10 Zizioulas, ibid., pp. 134–5.
11 Canon 34 reads: 'The bishops of every nation (*ethnos*) ought to know who is the first one (*prōton*) among them, and to esteem him as their head, and not to do any great thing without his consent; but everyone to manage only the affairs that belong to his own diocese and the territory subject to it. But let him (i.e. the first one) not do anything without the consent of all the other (bishops), for it is by this means that there will be unanimity, and God will be glorified through Christ in the Holy Spirit' (quoted in Zizioulas, ibid., pp. 135–6).
12 Zizioulas, ibid., pp. 137–8.
13 P. Bouteneff, a contemporary American Orthodox theologian, says that 'wherever the Church is not being actively missionary – preaching the Word to all (within and outside the Church's membership) – and not actively being socially responsible – ministering to and advocating for the poor, sick and oppressed, struggling for justice – it is *failing to be the Church*'. Aagaard and Bouteneff, op. cit., p. 33.
14 Zizioulas, op. cit., p. 198f.

Further reading

Anna Marie Aagaard and Peter Bouteneff, *Beyond the East – West Divide*, Geneva: WCC, 2001.

Nicholas Afanasiev, *L'Eglise du Saint Esprit*, Paris: Edition Cerf, 1975.

T. Best, and G. Gassmann, *On the Way to Fuller Koinonia*, Faith and Order Paper No. 166, Geneva: WCC, 1994.

Daniel Ciobotea, 'Holiness as Content and Purpose of Ecclesial Authority' in Tamara Grdzelidze (ed.), *One, Holy, Catholic and Apostolic*, Faith and Order Paper No. 197, Geneva: WCC, pp. 91–6.

Emmanuel Clapsis, 'Does the Church Have a Sacramental Nature? An Orthodox Perspective' in Tamara Grdzelidze (ed.), op. cit., 17–26.

K.M. George, *The Silent Roots: Orthodox Perspectives on Christian Spirituality*, Geneva: WCC, 1994.

——, 'Local and Universal' in *One World* (No. 180 Nov. 1992), 16–18.

——, *Light to the Nations: An Elementary Study of Church, Ministry and Sacraments*, Kottayam, 1989.

Paulos Mar Gregorios, *Glory and Burden: Ministry and Sacraments of the Church*, New Delhi/ Kottayam: ISPCK/MGF, 2005.

——, *The Church and Authority*, Delhi/ Kottayam: ISPCK/MGF, 2001.

P. Gregorios, W.H. Lazareth and N.A. Nissiotis (eds), *Does Chalcedon Divide or Unite? Towards Convergence in Orthodox Christology*, Geneva: WCC, 1981.

Alexey S. Khomiakov, *The Church is One*, N. Zernov (ed.), London: Fellowship of St Alban and St Sergius, 1968.

John Meyendorff, *Imperial Unity and Christian Divisions*, New York: St Vladimir Seminary Press, 1989.

V.C. Samuel, *The Council of Chalcedon Re-examined: A Historical and Theological Survey*, Madras: CLS, 1977.

Kallistos Ware, *The Inner Kingdom*, New York: St Vladimir Seminary Press, 2001.

——, *The Orthodox Way*, London and Oxford: Mowbray, Reprinted 1981.

John D. Zizioulas, *Being as Communion*, New York: St Vladimir Seminary Press, 1993.

9

LUTHERAN
ECCLESIOLOGY

Risto Saarinen

The emergence of Lutheran identity

During the initial phase of the Lutheran Reformation (1517–30), Martin Luther and his followers criticized the Roman Catholic church heavily. Not only problematic practices, such as indulgences and monastic customs but also, and indeed primarily, perceived theological errors in core doctrines regarding the Word of God, justification and the sacraments came into the focus of this criticism. In the Diet of Worms (1521), Luther defended his views but the so-called Edict of Worms declared him guilty of high treason and heresy. However, protected by the local princes, Luther could continue his teaching career at the university of Wittenberg, while the Reformation spread across Europe.[1]

Already during this initial phase Luther and his followers distanced themselves from many other and more radical Reformers who were often called 'enthusiasts' (*Schwärmer*). From Luther's point of view the more radical Refomers, for instance Ulrich Zwingli and Thomas Münzer, did not have enough respect for the sacraments, in particular the Lord's Supper. They also neglected the proper distinction between law and gospel as well as between earthly and spiritual power. Due to this neglect, the radical enthusiasts attempted to rule everything with recourse to the gospel, being both spiritualists and legalists at the same time. The Lutheran movement thus had to define its identity against two fronts: Lutherans[2] opposed the rigid institutionalism of Roman Catholicism, but they were also critical of the spirit-driven radical Reformation.

Lutheranism as a distinct church and confessional family was established at the Diet of Augsburg in 1530. Luther's Wittenberg colleague and collaborator Philip Melanchthon (1497–1560) composed a doctrinal text, the *Augsburg Confession*, to be defended on that occasion. It was not approved by the Catholic side, but a number of local leaders in Lutheran territories signed the confession and supported Luther's cause. Thus the Edict of Worms could not be implemented and Lutheranism continued to spread. In Northern Europe, the Danish and Swedish kings ordered their countries, which included Norway, Iceland and Finland, to become Lutheran. Lutheranism also spread to Baltic countries as well as to Moravia, Hungary and Transylvania.

It would be misleading or even anachronistic to call the Lutheran Reformation an 'ecclesiological' conflict. Luther and early Lutheranism opposed the institutional authority of the pope and pleaded for the right of the individual Christian to exercise a free judgement and to be guided by the Word of God. In this sense the Reformation was a conflict between authority and freedom of conscience in which the supreme authority of Rome was replaced with the authority of the Bible. It was not the apostolic and catholic church *per se* that was criticized. Already in the late 1520s it became clear to the more radical Reformers that Luther and his close followers wanted to retain much of the traditional structures and institution of the church, including the ordained ministry and in many cases also episcopacy. The division of labour between the earthly and spiritual rulers was not too different from the medieval idea of the two swords. Many recent studies have shown that the ecclesiastical laws of early Lutheran territorial churches took much material from the canon law which was abrogated in the initial phase of the Reformation.[3] In all these senses there was an ecclesiological continuity between medieval Catholicism and the Lutheran Reformation. At the same time one must bear in mind that the existing conflicts nevertheless had deep ecclesiological consequences.

Theologians who stress this continuity have sometimes also argued that the most radical ecclesiological changes did not take place between Catholics and Lutherans, but rather between Lutherans and more radical Reformers. It is true that the emerging Calvinism stressed more the individual local congregation and its leadership, whereas the greater Lutheran territorial churches were more centrally organized. Neither did early Lutheranism consider ethics and church order to be a mark of the church in the Calvinist sense. The really divisive doctrinal issues between Lutherans and Reformed were not, however, found in ecclesiology but in other topics, namely the Lord's Supper, christology and predestination. Modern ecumenical agreements, for instance the *Leuenberg Agreement* of 1973, consider that when these three divisive issues are settled, no doctrinal condemnation pertains to ecclesiology. In this sense the conflict between Lutheranism and Calvinism was not an ecclesiological conflict. At the same time it must be admitted that the early conflicts certainly contributed to the different ecclesiologies of these traditions.

The *Augsburg Confession* and its ecclesiology

In order to grasp the distinctive profile of Lutheran ecclesiology more closely, it is instructive to look at the most significant confessional documents. The seventh article of *The Augsburg Confession* (CA) describes the church as follows:

> . . . one holy church will remain forever. The church is the assembly of saints in which the gospel is taught purely and the sacraments are administered rightly. And it is enough for the true unity of the church to agree concerning the teaching of the gospel and the administration of the sacraments. It is not necessary that human traditions, rites, or ceremonies instituted by human beings be alike everywhere.[4]

This article continues to have an enormous importance for the self-understanding of the Lutheran churches. It is subject to various interpretations, both with regard to its actual content and with regard to the hermeneutical questions, such as how comprehensive this article is meant to be or what is its relation to CA V (Concerning Ministry in the Church) and CA VIII (What Is the Church?).[5] We can here only observe some basic characteristics of CA VII.

CA VII stresses that the one church will remain forever. The classical marks of apostolicity, unity, holiness and catholicity are embedded in this statement. Lutheran confessional writings also include the Nicene creed; thus it is clear that the four classical marks are present in Lutheran ecclesiology and the continuity of the church is emphasized. The principle of continuity also means that the Lutheran churches in their self-understanding continue the ancient and medieval orthodox Christianity.

The phrase 'assembly of saints' (*congregatio sanctorum*) raised the suspicion of Catholic critics who underline in their response to the CA that wicked persons and sinners cannot be separated from the church.[6] But this was not the sense intended by the Reformers, as Melanchthon says in the *Apology of the Augsburg Confession* (1531), which is also a confessional text of many Lutheran churches. The word *congregatio* does stress the communion of faithful persons and can thus be read as criticism of a merely institutional description of the church. At the same time, Melanchthon remarks in the *Apology* that 'we have not said anything new here'.[7] Thus the phrase is rather similar to the expression *communio sanctorum* in the Apostles' Creed. This is a catholic way of speaking. Thomas Aquinas, for instance, can say that 'the church is the same as congregation. Therefore the holy church is the same as the congregation of the faithful'.[8] It is theoretically possible to discuss whether Lutherans neglect the sacramental dimension of *communio sanctorum*, but the strong insistence of the real presence of Christ in the Lord's Supper should prove that this is not intended.

As the relative clause following this definition underlines, Lutherans understand the Word of God, that is, the gospel, and the two sacraments of baptism and the Lord's Supper to be the essential or even constitutive marks of the church. Whereas the four classical marks remain general and abstract characteristics, word and sacrament are criteria of concrete identification. When we hear pure teaching of the gospel message and find that baptism and the eucharist are administered 'according to the gospel', as the German text variant of CA VII formulates,[9] we can identify the true Christian church. It would be misleading, however, to understand word and sacraments as merely epistemic criteria of identification. They are rather the pillars on which the assembly of saints is founded.

One important reason why CA VII has gained new actuality in the age of ecumenism is that it seems to provide a flexible set of criteria which leave room for variation and even plurality. If the gospel is taught purely and the sacraments are administered rightly, other aspects in the life of the church can be organized in various ways, since they express 'human traditions'. The degree of this seeming flexibility has, however, remained a point of debate. Without entering this debate, some aspects of it should be noted. First, the Catholic critics of Luther agreed with the two last sentences of the text of CA VII quoted above.[10] Second, Lutherans did not and do not mean that literally everything else simply belongs to the 'human traditions'. In his writing *On Councils and Churches* (1539) Luther lists seven characteristics through which the church is known: the proclamation of the word of God, baptism, the Lord's Supper, the power of penance and forgiveness, the office of the ministry, worship and suffering.[11] In particular, the degree of flexibility with regard to the doctrine of ministry remains debated in much of Lutheranism.

Third, the theological extension of the gospel can be debated. The gospel comprises first and foremost the doctrine of justification which is the central issue of Lutheran theology. CA IV defines this doctrine as follows:

> Human beings cannot be justified before God by their own powers, merits, or works. But they are justified as a gift (*gratis*) on account of Christ through faith when they believe that they are received into grace and that their sins are forgiven on account of Christ, who by his death made satisfaction for our sins.[12]

Given this, the gospel includes the teaching on salvation. Lutherans certainly affirm the traditional trinitarian and christological doctrine, but the classical dogma is, at least in concrete proclamation, interpreted via the perspective of salvation through justification by faith. The definitions of CA IV and VII further display a tendency to disregard ethics as a mark of the church. Taken together, CA IV and VII bear witness to the Reformers' intention of articulating the fundamental core of Christianity. Such an intention may tend towards 'relegating' many ecclesiological considerations to a secondary role. In particular, issues of church order are considered to be 'human traditions' which do not belong to the essence of the gospel.

The *Augsburg Confession* and its *Apology* are the most important normative ecclesiological texts in Lutheranism. The *Smalcald Articles*, written by Luther in 1537, contain an article concerning the church, but this article only criticizes the Roman Catholics and concludes that the holiness of the church 'exists in the Word of God and true faith'.[13] Other confessional texts deal with the church mostly in the context of criticizing the false teachings and practices of the opponents. One historical problem of Lutheran ecclesiology is that most confessional formulations express a criticism that, in turn, forces Lutherans to steer their course among a variety of real and imagined enemies. As a result, confessional Lutherans often know what the church should not be, but they are less aware of what the church actually is. As an answer to this positive question, Lutheran theologians traditionally point towards CA VII and its immediate context.

Major developments after Reformation

European Lutheranism was shaped by the Catholic Counter-Reformation and especially by the Thirty Years War (1618–48). In university theology, this period was dominated by 'Lutheran Orthodoxy'. From about 1550 to 1650, the Lutheran Orthodoxy dominated the German and North European universities, seeking to establish the comprehensive doctrine and apply key ideas of the Reformation to all fields of theology and academic learning. The relative importance of university theology has always been great in Lutheranism, not only because Luther and Melanchthon were university professors, but also because in Continental Europe the territorial churches were formally led by political rulers who left doctrinal issues to be handled by academic theologians. Prominent theologians of Lutheran Orthodoxy include Martin Chemnitz (1522–86), Johann Gerhard (1582–1637), Abraham Calov (1612–86) and Johann Andreas Quenstedt (1617–88).[14]

At the same time, a distinctive spirituality and pastoral theology emerged. Johann Arndt (1555–1621) wrote *Four Books of True Christianity*, a devotional work which employed elements of mystical theology. Paul Gerhardt (1607–86) was the most influential hymn writer, whereas Johann Sebastian Bach (1685–1750) personifies the classical Lutheran organ music. Influenced by Arndt and other devotional writers, Philipp Jacob Spener (1635–1705), August Hermann Francke (1663–1727) and Nikolaus Ludwig of Zinzendorf (1700–60) transformed Lutheran Orthodoxy to Pietism, a devotional movement which underlines personal piety.

Pietism

The emerging Pietism of the eighteenth century led to ecclesiological controversies and new developments. Pietists opposed the rigid structures and institutions of territorial and state churches which now prevailed in Lutheran Germany as well as in Scandinavian countries. Pietists advocated the spiritual renewal of the local parish and often considered the worshipping community to be the heart of the true church. Given the opposition of the official church institution, this vision often meant the establishment of an *ecclesiola*, a small group of true and active believers which had a more or less visible presence inside the institutional *ecclesia*. Both the Pietists and the institutional church claimed that the 'assembly of the saints' (CA VII) theologically described their own respective group.[15]

Another Pietist initiative concerned the missionary work of the church. Since Lutheranism was structured in territories which did not have much opportunity for foreign travel and intercultural contact, Christian mission remained an underdeveloped theme. Pietists were more mobile people – and they were often forced to move away from the strictly Lutheran territories. Since they did not regard the true church in terms of established territories, they thus became more aware of the missionary needs of the church. August Hermann Francke's educational and social institutions in Halle, Germany, became an important centre for missionary training. Zinzendorf's Herrnhut settlement was another Pietist centre from which missionary impact spread to many parts of the world.

Pietism and its ecclesiology have remained a vital constituent of Lutheranism to this day, especially in some Nordic countries (Norway and Finland), parts of Germany (Wurttemberg) as well as in the Midwestern parts of the United States. The idea of a true and vital assembly of faithful Christians is very appealing in a state church setting in which everyone in the area belongs to Lutheranism, as has been the case in Norway and Finland until recently. In North European countries, Pietists have often remained formally within the structure of the territorial church, but have constantly criticized it, aiming at a self-critical renewal of the whole church. In practice, they have remained a small body (*ecclesiola*) within a larger church.

Pietists seek to be neither Donatist nor Novatian[16] in their ecclesiology, but they do claim to be the true followers of Lutheran doctrine. At the same time they regard inactivity, moral laxity and complicity in worldly structures to be the greatest problems of the territorial church. Although Pietists are often critical of modern developments, they are themselves a typical product of the Enlightenment in their stress on individual freedom and the inner light of personal conviction as well as in their understanding of community as an interest group. The stress on missionary work also reflects the modern understanding of humankind in terms of equal rights and global responsibility. As the institutionalized churches did not, at first, engage themselves in foreign missions, Pietists founded several missionary societies. Indeed, to this day Lutheran churches often practise mission work not as churches, themselves, but rather channel their efforts through missionary societies founded by the Pietists.

Pietist attitudes to sacramental theology vary considerably. Some groups, often connected with Reformed or Evangelical leanings, regard baptism and the Lord's Supper as rather impersonal rituals and lay more weight on the personal faith of the Christian. But many Lutheran Pietists have a strong theology of the sacraments. In keeping with this, they firmly advocate infant baptism and emphasize the real presence of Christ in the Lord's Supper. Pietists often consider that it is the territorial church which does not adequately respect the sacraments.

Indeed, it is fair to say that much of modern and even contemporary Lutheran ecclesiology can be understood as various mediating positions between territorial, institutional churches on the one hand and Pietists on the other. In Finland, it is still common today that future pastors come from Pietist youth movements that have a critical view of the institutionalized church. But in their first years of ministry the pastors become more moderate and begin to appreciate a larger variety of Christian lifestyles and organizational patterns safeguarded by the larger territorial church. In many African and Asian countries, the Lutheran churches have kept close contacts with the European missionary societies whose missionaries still advocate Pietist ideals. Thus many African and Asian Lutherans on the one hand stress the personal nature of the assembly of believers in a Pietist manner, but in their local inculturation and struggle for social justice they adopt other theological models present in contemporary Protestantism.

Lutheranism in America

American Lutheranism exemplifies the continuing influence of different historical periods. Lutheran migrants to North America often organized themselves on the basis of nationalities, thus reflecting the situation of European territorial churches. At the same time, Pietist groups were sometimes very critical of European circumstances and sought to develop other patterns of organization. Later, these cultural and ecclesiological differences became less significant and different groups eventually merged with one another to become what is now the Evangelical Lutheran Church in America (ELCA). But one can still today detect the different national influences and the more or less Pietist surroundings in different geographical areas. Due to the Norwegian immigration to Minnesota, for instance, many Lutheran theologians have kept their original low-church Pietist identity to this day.

A special case in this respect is the Missouri Synod, a denomination which today comprises around 2.5 million members in North America. They originate from German immigrants led by C.F.W. Walther (1811–87) who aimed to found a true church loyal to the Lutheran Confessions. Although the Missouri Synod has always been critical of European territorial church structures, its theology has not, however, been typically Pietist; rather, this church has sought to live in the spirit of Lutheran Orthodoxy. Ecclesiologically, this has been a most interesting venture because the Lutheran Orthodoxy of seventeenth-century Europe was closely connected with the territorial churches. Missourians, however, have sought to establish an assembly of saints in which the pure doctrine and right administration of the sacraments can identify the true church irrespectively of worldly rulers and territorial context. In practice, the Missouri Synod has firmly remained within the most conservative wing[17] of Lutheranism, a wing that is not in communion with the rest of the 66.2 million Lutherans on the global scene today.

Influential Lutheran philosophers

Many outstanding philosophers, for instance Immanuel Kant and G. F. W. Hegel, were Lutherans. It is not very plausible, however, to claim that their thinking was in any really significant way connected with Lutheran ecclesiology. There is, however, one philosopher and scientist about whom such a claim can be made, namely G.W. Leibniz (1646–1716). In his correspondence with Bishop Bossuet as well as in his *Systema theologicum* (1686) Leibniz outlines the idea of a universal, catholic church, in which the Protestants could accept the primacy of the pope and the doctrine of transubstantiation. The *Augsburg Confession* could serve as the confessional basis of this church. In Leibniz's view, even the Eastern Orthodox churches could adopt the *Augsburg Confession*. Although Leibniz's thinking remains idealistic, it provided inspiration for European rulers who wanted reconciliation and unification between different confessions. It has also provided ecclesiological models for the ecumenical movement of the modern era.

Another prominent philosopher with explicit views on Lutheran ecclesiology was Søren Kierkegaard (1813–55), who regarded the Danish state church as pompous and hypocritical. Kierkegaard advocates an existential understanding of Christianity which must take a 'leap of faith' in order to become genuine. In spite of his vehement criticism of the existing churches, Kierkegaard's radically individual understanding of faith remains actual in the postmodern reflection on Christian community.

Leuenberg and Porvoo as ecclesiological touchstones

The creation of Prussian Union in 1817 was an extremely important ecclesiological development for Germany. In this union, Lutheran and Reformed churches were to be merged by order of King Friedrich Wilhelm III. The union plan employed ideas taken from the Enlightenment as well as from the theology of Friedrich Schleiermacher. Many Lutherans vehemently opposed the union plan, and in the course of time it became somewhat moderated. The basic ecclesiological idea of the Prussian Union can be described in the following terms: the confessional basis of the Protestant union reflects the common convictions of different confessions. At the same time, historical confessions are not abandoned; they remain normative within a particular territory but should not hinder the broader ecclesial communion (*Kirchengemeinschaft, äusserliche kirchliche Gemeinschaft*) ordered by the king.[18]

In the very complex recent history of German Protestantism, this idea has remained vital. It allows the continuation of territorial church structures but creates at least a sense of unity and an ordered fellowship among them. After the First World War, when the remnants of the old monarchy-related territorial church system were abandoned, the Protestant Church of the Old Prussian Union (*Evangelische Kirche der altpreussischen Union*) emerged. In this church, the existence of different historical traditions within one Protestant church continued until the 1950s. In more recent times, this tradition has been called the Protestant Church of the Union (*Evangelische Kirche der Union*, EKU). Ecclesiologically, it is a fellowship of territorial churches coming from both Lutheran and Reformed traditions.

The German Lutheran churches outside historical Prussia came to be bound together in the so-called 'United Evangelical Lutheran Church' (*Vereinigte Evangelisch-Lutherische Kirche*, VELKD). After intensive negotiations, begun in the 1950s, EKU and VELKD were able to build an extensive church fellowship within the framework of the German Evangelical Church (*Evangelische Kirche in Deutschland*, EKD). In recent years, this 'fellowship' has increasingly proceeded towards the status of a 'merger'. Thus German Lutheranism is today characterized by a very complex institutional ecclesiology. Theologically, the territorial churches still remain churches in the strict sense. But both the VELKD and the EKD are very church-like institutions which can effectively take care of ecumenical relationships and many doctrinal matters. Furthermore, some Lutherans have remained united with the Reformed, since the days of Prussia, whereas other Lutherans are in church fellowship with them today only in the context of the EKD. As a result of this, the Lutheran tradition that exists within the EKU is not counted amongst the statistics of World Lutheranism, since the territorial churches of the EKU are not members of the Lutheran World Federation.

This German ecclesiological development has spread to European Protestantism in the framework of the so-called Leuenberg Church Fellowship. Its basic document, the *Leuenberg Agreement* (1973), has led to the formation of church fellowship (*Kirchengemeinschaft*) among the great majority of European Protestantism. With the exception of Anglicanism and Swedish and Finnish Lutheranism, in 2006 practically all the historically Protestant churches of Europe belonged to this fellowship. The Leuenberg Church Fellowship has been regarded as a tremendous ecumenical success and it exercises a considerable practical influence because it enables the exchange of ministers and effective co-operation in matters of doctrine, ethics and practical work.

The basic ecclesiological problem of the Leuenberg Church Fellowship is that the *Leuenberg Agreement* does not actually contain *any* ecclesiology. Thus the signatory churches commit themselves to a church fellowship without adopting any definite ecclesiology. It can also be noted that in English the Leuenberg Group does not call itself a 'communion', but a 'fellowship' or, more recently, a 'Community of Protestant Churches in Europe'. While this choice of language reflects the low-church tradition of Protestantism, it may also create difficulties for some Lutherans. The Lutheran World Federation, for instance, calls itself a 'Communion of Churches'.

The *Leuenberg Agreement* declares the traditional doctrinal condemnations between Lutherans and Reformed to be non-applicable today. It also lays out a common understanding of the gospel, that is, word and sacraments. But it does not outline an explicit ecclesiology and does not attempt to reconcile the very diverse set of ministries in the signatory churches. Deeply aware of its own ecclesiological deficit, the Leuenberg Fellowship has committed itself to do ecclesiological study. The most important fruit of this study is the document *The Church of Jesus Christ* (1995), a text which today represents the *opinio communis* of continental European Protestant ecclesiology.

This ecclesiological document holds that it is the nature of the church to be a 'community of saints', as the Apostles' Creed holds. The origin and foundation of the church is characterized by four aspects: first, the justifying action of the triune God which is the content of the gospel; second, the living witness of the gospel as an instrument of the Holy Spirit; third, the fellowship that springs from the living witness of the gospel; and fourth, the Christian freedom which has its origin in this foundation of the church. In all these four aspects, the church becomes defined in terms of its gospel message. More traditional phrases, such as the body of Christ and the four classical attributes of the Nicene Creed are dealt with under the general title 'The shape of the church'. Concerning ministry, *The Church of Jesus Christ* considers the so-called 'ordered ministry' of the public proclamation to be necessary. While the more traditional concept of 'ordained ministry' is also affirmed, it is to an extent subsumed under the broader idea of ordered ministry.[19]

Swedish and Finnish Lutheranism have preserved the historical episcopacy since the Reformation and emphasize the episcopal structures of church administration. The theological tradition of these churches has often been anti-Calvinist and they have remained outside of the Leuenberg Church Fellowship. During the twentieth century Swedish and Finnish churches have developed close ties with the Church of England. In 1920 and 1922 the Lambeth conference and the bishops of the Church of Sweden approved intercommunion between the two churches. They also decided to participate in each other's episcopal consecrations. Similar agreements were made with the Church of Finland in 1936 and 1951.[20]

After the fruitful results of global Anglican–Lutheran dialogue,[21] British and Irish

177

Anglican churches on the one hand and the Nordic and Baltic Lutheran churches on the other hand decided to negotiate an agreement of full communion. This agreement, the *Porvoo Common Statement* (Porvoo), was adopted by most of the participating churches between 1993 and 1995. For the Church of England the basic ecumenical and ecclesiological problem in negotiations with Nordic Lutherans was always the matter of the historical succession of bishops. Doctrinal orthodoxy in other matters was taken for granted. For this reason, Porvoo deals extensively with the issue of episcopacy. Porvoo does not, however, focus on bishops as such, but on the ministry of oversight, *episkopē*. Whereas *episkopē* is necessary for the church, historical episcopal succession is not an absolute necessity but a 'sign' which should be used in order to make the apostolic life of the church visible, although the sign alone does not guarantee the fidelity of the church to every aspect of apostolic faith.

On the basis of this view of *episkopē*, Porvoo affirms that each church has maintained a succession of episcopal ministry in the continuity of its pastoral life. In this way churches without historical episcopacy, for instance the Church of Norway, can also join the Porvoo Communion. It is assumed, however, that the participatory churches clearly affirm the episcopal order and use it as a 'sign' of their apostolicity. The Porvoo Communion has definitely increased the theological exchange between British and North European churches. In a similar, though not identical, fashion, agreements between the Anglican–Lutheran communions in the USA and Canada have been made in recent years. In France, Germany and Australia, far-reaching convergence between the two traditions has also been reached in regional agreements.[22]

The Lutheran World Federation and the Lutheran–Roman Catholic dialogue

In the twentieth century, Lutheran ecclesiology has not developed autonomously but as a result of three or four complex dialogue processes. The first of these was the process leading to Leuenberg, the second the one leading to Porvoo. A third process regards its relationship with Roman Catholicism. The fourth and most distinctively Lutheran process concerns the emergence of the Lutheran World Federation as the global communion of Lutheran churches. As indicated, due to their self-understanding as territorial churches, the Lutheran churches have traditionally displayed a very local and even a national self-understanding. For this reason, the relationships between differing Lutheran churches have not themselves been unproblematic. In the age of ecumenism, first efforts towards shaping a worldwide Lutheran fellowship were made in the meetings of the so-called Lutheran World Convention between 1923 and 1946. A more regular and effective co-operation was launched in Lund, Sweden, with the founding of the Lutheran World Federation (LWF) in 1947. The LWF grew rapidly; in 2006 it comprised 140 member churches representing 66.2 million Lutherans in all continents. With its headquarters in the Ecumenical Centre in Geneva, the LWF not only conducts extensive relief work but represents the Lutheran churches in bilateral dialogues with other world Christian communions.[23]

The ecclesiological self-understanding of the LWF has been extensively discussed from the beginning. The founding fathers of the organization were careful not to interfere with the ecclesiological convictions of the member churches. Therefore, the LWF defined itself in Lund 1947 merely as a 'free association' of the Lutheran churches. It soon became clear, however, that this solution was not theologically valid, since the membership involves the acceptance of the *Augsburg Confession* and Luther's *Small Catechism* as pure exposition of the Word of God. As the German theologian Peter Brunner argued, such a confessional obligation implies that the LWF is ecclesiologically much more than a free association.[24]

Although most Lutheran churches practised altar and pulpit fellowship with each other, it was nevertheless difficult to commit the churches to express such fellowship in the constitution of the LWF. Indeed, it was only in 1984 that the Lutheran churches finally took this step. Since 1990 the LWF has called itself a 'communion of member churches'.[25] In 2006, its constitution reads as follows: 'The LWF is a communion of churches which confess the triune God, agree in the proclamation of the Word of God and are united in pulpit and altar fellowship.' In keeping with the spirit of CA VII, the essential elements of this communion consist in agreement on the gospel as well as in the right administration of the sacrament at the altar.

One very important yet very complex discussion which prompted this development from association to communion concerned the suspension of membership of the South African churches that practised apartheid in the 1970s and 1980s. Such practice was considered to be contrary to the confessional basis of the LWF.[26] But in making this very consideration the LWF adopted the practice of making normative confessional judgements, which a free association could not make. Nonetheless, the LWF aims at respecting the autonomy of its member churches on most occasions. It is not and cannot become a 'Vatican' or even a 'Canterbury' of its member churches, since Lutherans continue to understand the territorial churches as self-regulating bodies. Yet the great ecclesiological importance of the LWF can be seen in the very fact that it has forced its member churches to think about common decision-making. In the ecumenical dialogues, for instance, the member churches as a rule follow the work of global commissions rather than enter into new bilateral efforts outside of coordination with the LWF. It can thus be claimed that the practice of ecumenical dialogues makes the LWF an ecclesial body that can represent Lutherans in the global context. This claim has been extensively debated with particular regard to the Lutheran–Roman Catholic dialogue.

The Lutheran–Roman Catholic dialogue, initiated in 1967, has been conducted from the Lutheran side by the LWF. In addition to this global dialogue, important regional conversations have been conducted in many countries, in particular Germany and the United States. Core ecclesiological issues were prominent throughout the very first global document to emerge from these discussions, the *Malta Report* (1972). This featured sections that dealt with ministry, papacy and intercommunion. In this report, both parties described the church in a manner fairly similar to that of CA VII:

> The church as a whole bears witness to Christ; the church as a whole is the priestly people of God. As *creatura et ministra verbi*, however, it stands under the gospel and has the gospel as its superordinate criterion. Its gospel ministry is to be carried out through the sacraments, and, indeed, through its total life.[27]

The most elaborate ecclesiological text of this dialogue is *Church and Justification* (1994). In this document an understanding of the church in the light of the doctrine of justification is attempted. The trinitarian and biblical dimensions of ecclesiology come more strongly into focus, as in the Lutheran Confessions. The document also receives substantial parts of the so-called ecclesiology of communion, as developed by Catholic theologians in and after Vatican II. Many traditionally controversial points are treated in detail, for example, the Catholic understanding of the church as 'sacrament', the concept and range of the 'local church', the distinction between the visible and 'hidden' church, as well as the 'sinfulness' of the church itself. The document also discusses the institutional role of ordained ministry in the church and the relationship of church jurisdiction to normative theological doctrine. One further substantial ecclesiological document is *Communio sanctorum* which emerged as a result of bilateral German dialogue.[28]

Perhaps the most debated text resulting from these dialogues is the *Joint Declaration on the Doctrine of Justification* (JD, 1999), a document in which the historical doctrinal condemnations regarding justification were declared to be non-applicable in today's churches. The JD text was officially approved by both Lutheran churches and the Vatican. Thus it possesses more normativity than other dialogue documents. Although JD does not deal with ecclesiology in the proper sense of the word, the rather heated process which led to its approval is symptomatic of many problems in Lutheran ecclesiology.[29] The process was steered by the LWF, but some member churches and individual theologians, especially in Germany, questioned the authority of the LWF to do this. In Germany, only the member churches of the VELKD and LWF participated in the process; the Lutheran tradition within the United churches was left outside. For this reason, the theological role of EKU and Leuenberg Church Fellowship was also an issue. One might well ask whether the lifting of condemnations by the Vatican applies to them as well.

From the perspective of ecclesiology, it was nevertheless significant that the great majority of the member churches of the LWF could agree with the outcome of JD. The success of this document shows that Lutherans can in many ways today act as a communion, although the territorial churches still remain the final decision-makers. In this sense, Lutheranism is no longer a 'free association' of churches, but a communion bound together by doctrinal consensus. Successful regional agreements, in particular *The Leuenberg Agreement* and *The Porvoo Common Statement*, also witness that this is the case in today's Lutheranism.

Prominent ecclesiological thinkers

Lutheran ecclesiology has not developed as a result of the intellectual achievements of prominent individual thinkers, but rather in the interaction with other traditions. It is fairly easy to name individual thinkers whose theology has influenced Lutheran ecclesiology. These include Friedrich Schleiermacher (1768–1834) and Rudolf Sohm (1841–1917) from the more liberal, Enlightenment surroundings, as well as Karl Barth (1886–1968) from the Neo-Orthodoxy. But it would be misleading to label their influence as a specifically *Lutheran* ecclesiology. It is rather the case that the Lutheran views concerning the church have been highly dependant on the broader theological currents in Protestantism. This state of affairs is related to the above-mentioned fact that the ecclesiology of Lutheran confessions has historically concentrated on criticizing the errors of Roman Catholics and radical Reformers. Positive and constructive ecclesiology has not come into focus in as prominent a fashion. Therefore, the actual positive ecclesiological developments offered by Lutheran theologians has varied considerably.

In the early ecumenical movement, Swedish Lutherans sought to develop an ecclesiology that would be both Lutheran and ecumenical. Nathan Söderblom (1866–1931), Swedish archbishop and the founding father of the ecumenical movement, advocated peace work and saw in ecumenism the mystical unity of humankind at work. Although his own theology reflected the liberalism of the early twentieth century, he also gave some impetus to the programme of 'evangelical catholicism', a movement that underlines the continuity of the church and pays serious attention to sacramental theology, liturgical renewal and ordained ministry. Evangelical catholicism has remained rather popular in Sweden and Finland. One reason for this is that these churches see themselves not only as Lutherans, but as representing the whole of Christianity in a particular area. Thus these territorial churches are considered to have a strong continuity with the Catholic heritage of medieval times.

Among the more recent evangelical catholic Lutheran theologians, Carl Braaten and Robert W. Jenson stand out as advocates of a Lutheranism that is very conscious of the legacy of Nicaea and Chalcedon and that distances itself from liberal Protestantism. In their work, the trinitarian dimension of theology and ecclesiology receives new actuality. For Jenson, the Christian soul appears as 'the *anima ecclesiastica*, that is, a personal self through whom the integral community of the church expresses itself'.[30] The liturgical interest of Lutheran evangelical catholicity has been outlined by Frank Senn.[31]

In his study *Christ and His Church*,[32] the Swedish systematic theologian and first president of the LWF, Anders Nygren, outlines a christocentric ecclesiology. Nygren discusses the Pauline picture of the church as the body of Christ and claims that the unity and diversity of the Christian life today should be understood in terms of this picture. He holds that the ecumenical movement has moved into its third period: after enthusiastic beginnings, followed by confessional awareness of the doctrinal truth, theologians can now move towards a christocentric understanding of the one church, a view which preserves unity but also allows for the diversity of its members. Nygren's christocentric vision was very influential in the ecumenical movement of the 1960s and 70s.

In recent decades, the most influential Lutheran theologian has been Wolfhart Pannenberg. His *Systematic Theology*[33] contains a broad ecclesiology in which the salvific presence of Christ determines the life of the church. For both Nygren and Pannenberg the church is defined as the body of Christ. Pannenberg considers the seven 'sacramental' realities of the church, which correspond to the seven sacraments of the Roman Catholic Church, to be signs through which this presence of Christ appears. Although he emphasizes the two traditional Lutheran sacraments, baptism and the Lord's Supper, he can thus also discuss, for example, marriage and ordination in terms of a broader sacramentality.

Although Jenson, Nygren and Pannenberg make extensive use of Lutheran theology, they do not aim at outlining a particularly Lutheran ecclesiology, but rather an ecumenical ecclesiology which is theologically adequate. Many Lutherans would consider the project of a 'Lutheran ecclesiology' to contain at least an inner tension if not a contradiction in terms. According to this line of thought, any theologically valid ecclesiology should become an ecclesiology of the one, holy, apostolic and catholic church, a vision which cannot serve particularist causes. For this reason, a narrowly confessional ecclesiology is not in fashion among academic Lutheran theologians and ecumenically minded church leaders.

In today's German Protestantism, sacramental approaches and evangelical catholicity are less popular. Rather, the church is considered to be a servant of the Word of God. In this service, the church is 'the pillar and bulwark of the truth' (1 Tim 3.15). Its purpose is not to be an autonomous, hierarchical entity, but a church that stands and falls with the truth of its gospel message. One recent example of such an ecclesiology is the work of Hans-Peter Grosshans.[34] Amongst other themes, Grosshans discusses the applicability of various theories of the truth in ecclesiology. He argues that whereas the consensus and coherence theories of truth may suit well for the purposes of Catholic ecclesiology, Protestants are called to highlight the ecclesiological relevance of the correspondence theory of truth.

Respect for this theory helps the church to be a genuine *ecclesia audiens*, a church that can listen to the Word of God and discern the truth of the gospel.[35]

Contemporary ecclesiological issues

Rome or Geneva?

An old but still very vital problem of Lutheran ecclesiology concerns the issue whether Lutheranism is closer to Rome or Geneva, that is, Catholicism or the Reformed tradition. In today's European scene, this problem is reflected in the two regional church fellowships, the Porvoo Communion on the one hand and the Leuenberg Church Fellowship on the other. While the Vatican has developed its relationships with the episcopal churches of England, Sweden and Finland, it has remained slightly more reserved towards the non-episcopal Protestantism of Continental Europe. Accordingly, the Lutheran–Roman Catholic JD was received very positively in Sweden and Finland, but many German Lutheran voices were raised against it.

Among the major Lutheran churches, the Church of Norway and the Evangelical Lutheran Church in America are in church fellowship with both Anglican/Episcopal and Reformed traditions. Most other Lutheran churches are in communion with either Anglicans or the Reformed. Among major Lutheran churches, only the Missouri Synod has remained outside all ecumenical agreements. These ecumenical preferences reveal some differences in the ecclesiology of Lutheranism. Often, however, the same differences can be found inside the churches as well. In its permissive ethical stance, the Church of Sweden joins the liberal wing of Reformed tradition, whereas many Swedish Lutherans approach Roman Catholicism in their tradition of evangelical catholicism. The Missouri Synod is very critical of Reformed theology, but at the same time many parts of it are permeated by the American evangelical movement which comes from Baptist and Calvinist sources. In these various ways, the Lutheran churches remain faced with the choice between the ecclesiologies of Rome and Geneva.

The theology of ministry is one especially delicate issue that influences how such a choice is made. For complex historical reasons, both episcopal and presbyterial-synodal structures of church government can be found in Lutheranism. While some ecumenically-minded Lutherans emphasize the threefold ministry of bishop, pastor and deacon, others prefer the model of one ordained ministry with a clear distinction from the laity. Still others underline the theological primacy of the 'priesthood of all baptized believers' and consider ordained ministry to be a secondary structure.

The LWF has been careful to avoid over-interference in this inner-Lutheran discussion. Only in 1993 did it publish the results of preliminary consultations and study projects dealing with episcopacy, the ministry of women and the theological meaning of ordination.[36] During the last twenty years, an increasing number of Lutheran churches have adopted the title of 'bishop'. At the same time, the number of Lutheran women pastors and bishops has grown rapidly. In spite of these developments, both episcopacy and the ordination of women continue to be debated in many Lutheran churches.

A more recent LWF statement[37] attempts to outline a convergence opinion with regard to the theology of ministry. This statement holds that the ordained ministry is 'essential and necessary for the church to fulfil its mission . . . The special ministry conferred by ordination is constitutive for the church.' The document further claims that 'there is a continuity or succession in the ordained ministry'. It also says that 'the Augsburg Confession assumes the continuation of the office of the bishop in the church'.[38] Although this new LWF text is thus rather episcopal in its theology of ministry, it emphasizes the 'ministry of oversight', *episkopē*, rather than the office of the bishop alone. Bishops are called 'to a special role of oversight in the church, but the wider community also is called to participate in oversight'. Synodal structures and institutions for sharing the task of oversight are thus 'consistent with Lutheran understandings of the church'.[39]

Ecclesiology and ethics

Another acute issue concerns the relationship between ecclesiology and ethics. Lutherans have traditionally denied that ethics, church discipline, or good moral behaviour in general, would be a theological 'mark of the church'. In this Lutherans have been different from much of the Calvinist tradition. In the age of ecumenism and secularization, however, Lutherans have realized that the theological neglect of ethics may also separate them from the Anglican and Roman Catholic traditions, in which a certain Christian morality is more or less consciously expected of church members. In addition, academic theologians have argued that church practice and communitarian activities necessarily belong to the identity of the church.[40] Whereas Lutherans may have taught that the church *has* a social ethic, they have not been familiar with the claim that the church *is* a social ethic.[41] At the same time, most Lutherans have, for the most part, lived in distinctly Christian societies. The challenge of the post-Christian secular world may have significant ecclesiological consequences for the Lutheran understanding of ethics.

One area in which this discussion has already led to a partial shift of opinion concerns the theology of marriage and sexuality. Lutheran churches have traditionally emphasized that marriage belongs to the secular and public sphere. Although Christian marriage and the religious education of children are promoted, the Lutheran view of two kingdoms considers marriage to be a fundamentally non-theological institution. Recently, however, some prominent Lutheran theologians have begun to argue that in our post-Christian world the traditional monogamous marriage which implies fidelity between the spouses and long-standing responsibility for the children may be a 'sign' of deeper theological and ecclesiological realities.[42] Thus a practised life-form may become related to a deeper Christian communion. Although such reflection is today hardly typical of Lutheranism, it may signify that the mutual relationship of ecclesiology and ethics is more complex than the Lutheran tradition has assumed.

Lutheran ecclesiology

Yet another vital discussion topic concerns the relative importance of structured ecclesiology in Lutheran theology. Liberal Protestant tradition has here claimed that the nature of the church as spiritual entity makes any institutional church law simply impossible.[43] In keeping with such claims it could be argued that CA VII favours a reductionistic ecclesiology in which the Word of God and the sacraments remain spirit-regulated and thus hardly need any institutional framework. On the other hand, confessional Lutheranism has argued that CA VII is nothing less than the first dogmatic definition of the essence and unity of the church in the whole of Christianity.[44] Given this, Lutherans do indeed have a unique ecclesiological legacy to preserve and spread.

The truth probably lies somewhere between the liberal and confessional extremes. While Lutherans certainly want to highlight the primacy of the gospel message of justification by faith, they also want to define the nature and purpose of the church in a manner which is not reductionist. While it is true that the Lutheran Confessions concentrate on criticizing other positions and do not contain an elaborate ecclesiology, it is also true that ecclesiology is a latecomer in Western theology as a whole. In Luther's times, comprehensive ecclesiological reflection had been initiated by Southern European theologians,[45] but there was no such received body of ecclesiological doctrine to which the Lutheran Reformers could have related. Instead, they related their criticism to the problematic practices of the existing Catholic church. It would therefore be anachronistic to claim that the Lutheran Reformation was a battle between different ecclesiologies. Whether today's ecumenical dialogue can nevertheless be described in terms of fundamental ecclesiological differences, remains another and very complex hermeneutical issue.

Notes

1 For this and the following historical details see Eric Gritsch, *A History of Lutheranism*, Minneapolis: Fortress, 2002; and *The Oxford Encyclopedia of the Reformation 1–4*, Oxford: Oxford University Press, 1996. See also Chapter 4 of this volume, 'Ecclesiology and the Religious Controversy of the Sixteenth Century'.
2 Lutheran theology often postulates theological differences between Luther and later Lutheranism. The usage of 'Luther' and 'Lutheranism' in this article does not, however, presuppose any specific view concerning their relationship.
3 John Witte, *Law and Protestantism: The Legal Teachings of the Lutheran Reformation*, Cambridge: Cambridge University Press, 2002; and Virpi Mäkinen (ed.), *Lutheran Reformation and the Law*, Leiden: Brill, 2006.
4 We use the new English translation: *The Book of Concord: The Confessions of the Evangelical Lutheran Church*, ed. Robert Kolb and Timothy Wengert, Minneapolis: Fortress, 2000, p. 43 (Latin original text).
5 For the historical and theological issues of interpretation, see the extensive new commentary by Gunther Wenz, *Theologie der Bekenntnisschriften der evangelisch-lutherischen Kirche 1–2*, Berlin: de Gruyter, 1996–8.
6 'The Confutation of the Augsburg Confession', in: *Sources and Contexts of the Book of Concord*, ed. Robert Kolb and James A. Nestingen, Minneapolis: Fortress, 2001, p. 110.
7 *The Book of Concord*, p. 174.
8 'Ecclesia est idem quod congregatio. Unde Ecclesia sancta idem est quod congregatio fidelium.' Thomas, *In Symbolum Apostolorum Expositio*, Art. 9. Quoted from *Confessio Augustana, Bekenntnis des einen Glaubens*, ed. Harding Meyer and Heinz Schütte, Paderborn: Bonifacius, 1980, p. 179. Dietrich Bonhoeffer's study *Communio sanctorum* (1930, English: Minneapolis: Fortress, 1998) has become an influential commentary on this idea.
9 *The Book of Concord*, p. 42.
10 *Confutation*, pp. 110–11.
11 Martin Luther's *Werke*, Weimarer Ausgabe, Weimar, 1883ff, vol. 50, p. 628–42.
12 *The Book of Concord*, pp. 39–41 (Latin text).
13 *The Book of Concord*, pp. 324–5 (§12).
14 For this and the following historical developments, see e.g. Gritsch, *A History* and Vilmos Vajta (ed.), *The Lutheran Church Past and Present*, Minneapolis: Augsburg, 1977.
15 Martin Brecht *et al*, *Geschichte des Pietismus 1–4*, Göttingen: Vandenhoeck & Ruprecht, 1993, and Johannes Wallmann, *Der Pietismus*, Göttingen: Vandenhoeck/UTB, 2005 offer the best updated information on Pietism. As these works aptly show, Pietism was not limited to Lutheran territorial churches but also influenced Reformed and other Protestant churches.

16 These ancient heresies denied the restoration of Christians after grave sins or apostasy. They are both condemned in the *Augsburg Confession* (CA VIII, XII).

17 Other very conservative Lutheran groups include the Wisconsin Evangelical Lutheran Church (400,000 members in the USA) and the so-called Laestadian Pietist movement inside the Scandinavian churches, in particular Finland (100,000 members).

18 For this and the following history, cf. Elisabeth Schieffer, *Von Schauenburg nach Leuenberg*, Paderborn: Bonifatius, 1983; and Tuomo Mannermaa, *Von Preussen nach Leuenberg*, Hannover: Lutherisches Verlagshaus, 1981. The websites www.ekd.de, www.velkd.de and www.leuenberg.net contain plenty of relevant information, also in English.

19 *Die Kirche Jesu Christi/ The Church of Jesus Christ*, Leuenberger Texte 1, Frankfurt: Lembeck, 1995, pp. 87–100 (bilingual edition, also available at www.leuenberg.net).

20 See Risto Saarinen, 'Porvoo Common Statement' in *The Encyclopedia of Christianity*, vol. 4, Grand Rapids. MI: Eerdmans, 2005, pp. 290–3; *Together in Mission in Ministry: The Porvoo Common Statement with Essays on Church and Ministry in Northern Europe*, London: Church House, 1993; *Apostolicity and Unity: Essays on the Porvoo Common Statement*, ed. Ola Tjorhom, Grand Rapids, MI: Eerdmans, 2002.

21 See the comprehensive collection *Anglican-Lutheran Agreements: Regional and International Agreements 1972–2002*, ed. Sven Oppegaard and Gregory Cameron, Geneva: LWF, 2004.

22 All texts are found in *Anglican-Lutheran Agreements*.

23 For this and the following, cf. *From Federation to Communion: The History of the Lutheran World Federation*, ed. Jens H. Schjorring et al., Minneapolis: Fortress, 1997, and the website www.lutheranworld.org.

24 *From Federation to Communion*, pp. 221–2. This chapter (pp. 216–46), entitled 'Affirming the Communion: Ecclesiological Reflection in the LWF' and authored by Michael Root, gives an excellent historical picture and good bibliography.

25 For an ecclesiological reflection of this development, see *The Church as Communion: Lutheran Contributions to Ecclesiology*, ed. H. Holze, Geneva: LWF, 1997.

26 *From Federation to Communion*, pp. 227–34.

27 *Malta Report*, § 48. All the documents of this dialogue are to be found in *Growth in Agreement: Reports and Agreed Statements of Ecumenical Conversations on a World Level* [1931–98], vols 1–2, ed. Harding Meyer et al., Geneva: WCC, 1984 and 2000.

28 English edition: *Communio sanctorum: The Church as the Communion of Saints*, Collegeville: The Liturgical Press, 2004.

29 The text: *Growth in Agreement 2*, pp. 566–82. André Birmelé, *Kirchengemeinschaft*, Münster: LIT Verlag, 2003, pp. 83–166, offers a detailed and balanced account of the process.

30 Robert W. Jenson, *Systematic Theology 2*, Oxford: Oxford University Press, 1999, p, 289.

31 Frank Senn, *Christian Liturgy: Catholic and Evangelical*, Minneapolis: Fortress, 1997.

32 Philadelphia: Westminster Press, 1956.

33 Grand Rapids, MI: Eerdmans, vols 1–3, 1991–8. Ecclesiology is dealt with in vol. 3.

34 Hans-Peter Grosshans, *Die Kirche – irdischer Raum der Wahrheit des Evangeliums*, Leipzig: Ev.Verlag, 2003.

35 Grosshans, *Die Kirche*, p. 293.

36 *Ministry – Women – Bishops*, Geneva: LWF, 1993.

37 *The Episcopal Ministry within the Apostolicity of the Church: A Lutheran Statement*, Geneva, LWF, 2003.

38 *The Episcopal Ministry*, §§14, 12, 27.

39 *The Episcopal Ministry*, §33.

40 E.g. Reinhard Hütter, *Suffering Divine Things: Theology as Church Practice*, Grand Rapids, MI: Eerdmans, 2000; and Hütter, *Bound to Be Free: Evangelical Catholic Engagements in Ecclesiology, Ethics, and Ecumenism*, Grand Rapids, MI: Eerdmans, 2004.

41 This claim is made by Stanley Hauerwas, *The Peaceable Kingdom*, Notre Dame: The University of Notre Dame Press, 1983, p. 99. See also *Ecclesiology and Ethics*, ed. T. F. Best and M. Robra, Geneva: WCC, 1997.

42 Jenson, *Systematic Theology* vol. 2, p. 265; Wolfhart Pannenberg, *Systematic Theology* vol. 3, Grand Rapids, MI: Eerdmans, 1991–8, p. 364.

43 Rudolf Sohm, *Kirchenrecht* 1, 1892, p. 700.

44 Hermann Sasse, *In statu confessionis*, Berlin: Luth. Verlagshaus, 1966, p. 51. Quoted from Gunther Wenz, 'Kirche VIII', *Religion in Geschichte und Gegenwart* 4th edn, vol. 4, p. 1016. Wenz agrees with this statement.

45 In particular John of Torquemada's *Summa de ecclesia* (1453).

Further reading

Anglican-Lutheran Agreements: Regional and International Agreements 1972–2002, ed. Sven Oppegaard and Gregory Cameron, Geneva: LWF, 2004.

Communio sanctorum: The Church as the Communion of Saints. Collegeville: The Liturgical Press, 2004.

The Book of Concord: The Confessions of the Evangelical Lutheran Church, ed. Robert Kolb and Timothy Wengert, Minneapolis: Fortress, 2000.

From Federation to Communion: The History of the Lutheran World Federation, ed. Jens H. Schjorring et al., Minneapolis: Fortress, 1997.

Eric Gritsch, *A History of Lutheranism*, Minneapolis: Fortress, 2002.

Die Kirche Jesu Christi/The Church of Jesus Christ. Leuenberger Texte 1, Frankfurt: Lembeck, 1995.

Carter Lindberg, *The Pietist Theologians: An Introduction to the Theology in the Seventeenth and Eighteenth Centuries*. Oxford: Blackwell, 2004.

The Lutheran Church Past and Present, ed. Vilmos Vajta. Minneapolis: Augsburg, 1977.

Anders Nygren, *Christ and His Church*. Philadelphia: Westminster Press, 1956.

The Oxford Encyclopedia of the Reformation 1–4, ed. Hans J. Hillerbrand. Oxford: Oxford University Press, 1996.

Wolfhart Pannenberg, *Systematic Theology 1–3*. Grand Rapids, MI: Eerdmans 1991–8.

Gunther Wenz, *Theologie der Bekenntnisschriften der evangelisch-lutherischen Kirche 1–2*, Berlin: de Gruyter 1996–8.

10

REFORMED ECCLESIOLOGY

Eddy van der Borght

Introduction

'Reformed' refers to the churches and theological tradition, as an expression of Christian faith of all times and places, that began with the sixteenth-century Reformation in Zurich, Strasbourg and Geneva. Due to the specific political situation in the Swiss region and the bordering regions of southern Germany, the reformation of the church was part of the emancipation of cities in these regions from the regional and ecclesial authorities during the first half of the sixteenth century. The local magistrates invited theologians to join them and to reorganize the church in their territory. Ulrich Zwingli in Zurich, Martin Bucer in Strasbourg and John Calvin in Geneva are the most famous examples. These theologians were inspired by the theology of Luther and his reformation of the church in Germany, but the differences that surfaced in relation to the understanding of the Lord's Supper became divisive in most cases. At the end of the sixteenth century, they had developed a reformation of their churches, under the name *ecclesiae reformatae*, that was related to the Lutheran model but at the same time separated from it. These distinctions were both in doctrine and in the form of the church. The Latin motto of many Reformed churches, 'Ecclesia reformata, quia semper reformanda'[1] – the Reformed church because it is always reforming – became programmatic. They displayed their awareness of belonging to a common tradition by accepting one of a relatively narrow range of positions on the doctrine of the eucharist, by endorsing one or more of a common set of confessions of faith, by inviting one another's theologians to their synods, and by sending future ministers for higher education to one another's universities.

From its origins in Switzerland and its border regions, the tradition spread into France, the Low Countries, parts of the Holy Roman Empire, Hungary and the Polish Lithuanian commonwealth. In Scotland the Reformed church would become the established church. England's national church assumed a Reformed cast under Edward VI (1547–53) and permanently joined the ranks of Europe's Protestant kingdoms when Elizabeth I succeeded Mary Tudor in 1558.

In the British Isles, the Reformed tradition would focus more on church polity as an instrument to safeguard the reformation of the church. Some favoured presbyterianism – church government through councils – while others favoured congregationalism, which focused almost exclusively on the local congregation. As a consequence, the churches of the Reformed tradition on the Continent would be called Reformed, while those in Great Britain and Ireland would become known as Presbyterian and Congregationalist/Independent.

Along the paths of exile and in the settlements of trade and empire, the European movement steadily expanded throughout the world. At present, the World Alliance of Reformed
Churches, the most important grouping of churches within the Reformed tradition, consists
of 215 member churches in 107 countries with more than 75 million members. Its centres of
strength, with numbers over a million each, are Australia, Canada, Germany, Hungary,
Indonesia, the Netherlands, the Republic of Korea, South Africa, Scotland and Switzerland.

In accordance with the phrase, *ecclesia reformata semper reformanda*, the church is called
to listen and respond to the word of God in all times and all places. Always referring beyond
itself to the word of God, each confession of the church is contextual *in tempo et in loco*,
never providing a full and definite response to God's call. As a consequence of this contextual nature of confessions within the Reformed tradition, a large variety of confessional
statements have been and are being produced, but none of them has risen to the status of
universal confession. Because of the use of confessions, the tradition can be labelled 'confessional,' but 'confessing' seems more accurate – the confessing act of the church has priority
over its confessional identity. The catholicity of the church is expressed in a diversity of
contextual confessions, not in one confession for all churches. Lukas Vischer enumerates
the following elements of the Reformed heritage:[2]

1   *Christus solus*: Jesus Christ is the only and exclusive source of salvation.
2   God to be glorified in all things. As a reformulation of the first commandment, it
    expresses the conviction that our salvation depends entirely on God's initiative. The
    doctrine of predestination has its ultimate root in this emphasis on God's exclusive
    initiative. Some Reformed confessions go so far as teaching that the effectiveness of
    Christ's saving work is limited to those whom God has chosen to save. The doctrine
    of predestination has been the subject of controversies among Reformed churches.
    Whatever the position taken, two points are not to be forgotten. The doctrine of
    predestination is not meant to exalt the sense of election, but rather to underline the
    mysterious character of God's dealings with humanity; and it does not reduce the
    urgency of sharing the good news of salvation with all people.
3   Reformed teaching confirms the trinitarian teaching of the creeds of the early church.
    Reformed theology emphasizes the saving and healing power of the Holy Spirit. The
    concept of covenant and a succession of covenants throughout history reveal the same
    focus on the Holy Spirit, expressing God's ever new initiatives to lead humanity and
    the whole creation to fulfilment in the coming kingdom.
4   The church. Throughout history God has always called people to be the church. It is
    not for humans to decide who is part of the chosen people, who belongs to the true
    church, since it is only God alone who knows who is part of the church. So the church in
    history can only be a mixed community of called and non-called. Only in the eschaton
    will it become visible who is truly part of the church. The Reformed use the two
    Lutheran marks for the true church: the pure preaching of the Word and the proper use
    of the sacraments. To be a Christian outside the community is not an option, since the
    church is like a mother who nourishes the faithful during the pilgrimage of their life.
5   Prayer and worship. The first response to the proclamation of God's gift of salvation in
    Jesus Christ is prayer and praise. Worship is primarily a corporate act that consists of
    prayer, reading scripture, proclamation, and the regular celebration of the Lord's
    Supper. In their reformation of the church, the Reformed opted for a reformation of the
    liturgy that removed everything that distracted from these essentials. Images in the

churches of the sixteenth century were especially targeted. The use of musical instruments and the type of hymns were also hotly debated. Today a variety of worship styles have developed within the Reformed churches.

6   Discipleship and discipline. Justified through God's saving grace, we are called to live a life in the church that is inspired by thankfulness and that leads to sanctification. The Reformed understand the law in scripture as a guide for a renewed personal and communal life (*tertius usus legis*). Since unholy lives lead to disintegration of the Christian community, the exercise of discipline against unholy practices and unsound teaching must safeguard the integrity of the church.

7   Ministries and church order. The Reformed theologians of the sixteenth century were convinced that a reformation of the church was to be sustained through a thorough revision of the order of the church in line with biblical directions. The order of ministries especially became essential. Calvin's influential model in Geneva recognized four permanent biblical ministries: pastors to preach the word and administer the sacraments, elders to assist the pastors and exercise discipline, deacons to take care of the poor, and doctors responsible for the pure teaching of the church. In the British Isles, the confrontation with the episcopal system of the Church of England led to the conviction that the presbyterian system was the only biblical way to order ministries. Church polity became identity marks *par excellence* for the various churches, and gave rise to divisions within the Reformed tradition itself. The Presbyterians opted for a strong emphasis on the collegial exercise of authority, while the Congregationalists stressed the primacy of the local community. In recent decades, a number of unions have taken place in which the polity of the new church combines presbyterian, congregationalist and episcopal elements.

8   Local and universal. The Reformed marks of the church – pure preaching and appropriate administration of the sacraments – focus on the local community, especially since the mediation of the hierarchical order is notably absent, and the Congregationalists have made this local focus the identity marker of the church. As a result, Reformed churches have developed a tradition of strong participation and responsibility among the members. Most Reformed churches have combined this local accent with a development of common decision-making at regional and national levels through a structure of representation in presbyteries (classes) and synods (assemblies). This system of representative collegial structures has become part of the Reformed heritage. The common decision-making has almost never exceeded the national level. None of the international bodies which have been set up by Reformed churches are synodal in nature, but serve as platforms of exchange. Awareness that a more universal structure of decision-making is needed is growing among the Reformed churches.

9   Missionary calling. The awareness of missionary calling was absent in the sixteenth century, but has grown strongly, especially through the revival movements in the eighteenth and nineteenth centuries, and has become prominent through the practice of mission since the nineteenth century.

10   Truth and unity. The Reformed churches have grown out of the call to return to scripture and to Christ. This call for renewal has often put strain on the commitment to the unity of the churches. This dilemma has caused many to abstain from the ecumenical movement, while at the same time the majority have become active in dialogue, collaboration and union. The search for unity requires serious debate about matters of doctrine and church structures.

11 Church and state. The relationship between church and state was a major issue of disagreement between Zwingli/Bullinger and Calvin in the sixteenth century; the former opting for responsibility for the magistrates in the internal disciplinary actions of the church, while the latter opposed this vigorously and called for an independent judiciary within the church. Basically, the strong emphases on a coherent, constitutionally established, internal order of the church and the secularization of society in many countries of the West have favoured autonomy from the state.

12 The witness of the church in society. A preoccupation with the reform of the church has not been understood as being in conflict with the conviction that a call for renewal extends to all aspects of life – the whole society included. In the sixteenth century Calvin already called on the magistrates in Geneva to protest against unjust laws and to advocate the protection of the poor. The Accra Confession of the 24th General Assembly of the World Alliance of Reformed Churches in August 2004 against neo-liberal globalization is an expression of the same concern for a societal witness that calls for justice, peace and integrity of creation. At the same time, societal witness is contested among Reformed churches.

Major ecclesiastical events and developments

In the first half of the sixteenth century, magistrates of various Swiss cities invited theologians with ideas of how to reform the church to put their insights into practice. In this context, discussion focused on the measure of the independence of the church in relation to the city authorities. In France, the Reformed church was a minority church that could, in general, not count on the support of the authorities and was always in danger of persecution. As a consequence, a pattern of independent churches was forced on the Reformed community. In 1559 the Reformed congregations in France gathered for a first *synode* and adopted the *Confessio Gallicana* with the intention to be recognized as a minority religion, and it accepted a church order, the *Discipline Eccléstique*, which described the synodal model for a Reformed church that was no longer confined to a city.

The growth of the Reformed tradition into a separate branch of Western Christianity was a gradual process that was illustrated by the different stages of the development of confessional statements. In the first stage, Reformed theologians defended their position in a number of theses in public disputations, after which the magistrates decided whether or not to join the Reformation. Examples such as Zwingli's *Schlussreden* of 1523 and the *Berne Theses* of 1528 pleaded for a reformation of the church in accordance with the Word of God. In a second stage, confessions tried to explain to the population and the authorities of the Empire the Reformed understanding of the gospel and of the church as a continuation of the true tradition over against both the deviations in the medieval papal church and the radical positions of the Anabaptists and later the Anti-Trinitarians. Zwingli's *Fidei Ratio*, which was addressed to the Diet of Augsburg in 1530, and the *First Helvetic Confession* of 1536 figure as examples. *The Belgic Confession* (1561), *the Heidelberg Catechism* (1563) and the *second Helvetic Confession* (1566) illustrate the third phase, offering a coherent account of the Christian faith as taught by the Reformed churches. Calvin explored a fuller development of Christian doctrine in his *Institutes*, various expanded versions of which appeared over a period of more than 20 years. His successor, Theodore Beza, together with other theologians of that period, organized the Reformed thinking into a coherent system that appealed to reason – the key concepts of which became the notions of double predestination and covenant. The resulting Reformed orthodoxy was less open than the previous stages.

The doctrine of double predestination would not remain uncontested. This type of predestination holds that God has not only appointed the eternal destiny of some to salvation (unconditional election), but by necessary inference, also the remainder to eternal damnation (reprobation). In other words, before the foundation of the world, God appointed his elect to eternal life, and condemned the rest to everlasting punishment. Jacobus Arminius (1560–1609), professor in Leiden, and his followers – the *Remonstranten* – held that God has destined those who believe for salvation, that Christ has died for the whole of humanity, and that grace is not within reach of human will but that it is not irresistible. Those who remained faithful to Reformed orthodoxy and who feared more state control called an international synod in Dordrecht (1618–19). *The Canons of Dordrecht* condemned Arminianism: election does not depend on faith, Christ's death brings salvation only to the elect, human nature is corrupted by sin, conversion is effected exclusively by God and the elect will persist in faith.

In the field of church order, a similar tendency to further define and limit the options can be observed. While Calvin's presbyterian order left room for other forms of church structure, as long as the preaching of the Word of God was assured, the presbyterian order became the only acceptable and biblically valid form of government of the church for the established Church of Scotland.[3] The Reformed in England – calling themselves 'Presbyterians' – contested the episcopal and liturgical forms of the established Church of England. In the growing dispute between king and parliament, the parliament decided in 1642 to reform the church and convened a synod that adopted guidelines for worship and church order (1645), the *Westminster Confession* (1647) and two catechisms (1648). The *Westminster Confession* as an expression of Reformed orthodoxy – stressing the doctrines of predestination and the covenant – would become the most widespread of all Reformed confessional writings. The Puritan movement among the Presbyterians strove for worship according to biblical prescriptions – cleansed from external rites, images and vestment. Persecuted for their convictions, many of them went to North America where they profoundly influenced the Reformed tradition. The congregationalists among the Presbyterians organized independent congregations, convinced that the local church was to be considered the ultimate authority in the life of the church and that discipline was not to be carried out by the state, bishops or synods, but by the local congregation as a whole. In 1658 they issued the *Savoy Declaration* that basically recognized the teaching of the *Westminster Confession*, but developed their own understanding of church order. Because of persecution many of them emigrated to the Netherlands and America. The independent minded congregationalist had a deep impact on the history of the church in North America.

The Enlightenment challenged the Reformed orthodoxy in two areas: predestination and the verbal inspiration of scripture. Could the doctrine of predestination be combined with the Enlightenment conviction that human, rational beings had to take responsibility for their lives? And how could a life under the ultimate authority of the divinely inspired scriptures be combined with the free exercise of human reason? At the end of the eighteenth century, some were of the opinion that the Reformed confessions had a definitive and unchangeable character; others felt challenged to formulate new answers on the basis of scripture and the confessions. These two approaches would become more and more divisive in the nineteenth century.

From the eighteenth century onwards Pietism in Lutheran Germany[4] and Methodism in England resulted in a call for more personal piety within the Reformed tradition – demanding personal conversion, spiritual renewal and sharing in fellowship. The powerful preaching of George Whitefield (1714–70) and Jonathan Edwards (1703–58) – calling for personal conversion – made a strong impact on the Presbyterian Church in England and America. In the nineteenth century, a new revival movement swept through the European and American churches of the Reformed tradition. A rationalist, apologetic argumentation supported the call for personal conversion and targeted anti-Christian forces.

This revival movement influenced the attitude to mission within the Reformed tradition. The Reformed tradition began as a movement to reform the existing church. It took almost three centuries, until the age of colonization in the nineteenth century, to realize the missionary mandate. It was not the churches, but faithful individuals who took responsibility for the organization of mission societies, such as the London Missionary society (1795), the *Nederlandsch Zendingsgenootschap* (1797) and the Basel Mission (1835). Only in the course of the nineteenth century did they establish links with the denominations to which they belonged. This lack of coordination lead to the establishment of separate churches in the same countries, reproducing and multiplying the divisions of the home countries. Many of these churches bear the characteristics of the revival movement.

In order to be more effective, the churches had to overcome their divisions. Some denounced a sectarian spirit in the Protestant churches, which led to the founding of the Evangelical Alliance (1846), the World Alliance of Reformed Churches (1875), and the International Congregational Council (1891).

World War I had a deep impact on the traditional confidence among European Christians. In many countries of the continent, it meant the end of the 'Christian society'. The Swiss Reformed theologians – Karl Barth, Eduard Thurneysen and Emil Brunner – rejected pietistic and liberal theology as attempts to encapsulate God in human projects and developed an understanding of Christian faith based solely on God's revelation in Christ as witnessed in scripture. Building on the growing social awareness in the nineteenth century and the theological work of the religious socialists Hermann Kutter (1863–1931) and Leonhard Ragaz (1868–1945), churches invested more in their social role in society. As a consequence of the rise to power of the Nazis in Germany in the 1930s, the German churches were pressed to bring their teachings in line with the nationalistic inspirations of the regime. Some who were not prepared to proceed on that road came together in an extraordinary synod of the Evangelical Church in Germany in 1934 and adopted a text prepared by Karl Barth – the *Barmen Declaration* – which, in six theses, rejected any compromise with Nazi ideology. Many members of the 'confessing church' that came out of this declaration would be persecuted in the years following. For the Reformed faithful, it was not only a tangible expression of resistance against an anti-Christian regime, but also served as a proof that the time of the confessions was not closed. Actual situations challenge the churches to witness in a confessing manner to the truth of the gospel in critical situations. The *Barmen Declaration* would become a model in the years to come, one most notable example occurring in 1986, when the synod of the Dutch Reformed Mission Church, the synod of the coloured churches within the Dutch Reformed family in South Africa, accepted the *Confession of Belhar* that declared that apartheid in church and society was anti-Christian and sinful.

As the United States began playing a more dominant role on the world arena, the influence of developments in America affected the life and witness of the Reformed churches worldwide. One influential movement was fundamentalism – referring to fundamental, indisputable convictions for Christians – which published *The Fundamentals*, a series of pamphlets published from 1910 to 1915. The inerrancy of the Bible, the divinity of Jesus, Jesus Christ as Saviour, the bodily resurrection of Jesus Christ and the second coming of Christ are its central convictions. The emphasis on verbal inspiration of scripture received a favourable reaction from many Reformed churches that had already been influenced by the revival movement in the nineteenth century. The movement eventually became a cause of many splits in Reformed churches.

More than fundamentalism, the evangelical movement would become the true heir of the revival movement, committed as it is to the authority of the biblical word and to the missionary mandate. In 1846, the foundation of the Evangelical Alliance was an important institutional expression of the movement, intended to find an answer to the political and spiritual recovery of the Roman Catholic Church and to coordinate Protestant mission activities. It rejected liberal views and was suspicious of social agendas in the churches that undermined the priority of the call to evangelize the world. In 1974 the establishment of the International Conference on World Evangelism in Lausanne stimulated the new missionary enterprise. Evangelicalism has become an integral part of the Reformed churches and has especially appealed to those in the Reformed pietistic tradition.

Pentecostalism is the third movement in the United States with an important impact on the churches of the Reformed tradition. William Seymour (1870–1922), the son of a black slave, is regarded as the founder of the Azusa Street Revival in Los Angeles (1906). Central to this revival was personal experience of the Holy Spirit, who provides self-respect to marginalized people. It influenced the existing churches and provided a stimulus for focus on the work of the Holy Spirit. Sometimes Pentecostalism found its way into the church; sometimes new churches were established.

After World War II, and particularly in the 1960s and 1970s, many Reformed churches in Western countries began to decline, while churches in the south expanded considerably. Two thirds of Reformed Christians today are to be found in Africa, Asia and Latin America. Indonesia, Korea and Nigeria especially serve as examples of countries with fast growing churches in the Reformed tradition.

Key ecclesiastical ideas and historical thinkers

By its nature, the Reformed tradition is challenged to describe the understanding and relevance of the gospel in every time and every place. As a living tradition, it yielded many contextual confessions, but also outstanding Christian theologians – such as Friedrich Schleiermacher at the beginning of the nineteenth century in Germany and Karl Barth in the twentieth century in Switzerland and Germany. Because it would be impossible in our limited space to give an adequate overview of the major Reformed theologians who substantially contributed to the development of Christian theology, this section will be limited to a description of one of the most import aspects of the theologian who has been most influential in forming the identity of the Reformed tradition: the ecclesiology of John Calvin.[5]

After more than two centuries of fighting, a growing number of self-governing cantons in the Alpine valleys, which were allied in the Swiss Confederation, had established a *de facto* independence of the Holy Roman Empire at the beginning of the sixteenth century. The civic authorities of the modestly sized cities in this region exercised substantial control over religious matters, taking seriously the ideal of the city as a Christian society. The establishment of Reformed churches within large parts of this territory depended upon the combined efforts of a group of interconnected humanists influenced by Erasmus.

The jurist John Calvin (1509–64), fleeing France after the suppression of the Protestants as a consequence of public controversy concerning the Mass in 1533, had drawn the attention of Geneva after the publication of the first edition of the *Institutio Christianae Religionis* in 1536 and was promptly invited to join Geneva in its efforts to reform the church in the city as part of their emancipation from submission to the Duke of Savoy and the papal church. The rest of his life would be devoted to the reformation of the church in Geneva and the development of his theology. His success in instituting an independent system of church discipline, the fame of his main work, *Institutio Christianae Religionis*, his involvement in the spreading of Reformed Protestantism – particularly in France but also in other parts of Europe – and the establishment of a theological academy all contributed to the fame of Calvin and Geneva's rise to prominence as the major centre of Reformed Protestantism in the second half of the sixteenth century.

His work on the completion of the Reformation in Geneva, begun by Guillaume Farel, would take about 20 years, during which time he was often at odds with the city government and was banned from the city between 1538 and 1541. During that period, Calvin ministered to the congregation for French refugees in Strasbourg at the invitation of Martin Bucer. The *Ecclesiastical Ordinances* were instrumental in the reorganization of the church, in which he tried to safeguard ecclesiastical prerogatives. They acknowledged four ministries with roots in the New Testament: *pastors*, who as ministers of the Word and the sacraments were to continue the ministerial care of the laity that was exercised by medieval parish priests and bishops; *doctors*, responsible for teaching on all levels – up to the most scholarly investigation of the Bible; *elders* chosen among the members of the various councils of the city and responsible for upholding discipline within the church; and the *deacons*, taking care of the charitable work. The *Ecclesiastical Ordinances* would become so successful because they contained a subtle balance of power between the ecclesiastical and civil power in the city. Central was the provision that attributed the power to test and nominate candidates for pastoral positions to the company of pastors, while granting the city government and the congregation final consent. Second, he made ecclesiastical and civil authorities co-responsible for upholding high moral and doctrinal standards through the creation of the consistory in which the pastors and the elders worked together and investigated issues such as irregular church attendance, inadequate knowledge of the catechism, suspected 'magical' or Catholic practices, moral offences – mostly sexual improprieties but also gambling, dancing and false business practices, and the defence of clerical authority. Punishment could range from private admonition before the consistory, to exclusion from communion, and referral of serious offences against civic legislation to the secular magistrates. The question of who had the power to excommunicate people from the church and city was contentious. Every week the ministers met in the *conférence* for common biblical and theological study, and sessions of fraternal corrections. All these measures created a new moral climate among the ministers and in the city at large that was illustrated by an astonishingly low rate of illegitimate births and prenuptial conceptions. The downside of this image of godly community was the growing number of excommunications and Genevans voluntarily leaving the town. This was compensated by a high influx of refugees entering the city. Calvin's theological teaching did not leave room for people with a fundamentally different view, as in the case of Hieronymus Bolsec who contested Calvin's views on predestination, nor the Italian anti-Trinitarians, who were all subsequently banned from the city. Most contested is Calvin's role in the execution of Michael Servetus, an Aragonese doctor with an idiosyncratic mille-narian religious vision. D. MacCulloch correctly observes: 'It was in fact much more like the high clericalism of the old Western Church. . . . A Church that stood alongside the civil authority and felt a God-given right to criticize it if necessary, while still aspiring to minister to the entire population which the civil authority administered, was a powerful expression of militant Catholic Christianity.'[6] Indeed, Calvin did not plan to start a denomination, but to reform the church.

As a prolific preacher and writer – including Bible commentaries, occasional writings and letters – he would continue to develop his first major text, *Institutio Christianae Religionis* (1536) from a catechetical handbook into a dogmatic work designed to familiarize students with the main points of Christian doctrine and later into a hermeneutical key for the study of scripture in the last of several Latin and French editions in 1559. This volume was expanded to four times the original of 1536. The fact that he kept the same title and merely expanded the original work indicates Calvin's own perception of the continuity in his thinking in many new contexts that made him develop the work.

In the first edition of 1536, he focuses on the church when explaining the words of the creed, *una sancta catholica*. He denies the identification claim of the hierarchical papal church with this church of the creeds. Instead, he emphasizes that the church of the creed is the invisible church. She is the sum of all those elected by God: those of previous ages, those living now and those to come in the future – humans as well as angels. Since the church has its foundation in the hidden election in Christ, only God knows who is part of it. Because God's calling is unrepentant, the elected cannot fall out of his hand, and this (invisible) church will always continue. This invisible church becomes visible where Word and sacra-ments are administered according to Christ's institution.

The work in Geneva immediately forced Calvin to be much more specific about the visible church. During the time of his banning between 1538 and 1541, he learned from Bucer in Strasbourg the need for organized church discipline and the possibility of discerning between a pluriformity of biblical ministries. These points would immediately become visible in the *Ecclesiastical Ordinances* that he presented to the magistrates upon his return to Geneva in 1541. And the next edition of the *Institutio Christianae Religionis* would present the theological justification. We will now proceed to a summary of the development of his ecclesiology, the fourth and most extensive part of the final edition of 1559.

While the third part of the *Institutes* concentrated on the internal working of the Holy Spirit in the heart of the individual believer, part four focused on the external means used by the Spirit to keep the faithful in communion with Christ: the church, its government, orders and power, and the civil order. The first chapter about the church begins with the invisible church grounded in election, but then goes on to the visible church, with the following introduction:

> But because it is now our intention to discuss the visible church, let us learn even from the simple title 'mother' how useful, indeed how necessary, it is that we should know her. For there is no other way to enter into life unless this mother conceive us in her womb, give us birth, nourish us at her breast, and lastly, unless she keep us under her care and guidance until, putting off mortal flesh, we become like angels (Matt. 22:30). Our weakness does not allow us to be dismissed from her school until we have been pupils all our lives.[7]

Calvin agrees with the insight of Cyprian that outside the church there is no forgiveness of sins and no salvation. This means that although for Calvin the visible church is not of the same rank as the invisible church of the elect, and as an external means is not salvation itself, yet this visible church is still an indispensable entrance into communion with Christ. And he adds another reason for not despising the visible church: she functions in accordance with an order instituted by God. He argues on the basis of Ephesians 4.11 that the educational task of the mother church is only instrumentally carried out in accordance with the will of God through the ministers' proclamation of the gospel. This *ordo* was God's *modus operandi* in Israel: he not only gave the law; he also provided priests to explain it. Although we do not know who the elect are, we can recognize the visible church as a community – a body – on the basis of the characteristics of purity in preaching the Word, being obedient, and administration of the sacraments in accordance with Christ's institution (IV.I.9).[8] It is important to note that Calvin does not mention discipline as one of the marks of the church.

Those who abandon the church in order to form a holy gathering without spot or wrinkle forget that the church stands in an eschatological perspective and is grounded in the justification of the godless.[9] They lack mercy. Calvin confronts this misplaced hankering for holiness by saying that the church is not just built on holiness in the Spirit, but is above all rooted in the reconciliation and justification of the cross. In this context, he again speaks about proclamation by ministers as it had been entrusted by Christ to the church and her servants from the time of the apostles; namely, as the power of the keys. With Paul, he characterizes this service as an ambassadorship of reconciliation (2 Cor 5.20). The theme of the proclamation by ministers is reconciliation with God in the name of Christ. The forgiveness of sins must be sought where God has placed it; namely, within the community of the church. This is confirmed in the creed: the forgiveness of sins is coupled to the church.

In addition to these marks, Calvin distinguishes different 'degrees' or levels in the visible church (IV.I.9). In the first place, he mentions the *ecclesia universalis*. This primary attention to the 'universal church' corresponds with his intensive ecumenical–ecclesiastical praxis. The question as to how this universal church is given concrete form remains unanswered. He mentions the local congregation as the second form taken by the visible church and emphasizes that this constitutes not a secondary, but a fully-fledged form of the church that is justified in claiming the name and the authority of the church. The third stage is formed by the individual people who are regarded as church on the basis of their profession of religion.

While Calvin intended to convince the Anabaptists to no longer detest the non-perfect church with its ministerial order and sacraments in the first chapter, in the second chapter he confronts the Roman Catholics when he distinguishes the false from the true church. The false church under the papacy tries in vain to claim legitimacy by pointing to an uninterrupted line of bishops, which allegedly started with the apostles (IV.II.2). Calvin rejects this claim that succession in the legal apostolic office is a mark of the true church because the Lord never recognizes anything as his own, except where his Word is heard and scrupulously observed. In the second part of this chapter, Calvin defends himself against the Roman Catholics' reproach that he and his followers behave like schismatics and heretics. The church's fellowship, held together by the bonds of sound doctrine and brotherly love, is broken when it is given form outside the Word of the Lord (IV.II.5). It is the Church of Rome that has broken communion with Christ – her head – and it is that church herself, with her *anathemas* against the followers of the Reformation, that has destroyed unity (IV.

II.6). But Calvin does not definitively write off this church. Some traces (*vestigia*) still remain. He particularly thinks of baptism as a mark of the covenant (IV.II.11).

In the third chapter Calvin develops his theology of ministry. The church's ministry finds its origin in the will of God to speak to us through the service of people. This also ensures the ministry's indispensability and dignity. There is a direct line from Christ to the minister. Christ uses ministry to offer the church his Word that brings salvation. Therefore, the leadership given by the minister is a symbol of christocracy. Ministers are only servants of Christ and his Word. They are not delegated by the congregation. And it is only as servants of the Word that they can be servants of the church, and not the other way around. On the basis of the New Testament, Calvin tries to distinguish four permanent ministries – pastor, doctor, elder and deacon – of which the first one, as ministry of the Word and sacraments, is central. He ends the chapter on ministry with much attention to orderly election and ordination.

From the fourth chapter onward, Calvin explores church governance in a historical perspective. After studying the way the New Testament offices functioned in the early church (Chapter IV) and their subsequent degeneration (V), he contemplates the assumptions for papal primacy (VI) and its historic growth (VII), and concludes by assessing the mandates to teach (VIII-IX), pass laws (X) and act with legal authority (XI-XII). Calvin rejects the papacy because the popes do not take up their task as shepherds who watch over their flocks by proclaiming the Word, administering the sacraments and exercising discipline. Just like other Reformers, he is horrified by the degeneration that took place in the way the ministry was exercised: they called themselves 'the vicars of Christ', they declared themselves to be head of the church, and instead of carrying out their ministry in a collegial way, they became dictators. The result was that they became so alienated from the believers that they were no longer able to speak on behalf of them. It is open to question whether the conclusion to be drawn, as far as Calvin is concerned, is that there can be no universal office whose aim is the unity of churches and believers. When describing Peter's task and function, he recognizes the need for a person who is a symbol of unity. His radical language is mainly aimed at how the papacy functioned in his own day, and it has a conditional, provisional character. In Calvin's judgement, this centre of unity is not based on divine law and scripture. Especially in Chapters 11 and 12, he understands the consistory where pastors and elders work together as the most appropriate way to exercise discipline – avoiding both arbitrariness as in the Roman Catholic Church and the relinquishing of ecclesiastical responsibility to the civil authorities as in the Lutheran and Zwinglian churches.

In his discussion of the sacraments, Calvin's formulation of his eucharistic teaching is especially important. Understanding sacraments in an Augustinian way as visible signs of an invisible grace, he attempted a middle ground between the symbolic understanding of Zwingli and the Lutheran doctrine of the real presence. Luther had not paid enough attention to the fact that a sign is different from the reality it refers to, while Zwingli – in Calvin's opinion – tended to separate the sign from the reality it refers to. Christ makes himself truly present to believers in the ritual, but only in the spirit – not as a real, substantial presence. The eucharist confirms and refreshes the faith of the believers, inspires them to greater thanksgiving and love for God, and binds them to one another in concord and affection. In 1549 Geneva, Zurich, Bern and other Swiss Reformed cities agreed on a common declaration on the sacraments – the 'Zurich Agreement' or *Consensus Tigurinus* – worked out by Calvin and Zwingli's successor, Heinrich Bullinger, in which they rejected the Lutheran understanding of the eucharist. By this agreement on the sacraments, the division between Lutheran and Reformed churches became almost permanent.

In the last chapter Calvin discusses the civil government as an external instrument of the Holy Spirit. Secular governments foster peace and tranquillity among men and uphold both tablets of the Ten Commandments. So they are obliged to punish idolatry, sacrilege and blasphemy. Although separate in jurisdiction, secular and ecclesiastical government were 'conjoined'.

Recent ecclesiological thought in the tradition and the place of the tradition in the ecumenical movement

Commitment to the ecumenical movement

Reformed churches were among the first to respond to the initiatives that ultimately led to the founding of the World Council of Churches in 1948 – Reformed Christians being active participants in the two movements of 'Faith and Order' and 'Life and Work' before World War II. The first two general secretaries of the council belonged to the Reformed tradition: Willem A. Visser 't Hooft (1948–66) of the Netherlands Reformed Church and Eugene C. Blake (1966–72) of the United Presbyterian Church in the USA. Many Reformed churches welcomed the new ecumenical initiative and joined the organization. Of the founding member churches, one third were Reformed, Presbyterian, or Congregationalist. The World Alliance of Reformed Churches (WARC) decided to deal with issues, as much as possible, in the context of the wider ecumenical family and moved its headquarters to Geneva, in the same building as the headquarters of the WCC.

But other Reformed churches were suspicious that membership of the WCC would lead to loss of confessional identity. A number of Reformed churches, mainly of Dutch origin and strongly committed to the classical Reformed confessions, established the Reformed Ecumenical Synod in 1946 as an international platform for an unambiguous Reformed witness. It was later renamed the Reformed Ecumenical Council (REC) and currently has 12 million members in 40 churches in 25 countries. However, its original ecumenical distrust has faded away. In the beginning of 2006, WARC and REC decided to begin the process of becoming one World Reformed Communion, representing more than 80 million Reformed Christians.

Some other churches took a vigorously anti-ecumenical stance, characterizing it as betrayal and apostasy. These churches were mainly influenced by the fundamentalist movement, who formed their own International Council of Christian Churches in 1948, and feared Roman Catholic and/or communist influence in the ecumenical movement. For many Reformed churches, participation in the ecumenical movement became a source of controversy and, in some cases, even division.

The opening up of the Roman Catholic Church to the world and to other churches since the Second Vatican Council (1962–5) challenged other churches to review their position towards this church. Some Reformed churches have explicitly modified their teaching by declaring certain anti-Roman sentences in the Reformed confessions obsolete. But other churches remain reserved or hostile toward the idea of closer contacts with the Roman Catholic Church and the relationship with the Roman Catholic Church continues to be a contentious issue among Reformed churches. In 1970 the Roman Catholic Church and the World Alliance of Reformed Churches started a formal dialogue that resulted in the report, *The Presence of Christ in Church and World*, which dealt with the question of the role and place of the church within the relationship between God and the world. The second phase focused on the doctrine of the church from a trinitarian perspective and published its final report, *Towards a Common Understanding of the Church*, in 1990. This interesting document begins with an attempt to reconcile memories and describe the common faith, and then proceeds to analyse the remaining differences caused by divergent conceptions of the church as *creatura verbi* or as sacrament of grace. These differing approaches produce varying answers to questions about whether the church can sin, whether the church is fundamentally visible, and the role of the ministerial order in the mission of the church. The third phase of the dialogue focuses on the church as a community of common witness to the Kingdom of God.

In 1973 the Leuenberg Agreement was signed between Lutheran and Reformed churches of Europe and marked the end of over 450 years of division between the churches. On the basis of their common understanding of the gospel, the past condemnations by the Reformation confessions in respect to the Lord's Supper, christology and predestination are no longer an obstacle to church fellowship (§ 27). The differences in forms of worship, types of spirituality and church order are also not a dividing factor (§28). The Leuenberg Agreement is the basic document of the Leuenberg Church Fellowship which in 2003 renamed itself as the Community of Protestant Churches in Europe. A similar agreement was adopted in the United States in 1997 and in the Middle East in 2006 (Amman Declaration). Various Reformed and Lutheran churches in countries such as Germany, the Netherlands, the United States, Indonesia, etc. have come into full mutual recognition of church, sacraments and ministries or have united. The first world-level dialogue resulted in the report *Toward Church Fellowship* (1989), followed by *Called to Common Witness and Communion* (2002).

The Anglican–Reformed dialogue focused on the unity of the church in the context of mission and the unity of humanity in its report, *God's Reign and Our Unity* (1984). *Together in God's Grace* was the title of the final report of the Methodist–Reformed dialogue of 1985–7, which evaluated whether doctrinal differences still have the power to divide the church in the context of the call to confess the gospel today. The dialogue between the Disciples of Christ and the Reformed resulted in *Towards Closer Fellowship* (1987), which dealt with issues such as the understanding of the church, baptism, Lord's Supper and ministry. The Mennonite–Reformed dialogue (*Mennonites and Reformed in Dialogue* 1986) covers the historic condemnation of the Mennonites by the Reformed, and issues that are relevant for Mennonite identity – such as baptism, peace and the state. During the seventies, the Baptist–Reformed dialogue discussed distinctive elements of Baptist and Reformed heritages; God's purpose for the world; scripture, church, baptism, mission, ministry; and the local and universal church. More recently, dialogue with the Pentecostal churches resulted in the report, *Word and Spirit, Church and World* (2001), which deals with various aspects of the work of the Holy Spirit. In that same year, the first dialogue session with the Seventh-Day Adventists was launched. Through their contacts within the WCC, the Orthodox and the Reformed started a bilateral dialogue that led to two agreed statements, one on the Holy Trinity (1993) and one on Christology (1994). Dialogue with the Oriental Orthodox began in 1992 with the objective of fostering mutual understanding and fellowship.

Challenges

Two issues have been hotly debated within and among the churches of the Reformed tradition since World War II. The first concerns the place of women in the church and has focused on the use of inclusive language, the participation of women in decision-making and the ordination of women to the ministry. Some Reformed churches have decided to allow women to exercise all ministries in the church – the ordained ministry included; others have refused them ordination. Both convictions defend their position with biblical arguments. The second issue relates to homosexuality, in particular the question of the place of homosexuals in the church, the blessing of homosexual relationships and homosexuals in (ordained) ministries. The discussion on this item has proved to be very difficult in many churches. One group even condemned the discussion of the topic itself. Here the various groups also defend their position on biblical grounds.

The history of the Reformed family since the sixteenth century expresses the vitality and dynamism of the tradition. It developed a strong missionary call and is rapidly growing in various places. Its call to sanctify all aspects of life as an expression of gratefulness for salvation in Christ stimulates social involvement. The challenge not to be only a confessional, but also – and even more – a confessing church favours much creativity in theological thinking. The result is a tradition with an impressive diversity of expressions of faith, ordering of the church and liturgical formulations.

But its strengths are at the same time its weaknesses. Many faithful do not consider the diversity as a richness, and instead experience a sense of estrangement. Controversies and splits have become a painful aspect of the tradition. How can the unity in all this diversity be strengthened? Are the classical elements for the unity of the church such as sound proclamation and administration of the sacraments, confessions and discipline not effective? The divisions within the tradition require a thorough investigation of its understanding of the church and its unity.

The experience that within the church contrasting points of view are equally defended on biblical grounds challenges the churches of the Reformed family to rethink their use of scripture. On the one hand, it proves that for everybody in the tradition the biblical authority is primordial. On the other hand, it reveals that scripture can be used to defend contrasting positions and that, as a consequence, a more balanced hermeneutical capacity has to be developed in order to use the scripture with authority in our actual situations.

More than ever, the churches within the Reformed tradition are challenged to understand their name as a programme: *ecclesia reformata semper reformanda*.

Notes

1 The motto was coined by the seventeenth-century Dutch churchman, Johannes Hoornbeek.
2 Lukas Vischer, 'The Reformed tradition and its multiple facets' in: Jean-Jacques Bauswein and Lukas Vischer, *The Reformed Family Worldwide: A survey of Reformed churches, theological schools and international organizations*, Grand Rapids, MI: Eerdmans, 1999, pp. 1–33.
3 See also Chapter 30 of this volume, on 'Governance'.
4 See also Chapter 9 of this volume, on 'Lutheran Ecclesiology'.
5 See also Chapter 4 of this volume, on 'Ecclesiology and the Religious Controversy of the Sixteenth Century'.
6 D. MacCulloch, *Reformation: Europe's House Divided 1490–1700*. London: Penguin Books, 2004, p. 240.
7 John Calvin, *Institutes of the Christian Religion* [1559], 2 vols, ed. John T. McNeill, trans. Ford Lewis Battles, Philadelphia: Westminster, 1960. The quote is from IV, I, 4.
8 The *Institutes* are traditionally referred to through reference to the book, the chapter and the paragraph.
9 Again cf. Chapter 4 and also Chapter 36 of this volume.

Further reading

Philip Benedict, *Christ's Churches Purely Reformed: A Social History of Calvinism*, New Haven, CT: Yale University Press, 2002.

Nicholas Lossky (ed.), *Dictionary of the Ecumenical Movement*. Geneva: WCC Publications, 2002, various entries.

Diarmaid MacCulloch, *Reformation: Europe's House Divided 1490–1700*, London: Penguin Books, 2004.

Alan P.F. Sell, 'The Alliance in dialogue, 1970–2003', *Reformed World*, 53/4 (2003), 210–27.

Eduardus Van der Borght, *Theology of Ministry: A Reformed Contribution to an Ecumenical Dialogue.* Leiden: Brill, 2007.

Lukas Vischer, 'The Reformed tradition and its multiple facets', in Jean-Jacques Bauswein and Lukas Vischer, *The Reformed Family Worldwide: A Survey of Reformed Churches, Theological Schools and International Organizations*, Grand Rapids, MI: Eerdmans, 1999, pp. 1–33. I have made extensive use of this work in writing this chapter.

Michael Weinrich, 'Confessing unity: a Reformed perspective on ecumenism', *Reformed World*, 53/4 (2003), 170–80.

11

ANGLICAN
ECCLESIOLOGY

Paul Avis

The character of Anglican ecclesiology

Introduction

At the beginning of the twenty-first century, Anglicanism is racked by internal argument and conflict over issues of sexual ethics, gender roles and – bound up with both of those – authority. This is not necessarily unhealthy, a sign of ecclesial pathology. In some ways, the 'normal' state of the Christian church is to be seething with argument and controversy. Conflict is endemic in Christianity and Anglicanism is not a special case.[1] Christians struggle to interpret the Bible and to apply its teaching to their current problems. They also wrestle with the question of the authority of tradition – in all its diversity. The Bible and tradition do not explicitly address some of these challenges in their current form, though there are some voices insisting that answers – generally negative ones – can be read off from the Bible or the unvarying practice of the church. However, that is not the Anglican way. Anglicans revere scripture and honour tradition, but they also take seriously what biblical criticism, historical scholarship and the human and social sciences have to say. Moreover, they believe in free and honest discussion, argument and debate and are averse to curtailing these by an arbitrary act of authority from on high: by and large censorship is not in the Anglican vocabulary. Anglicans are sustained through these intellectual and pastoral travails by the conviction that the truth will prevail, if only we 'listen to the Spirit' and maintain the bonds of charity and communion – and keep talking to each other, while aiming for the highest degree of communion that is possible between groups that have deep disagreements on grounds of conscience.

While the world around 'us' drifts further and further from the Christian church and is faced by urgent challenges of environmental degradation, global warming, HIV-Aids, global terror networks, overpopulation, hunger, disease and natural disasters, Anglicans spend as much time and energy arguing among themselves about whether women can be priests and whether or not homosexuality is acceptable. In the New Testament there are no priests or clergy as we know them and homosexuality was not a recognized condition. The appeal to unvarying tradition is largely an argument from silence. Genuine Anglican efforts to organize for mission and to rethink evangelism for our times are often eclipsed by public agonizing over matters that public opinion takes in its stride. The New Testament is gripped by the urgency of spreading the gospel of Christ, hastening the coming of God's kingdom and glorifying God in all that we do in our personal lives and in the common life of the church. Anglicans should have a bad conscience about squandering energy on internal squabbles while God yearns to redeem the world. People looking on, sometimes wistfully, from the sidelines draw their own conclusions about the relevance of the gospel.[2]

The ethos of Anglican ecclesiology

Anglican ecclesiology is modest – not in the sense that it does not make robust and sometimes rather grandiose claims for itself – but in the sense that it does not have grand intellectual pretensions. The quantum of official Anglican doctrine of the church is limited. This is probably true of Anglican doctrine as a whole: its character is to say what is necessary to keep the faithful on the road to salvation, and no more. Anglicanism is not a speculative faith: it does not erect conceptual superstructures. It is pastoral and, to that extent, pragmatic in character. It is concerned with what works in the Christian life and in the life of the community. Also, Anglicanism is not a confessional faith, as Lutheranism is, with its considerable body of official doctrine, including polemics, gathered together in *The Book of Concord*. Similarly, Anglicanism does not have the distinctive combination of scholasticism and an unchallengeable magisterium that the Roman Catholic Church has. Authority in Anglicanism can always be questioned. The legacy of the past is not systematized or codified, as in Denzinger's compendium of Roman Catholic doctrinal formulations, but is allowed to remain occasional, untidy and incomplete. Anglicanism presupposes the common tradition of the churches up to the sixteenth century and is open and receptive to what can be learned from other traditions: it draws particularly on Roman Catholic, Orthodox and Lutheran insights and resources. This inheritance can be appealed to selectively as it suits the needs of the moment. Anglicanism is frankly eclectic and is unlikely (in a rather disarming way) to deny it. Of course, other traditions are probably equally eclectic, but may be reluctant to admit this.

A second way in which Anglican ecclesiology is modest is that it does not make exclusive claims for itself. While the Roman Catholic and Orthodox Churches have traditionally seen themselves as the true church and have denied others the status of 'church' in the proper sense of the word (as the Roman Catholic Church has recently done in *Dominus Iesus* [2000] and in 'Responses to some questions regarding certain aspects of the doctrine of the Church' [2007]), Anglicanism has never made such a claim. In England it has seen itself as the original Catholic church in the land, in continuity with the mediaeval and patristic church. In the sixteenth, seventeenth and eighteenth centuries the Church of England recognized the Lutheran and Reformed churches on the mainland of Europe as sister churches and saw itself as part of the Protestant or Reformation family of churches – though not at the expense of being the Catholic church in England.

In more recent times some Anglican spokesmen (e.g. Stephen Bayne, Robert Runcie) have spoken of the provisionality of Anglicanism. They have described it as incomplete, temporary and destined to lose itself in a greater whole. This sounds rather noble and altruistic until we ask whether there are, in fact, any extant expressions of the church that should not be regarded as provisional but as final and permanent. Surely, no church, even the largest, can claim to be definitive. In a divided Christian church, there cannot be any church that is not provisional. They are all called into question by the existence of others. To deny this would be to embrace an ecumenical theology of 'return', implying that there is one church to which all others should revert – i.e. they are all provisional, except one, the 'mother' church. Anglicans would say that all churches are provisional in the light of the one, holy, catholic and apostolic church, which we confess in the creed. This means that those who affirm that the churches of the Anglican Communion are merely provisional churches are absolutely right – but it needs to be spelled out that this is said in the context of a fragmented universal church where there is no church that is not provisional when seen in an eschatological perspective.

These forms of theological modesty – the compact tool kit of doctrines about the church, the eschewing of any exclusive claims, and the confession of provisionality – help to give Anglican ecclesiology its distinctive character. But they are, of course, related. It is precisely because Anglicanism does not believe that it is the only true church and is able to affirm that it is a provisional expression of the church of Christ that it needs only a small quantity of specific doctrine, even on the subject of the church: the rest is a common inheritance. This brings us to the vexed question of whether Anglicanism has any special doctrines of its own.

Some distinguished modern interpreters of Anglicanism and apologists for it (Michael Ramsey, Stephen Neill, Henry McAdoo) have insisted that Anglicanism has no special doctrines of its own.[3] After frequent repetition, this has become unquestioned orthodoxy for many Anglicans. However, this assumption needs further probing. It goes without saying that the Anglican churches embrace the credal orthodoxy of the formative centuries of the church with regard to trinitarian and christological doctrine. The authority of the General Councils that produced these doctrines is acknowledged by Anglicans. The Nicene-Constantinopolitan Creed is rehearsed in the eucharist that is celebrated in Anglican churches. Is there any church that does not accept the ecumenical creeds, but manufactures its own? So far, then, what Stephen Sykes has branded the 'no special doctrines' gambit is a statement of the obvious, a platitude. It is integral to the self-definition of any church that it identifies itself with the doctrines articulated by the early church, because all churches see themselves as existing in continuity with the early church. All churches would disown with horror any suggestion that they might manufacture novel doctrines of their own. Even when churches appear to innovate (by ordaining women, or by recognizing same-sex relationships, for example), they appeal to biblical and traditional precedents and principles, as far as possible, in an attempt to show that what may appear to be an innovation is simply a development of what is latent in Christianity but has lacked the opportunity to be realized. The 'no special doctrines' or 'no doctrines of our own' mantra serves a purpose: it is symbolic of the intention of Anglicanism to be Catholic, to assert its claim to belong to the mainstream, to be part of the whole; it is saying, we are not like a schismatic sect, an aberration, we believe what the church believes.

Nevertheless the 'no special doctrines' claim is a fallacy. The divided state of Christendom decrees that every church should have at least one doctrine of its own – a doctrine of the church (i.e. ecclesiology) that legitimates its existence and affirms its integrity. While some churches continue to challenge (at least by implication) the right of other churches to exist, those latter churches will find it necessary to articulate a doctrine of the church that provides a place and a justification for their existence. The Anglican Communion cannot exist on the basis of Roman Catholic ecclesiology: that ecclesiology denies Anglicanism's ecclesial integrity. Anglicanism must have its own ecclesiology, and, of course, it does.

That does not mean that the Anglican doctrine of the church stands apart from all other ecclesiologies, that it does not overlap extensively with other churches' doctrines. In the eyes of faith there is only one church and because all the separated churches confess that fact and all orientate themselves towards it, they are bound to share extensive common ground when it comes to describing the church. To a significant extent, there is a general or ecumenical doctrine of the church: specific ecclesiologies are derived from that as it is expressed in diverse historical, political, social and cultural contexts. The existence of distinctive ecclesiologies does not call into question the existence of a Christian doctrine of the church, but rather affirms it.

The development of Anglican ecclesiology

The Reformation is not the beginning

Anglican ecclesiology did not begin at the Reformation. For Anglicans, the Reformation meant (and means), negatively, the repudiation of the jurisdiction of the Bishop of Rome within England and of several errors and corruptions of the medieval church. Positively, it meant (and means) the renewal of the church's life, worship and ministry by a return to the wellsprings of Christian doctrine and practice in the Greek New Testament and the writings of the early Fathers in the original languages. It did not (and does not) mean that a new church was born in the sixteenth century or that a line was drawn in the sand at that point, separating an 'old' church from a 'new' one. There was massive continuity as well as substantial discontinuity.[4] While at a popular level, the 'popish' past was often violently repudiated,[5] more considering minds, such as John Jewel (Bishop of Salisbury 1560–71) and Richard Hooker, knew that the integrity of the Church of England depended on its maintaining its visible continuity with the church through the ages, running back through the immediately preceding late medieval church to the early Fathers, bishops and martyrs. In reality, the reformed Church of England was formed, by addition or subtraction, from what it had inherited from the medieval church. The scriptures continued to be the final court of appeal and were (eventually) made available in the vernacular. The creeds were untouched (the *Filioque* of the Latin West being retained). The reformed liturgies were adaptations of medieval forms, and were written in the vernacular. The structure of parishes within dioceses remained. The round of parochial ministration continued through all the upheavals. Uniquely in Europe, the cathedrals remained as the mother church of the diocese, the seat of the bishop, with their own foundation, and more cathedrals were created. The Convocations of the Clergy still met, though they were now answerable to the king rather than to the pope. Large amounts of canon law were carried over. The first point to be made about the development of Anglican ecclesiology, then, is this: it did not begin with Anglicanism (the term is, in any case, an anachronism before the second half of the seventeenth century).

The reform (to use the received but admittedly tendentious term) of the English church was initiated by Henry VIII prior to the impact of Lutheran ideas in this country.[6] The Reformation in England was not triggered by Luther's teaching. Erasmus and his fellow Christian Humanists were the inspiration behind a reform programme that was aimed at the corruptions and excessive wealth, power and ignorance of the clergy, rather than at Christian doctrine or liturgy. This reforming tendency reflected the legacy of centuries of frustrated aspiration right across Europe with regard to reform, coupled with the thwarted Conciliar Movement that stemmed from the schism within the papacy itself in 1378. Reform and conciliarism went hand in hand in late medieval Christendom; they worked for a coherent programme: the remedying of abuses and corruptions, the elimination of heretical sects, and the unification of the church through a healed papacy and frequent councils at all levels of the church's life.

Thomas Cranmer (Archbishop of Canterbury 1533–53 under Henry VIII and Edward VI) provided the inspiration and guiding hand behind the production of several classic and defining texts of Anglicanism. The First and Second Books of Common Prayer (1549, 1552) provided a stripped-down form of worship, designed for lay people, rather than for religious. They pruned ritual to a minimum, emphasized the ministry of the Word and reshaped the eucharist as a communion rather than as a sacrifice (though this was not absent). They spoke of the universal church and the mystical body of Christ without mentioning the pope. The Forty-two Articles of 1563 (which became the Thirty-nine Articles of Religion, promulgated in their present form in 1571) affirmed the credal orthodoxy of the Church of England, rejected equally the errors of the Church of Rome and those of radical groups within the Reformation and highlighted the biblical route to salvation. The Ordinal of 1550 upheld the threefold ministry of bishops, priests (the word was intentionally retained) and deacons (dropping the minor orders), seeing them primarily as pastors and as ministers of the Word and sacraments. Cranmer was behind the first book of *Homilies* and also embarked on an abortive attempt to draw up a reformed canon law. Cranmer was guided by a heartfelt conviction about the divine mandate of kings to receive implicit obedience and the role of the 'godly prince', modelled on the just kings of the Old Testament, in reforming and governing the church.

During the reign of Elizabeth I, Jewel and Hooker respectively defended the reformed English church against Rome (externally) and the Puritans (internally). John Jewel proved the most successful exponent and advocate, on the grounds of patristic theology and the practice of the primitive church, of the reformed English church against Roman Catholic attacks.[7] His 'Challenge' sermon at St Paul's Cross appealed to the primitive church (the first six centuries) negatively: a catalogue of Roman Catholic practices could not be supported from patristic precedent. Formidable and not always scrupulous in disputation, he produced his *Apologia Ecclesiae Anglicanae* in 1562, which was translated and placed in parish churches. For Jewel, reform was imperative, but the Roman church frustrated all such attempts. The Church of England was continuous with the pre-Reformation church and had merely broken free from papal jurisdiction in order to institute the reforms that would save souls.

Richard Hooker (d. 1600) conducted his argument on an elevated and sometimes abstract level (grounding it in the first principles of law and reason, as expressing the mind of God). Hooker was a lethal and effectively unanswerable controversialist, magisterial in the scope of his arguments. In his *Of the Laws of Ecclesiastical Polity* (of which only the first five books were published in his lifetime), Hooker sought to vindicate what he perceived to be the rational, moderate reform under Elizabeth I against the more radical Puritan reformists who generally wanted to reject anything that was tainted with 'popery'. He delivered the Church of England from the threat of literal biblicism and liturgical poverty, while also safeguarding its liberties vis-à-vis the state. Hooker was beholden to no other theologian, ancient or modern, and though deeply influenced by both Aquinas and Calvin, ranged masterfully through the theological tradition and legal corpus. Hooker was a realist about the political nature of the church as a visible society, but did not allow this to obscure its mystical nature, its participation in the divine life through the sacraments. His polemic is shot through with fervent adoration. Almost contemporaneous with Hooker, Richard Field (d. 1616), the author of *Of the Church* in five books, was less accommodating to the Roman Catholic Church, believing it to have apostatized, as an institution, when the Council of Trent formally condemned the insights of the Reformation. His treatise is, along with Hooker's, a cornerstone of Anglican ecclesiology.

The Jacobean period (the first quarter of the seventeenth century) represents, in the eyes of many, the finest expression of Anglicanism, a time when theory and practice came closest together. Comparative political security at home and abroad (before the reign of King Charles I destabilized the regime) was combined with a harvest of Renaissance scholarship, effective polemic against the Roman Catholic Church from a reformed Catholic point of view, and the temporary recession of the Puritan threat to Anglican worship and polity. While Calvinist theology (not polity) was dominant, a new strand of moderate, tolerant and (as we might say today) liberal Anglicanism appeared in the writings of Lord Falkland, William Chillingworth and John Hales and this had implications for understandings of authority, the interpretation of the Bible and the nature of orthodoxy and heresy, unity and schism.

The abolition and restoration of Anglicanism

The most severe trial that Anglicanism (though the term is still, strictly speaking, anachronistic at this stage) has ever undergone was provoked by the attempt by Charles I and Archbishop William Laud to force the delicate counterpoise of Catholic and Reformation elements within the English church towards a more Catholic (but still reformed and certainly not a *Roman* Catholic) resolution. Charles and Laud enforced conformity to a 'high' view of liturgy, sacraments and church furnishing, in what many regarded as a return to 'popish' remnants, a closer approximation to the Church of Rome (which, through the Catholic nations, especially France and Spain, remained a serious political threat). English churchmen were traumatized by the execution of the Archbishop of Canterbury (Laud) and then the king (the divinely appointed Supreme Governor of the church), the abolition of the episcopate, the Prayer Book and the Christian year, and their replacement by Presbyterianism and Independency. When Charles II was restored to the throne in 1660, churchmen, whose views had hardened in the bitterness of exile, were determined not to compromise with the forces that had very nearly succeeded in eradicating Anglicanism once and for all. While the Restoration Anglican divines remained hostile to Roman Catholic claims, they were also more critical of the Lutheran and Reformed churches in mainland Europe for losing or renouncing the historical episcopate. The fact remains, however, that none of the seventeenth-century 'High Church' divines, from Hooker and Andrewes to Laud, Hammond, Cosin and Thorndike, go so far as to unchurch the continental Protestant churches on account of the deficiencies in their ministry. This new negative note is first struck with the schismatic Nonjurors, from 1689, certain of whom exaggerated the importance of episcopal ordination, regarding it as necessary even for valid baptism. From the Nonjurors, the denial of non-episcopal sacraments fed into the Oxford Movement.

Meanwhile, the sober but generally pious and dutiful Anglicanism of the eighteenth century was galvanized by the Evangelical Revival, which was broader than the Church of England. Certain Anglican clergymen, the Calvinist George Whitefield and the Arminians John and Charles Wesley, were primarily responsible for triggering the so-called 'Methodist' movement – a movement of fervent devotion, rigorous self-discipline, outreach to the unchurched through open-air preaching, and small-group shepherding of new converts.[8] The character of the Church of England was changed, to its detriment, by the fact that it could not accommodate the energies behind this movement. Anglican Evangelicalism remained strong through the nineteenth century, but made little positive contribution to the understanding of the church, ministry and sacraments. The Wesleys' Evangelicalism (if, indeed, that is what it was) was combined with High Church doctrines of the sacraments as means of grace and of the church's relation to the Sovereign (establishment). Through the force of his personal leadership, which was entirely autocratic, John Wesley developed a 'connexional', or unified and uniform, view of the Methodist movement, which shaped the church that it later became. Methodism was marked by a missionary fervour and an accompanying pragmatism that the more static Anglican understanding of ordained ministry has lacked. Anglican Evangelicalism has suffered from an ecclesiological deficit to the present day.[9]

The Oxford Movement and its critics

The Tractarian or Oxford Movement (launched in 1833) consisted of a cluster of High Church impulses that were generated partly by a the fruition of the Old High Church tradition in the form of a longing for a greater Catholic wholeness, connected to a sacramental understanding of the church, and partly by antipathy of the principal protagonist, John Henry Newman, to dominant popular Low Church Evangelicalism. Newman regarded it with distaste as coarse, superficial, lacking in reverence and mystery, and jingoistic.[10] The Tractarians attempted to redesign Anglican ecclesiology, grounding it on the apostolic nature of the church and the succession of faithful witnesses to apostolic faith and order, from the Fathers to the sound High Churchmen of the seventeenth and eighteenth centuries, rather than on the establishment of religion as a result of the 1688 settlement (though only the more radical spirits, such as R. H. Froude, questioned establishment). The Tractarians were an outcrop of Toryism among the prevailing Whiggery which assumed the authority to dismantle church structures (wealthy livings, cathedral foundations, Irish sees).

There were three areas of serious tension within Tractarian ecclesiology. First, they distorted the legacy of High Church Anglicanism, by denigrating their immediate predecessors or making them invisible: they alone, they claimed, had maintained the true faith.[11] Historians and the general reader have tended to believe the Tractarian propaganda and to read eighteenth-century Anglicanism in its light. Second, the rump of the Tractarians steadily moved away from the reformed identity of the Church of England, aiming to 'unprotestantize' it, as Froude put it. Thus they brought out the tensions between the Romanizers (Newman, W. G. Ward, Frederick Oakeley) and the successors of the Old High Churchmen (Hugh James Rose, John Keble, William Palmer of Worcester College, W. F. Hook and W. E. Gladstone). Third, although the Church of England appeared to reject Tractarianism – the more extreme tendencies, such as Ward and Newman's attempts to interpret Anglican formularies in a sense compatible with the teaching of the Council of Trent, being formally rejected by the bishops and the university of Oxford – the ethos of the movement profoundly reshaped the face of the Church of England and the Anglican Communion. It instilled a sense of the solemnity and beauty of worship and of the divine power contained in the sacraments to sanctify the Christian, a less hostile view of the Roman Catholic Church, for all its acknowledged deficiencies, and an increased wariness of the Lutheran and Reformed churches, who were becoming infected with sceptical biblical criticism. The Tractarians helped Anglicans to take the church, its mystical nature, its mission and unity, more seriously. Through colonial expansion, the Evangelical and Oxford movements were exported throughout the Anglican Communion as rival versions of Anglicanism and thus of Christianity itself.[12]

A current of ecclesiology within the nineteenth-century Church of England, that has received less attention than the Oxford Movement, is the so-called Broad Church tendency. Once again we have an alliance of original thinkers who were linked together by common influences and concerns. S. T. Coleridge (d. 1834) contributed to a renaissance of imaginative, poetic and empathetic theological method that had much in common with Keble and Newman. But Coleridge applied this to championing the Reformers, especially Luther, rediscovering the more Protestant classical Anglican divines, assimilating German biblical criticism, and developing a sophisticated theory of the relation between the Christian church and the culture and institutions of the nation. In such ways, Coleridge influenced not only Newman but also a succession of 'Germano-Coleridgeans'. F. D. Maurice (d. 1872) encouraged others to dig deep into the Christian tradition to ground their theology, inspired a vision of the universal church and its unity, pioneered a theology of communion, opposed the Tractarians and defended prophetic voices in the church, including Luther.[13] Thomas Arnold (d. 1842) attacked the Tractarians and their romanticizing of the Middle Ages and proposed a radical solution to the divisions within English Christianity: a broad national church that embraced differences of belief and liturgy. The influence of the Coleridgeans continued into the 'Cambridge Triumvirate' of J. B. Lightfoot, B. F. Westcott and F. J. A. Hort, who steadied biblical scholarship, adopting the more responsible elements of German biblical science, and combined this with an interest in a moderate but Catholic ecclesiology that did not make unsustainable claims for episcopacy and looked to the universal church in a broader sense than the Tractarians had done.

American voices

In the Protestant (as it then was) Episcopal Church of the USA major contributions to Anglican ecclesiology were made by William Reed Huntington (*The Church Idea*, 1870, which appears to have been influenced by F. D. Maurice and helped to shape the important ecumenical initiative, the Chicago-Lambeth Quadrilateral, 1886–8),[14] and in the late twentieth century by John Booty, an exponent of Jewel and Hooker, and J. Robert Wright, an ecclesiologist from the perspective of ecclesiastical history and a redoubtable ecumenist with a sceptical eye for the small print.

The twentieth-century Church of England

Charles Gore (d. 1932), a disciple of both Pusey and Westcott, was a third-generation Tractarian, a patristic scholar and a constructive theologian and apologist. Seeing the church as the extension of the Incarnation, Gore perpetuated the hierarchical view of ecclesiastical authority and an uncompromising insistence on episcopacy in relation to the Protestant churches, but combined this with acceptance of moderate biblical criticism, which led to some qualifying of traditional christology. Though uncompromising with Free Churchmen, Gore took part in discussions about unity with Roman Catholics. In his heyday, Bishop Gore was the most powerful influence on Anglican thinking and practice with regard to the church, its unity, ministry and mission. Though straining with internal tensions, Gore's stance promoted an incarnational, prophetic and redemptive ecclesiology, with a strong emphasis on the ordained ministry and continuity with the patristic (not the mediaeval or Reformation) church.[15]

A young admirer of Gore, A. M. Ramsey, produced in 1936 the most creative work of Anglican ecclesiology of the twentieth century: *The Gospel and the Catholic Church*. It showed the confluence of biblical theology, the Reformation impulse, and the liturgical and ecumenical movements. It attempted (not entirely successfully) to reconcile the Tractarian insistence on episcopacy with the Reformation's challenge to all institutionalizing of the Christian gospel. It took one of Luther's Ninety-five Theses (1517) as its watchword. It punctured the current triumphalism of the Anglo-Catholic movement and offered a more profound vision of catholicity in which all institutional expressions of the church would die for the sake of unity. In 1972, as Archbishop of Canterbury, Ramsey presided over the General Synod when, in spite of his pleas, it rejected a unity scheme with the Methodist Church.

Alongside Ramsey, as uniting biblical and mystical, Catholic and Reformation elements, with added Barthian eschatological urgency, should be mentioned Edwyn Clement Hoskyns, whose commentary on the Fourth Gospel, expositions of biblical theology, and sermons retain their value, not least for ecclesiology.[16] In the middle of the twentieth century Lionel Thornton of the Community of the Resurrection (founded by Gore) produced innovative work on communion ecclesiology, paralleling that of Roman Catholic theologians.[17]

On the eve of the 1978 Lambeth Conference of all Anglican bishops from around the world, the publication of Stephen Sykes' *The Integrity of Anglicanism* signalled a renewed concern for a more tough and self-critical approach to Anglican ecclesiology. Sykes distanced himself from a nebulous, lazy comprehensiveness and moved towards a more rigorous confessional position.[18] He was on the leading edge of a wave of Anglican ecclesiological renewal that was stimulated by ecumenical dialogue, especially that of the Anglican–Roman Catholic International Commission.[19] Sykes' subsequent writings on this theme were collected in *Unashamed Anglicanism* in 1995. He was the first to challenge the nostrum that Anglicanism has no doctrines of its own, or no special doctrines, and to point out that it must, perforce, have a doctrine of the church that is distinctive if it is to be able to say anything about itself.

Orientations and anchor points

The diversity of Anglicanism and the problem of selectivity

Because Anglicanism is neither confessional nor scholastic and lacks a strong magisterium (teaching office), any appeal to authoritative texts must be qualified. It is problematic to claim that certain texts or writers are 'typical' or 'representative' of Anglicanism. There is a serious methodological issue here, one that arises from several empirical factors that relate to the intellectual richness, the historical scope and the geographical extent of Anglicanism.

The first 'empirical' factor is that it is misleading to begin with the sixteenth century. Anglicans do not believe that their church originated with the Reformation and in this belief they are justified. A church would not be catholic and apostolic if it simply had been brought into being by a decision of Henry VIII or Elizabeth I. It is in the bones of Anglicans that they belong to a church that is continuous with the medieval church in the West and that goes back to the Apostles and early Fathers.

The second 'empirical' factor that contributes to the problem of selectivity in Anglicanism is that no single period of Anglican history is definitive, such as to serve as a paradigm of Anglican ecclesiology. The 'historic formularies' of the Church of England have shaped all churches of the Anglican Communion, while being adapted or revised in various ways by them. The Articles of Religion developed over an extended period in the sixteenth century, while the Book of Common Prayer and the Ordinal underwent a series of revisions for more than a century and then reached their final, classical form in 1662, when the climate was rather different after, first, the suppression and then the restoration of the Church of England. But we cannot stop there: Anglicanism has been continuously evolving and modern Anglican theology (and specifically ecclesiology) has been shaped by a number of subsequent developments, including the eighteenth-century High Church movement, Tractarianism and Anglo-Catholicism, the Broad Church tendency, Evangelicalism, the Ecumenical Movement, Protestant biblical theology and Vatican II. Anglicanism is a continuous story: we cannot freeze-frame it at any particular point and say, 'This is definitive Anglicanism.' It is still developing, in interaction with various cultures and with other Christian traditions.

The third empirical factor is that Anglicanism is a global phenomenon, existing in every part of the world. So we cannot take the Church of England as adequately representative of Anglicanism. Of course, the historic official texts from the sixteenth and seventeenth centuries, and the writings of the British and Irish divines of the period before the emergence of the world-wide communion, constitute a common inheritance. But Anglican theology has been developing its different emphases in various parts of the Communion, with the Episcopal Church of the USA making a particularly significant contribution. The churches or provinces that make up the Communion are constitutionally self-governing (autonomous), but spiritually and pastorally interdependent. The global spread of Anglicanism, into a Communion of around 75 million persons, makes it highly tendentious to select from the Anglican tradition. Nevertheless, there are ample theological resources that are sufficiently authoritative to enable us to pursue our question further. Where then should we look?

The principal sources (*indicative* rather than *definitive* texts) that are relevant to the ecclesiology of Anglicanism, are as follows:

- The 'historic formularies': the Thirty-nine Articles of Religion, the Book of Common Prayer, 1662, and the classic Ordinal (1550/1662). Although the provinces of the Communion are not bound to these and have adapted or archived them and produced their own doctrinal statements and liturgies, these historic formularies have shaped Anglican ecclesiology and are firmly lodged in the Anglican memory. They continue, officially or unofficially, to function as a touchstone of authentic Anglicanism.
- The ecclesiological teachings of the Lambeth Conferences from 1867 to 1998. Though these are not binding in a juridical sense on the provinces, they carry the authority of the collective episcopate of the Communion. They are a treasury of good theology and particularly of ecclesiology.
- The report of the Church of England's Doctrine Commission *Doctrine in the Church of England* (1938) deals extensively with the nature of the church, the ministry and the sacraments.[20]
- The statements produced in recent years by the Church of England's House of Bishops set out the ecclesiological principles and policy that guide the Church of England in its ecumenical discussions: *Apostolicity and Succession* (1994), *May They All Be One* (1997), *Bishops in Communion* (2000) and *The Eucharist: Sacrament of Unity* (2001).[21] Some other provinces of the Communion will have similar reports to turn to.

- The agreed statements of the Anglican–Roman Catholic International Commission (ARCIC) in its first phase on 'Ministry and Ordination' and 'Eucharistic Doctrine' have been acknowledged by the Lambeth Conference (and, as far as the Church of England is concerned, by the General Synod) as 'consonant in substance with the faith of Anglicans'. The first statement of ARCIC II, *Church as Communion* (1991), is also an indicative text, though its status is rather uncertain.[22]

- *The Dublin Agreed Statement* (1984) of the international Anglican–Orthodox Dialogue is an indicator of the broad affinity between Anglicanism and the Eastern churches: they both subsist as a family and communion of self-governing churches, without a central jurisdiction like that of the Roman Catholic Church.[23]

- The Lima Statement of the Faith and Order Commission of the World Council of Churches (WCC), *Baptism, Eucharist and Ministry* (1982), has been judged by Anglicans to reflect the faith of the church through the ages.[24]

- The famous statement on visible unity of the WCC Faith and Order Commission at the New Delhi Assembly in 1961 has been frequently invoked by Anglicans and has been, in effect, a benchmark for Anglican ecumenism. The fabric of visible unity is constituted when all in each place are in visible communion with all in every place. The Canberra statement of 1991 augments that of New Delhi: its sketch of visible unity has been echoed by Anglicans and their ecumenical partners in dialogue as they have looked for a common confession of the apostolic faith, a common baptism and eucharist, a single ordained ministry and shared structures of oversight and decision-making.

- The Porvoo Common Statement is the theological basis of an agreement that brought the British and Irish Anglican churches into communion with a number of Nordic and Baltic Lutheran churches in 1996: as such it has a place among the ecclesiological texts that are authoritative for English Anglicans.[25] By the same token, *Called to Common Mission*, which brought the Episcopal Church of the USA and the Evangelical Lutheran Church in America into 'full communion' in 2000, when seen in conjunction with the decades of work that led up to its predecessor *The Concordat*, provides an ecclesiological resource for Episcopalians.

- There is a useful section on the church in More and Cross's anthology of seventeenth-century Anglican writing *Anglicanism*, 1935 – though the unparalleled achievement of Richard Hooker is thinly represented (perhaps because Hooker wrote at the end of the sixteenth century).[26]

- *Love's Redeeming Work* (edited by G. Rowell, K. Stevenson and R. Williams) contains numerous relevant entries on the church, from the sixteenth century to the present, from the perspective of spirituality.[27]

The credal dimensions of the church[28]

Anglican ecclesiology aspires to embody the four credal dimensions of the church: one, holy, catholic and apostolic. Anglicans locate these not mainly in the empirical realm (Roman Catholics and Orthodox tend to emphasize the degree to which the eschatological perfection of the church is already realized on earth), nor mainly in the eschatological future, beyond this life (some Protestant churches play down the visible expression of unity, stressing the unity of the spirit and looking to the eschaton for its visible manifestation), but straddling both. Unity, holiness, catholicity and apostolicity are already instantiated in the life of the church. She has a real unity through faith and baptism, where these are mutually acknowledged, and a partial unity through the collegiality of her pastors. Nevertheless, her unity is imperfect; the church is currently fragmented; division has been a mark of the church since the beginning. She enjoys a real holiness through the Word and sacraments and her members and ministers are called to lives of charity and chastity, but all Christians fall short, lapse into sin and need to be forgiven and restored. In the same way, the church, as an institution, can become the instrument of injustice or oppression, even to its own members. The catholicity of the church is already apparent in the wholeness (the literal meaning) of the church's life and teaching. Each particular expression of the church must relate to and be conformed to the whole. The church already answers to the needs and aspiration of diverse human communities. Nevertheless, there are always some who feel excluded – the church does not rise to the challenge of welcoming them: then its catholicity is compromised. The apostolicity of the church is intrinsic: she is founded on the mission and message of the Apostles. But it is also an imperative: the church is called to be faithful to the Apostles' teaching (Acts 2.42) and to carry forward their mission in the present time and within the contemporary culture. In all this, the church as an institution is far from perfect and continually falls short of its calling. But the Christian virtue of hope sees the church in the light of God's purposes and God's promises that these purposes will one day be fulfilled. It is a libel, sometimes heard, to say that Anglicans do not believe that the one, holy, catholic and apostolic church exists. They believe that it is made up of the local communities gathered by their bishops and other pastors in the unity of the faith and of the sacraments. As well as affirming the church as a mystical entity, Anglicans acknowledge a universal church – a visible, structured and ordered community persisting through history – of the faithful, the baptized. But it does not confuse the two.[29]

The Reformation notes

In the late Middle Ages it became difficult for many Christians to see the mystical church in the institutional church.[30] The way of salvation was far from clear. But it was essential to belong to the church, to receive its sacraments, in order to be saved. The Reformation cry, 'How can I find a gracious God?' was matched by the search for the authentic church: 'Where can I find the true church?' The Reformers responded with the doctrine of the *notae ecclesiae*.[31] The notes or marks of the true church were, according to Luther and Calvin, the preaching of the Word of God and the administration of the sacraments. Article XIX of the Thirty-nine Articles echoes the Lutheran Augsburg Confession Article VII in stating that the visible community is to be found wherever the Word is truly preached and the sacraments rightly administered. The next generation of Reformers added the third note of discipline, the effective regulation and policing of Christian behaviour, and this is reflected also in the insistence of later Anglican divines that the church cannot be without its pastors and the ministry of oversight. For the Reformers, the notes were the sign of where salvation was to be had: the means of salvation were the gospel of justification by grace through faith, rediscovered at that time, and the sacraments of the gospel (baptism, the Lord's Supper administered in both kinds and not the ('sacrifice' of the) mass, and for the early Luther penance or sacramental confession). But, as stated by the Reformers, the notes are of limited value today, because churches disagree over the interpretation of the Word of God and have differing baptismal and eucharistic disciplines. Nevertheless, for Anglicans, the *notae ecclesiae* (though seldom invoked) underpin what Anglicans regard as the irreducible minimum of what makes the church the church: the church is constituted by Word and sacrament, ministered by its pastors.

The threefold ministry

The threefold ministry of bishops, priests (or presbyters) and deacons is a non-negotiable platform of Anglicanism in ecumenical conversations. There was no suggestion, in the English Reformation, that the episcopate should be by-passed or abolished and the historic succession of consecrations was preserved. The dropping of the minor orders left the three-fold ministry more clearly revealed. In 1662 the requirement for episcopal ordination became statutory and the distinction between bishop and priest was clarified. The diaconate has always been an ordained ministry, though in practice it was regarded as an apprentice-ship to the priesthood. Those who remained longer in deacons orders usually did so for prag-matic reasons such as retaining a college fellowship. Until recently, the diaconate lacked a cogent rationale beyond the rhetoric of 'servanthood'. The work of J. N. Collins in the 1990s on the meanings of the *diakon*-words in classical and New Testament Greek, bringing out the meaning of mandated or commissioned responsible agency, began to percolate through to the churches and to stiffen the theology of the diaconate. The Lambeth Quadrilateral insists on the historic episcopate (presupposing the threefold ministry) as one of the minimum conditions for reunion, but Anglicans have recognized the authenticity of the ministries of oversight (*episkope*) in non-episcopal churches.[32]

The Anglican experiment

A suspicious reading of Anglicanism sees it as a political expedient of the sixteenth century, to serve Henry VIII's dynastic and national ambitions – therefore as lacking in integrity and doomed to disintegrate under the pressure of internal contradictions. A more generous interpretation sees it as an inculturated expression of the Western form of the church Catholic, shaped by the conciliar and reforming movements of the late Middle Ages, to which the constitutional settlements under Henry and Elizabeth were subservient. Anglicanism does indeed attempt to hold together elements that are opposed in other tradi-tions – though not without strain. It defines itself as Catholic and reformed, orthodox in doctrine yet open to change. Its polity is both episcopal and synodical. It acknowledges an Ecumenical Council as the highest authority in the church, but is not opposed in principle to a universal primacy. It confesses the paramount authority of scripture, but reveres tradi-tion and hearkens to the voice of culture and science. It tries to be neither centralized nor fragmented, neither authoritarian nor anarchic. It is comprehensive without being relativ-istic. This interesting experiment has endured and evolved for nearly five centuries: in spite of the present difficulties, it is worth persevering with.

Notes

1 Cf. S.W. Sykes, *The Identity of Christianity*, London: SPCK, 1984.
2 For a discussion of mission in a changing culture see P. Avis, *A Church Drawing Near: Spirituality and Mission in a Post-Christian Culture*, London and New York: T&T Clark, 2003.
3 See the discussions in S.W. Sykes, *Unashamed Anglicanism*, London: Darton, Longman & Todd,

1995 and in P. Avis, 'The Identity of the Anglican Communion' in P. Avis, *The Identity of Anglicanism*, London: T&T Clark, 2008.

4 For discussion of continuity and discontinuity, with particular reference to the relationship between the conciliar and reforming movements of the late medieval period and their perpetuation through the Reformation, see P. Avis, *Beyond the Reformation? Authority, Primacy and Unity in the Conciliar Tradition*, London and New York: T&T Clark, 2006, passim and esp. Introduction and pp. 196–200.

5 The often extreme popular reaction against the recent (Roman Catholic) past is brought out in N. Jones, *The English Reformation: Religion and Cultural Adaptation*, Oxford and Malden, MA: Blackwell, 2002.

6 The unfolding of Anglican perspectives on the church is described, with bibliography, in P. Avis, *Anglicanism and the Christian Church: Theological Resources in Historical Perspective*, revised and expanded edn, London and New York: T&T Clark, 2002. The reader is referred to this work for detail and substantiation of the sketch given in the present section. The references that follow are recent works that supplement that biography. Chapter 16 consists of a commentary on the major twentieth-century works relevant to Anglican ecclesiology.

7 See the slightly jaundiced but stimulating study: G.W. Jenkins, *John Jewel and the English Church: The Dilemmas of an Erastian Reformer*, Aldershot and Burlington, VT: Ashgate, 2006.

8 For the Evangelical Revival or Awakening and the related rise of Methodism see J. Kent, *Wesley and the Wesleyans*, Cambridge: Cambridge University Press, 2002; David Hempton, *Methodism: Empire of the Spirit*, New Haven and London: Yale University Press, 2005; Kenneth Cracknell and Susan White, *An Introduction to World Methodism*, Cambridge: Cambridge University Press, 2005.

9 For an attempt at a modern Evangelical Anglican ecclesiology see T. Bradshaw, *The Olive Branch: An Evangelical Anglican Doctrine of the Church*, Carlisle: Paternoster Press, 1992.

10 For this dimension in Newman's life and thought see Frank M. Turner, *John Henry Newman: The Challenge to Evangelical Religion*, New Haven and London: Yale University Press, 2002.

11 See Peter Nockles, *The Oxford Movement in Context: Anglican High Churchmanship 1760–1857*, Cambridge: Cambridge University Press, 1994.

12 For an analysis of the various strands of the Oxford Movement, especially with regard to differing valuations of the Reformation, see P. Avis, *Anglicanism and the Christian Church*, Part 3.

13 On Maurice's ecclesiology see J. Morris, *F.D. Maurice and the Crisis of Christian Authority*, Oxford: Oxford University Press, 2005.

14 See Chapter 22, 'Ecclesiology and ecumenism', in this volume.

15 See further P. Avis *Gore: Construction and Conflict*, Worthing: Churchman, 1988.

16 E.C. Hoskyns and N. Davey, *The Riddle of the New Testament* (1931); ibid., *The Fourth Gospel* (2nd edn 1947; both London: Faber and Faber); ibid., *Crucifixion-Resurrection: The Pattern of the Theology and Ethics of the New Testament* (1981); E.C. Hoskyns, *Cambridge Sermons* (1938, 1970); both London: SPCK.

17 L. Thornton, *The Common Life in the Body of Christ*, 3rd edn, London: Dacre Press, 1950.

18 S.W. Sykes, *The Integrity of Anglicanism*, Oxford: Mowbray, 1978.

19 Anglican–Roman Catholic International Commission (ARCIC), *The Final Report*, London: SPCK and CTS, 1982.

20 *Doctrine in the Church of England: The Report of the Commission on Christian Doctrine appointed by the Archbishops of Canterbury and York in 1922*, London: SPCK, 1938. The report was re-issued in 1982 with a useful introduction by G.W.H. Lampe.

21 All published by Church House Publishing, London.

22 Anglican–Roman Catholic International Commission, *The Final Report*, London: SPCK/CTS, 1982.

23 *Anglican–Orthodox Dialogue: The Dublin Agreed Statement 1984*, London: SPCK, 1984. This also reproduces the Moscow Agreed Statement of 1976. *The Church of the Triune God*, London: Anglican Communion Office, 2006.

24 *Baptism, Eucharist and Ministry*, Geneva: WCC, 1982.

25 *Together in Mission and Ministry: The Porvoo Common Statement with Essays on Church and Ministry in Northern Europe*, London: Church House Publishing, 1992.

26 P. E. More and F. L. Cross (eds), *Anglicanism: The Thought and Practice of the Church of England Illustrated from the Religious Literature of the Seventeenth Century*, London: SPCK, 1935.

27 See also n 3.
28 Cf. J.R. Wright, 'Prolegomena to a Study of Anglican Ecclesiology' in D.S. Armentrout, ed., *This Sacred History: Anglican Reflections for John Booty*, Cambridge, MA: Cowley Publications, 1990, pp. 243–56; Sykes, *Unashamed Anglicanism*, Ch. 7: 'Foundations of an Anglican Ecclesiology'.
29 See further P. Avis, *The Anglican Understanding of the Church: An Introduction*, London, SPCK: 2000, Ch. 7.
30 For the tension between the mystical and the institutional dimensions of the Church in this period and during the Reformation, see P. Avis, *Beyond the Reformation?*
31 For an exposition of this concept in the Reformers see P. Avis. *The Church in the Theology of the Reformers*, London: Marshall, Morgan and Scott, 1982; reprinted Wipf and Stock, 2003.
32 Cf. P. Avis, 'The Revision of the Ordinal in the Church of England 1550–2005', *Ecclesiology*, vol, 1, no. 2 (2005), 95–110; ibid., *A Ministry Shaped by Mission*, London and New York: T&T Clark, 2005; J.N. Collins, *Diakonia: Reinterpreting the Ancient Sources*, Oxford: Oxford University Press, 1990.

Further reading

P. Avis, *The Anglican Understanding of the Church: An Introduction*, London: SPCK, 2000.

——, *Anglicanism and the Christian Church: Theological Resources in Historical Perspective*, rev. edn, London and New York: T&T Clark, 2002.

——, *The Identity of Anglicanism: Essentials of Anglican Ecclesiology*, London: T&T Clark, 2008.

A.E. McGrath (ed.), *The SPCK Handbook of Anglican Theologians*, London: SPCK, 1998.

S.W. Sykes, *Unashamed Anglicanism*, London: Darton, Longman & Todd, 1995.

S.W. Sykes, J. Booty, and J. Knight (eds), *The Study of Anglicanism*, rev. edn, London: SPCK, 1998.

R. Williams, *Anglican Identities*, London: Darton, Longman & Todd, 2004.

12

NON-CONFORMIST
ECCLESIOLOGIES

Michael H. Montgomery

'Non-conformist churches' may be described as Christian social movements that have adopted a model of church life which is at variance with the practices, governance and self-image of a (usually self-claimed) 'normative' church. That is usually a congregationally based model in which the congregation (and not a bishop, council or clergy) is viewed as the *sine qua non* of ecclesial existence. This serves to contain, defend and nurture religious movements that:

1   are centred upon particular beliefs and practices (e.g. Unitarians and Fundamentalists),
2   have doctrinal beliefs which privilege the position of laity (e.g. Quakers, Congregationalists and Baptists), and
3   emphasize religious experiences of the believer (Charismatic or Pentecostal Christians).

'Non-conformist ecclesiologies' are the theological reflections, groundings and identities of those communities and their practices. They are reflections upon ecclesial experiences, and as such are the 'third act' to the (first act) of the experience of Christians in community and the 'second act' of guiding theological meta-theories, the experience and practice of human liberation and the experience of the Holy Spirit. The most influential theological meta-theories emerged out of the Protestant Reformation: the priesthood of all believers, the importance of a direct relationship with God (rather than the church serving as an intermediary), God's covenant of grace, Jesus' call for discipleship, some (highly varying) degree of Biblical Restorationism (practicing church the way it is perceived to have been done in the New Testament). The modern 'children' of the Reformation movements include evangelicalism, social action-based liberalism, Pentecostalism and liberation theologies, all of which shape the way contemporary churches understand and practise 'being church'. If the practices of being 'church' do not precede formal ecclesiologies, then minimally they exist in a hermeneutical circle of belief, practice and theological reflection. More strongly put, an examination of non-conformist ecclesiologies show that for these Christian communities, practice precedes ecclesiological theory.[1]

The term 'non-conformist' is a misnomer in two senses: first in that it describes a variety of Christian movements which in their view seek to be conformist, albeit with the desires of God rather than those of a flawed society and established church. It is this 'divine conformity' that has energized their creation, shaped their form and challenges their future. The second sense in which this title is a misnomer is that in many parts of the world it is the 'non-conformist' churches which are in fact the dominant (and fastest growing) models of Christianity. Sociologically, in North America religion is lived at the ground level in a 'de facto congregationalism' in which people presume to join congregations, temples and mosques even when that very Protestant model is elsewhere foreign to the religion.[2] The mega-church phenomenon in the United States and elsewhere and the spread of entrepreneurial churches have added a new dimension to the 'normativity of non-conformity'.

This chapter will examine six 'ideal types' of non-conformist ecclesiologies that will help the reader identify and understand the varieties, blessings and perils of the non-conformist experience of being church. Some religious communities are non-conformist in some areas but not others (for example, the Church of Scotland and the Presbyterian traditions). Arguably, others were once non-conformist but are no longer so (the United Methodist Church in North America).[3] The selected expressions of non-conformity do not exhaust the field but do reflect paradigmatic experiences of ecclesial life. Each expression will be analysed through a presentation of (1) Introduction and identity, (2) Key concepts, (3) Social implications, (4) Ecumenical life and (5) Contemporary theologians. Having surveyed a sample of non-conformist ecclesiologies, I will then 'take a step back' to view what the experience of non-conformist ecclesiologies has to share with the wider church(es). The movements examined will be, in historical order, Anabaptist, Congregationalist, Baptist, Restorationist, an ecumenical church and the 'new paradigm church' movement.

Historic expressions: Anabaptists

The 'Anabaptist' movements emerged out of the same social, political, religious and economic ferment as the rest of Reformation churches in the late fifteenth and sixteenth centuries:[4] increasing literacy and affordable books, spiritual awakening and growing wealth. From these 'social seedbeds' came dozens of spiritual renewal movements that were born and evolved, either vanishing into the whispers of history, flourishing, or being crushed by the reaction of the established church and states. The 'radical reformers' of the early Reformation accepted the calls of their contemporary Luther for the rediscovery of the priesthood of all believers, justification by faith through grace, the primacy of the Bible over the traditions of the church and the importance of personal faith. They wanted to go much further than Luther was willing to go, calling not for reforming the existing church, but for its abandonment and the restoration of a new church modelled on what they saw as the practices of the early church as described in the teachings of the New Testament. Out of this new experience of 'church' came a new understanding of what being 'church' meant: a fellowship of believers gathered by religious belief and practice in a particular congregation with a focus upon obedience to the teachings of Christ. This was a stark contrast with the 'Christendom' model of a universal, national, city or state church to which all owed allegiance. It was this different gestalt of being church that guided reforms, energized participants and aroused murderous persecution.[5]

Such churches were different: constituted by people who had denied the legitimacy of their first baptism as infants and sought baptism as adults who had made a decision to accept Christ and follow His ways. In Switzerland, Michael Sattler wrote the Schleitheim Confession in 1527 defining the practices of what were to be called the Swiss Brethren:

1   believer's baptism in which only those who had freely come to faith would be baptized;
2   the ban (disciplining those who departed from the ways of faith (i.e. sinners) by shunning them and not calling upon the military powers of the state or church to enforce church doctrine);
3   communion in both kinds;
4   separation from the sinful world as much as possible;
5   clergy who will serve as pastors to guide and teach their flock and not rule over them;
6   pacifism;
7   the eschewal of oaths.[6]

The most enduring theologian of the early Anabaptists was Menno Simons (1496 – 1561), a Dutch priest who converted to Anabaptism in 1535 after experiencing increasing discomfort with the Roman Catholic understanding of the Mass, the primacy of church tradition over scripture in Catholicism and, ultimately, issues of baptism. He was part of the second wave of Anabaptists and was instrumental in recapitulating the religious beliefs of Anabaptists while also reining in perceived spiritual extremists who carried their religious perceptions beyond what the reason of the day could accept (open marriage, communal ownership of property, spiritualism and violent apocalypticism). His writings serve as the primary theological documents of early Anabaptism.

The followers of Menno, today's Mennonites, continue to practise a believer's fellowship model of church with a strong emphasis on non-violence and, as a contemporary extension of those beliefs, are well known for their missionary service programmes throughout the world through the Mennonite Central Committee.

It is the grounding concept of church as the fellowship of believers, a church that must remain distinct in a sinful world, that has been the dominant ecumenical influence of the Anabaptist movements. Mennonite theologian John Howard Yoder's *The Politics of Jesus* (1972) argued that simply being a Christian in an era of violence, greed and oppression ought to be a strong political statement and that authentic discipleship was more in keeping with the teachings of Jesus than were contemporary just war theories. Stanley Hauerwas was a student of Yoder's and has continued to articulate the call for Christian communities to be an alternative community in the world, defined not by how well they enable people to fit into society but by their fidelity to Jesus Christ.[7]

While Anabaptist churches have always been small groups of intent believers, the movement is arguably more influential today than ever before through their legacy of pacifism, service and consistent theological articulation. The conception of church as an alternative community to contemporary culture has found fresh homes in a wide range of theological perspectives. With popularity comes fresh challenges: liberation perspectives which challenge how the historic alternative community has itself been an oppressor (of minority positions, women, people who are gays and lesbians) and, more significantly, whether the very popularity of being an alternative community will mask how small a difference is often actually created.

Historic expressions: Congregationalists

Congregationalists emerged out of the Puritan movement of the English Reformation as an attempt to purify and reform church and society, chiefly along the lines articulated by John

Calvin. The Puritans who evolved into Congregationalists rather than Presbyterians differed from more orthodox Calvinists in a stronger emphasis upon the role of experience in theology, the understanding that faith could be expressed and judged but never compelled through creeds or mandated covenants and the firm conviction that individual congregations, although bound with other congregations in covenant, were themselves an independent and full expression of the visible church. Their ecclesiological foundation was not 'independency' as an end in itself, but the belief in a direct and accountable relationship between God and the individual believer. The church was expressive of that relationship, not an intermediary between God and believer. Congregationalists differed from the Anabaptists in that they did not understand the church as needing to separate from society or the state church but instead as called to reform both. They rejected rebaptism and practised the baptism of infants, following the teachings of John Calvin that baptism was to be understood as an expression of the covenant of grace. The significance of Congregationalism is threefold: they gave the fullest expression to ecclesiological understanding of the congregation; their experiments in church and societal governance had important ramifications for the understanding of both the doctrine of the priesthood of all believers and the establishment of democracy; and the mediating forms by which they sought to reform society are continued today by their religious tradition, institutions and resulting moral presumptions.

The congregational conceptions of what the church ought to be emerged out of the practices of reforming and 'purifying' congregations during the late sixteenth- and early seventeenth-century English Reformation. They may be divided between those who sought to withdraw from the established church of their day (John Smyth (see below) and, at times, John Robinson) and those who wished not separation but reformation and renewal (William Ames, Henry Jacobs and at times, John Robinson). The Cambridge Platform of the Congregational churches of the Massachusetts Bay Colony (1648) identified the movement's broad consensus of the church: 'A congregational church is by the institution of Christ a part of the militant visible church, consisting of a company of saints by calling, united into one body by a holy covenant, for the public worship of God, and the mutual edification of one another in the fellowship of the Lord Jesus'.[8] Congregationalists were people of 'faith, freedom and fellowship'.[9] Like the churches of the Anabaptist movement, the congregation was considered to be a fellowship of believers who had experienced the grace of God in their lives and who sought to live disciplined lives of faith in response. Each believer was responsible for their own relationship with God, but that freedom was a 'founded freedom' established by God's gift of grace in Jesus Christ. Church covenants, and the covenants between congregations, served to hold the respective entities together while at the same time promoting the freedom of each. Such covenants worked on three levels reflecting:

- God's covenant of grace given in Jesus Christ's atoning life, death and resurrection;
- God's covenant with the church in which the church sought to do God's will;
- the individuals of the church covenanting one with another for the support of the church and its mission and their own mutual admonition and support.[10]

The classic creeds (the Apostles' Creed, Nicene Creed, Athanasius Creed) were viewed at best as testimonies but not tests of faith and at worst as human contrivances that stood between the believer and God. The mark of a Christian was not someone who might make such a confession but rather the active covenanting and living out of the costs and joys of discipleship. The most famous example of a church covenant is the Salem Covenant of 1629, which affirms simply:

> We covenant with the lord and one with an other and doe bynd our selves in the presence of God, to walke together in all his waies, according as he is pleased to reveale himself unto us in his blessed word of truth.[11]

Such church covenants served as the models for social compacts in North America, by which new colonies legitimated their own self rule on the basis of the free consent of their citizens rather than the divine right of kings. Such churches were very focused upon the individual faith experiences but were surprisingly well equipped to adapt to address broader, societal issues, albeit not through congregations but through established 'instrumentalities' of the church, the first 'non-profit organizations' of the modern era. Note the rhetoric: mission organizations were instruments of the church, not the church itself. Instrumentalities were formed to address religious needs for missionary work and social reform at home and abroad. The logic of congregational autonomy led to an emphasis upon the creation of 'self supporting, self-governing and self-extension' by new churches in mission fields.[12] The emphasis upon the church as a collection of congregations meant that there were a great deal more leadership positions available for indigenous church members, and Congregational churches provided for greater leadership possibilities for non Euro-American leaders in nations that were colonized by England or America.[13] The empowerment of indigenous populations was often seen as contrary to the interests of colonial powers, which frequently led to governmental curtailment of Congregational missionary activities. A greater problem was that mission was seen in Congregational churches not as an expression of being church but as a consequence of the calling of some to do God's work. This was one of the great tensions within the congregational system, as to whether churches should be engaged in mission or rather focused upon the worship of God.

In the United States, the Congregationalists did not organize themselves into a formal denomination until 1871, after several failed plans of union and/or cooperation with their fellow Calvinists, the Presbyterians. Congregationalists in America moved steadily away from the orthodox Calvinism of their ancestors, so that by 1913 they could affirm in the Kansas City Statement of Faith:

> We hold it to be the mission of the Church of Christ to proclaim the gospel to all mankind, exalting the worship of the one true god, and laboring for the progress of knowledge, the promotion of justice, the reign of peace, and the realization of human brotherhood.[14]

The social gospel had found a home in Congregational churches! Significantly, this statement of faith was part of a new constitution and by-laws put into effect in order to create greater coordination and cooperation between local churches, regional associations and the various independent national agencies and instrumentalities of the still new denomination.

Congregationalists have been active participants in the ecumenical movement, joining both great ecumenical councils of the twentieth century, councils of churches and being active participants in church merger discussions. So long as the autonomy of congregations was secured, there was little to be lost and much to be gained. That caveat, however, proved to be a major issue for other ecumenical partners. The twentieth century's call for cooperation in mission, the neo-orthodox recovery of scripture and the press for ending the scandal of Christian division proved to be powerful motivators for organic union in the United States (United Church of Christ, 1957, see below), and in the United Church of Japan (1941), the Church of South India (1947), the United Reformed Church of Great Britain (1972), the United Church of Canada (1925), the United Church of Christ of the Philippines (1948) and other united and uniting churches. In some cases (the Church of South India), congregational autonomy was surrendered to the more pressing needs for common witness and mission. Not all Congregational churches have been in favour of organic union, however, with many in the 'continuing congregational' movement opting to remain independent. Today such churches remain independent for theological reasons, or because they are able to sustain their desired activities of fellowship and mission without formal relationships with other congregations.

P.T. Forsyth was the pre-eminent Congregational theologian of the early twentieth century,[15] He described the church as comprising a 'Holy Spirituality' revealed from the Cross of Christ. The freedoms of Congregationalism (freedom of conscience, congregational autonomy) were seen in this light as being 'founded freedoms', founded upon and in response to the Cross.[16] Douglas Horton (1891 – 1968), the General Secretary of the Congregational Christian Churches in the United States, was centrally important both in the recovery of Puritan theologians and also in clarifying the issues of the tradition as it explored unity with other ecclesiological forms, in particular the division between those who saw the congregation as purely the location for Christian formulation and worship and those who saw it as having a duty for mission in the world, and between those who viewed the essence of Congregationalism as independency from other churches and those who saw the tradition as engaged in a covenantal relationships with other churches (see United Church of Christ, below). Horton was an early translator of Karl Barth's work to the American scene and a leader in ecumenism throughout the twentieth century.[17] While other academic theologians were members of Congregational churches (H. Richard and Reinhold Niebuhr, for example), the theological work of the past century was focused upon the ethical and faith demands of wider society and the 'Great Church' rather than the confessional needs of congregational churches. Alan P.F. Sell, Theological Secretary of the World Alliance of Reformed Churches, has written a spirited defence of the 'Congregational way' as a positive contribution to the ecumenical movement, especially in the English context, focusing upon the church as a gathered community of believers that is gifted by God's grace to be visible saints, orderly in conduct and catholic in spirit.[18] Gabriel Fackre writes a 'narrative theology' of the church out of Congregational orientation (such narrative theology, while appropriating and expressing the historic faith, is a local endeavour).[19]

Today the Congregational form has spread around the world, but the Congregational substance has taken a willing back seat to the needs of ecumenicity, mission and witness. Time will tell if this was a wise move.

Historic expressions: Baptist churches

Contemporary Baptist movements had their genesis in two social movements: the elements of the English Reformation most influenced by Biblical Restorationism (pre-eminently the English proto-pentecostal John Smyth) and the evangelism campaigns of the Great Awakening (a period in the middle of the eighteenth century of spiritual renewal, chiefly American, led by preachers such as Jonathan Edwards, George Whitfield and the Wesley brothers and characterized by preaching aimed at awakening the religious life through conversion). Three religious presumptions are inherent to the movements: churches must be modelled upon the church structures of the Bible; the mission of the church is expressed in the Great Commission, to create new disciples for Christ; and an individualism reflects the emphasis upon personal religious repentance and faith. In one form or another, individuals having the 'born again experience' are expected to live their lives differently than before (with a historic emphasis upon personal righteousness reflected in sober living). Christian discipleship, and hence participation in the life of the church, is expected to make a difference in the believer's life.

The doctrine of the church is founded upon Jesus' promise in Matthew 18.20: 'For where two or three are gathered in my name, I am there among them'. The church is constituted by the presence of Christ, present through the believers' faith and discipleship. The church is known by its obedience to the will of God, constituted by covenantal association in the faith and fellowship of the gospel, right practices of biblical preaching and the correct administration of the 'ordinances' of Christ (chiefly believer's baptism but also a Zwinglian understanding of communion), and the biblical organization of the church: the congregation as the core organizational unit, clergy limited to those called to preach and rule, and deacons and elders for the organization and administration of the ministries of the church. While the covenantal understanding created a system where, after evidence of spiritual rebirth, there was room and expectation for considerable theological diversity, in the late twentieth century some of the larger Baptist movements (chiefly the Southern Baptist Churches) explicitly specified what had earlier been presumed: a mandate for the literal understanding of scripture. This is by no means universal within the broad range of Baptist churches, which have included the founders of the American 'Social Gospel' movement (Walter Rauschenbusch) and the champion of American theological liberalism, Harvey Cox. Baptist theologians, as with Baptist churches, 'multiply by division'.

African-American Baptist churches present a special case of ecclesiological development that has been particularly significant both in and outside of the Baptist movement.[20] Organized first under slavery and then under conditions of racial, legal and economic oppression that still echo with pain and suffering in American life, the 'Black Church' was the only social institution in which African-Americans could have control over their own organizations.[21] Significant for purposes of ecclesiological development are:

1 The conception of the church as a community whose purpose includes participating in the liberating work of God from sin, including personal, social and systemic expressions of alienation from God.
2 Church organization as an entrepreneurial activity, in which anyone who experiences a call to ministry may be ordained by a congregation and then seek to start 'their own' church.
3 Church practices as seedbeds of creativity and innovation in worship, organization and doctrine.

James Cone (*Black Theology and Black Power* (1969), *God of the Oppressed* (1975), *For My People* (1984)) is the most prominent African-American theologian today, bringing together a historical recovery of the practices of liberation experienced in many African-American churches, critical theory and the ethical call for the Black Church to be agents of liberation for all, but especially African peoples.[22] Marcia Y. Riggs adds an important voice in how women's organizations in the historic Black Church worked in ways that may now be seen as liberative under conditions of oppression.[23]

Considerable diversity does exist with the Baptist movements. While the world's most famous Baptist, evangelist Billy Graham, is known for his determined focus upon an individual's hearing and responding to the grace of God in the experience of spiritual rebirth without explicit social justice, an earlier generation of Baptists were leaders in the American 'social gospel' of the late nineteenth and twentieth century, which held that a genuine spiritual awakening had to entail work for social justice. The Rev. Dr Martin Luther King, Jr led the American civil rights anchored in the use of Baptist churches as organizing centres. The church as a community of human liberation was harnessed to be a community for changing society for human liberation. The social ethical positions of the largest Baptist churches focus upon issues of personal behaviour (don't smoke, don't drink or use non-medicinal drugs, etc.), often ignoring societal issues altogether either as an impediment to the essential work of conversion or contrary to the conversionist strategy by which social change occurs with the conversion of individuals.[24]

This diversity is also reflected within the ecumenical movement. Baptist leaders were early participants in ecumenical mission work and participated in the creation of several of the united and uniting churches (especially the Church of North India and the United Church of Christ of Japan). The largest Baptist body, the Southern Baptist Convention, however, while supportive of shared mission and evangelism programmes, is opposed to much of the work of the modern ecumenical movement as hostile to biblical representative Christianity. In the words of R. Albert Mohler, Jr, 'The only genuine basis of true Christian unity is a unity on the teachings of the Bible as commonly accepted and commonly understood.' Southern Baptists are committed to the unity of the churches, but this will remain a spiritual unity until there can be a joining based on common convictions which include free church polity, local church autonomy, and regenerate church membership. In Mohler's words, the ecumenical 'conviction of the Convention is *cooperation without compromise*'.[25]

While the beliefs of the largest non-conformist church can not be ignored or minimized, such sentiments are not dominant in the academic community, where the Baptist understanding of being church has in recent years enjoyed a renewal and recovery. German theologian Jürgen Moltmann adopted a Baptist ecclesiology in his 1977 opus *The Church in the Power of the Spirit*.[26] Writing in the context of European church decline, Moltmann adopts a believer's model of the church as a means to avoid becoming 'alienated from its foundation' under conditions of modernity. Such a move would allow authentic solidarity with people who are alienated from it: the poor, women and other peoples who are oppressed. The most eminent Euro-American theologian currently working within the framework of the larger Baptist movement is Miroslav Volf, whose 1998 *After our Likeness: The Church as the Image of the Trinity* compares the 'Free Church' understanding of church with both the Orthodox theologian John Zizioulas and the then Joseph Cardinal Ratzinger (now Pope Benedict XVI).[27] Volf grounds his ecclesiology in a historical recovery of the work of John Smyth, who serves as a 'proto-pentecostal' figure able both to unite the ecclesiological foundations of Congregational, Evangelical and Pentecostal churches and introduce the doctrine of the Holy Spirit into the conception of the church. This allows Volf to move into contemporary discussions of trinitarian theology and grounding a free church ecclesiology in a dialogical and non-hierarchical image of the Trinity.

The Baptist experience of being church remains the most contentious, creative and self-confident expressions of ecclesiology. The differences within the Baptist world are often greater than the unity of tradition that grounds them.

Historic expression: Restorationism

A significant issue for all churches is the question of what extent the models and practices of the New Testament church ought to be models and practices for churches of today. The Restorationist movement in ecclesiology represents one side of that balance, where the task of today's churches is to model as clearly as possible the models found in the New Testament. Ostensibly a simple reading of the Bible that privileges common-sense understanding above intellectual sophistication, the movement found its origins in highly educated pastors (such as Alexander Campbell) grounded in the presumptions of the philosophy of John Locke, which emphasized the capacity of each individual to make rational decisions based upon the individual's best interests.[28] The movement flourished in the aftermath of the Second Great Awakening among people who were disenchanted with the anti-democratic ethos of Calvinism (e.g. the doctrine of predestination and the complete depravity of humanity). In contrast, American pastors like Alexander Campbell and Barton Stone read from their Bibles a description of the church:

> That the church of Christ upon earth is essentially, intentionally, and constitu-tionally one; consisting of all those in every place that profess their faith in Christ and give obedience to him in all things according to the scriptures, and that mani-fest the same by their tempers and conduct, and of none else, as none else can be truly and properly called Christians.[29]

From this Campbell delineated twelve additional propositions, summarized as emphasizing:

1   the unity of the Church of Christ;
2   the supreme authority of the scriptures;
3   the special authority of the New Testament;
4   the fallacy of human creeds;
5   the essential brotherhood of all who love Christ and try to follow him and that if human innovations can be removed from the church, the followers of Christ will unite upon the scriptural platform.

Taking no name other than Christian, the Restorationists sought to model their worship upon what they read in the Bible: weekly communion services led by lay leaders and not clergy, believer's baptism and sermons rooted in the Bible, while suspicious of theology. There were divisions within the movement over whether the call to ecumenicism meant cooperation with churches that did not accept the Restorationist principles and whether the primacy of the Bible precluded the ethos of modernism and liberalism or could be main-tained within this new philosophical system. There are three primary groups. The congrega-tions of the Church of Christ, probably the largest of the three main groups of Restorationist Christianity, conceive themselves as a movement and not a denomination, but they are if anything an 'anti-denomination' (membership statistics are estimates since they refuse to count). They are most noted for the absence of musical instruments in their worship. Their inherent anti-modernism and resulting anti-intellectualism found fertile soil with many and led to the easy acceptance of American fundamentalism. The Christian Church (Disciples of Christ) combines the traditions of the Restorationist movement with the practices and values of mainstream Christianity. Members of the independent Christian Churches (non-Disciples of Christ) see the Disciples as having left the Restorationist movement through both their organization as a denomination in the 1920s and 30s and their openness to liberal and modernist influences. These Christian Churches are noted for their sponsorship of Bible Colleges and academies as alternatives to secular universities and schools.

The social ethics of the movement depend most crucially not on the ecclesiological principles of the church, but upon their stance in acceptance of or in opposition to modernism. The Disciples are the most liberal and hence the most likely to engage in broader social issues. The other two tend to be highly individualistic and view social justice as a matter of personal righteousness. With a touch of irony, the stances of the churches towards education lead the Disciples to be a church in favour of the poor, while the other two are (larger) churches of the poor.

While independent Christian Churches and members of the Church of Christ are open in theory to the ecumenical movement, their strict understanding of the essence of the church as following a particular form precludes their participation in an actual movement of genuinely different churches. The Christian Church (Disciples of Christ), despite being the smallest of the three Restorationist churches, has contributed significant leadership to the American and world ecumenical movement. After a long period of working cooperatively with the United Church of Christ, the two denominations formed a Common Global Ministries Board in 1996. A long period of discussion about organic merger led to the 1989 decision to adopt 'full communion' but not organic merger. Bilateral discussions have been held with the Vatican and Disciples personnel were active in the work of the US National Council of Churches and the World Council of Churches. But it is significant that it is the smallest branch of the Restorationist movement that has been the most engaged in the ecumenical movement while the other two expressions, truer to a purer (though perhaps naïve?) interpretation of Campbell's teachings, have flourished.

The Christian Church (Disciples of Christ) is most noted for its biblical scholars and practical theologians. Given the primacy given to the Bible and the latent suspicion of intellectualism, that is not surprising. Michael Kinnamon is a leading ecumenical theologian, having served on staff of the World Council of Churches' Faith and Order Commission and now teaching at a United Church of Christ seminary in St Louis, Missouri.[30] Paul A. Crow, Jr was a central leader in American ecumenical work for over twenty years in his capacity as the Disciples of Christ's ecumenical officer.

Contemporary expressions: the United Church of Christ, USA

By now it will have become obvious to the reader that all churches have glorious traditions and identities. These traditions and identities are shaped (more than we like to admit) by realities grounded in the forces of culture, human experience and the demands and possibilities of Christian discipleship. This vortex of experience and possibility brings twin challenges to ecclesiological reflection: the restatement of a particular tradition as authentic to contemporary existence and also its reshaping in the face of new difficulties.

Thus the twentieth century has seen a restatement of (Protestant Reformed) neo-orthodox biblical theology that challenged all traditions to take a fresh look at the scriptures and the meaning of the Christ event for these times. Liberation theologies challenged the complicity of Christian theology, especially ecclesiology, in the oppression of the poor, women and people understood as 'not normal'. The ecumenical movement raised with fresh passion the challenge of the 'scandal of the church's divisions' in the face of both the needs of the world and Jesus' prayer that 'all may be one'. Beginning with the World Missionary Conference of 1910, the 'Life and Work' movement challenged all churches to justify theological division in the face of what was seen as the biblical mandate for unity.[31]

The work of theologian H. Richard Niebuhr both reflects and guides the theological spirit of the age.[32] His 1929 *The Social Sources of Denominationalism* critiqued the American denominational system as more a reflection of social class than theological beliefs (which primarily served as ideological legitimization). *Christ and Culture* (1951) presented a highly influential, even paradigmatic, understanding of religious and ethical existence. The different Christian approaches to culture were expressed in five 'ideal types', with Niebuhr advocating a 'Christ transforming culture' approach in which an authentic Christian response seeks to change contemporary culture to ways fitting God's call. The call for Christians to be agents of social change was clear. This was written at a time in which American churches more often than not reflected the racial, class and political biases of the culture. Niebuhr called for the church to be a kind of social pioneer in the transformation of itself and society.

Out of this ethos came the aforementioned 1957 creation of the United Church of Christ (USA), the merger of the Evangelical and Reformed Church and the Congregational Christian Churches. The former were the 1934 merger of the (predominantly Lutheran) Evangelical Synod of North America and the (German) Reformed Church. The resulting denomination was the first merger in the United States reflecting different ethnicities, polities and ecclesiological backgrounds. Significantly, the Church of South India (1947), the United Church of Christ of the Philippines (1948) and the United Church of Christ of Japan (1941) both predate and reflect the ecumenical spirit of the age.[33]

This merger professed continuity with 'the' Protestant reformers and assured congregational polity, but left the important theological formulations for future work. This somewhat daring move was designed to force the new church to formulate its identity based on faithfulness to Christ in the present age rather than on fidelity to theological tradition. Four themes can be discerned in the denomination's emerging ecclesiology:

1   Continued congregational polity in which congregations have the right to call (select) their pastoral leadership and set their own policies and practices.
2   Understanding mission ('Missio Dei') to be joining God's mission on earth.[34]
3   Strengthening covenantal relationships between congregations and church structures rooted in the broader mission of the church.
4   A sense of the church as 'becoming the Beloved Community' of Christ which is characterized by radical inclusiveness of previously marginalized groups.

The adherence to the perceived mission of God for human liberation from the forces of sin has led the denomination to pioneering work in Civil Rights for African-Americans and women and now, through a congregational self-designation process, to being 'Open and Affirming' of people who are gay, lesbian, bisexual, or trans-gendered. The radicality of this work for justice was buffed for opponents on the grounds that the national church did not speak for the local church, but under the conditions of congregational polity it spoke to the local church and to the world, just as the congregations were encouraged to do. If a congregation did not choose to participate or support these programmes, it did not need to do so. This strategy for holding the church together while addressing controversial issues had worked well enough for the Congregationalists, but it remained to be seen how well it would succeed as this new church sorted out its 'future work'.

The United Church of Christ, as might be expected of a church whose motto is 'that all may be one', has been an enthusiastic participant in the modern ecumenical movement. It was expected in its creation that this would be the first step toward the eventual reuniting of all Protestant churches in the United States. Organic union, however, has been a step too far for most denominations, especially when key ecclesiological issues are addressed directly (e.g. is each congregation a full expression of the presence of Christ? Does the church require a broader representation of churches and people? Can bishops claim an apostolic succession, or is that succession reserved for the apostolic faith in the crucified and risen Lord?).

Internal critics within the denomination have noted an 'ecclesiological deficit' within the church, resulting in a denomination that at times has seemed to some not to know who it was (or perhaps more significantly, not liking what it was becoming). The UCC was challenged in ecumenical discussions as to whether it was a true church or 'merely' an alliance of churches. The Missio Dei identification of a church in mission in the world worked very well for the national mission agencies of the church, but were a much harder fit for congregations organized as fellowships of believers, leading to a sense of disconnection between the national agencies of the church and its member congregations. New understandings of being church could not be ignored, but would only slowly be appropriated by the members of congregations.

The denomination has suffered some from the gap between the theology articulated by the leadership and the beliefs of people in congregations. The leadership has espoused being a multi-cultural and multi-racial church. But since religion has a social function of legitimating ethnic differences in a here-to-now Anglo-dominated culture, and congregational polity presumes that each church is by definition a freely gathered community, under conditions of choice most congregations are mono-cultural and mono-racial. Covenants, while talked about, remain in practice elusive (and suffer from the lack of consensus on what the foundational covenant, of God with creation, is all about).

Illustrative of the growing pains of ecclesiological identity are a series of television ads which celebrated the United Church of Christ as welcoming people who may not have felt welcome in other denominations. Included in the ad, amongst pictures of many different people, were several couples of gay men or lesbian women. While the advertisements were banned from the major television networks as being too controversial, they enjoyed great visibility in national news debates. Missing from those debates was an important ecclesiological point: if the identity of a church on such a controversial subject could be made in the public's mind by the action of a national media campaign, what good is congregational polity?

The denomination has continued in the World Alliance of Reformed Churches, the World Council of Churches, the National Council of Churches, USA, and 'Churches Uniting in Christ' (CUIC), an American plan for common ministries without organic merger by the major mainstream Protestant denominations in the United States. More significant than these organizational forums have been the 'full communion' discussions and votes between the UCC and its primary ecumenical partners: the Christian Church

(Disciples of Christ) in the USA, the Evangelical Church of the Union of Germany (EKU), Lutheran–Reformed dialogue and other ecumenical discussions.

While the denomination has a rich theological heritage, most confessional ecclesiological work is being done by church leaders and not academic theologians. Barbara Brown Zikmund has led a seven-volume history of the theological work of the denomination and its predecessors, *Living Theological Heritage of the United Church of Christ*.[35] Current work may be found on the denomination's website, www.ucc.org.

Being faithful amidst venerable traditions and new challenges is not an easy task. Valued, even crucial, historical understandings may easily be subverted by contemporary issues as expendable losses. They may also prove to be essential to the viability of the church.

Contemporary expressions: 'New Paradigm Churches'

The congregational base of non-conformist ecclesiologies makes organizational innovation comparatively easy: the entire system does not have to change but only one entrepreneurial congregation or pastor. Successful innovations are rapidly adopted by other congregations as they seek to duplicate the success of the innovator. Such 'market sensitivity' has been a hallmark of congregationally based religion in America, and has carried with it theological implications for ecclesiology. Sociologist Donald Miller calls such churches 'New Paradigm Churches' because of the way that they have become some of the dominant religious communities (and in some areas, expression of the church) in North America.[36]

Such innovations have a demographic context: most of the churches which pioneered their use were founded in the 1970s in the United States in regions which were experiencing a high level of in migration from other parts of the United States but which were themselves comparatively 'unchurched'. There had been both an emerging counter-cultural religious movement in the 1960s in which young people reshaped Christian practices to fit that era's youth culture, and an organizational response by pastors who sought to establish new congregations with and out of that movement.[37] The contemporary innovations of these church pastors reflect an attempt to alleviate the cultural alienation that, they argued, separated people from the church. From that came the 'Seeker Church' phenomenon in which the practices and expressed theology of the church are reshaped with an eye to fitting the religious needs (and biases) of the local population. This can be done as part of a strategy for conversion, as with the justly famed Willow Creek Community Church where the elimination of Christian symbolism and traditional worship patterns is done as part of a calculated effort to bring people to conversion to Christ (as understood by evangelical Protestantism). The shape of the worship service (no hymns, religious rituals, religious symbolism like crosses) is determined in part by the intended audience. It can also be a part of wholesale cultural subversion, as is argued of 'prosperity churches' which organize around the theme of material and spiritual enrichment for believers, or where other cultural values are adopted wholesale. I witnessed a church where the preacher argued that they were counter to the (secular) culture and were for the values of patriotism, 'the traditional family', and the American free enterprise system. Usually the cultural proclamation is not so overt, but a number of scholars have pointed to the therapeutic, individualistic and anti-establishment ethos of such 'new paradigm churches', which, while they do cultural repair to the seeming narcissism of American culture, also accept and presume a cultural fit.[38]

A second cultural innovation championed by many contemporary churches is the adoption of modern business management techniques for the conception and operation of congregations. Common techniques include the use of marketing as a technique of ecclesiology or the adoption of a particular organization design model to 'guide' the organizational structure and operation of congregations. These become expressions of ecclesiology when they shape both operations and also the presumptions as to what a church can and should do. The adoption of a 'soft systems' model of organizational design (in which the boundaries of the organization are defined not by geography or formal act of membership but by participation in the life of the church and acceptance of the church's vision, mission and values) works well for a mission focused congregation but not so well for the less ideologically focused parish or congregation rooted in practices based upon presumptions of being a fellowship of believers. Overtly 'theologically neutral' organizational models carry implicit theologically agendas in the actions they favour and the identities they create. The classic marketing questions of: 'What is our business? Who are our customers? What are their needs?' carry with them theological presumptions about the nature of the church (a human enterprise engaged in value exchange by consumers whose loyalty must be continually won). Proponents argue (rightly, in my view) that such criticisms are overdrawn: churches have always implicitly done this. What is new is simply more creative and adaptive ways of bringing the gospel to current society. Methods, however, are not value neutral. The dependence upon 'cultural fit' by such models leads to a surrendering of a prophetic role for the church to speak gospel truth to power and a blurring of the values of the gospel with the values of a particular culture.

The key figures in the New Paradigm Church movement are primarily church pastors and not theologians, although they are well aware of the theological implications of what they are seeking to do. Rick Warren, the pastor of Saddleback Community Church (a Southern Baptist congregation) and author of *The Purpose Driven Church*, was one of the first to successfully adopt contemporary organizational design theory for churches. Bill Hybels is the founder of Willow Creek Community Church and a pioneer in what he calls 'seeker sensitive' churches. William Easum, a United Methodist pastor, popularized and adapted their approaches for a broader range of churches. Not professional theologians but pastoral innovators, they have extended and reshaped particular theological visions in ways that have profoundly shaped how Christianity 'is done' in America.[39]

Divine non-conformity: opportunities and challenges

Non-conforming ecclesiologies have much to commend them. By privileging a comparatively small level of Christian community, they maintain a normative status for both fellowship and discipleship. In principle (but not always in practice) they are able to unite the experience of the individual believer and the work of the church. There are few theological limits placed on what the church may and may not do. Such a doctrine is flexible, adaptive in changing situations and may be quite strong in the face of adversity. It remains the fastest growing part of the Christian community.

Such success notwithstanding, challenges remain for the non-conformists. The basic starting point of a non-conformist ecclesiology is the church as a fellowship of believers. The experiences of Christian communities would seem to indicate that this by itself is incomplete. It is too easy for a church to remain focused upon itself while looking at God (I see no difference between evangelical, liberal or Pentecostal churches in this regard). Fellowship and belief are incomplete without a mission of love for others.

The sticking point for many 'Fellowship of Believers' comes not with the fellowship but the believing part. At a shallow level, fellowship without believing is secularism, not Christianity. At another level, when such fellowships have been particularly vital there has been a clear consensus on what the covenant is between God and humanity and between God and the church. At the very least, most 'covenantal churches' lack a consensus on these points and thus lack the ability to mobilize themselves for significant witness in the world.

The challenges of the high or post-modern era have eroded the truth claims of non-conformists as well as other Christian expressions: treasured theological beliefs are shown to be more about social class maintenance; foundational understandings of 'what the Bible says' about how the early church lived prove less universal than any tradition would like. More significant than these challenges, however, is a foundational question for ecclesiology: the past century has seen a clear erosion of interest in ecclesiology itself in the face of both massive levels of human need in the developing world and religious restructuring elsewhere. Rather than theological identity, nature and purpose, the (formerly) mainstream churches have been focused upon issues of ethics and mission. Arguably these churches have become more relevant to the issues and less relevant to their members. Is the problem with the mission or the membership? How do we now know who we are? Has ecclesiology become the wrong topic for guiding the lives of real churches?

This is all the more striking when compared with the growth and material success of church movements which have been untroubled by modernity and its questions. The Congregationalists of India may have disappeared into the Church of South India out of self-sacrifice in the advance of Christian mission work, but that did not stop foreign para-church organizations from starting new, independent churches as 'their' mission. It is the smallest of the Restorationist and Baptist churches that are the most interested in the ecumenical movement. For the non-conformist social movements there remain twin challenges in the ecumenical age: how is their experience of faith life-giving and saving, and how is the ecumenical movement a part of this life-giving and saving experience of faith?

Finally, the key question for non-conforming churches (as well as the conforming churches) remains the same as the definitional puzzle with which this chapter began: conforming with whom? How do we conform today with the desires and delights of our God?

Notes

1 This differs from the traditional method of inquiry of examining theology by studying theologians, as exemplified by such different and accomplished theologians as Avery Dulles, *Models of the Church*, New York: Doubleday, 1978 and H. Richard Niebuhr's *Christ and Culture*, New York: Harper and Row, 1951. While maintaining an interpretive lens shaped by the great theologians, Roger Haight's *Christian Community in Context*, New York: Continuum, 2005, restores a measure of balance between theologian and context.

2 R. Stephen Warner, 'The Place of the Congregation in the Contemporary American Religious Configuration', *American Congregations: New Perspectives in the Study of Congregations*, edited by James Wind and James Lewis, Chicago: University of Chicago Press. 1994, pp. 54–99.

3 Eighteenth-century Methodism had distinctive conceptions of what it meant to be Christian, the purpose of the church and the social ethic of Christians in the world. Today this is only incidentally so. See David Hempton, *Methodism: Empire of the Spirit*, New Haven: Yale University Press, 2005.

4 See Chapter 4 of this volume, 'Ecclesiology and the religious controversy of the sixteenth century'.

5 Franklyn Littell offers the classical understanding of the origins of the Anabaptist movements, to be found in *The Anabaptist View of the Church*, Boston: Starr King Press, 1958. His approach has

been supplanted by James M. Stayer, Werner O. Packull and Klaus Deppermann, 'From Mono-genesis to Polygenesis: The Historical Discussion of Anabaptist Origins', *Mennonite Quarterly Review*, Vol. 49 (1975), 83–121, and Thomas Heilke, 'Theological and Secular Meta-Narratives of Politics: Anabaptist Origins Revisited (Again)', *Modern Theology*, Vol. 13:2 (April 1997), 227–52.

6 Found in Haight, *Christian Community in Context*, p. 225.

7 Stanley Hauerwas, *A Community of Character*, Notre Dame: University of Notre Dame Press, 1981. Stanley Hauerwas and William Willimon, *Resident Aliens: Life in the Christian Colony*, Nashville: Abingdon, 1989.

8 Chapter 2, ¶6, found in Williston Walker's *The Creeds and Platforms of Congregationalism*, New York: Pilgrim Press, 1991, reprint of 1893 original, pp. 194ff.

9 Daniel T. Jenkins, *Congregationalism: A Restatement*, New York: Harper, 1954, p. 40.

10 Classically put by John Smyth in his 'congregational period' before he developed into a Baptist and then 'proto-pentecostal'. See Haight, *Community in Context*, pp. 245 ff.

11 Walker, *Creeds and Platforms*, p. 116.

12 Francis M. DuBose, *Classics of Christian Missions*, Nashville: Broadman Press, 1979.

13 See Juanita De Barros, 'Congregationalism and Afro-Guianese Autonomy' in the CERLAC *Working Paper Series*, July, 1998.

14 Walker, *Creeds and Platforms*, p. 599.

15 Karl Barth, *The Church, the Gospel and Society*, London: Independent Press, 1962.

16 Samuel J. Mikolaski, editor, *The Creative Theology of P.T. Forsyth*, Grand Rapids, MI: Eerdmans, 1969; Marvin W. Anderson (ed.), *The Gospel and Authority: A P.T. Forsyth Reader*, Minneapolis: Augsburg, 1971.

17 See Douglas Horton, *Toward an Undivided Church*, New York: Association Press, 1967; *Congregationalism: A Study in Church Polity*, London: Independent Press, 1952.

18 Alan P.F. Sell, *Saints: Visible, Orderly and Catholic: The Congregational Idea of the Church*, Allison Park, PA: Pickwick Publications, 1986.

19 Gabriel Fackre, *The Christian Story: A Narrative Interpretation of Basic Christian Doctrine*, Grand Rapids, MI: Eerdmans, 1978.

20 See Chapter 24 of this volume, 'Black ecclesiologies'.

21 African-American churches are not all Baptist nor confined to non-conformist ecclesiology. Various kinds of Baptist churches predominate, however, and elements of Baptist practice have a deep resonance throughout most African-American communities.

22 James Cone, *Black Theology and Black Power*, New York: Seabury, 1969; *A Black Theology of Liberation*, Philadelphia; Lippincott, 1970; *For My People: Black Theology and the Black Church*, Maryknoll; Orbis, 1984.

23 Marcia Y. Riggs, *Awake, Arise and Act: A Womanist Call for Black Liberation*, Cleveland: Pilgrim Press, 1994.

24 While this has often meant that justice issues were completely ignored or worse, in some cases this strategy for social action has worked well. See Heidi Rolland Unruh, Ronald J. Sider, *Saving Souls, Serving Society: Understanding the Faith Factor in Church-Based Social Ministry*, New York: Oxford University Press, 2005.

25 'The Southern Baptist Convention and the Issue of Interdenominational Relationships' found at www.sbts.edu/mohler/FidelitasRead.php?article = fidel052.

26 Jürgen Moltmann, *The Church in the Power of the Spirit*, New York: Harper and Row, 1977. He adds a much stronger conception of the Holy Spirit in *The Source of Life: The Holy Spirit and the Theology of Life*, London: SCM Press, 1997.

27 Miroslav Volf, *After Our Likeness: The Church as the Image of the Trinity*, Grand Rapids, MI: Eerdmans, 1997.

28 Alan P.F. Sell, *John Locke and the 18th Century Divines*, Cardiff: University of Wales Press, 1997.

29 From the 'Declaration and Address of the Christian Association of Washington' found in Lester G. McAllister and William E. Tucker, *Journey in Faith: A History of the Christian Church (Disciples of Christ)*, St Louis: Bethany Press, 1975.

30 See Kinnamon, *The Vision of the Ecumenical Movement and How it has Been Impoverished by its Friends*, St Louis: Chalice Press, 2003. Kinnamon has also edited, with Brian Cope, the essential compendium of key texts of the ecumenical movement, *The Ecumenical Movement: An Anthology*, Geneva: WCC Publications, 1997.

31 See Chapter 22 of this volume, 'Ecclesiology and ecumenism'.
32 H. Richard Niebuhr, *The Social Sources of Denominationalism*, New York: Henry Holt, 1929; *Christ and Culture*, New York: Harper and Row, 1951; with James Gustafson and Daniel Day Williams, *The Purpose of the Church and its Ministry*, New York: Harper and Brothers, 1956.
33 For fuller discussions, see Louis F. Gunnemann, *The Shaping of the United Church of Christ*, New York: Pilgrim Press, 1977; *United and Uniting: The Meaning of An Ecclesial Journey*, New York: United Church Press, 1987; and Randi Jones Walker, *The Evolution of a UCC Style: Essays in the History, Ecclesiology, and Culture of the United Church of Christ*, Cleveland: United Church Press, 2005.
34 See Chapter 36 of this volume, 'Ecclesiology and world mission/*missio Dei*'.
35 See especially Barbara Brown Zikmund and Frederick Trost (eds), *The Living Theological Heritage of the United Church of Christ: United and Uniting*, Volume 7, Cleveland: Pilgrim Press, 2005.
36 Donald Miller, *Reinventing American Protestantism: Christianity in the New Millennium*, Berkeley: University of California Press, 1999.
37 Miller, *Reinventing*.
38 See Miller, *Reinventing*, for a scholarly and friendly introduction to the seeker church phenomenon. See Kimon Howland Sargeant, *Seeker Churches: Promoting Traditional Religion in a Nontraditional Way*, New Brunswick, NJ: Rutgers University Press, 1990, for a more critical view. For a hostile examination of church marketing and its implications, see Philip D. Kenneson and James L. Street, *Selling Out the Church: The Dangers of Church Marketing*, Nashville: Abingdon Press, 1997.
39 See Rick Warren, *The Purpose Driven Church*, Grand Rapids, MI: Zondervan, 1995; William Easum, *Sacred Cows Make Gourmet Burgers: Ministry Anytime, Anywhere by Anyone*, Nashville: Abingdon Press, 1995; and Gilbert Bilezikian, *Community 101*, Grand Rapids, MI: Zondervan, 1997.

Further reading

Roger Haight, *Christian Community in Context*, New York: Continuum, 2005.
——, *Christian Community in History*, New York: Continuum, 2005.
Stanley Hauerwas and William Willimon, *Resident Aliens: Life in the Christian Colony*, Nashville: Abingdon Press, 1989.
David Hempton, *Methodism: Empire of the Spirit*, New Haven: Yale University Press, 2005.
Lester G. McAllister and William E. Tucker, *Journey in Faith: A History of the Christian Church (Disciples of Christ)*, St Louis: Bethany Press, 1975.
Jürgen Moltmann, *The Church in the Power of the Spirit*, New York: Harper and Row, 1977.
——, *The Source of Life: The Holy Spirit and the Theology of Life*, London: SCM Press, 1997.
Kimon Howland Sargeant, *Seeker Churches: Promoting Traditional Religion in a Nontraditional Way*, New Brunswick, NJ: Rutgers University Press, 1990.
Miroslav Volf, *After Our Likeness: The Church as the Image of the Trinity*, Grand Rapids, MI: Eerdmans, 1997.
Randi Jones Walker, *The Evolution of a UCC Style: Essays in the History, Ecclesiology, and Culture of the United Church of Christ*, Cleveland: United Church Press, 2005.

And for fun:
Nathaniel Hilbrick, *Mayflower: A Story of Courage, Community, and War*, New York: Viking Press, 2006.

13

ROMAN CATHOLIC
ECCLESIOLOGY

Richard Lennan

Actors associated with a universally loved, or hated, character often experience both edges of the sword of success. Such a role might open doors to the rewards of 'celebrity', itself a mixed blessing, but can also keep the actors captive to the shadow of their alter ego, thereby circumscribing careers. The nineteenth-century historian Thomas Babington Macaulay (1800–59) portrayed the Roman Catholic Church in terms that function much like the unforgettable character does for actors: he lauds the church, while trapping it within one dimension. Abandoning critical restraint, Macaulay, who was not a Roman Catholic, wrote:

> There is not, and there never was on this earth, a work of human policy so well deserving of examination as the Roman Catholic Church. . . . The proudest royal houses are but of yesterday when compared with the line of Supreme Pontiffs. . . . The Papacy remains not in decay, not a mere antique, but full of life and youthful vigour. . . . [the Roman Catholic Church] saw the commencement of all the governments and of all the ecclesiastical establishments that now exist in all the world; and we feel no assurance that she is not destined to see the end of them all.[1]

That description helped to inculcate in the popular mind an image of the Roman Catholic Church as a formidable institution, a fixed point in a world of flux, and the product of sterling leadership. Only a decade after Macaulay's death, the First Vatican Council (1869–70) reinforced that image through its definition of papal infallibility. Once again, order and authority loomed large as the hallmarks of the Catholic Church – 'Now, what Christ the Lord, the Prince of Shepherds and the great Shepherd of the flock, established in the person of the blessed apostle Peter for the perpetual safety and everlasting good of the Church must, by the will of the same, endure without interruption in the Church.'[2]

Although the emphasis on authority produced a skewed view of the church, the dominance of that approach in the nineteenth century opens a window onto a basic fact about Roman Catholic ecclesiology: it has developed mainly in response to historical issues.

Indeed, until recent times, there has been little evidence of ecclesiology as a 'theoretical discipline'. Accordingly, since much of Catholic history has involved controversies over various aspects of the church's structure, 'authority' became a staple not only for reflections on the church, but also for the teaching of the bishops. This is not to imply, however, that Catholics thought of their church only in socio-political terms, a point that Macaulay perhaps failed to grasp. If there was less attention paid to more explicitly theological issues, it was because such matters did not seem to be problematic: there was, for example, no doubt that Jesus had established the church, whole and complete.

This chapter will track the development of a more systematic approach to ecclesiology in the Roman Catholic communion. This means that the focus will be on issues such as the relationship of the church to the Trinity and God's self-communication in history through Jesus and the Holy Spirit; the place of the church within the life of faith, including its relationship to scripture; possible shapes for the church's mission; and the eschatological orientation of the church. As part of establishing the history behind this shift in emphases, the next section of the chapter will survey the strands of theology that dominated Catholic thinking before the Second Vatican Council (1962–5), which remains the primary formative event in the life of the modern Catholic Church. Exploring Vatican II, through both its teaching and its reception into the church at large, will be a major focus of the chapter. The final section of the chapter will review contemporary trends, including contentious issues, in Roman Catholic ecclesiology.

An ecclesiology of primacy and perfection

As already noted, efforts to defend the authority of the Catholic Church claimed a firm basis in broader, long-standing ecclesiological principles. Above all, this meant an emphasis on Jesus as 'the founder' of the church and his establishment of Peter as the head of the church, the necessity of the church for salvation, and the right of the church to be free from control by any authority other than God. Those three principles, which are clearly identifiable from the time of the Council of Trent (1545–63), formed the core of Catholic ecclesiology until the advent of the Second Vatican Council.[3]

In addition, each of those principles relied on a scriptural warrant, particularly from Matthew's gospel – 'You are Peter, and on this rock I will build my church, and the gates of Hades will not prevail against it. I will give you the keys of heaven, and what ever you bind on earth will be bound in heaven, and whatever you loose on earth will be loosed in heaven' (Mt 16.18–19). Although contemporary biblical scholarship might argue that the appeal to such examples was a form of 'proof-texting', which involves mining the biblical text to provide support for pre-existing beliefs, the approach helped to reinforce for Catholics not only the validity of their church, but its superiority over the various Protestant incarnations.[4] Since Catholic ecclesiology operated in the post-Reformation era with a largely defensive mindset, such apologetic concerns were pre-eminent.

The certainty of Jesus' establishment of the church and his delegation of authority to Peter underpinned the defence of papal primacy which, for more than a millennium, was asserted in response to challenges from the churches of the East, from 'conciliarists', who promoted the rights of a council of the church over the pope, from Lutherans, who rejected many forms of ecclesial authority as contrary to the gospel, and from the philosophers of the Enlightenment, who argued for the supremacy of reason and the individual over faith and institution.[5] The clear implication was that Jesus' foundation of the church and its hierarchical structure provided Catholics with a sure means of truth that could sustain them in the face of all difficulties and lead them with certainty to the fullness of life in God.[6]

Complementing the emphasis on the church as God's unique vehicle for human salvation was the insistence on the church's right to freedom from control by secular authorities. That issue had loomed large in medieval controversies between popes and emperors, but received a new impetus when the notion of the church as a 'perfect society' developed after the Reformation, principally through the work of Robert Bellarmine (1542–1621), as a response to the first stirrings of what became the modern form of 'the state'.[7]

'Perfection' in this context was less about moral excellence than completeness. In other words, the church was competent, with a God-given competence, to rule itself without intervention by 'the state'. This was so because the church served a higher end than any pursued by secular society:

> God indeed even made the Church a society far more perfect than any other. For the end for which the Church exists is as much higher than the end of other societies as divine grace is above nature, as immortal blessings are above the transitory things of earth. Therefore the Church is a society *divine* in its origin, *supernatural* in its end and in the means proximately adopted to the attainment of that end; but it is a *human* community inasmuch as it is composed of men. For this reason we find it called in Holy Writ by names indicating a perfect society. It is spoken of as *the house of God*, the *city placed upon a mountain* to which all nations must come.[8]

Offsetting the value of the 'perfect society' as a vehicle for defending the church's integrity were two deleterious effects. First, it exacerbated the church's difficulty in finding a place within, rather than above, a rapidly-changing socio-political landscape. By the end of the nineteenth century, therefore, the image of the pope as 'the prisoner of the Vatican', to which Pius IX (1846–78) had retreated in protest against the unification of Italy, which had involved the expropriation of papal territory, expressed poignantly the place of the Catholic Church in the Europe whose shape had evolved through a century of revolution, industrial ferment, and urbanization. Although Leo XIII's (1878–1903) *Rerum novarum* (1891) was an attempt, albeit tentative and belated, to respond to the impact of socialism, the church was largely tangential to the discussion of social issues. Indeed, Johann Baptist Metz argues that, from the Reformation onwards, the Catholic Church was essentially a 'counter' church defining itself by opposition to the society of which it was a part.[9]

Secondly, the notion of the 'perfect society', connected as it was to a feudal model in which order derived from fixed relationships between unequal groups, was always in danger of implying that some members of the church were more important than others. This buttressed the division between 'the teaching church', made up of the bishops, and 'the learning church', constituted by everyone else. 'Perfection', then, could become a conscript of views of the church that privileged hierarchy, resistance to proposals for change and the disinclination to engage with the wider world.[10]

Vatican II and new possibilities

The beginnings of the twentieth century offered little prospect for alteration in the Catholic understanding of the church. The possibility of change seemed especially remote when suspicion, even repression, of theology became the norm in the wake of 'the Modernist crisis'.[11]

That clash, in the first decade of the new century, pitted against each other those desiring openness to 'modern' ways of thinking – '[the Catholic Church] has narrowed the borders of her tent . . . has shrivelled herself up to a waspish sect glorifying as none other in her rigidity and exclusiveness'[12] – and those, including the church's hierarchy, who were suspicious of new ideas or, at least, of the way that the proponents of modernity formulated such ideas – 'they lay the axe not to the branches and shoots, but to the very roots: that is to the faith and its deepest fibres . . . they proceed to disseminate poison through the whole tree'.[13]

Although Vatican II was the moment of change, the seeds that flowered at the Council had gestated 'underground' in the decades following the Modernist crisis.[14] Those seeds, which represented especially a retrieval, a *ressourcement*, of ancient perspectives on the church, via renewed methodologies in biblical, liturgical and patristic studies, contained ways of thinking that differed markedly from the prevailing ecclesiological emphases on order and authority. In addition, two encyclicals of Pius XII (1939–58), *Divino afflante Spiritu* (1943) and *Mediator Dei* (1947), offered some encouragement, although far from thoroughgoing enthusiasm, for the revival and broadening of biblical and liturgical studies respectively. Most significantly of all for ecclesiology, Pius XII's encyclical on the church, *Mystici corporis Christi* (1943), promoted the notion of the church as 'the mystical body of Christ', rather than as simply a 'perfect society'. Nonetheless, the emphasis of the encyclical did not stray far from the familiar themes of structure and the role of the pope as the foundations for ecclesiology – 'They, therefore, walk in the path of dangerous error who believe that they can accept Christ as the Head of the Church, while not adhering loyally to his vicar on earth.'[15]

John XXIII's (1958–63) opening address to the Second Vatican Council in 1962 signalled both that ecclesiology would be the main focus of the Council and that 'business as usual' was not the preferred outcome – 'Illuminated by the light of this Council, the Church, we confidently trust, will become greater in spiritual riches and, gaining the strength of new energies therefrom, she will look to the future without fear.'[16] Indeed, together with the *ressourcement* already mentioned, the word that has become most evocative of the work of Vatican II is *aggiornamento*, which suggests change, receptivity to what is new, and opening a sealed room to light and air.

The dynamism between *ressourcement* and *aggiornamento*, between seeking what continues to be life-giving and, therefore, Spirit-filled, in the richness of the past, while also being open to the presence of the Spirit in new ideas and ways of thinking, captures well the meaning of 'catholicity'. At the heart of authentic catholicity is the willingness to embrace the 'both . . . and', rather than to lapse into the more congenial 'either . . . or' – 'The Catholic spirit . . . continues to cherish the wisdom handed down from earlier centuries . . . it is prepared to learn from all parties, seeking out the truth in every opinion and the merit in every cause.'[17]

Even before the first session opened, the difference between Vatican II and previous Councils was evident in the composition of the bishops who formed it. Those attending Vatican II, which gathered as the 'post-colonial' world was beginning to emerge, represented the views and experience not simply of European and North American Catholics, but also of the 'new' churches of Africa, Asia and Oceania. Since most of the bishops were not European 'expats', but 'nationals', Vatican II became:

> a first assembly of the world-episcopate, not acting as an advisory body to the Pope, but with him and under him as itself the supreme teaching and decision-making

authority in the Church. There really was a world-council with a world-episcopate such as had not hitherto existed with its own autonomous function.[18]

In the midst of much tension, excitement, and struggle, the Council undertook the task of reconsidering the church both *ad intra* and *ad extra*.[19] This meant that its agenda was not simply to explore possibilities for reshaping the church's self-understanding and the relationships between members of the church (*ad intra*), it was also to re-imagine the church's relationship to those who were not 'in communion with the Roman Pontiff', which was a traditional rubric for expressing where the church ended and 'the world' began (*ad extra*).

One of the pillars that underpinned the ecclesiological shift that Vatican II initiated was its commitment to locating its subject in relation to other fundamental aspects of the Christian life. This was especially true of the relationship between ecclesiology and the theology of revelation, which was one of the areas where the Council's commitment to both *aggiornamento* and *ressourcement* was most productive.

Since the Council of Trent, Catholic theologies of revelation, as a counter to the Protestant stress on *sola gratia*, *sola fides* and *sola scriptura*, had emphasized that the church safeguarded and promulgated in its teaching the eternal truths about God necessary for salvation.[20] From the Catholic perspective, then, tradition, understood primarily in terms of the church's teaching office, was as necessary as scripture to an authentic understanding of revelation. While by no means rejecting a primary place for the church's teaching role, Vatican II, however, understood revelation in terms of the 'event' of God's self-communication, which took place in history, especially in Jesus Christ, through whom the church came into being.

Accordingly, the church did not possess the truth about God as an object, but as the heart of 'all that she herself is, all that she believes', the heart of the church's doctrine, life and worship.[21] The church, therefore, did not simply pass on a truth that remained external to it, but needed to grow in its appreciation of the mystery of God revealed in Jesus Christ. This required, pre-eminently, that the Bible take its place at the heart of the church's life. A principal vehicle for the church's immersion into the mystery of God's revelation was 'the contemplation and study of believers who ponder these things in their hearts', through 'an intimate sense of spiritual realities', and through 'the preaching of those who have received . . . the sure charism of the truth'.[22] Here was a church that was more than, other than, a perfect society. As the product of God's word, the church was invited to relationship rather than control, to ongoing conversion rather than mastery.

The Council's principal document on the church, *Lumen gentium* (1964), reinforced a similar idea by describing the church as an aspect of the mystery of God's self-revelation. Most particularly, that document summarized the purpose of the church as being 'in the nature of a sacrament – a sign and instrument, that is, of communion with God and of unity among all people'.[23] The joint application of 'mystery' and 'sacrament' to the church as a whole not only broke down the dominance of juridical understandings of the church, it also freed the notion of sacrament from the narrow definitions that had become the norm in the neo-Scholasticism that shaped the Catholic worldview in the centuries after Trent.

'Sacrament', therefore, no longer implied only an isolated moment of grace, one dependent on careful adherence to the conditions for validity, but expressed an invitation to encounter with God in history.[24] The use of 'sacrament' to describe the presence and purpose of the church in the world also broadened the understanding of the church's mission beyond the narrow focus on promulgation and defence of a fixed truth. The new emphasis thus reinforced the connection between the church and the purpose of God's revelation.

Similarly, the adoption of a sacramental framework for thinking about the church opened the way to a greater recognition of the role of the Holy Spirit in the church, including the link between the Spirit and the centrality of scripture.[25] This renewed pneumatology served to correct a tendency to christomonism, a one-dimensional focus on Jesus to the exclusion of the trinitarian reality of God, which had long been a feature of ecclesiology in the Western church. The possibility of such christomonism had been present in the exclusive stress on the historical acts by which Jesus 'founded' the church in all its important particulars, thus leaving no role for the Spirit except to 'animate' an institution that already existed in all its essentials.[26]

The newness of Vatican II, especially the alternative that it offered to a primarily juridical understanding of the church, was most evident in the second chapter of *Lumen gentium*, which is entitled 'The People of God'. Although this chapter sometimes falls victim to those seeking a weapon in the ideological disputes that scar the contemporary Roman Catholic Church – 'the chapter on the "People of God" comes before that on "the hierarchy", so Vatican II was implying that the people, not the hierarchy, are the most important part of the church' – such efforts usually misrepresent the chapter, while also diluting both its authentic lustre and the extent of its challenge. Indeed, far from being a partial view of the church, one that privileged either the hierarchy or the laity, the notion of the 'People of God' summoned all members of the church to recognize the implications that their common baptism had for both the communion and mission of the church.

The chapter addresses what all members of the church, those within the hierarchy no less than anyone else, have in common through their baptism; in other words, the focus is on what is prior to any distinctions that derive from particular roles in the church. Through their baptism, all the members of the church 'are consecrated to be a spiritual house and a holy priesthood'.[27] The application of 'priesthood' to all the baptized marked not only a fundamental shift in Catholic understanding of what had been a major point of divergence from the Reformers, it also identified baptism, rather than ordination, as the fundamental building-block of Christian holiness – Chapter Five of *Lumen gentium* echoed and expanded that theme, when detailing the call to holiness that applies to all the baptized. Although Chapter Two affirms that the baptized and ordained priesthoods differ 'essentially and not only in degree', it highlights their fundamental unity 'in the one priesthood of Christ'.[28] Like Christ, then, all the members of the church were to live in ways that reflected the centrality of their relationship to God, which would also enable them to be witnesses to Christ in the world.

Even more remarkable, in light of the strict division between the 'teaching' and 'learning' church that had long applied in Catholic life, is the document's recognition that all the baptized share also in Christ's 'prophetic office', that they are witnesses and teachers of the faith. *Lumen gentium* stresses that, in and through Christ, 'the whole body of the faithful who have an anointing that comes from the holy one cannot err in matters of belief. This characteristic is shown in the supernatural appreciation of the faith (*sensus fidei*) of the whole people, when "from the bishops to the last of the faithful" they manifest a universal consent in matters of faith and morals'.[29] Although the implications of this affirmation of the *sensus fidei*, the presence of the Spirit to all the baptized, have not been fully realized in the church in the forty years since Vatican II (a point that will recur later in this chapter), this teaching remains a landmark in moving Roman Catholic ecclesiology beyond a narrow focus on hierarchical office.

The backdrop against which the Council painted its understanding of this priestly people, all of whom share in the Spirit of Christ through their baptism, was the notion of communion. As already mentioned, this idea occurs in the opening section of *Lumen gentium* to identify the purpose of the church – 'sign and instrument of communion with God and of unity among all people'. The document locates communion as the fundamental expression of the life and mission of the Trinity.[30] Since the Trinity is the source of ecclesial life, 'communion' also describes the deepest reality of the church – 'Guiding the Church in the way of all truth and unifying her in communion and in the works of ministry, [the Holy Spirit] bestows upon her various hierarchic and charismatic gifts and in this way directs her.'[31]

The applications of communion in *Lumen gentium* include the relationship between the bishops and all other members of the church, but particularly the relationship between the bishops themselves, who together form a 'college', of which the pope is head.[32] Thus, without compromising papal primacy, Vatican II's ecclesiology broadened the understanding of the 'internal' dynamics of the church beyond a one-dimensional emphasis on papal prerogatives. The most significant flowering of this approach was the prominence that *Lumen gentium* gave to 'the local church'. No longer was the church at diocesan level regarded as simply a branch office of a Rome-based 'export firm'.[33] Instead, the Council opened new possibilities by teaching that:

> In [the local Church] Christ himself, his Gospel, his love and the unity of believers are present. The Constitution [*Lumen gentium*] recognises and explicitly states that the local and altar community, so far from being a mere minor administrative subdivision in a major religious organisation called the Church, is actually the concrete reality of the Church, the presence of Christ in which it achieves its highest fullness, and that too in the word, in the Eucharistic meal and . . . in the love which unites the hearers and those who celebrate the Eucharist.[34]

Ecumenism was the other major area of ecclesial life to which the Council applied the notion of communion. Given how deep and broad the divisions between the churches had become after the Reformation, ecumenism did not rate highly among the desiderata of Catholics in the first half of the twentieth century – 'There is but one way in which the unity of Christians may be fostered and that is by furthering the return to the one true Church of Christ of those who are separated from it; for from that one true Church they have in the past fallen away.'[35] Nonetheless, through its emphasis on baptism and the Word of God, the Council recognized that:

> [Those] who believe in Christ and have been truly baptised are in some sort of communion with the Catholic Church, even though this communion is imperfect. The differences that exist in varying degrees between [other communities] and the Catholic Church . . . do indeed create many obstacles, sometimes serious ones, to full ecclesiastical communion. The ecumenical movement is striving to overcome these obstacles. But even in spite of them it remains true that all who have been justified by faith in baptism are members of Christ's body and have a right to be called Christian, and so are deservedly recognised as sisters and brothers in the Lord by the children of the Catholic Church.[36]

This opening to the possibility of a deeper communion with Christians of other churches, instead of an unequivocal demand for their 'return' to 'the one true Church of Christ' had its basis in how Vatican II portrayed that latter church. Rather than the assertion of an exclusive identity between the Roman Catholic Church and 'the one true Church', the Council chose to say that the Church of Christ 'subsists in' the Roman Catholic Church, thereby leaving space to acknowledge that 'many elements of sanctification and of truth are found outside its visible confines'.[37] This option for the softer edge was in stark contrast to the uncompromising approach used earlier in the century.

A further service to ecumenism that Vatican II provided was its treatment of Mary, the mother of Jesus. In the decades after the Modernist crisis, Mariology was one of the few areas of Catholic theology that were 'safe' for speculation. Consequently, Mariology became a crowded field, with the resultant tendency to excessive claims. That tendency, together with the invocation of papal infallibility in 1950 to define Mary's Assumption into heaven, confirmed the worst of Protestant fears about devotion to Mary among Catholics. Although there was pressure at the Council to promulgate a separate document on Mary, the bishops opted to include a chapter on Mary within *Lumen gentium*. In so doing, they emphasized Mary's place within the communion of believers. Mary, then, came into relief as the one who received and pondered the word of God and, therefore, as the model of discipleship, the calling of all the members of the church. The Council did not shy away from endorsing the legitimacy of 'the cult of Mary', but was equally committed to discouraging its excesses – 'Let the faithful remember moreover that true devotion consists neither in sterile or transitory affection, nor in a certain vain credulity, but proceeds from true faith.'[38] After the Council, however, Paul VI gave a renewed fillip to Marian devotion by ascribing to Mary the title 'Mother of the Church', which the bishops at Vatican II had explicitly rejected.[39]

Echoing the Council's sensitivity to ecumenical issues was its concern to re-imagine the church's relationship with 'the world'. That concern had numerous manifestations: first, applying the notion of communion to embrace 'in various ways' those beyond the boundaries of the Catholic Church. In this context, the Council referred to the members of other world religions, which was not a group that had often registered on the Catholic radar, as well as to those with no knowledge of God, but whose lives reflected the goodness and truth that carried overtones of the gospel.[40] Secondly, there was the recognition that the church, like the world at large, was on pilgrimage to the fullness of God's kingdom. More explicitly, Vatican II acknowledged that the church's pilgrim way was not the path of unadulterated holiness, but always involved the need for purification, penance and renewal.[41] Admittedly, this was far from an unequivocal confession of the church's sinfulness, but it was a significant advance on the 'perfect society'.

Thirdly, and most importantly of all, the church's relationship with the world claimed its own document. This was a first in the history of Catholic ecclesiology, not simply because of its subject matter, but because it was a 'Pastoral Constitution', rather than a 'Dogmatic Constitution': grounded in the church's faith in Jesus Christ, the Constitution invited dialogue with 'the world', rather than instructing the world on how it ought to act.[42] The document, *Gaudium et spes* (1965), famously begins by affirming that 'the joy and hope, the grief and anguish of the people of our time' are those of the followers of Christ as well, since 'nothing that is genuinely human fails to find an echo in their hearts'.[43] The document committed the church to dialogue, a theme that Paul VI (1963–78) endorsed in *Ecclesiam suam* (1964), his first encyclical, as fundamental to the mission of the church. *Gaudium et spes* nominated as central to the church's concern about the future of humanity, and therefore as core matters for dialogue, issues of unbelief, marriage, peace and war, and the inequalities of economic development. Gone was the 'perfect' church above the world or condemnatory of the world; present was a church that understood itself in relation to the world and its needs, but that also recognized the hope that it had to share, the hope derived from its foundation in Jesus Christ. As the final document of the Council, *Gaudium et spes* encapsulated for many the *aggiornamento* at the heart of Vatican II:

> After more than a century of turning away from the world, this document resolutely turned the gaze of the church towards the world. Its tone was optimistic, yet marked by a realism about the nature of sin and the complexity of the world's problems. For many within the church, it mapped out a way of encountering the world pastorally. For those outside the church, it signalled a commitment to the world that had not been in evidence for generations.[44]

The mixed reception of Vatican II

At the conclusion of the Council, Karl Rahner (1904–84), who had been present as a *peritus*, a theological 'consultant', outlined his assessment of what lay ahead for the church as a result of Vatican II:

> God addresses to the Church the question whether it has the courage to undertake an apostolic offensive into [the] future and consequently the necessary courage to show itself to the world sincerely, in such a form that no one can have the impression that the Church only exists as a mere survival from earlier times because it has not yet had time to die. But even if it has the courage to change, time is needed and time must be taken. . . . For the Church cannot change into something or other at will, arbitrarily, but only into a new presence of its old reality, into the present and future of its past, of the Gospel, of the grace and truth of God.[45]

The first, albeit open-ended, task that the church needed to undertake in order to become 'a new presence of its old reality', which is a profoundly catholic formulation, was to receive Vatican II. Although the processes of reception, 'through which an ecclesial community incorporates into its own life a particular custom, decision, liturgical practice, or teaching', had followed every Council, the reception of Vatican II offered unique challenges.[46] This was so because of the volume of material and the breadth of themes that emanated from its documents.

For the purposes of this chapter, an awareness of the dynamics involved in the reception of Vatican II, which, as the following pages will illustrate, has been a complex exercise, is particularly helpful. Those dynamics underscore once again the extent to which ecclesiology in the Roman Catholic tradition has been a product of issues that have arisen from the church's place in history, rather than a 'chemically pure' application of theological principles.

Catholics at large seemed to be not only undaunted by the magnitude of the challenge involved in receiving Vatican II, but inspired particularly by the call to *aggiornamento*. Indeed, so evident was the enthusiasm that the period immediately following the Council ranks as a 'phase of exuberance', characterized by the belief that change was both possible and desirable.[47] One expression of that exuberance was the emergence of liberation theology in Latin America.

While commitment to the poor was the vehicle through which this theology read the Christian tradition, it nonetheless claimed Vatican II as a guiding force. In the work of the Council, the emerging liberation theologians found 'the best possible theoretical justification to activities developed under the signs of a theology of progress, of authentic secularization and human advancement'.[48] From that basis, however, they went beyond what the Council itself had imagined in developing new models for the operation of the church's structures and for the engagement of the church with the socio-political environment.[49]

Although the development of liberation theology was a particular instance of the convergence of theological insight, social analysis and a passionate commitment to live the gospel in the context of poverty, not all post-Vatican II phenomena reflected such richness of origin and intent. Indeed, it was not always clear what connection some practices and theologies in the immediate post-conciliar period bore to the Council or the wider life of the church – 'much of this could be likened to a spaceship that had lost contact with ground control'.[50] This applied particularly to the more fringe liturgical experiments, such as the use of 'soda and crackers', instead of bread and wine, and readings from magazines or other popular literature, rather than from the Bible, during eucharistic celebrations.

Contributing to this mixed character of the Council's reception was the fact that the church's history, particularly in the period after the Reformation, where the emphasis was on Jesus' definitive establishment of all that was central to the constitution of the church, left Catholics unskilled in discerning and negotiating possibilities for change. More specifically, there was no lived memory of how the dynamics of the *sensus fidei* might operate as the Council had advocated. Since descending models of authority had been so prominent, there was little awareness of either the theory or practice needed to nurture a communion of faith, including dealing with differences. Consequently, differences often became a source of division – 'Where one person talks about renewal, another sees only breakdown, crisis and loss of identity.'[51]

Furthermore, the problem with 'change' was not simply the lack of requisite skills to negotiate it, but its clash with particular theological notions. Thus, if 'tradition' represented an unbroken continuity with the apostolic church, it was unclear how anything new could express the faith that had underpinned the church from the beginning. Although theology offered expanded ways to think about issues such as apostolicity – 'it means being continuously and vitally the same Church as the Church of the apostles, led through history by the same Holy Spirit to proclaim the same Good News and to bring the same salvation' – these were far from common currency in the broader church.[52] As a result, changes in liturgical practices and popular piety at 'the ground level', for example, were often haphazard and damaging to the cohesion of local communities, as was the resistance to such changes.

This cohesion of the Catholic community, which had been a proud boast of the church during the centuries after Trent, when the existence of a common foe helped to buttress 'Catholic identity', suffered a major blow only a few years after the completion of Vatican II. That blow came via the dispute over *Humanae vitae* (1968), Paul VI's encyclical 'on the regulation of birth'. Although some of the points of controversy were explicitly theological – Christian conscience, the 'ends' of marriage, personal discernment of the Spirit, the implications of membership in the ecclesial community, and the role of the teaching authority – others were expressive of the church's irreducible connection to the modern world, the very world with which the Council had sought to dialogue – the emergence of the women's movement, new thinking on human sexuality, medical technology, and altered socio-economic expectations affecting families. The extent of the division over *Humanae vitae*, as well as the strength of feeling on both sides of the divide, signalled that the achievement of authentic communion in the church required more than the assertion of its importance.

If 1968 marks a watershed in the 'Sixties' in general, it perhaps serves the same function in the history of Vatican II's reception in the Roman Catholic Church. It is doubtful whether much of the immediate post-conciliar exuberance remained in the aftermath of *Humanae vitae*. Indeed, Walter Kasper speaks of the emergence of 'a phase of disappoint-ment', the second wave in the Council's reception.[53]

While much of that disappointment reflected the feeling of those who desired more consistent and widespread change in the church, it also expressed the dissatisfaction felt by those who experienced the immediate post-conciliar period as one of loss. Seen from this perspective, *aggiornamento* promoted vandalism, not authentic renewal. Even some socio-logical analyses of the church after the Council point to deleterious effects from Vatican II. Thus, for example, Vatican II's emphasis on the contribution of all the baptized is adduced as a reason for the vast number of resignations from the priesthood and the associated 'emptying' of seminaries, which were among the most obvious expressions of difference between the post-conciliar church and life prior to 1965. The argument here is that the Council reduced the 'rewards' of priesthood, especially its social esteem and sense of heroic sacrifice, leaving only the burdensome residue of compulsory celibacy, which became less attractive in the light of the Council's positive endorsement of marriage.[54]

Those dissatisfied with the shape of the post-Vatican II church often claim that the church's relationship with the world has been less about dialogue than surrender: 'It seemed as though the project was to "translate" uniquely Catholic doctrine, practice, and style into forms acceptable to the surrounding culture, always downplaying whatever might be seen as peculiar or "supernatural".'[55] As a result, according to this critique, the Catholic Church had become 'beige': 'somehow trapped between the solemn and empty ritual and the pervasive superstitions of the so-called confident Church and the bare bones of low-church Protestantism – not quite Catholic but not really Protestant either'.[56]

This suspicion of Vatican II's openness to the world has even found a place in papal teaching. Thus, John Paul II (pope from 1979–2005), while affirming that 'in its rich variety of teaching the Second Vatican Council contains all that "the Spirit says to the Churches" with regard to the present phase of the history of salvation', nonetheless stressed the need for careful discernment in reception of the Council. Such discernment, he argued, is 'espe-cially necessary in view of the fact that the Council *opened itself widely to the contemporary world*'.[57] Reflecting the complexity of his papacy, however, John Paul has also gone beyond Vatican II in acknowledging to the world the faults of the church, even stating that aspects of the church's history 'constitute a countertestimony to Christianity' and that 'our sin has impeded the Spirit's working in the hearts of many people'.[58]

In light of the chequered history of Vatican II's reception, it is perhaps no surprise that the last decade has witnessed an increase in 'revisionist' interpretations of the Council. These have presented Vatican II as primarily an exercise in gradualism and continuity, rather than significant change and disjunction.[59] On the other hand, there is also an expanding body of literature detailing the complex processes of the Council in the hope of 'rescuing' Vatican II from attempts either to minimize its significance or to portray it as a one-dimensional event.[60] What has become more evident as a result of the latter efforts is that Vatican II bequeathed to the church 'a building site', rather than a completed edifice.[61]

At the present moment, some in the church have moved beyond suspicion of Vatican II to a 'neo-exclusivism', which favours a renewed emphasis on a narrowly-defined orthodoxy, displays little sympathy for the virtues of dialogue, and seeks a retrieval of pre-Vatican II emphases in such areas of the church's life as its ordained ministry.[62] It is, however, difficult to reconcile aspects of these approaches with the need to wrestle with the 'both . . . and', which, as suggested above, is a manifestation of genuine catholicity. The alternative to such one-dimensional approaches is, as advocated by Walter Kasper, for the church as a whole to continue seeking how best to achieve 'the authentic, integral interpretation and implementation' of the Council.[63]

Possibilities for the future

This chapter has emphasized that a constant of ecclesiology in the Roman Catholic tradition has been the symbiosis between the church and history, between the church and happenings in the world. This has been true even though the church has often viewed 'the world' with suspicion, and responded to it from a particularly narrow understanding of 'church', with the usual result that defensiveness prevailed. This highlights that the church in Catholic understanding is neither simply a 'given', incapable of change, nor is it merely a 'religious' matter with no implications for life in the world. In fact, 'the church remains the difference that Jesus Christ makes in human history, in the world. Through the church he remains an historical agent.'[64] History and the church, then, are inextricably linked.

The Catholic perspective also stresses the centrality of the church to Christian life as a whole. In fact, believing within the church reinforces that Christianity is both a shared faith and a pilgrimage; it reinforces too that Christian discipleship involves making choices in the midst of an often complex world.[65] Within the church, Christians are involved in a constant process of reception of God's Spirit, seeking to discern the shape of an authentic response to that Spirit in the present. The church, then, is never less than a community of reception, which implies:

> the creative involvement of human beings in the decisions of history and in the creative interpretation of 'what God would want' the church of the future to be . . . the human receivers of revelation are to be portrayed as active participants in discerning the way forward, co-deciders with God's Spirit, assuring continuity through creative discontinuity . . . What has been given as the ultimate criterion, the *regula fidei*, is the life, death, and resurrection of Jesus, which must be received over and over in the power of that Spirit who 'will guide you into all truth' [Jn 16.13].[66]

This chapter has illustrated how, over an extended period, Catholic ecclesiology sought to fulfil this role of reception by emphasizing that the church, understood principally in terms of its instruments of authoritative teaching, was the guarantee of divine truth and order in the midst of what was perceived to be a hostile world. With the advent of Vatican II, broader ways of thinking became accessible: since both church and world could now be understood in terms of God's kingdom and the presence of God's Spirit, it was possible to conceive of new priorities for the church in the world and new forms of relationship within the church itself. The chapter has also detailed, however, that the reception of those new possibilities has been far from smooth, particularly for the internal cohesion of the church.

What, then, might be the way ahead for Catholic ecclesiology? More particularly, how might the church, in the key phrases of Vatican II, fulfil its mission both *ad intra* and *ad*

RICHARD LENNAN

extra? Although answers to those questions need to come in practice, not simply theory, the notion of the church as communion is able to provide raw material for answering them both. This explains why the focus on communion can lay claim to being 'the central and fundamental idea of [Vatican II's] documents'.[67]

Since all aspects of ecclesial communion derive from the trinitarian God, 'communion' is an appropriate expression for the church's mission in God's world. In order to achieve that communion, a constant challenge for the church is the inculturation of the Gospel:

> [Catholicism] has virtually always and everywhere taken shape in a way consonant with the idea that God can only be confessed in faith as creator and redeemer of humankind and of history to the extent that connections and linkages are made between rational truths and fundamental insights into secular realities, on the one hand, and the articles of faith, on the other. This involves the necessity of inculturating faith.[68]

Inculturating the Gospel in the contemporary environment of globalization and postmodernism presents unprecedented challenges, particularly when the globalized market locates virtue in innovation, efficiency and technical rationality, all of which promote 'the hyper-culture of consumption', which can be hostile to the very humanity that is the focus of the gospel.[69] Although the church does not have specific answers to every issue of social and economic policy, its theology of communion is 'in contrast to a society of competition and success, [the church] will understand itself as being on the side of those who drop out of this process since they can neither produce nor consume'.[70] The church can do this, can fulfil its mission of serving the kingdom, thereby offering an alternative to what is, ironically, the narrowness of globalization, only if all of its members are themselves open to ongoing conversion. A key to the future, then, is re-appropriating the implications of discipleship: 'Mission is not for the faint-hearted. It is for those whose hearts have been touched and healed by God's reconciling love, and who now burn that others might also experience it.'[71]

The conversion, *metanoia*, on which the authenticity of the church's mission in the world, its communion with the world, is contingent, also has its echo in what is necessary for the accomplishment of genuine communion within the church.

Although the theology of communion has been the most popular of post-Vatican II ecclesiologies, it has not been without its critics, particularly on the score of its use by the 'official' church.[72] In a nutshell, the critiques imply that the teaching authority's endorsement of communion is at odds with some of the practices of those in authority – the winding back of episcopal collegiality under John Paul II, the lack of authentic initiative accorded to local churches, the failure of accountability in responding to the issue of clerical sexual abuse, the denial of transparency in processes applied to censure theologians, the still-existing gap between ordained and lay members of the church, particularly its impact on women, and the absence of consideration for involving members of the local church in choosing bishops.

What those issues suggest is that the practices of those exercising authority in the church often express a narrow focus on the preservation of institution, rather than on communion and its implications for mission. As such, they not only fail to be evangelical, they become an obstacle to the church's mission in a world that is no longer receptive to absolutist forms of authority.[73]

The need for conversion to the implications of communion, however, applies not only to those exercising authority in the church, but to all its members. While there are, of course, complex human dynamics and relationships to be negotiated in the life of the church, it is important for every member of the church to keep in mind that the Spirit, who is at the heart of every process of reception, is also at the heart of ecclesial communion. It follows, then, that one indicator of the authenticity of openness to the Spirit is preserving and expanding that communion. The option for communion, therefore, can embody a response to divine initiative.

It is highly doubtful whether a present-day Macaulay would look on the Roman Catholic Church with the same benignity as his predecessor: a church scarred by the upheaval that has been characteristic of the decades since Vatican II hardly invites the donning of rose-coloured glasses. On the other hand, those interested in ecclesiology and the thriving of the church's mission are more likely to regard the contemporary context, with its dual challenge to the church (understood as all its members, not simply its bishops) to build its inner communion and its communion with the wider world, as the preferred time.

Notes

1 Thomas Babington Macaulay, 'An Essay on van Ranke's "History of the Popes"' in *Critical and Historical Essays Contributed to the Edinburgh Review*, London: Longmans, 1870, p. 548.
2 First Vatican Council, *Pastor aeternus*, Chapter Two (18 July, 1870) in *The Christian Faith* (rev. edn), ed. J. Neuner and J. Dupuis, New York: Alba House, 1982, p. 228.
3 For brief histories of the emphases in Roman Catholic ecclesiology, see Monika Hellwig, 'Ecclesiology' in *The Modern Catholic Encyclopedia*, ed. M. Hellwig and M.Glazier (rev. edn), Collegeville: Liturgical Press, 2004, p. 253; and Richard McBrien, 'Ecclesiology' in *The HarperCollins Encyclopedia of Catholicism*, San Francisco: HarperSanFrancisco, 1995, p. 448.
4 For a brief overview of the use of 'proof-texts' as support for the church's doctrine see Raymond Collins, 'Bible and Doctrine' in *The HarperCollins Encyclopedia of Catholicism*, ed. R McBrien, San Francisco: HarperSanFrancisco, 1995, pp. 170–1.
5 For a historical survey of the teachings of various popes and councils on the role and dignity of the papacy, see Neuner and Dupuis, *The Christian Faith*, pp. 217–35.
6 For an example of a textbook that presented the church in this way, see Adolf Tanquerey, *A Manual of Dogmatic Theology* (vol. 1), tr. J Brynes, New York: Desclee, 1959, pp. 95–168; this book was published originally in Latin in 1914.
7 For a summary of Bellarmine's ecclesiology, see Eric Jay, *The Church: Its Changing Image Through Twenty Centuries*, London, SPCK: 1977, pp. 202–4.
8 Leo XIII, *Satis Cognitum* (1896) in *The Papal Encyclicals: 1878–1903*, ed. Claudia Carlen, Wilmington: McGrath Publishing, 1981, p. 396; original emphasis.
9 Johann Baptist Metz, *A Passion for God: The Mystical-Political Dimension of Christianity*, tr. J.M. Ashley, Mahwah: Paulist Press, 1998, p. 46.
10 See Yves Congar, 'Moving Towards a Pilgrim Church' in *Vatican II Remembered By Those Who Were There*, ed. A. Stacpoole, Minneapolis: Winston Press, 1986, pp. 133–4.
11 For a detailed study of the major issues and figures of the Modernist period, see Gabriel Daly, *Tanscendence and Immanence: A Study in Catholic Modernism*, Oxford: Clarendon Press, 1980.
12 George Tyrrell, *Medievalism: A Reply to Cardinal Mercier*, Allen: Christian Classics, 1994, p. 37; originally published in 1908.
13 Pius X, *Pascendi dominici gregis* (1907) in *The Papal Encyclicals 1903–39*, ed. C. Carlen, Wilmington: McGrath Publishing, 1981, p. 72.
14 For an example of this 'underground' work, see Joseph Komonchak, 'Returning from Exile: Catholic Theology in the 1930s' in *The Twentieth Century: A Theological Overview*, ed. G. Baum, Maryknoll: Orbis, 1999, pp. 35–48.
15 Pius XII, *Mystici corporis Christi* (1947) in *Papal Encyclicals 1939–58*, p. 45; for a detailed contemporary evaluation of the encyclical's ecclesiology, see Karl Rahner, 'Membership of the Church

According to the Teaching of Pius XII's Encyclical "Mystici Corporis Christi'" in *Theological Investigations (vol. 2)*, tr. K-H Kruger, New York: Crossroad, 1975, pp. 1–88.

16 John XXIII's opening address in *The Documents of Vatican II*, ed. W. Abbott, London: Geoffrey Chapman, 1967, p. 712.

17 Avery Dulles, *The Catholicity of the Church*, Oxford: Clarendon Press, 1987, p. 180.

18 Karl Rahner, 'Basic Theological Interpretation of the Second Vatican Council' in *Theological Investigations (vol. 20)*, tr. E. Quinn, New York: Crossroad, 1986, p. 84.

19 There is a vast, and ever-expanding, amount of literature that deals with Vatican II from every conceivable angle. The most detailed analysis of the workings of the Council can be found in the five volumes of *The History of Vatican II*, ed. G. Alberigo and J. Komonchak, Maryknoll: Orbis, 1995 – 2006; the most helpful analysis of the documents themselves remains the five-volumed *Commentary on the Documents of Vatican II*, ed. H. Vorgrimler, London: Burns & Oates, 1967–9; for a valuable and accessible overview of the Council's ecclesiology see Joseph Komonchak, 'The Significance of Vatican II for Ecclesiology' in *The Gift of the Church: A Textbook on Ecclesiology*, ed. P. Phan, Collegeville: Michael Glazier, 2000, pp. 68–92.

20 See, for example, Chapter Three of *Dei filius* (1870), Vatican I's decree on revelation.

21 *Dei verbum* (1965), §8; unless otherwise indicated, all references to the documents of Vatican II are taken from *The Documents of Vatican II*, ed. A. Flannery, New York: Pillar Books, 1975.

22 *Dei verbum*, §8.

23 *Lumen gentium*, §1.

24 For a brief overview of the history of 'sacrament' as a category in ecclesiology prior to Vatican II, see Johann Auer and Joseph Ratzinger, *Dogmatic Theology (vol. 8)*, tr. M. Waldstein, Washington DC: The Catholic University of America Press, 1993, pp. 91–4.

25 See, for example, *Dei verbum*, §21 and §23.

26 This idea comes from Yves Congar, *I Believe in the Holy Spirit (vol. 2)*, tr. D. Smith, New York, Seabury, 1983, p. 9; for an extended discussion on how the focus on the Spirit broadens ecclesiology, see Denis Edwards, 'The Church as Sacrament of Relationships', *Pacifica*, 8 (1995), 185–200.

27 *Lumen gentium*, §10.

28 *Lumen gentium*, §10; for a detailed discussion of the meaning and implications of the difference in 'degree', see Melvin Michalski, *The Relationship Between the Universal Priesthood and the Ministerial Priesthood of the Ordained in Vatican II and Subsequent Theology: Understanding 'essentia et non gradu'*, *Lumen gentium no. 10*, Lewiston: Edwin Mellen Press, 1996.

29 *Lumen gentium*, §12; the implications of the baptized faithful's sharing in the 'office' of Christ as priest, prophet, and king are well explored in Ormond Rush, 'The Offices of Christ, *Lumen gentium*, and the People's Sense of the Faith', *Pacifica* 16 (2003), 137–52. For one of the foundational texts on the active engagement of the laity in discerning the faith of the church, see John Henry Newman, *On Consulting the Faithful in Matters of Doctrine*, ed. J. Coulson, New York: Sheed & Ward, 1962; originally published in 1859.

30 For a review of the sources of Vatican II's emphasis on communion, see Denis Doyle, *Communion Ecclesiology*, Maryknoll: Orbis, 2000, pp. 74–8.

31 *Lumen gentium*, §4.

32 See *Lumen gentium*, §21–24.

33 This phrase comes from Karl Rahner, 'Basic Theological Interpretation of the Second Vatican Council', p. 78.

34 Karl Rahner, 'The New Image of the Church' in *Theological Investigations (vol. 10)*, tr. D. Bourke, New York: Crossroad, 1977, p. 10; Rahner's comment applies particularly to *Lumen gentium* §26.

35 Pius XI, *Mortalium animos* (1928) in *Papal Encyclicals 1903–39*, p. 317.

36 *Unitatis redintegratio* (1965), §3.

37 *Lumen gentium*, §8; for an extended discussion of the implications of the Council's formula, see Peter Knauer, 'The "Catholic Church" Subsists in the "Catholic Church"', *The Way* 45 (2006), 79–93.

38 *Lumen gentium*, §67.

39 For details of the differences between the Council and Paul VI on the issue of Mary as 'Mother of the Church', see George Tavard, *The Thousand Faces of the Virgin Mary*, Collegeville: Liturgical Press, 1996, pp. 202–8.

40 *Lumen gentium*, §16.

41 *Lumen gentium*, §8. For discussion of the Council's understanding of the church's sinfulness see, Karl Rahner, 'The Sinful Church in the Decrees of Vatican II', *Theological Investigations (vol. 6)*, tr. K.-H. and B. Kruger, New York: Crossroad, 1982, pp. 290–2; and Francis Sullivan, *The Church We Believe In: One, Holy, Catholic and Apostolic*, Dublin: Gill & Macmillan, 1988, pp. 76–7, 82–3.

42 For discussion of the meaning of a 'Pastoral Constitution', see Karl Rahner, 'On the Theological Problems Entailed in a "Pastoral Constitution"', *Theological Investigations (vol. 10)*, tr. D. Bourke, New York: Seabury, 1977, pp. 293–317.

43 *Gaudium et spes*, §1.

44 Robert Schreiter, 'Culture and Inculturation in the Church: Forty Years of Dovetailing the Gospel with the Human Kaleidoscope', *New Theology Review* 18 (2005), 18.

45 Karl Rahner, 'The Changing Church' in *The Christian of the Future*, tr. W.J. O'Hara, London: Burns & Oates, 1967, p. 36.

46 Lucien Richard, 'Reflections on Dissent and Reception' in *The Church in the Nineties: Its Legacy, Its Future*, ed. P. Hegy, Collegeville: Liturgical Press, 1993, p. 6.

47 Walter Kasper, *Theology and Church*, tr. M. Kohl, London: SCM, 1989, p. 166.

48 Leonardo Boff and Clodovis Boff, *Introducing Liberation Theology*, tr. P. Burns, Tunbridge Wells: Burns & Oates, 1987, p. 68. See also Chapter 23 of this present volume, 'Liberation ecclesiology'.

49 See, for example, Leonardo Boff, *Church, Charism and Power: Liberation Theology and the Institutional Church*, New York: Crossroad, 1990.

50 Walter Kasper, 'The Council's Vision for a Renewal of the Church', *Communio* 17 (1990), 476.

51 Kasper, *Theology and Church*, p. 169.

52 John Wright, 'The Meaning and Structure of Catholic Faith', *Theological Studies* 39 (1978), 709.

53 Kasper, *Theology and Church*, p. 167; see also Hervé Legrand, 'Forty Years Later: What has become of the Ecclesiological Reforms envisaged by Vatican II?' in *Vatican II: A Forgotten Future*, ed. Alberto Melloni and Christoph Theobald, London: SCM, 2005 [*Concilium*, 2005/4], pp. 57–72.

54 See Rodney Stark and Roger Finke, *Acts of Faith: Explaining the Human Side of Religion*, Berkeley: University of California Press, 2000, pp. 177–82.

55 Robert Barron, 'Beyond Beige Catholicism', *Church* 16 (2000), 5–10.

56 Andrew Greeley, *The Catholic Revolution: New Wine, Old Wineskins and the Second Vatican Council*, Berkeley: University of California Press, 2004, p. 134.

57 John Paul II, *Dominum et vivificantem* (1986), §26 in *The Encyclicals of John Paul II*, ed. J.M. Miller, Huntington: Our Sunday Visitor, 2001, p. 261; original emphasis.

58 John Paul II, *Incarnationis mysterium* (1998), §11 in *Origins* 28 (10 Dec. 1998), 450.

59 See, for example, James Hitchcock, 'Version One: A Continuum in the Great Tradition', *Commonweal* 128 (9 Mar. 2001), 16, 18–19; and Avery Dulles, 'Vatican II: The Myth and the Reality', *America* 188 (24 Feb. 2003), 7–11.

60 A leading figure in this endeavour has been John O'Malley, see, for example, 'Vatican II: Did Anything Happen?', *Theological Studies* 67 (2006), 3–33; see also Ormond Rush, *Still Interpreting Vatican II: Some Hermeneutical Principles*, Mahwah: Paulist, 2004; Joseph Komonchak, 'Is Christ Divided?: Dealing with Diversity and Disagreement', *Origins* 33 (17 July, 2003), 140–7; and James McEvoy, 'Church and World at the Second Vatican Council: The Significance of "Gaudium et spes"', *Pacifica* 19 (2006), 37–57.

61 This image comes from Hermann Pottmeyer, *Towards a Papacy in Communion: Perspectives from Vatican Councils I and II*, New York: Crossroad, 1998, p. 128.

62 The notion of 'neo-exclusivism' comes from Gerard Mannion, 'Ecclesiology and Postmodernism: A New Paradigm for the Roman Catholic Church?', *New Blackfriars* 85 (2004), 314. For the difference in perceptions of priesthood between those ordained in the period immediately following the Council and those ordained in recent years, see Dean Hoge and Jacqueline Wenger, *Evolving Visions of Priesthood: Changes from Vatican II to the Turn of the New Century*, Collegeville: Liturgical Press, 2003; and Katarina Schuth and Frederick Maples, 'Character and Assessment of Learning for Religious Vocation: Interview Study of Roman Catholic Students and Faculty', *Theological Education* 40 (2005), 1–46.

63 Kasper, *Theology and Church*, pp. 169.

64 Joseph Komonchak, 'The Future of Theology in the Church' in *New Horizons in Theology*, ed. T. Tilley, Maryknoll: Orbis, 2005, p. 32.

65 For discussion of the implications of membership of the church, see Karl Rahner, 'Courage for an Ecclesial Christianity', *Theological Investigation* (*vol. 20*), tr. E. Quinn, New York: Crossroad, 1986, pp. 3–12; and Avery Dulles, 'The Ecclesial Dimension of Faith', *Communio* 22 (1995), 418–32.

66 Rush, *Still Interpreting Vatican II*, p. 76.

67 'Final Report', *Documents of the Extraordinary Synod of Bishops November 28–December 8, 1985*, Homebush: St Paul Publications, 1986, p. 35.

68 Peter Hünermann, 'Evangelization of Europe?: Observations on a Church in Peril' in *Mission in the Third Millennium*, ed. R. Schreiter, Maryknoll: Orbis, 2001, p. 65.

69 Robert Schreiter, *The New Catholicity: Theology Between the Global and the Local*, Maryknoll: Orbis, 1997, pp. 9–10.

70 John Fuellenbach, *Church: Community for the Kingdom*, Maryknoll: Orbis, 2002, p. 202; see also, T. Howland Sanks, 'Globalization and the Church's Social Mission', *Theological Studies*, 60 (1999), 625–51.

71 Robert Schreiter, 'Globalization and Reconciliation' in *Mission in the Third Millennium*, p. 143.

72 For examples of the critiques see José Comblin, *The People of God*, Maryknoll: Orbis, 2004; Clare Watkins, 'Objecting to *Koinonia*: The Question of Christian Discipleship Today – And Why Communion Is Not The Answer', *Louvain Studies* 28 (2003), 326–43; and David McLoughlin, '*Communio* Models of Church: Rhetoric or Reality', in *Authority in the Roman Catholic Church: Theory and Practice*, ed. Bernard Hoose, Aldershot: Ashgate, 2002, pp. 181–90. Again, see Chapter 6 of this volume, 'The Church in modern theology', for a further discussion of the ecclesiology of communion.

73 Hünermann, 'Evangelization of Europe?', pp. 67–71.

Further reading

John Fuellenbach, *Church: Community for the Kingdom*, Maryknoll: Orbis, 2002.

Walter Kasper, *Theology and Church*, tr. M. Kohl, London: SCM, 1989.

Richard Lennan, *Risking the Church: The Challenges of Catholic Faith*, Oxford: Oxford University Press, 2004.

Alberto Melloni and Christoph Theobald (eds) *Vatican II: A Forgotten Future*, London: SCM, 2005 [*Concilium*, 2005/4].

Peter Phan (ed.), *The Gift of the Church: A Textbook on Ecclesiology*, Collegeville: Michael Glazier, 2000.

Ormond Rush, *Still Interpreting Vatican II: Some Hermeneutical Principles*, Mahwah: Paulist Press, 2004.

Robert Schreiter (ed.), *Mission in the Third Millennium*, Maryknoll: Orbis, 2001.

14

ECCLESIOLOGIES
AT THE MARGIN

Henk de Roest

Marginal ecclesiologies is a non-judgemental term used to describe the ecclesiologies of ecclesial communities which have arisen out of, or are located on, the margins of mainstream (or 'traditional') churches. Marginal does not mean 'small' or 'non-influential'. Faith communities at the margin may have considerable size worldwide; their members may exercise a remarkable influence upon their respective contexts. They may energize the religious scene.[1]

'Ecclesiologies at the margin' contain major elements derived from mainstream doctrine, but can be discerned in contrast to mainstream modern ecclesiologies. The term refers to the fundamental perspectives in the narratives told by churches and ecclesial groups at the margin to articulate and justify their identity. These convictions belong to the 'theory' of their practices. Many can be found in documents, but they are also operative in activities, procedures, rituals, habits and structures.

In this chapter, we describe communities such as the pre-millenialist or Adventist churches, which emerged in the nineteenth century; critical–emancipatory churches like women churches and base communities that emerged in the late twentieth century; missional–contextual churches, including the so-called 'emerging churches', and youth churches, that came into being in the early years of the twenty-first century. The second category will be rather brief, since these communities have been described extensively in other chapters in this companion. One question demands our attention first: Is 'marginal' satisfactory as a common denominator by which we can group together the ecclesiologies of these churches and ecclesial groups when in fact many are as different as chalk and cheese? I hope to demonstrate, both in an introductory paragraph and throughout this chapter that concepts like 'margin', 'verge' and 'edge' contain a distinct semantic potential for the churches and for reflection upon their dynamics. This potential merits to be tapped.

The edge as space for innovation

What do pre-millenialist churches, critical–emancipatory ecclesial groups and missional–contextual church movements have in common? Do they share specific characteristics? At first sight, differences are more apparent.

Most pre-millenialist churches endorse and apply an approach in which boundaries are drawn that distinguish those who belong to their churches from the outside world. Beliefs are clearly articulated, behaviour is prescribed. They may use a test of orthodoxy, with verbal affirmations of belief in a specific set of doctrines, or a test of orthopraxy or right behaviour.[2] These churches advocate a bounded set. Missional–contextual and critical–emancipatory churches are either Christ-centred or 'fuzzy-centred'. Membership is based on relationship with Jesus Christ, not on knowledge or behaviour. When they are 'fuzzy-centred', there is no sharp line between Christians and non-Christians. They do not command loyalty to the Christian tradition. These communities embrace diversity. Both missional–contextual and critical–emancipatory churches stimulate belonging to a place of fellowship before believing, are inclusive without compromising, open to fresh insights and encourage a vivid exchange of experiences.[3]

Still, there are striking similarities and it is concepts like 'margin' and 'edge' which may help us to detect them. Marginal ecclesiologies have accompanied mainstream[4] ecclesiologies ever since the Christian church came into being. If we are able to consider them as *correlata* we see that the centrifugal force of the faith communities at the edges cannot be understood without noticing the centripetal tendencies of the believers in the centre.[5] Mainstream churches create a vacuum into which new ecclesial groups can move. This refers to practices, but also to teachings. The communities at the edges tend to focus upon one or two core beliefs or on practices with regard to community, mission and worship which are underemphasized in the mainstream churches. They aim at refocusing mission, reconfiguring community and refreshing worship, often initially concentrating on one or another.[6] They renew commitment to selected aspects of denominational histories and traditions. Marginal churches and peripheral ecclesial groups have been called the 'unpaid bill' of the church. They remind mainstream churches of relevant elements of their tradition and form a corrective to the shortcomings of the churches.[7]

Marginal communities typically emerge in times of religious ferment. They come into being in a context of competing religious claims, in an atmosphere that is ready for new ideas. The sense of embodying an alternative way is a critical component of their identity. They attract people who are discontented with 'mainline' expressions of faith; adherents are possibly deprived with regard to their social position, gender position or ethnic background; joining these groups may be also be connected with certain biographical events that are considered as turning points. Dealing with the point of recruitment in motivational terms, a selective focus on a predominantly 'negative' character of motivational profiles leads to an incomplete appreciation of the factors in community attraction. Times of religious ferment are likely to be periods of motivational fluidity. Ecclesial group characteristics may become 'appeals'. Marginal communities offer new ways of experiencing God, new social practices, new healing rituals, new creative communication forms and, in some cases, even new revelatory texts that can give meaning to one's life and the existence of the world. They forge a bond of solidarity and common commitment which enforces a strong community consciousness. Communities at the edge also have a strong self-awareness. At the edge a group or church notices its collective identity more poignantly.

The foregoing implies that the edges can be considered as a space of innovation,[8] in a theological, social, ritual, communicational and foundational sense. Emerging faith communities on the margins may challenge a variety of fundamental premises of the day with regard to beliefs, social practices, rituals, communication means and sometimes, as for example in the cases of the Latter-day Saints and Christian Scientists, with regard to sources as well.[9] Theological innovation is apparent in the Adventist churches. Social innovation can be observed in such diverse groups as the Shakers and the Peace Mission Movement. Ritual innovation occurs when ecclesial groups develop a negative critique of worship practices in established mainline churches, for example by rejecting formal, structured and liturgical patterns of worship in favour of free spiritual expressions. Both the Quakers and the Pentecostals provide striking examples of the power of the ritual setting, albeit that they carried their innovation in opposite directions.[10] Communicational innovation is a striking feature of the revivalist movements of the nineteenth century. As an example we mention the 'camp meeting' concept, originated in the USA on the frontier during the revival of 1800, when pioneers assembled for 'spiritual food' and camped for several days to enjoy preaching and fellowship. In the Adventist movement camp meetings contributed to a developing sense of community and identity. In other streams of Adventism, annual conferences contributed to the development of ecclesiological and theological doctrine.

In the last decades, theological, social, ritual and communicational innovation can be observed among such diverse ecclesial groups as critical churches (women churches, base communities) on the one hand and missional churches (youth churches, emerging churches) on the other hand. In these ecclesial groups new narrative approaches disclosing God's agency and new metaphors, symbols and rituals are created. Innovation in faith communication takes place when everyday life experiences shape the content and forms of sermons, conversations and worship. These communities also serve to correct, challenge, confront and transform complacent Christian self-understandings and practices. Communicational innovation becomes visible in the creative usage made of multi-media, like beamers, mobile phones and the internet.

Creativity does not seem compatible with 'mainline' or 'the middle'. The centre demands prudence and is inherently inert. Toynbee has demonstrated that the future of a community depends upon the creativity of minorities. Marginal communities can be regarded as creative minorities who contribute to Christianity in regaining and renewing its legacy or, as Leonardo Boff suggest, they provide the opportunity for an evangelical authenticity not found within the institution, with its time and energy spend to justify, defend, preserve and expand its structures.

Other features of marginal churches

Besides the innovative potential, and related to their origin in times of religious ferment, a common feature of emerging churches and ecclesial groups in the margin is the role of charismatic men and women and the influence of inspirational texts. It might even be argued that innovations are possible precisely because of these pioneers, who through their conduct and by means of their texts like sermons, articles, tracts, books and, in recent movements, website-pages and weblogs, exercise an animating influence upon the adherents. 'Charisma' refers to the following called forth by one who is able to catalyse latent discontents and extend the hope of overcoming them. Inspiring leadership and inspiring words, as well as impassioning songs,[11] contribute highly to the deepening of the motivation of the members and enable communities to open new avenues for the communication of faith and the experience of community. Inspiring men and women also enable spawning churches to seek the limelight.

Furthermore, a discourse on strictness or laxity in practices appears again and again in peripheral communities, which, combined with a sense of elitism and a genuine conviction of being called, often leads to the establishment of radicals and moderates, 'pliables' and 'stricts'. In some churches this can lead to a 'recurring decimal', whereby schisms are followed by schisms.

Peripheral ecclesiologies are also bound to be confronted with criticism put forward by established churches. Thus Adventists, critical churches and radical missional churches have attracted criticism with regard to the one-sidedness of their beliefs and the innovative nature of their practices.

We renounce the use of concepts like 'sects' or 'sectarian' in this chapter. Nobody takes such concepts into consideration with regard to their own religious community. It is always someone else who belongs to a sect.[12] In the sociology of religion, however, since its usage in contrast with 'church' by, first, Max Weber[13] and later Ernst Troeltsch,[14] the terminology has been common to describe churches and ecclesial groups at the periphery.[15] Later refinements of this contrast, for example by Milton Yinger, enabled the construction of a continuum, with 'universal church' and 'cults' as opposite poles.[16] According to Stark and Bainbridge the difference between 'church' and 'sect' is the difference between the degree of tension with society and culture.[17] Their conceptual framework and accompanying taxonomy have been proven useful. Yet, due to a range of historical events, the concept of 'sect' is heavily laden. In this chapter I prefer marginal or peripheral communities.

In this chapter we describe diverse examples of theological, social, communicational and ritual innovation at the margins. We offer some details with regard to the origins of several communities and ecclesial networks in the periphery; describe the theory that is operative in their practices; and highlight innovative teachings and practices.

Pre-millenialism churches

The first group of marginal ecclesiologies addressed is interpreted under the rubric of *pre-millenialism* or *Adventism*.[18] It includes the ecclesiologies of Seventh-day Adventists, Jehovah's Witnesses, Latter-day Saints, Brethren and Apostolics. They fit into the Advent Awakenings of the nineteenth century, marked by pre-millenialism, literalism and later also by separatism. The decisive dividing-line with mainstream churches is their attitude to the flow of time.[19] The belief in the nearness of judgement day looms in their thought. There is a focus on the *finis* of history, albeit that the inevitable succession of the generations, as Richard Niebuhr pointed out,[20] may have lead to a decay of the enthusiasm of the early period and to a lukewarmness among the members compared to the original mentality. Disappointments take their toll. Still, contra Niebuhr, in these movements there were always new members.[21] New converts joined and often served to keep old families in line. A loosening rigour, a loss of the sense of dissent and the muting of claims belong to movements in the margin, but some resist pressure better than others. In the ecclesiologies at hand, some practices and teachings have acted as 'insulating devices'. For the respective pre-millenialist ecclesiologies, believing in the imminent second coming of Christ and the emphasis on end-time events have remained distinctive features. As insulating devices one may point at, for example, the teaching of the seventh-day Sabbath and the dietetic code in Seventh-day Adventism, the hours of witnessing each week and the lengthy training and bible study at the halls of Jehovah's Witnesses,[22] the temple rituals and discipline of the Mormons[23] and the strict role of the offices of the Apostolics.

Adventist churches exhibit a remarkable capacity for innovation, especially when chiliastic expectations are not fulfilled. Members of Adventist churches often engage in unconventional actions. At the same time, especially when prophecies are publicly announced, conflicts are on the lurk. As we will see, the so-called Apostolic churches have undergone schism after schism, whereby each new branch has to legitimize itself as a valid expression of the church, designing new rituals and teachings.

In this chapter we will discuss the Seventh-day Adventists, which originated in the USA, and the so-called Work of the Apostles that came into being in Great Britain. Space, alas, does not permit a full discussion of Jehovah's Witnesses, the Church of Jesus Christ of Latter-day Saints and the Brethren.

The Seventh-day Adventist church

This church originated in New Hampshire in 1844 and in 2004 had approximately 15 million members. Its roots lie in the Millerite Adventist movement, with close affinities to the revivalist movements of the day.[24] Millerites came from nearly all Protestant churches and viewed themselves as 'unsectarian', by which they wished to express that they laid aside 'manmade' beliefs. In 1822, William Miller (1782–1849) wrote: 'I believe that before Christ comes in his glory, all sectarian principles will be shaken and the votaries of the several sects scattered to the four winds; and that none will be able to stand but those who are built on the word of God.'[25] Miller called for a literal interpretation of the scriptures, preparing the churches for Christ's return. In 1831 he stepped into the limelight with his calculations that the thousand-year reign of Christ would begin on March 21 in the year 1844, with the literal and visible return of Jesus Christ to earth.[26] His lectures were enthusiastically received or, as Everett Dick writes, 'eager listeners hung on his words, spellbound for two hours at a time, and packed houses were the rule'.[27] Millenialism became an effective revivalist theme. The revival movement gained momentum. 'Summer camp meetings' were organized throughout the country.[28] Large tents were constructed. Periodicals, like *Signs of the Times* and permanent newspapers, appeared. Networks of ministers spread the message. Leaders denied forming a new church, reflecting the antisectarianism of the time, but a dynamic built up that led toward separation. Disappointed when Advent leaders were called covenant breakers and were objects of mockery, in 1843 Miller broke with the churches, characterizing them as 'harlots'. In the year 1844 the return of Jesus would take place, but after the deadline passed on March 21 and particularly after October 22, the day chosen by a new and final calculation in August of that year, the year ended with what was afterwards labelled The Great Disappointment.[29] The Adventists experienced ridicule and antagonism, and many adherents abandoned the movement. Others stated that Christ had already come in a 'spiritual way'. These new ideas were published by George Storrs, later profoundly influencing Charles T. Russell, founder of the Jehovah's Witnesses.[30]

After these disappointments, a movement coalesced and became the Seventh-day Adventists, which was first officially used as a name in 1860. The movement included Ellen G. Harmon, her husband-to-be James White and a small band of followers. In December 1844 Ellen Harmon had the first of many visions in which she saw Adventists marching to the City of God.[31] At the time of her marriage, she and James White, took the issue of keeping the seventh-day Sabbath into serious consideration. A month later they began to keep Saturday as Sabbath. On April 3, 1847 Ellen White had a vision in which she saw the Ten Commandments, the fourth encircled by light. Ellen White's visions formed the basis of voluminous writing. She was soon accepted by many as a prophet. Her charismatic leadership contributed to the rapid growth of the movement. In 1849 James began a journal, using the media of the day to spread the message. Between 1860 and 1901, when clusters of local conferences were organized into unions, Seventh-day Adventists developed so-called 'societies', semi-independent units promoting church activities. After 1901 these societies became part of the General Conference. Para-church meetings, conferences and organizations contributed to the strength of the church and its internationalization.

Contemporary Seventh-day Adventists are known for a heavy emphasis on dietary laws and healthy living (members do not use tea, coffee, alcohol or tobacco), since the human body deserves respect because it is created perfect in God's image and, although marred by sin, is still the temple of God. Adventists encourage tithing and missional activities. Apart from their eschatological beliefs, the most important distinguishing factor is their practice of honouring the Sabbath on the seventh day of the week. The writings of Ellen White are authoritative. They form an innovative source, though they are not considered equal to the Bible.

Apostolic churches[32]

The Work of the Apostles has three roots: the so-called Albury conferences, starting in 1826, on the second coming of Christ;[33] several events (healings, *glossolalia*) in Scotland that were experienced as an outpouring of the Holy Spirit;[34] and, finally the public appearance of Edward Irving (1792–1834), who gave space to these experiences in his Scottish congregation in London. The Work of the Apostles has been understood as a reaction against the intellectual and moral doubt and accompanying relativism prevalent in early nineteenth-century Britain. The so-called Irvingite movement of the 1830s was highly charismatic and showed a longing for authoritative apostles, who were supposed to lead the churches back to unity and truth. They hoped for the 'revival of the gifts manifested in the primitive church'.[35]

From the conferences, a new 'para-church' phenomenon, the doctrine of the movement emerged. In addition, the movement grew in a converted art gallery at Newman Street, where *glossolalia* characterized Irving's services; he was discharged from his post in 1832, although still an ordained minister of the Church of Scotland.[36] Due to a prophecy by Henry Drummond, the initiator of the Albury conferences, the movement got the characteristic that distinguishes it from other pre-millenialist churches. In 1832, at a prayer meeting in Irving's house, Drummond walked up to the praying John Cardale[37] and called him to be an apostle. A month later Cardale appointed Drummond as the 'angel' of the community at Albury and called him to be an apostle in 1833. Others followed. In January 1832 a prophecy by Baxter referring to an imminent Advent was momentous for the movement.[38] Calculations by Cunnynghame were accepted by the members of the Albury conferences. By 14 July 1835[39] there were twelve apostles and they were selected, released from their task in their communities and after a year of training and study at Albury were sent to twelve 'tribal territories' in Europe, representing the tribes of a spiritual Israel.[40] The basic pattern of what they believed to be the originally restored church was now prepared for the whole of Christianity. The church is governed by apostles, served by prophets, evangelists, shepherds and teachers. Each local faith community is led by an angel, together with six elderly and local prophets, evangelists and shepherds.

The apostles addressed spiritual and worldly leaders with their so-called 'Testimonies'.[41] Their message fell on deaf ears. A crisis in the movement occurred in 1840, out of which the apostolic authority emerged with greater strength. By the end of the forties, the enthusiasm decayed. A new ritual was invented by the apostles at Albury. Prophets, evangelists and teachers were to be 'sealed'. The emphasis on ordinances grew.[42] A revival took place, possibly also caused by the tension of the times.

In 1855 three apostles passed away.[43] In his speech Cardale, the 'pillar among the apostles', stated that many a person had thought they would not die, but they were wrong. In 1859 two more apostles passed away, in 1862 another one. In 1859 a German evangelist, Charles Böhm, was called to be an apostolic messenger, interpreted by some as a call to the office of the apostle. The remaining apostles decided, however, that Böhm was called to be an assistant-apostle or *coadjutor*. The six could not find a mandate in scripture to replace the deceased apostles. In 1877 Cardale passed away, followed two years later by Armstrong, leaving Woodhouse as the only apostle left. The movement began to think that before or shortly after his death the second coming of Christ would take place.[44] In 1901 he passed away, thereby introducing a 'time of silence' (Rev 8.1) in which there could be no sealings, nor apostolic activities by the *coadjutors* or ordinations. The last angel of the German community of Siegen passed away in 1960, the last priest died in 1971. After his death, there was no Catholic Apostolic Church anymore, where the eucharist could be celebrated. Today, where Catholic Apostolic communities gather, services of praise and intercession are organized. Specific attention is given to the notion of confession of guilt due to the disunity of the church.

In Germany the development was different.[45] In 1862 German 'angel-prophet' Geyer and 'assistant-angel' Schwartz were deeply concerned when one apostle after another passed away. In the following year a schism happened. Schwartz and Geyer claimed to be called by the Spirit to become apostles. The Restored Apostolic Church came into being, raised out of the 'Old Order' (the 'English' apostles). Other apostles were called; the activities of the Apostolic Mission began, founding new apostolic communities and sealing individuals and small groups. With regard to the liturgy, 'old-apostolic' customs, like vestments, recitations and other so-called 'externals' were gradually abolished.

A new conflict in Germany and The Netherlands burst out after Schwartz's death in 1895, with regard to the hierarchical order of the offices and a new phenomenon: the new light.[46] Do the 'prophets' have authority apart from the apostles? Is scripture source and norm of faith? A new schism was the result. The adherents of the so-called 'new light' principle, containing the conviction that living apostles are the authorities of the Holy Spirit of the day, formed the Restored Apostolic Mission Church in the Unity of the Apostles or New Apostolic Church (1902). The older group called itself the Restored Apostolic Mission Church. This church later falls apart in three pieces.

The New Apostolic branch of the 'Work' displayed a tendency to identify the apostle with Christ. In a hymnal issued in 1933, out of 200 songs, 106 are devoted to the apostle. After World War II, a new crisis in this New Apostolic Church arose, driving the apostle even further upwards.[47] In the so-called Apostolic Society the conviction of a dualistic theism, implying a transcendent divine reality outside man, is dropped. Tang writes: 'After Christ-in-the-apostle it became Christ-as-apostle; now it is God-as-apostle.'[48] In the christological teachings of the Apostolic Society there is a complete evaporation of Jesus Christ into a 'life that is called Jesus' that has to be developed in souls. Members want to dedicate themselves to promoting the mentality of Christ. In the other, explicitly theistic, branch of the New Apostolic Church, the imminent Advent is still expected. In the 1950s, however, membership became inextricably connected to belief in the message of the tribe-apostle that Christ would come during his lifetime. This caused dissent among the New Apostolics and the emergence, once again, of a new church. Both wings united in 1964. The role of the apostle in this church is strictly functional, most of the hymns point at Jesus and the coming of the kingdom.

With regard the teachings of the Apostolics, as we have seen, the original order of the offices is the specific characteristic of the church. The metaphor of the church as body of Christ is foundational in providing an arrangement for the fourfold structure of the offices. It is more than a metaphor: it is ultimate reality. The distinction of a visible and an invisible church is rejected. A periodical division of history is common. With the exception of the Apostolic Society, history is regarded as an event that will soon find its end in the coming of Christ. In history, an increasing animosity between God and the Antichrist determines the course of events. Those who are sealed, including the children, will receive immortality. In Christ's thousand-year reign the Jews will be the second highest executives, being an instrument in God's hand for the conversion of the peoples.

Critical–emancipatory communities

The second group of marginal communities has its origin in the last decades of the twentieth century. We lump the reflections, groundings and identities of both 'women churches' and 'base communities' together as *critical* or *emancipatory* ecclesiologies.

We discuss them briefly. A striking feature is their critique of theology and tradition and their emancipatory ecclesial praxis. Theology and the church have to be liberated and humanized if they are to serve people and not oppress them.[49] In addition, women churches and base communities are actually undertaking the theological task of critique and reconstruction from the vantage-point of a concern to relate to the complexities of the experiences of women and the poor. These ecclesial groups explore creative avenues in 'creating and giving space'.

The *Comunidades Eclesias de Base* (CEB),[50] small neighbourhood groups of lay people, ranging from six to a hundred people who study the Bible and exchange experiences, began to appear in Brazil in the early 1960s. In Brazil they thrived in connection with the official church, providing a pastoral model for the Catholic Church, while in other Latin American countries they functioned as 'parallel' churches, independent of the hierarchy.[51] They were developed as a pastoral innovation, a means of revitalizing the church. At that time they were part of a non-politicized process. Parishes were divided into CEBs, the members living fairly close together as residential communities. Base communities, often located in the poorer neighbourhoods, emphasized lay initiative, opening up a space for the poor to express their experiences. They served to empower the poor. It involved 'plunging into' and listening to one's experiences in everyday life, a shared living as a small community and reflection upon both in the light of the Bible.[52] Often lay catechists acted as a facilitator or animator, in order to provoke dialogue and discussion.[53] Liturgical creativity, organizing great celebrations or *fiestas*, showed how a celebrating people is a people with hope.

Boff describes the CEB as a place where having a say is the first stage in shaping one's own destiny. It is a place where true democracy is practised.[54]

In the 1980s theologians focused more and more on God's presence in everyday life and particularly in the suffering and the struggles of the poor as a distinctive principle in acquiring knowledge about who God is and what constitutes a church. Notions like 'the crucified people' became central to reflection. Leonardo Boff typified base communities as an alternative to the hierarchical church, exhibiting characteristics like direct relationships, reciprocity, communion, mutual assistance, communality of gospel ideas and equality.[55] Boff witnessed the rising of a new church, in the form of bishops, priests and religious entering into the life of the marginalized, centres of evangelization headed by lay people, and so on. He observed the appearance of this new church, 'as in all renewal movements' on the periphery.[56] It contains an emancipatory potential and is highly critical toward the hierarchical church, especially criticizing all dominating power.

Outside Latin America, base communities remained confined to the margin, but they came into being in the 1970s throughout the world as they were rooted in distinctive experiences of, for example, African-Americans in the United States, Africans, Asians and women. Initiated in 1975 at an Americas conference in Detroit, the ensuing Ecumenical Association of Third World Theologians (EATWOT) provided an annual forum and an energizing network where theologians challenged each other. In 1980, at Sao Paulo, all the papers presented were contributions to the new understanding of base communities.[57] Since the 1970s base communities and so-called 'small Christian communities' (SCC) have spread over the world. Thus, for example, several different types of base communities were formed in the Philippines. Some remained limited to discussions, others initiated social activities, and in the third type villages were divided into groups that meet on a weekly basis.[58] In the United States and other Western countries, progressive, critical communities were founded, seeking to 'live the way Jesus lived' in forms of communal living. It is said that small Christian communities are a requirement if the church is to develop its common life.[59] Nowadays, SCCs are a recognized structure in many dioceses and are worldwide considered as an instrument to develop parishes as a 'community of communities'. In the Protestant churches small groups of eight to twelve members are considered to be an important source of life in the congregation. The internet shows numerous examples of SCCs in all the continents.

Women churches are also an offspring of the movement.[60] It was the development of a network[61] of women's base communities, small groups that gathered in the kitchens, sitting rooms and church halls of the members. In their self-definition, solidarity and sacrament characterize these groups as church.[62] The intention is to create a space for worship and spirituality in which an inclusive practice is fostered. Women churches are also considered as a religious safe place for women that have been spiritually abused in patriarchal churches. Their origins lie in the exclusion and marginalization of women and of women's experiences within the churches. Since the 1970s a generation of women has developed new rituals and practices.[63] Women churches draw on old traditions and juxtapose fragments and reinterpretations with new symbols in order to remember, celebrate and lament, as the occasion calls for, particular experiences.[64] Rituals also mark biological and social experiences of women in the present. Northrup has identified emerging patterns of women's ritualizing and names ritual images (the circle, nature, the body), ritual actions (naming, healing) and ritual characteristics (spontaneity, de-emphasis on formal leadership).[65]

Circulating among these groups is an array of liturgies, rites, songs and prayers. The God-talk and community-talk in these texts and rites actively shape experiences of God and community.

Missional–contextual ecclesial groups

The third group of marginal ecclesiologies has a radically different character. It contains the theological theories of new faith communities and ecclesial groups that have spawned in the margin in recent years. They are here interpreted under the rubric of missional–contextual ecclesial groups. These groups emphasize the missional dimension of the church, focusing on the necessity to radically transcend the spatial, temporal, traditional and sub-cultural boundaries of the churches. In this section we will discuss youth churches and emerging churches. Characteristic of these ecclesial groups is that they start where people are. They learn to look at the church from an outsider's point of view. Ecclesial groups start anew in interaction with the context. They earth worship, community and mission in popular culture (youth churches) or in a great diversity of informal surroundings (emerging churches).

One might contest their marginality as well. For example, the emerging church movement has mushroomed quickly and some authors predict it will become a dominant form of Christianity in an increasingly secularizing, individualizing and simultaneously religiously vibrant Western culture.[66] In pointing out their core practices like 'being missional', 'identifying with the life of Jesus', 'living as a community' and, particularly, 'transforming secular space',[67] one might argue in favour of their cultural relevance too. On the other hand, 'fresh' church expressions in informal surroundings are fragile, fluid, provisional and 'in an infant stage'.

'Marginal' also means that these ecclesial groups, like the nineteenth-century churches and critical churches, often define themselves in contrast to mainline churches, challenging them as functioning as 'privileged centres' (Pierre Bourdieu) that define whether an experience or a symbol counts as valid or not. They may share an anti-established-church sentiment. Some authors in the emerging church conversation express also an anti-ecclesiological sentiment, when ecclesiology is considered to be an active self-interest of the church, which ignores that mission is about crossing boundaries. The theological theories *behind* and *in* the practices of youth churches and emerging churches can be described as 'ecclesiologies-to-come' and as such are open to various influences.[68] These ecclesiologies are embryonic and developing.

Subsequent to the origin of these movements on the metaphorical margin, several of these communities have since expanded into networks across the world. Indeed, the whole concept of 'network' fits the character of this expansion very well. Travelling, personal visits, bilateral meetings and the internet (vivid email-contact, weblogs, websites and online chat rooms) contribute to the dynamics of these communities and to the ongoing conversation on their respective multi-faceted ecclesiologies. The internet especially acts as a medium for internal and external communication and for sharing news and information.[69] The developing identities of emerging churches, youth churches, house churches and new missional initiatives, as they are formed both by the principle of 'ecclesiality' (scripture and tradition) and the principle of 'contextuality', are highly communicative.[70] The emerging network lives through online discussions and blogs.[71]

The question of the meaning of 'community' is central to these missional churches. Zooming-in on the micro-level of the place where the members get together, we observe temporary, unstable, partial communities, in which people participate on a voluntary basis.[72] They are communities of choice, evolving around what people find interesting, attractive or compelling, bringing a wide diversity together.[73] These communities are imagined as networks, being based on communication rather than gathering. Ward asserts that meetings are of less significance than the quality and kind of communication that takes place in these ecclesial groups. In fact, communication within the group is supplemented by frequent communication. On the meso- and macro-level, networks that are imagined as community come into being.

Emerging church

'Emerging church' appeared in the USA, Great Britain, Australia, New Zealand and several countries in Western Europe at the end of the twentieth and the beginning of the twenty-first century and is variously described as a movement,[74] a process, a conversation, a mindset and a prism.[75] Sometimes it is called 'liquid church',[76] 'grassroots-church', 'organic church' or 'future church'. Often churches use these phrases at their own choosing. Although diversity is large and the emerging church takes various 'embryonic' forms, there are a number of common characteristics.[77] All the labels point to something dynamic, flexible and creative. 'Emerging church' starts with the missional desire to start a church in an informal surrounding, in the context or culture of the group involved: a workplace congregation in a restaurant; a pub church integrated into the pub community; a Thursday lunchtime discipleship course; a congregation that comes into being on Wednesday evenings in a real estate firm; church members meetings in a leisure centre; a mums and tots group evolving into a community with parenting courses, a series on 'spiritual resources that can help at home' and an Emmaus course; a community of older Christians on a large housing estate; a church born out of conversations between a few friends;[78] a diocesan web-based church;[79] an indigenous church in a community beyond the reach of mainline churches.[80] It is all about mission initiatives that in time may develop into congregations that may result in viable churches.[81] It is also about community churches offering 'zones' in its services. Emerging churches start without central planning. It is church from below, or even better, *from* and *in* the outside. The church goes out to others, breaks out of its boundaries and makes an outward movement. Its leaders want to search for appropriate expressions of church, suiting the people they want to reach. Their hope is for new processes of community-formation with people in their own context. The type of community that is longed for is 'oozy', welcoming people with opposing views and tolerant of diversity. The origins of emerging churches are Protestant, although its theologians may also be influenced by Catholic and secular thinkers.[82]

Emerging suggests dynamics, change and fluidity. It contains an anti-institutional sentiment and conveys the idea of being provisional and flexible. In its expressions it endorses a postmodern mentality. The phrase fits a society in which individuals are no longer confined to the communities in which they were born. It is a Christian answer to a culture in which the close bonds between the individual and one single institution, i.e. one church, one party, one company, one marriage, are gone. Emerging belongs to a culture in which mobility and selectivity widen the horizons.

According to Murray, emerging churches want to encourage belonging before believing.[83] Even the phrase 'member', suggesting a close way of belonging, is contested and proposals are developed for flexible and relational categories, honouring diverse groups of people at different stages in their journey of faith, bound together by their spiritual search.[84] The movement criticizes both 'seeker-churches' and 'megachurches'.

The outer envelope of the emerging church movement contains the legacies of Lesslie Newbigin,[85] David Bosch[86] and Johannes C. Hoekendijk,[87] who stimulated the formation of churches that link up with their respective culture and contexts. Hoekendijk wrote that church-centric mission is bound to go astray and stressed that mission does not take place between churches and the world but between the world and the kingdom. In their threefold dimensions, participation and sharing (*koinonia*), proclamation (*kerugma*) and service (*diakonia*), churches are but signs of the coming kingdom. Church members should go out and explore the temporal, local and cultural contexts in which the people they want to reach live their lives. Mission is the essence of the church. In their conversation, emerging church leaders and influential theologians also refer to Karl Barth,[88] Dietrich Bonhoeffer ('church for others', 'God winning power and space in the world by his weakness')[89] and Jürgen Moltmann, the latter being particularly understanding of the work of the Holy Spirit as 'the spirit of life' and arguing that the informal experiences of people should be taken seriously. The work of God is not limited to the institution of the church, nor to the congregation or parish.

The emerging church is heavily influenced by the concept of *missio Dei*.[90] Mission is regarded as the activity of God in the world, in which the church is an 'instrument', participating in God's initiative. There is a strong awareness of the need to break with the sender–receiver methodology. The concept of mission is relocated away from church structures and the organization of territories. The church becomes world-related because God himself is world-related. Mission becomes the participation of Christians in the activity of the Trinity.[91] The metaphorical language that grows out of this trinitarian theology is relational: solidarity, invitation, sharing, bear witness, love and community.[92] It involves both the movement of God towards humanity and the movement of humanity towards God. The church is part of God's gatherings of all things to himself. The purpose is the kingdom.

According to emerging church leaders, the understanding of God and Christian tradition is always partial, incomplete and fragmentary. Radicals criticize the *missio Dei* concept for its reduction of the context to a situation in which mission should 'land'. They emphasize the meaning of the context, in which the other contributes to a new understanding of the message by his or her experiences. Understandings of scripture can and should be complemented by a dialectical encounter with 'the other'.[93] Viewed at a meta-level, the expressions of church are shaped by their surrounding cultures.[94] This also has consequences for the design of ritual practices, with the desire to invite local alterity into the worship.[95] It implies a fostering of openness to the unexpected. Worship gatherings are designed as interactive experiences. Thus, in what is called an 'irrupted ecclesiology' a creed can be formulated that sees strength and value in a large socio-economically deprived housing estate. It asserts this housing estate as a place of God's presence and it asserts the people's struggle with poverty as a signifier of God's presence in a paradigm of mutual indwelling.[96] This principle of radical contextualization is informed by the incarnation, viewed as an immersion in cultures or, as McLaren writes: 'We follow Christ into the world'. If churches are to be mission churches, they must be incarnate churches. Other authors consider eschatology as the central point of reference to church and mission. The church is thus defined as a contextual-eschatological, continuing, open learning process, in lively interaction with the world outside the church.[97]

The emerging church is Christ-centred, thereby simultaneously and explicitly acknowledging that the 'expanding, deepening, resonant story of Christ' (McLaren) comes to the churches in many versions.[98] The inner core of the ecclesiology that emerges in the face-to-face conversations of participating theologians, i.e. their answers to the question 'What is the church?', is shaped by allegiance to Christ. Christians, it is said, are first joined to Christ and 'to be joined to Christ is to be joined to his church',[99] or the other way round: in belonging to Christ, one belongs to the other members of the body of Christ.[100] Life is considered as being lived in communion with Christ. Emerging churches try picturing the living words and deeds of Jesus, experiencing their dynamic and transformative power.[101] The gospel performs, catalyses and saves, and does so by convening and sustaining a community that seeks to live by it. The goal of knowing Christ, emerging-church theologians assert, is to partake in the presence of Christ. In this presence one discovers that the manyversioned and many-layered story of Christ centres on Jesus Christ, or, as McLaren writes: 'If Christianity has anything to say at all, if it has a message that is worth repeating at all, then at its core is Christ.'[102] The story that is told and retold in new ways is considered an invitation to encounter Jesus himself, and listening to the elders and others contributes to new understandings. In other words, the church is truly itself when it communicates Christ.[103] Furthermore, God is seen as the source of a post-individualistic community that teaches its participants to think and act in terms of mutuality and participation.

The emerging church is a major focus of evangelical interest. Criticism focuses particularly on its eclecticism, syncretism, relativism with regard to doctrine and its downplaying of the importance of individual conversion.

According to critics, emerging church draws from the Christian tradition, but shops in different outlets and connects the findings uncritically with a postmodern, foundationless or even anti-foundational, concept of truth.[104] Critics point to the risks of endless pluralism, in which churches may be left without certainties, and to the danger of giving relativism free play. Truth, they claim, is not paradoxical and personal. Evangelicals assert that truth is relational, but add that before it can be relational, it has to be understood as objective and knowable.

In addition, evangelical critics point to the minimal role attributed to sinfulness, both in a traditional, individual sense and in a social sense, as the source of injustice.[105] Consequently, concepts like 'conversion', 'justification' and 'rebirth' are redefined in corporate terms as participation in a new community and accepting a new pattern of values. The ground-note of grace and individual conversion is muted or lost. Critics challenge emerging-church theologians to answer the question why there has to be a church in relationship to God's active work in creating and sustaining the world. What is the relevance of the church, they ask, in relationship to God and his redeeming work? Is there a call to receive Christ and be born again?

Youth church movement[106]

Youth church is not only about 'pumping up' the local church or about monthly events; it is forming a congregation for youth, led by youth. Youth churches emerged in North America and Western Europe in the first years of the twenty-first century. They carry names like Thugz Church, Heartbeat, Impulse your Faith, Lighthouse, Deep Impact, etc. Over the years, the first youth churches have had ups and downs, but the movement is not on the wane. Para-church events,[107] like Christian youth festivals and nation-wide charismatic, New Wine and Pentecostal youth meetings, contribute to the dynamics of the movement. Participants read evangelical magazines and visit evangelical websites and weblogs. They listen to contemporary Christian music and worship music. Evangelicalism is *hot* among youth churches, since it embraces a secular popular culture and shares its fascination for the senses, corporality, experience and experiment.[108]

Popular culture was commonly regarded with suspicion by orthodox churches and the evangelical movement. Yet, in the 1970s, Jesus People in the USA, evangelists in jeans, showed a remarkable and creative missional application of the language, metaphors and sound of pop songs. Pop culture was regarded as part of God's creation. Evangelicalism and pop culture came to a synthesis. In the 1980s this synthesis expanded into a massive evangelical pop culture, with its own music industry, music labels, festivals, radio stations and websites. Secular pop culture was judged by evangelical theological criteria, but evangelicals also reached out to connect it with Christian identity. Young evangelicals developed an antenna to contextualize the gospel in the specific context of young people dominated by the world of music and the media, i.e. radio, television, film and the internet. According to researchers like Roeland, it is precisely the synthesis of religion and pop culture that makes 'young evangelicalism' (Webber) appealing to young people. It legitimizes an active participation in pop culture, offers the possibility of a religious world in which their 'language' is spoken and alternative expressions of the pop culture that cannot be accommodated within their own Christian persuasions.

The aforementioned synthesis also influenced worship and here we can observe striking innovations. Young evangelicals introduced new styles of worship (dance, rock, techno, trance, rap), new places of worship, ranging from coffee bars to stadiums, new styles of participation ('relaxed'), new media (beamer, lights, sounds), a new liturgical centre (stage), forms of entertainment in the service (theatre, *biblio*-drama), new styles of preaching and, finally, 'cool' language. Experience counts, worship is designed to evoke feelings and experiences. Worship, ministry and the sermon mediate God's presence. These are the 'sensational forms' that give access to the transcendental.[109] All the sensual receptors are to be opened. Thus one wholeheartedly longs for a feeling of the Holy Spirit: God being present. Roeland demonstrates that the experiences sought for are often described as a longing to be moved or touched by God, referring to feelings of calmness and acceptance and, on a physical level, experiencing goose pimples or warmness. These experiences, as phenomena to be compared with similar experiences during a pop concert, are understood as religious experiences.

One of the questions confronting youth churches refers to its missional range. Do they really reach so-called unchurched young people? Figures indicate that the number of churchless attendants hardly exceeds 10 per cent.[110] On the other hand, when 'the word gets out on the street', experience with youth churches indicates that participants take friends with them.[111] An ecclesial group can be formed that reads the Bible, prays, sings and becomes a community of its own in which believing and behaving follow belonging.

The influence of youth churches upon mainstream churches can be traced particularly in the renewal of elements of worship. The introduction of worship music, praise bands, ministry 'by youth for youth' and youth ecclesial communities *within* mainline congregations are pointers to this influence. In ecclesial practice, however, this is often the result of sometimes tough negotiations, in which young people search for space and traditional older church members look for limits. Churches are hesitant to give full support to youth churches. They are unwilling to change, which raises the question of whether these youth churches should try to develop themselves into viable churches and, consequently, whether their mainstream churches should bless them to break new ground.[112]

Afternote

In this chapter, we have seen how marginal communities and their respective ecclesiologies not only focus upon aspects of mainline churches, but can be considered to form a critical comment upon them as well. The margin of the 'main text' is, as Jacques Derrida has demonstrated, truly the space for comment, by which one may exercise influence upon the mainline. Pre-millenialist churches challenge the mainline churches on their rootedness in history and their need for a 'dash of chiliasm' in order to become oriented in their practices towards the coming kingdom. Critical–emancipatory churches challenge the mainline churches on their *presumed* catholicity and inclusiveness. Missional–contextual churches challenge the mainline churches on their traditional, bourgeois, sub-cultural captivity.

An interesting common feature of marginal ecclesial groups is that members go back and forth between the local and the trans-local. In Adventism, critical groups and missional groups we have observed a culture of participation in conferences, meetings and other 'events'. The appetite for these meetings and for the formation of networks that transcend local boundaries is likely to be stronger than in mainline or inherited churches. From a practical ecclesiological perspective, this 'commuting' explains some of the dynamics of movements at the edges. At the trans-local level, including in the accompanying media, adherents receive important impulses for the development of their communities. Parachurch initiatives stimulate activities that aim at renewal and renewed commitment. The bipolarity sparks energy and strengthens individual motivational structures. It is also an important mechanism for mediating identity. This seems an important lesson for the churches in the future.

Knowledge of marginal communities is both helpful and hopeful, since mainline churches in Western contexts are also getting marginalized in society. Mainline churches suffer drastic decline. Church developments at a local level may well be in the direction of the marginal communities discussed here. The shape and content of future ecclesial groups may resemble some of the features of Adventist churches, critical–emancipatory or missional–contextual ecclesial groups. Thus the 2004 report on 'Mission-shaped Church' suggests that Anglicans are allowing missiology to shape their ecclesiology. Developing missional networks may be a fruit of both inherited and emerging churches.

Notes

1 For example see R. Laurence Moore, *Religious Outsiders and the Making of Americans*, New York: Oxford University Press, 1986. Moore's essays aimed to 'shake up the denominational hierarchy that governs the way in which American religious history gets told' (p. vii). Moore underlined that statistics and the citation of numbers 'are of little help when we try to analyze the enormous popular attention that was focused on religious groups which on the basis of numbers should have occasioned little public comment' (p. xiii).

2 See missiologist Paul Hiebert on 'bounded sets', 'centered sets' and 'fuzzy sets', in Paul Hiebert, *Anthropological Reflections on Missiological Issues*, Grand Rapids, MI: Baker Book House, 1994, pp. 110–36.

3 See Stuart Murray, *Church After Christendom*, Carlisle: Paternoster 2004, 30.

4 We use the terms 'mainline' and 'mainstream' in this chapter, aware that these are loaded terms. It suits our purpose, however, to distinguish them from 'marginal'. Other terms are: 'traditional' or 'inherited' modes of church.

5 Cf. J. Lindeboom, *Stiefkinderen van het christendom*. 's-Gravenhage: Nijhof, 1929, p. 4.

6 According to Murray, this is characteristic of contemporary emerging churches. I think it is also recognizable in marginal churches in general. See Stuart Murray, *Post-Christendom. Church and Mission in a Strange New World*, Carlisle: Paternoster, pp. 254f.

7 Shortcomings of the churches can never be the only reason for emerging movements in the margin. Marginal churches embody alternative ways of Christian institutional practices, but their convictions and social arrangements have a binding force of their own.

8 See Stephen J. Stein, 'Religious Innovation at the Edges', in Peter Williams (ed.), *Perspectives on American Religion and Culture*, Malden, MA: Blackwell, 1999, pp. 22–33.

9 As authoritative revelations Mary Baker Eddy's *Science and Health* and Joseph Smiths's *Book of Mormon* form supplements to the Jewish-Christian Bible. On the other hand 'no two forms of Christianity could be farther apart than a corporealist, practical and very ritualistic Mormonism and an ultraspiritualist, nonsacramental and transcendentalist Christian Science'. See Paul

Conkin, *American Originals. Homemade Varieties of Christianity*, Chapel Hill, NC: The University of North Carolina Press, 1997, pp. 226f. Christian Science developed its own creed in which attunement to God is the goal of the individual's life. One may doubt whether these movements can be called 'church' in the true meaning of the word, given the fact that they acknowledge other revelations.

10 Stein, 'Religious Innovation at the Edges', p. 31.

11 In Christian theology little attention has been paid to the powers that are released when people sing together. Hymns are both expression and source of faith. According to Reich the hymn belongs to the core dimension of theology. The story of God and men has been handed down both by telling and singing. See Christa Reich, *Evangelium: klingendes Wort. Zur theologischen Bedeutung des Singens*, Stuttgart: Calwer Verlag, 1997, p. 22.

12 See Paul Schnabel, *Tussen charisma en stigma. Nieuwe religieuze bewegingen en geestelijke gezondheid*, Deventer: Van Loghum Slaterus, 1982, p. 75.

13 Max Weber did not follow Troeltsch in his typology with regard to the 'mystic' type. He sticks to the dualism 'church–sect', which he elaborates for the first time in 1905 in his *Protestant Ethic*. In his collected essays on the Sociology of Religion he writes: 'Eine "Kirche" ist eben eine Gnadenanstalt (. . .) zu welcher die Zugehörigkeit (der Idee nach!) obligatorisch, daher für die Qualitäten des Zugehörigen nichts beweisend, ist, eine »Sekte« dagegen ein voluntaristischer Verband ausschließlich (der Idee nach) religiös-ethisch Qualifizierter, in den man freiwillig eintritt, wenn man freiwillig Kraft religiöser Bewährung Aufnahme findet.' See Max Weber, 'Die protestantischen Sekten und der Geist des Kapitalismus', in: Max Weber, *Gesammelte Aufsätze zur Religionssoziologie*, Tübingen: Mohr, 1920, pp. 17–236, here p. 211.

14 The first time Troeltsch uses his typology 'church, sect and mystic' is in his speech at the First German 'Soziologentag' in 1910. See Ernst Troeltsch, 'Das stoisch-christliche Naturrecht und das profane Naturrecht', in *Verhandlungen des Ersten Deutschen Soziologentages vom 19.-22. Oktober 1910 in Frankfurt A.M.*, Tübingen 1911, pp. 166–92. He elaborated the distinction in Ernst Troeltsch, *Die Soziallehren der christlichen Kirchen und Gruppen*, Tübingen 1912. Together with Max Weber's 'church–sect' typology Troeltsch's typology gained enormous resonance. From the beginning, however, the meaning and range of the typology was contested. For a profound analysis see Arie L. Molendijk, *Zwischen Theologie und Soziologie. Ernst Troeltschs Typen der christlichen Gemeinschaftsbildung: Kirche, Sekte, Mystik*, Gütersloh: Gütersloher Verlagshaus, 1996. Molendijk asserts that Troeltsch's typology has gained influence in the USA and Great Britain primarily *via* Niebuhr's 'The Social Sources of Denominationalism' (1929) and, later, through the English translation of the 'Soziallehren' in 1931. See Molendijk, p. 28.

15 For example see Roland Robertson, *The Sociological Interpretation of Religion*, New York: Schocken Books,1970, pp. 113–49 ('Religious Collectivities'); Michael Hill, *A Sociology of Religion*, London: Heinemann Educational, 1973, pp. 47–70 ('Church and Sect'); Meredith B. McGuire, *Religion: The Social Context*, Belmont, CA: Wadsworth, 1992, 3rd. Reprint, pp. 133–72 ('The Dynamics of Religious Collectivities').

16 J. Milton Yinger, *The Scientific Study of Religion*, New York: Macmillan, 1970, pp. 251–81 ('Types of Religious Organizations').

17 First published in R. W. Stark and W.S. Bainbridge, 'Of Churches, Sects and Cults. Preliminary Concepts for a Theory of Religious Movements', in *Journal for the Scientific Study of Religion* 18/2 (1979), 117–33; R. W. Stark and W. S. Bainbridge, 'Towards a Theory of Religions. Religious Commitment', in *Journal for the Scientific Study of Religion*, 19/2 (1980), 114–28.

18 Bryan Wilson, 'Millenialism in Comparative Perspective', in *Comparative Studies in Society and History*, VI, 1963, 93–114; Graham Allan, 'A theory of millenialism: the Irvingite movement as an illustration', in: L. G. Jansma and P. G. G. M. Schulten (Red.), *Religieuze bewegingen*, 's-Gravenhage: Martinus Nijhof, 1981, pp. 159–77; Norman Cohn, *The Pursuit of the Millennium: Revolutionary Millenarians and Mystical Anarchists of the Middle Ages*, London: Maurice Temple Smith, 1970; Jerry Bergman, 'The Adventist and Jehovah's Witness Branch of Protestantism', in Timothy Miller (ed.), *America's Alernative Religions*, Albany, NY: State Univesity of New York Press, 1995, pp. 33–46.

19 Werner Stark, *The Sociology of Religion. A Study of Christendom. Vol. II, Sectarian Religion.* London: Routledge and Kegan Paul Ltd, 1967, p. 215.

266

20 H. Richard Niebuhr, *The Social Sources of Denominationalism*, first published 1929; cf. paperback ed., New York: Meridian Books, 1957, pp. 19f.

21 For the following, see Bryan R.Wilson, *The Social Dimensions of Sectarianism. Sects and New Religious Movements in Contemporary Society*, Oxford: Clarendon, 1990, pp. 108ff.

22 See Conkin, *American Originals*, p. 157.

23 The Mormons have many distinctive doctrines of their own. Adventism is only one of their distinguishing traits. See Conkin, *American Originals*, pp. 162–225.

24 For detailed descriptions of the events, see David T. Arthur, 'Millerism', in Edwin S. Gaustad (ed.), *The Rise of Adventism. Religion and Society in Mid-Nineteenth-Century America*, New York: Harper & Row, 1974, pp. 154–72; Everett N. Dick, 'The Millerite Movement', in Gary Land (ed.), *Adventism in America*, Grand Rapids, MI: Eerdmans 1986, pp. 1–35; cf. Rolf Pöhler, *Continuity and Change in Adventist Teaching. A Case Study in Doctrinal Development*, Frankfurt: Peter Lang, 2000, p. 21. Also see Donald C. Swift, *Religion and the American Experience. A Social and Cultural History, 1765–1997*, London: Sharpe, 1998, p. 91.

25 Quotation by David Arthur, 'Millerism', p. 154.

26 Miller based his fervent expectation on Dan 8.14, which mentions 2300 evenings and mornings. According to Miller's calculations, based upon commentators of the day, this meant 2300 years. Miller starts his count in 457 BC with the decree of Artaxerxes to rebuild the temple in Jerusalem. Other references to days in Daniel seemed to correlate with historical events too. Miller worked out a chart of world history. See Dick, 'The Millerite Movement', pp. 4f.; Conkin, *American Originals*, pp. 118f.

27 Dick, 'The Millerite Movement', p. 7.

28 Dick, 'The Millerite Movement', pp. 16ff.

29 For a description of the day, see Dick, 'The Millerite Movement', p. 29.

30 See Bergman, 'The Adventist and Jehovah's Witness Branch of Protestantism', p. 34.

31 See J. Gordon Melton, *Biographical Dictionary of American Cult and Sect Leaders*, New York: Garland Publishing, Inc., pp. 306–7.

32 For this paragraph I made extensive use of: M. J. Tang, 'Het Apostolische Werk in Nederland. Tegen de achtergrond van zijn ontstaan in Engeland en Duitsland' ('The Work of the Apostles in The Netherlands. Analyzed against its background in England and Germany'), Diss. Utrecht 1982. Also see Graham Allan, 'A theory of millenialism: the Irvingite movement as an illustration', pp. 168ff.

33 The first name to be mentioned with regard to the origins of the Apostolic Churches is not Edward Irving, but Henry Drummond, host of the first Albury Conference, November 1826, at Albury Park, Surrey. The parish vicar, Hugh McNeile, presided. Irving gave the thrust to the Work of the Apostles. See Tang, 'Het Apostolische Werk in Nederland', p. 19.

34 These events occurred at Port Glasgow, on the river Clyde, April 1830 – April 1831. See Tang, 'Het Apostolische Werk in Nederland', p. 23. In October 1830 a healing took place in London.

35 See Graham Allan, 'A theory of millenialism: the Irvingite movement as an illustration', p. 173.

36 The first person to experience a special expression of the Spirit was Edward Taplin, on August 25, 1831: 'A voice like thunder burst forth through him in a few words of an unknown tongue, followed by these in English; Jehovah, hear us!' See Tang, p. 24. Irving was discharged from office in March 1833, yet in open air meetings in the surroundings of Annan, in the county of Dumfries, thousands attended. A month later, Irving was ordained to be the 'angel' of the faith community in Newman Street. His community was the heart of the developing church.

37 John Bate Cardale, solicitor in London attended the first Albury conferences and travelled to Scotland with Taplin and a few others to investigate the expressions of the Holy Spirit, August 1830.

38 See Graham Allan, 'A theory of millenialism', p. 175.

39 This day is still celebrated as a feast day in Catholic Apostolic Churches.

40 Europe and Christianity did not coincide. Outer European territories were subsumed under European tribes as 'suburbs of Christianity': North America under Ruben, India and Australia under Gad, South America under Naphtali. See Tang, p. 35. By 1851 a faith community was founded in New York, 'prepared' by Millerite Adventism. In 1837 communities were formed in Kingston and Toronto, Canada. In 1850 a community was founded in Paris. In Germany the Work of the Apostles spread surprisingly fast. By 1899 there were 259 communities. Catholic Apostolic

Communities were also founded in Switzerland (39), Belgium (2), Sweden (12), Denmark (46), Norway (10) and The Netherlands (14). See Tang, p. 43.

41 King Friedrich Wilhelm of Prussia is supposed to have accepted the testimony with sympathy. See Tang, p. 37.

42 Davenport writes: 'Do we see here a further recession from the earlier stress on charismatic signs, and the growing emphasis on ordinances?' See R. A. Davenport, *Albury Apostles*, revised edn, London: The Free Society, 1973, p. 134.

43 Tang, 'Het Apostolische Werk in Nederland', p. 45.

44 Tang, 'Het Apostolische Werk in Nederland', p. 46.

45 Tang, 'Het Apostolische Werk in Nederland', p. 49ff.

46 Tang, 'Het Apostolische Werk in Nederland', p. 55f.

47 Tang, 'Het Apostolische Werk in Nederland', p. 65.

48 Tang, 'Het Apostolische Werk in Nederland', p. 69.

49 See Elisabeth Schüssler Fiorenza, *Discipleship of Equals. A Critical Feminist Ekklēsialogy of Liberation*, New York: Crossroad, 1993, p. 63. See, also, Chapter 25 of this volume.

50 The Portuguese *comunidades eclesiais de base* and the Spanish *comunidades eclesiales de base* are both abbreviated to CEBs. The term base ecclesial community became common in the literature after 1975. There are numerous indigenous terms.

51 See Manuel A. Vásquez, *The Brazilian Popular Church and the Crisis of Modernity*, Cambridge: Cambridge University Press, 1998, p. 48.

52 For an elaborate reflection of this approach, see Clodovis Boff, *Theology and Praxis: Epistemological Foundations* (trans. R. R. Barr), Maryknoll, NY: Orbis Books, 1987. See also the introduction to liberation theology by Leonardo and Clodovis Boff, *Introducing Liberation Theology* (trans. P. Burns), Maryknoll, NY, Orbis Books: 1987; Carlos Mesters, *Defenseless Flower. a New Reading of the Bible*, Maryknoll, NY: Orbis Books, 1989, p. 71. See, also, Chapter 23 of this volume.

53 See David Tombs, *Latin American Liberation Theology*, Boston: Brill, 2002, p. 168. See, also, Chapter 17 of this volume.

54 Leonardo Boff, *Church, Charism and Power: liberation theology and the institutional church* (trans. J. Diercksmeier), New York: Crossroad, 1985, p. 9.

55 See Leonardo Boff, *Ecclesiogenesis. The Base Communities Reinvent the Church*. Maryknoll, NY: Orbis Books, 1986, p. 4. For liberationist ecclesiology of the CEBs, see also L. Boff, *Church: Charism and Power*; J. Marins, T.M. Trevisan and C. Chacona, *The Church from the Roots. Basic Ecclesial Communities*, London: Catholic Fund for Overseas Development, 1989. For a Protestant perspective, see G. Cook, *The Expectation of the Poor. Latin American Basic Ecclesial Communities in Protestant Perspective*, Maryknoll, NY: Orbis Books, 1985.

56 Boff, *Church, Charism and Power*, p. 62.

57 Tombs, *Latin American Liberation Theology*, p. 220.

58 See Hermann Joseph Ingenlath, *Bausteine für eine Theologie der Basisgemeinden. Theologische Akzente christlicher Basisgemeinschaften*, Frankfurt A. M: Peter Lang, 1996, pp. 19f.

59 See Steven Croft, *Transforming Communities: Re-imagining the Church for the 21st Century*. London: Darton, Longman & Todd, 2002, p. 101.

60 See Chapter 25 of this volume.

61 Angela Berlis, Julie Hopkins and Hedwig Meyer-Wilmes, *Women Churches: Networking and Reflection in the European Context*, Yearbook of the European Society of Women in Theological Research, Eisenbrauns, 1995.

62 See Mary Hunt, *Fierce Tenderness: A Feminist Theology of Friendship*, New York: Crossroads, 1991, p.160.

63 Susan Ross writes: 'In the early 1970s, I was invited by a friend to participate in an informal gathering of women to celebrate a Eucharist without a priest. We met in her apartment, lit candles, read the Bible and prayed and blessed bread and wine together. It was an exhilarating experience, but also one that made us feel vaguely like criminals. I soon learned that we were not alone, and that women in many other places were doing the same.' Susan Ross, 'Church and sacrament – community and worship', in Susan Frank Parsons (ed.), *The Cambridge Companion to Feminist Theology*, Cambridge: Cambridge University Press, 2002, pp. 224–42, esp. 231.

64 See Ross, 'Church and sacrament – community and worship', p. 225.

65 See Lesley Northrup, *Ritualizing Women: Patterns of Spirituality*, Cleveland, OH: Pilgrim Press 1997, pp. 28–49.

66 Stuart Murray writes: 'Something significant is afoot which might recalibrate the church for post-Christendom', Stuart Murray, *Church After Christendom*, p. 71. In another book, Murray asserts: 'Talk of "new ways of being church" or "emerging church" indicates Christendom is fading.' See Stuart Murray, *Post-Christendom*, p. 252.

67 See E. Gibbs. and R.K. Bolger, *Emerging Churches. Creating Christian Community in Postmodern Cultures*, London: SPCK, 2006, pp. 43f.

68 Mark Mason, 'Impossible Ecclesiology? John D. Caputo and the Emerging Church Movement.' Unpublished lecture, Ecclesiological Investigations Network, 2007.

69 For the internet and new religious movements, see Jeffrey K. Hadden and Douglas E. Cowen (eds), *The Promised Land or Electronic Chaos?: Toward Understanding Religion on the Internet. Religion and the Social Order*, Greenwich, CT: JAI Press, 2000.

70 See Henk de Roest, *Communicative Identity. Habermas' Perspectives of Discourse as a Support for Practical Theology*, Kampen: Kok, 1998.

71 See, for example: The Ooze, an emerging-church forum; Acts29network.com, a site and a network; Emergent Village, the heart of the emergent stream of the emerging church movement; The Emerging Leaders Network, a community of ecclesiological conversation; ZoeCarnate, a site on emerging church; Emergingchurch.info is a site with storytelling and theological reflection.

72 See Gerrit Jan van der Kolm, 'De Verbeelding van de kerk. Op zoek naar een nieuw-missionaire ecclesiologie' ('The Imagination of the Church. Toward a new-missional ecclesiology'), Diss. Groningen, 2001, pp. 192ff.

73 Pete Ward, *Liquid Church*, Carlisle: Paternoster, 2002, pp. 89f.

74 Emerging church in the USA constitutes more than a perspective and can be considered as a movement. In the USA there is an 'emergentYS Books' publishing label – all books published by Zondervan, Grand Rapids, MI – websites facilitating conversations and regular meetings for emerging church leaders. 'Emerging' and 'emergent' are to be distinguished. Not everyone within the emerging churches identifies with 'emergentvillage', its conversation and authors/pastors like Brian McLaren, Steve Chalke, Steve Taylor, Frederica Matthewes, Dan Kimball, Doug Pagitt and others. In this introduction, however, I take 'emerging church' as an encompassing term.

75 See Michael Moynagh, *Emergingchurch.Intro*, Oxford: Monarch, 2004, p. 51.

76 See Ward, *Liquid Church*.

77 Pete Rollins, *How (Not) To Speak of God*, London: SPCK, 2006, p. 5. Numerous examples of emerging churches and sources of information are offered by Stuart Murray, *Changing Mission. Learning from the Newer Churches*, London: CTBI, 2005.

78 See Doug Pagitt, *Reimagining spiritual formation: a week in the life of an experimental church*, Grand Rapids, MI: Zondervan, 2003, pp. 37ff. This book describes the Solomon's Porch Community.

79 See www.i-church.org.; www.webchurch.org.

80 See Mats Rydinger, 'The vulnerable power of worship. A study of a power approach to contextualization in mission', Diss. Lund, 2006. Rydinger describes and analyses a Lakota Church. The basic theological orientation Rydinger identifies refers to the understanding that Christ is incarnated as the Word in Lakota culture and that Lakota culture should therefore be regarded as a locus of revelation. In worship, Lakota and Christian symbols, texts and actions are juxtaposed and thereby contribute to the formation of a loosely coherent belief system. They function as identity-mediating mechanisms.

81 For numerous examples: Michael Moynagh, *Emergingchurch.Intro*, Oxford and Grand Rapids, MI: Monarch, 2004. See also Church of England's Mission and Public Affairs Council, *Mission-shaped Church. Church planting and fresh expressions of church in a changing context*, London: Church House Publishing, 2004; J. Hinton and P. B. Price, *Changing Communities. Church from the Grassroots*, London: Churches Together in Britain and Ireland, 2003.

82 See for example the references to John Caputo in Brian McLaren, *The Church on the Other Side. Doing Ministry in the Postmodern Matrix*, Grand Rapids, MI: Zondervan, 2000, pp.190f. See also the use of the concept 'deconstruction' in Eddie Gibbs and Ryan Bolger, *Emerging Churches: Creating Christian Communities in Postmodern Cultures*, London: SPCK, 2006. Other academic influence on the emerging church movement includes the work of Michel Foucault, Jacques Derrida, Zygmunt Bauman ('liquid modernity'), John Howard Yoder and Stanley Hauerwas.

83 See Murray, *Church After Christendom*, pp. 27f.

84 See John Drane, *The McDonaldsization of the Church. Spirituality, Creativity, and the Future of the Church*, London: Darton, Longman & Todd, 2000, p. 159. Nigel Wright proposes an 'open community membership' and a 'core membership'. See Nigel Wright, *New Baptists, New Agenda*, Carlisle: Paternoster, 2002, p. 79.

85 See Lesslie Newbigin, *The Gospel in a Pluralist Society*, London: SPCK, 1989.

86 See David Bosch, *Transforming Mission*, Maryknoll, NY: Orbis, 1991.

87 J.C. Hoekendijk, *The Church Inside Out*, ed. L.A. Hoedemaker and Pieter Tijmes, Philadelphia: Westminster Press, 1964.

88 See for example Ward, *Liquid Church*, pp. 68ff.

89 See for example Brian McLaren's comment on Frederica Matthewes-Green, 'Under the Heaventree', in Leonard Sweet (general editor), *The Church in Emerging Culture: Five Perspectives*, Grand Rapids, MI: Zondervan/Youth Specialties, 2003, p. 181.

90 See Chapter 36 of this volume.

91 The emerging church is also inspired by contemporary theological reflection on the relationship between the Trinity and the defining pattern of the church. See John D. Zizioulas, *Being as Communion. Studies in Personhood and the Church*, Crestwood, NY: St Vladimir's Seminary Press, 1985; Colin E. Gunton, *The Promise of Trinitarian Theology* (2nd edn), Edinburgh: T&T Clark, 1997; Miroslav Volf, *After Our Likeness. The Church as the Image of the Trinity*, Grand Rapids, MI: Eerdmans, 1998; James Torrance, *Worship and the Triune God of Grace*, Carlisle: Paternoster, 1996; David S. Cunningham, *These Three Are One: The Practice of Trinitarian Theology. Challenges in Contemporary Theology*, Oxford: Blackwell, 1998; Paul S. Fiddes, *Participating in God. A Pastoral Doctrine of the Trinity*, London: Darton, Longman & Todd, 2000.

92 Prior to the shift to the trinitarian basis, missional language shared a predilection for military metaphors. See Robert J. Schreiter, 'Changes in Roman Catholic Attitudes towards Proselytism and Mission', in James A.Scherer and Stephen B. Bevans (ed.), *New Directions in Mission & Evangelization 2. Theological Foundations*. Maryknoll, NY: Orbis, 1994, pp. 113–25, esp. 117.

93 See Mats Rydinger, *The Vulnerable Power of Worship*, pp. 10ff. Also see Brian McLaren, 'The Method, the Message and the Ongoing Story', in Leonard Sweet (general editor), *The Church in Emerging Culture*, p.194. McLaren writes: 'The more I have changed my methods in preaching, evangelizing, discipleship, leading worship, and so on, the more experience I have gained sharing the good news with what are often called "the unchurched", and especially those we might call "postmodern seekers". These people have asked me new questions or old questions in new ways. The more I have interacted with them, the more questions I have had about not just my changing methods but my so-called unchanging message.'

94 Moynagh, *Emergingchurch.intro*, p. 43.

95 For an extensive description of the highly postmodern Allhellgona Service, Stockholm and the indigenous Lakota Church, see Mats Rydinger, *The Vulnerable Power of Worship*. The Allhellgona service addresses marginalized people and tries to create a communicative milieu that houses different images of and approaches to God and the gospel. People should be free to express their diverse feelings, experiences and thoughts about God and faith. There is spiritual knowledge among people and this 'capital' is valid in the Christian field. Their resources count. There is a worship service (outer circle) and there are several bible groups, art-groups, meditation-groups, kitchen group and a choir, a café, lunch spot, prayer meetings in the morning and at lunch time (second circle). The third, inner, circle refers to pastoral care groups. The service is held on a Sunday afternoon, 6 p.m., as an alternative to the main church of Katarina, 'which is loaded with tradition'. See Rydinger, p. 296.

96 For an extensive description of emerging churches in the housing estate of Ely, Cardiff, Wales, see Peter Cruchley-Jones, 'Living without walls. Mission in the rupture', in *Reformed World* 52/2 (2002), 94–104; Peter Cruchley-Jones, *Singing the Lord's Song in a Strange Land? Studies in the Intercultural History of Christianity*, Frankfurt: Peter Lang, 2001.

97 See Van der Kolm, 'De verbeelding van de kerk', pp. 211f.

98 See Brian D. McLaren, *A Generous Orthodoxy*, Grand Rapids, MI: Zondervan, 2004. See also Brian D. McLaren, *A New Kind of Christian: A Tale of Two Friends on a Spiritual Journey*, San Francisco: Jossey-Bass, 2001; Brian D. McLaren, *The Secret Message of Jesus: Uncovering the Truth that Could Change Everything*, Nashville: Thomas Nelson, 2006.

99 See Ward, *Liquid Church*, 33.
100 See Andy Crouch, 'Life After Postmodernity', in Leonard Sweet (general editor), *The Church in Emerging Culture*, p. 81.
101 See Frederica Mathewes-Green, 'Under the Heaventree', in Leonard Sweet (general editor), *The Church in Emerging Culture*, p. 159. Also see Mats Rydinger, *The Vulnerable Power of Worship*, p. 233. The Allhellgona service, see n. 117, is explicitly Christ centred. God is pictured as one who intervenes in people's lives. It is about restoring dignity and integrity among people who have lost it.
102 See Brian McLaren, 'The Method, the Message, and the Ongoing Story', in Leonard Sweet (general editor), *The Church in Emerging Culture*, p. 200.
103 See Ward, *Liquid Church*, p. 71.
104 See for example Donald A. Carson, *Becoming Conversant With the Emerging Church: Understanding a Movement and Its Implications*, Grand Rapids, MI: Zondervan, 2005. A discussion has started on the internet.
105 See Stefan Paas, 'Kerken vormen. De gemeenschappelijke structuur van het Evangelie anno nu', in *Soteria* 23/1 (2006), 26.
106 For this paragraph I draw extensively on Johan Roeland, 'God is a dj. Evangelicalisme en popular culture' in *Praktische Theologie* 34/2 (2007), pp. 194–206. See also John Hall, 'The rise of the youth congregation and its missiological significance', PhD thesis, University of Birmingham, 2003; Graham Cray, *Youth Congregations and the Emerging Church*, Cambridge: Grove, 2002.
107 Murray asserts that 'Church after Christendom' will possibly look like a para-church organization and suggests it is necessary to accept para-church organizations as authentically ecclesial, making the ungainly and inappropriate term 'para-church' obsolete. See Murray, *Church After Christendom*, p. 142.
108 'During our lifetimes, especially during the critical period of the 1980s, pop culture was the amniotic fluid that sustained us. For a generation of kids who had a fragmented or completely broken relationship to "formal" or "institutional" religion, pop culture filled the spiritual gaps.' See Tom Beaudoin, *Virtual Faith. The Irreverent Spiritual Quest of Generation X*, San Francisco: Jossey-Bass, 2000. According to Beaudoin popular culture took over the dominance of the churches in the fields of aesthetics, identity-formation, morality and the meaning of life. The spiritual longings of Generation X can be seen in pop songs.
109 See Birgit Meyer, *Religious Sensations. Why Media, Aesthetics and Power Matter in the Study of Contemporary Religion*, Amsterdam: Vrije Universiteit, 2006, p. 8.
110 See Ron Becker, 'Jongeren gaan voor', in *Soteria* 23/2 (2006), pp. 38–47.
111 For an example of a youth church in Rotterdam, The Netherlands: Daniël de Wolf, *Jezus in de Millinx. Woorden en daden in een Rotterdamse achterstandswijk*, Kampen: Kok, p. 128.
112 See Becker, 'Jongeren gaan voor', p. 47.

Part III

GLOBAL
PERSPECTIVES

15

THE CHURCH IN
ASIAN PERSPECTIVE

Peter C. Phan

Google 'Asian ecclesiology' and you will not find as many hits as when you type in, let's say, 'papacy' or 'episcopacy'. This is a signal that ecclesiology as a theological tractate on the church does not occupy a lion's share in Asian theology. On the other hand, it would be wrong to infer from this paucity of references that the church is not a major concern for Asian Christians. On the contrary, a 'new way of being church', to use a popular slogan among Asian theologians, arguably lies at the heart of the pastoral ministry of the Asian churches. To help understand why ecclesiastical or 'churchy' issues have not attracted the attention of Asian theologians and yet church mission and church life are the central focus of their reflections, this essay begins with a brief overview of Asian Christianity. It then presents the main elements of what may be called Asian ecclesiology. It concludes by noting how this ecclesiology can help Christianity shape the future of Asia as it assumes an increasingly significant role in the global village.

Which Asia? Which Christianities?

With two-thirds of the world's six billion population, Asia is the largest and most populous continent.[1] With Europe as a peninsula of the Eurasian landmass on its west, Asia lies, on its western limits, along the Urals, the Ural River, the Caspian Sea, the Caucasus, the Black Sea, the Bosporus and Dardanelles straits, and the Aegean Sea. On its south-western side, it is separated from Africa by the Suez Canal between the Mediterranean Sea and the Red Sea. In its far north-eastern part, i.e. Siberia, it is separated from North America by the Bering Strait. In the south, Asia is bathed by the Gulf of Aden, the Arabian Sea and the Bay of Bengal; on the east, by the South China Sea, East China Sea, Yellow Sea, Sea of Japan, Sea of Okhotsk, and Bering Sea; and on the north, by the Arctic Ocean.

As a continent, Asia is conventionally divided into five regions: Central Asia (mainly the Republics of Kyrgyzstan, Tajikistan, Turkmenistan and Uzbekistan); East Asia (mainly China, Japan, Korea, and Taiwan); South Asia (mainly Bangladesh, India, Myanmar, Nepal, Pakistan, and Sri Lanka); Southeast Asia (mainly Cambodia, Indonesia, Laos, the Philippines, Singapore, Thailand, and Vietnam); and Southwest Asia (the countries of the Middle East, Near East, or West Asia). Asia is the land of extreme contrasts. It has both the world's highest peak, Mt Everest, and its lowest point, the Dead Sea. Climatically, the continent ranges through all extremes, from the torrid heat of the Arabian Desert to the arctic cold of Siberia and from the torrential rains of monsoons to the bone-dry aridity of the Tarim Basin.

Asia's geographical and climactic extremes are matched by linguistic, ethnic, economic, political, cultural, and religious extremes. More than 100 languages are spoken in the Philippines and more than 600 in Indonesia, whereas Korea has only one. Ethnically, India and China are teeming with diversity, whereas Vietnam is predominantly homogeneous. Economically, Asia has one of the richest countries (Japan) and the poorest ones on Earth (e.g. North Korea, Cambodia and Laos). Politically, it contains the world's largest democratic government (India) and largest communist government (China). Along with linguistic, ethnic, economic and political diversity come extremely diverse cultures, which are also among the oldest and the richest. Religiously, Asia is the cradle of all world religions. Besides Christianity, other Asian religions include Bahá'í, Bön, Buddhism, Confucianism, Daoism, Hinduism, Islam, Jainism, Shinto and Zoroastrianism, and innumerable tribal religions.[2]

It is within the context of these mind-boggling diversities – geographic, linguistic, ethnic, economic, political, cultural, and religious – that the theme of 'The Church in Asian Perspective' should be broached. One of the bitter ironies of Asian Christianity is that though born in (Southwest) Asia, it returned to its birthplace as a foreign religion or, worse, the religion of its colonizers, and is still widely regarded as such by many Asians. But such perception of Christianity as a Western religion imported to Asia by Portuguese and Spanish colonialists in the sixteenth century, and later by other European countries such as Britain, France, Germany and the Netherlands, and lastly by the United States, belies the ancient roots of Christianity in Asia.

Of course, if Palestine is counted as part of (Southwest) Asia or the Middle East, as it must, then Christianity itself is an Asian religion. But apart from this geographical claim,[3] Asian Christians outside Southwest Asia can boast of an ancient and glorious heritage, one that is as old as the apostolic age. The conventional image of Christianity as a Western religion, that is, one that was born in Palestine but soon moved westward, with Rome as its final destination, and from Rome as its epicentre, sent missionaries worldwide, ignores the fact that in the first four centuries of Christianity's existence the most successful fields of mission were not Europe but Asia and Africa, with Syria as the centre of gravity.[4]

More specifically, Indian Christianity can claim apostolic origins, with St Thomas and/or St Bartholomew as its founder(s).[5] Chinese Christianity was born in the seventh century, with the arrival of the East Syrian/Nestorian monk Aloben during the T'ang dynasty.[6] Christianity arrived in other countries such as Japan, the Philippines, and Vietnam in the sixteenth century in the wave of Spanish and Portuguese colonialism.[7] For Korea, on the contrary, Christianity was first brought into the country towards the end of the eighteenth century, not by foreigners but by a Korean, Peter Lee Seung-hun (or Sunghoon Ri), upon his return from Beijing.[8] As for the Pacific Islands, Christianity reached them in the middle of the sixteenth century during the Spanish expeditions from Latin America to the Philippines and in the late seventeenth century to the Marianas.[9]

Today in Asia, Christians predominate in only two countries, namely the Philippines and East Timor – over 85 per cent of their populations are Catholic. In other countries, especially China, India and Japan, to name the most populous, and in countries with a Muslim majority such as Bangladesh, Indonesia, Malaysia and Pakistan, and in those where Buddhism predominates such as Cambodia, Hong Kong, Laos, Mongolia, Myanmar, Nepal, Singapore, South Korea, Sri Lanka, Taiwan, Thailand and Vietnam, Christians form but a minuscule portion of the population. However, despite their minority status (some 3 per cent of Asia's total population), the Christian presence is highly influential, especially in the fields of education, health care and social services.[10]

In addition to its minority status, Asian Christianity is also characterized by ecclesial diversity, so that it is more accurate to use 'Christianities' in the plural to describe it. Because of its past extensive missions in Asia, Roman Catholicism is the largest denomination.[11] Within the Roman Catholic Church, of great importance is the Federation of Asian Bishops' Conferences (FABC), which since the 1970s has served as a clearing house for theological reflection and pastoral initiatives through its general assemblies and several permanent offices.[12] Older than the Roman Catholic Church is the Malabar Church of India ('Saint Thomas Christians').[13] The Orthodox Church also has a notable presence in China, Korea and Japan.[14] The Anglican Church (including the Anglican Church of Canada) is well represented, especially in Hong Kong, India, Malaysia and Pakistan.[15] Various Protestant Churches also flourish in almost all Asian countries, e.g. the Baptists (especially in North India),[16] the Lutherans,[17] the Mennonites,[18] the Methodists,[19] the Presbyterians (especially in Korea),[20] and the Seventh-Day Adventists.[21] In addition, the number of Pentecostals and charismatics has recently grown by leaps and bounds, particularly among ethnic minorities and disenfranchised social classes.[22] The Yoido Full Gospel Church, located in Seoul, Korea, is the largest Pentecostal church in the world, with over half a million members.[23] Finally, there are numerous indigenous offshoots, inspired by nationalism, charismatic leadership, or by the 'Three Self Movement' (self-support, self-propagation and self-government). Among the most famous are the Iglesia Filipina Independiente (founded by Gregorio Aglipay in 1902),[24] and the Iglesia ni Cristo (founded by Felix Ysagun Manalo in 1914),[25] both in the Philippines, and the China Christian Council (and within it, the Three-Self Patriotic Movement of Protestant Churches in China and the Chinese Catholic Patriotic Association, founded in 1954 and 1956 respectively).[26]

Toward an Asian ecclesiology

From this extreme multiplicity of at times mutually conflicting ecclesial histories, canonical structures, denominational affiliations, liturgical traditions and theological orientations, it is obviously impossible to derive a common theology of the church that might be called an Asian ecclesiology. In what follows an attempt is made to identify some key elements of a vision of church among Asian church leaders and theologians. Such ecclesiology, as will be made clear, is geared not so much towards developing an idiosyncratic understanding of the institutional elements of the church as towards facilitating a new way of being a Christian *in* and *of* Asia.[27] Mention has been made of the fact that Christianity, though born in Asia, is still being regarded by many Asians as a foreign religion. This new 'way of being church' aims at erasing that perception by rooting the Christian faith in the Asian soil and creating a Christianity with an authentically Asian face while remaining true to the mission and teaching of Jesus.

A regnocentric church

One of the most curious features in Asian magisterial documents and theological writings on the church is the conspicuous absence of issues that have occupied much of the attention of European and American Catholics. One finds therein hardly any extensive discussion of staple ecclesiological topics such as papal primacy and infallibility, the Roman Curia, episcopal collegiality, ordination of women, mandatory clerical celibacy, institutional and canonical reforms, and the like. This lack of interest in in-house issues is not dictated by merely pragmatic considerations but is derived, I suggest, from what might be called 'ecclesiological kenosis', a moving away from the church *ad intra* to the church *ad extra*, from self-absorption to mission. This shift is predicated upon the theological conviction that at the heart of the Christian faith and practice there lies not the church and all its institutional elements but the reign of the Triune God. It is only by bearing witness to the reign of God and serving it among the Asian peoples that the church will truly become Asian, not by expanding its membership and socio-political influence. To be truly church, the Asian church must, paradoxically, 'empty' itself in the service of a higher reality, namely, the kingdom of God and cease to exist for its own sake. What the church is, is determined by what it must do; its essence is defined by its function. Ecclesiology, in the Asian perspective, must be essentially pastoral theology. It should not be given pride of place in theological discourse; it does not occupy a high position in 'the hierarchy of truths', to use an expression of Vatican II.

Recent Asian theology has vigorously urged this 'ecclesiological kenosis'. In his book, *Pentecost in Asia*, Thomas C. Fox has described well the evolution of the Asian Catholic Churches from their church-centred way of being church to a regnocentric or kingdom-centred ecclesiology. This conversion took place over three decades, from the foundation of the FABC in 1970 to the Special Assembly of the Synod of Bishops for Asia (the 'Asian Synod') which met in Rome from April 19 to May 14, 1998.[28]

In this kingdom-centred ecclesiology the church is no longer considered the pinnacle or centre of the Christian life. Rather, it has moved from the centre to the periphery and from the top to the bottom. Like the sun around which the earth and the other planets move, the reign of God is the centre around which everything in the church revolves and to which everything is subordinated. In place of the church the reign of God is now installed as the ultimate goal of all the activities within and without the church. Now both what the church is and what it does are defined by the reign of God and not the other way round. The only reason for the church to exist is to serve the reign of God, that is, to help bring about what has been commonly referred to as the 'kingdom values'. It is these values that the church must promote and not its self-aggrandizement, reputation or institutional survival. Every law and policy of the church must pass the litmus test of whether it promotes the reign of God.

The point of regnocentric ecclesiology is not to devalue the role of the church but to determine it correctly with regard to the kingdom of God. Needless to say, there is an intrinsic connection between the reign of God and the church, as is well expressed by Pope John Paul II in his apostolic exhortation *Ecclesia in Asia* promulgated after the Asian Synod: 'Empowered by the Spirit to accomplish Christ's salvation on earth, the Church is the seed of the Kingdom of God and she looks eagerly for its final coming. Her identity and mission are inseparable from the Kingdom of God which Jesus announced and inaugurated in all that he said and did, above all in his death and resurrection. The Spirit reminds the Church that she is not an end unto herself: in all that she is and all that she does, she exists to serve Christ and the salvation of the world.'[29]

There is therefore no intrinsic incompatibility between serving the kingdom of God and expanding church membership and influence – often euphemistically referred to as 'church growth' in missiological literature. Indeed, the two activities of Christian mission must go hand in hand. The issue is rather one of theoretical and practical priority. That is, when push comes to shove, which is to be favoured, the reign of God or the church? When, for instance, the choice is standing in solidarity with the poor and the oppressed and, as a consequence, forfeiting the church's privileges and favours among the powerful and the wealthy, what option must the church take?

The same problem can be framed in terms of the relationship between the reign of God and the church. Clearly, the church is not identical with the kingdom of God, nor is the kingdom of God confined to the church. The church is only, as Vatican II puts it, 'the seed and the beginning of that kingdom'.[30] Its constitution is defined by the kingdom of God, which acts as its goal and future, and not the other way round. The church is not an end unto itself; its *raison d'être* is to serve the kingdom of God. It is a means to an end. When this relationship is reversed, with the church turned into the goal of one's ministry, the possibility of moral corruption, especially by means of power, is enormous. Worse, one is tempted to protect one's personal advantages and interests under the pretext of defending the church! Asian theologians are particularly sensitive to this temptation, given past connections between Catholic missions and colonialism in their countries.

Church as missionary: a triple dialogue

A regnocentric church is by nature a missionary church, committed to promoting the 'kingdom values' preached by Jesus. But what are these? Or, more concisely, what does the kingdom of God stand for? Despite Jesus' frequent use of the symbol of the reign of God, he did not give it a clear definition. What is meant by the reign of God and the values it proclaims is implicit in Jesus' parables, miracles and above all in his death and resurrection. After all, the kingdom of God has come in and with Jesus, who is himself the *auto-basileia*. In a nutshell, the reign of God is nothing less than God's saving presence in Jesus by the power of the Holy Spirit, a presence that brings about gratuitous forgiveness and reconciliation and restores universal justice and peace between God and humanity, among humans themselves, and between humanity and the cosmos.

In the Asian economic, cultural and religious contexts, Asian bishops and theologians propose that the church's mission of realizing the kingdom values should take the form of a triple dialogue. The reason for this dialogical modality is the presence in Asia of many living religions and rich cultures, among which Christians are but a tiny minority; in order to survive, they must therefore, even on the purely human level, enter into dialogue with other believers in an attitude of respect and friendship. But more than pragmatic considerations, theological doctrine today, at least in the Roman Catholic Church, affirms that, as John Paul II says, 'the Spirit's presence and activity affect not only individuals but also society and history, peoples, cultures and religions. Indeed, the Spirit is at the origin of the noble ideals and undertakings which benefit humanity on its journey through history.'[31]

Given this religious pluralism, it is only natural that dialogue is the preferred mode of proclamation. As Michael Amaladoss puts it: 'As soon as one no longer sees the relationship of Christianity to other religions as presence/absence or superior/inferior or full/partial, dialogue becomes the context in which proclamation has to take place. For even when proclaiming the Good News with assurance, one should do it with great respect for the freedom of God who is acting, the freedom of the other who is responding and the Church's own limitations as a witness. It is quite proper then that the Asian Bishops characterized evangelization itself as a dialogue with various Asian realities – cultures, religions and the poor.'[32]

It is important to note also that dialogue as a mode of being church in Asia does not refer primarily to intellectual exchange among experts of various religions, as is often done in the West. Rather, it involves a fourfold presence:

> a. The *dialogue of life*, where people strive to live in an open and neighborly spirit, sharing their joys and sorrows, their human problems and preoccupations. b. The *dialogue of action*, in which Christians and others collaborate for the integral development and liberation of people. c. The *dialogue of theological exchange*, where specialists seek to deepen their understanding of their respective religious heritages, and to appreciate each other's spiritual values. d. The *dialogue of religious experience*, where persons, rooted in their own religious traditions, share their spiritual riches, for instance, with regard to prayer and contemplation, faith and ways of searching for God or the Absolute.[33]

In terms of areas in which dialogue must be carried out, the FABC suggests three: dialogue with the Asian people, especially the poor; with their cultures; and with their religions.[34] In other words, the three essential tasks of the Asian churches are liberation, inculturation and interreligious dialogue.[35] It is vital to note that for the FABC these are not three distinct and separate activities of the church; rather, they are three intertwined dimensions of the church's one mission of evangelization.[36] As the FABC's Seventh Plenary Assembly puts it concisely: 'These issues are not separate topics to be discussed, but aspects of an integrated approach to our Mission of Love and Service. We need to feel and act "integrally." As we face the needs of the twenty-first century, we do so with Asian hearts, in solidarity with the poor and the marginalized, in union with all our Christian brothers and sisters and by joining hands with all men and women of Asia of many different faiths. Inculturation, dialogue, justice and option for the poor are aspects of whatever we do.'[37]

A local church built on communion and equality

To be a kingdom-centred church, that is, an efficacious sign of the reign of God anywhere, the church must also be a truly local church built on communion and equality everywhere. And to achieve this goal, the church, according to the FABC, must be characterized by the following features.

1. First, the church, both at the local and universal levels, is seen primarily as 'a *communion of communities*, where laity, religious and clergy recognize and accept each other as sisters and brothers'.[38] At the heart of the mystery of the church is the bond of communion uniting God with humanity and humans with one another, of which the eucharist is the sign and instrument par excellence.[39]

2. Moreover, in this ecclesiology there is an explicit and effective recognition of the *fundamental equality* among all the members of the local church as disciples of Jesus, and among all the local churches in so far as they are communities of Jesus' disciples and their communion constitutes the universal church. The communion (*koinonia*) which constitutes the church, both at the local and universal levels, and from which flows the fundamental equality of all Christians, is rooted at its deepest level in the life of the Trinity in whom there is a perfect communion of equals.[40] This fundamental equality among all Christians,

which is affirmed by Vatican II,[41] annuls neither the existence of the hierarchy in the church nor the papal primacy. Rather it indicates the modality in which papal primacy and hierarchical authority should be exercised in the church, that is, in collegiality, co-responsibility and accountability to all the members of the church. Unless this fundamental equality of all Christians with its implications for church governance is acknowledged and put into practice through concrete policies and actions, the church will not become a communion of communities.

This vision of church as communion of communities and its corollary of fundamental equality are the sine qua non for the fulfilment of the church's mission. Without being a communion, the church cannot fulfil its mission, since the church is, as indicated above, nothing but the bond of communion between God and humanity and among humans themselves. As *Ecclesia in Asia* puts it succinctly, 'communion and mission go hand in hand'.[42]

3.   This pastoral 'discipleship of equals' leads to the third characteristic of the new way of being church in Asia, that is, the participatory and collaborative nature of all the ministries in the church: 'It is a *participatory* Church where the gifts that the Holy Spirit gives to all the faithful – lay, Religious, and cleric alike – are recognized and activated, so that the church may be built up and its mission realized.'[43] This participatory nature of the church must be lived out not only in the local church but also among all the local churches, including the Church of Rome, of course, with due recognition of the papal primacy. In this context it is encouraging to read in *Ecclesia in Asia* the following affirmation: 'It is in fact within the perspective of ecclesial communion that the universal authority of the successor of Peter shines forth more clearly, not primarily as juridical power over the local churches, but above all as a pastoral primacy at the service of the unity of faith and life of the whole people of God.'[44] A 'pastoral primacy' must do everything possible to foster co-responsibility and the participation of all the local churches in the triple ministry of teaching, sanctification and service in the church and must be held accountable for this task, so that these words do not remain at the level of pious rhetoric but are productive of concrete structures and actions.

4.   The fourth characteristic of the new way of being church in Asia is the *dialogical* spirit: 'Built in the hearts of people, it is a Church that faithfully and lovingly witnesses to the Risen Lord and reaches out to people of other faiths and persuasions in a dialogue of life towards the integral liberation of all.'[45] Ever since its first plenary assembly in Taipei, Taiwan, in 1974, the FABC has repeatedly insisted that the primary task of the Asian Churches is the proclamation of the gospel. But it has also maintained no less frequently that the way to fulfil this task in Asia, as pointed out above, is by way of dialogue, indeed a triple dialogue, with Asian cultures, Asian religions and the Asians themselves, especially the poor.[46]

5.   The fifth and last feature of the new way of being church in Asia is *prophecy*: The church is 'a leaven of transformation in this world and serves as a *prophetic sign* daring to point beyond this world to the ineffable Kingdom that is yet fully to come'.[47] As far as Asia is concerned, in being 'a leaven of transformation in this world', the church must now understand its mission of 'making disciples of all nations' not in terms of converting as many Asians as possible to the church (which is a very unlikely possibility) and in the process increasing its influence as a social institution (*plantatio ecclesiae*). Rather, being a 'small remnant' and likely to remain so for the foreseeable future, Christians must journey with the followers of other Asian religions and together with them – not instead of, or worse, against them – work for the coming of the kingdom of God.

This necessity to be local churches living in communion with each other was reiterated by the FABC's Seventh Plenary Assembly (Samphran, Thailand, January 3–12, 2000). Coming right after the Asian Synod and the promulgation of the Apostolic Exhortation *Ecclesia in Asia* and celebrating the Great Jubilee, with the general theme of 'A Renewed Church in Asia: A Mission of Love and Service', this assembly was of particular significance because it highlighted the kind of ecclesiology operative in the Asian churches. In the first place, the FABC took a retrospective glance over a quarter of a century of its life and activities and summarized its 'Asian vision of a renewed Church', seeing it as composed of eight movements which constitute a sort of Asian ecclesiology. Given its central importance, the text deserves to be quoted in full:

1. A movement towards a Church of the Poor and a Church of the Young. 'If we are to place ourselves at the side of the multitudes in our continent, we must in our way of life share something of their poverty', 'speak out for the rights of the disadvantaged and powerless, against all forms of injustice'. In this continent of the young, we must become 'in them and for them, the Church of the young' (Meeting of Asian Bishops, Manila, Philippines, 1970).

2. A movement toward a 'truly local Church', toward a Church 'incarnate in a people, a Church indigenous and inculturated' (2 FABC Plenary Assembly, Calcutta, 1978).

3. A movement toward deep interiority so that the Church becomes a 'deeply praying community whose contemplation is inserted in the context of our time and the cultures of our peoples today'. Integrated into everyday life, 'authentic prayer has to engender in Christians a clear witness of service and love' (2 FABC Plenary Assembly, Calcutta, 1978).

4. A movement toward an authentic community of faith. Fully rooted in the life of the Trinity, the Church in Asia has to be a communion of communities of authentic participation and co-responsibility, one with its pastors, and linked 'to other communities of faith and to the one and universal communion' of the holy Church of the Lord. The movement in Asia toward Basic Ecclesial Communities express the deep desire to be such a community of faith, love and service and to be truly a 'community of communities' and open to building up Basic Human Communities (3 FABC Plenary Assembly, Bangkok, 1982).

5. A movement toward active integral evangelization, toward a new sense of mission (5 FABC Plenary Assembly, Bandung, Indonesia, 1990). We evangelize because we believe Jesus is the Lord and Savior, 'the goal of human history, . . . the joy of all hearts, and the fulfillment of all aspirations' (GS, 45). In this mission, the Church has to be a compassionate companion and partner of all Asians, a servant of the Lord and of all Asian peoples in the journey toward full life in God's Kingdom.

6. A movement toward empowerment of men and women. We must evolve participative church structures in order to use the personal talents and skills of lay women and men. Empowered by the Spirit and through the sacraments, lay men and women should be involved in the life and mission of the Church by bringing the Good News of Jesus to bear upon the fields of business and politics, of education and health, of mass media and the world of work. This requires a spirituality of discipleship enabling both the clergy and laity to work together in their own

specific roles in the common mission of the Church (4 FABC Plenary Assembly, Tokyo, 1986). The Church cannot be a sign of the Kingdom and of the eschatological community if the fruits of the Spirit to women are not given due recognition, and if women do not share in the 'freedom of the children of God' (4 FABC Plenary Assembly, Tokyo, 1986).

7. A movement toward active involvement in generating and serving life. The Church has to respond to the death-dealing forces in Asia. By authentic discipleship, it has to share its vision of full life as promised by Jesus. It is a vision of life with integrity and dignity, with compassion and sensitive care of the earth; a vision of participation and mutuality, with a reverential sense of the sacred, of peace, harmony, and solidarity (6 FABC Plenary Assembly, Manila, Philippines, 1995).

8. A movement toward the triple dialogue with other faiths, with the poor and with the cultures, a Church 'in dialogue with the great religious traditions of our peoples', in fact, a dialogue with all people, especially the poor.[48]

This eightfold movement describes in a nutshell the new way of being church in Asia. Essentially, it aims at transforming the churches *in* Asia into the churches *of* Asia. Inculturation, understood in its widest sense, is the way to achieve this goal of becoming local churches. This need for inculturation in the church's mission of 'love and service', according to the FABC's Seventh Plenary Assembly, has grown even more insistent in light of the challenges facing Christianity in Asia in the next millennium, such as the increasing marginalization and exclusion of many people by globalization, widespread fundamentalism, dictatorship and corruption in government, ecological destruction and growing militarization. The FABC sees these challenges affecting special groups of people in a particular way, namely, young people, women, the family, indigenous people, and sea-based and land-based migrants and refugees.[49] To meet these challenges fully, the FABC believes that it is urgent to promote the 'Asian-ness' of the church which it sees as 'a special gift the world is waiting for': 'This means that the Church has to be an embodiment of the Asian vision and values of life, especially interiority, harmony, a holistic and inclusive approach to every area of life.'[50]

In sum, this Asian way of being church places the highest priority on communion and collegiality at all levels of church life and activities. At the vertical level, communion is realized with the trinitarian God whose *perichoresis* the church is commissioned to reflect in history. On the horizontal level, communion is achieved with other local churches and, within each local church, communion is realized through collegiality, by which all members, especially lay women and men, are truly and effectively empowered to use of their gifts to make the church an authentically local church.

The central role of the laity in Asian Christianity

Given the geographical vastness of Asia and its huge population, and given the small number of Asian Christians, it is clearly impossible for Christianity to fulfil its mission were it to rely primarily on its clergy and religious. Indeed, in many Asian countries, most if not all non-sacramental functions, especially evangelization and social services, are carried out by the laity. This is particularly true among Pentecostal and Charismatic churches, which do not require ordination for leadership and emphasize the duty of each and every member to spread the faith. Indeed, it is the work of the laity that accounts for the tremendous growth of these churches, especially in communist countries, which tend to control the activities of the clergy and ignore the lay people.

In the Roman Catholic Church, however, the role of the laity, in spite of Vatican II's reform, has been very restricted. The FABC is well aware of the extremely limited role to which the laity have been consigned both in the life of the church and in their specific ministry to the world. It has been advocating, repeatedly and vigorously, a greater involvement of the laity, especially women, in the church and in the world, corresponding to their baptismal vocation. Among its seven offices, the FABC has one dedicated to the laity, and of its seven general assemblies so far, two, the third and especially the fourth, focused on the laity, though of course discussions and statements on the laity are also found in the other general assemblies.[51]

At the third general assembly (1982) the FABC lamented the over-emphasis on the church as institution and the eclipse of the laity within it:

> The structures of our ecclesial organization (sometimes so large, amorphous and impersonal) often image-forth 'institution' in its less attractive aspects, and not 'community'; church groups not infrequently remain individualist in ethos and practice. Sometimes organs of lay participation and co-responsibility have not been established, or are left inactive and impeded, existing only in name. Often enough the gifts and charisms of the laity – both women and men – are not duly recognized, welcomed or activated in significant functions and tasks of ministry and apostolate.[52]

Four years later, in 1986, at its fourth general assembly, the FABC turned its full attention to 'the vocation and mission of the laity in the Church and in the world of Asia'. It examined the role of the laity with regard to the plight of Asian women, the family, education, mass media and work, business, and health care. Among the many recommendations the FABC made, two stand out with regard to the theme of this essay. First, it stressed 'renewal of structures: communion, collegiality, co-responsibility': 'The renewal of inner ecclesial structures does not consist only in strengthening and multiplying the existing parochial and diocesan organization, nor in creating new ones. It consists in creating the right atmosphere of *communion, collegiality and co-responsibility for an active and fuller lay initiation, participation and action.*'[53]

Secondly, with regard to the clergy–laity relationship, the FABC insisted that 'there is no one-sided renewal of clergy or laity. In a Church of communion we, clergy as well as laity, are mutually related and mutually conditioned. We feel the need for a basic change of heart. In a Church which is a communion that tries to liberate others from oppression and discrimination, *collegiality and co-responsibility are urgent.* . . . In this respect, the clergy leadership has a duty to make the initial moves to foster lay involvement and to recognize the emerging leadership of the laity.'[54] By linking the task of developing collegiality with, and co-responsibility to, the laity with that of liberation from oppression and discrimination, the FABC implicitly emphasized the need for the liberation of the laity both within and without the church.

It is only in a church that is truly participatory, 'in which no one feels excluded',[55] and in which everyone is co-responsible and accountable to everyone else, and whose sole *raison d'être* is to serve the kingdom of God, that any structural reform will lead to a greater transparency in church governance. In this task of church reform the experiences and teachings of the churches of Asia can lend their humble yet clear and firm voice, fully aware of their deficiencies, just as they too must learn from the experiences and teachings, and at times, the failures of the other churches.

Christianity with an Asian face

A theological critic, especially one trained in Western ecclesiology, might object that the various elements I have expounded above as essential parts of an Asian ecclesiology, important as they are, have not dealt with many other aspects that must be considered fundamental to a theology of the church, such as apostolic succession, hierarchical structure, the Petrine office, collegiality, the magisterium, ecumenicity and so on.

Such criticism would be well taken were a comprehensive ecclesiology to be developed. However, as pointed out above, the Asian bishops and theologians are not interested in elaborating a comprehensive dogmatic ecclesiology as such. While not denying the institutional aspects of the church, they are primarily concerned with the mission of the church and its pastoral ministry. Their overriding question is: How can we make the church into a living reality not only *in* but also *of* Asia? In other words, the task they set for themselves is forming a Christianity with an Asian face.

Recent demographical studies have noted that the future of Christianity seems to lie not in the West but rather in the non-Western parts of the globe. There has been a massive shift of the Christian population from the north (Europe and North America) to the south (Africa, Asia and Latin America), a fact long known among missiologists and recently brought to the attention of the larger public by Philip Jenkins in his *The Next Christendom: The Coming of Global Christianity*.[56] It is projected that by 2025 there will be 2.6 billion Christians, of whom 633 million will live in Africa, 640 million in Latin America and 460 million in Asia, whereas there will be only 555 million in Europe. In other words, by then half the Christians on the planet will be found in Africa and Latin America. Furthermore, it is projected that by 2050, only about one-fifth of the world's 3 billion Christians will be non-Hispanic Whites.

From the geopolitical and economic perspectives, Asian countries such as China, India, Japan and Korea (especially South Korea but also North Korea, for military reasons) will probably play a significant role on the global stage in the twenty-first century. The challenge for Asian Christianity at this juncture is how to help Asia achieve a beneficial impact on the world scene. It does not seem that the solution lies in converting individual Asians. Asian Christians still form but a tiny minority of the population, and even though the number of Pentecostals and Charismatics has been growing rapidly in recent decades, a drastic increase in the Christian population in Asia is highly unlikely. In fact, Asian churches, at least the mainline ones, do not seem to be overly concerned about augmenting their membership or even saving souls, as if Asian non-Christians were 'pagans' destined to eternal damnation unless they convert to Christianity. Rather, they see as their primary task the evangelization of Asian cultures and societies by imbuing them with the kingdom values.

This task cannot, however, be accomplished unless Christianity acquires an Asian face. This is of course a tall order, and the various steps the Asian bishops and theologians have suggested, i.e. focusing on the reign of God, evangelizing through dialogue, developing a church as communion of communities, and enabling the laity, will no doubt contribute greatly to shaping an authentically Asian face to Christianity.

Of these steps, I suggest that the triple dialogue is an especially appropriate means for contemporary Asian Christianity. Dialogue with the Asian poor, through liberation and integral development, is rendered more necessary and urgent than ever by globalization, which is arguably taking place more extensively in Asia than in any other continent. This economic process, while it has raised the standard of living in general, is creating a growing gap between the rich and the poor and between the wealthy and the impoverished countries. Unless the Asian churches stand in effective solidarity with the poor and the marginalized, who constitute the great majority of the Asian population, their preaching of the Good News is not credible. Similarly, dialogue with adherents of other religions, in particular Hinduism and Islam, is urgently called for to achieve peace and reconciliation, especially in India, Indonesia, Malaysia, Thailand, Sri Lanka and the Philippines, where religiously-inspired conflicts threaten to erupt. Finally, dialogue with cultures remains a permanent challenge since Christianity is still burdened by its linkage with Western colonialism and imperialism. This is true in particular in the case of Roman Catholicism since it is viewed not only as a foreign religion but also as part of a state (the Vatican), with all its diplomatic apparatus and political power.

In this 'dialogical ecclesiology', church issues such as communion and papal primacy, which have been a bone of contention in Western ecclesiologies, will, I submit, be approached rather differently. Communion will be seen in a context wider than that of eucharistic and intra-church unity. It will be enriched by the Asian concept of yin-yang harmony, which admits conflict and diversity as a vital and necessary component of unity. Furthermore, in a harmony (rather than communion) ecclesiology, church unity is directed *outward*, in the sense both of mission (which is relatively absent in current communion ecclesiology) and of collaboration with other religions (mission as dialogue). Similarly, papal primacy will be seen not so much as the pope's juridical power over his fellow bishops but as a reciprocal relationship of collegiality among them.

There is no doubt that for Christianity to acquire an Asian face is an arduous and lengthy process. But the stakes are high. A statement of the Federation of Asian Bishops' Conferences put it starkly 30 years ago: 'The decisive new phenomenon for Christianity in Asia will be the emergence of genuine Christian communities in Asia – Asian in their way of thinking, praying, living, communicating their own Christ-experiences to others . . . If the Asian Churches do not discover their own identity, they will have no future.'[57]

Notes

1 I am aware that in terms of physical geography (landmass) and geology (tectonic plate), Europe and Asia form one 'continent'. On the other hand, in terms of human geography, Europe and Asia have been conventionally treated as different continents, the latter divided into East Asia (the Orient), South Asia (British India), and the Middle East (Arabia and Persia). Here I use the term 'continent' of Asia in this generic sense. As mentioned below, today Asia is divided into five regions (geographers rarely speak of 'North Asia'). The adjective 'Asian' is also confusing. In American English, it refers to East Asian (Orientals), whereas in British English, it refers to South Asia (India). Sometimes the term is restricted to countries of the Pacific Rim. Here I use 'Asia' to refer to East Asia, South Asia, and Southeast Asia.
2 For a succinct presentation of the Asian context in which Christian mission is carried out, see John Paul II's apostolic exhortation *Ecclesia in Asia* (1999), nos 5–9. The text is available in Peter C. Phan, ed., *The Asian Synod: Texts and Commentaries*, Maryknoll, NY: Orbis Books, 2002, pp. 286–340.

3 Though in the modern period West Asia is dominated by Islam, it was, until the Arab conquest in the seventh century, the main home of Christianity.

4 For a comprehensive history of Asian Christianity, see Samuel Hugh Moffett, *A History of Christianity in Asia*. Volume I: *Beginnings to 1500*, Maryknoll, NY: Orbis Books, 1998; and *A History of Christianity in Asia*. Volume II: *1500–1900*, Maryknoll, NY: Orbis Books, 2005. See also the very helpful *A Dictionary of Asian Christianity*, ed. Scott W. Sunquist, Grand Rapids, MI: Eerdmans, 2001.

5 On early Christianity in India, see Leslie Brown, *The Indian Christians of St. Thomas: An Account of the Ancient Syrian Church of Malabar*, Cambridge: Cambridge University Press, 1956; rev. edn, 1982; A. Matthias Mundalan, *History of Christianity in India*, vol. I, Bangalore: Theological Publications, 1984; E.M. Philip, *The Indian Church of Saint Thomas*, Nagercoil: London Mission Press, 1950; and Placid J. Podipara, *Thomas Christians and their Syriac Treasures*, Alleppey: Prakasam Publications, 1976.

6 On Nestorian Christianity in China, see P. Yoshiro Saeki, *The Nestorian Documents and Relics in China*, 2nd edition, revised and enlarged, Tokyo: Maruzen, 1951; Charlotte E. Couling, *The Luminous Religion: A Study of Nestorian Christianity in China*, London: The Carey Press, 1925; Arthur C. Moule, *Christians in China before the Year 1550*, London: SPCK, 1930; idem, *Nestorians in China: Some Corrections and Additions*, London: China Society, 1949; John Foster, *The Church of the Tang Dynasty*, London: SPCK, 1939; Li Tang, *A Study of the History of Nestorian Christianity in China and Its Literature: Together with a New English Translation of the Dunhuang Nestorian Documents*, New York: Peter Lang, 2002.

7 For early Christianity in the Philippines, see John L. Phelan, *The Hispanization of the Philippines: Spanish Aims and Filipino Responses, 1565–1700*, Madison: University of Wisconsin Press, 1967; T. Valentino Sitoy, *A History of Christianity in the Philippines: The Initial Encounter*, Vol. 1, Quezon City, Philippines: New Day Publishers, 1985; Peter G. Gowing, *Islands under the Cross: The Story of the Church in the Philippines*, Manila: National Council of the Churches in the Philippines, 1967; Rafael Lopez and Alfonso Felix Jr., *The Christianization of the Philippines: The Orders of Philip II and the Basic Reports and Letters of Legaspi*, Manila: Historical Conservation Society, 1965. On Vietnam, see Louis-Eugène Louvet, *La Cochinchine religieuse*, 2 vols, Paris: Ernest Leroux, 1885; Peter C. Phan, *Mission and Catechesis: Alexandre de Rhodes and Inculturation in Seventeenth-Century Vietnam*, Maryknoll, NY: Orbis Books, 1998. On Japan, see Charles R. Boxer, *The Christian Century in Japan, 1549–1650*, Berkeley and Los Angeles: University of California Press, 1951; Joseph Jennes, *A History of the Catholic Church in Japan, from Its Beginnings to the early Meiji Era (1549–1873)*, Tokyo: Committee of the Apostolate, 1959; George Elison, *Deus Destroyed: The Image of Christianity in Early Modern Japan*, Cambridge, MA: Harvard University Press, 1988; Andrew C. Ross, *A Vision Betrayed: The Jesuits in Japan and China, 1542–1742*, Maryknoll, NY: Orbis Books, 1984; Neil S. Fujita, *Japan's Encounter with Christianity: The Catholic Mission in Pre-Modern Japan*, New York: Paulist Press, 1991.

8 For early Christianity in Korea, see Juan Ruiz de Medina, *The Catholic Church in Korea: Its Origins 1566–1784*, trans. John Bridges, Rome: Istituto Storico, 1991; Allen D. Clark, *A History of the Church in Korea*, rev. edn, Seoul: Christian Literature Society of Korea, 1971.

9 See Augusto V. de Viana, 'Filipino Natives in Seventeenth Century Marianas: Their Role in the Establishment of the Spanish Mission in the Islands', in *Micronesian: Journal of the Humanities and Social Sciences*, 3/1–2 (2004), 19–25; Ward Barrett, ed., *Mission in the Marianas: An Account of Fr. Diego Luis Sanvitores and his Companions, 1669–1670*, Minneapolis: University of Minnesota, 1975.

10 For an informative and lively survey of Asian Catholicism, see Thomas C. Fox, *Pentecost in Asia: A New Way of Being Church*, Maryknoll, NY: Orbis Books, 2002.

11 See 'Roman Catholic Church', in *A Dictionary of Asian Christianity*, pp. 707–14.

12 The FABC was founded in 1970, on the occasion of Pope Paul VI's visit to Manila, Philippines. Its statutes, approved by the Holy See *ad experimentum* in 1972, were amended several times and were also approved again each time by the Holy See. For the documents of the FABC and its various institutes, see Gaudencio Rosales and C. G. Arévalo (eds), *For All the Peoples of Asia: Federation of Asian Bishops' Conferences. Documents from 1970 to 1991*, New York and Quezon City, Manila: Orbis Books/Claretian Publications, 1992; Franz-Josef Eilers (ed.), *For All the Peoples of Asia: Federation of Asian Bishops' Conferences. Documents from 1992 to 1996*, Quezon City, Manila:

Claretian Publications, 1997; and Franz-Josef Eilers (ed.), *For All the Peoples of Asia: Federation of Asian Bishops' Conferences. Documents from 1997 to 2002*, Quezon City, Manila: Claretian Publications, 2002. These will be cited as *For All Peoples*, followed by their years of publication in parentheses.

13 On Malabar Christians, see Leslie W. Brown, *The Indian Christians of St. Thomas: An Account of the Ancient Syrian Church of Malabar*, Cambridge: Cambridge University Press, 1956; rev. edn 1982; and A. Matthias Mundadan, *History of Christianity in India*, vol. 1: *From the Beginning up to the Middle of the Sixteenth Century (1542)*, Bangalore: Theological Publications, 1984. In the seventeenth century, a large group of Malabar Christians joined communion with the Church of Rome (the 'Syro-Malabar Church', which uses the Liturgy of Addai and Mari). Those who did not join Rome attached themselves to the Syrian Orthodox, known as the Malankara Orthodox Church, and adopted the West Syrian Antiochene liturgy. In the nineteenth century, a group of these split and formed the 'Mar Thoma' Church. In 1930, a group of the Malankara Church united with Rome, known as the Malankarese Uniat Church. Currently, the Indian Catholic Church comprises 157 dioceses, of which 127 are of the Latin rite, 25 of the Syro-Malabar rite, and 5 of the Syro-Malankara rite.

14 See 'Orthodox Church', in *A Dictionary of Asian Christianity*, pp. 619–21.

15 See 'Anglican Church', in *A Dictionary of Asian Christianity*, pp. 25–33.

16 See 'Baptists', in *A Dictionary of Asian Christianity*, pp. 58–66.

17 See 'Lutheran Church', in *A Dictionary of Asian Christianity*, pp. 501–4.

18 See 'Mennonites', in *A Dictionary of Asian Christianity*, pp. 533–4.

19 See 'Methodism', in *A Dictionary of Asian Christianity*, pp. 535–46.

20 See 'Presbyterian and Reformed Churches', in *A Dictionary of Asian Christianity*, pp. 672–5.

21 See 'Seventh-day Adventists', in *A Dictionary of Asian Christianity*, pp. 746–52.

22 On the evangelicals, see *A Dictionary of Asian Christianity*, pp. 271–7. On the Pentecostals, see ibid., pp. 646–50. See also Allan Anderson and Edmond Tang, eds, *Asian and Pentecostal: The Charismatic Face of Christianity in Asia*, Carlisle: Regnum Books International, 2004; and John Mansford Prior, *Jesus Christ the Way to the Father: The Challenge of the Pentecostals*, Hong Kong: FABC Papers, 2006. Prior summarizes the rapid growth of Pentecostals in Asia succinctly: 'The past 30 years has witnessed Asian Pentecostalism move from marginality into the mainstream, from being a "third force" among Asian Christian communities to fast becoming the "first force" expanding more rapidly than both Protestant and Catholic Christianity. Since 1950 Pentecostal growth has outstripped the growth of all other branches of Christianity. During 1970–90 alone Pentecostal numbers tripled. Some 43 per cent of Asian Christians are now Pentecostal/charismatic' (p. 9).

23 See Myung Sung-Hoon and Hong Young-Di, eds, *Charis and Charisma: David Youngi Cho and the Growth of Yoido Full Gospel Church*, Carlisle: Regnum Books International, 2003.

24 See Pedro S. de Achútegui and Miguel A. Bernad, *Religious Revolution in the Philippines: The life and church of Gregorio Aglipay, 1860–1960*, Manila: Ateneo de Manila, 1961.

25 See Gerald H. Anderson, ed., *Studies in Philippine Church History*, Ithaca, NY: Cornell University Press, 1969; Ronald E. Dolan, ed., *Philippines: A Country Study*, Washington, DC: Federal Research Division, Library of Congress, 1993.

26 On the Three-Self Patriotic Movement of Protestant Churches in China, see Philip L. Wickeri, *Seeking the Common Ground: Protestant Christianity, the Three-Self Movement and China's United Front*, Maryknoll, NY: Orbis Books, 1988. On the Chinese Catholic Patriotic Association, see Donald E. MacInnis, *Religious Policy and Practice in Communist China: A Documentary History*, New York: Macmillan, 1972; idem, *Religion in China Today: Policy & Practice*, Maryknoll, NY: Orbis Books, 1989, pp. 263–312.

27 Given the importance of the FABC and the abundance of the theological literature emanating from it, my focus will be on the ecclesiology of Asian Roman Catholicism. This concentration on Roman Catholic ecclesiology, albeit dictated by my theological expertise, is not as narrowly denominational as it may at first appear. Of course it has distinctly Roman Catholic accents (such as the focus on sacramental life and collaboration between the hierarchy and the laity). However, to the extent that it emphasizes the centrality of the kingdom of God, mission as dialogue and the importance of the laity, this Roman Catholic Asian ecclesiology resonates with the concerns and approaches of other Christian churches in Asia.

28 Thomas Fox, *Pentecost in Asia: A New Way of Being Church*, Maryknoll, NY: Orbis Books, 2002.

29 *Ecclesia in Asia* (EA), no. 17. For the English text of *EA*, see Peter C. Phan, ed., *The Asian Synod: Texts and Commentaries*, Maryknoll, NY: Orbis Books, 2002, pp. 286–340.

30 *Lumen Gentium*, no. 5.

31 John Paul II, *Redemptoris Missio* [RM], no. 28. For the English translation of *RM*, see William Burrows, ed., *Redemption and Dialogue: Reading* Redemptoris Missio *and* Dialogue and Proclamation, Maryknoll, NY: Orbis Books, 1993, pp. 3–55.

32 Michael Amaladoss, *Making All Things New: Dialogue, Pluralism, and Evangelization in Asia*, Maryknoll, NY: Orbis Books, 1990, p. 59.

33 The Pontifical Council for Interreligious Dialogue and the Congregation for the Evangelization of Peoples, *Dialogue and Proclamation*, 42 (19 May, 1991). See also *For All Peoples* (1997), pp. 21–6.

34 See *For All Peoples of Asia* (1992), pp. 14–16; 22–3; 34–5; 107; 135; 141–3; 281–2; 307–12; 328–34; 344; *For All Peoples of Asia* (1997), pp. 196–203.

35 As Archbishop Oscar V. Cruz, Secretary General of the FABC, said at the Seventh Plenary Assembly: 'The triple dialogue with the poor, with cultures, and with peoples of other religions, envisioned by FABC as a mode of evangelization, viz., human liberation, inculturation, interreligious dialogue.' See *A Renewed Church in Asia: Pastoral Directions for a New Decade*. FABC Papers, no. 95, FABC: 16 Caine Road, Hong Kong, 2000, p. 17.

36 For reflections on the connection between evangelization and liberation according to the FABC, see Peter C. Phan, 'Human Development and Evangelization: The First to the Sixth Plenary Assembly of the Federation of Asian Bishops' Conferences', *Studia Missionalia* 47 (1998), 205–27.

37 *A Renewed Church in Asia: A Mission of Love and Service*, p. 8.

38 *For All Peoples* (1992), p. 287. The FABC applies this vision of church as 'communion of communities' to the church both at the local and universal levels: 'It [the church] is a community not closed in on itself and its particular concerns, but *linked* with many bonds *to other communities of faith* (concretely, the parishes and dioceses around them) and to the one and universal communion, *catholica unitas*, of the holy Church of the Lord'(*For All Peoples*, vol. 1, p. 56). In other words, not only the diocese but also the church universal are a communion of communities. The universal church is not a church above the other dioceses, of which the local churches are constitutive 'parts' with the pope as its universal bishop. Rather, it is a communion in faith, hope and love of all the local churches (among which there is the Church of Rome of which the pope is the bishop), a communion in which the pope functions as the instrument of unity in collegiality and co-responsibility with other bishops.

39 For an extended discussion of communion ecclesiology, see J.-M.R. Tillard, *Church of Churches: The Ecclesiology of Communion*, trans. R. C. De Peaux, Collegeville, MN: The Liturgical Press, 1992.

40 For a theology of the Trinity as a communion and *perichoresis* of persons, see Leonardo Boff, *Trinity and Society*, trans. Paul Burns, Maryknoll, NY: Orbis Books, 1986.

41 See *Lumen Gentium*, no. 32: 'All the faithful enjoy a true equality with regard to the dignity and the activity which they share in the building up of the body of Christ.'

42 *EA*, no. 24.

43 *For All Peoples* (1992), p. 287. See also ibid., p. 56: 'It [the Church] is a community of authentic *participation and co-responsibility*, where genuine sharing of gifts and responsibilities obtains, where the talents and charisms of each one are accepted and exercised in diverse ministries, and where all are schooled to the attitudes and practices of mutual listening and dialogue, common discernment of the Spirit, common witness and collaborative action.' The Exhortation also recognizes this participatory character of the church but emphasizes the fact that each person must live his or her 'proper vocation' and perform his or her 'proper role' (*EA*, 25). There is here a concern to maintain a clear distinction of roles in ministry, whereas the FABC is concerned that all people with their varied gifts have the opportunity to participate in the ministry of the Church.

44 *EA*, no. 25.

45 *For All Peoples* (1992), pp. 287–8.

46 For the intrinsic connection between the proclamation of the Gospel and dialogue in its triple form, see *For All Peoples* (1992), pp. 13–16.

47 *For All Peoples* (1992), p. 288.

48 *A Renewed Church in Asia: A Mission of Love and Service: The Final Statement of the Seventh Plenary*

Assembly of the Federation of Asian Bishops' Conferences. Samphran, Thailand, January 3–12, 2000, pp. 3–4. The document is available from FABC, 16 Caine Road, Hong Kong. E-mail: hkdavc@hk.super.net. For the Final Statement of the Seventh FABC Plenary Assembly, see For All Peoples (2002), pp. 1–16.
49 See For All Peoples (2002), pp. 6–12.
50 See For All Peoples (2002), p. 265.
51 For the final statement of the third general assembly, see For All Peoples (1992), pp. 53–61 and for that of the fourth, see pp. 178–98.
52 For All Peoples (1992), p. 57.
53 For All Peoples (1992), 193. Emphasis added.
54 For All Peoples (1992), p. 195. Emphasis added. Space does not allow a longer presentation of the FABC's teaching on the laity. For a fuller picture, see especially of the work of its Institute for Lay Apostolate (For All Peoples [1992], pp. 235–46) and its Office of Laity (For All Peoples [1997], pp. 75–139 and For All Peoples [2002], pp. 65–116).
55 EA, no. 45.
56 Philip Jenkins, The Next Christendom: The Coming of Global Christianity, Oxford University Press, 2002.
57 For All Peoples (1992), p. 70.

Further reading

Tom Fox, Pentecost in Asia: A New Way of Being Church, Maryknoll, NY: Orbis Books, 2002.
Peter C. Phan, Christianity with an Asian Face, Maryknoll, NY: Orbis Books, 2003.
——, In Our Own Tongues, Maryknoll, NY: Orbis Books, 2003.
——, Being Religious Interreligiously, Maryknoll, NY: Orbis Books, 2004.
Miguel Marcelo Quatra, At the Side of the Multitudes: The Kingdom of God and the Mission of the Church in the FABC Documents, Quezon City: Claretian Publications, 2000.

16

EARTH, WATER, FIRE AND WIND

Elements of African ecclesiologies

Steve de Gruchy and Sophie Chirongoma

At the start of the twenty-first century Africa is at the heart of global Christianity. An estimated 350 million Christians are found in its 54 countries, it has more recognized Christian denominations than any other continent, and worship takes place each Sunday in the majority of its many languages. Alongside this, Christianity in Africa has a long history that stretches back to the very beginnings of the church, and this history is deeply intertwined in the wider political, social and economic forces that have shaped the continent. This historical depth and contemporary breadth has given rise to an extremely wide diversity of Christian experience and church life on the continent, so much so that some speak of *Christianities* in Africa. To make sense of this diversity we begin this chapter with a brief survey of the history of Christianity on the continent and then reflect on those elements that offer African ecclesiologies an underlying sense of coherence: earth, water, fire and wind.

The Christian story in Africa

Five periods of expansion

The history of the church in Africa has been told in a number of recent books, with general agreement on five periods of Christian expansion.[1] The first is the establishment of the early church in North Africa and Ethiopia within the first century. Christianity became well established amongst the urban citizens of North Africa in cities such as Carthage and Alexandria; but a series of internal divisions and a lack of missionary engagement amongst the wider population did not give it the strength to withstand the arrival of Islam in the seventh century, save in small pockets in Egypt where it still exists today. Owing to its relative isolation and its alliance with the monarchy, the church in Ethiopia fared better, although it too was severely restricted by Islam. It has gone through various periods of growth and stagnation, and remains the dominant faith in the country today.

The second period of Christian expansion was a by-product of the European voyages of discovery. In 1462 the pope named a Missionary Prefect for all of West Africa, and Roman Catholic missionaries started to accompany the trading ships of the Portuguese. The church was planted in a few places on both coasts of Africa, and especially in the Congo, where the

291

conversion of the royal family in 1491 marked the beginning of Christian history in black and central Africa.[2] By the end of the eighteenth century the Portuguese had lost control of the water, and their presence in Africa, together with that of Catholicism, began to decline.

The third period, roughly a century from 1792 through to 1885, saw the establishment of Protestant missions in three key regions of Africa: West Africa, based in Sierra Leone and spreading eastwards through Ghana and into Nigeria; Southern Africa, based in Cape Town and spreading northwards into Namibia, Botswana and Zimbabwe; and East Africa, based on the Kenyan coast and spiralling outwards into Uganda, Southern Sudan and Tanzania.[3] The work involved a few European missionaries working for the many newly established Protestant missionary societies, but the rooting of Christianity in African society was mainly due to Christian communities from the African diaspora resettling in Africa, and the work of African converts and evangelists themselves – many of whom were freed slaves. The beginnings of Bible translation into indigenous African languages signalled an element that was to become crucial in later decades. Towards the end of this period, Roman Catholic missionaries returned to the continent and re-established a strong Catholic presence in various regions. Influenced by Henry Venn's three-self programme (a self-supporting, self-governing and self-propagating church), the vision of the missions was to build an indigenous church under the leadership of Africans.

These plans fell away in the next period, however, following the Berlin Conference of 1884/5 which marked the beginning of the formal colonial period in Africa. Colonial rule had clear advantages in terms of protection, communications networks and a need for educated people, and this enabling environment provided the context for 'one of the most remarkable stories of church growth in the annals of church history'.[4] Mark Shaw points to the statistics: in 1900 there were 4 million Christians in Africa, by 1914 there were 7 million, by 1930 there were 16 million, and by 1950 there were 34 million, a doubling of church membership roughly every fifteen years. Yet, as more and more African territory came under European rule, so the missions began to understand themselves in colonial terms. There was a racist hardening of attitudes towards the 'natives', and a feeling that only Europeans were capable of providing leadership. As Africans grasped the gospel while rejecting the racist and colonial package in which it was offered, there was a growing struggle for leadership within the missionary-initiated churches together with the emergence of African-initiated churches.

The fifth period was underway by 1960, the year of African independence. It is a period in which indigenous clergy took leadership responsibility in almost all of the missionary-initiated churches, Protestant and Catholic. The All African Conference of Churches (AACC) was founded in 1963, and the Roman Catholic Symposium of Episcopal Conferences of Africa and Madagascar (SECAM) in 1969, on the occasion of the first papal visit to Africa. In newly established seminaries and colleges there was an outpouring of theological reflection on what it meant to be both African and Christian, much of it engaging with the political and cultural critique of Christian missions in Africa. By 1990 Christianity was well and truly established as the dominant religion in Africa, with almost three hundred million Christians on the continent (compared to 34 million at the start of the period).

Current situation

It is likely that since 1990 we have entered a new period signalled by the fall of the Berlin Wall and the end of the last outpost of colonial rule in apartheid South Africa. It is a time of emerging democratic rule in Africa, but also of poverty in the context of the global economy, the devastating impact of the AIDS pandemic, renewed tension between Muslims and Christians due to conflict in the Middle East, and ongoing ethnic rivalry and civil war. African church leadership of the missionary-initiated churches is well into its second generation, more conscious of the difficulties of being the church in the African context and more aware of the power and presence of African Christianity in global terms. A Kenyan, Dr Sam Kobia, became General Secretary of the World Council of Churches in 2004 and African bishops are making a powerful impact upon both the Anglican and Roman Catholic Churches. This period has also seen the explosion of Pentecostalism onto the African ecclesial terrain, allied to rapid urbanization, migrancy and globalization. A new feature on the global Christian map is the churches of the modern African diaspora in Britain and Europe which are growing in size and significance.

This brief survey of the story of Christianity in Africa enables us to draw attention to the six dominant types of church that are found in Africa today.[5] The oldest are the churches of antiquity, the Orthodox of Egypt and Ethiopia who maintain an unbroken connection to the early church, and whose 40 million constitute 99 per cent of Christians in those two countries. The Roman Catholic Church is the largest single denomination, with 140 million members belonging to many dioceses throughout the continent. The third grouping is the mainline Protestant churches, including the Anglican, Lutheran, Reformed and Methodist churches, who make up the bulk of the membership of the All Africa Conference of Churches. The fourth grouping comprises those Protestant churches that understand themselves to be 'Evangelical' rather than ecumenical. Together these Protestant groupings have a membership of around 100 million. The African Initiated Churches, those churches that have grown up through the work of African prophets and leaders, which have no formal relationship to the historic churches of Europe or North America, and which seek a deep integration between Christian doctrine, rituals and symbols and African culture, are estimated to have a membership of 40 million. Finally, the newest type of churches in Africa are the Pentecostal or Neo-Pentecostal ministries that have emerged in the past twenty years, and which are growing apace in urban areas. They are estimated to have anything between 10 and 30 million members.

With this overview as a guide we suggest that all the churches in Africa are working with or are influenced by a set of four key elements that shape their character and their witness, namely, earth, water, fire and wind. These terms point to the abiding influence of certain trajectories that emerge out of the history and that continue to characterize contemporary church life. *Earth* introduces us to the extremely long history of Christianity on African soil as well as the contested role of African Traditional Religions in Christian life today; *water* points to the arrival of Western Christianity on the ships of missionaries and returning exiles from the West, events which have shaped the dominant ecclesial structures of Africa today. *Fire* symbolizes the struggle of African believers to remain Christian whilst rejecting the dehumanization implied in its received colonial guise, to be authentically African *and* authentically Christian at the same time; and *wind* points to the signs of the Spirit in Africa, in Revivalism and Pentecostalism and in initiatives that are emerging as the church seeks to respond to the *missio Dei* on the continent. The argument throughout is that none of the elements on their own is able to describe the richness and complexity of contemporary African ecclesiologies.

Earth

The Christian church is intrinsically tied to the African earth in two important ways: through the churches of antiquity, and the religious experience that African people bring with them into the church and through which they understand and embrace the Gospel.

Ancient churches

The church took root in Africa in ancient times. This very fact in itself provides a crucial key with which to understand the church in Africa, namely the heartfelt recognition that Christianity is not essentially a Western or European religion, but has its genesis in the Mediterranean world, a world in which Africa was an important participant. The continued witness of the church in Egypt and particularly in Ethiopia, which also maintained its political independence throughout the colonial period, provided a strong counterbalance to the assumption of cultural and racial superiority carried by much of mission Christianity in the twentieth century. Not surprisingly then, many African-initiated churches that emerged in the colonial period throughout the continent took the name 'Ethiopian', signalling their ideological connection to this non-Western church.[6]

Beyond this formal connection to the past is the fact that African theologians and church leaders in centres such as Alexandria and Carthage played a crucial role in shaping the contours of catholic Christianity in the first centuries of the new faith. Clement, Origen Tertullian, Cyprian and Anthanasius are amongst those Africans who made their mark on the world church, but it is Augustine of Hippo who did so most decisively, owing to the theology he developed in his struggle against the great heretical movements of his generation, Manichaeism, Pelagianism, and particularly Donatism.[7] Mention of these different and competing Christianities, to which can be added the Arianism of the conquering Germanic tribe, the Vandals, is a pointer to the contested nature of the faith in Africa even in those first centuries, reminding us that Africa has always been a place in which different forms of Christianity are tried and tested.

The continent has also served as an intense laboratory for the relationship between Christianity and Islam.[8] The appearance of this monotheistic rival in the seventh century has, in some instances, meant restriction and even elimination for the church, while in others it has meant aggression and military struggle. Throughout these thirteen centuries the church has been deeply shaped by a spectrum of attitudes that moves between creative toleration and violent disrespect, and thus it has much experience to contribute to a world in which Christian–Muslim tensions are rising. African Christian experience, and African theologians, have always contributed to an exploration of the meaning of the faith and the church in a pluralist world; it is frequently suggested that this is a resource that can serve the world church.

African religious experience

The second aspect of the *earth* in African ecclesiology is the inherent religious experience of those who are drawn into the church. As Tinyiko Maluleke puts it: 'African culture and African Traditional Religions (ATRs) have long been acknowledged as the womb out of which African Christian theology must be born.'[9] However, when the first Europeans arrived in Africa they did not find temples, priests and holy books and so made the assumption that Africans were not 'religious'. Against this wholly inadequate perspective, scholars today can point to a coherent sense of what constitutes the core elements of the wide diversity of ATRs,[10] the most important being that spirituality so infuses ordinary life that there is no separate thing called 'religion'. It is an 'all pervasive reality which served to interpret society and give wholeness to the individual's life and the community'.[11] Key elements include belief in a world of spirits and divinities and usually a supreme being or high God, the importance of rites of passage and community, belief that life is stronger than death and therefore that the living dead continue to play a role in the present, the presence of prophets and seers, and a focus on predicting and controlling divine causality around such crucial matters as rain-making and human health.[12]

Clearly then ATRs have a profound relationship to Christianity in Africa. Yet there remains a great deal of debate about how they do and should shape the life of the church today. For some they function as a *praeparatio evangelica*, their primal religious worldview providing a creative connection to the world of the Bible and thus the depth of the gospel. In this way, as Kwame Bediako has powerfully argued, the African Christian experience can serve as a reminder of the primal heart of Christianity, and it is here that 'the opportunity for a serious theological encounter and cross-fertilization between the Christian and primal traditions, which was lost in Europe, can be regained'.[13] On the other hand, there are those (like Maluleke) who argue strongly that Christians must respect the integrity and 'otherness' of ATRs, and share with them in mutual and humble dialogue, as with any other formal religious tradition. From either position, however, the significance of African religion for the church is crucial. Thus Sundkler and Steed note: 'A chapter, however brief, on African religion belongs in an African church history, not just as a background to be conveniently forgotten as the story of evangelization proceeds over the continent. It belongs there as an accompanying echo from the past and, perhaps, as a tempting exit in the future.'[14] From this perspective, the church in Africa, alongside ATRs and Islam, must understand itself as one of three religions of the African earth, and chart its way accordingly.

Water

Whereas *earth* refers to what has been in Africa since the beginnings of the Christian story, *water* refers to the new forms of Christianity that came to Africa from 'over the seas' in the period beginning with the fifteenth century. These forms, both Roman Catholic and Protestant, and their integration into the African experience have had a decisive but ambiguous impact upon the shape of the church in Africa. Here we point to some of the more significant themes.

Western Christian missions

The initial Roman Catholic presence in Africa began and ended with Portuguese naval fortunes. It was then further restricted by the suppression of the Jesuits in 1773 and the anticlerical impact of the French Revolution in 1789, so that by the end of the eighteenth century it had almost completely disappeared. Roman Catholic engagement in Africa started again, fifty years after Protestant missionary work, with the establishment of St Mary's mission in Gabon in 1844. Yet it only began to have an impact following the founding of three French orders, the Holy Ghost Fathers or Spiritans (1848), the Society of African Missions or Lyon Fathers (1856) and the Société de Notre-Dame d'Afrique or White Fathers (1868), and the Italian order, the Verona Fathers (1867).[15] Over the next decades, hundreds of missionary priests and nuns came to various regions in Africa, and by the start of World War I the Roman Catholic Church was well established throughout the continent, particularly in the French colonies. A key moment for the church was the visit of Pope Paul to Uganda in 1969, in which he challenged the church in the post Vatican II era to deeply enter the African experience: 'You may, and you must, have an African Christianity',[16] and this challenge to incarnate and indigenize the faith in Africa has been taken up with great seriousness in many Roman Catholic settings on the continent.

The Protestant presence in Africa came initially through three impulses. The first was via two communities of Protestant settlers who brought their faith with them. In 1652 the Dutch settled in Cape Town, and their Reformed faith was strengthened by the arrival of French Huguenots in 1688.[17] In West Africa it was returning exiles, freed slaves of African descent, beginning in 1787. The decisive settlement came in 1792 with 1190 black loyalists, all Christians, who had fought with the British in the American Revolutionary War. 'Their arrival was of epochal significance. It marked the establishment of the first black church in modern Africa.'[18] These two communities, one in South Africa and the other in Sierra Leone, provided the bridgeheads for the second Protestant impulse, the Western missionary societies that arrived at the start of the nineteenth century, with Europeans like David Livingstone, West Indians such as Thomas Birch Freeman, the 'Father of Ghanaian Methodism'[19] and African-Americans inspired by 'providential design', the idea that 'God in his inscrutable way, had allowed Africans to be carried off into slavery so that they could be Christianized and civilized and return to uplift their kinsmen in Africa'.[20]

By 1815 the Protestant missionary effort was firmly established in these two regions, and it was from here and through the knowledge gained in this early work that they could consider other areas, including East Africa.[21] Yet it should be borne in mind that Protestant-ism was spread more rapidly and more effectively throughout Africa by Africans themselves, either through powerful African evangelists or clergymen such as Samuel Adjai Crowther, a rescued slave who spearheaded Anglican work in Nigeria, and William Wade Harris who 'permanently re-wrote the geography of the Ivory Coast';[22] or through migrating communi-ties of converts who took their bibles and new faith with them. This third impulse has led Sundkler and Steed to propose a 'law': 'That first missionary arriving in a certain African village there to proclaim for the first time the name of Christ – was never first.'[23] In other words, when a European missionary arrived in a village assuming he was bringing something new, he would invariably find that people had heard about Christianity or the Bible through the networks of trade, travel and migration that characterize Africa.

Impact of the missionary movement

The arrival of these Christianities from over the water has left the African church with a number of enduring consequences. First, in terms of ecclesial relationships African churches have a very strong bond with the 'mother church', one that has continued today through links with mission societies, confessional communities, liturgical forms, scholarships and educational opportunities, and global identity. At the same time and for the same reason, rampant denominationalism is the order of the day in Africa. Whilst Hastings perhaps over-states the case, there is enough truth in his comment to make it stick: 'The denomination tag . . . is not something about which people feel a little ashamed, but rather something to glory in.'[24] Only in two countries in Africa, Zambia and Zaire, have initiatives to unite different Protestant traditions into a United Church come to fruition.

A number of other consequences can be noted. The reference above to 'freed slaves' is a reminder that in its origins in Africa, Christianity understood mission in holistic ways. The struggle against slavery was deeply rooted in missionary consciousness, and this in turn had a significant impact on the self-understanding of the church as a gathered community of the redeemed. The freed slaves who arrived in Sierra Leone over many decades (an estimated 67,000 by 1840)[25] drew themselves together into communities that knew and experienced the freedom they found in Christ. This paved the way for similar communities to be founded in Liberia, and in Bagamoyo and Freretown on the East Coast, the latter shaping its own expression of *kitoro* (refugee) Christianity.[26] This model of the gathered community of the redeemed also found expression in the 'Christian village' idea promoted by the missionaries, one which grew up around the mission station and its school and clinic, and which 'often reflected the belief that Africans could not practice a Christian life in a traditional environment, that it was necessary to make a clean break'.[27] The model of a holy city, a 'New Jerusalem', continues to be important in some African-initiated churches,[28] but it has not found a parallel in contemporary urban Africa.

A key task that the missionaries engaged in throughout the continent was both the introduction of the Bible as the key sign and symbol for African Christianity, and the overseeing of its translation into indigenous languages. This signalled a fundamental incarnation of the faith into the African cultural context, by shifting the foundational text from the element of *water* to the element of *earth*. In translating the text, the Bible became available for ordinary Africans in their own languages, but Andrew Walls, Lamin Sanneh and Kwame Bediako have noted that something else important happened.[29] The translations could not but rely on the existing African languages in which was embedded the pre-Christian religious framework of Africa; and so the African religious experience was taken up into the Bible and became the 'language' of the church. In this way Western Christianity has become African Christianity.

Because of the importance given to the Bible, Christianity was seen in Africa as a religion of the 'book', one that required literacy and thus education. One of the most significant legacies of the missionary period was the vast networks of schools and colleges that the churches developed in Africa in the twentieth century, and which contributed immeasurably to African independence by educating generations of leaders. This work was boosted by support and subsidies from the colonial powers, shaped (in the British colonies) by the two Phelps-Stokes Commissions in the period 1920–4, which promoted the idea that the colonial authorities should provide education for Africans through the missions rather than directly. Mission education was also crucial in promoting the colonial languages, English, French and Portuguese, as the dominant languages of national and pan-African communication, aiding the growth of both church and national identity in a continent that is home to a bewildering array of tribal languages. This role also opened the missions to the serious criticism of promoting 'cultural imperialism'.[30]

This point hints at the problems that the alliance between Christianity and colonialism caused for the church. In our historical survey we noted some of the benefits this had for the missionary enterprise, but as Ogbu Kalu points out, colonialism 'introduced a new spirit that overawed indigenous institutions and sought to transplant European institutions and cultures. Collusion with the civilizing project diminished the spiritual vigour of missionary presence and turned it into culture and power encounters.'[31] A great deal has been written about this; here we point to Shaw's summary of the criticisms: (i) collaboration with government, meaning that the missions came to be seen as the religious and ideological wing of colonial power and authority; (ii) cultural and religious imperialism, whereby colonial arrogance about the benefits of 'western civilization' became confused with the benefits of the gospel; (iii) paternalism in the church, because the European belief that Africans were 'not yet ready' for providing leadership in government spilled over into leadership in the church; and (iv) indoctrination in education, meaning that Africans were taught to admire all things European while disrespecting their own culture, history and traditions.[32] After 1886, as a whole, there was a fatal confusion between colonialism and Christianity in the minds of many Europeans and Africans. As David Bosch has it, 'there would no longer be any doubt about the complicity of mission agencies in the colonial venture. Parallels between the high imperial and the high missionary developments became more and more obvious.'[33] The full implications of this are captured in the third foundational element of the church in Africa to which we now turn.

Fire

The establishment of Western missionary Christianity in Africa generated a fundamental dissonance that would come to dominate church life on the continent in the twentieth century. On the one hand the preaching of the gospel, and work in education, health care and the anti-slavery movement led to a growing number of converts and the acceptance of the message that Africans were important to God; a message which resonated with traditional religious beliefs, imbued a sense of worth and dignity, and which implied an equality with other people. On the other hand, because Christianity came to be so deeply linked to Western racism and paternalism in tandem with the violence of colonialism, the African experience was contradictorily one of a loss of dignity, exploitation, and a negation of African community and culture at the hands of the very 'Christian' nations which sent the missionaries.[34]

Responding to this dissonance adds the element of *fire* to African ecclesiology: the flames of the anti-colonial struggle, the warmth and passion for the gospel from many theologians, church leaders and ordinary believers in difficult times, and the furnace of authenticity through which Christianity was (and still is) being refined by Africans themselves. There were many fires, and they burned with varying degrees of intensity. Here we can point to three of the most significant: the struggles for ecclesial authority, cultural respect and human flourishing.

Ecclesial authority

The first victim of the collusion with colonialism was the idea of a self-governing and self-propagating church, as the missionary leadership argued that local clergy were 'not ready' for leadership responsibility. The way in which Bishop Samuel Adjai Crowther of Nigeria, was stripped of his episcopal office through pressure from younger white missionaries in the mid-1880s provides a good example of this.[35] This kind of racist attitude was deeply resented by many in the churches, and led to two significant initiatives. The first was the formal establishment of black-led churches, in which charismatic pastors and evangelists separated themselves and their congregations in protest. Many of them found a welcome in the churches of the African diaspora, such as the African Methodist Episcopal Church; a number of them took the title 'Ethiopian', drawing on the long history of the church in

Africa which we have noted above, and thereby reminding the colonial missionaries that Christianity was not a Western religion; and a number of them simply started new churches.

The second African initiative towards ecclesial authority took place *within* the missionary-established churches, as African clergy began to clamour for greater responsibility and leadership opportunities rather than leaving them. To some extent this was the inevitable outcome of the demographic reality of the rapidly growing churches, but it also paralleled what was happening in national political life as African independence began to gather steam after 1957. The pressure led to the call for a missionary moratorium in Africa by some individuals, which was formally affirmed by the All African Conference of Churches meeting in Nairobi in 1974:

> To enable the African church to achieve the power of becoming a true instrument of liberating and reconciling the African people, as well as finding solutions to economic and social dependency, our option as a matter of policy has to be a moratorium on external assistance in money and personnel. [This] will necessitate the emergence of structures that would be viably African and programmes and projects of more urgent and immediate propriety. A moratorium on funds and personnel from abroad will also enforce the unifying drive of churches in Africa.[36]

While the moratorium was never formally adhered to, it was a very powerful symbolic statement of the depth of feeling about ecclesial authority. It signalled the fact that during the 1970s there was a fundamental shift of leadership towards Africans. By way of illustration, the Evangelical Lutheran Church of Tanzania appointed its first African president of a district only in 1959, yet within just sixteen years all eleven dioceses or synods were headed by Tanzanians.[37] Today hardly any missionary-initiated churches in Africa have white or expatriate leadership.

Cultural respect

The struggle for ecclesial authority went hand in hand with the struggle for cultural respect, for much of the disrespect for African Christian leadership was rooted in a profound arrogance towards African culture. Hastings, himself a missionary priest in East Africa, speaks of the 'largely inescapable cultural imperialism implicit in missionary practice'.[38] In too many instances European culture was taken to be the generic Christian culture, creating a disconnect between the gospel and African culture. There were many Africans who rejected the gospel because of this arrogance; but there were also a good number who became Christian and remained African, moulding the Bible and the symbols of Christianity into a profoundly African expression of the church.

In this way alongside the missionary-initiated churches, a whole range of hugely diverse African-initiated churches have grown up in Africa. These indigenous churches usually involve a focus on prophetic and charismatic leadership, special dress codes, rituals, song and dancing, and varied responses to aspects of traditional culture such as polygamy, ancestor veneration, food rules and healing practices.[39] Here the 'fire' of African agency involves rooting the church beyond just the element of 'water', by engaging seriously with the element of 'earth' that we noted above, an ongoing process that is at the heart of African ecclesiologies. There are thousands of such churches across Africa ranging from small worshipping congregations to huge institutional denominations. Some of the more important forms are the Zionist churches in Southern Africa, the Aladura churches in Nigeria, the Roho churches in Kenya, and the Kimbanguists in the Congo. There is much scholarly debate about why these churches emerged in the way that they did, but there is general consensus that they represent a search for cultural authenticity in African Christianity, and are a vital aspect of the church in Africa today.

Alongside this form of cultural resistance stands the African theology project of inculturation and indigenization that has gone on within the missionary-initiated churches, as leaders and theologians have contested the inherited negative 'Christian' view of African culture (see the discussion on *earth*). Scholars such as John Mbiti, John Pobee and Kwesi Dickson pointed the way to a more positive evaluation of African cultural practices from a biblical perspective, and this has spawned a whole theological project to find the connections between African culture and religion and the Christian gospel. In recent years African women theologians have developed creative ways of engaging with the patriarchal elements of this culture (see below).

Human flourishing

The third aspect of the struggle for African identity is the more political concern to witness to the gospel of life in the midst of the politics of death. Whilst early missionary initiatives linked to the struggle against the slave trade were a witness to the God of justice in the midst of dehumanization, this aspect of the gospel seemed to be lost after the work of the missions became subservient to the wider colonial project. There were exceptions in places such as Leopold's Congo; but it is perhaps the church in South Africa with its witness against apartheid that best illustrates this aspect of African Christian agency.[40] Apartheid, a form of repressive and overtly racist colonialism that served the interests of the expatriate population, was characterized by its strong ideological support from certain churches in South Africa. This gave to the struggle against apartheid a theological flavour undertaken with rigour and passion with leadership from people like the Nobel Laureate, Archbishop Desmond Tutu. The 1982 *Belhar Confession* and the 1985 *Kairos Document* were the culmination of the Christian witness for freedom and justice in which humans could flourish, a witness which bore fruit in 1994 when apartheid formally came to an end and South Africa became the last African country to throw off the legacy of colonialism.

The Christian struggle for human flourishing within Africa also engaged lay Christians in the wider political movement for independence and freedom. As noted above, Christian missions played a significant role in education in Africa in the middle of the twentieth century, and out of the 'narrow confines of the missionary school came the great leaders of Africa's first wave of independence such as Kenneth Kaunda of Zambia, Julius Nyerere of Tanzania, Hastings Banda of Malawi, Jomo Kenyatta of Kenya and Kwame Nkrumah of Ghana'.[41] To this could be added Nelson Mandela. Their witness, giving expression to what they had learnt from the missionaries about human dignity and the value of African people to God, remains a significant part of the legacy of the church in Africa.

Wind

One of the major shifts in missiology in the past fifty years has been the recognition that God is a missionary God, and that the church finds its meaning and existence in faithful response to what God is doing in the world. The *missiones ecclesia* is thus a response to the *missio Dei*. This is both a necessary corrective to any missionary-centred understanding of the church in Africa; and also a helpful lens through which to understand the fourth and final element of the church in Africa, namely, *wind*. For the story of the church in Africa is not just told with reference to its African roots (earth), the Western influence (water), or African agency (fire), but with reference to the work of the Holy Spirit (wind) empowering and equipping people to be faithful witnesses to the God of grace and truth.

Pentecostal movements

The most obvious sign of the work of the Holy Spirit in the church in Africa is the Pentecostal movement that has been present on the continent since its origins at the start of the twentieth century. There were earlier pointers to this in various holiness movements and spiritual revivals on the continent, for alongside the work of Catholics and Protestants there were also the faith missions and individuals inspired by Keswick piety who felt called to proclaim the gospel of holiness in Africa. Here the focus was on sanctification as a process by which one could reach a level of perfection 'where the entire focus is on Christ, and the power of sin in the believer is broken',[42] with evidence of this being shown in a striving for personal holiness. The most important of these were the Africa Inland Mission and the Sudan Inland Mission. The East African revival, sometimes known as the *Balokole* ('saved ones') revival, is possibly the most powerful of all the revival movements that both renewed the missionary churches and led to schism, and its emphasis on personal morality continues to be a strong mark of the churches in East Africa today.[43]

Yet it is the formal Pentecostal movement that is playing a crucial role in shaping the public profile of the church in Africa today. Like any religious expression, it has both its detractors and its supporters. Some see it as 'more part of the problem than part of the answer'.[44] Kwabena Asamoah-Gyadu is more positive. He sees its roots in the African-initiated churches, along with the Pentecostal revivals in the USA in the early 1900s, and a later explosion of a desire for a deeper experience of the Spirit amongst young people in movements like Scripture Union, the Student Christian Movement and Campus Crusade for Christ. He argues that 'The experiential and versatile nature of Pentecostalism has allowed African Christians to take their spiritual destiny into their own hands by deploying within local contexts a religion with a global outlook',[45] and thus it contributes to optimism and hope in a context of Afro-Pessimism.

While a final evaluation is still to be made about Pentecostalism, there is no doubt that it is a growing and vibrant religious element in Africa and in the churches of the modern African diaspora. Furthermore, the positive vibrancy and energy of Pentecostalism has an impact on all the churches, particularly on music and worship styles. Under the influence of television evangelists and successful mega-churches, many urbanized young people in the mainline churches are attracted to this form of Christianity and place pressure on their own communities to keep up with the changes. All-night vigils are common, and many church organizations such as youth movements and women's movements embrace such charismatic renewal.

Signs of the Spirit

We should not limit ourselves to Pentecostalism when talking about the work of the Holy Spirit in Africa today, for there are many signs of the wider church seeking to be faithful to the *missio Dei* in Africa in the power and presence of the Spirit. Three examples will illustrate this. The first is the work and witness of the All African Conference of Churches (AACC), which came into being in 1963 in Kampala. This ecumenical gathering of churches has sought over a period of almost half a century to unite the African Protestant witness, engage with the Roman Catholic bishops and other Christian churches, provide a channel for African theological reflection, engage with civil society, and contribute to the social and political life of the continent.[46] Through all of this, the AACC has been contributing to the search for Christian authenticity in Africa, and while it struggled with financial restrictions in the 1970s and 80s, the recent leadership of two General Secretaries, Jose Chipenda of Angola and Mvume Dandala of South Africa, has given it a greater profile.

Jesse Mugambi has written: 'As a witness to the rule of God in Africa, the African Church must confront face to face the concerns that contradict that rule throughout the continent.'[47] Thus our second example is this engagement of the church in matters of democracy, reconstruction and development.[48] Here a key issue is the devastating HIV/AIDS pandemic. Issues of stigma, inclusion, sexual morality, meaningless suffering, healing and death are pushing for rigorous and creative theological work by African theologians, those closest to the pandemic. The way people deal with the crisis is leading to new forms of the church, as people find the traditional structures discriminatory and exclusionary and seek fellowship and support amongst those on the margins.[49] In its response, from the lowest level of Home Based Care groups springing up all over the continent, through initiatives for Orphans and Vulnerable Children, to public health initiatives, the people of God are being prompted by the Spirit to explore new ways of being church in Africa.

A third example of the work of the Spirit amongst African Christians is the Circle of Concerned African Women Theologians, founded in 1989 under the visionary leadership of Mercy Amba Oduyoye. In an ecclesial context in which women's gifts, experience and theological insights have been hugely undervalued, the Circle is a space for women of Africa to do communal theology,[50] out of the experiences of African women in religion and culture.[51] The major objective or mission of the Circle is to undertake research, write and publish from the experiences of African women in religion and culture in so far as these affect women, as well as to mentor each other in this area. The Circle has expanded from the initial 69 women to 616 members in April 2006. It includes members from the Islamic and African Traditional Religion community as well as the church, and is involved in a number of cooperative projects with the church and theological institutions. It is playing a crucial role in shaping the struggle for an inclusive church for Africa in the twenty-first century.

Conclusion

With these examples of the work of the Spirit in the life of the churches in Africa today, we draw this essay to a close with a reminder that the story of the African church and its present diverse forms are shaped by the interaction of these four key elements that we have explored, namely, earth, water, fire and wind. Throughout the story the role and place of African believers is paramount, as they work with the elements to fashion and be fashioned into the Body of Christ in Africa. Earth, water, fire and wind provide the hermeneutical keys to understanding how we got to be who we are, and provide the resources for the ongoing struggle to be who we are called to be.

Notes

1 The reader is directed to the following: Adrian Hastings, *History of African Christianity: 1950 – 1975*, Cambridge: Cambridge University Press, 1979; John Baur, *2000 Years of Christianity in Africa: An African history 62 – 1992*, Nairobi, Paulines Publications Africa, 1994; Adrian Hastings, *The Church in Africa: 1450 – 1950*, Oxford: Clarendon, 1994; Elizabeth Isichei, *A History of Christianity in Africa from Antiquity to the Present*, London: SPCK, 1995; Mark Shaw, *The Kingdom of God in Africa: A short history of African Christianity*, Grand Rapids, MI: Baker Books, 1996; Bengt Sundkler and Christopher Steed, *A History of the Church in Africa*, Cambridge: Cambridge University Press, 2000; Ogbu U.Kalu (ed.), *African Christianity: An African Story*, Pretoria: Department of Church History, 2005.

2 Hastings, *The Church in Africa*, p. 73.

3 Note that these country names date from the later colonial or post-colonial period.

4 Shaw, *The Kingdom of God*, p. 207.

5 For the statistics on church membership I am following the tables in Baur, *2000 Years*, pp. 523–7, adjusted for the period 1994 – 2006 using the formula he has provided. He has based his data on David Barrett's *The World Christian Encyclopedia*. The latest edition is New York: Oxford University Press, 2001.

6 See Ogbu U. Kalu 'Ethiopianism in African Christianity' in Kalu (ed.), *African Christianity*, pp. 258–77.

7 Sundkler and Steed, *History of the Church*, p. 26. See Chapter 2 of this present volume.

8 See Akintunde E. Akinade, 'Islamic Challenges in African Christianity', in Kalu (ed.), *African Christianity*, pp. 117–38. He makes reference to Lamin Sanneh, *Piety and Power: Muslims and Christians in West Africa*, Maryknoll: Orbis, 1996; J. Haafkens, *Islam and Christianity in Africa*, Nairobi: Procmura, 1992; Lissi Rasmussen, *Christian-Muslim Relations in Africa*, London and New York: British Academic Press, 1993; and Noel Q. King, *Christian and Muslim in Africa*, New York: Harper & Row Publishers, 1971.

9 Tinyiko S. Maluleke, 'Half a Century of African Christian Theologies: Elements of the Emerging Agenda for the Twenty-first Century', in Kalu (ed.), *African Christianity*, p. 477.

10 For further information on African Traditional Religion see Placides Temples, *Bantu Philosophy*, Paris: Présence Africaine, 1945; E.G. Parrinder, *African Traditional Religion*, London: SPCK, 1962; J.S. Mbiti, *African Religions and Philosophy*, New York: Praeger, 1969; D. Zahan, *The Religion, Spirituality and Thought of Traditional Africa*, Chicago: University of Chicago Press, 1970; E.B. Idowu, *African Traditional Religion: A Definition*, London: SPCK, 1973; Benjamin C. Ray, *African Religions: Symbol, ritual and Community*, New York: Praeger Press, 1976; L Magesa, *African Religion: The Moral Foundations of Abundant Life*, Maryknoll: Orbis, 1997. T.G. Kiogora, 'Religious Pluralism in Africa' in D. W. Waruta (ed.), *African Church in the 21st Century: Challenges and Promises*, Nairobi: AACC, 1995, pp. 80–97.

11 Sundkler and Steed, *History of the Church*, p. 91.

12 Here I am drawing on summaries in T.G. Kiogora, 'Religious Pluralism in Africa' in D.W. Waruta (ed.), *African Church in the 21st Century: Challenges and Promises*, Nairobi: AACC, 1995, pp. 80–97.

13 Kwame Bediako, *Christianity in Africa: The Renewal of a Non-Western Religion*, Edinburgh: Edinburgh University Press, 1995, p. 261.

14 Sundkler and Steed, *History of the Church*, p. 91.

15 See Baur, *2000 Years*, p. 106; and Sundkler and Steed, *History of the Church*, pp. 100–9.

16 Quoted in Hastings, *African Christianity: An Essay in Interpretation*, London: Geoffrey Chapman, 1976, p. 59.

17 For an overview of the church struggle against apartheid in South Africa see John de Gruchy with Steve de Gruchy, *The Church Struggle in South Africa*, revised 3rd edn, London: SCM, 1994.

18 Jehu Hanciles, 'Back to Africa: White Abolitionists and Black Missionaries' in Kalu (ed.), *African Christianity*, p. 203.

19 Hastings, *The Church in Africa*, p. 179.

20 See Sundkler and Steed, *History of the Church*, pp. 120–3.

21 The detailed and diverse story of Protestant missions in Africa is covered in detail in all the major histories of African Christianity noted above.

22 Isichei, *History of Christianity in Africa*, p. 285.
23 Sundkler and Steed, *History of the Church*, p. 84.
24 Hastings, *African Christianity*, p. 19.
25 See Hanciles, 'Back to Africa', p. 205.
26 See Shaw, *The Kingdom of God*, p. 190.
27 Isichei, *History of Christianity in Africa*, p. 135.
28 See Hastings, *African Christianity*, p. 26.
29 See the discussion in Bediako's chapter, 'Translatability and the Cultural Incarnations of the Faith' in *Christianity in Africa*, pp. 109–25.
30 For more on missions and education see Baur, *2000 Years*, pp. 271–5; Sundkler and Steed, *History of the Church*, pp. 636–58; Shaw, *The Kingdom of God*, pp. 222–4.
31 Ogbu U.Kalu, 'African Christianity: An Overview' in Kalu (ed.), *African Christianity*, p. 36.
32 Shaw, *Kingdom of God*, pp. 208–10.
33 David Bosch, *Transforming Mission: Paradigm Shifts in the Theology of Mission*, Maryknoll: Orbis, 1999, p. 307.
34 The novels of African authors such as Ngugi wa Thiong'o and Chinua Achebe carry a great deal of this cultural criticism. See the book by J. Mugambi, *Critiques of Christianity in African Literature*, Nairobi: East African Educational Publishers Ltd, 1992.
35 See Sundkler and Steed, *History of the Church*, pp. 244–6; and Baur, *2000 Years*, pp. 121–2.
36 As quoted in Hastings, *African Christianity*, p. 23.
37 Hastings, *African Christianity*, p. 30.
38 Hastings, *African Christianity*, p. 39.
39 There are a number of books on this subject. For recent discussions of the topic see Graham Duncan and Ogbu U. Kalu, '*Bakuzufu*: Revival Movements and Indigenous Appropriation in African Christianity' in Kalu (ed.), *African Christianity*, pp. 278–308; and Afe Adogame and Lizo Jafta, 'Zionists, Aladura and Roho: African Instituted Churches', in Kalu (ed.), *African Christianity*, pp. 309–29.
40 See de Gruchy and de Gruchy, *The Church Struggle*.
41 Shaw, *The Kingdom of God*, p. 235.
42 Shaw, *The Kingdom of God*, p. 174.
43 See Sundkler and Steed, *History of the Church*, pp. 863–5; Isichei, *History of Christianity*, pp. 241–3; Shaw, *Kingdom of God*, p. 250.
44 Aylward Shorter and Joseph N. Njiru, *New Religious Movements in Africa*, Nairobi: Paulines Publications Africa, 2001, pp. 36, 38.
45 Kwabena Asamoah-Gyadu, '"Born of Water and the Spirit": Pentecostal/charismatic Christianity in Africa' in Kalu (ed.), *African Christianity*, p. 388.
46 For an overview of the work of the AACC to 1992 see Efiong Utuk, *Visions of Authenticity: The Assemblies of the All Africa Conference of Churches 1963 – 1993*, Nairobi: AACC, 1997.
47 Jesse Mugambi, 'Introduction' in J.N.K. Mugambi and Laurenti Magesa, *The Church in African Christianity: Innovative Essays in Ecclesiology*, Nairobi: Initiatives Publishers, 1990, p. 2.
48 See Paul Gifford, *African Christianity: Its Public Role*, London: Hurst and Company, 1998; Jesse Mugambi, *From Liberation to Reconstruction: African Christian Theology After the Cold War*, Nairobi: East African Educational Publishers, 1995.
49 For an example of the theological and ecclesiological responses to the HIV/AIDS pandemic see the various essays in the twin issues of the *Journal of Theology for Southern Africa*, Vol. 125 of July 2006 and Vol. 126 of November 2006.
50 Musimbi R.A. Kanyoro, 'Beads and Strands: Threading More Beads in the Story of the Circle' in Isabel Phiri and Sarojin Nadar (eds), *African Women, Religion, and Health*, Maryknoll: Orbis, 2006, pp. 19–41.
51 Isabel Phiri, 'African Women of Faith Speak Out in an HIV/AIDS Era' in Isabel Phiri, Beverley Haddad and Madipoane Masenya (eds), *African Women, HIV/AIDS and Faith Communities*, Pietermaritzburg: Cluster Publications, 2003, pp. 1–20.

Further reading

Kwame Bediako, *Christianity in Africa: The Renewal of a Non-Western Religion*, Edinburgh: Edinburgh University Press, 1995.

Paul Gifford, *African Christianity: Its Public Role*, London: Hurst and Company, 1998.

Adrian Hastings, *African Christianity: An Essay in Interpretation*, London: Geoffrey Chapman, 1976.

Elizabeth Isichei, *A History of Christianity in Africa from Antiquity to the Present*, London: SPCK, 1995.

Ogbu U Kalu (ed.), *African Christianity: An African Story*, Pretoria: Department of Church History, 2005.

John S. Mbiti, *African Religions and Philosophy*, New York: Praeger, 1969.

J.N.K. Mugambi, and Laurenti Magesa, *The Church in African Christianity: Innovative Essays in Ecclesiology*, Nairobi: Initiatives Publishers, 1990.

Bengt Sundkler, and Christopher Steed, *A History of the Church in Africa*, Cambridge: Cambridge University Press, 2000.

Efiong Utuk, *Visions of Authenticity: The Assemblies of the All Africa Conference of Churches 1963 – 1993*, Nairobi: AACC, 1997.

D.W. Waruta (ed.), *African Church in the 21st Century: Challenges and Promises*. Nairobi: AACC, 1995.

17

THE CHURCH IN A LATIN AMERICAN PERSPECTIVE

David Tombs

The church and its distinctive features

The historical position of the Roman Catholic Church[1] in Latin American societies is vividly symbolized by the central *plaza* (public square) of countless towns and cities designed on the classic Spanish or Portuguese template. An imposing building for the civil or political authorities stands on one side of the square. This is the town hall or city hall, or in the capital city it might be the Presidential Palace itself. On an adjacent side of the *plaza*, an equally imposing church building stands as an immediate neighbour. A church, a cathedral, or the National Cathedral, matches the government building with an ecclesial counterpart to the state or civil authority.

The close proximity of the Catholic Church to state power, attested by this shared presence on town and city *plazas* throughout Latin America, has been deeply influential on the development of both church and society since Christianity first arrived in the 'New World'. Sadly, for most of this time the Catholic Church's historical record has been deeply ambivalent. For much of its history the Catholic Church has been a bastion of social conservatism and support for the *status quo*. Throughout the colonial period (from the sixteenth century to the early nineteenth century), despite some honourable individual exceptions, the Catholic Church seemed largely indifferent to – or even acquiescent in – the cruellest and most exploitative social injustices. At other times, and especially in the last third of the twentieth century, the Catholic Church has been a leading voice – and sometimes virtually the only voice – raised in protest against violence and in defence of the oppressed.

The legacies of these past eras remain with the church today as it faces up to the new challenges of the twenty-first century. If they are taken seriously they will require a significant ecclesiological shift within both the Catholic Church and society as a whole. During the twentieth century the spread of industrialization and urbanization created new social and cultural challenges for the church. Secularism started to challenge the traditional religious authority of the church from one side, whilst a vibrant Pentecostalism started to compete with it from another.

Since the Catholic Church has played such a significant role in Latin American history, it is the main focus of this chapter, and rather less attention will be given to the so-called 'historical' Protestant churches that arrived in the nineteenth century, or to the rapidly growing Pentecostal churches of the twentieth century. However, there is little doubt that addressing the relationships between these three traditions and the church will be one of the biggest challenges that each of them faces in the twenty-first century. Latin American societies are likely to become increasingly pluralist and globalized as the century progresses. To work effectively in this new environment, the Catholic Church, the Pentecostal churches and the small 'historical' Protestant churches (including Anglicans/Episcopalians, Presbyterians, Congregationalists, Lutherans, Methodists, Baptists, Quakers and Mennonites) will need to develop better collegial and ecumenical relations if they are contribute to Latin America's rapidly changing societies.

So far, relations between the churches have generally been marked by suspicion and competition rather than respect and co-operation. There is a danger that the churches will fail to embrace the future and remain stuck in the patterns of the past. Hence, the ecumenical challenge of better relations between the churches, and the shared social challenge of helping to build new and better societies, are the two big issues that will need to shape ecclesiological thinking in the years to come. The history of the church in Latin America suggests that this will be a significant challenge for all concerned.

Major ecclesial events and developments

The Catholic Church

The conquest

The European 'discovery' of the New World in 1492, and the waves of conquest which soon followed, were driven by a mix of political and economic interests that were linked to explicitly religious convictions and justifications. This tension between Christian piety and the lust for wealth was never resolved. The Christian *conquistadores* that followed Columbus had no concern for the well-being of the local people. Obsessed by greed for gold, the Spaniards forced the native population of Arawak and Carib 'Indians' to labour in the mines and the fields. The population of Hispaniola (modern-day Haiti and the Dominican Republic) was halved in just two years. Estimates of the deaths during that period range from 125,000 to 500,000 people.

In 1519 Hernán Cortés set out from Cuba with about 600 men to conquer the Aztec kingdom of Mexico and inaugurate Spanish colonialism and Catholic faith on the mainland.[2] In contrast to the Caribbean islands where the inhabitants had basic subsistence economies, in Mexico the Spanish took over a sophisticated, wealthy and organized society with a developed religious system. They took control of a huge empire from which they could extract considerable riches. The amazing success of Cortés' adventure fuelled the drive of other *conquistadores* to explore and conquer similar prizes. From Mexico, Pedro de Alvarado launched the conquest of Guatemala and El Salvador (1524–34). Francisco Pizarro repeated Cortés' amazing achievement with the conquest of the Inca kingdom of Peru (1532–3).[3] From Cuzco the Spanish consolidated control over the central areas of the Inca kingdom (modern-day Peru and Bolivia) and moved out to strike at the north (modern Ecuador) and south areas (Chile). Within forty years of their first incursions on the mainland, the Spanish controlled a vast empire.

Although the pope and the Spanish crown saw the evangelization of the native population as a religious duty, it was for most part wishful thinking. Bitter experience taught the local people to avoid the Spanish wherever possible, making evangelization very difficult.

The legal framework for the work of the church was codified in 1508 by the *Patronato*

Real of Pope Julius II. This granted authority to the Spanish crown to appoint the bishops and other church personnel for its recently established settlements. In exchange the crown would pay all the church's expenses. Under this arrangement twenty Dominicans arrived in Cuzco in 1538 with the new bishop Vicente de Valverde, a Dominican who had accompanied Pizarro on the original conquest, and systematic organization of the church began with the First Provincial Council of Lima (1551–2).

Brazil, which had been colonized separately by the Portuguese, developed a similar arrangement. In 1500 Pedro Alvares Cabral had tried to lead a Portuguese expedition to India around Africa. He was badly off course, and then blown even further away from his proposed direction by a storm. Eventually he landed on undiscovered territory that under a treaty designed to demarcate Spanish and Portuguese claims to new lands designated this area to Portugal. It became known as Brazil. Although the land was claimed for Portugal as 'the land of the true cross' on 26 April 1500, the first group of settlers did not arrive until the 1530s. A similar *Padroado Real* was granted to the Portuguese monarchs temporarily in 1515 and confirmed permanently in 1551, when the diocese of Bahía was created.

Throughout the colonial period the Catholic Church and the political authorities worked in close alliance and their interests were usually the same. The system of royal patronage in Latin America brought great benefits to both the monarchy and the institutional church, but it severely limited the church's potential to oppose the state's power. It meant that Rome would not have direct contact with the Latin American church but would have to go through the mediation of the Spanish and Portuguese monarchs. Latin American church historian Enrique Dussel describes this arrangement as a unique form of 'colonial or dependent Christendom'. It was 'Christendom' inasmuch as the political and ecclesial powers were closely integrated, just as they were in the Roman and Byzantine empires. However, it was 'colonial' or 'dependent' because Latin American Christendom was always at the periphery and dependent on royal power.[4]

In colonial Christendom the Catholic Church and Spanish monarchy made an alliance of temporal and spiritual power for the glory of God and the Spanish crown. It was a political arrangement in which the church and state worked hand in hand for the governance of a Christian kingdom. The church had a position of unmatched institutional privilege and was a powerful landholder, second only to the crown in the colonial period. It benefited from Indian labour as well as a system of tithes and gifts. Some of the wealth it acquired went into adorning the magnificent churches and other buildings that it sponsored for elaborate worship services.

Above all, the position of the church rested on an official spiritual monopoly throughout Latin America, enforced by the Inquisition. Protestantism and other indigenous or African spiritualities were outlawed and their followers were liable to flogging or imprisonment. In return bishops and priests preached a conservative theology that emphasized respect for the state, the crown and all earthly authorities. Few in the church were moved to confront the suffering that the early *conquistadores* and later colonial settlers inflicted on the indigenous peoples. The problems of the poor were not seen as problems for the church. Although church teaching praised acts of charity that offered some relief for the poor, the wider structures of social injustice were never questioned. The church's predominant social teaching to those who suffered exploitation was an acceptance of hardship. Although there were some important exceptions, the church did little to protest or challenge the social conditions that created the misery.[5] The social virtues preached were obedience, endurance and patience.

Salvation was an otherworldly reward promised to those who meekly bore a life of trials and tribulations.

At a charitable level it supported education and medical facilities (albeit very unevenly) and was the main source of charity for the poor. Priests were often relatively poor but bishops could be fantastically wealthy and most enjoyed the full trappings of wealth and power. These attractions – combined with its traditional theology and Euro-centric confidence in the truth of its message – usually meant that the church as an institution was a willing collaborator in colonialist assertions of power.

From the centres of Spanish settlement itinerant missionaries went out to celebrate Catholic rites in the Indian settlements. However, efforts to 'evangelize' the indigenous peoples met with mixed success. Often the rites of Catholicism did not displace the Indian's traditional religious cultures but were added to them. The results were new forms of religious beliefs and behaviour. This folk religion defies easy classification to this day. The new amalgam of faith often showed a markedly Catholic appearance (with Latin rituals and the veneration of Christian saints) but the underlying religious outlook was often more complicated.

The apparition of the Virgin of Guadalupe at Mount Tepeyac, to the north-west of Mexico City, in 1531 is a good illustration of the cultural complexity and hybridity involved in evangelization. It is widely believed that Mary appeared to Juan Diego, a poor Indian, and told him to tell the local bishop that a church was to be built for her. The bishop dismissed Juan Diego's story and ignored his message until a miracle forced him to concede the authority of what the poor parishioner said. The appearance of the Virgin on Latin American soil, speaking the language of the colonized rather than the colonizer, addressing Juan Diego as son and taking the side of the peasant against the bishop, has been an icon of popular religion in Latin America ever since. The poor of Latin America have understood this appearance of Our Lady of Guadalupe as a sign of Mary's adoption of the native peoples and her solidarity with the oppressed. Devotion to the Virgin also facilitated the spread of the church through the integration of Catholicism with the worship of indigenous mothergoddesses. Mount Tepeyac, where the events occurred, was previously a place of pilgrimage to the indigenous mother-goddess Tonantzin-Cihuacóatl.

The nineteenth century and independence

Independence came to much of Spanish Latin America in the early nineteenth century. However, despite the rhetoric of the independence movement, and its appeal to liberal values, independence meant very little for the majority of the population. The colonial elite (the *peninsulares* – i.e. Spaniards who had been born back on the Iberian peninsular) were replaced with *creoles* but beyond this the political and economic structures were hardly changed. In many Latin American countries the almost feudal agricultural patterns inherited from the time of conquest remained. Societies remained sharply divided between a wealthy elite and an impoverished majority and labour practices were in many ways as coercive and brutal as slavery.

During the independence movements the church hierarchy sided with Spain. The crown had appointed all the bishops under the *patronato* and the vast majority were *peninsulares*. Their opposition to independence was firmly backed by the Vatican. Both Pius VII in *Etsi longissimo* (30 January 1816) and Leo XII in *Etsi iam diu* (28 September 1823) condemned the independence movement. In many countries, the clergy, who were usually *creoles* (who were born in Latin America to Spanish parents), were split on independence and tended to reflect whatever happened to be the prevailing sentiment. In areas such as Peru that were generally opposed to independence, the clergy also opposed it – especially clergy from religious orders who tended to be mainly *peninsulares*. Yet in Mexico and Central America some of the most prominent leaders of independence were clergy and independence found wider clerical support. In Mexico Father Miguel Hidalgo led the early independence movement until he was executed in 1810. In Central America Father Delgado was one of the first to call for Central America's independence, and along with thirteen other priests he put his name to Central America's declaration of independence in 1811.

The independence struggles took a heavy toll on the church. A substantial amount of church property was requisitioned and a significant number of priests who supported independence were killed. The wars left many missions in ruins and the credibility of bishops and clergy who had opposed independence was dramatically weakened. Furthermore, many bishops chose to return to Spain, leaving a gap in the leadership which was not filled for decades in some areas.

After independence most of the new republics initially recognized Catholicism as the state religion, but they abolished the Inquisition and granted some level of freedom for worship. The new republics were eager to claim for themselves the rights of the *patronato* to name the replacements of bishops, but Spain pressured the Vatican not to co-operate with such appointments. As a result many of the empty dioceses were left unfilled until Pope Gregory XVI (1831–46) finally gave formal recognition to independence and restored official relations. By then, however, it was hard for the church to recover its previous position.

As the century progressed, new political elites emerged under the banner of liberalism. They were sympathetic to European rationalism and as a result were inclined to anti-clericalism. Separation of church and state gathered speed as more liberal republics passed new constitutions. Colombia in 1849 was followed by Argentina in 1853 and then other countries during the 1850s. The church had difficulty coming to terms with the new situation. It remained dominated by the Christendom mentality of the bygone era in which it had taken a colonial 'option for power'. To maintain its institutional privileges it allied itself closely to conservative parties who rivalled the liberal parties for power. Not surprisingly, the fortunes of the institutional church rose when the conservatives were in power but often came under attack when liberals were in control. Even when it was favoured, the church's institutional fate made little difference to the Latin American poor during this period. The church's priority was more to protect the church's institutional interests than to present a prophetic voice on the suffering of the disadvantaged. Although the old Christendom model had broken down, it continued to remain the ideal to which the vast majority within the church clung and hoped to see restored. This failure of imagination prevented the church from finding a better way forward to confront the future. As liberalism gradually gained the ascendancy, the church's attachment to the Christendom model meant its position got weaker and weaker.

The twentieth century

By the early decades of the twentieth century the Catholic Church was the overwhelmingly dominant religious institution in Latin America, but it was no longer the force that it had been in previous centuries. For many in the new urbanized working class it seemed irrelevant to their daily lives. The church needed a new basis on which to engage with society. During the 1930s theological developments in Europe started to show how this might happen. The Lateran Treaty of 1929 signalled the Vatican's reluctant acceptance of the passing of old Christendom. Like the Wall Street crash the same year, it marked the transition from one era to another.

Slowly the church in Latin America started to find a new role for itself in society by making a move from a colonial 'Christendom' relationship to the political authorities to a 'Neo-Christendom' model in which it would seek to influence but no longer expect to control. It started to encourage Catholic laity to become more active in society, to take forward Catholic social teaching through Catholic Action and similar initiatives that strengthened its social role.

During the twentieth century, Latin American bishops formed themselves into national conferences and then into a unified body – the Conference of the Latin American Episcopate or CELAM (*Consejo Episcopal Latinoamericano* in Spanish or *Conselho Episcopal Latinoamericano* in Portuguese). The first joint meeting of this body – known as 'CELAM I' – was in Rio de Janeiro, 24 July to 4 August 1955. The primary challenge discussed at the meeting was evangelization. The central question was how to present Christian faith in an increasingly secular culture and it included attention to the competition from 'Protestant sects'. The outlook was still largely traditional, inward looking and defensive. There was little discussion of the church's wider social mission or positive engagement with social issues. However, things were starting to change and the Second Vatican Council (1962–5) had a particular impact in Latin America. The last third of the century was marked by an extraordinary experiment in church renewal that became known worldwide as Latin American liberation theology (see below).

The Protestant churches

During the colonial period Protestantism was a proscribed faith in Latin America. Protestants visiting Spanish and Portuguese areas were treated as heretics.[6] It was not until the nineteenth century, when Britain displaced Spain as the dominant economic power in Latin America, that this changed. Under pressure from the British, the new republics gradually passed legislation granting freedom for Protestantism. Private worship was protected and in the second half of the century Protestant churches sprang up in the ports and major trading areas. However, they mainly served expatriate British residents, and attracted very few local converts. Liberal parties were more likely to favour the work of Protestant missionaries and bible societies than Conservative parties, since they shared the sense of individualism, education and progress that were associated with Protestantism.[7] However, the impact of the Protestant missions was very limited and concentrated in areas associated with older forms of industrialization like the railways and mines. Statistics for 1903 suggest that the Protestant population of Latin America was only about 120,000.[8] This was a testimony to the difficulties they had in moving beyond the cultural constraints of their European or North American identities in the nineteenth century. Whilst there was a greater willingness to engage with the Latin American context in the twentieth century, the historical Protestant churches did not develop a truly popular appeal.[9] To this day the 'historical' Protestant denominations remain very small minorities. They still tend to be more urban than rural and appeal to a largely middle-class and better educated following who are sympathetic to more modern and liberal values.

311

By contrast, Pentecostalism, which arrived in the 1920s, has grown to an extraordinary degree since the 1960s. This has been a major shift that is transforming the religious demography of Latin America.

> During the past forty years, overall membership in Protestant churches has doubled in Panama, Venezuela, Paraguay, and Chile, tripled in the Dominican Republic, Nicaragua, and Argentina, quadrupled in Puerto Rico and Brazil, quintupled in El Salvador, Costa Rica, Peru, and Bolivia, and sextupled in Honduras, Colombia, and Ecuador. Approximately one-third of Guatemalans are now Protestant. Given current growth rates, Brazil may likely have a Protestant majority by 2030.[10]

Given the great number of different Pentecostal denominations and the different shape they take in different countries, it is dangerous to generalize on their character and it would be wrong to suggest that they all follow the same template. For example, some of these Pentecostal churches are highly influenced by North American models (which is where Pentecostalism first began in the early decades of the twentieth century) and some are actually dependent on US missions. However, the majority are more genuinely home-grown and independent and have proved much more adaptable to local culture than the historical Protestant churches.[11]

Despite the dangers of treating all Pentecostal churches as a homogeneous block, they usually share some important common features. They are typified by lively and participatory worship, a literalist biblical interpretation, a traditionalist theology of individual salvation, a strong sense of personal relationship with Christ, close ties with other members of the church, an emphasis on personal holiness and morality. Leadership is more a matter of a sense of calling and the congregation's acceptance of its authority than a matter of book study and training. At the more charismatic end of the spectrum there is an emphasis on speaking in tongues, healing and prophecy.

Many of the churches value their independence and guard it carefully. Ecumenical collaboration is viewed with suspicion and relationships with other churches are rarely better than polite and often marked by mutual distrust. The institutional dynamism and vitality of the Pentecostal churches is helped by the relative speed by which new churches can be created and new leadership can emerge. Although each congregation is in many ways its own self-sufficient unit, they also link together to form bigger organizations and networks. Even the potential disadvantage that comes with this organizational structure, its vulnerability to dissension and fracture during conflicts, has often proved to be a strength for Pentecostalism. Frequently disagreements in the churches lead to new churches being formed by dissident members and the further spread of Pentecostalism as a result.

There is little doubt that the Pentecostal churches meet an important need for many in Latin America. In a rapidly changing world they offer the security and certainty of absolute answers, an emotionally engaging spirituality, and a close-knit community of fellow pilgrims. On the social and political side the usual tendency is to stress spiritual matters in sharp contrast to the affairs of the world. There is a great emphasis on individual salvation and the need for evangelization. In fact, Pentecostals in Latin America are more likely to be known by the term 'evangelical' than Pentecostal. However, the world is something to be saved from rather than something to save. Participation in social and political affairs has traditionally been viewed with suspicion as potentially endangering to personal morality.

As the number of evangelicals increases, and they become a bigger proportion of the electorate, this reticence will start to change and they will take on a more active political role. Discovering the most helpful way to engage with wider society is therefore likely to be as much a challenge for the Pentecostal churches as for Catholicism.

Key ecclesiological ideas and thinkers

For most of its history the church in Latin America has shown little inclination to major innovation or the development of a consciously distinctive ecclesiology. The Catholic Church has taken its lead from Europe and the historical Protestant churches have been equally cautious. It is quite possible that in the century to come it will be the Pentecostal churches that offer the most distinctive ecclesiological ideas and thinkers but as yet this promise remains unfulfilled. This section looks at three innovative exceptions to this generally conservative history: the Dominican protests in the early sixteenth century; the Jesuit Mission experiments in the eighteenth century; and the liberation theology movement in the twentieth century. In each case they were founded on a social vision that drew the church into conflict with the political powers of the day. They raised distinctive ecclesiological questions on the social role of the church in Latin America that still remain unresolved. Furthermore, liberation theology had a significant ecumenical dimension that pointed to how closer collaboration on social issues might also help the churches in Latin America to address their own ecclesial relationships more constructively.

Sixteenth-century Dominican protests

In 1510 a Dominican mission had arrived in Hispaniola to join the Franciscans. The following year, 21 December 1511, the Dominican friar António Montesinos voiced the first recorded Christian protest against the oppression of the Indians. Preaching on Matthew 3.3 ('I am a voice crying in the wilderness') he berated the Spaniards for their cruelty and tyranny. He described their behaviour as a mortal sin and refused to absolve them for it. He argued that the exploitation of the Indians was incompatible with Christian duty and prevented any hope of evangelism.

Although very much in the minority, Montesinos was not entirely alone in his defence of the Indians. Three years after Montesinos' dramatic sermon, Bartolomé de Las Casas joined the Dominican order and made probably the most famous defence of the Indians.[12] By this time the situation in Hispaniola was especially dire. In his *History of the Indies* (*c*. 1540) Las Casas claimed that 90 per cent of the inhabitants were wiped out in the eight years that followed Isabel's decree of 1503. By 1515 there were probably no more than 10,000 native inhabitants left, and by 1540 they had been almost completely wiped out.

Las Casas was born in Seville in 1484 and witnessed Columbus's return from his first voyage to the Caribbean in April 1493. His father and two uncles sailed with Columbus on the second voyage and in 1502 Las Casas himself arrived in Hispaniola. He spent the next four years as a colonist. During this time, he trained for the priesthood whilst living on the labour of the Indians. In 1506 he travelled to Rome and the following year he was ordained as a diocesan priest. He then returned to the Caribbean in 1509 and began his life as a priest.

When the Dominicans first came to Hispaniola in 1510 under Pedro de Córdoba, Las Casas seems to have been unmoved by their criticism of the treatment of the Indians. However, as the Indian population collapsed from disease, overwork and cruelty, Las Casas became increasingly troubled. He had watched the genocide in Hispaniola and was distressed to see it repeated with such zeal in Cuba. In 1514, as he prepared his sermon for Pentecost, the words of Ecclesiasticus 34.18–22 struck him with full force. The judgement on those who make sacrifices and other religious rituals before God, and yet oppress their fellow human beings, spoke directly to his feelings about the ill-treatment of the Indians. He set free his Indian workers and from then on he sought to challenge the laws that governed the treatment of Indians throughout the new lands.

Las Casas sent his protests back to Spain and at the end of 1515 he went back to present his protest in person at the Spanish court. Unfortunately King Ferdinand died a short time later. Las Casas then saw Bishop Juan Rodríguez de Fonseca but found him unmoved by his concerns. When the Bishop's secretary tried to bribe him to drop his protests it was clear that he could expect little help from him. However, shortly afterwards a further change in fortune led to the official appointment of Las Casas as 'Protector of the Indies'. He returned to the Indies to continue his work and developed an elaborate settlement plan which he hoped would offer peaceful co-existence between Indians and Spaniards. In 1520 Charles V granted him land in Venezuela where he could try it out. He attempted to set up the settlement in 1521 but the outcome was disastrous because he was unable to stop slave raids by other colonists.

In 1522 he joined the Dominicans in order to advocate the Indian cause more effectively. He started a new Dominican monastery on the north of Hispaniola and started his great work *History of the Indies* to counterbalance the accounts recorded by conquistadors. His arguments that evangelization should only be carried out peacefully influenced Pope Paul III, who issued a papal Bull in 1537 that affirmed the rationality of the Indians and the importance of their evangelization. These were important affirmations in a time when apologists for conquest denied both.

The same year Las Casas started work as a missionary in northern Guatemala. He returned to Spain in 1540 to recruit further missionaries and stayed for a while to impress on the king the mistreatment of the Indians. For this purpose, he wrote the graphic *Short Account of the Destruction of the Indies* (c. 1540), a fierce attack on the suffering caused by the Spanish.[13] The passage of the New Laws (1542–3), which strengthened some of the Laws of Burgos, was partially in response to these efforts. In 1543 Las Casas was named bishop of Chiapas, where he worked diligently to improve the lot of Indians in his area until he returned permanently to Spain in 1547.

Back in Spain he wrote his *Defence of the Indians* in preparation for a debate in Valladolid with theologians from Salamanca including Juan Ginés de Sepúlveda (1550–1).[14] A critical element in this dispute was whether the Indians had souls or not. Their human identity – and therefore their shared human nature with the Spaniards – was seen to rest on the answer to this question. This, in turn, was seen as critical for whether it was legitimate for the Spanish to rule over them without their consent. The opponents of Las Casas argued that the Indians did not have souls, were therefore not fully human and might justifiably be compelled to serve the Spanish for their own good. Las Casas argued that they were equal in nature and the Spanish could only legitimately rule over them if they consented. The pope agreed with Las Casas; it was an important victory. Although it did not bring an end to colonialism or the suffering of the Indians, it did at least affirm the principle of universal human solidarity. Tragically, however, at one point Las Casas' concern for the Indians had led him briefly to ignore this principle and support the importation of slaves from Africa to replace Indians in their hard labours on *encomiendas*. This had been legal since 1501 and Las Casas and many of his contemporaries signed a petition to support it in 1516. However, it is clear that Las Casas came bitterly to regret this decision and he became one of the first to denounce the slave trade.

Las Casas died in 1566. He was the first colonist to distinguish between being Spanish and being Christian. The church and the state had merged this identity for their own reasons but Las Casas emphasized that Christianity should not be identified with the colonial culture or its burden of oppression.

Seventeenth- and eighteenth-century Jesuit missions

The Jesuit order was founded in 1540 and arrived in Bahía (Brazil) just nine years later, led by the Society's first Captain-General to serve in Latin America. They had been sent from Lisbon to start an official government for the country but friction with the first bishop of Brazil quickly forced them to travel south to the captaincy of São Vicente, where they helped to establish a new colony at São Paulo in 1554. Their work in Spanish America began in the following decade, with missions in Mexico and Paraguay starting in 1568. In many places (including Mexico, Paraguay and Brazil) the Jesuits gathered the Indians into special mission settlements, known as *reducciones*. The *reducciones* were intended to facilitate the evangelization and 'civilization' of the Indians. By the end of the seventeenth century there were at least thirty major reductions amongst the Guarani Indians (on the Paraguay and Paraná rivers) with a total population of more than 100,000. Unfortunately the settlements were vulnerable to Portuguese raiders from Brazil who were in search of Indian slaves. These raids increased markedly in the seventeenth century when the Dutch seized control of Angola (1641–9) and cut off the supply of African slaves. The Jesuits vigorously resisted these raids. After open warfare in 1641 they even armed the Indians for self-protection.

Enslavement of the Indians was a longstanding cause of conflict between the Jesuits and colonists in Brazil. Enslavement of Indians had been outlawed in Spanish America but was practised in Brazil despite vigorous opposition from the Jesuits. In 1570 the Portuguese king decreed that Indians were not to be enslaved unless they were cannibals. Unfortunately this was repealed under pressure from the colonists in 1574. In 1655 the Jesuits of the Amazon region persuaded the king to issue a new decree that outlawed the enslavement of Indians but it proved hard to enforce and led to new conflict with settlers, who expelled the Jesuits by force from the Amazon in 1661 and 1684.

The ethos of the *reducciones* was extremely paternalistic. They reflected the same arrogant confidence of Europeans that had marked relations with the local people since Columbus. The Jesuits, like all other settlers, took for granted that they should naturally be in a position of authority over the Indians and that their own civilization was superior. The settlements provided some level of protection from immediate dangers but over the long-term they deprived the Indians of opportunities to organize and govern themselves. This left the Indians more vulnerable than ever when they were finally abolished. However, despite their limitations the *reducciones* were a genuine attempt by the Jesuits to care for what they saw as their charges and to replace evangelization through threat and force with a more positive ethos that treated the Indians as real people. Their commitment to the work was to cost them dear. In 1750 a treaty assigned these areas to Brazil but the Jesuit missions refused to accept Portuguese authority. Jesuit relations with the powerful Portuguese first minister, the Marquis Pombal, were extremely difficult and open conflict broke out in 1754–6. The Jesuits, as a missionary order in contrast to the secular clergy, were more independent of the local bishops and therefore harder to control under the terms of the Portuguese *Padroado Real*. They were willing and able to appeal directly to the pope when they felt obliged to do so and this independence increased the crown's suspicion and hostility towards them. In the Amazonian region, the Jesuits of Para resisted the state's attempts to press Indians into labour service for the proposed plantations during the 1750s. In 1759 Pombal had the order expelled from all Portuguese territories. In 1767 Charles III banned them from Spain and all its territories and ordered the confiscation of their property. This was a serious blow to the Jesuit order, and also a huge loss for the Latin American church, but the institutional legacy of the work on the *reducciones* did not entirely disappear within the order. The Jesuits returned to Latin America in the twentieth century and it was no coincidence that many Jesuits were at the forefront of a further bold experiment within the church in the last third of the century, the liberation theology movement.

Twentieth-century liberation theology

At the end of Vatican II the Council of Latin American Bishops (CELAM) decided to hold a major meeting in 1968 at Medellín (Colombia) to discuss the implications of Vatican II for their continent. The meeting, known as CELAM II, was the single most important church event for the development of liberation theology.[15] Whilst it is important not to over-estimate the numerical strength of liberation theology within the church, since there were many in the church who actively resisted it, simply ignored it or just had little contact with it, it was nonetheless a major event in the history of the church in Latin America. It remains one of the great gifts that the church in Latin America has given to the global church.

Liberation theology originated in the revolutionary atmosphere of the late 1960s. It was 'born' through the work of progressive clergy and religious orders and 'named' in the writings of radical theologians like the Peruvian priest Gustavo Gutiérrez. It was 'baptized' by the bishops in 1968 at the second General Meeting of CELAM (the Latin American Bishops Conference) at Medellín and spread throughout Latin America during the 1970s and 1980s. Whilst it was always controversial and never universally supported – indeed in many places it was bitterly opposed – it is nonetheless by far the most regionally distinctive and influential ecclesiological model to have originated in Latin America, and arguably it was the most important church movement anywhere during the twentieth century.

Liberation theology continued to develop and deepen during the 1970s and reached maturity in 1980s. It entered a period of crisis during the 1990s but its legacies continue to be of importance. It is unlikely to regain its force within the church, or its coherence as a unified social movement in Latin American societies, but its achievements during very difficult times in many Latin American societies were truly inspirational for people both inside and outside the church.[16]

'Liberation theology' was a perfect name to represent the new course that progressive theologians and clergy tried to set for the church in the late 1960s. The language of liberation brought urgency to the church's involvement in social and political issues in countries disfigured by social division and economic exploitation.[17] However, since it was the *terminology* of liberation that was the major problem in the 1990s, it is important to be clear that liberation theologians never saw their work as just promoting the terminology of liberation. On the contrary, they stressed that liberation theology involved a whole new approach to theology. In his classic *A Theology of Liberation* the Peruvian priest Gustavo Gutiérrez, who is often referred to as the 'father' of Latin American liberation theology, described this new approach as 'critical reflection on historical praxis'.[18] This pushed theology's centre of gravity away form the internal world of the church out into the lives of the poor. The sufferings and struggles that were their daily experience became the starting point for theological reflections. For clergy and theologians who were willing to make this shift, this led to a transformation in pastoral practice and ultimately a new way of being the church.

The 1970s were difficult years in Latin America. Repression increased in countries already under military regimes (especially noticeable in Brazil after 1968, El Salvador after 1969 and Peru after 1975), and military coups in Bolivia, Chile and Uruguay (1973), and later in Argentina (1976), increased their numbers further. By 1978 only Colombia, Venezuela and Guyana in South America were free from military dictatorship. In Central America the military were in control in Honduras and El Salvador and the Somoza dictatorship held sway in Nicaragua.[19]

There were many who paid a high price for their solidarity with the poor. Liberation theologians came to a new understanding of persecution and martyrdom, which in turn strengthened their sense of their solidarity with the oppressed as a divine calling. In fact, for many liberation theologians the great surprise of the 1970s was that their experiences prompted a second transformation in their theology and their understanding of the church. Some speak of the unexpected 'conversion' of the church at this time.

Thus in 1980 Gutiérrez looked back on the changes liberation theology had undergone in the 1970s and noted the transformative influence of the poor on the church:

> After Vatican II and the stimulus of the Medellín Conference, we creatively reappropriated the gospel expression about evangelizing or 'preaching the good news to the poor'. Reinforced by an option for the oppressed and a commitment of solidarity with them, a series of rich and promising initiatives took place all over Latin America . . . Then came the irruption of the poor. At a terrible price the common people began to become the active protagonists of history. This fact gave us deeper insight into the whole matter of evangelization. Working in the midst of the poor, exploited people, whom we were supposedly going to evangelize, we came to realize that we were being evangelized by them.[20]

The Basque theologian Jon Sobrino SJ, who has spent his working life in El Salvador, described how the new contact and appreciation of the poor contributed to the shift within liberation theology in the 1970s:

> The important thing about the decade of the 1970s, then, was our rediscovery of the real life of the impoverished majorities, together with our evangelical rediscovery that it is to them that the good news of the gospel is addressed. In this perspective, the poor become the locus, the place, of the Christian life . . .[21]

The lives of the poor became not just an ethical priority for social work but also a historical *locus* where God was revealed in a special way. Sobrino expressed this clearly when he said 'This means that the poor are the authentic *theological source* for understanding Christian truth and practice.'[22] The epistemological commitment to the poor meant that Latin American liberation theologians like Gutiérrez and Sobrino judged their priorities and procedures in terms of their relevance to the poor and took the experiences of the poor as the starting point for their theological work.

As a result, during the 1980s liberation theology reached a new level of sophistication and maturity and many of the most thought-provoking works of liberation theology were written. Their approach during the 1970s had favoured more theoretical social and political analysis, and early works had drawn on Marxist analysis and dependency theory. By contrast, the theological reflections of the 1980s were guided much more by personal experience and took a more grassroots perspective on social issues. One result of this was that during the decade liberation theologians developed their thinking on less overtly political topics. Some of the best writing focused on spirituality and the meaning of faith in the face of injustice and adversity.

Furthermore, the understanding of oppression was also widened to recognize injustices created by race, culture and gender as well as class. Liberation theology also took on a more consciously global and ecumenical outlook at this time, encouraged by constructive discussions organized by the Ecumenical Alliance of Third World Theologians, which brought together Catholic and Protestant theologians from Latin America, Africa and Asia as well as black theologians from the United States. Each of these contextually rooted theologies helped liberation theology to address new areas and expand its vision of the challenges facing the church. This was particularly significant in relation to the experiences of women. Laywomen and women in religious orders had played a key role in liberation theology from its earliest times but in the early years they had not had a strong public profile. In the 1980s there was greater recognition of their importance and they were more likely to speak at conferences and have their work published. Just as Protestant male theologians had been particularly influential in the first years of liberation theology, women theologians like the Methodist biblical scholar Elsa Tamez made a similarly significant contribution to this phase of liberation theology.[23]

Nonetheless by the end of the decade liberation theology was facing serious problems. As the military regimes were gradually replaced and democracy returned, the earlier certainties became more complicated. The poor were still poor – and often even poorer than they had ever been – but the terminology of liberation and its political and economic analysis was less straightforward in neo-liberal and globalized economies. In addition local hostility from conservative bishops and centralized opposition in the Vatican put key liberation theologians like Gustavo Gutiérrez and the Brazilian Leonardo Boff under considerable pressure. Liberation theology was still a powerful theological influence in Latin America, and in progressive theological circles around the world, but as a social movement its ability to provide leadership in responding to the forces that were transforming Latin America had been severely weakened.

Liberation theology's strengths and weaknesses were illustrated in an ambitious project to systematize its contribution to theology. The *Theology and Liberation Series* was planned in the mid-1980s as a comprehensive statement on doctrinal areas in a 50-volume work that involved a number of the best-known liberation theologians. However, the project never realized its ambitious hopes and it was eventually suspended in 1993 with only twelve volumes published. The difficulties with the *Theology and Liberation Series* were a clear indication that despite the maturity of its theological writing, the liberation theology movement at the turn of the decade was entering a difficult phase.

With the fall of the Berlin Wall in November 1989 critics of liberation theology were quick to herald the demise of the movement amidst the triumph of global capitalism. Whilst much of the criticism missed the real point of liberation theology it was clear that the movement had reached something of a crisis. As the first generation of liberation theologians step into the background there are few signs of a new generation revitalizing and sustaining the liberation theology movement in its original form. However, even if liberation theology does not recover from the crisis as a movement, it would be misleading to think that it has no legacy.

Whilst liberation theology always had important limitations – and these certainly became more apparent in the 1990s – the same is true for any theological attempt to engage with social issues on the historical plane. Liberation theology's terminology may now seem dated in the neo-liberal world economy, its social analysis has often been too limited, and postmodernism raises questions about its underlying philosophical foundations. However, the same criticisms could be made of many other theologies. Liberation theology's difficulties in reading the signs of the current times and presenting a prophetic response do not belong to liberation theology alone. The terminology of 'liberation' (which was once a key strength) now makes liberation theology vulnerable to superficial and dismissive judgements. If the strong emphasis on liberation is no longer the helpful language that it once was – and others have co-opted it anyway – then the 'theology of liberation' may no longer serve the role it once did; but something else will need to take up its mantle. As Gustavo Gutiérrez has said, 'I was a Christian long before liberation theology and I will be a Christian long after liberation theology.'[24] New terminology may be needed to do justice to the complexity of the social realities of the present and future. Whether the new language will supplement the language of liberation or largely replace it remains to be seen. However, in an unjust world that remains far from the promise of the kingdom of God, much of liberation theology's legacy will continue to be relevant for a politically engaged Christian faith.

Distinctive ecclesial practices

One of the most significant aspects of liberation theology for the church in Latin America was the development of base communities as a distinctive ecclesial practice. The 'base ecclesial communities' (commonly referred to by their acronym in Spanish and Portuguese as 'CEBs') developed into impressive national movements in many countries, and especially in Nicaragua, Chile, Peru, El Salvador and most of all Brazil.[25] For many progressives the CEBs pointed towards a grassroots regeneration of the church in Latin America.[26] The Brazilian brothers, Clodovis and Leonardo Boff, are the theologians most associated with articulating the theological significance of the CEBs.[27] Leonardo Boff goes so far as to describe them as a new 'ecclesiogensis', in which the church is born from the poor, and regrettably this contributed to the controversy with the Vatican in the 1980s that eventually forced him to leave his order.[28]

The CEBs had their origins in a number of church initiatives in the 1950s and early 60s, prompted in part by a scarcity of clergy. However, it was not until CELAM II (Medellín, 1968) gave them institutional support that they started to take on their distinctive shape and role. During the 1970s they spread throughout Latin America and many became more politicized and radicalized through their relationship with liberation theology.

The communities played an important role in the dissemination of liberation theology amongst ordinary people and many base communities members were transformed into social activists through contact with the liberation theology they experienced in the CEBs. The communities showed that they were able to take over and live out the church's option for them with enthusiasm and dignity. The poor were active subjects who took the option forward in new ways. As noted above, an unexpected feature of the contact between liberation theologians and the communities was that liberation theology itself was transformed in the process.

The communities were not just a medium for the teachings of liberation theology 'down' to the base, but also a medium for ideas to flow 'up' from the base. This was developed in bible reading circles that valued the contribution of all participants in a mutual search for new understanding. The bible readings in base communities showed how the poor could bring their personal experiences to the Bible and offer theological insights that professional exegetes might miss.[29] A classic example of this is the record of the Solentiname community presented in the work of Ernesto Cardenal.[30] Contact with the communities encouraged theologians like Cardenal to develop their awareness not just as 'teachers' but also as 'students' with much to learn from the painful wisdom of the poor.

The new political context of the 1970s made this all the more important. The first phase of liberation theology had been set in the 'atmosphere of liberation' of the late-1960s. The second phase was marked by repression and persecution in the 1970s. The rise of authoritarian regimes throughout the region and escalating conflict between church and state provided a context of persecution and martyrdom. The church committed itself to the poor at a time when their suffering was most acute and it was particularly dangerous to challenge the powers of the militarized state.

The CEBs were known as 'base' level or 'basic' communities because they were smaller sub-divisions of the parish. A large or particularly active parish might be divided into many such communities. Many CEBs were in poor rural areas or in the working-class and shantytown areas surrounding larger cities. In these areas CEB members were likely to work with their hands as poorly paid labourers. Many were near the 'base' of the social pyramid and some were only marginally literate. However, even in poor neighbourhoods, the membership was unlikely to be composed of the most destitute. Most community members had sufficient means to get by most of the time; and enough stability in life to attend meetings on a fairly regular basis. The dispossessed homeless or entirely disenfranchised poor were less well-represented than the working poor. Furthermore, the CEBs often included more financially secure members as well – teachers or white-collar municipal workers who might provide lay leadership for the group.

As 'ecclesial', the groups were part of the official pastoral work of the church. The strength of commitment to the groups varied from parish to parish, diocese to diocese and country to country, but they were especially influential in Brazil and Central America. In 1975 crucial impetus to the term 'base ecclesial communities' was given by Paul VI's Apostolic Exhortation *Evangelii Nuntiandi* ('Proclaiming the Gospel') after the 1974 Synod of Bishops. Not only did *Evangelii Nuntiandi* use the term 'basic ecclesial communities' but it distinguished between communities which were critical of the institutional church (which it referred to simply as 'basic communities') and those which were supportive (which it described as 'basic ecclesial communities'). Thus the term CEB – Base *Ecclesial* Community – reflected official church approval.

Official support for the CEBs in Brazil was also reflected in the Brazilian Bishops' biennial plans of 1975–7 and 1977–9, which placed the CEBs among the top four pastoral priorities. This meant practical support for the communities in terms of resources and expertise. In most of Latin America it was usual for progressive bishops to promote CEBs and conservative bishops to resist them. However, Brazil was unusual for the shared consensus between conservatives and progressives that the church should promote base communities.

Support for base communities as a way of strengthening the church's presence in society was common in both the progressive and conservative wings of the Brazilian church. However, there was a marked difference on the social and political dimension to the activity of CEBs from diocese to diocese. For progressives, the orientation to social transformation was an integral part of the CEBs. For conservative critics, this 'politicization' was a serious deviation from the original purpose of the communities.

As a 'community' the people might meet once a week in small groups (anything from six to over a hundred people) to reflect on the Bible in the light of their local situation and their own lives. The active involvement of the laity was central to the CEBs. CEBs usually had someone who acted as a facilitator or 'animator' but this did not need to be a priest. The ideal type of facilitator was someone who could provoke discussion and dialogue rather than instruct. Progressive nuns and/or the local priest were often crucial in the establishment of a community but as the community developed it was likely to become increasingly dependent on lay leadership and often lay catechists took the role of facilitator. In practice, their effectiveness in this depended on their personalities, skills and commitment to the participatory ideal. It would be naïve to believe that every CEB lived up to these high ideals in every situation, but equally it would be unduly cynical not to recognize the dramatic change towards more equal relationships created within many of the communities.

In the process of sharing experiences a deeper awareness of common problems and their relation to wider causes often emerged. This process owed much to the pedagogical approach to consciousness-raising or 'conscientization' piloted in Brazil in the early 1960s by Paulo Freire.[31] After discussing a problem and diagnosing its roots the community could reflect on how they might solve it using their own means and initiatives. Community level solutions could range from pooling resources into a small credit fund for members, working together to build a shared centre, organizing a petition for traffic controls to protect pedestrians, or any manner of local community action.

Even at their high point in the 1980s the CEBs were never more than a significant movement within the Latin American church. They did not lead to a comprehensive recreation of the whole church. Nonetheless, they developed from fairly modest early origins to assume an important position in many countries. Had the CEBs not developed their remarkably constructive and mutually supportive relationship with liberation theology their ecclesial significance would have been much less dramatic. However, because the CEBs provided an outlet for liberation theology, and at the same time reshaped and reoriented the direction of liberation theology, they were much more important than they might have been at a different time of history. The CEBs meant that liberation theology became distinctive in terms of *who* did theology. The common split between the academic theologian and the people was rejected; instead the theologian was challenged to forge an organic solidarity with the people. Thus, after the mid-1970s liberation theology would often take place at at least three different levels: the professional, the pastoral and the popular. At each level there was a different emphasis in the theological forms, even though each level was interdependent on the others. In a classic image, Leonardo and Clodovis Boff refer to the different parts of a tree to explain the different parts of this single process:

> Liberation theology could be compared to a tree. Those who see only professional theologians at work in it see only the branches of the tree. They fail to see the trunk which is the thinking of priests and other pastoral ministers, let alone the roots beneath the soil that hold the whole tree – trunk and branches – in place.

The roots are the practical living and thinking – though submerged and anonymous – going on in tens of thousands of base communities living out their faith and thinking it in a liberating key.[32]

With the crisis in liberation theology the CEBs have also been on the decline, although impressive examples continue to flourish in some parts of Latin America. Given their achievements in the past, this is a pity. Rather than turning the clock back on the CEBs it would be better to see how a new approach to the CEBs might play a constructive role in the future. Despite their limitations the CEBs have much to offer if some of the problems associated with them can be overcome. In particular, the CEBs – and the church more widely – would benefit from better relationships with the Pentecostal churches, and a more respectful view of the achievements of Pentecostal churches in meeting people's needs. There is some truth to the observation that although liberation theology opted for the poor, the poor opted for Pentecostalism. Both progressives and traditionalists within Catholicism have criticized the Pentecostal churches but for rather different reasons. The progressives focused their criticism on the depoliticized gospel of heavenly salvation; whilst the traditionalists saw Pentecostals as a challenge to the institutional role of Catholicism. In either case, the tendency was to stereotype and dismiss the entire movement rather than recognize its diversity. There was little attempt to reflect on the factors that made the Protestant churches so organizationally effective, or consider why it was so attractive to converts in Latin America's new political and economic context.

This difficult relationship can only be improved if new ways can be found for the churches to work together in Latin America for the service of wider society. This is likely to remain the most important ecclesiological challenge that all the churches will face in the years ahead.

Notes

1 Henceforth 'Catholic Church'.
2 For a highly readable narrative account, see Hugh Thomas, *The Conquest of Mexico*, London: Pimlico, 1994 (1973). An interesting collection of sources giving the perspective from the indigenous peoples is offered in M. León-Portilla (ed.), *The Broken Spears: The Aztec Account of the Conquest*, trans. L. Kemp: Beacon: Boston Press, rev. edn. 1992 (1961).
3 A vivid account is offered by John Hemming, *The Conquest of the Incas*, London: Macmillan, 1970.
4 Enrique Dussel, *History and the Theology of Liberation*, trans. J. Drury; Maryknoll, NY: Orbis Books, 1976 (Spanish orig. 1973), pp. 75–109 (esp. 75).
5 For some important exceptions to this general tendency, see the section below on Bartolomé de Las Casas and the Jesuit *reducciones*.
6 The situation was different in much of the Caribbean, and also on the mainland in present day Surinam, Guyana and Guiana, which were Dutch, British and French colonies rather than part of Latin America.
7 For this reason some commentators use the term liberal Protestant churches rather than historical Protestant churches. In both cases it distinguishes them from the more evangelical Pentecostal churches.
8 José Míguez Bonino, *Faces of Latin American Protestantism*, Grand Rapids, MI: Eerdmans, 1997, p. 5.
9 Important developments in the early part of the century included a continental congress of Protestant churches in Panama in February 1916 and a subsequent congress in Havana in 1929.
10 Lee M. Penyak and Walter J. Perry (eds), *Religion in Latin America: A Documentary History*, Maryknoll, NY: Orbis, 2006, p. 214.
11 On the Pentecostal churches, see especially David Stoll, *Is Latin America Turning Protestant? The*

Politics of Evangelical Growth, Berkeley, CA: University of California Press, 1990; David Martin, *Tongues of Fire: The Explosion of Protestantism in Latin America*, Oxford: Basil Blackwell, 1990; David Stoll and Virginia Garrard-Burnett, *Rethinking Protestantism in Latin America*, Pennsylvania: Temple University Press, 1993; John Burdick, *Looking for God in Brazil: The Progressive Catholic Church in Urban Brazil's Religious Arena*, Berkeley, CA: University of California Press, 1993; Philip Berryman, *Religion in the Megacity: Catholic and Protestant Portraits from Latin America*, Maryknoll, NY: Orbis Books, 1996; Manuel A, Vásquez, *The Brazilian Popular Church and the Crisis of Modernity*, Cambridge: Cambridge University Press, 1998.

12 On Las Casas and his significance for liberation theology, see especially Gustavo Gutiérrez, *Las Casas: In Search of the Poor of Jesus Christ*, Maryknoll, NY: Orbis Books, 1993 (Spanish orig. 1992). For an account of Las Casas' life through his own writings at different points in his life, see G. Sanderlin (ed.), *Witness: Writings of Bartolomé de Las Casas*, Maryknoll, NY: Orbis Books, 2nd edn, 1992 (1971).

13 Bartolomé de Las Casas, *A Short Account of the Destruction of the Indies*, trans. N. Griffin; Harmondsworth: Penguin Books, 1992 (Spanish orig. 1542).

14 Bartolomé de Las Casas, *In Defence of the Indians*, DeKalb, IL: Northern Illinois Press, 2nd edn, 1992 (ET 1974, Spanish orig. c. 1549).

15 The origins of liberation theology as a cohesive social movement in the 1960s and its development in the 1970s have been superbly documented by Christian Smith, *The Emergence of Liberation Theology: Radical Religion and Social Movement Theory*, Chicago and London: University of Chicago Press, 1991. It should be stressed that although liberation theology was primarily a Catholic movement in Latin America, a few of its best-known earliest exponents were Protestant, including Ruben Alves in Brazil and José Míguez Bonino in Argentina. In addition many of the principles behind liberation theology had a significant impact on progressive Protestant pastoral workers and development agencies, and filtered down into Protestant churches.

16 See also Chapter 23 of this volume on 'Liberation Ecclesiology'.

17 At the same time, but entirely independently, James Cone was developing an equally prophetic black theology of liberation to address race and racism in the USA; see especially James H. Cone, *Black Theology and Black Power*, New York: Seabury, 1969; and *A Black Theology of Liberation*, Philadelphia: Lipincott, 1970.

18 Gustavo Gutiérrez, *A Theology of Liberation: History, Politics and Salvation*, trans. and ed. C. Inda and J. Eagleson; Maryknoll, NY: Orbis Books, 1973 (Spanish orig. 1971), p. 15.

19 See Penny Lernoux, *Cry of the People: The Struggle for Human Rights in Latin America – the Catholic Church in Conflict with US Policy*, New York: Penguin Books, rev. edn, 1982 (1980).

20 Gustavo Gutiérrez, 'The Irruption of the Poor in Latin America and the Christian Communities of the Common People' in S. Torres and J. Eagleson (eds), *The Challenge of Basic Christian Communities*, EATWOT International Ecumenical Congress of Theology, São Paulo, Brazil, 20 February – 2 March, 1980; Maryknoll, NY: Orbis Books, 1981, pp. 107–23 (120).

21 Jon Sobrino, *Spirituality of Liberation: Towards a Political Holiness*, trans. Robert R. Barr; Maryknoll, NY: Orbis Books, 1988 (Spanish orig. 1985), p. 3.

22 Jon Sobrino, *The True Church and the Poor*, trans. Matthew O'Connell; Maryknoll, NY: Orbis Books, p. 93.

23 See the writings of women theologians she edited as Elsa Tamez, *Through Her Eyes: Women's Theology from Latin America*, Maryknoll, NY: Orbis Books, 1989 (Spanish orig. 1986).

24 Robert McAfee Brown, *Gustavo Gutiérrez: An Introduction to Liberation Theology*, Maryknoll, NY: Orbis Books, 1990, p. 22.

25 The Portuguese *Comunidades Eclesiais de Base* and the Spanish *Comunidades Eclesiales de Base* are both commonly abbreviated to CEBs and translated in English as 'Base Church Communities' or 'Basic Christian Communities'. However, the communities are sometimes referred to as *Comunidades Cristãs de Base* (Portuguese) or *Comunidades Cristianas de Base* (Spanish), which is more literally translated as Base Christian Communities.

26 See Scott Mainwaring and Alexander Wilde (eds), *The Progressive Church in Latin America*, Notre Dame, IN: University of Notre Dame Press, 1989. It should also be noted that Base Communities also existed outside Latin America and were especially developed in the Philippines.

27 Clodovis Boff, *Theology and Praxis: Epistemological Foundations*, trans. R.R. Barr; Maryknoll, NY: Orbis Books, 1987 (Portuguese orig. 1977); Leonardo Boff, *Ecclesiogenesis: The Base Communities*

Reinvent the Church, trans. R.R. Barr; Maryknoll, NY: Orbis Books, 1986 (Portuguese orig. 1977); Leonardo Boff, *Church: Charism and Power: Liberation Theology and the Institutional Church*, trans. J. Diercksmeier; New York: Crossroad, 1985 (Portuguese orig. 1981).

28 See Harvey Cox, *The Silencing of Leonardo Boff*, Oak Park: Meyer Stone, 1988.
29 See especially Carlos Mesters, *Defenseless Flower: A New Reading of the Bible*, Maryknoll, NY: Orbis Books, 1989 (Portuguese orig, 1983). On the issues raised in such an approach, see Christopher Rowland and Mark Corner, *Liberating Exegesis: The Challenge of Liberation Theology to Biblical Studies*, London: SPCK, 1990.
30 See Ernesto Cardenal, *The Gospel in Solentiname*, trans. D.D. Walsh, 4 vols; Maryknoll, NY: Orbis Books, 1976–82.
31 See especially Paul Freire, *Pedagogy of the Oppressed*, trans. M. Ramos; New York: Continuum, 1970.
32 Leonardo Boff and Clodovis Boff, *Introducing Liberation Theology*, trans. P. Burns; Maryknoll, NY: Orbis Books, p. 12.

Further reading

María Pilar Aquino, *Our Cry for Life: Feminist Theology from Latin America*, trans. D. Livingstone; Maryknoll, NY: Orbis Books, 1993.

Phillip Berryman, *Religion in the Megacity: Catholic and Protestant Portraits from Latin America*, Maryknoll, NY: Orbis Books, 1996.

Leonardo Boff, *Ecclesiogenesis: The Base Communities Reinvent the Church*, trans. Robert R. Barr; Maryknoll, NY: Orbis Books, 1986 (Portuguese orig. 1977).

——, *Church: Charism and Power: Liberation Theology and the Institutional Church*, trans. John Diercksmeier; New York: Crossroad, 1985 (Portuguese orig. 1981).

Leonardo Boff and Clodovis Boff, *Introducing Liberation Theology*, trans. Paul Burns; Maryknoll, NY: Orbis Books, 1987 (Portuguese orig. 1986).

José Míguez Bonino, *Doing Theology in a Revolutionary Situation*, Philadelphia: Fortress Press, 1975. UK edn, *Revolutionary Theology Comes of Age*, London: SPCK, 1975.

——, *Faces of Latin American Protestantism*, Grand Rapids, MI: Eerdmans, 1997 (Spanish orig. 1995).

Edward L. Cleary, *Crisis and Change: The Church in Latin America Today*, Maryknoll, NY: Orbis Books, 1985.

Edward L. Cleary and Hannah W. Stewart-Gambino (eds), *Conflict and Competition: the Latin American Church in a Changing Environment*, Boulder, CO: Lynne Rienner, 1992.

——, *Power, Politics and Pentecostals in Latin America*, Boulder, CO: Westview Press, 1997.

Enrique Dussel, *A History of the Church in Latin America: Colonialism to Liberation (1492–1979)*, trans. and rev. A. Neely; Grand Rapids, MI: Eerdmans, 1981 (Spanish orig. 1964).

—— (ed.), *The Church in Latin America: 1492–1992*, Maryknoll, NY: Orbis Books, 1987.

Ignacio Ellacuría and Jon Sobrino (eds), *Mysterium Liberationis: Fundamental Concepts of Liberation Theology*, Maryknoll, NY: Orbis Books, 1993 (Spanish orig. 1990).

Virginia Garrard-Burnett and David Stoll (eds), *Rethinking Protestantism in Latin America*, Philadelphia: Temple University, 1993.

H. Goodpasture McKennie (ed.), *Cross and Sword: An Eyewitness History of Christianity in Latin America*, Maryknoll, NY: Orbis Books, 1989.

Gustavo Gutiérrez, *A Theology of Liberation: History, Politics and Salvation*, trans. and ed. Caridad Inda and John Eagleson; Maryknoll, NY: Orbis Books, 1973.

——, *Las Casas: In Search of the Poor of Jesus Christ*, trans. Robert R. Barr; Maryknoll, NY: Orbis Books, 1993 (Spanish orig. 1992).

Alfred. T. Hennelly (ed.), *Liberation Theology: A Documentary History*, Maryknoll, NY: Orbis Books, 1990.

Penny Lernoux, *Cry of the People: The Struggle for Human Rights in Latin America – the Catholic Church in Conflict with US Policy*, New York: Penguin Books, rev. edn, 1982 (1980).

David Martin, *Tongues of Fire: The Explosion of Protestantism in Latin America*, Oxford: Basil Blackwell, 1990.

Lee M. Penyak and Walter J. Perry (eds), *Religion in Latin America: A Documentary History*, Maryknoll, NY: Orbis, 2006.

Jon Sobrino, *The True Church and the Poor,* trans. Matthew O'Connell; Maryknoll, NY: Orbis Books 1984 (Spanish orig. 1981).

Elsa Tamez, *Through Her Eyes: Women's Theology from Latin America*, Maryknoll, NY: Orbis Books, 1989 (Spanish orig. 1986).

David Tombs, *Latin American Liberation Theology*, Religion in the Americas Series Vol. 1; Boston and Leiden: Brill, 2002.

Sergio Torres and John Eagleson (eds), *The Challenge of Basic Christian Communities*, EATWOT International Ecumenical Congress of Theology, São Paulo, Brazil, 20 February – 2 March, 1980; Maryknoll, NY: Orbis Books, 1981.

Manuel A. Vásquez, *The Brazilian Popular Church and the Crisis of Modernity*, Cambridge: University of Cambridge Press, 1998.

18

THE CHURCH IN A
NORTH-AMERICAN
PERSPECTIVE

Gregory Baum

Is it possible to write an article on the church in the North American perspective? It is well-known that the churches in the United States are manifold. The mainline churches[1] endorse what Americans call liberal values, and conservative Protestant churches, Pentecostal congregations and religious sects are suspicious of secular culture and fear that liberal values undermine faith in divine revelation. Yet despite this variety, past and present, there are social scientists who find common features in these churches and even employ the category of 'American religion'.[2] Because religion flourishes in the United States – the only western industrial society in which this is the case – sociologists have taken a special interest in American religion. Having studied and taught the sociology of culture and religion, I have become convinced that ecclesiology must enter into dialogue with sociology to become aware of the impact of church structures on culture and consciousness. Church structures do not remain external to believers; they are internalized by them, affect their perception of the religious reality and thus influence their theological self-understanding. Since ideas do not float above history but are in constant interaction with the social conditions of the people whom think them, I have argued that theology in general ought to be in dialogue with sociology.[3]

One sociological approach renders an account of the multiple divisions among the American churches in terms of class difference and the conflict between the disadvantaged and the elites. This approach was taken in Richard Niebuhr's *The Social Sources of Denominationalism*, published in 1929.[4] Following this perspective, the history of religion in America can also be interpreted as a series of challenges to Protestant cultural dominance offered by Catholics, Jews and followers of other religions. I have sympathy for analyses of this kind and readily acknowledge that religion and even spirituality participate in one way or another in the social conflicts produced by the unequal distribution of wealth and power. Yet the analysis of church developments in terms of social conflicts is unable to explain the extraordinary success of religion in the American Republic, a development at odds with the secularizaition initiated by industrialization in European societies.

The sociological approach that seems appropriate for this chapter focuses on the organization of the American churches. This approach recognizes that the self-definition of the American churches as 'denominations' has far-reaching religious and social consequences and may well be the principal reason why religion – all religions – thrive in the United States. Being social institutions, the churches define their self-understanding mainly by their practice and their relationship to the society in which they are situated. Even theological statements that articulate their ecclesiology must be interpreted in relation to their collective behaviour.

The major section of this article deals with the self-understanding of the churches in the United States of America. A briefer second section deals with the history of the churches in Canada, which is different from the American experience and internally differentiated between Quebec and English Canada. Like the countries of Western Europe, Canadian society has been subject to increasing secularization.

Churches in the United States of America

The American Revolution produced a profound change in the organization and the self-understanding of the Christian churches in the United States. Prior to the Revolution, the British colonies related themselves to the churches in different way. In some colonies Puritanism defined the public religion, in some the Anglican Church was the establishment, in some Congregationalism predominated, and in some religious pluralism had public recognition. During the vigorous revival movement of the eighteenth century known as the Great Awakening, Christians of the different colonies became acquainted with one another, discovered a spiritual bond that united them and experienced a new national awareness that was to become a significant cultural factor preparing the American Revolution.

The great majority of Christians supported the Revolution in 1776 and willingly embraced the radical separation of church and state introduced by the Constitution of 1780. According to Article 6, 'No religious test shall ever be required as a qualification to any office or public trust under the United States' and according to the provision of the First Amendment, 'Congress shall make no law respecting an establishment of religion, or prohibiting the free exercise thereof.'[5]

This radical break with the European tradition pleased the political leaders guided by Enlightenment ideas; it also pleased the great number of Christians who wished to organize their churches without reliance on the government. The new law demanded the restructuring of their ecclesiastical life. For the Anglican Church in particular, having been established in some of the colonies, the new historical situation called for a rethinking of its identity and the reorganization of its community. The church held its first General Convention in 1785, now calling itself the Protestant Episcopal Church of the United States.[6] Even the Roman Catholic Church was affected by the new democratic and egalitarian culture. While suffering from prejudice in many parts, it had a respected position in the colony of Maryland. Honouring the will of the Catholic priests not to have a foreigner as superior, the Vatican, persuaded by Benjamin Franklin, appointed John Carroll, an American, as their bishop.[7] Carroll believed in the compatibility of republicanism and Roman Catholicism; he respected the other Christian churches, created a constitution for his own diocese and assigned certain powers to the laity. We shall see further on that his ecclesiastical project was eventually suppressed.

The denominations

The American Revolution inspired a totally new ecclesiastical experiment. The American churches set themselves up as voluntary, self-supporting communities; and while each believed that it was the faithful expression of Christ's foundation, each was nonetheless willing to recognize the plurality of churches. Even though the churches were independent of the government and received no public funding, they offered cultural support for the Republic, were proud of being American, and thus contributed to the creation of a national consciousness. The new self-organization of the churches called for a new vocabulary: they became 'denominations'.

Denominations were a radical innovation. In the Middle Ages, the church was an integral part of the European national cultures, creating rites, symbols and loyalties that united the entire continent. Alternative religious movements were condemned as heretical and remained culturally marginal. After the Reformation and the wars of religion, the Peace of Westphalia of 1648 decided that the religion of the prince was to define the religion of his subjects, which meant that if the prince was Catholic, Protestants had to become Catholic or leave his realm, and conversely, if the prince was Protestant, Catholics had to convert or emigrate. In Britain the situation was different. The established Anglican Church did not succeed in enforcing its monopoly: thanks to the ideas of Enlightenment philosophers and the pressure exerted by dissident Christian groups, the Act of Toleration of 1689 recognized the right of dissent from the established church, except for Unitarian and Roman Catholics. It can be said that the free churches in Britain anticipated the new American ecclesiastical arrangement, yet they were not denominations, they were merely tolerated by the crown and the established church.

On the basis of the European experience, sociologists have made a clear distinction between 'church' and 'sect'. According to Max Weber, churches are identified with the communities in which they are located and hence people are born into them, while sects are small groups made up by people who have chosen to become their members.[8] He thus distinguished between the culturally established church (*Volkskirche*) and the so-called gathered communities. Ernst Troeltsch developed this distinction by exploring its cultural implications.[9] Churches, he proposed, are willing to make compromises to fit themselves into their society: they honour the public culture, they respect the social hierarchy, they accept secular learning, they appreciate works of art, they support the wars of their country, they are willing to water down the radical message of the gospel. By contrast, sects refuse to fit themselves into society, they are unwilling to make compromises, they prefer to remain marginal, they are suspicious of the dominant culture, they stay away from secular learning and works of art, and they may even oppose the war of their country.

The distinction between 'church' and 'sect' is useful in the study of European religion, but it does not shed light on the self-organization of Christianity in the United States of America. Richard Niebuhr has argued that by their willingness to regard themselves as minorities situated in a religiously pluralistic society, the European 'churches' located in America ceased to be churches in sociological terms; similarly, the European 'sects' present in America, by supporting the Republic and cooperating with other Americans, ceased to be sects in sociological terms.[10] Churches and sects have become denominations. They want to be faithful to their confessional tradition; and yet, despite interdenominational tensions, they are willing to recognize the plural structure of Christianity. They want to be independent of the state and do without government funding, yet they are patriotic and share a sense of the special destiny of the American Republic. They are ready to cooperate with other groups, Christian or secular, to alleviate people's needs or support certain public policies. Admittedly some sects continue as sects in America: they lay claim to exclusive truth, keep apart from public culture and prefer isolation. Yet they are subject to social forces that gradually transform them into denominations.

From the beginning there were tensions between the denominations. After all, each of them believed that its faith and its polity were the authentic expression of the gospel. Important also were ideological differences. Since the creation of the United States had been guided by Enlightenment principles as well as the ideal of Christian freedom, some denominations were willing to integrate Enlightenment ideas into their theology while others rejected them as incompatible with biblical faith. This tension has pervaded American church history: it has manifested itself in every age in new forms. The church historian Martin Marty distinguished between liberal denominations in dialogue with science and secular society, assigning religion a public role, and conservative denominations cautious in regard to science and secular society, emphasizing personal conversion to Jesus Christ.[11] We shall see further on that this distinction may no longer hold true today. According to Marty, both tendencies have shown evangelical passion and produced ardent missionary movements to save the world, some by spreading reformist ideas in the name of faith, others by preaching the gospel to people on other continents who do not know Christ. Students of American religion detect a certain messianic dimension in both the liberal and the conservative currents.

Despite these tensions, the denominational system has remained intact. The denominations respect one another and, even when they disagree, refuse to excommunicate one another. Sociologists have greatly admired the new self-organization of the American churches and attributed to it the enormous success of religion in the United States. Alexis de Tocqueville, who visited the United States in the 1830s, was amazed to find people's attachment to their faith in a pluralistic arrangement unknown and unimaginable in Europe.[12] He explained this attachment by arguing that religion exercised an important social function in the United States. In Europe, he argued, religion symbolized the unity of a country, yet people's identity was more concretely defined by the attachment to their village, their town or their region. In America, a society where people easily move from one part to another, it was membership in a denomination that gave people an identity allowing them to feel at home in all parts of the country. When they moved from one city to another, they joined the local church of their own denomination and found an environment familiar to them. In a society that fosters the pursuit of material self-interest, Tocqueville continued, the churches are socially significant cultural forces that tame people's selfishness and teach them the love of neighbour and concern for the community. Tocqueville even argued that in democracies where cultural egalitarianism allows public opinion to exert enormous power, religion mediating the wisdom of an ancient tradition actually protects people's freedom to think for themselves. Tocqueville was surprised that even the Roman Catholic Church in America fitted itself into the denominational system and tried to give itself a democratic image.[13]

Max Weber, visiting the United States at the beginning of the twentieth century, was also amazed by people's active participation in their churches, even though the churches enjoyed no public recognition nor received any public funding. He confirmed Tocqueville's observation that the denominational system fulfilled an important social function. Weber told many stories of how significant church membership was even in the world of business. One example presents a Baptist businessman who, moving from one city to another, introduces himself to the minister of the Baptist church in his new place, documents that he had been a member in good standing of the Baptist church in his previous location, and then, with a recommendation from the new minister, presents himself to the local bank manager to get credit.[14]

Sociologists have been puzzled by the success of religion in America. Since industrialization led to the secularization of society in Western Europe, Max Weber, writing at the beginning of the twentieth century, was convinced that secularization was the inevitable consequence of techno-scientific modernity,[15] a position shared by many European sociologists.[16] When Peter Berger and Bryan Wilson, writing independently in the 1960s, tried to demonstrate the theory of secularization scientifically by using empirical data gathered in European societies, they were embarrassed by the counter evidence of the thriving religion in America. Yet instead of looking for a sociological explanation for this development, they claimed that American religion was so secularized or so sentimental that it did not count as counter evidence.[17] This was not a persuasive argument. What these authors should have admitted was that the American experience disproves the universal validity of the theory of secularization.

A few years later, the American sociologist Andrew Greeley, basing himself on his own extensive empirical research, demonstrated that Christian denominational religion continues to fulfil an important social function in the United States.[18] He argued that since American society is highly mobile, people are able to find in the denominations a sense of belonging. Denominations are like tribes distributed across the United States that offer people a local community, a familiar context and a concrete identity. Greeley argued, moreover, that since the American population tends to be preoccupied with short-range business and labour concerns, the denominations offer people transcendent meaning, allowing them to make sense of their lives. Since, in the daily 'rat race' of American life, people easily suffer exhaustion and wonder whether their effort is worthwhile, they find rescue and a sense of purpose in the faith mediated by their church. Greeley also recognized that since Americans make great financial sacrifices to support their churches and religious organizations, they become attached to them, and even when they cease to be strong believers, remain loyal to the institutions in which they have invested so much money. A hundred and fifty years after Tocqueville's visit to the United States, Andrew Greeley offers empirical evidence that the Tocquevillian analysis still holds true, that the American type of religious pluralism suits people's needs and aspirations, and that active involvement in their churches makes them into good Americans.

Ecclesiology

What was the ecclesiology of the American churches? Ecclesiology as systematic theological reflection on the church in the light of faith is a fairly recent development. Still, in an unsystematic way, the church fathers interpreted the Christian church as distinct from the pagan world in terms of the biblical images for God's redeemed community – such as God's people, the true Israel, the heavenly Jerusalem, the bride of the Lamb, the body of Christ and many others. In his influential *Catholicism*, written in the 1940s, Henri de Lubac recovered and made available to the modern reader the collective self-understanding of Christianity in the patristic age.[19] Thanks to God's unmerited election, the church, while marked by repeated infidelities, was graced to repent, to be forgiven and ever to remain God's chosen people. The church was here the visible manifestation of a transhistorical reality. In times of discrimination and persecution, when the church's future appeared uncertain, patristic ecclesiology offered a source of hope for the believing community. Despite the evidence, the church had a promised place in history.

In the Middle Ages, reflection on the church tended to be apologetic. Clerical scholars wanted to demonstrate the legal foundation of the Catholic Church based on scriptural texts, historical events and imperial declaration. After the Reformation, ecclesiology remained apologetic: both Catholics and Protestants tried to reply to the question *ubi ecclesia*. Catholics argued that the true church had four marks – one, universal, holy and apostolic – marks that were found in the Roman Catholic Church and no other; while Protestants argued that the true church is found where the gospel is preached in its purity and where only two sacraments – baptism and the last supper – are celebrated. Wrestling for its place in post-Reformation Europe, the Roman Catholic Church defined itself increasingly in institutional terms and claimed to possess the full jurisdictional powers to take charge of its entire collective existence – the church as *societas perfecta*. Impatient with this institutional self-understanding, a few nineteenth-century Catholic theologians, best known among them Johann Adam Möhler and John Henry Newman, retrieved the patristic ecclesiology and revived a more mystical understanding of the church. This started a current of thought in theology that assumed importance in the twentieth century and eventually influenced the ecclesiology of the Second Vatican Council (1962–5).

This brief survey allows me to make a suggestion pertaining to the sociology of knowledge. Ecclesiologies are produced by theologians in an effort to solve certain concrete pastoral problems. Patristic ecclesiology sustained people's hope in the church's future in difficult times. The ecclesiology of the Middle Ages and post-Reformation Europe defended the legitimacy of the ecclesiastical institution. The emerging ecclesiology sparked by the work of Möhler and Newman aimed at the *spiritual* renewal of the church's self-understanding.

What was the ecclesiology of the Protestant denominations in America? This was not a topic that preoccupied them. As Protestants they regarded the church as the community of believers. Each of the denominations tried to show that its authority was apostolic, i.e. in keeping with the witness of the New Testament. While the churches carried on arguments on a variety of theological and ethical issues, their ecclesiological disagreement had to do with the revealed foundation of ecclesiastical authority. They searched the New Testament to defend and legitimate their own ecclesiastical polity – congregationalist, presbyterian or episcopal.[20] Yet despite these disagreements, the churches respected one another. Why? Because implicit in the denominational structure was the recognition that, in addition to the divine dispensation granted to one's own church, there is a wider notion of church that embraces Christians belonging to other denominations. Some theologians thought that this wider church included all baptized believers in Christ, possibly with the exception of Roman Catholics, while others preferred the idea of the invisible church embracing the saved across the ages.

The faithful in all denominations sang Samuel John Stone's beautiful hymn, written in 1866, celebrating the high ecclesiology of the New Testament and the patristic age. 'The church's one foundation is Jesus Christ her Lord, she is the new creation by water and by word; from heaven he came and sought her to be his holy bride, with his own blood he bought her, and for her life he died.' Yet this high vision of the church did not make American Protestants uncomfortable with the plurality of the churches. The denominational structure of American Christianity does not generate a spiritual yearning for the Christian unity announced in scripture. Implicit in denominational religion is a certain relativism. One's own church, faithful to its divine foundation, is believed to be situated in a wider economy of salvation that touches all the churches.

This lack of commitment to the unity of Christ's holy church was severely criticized by

Richard Niebuhr in the above-mentioned book, *The Social Sources of Denominationalism*. Deeply disturbed by the tendency of the churches to break up and multiply, Niebuhr thought that the American denominational system was rooted in infidelity. He argued that large churches have broken up into smaller ones because their fidelity to the gospel was not strong enough to reconcile Christians across class lines and cultural boundaries. Ruptures occurred between wealthy and poor congregations, between the urban North and the more rural South, between white and black churches, and between the settled East and the frontier regions of the West. This was a severe theological indictment. A sociological explanation for this behaviour points to the denominational system that reconciles believers to Christian pluralism and makes them overlook the New Testament teaching on Christian unity.

A certain anguish about the disunity of Christians was produced in the twentieth century by the ecumenical movement. A sign of the times was Paul Minear's book, *Images of the Church in the New Testament*,[21] which examined the high doctrine of the church in the New Testament, expressed in images and symbols, revealing the theological anomaly of the denominational divisions. The high ecclesiology of the church fathers, influential in recent Roman Catholic teaching, has also been honoured by the ecumenical movement in the hope of urging the divided churches to strive for greater unity. Some American churches did in fact become united in single bodies. Yet the majority of American Christians prefer to think of Christian unity simply as mutual recognition of the churches and cooperation in pastoral and social projects.

Behaving like denominations

Since denominational religion is so well-suited to the aspirations and practices of American Christians, Roman Catholics – as previously mentioned – also wanted to see themselves as a denomination. In this process they were stopped by the papacy, and it was only after Vatican II that the Roman Catholic Church in America was allowed to behave as a denomination, faithful to its unique calling yet recognizing a wider economy of salvation. The same movement toward denominational religion takes place in sects, i.e. in religious movements at odds with the dominant Protestantism, that regard themselves as the sole bearer of truth. As an example I shall take the Seventh-Day Adventists. Let us consider both 'case studies'.

I mentioned earlier that the Roman Catholic Church was affected by the democratic and egalitarian culture produced by the American Revolution. The first American-born bishop, John Carroll, welcomed the separation of church and state, had respect for the Protestant churches and introduced democratic practices into his own diocese. Carroll wanted lay trustees to build churches and assume responsibility for the material needs of the parish, and even when several bodies of trustees refused to accept the bishop's authority, he did not reject the system introduced by him.[22] In subsequent years, many Catholics, including priests and bishops, welcomed the First Amendment of the American Constitution as an advantage for their church and argued that Catholicism should adapt itself to the democratic culture of America. The Americanization of Catholicism was challenged by bishops in the second part of the nineteenth century, who believed that the church's first task was to serve the immigrant communities that were then arriving in great numbers from various Catholic regions of Europe. The Americanists also included highly-placed bishops. They supported democracy and the separation of church and state and wanted Catholics to exercise their faith by becoming responsible citizens. Their position was at odds with the church's official teaching and provoked a lively controversy in Europe. In 1898 Pope Leo XIII issued the apostolic letter *Testem benevolentiae* that condemned 'Americanism' as an activist misunderstanding of Catholicism inspired by semi-Pelagian trust in people's natural powers. The leading personalities who had advocated the adaptation of Catholicism to American democratic culture thought that the apostolic letter had caricatured their pastoral programme. According to Gerald Fogarty, the condemnation of Americanism had two major effects. 'First, American Catholic support for the First Amendment fell under suspicion until Vatican Council II, and second, American Catholic intellectual life, only in its infancy, was stifled for more than a generation, especially when Modernism, which bore some similarities, was condemned by Pope Pius X in 1907.'[23]

Two changes introduced in Roman Catholic teaching by Vatican II allowed the Catholic Church in America to behave like a denomination: first, the defence of religious liberty and human rights in general; and second, the recognition that the Catholic Church, though calling itself the one true church, was part of a wider economy of salvation that included all Christian churches and, more remotely, the whole of humanity. Without compromising its own self-understanding, the American Catholic Church now behaves like a denomination, promoting mutual respect, honouring difference, cooperating with other denomination in civil endeavours, and praying with other churches for Christian unity.

The Seventh-Day Adventists started as a sectarian movement, ridiculed by the Protestant churches, based on the prophecies of William Miller that the cleansing of the sanctuary predicted in Daniel 8.14 would take place before October 22, 1844. Miller interpreted this cleansing as the purification of the world by fire, initiating the second coming of Christ. This movement was joined by Christians from several churches. After the Great Disappointment of 1844, some of Miller's followers, in particular Ellen White, re-interpreted the cleansing of the sanctuary as an event in heaven that blotted out the sins on earth. They decided to found the Seventh-Day Advent Church in accordance with their reading of the Bible. They thought of their movement as a Protestant church, yet because they trusted in Christ's heavenly work of cleansing the sins after 1844, expected the Lord's imminent return and replaced the Sunday observance by the Sabbath, the movement was repudiated by the Protestant churches. Seventh-Day Adventists saw themselves at odds with American culture, suspected secular learning, abstained not only from alcohol but also from tea and coffee, and tried to convert Christians of other churches to their beliefs.

It has been observed that Protestant sects which are successful among the uneducated urge their members to work hard, live frugally and save their money, a practice that eventually raises them on the social scale and produces a second generation of educated middle class people who now demand a college-trained clergy and an intelligent presentation of their faith. According to Bryan Wilson, the genius of Protestant sects has been to give confidence to people belonging to a subservient class, teach them discipline and perseverance, and enable them to improve their social standing.[24] This social dynamics was operative among the Seventh-Day Adventists. They have become a successful church in America, supporting schools and colleges and having a wide international outreach. If we turn to their self-presentation on the internet, we learn how they now interpret the world and understand their place within it.

In 1995, their General Conference released the following statement:

> Seventh-day Adventists support the United Nations proclamation of 1995 as the
> *Year of Tolerance*. This proclamation comes as an opportunity when intolerance is

abounding on all continents – bigoted religious extremism, racism, tribalism, ethnic cleansing, linguistic enmity, and other forms of terrorism and violence. Christians carry their share of the blame for prejudice and inhumanity toward humans.[25]

The General Conference of 1997 made a statement on how Seventh-Day Adventists view Roman Catholicism:

Seventh-day Adventists regard all men and women as equal in the sight of God. We reject bigotry against any person, regardless of race, nationality, or religious creed. Further, we gladly acknowledge that sincere Christians may be found in other denominations, including Roman Catholicism, and we work in concert with all agencies and bodies that seek to relieve human suffering and to uplift Christ before the world. Seventh-day Adventists seek to take a positive approach to other faiths. Our primary task is to preach the gospel of Jesus Christ in the context of Christ's soon return, not to point out flaws in other denominations.[26]

The Seventh-Day Adventists have become a denomination. They are faithful to the unique divine call addressed to them through scripture and their tradition, and at the same time acknowledge the plurality of the Christian churches. They believe that their church has a truth that is all its own, but they also recognize an economy of salvation that touches believers in other churches and possibly even other religions. They now practise the ecclesiology implicit in the denominational system.

It can even be demonstrated that the denominational structure of American Christianity has made possible the social integration and institutional normalization of the Jews – and later of Muslims and the followers of other religions – who had arrived as immigrants. Since these religious communities are internally pluralistic, their self-organizations fit perfectly into the denominational pattern of American religion. While these religious communities include a small minority of sectarian groups – just as American Christianity does – the great majority of their members are affected by the denominational structure in which they find religious freedom, prompting them to advocate mutual respect, honour the differences, cooperate in the service of the common good, and silently acknowledge a wider economy of divine favour. It deserves to be mentioned that the mainline churches respect the non-Christian immigrants, make no effort to convert them to Christianity and defend their religious values against popular misconceptions, even if the churches have not formulated an ecclesiology that sanctions their practice. I am not suggesting that there exists in America no prejudice against non-Christians, no anti-Semitism or no Islamophobia (especially after September 11, 2001), yet when I compare the situation of religious minorities in Western Europe and the United States, I am impressed by the American experience: the rapid social integration of religious communities in institutional structures characteristic of American society.

Saving the world

The self-understanding of the Christian churches in America includes a certain messianic dimension. Robert Handy has shown in his history of the American churches that the missionary zeal characteristic of evangelicalism has affected all movements in American

Christianity: all felt called 'to save the world'.[27] In his *Righteous Empire*, Martin Marty recognizes the influence of evangelicalism on all American churches: 'I use Evangelical = Protestant virtually interchangeably most of the time.'[28] He means by this that most Protestant churches have a strong sense of mission: they believe that God is acting in them and through them to perform great things in human history.

Where does this messianism come from? The American Revolution, as the first successful self-determination of a people as an egalitarian and democratic society, generated the conviction among Americans that that their republic was God's own country, located at the vanguard of human history, appointed to be the model for all peoples subject to princes or subjugated as colonies. Americans came to believe that written into their history was the destiny – the manifest destiny – to exercise political power over the whole of the Americas and become the light and the liberator of all nations. The churches caught a whiff of this messianic spirit.

The article 'The Civil Religion of America',[29] written in 1966 by the sociologist Robert Bellah, produced a lively controversy in the United States. Bellah argued that examining the foundational documents of the American Republic, the ceremonies of handing on public office, and the speeches delivered at public holidays commemorating the important events of American history, obliges one to conclude that there exists an American civil religion with its worship, its rites and its divinity. According to Bellah, this civic religion combines two symbolic heritages, the Enlightenment trust in the laws of nature and nature's God, and the biblical faith in the high destiny of the chosen people in their promised land. This civil religion, Bellah argues, can be distinguished from the historic religions of the churches and synagogues. The traditional religions may be infiltrated by the civil religion, yet they retain their independence and autonomy, sometimes welcoming the civil religion and at other times repudiating it.

Readers differed greatly in their understanding of Bellah's article. Some interpreted civil religion as an ideology legitimating the American way of life. They related Bellah's article to Will Herberg's book *Protestant, Catholic, Jew*,[30] in which the author examined Protestant, Catholic and Jewish congregations in America and arrived at the critical conclusion that these congregations, while having different doctrines and following different rituals, actually endorse the identical ethos, namely the American way of life. Other readers regarded Bellah's civil religion as a dangerous idolatry that allowed a nation to worship itself and justify its aggressive foreign policies. Bellah's article, we note, was written during the American war in Vietnam. Yet what Bellah had in mind was quite different. He admitted that the civil religion could deteriorate and become a legitimating ideology or, worse, an idolatrous worship, yet the civil religion according to its true nature was the celebration of the highest values of the nation and thus provided transcendent norms for judging the actual collective life and the policies of the government. Civil religion, Bellah wrote, 'is the subordination of the nation to ethical principles that transcend it and in terms of which it should be judged'.[31] He believed that the student movement of his day, passionately engaged in defending civil rights and opposing the Vietnam war, was an expression of America's civil religion.

I have mentioned Bellah's study and the subsequent debate to show that America's civil religion can express itself on the political right, the political centre and the political left. It can add its energy to any Christian church in the pursuit of its own mission – mission on a world historical scale. Bellah's analysis offers a sociological explanation for the observation made by church historians that the American churches participate, despite their disagreements on many issues, in a certain messianic consciousness.

It was customary at one time to distinguish between mainline Christian churches that endorsed what Americans call liberal values, and conservative evangelical churches who see themselves as opponents of secular society and suspect liberal values of undermining Christian faith. For decades the mainline churches occupied the dominant place in American society while the conservative evangelical churches played a minor role in public life. Since their main concern was personal conversion to Jesus Christ, they denounced the efforts of mainline churches and ecumenical organizations to influence, in the name of faith, the country's political culture and the government's public policies. This changed dramatically in 1979 with the foundation of the Moral Majority, a political action group created by Jerry Falwell, composed of conservative Christians, many of them fundamentalists, who supported conservative candidates in the election of 1980 and advocated conservative cultural policies.[32] Evangelical Christians who had shunned political involvement now changed their mind and became politically active, organizing opposition to the liberal and secular values of American society. The new Christian Right became influential in the Republic Party and, in turn, was used by that party to attract the votes of conservative Christians. The Moral Majority was dissolved in 1989, yet after the re-election of President George W. Bush in 2004, a new organization, The Moral Majority Coalition, was founded 'to utilize the momentum of the November 2 elections to maintain an evangelical revolution of voters who will continue to go to the polls to vote "Christian"'.[33] In the culture war dividing the United States at the turn of twenty-first century, conservative Christians are making great gains, while the mainline churches, committed to liberal values, are now experiencing a certain decline.

Some social scientists believe that over the last decades the denominational character of American religion has been weakened.[34] They argue, first, that an ever increasing number of Americans leave their denomination and pursue a spiritual quest on their own and, second, that the conflict between conservative and liberals has invaded the mainline churches and produced dividing lines that no longer run along denominational lines. This may well be true. At the same time, the entry of sectarian Christian groups into public political debate transforms them into denominations, thus reaffirming the American pattern.

Churches in Canada

Canada is a British Dominion created in 1867 by uniting several British colonies. They including a francophone colony founded by France at the beginning of the seventeenth century and, after the British conquest of 1759, ceded to the British Crown by the Treaty of Paris in 1763. Canada was the creation of politicians, businessmen and representatives of the crown; it was not the product of a movement among the people. Canada never had a revolution; it moved gradually from colony, to dominion, to autonomous country. Gluing together two civilizations, British Protestant and French Catholic, produced an uncertain and unequal union devoid of common symbols. To this day Canada is the merger of two distinct histories. In each of them, the church has played a different role.[35]

Quebec

Under the French Crown the Catholic Church had a Gallican orientation: the bishop looked to the king as principal authority.[36] After the conquest, the bishops accepted the authority of the British king, an obedience facilitated by the remarkable Quebec Act of

1774 that recognized the Catholic Church in Canada and allowed it to collect the tithe, at a time when this church was still illegal in Britain. During the revolt of 1837, the bishops supported the crown and excommunicated the patriots. Soon after, the ecclesiastical leadership became increasingly ultramontanist: it supported the campaign of the papacy against the emerging liberal society and sought to control the culture of the francophone society. The bishops, after approval by Rome, favoured the confederation of 1867, trusting that it would protect the identity, culture and religion of *les canadiens*.

While the Catholic Church was never legally established in French Canada, it exerted enormous social and political influence. It successfully opposed liberal cultural movements as well as the invasion of Protestant ideas and practices. The people allowed this to happen. In a nation colonized by empire and thus deprived of its political autonomy, the church often becomes the symbol of identity and resistance, especially if the empire represents an alternative faith. This happened in Quebec, Ireland and Poland.[37] Moreover, several governments of the Province of Quebec refused to assume responsibility for social services and instead asked the Catholic Church to take charge of the school system, the hospitals, and the institutions taking care of the poor, the elderly, the orphans and the mentally disturbed. Thanks to this unusual arrangement, the Catholic Church enjoyed, in addition to its symbolic power, a bureaucratic omnipresence in Quebec for which there existed few, if any, parallels.[38]

A cultural upheaval, the so-called Quiet Revolution, started in June 1960 when the Liberal Party won the provincial election. Since the industrial, financial and business elites in Quebec were of British origin, the language of work throughout the province had been English, even though over 80 per cent of the population was francophone. The French-Canadian majority was economically disadvantaged, locked into a quasi-colonial inferior status. Reacting to this, the Quiet Revolution produced a political and cultural transformation of Quebec society. Quebecers wanted to be in charge of their own affairs, live and work in their own language, escape the inherited colonial mentality and prove to themselves that they were a gifted and resourceful people. They reacted negatively to the institutions that had defined their lives in the past, including the Catholic Church. Yet because Vatican II was taking place at the same time, Catholics felt free to oppose the power of the clergy and advocate a Catholicism more open to modern values.[39]

Disturbed by the upheaval and new vitality in the church, the bishops appointed a study commission in 1968, chaired by the sociologist Fernand Dumont, to hold hearings all over the province, to invite Catholic individuals and organizations to submit their ideas, and then, on the basis of the people's proposals, to formulate pastoral policies that promise the future flourishing of the church. The Dumont Report was published in 1971.[40] Among the recommendations was the democratization of church life within the papal-episcopal structure through new institutions that would allow the people to react to the policies adopted by their pastors. What the Dumont Report did not foresee was the rapid secularization of Quebec society. In the 1970s two thirds of the Catholic population stopped their religious practice, associated the church with *la grande noirceur*, the quasi-colonial situation prior to the Quiet Revolution, and embraced a passionate secularism. Because the church lost the symbolic power to define the Quebec identity and had its bureaucratic presence replaced by public institutions, it soon lost the majority of its members.

The chastened bishops accepted the new Quebec without nostalgia or resentment. They did not introduce the bold recommendation of the Dumont Report, yet they promised to remain in solidarity with the Quebec people, respect their aspirations, and continue to address public issues from a Catholic perspective, not as an exercise of authority but as participation in the democratic debate through which society defines itself. In keeping with Vatican II, the Quebec bishops became advocates of human rights and social justice. They offered ethical criteria for Quebec's nationalism. The remaining Catholicism in Quebec is anti-authoritarian, internally pluralistic and open to ecumenical and inter-religious cooperation without a clearly-defined ecclesiology that legitimates its behaviour.[41]

English Canada

As indicated with reference to Quebec, beginning in the eighteenth century the British conquered the North American colonies belonging to the French Crown, a military and political process that culminated in conquest of Quebec City in 1759 and the cession of the last French colony to Britain in 1763. The effort of the British Crown to establish the Anglican Church in the newly acquired colonies was not successful in the long run: the Protestant pluralism in these parts offered an effective resistance. Still, while there was no religious establishment in the strict sense, British North America was made up of conservative societies, loyal to the crown, in which the churches, in part supported by public funds, had a powerful cultural influence.[42] The Canadian sociologist S.D. Clark has shown that in the British North American colonies, and later in Canada, the protest of groups in the margin of society against the wealthy urban centres was carried on in religious language, opposing Protestant sects against the churches associated with the powerful.[43]

The foundation of Canada in 1867 had a profound impact on the churches. While they had previously been organized separately in the different colonies, they now supported the newly-created political unity and began to create their own national organizations. The quest for greater unity produced a movement among the churches that continued into the twentieth century. Early in the century an initiative began to unite Presbyterians, Methodists and Congregationalists in a single church, in part to foster the creation of a Canadian national identity. As French Canada was represented by a single church, so should the larger and more powerful English Canada.[44] In 1925, Presbyterians, Methodists and Congregationalists formed the United Church of Canada and envisaged negotiations for an eventual union with the Anglican Church – an effort that finally failed in 1970. A minority of Presbyterians refused to join the United Church: they preferred to remain an independent church, even if now greatly reduced in size. Thanks to these efforts to create greater church unity, the great majority of Canadian Christians belong to the three large churches, the Catholic Church, the Anglican Church and the United Church of Canada – an ecclesiastical pattern totally different from the multiple denominations in the United States of America.

The Canadian churches have been and still are different from their American sisters. Canadian Protestant churches were conservative, supported the monarchy, understood themselves as extensions of the British churches and, after Confederation, supported the as yet uncertain Canadian identity. Canada does not have a civic religion or national myth that unites French and English-speaking Canadians and might imbue the Protestant churches with a messianic passion. Since Confederation was based on a compromise involving two civilizations and several colonies, and since Canadians sought not revolution but a gradual entry into national autonomy without opposing the monarchy, Canadians have transformed compromise into a virtue. While the influence of American evangelicalism has often been strong in Canada, Christians with evangelical leanings have not left their churches. Even the small evangelical communities that do exist in Canada tend to be open to dialogue.

The difference between American and Canadian Christianity is even more dramatic: religion flourishes in the United States while in Canada secularization is progressing steadily, even in the English-speaking provinces. Reginald Bibby has carefully documented this.[45] The churches are shrinking, they are selling many of their houses of worship, they are in financial difficulties, and their voices cease to be taken seriously by the public. Is there a sociological explanation for this? It may be useful to examine the structural differences between religion in Canada and the United States. First, Canada has no civil religion, no national myth and no strong sense of its mission in the world. While Americans tend to be enthusiastic and idealistic, Canadians, surprised that their country still holds together, tend to be more cautious. Second, while the American churches are caught in a free market model where each church is promoting its own vision, the three major Canadian churches, occupying a government-assisted monopoly, did not have to rely on promotion. Third, just as Canadians have a polite respect for the monarchy as an ancient institution that has now lost its meaning, so do many of them look upon the church – an ancient institution no longer relevant. For them, monarchy and church belong to the same era. The Canadian Protestant theologian Douglas Hall, persuaded by the Canadian experience, announces in his work the end of Constantinian Christianity, calls upon the church to understand itself as a diaspora, and proposes that a mark revealing the church's identity is 'the mark of the cross'.[46] Like Jesus, the church will suffer rejection. The new historical situation demands that the church rethink its mission and boldly walk upon a new path.

Conclusion

This sociological look at the churches in North America reveals that they express their theological self-understanding in practice, in organizational forms and institutional decisions, though they have been unable to justify their practice in theological terms. The denominational structure of religion in the United States implies that the participant denominations acknowledge, in addition to their own claim to apostolic truth, the existence of a wider economy of salvation, even if this implies a certain relativism which they do not like. After the Holocaust, most of the churches in North America have rethought their relationship to the Jewish people. They now honour the Jewish faith and have no intention of converting Jews to Christianity, even though the doctrinal basis for this change of attitude is not clear. The American and Canadian churches also refrain from preaching the gospel to the non-Christian immigrant communities in their country. When, in the fall of 1999, the Southern Baptist Church announced that it would send a thousand missionaries to Chicago to convert the non-Christians living there to Jesus Christ, the Interreligious Council of Chicago, of which the mainline churches are active members, sent a letter to the Southern Baptist Church urging them not do this. Persuading the non-Christians in Chicago to change their religion, the letter said, would lead to social unrest and possibly even violence.[47] The churches approved of this letter, leaving the theological justification unclear. While in the past the American and Canadian churches repudiated the beliefs and rituals of the Amerindian peoples as pagan worship, many churches have decided to integrate certain Amerindian rites in their public liturgy. They have learnt to respect the spirituality of the Amerindians, even if they should decide to leave the church and return to their ancestral tradition. In all the churches, Christians are debating the nature of the church's mission. Must priority be given to the proclamation of the gospel or to the promotion of peace and justice in an unjust world torn apart by violence and structures of exclusion? The change in practice announces the eventual emergence of a new ecclesiology.

Notes

1 Ross Scherer, 'Mainline Churches', in William Swatos, Jr. (ed.), *Encyclopedia of Religion and Society*, London: Sage Publications Ltd, 1998, pp. 282–4.
2 Rhys Williams, 'American Religion', *Encyclopedia of Religion and Society*, pp. 15–19.
3 Cf. Gregory Baum, *Religion and Alienation: A Theological Reading of Sociology*, 2nd edn, Ottawa: Novalis, 2006.
4 Richard Niebuhr, *The Social Sources of Denominationalism*, New York: Henry Holt & Co., 1929.
5 The two texts are taken from Robert Handy, *The History of the Churches in the United States and Canada*, New York: Oxford University Press, 1977, p. 142.
6 Handy, p. 147.
7 Handy, p. 149.
8 Max Weber, 'The Protestant sects and the spirit of capitalism', in H.H. Gerth and C. Wright Mills (eds), *From Max Weber*, New York: Oxford University Press, 1958, pp. 302–22, 306.
9 Ernst Troeltsch, *The Social Teachings of the Christian Churches*, London: Allen & Unwin, 1931, vol. 1, pp. 331–43.
10 Niebuhr, *Social Sources*, pp. 124–34.
11 Martin Marty, *Righteous Empire: The Protestant Experience in America*, New York: The Dial Press, 1970, pp. 177–87.
12 Alexis de Tocqueville, *Democracy in America*, New York: Vintage Books, 1945, vol. 2, pp. 21–9.
13 Tocqueville, pp. 30–1.
14 Weber, 'Protestant sects', p. 305.
15 Max Weber, *The Protestant Ethic and the Spirit of Capitalism*, New York: Charles Scribner's Sons, 1958, p. 181.
16 Gregory Baum, *Religion and Alienation*, New York: Paulist Press, 1975, pp. 140–61.
17 Peter Berger, *The Sacred Canopy*, New York: Doubleday, 1967, p. 108; Bryan Wilson, *Religion in Secular Society*, London: Pelican Books, 1969, pp. 112, 122.
18 Andrew Greeley, *The Denominational Society*, Glenview, IL: Scott, Foresman & Co., 1972.
19 Henri de Lubac, *Catholicism, a Study of Dogma in Relation to the Corporate Destiny of Mankind*, London: Burn, Oates & Washburn, 1950.
20 D.A. Carson's article, 'Church, Authority in', in Walter Elwell (ed.), *The Evangelical Dictionary of Theology*, Grand Rapids, MI: Baker Book House, 1989, summarizes the biblical arguments offered by the congregationalist, presbyterian and episcopal denominations to defend their authority structure.
21 Paul Minear, *Images of the Church in the New Testament*, Philadelphia: Westminster Press, 1960.
22 Thomas McAvoy, *A History of the Catholic Church in the United States of America*, Notre Dame, IN: University of Notre Dame Press, 1969, pp. 61–122.
23 Gerald Fogarty, 'Americanism', in Richard McBrien (ed.), *Encyclopedia of Catholicism*, San Francisco: Harper, 1989, pp. 40–2, 42.
24 Bryan Wilson, *Religion in Secular Society*, London: Pelican Books, 1969, p. 42.
25 www.adventist.org/beliefs/statements/main_stat27.html, accessed May 25, 2005.
26 www.adventist.org/beliefs/statements/main_stat42html, accessed May 25, 2005.
27 Handy, *History of the Churches in the United States and Canada*, p. 279.
28 Martin Marty, *Righteous Empire: The Protestant Experience in America*, New York: The Dial Press, 1970, foreword.
29 Robert Bellah, 'Civil Religion in America', in W.G. McLoughlin (ed.), *Religion in America*, Boston: Beacon Press, 1966, pp. 3–23; reprinted with commentaries and rejoinders in D.R. Cutler (ed.), *The Religious Situation 1968*, Boston: Beacon Press, 1968, pp. 331–94; also republished in Robert Bellah, *Beyond Belief*, New York: Harper & Row, 1974, pp. 168–89.
30 Will Herberg, *Protestant, Catholic, Jew: an Essay in American Religious Sociology*, New York: Doubleday, 1955.

31 Bellah, *Beyond Belief*, p. 168.
32 Gabriel Fackre, *The Religious Right and Christian Faith*, Grand Rapid, MI: Eerdmans, 1982); David Bromley, *New Christian Politics*, Macon, GA: Mercer, 1884.
33 'What We are all About': www.faithandvalues.us, accessed May 25, 2005.
34 Robert Wuthnow, *The Restructuring of American Religion: Society and Faith Since World War II*, Princeton, NJ: Princeton University Press, 1988; Alan Wolfe, *The Transformation of American Religion*, Chicago: University of Chicago Press, 2003.
35 Terrence Murphy and Roberto Perin, *A Concise History of Christianity in Canada*, Oxford: Oxford University Press, 1996.
36 Terrence Fay, *The History of Canadian Catholics: Gallicanism, Romanism and Canadianism*, Montréal: McGill-Queen's University Press, 2002.
37 The same dynamics is taking place today in the post-colonial world of Asia and Africa: uncompromising religious dedication here becomes the symbol of identity and resistance.
38 Nive Voisine, *Histoire du catholicisme québécois*, Montréal: Boréal Express, 1984.
39 Gregory Baum, *The Church in Quebec*, Toronto: Novalis, 1991, pp. 15–48.
40 The Dumont Report consisted of five books, the principal one entitled *L'Église du Québec: un héritage, un projet*, Montréal: Fides, 1971.
41 Raymond Lemieux, Jean-Paul Montminy, *Le catholicisme québécois*, Québec: Les Presses de l'Université Laval, 2000.
42 John Moir, *The Church in the British Era, from the British Conquest to Confederation*, Toronto: McGraw-Hill Ryerson, 1872.
43 S.D. Clark, *Church and Sect in Canada*, Toronto: University of Toronto Press, 1948.
44 John Webster Grant, *The Church in the Canadian Era*, Birlington, ON: Welch Publication, 1988.
45 Reginald Bibby, *Fragmented Gods*, Toronto: Stoddart, 1987; *Restless Gods*, Toronto: Stoddart, 2002.
46 Douglas Hall, *Confessing the Church*, Minneapolis: Fortress Press, 1996, pp. 90–7.
47 See *National Catholic Reporter*, Dec. 10, 1999, p. 9.

Further reading

Anne Bayefsky, *State Support of Religious Education: Canada Versus the United Nations*, Leiden, Boston: Nijhoff, 2007.

Reginald Bibby, *Restless Gods: the Renaissance of Religion in Canada*, Toronto: Stoddart, 2002.

Jay Dolan, *In Search of American Catholicism, A History of Religion and Culture in Transition*, New York: Oxford University Press, 2002.

Dennis Doyle, *Communion Ecclesiology*, Maryknoll, NY: Orbis Books, 2000.

Terrence Fay, *A History of Canadian Catholics: Gallicanism, Romanism, and Canadianism*, Montreal: McGill-Queen's University Press, 2002.

Douglas John Hall, *Confessing the Faith in a North American Context*, Minneapolis: Fortress Press, 1996.

Pierrette Hondagneu-Sotelo (ed.), *Religion and Social Justice for Immigrants*, New Brunswick, NJ: Rutgers University Press, 2007.

Colleen McDannell, *Religions in the United States in Practice*, 2 vols, Princeton: Princeton University Press, 2001.

Quentin Schultze, *Christianity and the Mass Media in America: Toward a Democratic Accommodation*, East Lansing, MI: Michigan State University Press, 2003.

Derek Simon and Donald Schweitzer (eds), *Intersecting Voices: Critical Theologies in a Land of Diversity*, Ottawa: Novalis, 2005.

William Thompson-Uberuaga, *Jesus and the Gospel Movement*, Columbia, MO: University of Missouri Press, 2006.

Miroslav Volf, *After our Likeness: the Church as the Image of the Trinity*, Grand Rapids, MI: Eerdmans, 1998.

19

THE CHURCH IN AN
OCEANIC PERSPECTIVE

David Pascoe

Introduction

A global perspective is an apt expression in two ways for describing the content of this chapter. First, like other chapters in this part, there is the intention to describe the church in one particular region of the world. Second, however, the term global in large part describes the particular view of the church presented here for the region of Oceania. That is, the perspective itself is necessarily somewhat global. The necessity of the second is connected to the reality of the first for both geographical and ecclesial reasons. The expanse of the earth's surface defined by the term Oceania is different from other regions of the earth. This geographic area of approximately nine million square kilometres is dominated by the vastness of the Pacific Ocean. It is water, and at times vast distances across this body of water, rather than land, which 'connects' the immense number of islands and groups of islands that constitute the peoples of Melanesia, Micronesia, Polynesia and the people of New Zealand and those on the continent of Australia, as Oceania.[1]

This difference is important for offering a regional perspective of the church, because 'the accident of location tends to have an effect on the church and its message'.[2] The particular locational accident of the enormous geographic diversity of peoples and their relationships with one another in Oceania is significant for understanding the church in this region. Leaving Australia and New Zealand aside for a moment,[3] John Garrett makes the point with particular reference to the peoples of the Pacific Islands:

> Pacific Christian history is partly an essay in oceanography. . . . Pacific Islander Christians have a special way of comprehending the world. Most human beings look outward on solid earth. Islanders live on small pieces of earth surrounded by the wealth – and menace – of the sea. Travel and arrival, life and death, the Good News and the prospect of 'life among the stars' have distinctive meanings for Church and people.[4]

When Australia and New Zealand are included with the Pacific Islands, as they are for the region named as Oceania,[5] further dimensions of diversity, both geographical and ecclesial, are added to the complexity of presenting the distinctive nature of the church in this region. Ian Breward offers a critique of the notion of a unified identity of the region under discussion here. He uses the term Australasia and excludes the Polynesian and Micronesian Islands above the Equator in his work. Breward says:

> The terms Melanesia, Micronesia, Oceania and Polynesia all reflect Europeans' perceptions, imposed in a misleading unitive way. . . . Many islanders resent being given an identity constructed by outsiders which makes them part of a wider reality to which they feel no allegiance, but Australasia is a useful label.[6]

Likewise, the term Oceania is considered a 'useful label' for identifying and offering a unified perspective of the church in that place. Tony Swain and Garry Trompf uphold the reality of the identity of Oceania in their studies of religions in this region. They also recognize that until recently the original peoples of this region did not have an identity as Oceanians.[7] Further, like Breward they consider that the designation or idea of Oceania is European in origin; nevertheless, they state:

> A major part of the intellectual legitimacy of our domain of enquiry lies in the history of Western thought, our understanding of 'otherness' and of Europe's encounter with world cultures. This is not, of course, just a history of ideas, for ideas take political shape and so Oceania does emerge as a socio-political reality in recent centuries. This in turn has reshaped the identity of the original inhabitants of this region, so that today there is indeed much substance to the notion of religions in Oceania as a whole.[8]

Two issues are raised for developing a coherent perspective of the church in the region of Oceania and articulating its distinctive character. The first is the vastness of the geographic area, with the attendant cultural diversity of the many peoples of the region that combines with the diversity of Christian origins. Diverse denominational missionary endeavours constitute the origins of Christianity in Oceania. So as there is no singular original ecclesiological tradition, is it even possible to offer *a* coherent perspective of the church within the vast diversity of the region?

A second related issue is the reception of the above diversity. How have the diverse indigenous peoples who received the gospel and conversion to Christianity, along with those Christians from other parts of the world who have settled in this region over the last two centuries, developed and created a distinctive regional understanding of the church?

How might these questions be answered to offer *a* perspective of the church from the region of Oceania?

An ecclesiological thread: unity in mission

In light of the above it is important to recognize that this chapter presents *a* perspective of the church in Oceania. There could be other points of view and points of departure. Also, this presentation, in a sense, leaves out more about the church in the Oceanic region than it covers. However, I consider that a study of the inter-relationship between the two ecclesial elements of mission and unity provides a framework for locating the identity of the church in the region. They are two of many possible key ecclesial ideas. Nevertheless, they provide an understanding of how Christianity emerged and developed through the last two hundred years, both within the various church traditions and across them, and provide a framework to develop a standpoint by which the church can be understood in this part of the world.

Cyril Hally offers some helpful points of reflection in regard to the elements of mission and unity. In the context of the possible emergence of a new Oceanic identity, he acknowledges the Protestant origins of Christianity and so its dominant religious perception of the region. Also, that Christianity as a whole is imperfect in its diverse denominationalism in Oceania. However, the church could present a hopeful vision because, 'in an ecumenical environment colonial memories could be healed in a process of reconciliation – the emerging model of mission'.[9]

Hally offers a clue as to how we might provide a unified discussion about the church in Oceania. That is, while holding on to the reality of diversity, particularly with regard to a prevalent Christian denominationalism, it is possible to present an Oceanic perspective of the church in terms of the inter-relationship between the church's unity and its mission. The church's contemporary movement toward unity, which arose out of the modern missionary movement, becomes ground for the self-understanding of the church's mission in Oceania.

This particular perspective is affirmed in the context of a modern worldwide movement that posits the integral relationship of mission and unity for ecclesial self-understanding. Reflection on the consequences of missionary ventures provided a significant impetus for the rise of the ecumenical movement in the late nineteenth and early twentieth centuries.[10] The integral unity of the two elements of unity and mission for ecclesial self-understanding developed particularly with the formation and ongoing work of the World Council of Churches. For example, a paper submitted to its Central Committee at Rolle in 1951 is titled, *The Calling of the Church to Mission and to Unity*. It is noted:

> Our concern in this study is the recovery in thought, in action, and in organization, of the true unity between the Church's mission to the world (its Apostolate) and the Church's obligation to be one.[11]

A movement in the direction of this ecclesial self-understanding has more recently been taken up by the Roman Catholic Church in the Second Vatican Council and subsequent ecumenical theological developments in the later part of the twentieth century.[12]

The chapter proceeds in two sections. A framework of the inter-relationship between the elements of mission and unity will manage this approach. The first section of the chapter describes the emergence and early development of what is considered 'an' ecclesiological tradition of mission for the region of Oceania. It is in two parts. The first part describes the emergence and place of missionary activity as foundational for Christianity in the islands and island groups of the Oceanic region. The second part looks at the origins of Christianity in Australia with an emphasis on missionary activity. The distinction between the Pacific Islands and Australia is made on the grounds here of distinctive yet interlocked origins through the missionary movement in Oceania.[13]

The second section is concerned with the church in Oceania in the twentieth century. By the end of the nineteenth century questions had been raised as to the uncritical transportation of divisions in the church from their Western cultural setting through missionary endeavours. The rise and progress of the ecumenical movement was a direct result of this questioning. In what ways does the church in Oceania move with the changes toward unity in mission into and through the twentieth century?

The emergence of the church in Oceania

This section offers a broad descriptive overview of the origins and early development of the church in Oceania. It is not extensive in terms of covering all the missionary endeavours on all of the islands of Oceania. It has a particular emphasis on the early part of the nineteenth century and is generally historical in orientation. The origins of the church in Oceania through this period are formative for the church's identity in terms of mission and unity. The focus is on the intersection of the consequences of missionary activity and the birth of the church in Oceania with a particular consideration of the unity and more often its lack in this period. The issues addressed are the rise and influence of the Evangelical mission societies, the re-emergence of Catholic religious orders on mission in the region, and the missionary endeavour that arose internal to the Oceanic region by islander peoples themselves.[14]

Introducing Christianity to Oceania

Before the nineteenth century and in the time of European exploration and 'discovery',[15] the peoples of Oceania were introduced to Christianity via various forays of the Spanish, Dutch, British and French.[16] In 1493 Pope Alexander VI had divided the world outside Europe between Spain and Portugal – Spain to the west of Brazil and Portugal to its east.[17] In 1668, Mariana, Spanish Queen Mother and regent, sent a Jesuit mission to Guam and the Spanish Governor of Peru sent two Franciscan missionaries to Tahiti in 1772.[18] However, it was not until the impact of the renewal movements in the Church of England and Protestant churches of the eighteenth century in England and North America had been felt, and the call to worldwide mission made, that a more concerted effort brought and spread the gospel throughout the Pacific region.[19]

The Roman Catholic Church took to the South Seas again, thirty years after the Evangelical missionaries, with the revival of the Congregation for the Propagation of the Faith, the support and direction of successive popes in the nineteenth and early twentieth century, and the growth of both financial and spiritual support among Catholics.[20] Roman Catholics continued their missionary work substantially through the religious orders, as they had in the past,[21] but a new model of missionary endeavour emerged from the Evangelical renewal.

> One of the most significant developments to emerge out of this dynamic renewal movement was the founding of societies that were devoted explicitly to foreign missions. The key characteristic of this phenomenon was *voluntarism*. Instead of waiting for a signal from an official church, individual Christians, often across denominational affiliations, joined such societies to commit themselves to the task of world mission.[22]

The emergence and early consolidation of the church in Oceania coincides with a renewal in missionary thinking and endeavours in the nineteenth century by the churches in England, Europe and North America. The missionary enterprise to preach and spread the gospel and eventually to extend the church was the impetus for the emergence of the church in this region. It was not a mission that can be considered as conducted with a unified ecclesial vision, particularly between Catholics and Evangelicals.

Evangelical missionary endeavours

A variety of mission societies were formed in the eighteenth and early nineteenth century.[23] These provided the personnel and provision for the initial proclamation of the gospel for conversion to Christianity of the peoples in Oceania. They were both denominational (for example, the Baptist Missionary Society (BMS), 1792,[24] and Church Mission Society (CMS), 1799, formed within the Church of England[25]) and non-denominational (for example, the Missionary Society, 1795, which became the London Missionary Society (LMS) in 1818[26]). However, both the BMS and CMS, at least in their early formation, 'were not denominationally exclusive'.[27]

David Bosch describes three waves of general Protestant missionary endeavour; the first at the end of the eighteenth century, the second, more tied to a height of imperialism in the 1880s, and the third beginning with the end of World War II.[28] The period of the first wave is the primary focus here. The missionary endeavour of this time is Evangelical up to around 1830. The movement into a second wave of consolidation includes the initial Catholic missionary re-emergence in the Pacific Islands.

The first wave of Evangelical mission began with the LMS in 1797. They set up three missions in Tahiti, Tongatapu and Tahuata.[29] At the coaxing of Samuel Marsden, the Church of England chaplain in Sydney and representative of the LMS 'to look after their affairs in the South Seas',[30] CMS missionaries were sent to New Zealand in 1814. The latter were joined there by representatives of the Wesleyan Methodist Missionary Society (WMMS) in 1821.[31] It is worth noting here a remark by Charles Forman with regard to New Zealand in this period. He connects New Zealand with Hawaii as 'special' cases within the Pacific Islands.[32] In comments on the nineteenth-century missionary endeavours Forman states of his own work,

> New Zealand has not been included, even in this nineteenth century survey, for similar reasons: the predominance of white settlers early gave to mission and church an entirely distinct set of problems and directions.[33]

This is noted here not to exclude New Zealand from the discussion. Rather, it is to highlight the distinctive characteristics of interaction between missionaries and eventual colonial movements with all the peoples of Oceania. It is a reminder of the complex diversity of Christian origins in the region. This complexity is exemplified in the relationship between the CMS and the colonial church in New Zealand.[34] One example is the uneasy relations that existed between the CMS and the appointment of Bishop George Selwyn as the first colonial bishop. Even though the bishop accepted the position as a CMS vice president, 'he never identified himself fully with the movement'.[35] There is also the debate around the issue of forming either one church or two, one colonial and the other for the Maori.[36] Davidson makes the assessment in part that,

> [t]he ecclesiology of the early missionaries was shaped by their English culture and traditions, evangelical activism, and missionary pragmatism. These gave rise to Te Hahi Mihinare, a developing missionary church, in which the language and people were Maori but the forms and content were largely English and Anglican.[37]

As previously mentioned, another distinctive characteristic for missionary endeavour in Oceania that emerged from the earliest times is the activity by islander peoples themselves.

Neil Gunson notes that it was as early as 1822 that islander missionaries were sent to Vava'u in the Tongan group and similarly in '1826 Tahitian missionaries were sent to Lakeba in the Lau islands of the Fijian group'.[38] Pacific Island people quickly became missionaries within the region of Oceania. Often they preceded the coming of European missionaries. However, they also had key roles as missionary 'pastors' in the region:[39] Their role was crucial to missionary success.

> More Pacific Islanders than white missionaries spread Christianity across the Pacific. Their daily contacts proved deep and lasting. They slowly created a feeling of close kinship between the young churches of the region. Within two generations they were celebrated as pioneers of the faith, praised along with chiefs who had the wit to welcome them.[40]

Forman makes a distinction with regard to islander missionaries as *foreign missionaries* within Oceania. Those noted above by Gunson would belong to a group of foreign missionaries 'who went from one politically defined territory to another'.[41] That is, where political boundaries coincide with linguistic and cultural boundaries. However, as Forman points out, for Melanesia this is different.

> Melanesian tribes twenty miles apart may be totally foreign to each other in language and customs. The men who cross from one to the other are as truly foreign missionaries as those who cross a political boundary.[42]

The success of the first wave of missionary endeavour was not immediate. For example, of the three LMS missions, Tongatapu and Tahuata were soon abandoned. Tahiti eventually became the LMS's successful base of operations, but it too was vacated for a time. The reasons for the lack of success in these early days and later are complex. Ian Breward offers a general assessment of some difficulties, with particular reference to Polynesia, from the perspectives of the Polynesians and the European missionaries.

> For their part, Polynesians found Christianity hard to understand. Its invisible deity, who could not be seen nor heard, simply did not fit their religious world of *auta*, who appeared, spoke, and acted predictably. Christian morality was puzzlingly restrictive, its worship strange, and its explanations of evil, hell and disaster offensive. . . .
>
> Missionaries also had much to learn about Polynesian religion, and the problems of communicating their own religion effectively. Sharp disputes occurred over policy and methods for several decades. The relationship between civilizing and evangelizing, translation methods, linguistic issues, testing conversion, pastoral policy in matter of marriage and sexuality, attitudes to traditional religion, all had to be discussed outside the framework of conventional Protestant wisdom.[43]

Other difficulties to be overcome existed in relation to the particular differences between mission territories within the region of Oceania. Often distinctive characteristics within different groups of islands and islanders, which varied in their own religious and socio-political structures, were at issue for missionaries. For example, Darrell Whiteman argues that it was easier for missionaries to draw large numbers to Christianity when the chief from the

Polynesian hierarchical social structure was converted,[44] whereas this was more difficult in the area of Melanesia. The latter was characterized by 'a fragmentary, egalitarian social structure, where the local "big man" may have influence over no more than several hundred people'.[45] A second related difficulty was the numerous languages associated with the fragmented and isolated societies of Melanesia. This created a tremendous problem in communication, for if a missionary learned one of the languages he would frequently discover that at best he could communicate with only several hundred speakers.[46]

The missionaries had to learn the differences across the broad and diverse spectrum of the region to which they had been sent. Breward offers the assessment that it was 'to take a generation of failure and tribulation before some religious movement towards Christianity was discernible, and a theology of mission across cultures slowly began to emerge among the missionaries'.[47]

However, the movement towards Christian religious dominance continued and indeed succeeded in the region. Breward marks the period between 1830 and 1870, after the first initial wave of missionary endeavour, as a time of expansion and consolidation for the Pacific Island churches: they had essentially been established.[48] Garrett comments on the state of the mission in the Hawaiian Islands begun in 1820.

> Inevitably the whole period to 1830 involved busy, almost feverish activity for the American Board Missionaries and their pupils: translating, teaching, catechizing, instituting discipline, framing civil codes for the chiefs and explaining them to the people. Hymns were translated and composed . . . Modes of worship in the vernacular were devised and made familiar.[49]

As the Evangelical mission societies were consolidating their early positions in Oceania, the Roman Catholic Church re-emerged in the region. We now turn our attention to its initiatives.

Initial Roman Catholic missionary endeavours

Toward the end of the first wave of Protestant missionary endeavour the Roman Catholic Church entered the region of Oceania in 1830. The story of the arrival of the first Catholic missionaries is an intricate one.[50] It also differs somewhat in regard to personnel and provision from that of the Evangelical missionary societies. Wiltgen explains that '[t]he Sacred Congregation de Propaganda Fide founded in 1622 and since 15 August 1967 also called the Sacred Congregation for the Evangelization of Nations, supervises and directs missionary activity around the world'.[51]

Like the Evangelical societies for mission, the Catholic missionaries emerged from a renewal in the church. 'Coming out of the Catholic roots and heritage, the number of new orders and congregations, including many devoted implicitly or explicitly to mission, exploded.'[52] Bevens and Schroeder note a similar 'voluntarism' to that which is characteristic of the Evangelical societies of the period as a consequence of this renewal.[53]

There are, though, important differences. The Catholic missionaries were almost exclusively priests, brothers and sisters, and were strongly linked with the institutional church, particularly through the Vatican. There was not the movement of Catholic islander missionaries like those who responded to the Evangelical missionaries. However, it is important to recognize the place of local people as catechists for the Catholic missionary endeavours. Also, there were significant theological differences between Catholics and Evangelicals, which were compounded by nationalistic agendas. The latter is particularly clear where the missionaries 'were part of the competitive colonial enterprise of France and Britain claiming islands across the Pacific'.[54]

Indicative of the French missionaries, and the first to arrive in Oceania in the nineteenth century, was the Congregation of the Sacred Heart of Jesus and Mary (Picpus Fathers). They arrived in Hawaii in 1827 but were expelled in 1831.[55] They moved on to Mangareva in 1834 and the Marquesas in 1838. Gunson attributes limited success to their venture in the Marquesas.[56] Breward, however, offers a different assessment of one missionary's work in Mangareva.

> Gradually baptisms increased, then first communions, Christian marriages, and funerals. Leaders cut their hair breaking the *tapu* on their head, and speedily identified with Catholic views. Laval created a total Christian community, firmly disciplined in Tridentine style.[57]

Another significant Catholic presence in the region was the Society of Mary (Marists).[58] This group provided a significant presence in New Zealand from 1838 under the leadership of Bishop Pompallier. Further, seven priests and six lay brothers arrived in the Solomon Islands in 1845. Garrett suggests a possible thought that the missionaries may have had: 'Further west, New Guinea beckoned; the Solomon Islands would surely be suitable advance stations for its future conquest?'[59]

The Marists had sent 117 missionaries to the region by 1849.[60] However, like the Evangelical missionaries they experienced significant setbacks through the death of missionaries, both from disease and at times at the hands of islanders, and particular difficulties through the growing misunderstanding and disagreement between Bishop Pompallier himself, who lead the Marist missionaries from their base in New Zealand, and the Marist leader, Jean Claude Colin.

The above presents an introduction to the background of the arrival of Christianity into Oceania, particular to the island communities of the Pacific. Much more could be said. This could include the growing sense of acceptance by churches 'back home' of the missionary movement; the fact that the various church denominations were somewhat 'hidden' under the guise of the mission societies; the change in theological emphasis in the Church of England's missionary endeavours as the home church became more involved in missionary activity; the influence of the colonial governments and their association with missionaries (in both positive and negative ways); the movement of the mission societies and the missionaries themselves from 'east to west' across the Pacific, which explains why Melanesia was the last region within Oceania to be evangelized – the list could go on. However, another part of the Oceanic story, the rise of the church in Australia, requires our attention.

Origins of Christianity in Australia – mission and unity

The story of Christianity in Australia has it own distinctive characteristics especially when an emphasis is placed on mission activity. In 1788 the British established a colony on the continent of what is now called Australia. The movement toward colonization is coincidental with the emergence of the modern missionary movements. However, the movement in Australia virtually ignored the indigenous people. Breward notes that 'Christianity's future in Australia lay rather in the development of the colonists churches'.[61]

The efforts toward the colonization of the Pacific Islands generally and substantially followed the missionaries into the islands of the Pacific. The missionaries at times were torn between the need to accept the protection afforded by colonial powers and the desire to protect the new Christians from the advance of colonial influence. The missionaries, however, realized they needed the support of their home countries to sustain their missions and protect what they were forging in bringing Christianity to Oceania.[62]

The origin of Christianity in Australia is somewhat different. While British colonization coincided with the emergence of the activity of societies for missionary activity, unlike the Pacific Islands, the first colony was initiated through the establishment of a convict settlement. Also different was the attendant official religious presence in the initial stages of the Australian colony. The first presence was the evangelical and missionary ethos of the established Church of England in the person of the Revd Richard Johnson, who acted primarily as a military chaplain.[63] The first Roman Catholic priestly presence was unofficial in the persons of convicts, but became official with the appointment of two chaplains in 1819. They were Philip Conolly and John Joseph Therry.[64]

This is not to say that there was no concern for preaching the gospel and the conversion of the indigenous peoples. Rather, and over time, the effort of religious leadership focused primarily on the needs of the growing immigrant colonial population: both convicts and free settlers provided the focus for the establishment of the churches.

This being said, some degree of personnel and provision from both Evangelical and Catholic churches were supplied in the early history of Australia for missionary outreach to the Aboriginal people. The first official missionary, William Walker from the WMMS, arrived in 1821. George Clark from CMS, on his way to New Zealand in 1822, stayed in Australia for two years before continuing to his original goal, although he was somewhat disappointed with his efforts. The LMS was the third society to enter into missionary endeavour to the Aborigines in these early years.[65] Over time, with the expansion of colonization and the depletion of the Aboriginal peoples through disease, dispossession of their land and murder, various mission stations were set up around the country. These places were initiated more often than not 'by an outstanding person or family who single handedly created and sustained them by dedicated hard work and force of personality'.[66] Others were set up by the government and some of those initiated by Christians were taken over by the government under a policy of 'protection';[67] but most of these stations or Christian 'villages'[68] had disappeared by the end of the nineteenth century or shortly afterwards.[69] John Harris attributes the 'success' of these stations to their being places of survival: 'Aboriginal people's chances of *simply living at all* were greater in these missions than they were anywhere else.'[70]

Whatever 'success' is acknowledged needs, however, to be seen in the light of what is considered a general failure by the Christian churches in missionary endeavours to the Aboriginal peoples. The missionaries themselves considered their work a failure.[71] Harris lists a number of contributing factors, among them the belief of the Aboriginal peoples in the integrity of their own culture and world view; the opposing belief of the British in particular who understood their culture as vastly superior; a stance that saw Aboriginal peoples as inferior and degraded; the brutal treatment of the Aboriginal peoples by settlers; and the death of a large number of Aboriginal people.[72]

A prevailing attitude for first 150 years of mission to the Aboriginal peoples was to civi-

lize first in order to Christianize. This attitude provided the impetus for the practice of separating children from their parents.[73] Harris quotes from the *Sydney Morning Herald* in 1838,
'Before they are made Christians, you must make them men'.[74]

Samuel Marsden, as noted above, had a significant influence on the early missionary
endeavours in the Pacific. While he took the attitude of 'civilization first' toward missionary
endeavours in general, and saw this method as possible for the Pacific Island people, his attitude to the Aboriginals was different.

> The Aborigines are the most degraded of the human race . . . the time is not yet
> arrived for them to receive the great blessings of civilization and the knowledge of
> Christianity.[75]

It is difficult to summarize here in any detail the relationship between the British colonization of Australia, the attendant missionary endeavours of the churches, and the Aboriginal
people. Breward suggests:

> It was culturally impossible for most Europeans to move outside their ideas of reli-
> gion as public and book-related, to understand that Aborigines had a vastly
> different understanding of the sacred. Equally it was very difficult for Aborigines to
> understand the invaders' strange new religion.[76]

Certainly, with regard to missions and missionaries the notion of failure dominates. But
there has been at times a significant concern by individuals, churches and the government
of the day for the condition and welfare of Aboriginal peoples.[77] There is a complex history
of a very slow shift, by both government and the churches, away from 'civilization for
Christianization' to a policy of assimilation and then to one of integration. Michael Hogan
cites one example of the latter in the overwhelming acceptance by the Australian people in
1967 of granting Aboriginal people the right to vote.[78]

More recently both the Australian government and the churches have been concerned
about,[79] and begun to deal with, the issue of the separation of Aboriginal children from their
parents. In 1997 the Human Rights and Equal Opportunities Commission published the
findings of an inquiry established by the Federal Attorney General in 1995.[80] Their report is
dedicated to the 'stolen generations'.[81] One section of the report is 'The Roles of Churches
and Missions'. 'The Inquiry found churches played a major role in forcible removals by
providing accommodation and other services to the children in line with government
policy.'[82] The inquiry suggests to the churches that they acknowledge and apologize for their
role in the removal of Aboriginal children. While the government has not, many of the
churches have said they are sorry![83] In line with Hally's hope, this recognition by the
churches has placed the notion of reconciliation at the heart of Australian Christian
self-understanding.

Mission to the Aboriginal peoples in Australia has, however, been overshadowed by the
greater emphasis and energy that Christian churches have placed on those who colonized
the country. The first appointed chaplains and missionaries came with and followed the
significant immigrant populations that came predominantly from Britain, but also from
continental Europe, in the second half of the nineteenth century. As the various colonies in
Australia emerged and developed, the churches were simultaneously established as part of
the social fabric. Approximately 80,000 men, women and children were sentenced to be

transported by British courts before transportation to New South Wales ceased in 1840.[84] 'At the census of 1828 two in every three persons were either convict or ex-convict.'[85] Breward cites the figure of 70,000 people inhabiting the Australian colonies in 1830, and the increase between 1851 and 1901 as 405,356 to 772,210.[86] These numbers included members of the Anglican, Roman Catholic, Lutheran, Baptist, Congregationalist, and Presbyterian churches.[87]

Summary

The focus of this section has been on the origin and early spread of Christianity in Oceania as a result of missionary endeavour, both Evangelical and Catholic, across the great diversity of the region. Out of the Evangelical and Catholic revival movements of the late eighteenth and early nineteenth centuries the gospel was introduced to the region and by the end of the nineteenth century a variety of Christian churches were established. 'The Pacific Mission field provided some of the greatest successes of the nineteenth century. European evangelical impulse and Christianity virtually displaced the indigenous religions.'[88]

The inter-denominational and non-denominational missionary societies had provided an unconscious 'ecumenical' base for the rise of Christianity. Andrew Walls points out that the Evangelical societies provided a 'common ground' for the missionaries, a 'common means for people who start from different bases but have a common aim'.[89] Their common purpose was the individual conversion of those who had not heard the gospel.[90]

During the nineteenth century the various churches established by the mission societies began to emerge into an ecclesial denominational variety. Tolerance and harmony between the missions were maintained through the principal of comity,[91] where each denomination held to its 'own' island or group of islands.[92] However, it was critical reflection on this very division between the churches that eventually bore explicit fruit; the consequences of missionary endeavours were eventually ecumenical in result.[93]

It is to the explicit rise of the ecumenical movement and its consequences for the self-understanding of the church in Oceania that we now turn in the second section of this chapter. The integration of mission and unity is at the heart of a renewed self-understanding for the church.

Unity and mission in the twentieth-century church

The established churches of the nineteenth century were generally at first antagonistic to the non-denominational or inter-denominational character of the early Evangelical missionary movement. A consequence of this opposition was the exclusion of the notion of mission from ecclesial self-understanding:[94] mission was by the church, but not *necessarily* of the church's nature. A new understanding of the purpose of the church's missionary activity emerged in the middle of the nineteenth century, based on Henry Venn's principles of 'self-support, self-government and self-extension',[95] the more explicit intention being the creation of 'new' churches.[96] This practice reinforced a growing denominationalism and a stance of disunity. David Bosch argues that by the middle of the nineteenth century denominationalism was revived. He relates Venn's principles as aiding the movement to the 'planting' of denominational churches in the mission fields.[97]

However, it was also in this context that the preaching of the earliest missionaries of the 'Gospel without the church' was found to be inadequate. There was a growing acceptance by the established churches of their connection to the missionary movements and the essential place of mission in the church.[98] T.V. Philip argues that it was the growing encounter between missionary activity and the churches that developed 'within the missionary movement, the convictions and impulses for Christian unity'.[99]

The height of this renewed ecclesial self-understanding for the nineteenth-century missionary movement comes with the Edinburgh Conference of 1910 and the opening of the movement towards a sense of unity in mission.[100] Nevertheless, the integration took time.

> Edinburgh thought of the 'younger churches' as belonging to the domain of the mission and not in the region of the general church history. By Jerusalem in 1928, there was a greater appreciation of the place of the churches in the discharge of worldwide missionary responsibility. There was also greater recognition of the younger churches as the 'Body of Christ' in their respective places, to which all Christian activities in that place were to be ultimately related. This was the result of the theological emphasis which gradually emerged within the missionary movement that mission belongs to the church.[101]

This section again looks at the interaction of the ecclesial notions of mission and unity, focusing on the consequences for the church in Oceania of the new theological thinking of mission as it integrates with that of unity for ecclesial self-understanding. Our account of the Oceanic church's contemporary identity as based in unity for mission has two parts. First, there is a brief outline of Bevans and Schroeder's framework for understanding the notion of mission in the twentieth century. They base their understanding on Robert Schreiter's articulation of four periods of twentieth-century Catholic missionary movement,[102] but hold both the Protestant and Catholic churches together in their assessment.[103] How does the church in Oceania 'fit' within the general paradigm of missionary understanding? The second part looks at ecumenical cooperation as a concrete consequence of the integration of the principles of unity and mission for the church in Oceania in line with Bevans and Schroeder's framework. Ecumenical cooperation for mission emerges in a variety of ways in the region. One example is the issue of theological education.

Identifying something of the unique character of the church in Oceania in the twentieth century is no less complex than it was for the nineteenth. The general movement in the nineteenth century for Evangelical missionaries started out from common ground and purpose in missionary endeavour but then moved to greater denominational identity and a wide separation between Protestant and Catholic. The movement in the twentieth century has been something of a reversal. Out of a rising consciousness of the contradiction between missionary practice by a divided church and the gospel call to unity, there has been a deliberate movement towards seeking the church's unity in its mission. Bevans and Schroeder offer a framework in which this movement can be understood. Reflecting particularly on the Catholic Church, they see a movement from certainty, to ferment, to crisis and rebirth. These characteristics can also be found within other Christian churches, but for these the century is more generally split in two around the year 1961. This year separates the two periods, 'first, the life of the International Missionary Council (IMC); and second, Evangelical and Conciliar Protestants in Mission'.[104]

The period of certainty for the Catholic Church in general is from the turn of the century to 1962. At its simplest, this period was characterized by five papal encyclicals giving confident direction on mission over a forty year period, and an 'explosion' of mission activity.[105] The period of ferment for the Catholic Church came with the Second Vatican Council. A renewal in theology was presented by the Council which placed the church's mission within the nature of the church, having its origins in the Trinity. The Council also offered an ecclesial self-understanding which broke the explicit and exclusive identification of the Catholic Church with God's kingdom; openings were made for dialogue with other Christians, other religions and the world.[106] This renewal and shift in theological thinking provided the basis and impetus for the Catholic Church's participation in the ecumenical movement and dialogue with other religions.

The ferment turned into crisis[107] and some 'chaos' with the implementation of the Council's renewal of direction for the church. With regard to the place of mission within the renewal in ecclesial understanding, the security and sureness of the first half of the twentieth century was undermined. For example, a SEDOS conference in 1969 asked the basic question: 'Why mission at all?'[108]

After a time of crisis, however, a 'rebirth' for mission was initiated with Paul VI's encyclical *Evangelii Nuntiandi* (1975), and continued with John Paul II's *Redemptoris Missio* (1990).[109] These documents advance the understanding of the relationship between mission and unity as integral to the nature of the church. For example, John Paul states,

> Ecumenical activity and harmonious witness to Jesus Christ by Christians who belong to different churches and ecclesial communities has already borne fruit. But it is ever more urgent that they work and bear witness together at this time.[110]

The period of certainty for the Protestant churches was characterized by new ways for mission that focused on the 'corporate nature of the congregation and the church',[111] grounded in local circumstances, the rising consciousness of the need to engage with other religions,[112] the formation of the World Council along with the continued ecumenical missionary conferences,[113] and the turning point which linked the IMC with the World Council of Churches (WCC) in 1961.[114] Bevans and Schroeder also look to the 1960s as the period of ferment for Protestants. They highlight the emergence and impact of the 'radical' missiological views of Johannes Hoekendijk on the WCC, who saw 'the secular world and not the church as the primary locus of God's activity'; the growing distinction between Evangelical and Conciliar missionary emphasis was highlighted, each with their own theology of mission and relation to ecumenical endeavour.[115]

Toward unity in mission in Oceania

The year 1961 is a turning point with regard to the unity of the churches of the Pacific Islands within Oceania. The year coincides with the event on the world ecumenical-missionary stage of the coming together of the IMC, itself behind the explicit movement towards unity in the Pacific,[116] and the WCC. It was also the start of what Bevans and Schroeder see as a period of ferment in the churches. April 1961 saw the major Protestant churches and missions of the Pacific gather together and from this there emerged the Pacific Conference of Churches in 1966.[117] The Roman Catholic Church joined the Conference later in 1976.[118] There had been what Forman names as the 'tortured venture into church unity', in Tonga between 'the Free Church and the Wesleyan Church, both of Methodist extraction' achieved in 1926.[119] Generally, however, it is understood that ecumenism came late to the Pacific, although Solomone cites the Second World War as a significant event and precursor to more explicit ecumenical endeavours by virtue of the 'dire necessity of church co-operation', at least in Papua New Guinea.

> [D]uring the War we find cases of Catholics and Anglicans using each other's churches, entrusting their church to the priest of the other denomination, and even receiving communion from the other Pastor. Cases of co-operation between Lutherans, Catholics, Anglicans and Methodists during the war are reported in the records of these churches.[120]

Forman explains that there was an increase in missionary activity by both Protestant and Catholics in the Pacific after World War II, when missionaries returned in 'larger numbers than ever before'.[121] An important connection is made here between Australia and the peoples and churches of Oceania in the post-war period.

> Australia in particular had been made aware of its close relationship to the Pacific Islands as the bulwarks of its own security. Australians devoted themselves to foreign missions on a scale hitherto unknown. Over 2000 Australian Protestants were soon working as foreign missionaries and two-thirds of these were in the Pacific Islands. Australian Catholics, who hitherto had been absorbed in establishing themselves in their own land, likewise turned their attention outward. At the end of the war 278 foreign missionaries, a decade later over six hundred, and two decades later over a thousand, of whom three-fourths were serving in Oceania.[122]

This connection between Australia and the Pacific in the post World War II period is important when we consider the link between missionary endeavour and ecumenical activity in Oceania. Frank Engel argues for a significant advance in inter-church relations in Australia by the mid-1920s, particularly between Anglican and Protestant churches.[123] There is a considerable change in climate toward unity as a result of both particular local circumstances and global movements within the church.[124] Engel lists twenty factors that contributed to this movement toward Christian unity.[125] One of these is directly related to our purposes here:

> The size and complexity (evangelism, education, medicine, farming, language translation and literature) of the missionary task in the Pacific, Asia, and Africa, as well as within Australia, was a major cause of unity and united action.[126]

There is some coincidence between the period of global ecclesial certainty and the experience of the church in Oceania. Christian missionaries continued to act in some degree as they had done in the nineteenth century. However, there was movement toward unity of the churches connected with missionary activity in the Pacific. Forman notes that the conferences held in Australia and New Zealand in 1926 of missions working in the Pacific still focused on 'missions rather than churches', but the focus was changing.[127] Further, the Second World War brought a new impetus for unity in the churches.

From what has been said thus far it would be an overstatement to say that there was direct engagement in mission through a vision and action of unity among the churches. There was, however, a nascent development of an ecumenical environment and processes of reconciliation, 'the emerging model of mission', as noted by Hally. These developments continued in the second half of the twentieth century in Oceania through the stages of ferment, crisis and rebirth. The development of the Pacific Theological College provides one example of ecumenical endeavour for mission which we can draw on here to complete our somewhat cursory investigation. Forman notes, 'The cooperative relationships in theological education were one mark of an ecumenical revolution that swept through the islands from 1960 onward.'[128]

Ecumenical theological education

The idea for a central theological institution in the Pacific appeared in the 1944 minutes of the Methodist Overseas Mission Board, and was a recommendation from the Methodist United Synod in Fiji to this same board in 1956.[129] A discussion on the re-examination of a relevant theological education for ministry was a concern for the South Pacific Christian Conference at Morpeth, Australia in 1948. The idea of forming a council of churches to share experiences and mutual assistance was also discussed.[130] There was only one Pacific Islander present at Morpeth.[131] However, the need for an 'upgrade' of theological training for ministers and church workers of the Pacific was part of the agenda of the meeting of the Pacific churches and missionary agencies in 1961 at Malua Theological College in Western Samoa.[132] As a result of all these discussions, the establishment of the Pacific Theological College for ecumenical theological education was brought to fruition in 1965.[133]

Prior to shifts made after World War II, the emergence of ecumenical thinking in the Pacific, and the missions and churches gathering at Malua, Kambati Uriam argues that theological education for the various missions and churches of the Pacific was tied to training leadership for the maintenance and expansion of particular denominations.[134] This training was controlled by a Christian vision and mentality that was a legacy of 'missionization'. It was 'exclusive and self-centred, authoritarian and definitive, apologetic, local and sectarian, and dogmatic and hierarchical'.[135] These emphases changed as a direct result of the ecumenical thinking that brought the various churches of the Pacific together for the theological formation of ministers in an ecumenical setting and the formation of the Pacific Theological College.

Ilaitia Sevati Tuwere cites the three original aims of the college:

> to provide theological education orientated to the Pacific and its needs at a higher level than was previously available in the Pacific; to engage in research and reflection on issues facing the Pacific churches; and to provide a centre which would foster and express the unity of the Pacific churches, would encourage cooperation and sharing among churches.[136]

The Pacific Theological College was established to serve the major non-Roman Catholic denominations in the region: the Anglican, Methodist, Congregational, Lutheran, Presbyterian and Evangelical churches.[137] However, cooperation with the Roman Catholic Church and its respective seminaries is also evident. Kafoa Solomone explains with regard to the relationship with the Pacific Regional Seminary, established in 1972.

> They have a close working relation, which in the beginning was forced upon them by necessity; for example, lecturer shortage necessitated the exchange of lecturers

or students. This exchange has since developed into one of ecumenical conviction. This is also the way in which future leaders of the Pacific churches, both Catholic and Protestant, can get to know each other and become friends so as to facilitate ecumenical dialogue and co-operation.[138]

The language associated above with the ecumenical endeavour of this one example remains at the level of cooperation and sharing, and does not venture into explicit terms of common 'mission' in the unity of their common venture. Other examples could be multiplied in terms of various ecumenical associations of theological schools and ecumenical colleges of theology in the Pacific, New Zealand and Australia.[139] It also needs to be said that neither does the above deal with the multiple instances of official dialogue that occur between churches,[140] nor the multitude of practical local and national initiatives that exist among the people in the region that have emerged and developed in recent times. Further, the above does not address the continuing dis-unity between Christians that exists in Oceania, particularly, for example, with regard to what have been termed 'new religious groups' in the Pacific.[141]

However, I venture to suggest that this one example typifies the shift toward ecumenical endeavour that has occurred in Oceania in the twentieth century and provides an expression of the beginning of common mission that exists among the churches in this region. This shift in ecclesial self-understanding emerged from a recognition of the contradiction to the gospel that the very division of missionary endeavour expressed. A variety of events both international and regional in the twentieth century have given an impetus for the churches of Oceania to move with a growing ecumenical mind-set towards the goal of common mission.

Conclusion

The church in Oceania is distinctive in its origins, development and contemporary expression. It has its origins, like other churches, in the handing on of the Christian faith through mission. Unlike other regions is the great diversity of locations that constitute Oceania from its place in the Pacific, and the diversity of the missionaries who initially preached the gospel and established the church. The church in Oceania is like the church in other regions of the world in the global ecclesial influences that have impacted on it. It is distinctive in regard to how it has received these influences.

This work has selected one thread in the distinctive character of the church in Oceania: the relationship between mission and unity, which belongs to the nature of the whole church. It has exhibited something of the direction that the church in this region might pursue in order to be a uniting church in the one mission of Jesus Christ, which is its purpose.

Notes

1 'Oceania has traditionally been divided into four parts: Australasia (Australia and New Zealand), Melanesia, Micronesia, and Polynesia', Philip W. Goetz (ed.), *The New Encyclopaedia Britannica, Volume 8, 15th Edition*, Chicago: Encyclopaedia Britannica, 1988, p. 863.
2 Andrew Dutney, 'Postmark Australia', in Andrew Dutney (ed.), *From Here to Where? Australian Christians Owning the Past-Embracing the Future*, Melbourne: Uniting Church Press, 1988, p. 1.

3 In listing the countries and regions that constitute Oceania the United Nations has four group-ings: Australia and New Zealand, Melanesia, Micronesia and Polynesia. United Nations, retrieved 29 December 2005 from http://unstats.un.org/unsd/methods/m46/m49regin.htm#oceania

4 John Garrett, *To Live Among the Stars: Christian Origins in Oceania*, Geneva and Suva: World Council of Churches and Institute of Pacific Studies, University of the South Pacific, 1982, p. xi.

5 Ralph M. Wiltgen, *The Founding of the Roman Catholic Church in Oceania 1825–1850*, Canberra: Australian National University Press, 1979, p. 552. See note 46. Wiltgen shows the inclusion of New Zealand and Australia in the region of Oceania from early in the nineteenth century.

6 Ian Breward, *A History of the Churches in Australasia*, Oxford: Oxford University Press, 2001, p. 21.

7 Tony Swain and Garry Trompf, *The Religions of Oceania*, London: Routledge, 1995, p. 2.

8 Swain and Trompf, *Religions*, p. 2.

9 Cyril Hally, 'Oceania: A New Identity', retrieved on 30 September 2005 from www.columban.org.au/TFE/tfe_99janfeb_2.htm

10 T.V. Philip, *Edinburgh to Salvador: Twentieth Century Ecumenical Missiology – A Historical Study of the Ecumenical Discussions on Mission*, Delphi: Cambridge Press, 1999, p. 9; Konrad Raiser, '"That the World May Believe." The Missionary Vocation as the Necessary Horizon for Ecumenism'*, lecture at the SEDOS Seminar, Ariccia, 19 May, 1999; retrieved on 10 December 2005 from www.sedos.org/english/raiser_1.html

11 Lukas Vischer (ed.), *A Documentary History of the Faith and Order Movement 1927–1963*, St Louis, MO: The Bethany Press, 1963, p. 178.

12 Second Vatican Council, 'Decree on The Church's Missionary Activity', in Norman Tanner (ed.), *Decrees of the Ecumenical Councils: Volume Two, Trent to Vatican II*, London: Sheed and Ward, 1990, p. 1015.

13 Tony Swain and Garry Trompf make the point of a distinction between the traditions of Australia and the Pacific Islands and *within* each of these 'geographical' settings; *Religions*, pp. 1–2.

14 Neil Gunson uses the term Evangelical to describe the missionaries to the Pacific; the missionary societies were the 'direct outcome of the preaching of the revivalists Whitefiled and Wesley'; *Messengers of Grace: Evangelical Missionaries in the South Seas 1797–1860*, Melbourne: Oxford University Press, 1978, p. 2.

15 Stephen B. Bevans and Roger P. Schroeder offer the years 1492–1773. *Constants in Context: A Theology of Mission for Today*, Maryknoll, NY: 2004, p. 171.

16 Garrett, *To Live Among the Stars*, p. 3; Niel Gunson, *Messengers of Grace*, p. 11.

17 David J. Bosch, *Transforming Mission: Paradigm Shifts in Theology of Mission*, Maryknoll, NY, 1992, p. 227.

18 Garrett, *To Live Among the Stars*, pp. 2–3.

19 'Three factors converged to effect a spiritual change in the English-speaking world, . . . the Great Awakening in the American colonies, the birth of Methodism, and the evangelical revival in Anglicanism', Bosch, *Transforming Mission*, p. 277.

20 Bevans and Schroeder, *Constants in Context*, p. 222.

21 Bevans and Schroeder, *Constants in Context*, pp. 158–60, 173.

22 Bevans and Schroeder, *Constants in Context*, p. 210. Also Andrew Walls, *The Missionary Movement in Christian History: Studies in the Transmission of Faith*, Maryknoll, NY: Orbis Books, 1996, p. 242.

23 Andrew Walls pushes the origin back into the last year of the seventeenth century. *The Missionary Movement in Christian History*, p. 241.

24 Bevans and Schroeder, *Constants in Context*, p. 211.

25 Robert Glen, *Mission and Moko: Aspects of the Work of the Church Missionary Society in New Zealand 1814–1882*, Christchurch: Latimer Fellowship of New Zealand. 1992, p. 15.

26 Gunson, *Messengers of Grace*, p. 12. John Garrett lists Calvinistic Methodists, Wesleyan Methodists, Scottish Presbyterians and Congregational Independents along with Calvinist Anglicans coming together to form this Society. *To Live Among the Stars*, p. 9.

27 Bevans and Schroeder, *Constants in Context*, p. 212. '[T]he first CMS missionaries were seven German Lutherans', Allan K. Davidson 'Culture and Ecclesiology: The Church Missionary Society and New Zealand', in Kevin Ward and Brian Stanley (eds), *The Church Mission Society and World Christianity 1799–1999*, Grand Rapids, MI: Wm.B. Eerdmans, 1999, p. 205. Also Bosch, *Transforming Mission*, p. 330.

28 'Prior to the year 1900, a total of eighty-one mission agencies were founded in North America. During the subsequent four decades 1900–1939, another 147 were formed. The next decade, 1940–1949, recorded the creation of eighty-three societies, followed by no fewer than 113 new agencies during the decade 1950–1959, 132 in the period 1960–1969 and another 150 in the next ten years', Bosch, *Transforming Mission*, p. 327.

29 Gunson, *Messengers of Grace*, p. 12. Garrett, *To Live Among the Stars*, p. 12.

30 Garrett, *To Live Among the Stars*, p. 19.

31 Garrett, *To Live Among the Stars*, p. 66.

32 The divide between Australia and other countries of Oceania is evident here. However, I would include Australia with Forman's comments to some degree as it is a place where colonialism preceded substantial missionary activity.

33 Charles W. Forman, *The Island Churches of the South Pacific: Emergence in the Twentieth Century*, Maryknoll, NY: Orbis Books, 1982, p. 11. Also Steven Roger Fischer, *A History of the Pacific Islands*, Hampshire: Palgrave, 2002, pp. 123–30.

34 Davidson, 'Culture and Ecclesiology', pp. 198–227.

35 Davidson, 'Culture and Ecclesiology', p. 211.

36 'The missionaries' ecclesiology was shaped by their Anglican evangelicalism and their desire to protect the emerging Maori church', Davidson, 'Culture and Ecclesiology', p. 208.

37 Davidson, 'Culture and Ecclesiology', p. 227.

38 Gunson, *Messengers of Grace*, pp. 15, 18.

39 Doug Munro and Andrew Thornley explain the term pastor as the 'central person in the life of the local church'. They differentiate this title from those of minister, priest, catechist, evangelist, missionary or teacher, as these 'titles often imply ordination, pioneer evangelism or school work, none of which has been as universal as the shepherding role implied by the title pastor'. 'Retrieving the Pastors: Questions of Representation and Voice', *The Covenant Makers: Islander Missionaries in the Pacific*, Suva, Fiji: Pacific Theological College and The Institute of Pacific Studies, University of the South Pacific, 1996, p. 1.

40 Garrett, *To Live Among the Stars*, p. 302.

41 Charles W. Forman, 'The Missionary Force of the Pacific Island Churches', *International Review of Mission* 59 (1970), 219.

42 Forman, 'Missionary Force of the Pacific Island Churches', p. 219.

43 Breward, *History*, pp. 23–24.

44 See also Forman, *Island Churches*, p. 2.

45 Darrell L. Whiteman, 'From Foreign Mission to Independent Church: The Anglicans in the Solomon Islands', *Catalyst* 11 (1981), 76; Forman, *Island Churches of the South Pacific*, pp. 6–7.

46 Whiteman, 'From Foreign Mission to Independent Church', p. 76.

47 Breward, *History*, p. 25.

48 Breward, *History*, p. 65.

49 Garrett, *To Live Among the Stars*, p. 44.

50 Wiltgen, *The Founding of the Roman Catholic Church in Oceania 1825–1850*, pp. 1–116. Also Eusebius J. Crawford, 'Missionary Effort in the Pacific', *Australasian Catholic Record* 66 (1989), 131–47.

51 Wiltgen, *The Founding of the Roman Catholic Church in Oceania 1825–1850*, p. xxi.

52 Bevans and Schroeder, *Constants in Context*, p. 226.

53 Bevans and Schroeder, *Constants in Context*, p. 226.

54 Bevans and Schroeder, *Constants in Context*, p. 226.

55 Breward, *History*, p. 41; Gunson, *Messengers of Grace*, p. 26.

56 Gunson, *Messengers of Grace*, p. 26.

57 Breward, *History*, p. 41.

58 The stories of a variety of religious orders present and active in Oceania over the last two hundred years, both men and women, priests, brothers and sisters, could be multiplied. For example, Jesuits, Marist Brothers and Priests, Missionary Sisters of the Society of Mary, Sisters of Our Lady of Nazareth, Daughters of Mary Immaculate, Missionaries of the Sacred Heart, Daughters of our Lady of the Sacred Heart, the Christian Brothers, and Divine Word Missionaries. John Foliaki, with Patrick Casserly, Catherine Jones, Laurence Hannan and Peter Wood, *The Roman Catholic*

Organisations, in Kerry James and Akuila Yabaki (eds), *Religious Cooperation in the Pacific Islands*, Suva, Fiji: Institute of Pacific Studies, University of the South Pacific, 1989, pp. 10–19.
59 Garrett, *To Live Among the Stars*, p. 179.
60 Breward, *History*, p. 48.
61 Breward, *History*, p. 10.
62 David Hilliard, 'Colonialism and Christianity: The Melanesian Mission in the Solomon Islands', *The Journal of Pacific History* 9 (1974), 94.
63 Breward, *History*, p. 13.
64 Edmund Campion, *Australian Catholics: The Contribution of Catholics to the Development of Australian Society*, Ringwood: Penguin Books, 1987, pp. 1–13.
65 John Harris, *Christianity and Aboriginal Australia: Part 1. The Earliest Christian Missions*, Canberra: Zadok Institute for Christianity and Society, 1987, pp. 8–9.
66 John Harris, *Christianity and Aboriginal Australia: Part 3. Dispossession and Despair: The Missionary Response at the end of the 19th Century*, Canberra: Zadok Institute for Christianity and Society, 1988, p. 4.
67 Frank G. Engel, 'Australia: Its Aborigines and Its Mission Boards', *International Review of Mission* 59 (1970), 297–98.
68 Harris, *Christianity and Aboriginal Australia: Part 3*, p. 11. Engle notes: 'In these places missionaries learnt the language translated the scriptures and provided educational and health services', 'Australia: Its Aborigines and Its Mission Boards', p. 28.
69 Harris, *Christianity and Aboriginal Australia: Part 5. Owning the Gospel: From Aboriginal Missions to Aboriginal Churches*, Canberra: Zadok Institute for Christianity and Society, 1988, p. 2.
70 Harris, *Christianity and Aboriginal Australia: Part 3*, p. 4. My emphasis. Harris also makes a distinction here between the long-lived nineteenth-century missions and the revival of non-denominational missions of the early twentieth century.
71 Harris, *Christianity and Aboriginal Australia: Part 1*, p. 2.
72 Harris, *Christianity and Aboriginal Australia: Part 1*, pp. 4–5. Breward, *History*, p. 7.
73 Henry Reynolds, *Dispossession: Black Australians and White Invaders*, Sydney: Allen and Unwin. 1989, pp. 170–4.
74 Harris, *Christianity and Aboriginal Australia: Part 1*, p. 4.
75 Harris, *Christianity and Aboriginal Australia: Part 1*, p. 2.
76 Breward, *History*, p. 5.
77 For example, Harris lists sixteen missions initiated in the early twentieth century that are part of 'a massive increase in missionary interest among the mainline churches', *Christianity and Aboriginal Australia: Part 5*, p. 8.
78 Michael Hogan, *The Sectarian Strand: Religion in Australian History*, Ringwood: Penguin Books, 1987, p. 260.
79 'For most of the history of white settlement the attitudes of Christian leaders towards Aboriginal culture and religion have reflected attitudes of the general white community', Hogan, *The Sectarian Strand*, p. 260.
80 Human Rights and Equal Opportunity Commission, *Bringing Them Home: A Guide to the Findings and Recommendations of the National Inquiry into the Separation of Aboriginal and Torres Strait Islander Children from their Families*, Sydney: Human Rights and Equal Opportunity Commission, 1997.
81 *Bringing Them Home*, p. 3.
82 *Bringing Them Home*, p. 26.
83 A Statement by the Executive of the National Council of Churches. Retrieved 28th February 2006, www.ncca.org.au/natsiec/issues/stolen_generations
84 H.R. Jackson, *Churches & People in Australia and New Zealand 1860–1930*, Wellington: Allen & Unwin, 1987, p. 15.
85 Jackson, *Church & People in Australia and New Zealand*, p. 15.
86 Breward, *History*, pp. 66, 96.
87 Breward, *History*, p. 10.
88 Jabez Bryce, *Religious Cooperation in the Pacific Islands*, Suva, Fiji: Institute of Pacific Studies, University of the South Pacific, 1989, p. x.
89 Walls, *The Missionary Movement in Christian History*, p. 248.
90 Bosch, *Transforming Mission*, p. 331.

91 'By so-called comity arrangements, various mission groups, whether of the churches or independent of them divided new territories into spheres of operation', Tom Stransky, 'Common Witness', in Nicholas Lossky, *et al.* (eds), *Dictionary of the Ecumenical Movement*, Geneva: WCC Publications, 1991, p. 198.

92 For example of a dispute between LMS and Wesleyan missionaries in Samoa see Breward, *History*, p. 33. Charles Forman notes that there were no comity agreements between Catholics and Protestants; rivalry and hostility characterized the relationship of these 'branches of Christianity'; *The Island Churches of the South Pacific*, p. 203.

93 Philip, *Edinburgh to Salvador*, p. 55.

94 Philip, *Edinburgh to Salvador*, p. 6; Glen, *Mission and Moko*, p. 23.

95 Henry Venn, 'On Steps Towards Helping a Native Church to Become Self-Supporting, Self-Governing and Self-Extending', in Francis M. DuBose (ed.), *Classics of Christian Missions*, Nashville: Broadman Press, 1979, pp. 245–9.

96 Ward and Stanley, *The Church Mission Society and World Christianity, 1799–1999*, pp. 156–7.

97 Bosch, *Transforming Mission*, pp. 330–1; Philip, *Edinburgh to Salvador*, pp. 13–16.

98 This was coincident with the strengthening of colonial government's involvement in mission territories in the late nineteenth and early twentieth centuries: '[I]n the nineteenth century colonial expansion would once again acquire religious overtones and also be intimately linked with mission! . . . From the point of view of the colonial government . . . Who was better equipped than these missionaries to persuade unwilling "natives" to submit to the *pax Britannica* or the *pax Teutonica?*' Bosch, *Transforming Mission*, p. 303.

99 Philip, *Edinburgh to Salvador*, p. 55.

100 Philip A. Potter, 'Mission', in *Dictionary of the Ecumenical Movement*, p. 690. Also Ulrich Duchrow, 'The Conciliar Ecumenical Movement: Transcending Imperial Globalism and Parochial Tribalism' in Gregory Baum (ed.), *The Twentieth Century: A Theological Overview*, Maryknoll, NY: Orbis Books. 1999, p. 145. Two significant conferences preceded Edinburgh, both in 1900: the South India missionary conference at Madras and an ecumenical missionary conference in New York.

101 Philip, *Edinburgh to Salvador*, p. 56.

102 Robert Schreiter, 'Changes in Roman Catholic Attitudes toward Proselytism and Mission', in James A. Scherer and Stephen B. Bevans (eds), *New Directions in Mission and Evangelization 2: Theological Foundations*, Maryknoll, NY: Orbis Books, 1994, pp. 113–25.

103 Bevans and Schroeder, *Constants in Context*, pp. 244, 256.

104 Bevans and Schroeder note Benedict XV's teaching *Maxium Illud* (1919) as the first of the five encyclicals, *Constants and Context*, p. 245. However, *Maxium Illud*, 'On Spreading the Catholic Faith Throughout the World', is in fact an Apostolic Letter; five subsequent encyclicals leading up to Vatican II that I find include the issue of missions are: *Rerum Ecclesiae*, 'On Catholic Missions' (1926) and *Mortalium Animos*, 'On Religious Unity' (1928) by Pope Pius XI; *Evangelii Praecones*, 'On Promotion of Catholic Missions' (1951) by Pius XII; and *Princips Pastorum*, 'On the Missions, Native Clergy, and Lay Participation' (1959) and *Ad Petri Cathedram*, 'On Truth, Unity and Peace, in a Spirit of Charity' (1959) by John XXIII. Identification of *Maxium Illud* and excerpts from those by Pius XI and Pius XII in: The Benedictine Monks of Solesmes, *Papal Teachings: The Church*, Boston: St Paul Editions, pp. 414, 442, 449, 617. Encyclicals by John XXIII retrieved March 2003 from www.vatican.va/holy_father/john_xxiii/encyclicals/documents/hf_i-xxiii_enc_28111959_princeps-en.html and www.vatican.va/holy_father/john_xxiii/encyclicals/documentshf_i-xxiii_enc_29061959/ad_petri_en.html respectively.

105 Bevans and Schroeder, *Constants in Context*, p. 245.

106 Bevans and Schroeder, *Constants in Context*, pp. 249–51.

107 See Breward for a brief description of the consequences of Vatican II and the general time of 'crisis' in the Australian context: *History*, pp. 325–8.

108 Bevans and Schroeder, *Constants in Context*, p. 252.

109 Bevans and Schroeder, *Constants in Context*, p. 254.

110 John Paul II, *Redemptoris Missio: On the Permanent Validity of the Church's Missionary Mandate*, Homebush: St Paul's Publications, 1991, p. 83.

111 Bevans and Schroeder, *Constants in Context*, p. 256.

112 Bevans and Schroeder, *Constants in Context*, pp. 257–8.

113 For a brief survey see Potter, 'Mission', pp. 690–6.
114 Bevans and Schroeder, *Constants in Context*, p. 259. See also Lesslie Newbigin's inaugural sermon at the integration of the IMC and the WCC. Reprinted, 'The Missionary Dimension of the Ecumenical Movement', *International Review of Mission* 70 (1981), 240–6.
115 Bevans and Schroeder, *Constants in Context*, pp. 260–2.
116 The LMS initiated the move and the IMC was invited to organize the conference. Lorini Tevi and Akuila Yabaki, 'The Pacific Conference of Churches', in Kerry James and Akuila Yabaki (eds), *Religious Cooperation in the Pacific Islands*, p. 3.
117 Kambati Uriam, 'Doing Theology in the New Pacific', in Phyllis Herda, Michael Reilly and David Hilliard (eds), *Vision and Reality in Pacific Religion: Essays in Honour of Neil Gunson*, Christchurch: Macmillan Brown Centre for Pacific Studies, University of Canterbury and Pandanus Books, Research School of Pacific and Asian Studies, Australian National University, 2005, p. 301. Charles W. Forman, 'The Pacific Ecumenical Scene', *Pacific Journal of Theology* 4 (1990), 51; Kafoa Solomone, 'Ecumenism in Oceania', *The Pacific Journal of Theology* 24 (2000), p. 91.
118 Uriam, 'Doing Theology in the New Pacific', p. 302.
119 Charles W. Forman, 'Tonga's Tortured Venture in Church Unity', *The Journal of Pacific History* 13 (1978), 3–21.
120 Solomone, 'Ecumenism in Oceania', pp. 90–1.
121 Forman, *Island Churches*, p. 144.
122 Forman, *Island Churches*, p. 144; also Breward, *History*, pp. 334–52.
123 Frank Engel, *Conflict and Unity 1788–1926. Volume 1*, Melbourne: Joint Board of Christian Education of Australia and New Zealand, 1984, pp. 227–8.
124 With regard to the latter he cites Student Christian Movements that resulted from overseas influence and which had an understanding and commitment to Christian unity. Engel, p. *Conflict and Unity*, p. 227.
125 Engel, *Conflict and Unity*, pp. 228–31.
126 Engel, *Conflict and Unity*, p. 230.
127 Forman, *Island Churches*, p. 203.
128 Forman, *Island Churche*, p. 202.
129 Cyril Germon, 'Planning the Pacific Theological College', *South Pacific Journal of Mission Studies* 25 (2001), 24.
130 Uriam, 'Doing Theology in the New Pacific', p. 292.
131 Forman, *Island Churches*, p. 203.
132 Tevi and Yabaki, 'The Pacific Conference of Churches', p. 4.
133 Uriam, 'Doing Theology in the New Pacific', p. 302.
134 Uriam, 'Doing Theology in the New Pacific', pp. 288–96.
135 Uriam, 'Doing Theology in the New Pacific', p. 297.
136 Ilaitia Sevati Tuwere, 'The Pacific Theological College', in Kerry James and Akulia Yabaki (eds), *Religious Cooperation in the Pacific Islands*, Suva, Fiji: Institute of Pacific Studies, University of the South Pacific, 1989, p. 103.
137 Ilaitia Sevati Tuwere, 'The Pacific Theological College', p. 103.
138 Solomone, 'Ecumenism in Oceania', p. 99.
139 Australian and New Zealand Association of Theological Schools; New Zealand Association of Theological Schools; South Pacific Association of Theological Schools; Melanesian Association of Theological Schools; and, for example, various ecumenical consortia such as Melbourne College of Divinity, Sydney College of Divinity, Brisbane College of Theology and Adelaide College of Divinity.
140 For example, see Raymond K. Williamson (ed.), *Stages on the Way: Documents from the Bilateral Conversations between Churches in Australia*, Melbourne: The Joint Board of Christian Education, 1994.
141 Manfred Ernst, 'The Effects of New Religious Movements on Pacific Culture', *Pacific Journal of Theology* (1994), 7–14. Ernst makes the distinction between the new groups, 'basically evangelical and fundamentalist in nature', that have 'invaded' the Pacific Islands in the last thirty years, and the mainline churches, p. 7.

Further reading

Ian Breward, *A History of the Churches in Australasia,*. Oxford: Oxford University Press, 2001.

Andrew Dutney, *From Here to Where? Australian Christians Owning the Past-Embracing the Future*, Melbourne: Uniting Church Press, 1988.

Charles W. Forman, The *Island Churches of the South Pacific: Emergence in the Twentieth Century*, Maryknoll, NY: Orbis Books, 1982.

John Garrett, *To Live Among the Stars: Christian Origins in Oceania*, Geneva: World Council of Churches; Suva: Institute of Pacific Studies, University of the South Pacific, 1982.

Neil Gunson, *Messengers of Grace: Evangelical Missionaries in the South Seas 1797–1860*, Melbourne: Oxford University Press, 1978.

T.V. Philip, *Edinburgh to Salvador: Twentieth Century Ecumenical Missiology – A Historical Study of the Ecumenical Dimensions of Mission*, Delphi: Cambridge Press, 1999.

Tony Swain and Garry Trompf, *The Religions of Oceania*, London: Routledge, 1995.

Ralph M. Wiltgen, *The Founding of the Roman Catholic Church in Oceania, 1825 to 1850*, Canberra: Australian National University Press, 1979.

20

THE CHURCH FROM A EUROPEAN PERSPECTIVE

Peter De Mey

This book contains many valuable chapters on how the church has been understood in the course of history. In other chapters the history of the great ecclesial traditions has been presented. Because these historical overviews to a great extent cover the history of the church in Europe the present author will not here treat his subject from a historical point of view but will rather focus on the present challenges and opportunities for the Christian faith and for the churches in Europe.

In the first section we will look at the results of recent sociological analysis of this theme. The basic question governing such research is whether Europe is an exception to the desecularization thesis or not. In the second and third section the reader will be able to discover how the major ecclesial traditions in Europe look at this issue. At the same time we will introduce the work of the major intra- and inter-denominational church bodies which consider it as their particular task to reflect on the present situation of the church in Europe.

My next point of departure will be a substantial text issued on the very theme of the church in Europe by Pope John Paul II – the post-synodal apostolic exhortation *Ecclesia in Europa* (2003). Such texts are always written as a personal reflection by the pope on the results of one of the assemblies of the Synod of Bishops dealing with the same theme. The reader will also be introduced to the work of the Council of European Episcopal Conferences (CCEE) and the Commission of the Episcopates of the European Community (COMECE). The documents treated in sections two and three will also reflect on the political integration of Europe which has been a major issue during the last decade.

In the third section the Roman Catholic perspective will be compared with assessments of the church in Europe issued by other denominations. We will study the working document on *Churches in the Process of European Integration* (2001) by the Conference of European Churches (CEC), which is the largest cooperative body of Orthodox, Protestant and Old Catholic Churches in Europe. Thereafter we will turn the attention to the Community of Protestant Churches in Europe (CPCE) and their recent document, *Evangelising: Protestant Perspectives for the Churches in Europe* (2006). As far as the Orthodox Church is concerned we will especially focus on the work of the Representation of the Russian Orthodox Church to the European Institutions.

In the last section of this chapter, as a complement to the other chapters of this book dealing with ecumenism, special attention will be paid to the *Charta Oecumenica* (2001), a short document containing 'Guidelines for the Growing Cooperation of the Churches in

Europe'. The document is the result of the intense cooperation between the Conference of European Churches and the Council of European Episcopal Conferences.

The results of recent sociological research on church and faith in Europe

Before analysing a number of recent documents issued by authoritative voices or consultative bodies from different churches in Europe on the same theme, it seems useful to summarize the results of recent sociological reflections on the current situation of church and faith in Europe. These studies have been written from a Western European perspective, but the tendencies described apply to some extent to Eastern European countries as well.[1]

Usually the point of departure of contemporary sociology of religion is the self-criticism by Peter Berger and Harvey Cox as regards the secularization thesis which they have strongly defended since the 1970s.[2] This thesis made use of the 'zero-sum-theory', arguing that the sum of modernization and religion is always zero. In the meantime it has become clear that in most countries of the world, a new resurgence of religious life in its rich variety has gone hand in hand with economic growth. Berger and Cox, however, believe that Europe is an exception to the desecularization thesis, in view of the absence of a clear religious revival.

European sociologists and theologians who comment upon the results of their research present a more nuanced view on religion in Europe. A comparative analysis of the results of the 1981, 1990 and 1999 surveys of the European Values Study allowed the French sociologist Yves Lambert in a recent article to speak of a religious mutation in Europe.[3] The process of 'un-churching' still continues, but among the younger generation the quest for religiosity, or, more precisely, for different forms of spirituality, is increasing. However, because this certainly does not lead to a greater attachment to the traditional religions, Lambert carefully concludes that Europe has become a little bit less of an exception to the desecularization thesis. There is also a great difference among European countries with regard to the question whether the public presence of churches and religious communities is being encouraged rather than hindered by the political authorities. Lambert observes signs of desecularization in his own previously vehemently laicist country, France, whereas a confessional country like Sweden is further secularizing. In view of the fact that the secularization thesis is no longer applicable in an undifferentiated way to Europe, the Belgian theologian Lieven Boeve believes that it is legitimate to speak about a 'post-secular Europe', characterized by the individualization, detraditionalization and pluralization of religion.[4]

I will pay special attention to the research of the British sociologist Grace Davie, because she believes that the historic churches – at least for the moment – still fulfil an important role in the lives of the majority of European citizens. Davie coined the very useful expression 'believing without belonging' to indicate that 'the falling-off in religious attendance has not yet resulted in a parallel abdication of religious belief'.[5] At the same time Davie is convinced that such an attitude towards the Christian tradition can only last for about one generation. Therefore she prefers to leave open the question whether or not Europe is an exceptional case with regard to the desecularization thesis.[6]

As a sociologist Davie believes that there is strong evidence that the historic churches still fulfil an important role in contemporary Europe, even if they have become a minority organization – with a strong presence of women and elderly people – whose active members belong not by tradition but by opting in. Large segments of society, however, expect this minority to be continuously available with its offer of meaningful rituals at key moments of life, especially at the moment of death. Davie makes this clear by analysing the examples of the funeral services for Princess Diana and François Mittérand.[7]

Davie believes that the group of active participants in church life has become a minority but that this minority remains faithful to its choice 'on behalf of a much larger number, who (implicitly at least) not only understand, but, quite clearly, approve of what the minority is doing'.[8] This is Davie's definition of 'vicarious religion', the key term in her argument.[9] She convincingly argues that the larger portion of society expects believers, and especially religious leaders, to remain faithful to the ethical ideals prescribed by their churches and not to question the doctrinal tradition – in Davie's terminology, the 'authorized memory' – of their church in public. If this happens, it is followed by a storm of indignation.[10]

The largest part of her book deals with the mutations of this memory in contemporary society. Among the examples studied are religious innovations such as the greater involvement of the laity in Catholic Europe and the opening up of ministry to women in almost all Protestant churches;[11] the rejection by Christians in modern Europe of parts of the teaching of their church – such as those dealing with sexual ethics – without 'necessarily rejecting religion, even the Christian religion, *per se*';[12] the growing success of adult baptism and adult confirmation as an example that '[v]oluntarism is necessarily, if not legally, asserting itself';[13] the concern about 'religious illiteracy amongst younger generations', even if the success of World Youth Days shows that 'certain forms of religious activity do still appeal to young people';[14] the growing success of new religious movements and other-faith communities;[15] and the fairly intact 'aesthetic or cultural memory associated with the Christian tradition'.[16]

I want to end this section on a positive note by quoting Davie's still relatively optimistic overall view on the future of the presence of religious life in Europe: '[T]he combination of all these factors will increase rather than decrease the salience of religion in public, as well as private, debate – a tendency encouraged by the ever more obvious presence of religion in the modern world order. In this respect, the world is more likely to influence the religious life of Europe than the other way round.'[17]

The Roman Catholic view on (the church in) Europe: John Paul II and *Ecclesia in Europa* (2003)

During his long pontificate (1978–2005), John Paul II expressed a profound interest in Europe. In several hundred of his speeches, letters and other documents, he reflected on Europe's past and future and on its necessary unity. Studies make reference to the existence of a characteristic 'Wojtylian geopolitics'.[18] From the very beginning of his pontificate, he alluded regularly to General de Gaulle's renowned statement that the borders of Europe extend from the Atlantic to the Urals. Since his first pilgrimage to Poland in 1979, Pope John Paul II was instrumental to some degree in stimulating the interest of Western European Christians and politicians in Eastern Europe. In 1980, he proclaimed Saints Cyril and Methodius as co-patrons of Europe, some fifteen years after Pope Paul VI had done the same with St Benedict of Nursia.

According to many analysts, the pope's vivid, 'quasi-obsessive'[19] interest in Europe was due to the fact that he could not imagine the 'old continent', which had once been the point of departure for the proclamation of the gospel in the most remote parts of the globe, ever ceasing to cultivate its Christian roots. In 1991, shortly after the collapse of the Berlin wall, Pope John Paul II convened a special assembly of the Synod of Bishops in order to focus specifically on the urgent need for a 'new evangelization' of Europe. With this programme the Pope hoped to counter the crisis of secularism and laicism in Europe. In 1999 a second special assembly of the Synod of Bishops was convened on pretty much the same theme, as 'the last of a series of continental Synods celebrated in preparation for the Great Jubilee of the Year 2000' (EE 2).[20]

John Paul II was aware that there were many places in Europe in which 'a first proclamation of the Gospel [was] needed' (EE 46), due either to the prohibition of the work of evangelization, a spirit of religious indifferentism, or practical agnosticism. At the same time 'a renewed proclamation [was] needed, even for those already baptized' (EE 47). However, this challenge was taken up during the synod not by criticizing Europe but by offering a constructive, hopeful alternative, as was already evident in its title: 'Jesus Christ, alive in his church, the source of hope for Europe'. In his post-synodal exhortation, which the pope published in 2003 as a personal reflection on the interventions of the bishops and other synod guests, he demonstrated the urgency of the task of proclaiming the gospel anew in Europe by selecting passages from the Book of Revelation as the motto for each chapter.[21]

I believe it makes sense to take a closer look at John Paul II's views on the challenges and signs of hope for the church in Europe, as reflected in the post-synodal exhortation *Ecclesia in Europa*.[22] We have to realize, of course, that a substantial amount of frustration exists with the way the synod of bishops functions concretely as an instrument of episcopal collegiality. Michael Fahey's observations with regard to the Synod of America are also applicable to the results of the two synods on Europe: 'Unfortunately, despite high hopes for their success, results of synods have been negligible. Each new synod attracts less and less attention; the structure of their sessions has become unwieldy; they have become rituals with little practical impact on the life of the Church. In the last 30 years the institution has not been notable as a wellspring of new ideas and strategies.'[23] It should also be noted by way of critique that the footnote references in *Ecclesia in Europa* draw exclusively on the teaching of the universal magisterium of the church, whereas there can be little doubt that valuable contributions from individual European bishops and theologians or their collaborative gatherings are also available. In the present author's opinion, it is sad – and perhaps some indication of a lack of ecumenical engagement on behalf of the Catholic Church – that there is no single reference in *Ecclesia in Europa* to the *Charta Oecumenica* (2001), a major result of cooperation between a Roman Catholic body, the Council of European Bishops' Conferences (CCEE), and the Conference of European Churches.

Finally, it is curious that the list of propositions offered to the pope in preparing his post-synodal exhortation has not been made public.[24] Is this based on a fear that the said *propositiones* do not really do justice to some of the more critical interventions of individual participants during these synods?

What are the 'challenges and signs of hope for the Church in Europe' (EE 7–17) according to the analysis given by John Paul II? Firstly, the pope mentions 'the loss of Europe's Christian memory and heritage, accompanied by a kind of practical agnosticism and religious indifference whereby many Europeans give the impression of living without spiritual roots' (EE 7). This loss of Christian memory, according to the pope, 'is accompanied by a kind of fear of the future', the 'signs and fruits' of which include 'the diminishing number of births, the decline in the number of vocations to the priesthood and religious life, and the difficulty, if not the outright refusal, to make lifelong commitments, including marriage' (EE 8). The pope believes that a worldview in which the human person is considered 'apart from God and apart from Christ' lies at the root of this loss of hope, even if it pertains to a non-reflexive form of atheism: 'European culture gives the impression of "silent apostasy" on the part of people who have all that they need and who live as if God does not exist'[25] (EE 9). Among the signs of hope (EE 11–17), the pope mentions growing contact between Western and Eastern Europe, progress made in the journey of ecumenism and the flourishing of new movements and new ecclesial communities. The pope adds some additional challenges and signs of hope to this list when he introduces the chapter on 'Celebrating the Gospel of hope'. The pope sounds (too?) optimistic when he states that 'despite the dechristianisation of vast areas of the European Continent, there are *signs* which suggest an image *of a Church which, in believing, proclaims, celebrates and serves her Lord*' (EE 67). Sociologists, as we have seen, tend rather to point to the resurgence of new forms of religiosity, in Europe and elsewhere, which cast doubt on the persistence of the secularization paradigm, although it can be doubted whether this always pertains to Christian religiosity. Perhaps some of these forms are being alluded to when the pope introduces some challenges:

> Together with the many examples of genuine faith, there also exists in Europe a *vague and at times deviant religiosity*. Its signs are often generic and superficial, or even contradictory, in the very persons who manifest them. There are evident signs of a flight to spiritualism, of religious and esoteric syncretism, of a frantic search for extraordinary events, even to the point of making aberrant decisions, such as joining dangerous sects or engaging in pseudoreligious experiences. (EE 68)

One might be inclined to wonder whether the World Youth Days, which the pope recalls with profound joy (EE 62), do not reflect a similar search for extraordinary events by young Catholics. A concluding series of challenges pertain to the Christian call to serve the gospel of hope in a society characterized by problems such as unemployment (EE 87), the crisis of the family (EE 90) and, especially, the culture of death (EE 95). The pope particularly deplores the fact that legislation in a number of European countries permits abortion and in some instances even euthanasia.

The pope points not only to the specific task of ordained ministers, consecrated people, laity and women with regard to the proclamation of the gospel in Europe (EE 33–43), but also to the specific role of two 'continental ecclesial bodies' involving 'cooperation between all the particular churches of the continent as an expression of their essential communion' (EA 53). The pope makes explicit mention of the Council of European Episcopal Conferences (EA 53, 118)[26] and the Commission of the Episcopates of the European Community (EA 118).[27] The description of the work of the former throws some interesting light on the discussion on whether episcopal conferences are an instrument of affective or effective collegiality among bishops. In paragraph 23 of Vatican II's dogmatic constitution on the Church, *Lumen Gentium*, it is explained how 'episcopal conferences can today make a manifold and fruitful contribution to the concrete application of the spirit of collegiality'. The Council fathers, however, left the precise juridical status of these episcopal conferences undecided.

In his *Motu proprio Apostolos Suos* (1998) John Paul II distinguished between 'collegialis affectus' mentioned in LG 23 and 'collegialis actio' – and thus between 'affective' and 'effective' collegiality – and stated that 'collegial actions cannot be carried out at the level of individual particular Churches or of gatherings of such Churches called together by their respective Bishops'.[28] Even if recent theological research has argued that it would be better to refrain from using these terms because they are too ambiguous,[29] magisterial texts such as

Ecclesia in Europa mostly speak about episcopal conferences and about councils of episcopal conferences in terms of 'affective collegiality'.

The first line of the description of the work of the CCEE may leave room for some ambiguity, but the precise terminology of the final line leaves no doubt on the juridical status of the CCEE:

> The Council is an effective means for exploring together appropriate ways of evangelizing Europe. Through an 'exchange of gifts' between the various Particular Churches, the experiences and the reflections of Western and Eastern, Northern and Southern Europe are shared and common pastoral approaches emerge. The Council is becoming an increasingly significant expression of the collegial sentiment linking the Bishops of the Continent, aimed at proclaiming together, boldly and faithfully, the name of Jesus Christ, the sole source of hope for everyone in Europe. (EE 53)[30]

Quite remarkably, however, another paragraph of *Ecclesia in Europa* dedicated to the work of the CCEE makes reference to an earlier address given by John Paul II in 1993, several years before *Apostolos Suos*, stating that 'the strengthening of affective and effective collegiality and of hierarchical communion' (EE 118) is part of the task of the CCEE.

The lines that follow deal with the significance of COMECE:

> Together with the Council, acknowledgment must also be made of the service provided by the Commission of the Episcopates of the European Community, which, in following the process of consolidation and enlargement of the European Union, favours the sharing of information and coordinates the pastoral initiatives of the European Churches involved. (EE 118)

John Paul II appears at times to comment on the difficult preparatory process lying behind the Treaty Establishing a Constitution for Europe. The pope expresses the hope that a united Europe would be built upon important values such as the inalienable dignity of the human person and the sacredness of human life. He refers to 'the spirit of ancient Greece and Rome, the contributions of the Celtic, Germanic, Slav and Finno-Ugric peoples and the influence of Jewish and Islamic culture' as important factors in the development of these values. The text concludes with what can be described as an inclusivist argument, ending with an implicit plea that the Constitution should recognize the full elaboration of these values in Christianity.[31] The following line contains an implicit plea for a clear reference to the Christian roots of Europe in the preamble of the Constitution: 'Europe's history would be incomprehensible without reference to the events which marked first the great period of evangelization and then the long centuries when Christianity, despite the painful division between East and West, came to be the religion of the European peoples' (EE 24). A further argument in support of the same plea seems to be that 'Europe drew the best of its humanistic culture from the biblical conception of man' (EE 25). The final version of the preamble to the 2004 Treaty Establishing a Constitution for Europe – an enterprise which might well be abandoned in the near future because of the lack of sufficient recognition among the member states – only mentions that the constitution draws 'inspiration from the cultural, religious and humanist inheritance of Europe'.[32]

The most explicit attempt of John Paul II to influence the text of the Constitution is to be found in EE 114, which is in turn a paraphrase of one of his annual addresses to the diplomatic corps, given on January 13, 2003. The text of *Ecclesia in Europa* reads as follows.

> In the light of what I have just emphasized, I wish once more to appeal to those drawing up the future European constitutional treaty, so that it will include a reference to the religious and in particular the Christian heritage of Europe. While fully respecting the secular nature of the institutions, I consider it desirable especially that three complementary elements should be recognized: the right of Churches and religious communities to organize themselves freely in conformity with their statutes and proper convictions; respect for the specific identity of the different religious confessions and provision for a structured dialogue between the European Union and those confessions; and respect for the juridical status already enjoyed by Churches and religious institutions by virtue of the legislation of the member states of the Union.[33]

To all intents and purposes, Pope John Paul II appears to repeat the proposal jointly made by the Church and Society Commission of the Conference of European Churches[34] and the Commission of the Bishops' Conferences of the European Community in a letter to the president of the drafting body of the European Convention, Valérie Giscard d'Estaing, on September 27, 2002. The text proposes three sections for an article on 'Churches and Religious Communities'.

> 1. The European Union recognizes and respects the right of the churches and religious communities to freely organize themselves in accordance with national law, their convictions and statutes and to pursue their religious aims in the framework of fundamental rights; 2. The European Union respects the specific identity and the contribution to public life of churches and religious communities and maintains a structured dialogue with them; 3. The European Union respects and does not prejudice the status under national law of churches and religious communities in the Member States. The European Union equally respects the status of philosophical and non-confessional organizations.

Article I-52 of the Treaty Establishing a Constitution for Europe has clearly been influenced by either one or both texts:

> 1. The Union respects and does not prejudice the status under national law of churches and religious associations or communities in the Member States. 2. The Union equally respects the status under national law of philosophical and non-confessional organizations. 3. Recognizing their identity and their specific contribution, the Union shall maintain an open, transparent and regular dialogue with these churches and organizations.[35]

The Roman Catholic perspective compared with assessments of the church in Europe issued by other denominations

In this relatively brief section I intend to analyse some representative views on the church in Europe that have been published by other Christian churches and their cooperative bodies. I will only highlight those aspects that are missing from, or have been treated differently in, *Ecclesia in Europa*.

The Conference of European Churches

The Conference of European Churches (CEC) is the largest cooperative body of Orthodox, Protestant and Old Catholic Churches in Europe. There is a close cooperation between the CEC and both the CCEE and the COMECE but – in like fashion to the decision regarding membership of the World Council of Churches (WCC) – the Roman Catholic Church is not a member of this fellowship. The main task of the 'Church and Society Commission' of the Conference of European Churches is to follow the activities of European institutions. In 2001, its 'Working Group on the Process of European integration' published a working document entitled *Churches in the Process of European Integration*[36] to which we will now briefly turn our attention.

The theme of diversity is certainly not absent from *Ecclesia in Europa*. The term is only used three times, however, in a document three times as long as *Churches in the Process of European Integration*, and the most relevant passages emphasize 'unity in diversity'.[37] In *Churches in the Process of European Integration*, respect for diversity is presented as the major challenge facing the European integration process. Some fear exists that European politicians are only interested in economic values, whereas 'at least equal attention must be paid to the protection of the rich cultural, ethnic and spiritual diversity of the continent' (2.2). If there are grounds for this fear, then there is a danger that one part of Europe – read Western Europe – will impose its own – read materialistic and secular – values upon the whole of Europe. If one wishes to create a 'genuine European community', then more attention must be given to the diversity of values that are found at the level of 'the particular, regional or national' (2.2). The text returns to this issue when it states that 'respect for diversity' has often been called 'a substantive element of European identity' in European circles (3.2). What Europe needs is 'a mutual interplay between unity and diversity' (3.5).[38]

Whereas this very specific plea for diversity seems to have been inserted in the text on the insistence of the Orthodox churches, the example of the protection of minorities seems to reflect a Protestant sensitivity.[39] The text recognizes that respect for minorities is at times a challenge for the churches:

> On various occasions, churches contributed to developing tensions, misunderstandings and even conflicts. Not always were churches consistently following basic rights of respecting minorities' opinions, respecting each other and religious freedom. This did not only happen in the remote past. In our current situation tensions still persist which are revealed on various occasions in the ecumenical movement. (4.1)

There is an obvious contrast with *Ecclesia in Europa*, where the terms 'minority' and 'minorities' are only mentioned three times in passing (EE 57, 63, 115). Furthermore, in contrast with *Ecclesia in Europa*, the CEC document refers towards the end to the *Charta Oecumenica* in which all the churches in Europe committed themselves to support the process of European integration (4.3).

The Community of Protestant Churches in Europe (CPCE)

At present, more than 100 Protestant churches in Europe grant each other pulpit and table fellowship on the basis of the Leuenberg Agreement of 1973. In their search for visible unity, these churches prefer the model of *Kirchengemeinschaft*.[40] The Leuenberg Agreement makes a distinction between the message of justification and the plurality of legitimate doctrinal expressions of this message.[41] In the 1990s, the model of church fellowship was also accepted by the Anglican churches. The *Declaration of Meissen* between the Evangelical Church in Germany (EKD) and the Church of England (1988) is an example of a form of limited church fellowship, also termed 'interim eucharistic sharing'. Eucharistic hospitality is possible, but it does not yet include full interchangeability of ministries because of a continuing lack of consensus on episcopacy. Since the approval of the *Porvoo Declaration* (1992), full church communion has been realized between the Anglican churches in the British Isles and most Lutheran churches in Scandinavia and the Baltic countries.[42] The relatively thin structure of the Communion of Protestant Churches of Europe is deplored on occasion, even if attempts to strengthen these structures often meet with negative reactions from the signatory churches out of fear of being governed by a 'super-church'.[43] A specific problem consists in the fact that individual Protestant churches can be members of different communions of churches, each with their own policies and ecumenical agendas.[44] In this section, we will discuss the document *Evangelising: Protestant Perspectives for the Churches in Europe*,[45] which was accepted by the General Assembly of the Community of Protestant Churches in Europe in Budapest in September 2006.

At a number of crucial places in the document, the theological awareness is expressed that the work of mission is ultimately God's work: 'Mission is *missio Dei*, i.e. a movement of God to human beings which God makes through the church.'[46] An important methodological decision made by the drafters of the text was to avoid the term 'evangelism'. Instead of this term, which expresses 'an isolated word-event with no reference to social experience', the term 'evangelising' was chosen, 'which we take to mean a life-process of the whole church in word and deed; a process that opens up to people the Gospel's space for freedom in which it is made possible for them to meet with the God who became human in Jesus Christ' (1.4).

While it is true that the apostolic exhortation *Ecclesia in Europa* also pays attention to both challenges and signs of hope for the proclamation of the gospel in Europe, the reader is aware of the many crypto-condemnations of a number of these challenges. The third chapter of *Evangelising: Protestant Perspectives for the Churches in Europe*, 'What challenges do the European contexts pose for evangelising?', contains a remarkable introduction which deserves to be quoted in full, and which illustrates the way in which the fifteen challenges have been approached in this chapter.

> God approaches people of all times and contexts. No context in itself is categorically closed to God or in itself particularly near to him. Every context has specific affinities to the Gospel and at the same time particular barriers to it. This ambivalence is plain everywhere, including the contexts of present-day Europe. We maintain that these contexts are not in principle resistant to the Gospel and in consequence we do not meet them with any pessimism about the culture or the Zeitgeist. In what follows, we will highlight some ways in which the European contexts challenge our churches to missionary activity and the new opportunities which they open up for the offer of the Gospel. (3)

372

After the introductory chapter entitled 'Why is evangelising a challenge for Protestant churches in Europe?' had already stated unambiguously that 'Europe is the most strongly secularised continent' (1.5), it comes as no surprise that 'secularisation' is mentioned as the first challenge in Chapter 3. Whereas an 'ideologised secularism' is certainly not encouraged, the document pays equal attention to the beneficial aspects of secularization.[47]

Compared to John Paul II's fierce critique of 'deviant religiosity', this document is certainly less afraid of the 'new religious longing', which is treated as the second challenge and as almost the natural counterpart of secularization.[48] The (misinterpreted?) Roman Catholic approach towards evangelization is certainly no option: 'Great as the passion for evangelising may be, a "re-Christianising" of Europe in the sense of a so-called *Corpus Christianum* is neither realistic nor from a Protestant perspective desirable.' It is their conviction that '[a]ll churches have a duty to be humble and to abandon any "missionary imperialism"'.

Chapter 4 is entitled: 'How can evangelising become a reality?' It contains some recommendations for individuals, local parishes, member churches and the entire Community of Protestant Churches in Europe. The advice for local churches reminds us of Grace Davie's reflections on 'believing without belonging':

> For this reason, we need local churches which value the seekers and enquirers, the undecided and sceptics, without putting undue pressure on them. The traditional sequence, 'first find the way to faith, then into a church', seems to be being reversed: finding a home in a church often precedes finding oneself at home in faith in Christ. So we need churches which can put up with the stressful conjunction of belief and unbelief and do not draw distinctions too quickly. (4.1)

The Orthodox Church and (the church in) Europe

The Orthodox Church has already been introduced in this chapter insofar as the majority of Orthodox churches are members of the CEC, with the exception of the patriarchates of Georgia and Bulgaria, the autonomous Estonian Apostolic Orthodox Church and the three Orthodox jurisdictions in Ukraine.[49] While a Liaison Office of the Orthodox Church to the European Union has been set up to work on behalf of the ecumenical patriarchate, I believe the Orthodox churches in Europe have not yet produced a common statement that can be compared to those studied above. The major reason for this may be the difficulty they encounter in making decisions at an international level, bearing in mind their autocephalous and autonomous character.[50] It is significant, for example, that three Orthodox churches have their own office in Brussels: the Romanian Orthodox Church, the Representation of the Church of Greece to the European Union[51] and the Representation of the Russian Orthodox Church to the European Institutions.[52]

The website of the latter contains a banner with a message from Patriarch Alexy II of Moscow and All Russia:

> The Russian Church, which has several dioceses, hundreds of parishes and millions of believers on the territory of the European Union, is taking an active part in the creation of the new face of our continent. It is the task of our Church to remind Europe[53] of its Christian roots, to resist the attack of aggressive secularism and to defend traditional values. An active role in the realization of this noble task is

fulfilled by the Representation of the Russian Orthodox Church to the European Institutions.

Allusions to the attack of aggressive secularism are a constant feature in the official discourses of Orthodox authorities.[54] In the opening speech of a conference organized jointly by the Department for External Church Relations of the Moscow Patriarchate and the Pontifical Council for Culture of the RCC (Vienna, 2006), Metropolitan Kirill of Smolensk and Kaliningrad paid attention in his criticism of secularized Europe to the analogy with the secularization of traditional Orthodox values which the Russian Orthodox Church experienced during Communist times.[55] Metropolitan Kirill is also convinced that extremist reactions by Muslims in the wake of the publication of the so-called 'Mohammed cartoons', were not a reaction against Christianity as such, but against the secularized life-style of Western Europe.

In an article on 'Traditional and liberal values in the debate between Christianity and secularism' in the same electronic journal, Bishop Hilarion mentions that two different reactions are possible against the challenge of secularism, apart from the already mentioned reaction of Islamic extremism. Here we observe for the first time a very strong anti-Protestant inclination among representatives of the Orthodox Church, as well as a tendency to consider the Roman Catholic Church as a partner:

> Another variation of the religious answer to the challenge of secularism is the attempt to adapt religion itself, including dogma and morals, to modern liberal standards. Some Protestant communities have already followed this path, single-mindedly instilling liberal standards into their doctrine and church practice over the course of several decades. (. . .) Finally, the third variation of the religious answer to secularism is the attempt to enter into a peaceful, non-aggressive, though obviously unequal, dialogue with it, with the aim of achieving a balance between the liberal-democratic model of Western societal structure and the religious way of life. Such a path has been chosen by Christian Churches that have remained faithful to tradition, namely the Roman Catholic and Orthodox Churches, as well as several non-Christian religions such as Judaism, Buddhism and moderate Islam.[56]

Bishop Hilarion concludes his intervention with a call to engage in a constructive dialogue with the reality of secularism and in doing so he repeats a position that was defended almost twenty years ago by the renowned French Orthodox theologian Olivier Clément, in an article on 'Witnessing in a Secular Society'.[57] While the latter is aware that many people in Western Europe consider the Orthodox Church to be a safe place against the decadency of history and modernity, he believes that secularization will be a lasting event and that all churches in Europe, and especially in Western Europe, will ultimately have to find a new place for themselves in a secularized society.

Ecumenism in Europe: *The Charta Oecumenica*

Ecumenical dialogues between the Christian churches do not often take place at the level of each continent. This is not to say, however, that ecumenical dialogue at a pan-European level is fully absent. The cooperation between the CCEE and CEC resulted in 2001 in a relatively short and practical document, *Charta Oecumenica*,[58] to which I will now briefly turn our attention.[59] The intention of the churches initiating the *Charta Oecumenica* was that it would contain, as its subtitle states: 'Guidelines for the growing cooperation among the Churches in Europe'. The churches in Europe received the task to prepare such guidelines during the Second European Ecumenical Assembly, organized conjointly by CEC and CCEE in Graz in 1997, which had as its central theme: 'Reconciliation: Gift of God and Source of New Life'.[60]

The drafting committee was confronted with the delicate task of composing a text which on the one hand was not entitled to have a doctrinal character and on the other hand would express the clear commitment of the churches to cooperate. At its first meeting the drafting committee coined the term *Charta Oecumenica*. By analogy with a political charter, which is explicitly binding for the subscribing nations, the *Charta* would be binding for the participating churches and their members in Europe. The preamble contains the following reflection on the status of the document:

> [W]e adopt this charter as a common commitment to dialogue and co-operation. It describes fundamental ecumenical responsibilities, from which follow a number of guidelines and commitments. It is designed to promote an ecumenical culture of dialogue and co-operation at all levels of church life, and to provide agreed criteria for this. However, it has no magisterial or dogmatic character, nor is it legally binding under church law. Its authority will derive from the voluntary commitments of the European churches and ecumenical organisation.

The preamble also contains the same broad understanding of Europe which we have met already in other documents: 'Europe – from the Atlantic to the Urals, from the North Cape to the Mediterranean – is today more pluralist in culture than ever before. With the Gospel, we want to stand up for the dignity of the human person created in God's image and, as churches together, contribute towards reconciling peoples and cultures.'

The *Charta Oecumenica* contains 12 paragraphs which each treat a different topic. Each paragraph exhibits the same structure: a descriptive introduction is followed by a number of resolutions introduced by the words: 'We commit ourselves'. The document as a whole contains three chapters which I will now briefly introduce.

The first chapter, 'We Believe in "One, Holy, Catholic and Apostolic Church"', contains one single paragraph, 'Called together to unity in faith', which describes the foundation of cooperation between the churches in Europe. This foundation consists in faith in the Triune God as formulated in the creed of Nicaea-Constantinople (381).

The second chapter describes important activities of the Christian Churches 'On the Way towards the Visible Fellowship of the Churches in Europe': 'Proclaiming the Gospel together' (CO 2), 'Moving towards one another' (CO 3), 'Acting together' (CO 4), 'Praying together' (CO 5) and 'Continuing in dialogue' (CO 6).

In the final version, the opening paragraph of Part II has become: 'Proclaiming the Gospel Together' (CO 2), moving the paragraph 'Coming to meet one another' in the draft document into second place (CO 3). This is clearly the result of the strong desire, reflected in many Protestant responses to the draft document, to give the task of a common mission a more dominant place in the document. As it is stated in this paragraph, '[t]he most important task of the church in Europe is the common proclamation of the Gospel, in both word and deed, for the salvation of all' (CO 2). The commitments which follow this opening paragraph are an attempt to make this goal more concrete. The first commitment states that the churches have to discuss their 'plans for evangelisation with other churches, entering into agreements with them and thus avoiding harmful competition and the risk of fresh divisions'. In the second commitment, the prohibition of proselytism is implicitly affirmed – a strong desire of the Orthodox delegates – but complemented by two statements about freedom of conscience. 'We commit ourselves to recognise that every person can freely choose his or her religious and Church affiliation as a matter of conscience, which means not inducing anyone to convert through moral pressure or material incentive, but also not hindering anyone from entering into conversion of his or her own free will.'

The churches in Europe have to enter a learning process of 'Moving towards one another' (CO 3). They have to become appreciative of the rich traditions of other churches. This learning process involves an element of conversion and a healing of memories. The reality of the divisions and schisms of the past[61] has implications for the proclamation of faith in the present.

The paragraph 'Acting together' (CO 4) contains the recommendation 'that bilateral and multilateral ecumenical bodies be set up and maintained for co-operation at local, regional, national and international levels. At the European level it is necessary to strengthen co-operation between the Conference of European Churches and the Council of European Bishops' Conferences and to hold further European Ecumenical Assemblies' (CO 4).[62] I deplore that a line was removed from the draft version which would have implied the recognition by the churches in Europe of what is known as the method of 'differentiated consensus'.[63] The original commitment read as follows: 'to clarify, at local, regional, national and international levels, in bilateral and multilateral conversations, on which statements of principles agreement is indispensable, and in which issues difference need not lead to division and can be mutually tolerated'.[64]

The discussions on the paragraph on common prayer (CO 5) have not been easy. Even if it sounds like a contradiction in view of the first commitment – 'to pray for one another and Christian unity' – I am pleased that the final version kept the title 'Praying together'. One can also appreciate that the drafting committee decided to add to this paragraph an observation which was believed to be an important lacuna by many respondents, namely, that a particularly 'painful sign of the divisions among many Christian churches is the lack of Eucharistic fellowship'. Also, a new commitment was added in the final text which refers to the necessity of moving 'towards the goal of Eucharistic fellowship'.

Although the CO does not deal with the content of the ecumenical dialogues, it does offer a formal plea to pursue such dialogues. The *Charta* acknowledges the existence of 'differing theological and ethical positions' between the churches and that the current 'separations between churches' are the consequence of 'differences of opinion on doctrine, ethics and Church law' (CO 6). These observations, however, are only the second part of the first and second line of paragraph 6. The first idea in each sentence draws attention to what is more important than the divisions between the churches. In the first line it is the fact that we 'belong together in Christ'. The second line opens with the belief that there exists a plurality of theological, ethical and canonical opinions that do not lead to church divisions, but which constitute legitimate diversity.[65]

The text of the CO continues by insisting that the dialogue between the churches should be oriented towards a consensus. Churches that enter into dialogue are already, to some degree, in communion with one another. This communion is deepened by the dialogue process. The goal of full ecclesial communion between churches, however, presupposes 'unity in faith'.[66] One can ask whether this line is not an implicit rejection of the tradition which has developed among some Protestant churches that restoring or realizing church communion can be done on the basis of a 'differentiated consensus'. Fortunately, the commitment to promote the reception of the results of ecumenical dialogue is still found in the final version of the CO. The text exhorts the churches 'to examine the question of how official Church bodies can receive and implement the findings gained in dialogue' (CO 6).

The third chapter describes 'Our Common Responsibility in Europe' under six headings: 'Participating in the building of Europe' (CO 7), 'Reconciling peoples and cultures' (CO 8), 'Safeguarding the creation' (CO 9), 'Strengthening community with Judaism' (CO 10), 'Cultivating relations with Islam' (CO 11) and 'Encountering other religions and world views' (CO 12).

The churches 'support an integration of the European continent' (CO 7) but only one which is based upon individual rights and social values. 'On the basis of our Christian faith, we work towards a humane, socially conscious Europe, in which human rights and the basic values of peace, justice, freedom, tolerance, participation and solidarity prevail. We likewise insist on the reverence for life, the value of marriage and the family, the preferential option for the poor, the readiness to forgive, and in all things compassion.' Europe should not only be concerned about just economic relations between East and West: 'At the same time we must avoid Eurocentricity and heighten Europe's sense of responsibility for the whole of humanity, particularly for the poor all over the world.' This paragraph also contains the important commitment 'to resist any attempt to misuse religion and the church for ethnic and nationalist purposes'.

In the paragraph on 'Reconciling peoples and cultures' (CO 8), the churches in Europe commit themselves 'to work for structures of peace, based on the non-violent resolution of conflicts'. The churches are also convinced that 'migrants, refugees and asylum-seekers' deserve 'a humane reception in Europe'. Another concern pertains to 'the position and equal rights of women in all areas of life' (CO 8). This is followed by a paragraph which expresses the commitment of the churches in Europe to 'Safeguarding the creation' (CO 9).

In the draft version, the final paragraph of the *Charta Oecumenica* focused on 'Fostering relations with other religions'. In the final version a certain hierarchy in the relations of the churches in Europe with other religions and worldviews has been installed. The first duty in this respect is that of 'Strengthening community with Judaism' (CO 10). Apart from supporting 'Christian-Jewish co-operation' the document also contains a recognition of guilt. 'We deplore and condemn all manifestations of anti-Semitism, all outbreaks of hatred and persecutions. We ask God for forgiveness for anti-Jewish attitudes among Christians, and we ask our Jewish sisters and brothers for reconciliation.'

The paragraph on 'Cultivating relations with Islam' (CO 11) is equally aware that 'there are still strong reservations and prejudices on both sides' which 'are rooted in painful experiences throughout history and in the recent past'. Thereafter the document expresses the commitment 'to intensify encounters between Christians and Muslims and enhance Christian–Islamic dialogue at all levels' (CO 11).

The final paragraph on 'Encountering other religions and world views' (CO 12) offers a realistic description of important changes in the religious situation of Europe without approving these changes.

> The plurality of religious and non-confessional beliefs and ways of life has become
> a feature of European culture. Eastern religions and new religious communities are

spreading and also attracting the interest of many Christians. In addition, growing numbers of people reject the Christian faith, are indifferent to it or have other philosophies of life. We want to take seriously the critical questions of others, and try together to conduct fair discussion with them. Yet a distinction must be made between the communities with which dialogues and encounters are to be sought, and those which should be warned against from the Christian standpoint. (CO 12)

Conclusion

Is there a future for church and faith in Europe? The resurgence of religion, manifestly present in other continents, seems to appear in Europe under the form of pluriform expressions of renewed interest in religiosity, but not of a renewed attachment to the historic churches. Still, as we have seen in the research of Grace Davie, these churches continue to exercise a vicarious role on behalf of the larger society.

The major denominational traditions assess the future of church and faith in Europe in a different way. We have preferred in this chapter to focus on the official view of the churches, as expressed in a number of documents or in statements by church leaders. The Roman Catholic Church clearly observes signs of hope, but is at the same time quite critical of the effects of the secularization of Christian values in Europe. Both Pope John Paul II and Pope Benedict XVI have used the term 'apostasy' in this regard. The Orthodox Church is also clearly opposed to the evil of secularism. The Protestant churches are not so critical of the effects of secularization but are looking for ways to adapt their methods of evangelization to the changed worldview. This approach in turn has received severe criticism on behalf of the Orthodox Church.

We have also become familiar with the work of some of the major ecclesial bodies in Europe. The Roman Catholic Church pays special attention to the challenges of the church in Europe through two instruments, one oriented towards the membership of the European Union, the other towards the membership of the Council of Europe. Ecclesiologists want to strengthen the structures of decision-making within the Roman Catholic Church at regional and continental level and are, therefore, no longer satisfied with seeing these bodies only as an expression of the affective collegiality of bishops. The Community of Protestant Churches in Europe represents the churches who have signed the Leuenberg Agreement. A number of Protestant ecclesiologists would like this body to receive greater authority. Unfortunately, the level of cooperation between the different Orthodox churches in Europe does not yet appear to be quite so intense.

Finally, we have also observed that the churches have tried to exercise some influence on the process of integration in Europe through joint ecumenical efforts such as the ecumenical dialogue of the Council of European Episcopal Conferences and the Conference of European Churches which lead to the *Charta Oecumenica* (2001) and the joint letter by the Church and Society Commission of the Conference of European Churches and the Commission of the Bishops' Conferences of the European Community (2002).

Notes

1 The opening article by Ioan Horga and Mircea Brie, 'Religion in the Context of Secularization and Globalisation', in Maria Marczewska-Rytko (ed.), *Religion in a Changing Europe: Between Pluralism and Fundamentalism*, Lublin: Maria Curie-Skłodowoska University Press, 2003, pp. 23–32,

points e.g. to a great similarity between Eastern and Western Europe as far as the process of secularization is concerned: 'After 1990, political transformations in the former Communist Europe and the passage to a democratic way and to a market economy have allowed the return to a normal religious economy (that is a free manifestation) in most of the Eastern countries. This socio-political and economic situation is pretty new. Consequently, the opening of the new states to mondialisation and globalisation gives birth to mutations and recompositions on the level of religious feeling and thus, it creates the premises for the acceleration of the process of secularisation of the society' (p. 28).

2   Harvey Cox, 'The Myth of the Twentieth Century. The Rise and Fall of Secularization', in Gregory Baum (ed.), *The Twentieth Century: A Theological Overview*, New York: Orbis, 1999, pp. 135–43; and Peter Berger (ed.), *The Desecularization of the World: Resurgent Religion and World Politics*, Grand Rapids, MI: Eerdmans, 1999.

3   Yves Lambert, 'A Turning Point in Religious Evolution in Europe', *Journal of Contemporary Religion* 19 (2004), 29–45.

4   Lieven Boeve, 'Religion after Detraditionalization: Christian Faith in a Post-Secular Europe', *Irish Theological Quarterly* 70 (2005), 99–122.

5   Grace Davie, *Religion in Modern Europe: A Memory Mutates*, Oxford: Oxford University Press, 2000, p. 8. At the same time she is aware that, even if the situation is slowly changing, in the Lutheran state churches of Northern Europe, the majority of Christians seem 'to belong but not to believe' (p. 17). By way of comparison she also indicates that 'approximately 40 per cent of the American population declare that they both believe and belong' (p. 8). Or, in terms of the central argument of her book: 'Americans are anything but vicarious in their religious life' (p. 49). For a comparative study of the influence of consumer culture on religion in America and Europe, see Lieven Boeve (ed.), *Consuming Religion in Europe? Christian Faith Challenged by Consumer Culture* (= *Bulletin ET* 17 (2006), 1–178). This book is the result of a conference on the occasion of a book written by the American Catholic theologian Vincent Miller, *Consuming Religion. Christian Faith and Practice in a Consumer Culture*, New York: Continuum, 2004.

6   Cf. Grace Davie, 'Is Europe an Exceptional Case?', *The Hedgehog Review* (Spring and Summer 2006), 23–34.

7   *Religion in Modern Europe*, pp. 78–80.

8   'Is Europe an Exceptional Case?', 24.

9   Cf. *Religion in Modern Europe*, p. 59: '[I]t seems that significant numbers of Europeans remain grateful to rather than resentful of their churches at the turn of the millennium, recognizing that these churches perform, vicariously, a number of tasks on behalf of the population as a whole. From time to time they are asked to articulate the sacred in the life-cycle of individuals or families or at times of national crisis or celebration. It is significant that a refusal to carry out these tasks would violate both individual and collective expectations.'

10   *Religion in Modern Europe*, p. 179.

11   *Religion in Modern Europe*, pp. 46, 48, 149. Davie is well aware that, as a sociologist, she can only notice and observe certain mutations. She can only raise the open question whether such mutations are in the long run not threatening for the tradition, but it is up to theologians to reflect on this; p. 155: '[A]re such innovations truly Christian? How malleable, in other words, is the Christian tradition in terms of innovation and who is going to decide where the limits lie? Or to put the question in a different way, when does a mutation become a distinct, different, and possibly competing species? A sociologist can indicate the nature of the tension; setting the limits, however, must be the task of a different discipline.'

12   *Religion in Modern Europe*, p. 64. Davie again realizes that this may imply serious dangers in the long run. 'The tendency to bracket out certain aspects of its teaching is, however, more damaging to the authority of the church than is sometimes realized, in that it becomes an ongoing process. If some formulations can be bracketed out for particular reasons, so too can others – the slippery slope is difficult to resist.'

13   *Religion in Modern Europe*, p. 72.

14   *Religion in Modern Europe*, p. 97. Davie is aware that this may have some influence on the future of religious belief in Europe. Therefore, in the subtitle of this section religion is called a 'precarious memory' for young people. 'With this [the growing religious illiteracy] in mind, it seems entirely possible that the religious memory of Europe – at least in its traditional form of a basic under-

standing of Christian teaching – might simply cease to exist, except as a branch of specialist knowledge; it is indeed precarious.'

15 *Religion in Modern Europe*, p. 116–34. Davie pays special attention to the growth of Muslim communities, who are mostly new arrivals in Europe, and also discusses some cases of serious tension between these groups and the population at large: the 'Rushdie controversy' and the 'affaire du foulard'.

16 *Religion in Modern Europe*, p. 172.

17 'Is Europe an Exceptional Case?', 34.

18 Jean-Dominique Durand, 'Giovanni Paolo II e l'Europa Occidentale. Al di là della secolarizzazione', in E. Guerriero and M. Impagliazzo (eds), *I cattolici e le chiese cristiane durante il pontificato di Giovanni Paolo II (1978–2005)*, Storia della Chiesa, 26, Cinisello Balsamo: San Paolo, 2006, pp. 39–69, p. 40. See also Maciej Drzonek, 'John Paul II's Vision of Europe', in Maria Marczewska-Rytko (ed.), *Religion in a Changing Europe: Between Pluralism and Fundamentalism*, Lublin: Maria Curie-Skłodowoska University Press, 2003, pp. 89–104.

19 Durand, 'Giovanni Paolo II', p. 44.

20 John Paul II, 'Apostolic Exhortation *Ecclesia in Europa*', Origins 33 (2003–4), 149–76, § 6. All references to this document will be indicated between brackets in the main body of the text using the Latin abbreviation EE followed by the paragraph number.

21 John Paul II's programme of new evangelization has not been free of criticism. See, e.g. Ottmar Fuchs, 'Was ist Neuevangelisierung?', *Stimmen der Zeit* 210 (1992), 465–73.

22 In its tri-annual conferences, the European Society of Catholic Theology (ESCT), founded in 1989, also pays special attention to evolutions in Catholic Theology and in the Catholic Church in Europe. The 6th international congress (Leuven, 2007), for example, focused on *Religion and the European Project: Theological Perspectives*. The conference proceedings and contributions by members are published in *Bulletin ET*. More information can be found on the organization's website: www.kuleuven.ac.be/eurotheo/index.php

23 Michael Fahey, 'The Synod of America: Reflections of a Non-Participant', *Theological Studies* 59 (1998), 486–504, 489.

24 An exception was made for the 11th Ordinary General Assembly of the Synod of Bishops, Rome, October 2–23, 2005, the first synod presided over by Pope Benedict XVI on 'The Eucharist: Source and Summit of the Life and Mission of the Church', as is evident from the following communication: 'The official Latin text of *The Final List of Propositions* of the Eleventh Ordinary General Assembly of the Synod of Bishops, subject to individual vote by the synod fathers, is intended for the Supreme Pontiff, to whom it will be duly submitted. By its very nature, this text is confidential and will not be published, in keeping with the consultative character of the synod's work, since the text decidedly contains recommendations. This time only, the Holy Father, Pope Benedict XVI, has graciously allowed the provisional and unofficial Italian-language text, done by the General Secretariat of the Synod of Bishops, to be published in the Holy See Press Office Bulletin.'

25 The harsh tone of a speech given by Pope Benedict XVI on March 24, 2007, on the occasion of a congress organized by the Commission of the Episcopates of the European Community to commemorate the 50th anniversary of the signature of the Treaties of Rome, however, may offer some indication of the fact that the present pope prefers to deal with challenges rather than to focus on signs of hope, as John Paul II did in *Ecclesia in Europa*. Benedict XVI elaborated further on John Paul II's reflection on the silent apostasy of many people in Europe who are living as if God does not exist, even if they are not self-proclaimed atheists. Pope Benedict wonders whether Europe, apart from this 'apostasy from God', does not also run the risk, 'in this historical hour', of committing another form of apostasy, namely 'apostasy from itself', since it apparently no longer recognizes 'the very existence of universal and absolute values', including the 'truth of the human person'.

26 The abbreviation CCEE is based on the Latin name of the institution: Consilium Conferentiarum Episcoporum Europae. The CCEE corresponds to the member countries of the Council of Europe, whose seat is in Strasbourg. Their secretariat is located in Sankt Gallen. For more information, see their website: www.ccee.ch/english/default.htm

27 The abbreviation COMECE is based on the French name of the institution: Commission des Épiscopats de la Communauté Européenne. COMECE brings together the bishops delegated by

the episcopal conferences in those countries that are members of the European Union. Its secretariat is located in Brussels. See their website for more information: www.comece.org

28 John Paul II, 'Apostolic Letter issued "Motu Proprio" on the Theological and Juridical Nature of Episcopal Conferences', *Origins* 28 (1998–9), 152–58, § 10.

29 Cf. the recent dissertation by Klaus Winterkamp, *Die Bischofskonferenz zwischen 'affektiver' und 'effektiver Kollegialität'* (Studien zur systematischen Theologie und Ethik, 43), Münster: LIT, 2003 and my own 'Is "Affective" Collegiality Sufficient? A Plea for a More "Effective" Collegiality of Bishops in the Roman Catholic Church and Its Ecumenical Implications', in *Friendship as an Ecumenical Value: Proceedings of the International Conference Held on the Inauguration of the Institute of Ecumenical Studies (Lviv, 11–15 June 2005)*, Lviv: Ukrainian Catholic University Press, 2006, pp. 132–53.

30 This definition is in line, however, with the first statutes which the CCEE received in 1971, the year of its foundation, which hold that 'the purpose of the CCEE is that the *affectus collegialis* and a closer connection among the European conferences of bishops is practiced'. The revised statutes of 1991 even make it clear that the CCEE does not have the same authority as an episcopal conference. It is an 'instrument of communion (*organum communionis*) of the conferences of bishops of Europe'. Nevertheless, Myriam Wijlens, in her article 'Exercising Collegiality in a Supra-national or Continental Institution such as the FABC, CCEE, and ComECE', *The Jurist* 64 (2004), 168–204, wonders 'whether the cooperation of the diocesan bishops in a continental or supra national structure differs theologically very much from their cooperation in an episcopal conference' (191).

31 'Yet it must be acknowledged that these inspiring principles have historically found in the Judeo-Christian tradition a force capable of harmonizing, consolidating and promoting them. This is a fact which cannot be ignored; on the contrary, in the process of building a united Europe there is a need to acknowledge that this edifice must also be founded on values that are most fully manifested in the Christian tradition. Such an acknowledgment is to everyone's advantage' (EE 19).

32 Compare Joël-Benoît d'Onorio, 'Religions et constitutions en Europe: A propos d'un préambule contesté', *Revue du Droit Public* 122 (2006), 715–36.

33 Compare with paragraph 5 of the Address of His Holiness Pope John Paul II to the Diplomatic Corps (January 13, 2003): 'In recalling this patrimony, the Holy See and all the Christian Churches have urged those drawing up the future Constitutional Treaty of the European Union to include a reference to Churches and religious institutions. We believe it desirable that, in full respect of the secular state, three complementary elements should be recognized: religious freedom not only in its individual and ritual aspects, but also in its social and corporative dimensions; the appropriateness of structures for dialogue and consultation between the Governing Bodies and communities of believers; respect for the juridical status already enjoyed by Churches and religious institutions in the Member States of the Union. A Europe which disavowed its past, which denied the fact of religion, and which had no spiritual dimension would be extremely impoverished in the face of the ambitious project which calls upon all its energies: constructing a Europe for *all*!'

34 The Conference of European Churches (CEC), founded in 1959, is a fellowship of 127 Orthodox, Protestant and Old Catholic churches from all countries on the European continent. The Roman Catholic Church maintains cordial and intense relations with the CEC through the joint committee of CEC–CCEE. The 127 member churches grant certain responsibilities to this coordinating body, while remaining autonomous. The Church and Society Commission was established in order to follow critically the decisions made by the European institutions. It also formulates suggestions on how the member churches of CEC should assess the direction taken by 'Europe'.

35 See for more background information Thomas Jansen, 'Europe and Religions: the Dialogue between the European Commission and Churches or Religious Communities', *Social Compass* 47 (2000), 103–12; Silvio Ferrari, 'From Tolerance to Rights: Religions in the Unification Process', in Alberto Melloni and Janet Soskice (eds), *Rethinking Europe*, London: SCM Press, 2004 (= *Concilium* 2004/2), pp. 42–50.

36 Cf. www.cec-kek.org/English/IntegrationprocE.htm

37 EE 109: '[Europe] needs to build a new model of unity in diversity' and E 116: 'The Catholic Church in fact provides a model of essential unity in a diversity of cultural expressions'.

38 The approach of the CEC does not lack its critics. Cf., for example, Friedemann Walldorf, 'Towards a Missionary Theology for Europe: Conclusions from the Ecumenical Debate on the New Evangelization of Europe between 1979–92', *European Journal of Theology* 13 (2004), 29–40.

This journal is closely linked to the Fellowship of European Evangelical Theologians. The author wants to present the 'bibliocentric-communicational' approach towards evangelization, which is characteristic for evangelicals, as an alternative to both the 'ecclesiocentric-inculturational' model of Roman Catholicism and the 'cosmocentric-liberational' model defended by the Conference of European Churches. One of his criticisms pertains precisely to the defence of diversity by the CEC: 'While the Evangelical contextual model gives prominence to the Bible as normative factor (*norma normans*) in this transformational process, the KEK-Model tends to see European society in its diversity as the main "agent of change" for the churches' mission. The ecclesiocentric Roman-Catholic model is more intransigent and finds it more difficult to change and renew itself, since it does not acknowledge any authority outside the normative ecclesiastical teaching tradition' (Walldorf, 34).

39 This idea is taken up in many places of the document.

40 This term was intended initially to be translated into English as 'church fellowship', whereas preference is now given to 'communion'. The official name of the 'Leuenberg Church Fellowship' is now 'Community of Protestant Churches in Europe'. There is a similar evolution in World Lutheranism. The Lutheran World Federation describes itself as 'a global communion of Christian churches in the Lutheran tradition'. See also Jens Holger Schjorring (ed.), *From Federation to Communion: The History of the Lutheran World Federation*, Minneapolis, MN: Fortress, 1997.

41 For additional information on this agreement see especially Chapter 9 of this volume, and also Chapter 10. Cf. also André Birmelé, 'La Concorde de Leuenberg et sa réception', *Irénikon* 72 (1999), 479–501.

42 Cf. Günther Gassmann, 'Leuenberg, Meißen, Porvoo – Bedeutung, Chancen und Risiken gegenwärtiger ökumenischer Entwicklungen', *Materialdienst des Konfessionskundlichen Instituts Bensheim* 54 (2003/2), 23–27 ; and Wilhelm Hüffmeier and Colin Podmore (eds), *Leuenberg, Meissen and Porvoo. Consultation between the Churches of the Leuenberg Church Fellowship and the Churches involved in the Meissen Agreement and the Porvoo Agreement* (Leuenberger Texte, 4), Frankfurt am Main: Lembeck, 1996. See also Chapter 22 of this volume, on ecumenism.

43 Cf. also the following publications by André Birmelé, 'Zur Ekklesiologie der Leuenberger Kirchengemeinschaft', in Peter Walter *et al.* (eds), *Kirche in ökumenischer Perspektive. Kardinal Walter Kasper zum 70. Geburtstag*, Freiburg-Basel-Wien: Herder, 2003, pp. 46–61 and 'Sichtbare Einheit: eine bleibende Aufgabe für die Leuenberger Kirchengemeinschaft', in Jari Jolkkonen *et al.* (eds), *Unitas visibilis. Studia oecumenica in honorem Eero Huovinen episcopi Helsingiensis*, Helsinki, 2004, pp. 42–54.

44 The United Protestant Church of Belgium, to mention but one example, is not only a member of the Community of Protestant Churches in Europe and the Conference of European Churches, but also of the World Alliance of Reformed Churches and the World Council of Churches.

45 See: http://lkg.jalb.de/lkg/documents/lkg_doc_en_2089.pdf

46 The quotation is to be found in the preface of the document. The idea is also present in sections 2.13 and 2.16. See also Chapter 36 of this volume, on *Missio Dei*.

47 See e.g. 3.1: '[S]ecularisation can also be understood as a process of emancipation. Indoctrination is rejected, ideologies are unmasked, comfort from another world and a flight into it have disappeared. Secularisation is creating new room for an authentic rendering of faith, often with a biographical stamp.'

48 Cf. 3.2: 'The churches see themselves faced with the task of bringing out the religious dimensions of such phenomena without condemning them over-hastily, and at the same time building bridges between people's religious longing and Christian spirituality.' The document also hopes that the churches will be able to see the end of the 'grand narratives' as a positive challenge (3.6) and the growing 'antipathy to institutions' also has to be turned into a positive task (3.11).

49 See the list of member churches on the CEC website: www.cec-kek.org/content/churches.shtml

50 See Jivko Panev, 'Quelques remarques sur l'autocéphalie', *Contacts* 47 (1995), 125–34, with reference to a famous speech delivered by the prominent Serbian theologian Popovic dating from 1923: 'The time approaches when our Church representatives must cease of exclusively being the servants of nationalism, in order to become priests and archpriests of the One, Holy, Catholic and Apostolic Church' [my translation].

51 See www.regue.org

52 See www.orthodoxeurope.org. The office and in particular its supervising bishop, Metropolitan Hilarion of Vienna and Austria, also provide an informative newsletter entitled *Bulletin Europaica*.

53 While the Orthodox churches do their best to exercise some degree of influence on the work of the European institutions, they are very much aware that Europe is much larger then the EU. See, for example, Athanasios Basdekis, 'Wird das vereinigte Europa orthodoxer? Die Orthodoxie, ihre Traditionen und aktuelle Lage', *Orthodoxes Forum* 18 (2004) 189–212, 188.

54 See also contributions from individual Orthodox theologians, including Konstantin Nikolak-opoulos, 'Europa und Byzanz: Die Rolle der Orthodoxie in Europa gestern und heute', *Orthodoxes Forum* 18 (2004), 175–88, 185: 'All Christians of Europe are appealed to resist the continuing secularization, spiritual changes and a unilateral rationalization of daily life' [my translation].

55 Cf. *Bulletin Europaica*, No. 96, May 11, 2006: '[T]he forms of social relations that were shaped in the twentieth century were to a significant extent a secularized variant of values characteristic of the Russian spiritual tradition: collectivism became the secularized version of conciliarity ("sobor-nost") and the community-centred life, a single state ideology replaced the spiritual authority of the Church. The effects of this substitution are well known to everyone. Thus, secularism, the break with spiritual traditions, represents a great threat to the existence of European civilization.'

56 For a similar attack on Protestantism see Métropolite Cyrille de Smolensk, *L'évangile et la liberté: Les valeurs de la tradition dans la société laïque*, Paris, Cerf, 2006, esp. pp. 103–5. Another critic of 'the world of secularization and pluralism, which is pressing on for globalization' is George D. Dragas, 'Orthodox Theology in the Contemporary World', in *Orthodoxy and the World Today: Sixth Congress of the Higher Orthodox Schools of Theology*, Sofia: St Kliment Ohridski University Press/ Omophor Publishing House, 2006, pp. 96–108. Starting from his definition of Orthodox theology as 'church theology, i.e. it is tied to the Church's existence and mission in the world' (p. 98), Dragas makes a firm distinction between Orthodox theology and Roman Catholic theology, on the one hand, and Orthodox and Protestant theologies on the other: 'It does not develop, as for instance Roman Catholic Theology does, nor does it change with the changes that occur in the world, as it happens with the various Protestant Theologies' (p. 99). His final appeal to Orthodox theology to remain faithful to its biblical, doctrinal and liturgical traditions is followed by another critical comparison with 'the Heterodox'. 'We need to do this so that we may not enter into the same crisis, which has led the heterodox to their present decline. We should never lose sight of the fact that Orthodoxy is the criterion of Heterodoxy and not its ally or partner' (p. 108).

57 Olivier Clément, 'Témoigner dans une société secularisé', *Contacts* 40 (1988), 277–95. Rowan Williams, the current Archbishop of Canterbury, aptly characterizes this theologian in an article entitled 'Eastern Orthodox Theology', in David F. Ford (ed.), *The Modern Theologians. An Introduction to Christian Theology after 1918*, third edn, Oxford: Blackwell, 2005, pp. 572–88, p. 584: 'Orthodoxy in France is now overwhelmingly Francophone, and its leading constructive theologian, Olivier Clément, is of French birth. A friend and pupil of Lossky, he has developed Lossky's critique of the abstract foundations of Western theism, and written of the dialectical necessity of European atheism as a step to recovering the vision of a living God. He has succeeded in constructing an Orthodox theology very deeply engaged with the mainstream of Western European culture, and free from either Byzantinist or Slavophil nostalgia.'

58 Viorel Ionita and Sarah Numico (eds), *Charta Oecumenica: A Text, a Process, and a Dream of the Churches in Europe*, Geneva: WCC, 2003. The English translation of the document is found on pp. 7–16. Reinhard Frieling, who was a member of the drafting committee, discusses the relevance of the document in the light of the current ecumenical situation in Europe in his article 'The Ecumenical Movement in Europe: Challenges and Conflicts', *Concilium* 2004/2, 57–66.

59 For a more lengthy treatment of the *Charta Oecumenica* including an analysis of the reactions to the first draft see my 'Ecumenism in Europe: A Presentation of the Charta Oecumenica', in Jaroslav Skira and Michael Attridge (eds), *In God's Hands. Essays on the Church and Ecumenism in Honour of Michael A. Fahey, S.J.* (Bibliotheca Ephemeridum Theologicarum Lovaniensium, 199), Leuven: Peeters, 2006, pp. 227–46.

60 CEC-CCEE, *Reconciliation: Gift of God and Source of New Life*, Graz, Styria, 1998. The theme of the first assembly, which took place in 1989 in Basel after the end of the Cold War, was: 'Peace and Justice for the Integrity of Creation'. The Third European Ecumenical Assembly held from 4–8 September 2007 in Sibiu, Romania. The theme of this meeting was 'The Light of Christ shines upon all. Hope for renewal and unity in Europe'.

61 The earliest schism is that of the Assyrian Church of the East, which rejected some aspects of the third ecumenical council of Ephese (431). The other Oriental Orthodox churches separated from Chalcedonian Orthodoxy. Growing tensions between the Patriarch of Byzantium and the Pope of

Rome reached its climax in 1054, even if it would still last a few centuries before one can speak of a formal schism between the Byzantine Orthodox Churches and the Roman Catholic Church. Another series of mutual condemnations took place between the churches of the Reformation and Rome in the sixteenth century.

62 Cf. also Chapter 35, on ethics and ecclesiology.

63 In the last decades this hermeneutical method has been successfully applied in a number of ecumenical dialogues, e.g. the *Joint Declaration on the Doctrine of Justification* (1999). In the introduction of the latter statement the common understanding is explained as follows: 'It does not cover all that either church teaches about justification; it does encompass a consensus on basic truths of the doctrine of justification and shows that the remaining differences in its explication are no longer the occasion for doctrinal condemnations.' Cf. Hervé Legrand, 'Le consensus différencié sur la doctrine de la Justification (Augsbourg 1999). Quelques remarques sur la nouveauté d'une méthode', *Nouvelle Revue Théologique* 124 (2002), 30–56.

64 Conference of European Churches and Council of European Bishops' Conferences, *Charta Oecumenica for the Co-operation of Churches in Europe. Draft*, Geneva and Sankt Gallen, 1999, § 6.

65 The full text reads as follows: 'We belong together in Christ, and this is of fundamental significance in the face of our differing theological and ethical positions. Rather than seeing our diversity as a gift which enriches us, however, we have allowed differences on doctrine, ethics and church law to lead to separations between churches, with special historical circumstances and different cultural backgrounds often playing a crucial role.' The source of inspiration for the first line is the document of the WCC's Joint Working Group with the Roman Catholic Church on *The Ecumenical Dialogue on Moral Issues* (1995). Of the ten guidelines formulated at the end of the text, I quote the last one in full: 'When the dialogue continues to reveal sincere but apparently irreconcilable moral positions, we affirm in faith that the fact of our belonging together in Christ is more fundamental than the fact of our moral differences. The deep desire to find an honest and faithful resolution to our disagreements is itself evidence that God continues to grace the *koinōnia* among disciples of Christ' (*Growth in Agreement II: Reports and Agreed Statements of Ecumenical Conversations on a World Level, 1982–1998*, Geneva: WCC, I, p. 910). Both texts, however, reflect a different dynamic. *The Ecumenical Dialogue on Moral Issues* speaks about the existence of 'irreconcilable moral positions' in ecumenical dialogues which should not be considered threats to the basic communion in Christ. The CO affirms that differences between the churches are not irreconcilable. On the contrary, the very fact of their communion in Christ should encourage the churches to continue dialogue.

66 The official English translation here is unreliable. It states, 'Only in this way can Church communion be given a theological foundation' (CO 6). The original German text of this phrase reads as follows: 'Ohne Einheit im Glauben gibt es keine volle Kirchengemeinschaft.'

Further reading

Lieven Boeve (ed.), *Consuming Religion in Europe? Christian Faith Challenged by Consumer Culture* (= *Bulletin ET* 17 (2006), 1–178).

Timothy A. Byrnes and Peter J. Katzenstein (eds), *Religion in an Expanding Europe*, Cambridge: Cambridge University Press, 2006.

Grace Davie, *Religion in Modern Europe: A Memory Mutates*, Oxford: Oxford University Press, 2000.

Viorel Ionita and Sarah Numico (eds), *Charta Oecumenica: A Text, a Process, and a Dream of the Churches in Europe*, Geneva: WCC, 2003.

John Paul II, 'Apostolic Exhortation Ecclesia in Europa', *Origins* 33 (2003–4), 149–76.

Maria Marczewska-Rytko (ed.), *Religion in a Changing Europe: Between Pluralism and Fundamentalism*, Lublin: Maria Curie-Skłodowoska University Press, 2003.

Alberto Melloni and Janet Soskice (eds), *Rethinking Europe*, London: SCM Press, 2004 (= *Concilium* (2004/2), 42–50).

Tim Noble *et al.* (eds), *Charting Churches in a Changing Europe: Charta Oecumenica and the Process of Ecumenical Encounter* (Currents of Encounter, 28), Amsterdam and New York: Rodopi, 2006.

Mario Spezzibottiani (ed.), *Giovanni Paolo II. Profezia per l'Europa*, Casale Monferrato: Piemme, 1999.

Part IV

METHODS AND DEBATES

21

COMPARATIVE
ECCLESIOLOGY

Roger Haight, S.J.

Comparative ecclesiology studies the church in a way that takes into account the various levels of pluralism which mark its existence today. As an academic discipline it employs a method that explicitly recognizes the diversity of religious traditions, whether among Christian churches, as in ecumenical reflection on the church, or among the various religions of the world, as in interreligious dialogue and comparative theology. Comparative ecclesiology may be distinguished from denominational ecclesiologies which pursue a study of the church entirely within the boundaries of a particular church, communion of churches, or ecclesial tradition. By contrast a comparative ecclesiology seeks an understanding of the church through an explicit appeal to religious sources that transcend a particular church. An understanding of the church in question is achieved by some form of implicit or explicit comparison with other religious communities.[1]

Although one may rightly draw particular attention to the need for comparative ecclesiology in our time, it would be a mistake to ignore various instances and ways in which recognition of pluralism within the church and among the religions has entered into the reflective self-understanding of the Christian church across its history. Recalling the manner and degree to which this interaction has influenced the discipline of ecclesiology will soften what may otherwise appear as a novelty. Moreover, history shows that the designation 'comparative ecclesiology' is analogous and can legitimately characterize several different modes of reflection on the church. The point of this discussion is formally to thematize various manifestations of comparative ecclesiology as a collection of diverse methods and goals that together form part of the wider field of ecclesiology. This entails some overlapping and inclusion of matter treated under other titles in this book. The thematic that constitutes an ecclesiology as comparative is precisely the various ways in which ecclesiology explicitly interacts with pluralism.

The treatment which follows is divided into three sections. The first traces briefly and broadly certain landmarks in the history of the church that indicate the shifting ways in which pluralism has commanded attention within the discipline of ecclesiology. The second section enumerates certain premises upon which a positive discipline of comparative ecclesiology is built. And the third analyses five variations of comparative ecclesiology according to different sources, goals and methods of comparison. The conclusion underlines the place of comparative ecclesiology in ecclesiology more broadly conceived, and the necessary tension that must obtain between particular and more universal modes of understanding the church.

Historical context

Certain key events in the genesis and historical development of the Christian church provide perspective on what today is called comparative ecclesiology. The earliest church, which was founded upon the event of Jesus Christ, evolved as a product of historical development. The genesis of the specifically Christian church consisted in establishing its unique historical identity vis à vis the synagogues of Judaism on the one hand and the polytheism and mystery religions of the Mediterranean region on the other. Moreover, the gradual inculturation into the Greek East and the Latin West involved constant absorption of religious elements from these cultures that required comparing, weighing propriety, and deciding. In the beginning there was no single clear identity that could close in upon itself for protection: Christianity was born in a dialogue between faith in Jesus as the Christ and the parent religion of Judaism and other religions and cultures. Gradually, in the course of the earliest centuries, the Christian church grew spontaneously into different Greek and Roman churches in communion.

The early patristic period of the church in the West produced among many others two figures and protracted events that contain basic principles relevant to comparative ecclesiology. The first is Augustine's engagement with the Donatists. In a sense Augustine's *De Baptismo* represents a major, public exercise in comparative ecclesiology, in this case one that is negative or polemical, in which two fundamentally different ecclesiologies were contrasted, each with its own tradition and a set of authorities and practices to which it could appeal. Augustine's polemics and the Donatists' tenacity show that there can be differences in ecclesiology that make a difference. The second example is one of openness and forbearance in the claim and exercise of authority. Gregory I may have thought that Roman primacy entitled him in certain spheres to some kind of universal juridical authority, but, if he did, he absolutely refused to claim it or try to exercise it. He had been a liaison to the Greek church before becoming pope, and he could not conceive of exercising universally the juridical authority he actually possessed in his own sphere, but insisted on the autonomy of the other patriarchs.[2] Here an implicit comparative judgement yielded a macro ecclesiology of communion that transcended juridical power.

The Gregorian Reform of the second half of the eleventh century may have been the most significantly defining period of the Roman Catholic Church in its long history. It stands at the source of many lasting traits, some of which bear comment especially in relation to the Greek church. Through a concatenation of many historical factors the position of the papacy as the head of the Roman Church was solidified in the course of the Reform and its aftermath: the clergy were drawn together into a body and state of life distinct from the laity and the whole structure was regulated by law and an administration that gave the church a commanding status across Europe. But this juridical authority could not be extended to the Eastern church; the bonds of legal authority between the Eastern and Western churches were broken by the forces of culture, politics and war, and by the deeper differences of piety and church life. Once again the lesson is clear: juridical authority alone cannot hold churches together; only denser and subtler bonds of faith and love manifested in respect can keep different churches in communion with each other. Looking back it becomes plain that positive constructive dialogue and comparison are a better way to forge communion than polemics or claims to juridical authority.

The late medieval period gave rise to the first focused, multifaceted and intense discussion of ecclesiology across the Western church during the Western Schism. The comparison was not between churches but ecclesiologies. Two broad positions seemed to stand as alternatives: the one, centrist, revolved around the papacy; the other, conciliarist, positioned the pope at the head of a communion. The two were pitted against each other in a debate in which the unity of the Western church and the papacy itself were at stake. The debate engaged all quarters and employed arguments that were at once legal, social, political, philosophical and theological. In the end, it was not resolved theologically but historically and politically. But during the course of the fourteenth and fifteenth centuries ecclesiology began to emerge as an autonomous or distinct discipline.

The Protestant Reformation in the sixteenth century completely transformed the nature of ecclesiological discussion: it ceased as simply a discussion within a single Western church to become self-definition within the context of a larger polemical debate among the churches. What we know today as comparative ecclesiology in an ecumenical form, exemplified in the East-West dialogues, became the status quo of the whole church. The church became a pluralistic reality in a formal sense, and every church understood itself over against others. The Reformation produced two great comprehensive and systematic ecclesiologies by single authors in Calvin's *Institutes* and Hooker's *Laws*, and a host of less extensive but still distinctive ecclesiologies. No church was as institutionally developed as the Roman Catholic Church, but Trent did not attempt an integral comprehensive ecclesiology. The new feature in all of these ecclesiologies was pluralism: every ecclesiology now had to be developed against the background of a divided church or 'the churches'. For the most part the comparative thrust was carried by polemic, but with some major exceptions. Calvin and other reformers remained open to pluralism in principle with a definition of the church that was open: wherever the word of God was purely preached and heard, and the sacraments authentically administered, there the true church existed. But Hooker more than others explicitly recognized a whole–part distinction in the great church: the catholic church is like the sea, but various parts of it bear their own names and are churches within themselves. In Hooker comparative ecclesiology transcended polemic in the sense that he sought only to justify the Anglican formula, not disenfranchise others. But sixteenth-century Europe still did not tolerate different churches in the same place.

The modern period produced the most significant intellectual development in Western theology that in turn led to the flourishing of comparative ecclesiology. The rise of critical historical method applied to religious sources and an attendant historical consciousness transformed the discipline of ecclesiology as it did the whole range of humanistic disciplines. Both are explicit in F. Schleiermacher's turn to the religious experience of the community as the basis of theology and his definition of dogmatics as the systematization of 'the doctrine prevalent in a Christian Church at a given time'.[3] Schleiermacher's ecclesiology itself was ecumenically Protestant as he appealed to the confessional documents of a variety of church traditions. In it he formulated a number of principles that explained why pluralism among church traditions was necessary in a historical church and at the same time opened up narrow denominational ecclesiologies to common dimensions of truth and practice amid diversity that prohibited division in the church.[4] At the turn of the twentieth century, E. Troeltsch expanded historical consciousness to include the world's great religions: all religious knowledge of all religious traditions are particular and mediated by history. With Troeltsch the horizon of ecclesiology was opened still further beyond the limits of multiple churches to that of the other world religions.

During the course of the twentieth century the ecumenical movement mediated an explosion of comparative ecclesiology. One can distinguish various degrees in the implicit or explicit formality of the variety of impulses that made up the ecumenical movement. For example, participation itself in the movement's quest for unity required of churches an implicit comparison of their ecclesiological status and its compatibility with other churches. After the First World War a good number of churches came together to negotiate union churches that required comprehensive comparative analysis. Still another form of comparative ecclesiology was pursued by Faith and Order, beginning with its first Conference in Lausanne in 1927 when it attempted a statement of ecclesiological positions shared in common by the participating churches, a quest that continues to this day.

Finally, the broad interreligious perspective opened up by Troeltsch also developed in the course of the twentieth century, despite the inhibiting factor of the neo-orthodox theology associated with the commanding synthesis of K. Barth. Comparative theology as a distinct form of Christian theology emerged in the last quarter of the twentieth century, and it has been applied to the discipline of ecclesiology.

Before presenting an analytical account of these various forms of comparative ecclesiology, however, it is important to consider certain presuppositions upon which a constructive engagement with this form of theology depends.

Premises for a comparative ecclesiology

Consideration of the history of the church and its ecclesiology reveals a gradual opening up of the churches' theological imagination beyond denominationalism to a positive recognition of other churches, a desire to learn from them, and in some cases to enter into communion with them. Such a development was gradual and uneven; far from being inevitable, it was and continues to be resisted by many churches. This prompts an analysis of the suppositions of a comparative ecclesiology, the more or less necessary conditions of the possibility of recognizing its necessity and importance. Five themes may function as a set of qualities that together define a new requirement that ecclesiology be open to other churches and religions in its way of proceeding.

Historical consciousness   Historical consciousness consists in a heightened awareness of the particularity and historical limitations that surround all human thinking. Revelation of God, which is mediated through the particular religious symbols of a specific location in history, bears the limits of the individual time, place and culture of its appearance. Human intelligence certainly transcends the particular, but despite its transcendent dynamism and finality, human knowing is not infinite in its actual scope but simultaneously bound to the limits of its finite and particular horizon even in its transcendence of it. This bond to history attaches to all human knowledge, and hence to theological expression, an acknowledgment that there is more truth in all domains than can be attained from a particular perspective. It encourages an openness to other points of view and achievements, an expectation that what is and will be discovered by others shares a validity that exceeds or adds to the cumulative knowledge up to this point, and hence, finally, a certain humility before the unknown that continually beckons from the future. Historical consciousness can exist in different degrees, but some level is necessary for an appreciation of the value of the truly other.

Positive appreciation of pluralism   Pluralism refers not simply to multiplicity and diversity, but to differences shared within a common field of unity. Some form of diversity has always been part of the social human condition, and in a sense the polemical dimension of ecclesiology can be counted as comparative in nature. But the rise of historical consciousness mediated the possibility of a simultaneous shift in valuation relative to the fact of pluralism. Recognition that one set of human ideas and values does not exhaust the mystery of the human allows for a positive appreciation of difference as adding depth and breadth to human self-knowledge – a fortiori relative to the incomprehensible mystery of ultimate reality. The dynamics of interchange that lead to genuine learning inculcate attitudes that transcend competition. This passage from mere tolerance of the other to positive curiosity and active interchange is a requirement for constructive comparative ecclesiology.

A whole–part conception of the church   The epistemological a prioris just listed when applied to ecclesiology lead to what may descriptively be called a 'whole–part' framework for appreciating the nature of the church. A whole host of more subtle or ambiguous distinctions revolve around this basic conception, such as the visible and invisible church, or the church as community of faith and the church as organization or institution. But a 'whole–part' distinction is both simpler and more telling. The distinction is based on the insight and conviction that the term 'church' refers to the whole Christian movement, which is divided into many churches which are parts of the whole church. At the same time, each of these parts contains the 'whole church' in the sense that, despite their particularities, limitations and defects, all that it takes to be a church is contained in the 'part'. It follows that no single church exhausts in itself all the possible qualities of what it may mean to be 'church'. Since members of the church do not belong merely to some particular church but through it to the universal church as well, an internalization of a distinction such as this becomes essential for the constructive possibilities of comparative ecclesiology.

Religious pluralism   Since the work of Troeltsch, and increasingly during the course of the twentieth century, the awareness that Christianity is one religion among many vital religious traditions began to affect Christian theology as such. The same dynamics of a historical consciousness leading to a recognition of the positive character of pluralism was gradually incorporated into the study of other religions, interreligious dialogue and the emergence of comparative theology as a subdiscipline of Christian theology. As Christian theology, comparative theology seeks to understand the content of Christian faith and reality in the light of Christian symbols. But it pursues this goal by entering into dialogue with the texts and positions of other religions and rereading Christian faith in the light they throw on the subject matter. Since coexistence with other religions is part of the actual situation of Christianity today, taking account of other religions' traditions expands the comparative horizon of Christian ecclesiology.

Retaining a confessional or particular ecclesial identity   Finally, the supposition of comparative ecclesiology is that, as Christian theology, it unfolds from a location within the Christian church and, in fact, from a particular denominational membership and affiliation. Negatively, comparative ecclesiology does not transpose the discipline into an objective, neutral, or scientific sphere that surrenders or brackets the faith claims of the theologian and his or her community. Rather, comparative ecclesiology consists not in overcoming denominational Christianity or Christianity itself, but in transcending the limits of individual churches by expanding the sources brought to bear on the task of understanding Christian faith – in this case, the church. What is learned from these sources is brought back as further light on the particularities of any given church. The concern for the truth contained in one's own community guarantees that the discipline remains Christian theology.

These five premises or suppositions lie behind or beneath the various forms of the discipline of comparative ecclesiology. Certainly they do not exhaust the assumptions of this subdiscipline. But it would be difficult to imagine the several comparative theological initiatives without the internalization of these basic insights. In their turn they provide a groundwork that has opened up several distinct forms of comparative theology.

Five variations of comparative ecclesiology

Comparative ecclesiology was initially defined so as to admit a number of variations in the focus of its subject matter, the sources appealed to, the goals that are aimed at, and the theological method used to achieve them. What follows then is an account of various forms of comparative ecclesiology. These different forms may function as a typology, but it is one generated not by a theoretical imagination but, more concretely, by a description of what various theologians have been doing. What makes each of these projects distinct and able to be distinguished from others is usually the integration of the goal or point of the work with its attendant method and the sources to which a given theologian appeals. The analysis which follows distinguishes five variations of comparative ecclesiology without any claim to being exhaustive. In each case the development will attach a name to this project, sometimes quite arbitrarily, and present a schematic analysis of its logic. This will be followed by a more pointed description of one or two practitioners of this kind of comparative ecclesiology. The analysis will conclude in each case with a summarizing appropriation of this particular method of comparative ecclesiology.

Objective analysis and comparison

A rather basic form of comparative ecclesiology consists in laying out the ecclesiologies of two or more churches in order to compare them. The sources for such an ecclesiology would be those to which the particular churches ordinarily appeal: scripture; various warrants in their history such as classical figures and credal or confessional statements of the church; and, finally, contemporary officials or theologians able to define or explain the church to its constituents with some degree of authority. The goal of such a comparative method is so to represent the ecclesiologies alongside each other that their similarities and differences become highlighted. This can be accomplished by the use of a historical critical method that represents the churches accurately. The comparison may be facilitated by an organizational scheme that allows for comparison across particular dimensions or elements that make up an integral ecclesiology.

One example of such a comparative ecclesiology is *The Christian Church: An Introduction to the Major Traditions*, edited by P. Avis.[5] Avis enlisted a group of Christian scholars to represent their own churches in an orderly way in response to several key questions regarding the nature, mission, polity and ministry of the church, and its relationship to other churches. The explicit aim of the collection is 'to bring out the distinctiveness of the churches and to exhibit the living traditions in their strength and integrity' (p. ix). More explicitly, the goal is to counter certain spurious ecumenical attitudes which, by seeking some common denominator in ecclesial life, short-change the distinctive features of the traditions that in their concreteness actually energize the members of each particular church. Comparison is built into the presentations themselves as each author describes his or her own church's ecclesiology and 'its standpoint in relation to other churches' (p. xi).

Another example of a comparative ecclesiology of this kind is *Christian Community in History, II: Comparative Ecclesiology* by R. Haight. Here too a series of ecclesiologies are laid out by the author, using a historical critical method that reconstructs the ecclesiology of a particular author who enjoys some authority in a tradition and can be taken as representative. The ecclesiology is situated in a historical setting and represented according to a grid that systematically portrays central theological and organizational topics that are typical in a comprehensive ecclesiology. The goal of this analysis overlaps with the first example in showing the distinctiveness and integrity of each ecclesiology. It has the added goal of illustrating not only differences but also what the compared churches share in common in a dialectic of sameness and difference. The analysis intends to illustrate the breadth and depth of the whole Christian church by showing the many differences and variations it can sustain within a broad, overall common structure (pp. 6–7).[6]

In sum, this first and most elementary form of comparative ecclesiology consists in laying side by side objective historical representations of two or more ecclesiologies so that their differences may appear across the common field of their being Christian churches. The expanded horizon of understanding provides a deeper insight into the distinctiveness of each church and the depth of the whole church.

Constructing the foundations of ecclesial existence

'Ecclesial existence' refers to the kind of social historical existence lived by a member of a Christian church. Ecclesial existence is simultaneously historical, because it designates the actual lives of Christians in church communities, and ideal, because it points to those features of human existence that are constant or continuous across history and across denominations at any given time. This mixture of the actual and ideal can only be determined by examining the common features of churchly existence across the boundaries of historical churches. The range of churches, therefore, makes up the sources of this comparative ecclesiology. But a grasp of this ecclesial existence requires a method that transcends historical critical examination of sources. It demands a combination of historical phenomenology and transcendental hermeneutics of what is going on in the historical lives of the churches that combines historical, existential, sociological and theological interpretation. The phrase 'constructing the foundations of historical existence' states the goal of this analysis and interpretation, namely, to characterize the social anthropology entailed in a distinctively Christian existence.

A good example of this kind of comparative ecclesiology is found in E. Farley's *Ecclesial Reflection*.[7] In this work he defines ecclesial existence, explains his method of constructing it and provides an outline of its content.

Ecclesial existence refers to a corporate historical form of social being that is not identical with any given church but prior to all of them as a universal type of existential, historical existence. It does not designate 'a single treasure to be unearthed once for all but is a living, changing reality portrayable through many types of inquiries. Even that which is grasped as an enduring feature has a historical character' (p. xvi). Ecclesial existence is simultaneously a historical phenomenon and a type of ideal Christian existence (p. 205). As theological reality, it cannot be circumscribed by the discipline of history, and as a historical reality it is always shifting in its actuality. Therefore, ecclesial existence is itself always in process so that no historical instantiation or concatenation of churches can definitively characterize it (pp. 200–5).

The method for characterizing ecclesial existence is historical, comparative and theological. Ecclesial existence as a unified type of corporate existence bears a historical and an ideal or theological character. It can only be determined historically through a variety of different kinds of inquiry because 'its subject matter, whatever it is, is a historical phenomenon' (p. 200). History then is the most basic route to determining ecclesial existence. It is gradually constructed in the course of multiple inquiries (pp. 200–1).

The content of ecclesial existence in Farley's reconstruction can be summarized in four features.[8] First, it is a theological and historical mode of existence defined by the initiating and normative event of Jesus Christ. The normativity of the event of Jesus Christ consists in its universal relevance of bearing salvation or liberation for human existence that thus transforms all human spaces and times and is not bound to any particular ethnic or cultural determinants.

Second, the normative event can be and is normative for subsequent situations of the community it forms by its being expressed in language, codified in writings and gathered together in a canon of scripture. Other sedimentations of this historical-theological existence are also objectified into written forms or traditions. The message is continually made relevant for ecclesial existence by interpretation.

Third, this ecclesial existence entails certain activities that are needed for maintaining it across successive generations. Three of these activities appear to be essential and consistent: proclamation, sacramental celebration and mediation of the message, and care of individuals and groups.

And, fourth, for these activities to be readily available, ecclesial existence must have institutional forms to serve as their vehicles. The elemental structuring of the community institutionally thus requires (a) leadership and various forms of expertise related to the activities. (b) There is need of assembly and an on-going face-to-face community or congregation. (c) One also finds an impulse in ecclesial existence for these communities to be united with others to form a larger unit of ecclesial existence, and not to have the communities in isolation from one another.

In sum, this second form of comparative ecclesiology builds on objective historical-comparative ecclesiology of the first kind. It seeks to formulate the common ecclesial existence that subsists within the various churches across time and at any given time. Comparison is the constant internal heuristic by which the historical data are considered. Within the comparative historical context this ecclesiology strives to formulate the common social form of Christian existence. Common existence does not compete with the differences among traditions but subsists within them. This type of comparative ecclesiology, therefore, stands in a dynamic, reciprocal and dialectical relationship to the display of difference achieved in the first form of comparative theology.

Ecumenical and dialogical analysis

A third subtype of comparative ecclesiology is found in the ecumenical dialogues between Christian churches. The pattern of these dialogues may vary slightly, but they follow a generically common set of methods and techniques.[9] They involve both a historical critical understanding of each church tradition and a systematic doctrinal command of its current ecclesiology. These understandings of the church are then compared with each other with attention to difference and commonality. Normally this would involve distinctions between unity-breaking differences and those which could be absorbed in some form or degree of communion between the churches. It is frequently noted that such communion is not a matter of all or nothing, because churches can recognize various degrees of partial communion. Dialogues presuppose that 'there exists a common faith behind the divisions, and that it can be reached by going behind the barriers of differences of view of tradition which make it difficult to see clearly'.[10] This whole process makes sense in relation to the particular goals of ecumenical dialogue, and it is important to recognize distinctions among these as well. For example, most ecumenical activity reaches forward towards a long term and ideal goal of some form of visible communion among the churches. But, short of that, dialogues serve a number of other immediate purposes such as promoting mutual understanding among the churches. It also adds a broader horizon, a deeper insight, and a heightened differentiation to the understanding of a particular church.

Hundreds, or perhaps thousands, of examples of local, regional and international dialogues between churches can be called upon to illuminate this type of comparative ecclesiology. Two bilateral dialogues, one between Roman Catholics and Lutherans in the United States on two distinct ecclesiological issues and another between Roman Catholics and United Methodists, are here called as witnesses.[11]

One can see the logic of comparative ecclesiology going on in every phase of the Lutheran–Catholic Dialogue on eucharist and ministry. The volume contains papers on historical and contemporary issues, discussions which include formal questions posed by the participants representing one church to those representing the other, explicit responses to those questions, a common statement representing the consensus of the theologians of both churches, and the statements of the participants representing each church. Each phase of the process is comparative. This means that each church and its history is scrutinized within the context of its relationship to the other church, its dissimilarity on the one hand, or the degree of its similarity on the other hand. In the case of each issue, or specificity, or question concerning one church, the response is framed with the position of the other church as a quite explicit background. Comparison thus provides a lens or optic for understanding; one understands the one church in relation to the other, by contrast, by analogy, by common function. In this way the understanding of one's own church is, on the one hand, expanded and enlarged because the field or horizon for understanding is enlarged; but it is also, on the other hand, rendered more precise in its difference from the other, even when the two approach each other in commonality.[12]

The suppositions of comparative ecclesiology often rise to the surface of bilateral dialogues because they are so straightforward. The whole–part distinction regarding the church is operationally evident in the mutual respect for the coherence of the positions of others against the background of 'one large church'. Historical consciousness is sometimes explicitly underlined: 'Historical criticism has significantly altered understandings of divine and human law and criteria for distinguishing them. Especially in relation to the papacy, but also in relation to other traditionally controversial questions relating to ministry, the categories of divine and human law need to be re-examined and placed in the context of ministry as service to the *koinonia* of salvation' (LCD-X, p. 74). The quest for understanding what is shared in common often allows the theological imagination to cut through canonical understanding to a deeper existential level. This is exemplified in Lutheran–Catholic discussions: 'With respect to Roman Catholics, the international Roman Catholic-Lutheran

Joint Commission has noted that, despite the definition of the local church as the diocese, "in actual fact it is the parish, even more than the diocese, which is familiar to Christians as the place where the church is to be experienced'" (LCD-X, p. 84).[13] Frequent appeal is made to functional equivalence between different formal institutions or different names of offices and operations. Juridicism or fixation on historical institutions as absolute is a permanent blockage to elementary religious and theological perception (see LCD-X, p. 121).

In sum, this third, simplest, and purest form of comparative ecclesiology combines the historical critical method of the first type and the concern for what is shared existentially and theologically of the second type. It is the most explicitly comparative of all the methods catalogued here in its overt search for a commonality that respects differences.

Convergence on a common ecclesiology

This fourth instance of comparative ecclesiology strives to define more than a fundamental ecclesial existence but less in terms of detail than a denominational ecclesiology. The goal of this ecclesiology is asymptotic, namely, an approachable but unattainable common Christian ecclesiology. It aims to characterize an ecclesiology in lines broad enough that the many churches can identify themselves in it and thereby lessen any essential or major differences with other churches. But this effort perforce must remain ideal and general enough to disable any possibility of its being the ecclesiology of a particular church and thus a rival of the denominations. Such an ecclesiology requires multilateral comparison between the ecclesiologies of the many churches. It must combine generalized, reconciling language with enough specific detail to formulate the many aspects of the church in a way that is not flat, bland, or a mere abstraction.

This kind of ecclesiology is best illustrated by the process begun by the Faith and Order movement in its Conference at Lausanne in 1927, and continued by the Faith and Order Commission of the World Council of Churches. Its most significant achievements are *Baptism, Eucharist and Ministry* (1982) and the collection of the responses of the churches to that document during the 1980s. Another major document published in 2005 describes the nature and mission of the church.[14]

The goal of this instance of this kind of comparative ecclesiology is succinctly stated in Faith and Order's statement on the church: 'to give expression to what the churches can now say together about the nature and mission of the Church and, within that agreement, to explore the extent to which the remaining church-dividing issues may be overcome' (NMC, p. 5). More specifically, it attempts to develop specific documents which can be recognized by the churches as the 'faith of the church through the ages' (FO-149, p. 8). The subject matter is not any denomination's ecclesiology but 'our' Christian ecclesiology. It does not strive to determine the developed ecclesiology of a particular church but seeks recognition of a formulation of something that can be agreed upon and held in common as authentically Christian by all parties. The phrase 'convergence document' is used to describe 'the fruit of what all of [the churches], after a long period of dialogue, [are] now able to affirm together beyond their different theological perceptions' (FO-149, p. 9).

But this goal cannot be achieved by a method of mere comparison and negotiation. Prior to the composition of BEM, the process shifted from a positivistic 'comparative method to a common biblically and christologically centered reflection and referred to the hermeneutical problem in terms of different "language" and thought-forms concerning the subject under discussion' (FO-149, p. 7). If comparative ecclesiology is to generate judgements, it needs the criteriological dimension of relating to the normative sources of all ecclesiology in bible and tradition. A genetic and constructive process is thus built into the comparative ecclesiology of BEM and NMC.[15]

A defining characteristic of this form of comparative ecclesiology is the tensive or dialectical character of the way it proceeds and its resultant language. The favoured image and concept for the church is *koinonia* or communion, because it captures the tension of unity amid diversity; communion by definition is not uniformity but pluralism. 'There is a rich diversity of Christian life and witness born out of the diversity of cultural and historical context' (NMC, p. 61). Not only unity but also diversity is a gift of God to the church because the whole is enriched by the parts (NMC, p. 60). The tensive character of these two dimensions is addressed explicitly:

> Each local church must be the place where two things are simultaneously guaran- ·
> teed: the safeguarding of unity and the flourishing of a legitimate diversity. There
> are limits within which diversity is an enrichment but outside of which diversity is
> not only unacceptable, but destructive of the gift of unity. Similarly unity, particu-
> larly when it tends to be identified with uniformity, can be destructive of authentic
> diversity and thus can become unacceptable. (NMC, p. 62)

To preserve this tension the conceptualization of this ecclesiology must be such that it captures the unity among the churches by recognizing legitimate differences in particular churches. It reaches for the deepest sources of unity with God and among the churches. It thus challenges the churches to assume critical responsibility for what they consider obstacles to various levels of communion.

In sum, this form of comparative ecclesiology is also constructive; it transcends report and analysis of the actual churches by proposing that which is both constitutive of the existing churches and simultaneously ideal in the communion between them. It appeals to the normative origins of the church and the eschatological fulfilment that together judge division and urge communion in what transcends particular traditions but exists in all of them because it can be recognized theologically as representing the apostolic tradition.

Interreligious comparative theology of the church

Finally, a fifth mode of comparative ecclesiology consists in the application of a method of comparative theology to the area of the church, that is, ecclesiology. Comparative Christian theology counts other religious communities and traditions among its sources for understanding Christianity. It rests on the premise that we live in a religiously pluralistic world and that, viewed from a Christian perspective, God's revelation cannot be confined within the boundaries of Christianity. It therefore broadens the horizon of *Christian* self-understanding by taking into account the positions of other faith traditions in reflecting on the symbols of properly Christian faith. This form of reflection remains Christian theology because it does not abandon the point of view and confession of Christian faith. But it returns to a critical understanding of Christian faith only after passing through an objective and appreciative study of one or more texts or positions from other religious traditions. The point of this form of theology is three-fold: it generates understandings of a given subject matter in multiple religions traditions, allowing a comparison of their sameness and differences; it contributes to a synthetic interreligious understanding of a particular subject matter; and it generates a new and transformed specifically Christian understanding of the Christian church by reason of the broader horizon of consideration and the specific comparisons that are implicitly made in the returning critical reflection on Christian symbols.

Two practitioners of comparative theology, F. X. Clooney and K. Ward, can help shed light on the method and goals of this kind of comparative ecclesiology.[16] Although one can distinguish certain differences between these two authors, they share enough to align them in a common cause.

In Clooney's view, comparative theology when applied to the church would draw into itself the study of religious communities of other faiths, principally but not exclusively through a reading of their texts. This would, in turn, entail rethinking ecclesiologies which were developed in a narrow, denominational or even a larger Christian framework (TAD, pp. 6–7). This comparative theology has three qualities. It is *interreligious* or conversational across religions traditions. It is *dialogical* in the sense that theologians 'explain what they believe in a way that others, even believers in other religious traditions, can understand' (HGCG, p. 10). It is *confessional* in the sense of 'truth affirming' within the context of one's commitment to one's own faith tradition (HGCG, p. 11).

> Comparison retains a confessional dimension, while confession is disciplined by comparative practice. My model of theology as interreligious, comparative, dialogical, and confessional . . . might be described more dynamically as moving from a confessional base through intervening intellectual inquiries to a renewed and transformed reappropriation of confessional views. Neither theological comparison nor confession can flourish in separation from the other, and each constantly transforms the other. (HGCG, p. 26)

Ward, for his part, tends to distinguish and contrast comparative theology from confessional theology on the basis of the sources from which they draw (RR, pp. 39–40).[17] But he also has a view of comparative theology that proceeds from and returns to a confessional base.

> Seen from this perspective, comparative theology must be a *self-critical discipline*, aware of the historical roots of its beliefs; a *pluralistic discipline*, prepared to engage in conversation with a number of living traditions; and *an open-ended discipline*, being prepared to revise beliefs if and when it comes to seem necessary. There is nothing to prevent a comparative theologian from being committed to one religious tradition, even a very authoritarian one, unless that authority prohibits such a study. (RR, p. 48)[18]

Indeed, Ward's own comparative ecclesiology consists in applying this method of comparative theology to the church.

> By placing this conception of a religious community [the church] within the global context of human religious life, it may be possible to discern both the distinctiveness of the Christian community, and its basis in a general human concern to establish and sustain appropriate ways of being human, and of attaining the highest human goal, in relation to one or more superior spiritual beings or states. (RC, p. 5)

In sum, this form of comparative ecclesiology is inherently creative for several reasons. The breadth of the horizon of data and interpretation is vast; the tradition and the texts with which an understanding of the Christian community is compared is arbitrary (Clooney, TAD, p. 154); the ways the texts are compared beyond simple notation of similarity and difference are many and offer countless possibilities for new critical interpretation.

Conclusion

Comparative ecclesiology is an analogous notion that includes a variety of subdisciplines that address with distinct methods and goals the various levels of pluralism that characterize Christian social existence in our time. Comparative ecclesiology in all its forms explicitly addresses the tension between particularism, in the sense of a withdrawal into denominationalism, and universalism, in the sense of a concern for religious community as such. All ecclesiology need not be explicitly comparative in nature. There will always be a demand for denominational studies. But given globalization and the new sense of connection between religious communities at all levels, one may expect that various forms of comparative ecclesiology will assume a more important role in the self-understanding of the Christian churches.

Notes

1 See David Tracy, 'Comparative Theology', in *The Encyclopedia of Religion*, 14, ed. Mircea Eliade, New York: Macmillan Publishing, 1987, pp. 446–55.
2 Gregory I, *Register of the Epistles of Saint Gregory the Great*, in *Leo the Great and Gregory the Great, Nicene and Post-Nicene Fathers*, 12, ed. P. Schaff and H. Ware, Peabody, MA: Hendrickson Publishers, 1994, Book VII, Letter 40 and Book VIII, Letter 30.
3 Friedrich Schleiermacher, *The Christian Faith*, New York: Harper & Row, 1963, #19, p. 88.
4 Roger Haight, *Christian Community in History, II: Comparative Ecclesiology*, New York: Continuum, 2005, pp. 334–5, p. 364.
5 Paul Avis (ed.), *The Christian Church: An Introduction to the Major Traditions*, London: SPCK, 2002.
6 Another essay of this type is Edward LeRoy Long's *Patterns of Polity: Varieties of Church Governance*, Cleveland: Pilgrim Press, 2001. This book analyses three broad types of church organization or government, by bishops, by elders, by congregations, and distinguishes three subtypes in each of these. This provides a striking comparative view of the varieties of church organizational structure.
7 Edward Farley, *Ecclesial Reflection: An Anatomy of Theological Method*, Philadelphia: Fortress Press, 1982. This work was preceded by an earlier foundational reflection which is propaedeutic to this one and was entitled *Ecclesial Man: A Social Phenomenology of Faith and Reality*, Philadelphia: Fortress Press, 1975.
8 What follows paraphrases Farley's own summary at p. 299.
9 See G.R. Evans, *Method in Ecumenical Theology: The Lessons so far*, Cambridge: University Press, 1996, for an analysis of the various techniques used in ecumenical theology to find common understanding and agreement within difference.
10 Evans, pp. 134–5.
11 Paul C. Empie and T. Austin Murphy (eds), *Eucharist and Ministry: Lutherans and Catholics in Dialogue IV*, Minneapolis: Augsburg, 1970 (cited as LCD-IV); Randall Lee and Jeffrey Gros (eds), *The Church as Koinonia of Salvation: Its Structures and Ministries: Lutherans and Catholics in Dialogue*, X, Washington, DC: United States Conference of Catholic Bishops, 2005 (cited as LCD-X); *Through Divine Love: The Church in Each Place and All Places: United Methodist-Roman Catholic Dialogue*, Washington, DC: United States Conference of Catholic Bishops, 2005 (cited as UM-RC).
12 The comparative structure of theological reasoning is clearly displayed in the way the dialogue

unfolds in UM-RC. On a given issue, for example, the church as communion, the understanding and emphases of the United Methodist Church are laid out schematically and analytically. This is followed by a parallel statement concerning the Roman Catholic Church. This allows a third and fourth step of stating what the two churches share as more or less common understandings and the various points at which they differ.

13 This statement is balanced by another statement expressing the regional side of ecclesial existence: 'The local church is not a free-standing, self-sufficient reality. As part of a network of communion, the local church maintains its reality as church by relating to other local churches' (LCD-X, 90, citing the 'Joint Working Group of the World Council of Churches and the Roman Catholic Church', #13).

14 World Council of Churches, *Baptism, Eucharist and Ministry*, Faith and Order Paper 111, Geneva: WCC Publications, 1982 (cited as BEM); WCC, *Baptism, Eucharist and Ministry 1982–1990: Report on the Process and Responses*, Faith and Order Paper 149, Geneva: WCC Publications, 1990 (cited as FO-149); WCC, *The Nature and Mission of the Church: A Stage on the Way to a Common Statement*, Faith and Order Paper 198, Geneva: WCC Publications, 2005 (cited as NMC).

15 Ormond Rush expresses what is going on here in the context of a bilateral ecumenical discussion: 'Instead of comparing and contrasting traditions, both parties attempt to interpret together the apostolic tradition. If each can recognize in the other's interpretation "the apostolic faith", then surprising agreement and common ground can be achieved' (Ormond Rush, *Still Interpreting Vatican II: Some Hermeneutical Principles*, New York: Paulist Press, 2004, p. 67). This describes the intention of the convergence documents of Faith and Order: they aim to state in a commonly accepted language the common apostolic faith.

16 Francis X. Clooney, *Theology after Vedanta: An Experiment in Comparative Theology*, Albany: State University of New York Press, 1993 (cited as TAD); idem, *Hindu God, Christian God: How Reason Helps Break Down the Boundaries between Religions*, Oxford: University Press, 2001 (cited as HGCG); idem, 'Comparative Theology', in *Oxford Handbook of Systematic Theology*, manuscript, in preparation (cited as CT); Keith Ward, *Religion and Revelation: A Theology of Revelation in the World's Religions*, Oxford: Clarendon Press, 1994 (cited as RR); idem, 'Keith Ward: A Guide for the Perplexed', in *Comparative Theology: Essays for Keith Ward*, ed. T.W. Bartel, London: SPCK, 2003, pp. 190–8 (cited as GP); idem, 'Comparative Theology: The Heritage of Schleiermacher', in *Theological Liberalism: Creative and Critical*, ed. J'annine Jobling and Ian Markham, London: SPCK, 2000, pp. 60–74 (cited as CT); idem, *Religion and Community*, Oxford: Clarendon Press, 2000 (cited as RC).

17 'In a full comparative study, the adherents of many faiths would need to co-operate in an interactive analysis of their diverse communities' (RC, pp. 5–6). 'Comparative theology is a co-operative enterprise. It is a way of doing theology in which scholars holding different world-views share together in the investigation of concepts of ultimate reality, the final human goal, and the way to achieve it' (RC, p. 339). This idea of a 'comparative theology' approaches the notion of what Wilfred Cantwell Smith called a 'world theology'; in *Toward a World Theology*, Philadelphia: Westminster, 1981.

18 This theology 'is comparative, because it compares and contrasts, in a broadly descriptive way, various religious beliefs about revelation, God, human nature and the right way to live. It is theological, because it is concerned with issues of rationality and truth. Thus it is normative, providing constructive suggestions about how to understand one particular faith tradition in a rationally justifiable way' (GP, p. 195).

Further reading

Paul Avis, (ed.), *The Christian Church: An Introduction to the Major Traditions*, London: SPCK, 2002.

Francis X. Clooney, *Theology after Vedanta: An Experiment in Comparative Theology*, Albany: State University of New York Press, 1993.

——, *Hindu God, Christian God: How Reason Helps Break Down the Boundaries between Religions*. Oxford: University Press, 2001.

——, 'Comparative Theology', in *Oxford Handbook of Systematic Theology*; manuscript, in preparation.

Paul C. Empie and T. Austin Murphy (eds), *Eucharist and Ministry: Lutherans and Catholics in Dialogue IV*, Minneapolis: Augsburg, 1970.

G.R. Evans, *Method in Ecumenical Theology: The lessons so far*, Cambridge: CambridgeUniversity Press, 1996.

Edward Farley, *Ecclesial Reflection: An Anatomy of Theological Method*, Philadelphia: Fortress Press, 1982.

——, *Ecclesial Man: A Social Phenomenology of Faith and Reality*, Philadelphia: Fortress Press, 1975.

Roger Haight, *Christian Community in History*, I-III, New York: Continuum, 2004–8.

Randall Lee and Jeffrey Gros (eds), *The Church as Koinonia of Salvation: Its Structures and Ministries: Lutherans and Catholics in Dialogue*, X, Washington, DC: United States Conference of Catholic Bishops, 2005.

Edward LeRoy Long, *Patterns of Polity: Varieties of Church Governance*, Cleveland: Pilgrim Press, 2001.

Ormond Rush, *Still Interpreting Vatican II: Some Hermeneutical Principles*, New York: Paulist Press, 2004.

Through Divine Love: The Church in Each Place and All Places: United Methodist-Roman Catholic Dialogue. Washington, DC: United States Conference of Catholic Bishops, 2005.

David Tracy, 'Comparative Theology', in *The Encyclopedia of Religion*, 14, ed. Mircea Eliade. New York: Macmillan Publishing, 1987, pp. 446–55.

Keith Ward, *Religion and Revelation: A Theology of Revelation in the World's Religions*, Oxford: Clarendon Press, 1994.

——, 'Keith Ward: A Guide for the Perplexed', *Comparative Theology: Essays for Keith Ward*, ed. T. W. Bartel, London: SPCK, 2003, pp. 190–8.

——, 'Comparative Theology: The Heritage of Schleiermacher', in *Theological Liberalism: Creative and Critical*, ed. J'annine Jobling and Ian Markham, London: SPCK, 2000, pp. 60–74.

——, *Religion and Community*, Oxford: Clarendon Press, 2000.

World Council of Churches, *Baptism, Eucharist and Ministry*, Faith and Order Paper 111, Geneva: WCC Publications, 1982.

——, *Baptism, Eucharist and Ministry 1982–1990: Report on the Process and Responses*, Faith and Order Paper 149, Geneva: WCC Publications, 1990.

——, *The Nature and Mission of the Church: A Stage on the Way to a Common Statement*, Faith and Order Paper 198, Geneva: WCC Publications, 2005.

22

ECCLESIOLOGY
AND ECUMENISM

Thomas F. Best

'Ecclesiology' points to reflection on the church and its nature and mission in the world. It encompasses the churches' reflection on the church, and the reflection of each church on its own ecclesial identity. 'Ecumenism' points to the engagement of the churches with one another, so far as is possible, in common confession, worship, witness and service. It expresses both the churches' spiritual bonds, and their material solidarity and sharing, with one another as members of the one body of Christ.

The churches' ecumenical experience has shaped both the practise and results of ecclesiological reflection. Through the ecumenical movement churches experience what they deem to be authentic ecclesial life in a variety of forms, some different from their own; this challenges their own thinking on what it means to be the church and what the church is for. The encounter with other churches also helps each to grow in its own self-understanding, to deepen its relationships with other churches, and to discover new possibilities for common confession and life.[1] This article will explore the relationship of ecclesiology and ecumenism, tracing some of the central factors and issues in their interaction.

Background, emergence and development

Ecclesiology is inherently 'ecumenical', dealing as it does with the one body of Christ composed of many members, each integral to the whole (cf. 1 Cor 12.12–26). The liturgies of many churches express this fact through prayers for the unity of Christians and the church. The primal ecclesiological fact is the unity of Christ's body, and the ecumenical movement is a response to the division and fragmentation of that body. It has arisen from the churches' conviction that they are part of the church; that harmful divisions among the churches are wounds in Christ's body, the whole of which they are a part; and that it is their duty to overcome those divisions.

This is not to say that early institutional ecumenism focused on ecclesiology. Indeed ecclesiology itself was sometimes identified as a factor dividing the churches and in that sense a hindrance to ecumenism; energy was put rather into joint diaconal work, or common witness on social ills such as alcoholism, where the churches could set aside their internal differences and offer a common witness and service to the world. Some leaders were more interested in promoting a broad, bold vision of unity than in pursuing the niceties of ecclesiological dispute. Thus for the great pioneer John Mott, speaking at the conclusion of the World Missionary Conference in Edinburgh in 1910, the ecumenical advance lay in the energy and resources generated by the encounter among previously-separated Christians, recognizing themselves for the first time as a world-wide community: 'we go out . . . with a larger acquaintanceship, with deeper realization of this fellowship . . . Our best days are ahead of us because we have a larger Christ.'[2] Other leaders sought a broad-spectrum approach to overcoming divisions, as seen in the path-breaking Encyclical of the Ecumenical Patriarch which already in 1920 called for 'a contact and league (fellowship) between the churches'. This vision stressed the building of mutual understanding and respect; in this process the study of 'doctrinal differences' had its place, but was just one of 11 areas in which common work was called for.[3]

Nevertheless ecclesiological work has been at the heart of the ecumenical movement from its beginning. Three decisive expressions of the ecumenical ecclesiological quest will be traced through this article. Continuing to the present, they are seen already in the period from 1920: Faith and Order's early *multi-lateral work* at its first World Conference in Lausanne in 1927; *church unions* formed in Canada (1925), Hong Kong (1927) and Thailand (1934); and early *bi-lateral dialogues*, leading for example to the 1931 Bonn Agreement establishing full communion between Anglican and Old Catholic churches.

As for the content of this ecclesiological work, three enduring themes may be traced. These have received varying degrees of attention from one ecumenical context and historical period to another. The first is *the nature of the church*. Broad agreement in this area is typically expressed, as already at Lausanne, in two ways: first through biblical images such as the Body of Christ and the Temple of God,[4] and second in terms of the 'characteristics by which [the church] can be known'. These characteristics include the presence of the Word, profession of faith, commitment to mission, observance of the sacraments, 'a ministry for the pastoral office', and a fellowship in worship and the means of grace. Beyond this point the churches differ in their understanding of the church, and particularly of 'the nature of the church visible and the church invisible, their relation to each other, and the number of those who are included in each'.[5]

A second enduring ecclesiological theme has been *the nature of the unity we seek*. This has been addressed in terms of church order (Lausanne already identified the three classic dimensions of the episcopate, the councils of presbyters, and the congregation of the faithful as essential aspects 'in the order of life of a reunited Church'[6]) and of models of unity (beginning with 'organic unity', proposed at the second world conference on Faith and Order in Edinburgh in 1937).[7] A point to both themes is that ecclesiological work in the ecumenical context includes not only churches which understand themselves as one among several different, but fully valid, expressions of the church, but also churches which understand themselves as being, in some sense, its 'true' and 'normative' expression. Ecumenical ecclesiological dialogues have proved remarkably resilient in incorporating these radically divergent views. But this should not be taken for granted; indeed, it is a miracle of the ecumenical movement.

A third enduring ecclesiological theme has been *the relation of church and world*. Churches within the ecumenical movement have agreed that the church must witness to society. More problematic has been the question of how far the 'world' may be said to influence, or be present within, the church.[8] 'Non-theological' factors were recognized from the beginning as playing a role in division, and therefore as being ecclesiologically significant. It is thus no accident that the By-Laws of Faith and Order direct it to study both 'such questions of faith, order, and worship as bear on [the search for visible unity]' *and* 'such social, cultural, political, racial, and other factors as affect the unity of the Church'.[9] Ecumenical work has sought to integrate these aspects of the search for visible unity, but it has not always proved easy in practice.

With these themes in mind, we move to the next stage in the development of the ecumenical movement. In 1948 the Faith and Order and Life and Work movements joined to found the World Council of Churches (WCC). Despite the diversity among the 147 churches present at its founding assembly in Amsterdam, initially the WCC reflected the Christo-centric theology of its architects: the WCC Basis stated simply that it was 'a fellowship of churches which accept our Lord Jesus Christ as God and Saviour'. (In the next 15 years this was developed through references to the scriptures and the Trinity, so that the Basis more accurately reflected the fullness of the faith of the WCC's member churches.)[10] Fundamental ecclesiological questions emerged about the nature of that fellowship: what was the ecclesial status of the WCC; what were the ecclesiological *implications* of membership; and did membership entail recognition of other WCC member churches *as* churches?

The 1950 'Toronto Declaration' insisted that the WCC is not and cannot be a church; that it 'cannot and should not be based on any one particular conception of the church'; and that membership 'does not imply that each church must regard the other member churches as churches in the true and full sense of the word'. Yet the Declaration is not minimalist: pointing to Christ as the 'divine head of the body', it insists that membership in the one church of Christ 'is more inclusive than the membership of their own church body'.[11] This appeal to a higher ecclesial standard, to the one Body of which each church is but a part, was to become a recurring theme in ecumenical work on ecclesiology.

In the first half of the twentieth century, dialogues were based on a comparative method corresponding to the need for greater understanding among the partners: centuries of separation, misinformation and distrust had to be corrected. Characterizing this period – and pointing beyond it – Faith and Order Commission Secretary Oliver Tomkins suggested in 1952 that the churches had come

> to the end of what I would call a *mere comparative ecclesiology*. It was an essential and pioneer task ... As a result of forty years of patient and careful work, there now exists a considerable literature setting forth the distinctive theological convictions of the main Christian traditions on such themes as ... the nature of the Church ... I would yet suggest that we who are called by our churches to work at the heart of this enterprise have reached a limit in what can be profitably done in mutual explanation.[12]

The seeds of the next stage of reflection were inherent in the conference at Lund itself, as seen in the famous 'Lund Principle':

> A faith in the one Church of Christ which is not implemented by acts of obedience is dead. There are truths about the nature of God and His Church which will remain for ever closed to us unless we act together in obedience to the unity which is already ours ... Should not our churches ask themselves ... whether they should not act together in all matters except those in which deep differences of conviction compel them to act separately?[13]

This quietly startling suggestion – that common action by the churches should be the *norm*, rather than the exception – reflected the conviction that the groundwork had been done, and the churches were now called together to a more active engagement in the ecclesiological task.

This meant that the focus was no longer on the distinctive positions of the particular churches, but upon what they might say *together* about the nature and mission of the church. This 'convergence' method focuses on points at which the churches are approaching one another in their understanding and practise. Those involved are expected to remain true to their ecclesial identities and convictions, even as they seek understandings and formulations to express ecclesial truths which are yet deeper than the issues which divide us; and 'differences are to be clarified and recorded as honestly as agreements'.[14]

This method has brought a new focus on the churches' common ecclesial convictions, and encouraged them to appreciate the convictions of others. Some have enlarged their ecclesiological vocabulary, drawing on insights from other churches. Sometimes the method has revealed the function which certain ecclesiological ideas play within a church; sometimes it has become clear that certain ecclesiological notions – whatever their original value – function today mainly to maintain divisions. In other cases a re-examination of centuries-old language has led to the discovery of unexpected ecclesiological agreement, as in the Eastern Orthodox–Oriental Orthodox dialogue:

> In the light of our four unofficial consultations (1964, 1967, 1970, 1971) and our three official meetings which followed on (1985, 1989, 1990), we have understood that both families have loyally maintained the authentic orthodox christological doctrine, and the unbroken continuity of the apostolic tradition, though they may have used Christological terms in different ways.[15]

Such a method places a premium on the human dimension. As ecclesiological texts are hammered out in meetings ideas are exchanged, formulations tried, and differences noted, all within a context of common life and growing personal relationships: worship is shared to the extent possible, meals are taken together, experiences of church, community and family are shared – and the next day the group sits down again to its work. This community of common work now extends over several ecumenical generations; many of today's church leaders and theologians, ecclesiologists and liturgists have experienced and been influenced by it. The dialogue results must, of course, be convincing in their own right since the experience of the dialogue cannot be fully shared with those who were not involved.

It has been said that that we are on the brink of a new period, in which a new method for ecumenical ecclesiological work will emerge. If so it would, I expect, foster a stronger interaction between the dialogue process and the churches which are taking its results into their own lives. This leads to the crucial question of *reception*, for ecclesiological work becomes effective only insofar as it is 'received' by the churches. The term, which was originally applied to the centuries-long process of the churches' appropriating the historic councils of the early Christian period, means far more than formal adoption of a text.

In this broader and deeper sense of the term, 'reception' means that a church not only adopts a text but takes that text into its own life, studying and absorbing it and, in the most complete expression of reception, allowing it to shape the church's own self-understanding and practice. Few ecclesiological texts produced within the ecumenical movement (or indeed within individual churches) actually attain this. Those which *are* being 'received' (pre-eminently *Baptism, Eucharist and Ministry*) have been offered at a strategic moment in the lives of the churches; have been marked by clarity and vigour of expression; and have addressed real needs, both practical and theoretical, in the lives of the churches.

Major related ecclesial and intellectual events and developments

In addition to the formation of the WCC, two events had a special impact on ecclesiological reflection within the ecumenical movement during the second half of the twentieth century. The first was the Second Vatican Council, especially its Decree on Ecumenism which declared ecumenical engagement a duty of Roman Catholics and of the Roman Catholic Church and stressed the ecclesiological principle that *all* the baptized have been incorporated into Christ.[16] Following the Council, Roman Catholic theologians and ecclesiologists became officially engaged with Faith and Order's multilateral work for visible unity (there had been unofficial collaboration on the Week of Prayer for Christian Unity even before the Council). This was paralleled by the Roman Catholic Church's entry into many bilateral dialogues, and its entry into national (as of 2001 some 58) and regional (at least 3) councils of churches world-wide.

A second decisive event was the WCC's 4th assembly at Uppsala in 1968. Marked by the accession of many churches from the South and the presence of many young people, meeting in the context of the civil rights movements and the world-wide social upheavals of the late 1960s, and following shortly upon the Geneva Conference on Church and Society of 1966, it put issues of justice squarely on the ecumenical agenda. A corollary was the call for churches to practise justice within their own lives, refusing, for example, to 'allow their membership to be determined by discrimination based on race, wealth, social class or education'. Strikingly, Uppsala put this call in ecclesiological language: the church in its unity is 'the sign of the coming unity of mankind'; to practise discrimination amounts to 'refusing the gift of catholicity both individually and corporately'.[17] A series of studies at the interface of church and world followed (for example, on Theology and Racism in the 1970s, the Unity of the Church and the Renewal of Human Community through the 1980s, and Ecclesiology and Ethics through the 1990s[18]), all treating divisions in the human community as threatening the unity of the churches – composed of human beings as they are – and thus ecclesiologically significant.

Two quite different groupings of churches have proved of special significance in this connection. The first, the United and Uniting Churches, are those formed or under formation through the structural union of separated churches, usually at the national level.[19] They are the most complete embodiment of the 'organic union' envisioned by the second world conference on Faith and Order in 1937,[20] and of the vision of unity from the WCC's New Delhi assembly in 1961, whereby 'all in each place who are baptized . . . are brought by the Holy Spirit into one fully committed fellowship'.[21] In addition they have been widely identified with the 'local churches truly united' referred to in the statement on conciliar fellowship from the Nairobi assembly in 1975.[22]

Inspired by New Delhi's prophecy that 'the achievement of unity will involve nothing less than a death and rebirth of many forms of church life as we have known them. We believe that nothing less costly can finally suffice',[23] the United and Uniting Churches have understood themselves through a 'kenotic ecclesiology' whereby divided denominations have 'died' to their separate identities in order to 'rise' together into a single new, united church. They are linked by the common experience of structural (and not only 'spiritual') union as the fullest expression of *mutual accountability*, as all aspects of church life, from decision-making on issues of faith to common social witness, are lived out henceforth within a single, new ecclesial structure. As D.T. Niles famously said at the WCC's founding assembly, 'No "schemes of union" have come about, *the churches had united*'.[24]

United churches form the most widely-diverse family of churches world-wide, as a brief survey shows. The earliest unions, from the Old Prussian Union of 1817, were those in Germany, Austria and Czechoslovakia uniting Lutheran and Reformed elements.[25] A second group, beginning with the United Church of Canada in 1925 and mainly in North America, the United Kingdom and Australia, united various combinations of Protestant churches (most often Presbyterians, Congregationalists, Methodists and Disciples of Christ). A third group, including the Church of Christ in Thailand (1934) and the United Church in Jamaica and the Cayman Islands (1992), includes these denominations in 'third world' contexts; they are often a force for indigenization of the gospel as mission-founded churches give way to a single locally led and funded church. A fourth group, beginning with the Church of South India (1947) and so far limited to the Indian sub-continent, incorporated Anglican churches and thus episcopal structures. (This group also includes the most comprehensive union, the Church of North India, incorporating former Anglican, Baptist, Congregational, Disciples, Methodist, Brethren and Presbyterian churches.) A fifth group includes unions among churches within the same confessional tradition (such as the Evangelical Lutheran Church in America, uniting three national Lutheran denominations in 1988).[26] Thus these churches incorporate an astonishing variety of ecclesial types; their significance lies in their having overcome divisive ecclesiological issues to make union possible.

Notably, United Churches have insisted that 'non-theological' factors have ecclesiological implications; even when the churches have few ecclesiological differences, the very act of union offers a powerful witness to reconciliation within Christ's body, the church. The Uniting Presbyterian Church in Southern Africa united White and Black Presbyterian churches in the context of post-apartheid South Africa; the promise – and costs – of such a union are suggested in this comment on its formation:

> this union is a step in faith. It does not mean that the old divisions and all the hurts, suspicions and fear that go with them have suddenly been overcome, but it does demonstrate a willingness to allow God to take us a stage further in the healing process.[27]

A second grouping of ecclesiologically significant churches has been the Christian World Communions (CWCs). These vary greatly in self-understanding (from the Anglican Communion, linking Anglican churches world-wide spiritually through the Archbishop of Canterbury, to the Baptist World Alliance, an association promoting sharing among self-contained Baptist churches world-wide), organization, and relationship to their member churches. The Roman Catholic Church participates actively in the CWCs movement, as do both Eastern and Oriental Orthodox families of churches. Some United Churches are members of those CWCs which incorporate their constituent denominations.

Since the 1960s CWCs have gained in self-confidence and influence, not least through organizing bilateral church dialogues at the global level.[28] These bring pairs of churches together for dialogue, with ecclesiological issues having pride of place. Again they vary greatly, from the Anglican–Roman Catholic dialogue (linking churches with a direct history of separation, and with the potential goal of union) to the Disciples–Roman

Catholic dialogue (where there is no direct history of division, and the dialogue reflects a search for understanding and mutual enrichment rather than an aspiration for union). Significant dialogues have also been held at the national and regional level.[29]

The bilaterals focus upon specific issues which divide the churches concerned, or are otherwise of mutual concern. Their official character means that agreements made should have an actual impact upon the churches involved. They may touch on matters requiring the 'healing of memories' of bitter past conflicts, in order that reconciliation can take place. A notable example is the Leuenberg Church Fellowship in Europe agreed in 1973 and known since 2003 as the Community of Protestant Churches in Europe.[30] This achieved mutual recognition of ministries and presidency at the eucharist among Lutheran and Reformed churches; it now encompasses 104 Waldensian, Hussite, Czech Brethren and United Churches (including some in South America). Through a Joint Declaration of Church Fellowship, seven Methodist churches are now involved.

The most famous recent bilateral result is the Lutheran–Roman Catholic 'Joint Declaration on the Doctrine of Justification'[31] signed in Augsburg, Germany in 1999. Building upon bilaterals in the United States and Germany, this has overcome theologically one of the fundamental issues which had divided these churches at the time of the Protestant Reformation. The churches declared a consensus in basic truths of the doctrine of justification and agreed that, in view of their current understandings of the doctrine, their historic mutual condemnations no longer applied.

Some have hoped that as other churches signed the Declaration it might come to represent a general healing of the theological divisions underlying the Reformation. Methodist churches have signed at the Methodist World Alliance meeting in Seoul in July, 2006; but some church families, notably the Reformed, have resisted on the grounds that the Declaration does not address the specific issues decisive in their separation from the Roman Catholic Church. And it must be noted that this theological breakthrough did not solve the *ecclesiological* issues which continue to divide the Lutheran and Roman Catholic churches: the Declaration does not enable mutual participation in the eucharist, since this requires the reconciliation of ministerial orders.

The most significant ecclesiological development in the ecumenical context, however, has undoubtedly been *Baptism, Eucharist and Ministry* (BEM).[32] This multilateral convergence text, approved by the Faith and Order Plenary Commission in Lima, Peru in 1982 for study and response by the churches, was unique in its scope:

> This Lima text represents the significant theological convergence which Faith and Order has discerned and formulated . . . That theologians of such widely different traditions should be able to speak so harmoniously about baptism, eucharist and ministry is unprecedented in the modern ecumenical movement. Particularly noteworthy is the fact that the Commission also includes among its full members theologians of the Roman Catholic and other churches which do not belong to the World Council of Churches itself.[33]

By the year 2000 BEM, translated into almost 40 languages, had become the most widely studied of all ecumenical texts. It had received official responses from about 190 churches (and many more from other sources) and had been studied in faculties, lay academies and church education classes around the world. It continues to inspire formal agreements among churches, and to inform ecclesiological work done ecumenically and within individual churches. These are signs that BEM has been 'received' in a substantial way by the churches and within the ecumenical movement.[34]

This was possible first because BEM was a process as well as a text, with its production taking place over some 20 years. The 'embryo texts'[35] on eucharist (1967), baptism (1968) and ministry (1972) were sent from the Accra Plenary Commission meeting in 1974 to the churches for reaction; on the basis of the 150 official responses received, the texts were further developed for approval at Lima in 1982. All the official church responses were published,[36] as were a penetrating analysis of the responses and, now, a critical appreciation of BEM on the twenty-fifth anniversary of its publication.[37]

A second factor enabling this reception was the text itself. In contrast to many ecumenical and church texts, it is well-written and engaging, laced with scriptural references, and shows the relevance of theological and ecclesiological reflection for the life of the church: 'Baptism is related not only to momentary experience, but to life-long growth into Christ';[38] 'The eucharist embraces all aspects of life . . . All kinds of injustice, racism, separation and lack of freedom are radically challenged when we share in the body and blood of Christ';[39] 'In the fulfilment of their mission and service the churches need people who in different ways express and perform the tasks of the ordained ministry in its diaconal, presbyteral and episcopal aspects and functions'.[40] BEM includes a commentary set parallel to the text, explaining terms and setting divisive issues in theological and historical context.

A third, and most significant, aspect of the reception of BEM was the way in which it was sent to the churches for official response 'at the highest appropriate level of authority'. Churches were asked to indicate *not* how far BEM corresponded to their own doctrines and practises, but rather 'the extent to which your church can recognize in this text the faith of the Church through the ages'[41] – a quietly revolutionary question which made clear that the BEM process was about the common core of the Christian faith, about the church rather than the particular beliefs and practices of the churches. This approach drew on the seminal distinction made at the Faith and Order World Conference in Montreal in 1963 between the Tradition ('the Gospel itself, transmitted from generation to generation in and by the Church') and the traditions ('both the diversity of forms of expression and also what we call confessional traditions, for instance the Lutheran . . . or Reformed').[42] Additional questions were equally direct, asking, for instance, about 'the consequences your church can draw from this text for its relations and dialogues with other churches' and 'the guidance your church can take from this text for its worship, educational, ethical and spiritual life and witness'.[43] Such questions invited change in the lives of churches committed to the response process.

To be sure, many churches judged BEM mainly by its degree of correspondence with their own positions. Some critics felt that BEM favoured the ecclesiological positions of episcopally ordered churches with a strong sense of tradition; others objected that scripture was not given sufficient weight as a structural principle of the Christian faith.[44] Yet these critiques were not the burden of the response process. Through 'receiving' BEM many churches gained a new appreciation of how much the churches do hold in common. In some cases BEM solidified a consensus which had been building within a church.[45] Where churches did not agree with BEM, some undertook the 'ecumenical discipline' of reconsidering their own views in light of the consensus expressed there.

The analysis of the responses to BEM identified three areas urgently needing further study: the relation of Scripture and Tradition, the question of Sacrament and Sacramentality, and the understanding of the church itself.[46] This result of the BEM process inspired ecumenical work in all three areas but especially in the last, the understanding of the church. Recent Faith and Order work on ecclesiology has built on the convergence reflected in BEM, while tackling disputed issues such as episcopacy and ordination more directly than had been done before. This has culminated in two Faith and Order texts: first, the study document *The Nature and Mission of the Church: A Stage on the Way to a Common Statement* (2005) [47] and second, 'Called to be the One Church',[48] the complementary text on ecclesiology from the WCC's Porto Alegre Assembly (2006). As we will see below, both texts are now before the churches for study and response by early 2010.

Some key ecclesiological ideas

Churches within the ecumenical fellowship have not felt the appeal of the purely 'spiritual' unity so dear to many evangelistic and Pentecostal churches. Generally the ecumenical fellowship has agreed that unity is for the glory of God; that it must be visible and not merely spiritual; that it must allow for legitimate diversity in the faith and life of the churches; that it means renewal in the life of the churches; that it is for the sake of the churches' witness and service in the world; and that it is 'for the sake of the salvation and the renewal of all humanity according to God's purpose'.[49]

But what would visible unity *look* like? What structural form might it take, what would be its constituent organs, and what ligaments and sinews would bind it together? Such questions have given rise to 'models of unity' which have shaped ecumenical reflection on the church. While not having the predictive power of scientific models, they have been helpful in focusing discussion and clarifying alternatives.[50]

The first of the models, *organic unity*, has been associated with the Faith and Order movement since its second world conference in Edinburgh in 1937. Such unity does not mean uniformity, but rather

> the unity of a living organism, with the diversity characteristic of the members of a healthy body . . . In a church so united the ultimate loyalty of every member would be given to the whole body and not to any part of it. Its members would move freely from one part to another and find every privilege of membership open to them. The sacraments would be the sacraments of the whole body. The ministry would be accepted by all as a ministry of the whole body.[51]

Organic union has been associated with the full structural union of the United and Uniting Churches, but other forms of 'union' may also fall within its scope. The word 'organic' guards the *diversity* of the body; the text speaks of '*some measure* of organisational union', and preserving 'the relative autonomy of the several constituent parts' through the 'federal' principle.[52]

The WCC's New Delhi assembly in 1961 sought to identify the elements of an 'organic union'; typically, structural principles were not offered, but rather practices which would mark the life of a church united. Unity is

> being made visible as all in each place . . . are brought . . . into one fully committed fellowship, holding the one apostolic faith, preaching the one Gospel, breaking the one bread, joining in common prayer, and having a corporate life reaching out in witness and service to all.[53]

This local fellowship is 'united with the whole Christian fellowship in all places and all ages in such wise that ministry and members are accepted by all, and that all can act and speak together as occasion requires for the tasks to which God calls his people'.[54] Thus the fundamental elements of a church united would include unity in faith rooted in the scriptures, a common eucharistic and other worship life, acceptance of ministries and members, common witness and service, and organs for common decision-making.

Organic union was further developed through the notion of *conciliar fellowship* defined at the WCC assembly in Nairobi in 1975, drawing on Faith and Order discussions at Salamanca in 1973.[55] Nairobi noted that:

> The one Church is to be envisioned as a conciliar fellowship of local churches which are themselves truly united . . . each local church possesses, in communion with the others, the fullness of catholicity, witnesses to the same apostolic faith, and therefore recognizes the others as belonging to the same Church of Christ and guided by the same Spirit . . .[56]
>
> Conciliarity expresses this interior unity of the churches separated by space, culture or time, but living intensely this unity in Christ and seeking, from time to time, by councils of representatives of all the local churches at various geographical levels to express their unity visibly in a common meeting.[57]

The WCC assembly, at Vancouver in 1983, building upon work at the Faith and Order Plenary Commission in Bangalore in 1978,[58] spoke of three 'marks' proper to 'a strong Church unity': a common understanding of the apostolic faith; a common confession of the apostolic faith including full mutual recognition of baptism, the eucharist and ministry; and common ways of decision-making and teaching authoritatively.[59] The final point raises the complex issue of authority in the church,[60] reflecting a determination finally to deal concretely with the structural implications of conciliarity: how would common decisions of a conciliar gathering be implemented – and how would churches hold one another mutually accountable for implementing them? Strikingly, Vancouver also brought a fresh stress on the unity of the church in relation to its witness and service to the world, calling for 'a witnessing unity, a credible sign of the new creation' in which 'overcoming church division' meant also 'binding us together in the face of racism, sexism, injustice'. Not just confessing, but 'living [the] apostolic faith together' would enable the churches to 'help the world to realize God's design for creation'; their 'visible communion' would allow 'the healing and uniting power' of the gifts of baptism, eucharist and ministry to offer a true sign of unity 'amidst the divisions of humankind'.[61]

Neither organic unity, nor its development through conciliar fellowship, had clarified fully the place of the historic churches within a future church united; but two other models of unity clearly foresaw the continued existence of the historic confessional and denominational expressions of the church. The first, the *communion of communions* proposed in 1970,[62] saw each of these as a '*typos*' (a distinct constellation of theological foci and methods, church discipline, and liturgical and spiritual life) to be preserved for the enrichment of the church as a whole, but to be set within a larger ecclesial framework. In its original formulation this included common sacraments and dogma, as well as a basic structure for ministry – in which the bishop of Rome would exercise a unique ministry on behalf of unity.

The second such model, *reconciled diversity*, was proposed originally by the Christian World Communions in 1974 as an alternative to the organic unity and conciliar fellowship 'trajectory' developed by Faith and Order.[63] For reconciled diversity, the present confessions are legitimate expressions of diversity within the one body of Christ, each preserving certain aspects of Christian faith and life for the benefit of the church as a whole. These qualities, however, should not be 'maintained unaltered' but should 'lose their divisive character and [be] reconciled to each other'.[64] While no overarching ecclesial framework is specified, such a 'unity in reconciled diversity' should be 'ordered in all its components in conciliar structures and actions'.[65]

Despite efforts to show how organic union and reconciled diversity were complementary, the two approaches stood inevitably in tension: one foresaw the possibility of the disappearance of denominational expressions of the church, while the other was committed to their survival (albeit in 'renewed' form). Furthermore, none of the models had shown how the language of conciliarity could be put into practice structurally in the current church and ecumenical situation.

At this moment the notion of *koinonia* emerged as a framework within which ecumenical ecclesiological work could continue. *Koinonia* has even less structural content that most other models; it rather evokes the special *quality of relationships* which should obtain among Christians and the churches, pointing to 'the intimate, mutually sustaining and challenging bonds – both spiritual and material – linking them within, and to, the one Body of Christ'.[66] Originally a secular term, it was used by the early Christian movement to indicate sharing or participating in *spiritual things* (the gospel, Phil 1.15; faith, Philem 6; Christ's body and blood, 1 Cor 10.16; the divine nature, 2 Pet 1:4; sufferings, either those of other Christians, 2 Cor 1.7, Heb 10.33, or, strikingly, of Christ, Phil 3.10, 1 Pet 4.13) but also in *material things* (Paul's collection for the 'Saints' in Jerusalem, Rom 12.13, 15.26–27, 2 Cor 8.4, 9.13, also 1 Tim 6.18).[67] Thus *koinonia* offers a biblical basis for both the churches' spiritual bond with Christ and one another, and their material support of each other and of a world in need.

This double focus has enabled *koinonia* to bridge various approaches to unity. In the form of 'communion' or 'fellowship' it had long been important for Faith and Order's multilateral work (indeed since Lausanne in 1927); and had emerged at the WCC's New Delhi assembly as a preferred description of the nature of the church:

> The word 'fellowship' (*koinonia*) has been chosen because it describes what the church truly is. 'Fellowship' clearly implies that the church is not merely an institution or organization. It is a fellowship of those who are called together by the Holy Spirit and in baptism confess Christ as Lord and Saviour.[68]

But *koinonia* had also been a central term in the bilateral discussions of the CWCs: for example, the Anglican–Roman Catholic dialogue (ARCIC I, 1981) made *koinonia* 'fundamental to all reflection on the nature of the church' and 'the base on which the whole report rests'.[69]

The multilateral and bilateral work for unity came together at the WCC's seventh assembly at Canberra in 1991. The assembly's unity statement, prepared by Faith and Order and entitled 'The Unity of the Church as Koinonia: Gift and Calling', integrated the themes from almost a century of ecumenical ecclesiological work in identifying the unity of the church as:

> A koinonia given and expressed in the common confession of the apostolic faith; a common sacramental life entered by the one baptism and celebrated together in

one eucharistic fellowship; a common life in which members and ministries are mutually recognized and reconciled; and a common mission . . . full communion is realized when all the churches are able to recognize in one another the one, holy, catholic and apostolic church in its fulness. This full communion will be expressed . . . through conciliar forms of life and action. In such communion churches are bound in all aspects of their life together at all levels in confessing the one faith and engaging in worship and witness, deliberation and action.[70]

With this a vision of unity is reached which involves 'all but' structural union. Without excluding, in particular local circumstances, the United churches' structural witness to union, Canberra clearly anticipates the continued existence of present denominational identities. But what has come to the fore is the depth and extent of the bonds among the churches, and their mutual accountability to one another. The notion of *koinonia* is used to develop unity as a full integration of the churches into a truly common confession, life and witness, supported and expressed through conciliar life at all levels. Even as they remain structurally separate, the churches 'are bound in all aspects of their life together at all levels': 'All'.

But what does it mean to be 'bound . . . together'? As we have noted, because *koinonia* does not address issues of structure it could not help develop the promise of the 'common ways of decision-making and teaching authoritatively' announced at Vancouver. This in turn has delayed the development of conciliarity, especially in relation to the exercise of authority within conciliar structures of unity.

Recent developments and debates

Recent developments have posed a number of challenges to ecclesiological work being done in the ecumenical context. We may note seven of these. A first area of challenge involves the United and Uniting Churches. Here the crucial ecclesiological issue remains the incorporation of episcopal structures into new church unions. Three union processes have stalled on this issue as of 2006;[71] the most dramatic recent setback in union efforts was due to a failure to reach agreement in this area;[72] and the failure of the memorable proposal for an 'ecumenical bishop' for East Cardiff in Wales also attests to the current intractability of this question for the United and Uniting Churches movement.[73] The success in including episcopacy within the United churches in the Indian sub-continent has not proved 'exportable' to other situations in which both Anglicans/Episcopalians and Presbyterians are involved, not least because the current stress on denominational identity does not encourage creativity in reconciling divergent understandings of church order and ordination.

These churches are also facing challenges to the understanding of union itself: can the term be applied more widely, to 'anticipatory' partnership and full-communion agreements? Moves in France in 2006 to create the Union of Protestant Churches in Alsace and Lorraine press the point: the two churches involved[74] continue joint programming, and will hold pastoral resources in common. Each maintains its distinctive doctrinal profile; no structural changes are made – and the churches proclaim this to be 'union'. Is it? An even more radical question is whether a newly-formed United Church is truly a 'new' church, deriving its identity from its relation to Christ and its own authentic sacramental life – or does it simply continue the ecclesial identities of its constituent churches, if in a new form?

A second area of challenge involves the bilateral dialogues pursued by the Christian

World Communions. Here the most interesting question ecclesiologically is that of 'transitivity': what is the significance of agreements reached between two churches, for the other relationships in which each is involved? Could a church enjoy full communion with one church which ordains women to the ministry of word and sacrament, and also with another church which does not do so? The Old Catholic Church has explored related questions in a nuanced way in its dialogue with the Orthodox, for the benefit of the whole ecumenical movement.[75]

A third area has to do with the scope of ecclesiological study itself. The location of ecclesiology within the ecumenical context is not innocent. The point has been sharpened through recent study on ecclesiology and ethics, in which the following question has been asked:

> Is it enough to say . . . that ethical engagement is intrinsic to the church *as* church? Is it enough to say that, if a church is not engaging responsibly with the ethical issues of its day, it is not being fully church? Must we not also say: if the churches are not engaging these ethical issues *together*, then *none of them individually is being fully church?*[76]

A related, even more challenging question was posed in a working session at the fifth world conference on Faith and Order in 1993:

> We affirm that, in many places . . . koinonia-generating involvement in struggles of humanity is taking place. We recognize in these common involvements an urgent, real, but imperfect koinonia, and urge the Faith and Order Commission to give priority to . . . clarifying their ecclesiological implications.[77]

The discussion was careful *not* to speak of 'ecclesio-genesis', nor did the Commission rush to take up the issue; but the question remains. Again: 'We see that moral struggle, discernment and formation are not optional "extras" alongside the understandings of church . . . from our various traditions. They also *challenge* those traditional understandings, helping us learn from God's world how better to be church'.[78] Is our ecclesiological reflection prepared to take up these challenges? And how far is the ecclesiological enterprise itself prepared to be challenged – and changed – in the process?

A fourth area is a new determination to tackle sensitive and difficult ecclesiological issues. This is seen not least in the Papal Encyclical *Ut Unum Sint* issued in 1995, calling for 'a patient and fraternal dialogue'[79] on the nature and exercise of the papal office and renewing interest in the thorny issues of primacy and succession in the church. An example from the Orthodox context is the fresh discussion of 'oikonomia' in relation to the limits of the church and the 're'-baptism of persons entering the Orthodox church from another.[80] Yet another example is the readiness by private or semi-official parties to offer fresh, sometimes bold proposals for the search of unity – for example, the call of the French Protestant–Roman Catholic *Groupe des Dombes* for a 'conversion' not only of Christians, but of the churches themselves.[81]

A related fifth area is a new readiness finally to take up the question of authority and its exercise in the churches.[82] As noted above, the absence of such work has hampered progress on conciliarity and thus on the structural form of visible unity. In the bilateral context, the Anglican–Roman Catholic dialogue has produced material (controversial within both ecclesial contexts) on 'the gift of authority';[83] and Faith and Order, approaching the issue from earlier work on hermeneutics, has made a new commitment to tackling the question of authority and its exercise in the churches.[84]

A sixth area is a shift in the focus of ecclesiological reflection in the ecumenical context. Since the middle of the twentieth century this had concentrated on the nature of the unity we seek and the elaboration of models of unity. In addition much attention was paid to specific aspects of the church and its life – for example baptism, eucharist, ministry, intercessory prayer,[85] and the distortions in the life of the church threatened by sexism.[86]

There is now a clear trend towards the study of the *nature of the church itself*. This was spurred by the churches' responses to BEM, published from 1986–90 and (as noted above) identifying ecclesiology as one of the crucial topics for further work. Another factor concerned issues raised by a series of church unions in Jamaica (1992), South Africa (1994 and 1999), the Netherlands (2004), and the formation of the Communion of Churches in India (2004), as well as positive developments in the bilateral dialogues (for example, that on justification). The Report of the Special Commission on Orthodox Participation in the WCC, published in 2002, proposed a distinction between two fundamental ways of understanding the relationship of particular churches to the church.[87] Although the language used (of either 'identifying' oneself with, or of seeing oneself as 'part[s] of', the One, Holy, Catholic and Apostolic Church) is not the happiest, the Report has served to focus attention on the nature – and limits – of the church as an ecumenical issue.[88]

The most striking example of this trend, however, is the fact that (as noted above) two substantial, complementary Faith and Order texts on ecclesiology are now before the churches for response by early 2010. The first and longer text, *The Nature and Mission of the Church: A Stage on the Way to a Common Statement*, aims 'to give expression to what the churches can now say together about the nature and mission of the Church and, within that agreement, to explore the extent to which the remaining church-dividing issues may be overcome'.[89] Its role as a nascent convergence text is indicated by the questions asked of the churches: 'Does this study document correctly identify our common ecclesiological convictions, as well as the issues which continue to divide us? Does this study document reflect an emerging convergence on the nature and mission of the Church?' Thus it aims to draw the churches into a process aimed at developing the text itself. Notably, it seeks to move beyond present impasses by clarifying the 'structure' of divisive issues – that is, by identifying the ecclesiological assumptions lying behind the diverse positions, and indicating what would need to change on each side for agreement to be reached.[90]

The second, concise text, 'Called to be the One Church', was adopted by the WCC assembly in Porto Alegre in 2006 as 'an invitation to the churches to renew their commitment to the search for unity, and to deepen their dialogue'.[91] It stands in the line of unity texts from the assemblies at New Delhi (1961), Nairobi (1975), Vancouver (1983) and Canberra (1991). But rather than offering another vision of the unity we seek, the Porto Alegre text asks a series of unusually direct questions. The burden of these is the degree of actual, practised mutual recognition among the churches as expressed not in terms of ecclesiological theory but concretely, in the daily interaction of the churches with one another: 'Why does your church believe that it is necessary, or permissible, or not possible to share the Lord's Supper with those of other churches? . . . How fully can your church share in prayer with other churches?' The questions are not aimed at developing the text itself, but rather at stimulating a process among the churches themselves to see how far they are able to recognize one another as expressions of the church of Christ. The fact that two such texts are now before the churches, and that the churches at Porto Alegre committed themselves to respond formally to them, speaks volumes about the interest in ecclesiology in the current ecumenical scene.

With a seventh and final area we reach a fundamental question – something hardly asked as yet, yet inevitable in view of the churches' growing and deepening ecumenical experience: Is there more than an ecumenical *method* for doing ecclesiology? Can one speak of an *ecumenical ecclesiology*, in the sense of an ecclesiology rooted in and developed from the ecumenical experience itself? Analogous questions may be asked in other areas of ecumenical experience: Does 'ecumenical worship' have its own authenticity, arising from the ecumenical nature of the community gathered for praise and prayer; or is its 'content' only the sum of the worship life of the historic communions represented? Do councils of churches have an ecclesial significance in and of themselves; or are they only the sum of – or indeed less than – the ecclesial identities of their constituent member churches?

These are various ways of asking the question: is the ecumenical whole greater than the sum of its ecclesial parts? Is there any 'ecclesial density' in the experience of Christians, separated for centuries by hostility or indifference, coming together for a century now in common confession, worship, witness and service? If so, could ecclesiological reflection begin from this experience, from the presumption and foretaste of unity rather than from our present divisions? What would this mean for our understanding of ecclesiology – and of the nature and mission of the church?

Notes

1 Here cf. also Chapter 21 of this volume, on 'Comparative Ecclesiology'.
2 *The International Missionary Council: Addresses and Papers of John R. Mott*, vol. 5, New York: Association Press, 1947, pp. 19–20.
3 In *The Ecumenical Movement: An Anthology of Key Texts and Voices*, ed. Michael Kinnamon and Brian E. Cope, Geneva: WCC Publications, and Grand Rapids, MI: Eerdmans, 1997, pp. 11–14.
4 'Report of Section III, The Nature of the Church', in *Faith and Order: Proceedings of the World Conference, Lausanne, August 3–21, 1927*, ed. H.N. Bate, London: Student Christian Movement, 1927, p. 463.
5 'Report of Section III, The Nature of the Church', p. 464.
6 *Proceedings of the World Conference, Lausanne*, p. 469.
7 See *The Second World Conference on Faith and Order: Edinburgh 1937*, ed. Leonard Hodgson, New York: MacMillan, 1938, pp. 252–3.
8 See for example 'Obstacles not restricted to "Faith" and "Order"', in *The Second World Conference on Faith and Order*, pp. 258–9.
9 'By-Laws of the Faith and Order Commission', 3.2(a), p. 98 (emphasis mine).
10 See T.K. Thomas, 'WCC, Basis of', in *Dictionary of the Ecumenical Movement*, 2nd edn, ed. Nicholas Lossky *et al.*, Geneva: WCC Publications, 2002, pp. 1238–9.
11 For the citations in this paragraph see W.A. Visser 't Hooft, *The Genesis and Formation of the World Council of Churches*, Geneva: WCC Publications, 1982, III.3, p. 114; IV.4, p. 117; IV.1, p. 116; and IV.3, p. 117 respectively.
12 'Implications of the Ecumenical Movement', in *The Ecumenical Review*, vol. 5, no. 1 (January 1952), 19–20. Tomkins was speaking to the Third World Conference on Faith and Order at Lund.
13 'A Word to the Churches', *Third World Conference on Faith and Order, Held at Lund August 15th to 28th, 1952*, London: SCM Press, 1953, p. 16.
14 This formulation of this principle is taken from the 'By-Laws of the Faith and Order Commission', 3.2.ii, see *Minutes of the Standing Commission on Faith and Order: Faverges, Haute-Savoie, France, 14–21 June 2006*, Faith and Order Paper 202, Geneva: World Council of Churches, 2006, p. 120.
15 Proposals for the Lifting of Anathemas, 1, in 'Communiqué, Joint Commission of the Theological Dialogue Between the Orthodox Church and The Oriental Orthodox Churches Geneva, November 1–6, 1993', in *Growth in Agreement III: International Dialogue Texts and Agreed Statements 1998–2005*, ed. Jeffrey Gros, FSC, Thomas F. Best, Lorelei F. Fuchs, SA, Faith and

Order Paper 204, Geneva: WCC Publications and Grand Rapids, MI: Eerdmans, 2007. For earlier stages of the dialogue see 'Communiqué: Chambésy, Geneva, Switzerland, 15 December 1985'; 'Communiqué: Anba Bishoy Monastery, Egypt, 24 June 1989'; 'Second Agreed Statement and Recommendations to the Churches: Chambésy, Switzerland, 28 September 1990'; in *Growth in Agreement II: Reports and Agreed Statements of Ecumenical Conversations on a World Level, 1982–1998*, Faith and Order Paper 187, ed. Jeffrey Gros, FSC, Harding Meyer, William G. Rusch, Geneva: WCC Publications; Grand Rapids, MI: Eerdmans, 2000, pp. 190, 191–3, 194–9 respectively.

16 *Unitatis Redintegratio*, §3. Here, cf. also Chapters 6, 13 and 36 of this volume.
17 For the quotations in this paragraph see 'The Holy Spirit and the Catholicity of the Church: The Report as Adopted by the Assembly', in *The Uppsala Report*, ed. Norman Goodall, Geneva: WCC, 1968, §10, p. 14; §20, p. 17; §10, p. 14 respectively.
18 See *Racism in Theology and Theology against Racism: Report of a Consultation organized by the Commission on Faith and Order and the Programme to Combat Racism*, Geneva: WCC, 1975; *Church and World: The Unity of the Church and the Renewal of Human Community*, Faith and Order Paper 151, 2nd, rev. printing, Geneva: WCC Publications, 1992; and *Ecclesiology and Ethics: Ecumenical Ethical Engagement, Moral Formation and the Nature of the Church*, ed. Thomas F. Best, Martin Robra, Geneva: Units I and III, WCC, 1995.
19 For these churches see the documentation of their international consultations held since 1967, most recently *'With a Demonstration of the Spirit and of Power': Seventh International Consultation of United and Uniting Churches*, ed. Thomas F. Best, Faith and Order Paper 195, Geneva: WCC Publications, 2004; and the Surveys of Church Union Negotiations published in various formats since the 1930s, most recently Thomas F. Best and Union Correspondents, 'Survey of Church Union Negotiations 2003–2006', in *The Ecumenical Review*, Vol. 58, No. 3 (July/October 2006), pp. 297–385.
20 See *The Second World Conference on Faith and Order: Edinburgh 1937*, ed. Leonard Hodgson, New York: MacMillan, 1938, p. 252.
21 'Report of Section: Unity', *The New Delhi Report*, ed. W. A. Visser 't Hooft, London: SCM, 1962, §2, p. 116.
22 'Report of Section II: What Unity Requires', in *Breaking Barriers, Nairobi 1975: Official Report, Fifth Assembly, World Council of Churches*, ed. David M. Paton, London: SPCK, and Geneva: WCC, 1976, §3, p. 60.
23 *The New Delhi Report*, §3, p. 117.
24 *The First Assembly of the World Council of Churches*, ed. W. A. Visser 't Hooft, London: SCM Press, 1949, p. 62 (emphasis mine).
25 See also Chapter 9 of this volume.
26 This typology owes much to the work of Martin Cressey, see for example his 'Where and whither? An Interpretative Survey of United and Uniting Churches, with a View to their Contribution to the Fifth World Conference on Faith and Order to be held in 1993', in *Minutes of the Meeting of the Faith and Order Standing Commission, Rome, Italy, 1991*, Faith and Order Paper 157, Geneva: World Council of Churches, 1991, pp. 58–9. On this topic, again see Chapter 9 of the present volume.
27 Alastair Rodger, 'Uniting Presbyterian Church in Southern Africa', in Thomas F. Best and Church Union Correspondents, 'Church Union Survey 1996–9' in *The Ecumenical Review*, vol. 52, no. 1 (January 2000), 29.
28 See *Growth in Agreement: Reports and Agreed Statements of Ecumenical Conversations on a World Level*, ed. Harding Meyer and Lukas Vischer, Faith and Order Paper 108, Ecumenical Documents 2, New York: Paulist Press; Geneva: World Council of Churches, 1984; reprinted as *Growth in Agreement I*, Geneva: WCC Publications, 2007; *Growth in Agreement II: Reports and Agreed Statements of Ecumenical Conversations on a World Level, 1982–1998*; *Growth in Agreement III: International Dialogue Texts and Agreed Statements to 1998–2005*.
29 See *Growing Consensus: Church Dialogues in the United States, 1962–1991*, Ecumenical Documents V, ed. Joseph A. Burgess and Jeffrey Gros, FSC, New York/Mahwah, NJ: Paulist Press, 1995; and *Growing Consensus II: Church Dialogues in the United States, 1992–2004*, Ecumenical Documents VII, ed. Lydia Veliko and Jeffrey Gros, FSC, Washington, DC: Bishops' Committee for Ecumenical and Interreligious Affairs, United States Conference of Catholic Bishops, 2005.
30 Cf. Chapters 9 and 20.
31 Lutheran World Federation and the Roman Catholic Church, Grand Rapids, MI: Eerdmans, 2000.

32 Faith and Order Paper 111, Geneva, World Council of Churches, 1982; 25th anniversary [39th] printing with additional introduction, Geneva: World Council of Churches, 2007.
33 *Baptism, Eucharist and Ministry*, Preface, p. ix.
34 For a recent critical review of the origin and lasting effect of BEM see Lukas Vischer, 'The Convergence Texts on Baptism, Eucharist and Ministry: How Did They Take Shape? What Have They Achieved?' in *The Ecumenical Review*, Vol. 54, No. 4 (October 2002), pp. 431–54.
35 See Max Thurian, 'Baptism, Eucharist and Ministry', in *Dictionary of the Ecumenical Movement*, p. 92.
36 *Churches Respond to BEM: Official Responses to the 'Baptism, Eucharist and Ministry' Text*, Vols. I-VI, Faith and Order Papers 129, 132, 135, 137, 143, 144, ed. Max Thurian, Geneva: WCC, 1986–8.
37 *Baptism, Eucharist and Ministry 1982–1990: Report on the Process and Responses*, Faith and Order Paper 149, Geneva: WCC Publications, 1990; and *BEM at 25: Critical Insights into a Continuing Legacy*, ed. Thomas F. Best and Tamara Grdzelidze, Faith and Order Paper 205, Geneva: WCC Publications, 2007.
38 BEM, 'Baptism', §9.
39 BEM, 'Eucharist', §20.
40 BEM, 'Ministry', §22.
41 BEM, 'Preface', p. x.
42 'Report of Section II: Scripture, Tradition and Traditions', in *The Fourth World Conference on Faith and Order: Montreal 1963*, ed. P. C. Rodger and Lukas Vischer, Faith and Order Paper 42, London: SCM Press, 1964, §39, p. 50.
43 BEM, 'Preface', p. x.
44 On the latter point see 'Evangelical-Methodist Church: Central Conference in the German Democratic Republic', in *Churches Respond to BEM*, Vol. IV, pp. 167–8.
45 For example, the response of the Christian Church (Disciples of Christ) consolidated its rejection of 're-baptism'. See 'Christian Church (Disciples of Christ)' in *Churches Respond to BEM*, Vol. I, pp. 115–16.
46 See *Baptism, Eucharist and Ministry 1982–1990*, pp. 131–51. On BEM, see also Chapters 6, 9, 20 and 31 of this volume.
47 Faith and Order Paper 198, Geneva: WCC Publications, 2005. The text is available on the WCC website at www. oikoumene.org/index.php?id=2617&L=0.
48 The text is available from Faith and Order, WCC, 150, rte. de Ferney, 1211 Geneva, Switzerland, and on the WCC website at www.oikoumene.org/en/resources/documents/assembly/porto-alegre-2006/1-statements-documents-adopted.html.
49 Cf. for all but the penultimate of these points Günther Gassmann, 'Unity', in *Dictionary of the Ecumenical Movement*, p. 1173.
50 A helpful survey up to the emergence of the *koinonia* 'model' is Paul A. Crow, Jr., 'Ecumenics as Reflections on Models of Christian Unity', in *The Ecumenical Review*, Vol. 39, No. 4 (October 1987), 389–403.
51 *The Second World Conference on Faith and Order*, p. 252.
52 *The Second World Conference on Faith and Order*, p. 253 (italics mine).
53 *New Delhi Report*, §2, p. 116.
54 *New Delhi Report*, §2, p. 116.
55 'The Unity of the Church – Next Steps', Report of the Consultation on 'Concepts of Unity and Models of Union', in *What Kind of Unity?*, Faith and Order Paper 69, Geneva: WCC, 1974, p. 121.
56 'Report of Section II: What Unity Requires', in *Breaking Barriers, Nairobi 1975*, §3, p. 60.
57 'Report of Section II: What Unity Requires', in *Breaking Barriers, Nairobi 1975*, §§5–6, p. 61.
58 *Minutes and Supplementary Documents from the meeting of the Commission on Faith and Order*, Faith and Order Paper 93, Geneva: WCC, Commission on Faith and Order, 1979, pp. 40–2.
59 *Gathered for Life: Official Report, Sixth Assembly, World Council of Churches*, ed. David Gill, Geneva: WCC, and Grand Rapids, MI: Eerdmans, 1983, §§5–8, p. 45.
60 See Chapters 27 and 29 of this volume.
61 *Gathered for Life*, §§5–9, p. 45.
62 See the address of Cardinal Johannes Willebrands at Great St. Mary's Church, Cambridge, England, January 18, 1972 during the Week of Prayer for Christian Unity, in *Called to Full Unity: Documents on Anglican-Roman Catholic Relations 1966–1983*, Washington, DC: United States Catholic Conference (for the Bishops' Committee for Ecumenical and Interreligious Affairs, National Conference of Catholic Bishops, and the Ecumenical Office, Executive Council of the Episcopal Church), 1986, pp. 45–53.

63 Harding Meyer, 'Reconciled Diversity', in *Dictionary of the Ecumenical Movement*, pp. 960–1.

64 'Statements of the Assembly: 3. Models of Unity', in *In Christ – A New Community: The Proceedings of the Sixth Assembly of the Lutheran World Federation Sixth Assembly*, ed. Arne Sovik, Geneva: Lutheran World Federation, 1977, §15, p. 174.

65 'Statements by the Seventh Assembly: Statement on "The Unity we Seek"', in *Budapest 1984: Christ – Hope for the World, Official Proceedings of the Seventh Assembly of the Lutheran World Federation*, ed. Carl H. Mau, Jr., LWF Report 19/20, Geneva: Lutheran World Federation, 1985, p. 175.

66 Thomas F. Best, 'Unity, Models of', in *Dictionary of the Ecumenical Movement*, p. 1174.

67 Thomas F. Best, 'The Issues Beyond the Issues: Possible Futures for the Faith and Order World Conference', *The Ecumenical Review* 45, 1 (January 1993), 59–60.

68 *New Delhi Report*, §10, p. 119.

69 J.-M.R. Tillard, 'Koinonia', in *Dictionary of the Ecumenical Movement*, pp. 646–52.

70 *Signs of the Spirit: Official Report, Seventh Assembly, World Council of Churches*, ed. Michael Kinnamon, Geneva: WCC Publications, Grand Rapids, MI: Eerdmans, 1991, pp. 172–4.

71 That is, The Church Unity Commission (CUC) in South Africa, the Commission of the Covenanted Churches (CYTUN) in Wales, and Churches Uniting in Christ (CUIC) in the United States.

72 The disillusion of the Scottish Churches Initiative for Union. See Sheilagh Kesting, 'United Kingdom – Scotland', in Thomas F. Best and Union Correspondents, 'Survey of Church Union Negotiations 2003–2006', pp. 42–44.

73 See Siôn Rhys Evans, 'United Kingdom – Wales', in Thomas F. Best and Union Correspondents, 'Survey of Church Union Negotiations 2003–2006', pp. 45–48.

74 The Reformed Church of Alsace and Lorraine, and the Church of the Augsburg Confession of Alsace and Lorraine.

75 Martin Parmentier, 'Old Catholic-Orthodox Dialogue', in *Dictionary of the Ecumenical Movement*, pp. 843–4.

76 'Costly Commitment: Report of the Consultation at Tantur Ecumenical Institute, Israel, 1994', in *Ecclesiology and Ethics: Ecumenical Moral Engagment, Moral Formation and the Nature of the Church*, ed. Thomas F. Best and Martin Robra, Geneva: WCC Publications, 1997, §17c, p. 29. See also Chapter 36 of this volume.

77 'Report of Group IV', in *On the Way to Fuller Koinonia: Official Report of the Fifth World Conference on Faith and Order*, Faith and Order Paper 166, ed. Thomas F. Best and Günther Gassmann, Geneva: WCC Publications, 1994, §32, p. 260.

78 'Costly Commitment', §73, p. 47.

79 §96.

80 For a recent helpful survey of this complex theme see Tamara Grdzelidze, 'Using the Principle of Oikonomia in Ecumenical Discussions: Reflections on "The Limits of the Church" by George Florovsky', in *The Ecumenical Review*, Vol. 56, No. 2 (April 2004}, pp. 234–46.

81 *For the Conversion of the Churches*, trans. from the French by James Greig, Geneva: WCC Publications, 1993.

82 See again Lukas Vischer, 'The Convergence Texts on Baptism, Eucharist and Ministry', p. 450. Once more, cf. Chapters 27 and 29 of this volume.

83 See 'The Gift of Authority (Authority in the Church III), 3 September 1998, Anglican Roman Catholic International Commission', in *Growth in Agreement III: International Dialogue Texts and Agreed Statements 1998–2005*.

84 See 'Report on Work Planned by the Faith and Order Standing Commission', in *Minutes of the Standing Commission on Faith and Order, 12–19 June, Crans-Montana, Switzerland*, Faith and Order Paper No. 206, Geneva: WCC Commission on Faith and Order, 2007, pp. 41–42. See Chapter 34 of this volume.

85 See Lukas Vischer, *Intercession*, Faith and Order Paper 95, Geneva: WCC, 1980.

86 See *The Community of Women and Men in the Church: A Report of the World Council of Churches' Conference, Sheffield, England, 1981*, ed. Constance F. Parvey, Geneva: WCC, 1983.

87 See 'Final Report of the Special Commission on Orthodox Participation in the WCC', Geneva: WCC, 2002, B.3, §15.

88 The Special Commission was writing, of course, in the context of two documents published in 2000: the Roman Catholic text *Dominus Iesus*, and 'Basic Principles of the Attitude of the Russian Orthodox Church towards the Other Christian Confessions', adopted by the Jubilee Bishops' Council of the Russian Orthodox Church, 14 August 2000. See Geoffrey Wainwright, 'Church', in *Dictionary of the Ecumenical Movement*, p. 180.

89 §5, p. 10. See n. 47, above.
90 See for example the 'boxes' (sidebar text) on 'Church as Sacrament?' following §48, pp. 29–30; and 'Limits of Diversity' following §63, pp. 37–9. For the questions see §8, p. 5 of the text.
91 See n. 48, above. For the questions see §14 of the text.

Further reading

Baptism & the Unity of the Church, ed. Michael Root and Risto Saarinen, Institute for Ecumenical Research, Strasbourg, France, and Grand Rapids, MI: Eerdmans, and Geneva: WCC Publications, 1998.

Baptism, Eucharist and Ministry, Faith and Order Paper 111, Geneva: World Council of Churches, 1982.

Baptism, Eucharist and Ministry 1982–1990: Report on the Process and Responses, Faith and Order Paper 149, Geneva: WCC Publications, 1990.

BEM at 25: Critical Insights into a Continuing Legacy, ed. Thomas F. Best and Tamara Grdzelidze, Faith and Order Paper 205, Geneva: WCC Publications, 2007.

'Called to be the One Church' [the Porto Alegre ecclesiology text], adopted by the World Council of Churches Porto Alegre Assembly as a basis for study and dialogue among the churches, Geneva: World Council of Churches, 2006.

Church and World: The Unity of the Church and the Renewal of Human Community, Faith and Order Paper 151, 2nd, rev. printing, Geneva: WCC Publications, 1992.

Dictionary of the Ecumenical Movement, 2nd edn, ed. Nicholas Lossky *et al.*, Geneva: WCC Publications, 2002.

The Ecumenical Movement: An Anthology of Key Texts and Voices, ed. Michael Kinnamon and Brian E. Cope, Geneva: WCC Publications, and Grand Rapids, MI: Eerdmans, 1997.

G. R. Evans, *The Church and the churches: Towards an Ecumenical Ecclesiology*, New York: Cambridge University Press, 1994.

Faith and Order at the Crossroads: Kuala Lumpur 2004, The Plenary Commission Meeting, ed. Thomas F. Best, Faith and Order Paper 196, Geneva: WCC Publications, 2005.

Georges Florovsky, 'The Limits of the Church', in *Church Quarterly Review*, Oct. 1933, 117–31.

Ernst Lange, *And Yet it Moves: Dream and Reality of the Ecumenical Movement*, Geneva: World Council of Churches, 1979.

The Nature and Mission of the Church: A Stage on the Way to a Common Statement, Faith and Order Paper 198, Geneva: World Council of Churches, 2005.

On the Way to Fuller Koinonia: Official Report of the Fifth World Conference on Faith and Order, ed. Thomas F. Best and Günther Gassmann, Faith and Order Paper 166, Geneva: WCC Publications, 1994.

Orthodox Perspectives on Baptism, Eucharist and Ministry, ed. Gennadios Limouris and Nomikos Michael Vaporis, Faith and Order Papers 128, in *The Greek Orthodox Theological Review*, Vol. 30, No. 2, Summer 1985.

G. H. Tavard, *The Church, Community of Salvation: An Ecumenical Ecclesiology*, Collegeville, MN: Liturgical Press, 1992.

J.-M. R. Tillard, *Church of Churches: The Ecclesiology of Communion*, Collegeville, MN: Liturgical Press, 1992.

W. A. Visser 't Hooft, *The Genesis and Formation of the World Council of Churches*, Geneva: WCC Publications, 1982.

Miroslav Volf, *After our Likeness: The Church as the Image of the Trinity*, Grand Rapids, MI: Eerdmans, 1998.

Geoffrey Wainwright, 'Church', in *Dictionary of the Ecumenical Movement*, 2nd edn, ed. Nicholas Lossky, *et al.*, Geneva: WCC Publications, 2002, pp. 176–86.

J. Zizioulas, *Being as Communion: Studies in Personhood and the Church*, Crestwood, NY: St Vladimir's Seminary, 1985.

23

LIBERATION
ECCLESIOLOGY

Gerard Mannion

The monumental importance of liberation theology, and the ecclesiological perspectives that have emerged from its numerous forms, has been captured very well by the Vietnamese-American theologian, Peter Phan, who tells us that,

> Future historians of Christianity will no doubt judge liberation theology to be the most influential movement of the twentieth century, possibly even since the Reformation. They certainly will painstakingly document its emergence as independent theological movements in the late 1960s and will marvel at its spectacular expansion throughout the entire ecumene in a matter of just a couple of decades. The profound influence of liberation theology will be evident not only from the way it has penetrated far-flung countries and continents and permeated all branches of Christian theology, from biblical studies through systematics to ethics, but also from the vigorous attacks orchestrated against its proponents by the ecclesiastical establishment as well as political authorities who have regarded it as the most pernicious threat to orthodoxy, democracy, and the capitalistic system.[1]

Despite its many academic, ecclesial and political critics and those (largely European and North American) studies that have depressingly declared liberation theology to be 'yesterday's news' and a failure now proved to be ultimately ineffective, the church and ecclesiology in the twenty-first century would be literally inconceivable without liberation theology. Even those who would list themselves amongst its critics will nonetheless have had their own theological, ecclesial and ecclesiological ideas and practices influenced in numerous ways by the achievements of liberation theology. Indeed, for at least 80 per cent of the world's Christians, liberation theology constitutes one of the most formative influences upon their 'way of being church' today.

Elsewhere in this volume various aspects of liberation ecclesiology in general and indeed particular forms, such as Latin American, feminist, womanist and *mujerista* ecclesiology, as well as Black ecclesiology, are discussed. So too are concepts such as 'woman-church', the Base Communities movements etc., as are the particular liberationist perspectives developed in Africa and Asia.[2] Liberation theology here will be taken as an umbrella concept that includes such approaches in general, as well as contextual theology, certain forms of practical theology, political theology and so on. The purpose of this chapter, then, is not to repeat what has been covered elsewhere but rather to explore some of the more theoretical and critical debates concerning liberation ecclesiology, as well as to touch upon some more recent developments that offer great potential for the future of ecclesiology in general. As Latin American liberation theology has played such a formative role in the development of these and many other ecclesiologies of liberation, such will form the basis of much of our reflection here, although aspects of other ecclesiologies of liberation will be touched upon as well.

After introducing the history and development of liberation theology and its ecclesiological implications, we will briefly identify the numerous other forms of liberation theology and then move on to explore some of the predominant themes in liberation ecclesiology itself by examining the work of but a few prominent theologians in this field, again focusing in particular upon such visions of the church as found in Latin America. Following this, we will touch upon some of the critical debates surrounding liberation ecclesiology before turning to consider what liberation ecclesiology in general has to offer the wider church today. This will be discussed with reference to a case study from Asian liberation ecclesiology. Finally, we will illustrate how the various forms of liberation ecclesiology have collectively helped to demonstrate the need for a 'Copernican revolution in ecclesiology', whereby a renewed emphasis upon the trinitarian dimensions of ecclesiology can help inform a renewed church mission for today that puts human liberation, dialogue and praxis at its heart.

From theology to ecclesiology of liberation

The theologian generally recognized as the 'founding father' of modern liberation theology, Gustavo Gutiérrez, summarizes the primary orientation of this approach to theology thus,

> The theology of liberation attempts to reflect on the experience and meaning of the faith based on the commitment to abolish injustice and to build a new society; this theology must be verified by the practice of that commitment, by active, effective participation in the struggle which the exploited social classes have undertaken against their oppressors. Liberation from every form of exploitation, the possibility of a more human and more dignified life, the creation of a new man – all pass through this struggle.[3]

Latin American Liberation theology arose out of 'an ethical indignation at the poverty and marginalisation of the great masses of our continent' (L. Boff). Recognizing that history is always written from the perspective of the victors, it is a way of doing theology 'from the underside of history' (Gutiérrez) – from the perspective of those who are not the 'victors', the triumphant, the powerful. Let us briefly provide an account of the origins and development, as well as the key themes, of liberation theology.[4]

Origins

Liberation theology thus builds upon the concept of human liberation that, in one guise or another, has been integral to much Christian theology throughout its long history but, in particular, came to be a dominant theme in the discourse of the oppressed Latin American peoples, especially from the nineteenth century onwards. Thus the origins of liberation theology per se go back to the time of the missionaries and colonizers in Latin America and the struggles of (and sometimes against) the former to live out the gospel truly and therefore to be able to bring the 'good news' to the peoples of those lands being ruthlessly colonized and exploited by the major European powers of the colonial era.

Informed by and further developed alongside the differing forms of political theology and theologies 'of hope', liberation theology per se emerged as a discipline in its own right particularly from the 1960s onwards, in the context of the various struggles for freedom and self-determination across Latin America. It builds upon the notion of the 'church as servant' that emerged in Roman Catholic discourse at Vatican II and in the many documents of the World Council of the Churches in the decades following World War II.

Indeed, Vatican II (1962–5), with its ecclesiologically revolutionary call to church renewal and *aggiornamento* (bringing up to date) and, in particular, its affirmation of the necessity for the church to enter into dialogue with the contemporary world, helped sow the seeds for the rapid theoretical and practical development of liberation theology in a very positive and practical direction. So, too, did the political climate and events of the 1960s and 1970s, and the ecumenical initiatives of these decades also helped play a fundamental part in the spread of its popularity.

A groundbreaking assembly of the Latin American Roman Catholic Bishops' Conference – *Consejo Episcopal Latinoamericana* (CELAM) – met at Medellín, Columbia, in 1968. It focused upon the profound inequality prevalent across Latin America, spoke of 'First world' abuses, and tackled head-on the issue of institutionalized violence. This was followed up by a further milestone meeting in Puebla, Mexico, the year after, at which the bishops stated that 'We affirm the need for conversion on the part of the whole church to a preferential option for the poor, an option aimed at their integral liberation.'

However, liberation theology was to offer not just a critique of society but also of the church and of the power structures and oppression within it, as we shall see.

The shape of liberation theology

Firstly, liberation theology has developed a distinctive *method*, one which is critical of the European and North American 'armchair theologians' and 'bourgeois theologians', one which is attentive to the situation, the context of where theologians are 'at', where they 'live out' their theology (or not as the case may be).

Secondly, above all else liberation theology is a *constructive* theology, a theology that seeks to be transformative and revisioning. Amongst its most discerning features are an emphasis upon *faith* – in its attention to salvation, to the objective elements of the faith, the revelation of God and the 'givenness' of many aspects of the faith. It is, by and large, doctrinally orthodox, despite the impression given by some of its critics. It does not deny but rather affirms a 'formal' starting point.

But liberation theology equally emphasizes the importance of *experience* – which must go hand in hand with faith. Hence this balances those objective aspects mentioned above with due attention to the concrete, the subjective, indeed to the *practice* of faith. Hence central to liberation discourse is the notion of *praxis*: right praxis, *orthopraxis*, is to be preferred over 'right belief or worship' that fails to give due attention to the concrete and to the practical, i.e. 'mere' *orthodoxy*. Naturally, there are major ecclesiological implications of such a shift in focus.

Liberation theology thus stresses the need for a 'material' starting point. Central to its task is a process of *conscientization* – raising awareness amongst ordinary people of the origins and causes of their oppression on the one hand, and of the ways and means by which they might work towards their own liberation on the other. In liberation ecclesiology, the Bible is seen as a living text, speaking directly to the plight of the poor, the marginalized and oppressed of today.

Thus *social criticism*, analysis of the ills of various societies and structures, forms a key part of this method. Yes, Marxism (the political and economic philosophy inspired by Karl Marx, 1818–83) and the understanding of social, economic and political realities in terms of the clashing of differing groups and economic 'forces', i.e. dialectical materialism, have been employed by liberation theologians in order to help explain the deep oppression and divisive class structures in Latin America. But Marxism is only one influence upon their social analysis amongst many. Indeed, Joseph Ratzinger, long-time critic of liberation theology, once said that its biggest problem was that the Latin Americans had studied too much German *theology*.

But liberation theology also offers a challenging critique of European theology – of what it calls 'classical theology' and hence also of Eurocentric *ecclesiology*. Liberation theology sees itself as consisting of 3 different forms of theological undertaking, namely, the professional (e.g. university based), the pastoral (e.g. church and ministry oriented) and finally the popular (whereby everyone is seen to be a theologian – their everyday lives forming a rich source of theological refection and insight). The key challenge is how best to achieve the *integration* of these three different forms of theology.

Rapid expansion and development: other forms of liberation ecclesiology

From Latin America these ideas spread rapidly, long before Jürgen Moltmann's call for a 'global liberation theology'. Other liberationist theologies soon emerged and developed across the globe, helped in large part by the foundation of the *Ecumenical Association of Third World Theologies* (EATWOT) in 1976. Furthermore, it became apparent very quickly that fundamental to theology is the question of who is doing that theology, where it is being done and on whose 'behalf'. Thus *context* moved centre stage and *contextual* theology emerged as a further sub-discipline in its own right. However, it is a positive matter of fact that there is no clear dividing line between liberation theology and contextual theology.

Marc Reuver has illustrated how *resistance* to dehumanizing forces has been the common denominator in the emergence of these various forms of theology. People come to a greater understanding of God through their *experiences* of God's liberating power. Such theology is firmly wedded to history in its making. In particular, Reuver outlines three groundbreaking 'families' of such theologies of resistance. First, Latin American liberation theology with its overriding emphasis upon *praxis* and upon love, peace and justice over oppression and death. Second, 'prophetic theology' in Africa, which seeks to relate theology to the most pressing events in daily life here and now. Third, Reuver discusses the Asian context and 'contemplative commitment' which finds expression in a 'spirituality of action'. Reuver suggest that the so-called 'developed' world can learn much from these new ways of doing theology which derive their authority from the struggles of the downtrodden.[5]

The enormity of such developments can be illustrated with reference to just one example, the Asian context, and the recent publication of a massive three-volume survey and overview of Asian Christian Theologies alone.[6] Even in a country where Christians represent but a tiny minority, such as Pakistan, the contextualized Christian experience, informed by a very particular liberationist perspective, has given rise to studies such as John O'Brien's 700-page tome, *The Construction of Pakistani Christian Identity*.[7] This penetrating study embraces history, ethnography, hermeneutics and the social sciences to chart the story of an 'oppressed and excluded people', largely from one tribe, 'who found in Christianity a new identity which offered them the human dignity and the emancipation that had been denied them for millennia'.[8] Peter Phan has comprehensively demonstrated that inculturation, the two-way process whereby a particular culture and context will receive from and in turn further shape and develop Christianity and the church, has now itself also entered a new and distinctive stage whereby *migration* becomes a starting point for theological and ecclesiological reflection. Thus the minorities who come from the corners of the earth to live in very different societies bring with them rich resources for developing further perspectives – the latter necessitated not least by the persecution, exclusion, racism and oppression these migrants suffer from the wider societies and Christian communities alike in their 'new homes'.[9] Phan speaks of the need for and the reality of an 'Inter-Multicultural theology' informed by a 'seeing from the margins'.[10] Of course, this reminds us of the formative influence upon Christianity of generations of migrants in the eighteenth, nineteenth and twentieth centuries as well, such as the African slaves in the United States and Irish people first fleeing from famine and then driven from home by economic necessity to hostile places such as numerous parts of Britain, where the phrase, 'no blacks, no dogs, no Irish' was as applicable in many churches as it was in boarding houses and workplaces.

Hence the development of a diversity of liberation theologies, from Black Theology to theologies of liberation and emancipation relevant to, for example, the South African, the Indian Dalit, the Korean (*Minjung* theology) and the Sri Lankan contexts, from 'tribal' and 'homeland' theologies to theologies of liberation applied in contexts as diverse as Sheffield, England, or the North of Ireland. Following the initial wave of developments in liberationist perspectives, there came, from the 1980s onwards, a critical era (from right and left alike) and then a further developmental phase with innovative approaches developed by people such as Sharon Welch, who helped transform not simply perspectives on liberation theology and ecclesiology in general, but also held up a critical mirror to feminist thought itself, as well as to 'western' ethical discourse with her groundbreaking approach first set forth in *Communities of Resistance and Solidarity: a Feminist Theology of Liberation*.[11] A 'second generation' of liberation theologians emerged in the 1980s and 90s, who built upon the foundational and reactionary struggles of the 'first generation' and who now set their sights upon more constructive and less reactionary theological pursuits.[12]

Further issues of gender and identity have increasingly emerged from the theological and ecclesiological 'closet' with the development of gay and lesbian theologies of liberation, championing the rights, perspectives and experiences of gay, lesbian, bisexual and transgender communities. These theologies have become increasingly more developed in recent decades and the ecclesiological campaigns and challenges of these communities have come to dominate discussions across many different denominations. Such approaches have offered a new ecclesiological hermeneutic to a long hidden and denied form of sinful oppression and prejudice across the churches.[13]

Animal theology poses an additional and very particular challenge to the churches today as discrimination against other animals, 'speciesism', rapidly becomes one of the last remaining forms of prejudice that Christians, by and large, seem very reluctant to acknowledge, confront and defeat.[14]

All these forms share what has been called the 'particular perspective' of liberation. Thus, as indicated, it is strictly speaking more correct to speak of 'theologies' of liberation, as opposed to 'theology' of liberation in the singular. But these differing theologies focused upon liberation share sufficiently common themes, methods and aims to warrant their grouping under a collective umbrella. All, for example, seek dialogue, debate, cooperation. All look towards establishing particular projects aimed at liberation and at the renewal of the church and wider society alike. Peter Phan speaks of 'A Common Journey, Different Paths, the Same Destination'.[15]

Let us now turn to explore some of the predominant themes in liberation ecclesiology itself by examining the work of a few prominent theologians in this field.

Ecclesiology and human liberation: major themes and perspectives

On the one hand, it could be said that liberation theology is a form of theology that is 'trans-ecclesial', some might even say anti-ecclesiological. For central to the liberationist approach is the belief that theology and Christian practice should not have the church itself as its primary focal point or indeed agent. Rather, the kingdom or reign of God should be central – building communities of love, justice, solidarity and equality.

But on the other hand one can equally suggest that, first and foremost, liberation theology is a deeply ecclesiological way of doing theology. Central to its fundamental reflections and practices is the notion of Christian community, of church, and how we can and should transform our way of being church. Liberation theology realizes that, sufficiently transformed from the sinful ways present throughout its own structures and ways, the church can be one of the most powerful agents for human liberation and for building that kingdom. In essence, liberation ecclesiology seeks an understanding and structure of church that is non-hierarchical, viewing all leadership purely in terms of, and as service to, the community. Although many of the leading pioneer theorists in Latin American liberation theology and ecclesiology alike were Roman Catholics, the key ideas and debates swiftly embraced those of numerous other churches and confessions. It should be emphasized, then, that liberation ecclesiology swiftly became an *ecumenical* way of reflecting upon and of being church.[16] Critics of liberation theology have come from both within the churches of its leading proponents (right up to the 'highest' levels of leadership and authority in the case of the Roman Catholic Church) and without. In recent decades, one of the key challenges for the theology of liberation, and to its new forms of ecclesial being in general, has been the rapid growth and spread of particular forms of Pentecostal Christianity across Latin America and indeed other continents as well.

'New ways' of being church

Re-integrating church with the reign of God and the world

The Mexican ecclesiologist Alvaro Quiroz Magaña has provided a survey of the key themes and perspectives which liberation theology has brought to ecclesiology. The changing historical and socio-political realities are what dictate the need for a new self-understanding of church, indeed a renewed way of *being* church. Such theologians have sought to reflect upon existing models of the church and to see how they might form an ecclesiology which would better capture the experience of the peoples of their continent, serve their needs and, above all, 'incarnate for present history the response of fidelity to the call of the gospel'.[17]

In this, they sought to interconnect the core categories of 'church', 'reign of God' and 'world'. Liberation ecclesiology seeks to show that the church brings the reality of the liberative gospel to the lives of the poor, for the church accompanies the poor on the road to social and historical transformation.

Magaña notes the importance of ecclesiological reflection to liberation theology as a whole and recognizes that liberation ecclesiology is a task that is never complete, constantly demanding responses to the ever-changing situation of the people of God. Theologians and church leaders are actually evangelized *by* the poor, who constitute 'the most important agent of this evangelizing liberation'.[18]

The key themes of liberation ecclesiology are identified as the church being understood as the sacrament of historical liberation; the church as sign and servant of the reign of God; the church as the People of God; the need to recognize and overcome divisions in the church; and the importance of new forms of service and ministry in the church, along with new forms of church structure.

The church seeks to make God's reign a reality by proclaiming a gospel in solidarity with exploited classes. In all this we see the profound influence of the ecclesiological themes which came to prominence at Vatican II.[19]

'Re-inventing the church'

There is little doubt that liberation ecclesiology has helped 're-invent' the church (as the Brazilian theologian Leonardo Boff has put it) in many parts of the world. In such visions there is a Spirit-centred, i.e. 'pneumatological', character to the ecclesiologies, to complement the Christ-centred, i.e. 'christological', emphasis found in many other ecclesiologies, in addition to a strong emphasis upon biblical themes and teachings. Such approaches are typified by the Base Communities movement in Latin America, which is central to liberation ecclesiology and is explored elsewhere in this volume at greater length.[20] Suffice to say here that it is a transformative means of organizing the church around small local communities and making sure the church gives due attention to their needs and hopes and fears, all the time interpreting the gospel in its relevance for their day-to-day lives in the here and now.

One of the most famous of all liberation theologians, and one who has devoted a considerable amount of his ministry and life in general to ecclesiological issues and to developing 'new ways of being church' is, of course, Boff himself. Boff excels in identifying many important issues in the attempt to make the church more relevant to the day-to-day lives of the poor, oppressed and marginalized, especially in his influential (and controversial) work entitled *Ecclesiogenesis – The Base Communities Reinvent the Church*.[21] Although this work is now well over two decades old,[22] many of the pressing issues that it raised have continued to be dismissed or ignored in ecclesial circles and by church authorities in many parts of the Catholic world.

From the outset of that work, Boff speaks of 'a new *experience* of church'. He outlines the gradual formation and development of the 'basic church community' movement, from its beginnings through initiatives in Brazil in the 1950s and 1960s in response to the shortage of priests. Obviously there are parallels to draw and lessons which the church elsewhere can learn here, whether the shortage is due to too few vocations or too many Christians in given areas. In Brazil lay people were trained and empowered to fulfil as many ministerial functions as possible in the church, short of carrying out those duties reserved for the priest. Boff believes the time has now come for even those tasks to be carried out by lay people. Let us consider further aspects which help illustrate why this ecclesiological vision is still of continued and wider relevance for the contemporary church.

Among the major problems that Boff discusses is that of the 'atomization of existence' characteristic of modern society (by which he means its fragmentation and compartmentalization – i.e. when peoples' lives lose any sense of wholeness and unity). This, in turn, depersonalizes individuals and leads to the predominance of uniformity over independence and originality. Community breaks down and withers away. One might argue that Boff's writings display an *increased*, as opposed to diminishing, relevance for us in our 'postmodern societies' and in an era where globalization has emerged as the new dominant 'grand narrative'. Such developments have worsened all the more.[23]

Boff believes that the base communities represent a grassroots response to modernity's assault upon community. They represent a new way of being church which can help rejuvenate the wider church itself. Indeed, the base communities are also a *charismatic* (i.e. Spirit-oriented) response to many of the problems of the institutional church itself.[24]

The new movement helps to build a truly living church, true to the central mission of the church of bringing to society the 'communitarian spirit'. Boff does not, however, speak of the relation between institutional and charismatic sectors of the church in terms of opposition. He rather speaks of their convergence. Nonetheless, he recognizes that there will always be a 'dialectical tension' between the global church and the localized base communities movement.

Liberating ministry: a church of service

Later in the same work Boff further employs a hermeneutics of suspicion with regards to the dominant organization, as well as the self-understanding, of the church in Europe and North America. He thus goes on to speak about the 're-invention of the church'[25] and outlines how the base communities movement seeks to transform the structures of authority, governance and ministry in the church. Rejecting the outdated and oppressive hierarchy-centred model of church organization and authority, Boff draws upon much social analysis (by social scientists and philosophers alike) to demonstrate how such ventures as the basic Christian communities allow for much greater consultation, collaboration and lay participation in the church. Structures are transformed and new ministries come to the fore.

In short, for Boff the church has been reformed and re-invented by these groups and their imagination and commitment, to become a church driven as much by the Holy Spirit as by ecclesiastical structures. Great diversity in ecclesiology results, even throughout the base communities themselves, for each community has its own special identity and structure. Thus such developments help pull the church away from an overt obsession with a *juridical* understanding of church authority, focused solely on a view of the church's relation to Christ as a society to its founder. Boff does not reject the need for the hierarchy, but he believes that the self-understanding of the church must be ordered correctly; first the flock, then the shepherds for the sake of the flock. That is to say, the people of the church must come first – the bishops and leaders are only there to serve the people and to be part of the wider community in the church. Of course, here we might add that this echoes much of the spirit of Vatican II.[26]

For Boff, then, the old hierarchy-centred ecclesiology reverses the natural order. A focus upon the church as being driven by the spirit and presence of the risen Christ leads to a conceptualization of the church 'more from the foundations up than from the steeple down'.[27] This is a vision of the church where all are equal, though people will have different charisms (callings/gifts) and therefore different roles, including those of the socially inevitable hierarchy and of especial leaders, including the pope, in the service of (rather than presiding over) the unity of the whole community. One might add that this reflects one of the traditional titles of the pope as *Servus servorum Dei* – the Servant of the Servants of God, a title which John Paul II emphasized in his own teachings.

All services come from *within* the community and are *for* the community. Boff calls this a 'more evangelical sense of church' which recognizes diversity. In turning back to wider current ecclesial challenges and discussions, we are reminded that the laity have both the opportunity and the duty to act, just as in other times of challenge for the church. For example, consider St Francis of Assisi's original calling to 'rebuild' the church or Newman's famous observation of how it was the faithful laity, rather than the bishops, who ensured that christological orthodoxy finally prevailed during the Arian crisis. A much more recent example is how the lay faithful, through their sheer perseverance and endurance, finally managed to force the institutional church leaders to acknowledge the awful truth of the sexual and physical abuse scandals in the church. And it is primarily the laity who are trying to ensure that such leaders face up to their responsibilities in the light of these sorry revelations.

Boff argues that the rigidity of current church structures can be overcome and decision-making processes can be transformed into ones which are truly more inclusive of the whole community. As numerous scholars have argued in recent decades, the exclusion of the laity from participation in such decisions is a fundamental problem for the church in our times. Hence the base communities help to develop a new form of church structure where the roles of all, including priests and bishops, are transformed. The church moves towards a process of declericalization, as the ecclesiological emphasis switches to the whole 'people of God', to whom collegiality now belongs.

Nonetheless, Boff takes care to stress that all this offers not a 'global alternative', nor a blueprint for the entire church, but instead a 'leaven of renewal' for the church. As Boff states in another work, the challenge we still face is to make our ecclesial teachings and aspirations a reality,

> The true difficulty involves the theological implications present in the basic statement: the Church is the People of God. There is a fundamental equality in the Church. All are People of God. All share in Christ, directly and without mediation. Therefore, all share in the services of teaching, sanctifying, and organising the community. All are sent out on a mission; all are responsible for the unity of the community; all must be sanctified. . . . The concept of Church as People of God inverts the relationships with regard to ministries. In classical ecclesiology there is a Church that only takes the hierarchy into account . . . Anyone who opts for the Church as People of God must take it to its logical conclusion: to be a living Church, with flexible and appropriate ministries, without theological privileges.[28]

Boff nonetheless recognizes that equality does not mean that everyone must be able or permitted to perform every task, just as he also recognizes the need for a particular role of 'giving unity to all of the services so as to maintain harmony'. The priest and bishop fulfil such a role on the local and regional levels, and the pope fulfils the role at the universal level. But these ministries are ones of 'unification and not of sanctification'.[29]

Of course, the experiments with the base communities have also had their difficulties – one would not seek to paint a utopian picture here, and their actual success has been limited in some areas.[30] Nonetheless, in reflecting upon the 'leaven' that such an emerging ecclesiology might provide, we can express full agreement with Paul Lakeland, who has sought to incorporate the achievements of Latin American liberation theology into wider (particularly North American) ecclesiological thinking, when he suggests that

> [t]he phenomenon of base Christian communities offers the church at large a model for lay ministry that needs to be taken seriously. For one thing, the church as a whole is becoming more and more like the Latin American church in its dire shortage of ordained ministers. But more importantly, the base communities working at their best show a serious degree of lay involvement in the worship and leadership of the local community, coupled with an equally vigorous outreach to the world. The social and political realities of life in the secular world come to be seen as genuine concerns of the church. They are also obviously the prime task of laypeople. . . . Liturgical life and the struggle for justice become intertwined in liberation theology in a way that has not occurred elsewhere in the Catholic world.[31]

In reflecting upon what we have considered thus far, we can see that liberation ecclesiology has helped build a strong case that the laity today must take up the challenge of ensuring that the ecclesial vision of the church as the people of God is allowed to flourish at every level of the church.[32] Liberation ecclesiology challenges those in the wider church, particularly in numerous European and North American societies, to be honest and ask themselves in exactly how many dioceses and parishes, and in the analogous forms of ecclesial community across other churches, can we say that the laity is allowed to do so?

Spirituality, equality, and practical ecumenism

As a further example of these contextual and particularly liberationist perspectives of ecclesiology, let us briefly consider the work of two theologians, Pedro Casaldáliga, and José María Vigil, who have focused upon the spiritual aspects of such visionary developments. In their work, *The Spirituality of Liberation*,[33] in particular, they consider the spiritual implications of 'a new way of being church'. As Bishop of São Félix do Araguaia in Brazil, Casaldáliga came to offer great ecclesial vision and leadership in trying to put such a new ecclesiology into practice.[34]

Here Casaldáliga and Vigil describe a church of the poor and marginalized – where these people have 'rights and authority', in opposition not to the hierarchy but to the bourgeois church, a church 'taken over by elites which dominate people'. Once again, the emphasis is not upon the church as institution/society, but upon the reign of God and the church's sacramental role in serving this reign and bringing about human communion. They equally espouse an ecclesiology based upon those teachings of Vatican II where the local church is seen as primary, and where the church is inclusive and egalitarian, with a 'circle of sharing' – stressing, like Boff, a horizontal over a vertical, hierarchical model of authority.

Finally, and crucially, they highlight the importance of *practical* ecumenism in Latin America in building up the church, serving the people and facilitating the reign of God.[35] The practical necessity of ecumenism, of cooperation amongst different Christian denominations (as well as amongst people of different faiths) is a crucial lesson which the churches in Latin America, Asia and Africa alike have offered the church in European and North American societies today, where many continue to be particularly poor at encouraging and developing such cooperation.

So, in reflecting upon such visions of the church, we see further affirmation that the laity are thus, in so many ways, the key to the future life of the church, to the development of new ways of ecclesial living, new structures and new visions which further develop the self-understanding of the church. The gospel is good news about justice, human well-being, truthfulness and hence freedom. In Latin America, to speak of a theology of liberation is simply shorthand for this, i.e. freedom from all that oppresses, that stifles human being and prevents us from being our true selves and from being closer to one another and hence to God.

Furthermore, liberation ecclesiological method shows us, as Magaña argues, that it is not a question of mutually exclusive ecclesiologies. Liberation ecclesiology is never a 'closed system'.[36] This is one very important lesson we can learn from these still-emerging ecclesiologies: prescriptive ecclesiology is something of a contradiction in terms.

Critique: the liberation ecclesiology debates

Of course, liberation theology and the ecclesiologies it has informed, which were once celebrated throughout the Roman Catholic church, fell foul of the Vatican doctrinal authorities in a quite spectacular fashion. Paul Lakeland has argued that, whilst it is difficult to pin down precisely what the Vatican found most problematic in liberation theology (its complaints against it frequently fluctuated), it would appear likely that the root problem was, indeed, primarily ecclesiological and pertained to the vision of liberation theology for the laity, i.e. 'the spectre of an alternative ecclesiology in which laypeople play a profoundly important animating role in the local community'.[37]

But for some today, liberation theology seems not a little passé, whether in ecclesial, methodological or even epistemological terms. Granted, some elements of the critique of the method and epistemology of liberation may have proved justified, but liberation theology has moved on and developed a great deal since then. Indeed, against those who feel that it has had its day and failed, one could rather argue that its day has yet to come. Liberation theology was stifled just as it began to make a transformative difference to ecclesial and societal communities and structures alike. This does not mean, just as with Vatican II's ecclesiological vision (out of which, as we have noted, much liberation ecclesiology emerged), that its day cannot still come. As Lakeland suggests, the concept of 'faithful sociality' has much to offer the church in our times and the church of the future.[38]

With regard to the liberationist movements in particular, Lakeland has perceived their form of response to the postmodern world to be preferable to other forms of 'faithful sociality' such as postliberalism and Radical Orthodoxy.[39] And to this I would add all other forms of what we might term 'neo-exclusivism'.[40] Indeed, liberation ecclesiology is a positive antidote to any world-renouncing ecclesiologies, particularly those that shun dialogue with the social sciences. Furthermore, liberation ecclesiology continues to pose challenging and practical questions to political authorities everywhere.

Lakeland's suggestions here further illustrate the enormous potential for liberation ecclesiology to help shape the more constructive vision of being church that many ecclesiologists deem necessary for these postmodern times:

> Though it is not often noticed, liberation theology and its sister movements incorporate a critique of modernity. The challenge to the church is expressed against the totalizing instincts of traditional theology and the theologico-cultural hegemony of white patriarchal/Roman/Eurocentric ecclesiality. The challenge to the secular world is aimed at a whole panoply of factors – geopolitics, free market economics, Eurocentrism, scientism, technologism, and economism – which together represent the metanarrative of the West. Both, religious and secular, reflect the dark side of modernity's triumph in the West. The alternative vision that liberation theology proposes is centrifugal, grass-roots oriented, community-based, non-hierarchical, intersubjective, devolutionary, in a phrase, 'small-scale'. Whilst liberation thought reflects the small-scale, devolutionary and intersubjective emphases of postmodern social thought, it also has the potential to extend its critique of modernity to challenge the darker side of postmodernity itself.[41]

Lakeland believes that radical theologies echo Habermas' critique of much postmodern thought as 'neo-conservative'. However, such radical religious thought, including in an exemplary fashion the theologies of liberation, although 'voiced in postmodern communities and alliances', remains 'with at least one toe, if not a whole foot, well within the sea of enlightenment'.[42] Liberationist thought and practice can thus, he declares, mirror the best of postmodernity, whilst challenging the worst.[43] We might here add that such ecclesiologies make it something of an imperative that all in the church must continuously learn the lessons of history.[44] Today, as before, we must 'discern the signs of the times'. Recall that the subtitle of Gutíerrez's classic A Theology of Liberation was History, politics, salvation.[45]

Let us consider some methodological, practical and concrete examples of how liberation ecclesiologies continue to offer the wider church much constructive food for ecclesial thought.

Promising comparative pathways – the power of liberationist ecclesial hermeneutics

Transforming traditional ecclesiologies

Many may well say, however, that it is all very well dealing with such abstract and theoretical ecclesiologies from elsewhere, but how might such liberationist thinking inform fresh ideas in societies elsewhere, particularly in the contemporary European and North American churches? For example, some might feel that the vision of the Latin American liberationists is not applicable elsewhere at all or, indeed, that such thinking is now passé. Or they may suggest that forms of liberation ecclesiology such as feminist, womanist and mujerista thinking have only limited application with regard to certain interest groups. In seeking to suggest that the contrary is rather the case, one could point towards numerous recent attempts to build upon and develop the work of the pioneers of liberation theology, along with the pioneers of the modern theologies of the laity. The debt that inspirational ecclesiological work in Europe and North America in recent times owes to these still-emerging liberation ecclesiologies is immense.

Of course, as already suggested, one must acknowledge that all forms of ecclesiology and the methods, epistemologies and theologies underpinning them are open to criticism, often justifiably so. I make no challenge to the fact that there may well be a multitude of additional critical debates to be had in relation to all we have considered thus far. No rose-tinted spectacles here, then. But no unnecessary cynicism or debilitating pessimism either, because, allowing for whatever deficiencies there may be in some emerging pathways (for do not all theological pathways contain numerous deficiencies?), one does not have to have fastened upon 'the' definitive method, epistemology, theology or, of course, ecclesiology (something which the neo-exclusivists, perhaps evidenced in a most unappealing manner in the writings of certain proponents of radical orthodoxy, appear not to have realized) in order to contribute something to the shared efforts of Christians to discern the signs of the time and to interpret and put the gospel into practice in ever new and challenging contexts.

So, in offering just some brief 'comparative' conclusions here, can we identify particular inspiring lessons that those working in ecclesiology elsewhere might take from these liberating ecclesiologies?

One could list numerous instances of where this is the case. But above all, it is important to emphasize how those working in ecclesial settings of Europe, North America and Oceania can take from these ecclesiologies of liberation the sense that openness is a virtue and hence an open ecclesiology is necessary in order to build and proclaim an open church. These ecclesiologies return us to the gospel, to its meaning in new contexts and situations, to questions of praxis, to attentiveness to the poor, oppressed and marginalized – the least of society to whom Christ was so concerned to reach out. Social and political issues are to the fore, as the gospels demonstrated that they were in the mission and teaching of Christ and the early church. They encourage an ongoing and self-critical attentiveness to our ways of being church, our ecclesial structures and models of ministry, authority and governance. They point towards the priority of caritas and honest dialogue.[46]

Such ecclesiologies can help the churches elsewhere free themselves from particular and long-standing cultural, intellectual and indeed religious strictures. How? Let us briefly consider perhaps the two most significant ways.

Liberative ecclesial hermeneutics

One very important lesson to be learned concerns the priority which ecclesiologies of liberation give to hermeneutics, to engaging the other, indeed to true catholicity, in ways which often leave the churches and their theological servants in the Euro-North American world lagging far behind. As Tracy has said, the 'new hermeneutics as discourse analysis'[47] shifts the focus from historical context to social location. In the economically poorer parts of the world and where pluralism is a day-to-day reality, this is a necessity that has been known long before its complex articulations in the philosophical analysis of what is variously and frequently erroneously termed the 'north' or 'west'. The engagement with the other *as* other comes far more naturally to those in many other continents than it does to the so-called 'first world' theologians.[48] And this should be no surprise. Did not the Latin American liberationists label their European and North American counterparts mere 'armchair theologians'?[49] And in many ways, for Roman Catholics, they may help the church to harness better and try to implement – at long, long last – the vision of the Second Vatican Council which waits, over 40 years after its triumphant close, to be fully implemented throughout the whole Roman Catholic Church.

For Tracy, the emerging theologies in liberationist, political, feminist and practical forms have actually so transformed and widened the historical consciousness of theological work, that they have helped bring about two fundamental developments:

> First, the widespread recovery of practical philosophies (such as Aristotelian notions of *phronesis*, virtue, and community; Hegelian and Marxist notions of praxis; the new North American and German neopragmatism as the necessary ally to hermeneutical theory). Second, there exist in post-Heideggerian and post-Gadamerian hermeneutics less purely culturalist notions of historicity. Indeed, the use of critical theory in Habermas as well as Ricouer's development of a hermeneutics of suspicion (Freud, Marx, Nietzsche) to parallel Gadamer's earlier hermeneutics of retrieval may now justly be viewed as philosophical parallels to the emergence of political and practical theologies in our period.[50]

Thus here I suggest that these emerging ecclesiologies of liberation help further demonstrate that any imposed and 'blueprint' ecclesiology for our times will fail because it will stifle the very church it seeks to articulate and enhance. Indeed, as with Yves Congar's timely reminder that 'institutions also speak', these emerging theologies and their (sometimes precursory and sometimes subsequent) ecclesiologies help us to unmask, bring to light and critique the consequences of the 'discourse of institutions'.[51] Tracy believes we can especially thank political, liberation and feminist theologies for helping us to embrace the need for a hermeneutics of suspicion – for they have demonstrated that

> our problems *with* history (the tradition) and *in* history (our present social, economic, political, and ecclesiological situations) are not confined to corrigible conscious errors (i.e. corrigible through better inquiry, better conversation, better argument, better hermeneutics of retrieval). Rather, our present problems include the need to suspect (the verb is accurate) that we are likely to find not merely conscious errors but also unconscious systemic illusions in all history, all traditions, all texts, all interpretations.[52]

Consider the ecumenical implications of such a statement here. For Tracy, the attention to 'social location' means that 'explicit attention' to questions of gender, race and class become inescapable.[53] And in a hermeneutical shift from text to discourse, so too is attention to 'explicit or implicit power realities' inescapable,[54] for in analysing any form of discourse we must therefore pay due attention to the power relations going on within that discourse and, therefore, be particularly attentive to questions of gender, race and class implicit in those power relations. Hence the hermeneutics of suspicion moves beyond its earlier manifestations (its early Frankfurt forms focusing on psychoanalytical and revisionary Marxist models) to one which focuses upon these issues and thereby can enable theology (and so, for our debates here, ecclesiology) to become 'yet more practical and ethical-political without ceasing to be fundamentally hermeneutical'.[55] Which can thus help construct a 'fundamental theology' of the most practical relevance of all.

Liberation ecclesiology and the triune God

Of much wider and greater ecclesial implication, these liberating ecclesiologies also point towards an emphasis upon our actual understanding and, indeed, experience of God in our ecclesiological undertakings – and most of all, upon attentiveness to the fact that Christians proclaim and are called to communion with God understood in a threefold sense. Liberating ecclesiologies help us appreciate that attentiveness to the triune communion of persons (or ways of divine being) obliges us simultaneously to be attentive to the moral and practical ways of being church; in other words, such attentiveness throws our ecclesial virtues and vices alike into sharp relief. Of particularly great value for future ecclesiological developments is the attentiveness to the pneumatological, i.e. Spirit-filled and Spirit-oriented, dimensions that many liberation ecclesiologies share in common. With such a dimension comes greater ecclesial freedom, greater innovation, greater renewal and even, at times, revolution.[56]

But are our aspirations here still too idealistic?

Elsewhere, I have sought to illustrate the relevance of virtue theory and how this also relates to the 'trinitarian turn' in ecclesiology and the still very untapped potential of both for the church and ecclesiology in our times.[57] But to further illustrate our case that emerging ecclesiologies may offer us a great deal today, let us now finally consider a 'more concrete and practical' example and explore the vision of being church in one area where such aspirations are deemed not only to be possible, but also necessary. It illustrates a very particular instance of where the achievements of one regional set of emerging ecclesiological principles have recently been applied to a set of difficulties experienced by those 'northern' churches.

A 'Copernican revolution' in ecclesiology? Lessons from the global 'south'

Thus, for those who may perhaps still ask why the church in the Euro-North American world should seek to learn from ways of being church developed elsewhere, we turn to the work of Peter C. Phan, who has illustrated in an impressive array of publications how ecclesiologically fruitful it can be when we give significant attention to context and, above all else, the theme of human liberation.[58]

Through focusing on the ecclesial fault-lines in the church of Europe and North America, uncovered in the wake of the clerical sex abuse scandals, Phan has also made a thoroughly convincing case for learning from elsewhere. He suggests that the problems uncovered and the disastrous tactics employed by bishops and diocesan personnel for dealing with offenders and their victims betrayed an ecclesiology that did not serve the church well. By and large it is a 'church-centred' ecclesiology, where the institutional church takes priority over all else, including pastoral provision and care for the welfare of the faithful. He also points to the incontrovertible figures that illustrate stagnation in the 'north' and massive growth in church membership in the south. In the not very distant future the vast majority of the world's Roman Catholics (at present totalling over 1.6 billion) will be located in Latin America, Africa and Asia.

Furthermore, he argues that it is not that the church in other parts of the world is perfect and suffers from fewer problems than its sister churches in Europe and North America. It is simply that the churches elsewhere have had to take stock and rethink their ecclesiologies in the light of very different situations and particular challenges. What has come about, Phan suggests, is nothing short of a 'Copernican revolution in ecclesiology' – a revolution that the churches of the 'north' must embrace or risk further decline.[59]

But what transformations come about in such a revolution? Phan's work in general, and here in particular, touches upon each of the major themes in liberation ecclesiology in an exemplary fashion and clearly shows their practical relevance and thus their further and wider potential. Focusing upon the church in Asia, Phan points to how, in recent years, the church in Asia has shifted its focus and its priorities, helped by the work of the Federation of Asian Bishops' Conferences (FABC), founded in 1970, as well as events such as the 1998 Asian Synod of Bishops and the emergent papal document, *Ecclesia in Asia*. No longer is the institutional church at the heart of its priorities. No longer does it come first. Instead, the kingdom of God (or of heaven) comes first. After all, the word church only occurs in the gospels twice (and then only in Matthew), whereas the theme of building the kingdom is a constant presence in all four gospels. Thus, as Phan states, the church's constitution becomes 'regnocentric' – defined by the kingdom of God rather than vice versa.[60]

A kingdom-centred ecclesiology works in accordance with kingdom-centred values and strives to promote these in the wider world. In several writings, Phan has expanded on the ecclesiological implications of this shift away from an ecclesiocentric to a 'reign of God-centred' ecclesial vision, arguing that 'This single-minded and total commitment to the reign of God is *the* essential and distinctive feature of Christian social spirituality in general and of liberation spirituality in particular. It informs the way Christian social spirituality understands the ministry of the historical Jesus, the Trinity, and the Incarnation'.[61]

From the various documents to emerge from the collective deliberations of the churches in Asia, Phan identifies many particular ecclesiological priorities, but pre-eminent amongst them is a trinitarian emphasis through which ecclesial structures and offices, even the primacy of the pope, are understood in their rightful terms – i.e. authority is exercised in terms of collegiality, co-responsibility and accountability to all the faithful.[62] Phan notes that such a trinitarian emphasis was also echoed in the 'Asian Vision of a Renewed Church', which describes 'eight movements' of the churches in Asia towards this renewed ecclesiology since 1970.[63] The picture Phan sketches is of the desire of the Asian churches to develop and live out a *true* ecclesiology of communion.[64]

Throughout his many works, Peter Phan shows us how liberation ecclesiology in general, and Asian perspectives on the church and the Asian context in particular, can offer so much to a much wider debate concerning the transformation not simply of fundamental ecclesiology, the self-understanding of the church itself, but also of *mission*, the very purpose and business of the church today.[65]

The importance of such ecclesiological concepts as true communion, the importance of the local church, the need for renewed and reformed ecclesial structures, co-responsibility, participation, the 'liberation of the laity', accountability, collegiality, equality, dialogue and prophecy are themes of fundamental importance for the church today. The necessity and importance of the church today and in the future being open to a greater 'complementarity' of Christianity with other faiths in promoting the 'reign of God' also needs to be emphasized, despite the controversy that certain interpretations of such a concept have generated. For surely this must logically be in accordance with what can be discerned of the will of God and *Missio Dei*? Peter Phan's works demonstrate just how grateful we must therefore be, that our Asian sisters and brothers have already sought to demonstrate that attention to such important themes and features of the church in our times can prove fruitful.

Conclusion: the liberating promise of trinitarian ecclesiology

So our comparative explorations have underlined a common theme in these emerging ecclesiologies which may provide grounds for great ecclesiological hope across the wider church. We have illustrated such here with reference to that 'new way of being church' encountered in Asia but we could have used examples from Asia, Latin America or Africa, or from a feminist, ecological or political perspective. For one of the most positive and promising ecclesiological themes that occurs in much of the liberationist ecclesiological thinking is an emphasis upon communion that seeks to be truly reflective of the reality of the love of the triune God, the God who *is* radically equal community. Of course, trinitarian theology has enjoyed a renaissance in general in the second half of the twentieth century, but it is in raising anew awareness of the social, ethical and practical implications of the doctrine of the Trinity, and therefore the ecclesiological implications, that the particular achievements of liberation ecclesiology lie.[66] In the feminist approaches to such ecclesiological themes and realities there is a shift, as Natalie Watson again illustrates, from institution to community:

> That women, men and children begin to find spaces in which they can flourish and enable each other to flourish and live in relationships of justice, is rooted in the story of the triune God sharing God's own being with humankind and in doing so sharing their being. The triune God became a particular human being so that particular human beings might flourish as the people they are and share their lives with each other as they are sharing in God's life. Such sharing is possible as human beings live in the tension of being fully themselves and transcending the limitations and boundaries of their own lives and they share the lives of others and of God. *This is where being church begins to happen.*[67]

Miroslav Volf's own groundbreaking and, indeed, comparative study in trinitarian ecclesiology, was itself very much inspired by feminist ecclesiology, along with reviving the idea of John Smyth, the first Baptist, of the church as a 'gathered community'. Volf's aim was to counter individualistic emphases in Protestant ecclesiology, and along the way he engages with a variety of conversation partners such as Joseph Ratzinger and John Zizioulas. However, even in 'mainstream' Catholic and Orthodox thought, he believes that the connections between 'divine community' and 'ecclesial community' have been, with the exception of more recent scholars, 'more affirmed than carefully reflected upon'.[68] Hence he describes the purpose of his book as being

> to suggest a viable understanding of the church in which both person and community are given their proper due. The ultimate goal is to spell out a vision of the church as an image of the triune God. The road I have taken is that of a sustained and critical ecumenical dialogue with Catholic and Orthodox ecclesiology in the persons of their more or less official representatives.[69]

But Volf not only engages with and draws upon such 'official' representatives, but also, in addition to the emerging feminist ecclesiologies, the emerging ecclesiologies of what he calls the 'thriving churches' to be found in other parts of the world where Western ideas do not dominate.[70] In other words, liberation ecclesiology.

And as both Marie-Dominique Chenu and Gregory Baum have shown, it is the re-emergence of a trinitarian emphasis in Roman Catholic ecclesiological understanding at

437

Vatican II that has helped inspire so many ecclesiologies of liberation, and pastorally sensitive ecclesiologies in general that are mindful of the actual lived experience of the faithful.[71] Thus the potential for future ecclesiological investigations posed by such comparative undertakings, particularly with respect to the increasing awareness of this common emphasis in progressive ecclesiologies upon the church as image of the Trinity, is immense.

Notes

1 Peter C. Phan, *Christianity with An Asian Face: Asian American Theology in the Making*, Maryknoll, NY: Orbis, 2003, p. 26.
2 See Chapters 7, 14–17, 24 and 25 of this volume.
3 Gustavo Gutiérrez, *A Theology of Liberation*, London: SCM, 1973, p. 307.
4 Here following the core themes and milestones typically discussed in such 'foundational' texts as Leonardo and Clodovis Boff, *Introducing Liberation Theology*, Tunbridge Wells: Burns & Oates, 1987; and Rosino Gibellini, *The Liberation Theology Debate*, London: SCM, 1987.
5 Marc Reuver, 'Emerging Theologies: Faith Through Resistance', in *The Ecumenical Movement Tomorrow*, eds Marc Reuver, Friedrich Solms and Gerrit Huizer, Kampen: Kok Publishing, 1993, pp. 263–80.
6 *Asian Christian Theologies: A Research Guide to Authors, Movements and Sources*, eds John C. England, Jose Kuttianimattathil, John M. Prior, Lily A. Quintos, David Suh Kwang-sun, Janice Wickeri, 3 vols, Delhi, Quezon and Maryknoll, NY: ISPCK/Claretian Publishers/Orbis, 2002.
7 Lahore: Research Society of Pakistan, 2006.
8 O'Brien, *Pakistani Christian Identity*, p. xiii.
9 Cf., for example, Peter C. Phan, *Christianity with An Asian Face*. Cf. also Chapter 15 of the present volume.
10 Phan, pp. 12ff.
11 Maryknoll, NY: Orbis, 1985.
12 Cf. Chung Hyun Kyung, *Struggle to be the Sun Again: Introducing Asian Women's Theology*, Maryknoll, NY: Orbis, 1990, esp. pp. 190–114, given in an adapted form as 'The Future of Asian Women's Theology' in Reuver, Solms and Huizer (eds), *The Ecumenical Movement Tomorrow*, pp. 256–61.
13 Cf. Elizabeth Stuart, *Religion is a Queer Thing: A guide to the Christian faith for lesbian, gay, bisexual, and transgendered people*, London: Cassell, 1997; and Lisa Isherwood and Marcella Althaus Reid (eds), *The Sexual Theologian*, London: T&T Clark, 2005. On ecclesial neglect and discrimination against gay, lesbian and transgender people, cf. Kevin T. Kelly, 'Sexual Ethics – Denying the Good News to Gay Men and Lesbian Women?' in his *New Directions in Sexual Ethics: The Challenge of HIV/AIDS*, London: Continuum, 1997, pp. 75–108. For discussions of the ecclesiological implications of these approaches cf. Steven Shakespeare and Hugh Rayment-Pickard, *The Inclusive God: Reclaiming Theology for An Inclusive Church*, London: Canterbury Press, 2006; and also Steven Shakespeare, 'A Community of the Question: Inclusive Ecclesiology', in Gerard Mannion (ed.), *Church and Religious Other: Essays on Truth, Unity and Diversity*, London: T&T Clark, 2008.
14 Cf. Celia Deane Drummond, 'Animal Theology: Where do we go from here?' in *Moral Theology for the 21st Century: Essays in Celebration of Kevin Kelly*, eds Julie Clague, Bernard Hoose and Gerard Mannion, London: T&T Clark, 2008.
15 Cf. Phan, *Christianity with An Asian Face*, pp. 26–46.
16 Cf., e.g. the work of the Argentine Methodist, José Miguez Bonino, *Revolutionary Theology Comes of Age*, London: SPCK, 1975, esp. Ch. 8, 'Church, People and the Avant Garde', pp. 154–74.
17 Magaña, 'Ecclesiology in the Theology of Liberation'. in *Systematic Theology – Perspectives from Liberation Theology*, eds Jon Sobrino and Ignacio Ellacuria, London: SCM, 1996, p. 183. See also Roger Haight, 'Liberation Ecclesiology and Basic Ecclesial Communities', in his *Christian Community in History*, New York: Continuum, 2004, vol. 2: Comparative Ecclesiology, pp. 408–19.
18 Haight, p. 180.
19 Magaña, 'Ecclesiology in the Theology of Liberation', pp. 186ff.

20 Cf. Chapters 14 and 17 of the present volume.

21 London: Collins Flame, 1986.

22 From its original publication date.

23 Cf. Chapter 7 of the present volume.

24 For more on the base communities movement, see Leonardo Boff, 'The Base Ecclesial Structure: A Brief Sketch' and 'Underlying Ecclesiologies of the Base Ecclesial Communities', Chapters 9 and 10 of his *Church, Charism and Power*, London: SCM, 1985 (pp. 125–30 and 131–37, respectively). See also Margaret Hebblethwaite, *Base Communities – An Introduction*, London: Geoffrey Chapman, 1993; and Andrew Dawson 'The origins and character of the base ecclesial community: a Brazilian perspective', in Christopher Rowland (ed.), *The Cambridge Companion to Liberation Theology*, Cambridge: Cambridge University Press, 1993. Again, see also Chapters 14 and 17 of the present volume.

25 See especially Chapter 3.

26 The problem thus being the stalled full implementation of Vatican II.

27 Cf. the discussion of ecclesiologies 'from above' and 'from below' in Mannion, *Ecclesiology and Postmodernity*, Chapter 2, pp. 25–40.

28 Leonardo Boff, *Church, Charism and Power*, p. 133.

29 Ibid.

30 Not least due to restraints placed upon such experiments by the influx of more conservative bishops. And, of course, Boff's own very public disagreements with the Roman authorities and their continued investigation into his work and restrictive interference led to his leaving the active ordained ministry to work with the poor in the shanty towns of Sao Paulo and to an increasing involvement in environmental issues and campaigns instead. Cf., Harvey Cox, *The Silencing of Leonardo Boff*, London: Collins Flame, 1988; Peter Hebblethwaite, *The New Inquisition*, London: Fount, 1980; and Rosino Gibellini, *The Liberation Theology Debate*, London: SCM, 1987.

31 Paul Lakeland, *The Liberation of the Laity: in search of an accountable church*, New York: Continuum, 2003, p. 142.

32 Cf. Gustavo Gutiérrez, *We Drink from Our Own Wells: the spiritual journey of a people*, Maryknoll, NY: Orbis, 1984.

33 London: Burns & Oates, 1993, pp. 181–91.

34 See his more recent reflections upon such questions in Pedro Casaldáliga, 'Another Way of Being Church', in *Crie* (Mexico) nos 351 (March 1997) and 352 (April 1997), also available via the SEDOS website, www.sedos.org/english/20_10_97.htm (accessed 3 April, 2007).

35 Recall our discussion of their account of 'macro-ecumenism' in Chapter 12.

36 'Ecclesiology in the Theology of Liberation', p. 184.

37 Lakeland, *Liberation of the Laity*, p. 141. See also Peter Hebblethwaite, 'The Vatican and Liberation Theology', in Chris Rowland, *The Cambridge Companion to Liberation Theology*, Cambridge: Cambridge University Press, 1999; and Juan Luis Segundo, *Theology and the Church – A Response to Cardinal Ratzinger and a Warning to the Whole Church*, London, Geoffrey Chapman, 1985. See also again Harvey Cox, *The Silencing of Leonardo Boff*; Peter Hebblethwaite, *The New Inquisition*; and Rosino Gibellini, *The Liberation Theology Debate*.

38 Lakeland defines 'faithful sociality' thus, '"Sociality" stresses the inevitably social and political presence of the members to one another and within the larger society. But the qualifier "faithful" reminds us that spirituality is as important as political praxis', Paul Lakeland, *Postmodernity: Christian Identity in a Fragmented Age*, Minneapolis: Fortress Press, 1997, p. 63.

39 Lakeland, *Postmodernity*, pp. 60–4. See also his *Liberation of the Laity*, on Lindbeck, pp. 88–9, on radical orthodoxy, pp. 232, 244, 249.

40 Cf. Mannion, *Ecclesiology and Postmodernity*, esp. Chapters 2–4, pp. 25–101.

41 Lakeland, *Postmodernity*, pp. 62–3.

42 Lakeland, *Postmodernity*, p. 63.

43 Lakeland, *Postmodernity*, p. 63 (note a parallel with what Gregory Baum states about the church of Vatican II's response to modernity and its similarities with critical theory (*Amazing Church*, Maryknoll, NY: Orbis, 2005, p. 142); see Mannion, *Ecclesiology and Postmodernity*, pp. 21, 51).

44 Robert Ombres, 'What Future for the Laity? Law and History', in Noel Timms and Kenneth Wilson (eds), *Governance and Authority in the Roman Catholic Church: Beginning a Conversation*, London: SPCK, 2000, p. 95.

45 London: SCM, 1974.

46 Tracy notes that the theologies behind these ecclesiologies have helped historical consciousness move beyond merely cultural bounds and into the economic, social and political realms, a move further assisted by the emergence of new forms of practical theology; David Tracy, 'Beyond Foundationalism and Relativism: Hermeneutics and the new ecumenism', in Tracy, *On Naming the Present. God, Hermeneutics, and* Church, Maryknoll, NY: Orbis, 1994, Ch. 12, pp. 131–40, p.134 (originally published in Norbert Greinacher and Norbert Mitte (eds), *The New Europe: Challenge for Christians; Concilium* 1992/2).

47 Tracy, 'Beyond Foundationalism and Relativism', pp. 133, 135–6.

48 Cf. the central arguments of Phan in *Being Religious Interreligiously: Asian Perspectives on Interfaith Dialogue*, Maryknoll, NY: Orbis, 2004.

49 Of course, much very good work in all these areas has been and continues to be done in Europe, North America and Oceania. And indeed much pioneering work has emerged from these areas. But here one can generalize enough to suggest that theologians there still have much to learn from the emerging ecclesiologies. Not least because they have constantly flirted with, borrowed from and usurped their achievements, only to then go on and be complicit in their being undermined either at the hands of reactionary intellectual, cultural or, of course, ecclesial forces. Nowhere is this illustrated more vividly than in the case of Latin American liberation theology, itself.

50 Tracy, 'Beyond Foundationalism and Relativism', pp. 134–35.

51 Cf. Paul Lakeland, *Theology and Critical Theory: the Discourse of the Church*, Nashville: Abingdon, 1990.

52 Tracy, 'Beyond Foundationalism and Relativism', p. 135.

53 Ibid.

54 Ibid.

55 Ibid., p. 136. For a discussion of the ecclesiological implications of hermeneutics in general, including a discussion of Tracy's particular contribution to theological hermeneutics, see Gerard Mannion 'Hermeneutical Investigations: Discerning Contemporary Christian Community', Chapter 4 of Paul Collins, Gerard Mannion, Gareth Powell, Kenneth Wilson, *Ecclesiological Investigations* (London: T&T Clark, forthcoming, 2008).

56 I am grateful to Peter Phan here for his helpfully suggestive comments on the pneumatological dimension.

57 *Ecclesiology and Postmodernity*, Chapters 8, 9 and Conclusion.

58 See Chapter 15, above. Cf. also, for example, his trilogy, Peter Phan, *Christianity with An Asian Face: Asian American Theology in the Making; In Our Own Tongues: Perspectives from Asia on Mission and Inculturation*, Maryknoll, NY, Orbis, 2003; and, finally, *Being Religious Interreligiously: Asian Perspectives on Interfaith Dialogue*. See also his 'Christian Social Spirituality: a Global Perspective', in *Catholic Social Justice: Theological and Practical Explorations*, eds Philomena Cullen, Bernard Hoose and Gerard Mannion, London: T&T Clark/Continuum, 2007, pp. 18–40.

59 Peter Phan, 'A New Way of Being Church: Perspectives from Asia', Chapter 14 in *Governance, Accountability and the Future of the Church*, eds Francis Oakley and Bruce Russet, New York: Continuum, 2003, pp. 178–90. See also Chapter 15 above, and Phan, *Christianity With an Asian Face*.

60 See above, Chapter 15, pp. 281–83, and Phan, 'A New Way of Being Church', p. 184. Note that some tension is thereby shown between such a vision and its apparent official recognition in *Ecclesia in Asia*, and the document issued by the CDF in 2000, *Dominus Iesus* which, although commenting that the church does not supersede the kingdom, nonetheless offers a very church-centred ecclesiology indeed.

61 Phan, 'Christian Social Spirituality' in Cullen *et al.* (eds), *Catholic Social Justice*.

62 Phan, 'Christian Social Spirituality'.

63 'Asian Vision of a Renewed Church', no. 4, as quoted in Phan, 'A New Way of Being Church', p. 187.

64 Phan, 'A New Way of Being Church', p. 188. Cf. also his own 'Christian Social Spirituality', where he states: 'Christian social spirituality also professes faith in the triune God, but it sees the problem of faith today to consist not so much in atheism as in idolatry. The real issue for Christian social spirituality is not whether God *exists* but whether the God one worships is the *true* God, a masked idol or the God who reveals himself as the Father of Jesus and the Sender of the Spirit and

whose reign is one of truth and justice and peace, especially for the poor and the marginalized. This triune God, constituted by the three divine Persons in absolute equality, perfect communion, and mutual love, is Christianity's social agenda in a nutshell. Like the all-embracing Trinity in Andrej Rublev's famous icon, Christians welcome all, especially those deprived of human dignity, to the table of life, peace, justice, and love', p. 24.

65 Cf., e.g., 'Christian Social Spirituality' and *Christianity with An Asian Face*.

66 Cf. Mannion, *Ecclesiology and Postmodernity*, Chapter 8.

67 Watson, *Introducing Feminist Ecclesiology*, p. 118 (my italics), and cf. also p. 120; and Natalie Watson, 'Feminist ecclesiology', Chapter 25 of the present volume.

68 Miroslav Volf, *After Our Likeness: the church as the image of the Trinity*, Grand Rapids, MI: Eerdmans, 1998, p. 4. Dennis Doyle provides a critique of Volf's approach in *Communion Ecclesiology: Visions and Versions*, Maryknoll, NY: Orbis, 2000, pp. 161–7.

69 Volf, *After Our Likeness*, p. 2.

70 Volf, *After Our Likeness*, pp. 5–6.

71 Marie-Dominique Chenu has provided a wonderful sketch of how, largely thanks to influences from the 'east', the council fathers at Vatican II came to re-embrace the trinitarian implications of ecclesiology, 'The New Awareness of the Trinitarian Basis of the Church', in Giuseppe Alberigo and Gustavo Gutiérrez (eds), *Where Does the Church Stand? Concilium* 146, New York: Seabury, 1981, especially pp. 19–20; Gregory Baum, 'The Pilgrim State of the Christian Church', in Giuseppe Ruggieri and Miklós Tomka (eds), *The Church in Fragments: Towards What Kind of Unity?*, *Concilium*, London: SCM (1997/3), p. 116: 'The ecclesiology of Vatican II tried to overcome the institutional understanding of the church as *societas perfecta* by emphasizing its spiritual or mysterious character. The church is created by the gifts of God: Christ present in Word and Sacrament, and the Spirit uniting the faithful in a single communion'; also cf. Chenu, p. 18. Note that both realize that Vatican II also left much work to be done.

Further reading

K. C. Abraham, *Third World Theologies: Commonalities and Divergences*, Maryknoll, NY: Orbis, 1983.

Leonardo Boff, *Church, Charism and Power*, London: SCM, 1985.

——, *Ecclesiogenesis – The Base Communities Reinvent the Church*, London: Collins Flame, 1996.

——, *Trinity and Society*, London: Burns and Oates, 1988.

Robert McAfee Brown, *Kairos: Three Prophetic Challenges to the Church*, Grand Rapids, MI: Eerdmans, 1990.

Chung Hyun Kyung, *Struggle to be the Sun Again: Introducing Asian Women's Theology*, Maryknoll, NY: Orbis, 1990.

Harvey Cox, *The Silencing of Leonardo Boff*, London: Collins Flame, 1988.

Andrew Dawson, 'The origins and character of the base ecclesial community: a Brazilian perspective', in Christopher Rowland (ed.), *The Cambridge Companion to Liberation Theology*, Cambridge: Cambridge University Press, 1993.

Elisabeth Schüssler Fiorenza, *Discipleship of Equals. A Critical Feminist Ekklesia-logy of Liberation*, London: SCM, 1993.

——, (ed.), *The Power of Naming: a Concilium Reader in Feminist Liberation Theology*, London: SCM, 1996.

Rosino Gibellini, *The Liberation Theology Debate*, London: SCM, 1987.

Gustavo Gutiérrez, *A Theology of Liberation*, Ch. 12, 'The Church: Sacrament of History', London: SCM, 1974, pp. 255–85.

——, *Gustavo Gutiérrez: Essential Writings*, Part 5, 'Liberating Evangelization: Church of the Poor', ed. with an Introduction by James Nickoloff, London: SCM, 1996, pp. 236–85.

Margaret Hebblethwaite, *Base Communities – An Introduction*, London: Geoffrey Chapman, 1993.

Alvaro Quiroz Magaña, 'Ecclesiology in the Theology of Liberation', in *Systematic Theology – Perspectives from Liberation Theology*, eds Jon Sobrino and Ignacio Ellacuria, London: SCM, 1996.

Peter Phan, *Christianity with An Asian Face: Asian American Theology in the Making*, Maryknoll, NY: Orbis, 2003.

——, *In Our Own Tongues: Perspectives from Asia on Mission and Inculturation*, Maryknoll, NY: Orbis, 2003.

Peter C. Phan, *Being Religious Interreligiously: Asian Perspectives on Interfaith Dialogue*, Maryknoll, NY: Orbis, 2004.

Anthony G. Reddie, *Black Theology in Transatlantic Dialogue*, London: Palgrave Macmillan, 2006.

Marc Reuver, 'Emerging Theologies: Faith Through Resistance', in *The Ecumenical Movement Tomorrow*, eds Marc Reuver, Friedrich Solms and Gerrit Huizer, Kampen: Kok Publishing, 1993, pp. 263–80.

Rosemary Radford Ruether, *Women-Church. Theology and Praxis of Feminist Liturgical Communities*, San Francisco: Harper & Row, 1985.

Letty M. Russell, *The Church in the Round: Feminist Interpretation of the Church*, Louisville: Westminster John Knox Press, 1993.

Lamin Sanneh, *Whose Religion is Christianity? The Gospel Beyond the West*, Grand Rapids, MI: Eerdmans, 2003.

Steven Shakespeare and Hugh Rayment-Pickard, *The Inclusive God: Reclaiming Theology for an Inclusive Church*, London: Canterbury Press, 2006.

Natalie Watson, *Introducing Feminist Ecclesiology*, London: Sheffield Academic Press, 2002.

Sharon Welch, *Communities of Resistance and Solidarity: a Feminist Theology of Liberation*, Maryknoll, NY: Orbis, 1985.

24

BLACK ECCLESIOLOGIES

Anthony G. Reddie

Introduction

This chapter is a Black theological reading of the development, intent and characteristics of Black ecclesiologies across the African Diaspora. It is based upon a clear theological rationale for the ideological and intentional collective agency of Black people in Black ecclesial spaces.[1] My notion of Black ecclesiologies is predicated on the notion of 'the Black church' in the African Diaspora.[2]

Not all Black churches in the African Diaspora will either wish to be identified as being Black or perceived as being related to the liberative theological agenda within which this essay is constructed. Despite such sensitivities there is, nonetheless, the substance of Black Diasporan history, which gives weight and credence to the nature, purpose and intent of Black ecclesiologies across the past four centuries and into the present day.

Historic roots

In this chapter I shall analyse the development of Black ecclesiologies in the African Diaspora. This development has grown out of the ongoing struggles of Black peoples to affirm their identity and very humanity in the face of seemingly insuperable odds.[3] The 'invention' of Blackness, as opposed being 'African', is a construction of the Enlightenment.[4] Deeply racialized depictions of people of darker skin already existed within the cultural imagination of Europeans, influenced in no small measure by Greek philosophical thought; nevertheless, the construction of an overarching doctrine of racial inferiority ascribed to people of African descent reached its apotheosis during the epoch of slavery, aided and abetted by specious notions of pseudo-science.[5] In short, somewhere across the 'Middle Passage' and the 'Black Atlantic', Africans became 'Negroes'.[6]

The use of the term 'Black' as a qualifying nomenclature for any particular theological or ecclesiological entity remains a contested and even controversial notion. In using the term 'Black' with reference to a particular understanding, development and intent of church, embodying the Body of Christ, I am drawing upon a particular theological, philosophical and ideological tradition that finds its roots in the epoch of slavery. This particular understanding of the term 'Black', with its roots in the slave epoch, became an academic concept with the development of Black Theology in the 1960s, during the Civil Rights and Black Power era in the United States of America.

In seeking to define a notion of Black ecclesiology, I am drawing upon a body of literature that has identified African Diasporan Christian religious experience as a struggle for a humanity that is more affirmed, realized and nuanced than the crude construction of racialized inferiority imposed upon Black people by White Christian hegemony. Anthony Pinn has called this ongoing struggle the 'quest for complex Subjectivity'.[7] Complex subjectivity is the attempt by Black people of the African Diaspora to construct notions of their own humanity on terms that are more amplified and nuanced than the reified strictures of fixed objectification that was a feature of the construction of the 'negro'.[8]

The roots of Black ecclesiologies lay in the counter-hegemonic struggles of Black peoples in the Americas, the Caribbean and Britain to challenge the worst excesses of oppressive, Christian-inspired supremacist practices through a radical reinterpretation of the central tenets of the Christian faith. This dialectical tension between White normalcy and the Black subversive hermeneutical response can be found in the apposite words of John Wilkinson, who writes:

> the heart of Black Christianity lay not with the teaching of the white missionaries but with the form of Christianity which the slaves fashioned for themselves arising out of their *own* experience and needs.[9]

The roots of Black ecclesiologies can be found in the radical and subversive reinterpretation of Christianity by Black slaves in the so-called New World during the eighteenth and nineteenth centuries. Black people, having being exposed to the tendentious Christian education of the exploitative planter class in the Americas and the Caribbean, began to 'steal away' from beneath the close confines of their slave masters to worship God in their own existential spaces.[10]

The desire of Black people to form their own ecclesial spaces was the process of a long period of history, arising from the 'Great Awakening' in the middle of the eighteenth century.[11] It is beyond the scope of this essay to mount a detailed analysis of the historical development of Black churches in the African Diaspora, but it is worth noting the importance of Black existential experience and context to the historical manifestation of such ecclesial bodies. Black ecclesiological method begins with Black existential experience, not with historic mandates born of often abstract philosophical musings as to the nature of the 'Body of Christ'. Black churches were born of the existential need to create safe spaces in which the Black self could rehearse the very rubrics of what it meant to be a human being.[12]

The birth of the independent Black church in the Caribbean can be traced to the arrival in Jamaica in 1783 of approximately four hundred White families, who migrated from the United States, preferring to live under British rule than the newly independent thirteen colonies. Amongst such White migrants were two freed Black slaves, George Liele and Moses Baker.[13]

In the United States, activists such as Richard Allen used Christian teachings and a nascent Black existential theology as their means of responding to the need for Black subjectivity. Richard Allen, a former slave, became the founder of the African Methodist Episcopal Church (AME), which seceded from the American Episcopal Church due to the endemic racism of the latter ecclesial body.[14] Henry McNeal Turner, a descendant of Allen in the AME church, began to construct an explicit African-centred conception of the Christian faith, arguing that an alignment with Africa should become a primary goal for Black Americans. This focus upon African ancestry would enable subjugated objects of

Euro-American racism to find a suitable terrain for the subversive activism that would ultimately lead to liberation.[15] Anthony Pinn acknowledges the link between the African-centred strictures of the AME church and the later Black nationalism of Marcus Garvey and the Black Star Line 'Back-to-Africa' movement of the early twentieth century.[16]

Responding to the ongoing threat of non-being has been one of the central aims of the Black church that has emerged from the existential experiences of oppressed Black peoples of the African Diaspora. Harold Dean Trulear, discussing the importance of Black Christian religious education within the Black church in the United States, writes:

> Rather it [religious education] has carried upon its broad shoulders the heavy Responsibility of helping African Americans find answers for the following question: What does it mean to be Black and Christian in a society where many people are hostile to the former while claiming allegiance to the latter?[17]

So the historic roots of Black ecclesiologies emerge from the Black experience of struggle and marginalization during the era of slavery and was a determined and self-conscious attempt to create liminal spaces where the subjected and assaulted Black self could begin to construct a notion of selfhood that extended beyond the limited strictures of the objectified and absurd nothingness of fixed identities.[18]

What is a Black church?

Perhaps one of the thorniest problems when trying to talk about the Black church is the question of definition. What do we mean by the term 'The Black church'? For reasons that will soon become readily apparent, the question is somewhat easier to answer within the US context than it is in Britain or the Caribbean. In the United States the notion of the Black church is an ingrained historical, theological, sociological and experiential reality for many African Americans. 'The Black church' has an automatic efficacy that finds expression in myriad forms of discourse and academic courses.[19]

The Black church has been perceived by many scholars as the key social, political, educational and organizational entity in the collective and communitarian experience of Diasporan people of African descent.[20] In Britain, the Black church is often seen as the key location for the intimations of Black selfhood and collective solidarity.[21] Within the United States the Black church is a normative context out of which the Black religious experience has arisen.[22]

Black self-determination in the US experience

The term Black church when used in the United States is a generic one, seeking to denote and describe particular faith communities in which Black leadership, culture, traditions, experience and spirituality represent the norm and from which White, Euro-American traditions and expressions are largely absent. These churches are termed 'generic' because, unlike in Britain, they are not confined to any one denominational or theological slant (of which more shortly).

These churches cut across the whole spectrum of church affiliation and the multiplicity of settings in which Black life is experienced. The development of the 'Black church' in the United States of America grew out of the racism of the established churches of White,

445

European origin. The worshipping life of these churches displayed discriminatory practices, convincing Black people to leave in order to form their own churches. The denominations most commonly identified with the Black church are the African Methodist Episcopal Church (AME), the African Methodist Episcopal Zion Church (AMEZ), the Christian Methodist Church (CME), the National Baptist Convention Incorporated, the National Baptist Convention of America and the Progressive Baptist Convention.[23]

Black churches in Britain and the Caribbean

Black churches in Britain, like their counterparts in the United States, are not confined to any one denomination. Black churches can be divided into three broad categories.

1   The first category and by far the most visible are Black majority Pentecostal denominational churches. These churches owe their origins to Black migrants travelling from the Caribbean mass movement of the last century after the Second World War. The first churches were offshoots of predominantly White Pentecostal denominations in the United States and were first planted in the early 1950s. The largest and most established of these churches are the New Testament Church of God and the Church of God of Prophecy.[24]

2   The second strand is that of independent Black majority Pentecostal churches or neo-Pentecostal churches. This group is in many respects a dynamic development of those in the first category. These churches tend to be 'stand-alone' entities that operate as independent communities of faith outside any established national denominational structure. One of the most significant differences between the first and second categories is that while the first is almost exclusively Black Caribbean, those in category two are a mixture of Black Caribbean and Black African, with the latter the more expressive and growing constituent.

3   The final strand is Black majority churches in White historic denominations. These churches are demographically determined, as their Black majority membership has grown out of Black migrants moving into inner city, urban contexts, coupled with the 'White flight' of the middle class.[25]

Within the literature of Black religious studies particular emphasis is placed on the role of the Black church as the major (in some respects, the only) institution that has affirmed and conferred dignity upon the inhibited and assaulted personhood of Black people.[26] To put it quite simply, Black folk in the African Diaspora might not have survived up to this point were it not for their 'inspired ability' to create their own ecclesial spaces, which provided some safety from the ravages of racism.

Black majority Pentecostal denominational churches

The origins of these churches in Britain date back to the mass migration of predominantly Black people from the Caribbean after the Second World War. Whilst some of these people came as communicant members of historic (White) denominations,[27] many of them arrived as members of established Pentecostal denominations in the Caribbean. For many, their arrival in Britain was born of an intense missionary desire to plant and establish their own churches in this new cultural and social context. A detailed history of this largely untold narrative can be found in the work of Black British scholars such as Joe Aldred,[28] Mark Sturge[29] and Doreen McCalla.[30] This new narrative is challenging and dismantling the old discourse, which asserted that Black Pentecostalism was a historical (and by definition unfortunate) accident, borne of English racism that forced Black people to leave White historic denominations to found their own churches. This narrative was at best always a 'half-truth'.

Due to their origins and development from within a Black experience, the churches in this category have often been perceived the natural equivalents of the Black church tradition in the United States. What complicates this particular perspective, however, is the fact that many of these churches, although emerging from within a Black experience, were nevertheless founded by conservative White Americans in the United States and then planted in the Caribbean by means of missionary work.

Ironically, we now have Black majority Pentecostal churches in Britain which are often seen as the natural equivalents of Black churches in the United States due to their Black majority, self-determined status, yet whose historical development is linked to a form of US White ecclesial exclusivism from which Black people had to separate in order to create a version of Christianity that did not oppress them.

For many years, these churches have been defined using the terms 'Black-led'. This term (often used by White commentators and not by the adherents themselves) has been a highly contested one for many years. A number of Black Pentecostal writers, such as Arlington Trotman, have challenged the use of such terms as 'Black-led' for predominantly Black British Pentecostal churches. They reject this term because they feel it does not cohere with the self-understanding of the people who attend these churches; it defines such ecclesial bodies in 'racial terms' and not on the basis of denomination or doctrine.[31]

One of the defining characteristics of Black Pentecostal churches is their worship style, which draws upon a range Black Diasporan (and continental) African traditions, some of which are African American in style. The invocation of the spirit within Black Pentecostal worship, for example, fused with an expressive, informal liturgy has been one of the defining hallmarks of Black religiosity. Robert Beckford offers a carefully constructed Black British Pentecostal perspective on this creative dynamic in which participation and movement are important means by which the liberative impulse of Black life is expressed.[32]

Independent or neo-Pentecostal Black churches in Britain

The second typology for Black ecclesiologies in Britain emerges from within the comparatively newer movement of neo-Pentecostalism in Britain. There are a good many similarities between churches in these contexts and those found in category one. Both are based upon an explicit rendering of Black religious cultural expression in terms of music, preaching and liturgy; in which the practice of 'being church' is reflective of the experiences of the Black people who attend these ecclesial bodies.

In short, to be in the worship services of one of these churches is to find oneself immediately located in a cultural setting removed from the normative, mainstream expression of White Christianity, particularly as it is expressed in most White majority historic churches of European origin. Charismatic worship and a strong emphasis upon the outworking of the Holy Spirit (pneumatology), coupled with African and Caribbean musicology, characterizes the distinctive contribution of many of these churches to British Christianity.[33]

There are a number of differentiations one can deduce between churches in the first and second categories. I want to highlight two of them. The first, to which I have already alluded, is that these churches, whilst retaining an overwhelmingly Black constituency, tend to have a greater proportion of members who are Africans as opposed to the majority Caribbeans who make up the first group. Secondly, these churches are much younger than those in the first category. Whilst many of the older Black majority Pentecostal churches are now approaching or have passed the half century mark in terms of longevity, some of the newer neo-Pentecostal churches are between ten and twenty years old. Amongst the best-known exponents of these churches in the second category are Kingsway International Christian Centre,[34] Glory House[35] and Ruach.[36]

Historically, Black churches of whatever denomination or theological perspective have suffered from two particular flaws. The first is a tendency to spiritualize the central tenets of the Christian gospel, which has led as a corollary to a disengagement from socio-political matters as they affected Black people in Britain.[37] The excellent work of such projects as 'Black Boys Can' of the Church of God of Prophecy or 'Bringing Hope', the ecumenical initiative against gun crime and violence, has tempered this age-old tendency.

The second flaw is a tendency towards factionalism, separation and mutual mistrust, which has been challenged by the pioneering work of such individuals as Philip Mohabir, Joel Edwards, Ron Nathan and Mark Sturge of the Evangelical Alliance.[38] More recently, Joe Aldred, who is chair of the Council for Black-Led Churches and also Minority Ethnic Christian officer for Churches Together in Britain and Ireland,[39] has also done a great deal to overturn the suspicions of the past.

The Black ecclesiologies that can be identified within these first two typologies can trace their roots to the birth of the Pentecostal movement in Azusa Street, Los Angeles in 1906. It is believed by many that the manifest outworking of the Holy Spirit gave rise to a new form of church, which in its earliest years attempted to move beyond the racialized division in ecclesial bodies within the Body of Christ that has so far been a feature of the discourse in this chapter.[40] To my mind, one of the major tragic occurrences in the ongoing development of Black ecclesiologies from within this Pentecostal typology has been the extent to which they have lost the implicit and explicit radicalism of their birth at the dawn of the last century in favour of an abstracted, contextless spiritualized existence. This existence is one that runs counter not only to the substantive historical experience of Diasporan Black people, but also to the general liberative and materialist transformative theological thrust of all Black ecclesiologies in their original incarnation.

White majority churches and Black people in Britain

The third broad typology is that of Black churches in White majority historic churches in Britain, such as the Roman Catholic Church, the Church of England (Anglican), and the Methodist, Baptist and United Reformed Churches.

For many years, it has been assumed that Black members of these White majority churches were not part of a Black church tradition. The Black experience was seen to reside within Black majority Pentecostalism.[41]

The majority of the Black members in White majority historic churches in Britain can trace their roots to Africa and the Caribbean. The majority of these church adherents attend Black majority churches in predominantly inner city urban contexts.[42] These churches operate, in effect, as Black enclaves within the overall White majority structure and membership of the church. Among the most significant churches in this category are

Walworth Road Methodist Church (in South London) and Holy Trinity Birchfield Church of England (Birmingham).

The development of Black majority churches within these White majority historic bodies has emerged due to demographic changes in inner city areas within the larger cities and towns in Britain, and not through a self-conscious separation along the lines of 'race', as has been the case in the recent United States. Research by Peter Brierley has shown that the majority of Black Christians in Britain belong to White majority historic churches (by a factor of almost 2 to 1).[43]

The place and role of Black churches in predominantly White majority historic denominations remain deeply contentious issues. David Isiorho, a Black Anglican priest in Britain has written on the dominant images of 'Whiteness' and 'Englishness' (the latter often taken as a synonym for the former) in the Church of England, which fails to acknowledge the plural and multi-ethnic nature of the church.[44]

Writing about the seemingly inextricable link between the overarching construct of 'Englishness' and 'Whiteness' and that of the Church of England, Isiorho argues that these twin seminal building blocks in the self-understanding of the established churches combine to exclude Black people.[45] This combination of Whiteness being associated with Englishness (and the established church being the 'Church of England') means that it becomes structurally and symbolically difficult for Black people to feel a representative part of this White dominated edifice.

Defining characteristics of Black ecclesiologies

Adherence to the Bible

One of the important characteristics of Black ecclesiologies is the centrality of the Bible. This is not to suggest that the Bible is not central to other formulations of the Christian church, but it is a generalized truth that every branch of the Black church across the world hold scripture to be the supreme rule of faith and central to their understanding of God's revelation in Christ.

Despite their radical roots in countering racism and Black dehumanization, many Black ecclesiologies, whether in the United States, the Caribbean or Britain, have remained wedded to a form of nineteenth-century White Evangelicalism. A number of Black scholars have demonstrated the extent to which Christianity as a global phenomenon has drunk deeply from the well of Eurocentric philosophical thought at the expense of African or other overarching forms of epistemology.[46]

Black ecclesiologies world-wide largely adhere to a form of pre-modern White European Evangelicalism that is a product of a post-Reformation biblicism. Black people on both sides of the Atlantic may have learnt how to utilize a 'hermeneutic of suspicion' of White supremacist overlays on the gospel, in terms of the existential experiences arising from slavery, but they have been reluctant to challenge the evangelical basis of faith they received from the Great Awakening in the eighteenth century.

For most part, the heart of Black ecclesiologies are built upon quasi-literalist readings of scripture, in which Jesus and salvation are conceived solely in terms of adherence to Jesus Christ as the only means of salvation. One of the important defining qualities of Black ecclesiologies is the christocentric nature of their doctrine and worship. Within parts of Black Pentecostalism in Britain, for example, there remains a powerful 'Oneness Tradition' which does not recognize the allegedly speculative trinitarian formulation of the historic church.[47]

In terms of christology, Black churches on both sides of the Atlantic have adhered to an orthodox Johannine christology. Through a-historical and de-contextualized readings of John 14.6, Jesus becomes the only means by which people can be saved. The extent to which the Black church has traditionally been loath to engage in interfaith dialogue has been largely influenced by the strictures of this normative, classical Christianity, in which the benefits of salvation are confined to those who acknowledge Christ's atoning work on the cross.

In the literature of Black theology a number of writers have located within the suffering of Jesus a sense of divine solidarity with their own historical and contemporary experiences of unjustified and unmerited suffering. Scholars such as Douglas,[48] Cone[49] and Terrell,[50] to name but a few, have all explored the theological significance for Black people of Jesus' suffering on the cross. Writing on this theme, Terrell states,

> Yet the tendency among Black people has been to identify wholly with the suffering of Jesus because the story made available to them – Jesus' story – tells of his profound affinity with their plight. Like the martyrs, they are committed to him because his story is their story. Jesus' death by crucifixion is a prototype of African Americans' death by *circumscription*.[51]

This radical identification with the undeserved suffering of an innocent individual has exerted a powerful hold on the imagination of many Black people and other marginalized and oppressed groups in the world.[52] The christocentrism of Black ecclesiologies in affirming Jesus (as opposed to God) as the central point of departure in its ecclesial method have led to an over-reliance on notions of orthodoxy in their doctrinal and missiological practices. In placing less emphasis upon the Trinity, the 'Jesus-ology' of Black ecclesiologies has seen many Black churches fall into the unwitting trap of emphasizing a single-trajectory notion of faith (in Jesus only), which loses the inter-penetrative reflections of perichoresis that have been one of the hallmarks of Christian trinitarian theology.[53]

In claiming a 'high christology' of Jesus in light of the seeming exclusivism of John 14.6, Black ecclesiological development in the twentieth and twenty-first centuries has become trapped in the cul-de-sac of doctrinal adherence and dogmatic certitude. One of the problems of this adherence to neo-orthodoxy is that it runs contrary to the historic development of Black ecclesiologies, in that the majority of Black churches came into existence not to replicate the arcane sterility and anti-modernist resistance of many forms of White Evangelicalism,[54] but rather as an oppositional response to the corruptions of White Christian hegemony and its tendencies towards spiritualized abstraction in the face of Black oppression.

The roots of the Black church lie in a radical appropriation of the gospel in order that those who are the 'least of these' (Mt 25.31–46) might live and have that life in all its fullness (Jn 10.10). That work was praxis orientated and not mindful of either doctrinal purity or biblical literalism.[55]

What is instructive about the continued rise of Black churches on both sides of the Atlantic is the fact that it is not culturally or ethnically specific.[56] With reference to fundamentalist approaches to reading the Bible, Wimbush writes,

The intentional attempt to embrace Christian traditions, specifically the attempt to interpret the Bible, without respect for the historical experiences of persons of African descent, radically demarcates this reading and this period from all others [that have preceded it].[57]

The Black church, in terms of strict adherence to classical Christian doctrines, aided and abetted by a literalist reading of the Bible, has become (at worst) a thinly coloured coating of the White Christianity to which it was once in opposition.

Black worship

The invocation of the Spirit within Black worship, fused with a decorative and expansive display of 'theatricality', has been one of the defining hallmarks of Black religiosity, in which ritualized drama has played a central part. Robert Beckford offers a carefully constructed Black British Pentecostal perspective on this creative dynamic, in which informal drama is an important means of expressing the liberative impulse of Black life.[58] Dale P. Andrews notes the inherent dynamism of Black religiosity, in which the dramatic encounter with the 'otherness of God' is often a common feature, particularly in the area of worship and preaching.[59]

Anthony Pinn's highly influential book, *Terror and Triumph*, highlights the evocative power of ritual and decorative display in Black religious and liturgical life.[60] Pinn contends that the elaborate, decorative display that is often exemplified in Black religiosity (many Black Christians still remain wedded to reserving their 'best clothes' for Sunday worship) was a conscious attempt to create an embodied text on which to construct their own quest for 'complex subjectivity'.[61] This phenomenon is not the sole preserve of Black peoples, of course; it can be argued that *all* immigrant communities have used their embodied text as a means of achieving 'complex subjectivity'. In the case of Black people, however, so often degraded, dehumanized and destroyed by White power and oppression, religiosity became the site for decorative dress and complex human emotions and expression, in order to assert the humanity and subjectivity of the Black self.

One of the strengths of Black ecclesiologies is their ability to embody another world within their liturgical practices. One of their common features is the use of a dialectical method for fusing personal experience within their pneumatological perspectives on divine agency in order to transcend the limitations placed upon the Black self. In short, Black people are able to play with reality by means of an immanentist realization of the Holy Spirit in worship in order to remake their social realities.

Within the broader literature of Black theology this transformative inner quality of Black existential experience has been the 'locomotive fuel' that has inspired the Black self to transcend the limitations placed upon it by White hegemony. For example, Robert Beckford has spoken of the liberative facets of Black spirituality in his analysis of Black British Pentecostalism.[62]

The claims to direct access to God by means of divine knowledge through pneumatological experience enable individuals and communities to transcend the traditional, patrician-inspired hierarchical divide as to the possession of knowledge and truth.[63] Black ecclesiological spaces have always embodied a distinctive counter-cultural element in which Black people have been enabled to counter the worst excesses of White hegemony through their pneumatologically inspired genius for creating 'safe spaces' – spaces in which Black life and cultural expression have been normalized and legitimated.

Black ecclesiologies and preaching

Within many models of Black ecclesiology, the art of preaching – homiletics – remains a hugely significant arena in both the definition of the church and its nature and intent. The struggles of Black peoples across the world have required the preacher to occupy the multifarious roles of social commentator, cultural critic, prophet, teacher and exhorter. Black preaching within Black churches remains a highly distinctive and carefully crafted theological art form.[64]

The preacher within Black ecclesial settings is a mediator who brings forth the established presence of God as revealed in the 'Word' and attested through tradition, tempered by reason and affirmed by experience. Given the relatively non-sacramental nature of a good deal of Black ecclesiology within the African Diaspora (often a product of their roots in the Evangelical Revival of the eighteenth and nineteenth centuries), Black preaching remains the central defining feature and liturgical heart of Black worship. The preacher is asked to be a prophetic chronicler of the times and to offer an impassioned word that speaks to the often problematic and troubled nature of Black existence.

For many Black preachers, the biblical text is the point of departure for a hermeneutical exploration of the relevance of Holy Scripture to the existential realities of the largely Black congregation. The encounter that exists in Black worship is an engagement between the text and the context. The text, that is scripture, is not a fixed entity even within largely neo-conservative settings. The preacher is a negotiator between that which stands in and of itself and that which is yet to be. The former is the 'Word of God', the latter is the word that speaks to the moment. This is a movement from the established to the newly becoming. The driving force is not some vague notion of inspiration, but the mediated presence that lies within the Godhead, namely the Holy Spirit. The preacher is attempting to bring to life all the exhaustive riches and resources that have inspired and challenged countless earlier generations.[65]

Within Black liturgical traditions, particularly within African American religious culture, many scholars have spoken of the dynamic interchange that exists between the preacher, the congregation and the Holy Spirit. The Spirit of God that mediates between the different parties enables both the preacher and the congregation to respond to the creative moment and space that exist within the sanctuary at that precise time in history.[66]

The 'Call and Response' tradition of African American worship is a time-honoured means by which the congregation can engage and interchange with the preacher in order that the latter may be enabled to go beyond the written text of the prepared sermon.[67] Essentially, that which has been prepared is energized and given new meaning and expression by means of the performance of preaching. The congregation becomes an essential ingredient in the performative act of bringing new wisdom and knowledge to life.[68]

Dale Andrews argues that Black preaching and the use of scripture has always been a multilayered engagement between preacher, congregation, the Bible and Holy Spirit.[69]

Whilst Black preaching comes in many forms and incorporates a wide variety of styles,[70] the expectations placed on Black preachers by their congregations are always high. Preachers are expected to be socially engaged, linking the story of the negated and troubled

Black self with the ongoing narrative of redemption and salvation that comes from God's very own self.[71]

The need to bring new meaning and fresh insights from the Bible, whilst remaining connected to the traditions that have informed the collective whole that is 'Holy Scripture', has always been the high challenge presented to Black preachers. It is the challenge to 'bring a fresh' word for the immediate context without doing violence to the text from which one's inspiration is drawn.[72]

Black preaching within the context of Black ecclesiologies harnesses the ongoing dynamic that is Black worship. One of the challenges, therefore, for Black homiletics is the need to engage with the challenge of postmodernity. How can Black preaching within Black churches meet the challenges of social and cultural diversity and plural epistemologies? I believe that the best of Black preaching has always responded to the prevailing Zeitgeist by means of a dialectical spirituality of improvisation. The process of moving between the seeming fixity of the 'Word of God' and the provisionality of the social and cultural milieu in which the preacher is located has always demanded that Black preachers adopt a spirit of improvisation in their homiletics. Identifying Black preaching as an improvisational art is to understand that this form of heuristic provides a helpful framework for assisting us to move beyond the limited binary of evangelical and liberal arguments around biblical authority. Black ecclesiologies at their historic best have always been the incubators for the budding shoots of liberation and social transformation that has transformed and continues to transform Black lives across a world of globalized White hegemony.

The importance of prayer

If Black worship and preaching are distinctive hallmarks of Black ecclesiology, then the aforementioned factors are informed and transformed by the dynamic theological reality of prayer. Prayer remains an essential hallmark of Black Christian spirituality. For generations, Black Christians have appropriated a literal understanding of God intervening in the life affairs of God's people – within Black theological thought this means Black people – in order to rescue them from their existential crises.[73]

The contemporary survival of Black ecclesiologies in Britain owes much to the continued fortitude and perseverance of older Black, Caribbean peoples, many of whom have sustained their churches in difficult inner city contexts for over forty years. For many of these individuals, their formative socialization into the Christian faith was achieved during their time in the Caribbean.

The Caribbean of the 1950s and 60s was passing through a colonial, pre-independence epoch of extreme poverty and struggle.[74] For the greater majority of peoples living in the diverse islands of the Caribbean, amelioration of the concrete realities of poverty and marginalization emanated from the Black church. This identification with the Christian faith as a means of liberating praxis has a historic dimension. The literal appropriation of prayer as a means of overcoming contextual struggles find echoes in the actions and beliefs of slaves on the Caribbean islands.

Kortright Davis asserts that slaves never accepted a transcendent construct of God that was remote and above the sufferings of Black people. Conversely, the slaves held on to a concept of an immanent God that was alongside them in their struggles.[75] Davis continues by reminding us that African people believe strongly in the immediacy of supernatural beings that exist alongside ordinary human beings in their common existence.[76]

The importance of prayer as a concrete resource for surmounting struggle and achieving liberation resonates very firmly within the Diasporan Black experience. From the time of slavery through to the present day the facility of prayer has given substance and cohesion to the liberation impulse within the exilic experience of Diasporan Africans. For Black women, prayer has been the means of instilling hope in their children.[77]

Ongoing challenges for the future

The historic development of Black ecclesiologies over the past four centuries has not been without its troubles. Gayraud Wilmore has asserted that the radicalism of the early Black church movement in the United States was ceded to the strictures of conventional, normative, pseudo-White social mores and theological and ecclesial respectability.[78]

Within the British context there are issues pertaining to the ongoing struggles for familial cohesion and a sense of the loss of cultural and historical memory. Contemporary post-colonial Britain is a context where lives are governed by the all-pervasive influence of postmodernism. The old assumptions surrounding family life and collective identities are fast disappearing. In this particular epoch the realities of social and geographical mobility are constantly challenging the traditional notions of collective and communitarian cohesion. These social and cultural factors have been the bedrock on which Black ecclesiologies have gained their traditional strength, and from which the majority of their adherents have been drawn.

The challenge facing Black churches in their historic task of offering safe ecclesial spaces for affecting the liberative impulse for Black existential freedom can be seen in my own formative experiences. I was born into a Black Caribbean Christian family, and although my family attended a White majority church for a good deal of my formative years, the values of Black Christian traditions, learnt from the Black church of mother's childhood in Jamaica, were nevertheless highly visible in my Christian nurture and socialization.

Prayer remained an important component in my Christian nurture and formation. I still retain distinct memories of being taught the traditional prayer of 'Gentle Jesus' at my mother's knee at a very young age.[79] An informal survey amongst a group of forty-something Black Christians a few months ago revealed that this prayer seems to represent some form of signifier in connoting aspects of an African Caribbean religio-cultural heritage. Learning this prayer was an important moment in my own sense of identity in religio-cultural terms.

In God, who is defined in psychological terms as the 'Ultimate Reality'[80] Black people have found through the facility of prayer a constant and accessible mediator for their troubles and hardships.[81] In this particular understanding of prayer, God is identified in immanent terms. God, through the life, death and resurrection of Jesus, and by and through the power of the Holy Spirit, is manifested in God's own creation, mediating alongside humankind, who are created in the image of God.

Reference to the importance of a literal, immanentist approach to prayer has been highlighted in a previous publication.[82] For example, my own mother, in particular, inculcated the importance of praying to God at all times. Accompanying this approach to prayer was the literal, almost eager expectation that God would answer one's petition. There was never any doubt within my mother's concept of God that this God was in the business of assisting and supporting the presence of God's own people. The faithful would be upheld and no forces of evil, such as racism, would overpower them. In this respect, the words of Romans 8.37–39 ring true:

In everything we have won more than a victory because of Christ who loves us. I
am sure that nothing can separate us from God's love – not life or death, not angels
or spirits, not the present or the future, and not powers above or powers below.
Nothing in all creation can separate us from God's love for us in Christ Jesus our
Lord![83]

One of the central challenges facing Black ecclesiologies as we walk hesitantly into the
twenty-first century is the ability to continue to meet the existential concerns of Black
people, whether in Kingston, Jamaica, New York or London, Amsterdam or Paris. The challenge that faces Black ecclesiologies is the need to harness the historic resources that have
informed and governed her existence to date, juxtaposed with the possibility of discerning
new ways of being and doing.

In order to address the challenge of postmodernism the Black church, inspired by an
improvisatory approach to Black theology, will gain the confidence to move beyond the
strictures of a stultifying form of conformity into which so many of us have been herded. In a
previous work I have questioned the conformist strains of many Black churches, influenced
by a strict 'holiness' code and governed by the twin concerns of 'shame' and 'racism'.[84]
Scholars such as Kelly Brown Douglas,[85] Robert Beckford,[86] Jacquelyn Grant[87] and, indeed,
my own writings in this field,[88] have all explored in our many differing ways the challenges
faced by the Black church to move beyond the seemingly endemic forms of conservative
thinking and practice that have limited the scope of its prophetic agency.

The challenge that faces Black ecclesiologies is one of attempting to connect with the
postmodern realities that presently face Black people and to construct new ways of engaging
in the historic mission of not only saving individual souls but also challenging racism and
transforming the world so that it better reflects the qualities and attributes of the Kingdom
of God.

In this respect, Black ecclesiologies need to re-learn the strident and polemical forms of
radical Christian praxis that galvanized Diasporan African peoples in previous epochs. This
form of a newly imagined paradigm of the Black church is one that will continue to work
within the historic tradition that has sustained countless generations of Black people of the
African Diaspora, and younger generations born and socialized in this country. The challenge is to model examples of good praxis that inspire prayerful dedication and discipleship,
so that Black children and young people can begin to reflect some of the factors, both immanent and transcendent, that have enabled people of African descent to survive the many
travails of the past. Janice Hale says something to this effect when reflecting upon the
importance of re-telling stories of experience, by word and example. She writes,

These stories transmit the message to Black children that there is a great deal of
quicksand and the many land mines on the road to becoming a Black achiever . . .
They also transmit the message that it is possible to overcome these obstacles.[89]

If this Black ecclesiological praxis can be developed and shared between Black people of
differing generations, then the substantive claims of the Christian faith will come alive for
succeeding generations and not be perceived as fatuous and inane religious discourse.

Black ecclesiologies of the twenty-first century must develop a model of Christian
mission that inspires and transforms. This cannot be the kind of theological moribund
framework that seeks to offer a simplistic and spiritualized placebo for the contemporary and

more historic ills that have plagued Black people for the past half millennia. This cannot be the type of Christian practice that seeks refuge in certain forms of abstractions that describe a personal piety, which retreats from the world rather than seeking to transform it.

The kind of Black ecclesiological Christian praxis of which I speak, is the facility that connects with the very heart of God. It is a form of praxis that demands reflective action. The kind of action that is an integral component of faith, whose practical demonstrable consequences, are described in James Chapter 2: verses 14–26. The demand for praxis (action and reflection) finds expression in the salient words of Paulo Freire who opined that 'Action without reflection is mere activism, and reflection without action is pure verbalism'.[90]

The search for and location of appropriate strategies for surviving and thriving within a racially oppressive, seemingly secular, post Christian society cannot be anchored upon solely rationalistic, cognitive processes, however. Whilst the search for wholeness and holistic living, has been influenced by important discoveries within developmental psychology, emancipatory theologies and transformative education, there remains, however, the crucial import of the transcendent. The numinous power of God! The aforementioned approaches to transformative Christian praxis should include the latter, but there can be a tendency to forget that our journey of faith is essentially a God-centred pilgrimage that is governed by grace and redemption. There must be the realization that God is beyond the finite limits of our cognition. Yet that same God enters into our struggles and travails, in order that we might experience life in all its fullness.

At their very worst, poorly conceived models of Christian praxis emerging from predominantly contemporary neo-Pentecostal examples of Black ecclesiologies simply lead to the false consciousness of learned piety, enforced religiosity and vacuous rhetoric. Many of the newer Pentecostal churches in the United States, the United Kingdom, the Caribbean and Africa can be accused of glorying in the rhetoric of affiliative faith[91] – a 'hand me down', imitative faith that is not grounded in the contextual realties of the 'here and now'.

In conclusion, Black ecclesiologies have emerged from dispiriting and dehumanizing contexts in the so-called New World to now occupy significant cultural and social spaces within the globalized economy of many Western nations. The growth and development from the submerged 'underground railway' and concealed gatherings to the 'mega-church' phenomenon of postmodernity is testament to the tenacity and perseverance of Black people across the world. Yet the challenge that now confronts Black churches is the need to constantly re-engage with the existential realities of the bulk of Black peoples across the world, whose life experiences and realities remain stunted and blighted by the twin terrors of racism and economic poverty. Black churches are challenged with locating once again, as they have in former epochs, their God-inspired genius for developing faith-based frameworks that provide the liberative praxis that can offer life in all its fullness to those who are often deemed the least of these in a world of extravagance and plenty.

Notes

1 My initial foray into academic theology came via the persuasive powers of Robert Beckford, whom I met for the first time in the early 1990s when I undertook a course in Black Christian studies in Birmingham. It was from Beckford that I gained the inspiration to undertake my doctorate at the University of Birmingham. It was also courtesy of Robert Beckford that I was introduced to the searing inconoclastic work of James Cone. From my reading of James Cone's work I gained the confidence to articulate my hitherto subversive version of Christianity, which did not reflect the

broader strains of evangelicalism into which I had been born and socialized. Reading James Cone enabled me to move out from the stultifying constraints of conservative Christianity to embrace my Blackness as not only a physical identifier but, of equal import, a theological point of departure for interpreting Christianity. Finally, Grant Shockley, perhaps the least well known of the three, offered me a flexible and inter-disciplinary means of undertaking Black theological scholarly work by means of transformative education and pedagogy. Further details on the work of the three important scholars can be found in the writings of Robert Beckford: *Jesus Is Dread*, London: Darton, Longman and Todd, 1998; *Dread and Pentecostal*, London: SPCK, 2000; *God of the Rahtid*, London: Darton, Longman and Todd, 2001; *God and the Gangs*, London: Darton, Longman and Todd, 2004; and *Jesus Dub: Theology, Music and Social Change*, London: Routledge, 2006. See James H. Cone, *God of the Oppressed*, San Francisco: Harper, 1975; and idem, *A Black Theology of Liberation*; New York: Orbis. 1986; Charles R. Foster and Fred Smith, *Black Religious Experience: Conversations on Double Consciousness and the work of Grant Shockley*, Nashville: Abingdon, 2003.

2 I am a Black Liberation theologian and educator. It is important that the reader is aware of this fact for it informs my highly tendentious and politicized theological analysis of Black ecclesiologies. I make no pretence to normativity in my account. Clearly, given the nature of this work and the stature of the publication in which it is located, I have made assiduous attempts to ensure the veracity and the legitimacy of my account. I have sought to locate my work within the best traditions of Black Atlantic religious scholarship and intellectual thought. I hope that I have not 'taken liberties' with the truth nor sought to obfuscate or disguise my true intent and underlying agenda, which is one of locating a liberationist approach to understanding the identity and intent of Black ecclesiologies. I am writing on the firm premise that there are a number of distinctive cultural and theological markers for Black churches in the African Diaspora.

3 See Dwight N. Hopkins, *Down, Up and Over: Slave Religion and Black Theology*, Minneapolis: Fortress, 2000, pp. 11–36.

4 See Emmanuel C. Eze, *Race and the Enlightenment*, Cambridge, MA, and Oxford: Blackwell, 1997.

5 See Dwight N. Hopkins, *Being Human: Race, Culture and Religion*, Minneapolis: Fortress, 2005, pp. 113–60.

6 See Anthony B. Pinn, *Terror and Triumph: The Nature of Black Religion*, Minneapolis: Fortress, 2003, pp. 1–5.

7 Pinn, *Terror and Triumph*, pp. 82–107.

8 Ibid.

9 John Wilkinson, James H. Evans Jr and Renate Wilkinson, *Inheritors Together: black people in the Church of England*, London: Race, Pluralism and Community Group, 1985, p. 10.

10 Henry H. Mitchell, *Black Church Beginnings: The Long-Hidden Realities of the First Years*, Grand Rapids, MI: Eerdmans, 2004, pp. 24–45.

11 See Anne H. Pinn and Anthony B. Pinn, *Fortress Introduction to Black Church History*, Minneapolis: Fortress, 2002, pp. 6–8.

12 Mitchell, *Black Church Beginnings*, pp. 8–45.

13 Noel L. Erskine, *Decolonizing Theology: A Caribbean Perspective*, Maryknoll, NY: Orbis, 1983, pp. 41–5.

14 Pinn and Pinn, *Fortress Introduction*, pp. 32–43.

15 Pinn, *Terror and Triumph*, pp. 90–3.

16 Pinn *Terror and Triumph*, p. 93.

17 Harold Dean Trulear, 'African American Religious Education', in Barbara Wilkerson (ed.), *Multicultural Religious Education*, Birmingham, Alabama: Religious Education Press, 1997. p. 162.

18 Pinn, *Terror and Triumph*, pp. 52–77.

19 Foster and Smith, *Black Religious Experience*, pp. 64–5.

20 See Dwight N. Hopkins, *Introducing Black Theology of Liberation*, Maryknoll, NY: Orbis, 1999, pp. 43–4. See also C. Eric Lincoln and Lawrence H. Mamiya, *The Black Church in the African American Experience*, Durham and London: Duke University Press, 1990; Peter J. Paris, *The Social Teaching of the Black Churches*, Minneapolis: Fortress, 1985; and Anne H. Pinn and Anthony B. Pinn, *Black Church History*, Minneapolis: Fortress, 2002.

21 See Beckford, *Dread and Pentecostal*; and also Nicole Rodriguez Toulis, *Believing Identity*, Oxford and New York: Berg, 1997.

22 See James H. Harris, *Pastoral Theology: A Black-Church Perspective*, Minneapolis: Fortress, 1991.

See also Dale P. Andrews, *Practical Theology for Black Churches: Bridging Black Theology and African American Folk Religion*, Louisville: John Knox Press, 2002.

23 See Pinn and Pinn, *Black Church History*, 2002.

24 For further details see Joe Aldred, *Respect: understanding Caribbean British Christianity*, Peterborough: Epworth Press, 2005.

25 For further information see John L. Wilkinson, *Church in Black and White: The Black Christian Tradition in 'Mainstream' Churches in England: A White Response and Testimony*, Edinburgh: St. Andrews Press, 1993.

26 See Lincoln and Mamiya, *African American Experience*; and Paris, *Social Teaching*. See also Pinn and Pinn, *Black Church History* for a brief selection of an extensive literature in this area of Black theological work.

27 See Wilkinson, *Church in Black and White*.

28 See also Aldred, *Respect*.

29 See Aldred, *Respect*; and Mark Sturge, *Look What The Lord Has Done!: An Exploration of Black Christian Faith in Britain*, London: Scripture Union, 2005.

30 See also Doreen McCalla, 'Black Churches and Voluntary Action: Their Social Engagement with the Wider Society', *Black Theology: An International Journal*, Vol. 3, No.2 (July 2004).

31 Arlington Trotman, 'Black, Black-Led or What?' in Joel Edwards (ed.), *'Let's Praise Him Again': An African Caribbean Perspective on Worship*, Eastbourne: Kingsway Publications, 1992, pp. 12–35.

32 Beckford, *Dread and Pentecostal*, pp. 176–82.

33 See Sturge, *Look What The Lord Has Done!*, pp. 123–5; also Beckford, *Jesus Is Dread*, pp. 103–7.

34 For further details see *Black Majority Churches UK Directory*, London: African Caribbean Evangelical Alliance and Churches Together in Britain and Ireland, 2003, p. 67.

35 *UK Directory*, p. 59.

36 *UK Directory*, p. 112.

37 See Beckford, *Dread and Pentecostal*, pp .178–82.

38 See *Focus: The African Caribbean Evangelical Alliance Magazine*, 21st Anniversary Edition (May-August, 2005), 8–9.

39 For more information see the 'Minority Ethnic Christian Affairs' page of Churches Together in Britain and Ireland – www.ctbi.org.uk

40 See Beckford, *Dread and Pentecostal*, pp. 119–20.

41 See Beckford, *Jesus is Dread*, pp. 42–58. See also Roswith I.H. Gerloff, 'A plea for British black theologies: the black church movement in Britain', 2 vols, unpublished PhD thesis, University of Birmingham, 1991.

42 See M. Byron, *Post War Caribbean Migration to Britain: The Unfinished Cycle*, Aldershot: Averbury, 1994. See also R.B. Davidson, *West Indian Migrants*, London: Oxford University Press. 1962; and R. Glass (assisted by Harold Pollins), *Newcomers: The West Indians in London*, London: George Allen and Unwin, 1960, for a historical analysis for the presence of disproportionate numbers of Black people living in inner urban conurbations in Britain.

43 Peter Brierley, *The Tide Is Running Out: What The English Church Attendance Survey Reveals*, London: Christian Research, 2000, p. 136.

44 David Isiorho, 'Black theology in urban shadow: combating racism in the Church of England', *Black Theology: An International Journal*, Vol.1, No.1 (November 2002), 29–48.

45 David Isiorho, 'Black theology in urban shadow', 47.

46 See Robert E. Hood, *Must God Remain Greek?: Afro-Cultures and God-Talk*, Minneapolis: Fortress, 1990; and also Gay L. Byron, *Symbolic Blackness and Ethnic Difference in Early Christian Literature*, New York: Routledge, 2002.

47 See Sturge, *Look What The Lord Has Done!*, pp. 134–5.

48 See Kelly Brown Douglas, *The Black Christ*, Maryknoll, NY: Orbis, 1993.

49 James H. Cone, *God of the Oppressed*, pp. 108–95.

50 JoAnne Marie Terrell, *Power in the Blood?: The Cross in the African American Experience*, Maryknoll, NY: Orbis, 1998.

51 Terrell, *Power in the Blood?*, p. 34. Terrell uses the term 'circumscription' to describe African American's connection with Jesus' death. This term refers to the ways in which African Americans believe that just as Jesus' death was bound up and synonymous with the socio-historic restrictions

of first-century colonization in Galilee, which meant that his suffering and death was inevitable, so too was that of African Americans in the context of a slave economy in the United States.

52 See Beckford, *Jesus is Dread*; and Riggins R. Earl Jr, *Dark Salutations*, Harrisburg, PA: Trinity Press International, 2001, pp. 1–16.

53 See Stanley J. Grenz, *Rediscovering The Triune God: The Trinity in Contemporary Theology*, Minneapolis: Fortress, 2004, pp. 16–32.

54 Gayraud S. Wilmore, *Black Religion and Black Radicalism*, Maryknoll, NY: Orbis, 1983, pp. 103–35.

55 Vincent L. Wimbush, *The Bible and African Americans: A Brief History*, Minneapolis: Fortress, 2003, pp. 63–7.

56 This essay has concentrated on the development of Black ecclesiologies in the Americas and Britain. The author approached the writing of this chapter in this way in order to foreground the liberationist intent and ideals within the formation of Black churches that arose from the epoch of slavery in the eighteenth and nineteenth centuries. There are, of course, developments in Black ecclesiologies that can be discerned in mainland Europe, in countries such as Holland, Germany, France and Sweden. Further information on this phenomenon can be found in Roswith I.H. Gerloff, 'The African Diaspora in the Caribbean and Europe: from Pre-emancipation to the Present Day', in Hugh McLeod (ed.), *The Cambridge History of Christianity Vol.9 World Christianities c. 1914–c. 2000*, Cambridge University Press, 2006, pp. 219–35.

57 Wimbush, *The Bible and African Americans*, p. 66.

58 Beckford, *Dread and Pentecostal*, pp. 176–82.

59 Andrews, *Practical Theology*, pp. 16–23.

60 See Pinn, *Terror and Triumph*.

61 Pinn, *Terror and Triumph*, pp. 139–73.

62 See Beckford, *Dread and Pentecostal*.

63 Beckford, *Dread and Pentecostal*, pp. 168–76.

64 Carol Tomlin, *Black Language Style In Sacred And Secular Contexts*, New York: Caribbean Diaspora Press, 1999, pp. 103–65.

65 See James H. Harris, *The Word Made Plain*, Minneapolis: Fortress, 2004, pp. 1–50.

66 See Henry H. Mitchell, *Black Belief*, New York: Harper and Row, 1975.

67 William A. Jones Jr, 'Confronting the System', in Gayraud Wilmore (ed.), *African American Religious Studies: An Interdisciplinary Anthology*, London: Duke University Press, 1989, pp. 429–57.

68 Grant Shockley, 'From Emancipation, to Transformation to Consummation', in Marlene Mayr (ed.), *Does The Church Really Want Religious Education?* Birmingham, AL: Religious Education Press, 1988, pp. 234–6.

69 See Andrews, *Practical Theology*.

70 See Joe Aldred (ed.), *Preaching with Power*, London: Cassell, 1998.

71 Ermal Kirby, 'Black preaching', *The Journal of the College of Preachers* (July 2001), 47–9.

72 Ibid., 48.

73 Harold A. Carter, *The Prayer Tradition of Black People*, Baltimore: Gateway Press, 1984, pp. 80–109.

74 See Eric Williams, *From Columbus to Castro: The History of the Caribbean–1492–1969*, London: Andre Deutsch, 1970; Ian Randle, *Caribbean Freedom: Society and Economy from Emancipation to the Present*, London: James Currey, 1993; Douglas Hall, *Free Jamaica: 1838–1865: An economic History*, Aylesbury: Ginn, 1981.

75 Kortright Davis, *Emancipation Still Comin'*, Maryknoll, NY: Orbis, 1990, p. 59.

76 Davis, *Emancipation Still Comin'*, p. 59.

77 Carter, *Prayer Tradition*, pp. 80–109.

78 Wilmore, *Black Religion and Black Radicalism*, pp. 187–227.

79 This event and the memory of it remain hugely significant in my Christian development. From my mother I have learnt the importance of prayer and the need to see this as a literal resource in my Christian discipleship.

80 See James Fowler, *Stages of Faith*, San Francisco: HarperCollins, 1981.

81 See Earl, *Dark Salutations*, pp. 1–16.

82 Anthony G. Reddie, 'Jesus in the spaces in my life', in Ruth Harvey (ed.), *Wrestling and Resting: Exploring stories of spirituality from Britain and Ireland*, London: CTBI, 1999, pp. 72–82.

83 *The Contemporary English Version Bible*, Nashville, TN: Thomas Nelson Publishers, 1995, p. 1363.

84 See my post-sketch reflections to 'It Could Have Happened Like This?' in Anthony G. Reddie, *Acting in Solidarity: Reflections in Critical Christianity*, London: DLT, 2005, pp. 45–53.
85 See Kelly Brown Douglas, *Sexuality and the Black Church: A Womanist Perspective*, Maryknoll, NY: Orbis, 1999.
86 Beckford, *Jesus Is Dread*, pp. 61–78.
87 Jacquelyn Grant, 'Freeing the Captives: The Imperative of Womanist Theology', in Iva Carruthers, Frederick D. Haynes III and Jeremiah A. Wright Jr (eds), *Blow the Trumpet in Zion: Global Vision and Action for the 21st century Black Church*, Minneapolis: Fortress, 2005.
88 See my dramatic sketch entitled 'Black Voices', in Reddie, *Acting in Solidarity*, pp. 109–19.
89 Janice Hale, 'The Transmission of faith to young African American children', in Randall C. Bailey and Jacquelyn Grant (eds), *The Recovery of Black Presence*, Nashville, TN: Abingdon, 1995, p. 207.
90 Paulo Freire, *Pedagogy of the Oppressed*, New York: Herder and Herder, 1972, p. 68.
91 The Consultative Group on Ministry among Children, *Unfinished Business: Children in the Churches*, London: CTBI Publications, 1995, p. 34. See also John Westerhoff III, *Will Our Children Have Faith?* New York: Seabury Press, 1976.

25

FEMINIST
ECCLESIOLOGY

Natalie K. Watson

Beyond patriarchal institutions: starting points for
feminist explorations in ecclesiology

In 1893, Matilda Joslyn Gage, the leader of the National Women's Suffrage Association, described the Christian church as the 'prime source of oppression for women'. In order to be liberated, so Gage believed, women must throw off both Christianity itself and all patriarchal legal codes shaped by it.

In 1971, on the occasion of being the first woman to be invited to preach the Sunday morning sermon in Harvard Memorial Church, Mary Daly, then still working as a Christian theologian, staged a symbolic exodus. She invited all present, women, men and children, to join her in leaving the church behind by symbolically walking out of the building. This symbolizes that the churches' identification with patriarchy can and does lead to women being disaffected with the church. Daly came to understand the church and all expressions of Christianity, and indeed all organized religion, as the prime means of patriarchy to generate, enforce and perpetuate the subordination of women. She speaks of 'sisterhood as the "cosmic antichurch"', the ultimate denial of all religion.[1]

For many women and feminist theologians the question is: why bother with ecclesiology? Or even more profoundly: why bother with the church? There are those (like Mary Daly and Daphne Hampson) who have written off the Christian church as an irredeemably patriarchal institution which can under no circumstances be the site of women's liberation. Yet, there are others (like Elisabeth Schüssler Fiorenza, Rosemary Radford Ruether, Letty Russell, Mary Grey and myself) who regard the church as too important to leave it to the devices and desires of hetero-patriarchy. To reject it as irredeemably patriarchal would mean to deny that women are church and have always been church.

Historical, denominational and methodological
considerations

Feminist theology is the critical, contextual, constructive and creative re-reading and re-writing of the Christian tradition which regards women – and their bodies, perspectives and experiences – as relevant to the agenda of Christian theologians and advocates them as subjects of theological discourses and as full citizens of the church. Until the second half of the twentieth century, women were largely excluded from the process of writing Christian theology in a formal, academic context in general and from developing ecclesiological

461

patterns of thought in particular. This may be the case because the study of ecclesiology is somehow even more closely connected with the male clerical power structures of the church than other parts of Christian theology. Yet these traditional ecclesiological texts claim to speak for the church as a whole and therefore claim to make statements about women's reality as part of the church. Women therefore claim and reclaim their part in these discourses as critical and resistant readers. In doing so, they refuse to assume the role of the generic, supposedly normative hetero-patriarchal male and claim their role as women readers of texts largely written by men. They must name their exclusion and identify how the texts and metaphors used traditionally to describe the church have shaped women's experiences of being church in a way that is oppressive and exclusive.

One of the main reasons for engaging in ecclesiological discourse is that the church as the community of women and men is an important transfer point of power between men and women. One of the key tasks of a feminist ecclesiology is to reclaim and subvert the institutional power-centres within the church: the reading of scripture and tradition, sacramental celebration and ministry. A feminist analysis of the language that shapes the space where such transactions of power take place is necessary to identify the gender-power interaction between human beings in an institution as central to the lives of human beings as the church. Feminist ecclesiology seeks to identify sexuality as a hitherto neglected dimension of ecclesiology and identifies this neglect as the reason why oppressive power structures could develop within the church.

Throughout the history of Christianity, women have experienced the church as a space of profound ambiguity. While in most, if not all, churches, women are in the majority among those who attend worship, they have been, and in some cases still are, excluded from major positions of leadership and have traditionally not been involved in the writing and shaping of the churches' theological reflection on their own nature and identity. At the same time, women have experienced and still experience the church as a space where they can create their own discourses of faith, sometimes alongside and sometimes in spite of male domination. Feminist ecclesiology is essentially about reclaiming the Christian church as a space where women's discourses of faith are possible and a conscious choice to claim and reclaim being church for women.

The task of feminist ecclesiology is a two-fold one: on the one hand it means a critical and constructive feminist critique of existing ecclesiologies and on the other the critical reflection on the praxis of the church as it is experienced by women which may lead to alternative structures and ritual practices.

While for most of Christian history women on the whole tacitly accepted their exclusion from ecclesiological discourse, a number of events during the second half of the twentieth century challenged women to claim for themselves participation and a voice in reframing not only the life of the churches but also the ecclesiological debate itself. Three events/movements must be named in particular: (1) the Second Vatican Council which invited a more open debate on all aspects of the life of the Roman Catholic Church; (2) the emergence of the Feminist Movement (and its Second Wave in particular); and (3) the development of the debate on the ordination of women in the Reformed traditions and the rejection of this debate in the Roman Catholic tradition. These three trigger events indicate that up to this day, the feminist debate about the nature of the church has primarily taken place in the context of the churches in the Christian West, while many Eastern Orthodox women regard feminism as an aspect of Western secular culture that has no relevance for women and the church in the Christian East.[2] For women in the Western Christian traditions of Roman Catholicism, the Reformed traditions and Anglicanism, each of these trigger events reflects the profound ambiguity which is not only characteristic of women's experience of church life but also of the history of the feminist ecclesiological debate itself.

The Second Vatican Council signified a major paradigm shift in the life of the Roman Catholic Church which expressed its intention for renewal and opening to the modern world and not least to Christians and churches outside the Roman Catholic tradition. Yet it must also be recognized that the Council remained, in the tradition from which it originated, an essentially clerical and therefore essentially male event. Not until later in the Council were women admitted even as auditors to the Council and the Council or the movement of opening and renewal which emerged from it left the situation of women in the Roman Catholic tradition largely unaltered.[3] The same church which proclaimed its openness to the modern world and to renewal from within the church was later able not only to refuse women's participation in the ordained ministry as such but to close and forbid the debate as such.

The Second Wave of the Feminist Movement invited women to become aware of their own oppression and exclusion within male-dominated discourses and institutions and to demand access to them.[4] Feminism as such, however, remained a secular movement which throughout its history has shown little to no interest in Christianity or any other religious discourse and has largely regarded the Christian churches as supporters of the historical oppression of women which needs to be overcome. Feminist theologians are aware that the ideas of feminist philosophy and social theory cannot be simply applied to Christianity and its institutions, but that they provide a framework for a critical reading and re-reading of the tradition which then enables us to find and uncover within the Christian tradition resources for the liberation of women and the transformation of religious discourse.

The emerging debate with regard to the ordination of women developed in most of the Reformed traditions in the course of the twentieth century. The first woman to be ordained to the ministry of word and sacrament was the Congregationalist Constance Coltman in 1917.[5] Most of the Reformed churches on the Continent of Europe admitted women to the ordained ministry during the 1960s and 1970s, while the first women in the Church of England were ordained to the diaconate in 1987 and to the priesthood in 1994. The Episcopalian Church in the USA witnessed the first irregular ordinations of women to the priesthood in 1974 and officially admitted women to the priesthood in 1976. The Roman Catholic Church and the Eastern Orthodox churches to this day regard women's admission to the priesthood as contrary to the Christian gospel itself and thus as an obstacle to Christian unity.[6] It is, however, important to bear in mind that feminists hold different positions about the ordination of women as a goal. A significant number of feminist theologians argue that a feminist ecclesiology must go much further than the mere request for the admission of some women to unchanged patriarchal structures and offices, while others object to clericalism – domination by the exclusive exercise of power by a small male clerical oligarchy – as an expression of patriarchy but accept and affirm the ordained ministry as part of the Christian tradition to which some women may be called. The ordination of women can then also become a way of subverting and transforming the church from within.

The concept of Women-Church

The first significant historical development with regard to feminist ecclesiology was the emergence of the Women-Church movement in the early 1980s. This signifies a paradigm shift from requesting admission to an unchanged patriarchal institution to the bold state-ment that 'women are church and have always been church'.[7] As such, women can and do claim their own right to full participation and citizenship in the *ekklesia* of women. The ecclesiological paradigm used by the feminist theologians in the 1980s was that of Women-Church, a loose network of small feminist liturgical communities and civil rights organiza-tions. Women-Church uses the model of base ecclesial communities which originated from Latin American liberation theology.[8] All over the United States and also in other parts of the world, small groups of women began to emerge who met to worship, to read scripture and to discuss their own experiences of the church.

Women-Church is focused on ritual (the creation of liturgies and acts of worship which reflect women's experiences), justice (a strong commitment to social justice) and the creation of an alternative hermeneutical space.

It is important that the Women-Church movement does not see itself as a schismatic movement. Within Women-Church there are a wide range of different attitudes to the existing institutional churches. Some women indeed no longer participate in the life of the mainstream institutional churches, while others see Women-Church as a space where they can experience the liberation of which they dream and for which they work in mainstream Christian churches. Women-Church is rooted in the American philosophical tradition of pragmatism and voluntarism. By participating in Women-Church, women take their being church into their own hands and shape and reshape their own experiences of worship and the struggle for liberation. Women-Church is part of a wider cluster of civil rights and voluntarist organizations within the North American churches, such as Call to Action.

More recently the WomenEucharist movement has emerged in which women meet to celebrate the Eucharist together. They reject that celebrating Holy Communion is a prerog-ative of the male clerical elite from which they or anyone else can be excluded.[9] In her seminal book *Women-Church*, Rosemary Radford Ruether spoke of the 'eucharistic famine' in the church. She describes the eucharist as 'the sacramental symbol that has been most radically alienated from the people and transformed into a clerical power tool'.[10] She argues for a re-appropriation of the sacraments to the people where they can once again become a place for embodied celebration and a source of mutual empowerment.

While the Women-Church and WomenEucharist movements have developed their feminist ecclesiology in the context of particular aspects of ecclesial institutional praxis, a feminist reflection on ecclesiology would be incomplete without taking into account three further ways into rethinking and reshaping ecclesiology from a feminist theological perspec-tive. These are a feminist critical re-reading of more traditional ecclesiological texts which involves a challenge to the kind of metaphorical theological language used in these texts and the development of a feminist narrative ecclesiology which reconsiders the church as the space where women, men and children tell and embody the story of God through worship and mission.

A feminist reading of ecclesiology: three key metaphors of ambiguity and alienation

Here I want to concentrate on three metaphors traditionally used to describe the church in theological discourse. These are: the church as feminine/bride of Christ, the church as servant, and the church as the body of Christ.

Janet Martin Soskice defines metaphor as a 'figure of speech whereby we speak about one thing in terms which are seen to be suggestive of another'.[11] We need to ask whether the theological language and ideas traditionally used by male theologians speak about the church in a way which is meaningful for women and describes the church as a liberating and life-giving reality for women and enhances the celebration of women's being church. This involves the search for counter-patriarchal and subversive readings of traditional ecclesiologies in order to reclaim the church as a space where women's discourses of faith can and do take place. In our feminist critical reading of the core metaphors of ecclesiological discourse, we make the assumption that these core metaphors are contingent and therefore changeable because they are influenced by particular cultural and social contexts in order to create and establish a hetero-patriarchal socio-symbolic order which is contrary to the gospel of liberation. A feminist reading of ecclesiology seeks to bring traditional ecclesiological concepts into creative dialogue with the ideas of feminist theologians as part of a creative and constructive re-reading of the Christian tradition which I understand to be at the heart of feminist theology.

The church as feminine/bride of Christ

In his letter to the Ephesians the Apostle Paul exhorts husbands to love their wives as Christ loved the church. Women in turn are asked to submit to their husbands as to the Lord. Subsequently, the church has often been portrayed as the feminine submissive bride submitting to Christ her husband. This metaphor, which may say something about the relationship between the human church and its divine creator and redeemer, has also frequently been used to justify, establish and foster hetero-patriarchal structures of oppression and exclusion both in the church and in the wider society. It has primarily been the latter image which throughout Christian history has dominated the experiences of most married women: the female is ordered to be humble and submissive to the male. This is modelled in the relationship between Christ and the church which theologians such as Louis Bouyer and Hans Urs von Balthasar describe as the fundamental structure of the universe which is ultimately beyond metaphor. This means that the hetero-patriarchal ordering of society, and of the church as the ideal society, is beyond question. Such a static ordering of society has been used to justify heterosexual marriage as the only acceptable form of sexual relationship between two people. Even those who by ecclesiastical law or choice are compelled to abstain from any committed relationship with another human being are defined in terms of the absence of heterosexual partnership or the substitution of a human partner through a disembodied spiritual one, be it the church for the celibate priest or Christ for women religious.

This is coupled with the idea of women's ritual impurity. Even though the church is portrayed as feminine, even at times as a woman, it is one of her most fundamental characteristics that she is not like other women. The church as feminine and bride of Christ does not have a woman's body. The male-defined and male-dominated church of hetero-patriarchy has throughout its history shown ample inability to cope with the reality of women's bodies within it. The bride of Christ does not menstruate and is not defiled by the blood shed in childbirth.

In recent Roman Catholic moral theology the image of the church as the bride of Christ has been used to establish the rhetoric of the supposed 'dignity' of women as long as they perform their childbearing function or fit into the patterns of either hetero-patriarchal marriage or the denial of their female sexuality. It has also been used as a means of silencing the debate about the ordination of women in the Roman Catholic Church by constructing a theological and ecclesiological framework which renders such a debate impossible.

Another variation of the church being portrayed as submissive and feminine is the concept of Mary as the supreme personification of the church, the ideal disciple and yet its mother. A long tradition of theologians in the Western tradition, beginning with Ambrose and Augustine, has seen Mary as the 'type of the church'. Both Mary and the church are seen as the 'new Eve'. Standing under the cross, Mary becomes not only the mother of Christ but also gives birth to his body, the church.

While Mary on the one hand represents the 'feminine aspect of the divine', she also represents an ideal which real women are unable to reach. On the one hand, Mary acts as an 'intercessor', as the one who is closer to her son, who will not reject her requests on behalf of human beings; on the other hand, she is also virgin and mother at the same time: female but non-sexual. As such, Marian symbolism can be and is abused as an instrument of male power over women, as a means of disciplining women through an unattainable ideal. Such a form of Marian ecclesiology allows Mary to be church but not women.

Some male theologians see the personification of the church in Mary as a counterbalance to a concept of church which is dominated by an emphasis on structures, hierarchies and institutions. These aims are similar to those pursued by feminist theologians working on the transformation of the church. Yet we have to ask whether an understanding of Marian symbolism which essentially serves to deny women's sexuality and support the existing male-dominated hierarchical structures can really be a means of transforming structures which would allow women full participation in the life of the church. This can be seen, for example, in the fact that such idealized Marian ecclesiology is used as an argument against women's admission to the ministerial priesthood. It is argued that Mary herself, the highest of all human beings and the supreme personification of the church, never demanded to participate in the hierarchy or to be ordained priest. One could for example think of her submission to her son at his first miracle recorded in John's Gospel, the wedding at Cana. So, the argument goes, if Mary was not granted admission to the priesthood, why should women? Thus the idea of Mary as the supreme personification of the church can only serve for women to take their place where patriarchal ecclesiology wants them to be, within a church with which they cannot identify on their own grounds.

The church as servant

Another metaphor of ambiguity and alienation used in traditional ecclesiological discourse is that of the church as the servant of the world. From a feminist point of view such a separa-tion between church and world does not make sense. Yet it is the idea of servanthood as such which must be reconsidered in the light of women's experience. Women have often found themselves called to subservience and service and have experienced their lives being regarded as of no value other than to exist for the sake of others, be it their husbands, their children or even the church.

The servant metaphor has been used to identify the life and ministry of the church with that of Christ: Christ was the one who gave his life for the salvation of the world and so should those who are church. We have to ask whether this can indeed be a useful role model for women. Women seeking help in cases of abuse and violence at the hands of their husbands are frequently told to identify with the suffering of Christ rather than to challenge the behaviour of their abusers and withdraw from situations of abuse. We therefore have to ask whether an understanding of the church as servant is not in danger of becoming a means of perpetuating, rather than challenging and subverting, structures of sin, injustice and abuse within the church and society.

One of the main representatives of servant ecclesiology is the twentieth-century German theologian Dietrich Bonhoeffer, who argued that the church could only be the church if it was for others. A feminist ecclesiology can only conceive of a church 'with others' and essentially a church 'of others'. The church is not a self-contained club which leaves the poor in their poverty and extends only charitable giving to them, but a community in which all are welcome as the people they are, where human beings are valued and celebrated in their diversity as being in the image of the divine. It is essentially a community of justice. Such justice is, however, not merely the more or less equal distribution of goods by those in power but the core value of the *ekklesia* of women and men where each body is celebrated as part of the body of Christ.

The church as the body of Christ

The third metaphor of ambiguity and alienation challenged by feminist ecclesiological discourse is that of the church as the body of Christ. Bodies, and women's bodies in particular, are central to feminist theological discourses. Feminist theology seeks to reclaim women's bodies from being constructed as impure and deficient by male hetero-patriarchal theologians. Yet the idea of the church as the body of Christ is not without problems for women. Even though the church is described as feminine, when it comes to using body imagery, it is a *male* body which becomes the site of salvation. This is an expression of the alienation which women often experience: they are required to deny their sexuality, their bodies, their humanity, their womanhood in order to be part of the church. Salvation is regarded as only possible through the body of a man. The church is only the body of Christ because she is also the mystical bride of Christ. Such a mixing of metaphors reflects the confusion and utter repulsion with regard to women's actual bodies which some forms of traditional ecclesiology express. It shows the dependence of the feminine church on its male head, Christ, a disembodied man. Such negative body theology can be and has become a means of alienating women from their own bodies and essentially from each other.

The use of metaphorical language in ecclesiological discourse cannot be separated from women's experience of the life of the church, for example in the liturgy. What does it mean for women that on the one hand they have, through the symbolic new birth of baptism, become part of the body of Christ, but are then on the other hand denied access to the eucharist (as is still the case in the Eastern Orthodox churches) after they themselves have given birth?

In order to reconsider the idea of the church as the body of Christ it has to be defined in a way which affirms and celebrates women's bodies as part of this corporate body, which understands the church as incomplete without the presence of women, and which celebrates their sacramental presence within it.

Towards a critical ecclesiology: transformative feminist readings

Our feminist critical analysis of ecclesiological discourses takes place in a space of fundamental ambiguity between identification with the church and the necessity of developing

alternative structures, between claiming that women are church and the demand to participate in defining what the church is. Traditional ecclesiological concepts still hold some
relevance for women because they are expressions of a church with which women identify at
least in part, even though they have not been participating in its process of self-reflection. A
feminist critical reading of ecclesiology is both *subversive* and *constructive*. Its purpose is not
to define the church in terms of its timeless essence or even to identify the theology of the
church of a particular author, but to overcome the notion of there being 'legitimate' ways of
doing ecclesiology by reclaiming the significance of women as authors, as reader and writers/
poets with authority, and to develop an ecclesiological *écriture feminine*.

Such a feminist reconstruction of traditional ecclesiological language can be seen in a re-
reading of the 'marks of the church', to be found in the ancient Creeds. Here the church is
defined as one, holy, catholic and apostolic.

The unity of the church is often expressed as the supreme desirable characteristic, yet in
women's experience it is also often used as an excuse not to hear the voices of women and as
permission to deny the gifts and vocations of women in the church, for example in the
debate on the ordination of women. Is this the unity which is meant or is even desirable in
the context of a feminist reconsideration of ecclesiology? Or are we talking about a different
kind of unity, a unity in diversity which is found in God's own being in relation, a unity
which celebrates the diverse expressions within the Christian tradition and the diverse
stories and lives which perform and manifest the story of God with the church and the
whole of creation?

The idea of the church as holy has often been used as a means to exclude women on the
grounds of their supposed impurity. Holy men, clerical or other, are those who stay away
from women as sources of defilement, and holy women are those who manage to deny or
reject their female sexuality. Yet we have to ask: whose holiness is the holiness of the
church? Is it that of a community which withdraws from the rest of the world and accountability to it and as a result creates its own sinful hetero-patriarchal structures of oppression?
Is it the holiness that withdraws from the world and therefore from its responsibility to challenge sinful structures of injustice? Or is it the holiness of God creative and incarnate, who
became a sexual human being and manifests God's own being in the lives of women and
men? God's holiness and that of the church manifests itself in living as God lives in the
world, in a commitment to those to whom God is committed, the poor and the oppressed
and the whole suffering creation.

Catholicity with regard to the church means universality: the church is the same wherever, whenever and by whomever it exists and manifests itself. The church knows no
geographical, racial or sexual boundaries and yet it is profoundly contextual: its particular
manifestations are deeply rooted in the local cultures in which they take place. Yet women's
experience of the church has often been one of boundaries, limitations or glass ceilings, of
being the Other rather than being fully affirmed in their belonging to the body of Christ.
Catholicity is sometimes understood as an eschatological reality which is used to verify
authority rather than affirm those who are church. From a feminist point of view, the catholicity of the church is its profound openness to all and its ability to break the boundaries of
race, class and sex. This is not merely a reality which will ultimately only be fulfilled in the
next world but something which has to become real in this world for the church to be the
church. By claiming that they are church and have always been church, women remind the
church of its catholicity, of the universality of its vocation.

The idea of apostolicity and the apostolic succession in particular has frequently been used as a means of rejecting and excluding women from parts of the life of the church. The apostolic succession of ministries is often falsely understood as a chain of the 'right' hands being laid on someone at their ordination. Extreme groups not only refuse to recognize the ministries of women bishops, priests and deacons, but sometimes also the ministry of those who, in their eyes, have defiled themselves by ordaining women and thereby have stepped outside the line of the church catholic and apostolic. Again we need to ask: whose apostolicity is it? True apostolicity is always the apostolicity of the whole church and not restricted to its ordained ministers. It is the life of the church as the continuation of the vision of the earliest Christian communities which feminist theologians such as Elisabeth Schüssler Fiorenza reconstructed as one of equality and justice for all, a vision in which women's ministries and lives are affirmed and celebrated.[12]

Development and application of the concept of Women-Church

While the early feminist theologians like Fiorenza, Ruether and Russell in the early to mid-1980s concentrated on the life and praxis of the church as their starting point, and on creating alternative worship spaces such as Women-Church, my own work has sought to reflect on re-reading ecclesiological texts and language as such. Fiorenza, Ruether and Russell are firmly rooted in the liberation theology paradigm and in their work develop the base ecclesial community model in a feminist context. In my own work, I have sought to show the limitations of the base community model for an ecclesiology that seeks to take account of sexual difference in a constructive way. Rather than commending one particular model of church as more liberating than others, I have sought to identify a range of criteria and aims which help to develop a vision of church which can indeed be a space of liberation and redemption for women.

Women-Church is a movement, a loose network of groups and organizations, most of which were in one way or another connected with the Roman Catholic tradition. The two theologians who have reflected most extensively on the life of Women-Church and developed the first models of feminist ecclesiological writing were Elisabeth Schüssler Fiorenza and Rosemary Radford Ruether.

Elisabeth Schüssler Fiorenza

Fiorenza is a Roman Catholic and a New Testament scholar and Early Church historian. Her ideas are based in her studies of the Jesus movement and the earliest Christian communities, where she finds a vision of radical equality and liberation. Although the reality of this vision being implemented, for example in equal access to ministry in the church, was later overtaken by the inevitable patriarchalization of the church in its Graeco-Roman context, remnants of this vision have survived and subverted the church in every generation. The life of the Jesus movement and the earliest Christian communities is therefore not an *archetype* which must be imitated but the *prototype* of a radically inclusive and radically egalitarian community which inspires the life and the renewal of new and different Christian communities throughout the ages. Women's experiences of struggling against patriarchal oppression must be recovered as a source of empowerment for women in the church today.

Fiorenza uses the term 'ekklesia of women'. *Ekklesia* for Fiorenza is a dynamic term which describes a community where radical democracy is practised and where women participate fully and on equal terms in the life of the church. The vision of radical democracy inherent in both the *ekklesia* of women and the Jesus movement (which is not to be confused with present-day kyriarchal actualizations of democracy such as democratic societies like the USA or Britain, in which women are still not fully equal to men with regard for example to representation in parliament) enables Women-Church to become a space for alternative, counter hegemonic discourses of faith and political commitment. Fiorenza argues that women must reclaim the centre of hermeneutical and ecclesiological discourses for the vision of the *ekklesia*. The self-affirmation of women in the Jesus movement as human beings no longer defined by patriarchy and no longer subject to its structures is the primary goal of the feminist movement in which the creation of the '*ekklesia* of women' is located. Women-Church is the hermeneutical centre where the process of discernment of tradition takes place. The '*ekklesia* of women' is a women-defined place where hermeneutical processes of reading, discernment and re-construction can take place in order to renew the vision of radical democracy within the church of today.

Fiorenza is not so much concerned with the particular forms in which the vision of Women-Church is implemented. For her, ecclesiology and hermeneutics are closely linked in rejecting the exclusive claim made by patriarchy on the 'church'.

Women-Church for Fiorenza is a manifestation of the universal church in which all man-made boundaries are transcended and where a vision of radical justice is implemented. Fiorenza's contribution to feminist ecclesiology is the mapping out of a radical alternative vision of church.

Rosemary Radford Ruether

While Fiorenza develops a vision of the kind of hermeneutical spaces and processes that will make Women-Church possible, Rosemary Radford Ruether's work is rooted in the experience and praxis of feminist liturgical base communities, as well as the experience of women being marginalized in the institutional church. Working essentially in a liberation theological paradigm, the experience and praxis of women in the church and as church is prior to any academic ecclesiological discourse about the nature of the church. She sees feminist liturgical communities as liberated zones which are in dialectic tension with the mainstream patriarchal church. Base communities provide spaces for women to explore and develop their own spirituality and work for justice without entirely separating from it, but at the same time in a space beyond its control and power mechanisms. For Ruether, Women-Church is a way to ensure the spiritual survival of those who find themselves marginalized and excluded by the patriarchal institution of the church. Feminist liturgical communities as liberated zones within the patriarchal church anticipate and work for the vision of a liberated co-humanity of women and men.

For Ruether the church is an 'exodus community': it is a community on its way from patriarchy to liberation. In order to implement the vision of liberation, Ruether argues for a dismantling of clericalism and the divisions and hierarchical binary structures of oppression which it creates. Clericalism is the realization of sinful patriarchal ideologies within the church. The existing clerical structures should be replaced by a framework which enables ministries of mutual empowerment and liberation. According to Ruether the church always lives in the tension of being an established historical institution (which is in danger of becoming static and oppressive) and a spirit-filled charismatic community (which is capable of renewal and transformation). Jesus founded a movement, not an institution. Institutionalization occurs as a matter of historical necessity, but all institutional structures within the church are by nature historically contingent and therefore changeable, particularly if they are oppressive and patriarchal rather than liberating. No church can therefore claim a monopoly to represent salvation or an infallible teaching of truth. To acknowledge the possibility of being in error as well as rejecting the need for such certainties in favour of a multiplicity of perspectival truths is a necessary step towards maturity which the church needs to take and an important growing process for women in becoming agents of their own faith.

Ruether challenges women to re-read the Christian tradition and to uncover and reclaim alternative traditions which were often silenced by the dominant institution, not least because they allowed women to participate more fully in all aspects of church life.

Letty Russell

While Fiorenza and Ruether originate from a Roman Catholic background, Letty Russell's feminist ecclesiology, most explicitly developed in her book *The Church in The Round. Feminist Interpretation of the Church*,[13] draws on her experiences as an ordained minister in a Presbyterian church in Harlem, New York, as well as her involvement in the life of the World Council of Churches. Russell develops an ecclesiology of liberation which seeks to apply a feminist spirituality of connection to her reconstruction of the Christian community. Ecclesiology for her is an interpretation of the experience of gathering in Christ's name and then the experience in Christ's service. She describes the church as the community of Christ where everyone is welcome. The praxis of Jesus as found in the synoptic gospels is the model for the life of the church. It is the praxis of fundamental openness to the marginalized and excluded in society which is to be continued in the practice of hospitality. The life of the church is the continuation of the liberating praxis of Jesus and of the life of God's trinitarian activity.

The core metaphor in Russell's ecclesiology is that of table fellowship. Around the table where everyone is welcome the pattern of margin and centre is overcome and work for radical equality is possible.

This leads to new models of leadership which are based on partnership rather than hierarchy and which aim for the ultimate abolition of all clerical structures. Authority is held not in the institution or in particular offices within it but in the community. It is a shared functional authority, an authority which is no longer exercised *over* the community but *in* community. True leadership sees its primary task in empowering those on the margins of the community and integrating them in the life of the community.

Russell presents an 'open ecclesiology' which integrates a wide variety of possible shapes of church in response to its calling to work and live by the promises of God who works in and through history.

The church for Russell is one place where God is present but by no means the only one. It is not a closed institution but open to the world and its needs.

Russell's ecclesiological work, like that of Fiorenza and Ruether, is closely connected with working for social justice. She argues for justice to become a fifth mark of the church. According to Russell, the church can only claim to be a place of salvation if it understands its primary task as taking sides for the poor and the oppressed: there can be no salvation outside the poor.

Constructive dialogue with the Christian tradition: developing a feminist narrative ecclesiology

My own work on reconsidering ecclesiology from a feminist perspective proposes a constructive dialogue with the Christian tradition and is indebted to Fiorenza and Ruether. While Fiorenza, Ruether and Russell work in a North American context, I write as an Anglican and as a theologian whose thinking was developed in both German and English universities and churches.[14]

What feminist theology at the beginning of the twenty-first century can provide is not so much a new and different model of being church or an alternative institutional structure, but rather a framework of criteria which allow for a constructive critique of all ecclesiologies and aspects of church life. The Women-Church movement attempted to provide an alternative framework of praxis as well as an alternative hermeneutical space where the alternative vision of the Jesus movement can be re-modelled. This does not, however, essentially resolve the question of sexual difference and is as culturally contingent as any other model of church.

What feminist ecclesiology can offer, and this is in the spirit of the early work in this area by Fiorenza and Ruether, is a visionary framework for the struggle towards a full affirmation and celebration of women's being church. At the heart of feminist ecclesiology is the struggle for justice and the creation of right relationships, relationships of mutual respect and justice. It is in this struggle, embodied in a variety of different historical patterns and institutional and para-institutional bodies, that the *ekklesia* of women, men and children exists and has always existed.

I propose a narrative ecclesiology where the story of the triune God is told/ embodied in the stories of women's lives. The church has the potential to be the space where such stories can be told and where women can hear each other into speech. This 'hearing into speech' is essentially sacramental and as such creates the fabric of the church.

A feminist ecclesiology is essentially rooted in a shift of focus from the disembodied institution to those who are church. The question shifts from 'What is the church?' to 'Who is the church?' The church, re-visioned in a feminist paradigm, is a space where women can flourish and celebrate their being in the image of the divine. Catherine Mowry LaCugna writes that the life of the church together with 'sacramental life, ethical life, and sexual life will be seen clearly as forms of Trinitarian life: living God's life with one another'.[15] It is the continuation of the incarnation of the Triune God in the concrete, embodied and sexual lives of women, men and children. The focus shifts from the church being a hetero-patriarchal institution which seeks to control and essentially to deny women's sexualities to the church being a space of liberation and celebration where women can receive and share their own bodies as a gift and thereby reject those forces inside and outside the church which deny the goodness of their sexuality. Feminist ecclesiology proclaims the church as an embodied community which enables sacramental celebration of the story of God embodied in the lives of women past and present. It needs to work for a church which is affirmative and open to the bodies of those often constructed as outsiders on the grounds of their race, sexuality or disability. It works towards the celebration of embodiment in all aspects of life, starting with the construction of the spaces in which church celebrations and meetings take place. It also needs to take into account the different voices of human beings at different stages in their lives, such as children and young people. Children are not merely the church of tomorrow, but are church as the people they are now, and therefore need to be included and heard into speech.

This means that the focus shifts from being a disembodied institution to being communities where diversity can be celebrated. This does not, however, mean an unrealistic ideal of community but one that acknowledges the significance of the continuity with the Christian tradition and the reality of pain and suffering both within the community and outside it. Such communities are not so much safe places of retreat as a subversive leaven in the lump of the church.

Feminist ecclesiology seeks to re-vision the church as a community of justice. In working towards justice for all, it performs God's work in the world. Serene Jones writes:

> This church . . . seeks practices that honour the bodies of all people. Health-care reform, adequate state aid for children, excellent public child care, livable (sic!) workplace regulations – the church is an advocate for these in the broader culture as well as in its own midst. It has a positive vision of the kind of space human beings need to flourish. Recognizing the grace that envelops and defines the integrity of all creation, this church contests institutions and practices that fracture and diminish, such as economic exploitative structures, hazardous ecological practices, and degrading cultural representations.[16]

One of the key characteristics of feminist ecclesiology is that it is essentially an open ecclesiology. The church is not a closed community in which some are in and others are out, but it is a round-table community where everyone, regardless of gender or sexuality, is welcome and affirmed. Hospitality and justice are to be added to unity, catholicity, holiness and apostolicity as marks of the church. Feminist ecclesiology rejects the patriarchal notion of being 'in' or 'out' of the institution. At its heart is the open invitation to all to participate in the life of the church as the people they are, but also an openness to the future, to transformation and change. Feminist ecclesiology is not focused on a static institution, but is reflection on an open process of participation and belonging. It is also essentially open to the whole of creation. It is an ecological church. It is a church committed to inter-connectedness and inter-dependence among human beings and with the whole of creation.

Feminist ecclesiology is about providing open spaces in which women's diverse embodied discourses of spirituality, in dialogue with the Christian tradition, are valued and shared as part of that tradition and yet also as a subversion of the institutions and boundaries which that very tradition has created for women. It is important that such communities remain self-critical and keep alive within them the spirit of the charismatic community which is open to and inclusive of all. Women's communities must be careful to remain connected to the actual and concrete lives of women and not see the lives and experiences of some women as representative of all.

Feminist ecclesiology, like liberation ecclesiology, is essentially political. The nature of the church cannot be discussed apart from the concrete and contextual praxis of the church. In reframing the ecclesiological debate, feminist theologians affirm the church as one, holy, catholic and apostolic, as the church which celebrates diversity, which is committed to a vision of justice and equality which is God's vision, a church which is open to all and the whole of creation, and a church which seeks to embody the vision of the earliest Christian communities and to re-enact it in a multiplicity of different contexts.

Notes

1 Mary Daly, *Beyond God the Father: Toward a Philosophy of Women's Liberation*, London: The Women's Press, 1973, p. 172.
2 For a reflection on being a woman in the Orthodox Church see for example Katerina Karkala Zorba, 'Women and the Church: A Greek Orthodox Perspective', *Concilium* 2006: 3, 36–45.
3 The experiences of the women who attended the Council are documented in Carmel McEnroy, *Guests in Their Own House. The women of Vatican II*, New York: Crossroad, 1996. It is interesting to note that the issue of *Concilium*, a journal which was founded to promote the new and renewed theology of the Council, which sought to commemorate the fortieth anniversary of the end of the Council in 2005 did not contain a single contribution by a female theologian. For a critical feminist reading of the ecclesiology of *Lumen gentium*, the major ecclesiological document of the Council, see Natalie K. Watson, 'A Feminist Critical Reading of the Ecclesiology of "Lumen Gentium"', in *Is There a Future for Feminist Theology?* ed. Deborah Sawyer and Diane M. Collier, Sheffield: Sheffield Academic Press, 1999, pp. 74–83.
4 A classic example of the application of Second Wave feminist thinking to the life of the Christian church is Mary Daly's *The Church and the Second Sex*, New York: Harper & Row, 1968, which is sometimes regarded as the first feminist theological work as such.
5 On women's ministry in the Free Churches see Elaine Kaye, Janet Lees and Kirsty Thorpe (eds), *Daughters of Dissent,* London: United Reformed Church, 2004; and Janet Wootton (ed.), *This is Our Story: Free Church Women's Ministry*, Peterborough: Epworth, 2007.
6 For an extensive documentation of the debate in the Roman Catholic Church see John Wijngaards, *The Ordination of Women in the Catholic Church. Unmasking a Cuckoo's Egg Tradition*, London: Darton, Longman and Todd, 2001, and www.womenpriests.org.
7 Elisabeth Schüssler Fiorenza, *Discipleship of Equals. A Critical Feminist Ekklesia-logy of Liberation*, London: SCM, 1993.
8 Mary Hunt in her unpublished PhD thesis, 'Feminist Liberation Theology. The Development of Method in Construction' (Ann Arbor: UMI, 1980), was the first to identify feminist theology as a liberation theology. The first documented use of the women-church concept is in Elisabeth Schüssler Fiorenza, 'Gather Together in My Name . . . Toward a Christian Feminist Spirituality' in: *Women Moving Church*, eds Diann Neu and Maria Riley, Washington: Centre for Concern, 1982. For a more extensive development see Rosemary Radford Ruether, *Women-Church. Theology and Praxis of Feminist Liturgical Communities*, San Francisco: Harper & Row, 1987, and Natalie K. Watson, *Introducing Feminist Ecclesiology*, London: Sheffield Academic Press, 2002, esp. Ch. 4.
9 See Sheila Durkin Dierks, *WomenEucharist*, Boulder, CO: Woven Word Press, 1997.
10 Rosemary Radford Ruether, *Women-Church*, p. 77.
11 Janet Martin Soskice, *Metaphor and Religious Language*, Oxford: Clarendon Press, 1985, p. 15.
12 Elisabeth Schüssler Fiorenza, *In Memory of Her: A Feminist Theological Reconstruction of Christian Origins*, 2nd edition, London: SCM, 1993.
13 Letty M. Russell, *The Church in the Round. Feminist Interpretation of the Church*, Louisville: Westminster John Knox Press, 1993.
14 Watson, *Introducing Feminist Ecclesiology*; Natalie Knödel, 'Reconsidering Ecclesiology: Feminist Perspectives', unpublished PhD thesis, Durham, 1997.
15 Catherine Mowry LaCugna, *God For Us: The Trinity and the Christian Life*, San Francisco: Harper, 1991, p. 411.
16 Serene Jones, *Feminist Theory and Christian Theology: Cartographies of Grace*, Minneapolis: Fortress Press, 2000, p. 173.

Further reading

Sheila Durkin Dierks, *WomenEucharist*, Boulder, CO: Woven Word Press, 1997.
Elisabeth Schüssler Fiorenza, *Discipleship of Equals: A Critical Feminist Ecclesia-logy of Liberation*, London: SCM, 1993.
Mary Grey, *Beyond the Dark Night: a Way Forward for the Church*, London: Cassell, 1997.

Susan A. Ross, *Extravagant Affections: Feminist Perspectives on Sacramental Theology*, New York: Continuum, 1998.

Rosemary Radford Ruether, *Women-Church: Theology and Praxis of Feminist Liturgical Communities*, San Francisco: Harper & Row, 1988.

Pamela Dickey Young, *Re-creating the Church: Communities of Eros*, Harrisburgh: Trinity Press International, 2000.

Natalie K. Watson, *Introducing Feminist Ecclesiology*, London: Sheffield Academic Press, 2002.

26

ECCLESIOLOGY AND RELIGIOUS PLURALISM

Hans Waldenfels, S.J.

Historical setting

From a religious point of view, we can divide Western modernity (thus far) into two distinct periods: Western European Enlightenment and post-Christian modernity.[1]

Western European enlightenment

This refers to that era which began after the Reformation period as a movement for emancipation by which human persons sought to free themselves from ecclesial authority and insisted, instead, upon the authority of human reason. However, in many ways people remained connected with the Christian roots of Western culture, despite the negative rejection of elements of the same.

Basic concerns of the Enlightenment included:

- *individualism* – connected with a strong tendency towards privacy and subjectivism; 'everybody should be saved in his own manner' (Frederick II);
- *rationalism* – putting everything under the sole judgement of human reason;
- *secularism* – i.e. the removal of religious influences from public life, education, politics, etc., aiming at a total separation of religion and state, and changing religion from a public to a private affair.[2]

Post-Christian modernity

In the middle of the twentieth century (if not earlier) a second period of modernity sprang up, when pluralism in its various forms began to dominate the life of human societies. Central topics of concern which arose included:

- the ambiguity of human reason and loss of confidence in the priority and power of human reason to lead to progress in all fields of human life;
- the shift of economic centres from the western hemisphere to other parts of the world, especially South-East Asia (China and India);
- notwithstanding the secularizing tendencies in society, a revival of religion, an upsurge of new religious movements, a growing religious influence in the various fields of public life such as education, health care, ministry among marginalized people, etc.: the 'return of the Gods'[3] (polytheism instead of monotheism);

476

- the awareness of many forms of pluralism (ethnic, cultural, religious, political), combined with a growing strength of radical forms of relativism and the loss of a sense of the absolute (cf. Friedrich Nietzsche: 'God is dead').

Throughout this era, Christianity has increasingly lost its 'normative strength' in Western culture and has been transformed into simply one feature of religious inspiration and moral directives among several others. At the same time European predominance over the wider world came to an end. Western colonialism ended. The former colonies changed into independent states which reconsidered their origin and history, their cultures, their languages, their religions. Indeed, many countries of the world have since developed their own strengths in technologies and will probably overtake the Western world in due course, both in demographical and technological terms.

On the one hand, such developments have led to an emphasis upon ethnic and local particularities; on the other hand, because modern technologies, especially in the field of communication and mobility, are reaching almost every corner of the world, a new and varied network of connections has come into existence covering the whole world. This all points towards the phenomenon of what has become known as the process of *globalization*. Unity and variety, even uniformity and pluralism, have been in tension ever since. In this changing situation, religious pluralism, too, has received increasing attention, since the phenomenon itself is part of the greater context of pluralism in general.

Religious pluralism

The actual development of religious pluralism itself needs special attention here, not least because the history of the various Western nations shows little conformity. Countries like the USA were from their beginning formed by historical developments and tendencies which led to different forms of common life, tolerance or even 'ghettos', and became models from which other nations could learn.

In Europe, almost to the present day, the state church system prevailed in certain countries such as Scandinavia or Great Britain. In Germany the pluralistic view did not become very widespread until the end of World War II, because the consequences of various religious peace treaties, such as Augsburg 1555 (*'cuius regio, eius religio'*) were still in operation. The various regions of the country were divided according to the various Post-Reformation religious affiliations, especially between the mainstream Protestant churches (Lutherans, Reformed, Zwinglians) and the Roman Catholic Church. The Prussian Union proclaimed by Friedrich Wilhelm III of Prussia in 1817 led to the federation of Lutheran and Reformed communities in provinces governed by the Prussian government; this changed the situation within German Protestantism, but not between Protestants and Catholics in Germany.

Thus it was due more to external reasons that a mingling of the different denominations came about. One early causative factor was the start of industrialization and urbanization in the eighteenth and nineteenth centuries, when many people moved from the countryside into the newly developing urban regions – relocations which were not chosen according to religious affiliations. This tendency grew stronger at the end of World War II, when thousands of people were expelled from Eastern Europe and moved into German villages and towns, and there was little care taken whether they fitted in with the local religious affiliation. In the fifties and sixties of the last century many new churches had to be built, Protestant churches in Catholic regions and Catholic churches in Protestant districts. A third reason for the rise of religious pluralism was the call by various West European nations for immigrant labour forces. The situation changed insofar as a growing percentage of jobseekers came not only from other European countries, but also from countries with Islamic populations such as Turkey.

Ecclesial events and reactions

Shifts in Protestant and Orthodox perspectives:
After Edinburgh 1910

When the First World Mission Conference convened in Edinburgh in 1910, two significant factors emerged: First, dissension between the various Christian communities in the mission fields was perceived as *the* decisive reason for the Christian message's growing lack of credibility throughout the world. Second, the gathering together of representatives of various Protestant missionary societies has to be considered one of the founding events of the modern ecumenical movement.

In 1948, in the aftermath of World War II, 147 Protestant and Orthodox churches founded the World Council of Churches (WCC) in Amsterdam. Although the Roman Catholic Church did not join the WCC, the latter should nonetheless be rightly considered a representative body of ecclesial organizations which, in its later plenary assemblies, among them New Delhi (1961), Nairobi (1975), Canberra (1991) and Harare (1998), demonstrated a truly global outlook and facilitated the development of a new process in dealing with non-Christian religions. Undoubtedly the influence of non-European churches and theologies left its mark in Protestant circles much earlier than in the Roman Catholic Church. Nonetheless, the influence of the non-European continents also grew in its own way upon the Roman Catholic Church.

Shifts in Roman Catholic perspectives: After Vatican II

The transformed ecclesial outlook that emerged between the two World Wars has frequently been described in terms of 'from West mission to World mission' (H.-W. Gensichen[4]). With the encyclicals *Maximum illud* of Pope Benedict XV, published in 1919, and *Rerum ecclesiae* of Pius XI (1926), the constitution of local churches and the appointment of indigenous bishops moved firmly onto the agenda of the Roman Catholic Church. The first six Chinese bishops of modern times were ordained in Rome in 1926.

Nowadays the attitude of the Roman Catholic church towards the complexity of the modern world is mostly determined by the Second Vatican Council (1962–5) and its various documents. For the first time a council dealt with the non-Christian religions (cf. *Lumen gentium* n. 16; *Nostra aetate*; *Dignitatis humanae*). Missionary activity (cf. *Ad gentes*), ecumenism (cf. *Unitatis redintegratio*), and the church's position in the modern world (cf. *Gaudium et spes*) were other topics that should also be mentioned in this context.

With regard to the 'religious question', dialogue and religious freedom became the two outstanding topics for consideration. Indeed, the discussions first raised at the Council continued throughout the following decades and can be witnessed in ecclesial debates even today, over 40 years after the closing of the Council. From the outset, two main questions were discussed – just as they were being discussed by the other various Christian denominations: (a) from a Christian point of view, the question of the salvation of all people in relation to the importance of Christ's redemptive action, and (b) the significance of the variety of religions in human and religious history.

The salvation of all people

Religious pluralism is experienced today in former missionary countries across Africa and Asia as well as in countries with long established Christian church structures. For centuries an urgent question for Christians was: How will people be saved who have never heard about Jesus Christ and have never had the chance to be baptized? The threat of final condemnation made missionaries work for the salvation of the people they encountered.[5] Cyprian's slogan '*Extra Ecclesiam nulla salus*' prevailed throughout the church. At the same time theologians were searching for ways to broaden 'entry' to the church. From the time of the Fathers the opinion was expressed that people might be saved by desire (cf. the terms *baptismus flaminis*, *votum Ecclesiae*, *votum baptismi*). What in the beginning was presupposed in an explicit way, later on turned into a *votum implicitum*,[6] a desire included in an act of perfect surrender to God, an act of perfect contrition and love by which human beings abandon themselves completely and give themselves fully into the hands of – what Christians call – 'God'.

One of the best known concepts along such lines was that of the 'anonymous Christian' or 'anonymous Christianity', as articulated by Karl Rahner.[7] In doing so, he combined two concepts: 'anonymous Christianity' and 'legitimate religions'. Because humans by nature are social beings, their way of life cannot be limited to their individualities. As social beings humans are formed by language, culture and religion. However, where Christianity does not exist or influence a human person in his very existence, other existential factors must be taken into consideration. According to Rahner, a religion is 'legitimate' until the Christian message becomes a real challenge for a person so that in his existence he has to decide for or against it.

At the same time a human person can decide in her or his life to fulfil the requirements which are expected from him for his salvation. For Karl Rahner, human history is coextensive with God's universal will of salvation. This means that wherever and whenever a person lives, God gives him the gifts and the grace which enable him or her to correspond to the will of God. According to our understanding, the background to Rahner's thinking is Christian theology combined with philosophical ideas and concepts found both in ancient and modern European history alike.

The basic criticism of Rahner's concept referred to the fact that his ideas were developed *from within* the boundaries of Christian thinking, without any explicit interest in the standpoints of other religions. In fact, the concept of 'anonymous Christianity' can be explained without any knowledge of, or reference to, other religions. The question remains: Do we really do justice to the others, as long as we are only searching for ways to include them within our own system or give them a place within our own conception of salvation? In a way, Rahner's point of view was rather neutralized when others began to refer to Christians as 'anonymous Buddhists', 'anonymous atheists', etc.

Against the approach of '*extra . . . nulla salus*', which is usually referred to as 'exclusivism', Rahner's and similar concepts could be termed 'inclusivism'. Such terminology, I suggest poses little difficulty provided we insist on the possibility of '*mutual* inclusivism'.[8] In engaging with such an approach, we can explore further the question of the various forms of self-understanding.[9]

HANS WALDENFELS, S.J.

A Pluralist Theology of Religions

In recent decades some Protestant[10] and Roman Catholic theologians[11] have offered their solution to these problems by expounding a so-called 'Pluralist Theology of Religions' (PTR – occasionally reduced to a Pluralist Theory of Religion). The authors, in general, reject both an exclusivist and an inclusivist attitude and replace them with a pluralist attitude. Accordingly, each religion offers a valid way to salvation in its own right. However, critics suggest that even if this proposed approach seems to give credit to all other major religions, it can hardly be realized without the loss of a truly dialogical attitude and the sacrifice of one's own point of view. In fact, true dialogue implies a deep respect for the standpoint of the other and an adequate effort towards a profound understanding of the other – as other – and, at the same time, maintaining an equal adherence to one's own religious way. Where this is missing the universal value of truth gets lost.

Here space does not permit a full account of all the various forms of PTR. It suffices to mention that there are philosophical as well as theological questions which need to be discussed in relation to it. Protestant authors often refer to Kantian and post-Kantian philosophical presuppositions by which, for example, the approach to the God-question is predetermined. So J. Hick is inclined to distinguish strongly between the various 'names' or 'phenomena' called 'God', and the inscrutable reality behind the variety of names and concepts which he simply calls 'the Real'. Thus he avoids the term 'God' in order to accommodate the various indications of a final reality which lies beyond any human expression. Whether we deal with Jewish-Christian God-talk or Buddhist or other Asian renunciations of it, the term 'God' is avoided. However, whilst this approach might accommodate philosophical thinking and stand for the final end of human search, Christian critics suggest that it does not respect God's own possibilities and power. What Christians confess whenever they refer to God's revelation and total self-communication in Jesus Christ is beyond human imagination and disposal. Such revelation is God's free action which cannot be deduced from God's work of creation.

Therefore, the boundaries of human knowledge do not limit God's own freedom. Human thinking may end in silence, but that does not mean that *God* is unable to speak of that which limited humans cannot. Human dealings with the transcendent reality imply respect for the fact that human beings do not reject this notion but, instead, are open to God's own actions – or in Christian terms, to God's almightiness, mercy and love. In a way Hick's hypothesis seems to be closed against the expectations and content of Christian profession of faith. Theologically, for this writer at least, it would, indeed, appear that Hick's proposals lead to a negation of the uniqueness of Christ's salvific work. For example, if we consider the testimony of 1 Tim 2.3–6, where we see two principles are combined:

- It is God's will that all humans will be saved and will come to the knowledge of truth.
- God is one and there is but one mediator between God and humanity, i.e., the man Christ Jesus.

It is the second principle which poses difficulties to a pluralistic perspective. The theologians of the early church were struggling to bring together both divinity and humanity in the one human person Jesus of Nazareth. A solution was found in the Council of Chalcedon (451) where in terms of a 'negative christology' (W. Kasper), i.e. in four negative terms 'unmixed, unchangeable, undivided, indivisible' (DH 302), Jesus Christ was declared 'true

God and true man' (DH 301). Likewise the Second Vatican Council refrained from explaining 'the two natures in one person' in a positive way, but by negatively stating what it is not.[12]

Here a footnote must be added: When comparing the two fields of philosophy and Christology, ecclesiological considerations become of secondary importance. It might thus be more helpful first of all to determine the point of view from which the ecclesiological question, itself, is being considered. After all, there are crucial differences involved when we contemplate the church from the internal perspective of a believer or when from the outside view of a spectator. Or, again, whether we consider the church as a visible organization and system or choose rather to focus upon its invisible essence, or, indeed, according to the Protestant distinction reintroduced at the beginning of the twentieth century, between the visible and the invisible church. Pluralism, therefore, and not simply *religious* pluralism, admits a variety of church views. Thus the fact of ecclesiological pluralism, itself, would appear to have a bearing upon our considerations of religious pluralism.

'Dominus Iesus'

Roman Catholics have recently been repeatedly admonished anew by the ecclesial magisterium to maintain that the salvific action of Jesus Christ is the only path to salvation. Particular attention should be given here to the Roman declaration *Dominus Iesus* published by the Congregation for the Doctrine of the Faith (CDF) on Sept. 5, 2000.[13] Although in their understanding of Jesus Christ Protestants and Catholics share much in common, the Roman evaluation of the *ecclesial character* of Protestant churches in *Dominus Iesus* §§16f. nonetheless caused much offence amongst Protestant Christians, particularly the document's statement that, 'The ecclesial communities . . . which did not preserve the valid episcopacy and the original and entire reality of the Eucharistic mystery, are not Churches in the proper sense.'

And yet the declaration was, in part, aimed at problems raised by the numerous differences in religious language that have become increasingly acute in an age of general linguistic confusion which stems from the sheer diversity and multiplicity of languages and cultural differences prevalent in our immediate world today. In fact, there are many cultural–linguistic forms today that appear to be limited and closed systems. So *Dominus Iesus* was seeking to criticize certain philosophical and theological opinions which the CDF believed lead to false conclusions. Thus, for example, it challenged,

- the conviction that divine truth is incomprehensible and unpronounceable, even in Christian revelation;
- the attitude of relativism whereby truth for one individual is true, whilst for another it may not be;
- the radical antagonism between the logical thinking of the Occident and the symbolic thinking of the Orient;
- the subjectivism of those who accept reason as the only source of knowledge;
- the metaphysical evacuation of the historical event of the Incarnation;
- the eclecticism of those who in their theological research accept ideas taken from various philosophical and religious sources without concern for the different logical and contextual factors in play and without examining their compatibility with 'Christian truth';

- the tendency to interpret Holy Scripture irrespective of various ecclesial traditions and the history of ecclesial reception.

Undoubtedly, Christianity as a whole, with its variety of ecclesial entities, is confronted with many different societal, ethnic, cultural and religious contexts, languages and life-patterns, which influence the life of the church in liturgy, biblical exegesis and preaching. The situation is widened still further as soon as we pay attention to the various difficulties faced in human societies or in certain segments of human life: the unjust relationships between men and women (feminism), the disorder between poor and rich, free and oppressed people (liberation), and the relics of colonialist thinking (inculturation). If we wish to address this contemporary situation, two things need to be observed:

- We need a thorough reflection on the various methodologies applied at large in an age of pluralism. Such a reflection would also encompass the use of methods borrowed from other sciences and fields of research, as well as a reappraisal of older methodologies which may still have something to offer today.
- It is not enough to restrict our attention to *methodological* perspectives, we also need to be concerned for the *content* of Christian faith.

In a way, ecclesiology belongs to *both* parts. It is concerned with methods of self-realization and theological self-understanding. In this sense the church is always part of the profession of faith and Christian doctrine.

Key ideas

From the previous observations we can easily gather a number of important key ideas which have to be applied. We shall take into account four basic concepts: contextuality, dialogue, liberation, and inculturation. The application of these four concepts has consequences for the appearance and formation of the church and, consequently, for ecclesiology.

Contextuality

The concept

The term 'contextuality' includes the basic term 'text'. 'Text' is connected, on the one hand, with literary texts, and on the other hand, with 'textiles'. In either case, it refers to structural elements, whether we deal with literary texts or with textiles. Dealing with literature, the more recent analysis of literary texts has led to the observation that involved in the texts, often hidden and beyond the explicit expressions, there are elements which are easily over-looked: the author, and his or her time, style, his or her intention, the circumstances of life, and linguistic capabilities and many more things besides. But we must consider also the reader, his capacity to understand, his time and place. In our reflection we may suddenly realize how much our own personal situation can contribute to the study and understanding of a text. These elements connected with the text we call 'contexts'.

Christian theology grounded upon a historical event, viz., the birth, life and death of the Jew Jesus of Nazareth, the reports on his life, and the first theological reflections on it, and connected with the Holy Scripture of his life as a Jew, the Torah or Old Testament, is therefore very much bound to texts. Little wonder, then, that contextual awareness and thinking began in the field of biblical, and especially Old Testament, exegesis. Dealing with history, historical settings, ethnology, the formation of societies, foreign religiosity and symbolism, the distance between the author's intention and later views led to a growing awareness of the problematic of contexts. This awareness led to a variety of criticisms or critical deliberations: textual, literary, historical, religious and others. A main point of consideration became the so-called 'Sitz im Leben' (M. Gunkel).

Application

The different approaches to the concept 'text' – whether in terms of literary texts or in terms of textiles – prove that the term, as well as its complementary concept 'context', can be applied to different fields of human life, and so to different fields of theology and scholarly research as well – even to non-verbal content. Theological conceptions that are concerned in a special way with local, cultural and other contexts in which the basic theological text is reflected, are called 'contextual theologies'.[14] In concrete terms, different settings combined with corresponding methodologies have today produced new fields of theology such as African, Asian (especially Indian), feminist, and ecumenical theology, theology of religions and the like. One main consequence is that theology is studied in a more inductive manner, rather than deductively.

Because contextual theologies imply a change of standpoint, they require the application of different methodologies borrowed from other fields of scientific research such as the history, sociology, ethnology, and anthropology of religion, etc. One danger to be avoided in all this is the potential loss of the 'text' proper to theology and its ecclesiology in favour of a focus upon contexts alone. The Vatican II Pastoral Constitution, *Gaudium et spes* (n. 4), calls for 'the research of the signs of the time and their interpretation in the light of the gospel'. And certainly, the gospel should likewise be perceived in the light of the 'signs of the times'. However, here the key question becomes whether the context should be the norm by which the text is judged and transformed, or, rather whether it should be the other way around. That is to say, whether the text is the *norm* which should retain its 'authority', even in any attempt to discern its rightful place in the variety of different contexts. Christian theology, it would appear, is obliged to follow this second path.

Ecclesiological consequences

Considering that the 'concrete form' of the institutional church is shaped, in many respects, by local forms of socialization and has equally been transformed, over the course of time, by cultural developments within various human societies, our ecclesial structures also need to be reconsidered today. In Roman Catholic theology we distinguish between elements which are *iuris divini*, i.e. perceived as unchangeable because they are grounded in God's 'constitutional will', and those elements which are *iuris ecclesiastici resp. humani* and therefore can be changed. The borderline between these two groups is less clear than might be presumed, for throughout much of church history, certain elements have been considered to be *iuris divini*, and yet, when they were later in fact changed, it became clear that they were not.

A good example here is the determination of the role of women in the church. Whereas many denominations, especially the Protestant churches, have reached positive conclusions with regard to the possibility of women's ordination and have consequently ordained women as liturgical ministers, the Roman Catholic Church has declared that the possibility of doing likewise is not in the church's gift to decide and, therefore, discussion about the subject is closed. Nevertheless, even this decision has not been pronounced in a way that makes it an infallible statement. Thus a stalemate of sorts has been reached and the great majority of the community remains silent on the question whilst waiting for future developments.

Dialogue

One of the most influential concepts in the period of church history following Vatican II is, of course, that of *dialogue*. Pluralism calls for peaceful ways of communication. The numerous negative experiences of 'outsiders', people perceived as foreigners and strangers; and wars waged with conventional weapons and modern arms alike that end in the blood-shed of innumerable soldiers and innocent civilians and leave much destruction, whether of razed cities or scorched earth in their wake, have eventually come to be seen for the barbarous, cruel and inhuman realities that they were and are. It was thus that people eventually came to cry out for peace and to seek to develop new forms of discourse and interaction between peoples of different nationality, origin, race and religion. 'As long as people are talking to each other, they will not be killing each other', is a very true saying indeed.

The concept

In the meantime, 'dialogue' has become a term which is used in an almost inflationary way. And yet, strictly speaking, not every form of speech and even less every form of encounter can be called 'dialogue'. The term itself brings together the Greek '*logos*' = word, speech, language[15] + '*dia*' = through, back and forth. Consequently, 'dialogue' is an affair between people, not so much between organizations and institutions. Talk about 'interreligious dialogue' is to be understood as a discourse between adherents of *different* religions. Here again we have to distinguish between two different aspects:

- We need, first, to make a distinction between the various kinds of meetings and encounters, conversations, colloquies, discussions and planned events which could all be gathered together as instances of 'dialogue'. Of course, just as not every encounter in day-to-day life that leads to an exchange of greetings and a few words of small-talk deserves to be considered worthy of the name dialogue, by the same token not all conferences, deliberations or negotiations that take place with the aim of clarifying certain questions, resolving certain problems, or overcoming particular quarrels (for example, the religious implications of terrorist actions) are to be considered as 'dialogue' in the sense meant here.
- A second question here addresses the issue of the *participants* in an encounter. It is significant whether people who represent different religious *organizations* enter into a religious conversation, or whether people ('believers') from different faiths enter as such into an interreligious discourse. In recent times it is often the case that officially appointed representatives of a religion engage in dialogue with representatives of one or more other religions. Sometimes such conversations result in summit talks and a mutual encounter on the part of religious leaders.

Essential elements

Summarizing the various aspects and elements of a real dialogue, the following points can be raised:

- Dialogue requires an encounter between different persons who are able and willing to meet face-to-face in true partnership. One of the basic prerequisites for this is the knowledge of different languages, and where this is not the case, the presence of sufficient means placed at the disposal of the interlocutors, such as translators and the like.
- Of even greater importance is the need for human beings to be able to see and judge things from both their own and other points of view. Such an opportunity implies the ability to move from the position of one's own perspective to the understanding of others – mindful of the need for an ability to discern between these different points of view. Whoever wishes to enter into true dialogue must also be willing to contemplate things from a different point of view, in addition to their own perspective. Nonetheless, this does not mean that the participants in a dialogue simply abandon their own standpoint: they simply need to be willing to appreciate things from different 'sides' and, where necessary, to correct their own understanding. Thus in interreligious dialogue the supreme criterion has to be truth.
- The fundamental attitude demanded of participants in interreligious dialogue is a deep respect for other human beings as human subjects in their own right. For example, the Roman Catholic Church has come to appreciate this necessity in its engagement with those members of the Jewish faith who survived the atrocities of the German concentration camps during the Nazi era. Since then, Roman Catholics and other Christians cannot undertake any research in the field of Judaism without engaging with contemporary Jews as both their companions in conversation and as being in a position to offer a corrective to their efforts to understand the Jewish faith and its traditions.[16]

   The same applies equally today in relation to dialogue with Muslims, as well as with members of the leading Asian faiths and numerous other religious traditions. As long as we respectfully engage with one other as witnesses to a particular religious conviction, and do so with a readiness to open ourselves to the fundamental convictions of others – indeed to *learn* from them – then our encounters may result in deeper mutual understanding and cooperation on the part of both 'sides' of any such encounter. The question of truth, then, will be less a point of separation and dissension than of mutual enrichment, as long as all sides are working towards peace and justice.
- There is a further essential element presupposed in any successful dialogue: the partners in conversation have to meet in a spirit of religious freedom. Returning again to Vatican II, for example, we need to realize that the conciliar documents *Nostra aetate* and *Dignitatis humanae* are both deeply connected: the attitude of the church towards other religions and towards religious freedom are intertwined.

   In an age when China is undergoing tremendous economic and political change and is growing in influence in both spheres, it cannot be overlooked that religious freedom is a component of the agreed corpus of fundamental human rights and, indeed, of human dignity itself. The same applies to the situation in certain Islamic countries, in Turkey and in some of the Arabic states. There can be no real dialogue unless people meet on the basis of free speech and religious freedom.

Indeed, *Nostra aetate* identifies dialogue itself as the most important means of dealing both with other individuals beyond Christianity and with other religions themselves. It is thus necessary that the conditions of any true dialogue are more closely examined and elaborated. In this connection religious freedom must again be perceived as one of the main preconditions.

- Special attention needs to be given to the *purposes* of interreligious dialogue, which can be both theoretical and practical. Accordingly, we can distinguish between different levels of dialogue:

  - Day-to-day dialogue between peoples of different origin and religion in a common *location:* living together with respect and tolerance and, where necessary, a spirit of cooperation.
  - Dialogue in a given state and society in order to find solutions and encourage cooperation wherever particular problems in public life have been identified.
  - Dialogue on an intellectual and scholarly level with the aim of fostering and deepening a mutual understanding between adherents of different religions.
  - Dialogue on the basis of philosophical and 'theological'[17] reflection which includes deliberations concerning fundamental questions of human life and destiny, the origins and aim of creation, the 'power' behind all that exists, and other, deeper mysteries that remain perennial.
  - Finally, dialogue as an exchange of spiritual experiences and as mutual participation and sharing in words or even, indeed, in silence.

Ecclesiological consequences

The proof of an attitude of truly *inter*religious dialogue toward believers of other faiths and religions is an atmosphere of truly *intra*religious dialogue. More concretely, unless there exists a real dialogue *inside* the church, a commitment to brotherly/sisterly exchange and cooperation, we can hardly presume that an honest and open attitude will be extended towards others. For far too long within the church there prevailed an atmosphere dominated by command and obedience. The image of the Good Shepherd was projected onto the various tiers of the hierarchical order, so that the image of shepherd and flock, shepherd and sheep became deeply rooted in the consciousness of the faithful. Of course, in different communities the synodal elements are strongly developed. And, we must not forget that Vatican I's pronouncements concerning papal supremacy and infallibility were followed in the 1960s by the Roman Catholic Church's convocation of Vatican II, followed by the convocation of various synods, central, regional and national.

Nonetheless, there are some other features that indicate just how slowly changes in ecclesial mentality have progressed. The church per se is considered as *communio* – i.e. both communion with God and communion among the members of the church. But what is thought to be essential for the self-understanding of the church still needs concrete fulfilment in various aspects of church life: in its means of communication, the character of its communicative intercourse and the quality of relationships throughout its life – all such need to be informed by the words of Jesus Christ: 'I do not call you slaves any more, because the slave does not know what his master does. Rather I call you friends; for I have communicated to you everything that I have heard from my Father' (Jn 15.15f.). An atmosphere of dialogue implies partnership, trust and confidence, a mutual relation of giving and receiving, listening and speaking – an atmosphere which also needs to be inculcated between church leaders and the other members of any given church community.

Liberation

Key religious concepts

Redemption and salvation are key words for Christian theology. In the Old Testament especially, redemption had to do with the fact that, from the very beginning, human beings were enabled to counteract and even to contradict God's will and intentions for the world. God had created humanity in God's own likeness, and this means as beings who are free – and such freedom extends even to our decision to follow the path of God or to turn away from it. One of the most fundamental problems facing human beings is the difference between the order of creation and the evident disorder within the world which we experience in a double way: in the many natural catastrophes and calamities, floods and earthquakes, and in disasters caused by human decisions and behaviour with their consequences witnessed in public and social life, such as wars, expulsions, extermination and homicide.

The Old Testament, which reports many cases of natural and moral evil, describes God not only as Creator, but at the same time also Redeemer and Saviour. From the fall of humanity described in Genesis 3, God manifests Godself as a God who pursues a plan aimed towards the salvation of humanity – a plan which leads to the Incarnation of God's own very self in Jesus Christ and his death at the cross. What in the Old Testament seemed to refer more to earthly life, first communal and, later, also individual, is focused in Christian theology more upon the final destiny of humanity and our post-mortal situation.

Liberation theology

As explored in more detail in other chapters in this volume, the 1960s witnessed the emergence of a movement in various parts of Latin America which combined opposition against various kinds of socio-political, economic, cultural, sexist and racial oppression and unjust dependency with religious initiatives for liberation inspired by the life and teachings of Christ. Basic ecclesial communities cooperated with theologians of various denominations. Because of Marxist input in the various forms of social analysis employed in liberation theology, ecclesial reactions to it were divided. However, the three meetings of the *Consejo Episcopal Latinoamericano* (CELAM) in Medellín (1968), Puebla (1979) and Santo Domingo (1992) strengthened the effect of these liberation theologies[18] in both praxis and theory. The main aims of such theologies were a deepening of communicative action; reflection upon the common social and economic problems of the day; coordination of activities in the fields of catechesis, education and the formation of both laity and clergy; liturgical and social activities (option for the poor); ecumenism; and pastoral deliberations about culture, youth and family life, etc. This enormous variety of concerns and objectives were expressed in concise form in a collaborative treatise which featured the best known and most important authors of liberation theology (among them G. Gutiérrez, Clodovis and Leonardo Boff, José Comblin, Enrich Dussel, Ignacio Ellacuría, Juan Luis Segundo, Jon Sobrino and Paulo Suess): *Mysterium Liberationis*.[19]

Indeed, in due course, the inspirations and motivations of liberation theology spread throughout the whole world, to Asia and Africa and even to Europe and the 'Western' world, because oppression was, of course, not limited to certain regions, and thus similar phenomena suppressing liberty could be discovered in almost every part of the world and in the relation of many social groups, castes and their different estimation.

Ecclesiological consequences

Such research and investigations into the roots of oppression did not restrict itself to examining the 'surface' of human life, to economics and politics, but was also extended to *weltanschauung*, ideologies and religions and even to Christian ecclesiology. Ever since the discovery of Latin America, when colonial powers and certain Christian missionaries cooperated in the conquest and submission of the various countries, both worldly and ecclesial powers have met with criticism. Hence, if the church, including its organizational elements, was forced to reflect upon her situation anywhere at all, it would have been in Latin America.

Thus, in a way, the Roman Catholic church, in particular, and her constitution were reconsidered from the standpoint of the common people, as opposed to the standpoint of the pinnacle of the hierarchical order. In Vatican II's Dogmatic Constitution on the Church, *Lumen gentium*, Chapter 2, the church was newly defined as the people of God on pilgrimage. The Old Testament notion of the exodus of God's chosen people from Egypt became a central symbol for the self-understanding of the church community. However, this became not only a theoretical symbol, but a symbol that also began to work in ecclesial practice.

Hence it was in Latin America, more than anywhere else, that church life began to be transformed 'from the base' and that models of so-called 'basic communities' came into existence. The religious life of the 'ordinary' people became significant, including their popular devotions. At the same time many began to investigate the religious roots of traditions and practices inherent in the lives of descendants of the African slaves who had been transported to the Latin American colonies, and also of Asian immigrants. These included African-American and Asian-American cults that continued to exist alongside the predominant Christian religion which often penetrated only the surface, and not the depths, of the lives of such peoples. In the meantime, the new colonialists, especially the United States of America, took an active interest in supporting the interests of different Christian groups coming from the States to Latin America and thus began to exercise a strong influence upon Latin American life in general. Issues pertaining to Christian and religious pluralism became a difficult problem, in particular for the formerly predominant Roman Catholic Church whose influence began to decrease at a rapid rate. Indeed, there is no continent where the church as such is undergoing such extensive change as in Latin America.

Wherever the church is striving today for human freedom and flourishing in society, she is called to work and struggle for human dignity, which includes equal rights and autonomy aimed towards fulfilment and well-being for all human beings, regardless of nation, gender, race and religious affiliation. Although for a long time in Western history the notion of liberation had been applied more to the individual person and its final destination, in its renewed and continued reflection upon God's redemptive action in favour of God's elected Jewish people and upon Jesus' healing and consoling deeds during his life time, the church finally, albeit not without cost, also began to proclaim anew the political and societal, and thus the 'this-worldly' elements of God's salvation in human history and society.

However, what is valid for dialogue must also apply to freedom and liberty. The church cannot convince others with its message of freedom unless the church itself becomes visibly a place of freedom. For example, the procedures followed by those in authority in dealing with those who live in fundamental contradiction and opposition to 'official' church teachings on faith and morality, as well as with those whom the Roman Catholic Church calls 'heretics' and 'schismatics', need to be re-examined. Of course, some people who feel totally unable to live and think in accordance with certain seemingly fundamental Christian convictions decide, in all honesty, to leave the Christian community. And yet there are many questions discussed *within* Christianity about which different Christian communities differ in their understanding and interpretation. But even with regard to such issues, all Christian communities need to be able to 'find their way' and to live and act with conviction and in a spirit of true freedom.

'In God's likeness'

Liberation aims at the rediscovery and restoration of human freedom. As already mentioned, humanity is created in the likeness of God, and one of the fundamental features of the very being of God is *freedom*. Before entering into any discussion of liberation, we need to return to the fundamental topics involved in the doctrine of creation. No wonder that, in a period of interreligious dialogue, Christian theology also displays a renewed interest in the theology of creation. Indeed, the fundamental elements of theological anthropology are also to be discovered in the theological explication of the belief that creation, even before the Incarnation of Christ for the salvation of humanity, required such redemption because of humanity's turn away from God, a decision made in free will against humanity's creator, in other words, on account of what is called 'sin'.

At this point of our reflection we realize that dealing with pluralism implies an awareness of very real differences across the various traditions in human thinking, which are not only a question of methodology, but even more a difference of understanding and interpretation of evident facts that we experience in our lives. Being made 'in the image and likeness of God', however, leads humans to make use of intellect/reason and will, and not to accept everything as fate and a destiny imposed by necessity. As we know, many religions do not share the conviction that God is Creator and, consequently, the Redeemer. But in view of God's essential freedom, it is all the more the duty of Christians to fight for human freedom as well. For Christianity, the history of human liberation reaches its pinnacle, though not its completion, in Christ's death on the cross. There are many more stations on the way towards the final liberation of humankind along with the rest of creation.

Inculturation

The concept

The term[20] is a neologism mainly used in cultural anthropology and theology. A more detailed explication must distinguish between *enculturation, acculturation, accommodation, adaptation, indigenization,* in addition to *syncretism,* etc. Theologically speaking, 'inculturation' represents a missiological programme which refers to the mutual influence upon one another of the Christian message and the plurality of cultures in which it finds itself expressed. Through such interaction the gospel is transferred into different socio-political, cultural and religious situations, and expressed in different languages, without losing its fundamental identity. In brief, in a pluralist society and amidst a plurality of cultures and religions the church becomes aware of the fact that many of its most fundamental features have been inherited from its Mediterranean and European background, from Greek philosophy and mythology, and from Roman law and art. The relation of the Semitic-Jewish background and the process of Hellenization, which became effective in Christian dogma and church law, obviously form the basis of much discussion here.

In reflecting upon its own history, the church feels invited to find the right way of translating the gospel into new and unaccustomed circumstances and how it can adapt to new ways of linguistic, symbolic and other forms of expression. History also teaches us, however, that from the very beginning the divine message entered human life at a specific time and in a specific place, as well as in a language spoken and understood by a limited number of people.

In other words, Christianity was inculturated from its very beginnings. However, since we are dealing with translation from one culture to another, the question needs to be raised whether, instead of talking about 'inculturation', we should not prefer to discuss 'interculturation'. Furthermore, the question once again arises concerning the extent to which, in view of linguistic complications and limitations, the meaning intended in the original contents might be lost during the process of reproduction and translation. It is my belief that when theologians encounter the other, the strange, the foreign, in a new way, they must not only insist upon the mystery of God in God's divine self (divine immanence), but also upon the mystery which is hidden within another human person and behind the multitude of cultures and religions in the world.

Ecclesiological consequences

The situation we are heading for in the present time calls for pioneers, and we cannot even be certain whether, with the best of intentions, people who dare to take the way of pluralism will not fail. And yet the situation is clear: The mission of the church no longer consists in the simple transfer of its Western appearances into other countries across the globe with their own history and culture, in the destruction of their temples and sanctuaries and the extirpation of old religious customs and norms. The 'Western' church and all its communities are challenged to respect the cultures and traditions of these others, and at the same time to allow the church itself to be transformed through such engagement. That does not mean that the church loses its right to initiate conversion and transformation; however, it does mean that throughout the church there must be a growing conviction that the church herself is *ecclesia semper reformanda*, a church which needs continuously to change, reform and, indeed, undergo conversion. This applies to the various Christian churches and communities, including the Roman Catholic Church. For the latter, even the claim to speak and act in an infallible way is only given under very limited conditions and leaves ample space for manoeuvring in order to bring about the changes called for by today's world, as well as space for human error and fallibility. The church is a church of saints and sinners as, amongst many others, Karl Rahner reminds us.

In any case, the process of inculturation will be more fully realized in the time to come. It includes 'constructing local theologies' (Robert Schreiter) or, as the German title of the same book indicates, a 'farewell to the God of the Europeans',[21] a new view of the catholicity of the church which comprises the richness of non-European, i.e. non-Western, cultures and is open to the multitude of expressions to be gleaned from other approaches to the mystery of God's salvific action through Christ and the Spirit in the world of creation. We only need to look at the many faces at the international meetings of the WCC, the Roman Catholic members of the College of Cardinals, and the bishops to gain a small indication of just how greatly the church is changing and being enriched through all such interaction.

The Church of the future

To conclude, I would like to offer a short sketch of some of the moments that illustrate a church that is undergoing transformation through this increasing awareness of plurality all over the world. Plurality is more than the loss of unity and uniformity. It is the experience of multitude and plenitude, in a way a foretaste of the promised eternal life. Three metaphors are frequently used to describe the future church: the growing seed, marriage, and dialogue, foremost among them, perhaps, that biblical image of the growing seed. Each of these images presupposes different aspects of the church which have been mentioned in our discussions above. In dealing with plurality and pluralism, more attention needs to be given to the external appearance of the church than to its inner foundation in the love and benevolence of God, i.e. to that mystical union as portrayed through the image of marriage.

Four distinctive marks

In the common Creed of the Christian community four distinctive marks are mentioned, which will be equally characteristic for the life of future church: The church is one, holy, catholic and apostolic.

- Oneness refers to the common profession of the basic data of the Creed, which is a confession to the triune God, the Father as Creator of heaven and earth, the Son revealed in Jesus of Nazareth, his life, death and resurrection, the Holy Spirit as God's continuous presence in church and world. Unity in faith does not mean uniformity. It remains open to debate precisely where and when union is fully realized and where and when it is more appropriate to speak of only partial communion. Moreover, we must also ask who is entitled to decide the question of total or partial union and thus to define the 'true' identity of the Christian community and communion? In Eph 4.2–6 we find a description of unity that follows the unity of the triune God: 'one body and one Spirit as a common hope is given to you through your vocation, one Lord, one faith, one baptism, one God and Father who is above all and through all and in all.'
- The holy church is holy only and uniquely through the presence of the Holy God, a presence which we call the working of the Holy Spirit, who is the Spirit of God the Creator and Jesus Christ the Redeemer. One of the key questions still open to debate today concerns God's activity both within and without the confines of the 'visible' church. The history of theological speculation on this question dates back to the Patristic period, when, for example, Augustine spoke about the 'Ecclesia ab Abel', an idea that was recalled in Lumen gentium §2.

  Today we must also discuss what role other religions play in God's plan of salvation and in the course of the history of salvation. Some authors connect the limited exis-tence of the visible, historical church with the limited human existence of Jesus of Nazareth. There is a certain tendency to separate the activity of the Spirit of Creation and that of Jesus of Nazareth, the Logos and Jesus, the Kingdom of God and the church.

No doubt some such approaches may occasionally fall prey to the danger of bypassing the teaching of the Council of Chalcedon, but a further question arises here – against the common conviction of mainstream Christianity – as to whether this leads to salvation 'extra Christum'. Such problems remain unsolved and will no doubt preoccupy theologians for the foreseeable future, involving as they do the further question of whether or not, and in what sense, the church is to be considered a 'necessary means of salvation'. Indeed, here the very role of the church, itself is under consideration.

- Catholicity is to be understood in a double sense: quantitatively as extending over the whole globe and qualitatively as penetrating all fields of human expression and development. In fact, the Christian message has already reached the ends of the earth. However, if we understand catholicity as fullness and plenitude, there remain a multitude of possibilities concerning the 'way' towards perfection. In its catholicity Christianity can discover new styles of realization, a deepening of self-understanding, a new openness to further ecclesial development. Moreover, as mentioned before, under this heading of catholicity the future church will experience herself not only as 'mater et magistra' (John XXIII), but even more as a *disciple* who learns from others.

- The strong tendency towards conservatism apparent in the mainstream church(es) in recent times has much to do with a fear that the church might lose its own identity in these precarious postmodern times. Indeed, living through such a time of exploration and new experiences might well lead some individual Christians to lose their way and go astray. In this situation apostolicity can serve as a kind of compass. Here we need not explain the notion of apostolicity in detail, referring as it does to the apostles as eyewitnesses and Paul as a 'first witness'. Suffice to say that in a time when the church is finally on its way from being primarily a Western church towards a truly world church, experimenting with new pathways and preserving the core ecclesial identity obviously need to be finely balanced. This leads us back to the basic Christian belief that we do not trust in ourselves, but in God. The road that leads to God first leads away from ourselves in order to discover that God works in us as God works in the world and in humanity in general.

Other religions

In our reflections here upon ecclesiology and religious pluralism we have mostly been concerned with questions of a general nature. Hence we have not been able to dwell upon particular characteristics of other particular faiths. In this final analysis I wish to suggest that we might profitably expand our considerations by concentrating upon each of the main religions in today's world, first paying particular attention to the way they operate within and relate to our societies, and then engaging in a comparative analysis of the church in relation to, for example, the synagogue, the *umma*, the Buddhist *sangha* and other forms of religious community.

Whenever we seek to engage in 'official' interreligious encounters, we must do so through 'official' representatives. Hence the question of religious representation is one which also requires further attention today, and which is also relevant to unresolved tensions in the arena of state–religion relations. In various states such as China and Turkey, alongside the original religious communities we also find associations or offices organized by the governments themselves. For example, in Turkey the government is in charge of the office of religious affairs which also supervises the Islamic activities of Turkish citizens in foreign countries. In the People's Republic of China, the government plays a significant role in China's five officially sanctioned religious organizations (Buddhism, Daoism, Islam and two branches of Christianity, Catholicism and Protestantism) through their approval of the corresponding associations. With regard to Christianity, deciding how to respond in the light of such developments remains a pertinent question for the various churches and ecclesial communities both within and without that Republic. There is little doubt that the religious landscape will change in the future and that all religions, including Christianity, will take part in the progress of time.

Notes

1 See H. Waldenfels, *Kontextuelle Fundamentaltheologie*, Paderborn: Schöningh, 4th edn 2005, pp. 484ff.; idem, *Phänomen Christentum*, Bonn: Borengässer, 2002, pp. 15–28.

2 I will refrain from explaining the different forms and degrees of separation of church–state relationships in Germany, France, England and other countries, which can vary considerably.

3 See F.W. Graf, *Die Wiederkehr der Götter. Religion in der modernen Kultur*, München: Beck, 2004.

4 Cf. H.-W.Gensichen, 'Missionsgeschichte des Christentums III', LThK³ VII, 309.

5 For the following discussion see Waldenfels, *Kontextuelle Fundamentaltheologie*, pp. 427–32; J. Dupuis, *Toward a Christian Theology of Religious Pluralism*, Maryknoll, NY: Orbis, 1997.

6 The doctrine of the *votum implicitum* was applied in a letter of the Holy Office to Archbishop Cushing of Boston, August 8, 1949; cf. H. Denzinger, *Enchiridion symbolorum, definitionum et declarationum des rebus fidei et morum*, ed. P. Hünermann (DH), 37th edn, Freiburg: Herder, 1991, nn. 3866–73. The letter was directed against L. Feeney SJ, who declared that anybody who was not a member of the Roman Catholic Church (or at least a catechumen) was excluded from salvation. Feeney himself was excommunicated and only reconciled on his deathbed.

7 For more detail see Waldenfels, *Kontextuelle Fundamentaltheologie*, pp. 430–2; idem, *Begegnung der Religionen. Theologische Versuche I*, Bonn: Borengässer, 1990, pp. 53–74.

8 See R. Bernhard (ed.), *Horizontüberschreitung. Die Pluralistische Theologie der Religionen*, Gütersloh: Bertelsmann, 1990.

9 One of the best examples is the document *Dominus Iesus* published by the Roman Congregation of Faith on Sept. 5, 2000. See below p. 481.

10 See, for example, John Hick (ed.), *Truth and Dialogue. The Relationship between World Religions*, 2nd edn, Philadelphia: Westminster Press, 1975; idem (ed.), *The Myth of God Incarnate*, Philadelphia: Westminster Press, 1977; idem, *God has Many Names*, London: Macmillan,1980; idem, *An Interpretation of Religion. Human Responses to the Transcendent*, London: Macmillan, 1989; idem, *The Metaphor of God Incarnate*, London: SCM, 1993; W.C. Smith, *Questions of Religious Truth*, London: Gollancz, 1967; idem, *Faith and Belief*, 2nd edn, Princeton: Princeton University Press, 1987; idem, *Towards a World Theology*, 2nd edn, Maryknoll, NY: Orbis, 1989.

11 Cf. P.F. Knitter. *No Other Name? A Critical Survey of Christian Attitudes Toward the World Religions*, Maryknoll, NY: Orbis, 1985; idem, *Horizonte der Befreiung. Auf dem Weg zu einer pluralistischen Theologie der Religionen*, Frankfurt: Lembeck/Paderborn: Bonifatius, 1997; P. Schmidt-Leukel, *Theologie der Religionen. Probleme, Optionen. Argumente*, Neuried: Ars una, 1997; idem, *Gott ohne Grenzen. Eine christliche Kirche und pluralistische Theologie*, Gütersloh: Bertelsmann, 2005; L. Swidler, *After the Absolute. The Dialogical Future of Religious Reflections*, Minneapolis: Fortress Press, 1990.

12 Cf. G.M. Hoff, 'Chalkedon im Paradigma Negativer Theologie, Zur aporetischen Wahrnehmung der chalkedonensischen Christologie', in *Theologie und Philosophie (Frankfurt)* 70 (1997), 355–72.

13 Cf. H. Waldenfels, *Auf den Spuren von Gottes Wort. Theologische Versuche III*, Bonn: Borengässer, 2004, pp. 409–28, 439–54.

14 As an example see my own *Kontextuelle Fundamentaltheologie* (note 1), and the preface.

15 Although the term implies many more significations like reason, meaning, etc., we restrict ourselves to the vocal sense of speech and speaking. For the following paragraph see in more detail H. Waldenfels, *Gottes Wort in der Fremde. Theologische Versuche II*, Bonn: Borengässer 1997, Part I, 'Languages as bridges to foreign land'.

16 See Waldenfels, *Kontextuelle Fundamentaltheologie*, pp. 424–7: 'Dialogue as respect for strange subjectivity'.
17 The Jewish-Christian term is used as substitution for analogous terms in other religions.
18 For a summary see G. Collet, Th. Hausmanniger, G. Gutierrez and N.Mette, 'Befreiungstheologie', in *Lexikon für Theologie und Kirche*, 3rd edn, Freiburg: Herder, 1996, Vol. 2, pp. 130–7.
19 Cf. I. Ellacuría and J. Sobrino (eds), *Mysterium Liberationis. Conceptos fundamentales de la teología de la liberación*, Madrid: Trotta.S.A, Editiorial, 1990.
20 For more information and literature see G. Collet, A. Feldtkeller, K.Schatz, R.J. Schreiter and T. Groome, 'Inkulturation', in *Lexikon für Theologie und Kirche*, 5, pp. 504–10.
21 Cf. R.J. Schreiter, *Constructing Local Theologies*, Maryknoll, NY: Orbis, 1985; in German: *Abschied vom Gott der Europäer. Zur Entwicklung regionaler Theologien*, Salzburg: A. Pustet, 1992.

Further reading

R. Bernhard (ed.), *Horizontüberschreitung. Die Pluralistische Theologie der Religionen*. Gütersloh: Bertelsmann, 1990.
Jacques Dupuis, *Toward a Christian Theology of Religious Pluralism*. Maryknoll, NY: Orbis, 1997.
Ignacio Ellacuría and Jon Sobrino (eds), *Mysterium Liberationis: Fundamental Concepts of Liberation Theology*. Maryknoll, NY: Orbis Books, 1993 (Spanish orig. Madrid: Trotta. S.A, Editiorial, 1990).
F.W. Graf, *Die Wiederkehr der Götter. Religion in der modernen Kultur*, München: Beck, 2004.
John Hick (ed.), *Truth and Dialogue. The Relationship between World Religions*, 2nd edn, Philadelphia: Westminster Press, 1975.
—— (ed.), *The Myth of God Incarnate*, Philadelphia: Westminster Press, 1977.
——, *God has Many Names*, London: Macmillan, 1980.
——, *An Interpretation of Religion. Human Responses to the Transcendent*, London: Macmillan, 1989.
——, *The Metaphor of God Incarnate*, London: SCM, 1993.
P.F. Knitter. *No Other Name? A Critical Survey of Christian Attitudes Toward the World Religions*, Maryknoll, NY: Orbis, 1985.
P. Schmidt-Leukel, *Theologie der Religionen. Probleme, Optionen. Argumente*, Neuried: Ars una, 1997.
——, *Gott ohne Grenzen. Eine christliche Kirche und pluralistische Theologie*, Gütersloh: Bertelsmann, 2005.
R.J. Schreiter, *Constructing local Theologies*. Maryknoll, NY: Orbis, 1985.
W.C. Smith, *Questions of Religious Truth*, London: Gollancz, 1967.
——, *Faith and Belief*, 2nd edn, Princeton: Princeton University Press, 1987.
——, *Towards a World Theology*, 2nd edn, Maryknoll, NY: Orbis, 1989.
L. Swidler, *After the Absolute. The Dialogical Future of Religious Reflections*, Minneapolis: Fortress Press, 1990.
H. Waldenfels, *Begegnung der Religionen. Theologische Versuche I*, Bonn: Borengässer, 1990.
——, *Gottes Wort in der Fremde. Theologische Versuche II*, Bonn: Borengässer, 1997.
——, *Phänomen Christentum*. Borengässer: Bonn, 2002.
——, *Auf den Spuren von Gottes Wort. Theologische Versuche III*, Bonn: Borengässer, 2004.
——, *Kontextuelle Fundamentaltheologie*, 4th edn, Paderborn: Schöningh, 2005.

Part V

CONCEPTS AND THEMES

27

AUTHORITY

Mark Chapman

Introduction

The British Congregationalist theologian P.T. Forsyth wrote at the turn of the twentieth century that 'The question of authority . . . in its religious form, is the first and last issue of life. . . . As soon as the problem of authority really lifts its head, all others fall to the rear.'[1] While this might be something of an overstatement, the problem of authority undoubtedly forms one of the most contested of all areas of Christian theology, since it relates directly to the vexed questions of decision-making and the exercise of power in the church. In recent years many denominations have been deeply divided about different understandings of the sources of authority used to make changes in the order and teachings of the church. The legitimacy of certain developments (including, for instance, the ordination of women as priests and bishops or the appointment of practising homosexuals to ecclesiastical offices) has created tensions which threaten unity within and between the different denominations.

With its background in political and legal discourse, the problem of authority leads on to many of the most controversial areas of Christian ecclesiology, in particular the use and interpretation of scripture and tradition, the role and status of the different orders of ministry, as well as the relationships between church and state. Indeed, the problem of authority crystallizes many of the disputes which led to the division of Western Christendom in the sixteenth century and it still forms the most fundamental stumbling-block in attempts to resolve the remaining differences between the denominations.[2]

Perhaps most centrally, the question of authority is tied up with the claim to speak and act in the name of God. For Christianity, this is naturally founded upon the divine commission of Christ and, following on from him, it relates to the purported supernatural origins of the institutions and leaders of the church, particularly its bishops, who are entrusted with the task of proclamation and handing on the church's teachings and traditions. Søren Kierkegaard summarized the problem in addressing his own question: 'Is authority the profundity of the doctrine, its superiority, its cleverness?' 'Not at all;' he answered, 'authority is the specific quality which comes from another place.'[3] How the authority that comes from 'another' place relates to the institutions of this world, both ecclesiastical and civil, is at the heart of the problem of authority. An institution which claims to be founded on the divine word gains an authority equivalent to that word. It thereby becomes what Mikhail Bakhtin called an 'authoritative word', which 'demands that we acknowledge it, that we make it our own; . . . it is, so to speak, the word of the fathers. Its authority was already acknowledged in the past'.[4] 'Authoritative discourse' presupposes a point of origin and a receiver, which immediately connects the problem of authority with that of tradition and reception.

However, as Rowan Williams notes, this task of handing on an authoritative discourse carries with it enormous dangers. The totalizing claim of an authoritative discourse means that the bearers of that discourse can easily become immune from criticism: 'The idea of being "authorized" to speak of God is fraught with risk, and has frequently been put to deeply corrupt use.'[5] The problem of authority points to questions of divine and human legitimacy, sovereignty and status, as well as the use and abuse of coercive power in both church and state.

Supernatural 'authority' was frequently used to legitimize political rulers who were sacramentally anointed to perform their duties by divine right. Theories of consent and popular will usually played second fiddle to a divinely-grounded absolutism expressed in both church and state. Indeed, for much of the history of the church, there was a complex interplay (and frequently an interchangeability of persons) between political and ecclesiastical authority. In much of the modern world, however, the shape of political authority has changed, and it is now closely related to popular legitimacy and democratic accountability. In a world where legitimacy has to be voluntarily conferred before authority is obeyed, this has inevitably affected ecclesiastical authority which has been traditionally legitimized through supernatural claims.

When church allegiance is a matter of voluntary choice, as has become the norm in most modern states, obedience to the church can no longer rely on the unquestioned authority and coercive power of the state. Instead, the state has become neutral towards religion, and religion has to rely on the voluntary commitment of its members. Rather than being part of any wider system of authority, authority in the church is now usually exercised in relation to those who voluntarily choose to accept its authority. While many in positions of authority in the church might still demand obedience and many churchgoers might be willing to submit to their authority, the exercise of authority can never be quite as straightforward in a situation where churchgoers are free to leave and to withdraw their support, both material and spiritual. Authority is more likely to be negotiated rather than simply accepted. Whether they like it or not church leaders are frequently forced to consult the laity as they seek to exercise authority. Many churches have sought to introduce forms of popular representation which recognize the voluntary nature of the church and allow a voice to all who participate. Others have been slower to accept the consequences of voluntarism, assuming that the 'command' structures of the past will persist into the future. The relationship between lay synods and traditional forms of episcopal (and papal) authority, however, is by no means straightforward, and creates significant new problems for the churches.

Meanings

There are at least two related senses of the word 'authority'. First is the sort of authority displayed by those who have a particular learning or expertise. This can be called authority in matters of belief. This is used of those people who are deemed to be 'authorities' and who make authoritative decisions in virtue of their superior wisdom, learning or academic status. This amounts to what the French political theorist, Bertrand de Jouvenel, called 'the faculty of gaining another man's assent'.[6] An authority on Shakespeare, for instance, will be respected by his or her peers, and most inferiors will simply assent to his or her judgements, which will carry weight and help sway arguments. The counterpart to this is that those who are not authorities in a particular area are expected to subordinate themselves to those who display authority. The English statesman, George Cornewall Lewis, suggested that this principle of authority rested in 'adopting the belief of others, on a matter of opinion, without reference to the particular grounds on which that belief may rest'.[7] Authority is thus a matter of personal trust and implies voluntary obedience.

The history of the word 'authority' illuminates this first meaning: the English word derives ultimately from the Latin *auctoritas*. In ancient Rome the concept of *auctoritas* originated in the law of inheritance: the person disposing of property (who was known by the cognate word *auctor*) guaranteed the help of the law to the inheritor against the claims of any third parties on that property. The guarantee itself gradually came to be known as the *auctoritas*. In this way it came to be associated with particular people whose opinions carried special weight, sometimes on account of their position within the community, and sometimes because of their learning or the strength of their personality. In Roman politics this meant that the concept of *auctoritas* was quite different from that of power (*potestas*). Power was something associated with the magistrate and carried with it the possibility of coercion and force. In distinction, *auctoritas* was used in relation to the advice offered by the Senate, thereby functioning as a check on the unfettered power of the magistrates: whatever power such a form of authority could command had to be earned through respect and guaranteed by the wisdom of those who were held to have authority. This sense of authority is reflected in the so-called 'authorities' of the English Legal tradition: a judge, whose sentence carries with it legal and coercive power, is nevertheless wise to base his or her decision on the 'authorities' of the legal tradition, even though there is no absolute requirement to do so. This might be referred to as 'enabling' authority rather than coercive power. To be most effective, the coercive power of the magistrate had to be based on his or her use of the accepted authorities.

The second meaning of authority relates to those people who are *in* authority in virtue of an office they hold rather than because of any personal qualities (although they might also be authorities in the first sense). They will have authority because of their position, status or role. Those with this form of authority will claim obedience from those over whom they exercise authority, and they may well have coercive power at their disposal. In this sense they can be said to have a commanding authority which does not need to be justified or proved, and is much closer to the related concepts of power and sovereignty. It derives primarily from the role: as the political philosopher, Thomas Hobbes, put it in the seventeenth century:

> Command is where a man saith, 'Do this,' or 'Do not this,' without expecting other reason than the will of him that says it. From this it followeth manifestly that he that commandeth pretendeth thereby his own benefit: for the reason of his command is his own will only, and the proper object of every man's will is some good to himself.[8]

Central here is the relationship between authority and power, a subject that has been much discussed among social scientists.

This second understanding of authority also derives from the Roman world. The Emperor Augustus claimed to be the leading citizen or *princeps* of the empire. It was from his primary position of authority that the power of the other magistrates was derived. This meant that all authority was vested in the person of the emperor. This could easily lead to some confusion as *auctoritas* came to be associated with the legal *power* of the magistrate and depended on office rather than status or wisdom. Power and authority became difficult to distinguish in practice. However, significant differences remain between the two terms: authority, which the sociologist Talcott Parsons described simply as 'an institutionalized complex of norms'[9] requires some form of legitimacy (on Max Weber's analysis, either charismatic, traditional or rational), whereas power does not rely on any form of consent of the governed.

Authority in the New Testament

The confusion between power and authority is already present in the New Testament; there is no direct equivalent of the Latin word *auctoritas* in the Greek text. The word which is often translated as 'authority' (*exousia*) is far closer to the English word 'power' (Latin *potestas*) which is also used to translate the word *dunamis*. There are, however, obvious similarities between Jesus' role as an 'authoritative' interpreter of his own religious tradition in virtue of his learning and status as a charismatic leader, and the claims made to speak with 'power' (*exousia*), a word which is used ninety-five times in the New Testament. Jesus claims a legitimacy in relation to the traditions of his elders and also his own charismatic gifts. The most important usage of the word *exousia* in the synoptic gospels connects Jesus' power with the power of God: what he does, especially when he speaks and acts as one 'with authority' (Lk 4.32),[10] he does in the name of God. Thus, at the outset of the Gospel of St Mark, it is the Son of Man who is given the authority on earth to forgive sins (Mk 2.10). This claim to be acting in the name of God is the cause of many of the conflicts with his opponents: for instance, Jesus is asked by his detractors: 'By what authority (*exousia*) are you doing these things?' (Mk 11.28; cf. Mt 21.23, where the same question is asked by the chief priests at Jesus' trial). Jesus is usually cryptic in his answers, leaving it up to his detractors to decide for themselves. He frequently answers questions with further questions. Thus at Mark 11.30–33, he asks, 'Did the baptism of John come from heaven, or was it of human origin? Answer me.' When the priests answer that they do not know, Jesus responds, 'Neither will I tell you by what authority I am doing these things.' The answer is presumably implied in his actions which are seen as displaying the power of God at work in Christ and legitimized by his miraculous abilities. At one point this power that comes from God is contrasted with the power of Beelzebul and Satan (Mk 3.22).

This notion of authority legitimized by supernatural power (*exousia*), which was exercised by Jesus, is akin to what Weber called 'charismatic authority', which he defined as

> a certain quality of an individual personality, by virtue of which he is set apart from ordinary men and treated as endowed with supernatural, superhuman, or at least specifically exceptional powers or qualities. These are such as are not accessible to the ordinary person, but are regarded as of divine origin or as exemplary, and on the basis of them the individual concerned is treated as a leader.[11]

The sort of authority displayed by the charismatic leader (among whom Weber ranks Napoleon as well as Jesus) is almost entirely personal and depends on a perceived legitimacy which is often based on religious or supernatural claims. The effects of the charismatic leader are often revolutionary in the sense that they challenge traditional patterns of behaviour: 'The genuine prophet, like the genuine military leader and every true leader in this sense, preaches, creates, or demands *new* obligations.'[12] Not surprisingly, however, such a form of authority can easily dissolve when the leader is removed from the scene.

The question that has attracted much debate among New Testament scholars is how the personal and charismatic authority of the founder (or founders) of Christianity is transmitted to the next generation. In this context it is important to note that the word *exousia* continues to be used in the New Testament of those who follow Jesus. At Mark 3.15, for instance, *exousia* is granted by Jesus to the twelve apostles so that they can cast out demons: Jesus' 'charismatic authority' is thus extended to those whom he has chosen as his disciples. Charisma is shared among a group.[13] Disciples, who undergo a form of religious rebirth (for example, by leaving occupations and family), share something of the charismatic authority of their leader. This creates what Weber called a 'charismatic aristocracy composed of a select group of adherents who are united by discipleship and loyalty and chosen according to personal charismatic qualification'.[14] Similarly, St Paul, while not one of those originally chosen, claims authority on the basis of what he has received from Jesus. He uses the word *exousia* in relation to the power coming from the Lord: 'Now, even if I boast a little too much of our authority, which the Lord gave for building you up and not for tearing you down, I will not be ashamed of it' (2 Cor 10.8; 13.10). The power of God thus resides in the apostle in order that he might undertake his task of proclamation, 'for it is not those who commend themselves that are approved, but those whom the Lord commends' (2 Cor 10.18). For Paul there is a close connection between the power of God and the authority of the apostle to carry out his pastoral duties. Like Jesus, Paul claimed charismatic authority for himself, understanding his mission in terms of authoritative interpretation of the scriptures which challenged the traditional forms of authority of the past. The law of Moses thus gave way to what had been received from Christ (1 Cor 11.23). Similarly in 1 Thessalonians 4.1, Paul connects obedience to his own message (and thus its authority) with obedience to Christ: 'as you received from us how you ought to live and to please God, just as you were doing, you do so more and more; for you know what instructions we gave you through the Lord Jesus'.

As charismatic authority was shared out among a 'charismatic aristocracy', so the problem of succession gradually became more pressing. Although the early Christians expected the imminent return of Christ, when this failed to materialize it became necessary to regularize a system for handing on the faith and to ensure that there were functionaries who possessed the authority to teach and who could claim legitimacy. In the later New Testament writings it is possible to detect the emergence of institutions for what Weber called the 'routinization of charisma' whereby new legal and traditional patterns of authority were established. Charismatic authority, according to Weber, could not remain 'stable, but becomes either traditionalized or rationalized, or a combination of both'.[15] The adaptation of charisma to routines (literally, in the German, 'everyday life') marked the 'turning point' where disciples become 'fiefholders, priests . . . all of whom want to live off the charismatic movement'.[16]

Elsewhere in the New Testament it is possible to detect the handing on of authority in terms of a commissioning of the next generation, which also leads to the creation of new traditions and primitive institutional and legal arrangements. Thus in 1 and 2 Timothy, the eponymous apostle is entrusted by Paul to 'guard the deposit' of faith (1 Tim 6.20) or the 'good treasure' (2 Tim 1.14) in order to hand it on. As Paul entrusts this charge to Timothy (1 Tim 1.18), so Timothy in his turn hands it on to others: 'what you have heard from me through many witnesses entrust to faithful people who will be able to teach others as well' (2 Tim 2.2). By the end of the New Testament period there is an institutional authority where the apostolic tradition, the faith 'once for all entrusted to the saints' (Jude 1.3), is passed from generation to generation. The charismatic authority of the first Christians thus 'actively seeks institutional manifestation, albeit a radically new one in contrast to existing patterns of authority'.[17] Paul's justifications for what he is doing, and the justifications given by his successors in the post-Pauline writings, help institutionalize the authority of the apostolic office, legitimized by what becomes the doctrine of apostolic succession. From the New Testament onwards the question of succession has remained important. Bishops, who were seen as holding the office of successor to the apostles, became authoritative interpreters and handers on of tradition. An early form of this institutionalization can be seen in the list of qualities required of a bishop in 1 Timothy 3.1 – 4.1, who 'must be above reproach, married only once, temperate, sensible, respectable, hospitable, an apt teacher, not a drunkard, not violent but gentle, not quarrelsome, and not a lover of money'.

Authority in the early church

The jurist Tertullian, at the turn of the third century, was the first to use the Latin word *auctoritas* in theology. Just as it had changed its use in imperial Rome to reflect the plenitude of power exercised by the emperor, so he used it to refer to the absolute authority of God, which was identified with the authority of Christ, which was embodied in the tradition which had been received from the apostles. In turn the tradition (which amounted to the canon of 'inspired' scripture understood in the light of the Creeds) was guaranteed by the institution Christ set up on earth. This institution was legitimized by the authority of the apostles as *auctores*:

> We Christians are forbidden to introduce anything on our own authority or to choose what someone else introduces on his own authority. Our authorities are the Lord's apostles, and they in turn chose to introduce nothing on their own authority. They faithfully passed on to the nations the teachings they had received in Christ. So we would anathematize even an angel from heaven if he were to preach a different Gospel.
>
> (*De Praescriptiones* 6)

The bishops, as successors to the apostles and ritually legitimized by an anointing with the Holy Spirit, became guarantors of the truth and the focus of unity. Charisma was routinized in the apostolic office which spoke in the name of the Holy Spirit. This theory was well described at Vatican II: the Spirit 'guides the church in the way of all truth and, uniting it in fellowship and ministry, bestows on it different hierarchic and charismatic gifts, and in this way directs and adorns it with his fruits' (*LG* 4). By the time of St Cyprian (d. 258), authority had become almost wholly identified with the person of the bishop, who began to resemble an earthly monarch. The church was understood as the bishop's church (*Ep.* 33:1): it was 'the people united to its pontiff, and the flock abiding with its shepherd' (*Ep.* 66:8). It became easy to equate episcopal authority with the power of the magistrate and, although there was always a claim to share authority with the wider church ('I decided to do nothing of my own opinion privately without your advice and the consent of the people' (*Ep.* 14:4)), the bishop became effectively invested with an almost unfettered power (*Ep.* 45:2; 68:5). The authority of the bishop as guardian of the Christian faith, legitimized by the Holy Spirit and succeeding from the apostles, could easily be identified with the power (and judgement) of God. This understanding continues the earlier tradition of Ignatius at the beginning of the second century: being subject to their bishop, the Magnesians (*Magn.* 3:1–2) and the Trallians (*Tral.* 2:1) are subject to God himself.

Augustine (354–430) later used the word *auctoritas* frequently, although he was never systematic. He based his theories on a traditional pattern of authority, which he saw as the foundation of all human life. Authority was something learned and legitimized through education in the distinctive pattern of communal life. The community was bound together by certain mores and rules which were themselves manifestations of God's love. The role of the leader in such a community was to teach Christian language and lifestyle through passing on the traditions and authorities (*auctoritas*) of the faith. For Augustine, learning, assimilating, reshaping and passing on a tradition were essential human characteristics, which went far beyond the mere emptiness of grammatical rules. The only means to overcome the inherited temptation towards pride was to trust in the authority of Christ passed down to the present generation through the church which functioned as his authoritative interpreter. In a famous quotation Augustine could write: 'I would not believe the Gospel unless the authority of the Church moved me to do so' (*C. Ep. fund.* 5, 6). The Spirit of Christ thus survived in the scripture and traditions and institutions of the church. However, Augustine was reluctant to identify any particular office, such as those bishoprics which claimed to have been established by the apostles themselves, with the utter certainty of divine power. Instead, all people were to return to the scriptures as the ultimate guarantee and test of their authority, and the bishop was always to exercise his authority in relation to his flock: 'When I am frightened what I am for you, then I am consoled by what I am with you. For you I am the bishop, with you I am a Christian. The first is an office, the second a grace; the first a danger, the second salvation' (*Sermo* 340:1).

Following the establishment of Christianity as the official religion of the Roman Empire in the fourth century, the concept of authority underwent significant change. Christian theology had to work out a theology of the Christian state, and of the relationships between secular and ecclesiastical authority. The authority exercised by both church and state was legitimized by a theory of divine origins. Matters were complicated still further as the church began to play a major part in the administration and bureaucracy of the state, which was emphasized after the decline of the Roman Empire. This can be understood in terms of Max Weber's typology as the introduction of a form of bureaucratic domination, whereby a form of legal authority is established as the rational basis for the exercise of power.[18] While this is always related to the traditional and charismatic authority claimed by the church, it nevertheless decisively alters the way in which the authority of the church is exercised.

The later Middle Ages were characterized by frequent conflicts between the authority of the church and that of the state. A well-known early example is that of Pope Gelasius I, who wrote to the emperor in 494, stressing the church's rule over the world: 'There are two principal authorities by means of which the world is ruled: the sacred authority of the bishops and the power of the royal office' (*DS* 347). In a theory which reasserted itself at various points, the authority of the bishop, which was equated with the authority of God, could hold the power of the emperor to account. At other times, however, the church was readily brought under the emperor's control. Even after the Reformation the civil ruler could be given a great deal of authority. In England, the king was elevated into the position of head of the church. An English archbishop (John Whitgift) wrote in the sixteenth century: 'The Archbishop doth exercise his jurisdiction under the prince and by the prince's authority. For, the prince having the supreme government of the realm, in all causes and over all persons, as she doth exercise the one by the Lord Chancellor, so doth she the other by the archbishops.'[19] Similarly for Luther, there was a duty to obey the magistrate in worldly matters primarily on account of the need to restrain the wicked, and for the Swiss reformer,

Zwingli, the Christian magistrate was understood as 'God's agent, no less than the prophet'.[20]

The centralization of authority

The history of the church is a history of conflict, much of it over the relative degree of weight which was to be attached to the authority of the different bishops (for instance, those of the ancient sees of Alexandria and Antioch in the East, and Rome in the West) in their efforts to find a solution to a disagreement. A good early example is the third-century conflict between St Cyprian and Pope Stephen over the validity of baptism by heretics, where the pope and Cyprian argued over the equality of bishops. For Cyprian, all bishops were equal, since:

> The episcopate is one; it is a whole in which each enjoys full possession. The church is likewise one, though she be spread abroad, and multiplies with the increase of her progeny. . . . Thus the Church, flooded with the light of the Lord, puts forth her rays through the whole world, with yet one light which is spread upon all places, where its unity of body is not infringed. She stretches forth her body over the universal earth, in her riches of plenty, and pours abroad her bountiful and onward streams; yet is there one head, one source, one Mother, abundant in the results of her fruitfulness. It is of her womb that we are born; our nourishing is from her milk; our quickening from her breath.
>
> (*De Unitate* 1)

The sole source of unity was Jesus Christ, which meant that no bishop had the right to interfere in another's business (*De Unitate* 5).

If that was the case then there could be no ecclesiastical equivalent of an appeal court, which meant that conflicts would remain unresolved unless a council of all the bishops ('ecumenical councils') could be summoned, which was both expensive and time consuming. While a gathering of bishops often took on special authority, it was far from true that the rulings of ecumenical councils were accepted without controversy, especially as there were few disciplinary powers available to the councils. Similarly, there was often conflict over the role of the civil authorities in summoning the councils in the first place.

The perceived need for central authority led to the increasing supremacy of the Roman See, which had earlier been regarded by Ignatius as a church 'foremost in love' (*Romans* 4) and by Irenaeus as a church 'of most excellent origins' (*Adv. Haer.* 3.3.2). Its claims to have been founded by both Peter and Paul proved useful in pointing to the power of the keys given to Peter in Matthew 16.18–19: 'I tell you, you are Peter, and on this rock I will build my church, and the gates of Hades will not prevail against it. I will give you the keys of the kingdom of heaven, and whatever you bind on earth will be bound in heaven, and whatever you loose on earth will be loosed in heaven.' By 343 Latin representatives at the Synod of Sardica claimed that deposed bishops could appeal to the bishop of Rome. This was put into practice, since by the time of Pope Damasus (366–84) there were complaints about his heavy-handed use of coercive authority.

In the Middle Ages, particularly after the reforming pontificate of Hildebrand (Gregory VII, 1073–85), authority and power were increasingly focused on the papacy, which began to expand its legal bureaucracy with the rise of the curia. The power of the keys was identified with the monarchical and legal authority of the pope, who alone gained the rights to dispense from certain laws, which frequently brought popes into conflict with secular rulers. The pope also gained significant material wealth. Since his power stemmed from God, he had authority over matters temporal (plenipotentiary power) as well as matters spiritual. By the time of Innocent III (1198–1216) the pope was beginning to adopt the title 'vicar of Christ'. The two aspects of authority were later differentiated into the *ius administrationis* (those aspects of episcopal authority which could be exercised before ordination) and the *ius actoritatis*, which required sacramental ordination. Popes gained the right to confirm bishops in their sees and could assert an unprecedented degree of unilateral power over the whole of the Western church, although this frequently brought them into conflict with the civil rulers, many of whom claimed authority over ecclesiastical preferment. The supernatural authority assumed by the papacy (occasionally challenged by an equivalent authority assumed by the rest of the bishops meeting in council ('conciliarism'), which was especially prominent in the fourteenth and fifteenth centuries) was exercised primarily through the use of legal power.

This concentration of ecclesiastical power in the papacy was accompanied by an increasingly centralized teaching office (*magisterium*) associated with the authority of the papacy, particularly in matters of faith. This meant that the tradition of the faith could be 'increased' through the definition of new dogmas. The pope gradually became the ultimate authority in doctrinal matters and, as the earthy representative of Christ, could not err in matters pertaining to human salvation. This led to a fully-fledged doctrine of papal infallibility which was based on a theory that Christ founded a perfect society represented by the church, headed by the pope as successor to Peter. The papacy was thus charged with the *authorization* of doctrine, a theory which was expanded at the Council of Trent, receiving its doctrinal formulation at the First Vatican Council of 1870:

> The Roman Pontiff, when he speaks *ex cathedra* – that is, when in the exercise of his office as pastor and teacher of all Christians he defines, by virtue of his supreme Apostolic authority, a doctrine of faith or morals to be held by the whole Church – is, by reason of the Divine assistance promised to him in blessed Peter, possessed of that infallibility with which the Divine Redeemer wished His Church to be endowed in defining doctrines of faith and morals; and consequently that such definitions of the Roman Pontiff are irreformable of their own nature (*ex sese*) and not by reason of the Church's consent.
>
> (DS 1839)

Although there has been sparing use of *ex cathedra* papal infallibility (limited to the two Marian dogmas of the Immaculate Conception and Assumption), the very possibility of infallibility has elevated the status of all papal pronouncements. As the papacy lost its temporal power, so papal authority was exerted against the claims of national churches, even extending to the choice of bishops. While some emphasised the equivalent magisterial authority of bishops in council, many continued to elevate the claims of the papacy. Pope John Paul II, for instance, restated the theory of infallibility more moderately in 1979: 'The Church's teaching, liturgy and life spring from [the Bible and the Gospels] and lead back to it, under the guidance of the pastors and, in particular, of the doctrinal Magisterium entrusted to them by the Lord' (*DN* 259.27).[21] In practice it is difficult to discern limits to papal authority, even when it is not exercised *ex cathedra*. For instance, the papal document

Ordinatio Sacerdotalis (1994), which reserves priestly ordination to men alone, concludes unambiguously 'that the Church has no authority whatsoever to confer priestly ordination on women and that this judgment is to be definitively held by all the Church's faithful'. The very discussion of the possibility of the ordination of women was definitively ruled out by papal decree.

Authority and the Reformation

The Reformation was directed in part against the centralization of power and authority in the Petrine office to the exclusion of other sources of authority, perhaps most importantly that derived from reading the plain text of scripture.[22] The traditional authority of the church – in particular its scripture and to a lesser extent the traditions embodied in the Creeds – were pitted against the bureaucratic and legalistic authority of the papacy, which had been reiterated at the fifth Lateran Council of 1512–17 (*DS* 1445). Among scholars like Erasmus, who pioneered textual criticism, Christ once again 'lived, breathed and spoke for us'. The 'Word of God' was not to be identified with the word of the pope or the priest as God's representatives. Instead, according to the cardinal reformation doctrine of the absolute sovereignty of God, there could be no intermediary between God and the world, which meant that no ecclesiastical or political authority could stand between God and the human being.

Martin Luther challenged the office of the priesthood and the independent authority of the church in the controversies of 1517–20, which were epitomized by his three treatises of 1520. Luther claimed authority for the Word of God as the judge of all human authority. This meant that Christ alone was head of the church, and the only law was the law of the gospel. The Word of God existed externally to the church and acted as its critic. The rational forms of legal authority which had been upheld by theorists of reason, including Thomas Aquinas, were also challenged in the light of the Word of God. Like Luther, John Calvin also understood the church as subject to the word of the Lord: 'the only authorized way of teaching in the church is by the prescription and standard of [God's] Word'.[23]

Such a view has continued to shape Protestant understandings of authority until the present day, as the Barmen Declaration bore witness when the Confessing Church made a stand against the National Socialists in Hitler's Germany. All institutions and authorities, both ecclesiastical and political, were open to judgement in the light of the Word of God: 'We reject the false doctrine that, apart from this ministry, the Church could, and could have permission to, give itself or allow itself to be given special leaders [*Führer*] vested with ruling authority' (*Barmen Declaration* 4). With the rise of Protestant Orthodoxy in the seventeenth century and the development of doctrines of verbal inspiration in the nineteenth, the authority of scripture itself was amplified to the extent that God himself was seen as its *auctor*. This conferred on the letter of scripture a quasi-juridical role in questions of faith, something still maintained by many conservative Evangelicals.

To some extent, the principle of the authority of scripture was paralleled in the Catholic Reformation with the reassertion of the teaching authority of the pope, enshrined in the elevation of an oral tradition expounded by the teaching office and elevated to a similar status to scripture. This led to the 'two-source' theory, with equal weight being given to proofs from both scripture and tradition. This was clearly stated in the sixteenth century at Trent:

> The Holy ecumenical and general council of Trent . . . receives and venerates with the same sense of loyalty and reverence all the books of the Old and New Testaments – for God alone is the author of both – together with all the traditions concerning faith and morals, as coming from the mouth of Christ or being inspired by the Holy Spirit and preserved in continuous succession in the Catholic Church.
>
> (*DN* 210; *DS* 1501)

The authority of the original apostles was extended to the present by a theory of living succession which gave to the bishops, as guardians of the tradition, something approaching the authority of Christ himself.

Authority in the modern world

The concept of authority has changed fundamentally since the Enlightenment of the eighteenth century. The liberation of human reason, as a self-legislating authority which did not rely on the traditional authorities of the past, decisively reshaped the nature of political authority. This had profound effects on the nature of ecclesiastical authority, challenging the comprehensive authoritarianism of the church-state unions of Europe. With the demand for self-legislating autonomy, which Peter Gay has called a 'recovery of nerve',[24] the supernatural authorities which legitimated the structures of power (which included the institutions of the church and its traditional interpretations of scripture) were themselves called into question. All traditional authority was challenged, whether the scriptural principle of the Reformers, the rule of the Christian magistrate, or the Catholic *magisterium*.

In England, for instance, the increasing democratization of political authority challenged the Anglican Settlement, which provoked many conservative church leaders into a clamour to repristinate the traditional models of church authority, most importantly the concept of 'apostolical succession', which was proclaimed by John Henry Newman in the first of the polemical pamphlets published as *Tracts for the Times* in 1833. A similar clamour can be found in other churches: there was a resistance towards liberalism and a desire to return to the supernaturally based certainties which legitimized the unquestioned authorities of the past. The success of liberalism in the very homeland of the papacy can be understood as one of the most important reasons behind the declaration of papal infallibility in 1870. Similarly, biblical fundamentalism in the United States can be seen as a clamour for certainty against the insecurity and doubt that come with the critical method of the Enlightenment.[25] In some denominations there has been a resort to 'experience' of the Holy Spirit as a source of authority and power, which some have seen as a rejuvenation of charismatic forms of authority, but which many have criticized on psychological grounds.[26]

The return to traditional patterns of authority sets the church against the modern world, where authority is usually understood as having to be negotiated rather than relying on supernatural forms of legitimation. It becomes a two-way process. Some critics have gone further, seeing the demands for traditional authority as evidence of the survival of a form of oppression that denies human freedom. If authority demands a form of absolute obedience then Graham Shaw's question is surely relevant: 'Is all religious authority of its nature oppressive, evading criticism by divisive social attitudes? Is the Christian gospel inherently self-contradictory, promising freedom but enforcing obedience, promising reconciliation but sanctioning division? Is the language of Christianity a device for disguising the exercise of power?'[27] The Christian vocabulary of obedience (restated by Luther), which has often focused on 'bondage' and 'slavery' and the denial of free-will, invites careful theological and psychological critique.[28]

Authority and the voluntary church

In much recent Roman Catholic theology there has been talk about the *sensus fidelium*, as the 'holy people of God' are called to share in 'Christ's prophetic office'. The people of God 'guided by the sacred *magisterium* which it faithfully obeys, receives not the words of human beings but truly the word of God' (*LG* 12). While this hardly amounts to a democratic vision, it does at least affirm the inter-relationship between the traditional authorities of the church and the 'people of God'. This can be read as a (perhaps reluctant) concession to modernity and the need to win legitimacy not through traditional or supernatural means but by a form of consent. John Henry Newman referred to this as a 'breathing together',[29] by which he meant that the whole church participated in the handing on of the faith. Similarly the great Catholic theologian of authority and tradition, Yves Congar, claimed that the authority of the bishop was always exercised in the service of the laity, which was later restated in the 1994 Catholic Catechism.[30]

Other churches have set up formal processes of consultation, having introduced various types of synodical government (or, as with many Reformed churches, developing them from their reformation roots). Most churches in the Anglican Communion, for instance, seek to legitimize the authority of the church leadership through votes in legislative chambers. This can be seen as a rationalization and de-traditionalization of authority, which does not always sit easily with the survival of apostolic succession and episcopal authority. In many denominations, church leaders are elected by more or less democratic franchises, even when this provokes serious disagreement (as with the election of an openly homosexual bishop in the American Episcopal Church). While there have been surprisingly few theorists of synodical authority, it is clear that there is a need to renegotiate the basis of authority when members of churches no longer place much weight on traditional structures or legitimations of authority. The fact that there has been widespread disobedience of many pronouncements by church leaders (not least the rulings on contraception by Pope Paul VI) points to the complexity (and pointlessness) of any system of authority which cannot command obedience.

One of the most thoroughgoing theorists of negotiated authority was the Anglican writer J. Neville Figgis, who sought to draw out the implications of post-Enlightenment voluntarism for the church. Authority was not about passive obedience but an active participation in a form of authority intimately bound up with the conscience of each individual who decided to join in the first place:

> What we most need to realise is that authority in the Church of God is the expression of the life of the whole Christian community, and no single member but plays his part. Of all dangers which beset the statement of the idea of authority, none at this moment is so serious as that which views it purely as external command. The moment that notion is accepted, we are far on the way to the notion that the duty of the majority is merely passive.[31]

The idea of participation has been a key theme among many writers, including Roman Catholics. How this form of mutual and voluntarily negotiated authority might develop is an open question. What cannot be denied, however, is that the problem of authority remains very much a live issue in the churches today.

Notes

1 P.T. Forsyth, *The Principle of Authority in Relation to Certainty, Sanctity, and Society; an essay in the philosophy of experimental religion*, London: Hodder and Stoughton, 1913, p. 1. Cf. T.A. Lacey, *Authority in the Church*, London: Mowbray, 1928.
2 See the enunciation of the problems, particularly over papal primacy, in the ARCIC agreed statement *Authority in the Church* I, London: SPCK, 1977, esp. §24. These issues were taken up in *Authority in the Church* II, London: SPCK, 1981; and *The Gift of Authority: Authority in the Church III*, London: CTS, 1999.
3 Kierkegaard, *On Authority and Revelation: The Book on Adler, or A Cycle of Ethico-religious Essays*, Princeton: Princeton University Press, 1955, p. 110.
4 Mikhail Bakhtin (ed. Michael Holquist), *The Dialogic Imagination: Four Essays by M. M. Bakhtin*, Austin, Texas: University of Texas Press, 1981, p. 342.
5 Rowan Williams, *On Christian Theology*, Oxford: Blackwell, 2000, p. 231.
6 Bertrand de Jouvenel, *Sovereignty*, Cambridge: Cambridge University Press, 1957, p. 29.
7 George Cornewall Lewis, *An Essay on the Influence of Authority in Matters of Opinion*, London: Parker, 1849, p. 7.
8 Thomas Hobbes, *Leviathan* (Ch. 25), London: Fontana, 1962, p. 237.
9 Talcott Parsons, *Essays in Sociological Theory*, New York: Free Press, 1954, p. 205.
10 All Bible references are to NRSV.
11 Weber, *Economy and Society: an Outline of Interpretative Sociology*, New York: Bedminster, 1968, p. 241.
12 Weber, *Economy and Society*, pp. 243–4.
13 Bengt Holmberg, *Paul and Power: the Structure of Authority in the Primitive Church as Reflected in the Pauline Epistles*, Minneapolis: Fortress Press, 1978, p. 141. See also Nicholas Taylor, *Paul, Antioch and Jerusalem: A Study in Relationships and Authority in Earliest Christianity*, Sheffield: JSOT Press, 1992, pp. 32–43.
14 Weber, *Economy and Society*, p. 1119.
15 Weber, *Economy and Society*, p. 246.
16 Weber, *Economy and Society*, p. 1122.
17 Holmberg, *Paul and Power*, p. 165.
18 Weber, *Economy and Society*, p. 213.
19 John Whitgift, *The Works*, Cambridge: Cambridge University Press (Parker Society), 1853, ii, p. 248.
20 G.R. Potter (ed.), *Huldrych Zwingli*, London: Arnold, 1977, p. 124.
21 English translation of *Catechesi Tradendae* in J. Dupuis and J. Neuner (eds), *Christian Faith: Doctrinal Documents of the Catholic Church*, London: HarperCollins, 1992 (hereafter *DN*). For a selection of texts see Gerard Mannion *et al.*, *Readings in Church Authority: Gifts and challenges for contemporary Catholicism*, Aldershot: Ashgate, 2003.
22 See G.R. Evans, *Problems of Authority in the Reformation Debates*, Cambridge: Cambridge University Press, 1992.
23 John Calvin, *Institutes of the Christian Faith* (IV.8.8), Philadelphia: Westminster Press, 1960, vol. ii, p. 1155.
24 Peter Gay, *The Enlightenment*, New York: A. Knopf, 1967, ii, pp. 3–8.
25 See James Barr, *Fundamentalism*, London: SCM, 1978.
26 See Martyn Percy, *Power and the Church*, London: Cassell, 1998.
27 Graham Shaw, *The Cost of Authority*, London: SCM, 1983, p. 12.
28 See Paul Avis, *Authority, Leadership and Conflict in the Church*, London: Mowbray, 1992, Ch. 2.
29 John Henry Newman, *On Consulting the Faithful in Matters of Doctrine*, London: Chapman, 1961, p. 163.
30 Yves Congar in J. M. Todd (ed.), *Problems of Authority*, London: DLT, 1962, Ch. 7; cf. Congar, *Lay People in the Church*, London: Chapman, 1959. The teaching office 'serves' the laity (*Catechism of*

the Catholic Church, London: Chapman, 1994, § 2235–6). See also Bernard Hoose (ed.), *Authority in the Roman Catholic Church*, Aldershot: Ashgate, 2002.
31 J. N. Figgis, *Fellowship of the Mystery*, London: Longmans, 1914, p. 193. See also *Churches in the Modern State*, London: Longmans, 1913.

Further reading

Authority in the Church I, London: SPCK, 1977, esp. §24.

Authority in the Church II, London: SPCK, 1981; and *The Gift of Authority: Authority in the Church* III, London: CTS, 1999.

Paul Avis, *Authority, Leadership and Conflict in the Church*, London: Mowbray and Philadelphia: Trinity Press International, 1992.

Mark D. Chapman, *By What Authority?* London: Darton, Longman and Todd, 1997.

Gillian Evans, *Problems of Authority in the Reformation Debates*, Cambridge: Cambridge University Press, 1992.

Bengt Holmberg, *Paul and Power: the Structure of Authority in the Primitive Church as Reflected in the Pauline Epistles*, Minneapolis: Fortress Press, 1978.

Bernard Hoose (ed.), *Authority in the Roman Catholic Church*, Aldershot: Ashgate, 2002.

Gerard Mannion et al., *Readings in Church Authority: Gifts and Challenges for contemporary Catholicism*, Aldershot: Ashgate, 2003.

Nicholas Taylor, *Paul, Antioch and Jerusalem: A Study in Relationships and Authority in Earliest Christianity*, Sheffield: JSOT Press, 1992.

John M. Todd (ed.), *Problems of Authority*, London: Darton, Longman and Todd and Baltimore: Helicon Press, 1962.

28

THE LAITY

Paul Lakeland

Introduction

A discussion of the role of the laity in the Christian church must face from the beginning the ambiguities of the term 'laity' and, frankly, the questionable reference of a word which has served for most of the history of the church to denote those who are thought to have nothing special about them, and to distinguish them from the ordained who by the very fact of their ordination are, indeed, special. There is a certain irony, as peculiar as it is revealing, to the fact that theology is almost bereft of sustained reflection on the history and theological significance of these 'laity', over 95 per cent of the members of the Christian church through the ages. Theologically speaking, the Christian laity have been all but invisible for most of the last fifteen hundred years.[1]

There are three exceptions to the theological invisibility of the laity. The first and most extended is the early centuries of the Christian church when the whole people were materially involved in the governance and leadership of the community of faith. The second is the consequence of the Protestant reformers' distaste for the hierarchical ministry of the Roman Catholic Church.[2] And the third is the twentieth century renascence of a vital Christian laity and the concomitant efforts to reflect theologically on what that might mean. Each has its own contribution to make to understanding the idea of the laity.

The early church

Let us begin with scripture. While the word *laikos* (lay person) does not occur anywhere in the Bible, the word *laos* (people) is found frequently in both Hebrew and Christian scriptures, referring to the people of God. It is the *sacred* people that *laos* signifies, those who are consecrated to God, whether Israel or, later, the priestly people of the new covenant. The use of the word has the twin significances first that it denotes the faithful people over against those who do not share this faith, and second that it refers to all of them, without any distinctions within the faithful community. All are a consecrated *laos*. This usage of the term *laos* can be found today in the ecclesiology of the Second Vatican Council (1962–5), where the Dogmatic Constitution on the Church makes much of the idea of the 'people of God' as a central image for the entire community, ordained and non-ordained together. While it has fallen into disuse for long periods of time between the early church and the present day, the idea common to all Christian confessions that it is baptism which makes the faithful people is an at least implicit reference to the fundamental equality of all the faithful people, the *laos* of God.

The growth of early church leadership into the historic tripartite ministry of bishops, priests and deacons was a long-drawn-out affair, taking some three centuries to emerge fully in a form that continues mostly unchanged in Orthodox and Catholic traditions up to the present day. Among the very earliest Christians the apostles formed the only formal leadership. These were a small group of men who had been close to Jesus during his life, and who emerged after his death as a kind of council of elders whose deliberations together, under the leadership of Peter and James, seem to have been unquestioningly accepted as the rule of the community. It is of course impossible to say how historically accurate such a picture is, but it is certain that these men had a sufficiently central role that the gospels represent them as having been selected by Jesus himself. This, of course, further attested to their authority or, if you will, consolidated their power. However, by the time the gospels were written many if not all of the original apostles were dead and the Jerusalem church which had been their focus was pretty much a thing of the past. The gospel story of apostolic authority is, then, in truth an attestation of the apostolic tradition, of the sense that leaders in the church – bishops if you will – were continuing the apostolic tradition and shared somehow in the authority of the apostles themselves.[3]

In the early church the whole people seem to have been materially involved in what today we would call governance. This is evident in the opening verses of the Acts of the Apostles where the number of the apostles must be restored to the symbolic twelve with the replacement of Judas. The text is absolutely clear that Matthias is chosen by the 120 people present, who pray and then cast lots to determine which of the two candidates is most suited, 'and he was enrolled with the eleven apostles' (1.26). Thus is established a most important principle in early Christianity that lasts at least until the fourth century, and in some places longer. The entire *laos* plays a central role in the selection of those who will exercise leadership of and authority over the whole community. The late first-century *Didache* instructs its community to 'elect therefore for yourselves bishops and deacons of the Lord'. In succeeding centuries Origen, Hippolytus, Cyprian and many others show conclusively that while the procedures for the selection of bishops varied from place to place, and while there was a slow development towards the eventual exclusion of the non-ordained from any serious voice in their selection, it was the standard pattern of the church of the first three centuries for the whole people to be involved in elections.[4]

The flowering of monasticism is often linked to the Constantinian revolution that so deeply affected the church in the fourth century, but it also marks an important step in the development of the Christian laity. With the legitimation and domestication of the church occasioned by the pagan emperor Constantine's new-found affection for it, something of its edge was in danger of being lost, and monasticism is rightly seen as in part a critique of this loss of the prophetic. But it is at least as important as a sign of the changing roles of lay people. Early monasticism was largely a lay phenomenon, perhaps one response to their growing exclusion from roles in governance. Of course, prominent lay people continued to serve for a time as theologians and never lost their place as principal benefactors of the church. However, the fourth century was the last in which Christian lay people (at least in the churches along the northern shores of the Mediterranean) could be relied upon to cherish the classical traditions and to have a degree of classical education that equipped them for theological speculation.[5] Naturally, such roles could not be assumed by everyone, and so the decline in the importance of lay people continued even as a few prominent laity acquired significant roles. But it is also true, if we are to believe the Emperor Julian (who died in 363), that the works of charity of ordinary Christians were such that they could impress a good pagan. At the beginning of the fifth century, with the fall of Rome, all this changed. The classical tradition was all but lost to the world, and both an apocalyptic mentality and a more ascetic temperament replaced the urbane sensitivities of late antiquity, above all in the Latin West.

A sociologist might reasonably see the first three or four hundred years of the church as a time in which the professional specialization of clergy was slowly forming, and think that as this took place, the laity naturally receded from the realm of decision-making. A theologian would want to point out, however, even if the sociologist's picture were acceptable, that there is a problem with this development, if development it was. For while it is possible to assert that leadership lies with the clergy – the Catholic tradition has mostly followed this approach – it ought not to follow that therefore there is nothing to say, theologically, about what it means to be a lay person. What happens in the early church, theologically speaking, is that by degrees the significance of baptismal equality is displaced by a focus on the power of orders. The *laos*, the people, goes from being a designation of the whole community to applying to the remainder, the silent 'lay' majority, about whom there is apparently nothing special to say.

Protestants and Catholics

While it may seem preposterous to sum up the next thousand years in a couple of paragraphs, it is fair to say that the time between the end of the sixth century and the age of Luther and Calvin was one in which the laity went into eclipse in the church. Of course, there were lay rulers and emperors who at times controlled the church, and lay men and women occasionally exercised enormous influence over the church (one naturally thinks of a person like Catherine of Siena, but there were many more), and there were even lay theologians of some distinction (Henry VIII of England, for example), but by and large the laity were not on the radar screen of ecclesiastics, other than as the great masses on whose behalf the church administered the sacraments. Indeed, Yves Congar accurately described them as 'negative creatures'. That is, they were 'not clerics' and 'not monks and nuns'. They were thus of no theological interest to a church which stressed the visible institution and its hierarchical constitution. While this was to change to a degree among the new Protestant churches from the sixteenth century onwards, reaction to the Reformation, if anything, intensified this view of the laity in the Catholic tradition. There the laity perhaps reached the nadir of their fortunes as recently as 1910, in the words of Pope St. Pius X (1901–14):

> It follows that the Church is essentially an unequal society, that is, a society comprising two categories of person, the Pastors and the flock, those who occupy a rank in the different degrees of the hierarchy and the multitude of the faithful. So distinct are these categories that with the pastoral body only rests the necessary right and authority for promoting the end of the society and directing all its members towards that end; the one duty of the multitude is to allow themselves to be led and, like a docile flock, to follow the Pastors.
>
> (*Vehementer Nos*, para. 8)

The sixteenth-century re-emergence of the laity in the thinking of the Protestant reformers, whether seen in Luther's renewed attention to the baptismal priesthood or in Calvinist congregationalism, was a long overdue reminder that the rights, responsibilities and powers of the clergy were meant to be at the service of all the faithful people. Inspired by the famous passage in Galatians 3, which proclaims that 'there is neither Jew nor Greek, slave nor free, male nor female, for you are all one in Christ Jesus', Luther made the fundamental equality of all Christians through baptism absolutely central to his vision. Indeed, lest anyone doubt the application, he rewrote the passage very pointedly to read, 'There is neither priest nor layman, canon or vicar, rich or poor, Benedictine, Carthusian, Friar Minor or Augustinian, for it is not a question of this or that status, degree, order.' John Calvin was essentially in agreement with Luther on the baptismal priesthood, though his concern that the consent of the whole community was needed to confirm the call of the Spirit upon individuals was an important check on exaggerated individual claims to inspiration that were erroneously thought to have been encouraged by Luther's position.[6]

The changes wrought by the Reformation, however, involved no sustained theological reflection on what it meant to be a lay person. They were for the most part steps which led to a variety of church orders at variance with the Catholic model, but not implying much if anything about what being 'lay' might mean. It was not long, in any case, before a renewed clericalism affected the Protestant churches in some quarters, and a virulent anticlericalism in others. But the curious fact is that the attempted destruction of the Catholic understanding of hierarchical ministry and the reassertion of the baptismal priesthood inevitably has the effect of removing, at least theoretically, the very category of 'laity'. Just as in the early church, everyone is part of the people, the *laos*. For this reason if for no other, a theology of the laity is more likely to emerge in the Catholic tradition, where the clergy/laity distinction is maintained, however modified, even up to the present day. At the same time it has to be said that the changes in the Catholic tradition which we shall discuss later have brought that tradition too to the same set of issues. If we re-emphasize baptism in order to restore the balance lost in the privileging of hierarchical ministry, and turn simply instead to thinking of a range of different ministries, do we not run the risk of what John Paul II frequently called 'the clericalization of the laity and the laicization of the clergy'? And, *pace* the late pope, is that such a bad thing anyway?

The 'primitivist' or 'restitutionist' implications of the Protestant position on the baptismal priesthood demand and certainly elicited a response from the Catholic wing of the church. At first, the polemical climate of the Reformation and Counter-Reformation inevitably meant that the Roman Catholic Church simply rejected the Lutheran position.[7] However, Roman Catholicism since Vatican II has asserted much more strongly than ever before the importance of lay mission and ministry, and has placed the baptismal priesthood at the centre of all discussions of church. Nevertheless, it has also maintained equally strongly its commitment to a hierarchical church order in which, when all is said and done, lay people have no formal voice whatsoever. This equality in mission and hierarchical subordination in church order is grounded, in the Roman Catholic vision of things, in the New Testament. The standard Roman Catholic position is that hierarchy is given with the foundation of the church. As Jesus calls his disciples around him, he also selects leaders. Apostolic authority is thus on the one hand absolutely fundamental to church order, and on the other – most importantly for the Catholic vision – a commission that comes directly from Christ and not a function of the community itself. Protestant theology would be inclined too, in particular before the advent of the historical–critical method, to recognize separate establishment of the college of the apostles. But it would not conclude in as sanguine a fashion as the Catholic tradition that this apostolic foundation extends to the bishops. While ministerial leadership in the Protestant tradition is understood as a function quite other than that of apostolic authority, the Roman Catholics see it as a continuation of that apostolic authority.

While attending to theological issues of ministry and orders gives some coherence to the historical fortunes of the *idea* of the laity, it does not do justice to the rich contribution that lay people themselves made to the life of the church in the centuries between Luther and, say, the advent of the First Vatican Council in the Roman Catholic Church (1870). It is here that the vitality of the lay contribution shows up to such a profound degree that, sometimes, the theological disputes among church divines pale by comparison. What, for example, of the heroic efforts of Joseph Schaitberger (1658–1733), who led a virtual lay person's church of Lutherans in the midst of Catholic Salzburg until their expulsion from Austria in 1732? Or, in nineteenth-century Germany, Richard Rothe's (1799–1867) efforts to promote a kind of secular Christianity in which the clergy were no longer necessary and the work of evangelization fell entirely to the laity? For a more decorous and entertaining story we could turn to the life of Selina Countess of Huntingdon (1707–91),[8] who used her aristocratic status as a licence to evangelize her fellow English blue-bloods, a thankless task if ever there was one. The Roman Catholic tradition can boast major figures like Joseph de Maistre (1751–1821), Charles de Montalembert (1810–70) and Frederic Ozanam (1813–53).[9] But perhaps there has been no more influential Catholic lay person in recent centuries than Baron Friedrich von Hügel, a figure at the heart of the Modernist crisis in the Roman Catholic Church at the turn of the twentieth century.[10]

The Christian laity in modernity

In the twentieth century many factors came together to make it inevitable that the laity would emerge as the object of theological scrutiny. Among them were the rise of an educated laity, democracy, the perceived threat of secularism particularly in European societies, and the decline in the number of clergy, this last especially in the Roman Catholic Church. But there were also other than sociological reasons, among them the rise in scriptural and early church scholarship, the renewal of liturgical and sacramental theology, and the opening to the world that had no better symbol than Pope John XXIII's calling of the Second Vatican Council for the express purpose of *aggiornamento* (updating) of the church. Better ecumenical relations have also meant that the approaches to ministry in Protestant and Catholic traditions have, at least to a degree, been enlightening to those of the 'other persuasion', rather than demonized. All of these developments have meant that in the early years of the twenty-first century real progress is finally being made in understanding just what it is to be a lay Christian.

'Coming of age' is a term we use from time to time to designate moments at which the rights and responsibilities of adulthood are acquired. Dietrich Bonhoeffer's use of the phrase 'a world come of age' (borrowed from Immanuel Kant) issued a challenge to Christians to find their way to theological reflection that took the modern world seriously, and has some softer echoes in Vatican II's call to attend to 'the signs of the times' in thinking theologically. But we can also use the language of coming to adulthood a little more aggressively, to designate the demands of modern human beings for a full say in the decisions and structures that determine so much of their lives. The thirst for democracy is one such development in recent history. In the churches, lay people have similar concerns for the end of ecclesial structures that enforce a kind of infantilization upon the non-ordained. For Roman Catholics, this status has been a matter of theology, while for Protestants it has sometimes been a case of practice contradicting theology (the baptismal priesthood, congregational autonomy, and so on).

There is no question that in the years since Vatican II the Roman Catholic laity has come of age in terms of the kinds of roles that some at least have been asked to play. There are far more lay people in positions of responsibility in chancery offices, in the Vatican, and above all in the parishes, than could ever have been envisaged only fifty years ago. However, there is a deeper meaning to adulthood than simply being given jobs. Adulthood implies ownership, and requires the recognition on the part of all that adults make decisions for themselves. Where adults do not make their own decisions, they are either phantom adults or they live in a paternalistic culture in which adulthood is not really recognized. But because lay subordination is a product of hierarchical theologies, the shift towards adulthood requires a theological foundation. The language of 'human rights' seems not to be persuasive in the context of the Roman Catholic Church, whether it has to do with the ordination of women or a lay voice in the selection of bishops.

It seems pretty clear that in today's church Christians are trying to find their way to adulthood in this deeper sense. Of course, the church is an organism in which different people exercise different gifts, and not all are called to leadership or to preaching, or to presidency at the eucharist. But at the same time we all of us know what an adult society is like. It is one in which we have leaders with particular responsibilities, but this does not preclude a vigorous public forum in which all the adult members of the given society exercise their adult rights and responsibilities. In other words, while the church is certainly not the state, nor needs to be modelled on the state, a church which recognizes the adulthood of its members is going to look like any other open society. In this sense at least, the church needs to be much more democratic. The only alternative to that is the prolongation of a paternalistic culture of clericalism in which adult lay people settle for the ecclesiastical status of children, however complex, professional and 'adult' their secular responsibilities may be.

The most significant modern efforts to think about the theological status of lay people in the Christian church have taken place in the work of the Roman Catholic bishops at the Second Vatican Council (1962–5).[11] While there were great Catholic theologians in the first half of the twentieth century, particularly in France and Germany, who began to lay the foundations for a genuine theology of the laity, it was not until Vatican II that the institutional church itself found a way to correct the imbalances of the previous 1700 years. In three documents of the Council, on the Church, on the Apostolic Activity of Laypeople, and on the Church in the Modern World, the bishops recognized the equality of all the faithful in virtue of their baptism, they reasserted the priestly character of the whole people of God, and they wrote eloquently of the rights and responsibilities of lay people to evangelize, to share in the mission of the church, and to speak up courageously for the good of the church.[12] Vatican II was an enormous step forward in an understanding of the roles of lay people in the church, and it has borne fruit in the wonderful proliferation of lay ministries, nowhere more in evidence than in the Roman Catholic Church in America, where the number of full-time lay ministers will soon exceed the number of ordained priests.

While the Vatican Council's contribution was remarkable, it was at the same time something of a missed opportunity. On the whole, the bishops preferred to discuss the lay apostolate rather than examine the theological status of lay people. The reasons are obvious. You cannot separate a theology of the laity from a theology of the church, a theology of priesthood, a theology of authority, and so on. At Vatican II the assembled bishops were not ready to tackle the kinds of questions that a theological reflection on laity would rapidly have led to. So, in those remarks they did make about the theological status of the laity, they fell back for the most part on the language of 'secularity'. Lay people were those in the church whose vocation was understood to be in the secular world. Some lay people, of course, held some kinds of positions within the church, but these 'ministries' were understood more as auxiliary to those of ordained priesthood than as proper to the lay state itself. The proper sphere of the laity, still, was the secular world. The proper sphere of the clergy was the church. And so, inevitably, the divide between clergy and laity persisted, for all the advances of Vatican II.

In the United States particularly, one cannot overstate the significance of the scandal of clerical sexual abuse of minors in energizing the Roman Catholic laity.[13] The problem of sexual abuse is not an exclusively Catholic problem, nor is it a concern only for the American church. England, Ireland and Poland, Canada and Australia and Austria, to name but a few, have all had major crises of their own. But most public scrutiny has been given to the American context. And the Roman Catholic situation has been most challenging for two reasons. First, the fact that all the clergy are male and almost all are celibate, and that most victims of sexual abuse were adolescent boys, has strained the traditional trust in the priesthood. Second, the scandal of sexual abuse led to an equally serious crisis of trust in episcopal authority, since the bishops have in many cases done a particularly poor job of dealing with offenders, often in fact enabling them, and seem as a whole to have taken insufficient responsibility for the pain and suffering of the victims. For both these reasons, many lay people have organized as never before to challenge the leaders of their church. The principal organization founded as a direct response to the scandal was the Boston-based Voice of the Faithful, which began as a handful of people in early 2002 and grew in about a year to around 25,000 members. While not an activist organization on neuralgic issues like the question of mandatory celibacy for priests or the possibility of ordaining women, Voice of the Faithful does stand for structural changes in the church that would lead to considerably more of an active role for laity in the governance of their parishes and the local church.

Baptism and hierarchy

Implicit in the scripturally based theology of the people of God is the sense that at its root the Christian body is a *communio*, a union of those who share the same beliefs in God's saving acts in and through their Lord Jesus Christ, and who have entered into this community of faith through their baptism. In baptism they form a new creation, the Body of Christ, in which, in the words of Paul in Galatians, there is no longer slave nor free, Jew nor Gentile, male nor female, 'for you are all one in Christ Jesus' (3:28). While, therefore, Christ is the head of the body which is his church, the church itself is conceived in radical equality, a community in which old notions of 'us' and 'them' must be left behind. This is a *communio* of equals. Moreover, in virtue of baptism this body of the faithful is priestly, prophetic and royal in a more than analogous relationship to Christ who is priest, prophet and king. Baptismal priesthood is not a metaphor or an analogy. It is a reality which implies involvement in Christian discipleship and in the mission of the church.

If indeed the community of faith that scripture seems to envisage is one of the utter equality of its members, then the question immediately arises of the source of difference within the community, particularly those differences which have the potential in the end to become new forms of 'us' and 'them' disparities of power, influence or status. If all the baptized constitute the *laos* of God, then what is the warrant for hierarchy? And once some have been distinguished by particular roles, what prevents the idea of 'the laity' becoming little or nothing more than a remainder concept? In historical terms, the laity emerge from the *laos* just as church leaders are beginning to acquire cultic characteristics. The more the cultic separation of the clergy is emphasized, the more subordinated do the laity seem to become. If all power is vested in the ordained, what is there for the laity to do but 'pray, pay and obey'? Eventually the Protestant Reformation sets out to overcome this dualism and succeeds to a degree. However, to the extent that the cultic separation is ended, the difference between ordained and laity becomes simply one of function and, in the case of the ordained, functions to which they have been called by the (mostly lay) community of faith. It is above all in the Roman Catholic Church, where the cultic separation is maintained even to the present day, that a theological rather than functional reflection on clergy and laity is most fruitful. However, it has to be said that in practice the day-to-day challenges to lay life in the different churches are very similar to one another, however much or little the particular community employs a cultic understanding of priesthood. A glance at the 1997 WCC document on the laity makes clear that a different understanding of ministry does not always materially affect the position lay people hold in their churches. This document, which Roman Catholics were not involved in producing at all, makes a telling point:

> Further study needs to be made of the issue of baptism in relation to the laos, that is to say the whole Body of Christ. For example, common reference is made to baptism as a *universal* ordination 'to' the 'people of God'. This is helpful, but what does it imply about the 'second' ordination of the clergy to their particular functions? Is it possible to use this language without implying that the 'second' ordination is more 'complete', or a 'perfection' of the first? Can we speak of baptism of all Christians as a 'general' ordination without implying that clerical ordination is a *second* ordination?[14]

Attention to baptism is an important contemporary avenue for overcoming clericalism and clarifying the role of the laity. Under the influence of the Orthodox theologian John Zizioulas, Catholic theologians like Richard Gaillardetz and Edward P. Hahnenberg are drawing attention to the way in which baptism incorporates the new Christian into what is already an ordered communion.[15] Baptism, in other words, is not merely or even mainly a rite of initiation. It is entry into a community in which all have a particular place. It is a community constituted by relationships. So, the particular place I have in the community can be described in terms of the web of relationships which accompany it. If I am a bishop or a catechist or a church administrator, I am differently related to the whole body of the faithful because of the place I occupy. And the place I occupy is also the ministry I exercise, because this ordered community that is the church is a community constituted by mission. Thinking along these lines, it is possible to envisage the replacement of the idea of clergy and laity with the concept of 'different ministries', some of which involve leadership of the local community of faith or, perhaps, the regional or even global community, and some of which pertain in different ways to the good order of the local community, and some of which address the mission of the church to the world beyond it, in service of Christian discipleship. This was the approach that Yves Congar was following some forty years ago, but the challenge that such a path represents for his own Roman Catholic community may explain why the institutional church preferred his earlier thought, where he preserved attention to the

518

clergy/lay distinction, over the later theology in which these distinctions seemed open to radical relativization.

A focus on the baptismal priesthood and a relational understanding of ministry not only presents challenges for those churches which favour a high theology of ordained priesthood. They also throw the very notion of 'laity' into doubt. For if what is common to all Christians in virtue of their baptism is a ministry within the ordered community, then upon what is the distinction between clergy and laity, and hence the distinctiveness of lay life, to be based? If leadership in the churches is not to be a cultic priesthood but to be one ministry among others, albeit a particularly important one, then what is the basis for any notion of laity at all? As Edward Schillebeeckx has written, it is pretty easy to come up with a definition of a Christian, perhaps by focusing on the commonality of baptism, but how do you derive a definition of the lay person which is not couched in negations? Are we in fact returned to the early church, where everyone is laity while all exercise different charisms? Is there any way to rescue the idea of 'laity', other than to use it as a descriptor of all those Christians in all the churches who prefer a minimalist if not purely passive appropriation of discipleship? To examine this important question we need to turn to the popular notion, at least in Roman Catholicism, that what distinguishes the laity is their 'secular character'.[16]

Secularity

While the Protestant Reformation's emphases on the baptismal priesthood (Luther) and congregationalism (Calvin and the radical reformers) produced an understanding of the laity that directly challenged that of the Catholic tradition, the impact of the Enlightenment sowed the seeds of similar developments within the Church of Rome itself. To quote Yves Congar once again, there really is no such thing as the laity until the concept of the secular takes root. Of course there are people who are 'not ordained' and in that sense there are laity or non-clerics, but they are of no theological significance when the focus on baptism has been lost. But once the church accepts the reality of a distinction between secular and sacred, then the secular becomes the 'proper' realm of the laity and of lay apostolic activity, and at least a kind of distinct and even positive role for the laity emerges. However, the Roman Catholic Church initially received the notion of the secular through Lutheran two-kingdoms theology and in the writings of Enlightenment philosophers, neither of which would recommend itself. In consequence, the defensive intransigence of the nineteenth-century papacy in the face of modernity could not allow for a reconsideration of the place of the laity. But the reality of the secular world both demanded and allowed for it. In particular, French theology in the early and mid-twentieth century took up these themes, and they came to flower in Roman Catholicism in the documents of the Second Vatican Council.

The emergence of a positive theological valuation of the laity is a phenomenon of modernity, and principally to be found in the Catholic tradition. Protestant churches, in theory if not always and everywhere in practice, have for the most part so removed the cultic separation of clergy and laity that they do not assign the same priority to a theology of orders. Thus the baptismal priesthood grounds the unity of all Christians, laity and ministers alike, and laity are distinguished from ministers, if at all, principally in terms of their functions. In the Roman Catholic Church, however, because the cultic priesthood remains so much in evidence and is buttressed by a distinctively clerical lifestyle, the theology of a hierarchical ministry remains prominent. This focus on the special status of the clergy is only intensified by traditional approaches to the sacrificial understanding of the Mass and the priest as its special minister, though more recent Catholic theologies have tried to explain the role of lay people also in sacrificial categories.[17] Thus the question of a theology of the laity, when it comes to be asked at all, is answered in terms of the nature and mission of the laity as distinct from that of the clergy. Because, that is, the power of orders in Roman Catholicism has traditionally been understood as involving substantial ontological change in the ordinand, the theological question of the status of those 'only' admitted to baptismal priesthood remains a weighty one. The post-Enlightenment emergence of the secular world as an autonomous realm of human activity, beyond the power of the church, is a gift to theology, at least when the point is reached at which it can be seen as good or at least neutral.

While there is a natural and even inevitable association of the laity with the secular world, which is after all where the laity, for the most part, live their lives and do their work, this identification contains within it the dangerous tendency towards a persistent dualism of sacred and secular. At its worst, such a dualism intensifies the differences between clergy and laity by assigning the sacred realm to the ordained and consigning the non-ordained to the secular world. This is evidently not what was intended either by the discussions of the secularity of the laity in the documents of Vatican II, or in the parallel considerations offered, for example, in the 1997 WCC Consultation, *Towards a Common Understanding of the Theological Concepts of Laity/Laos: The People of God*.[18] Both Protestant and Catholic considerations make the point that the church itself is enmeshed in the secular, that secularity is one dimension of its reality, and consequently such an easy dualism of secular and sacred needs to be eschewed.[19] One of the best images for appreciating the sea-change in the attitude to the world that has come about in twentieth-century theology can be found in the opening words of Vatican II's final major document, the Pastoral Constitution on the Church in the Modern World, where the conciliar bishops proclaim that 'the joys and hopes, the griefs and anxieties of the people of this world, they are the joys and hopes, the griefs and anxieties of the church'. Once solidarity with the world is asserted, the work of lay people in the world becomes much more than a rescue operation.

A theology of the laity that takes their secularity seriously is best developed by linking this idea to that of the baptismal priesthood. Thus the laity come to be understood as exercising a priestly and apostolic role relative to the secular world. Here the older notion of the priest as mediator between God and the people needs to be recalled, not now in the sense that an ordained priest exercises this role on behalf of a passive laity, but with the far more fruitful insights that the laity express the priestly character of the community of faith in their mediation between the God who loves the world and the world which deserves to know this fact. In their daily lives the laity are the principal bearers of the mission to the world. In worship they bring the world in which they live before the God who wills its salvation. On this kind of understanding, to designate the laity as secular is to place them at the heart of the mission of the church, not to sideline them in the kind of pious passivity to which they have been consigned for the greater part of Christian history. At the same time, it has to be said that furthering this understanding of the role of the laity may entail, even in Catholicism, reserving the term 'priestly' for reference to the baptismal priesthood of the whole people of God, and distinguishing between different ministries within the people, some of them 'ordained', others perhaps 'commissioned' (Gaillardetz), and still others – especially those 'in the world' – following directly from the possession of baptismal priesthood and thus requiring neither special rites to establish them nor ecclesiastical sanction for their enactment.

Lay ministry

One of the more significant recent developments that has pushed at least the Roman Catholic Church in the direction of examining lay mission is the enormous flowering since the end of Vatican II of what is termed 'lay ecclesial ministry'. The dramatic decline in the numbers of priests in the church has been matched by the growth in numbers of lay people working, paid or voluntary, full or part-time, in ministries within the church which in former terms would have been the work of priests or at least of religious sisters. So the lay ecclesial minister is an unordained person whose mission is wholly or mainly within the community of faith, perhaps as a parochial Director of Religious Education, or as a parish administrator or as the Chancellor of a diocese. In terms of the work done, this person seems like clergy. But in the Roman Catholic context, she or he remains lay because this person stands outside the ranks of the male, celibate clergy.

We can learn a lot about the lay status by reflecting on this lay ecclesial minister. Much of the language of the church's documentation suggests that the lay minister is in essence a substitute, a stand-in for essentially priestly work that historical circumstance has necessitated. Sometimes irreverently referred to as 'the apostolate of the second string', this line of thinking assumes that in an ideal world these works would be done by the clergy and, at least implicitly, hopes for a future in which such 'right' relations between the work of clergy and laity will be re-established. Obviously, some of this work seems more 'priestly' than other parts of it. There is not much concern, for example, about catechesis of the young (in the pre-Vatican II church mostly accomplished by religious sisters) or about minor administrative functions or church music. But there is considerable nervousness about the increasingly common phenomenon of so-called 'priestless parishes', which are led by lay people with titles like 'pastoral assistant' (though never 'assistant pastor'). And in the Roman Catholic Church preaching by the non-ordained is still anathema, at least officially. However, the point can perhaps best be made by thinking of the common role of lay people today as 'eucharistic ministers', that is, people designated and sometimes formally 'commissioned' to assist the priest with the distribution of Holy Communion. This entirely post-Vatican II phenomenon came about in part because of the sheer numbers of people receiving communion, especially when – as is commonly the case since the end of the Council – communion was distributed under the two forms of bread and wine.

'Eucharistic ministers', a product of the Vatican Council, seem to threaten elements of the ecclesiastical establishment today. The theological question is a straightforward one: is the lay person distributing Holy Communion a living sign that the Mass is a liturgical act of the whole faithful people, or is she an expedient, to be set aside if there are enough priests available to distribute communion? The cultural or political dimension of the problem follows immediately. If the answer is that lay people distribute communion as part of the recognition that the Mass is not the priest's celebration but that of the whole church (a point made frequently in the liturgical renewal stimulated by Vatican II), then they are going to be up there at the altar with the priest a lot more than they used to be. (It is not so many years since women at least were never allowed beyond the altar rails during worship.) And if this is what is going to happen, and it does, then isn't it the case that slowly but surely the lay people in the pew will become 'confused' about the 'essential' distinction between clergy and laity? In recent years, several documents have been issued by Rome which seek to reassert this 'essential' distinction, for example by requiring that lay ministers of the eucharist are only used when the numbers are really overwhelming, or are not used at all if extra priests are available to assist with communion. These documents also prohibit lay people picking up the communion plate from the altar – the priest must give it to them – or receiving communion simultaneously with the priest. In detail after detail, the same point is being made. Lay people do not assist in these roles in any other way than as a temporary expedient, as 'extraordinary' ministers of the eucharist. However, the resistance to this relegation to extraordinary status suggests that the institutional church is attempting to shut the ecclesiastical stable door after this particular horse has bolted. Lay people in general, and many of the parish clergy, have passed the point at which they are ready to accept any efforts to return to the *status quo ante*.

The irony of the Roman Catholic Church's situation is one that the Protestant experience might enlighten. In Catholicism, while the institution is currently seeking to limit lay visibility in what have traditionally been 'priestly' roles, the dramatic decline in the numbers of clergy means that more and more lay people must be involved if the church's capacity to meet the sacramental needs of its people is not to be irreparably compromised. Protestants have not generally had this kind of problem, since the demarcation between ministers and laity is not characteristically so absolute as the traditional understanding of hierarchical ordination makes it in Roman Catholicism. Protestant churches also provide examples of the pros and cons of electing ministers, as well as part-time and temporary ministry. It may well be that the future of the laity even in Catholicism lies more in this Protestant direction. In other words, the study of the baptismal priesthood and the uncertainty about the future of the language of 'substantial ontological change' to explain what happens in priestly ordination may lead Roman Catholics to a greater stress on the apostolic responsibilities of all the faithful. They may come to accept their own Yves Congar's considered judgement that the language of 'different ministries' is a more hopeful way forward than maintaining the cultic separation between laity and clergy.

Notes

1 The principal historical study of the place of the laity in Christian history is Yves Congar's magisterial work, *Laypeople in the Church*, which should be read in the second and revised edition, Westminster, MD: Newman, 1965. For those who read French there is the same author's lengthy contribution, 'Laic et laicat', in the *Dictionnaire de spiritualité ascétique et mystique*, edited by Marcel Viller et al., Paris: Beauchesne, 1976, vol. 9, cols 79–108. Both works consider the apostolic and post-apostolic church quite comprehensively, but their treatment of more modern times is principally focused on the Roman Catholic Church.

2 Throughout this essay I have used both the terms 'Catholic' and 'Roman Catholic'. I have tried to reserve the former for the more diffuse Episcopal and sacramental tradition that would include Episcopalian theology if not polity, while specifying 'Roman Catholic' when I am discussing that particular church.

3 In addition to Congar's works mentioned in n. 1 above, there are two useful sources for the discussion of the emergence of the concept of the laity in the very early church. Alexandre Faivre, in *The Emergence of the Laity in the Early Church* (New York/Mahwah, NJ: Paulist, 1990), argues 'the laity' are a third-century development, while an earlier date and a more positive evaluation of 'laity' is offered by Ignace de la Potterie, 'L'origine et le sens primitif du mot "laic"', in *Nouvelle revue théologique* 80 (1958): 840–53. See also the same author's book, *La vie selon l'Esprit*, Paris: Cerf, 1965.

4 There is unavoidable terminological clumsiness in the use of 'lay' and 'laity' throughout this chapter, but I will use it throughout in the modern sense as employed in the Catholic tradition, to denote those who have not been ordained to ministry, though in a sense this is to perpetuate a reductionist understanding of the role of baptismal ordination.

5 While Pelagius is the best-known of the lay theologians of this time, there were many others including Ambrosiaster (a great influence on Pelagius) and lesser-known individuals like Cresconius (who was sufficiently significant to Augustine that he wrote four books to combat Cresconius' ideas), Tyconius, and Jovinian (one of the objects of Jerome's wrath but nevertheless a man whom Jerome declared to be 'thoroughly learned in the law of the Lord').

6 See the paper submitted to the 1998 General Assembly of the Presbyterian Church of Canada on the subject of the laity in Calvinist traditions (www.presbyterian.ca/mcv/resources/laity.pdf).

7 See my essay on 'The Laity' in *From Trent to Vatican II: Historical and Theological Investigations*, ed. Raymond F. Bulman and Frederick J. Parella, Oxford: Oxford University Press, 2006, pp. 193–207.

8 For those who would like to follow the stories of these and countless other fascinating individuals, there is no better to place to start than in a wonderful survey, long out of print, of the lay role in the church. See *The Layman in Christian History*, ed. Stephen Charles Neill and Hans Ruedi Weber, Philadelphia: Westminster, 1963. There is little or nothing available in English on either Schaitenberg or Rothe, but see Alan Harding, *The Countess of Huntingdon's Connexion* for a useful study of the movement which she founded in eighteenth-century Methodism (Oxford: OUP, 2003).

9 The works of de Maistre and Montalembert are widely available in English. For Ozanam see *Apostle in a Top Hat*, by James Patrick Derum, Garden City, NY: Hanover House, 1960.

10 Von Hügel is unaccountably absent from *The Layman in Christian History* but his own work is widely available and there is an excellent study of his influence in *Baron Friedrich von Hügel and the Modernist Crisis in England*, by Lawrence F. Barman, Cambridge: CUP, 1972.

11 The literature on Vatican II is enormous and reflects the wide range of ideology and opinion on the meaning of the Council. One seminal early work that takes the place of lay people particularly seriously is *Coresponsibility in the Church*, by Leon Joseph Cardinal Suenens, a principal actor in the dramatic events of the Council and a major influence on its eventual direction (New York: Herder & Herder, 1968).

12 *The Documents of Vatican II*, ed. Walter M. Abbott, New York: Herder & Herder, 1966.

13 Many recent books have looked more or less sensationally at the implications of the sex abuse scandal for the life of the church. Among the less sensational are: David Gibson, *The Coming Catholic Church: How the Faithful Are Shaping a New American Catholicism*, San Francisco: Harper, 2003; Paul Lakeland, *The Liberation of the Laity: In Search of an Accountable Church*, New York: Continuum, 2003; and Peter Steinfels, *A People Adrift: The Crisis of the Roman Catholic Church in America*, New York: Simon & Schuster, 2003. There are also two particularly useful collections of essays on the historical background to the crisis, namely, Francis Oakley and Bruce Russett (eds), *Governance, Accountability and the Future of the Catholic Church*, New York: Continuum, 2004; and Stephen J. Pope (ed.), *Common Calling: The Laity and Governance of the Catholic Church*, Washington, D.C.: Georgetown, 2004.

14 www.wcc-coe.org/wcc/what/education/laity.html

15 John Zizioulas' major work is *Being as Communion: Studies in Personhood and the Church*, New York: St Vladimir's Seminary Press, 1997. See also Edward P. Hahnenberg, *Ministries: A Relational Approach*, New York: Crossroad, 2003; and Richard R. Gaillardetz, 'The Ecclesiological Foundations of Ministry Within an Ordered Communion', in Susan K. Wood (ed.), *Ordering the Baptismal Priesthood: Theologies of Lay and Ordained Ministry*, Collegeville, MN: Liturgical, 2003.

16 See the essays by Zeni Fox and Aurelie Hagstrom in *Ordering the Baptismal Priesthood* (n. 15 above).

17 Yves Congar was one of the first to make this case. See *Laypeople in the Church*.

18 See n. 6.

19 There are many who would contest this position, including the postliberal theology of George Lindbeck and the proponents of Radical Orthodoxy, a movement with some clout in academic circles though none at all, as far as I can see, in the life of the churches, and of course the immensely influential work of Stanley Hauerwas.

29

MAGISTERIUM

Michael A. Fahey, S.J.

A Christian or simply a Roman Catholic concept?

Notably, one theological concept that receives considerable attention in the Roman Catholic community, namely 'magisterium', is rarely alluded to – at least under that nomenclature – in the Orthodox, Anglican, or Reformation churches. English-speaking Catholics generally continue to use the Latin term '*magisterium*', whose original meaning was simply a task undertaken by a magister (a teacher or 'master'). A brief attempt to employ the term 'magistery', especially in British usage, never caught on widely in theological circles, probably because the esoteric term has notable secular or juridical connotations. Since the Latin language does not make use of the definite or indefinite article, a reader who comes upon the term *magisterium* cannot tell at first glance whether its proper translation should be 'a magisterium' (something taught) or 'the magisterium' (those persons forming a group entrusted with authorization to decide what is correct ecclesiastical teaching or discipline).

After the birth of the modern ecumenical movement and the increased willingness of the various confessional bodies to discuss doctrinal differences dispassionately under the aegis of official bilateral dialogues, what emerged was the realization that the topic really applies to every church. What emerged were equivalent nomenclatures such as 'doctrinal authority' or 'teaching authority'. As such, the notion magisterium suggests a conclusion or teaching. But more and more during the last century and a half, the word has come to be used to identify those persons authorized to formulate official, orthodox doctrinal teaching within one's church. The German term *Lehramt* (teaching office) suggests elements of both meanings. Other Christians besides Catholics wrestle with this reality in unique ways.

Modern documents emanating especially from the Vatican attempt to remove ambiguity regarding the sense in which the term is used, by printing the word in upper-case, using a capital letter 'M' for Magisterium in order to make clear that what is being referred to is the authorized person or persons exercising the legitimate teaching authority. To avoid further confusion, the Vatican typically combines this capitalized noun with the Latin adjective 'authenticum' which leads those not familiar with Latin to translate the combination as 'authentic Magisterium' (as opposed to inauthentic magisterium?), whereas more accurately the Latin adjective should be translated as 'authoritative'. Other adjectives also linked to Magisterium in Vatican documents include 'sacred', 'solemn', or 'ecclesiastical'.

In the 1970s there was a brief attempt by theologians to argue that it would be helpful to restore the medieval distinction of two kinds of magisteria, one pastoral, the other academic, the first exercised by bishops, the second by theologians. Despite the enhancement that such terminology afforded the work of theologians, it was quickly decided that such language would confuse the faithful and obscure the different finalities of two distinctive ministries in the church.

There are, of course, multiple levels of magisterial teaching, each of which requires a different level of adherence or 'obsequium' (a term notoriously difficult to translate). The Roman Catholic Church recognizes and teaches that there are degrees of binding force applicable to teachings, depending on the immediate source of the teaching, or the literary form in which it is formulated. One crucial distinction is that between dogma and doctrine. A dogma refers to a 'core, central affirmation of the faith' (such as a declaration on a critical issue by an ecumenical council of bishops that, for instance, Jesus Christ is 'consubstantial' with God the Father). When the magisterium re-states such a traditional teaching it is legitimately exercising its responsibility of guarding and proclaiming a critical dimension of the Christian faith at the core of the creed, which obtains its importance from the original source, which may be scriptural or conciliar. A doctrine, on the other hand, is an 'official' teaching but one which requires of the believer a somewhat lesser degree of adhesion.

Besides the proclamation of the gospel, namely the revelation communicated in Sacred Scripture which is the central faith of the believing community, those who are responsible for teaching authoritatively in the church also formulate doctrines, with the assistance of specialists and the insights of the faithful, that assist the believer to adhere to the faith and to practise Christian virtues. These doctrines are found, for instance, in catechisms, papal encyclical letters, pastoral letters of national hierarchies, apostolic exhortations based on discussions at international synods, etc. There are various levels of authority behind these forms of teaching. Sometimes, despite using a literary genre that seems informal, ecclesiastical teachers may be reiterating something that is at the very core of the gospel, such as the teaching of the Johannine Gospel that God is love. But it is also possible that what is being stated 'officially' is simply the result of a prudential judgement, based on a particular theological school of thought, regarding, for instance, a complicated bio-medical procedure, an international economic situation, or an aesthetic assessment, a judgement which conceivably could evolve with the passage of time. Serious minded and well disposed believers naturally take note of what exactly is stated in such doctrinal teachings, weigh the arguments proffered, but may ultimately find that their conscience permits them – or even requires them – not to accept every nuance of such teaching.

Traditional manuals of theology typically distinguished between two groups in the church, the *ecclesia docens* (the teaching church) and the *ecclesia discens* (the learning church). This usage has largely died out since the distinction was artificially neat and many argued that the best teachers were those who were continually learning. Where teaching in the church occurred it was subdivided between (a) the extraordinary magisterium and (b) the ordinary (and universal) magisterium. These terminologies appear in Vatican II documents and later in the revised Code of Canon Law (1983). The extraordinary magisterium includes a teaching of an ecumenical council which articulates the weighed views of the world-wide Catholic episcopate in union with the Bishop of Rome. The sixteen documents published by the fathers of Vatican II can be referred to as the work of the extraordinary magisterium, although, by their own desire, they abstained from formulating new, defined dogmas. Another form of extraordinary magisterium is a rare infallible papal teaching *ex cathedra*. On the other hand, the ordinary and universal magisterium of the church is a more elusive concept. It refers to consistently and uniformly taught doctrines among the world-wide bishops in association with the pope. What makes the concept difficult to assess is how this universality is determined, especially if individual bishops or even national episcopal conferences may be reluctant to distance themselves from a common teaching. Likewise, this understanding of the magisterium does not address what share in this universality might be found for other bishops (or their equivalents) in non-Catholic churches or ecclesial communities. The ordinary magisterium of the world-wide episcopacy does not spring *ex nihilo*, but presupposes that the bishops have been in creative dialogue with theologians and with the faithful at large to discern what is already de facto the convictions of the faithful. It is not clear how Christians who are not actively practising their faith or who are not fully responsive to the exigencies of the magisterium can or might contribute to the teaching of the church. In other words, if Christians are recognized as sinners or are identified by leadership in their church as unfaithful to an aspect of the gospel or to a specific moral teaching of the church, how can they still be regarded as inspired and led by the Spirit and thus worthy of being heard?

After deliberation, the faithful may come to judge that the teaching of the bishops or the pope on a particular issue is incomplete or ambiguous. Professional theologians who are not intimidated may express their convictions in specialized journals or reviews or at conferences. In doing so, these theologians see themselves as inviting the magisterium to be more comprehensive and to take into further consideration something that has been forgotten or overshadowed. As such, when done respectfully and intelligently, the response of theologians to official teaching should be taken seriously and become part of the dialogue. During the preparatory sessions for Vatican II, and even during its sessions, there was a wide range of disagreement and discussion among bishops and their advisers (*periti*). In subsequent years, however, theologians and other members of the faithful who have found fault with a formulation of teaching came to be described as dissenters. Dissatisfaction with the way a teaching was formulated came to be regarded pejoratively in official quarters as dissent, something similar to disobedience. Disagreement came to be regarded as a lack of solidarity or loyalty.

Some have argued that the magisterium's hardening of attitudes toward theologians and others who challenge magisterial formulations of teaching is somehow connected with the present method of appointing bishops, which is based on a narrower list of qualifications. It is said that people who show special competencies of leadership are sometimes passed over because they are perceived as too independent or venturesome, qualities that are seen to be incompatible with loyalty and conformity to official church teaching. Added to this is what is judged to be the ineffectiveness of some bishops, not merely in one country but in an assortment of countries, a judgement that has created a crisis of confidence about the bishops' effectiveness. Bishops have come to be seen as too ready to set aside the good intentions of their own flock, especially in matters of liturgical style, translations of biblical and liturgical texts, or legitimate local customs. In contrast to the discussions at Vatican II, when bishops displayed creativity and some independence of thought, it is now widely seen that their number one priority is conformity to the preferences of a highly centralized administration. The disenchantment toward bishops by the faithful, who judged them ineffective in dealing with cases of sexual abuse, has certainly lessened the level of cooperation between faithful and bishops, and ultimately has had an impact on the way magisterial statements are heard.

After Vatican II Pope Paul VI decided to set up regular meetings of international episcopal synods as a means of advising the papal magisterium about decisions central to the life of the church. After a shaky beginning and some degree of success, these international synods of bishops eventually lost their impact because the agendas were tightly controlled from on high, and even the eventual publication of the synodal recommendations was often truncated. Another institution that was promoted by Vatican II was the formation (where they did not already exist) of national episcopal conferences. Some countries achieved remarkable position statements and background papers. The American episcopal conference, the United States Conference of Catholic Bishops, after extensive and varied consultation and input from a broad spectrum of the faithful, published two brilliant pastoral statements: 'The Challenge of Peace' (1983) and 'Economic Justice for All' (1986). Eventually, Pope John Paul II in a motu proprio, *Apostolos Suos*, on 'The Theological and Juridical Nature of Episcopal Conferences' (1998), stated – perhaps in part because different national groups of bishops were taking somewhat different positions – that what the national episcopal conferences taught in such pastoral letters was strictly speaking not an exercise in magisterial teaching. For many of the faithful, however, these national episcopal texts were eminently insightful. Where then are magisterial teachings most frequently conveyed? Canadian theologian Gregory Baum once remarked in an unpublished lecture that the voice of the magisterium is not found principally in curial or papal or episcopal documents but rather in the responsible and scripturally based preaching of the church.

Some churchgoers have the mistaken view that the leadership in the church, from the pope on down to the bishops, especially when acting in concert, has an answer for every question, no matter how complex and intricate the issue. These faithful fail to understand that sometimes what is provided by ecclesiastical teachers is simply a prudential judgement based on the present insights in this matter. With the present-day multiplication of instant, world-wide communication and increased media interest in papal or episcopal opinions, one is inundated with comments from church leaders on a more or less daily basis. It is not clear the extent to which these statements represent official, perhaps even binding, teachings.

The teaching of the magisterium, as will be further explained later, has become more closely associated with canon law regulations and the penal ramifications of the situation. This has led to a closer association of the concepts of magisterium and obedience. With regard to the vocations of teaching and writing as a Catholic theologian, the Vatican has reserved the right to forbid a particular writer to publish, especially on a specific topic. The Vatican may also remove a person's licence (*mandatum* or *missio canonica*) to teach as a Catholic theologian at a university or seminary. In the forty years since Vatican II there have been high profile theologians who have run into difficulty with various Vatican curial offices, especially the Pontifical Congregation for the Doctrine of the Faith. Individual bishops may also ban a speaker or teacher in his diocese.

Major ecclesial and intellectual events and developments in relation to the magisterium

In the last 150 years a number of internal church events have taken place that have influenced the way the notion of magisterium is understood in the Catholic community. These events have often been actions that enhanced centralization by the papal office and its curial structures. First among these was the gathering of Catholic bishops at what was called the First Vatican Council (1869–70), convened to update their teaching on the virtue of faith and doctrinal authority. In order to afford the pope a degree of freedom from political interference, Vatican I affirmed that the bishop of Rome, when solemnly formulating a teaching as supreme pontiff (*ex cathedra*) on a matter of 'faith and morals' is gifted with infallibility. This form of papal magisterial teaching, or teaching of the bishops at a general council, came to be known, as we have seen, as the *magisterium extraordinarium*.

In the first decade of the twentieth century the role of papal teaching became more pronounced through a series of condemnations regarding a congeries of theological attitudes labelled by Rome as 'Modernism'. On September 8, 1907, Pope Pius X's encyclical *Pascendi dominici gregis* condemned Modernism as 'the compendium of all heresies'. Vigilance committees were set up in every diocese to ferret out suspected Modernists. Obviously, this created an atmosphere of fear in academic circles, especially seminaries, which discouraged creativity and hindered access to theological literature judged to be suspicious, especially publications by non-Catholics. These stringent measures inevitably promoted waves of anti-intellectualism and a ghetto mentality, especially among candidates for the priesthood. Obedience became more valued than understanding.

The Catholic Church's 'Holy Office' as a Vatican 'congregation' or dicastery oversaw the orthodoxy of what was taught and published by Catholics to determine whether erroneous or detrimental teachings were being disseminated. This bureau, now known as the Congregation for the Doctrine of the Faith, has been particularly concerned about what is published, although the office sometimes heard complaints about what was being taught in the classroom. Since it was conceivable that reports filed with the CDF were mistaken or incorrect, concern grew, especially among those criticized for their lack of orthodoxy, for fair and comprehensive norms for due process.

In subsequent decades of the twentieth century, especially in the 1940s and 1950s, and after the publication of Pope Pius XII's encyclical *Humani generis* (1950), the role of the magisterium became further enhanced. The encyclical focused on 'False Opinions of Catholic Doctrine' and argued that 'the most noble office of theology is to show how a doctrine defined by the Church is contained in the source of revelation . . . in that sense in which it has been defined by the Church' (no. 21).

Earlier in the post World War II context, especially in Europe and to a lesser degree in North America, at the height of the so-called *ressourcement* theology or *nouvelle théologie* – an effort to centre modern theology on scripture, patristics and liturgical texts – a number of theology professors were prevented by Roman authorities from publishing or lecturing, at least on certain sensitive topics. Ironically, several of those who had been under a cloud of suspicion, such as Henri de Lubac, Yves Congar, Karl Rahner and John Courtney Murray, turned out to be vindicated and honoured at the close of Vatican II. This form of censorship had the unfortunate result of silencing some of the major theologians who were wrestling with the challenge of how to have the teachings of the church in dialogue with modern, contemporary thought. Although some of the theologians were 'silenced' to prevent their lecturing and writing, for instance on the role of the laity in the church, the church in the modern world, and religious freedom, these restrictions were ultimately rescinded and key elements of their teaching were finally accepted and incorporated into the decrees of Vatican II.

Following the publication of Pope Paul VI's encyclical on marriage, *Humanae vitae* (1968), disciplinary actions were taken by Rome against specific professors who publicly disagreed with parts of the encyclical relating to artificial methods of contraception. From time to time there are interventions against writers who advocate suspicious theological viewpoints. These criticisms and punitive actions are sometimes reversed or revised depending on subsequent information. Because of the seriousness of these disciplinary actions, theologians and other involved Catholics argued for the need for clear guidelines regarding due process. In the United States, the Catholic Theological Society of America (CTSA) and the Canon Law Society of America (CLSA) jointly produced a series of guidelines on how such cases should be adjudicated. The suggested guidelines were not formally adopted by the US Catholic bishops, which heightened a sense of urgency and vulnerability among theologians.

Further ecclesial, conciliar and ecumenical treatments of magisterium

In its various documents Vatican II refers several times to the concept of magisterium. To appreciate the full flavour of the final texts, it would be helpful to compare them with the preliminary draft prepared by the conservative members of the Council's Preparatory Doctrinal Commission. The notable rejection of this preliminary draft illustrates that some of the standard formulae elaborated in the manuals of theology of the time no longer corresponded to the thinking of the church at large. Especially enlightening is the following passage from the Dogmatic Constitution on Divine Revelation, *Dei Verbum*:

> Sacred tradition and sacred Scripture form one sacred deposit of the word of God, which is committed to the church. Holding fast to this deposit, the entire holy people united with their shepherds remain always steadfast in the teaching of the apostles, in the common life, in the breaking of the bread, and in prayers (cf. Acts 2,42), so that in holding to, practicing, and professing the heritage of the faith, there results on the part of the bishops and faithful a remarkable common effort. The task of authoritatively interpreting the word of God, whether written or handed on, has been entrusted exclusively to the living teaching office of the church, whose authority is exercised in the name of Jesus Christ. This teaching office is not above the word of God, but serves it, teaching only what has been handed on, listening to it devoutly, guarding it scrupulously, and explaining it faithfully by divine commission and with the help of the Holy Spirit; it draws from this one deposit of faith everything which it presents for belief as divinely revealed.
>
> (no. 10)

After the high level of cooperation at Vatican II between the *periti* or theological advisers and the bishops, it was anticipated that this level of cooperation would continue not only through the creation of the International Synod of Bishops, but also by means of the International Theological Commission made up of some 30 experts from around the world. The high hopes for the Commission were rarely realized, perhaps because of the workings of the team. In 1976 the Commission published a study entitled *Theses on the Relationship between the Ecclesiastical Magisterium and Theology* (1976), a series of twelve theses designed to promote acceptance of the teaching of the magisterium as understood by the Vatican. The text received very little attention either inside or outside the Roman Catholic Church and appears to be little more than a restatement of earlier terminology and perspectives. Two members of the Commission, Otto Semmelroth and Karl Lehmann, appended an insightful commentary, but this was described as personal and unofficial.

When the new *Code of Canon Law* was published for the Latin Church (1983) and several years later the *Code of Canons of the Eastern Churches* (1990), much of the terminology of Vatican II's documents about the magisterium was retained but formulated into juridical contexts. The canons in both codes included references both to the obligation to adhere to the '*credenda*' as outlined by the authoritative magisterium, and to appropriate disciplinary penalties for those who failed to do so. These canons seemed to suffice at the time.

To understand why it was later determined that these canons needed to be somewhat expanded, it is necessary to go back to the publication of a Profession of Faith created by the Congregation for the Doctrine of the Faith on March 16, 1989, as well as its Oath of Fidelity on Assuming Office in the Church. The Profession of Faith added three paragraphs to the Nicene-Constantinopolitan Creed, attesting, first, that: 'With firm faith, I also believe everything contained in the Word of God, whether written or handed down in Tradition, which the Church, either by a solemn judgment or by the ordinary and universal Magisterium, sets forth to be believed [*credenda*] as divinely revealed.' The Profession of Faith then continues in a second paragraph: 'I also firmly accept and hold each and everything definitively proposed by the Church regarding teachings on faith and morals.' Finally, in the third paragraph it adds: 'Moreover, I adhere with religious submission [*obsequium religiosum*] of will and intellect to the teachings which either the Roman Pontiff or the College of Bishops enunciate when they exercise their authoritative Magisterium, even if they do not intend to proclaim these teachings by a definitive act.'

John Paul II's *motu proprio* on protecting the church from the errors of theologians, entitled *Ad tuendam fidem* (1998), sought to extend the notion of obedience incumbent on believers, especially theologians, to include not simply dogmas that are to be believed (*credenda*) but teachings that are to be held (*tenenda*). No specific appropriate penalty was provided for this second scenario. The pope, doubtlessly urged on by his advisers in the Congregation for the Doctrine of the Faith, rushed to 'clarify' loose ends in disciplinary zones. *Ad tuendam fidem* was seen as necessary for the good housekeeping of the Roman curia. Yet the canonist Ladislas Örsy had already noted in 1990 that the profession of faith promulgated by the Congregation for the Doctrine of the Faith was somewhat of an anomaly because it rode roughshod over Rome's traditional prudence which keeps 'a profession of faith apart from other affirmations of a lesser nature'.

In the *motu proprio* and its accompanying, non-official, non-curial (but nonetheless highly influential), commentary by Cardinal Ratzinger, changes were indicated. In the *motu proprio*, the changes to the Latin code of canon law read as follows:

> Canon 750 now consists of two paragraphs; the first presents the text of the existing canon; the second contains a new text. Thus, canon 750, in its revised, complete form, now reads:
> Canon 750 – § 1. Those things are to be believed [*credenda*] by divine and catholic faith which are contained in the word of God as it has been written or handed down by tradition, that is, in the single deposit of faith entrusted to the Church, and which are at the same time proposed as divinely revealed either by the solemn Magisterium of the Church, or by its ordinary and universal Magisterium, which in fact is manifested by the common adherence of Christ's faithful under the guidance of the sacred Magisterium. All are therefore bound to avoid any contrary doctrines.
> § 2. Furthermore, each and everything set forth definitively [*definitive*] by the Magisterium of the Church regarding teaching on faith and morals must be firmly accepted and held [*amplectenda ac retinenda*]; namely, those things required for the holy keeping and faithful exposition of the deposit of faith; therefore, anyone who rejects propositions which are to be held definitively [*definitive tenendas*] sets himself against the teaching of the Catholic Church.

Canon 1371, n. 1 of the Code of Canon Law, consequently, receives an appropriate reference to canon 750 § 2, so that it now reads:

Canon 1371 – The following are to be punished with a just penalty:

1° a person who, apart from the case mentioned in canon 1364 § 1, teaches a doctrine condemned by the Roman Pontiff, or by an Ecumenical Council, or obstinately rejects the teachings mentioned in canon 750 § 2 or in canon 752 and, when warned by the Apostolic See or by the Ordinary, does not retract;

2° a person who in any other way does not obey the lawful command or prohibition of the Apostolic See or the Ordinary or Superior and, after being warned, persists in disobedience.

In brief, the altered texts amend the canon law to include theological dissent from 'definitive' but non-infallible teachings under the heading of actions deserving of punishment by an 'appropriate penalty'. Similar adjustments were made at the same time to the corresponding canons for the Eastern churches. All teachers of the faith are required to accept without further discussion doctrines which are not defined truths of the faith, and doctrines not even proposed as definitive but reaffirmed by the 'ordinary magisterium'. Before *Ad tuendam fidem*, as Richard McBrien noted, the church's theologians had been 'warned, scolded, chided and admonished' to toe the magisterial line in their writings and public utterances, even on matters not infallibly defined by a pope or ecumenical council. There was never any mention in church law of formal punishment, however mild it might be, for dissent against non-infallible teachings. What has resulted now is a smudging of the distinction between infallible and non-infallible teaching by means of a creative use of the word 'definitive'. Now non-infallible but 'definitive' teachings are to be regarded, so it would seem, as though they too were infallible. Difficulties about the present document may be traced in part to confusion over the terminology. Can the magisterium speak 'definitively' without engaging its infallibility? Can the faithful be bound to assent 'definitively' to doctrines that could eventually be reversed? There is a need for more clarification of these issues on the official level.

Writing in the US journal *America*, canonist James Provost of Catholic University of America noted several inconveniences in the *motu proprio*:

> In an attempt to safeguard the faith, the Pope has canonized a category of response that is relatively new in official teaching. This carries with it the inconvenience that clear criteria to determine what is 'definitively' taught have yet to be developed. . . . Safeguards need to be clear if they are to guard safely. The incorporation of these new categories of teaching and response into the codes before a consensus has developed on how they are to be applied could weaken rather than strengthen the desired protection of the faith.[1]

One of the strongest critiques of the document emerged from France, written by the Jesuit Bernard Sesboüé, a member of Le Groupe des Dombes, former member of the International Theological Commission, and professor of theology in Paris. No bishop, priest, or cleric, he wrote, can avoid feeling very concerned by a document that is potentially heavy with weighty consequences for ecclesiology. He strongly objected to the negative tone of the opening sentence of *Ad tuendam fidem* which singles out theologians as though they were a danger to the church. Commenting on the opening phrases of the text: 'to protect the faith of the Catholic Church against errors arising . . . especially from among those dedicated to the various disciplines of sacred theology', the French Jesuit observes that 'no theologian can read such a sentence without pain. This negative assessment is a serious warning; but do theologians represent a danger to the Church?' This, he says, is a far cry from the fruitful collaboration during Vatican II between theologians and bishops. Certainly theologians have made mistakes, but what is so disquieting is this obsession, this refusal of any debate in the church on so many important points.

These documents and decisions that have emerged from the Vatican since the council have tended to harden the standard terminology and assign a further juridical force to them. For progress in creative systematic theology regarding doctrinal authority, we need to look at various consensual ecumenical statements, and these will now be discussed.

Important historical and contemporary thinkers on magisterium

To understand how the Roman Catholic doctrine of magisterium is being articulated today, we naturally look to several major theologians and church historians who are researching this area. Individuals who have made contributions to this topic in recent years include Francis A. Sullivan, John Boyle, Richard Gaillardetz, Yves Congar and Karl Rahner. The theological community is much indebted to them and to other individuals. But the real pioneering work on magisterium over the last few decades seems to have been the coopera-tive, collegial work achieved by members of the official ecumenical consultations which began towards the end of the 1960s. These ecumenical explorations have treated the topic largely under the heading of 'teaching authority' in the church. Teaching authority is described as part and parcel of the life of the church, given the nature of divine revelation, the inspiration of Sacred Scripture, and the responsibilities that were bestowed upon the earliest apostles and disciples to maintain the 'deposit of the faith'. Churches that preserve the notion of apostolic succession see authority especially conferred on bishops who are in continuity with the founding apostles. And even churches that do not ordain bishops, as the Groupe des Dombes has argued, do in fact recognize the responsibility of *episkope* (oversight) among some designated members of the church.

All Christian believers who feel uncomfortable regarding the role of a living magisterium in the life of the church are typically uneasy not with the institution itself but rather with the way it is sometimes exercised. These faithful believe strongly that authority must be exercised in conjunction with other realities in the life of the church. They appeal, for instance, to the need to respect the *sensus fidelium* (the way the Holy Spirit guides believers to preserve them in the faith); to attend to the role of reception (the fact that one of the norms for identifying the aptness of a particular teaching is the degree to which it is subse-quently assumed concretely into the life of the church); and to see how the leadership in the church respects and heeds charisms present in the church since Vatican II stressed that all Christians receive charismatic gifts from the Holy Spirit for the building up of the church.

Francis Sullivan, long-time professor at the Gregorian University, Rome, and an expert in ecclesiology, has written extensively on magisterium. In his several books on the topic he displays a clear understanding of manual theology, modern ecumenical progress in consensus statements, and the thrust of the new canon law of the Catholic Church. His studies are useful because he takes up the terminology of Vatican curial office and shows its inconsis-tencies and occasional ambiguities. The contribution of Yves Congar, who has been a strong force in the renewal of ecclesiology since his pioneering work, *Jalons pour une théologie du laïcat* (1954), has centred more on a series of detailed historical studies, showing how the term magisterium fluctuated in the High Middle Ages, sometimes referring to the teaching of theologians at major universities such as Paris, and sometimes to the teaching of the Roman pontiff. Congar's historical research has demonstrated that the term magisterium, used in its more restrictive sense to describe a 'living magisterium', a specific person or group of people exercising a responsibility, is relatively recent and appears for the first time in an encyclical of Pope Gregory XVI published in the year 1830. Another detailed study on the history of the term 'ordinary magisterium' has been done by John Boyle, based on a thorough study of the Vatican archives.

Karl Rahner, in his occasional articles in *Theological Investigations* and at various conferences, has explored *Lehramt* not in the more restricted usage of Vatican documents, but in the widest possible sense to include how revelation is preserved and handed on through the whole church. He did not simply adopt the terminological usage that has become current in Vatican circles, but broadened it considerably. One particularly provocative study was his address in Frankfurt to a group of Jesuit ecumenists, entitled: 'Open questions in dogma considered by the official Church as definitively decided'.[2]

Two consensual ecumenical statements, which are arguably the most comprehensive articulations of the notion of magisterium or teaching authority, are those produced by the United States Lutheran/Roman Catholic study group and the more recent lengthy study on doctrinal authority in French by the Groupe des Dombes, a long active Catholic/Eglise Réformée dialogue partnership.

The US Lutheran/Catholic text on *Teaching Authority and Infallibility in the Church* (1978) is one of ten splendid volumes published jointly by Lutherans and Catholics since the consultation's foundation after Vatican II. The 'Common Statement' segment of this particular agreement comprises 58 lengthy sections and is a model of comprehensiveness. Providing what it calls a 'fresh look' at doctrinal authority, it focuses on the gospel, seen first and foremost as God's saving action in Jesus Christ who emerges as the authority *par excellence*, as the primordial source and ground of authority. The term gospel is subsequently described as the kerygma of the saving deeds of Christ, proclaimed by the first witnesses, recorded in the scriptures, made living from age to age by reception and further reception of the good news, served by ministers. As centuries went by, the church remained committed to preserving the 'deposit of the faith', seen as an unbroken line of apostolic teaching. The agreed statement goes on to provide what ultimately comes down to a definition of magisterium, understood in its most basic sense of those who have been assigned ministries and structures and who are charged with the teaching of Christian doctrine and with supervision and coordination of the ministry of the whole people of God, including the mandate for bishops or other leaders to judge doctrine and condemn doctrine that is contrary to the gospel. This priceless document is arguably the best articulation of teaching authority in the postconciliar time frame.

The most recent text on the nature of magisterium has been published by the ecumenical Groupe des Dombes under the title: *'Un Seul Maître': L'Autorité doctrinale dans l'Église*. This lengthy 247-page tome, whose title alludes to the pericope in Matthew 23.8–11 where Jesus is speaking to his disciples, covers an enormous amount of preliminary and background material drawn from the church's long history, which is described as a sort of exercise in *anamnesis*. It is not possible to summarize here the richness of the study but only to refer briefly to one of the central portions of the volume. Chapter Four addresses 'Doctrinal Propositions' and recognizes a consensus with regard to: [a] the authority of texts (nos 317–30);

[b] the authority of communities and persons (nos 331–41); and [c] the authority of institutional levels of appeal (*instances*) (342–6). The authority of texts includes first of all scripture, credal formulas, conciliar documents (especially those of the first four councils), liturgical prayers, catechisms, disciplinary texts, and even some ecumenical texts. Not all the texts bear the same level or degrees of authority but all are important in their own way. Obviously scripture is the *norma normans*; everything else is *norma normata*. Secondly, these texts require a living community to receive them or they remain simply dead letters. They need to be taken up and given life by communities and individuals. The lived tradition is reflected in the lives of the Christian faithful by the phenomenon known as reception, the authority of personal conscience, the teaching of the fathers of the church, as well as the teachings of the church's doctors and theologians. Thirdly, there is the authority associated with institutional, quasi-juridical places or levels of appeal charged with protecting the community in the unity of the faith. For the multiplicity of churches today there exist multiple instances, whether they be bishops, presbyteral conferences, councils or synods. But every church faithful to its calling needs to have access to appeals at three levels: communitarian, collegial and personal. It is to be hoped that this splendid study will soon be translated into several languages.

The fact that it is impossible to write a theological essay on magisterium without focusing predominantly on Roman Catholic practices, documents and attitudes illustrates the extent to which post-Tridentine Catholicism has become more and more centralized and preoccupied by doctrinal and theological uniformity. These traits, which are exemplified in the protective policies of the papacy and its administrative congregations or councils, the strict and cautious selection of candidates for the episcopate, concern for doctrinal and theological unanimity, and its uneasiness in moving to a new level of ecumenical engagement, are important factors in the search for Christian unity. Modern interchurch dialogue groups which stress the need for conversion of heart or changes in entrenched practices are correct, for without such *metanoia* true coming together will be unrealizable. It may be true in the first decade of the twenty-first century that the tensions between the living official magisterium and Catholic theologians, women and men, are not as extensive as the media might suggest. But the reluctance of those charged with producing official magisterial statements, whether definitive or not, on nearly every aspect of life and death, to allow greater tolerance for ambiguity and diversity will only harden the divisions and separations existing in the broader Christian family. Two central questions to address in the coming years are: to what extent is the Roman Catholic understanding of magisterium purely doctrinal or largely cultural? And secondly, how can the exercise of magisterium be more integrated into the other dimensions of decision making so that it is more comprehensive?

Notes

1 'Safeguarding the Faith', *America*, (August 1, 1998), 8–12.
2 Karl Rahner, 'Open questions in dogma considered by the official Church as definitively decided', *Journal of Ecumenical Studies* 15/2 (1978).

Further reading

John Boyle, *Church Teaching Authority: Historical and Theological Studies*, Notre Dame, IN: University of Notre Dame, 1995.

Yves Congar, 'Pour une histoire sémantique du terme "magisterium"', *Revue des sciences philosophiques et théologiques* 60/1 (1976).

Charles E. Curran and Richard A. McCormick, eds, *The Magisterium and Morality*, Readings in Moral Theology no. 3, New York: Paulist, 1982.

Paul C. Empie, T. Austin Murphy, and Joseph A. Burgess (eds), *Teaching Authority and Infallibility in the Church*, Lutherans and Catholics in Dialogue VI, Minneapolis: Augsburg, 1980.

Richard R. Gaillardetz, *By What Authority? A Primer on Scripture, the Magisterium, and the Sense of the Faithful*, Collegeville: Liturgical, 2003.

Groupe des Dombes, *'Un Seul Maître': L'Autorité doctrinale dans l'Église*, Paris: Bayard, 2006.

International Theological Commission, *Theses on the Relationship between the Ecclesiastical Magisterium and Theology* [dated June 6, 1976], with a commentary by Otto Semmelroth and Karl Lehmann, Washington: United States Catholic Conference, 1977.

John Paul II, Motu proprio, *Ad Tuendam Fidem*, Boston: Pauline, 1998. Contains in appendix the earlier Profession of Faith and the Oath of Fidelity dated March 1989.

——, Motu proprio, *Apostolos Suos*, 'The Theological and Juridical Nature of Episcopal Conferences', *Origins* 28 (July 30, 1998).

Gerard Mannion, Richard Gaillardetz, *et al.* (eds), *Readings in Church Authority: Gifts and Challenges for Contemporary Catholicism*, Aldershot: Ashgate, 2003.

André Naud, *Le magistère incertain*, Montreal: Fides, 1987.

Leo J. O'Donovan, SJ, *Cooperation between Theologians and the Ecclesiastical Magisterium: A Report of the Joint Committee of the Canon Law Society of America and the Catholic Theological Society of America*, Washington: Catholic University of America, 1982.

Ladislas M. Orsy, *The Church: Learning and Teaching: Magisterium, Assent, Dissent, Academic Freedom*, Wilmington, DE: M. Glazier, 1987.

Karl Rahner, 'Open Questions in Dogma Considered by the Official Church as Definitively Decided', *Journal of Ecumenical Studies* 15/2 (1978).

Joseph Cardinal Ratzinger, 'Commentary on the Concluding Formula of the "Professio Fidei"', *Origins* 28 (July 16, 1998).

Bernard Sesboüé, *Le magistère à l'épreuve: Autorité, vérité et liberté dans l'Église*, Paris: Desclée de Brouwer, 2001.

——, 'A propos du Motu proprio de Jean-Paul II *Ad tuendam fidem*', *Études* 389/4 (Octobre 1998).

Francis A. Sullivan, *Creative Fidelity: Weighing and Interpreting Documents of the Magisterium*, New York: Paulist, 1996.

——, *Magisterium: Teaching Authority in the Catholic Church*, New York: Paulist, 1983.

Norbert Trippen, *Theologie und Lehramt im Konflikt: Die kirchlichen Massnahmen gegen den Modernismus in Jahre 1907*, Freiburg: Herder, 1977.

J.-M.-A. Vacant, *Le magistère ordinaire de l'Église et ses organes*, Paris: Delhomme et Briguet, 1887.

30

GOVERNANCE

Adam Hood

This essay aims to provide a brief introduction to 'governance'. After some introductory comments, the first section maps out some points of debate and difference amongst churches on the question. Section two gives an overview of various systems of church governance. Section three touches on important historical events, thinkers and documents.

The concept of governance refers to 'the act or manner of governing'.[1] Any organization, including the church, that wishes to exist over time needs to find ways of ordering its life. Admittedly the communal existence of the early church (AD 27–70) appears relatively harmonious,[2] depending on direction by charismatic leaders like Peter, whose authority was authenticated by healings, other miracles, inspirational preaching and an association with the earthly Christ.[3] It is not long, however, before the exercise of power begins to be routinized through the establishing of decision-making procedures.[4] The need for such structures was related to dispersal and growth, so that by the late first century there is a fairly developed leadership structure,[5] though this should not be overstated.[6] The dispersal of Christians raised issues of the legitimacy of local church life, leading to attempts to define orthodoxy.[7]

Power and authority

In approaching the question of church governance it is helpful to make a distinction between power and authority. Power is, in Weber's words, 'the chance of a man or a number of men to realize their own will in a communal action even against the resistance of others who are participating in the action'.[8] Power, in this sense, may be nakedly coercive. Legitimate power, on the other hand, is exercised with the agreement or acquiescence of those who are on the receiving end of decisions. The focus here is on the exercise of legitimated power.

In Weber's view, there are three sources of legitimated power or authority: legal–rational, traditional and charismatic.[9] The first is characteristic of the exercise of power through occupancy of a post. Bureaucrats might be examples here. Traditional legitimacy is to do with power hallowed by custom. A hereditary monarch is an example. Charismatic legitimacy attaches to the perceived charisma or 'giftedness' of a leader. Jesus himself is an instance of this kind of authority.

In Weber's terms, the present essay is concerned with the exercise of ecclesial authority of a legal–rational character. Though, of course, there are elements of the charismatic and traditional in ecclesial authority, the question of governance focuses attention on the legal–rational dimension.

One of the Greek words from which 'church' is derived, *kuriake*, literally means 'belonging to the Lord'.[10] All Christian churches would agree that the governance of the church belongs to the Lord. However, the divine Lordship requires mediation through institutional structures. Such arrangements typically provide answers to several interrelated questions, including: who is to govern; the limitations on authority; the social and theological legitimation of authority; and the relationship between ecclesial and political power?

The scope of governance

The exercise of authority in the church focuses on at least three distinct areas. First, there is the identification and articulation of the normative beliefs and practices of the faith, which implicitly involves judgements on who may be a fully accepted part of the Christian community. Churches have mechanisms for deciding these issues. Within the Roman Catholic Church, for instance, the official teaching role (magisterium) of the church has a four-fold manifestation: the teaching of 'individual bishops in communion with the Roman Pontiff'; 'the authoritative teaching of the bishop within his own diocese'; 'the authentic teaching of the Roman Pontiff when it is manifested without the conditions and guarantees of infallibility'; 'the case of an infallible teaching'.[11] Again in churches with a congregationalist polity, such as the United Church of Christ and the Baptist churches, which view the local congregation as the primary expression of the visible church, a considerable degree of local autonomy is exercised in defining faith and practice.

Second, there is the question of the financial, educational, welfare and property assets of a church. There have, it is true, been movements within the church that have eschewed 'worldly' attachments.[12] But mostly there has been the recognition of the value of tangible assets; their importance is borne out by the sometimes bitter feuding over property that is associated with church reorganizations. A key contemporary issue here is the degree to which authority is exercised transparently and accountably, a responsibility that the church shares with all voluntary organizations.[13]

Third, a far-reaching authority is that exerted in the selection of leaders, which can shape the theological and liturgical character of a church far into the future.[14]

Challenges to patterns of ecclesial governance

There have been many challenges to patterns of ecclesial governance in modern times. The development of opportunities for mass travel and information sharing has encouraged a comparative and critical approach to ecclesial authority.[15] One example is the role of feminism in calling into question patriarchal and hierarchical practices within the church.[16] Schüssler Fiorenza, for instance, argues that the 'ekklēsia of women is critical of patriarchal elements within the church, expressed in class, gender, racial and age stratifications'. Feminist Theology, she argues, has an important role to play in transforming Western patriarchy, through a new kind of 'democratic discursive practice'.[17]

Pressures towards more democratic governance have also been important. It has been argued, for instance, that the base communities movement in Latin America has offered a practical challenge to hierarchical forms of church governance, by encouraging the demand for a mutual and egalitarian collegiality inclusive of bishops, priests and laity.[18] Instead of mirroring in its structures the power arrangements of the world, the church is called to be an exemplary community which gives particular attention to the empowerment of the marginalized.[19]

Events as well as ideas have been important. It is claimed, for example, that the abuse of public power by states and churches – we might think of sexual abuse by clergy – has encouraged a critical attitude.

Points of debate and difference

Who governs: communitarian and personal authority

Who can legitimately claim the right to authority is a key issue. This deceptively straightforward question contains within it a number of areas upon which churches disagree, including that of whether authority should be located in particular offices or exercised through communitarian bodies.[20]

All churches include elements of the personal and communitarian in their governance structures, and the balance between these elements is likely to be fluid, changing in response to the people involved and the circumstances in which churches find themselves. One example of context shaping the governance of a church is the development in the second century of what has been called 'monarchical episcopacy' in response to the challenge of certain 'heretical' movements.[21] The question, then, is whether churches tend in one direction or the other.

The numerically dominant churches are episcopal in their governance, which is to say that they are organized hierarchically and place chief authority in bishops, though they also have communitarian dimensions. In the Eastern Orthodox Church, for instance, though there are autocephalous primates for each of the sixteen constituent churches, yet the governance of the church as a whole is entrusted to the primates as a group. In the Scottish Episcopalian Church, by contrast, bishops are elected by representatives and clergy in their respective dioceses and are constrained in matters of policy and finance by an elected synod.[22]

Non-episcopal churches tend to emphasize communitarian forms of decision making. Good examples of this are the churches of the Reformed tradition, both congregationalist and presbyterian.[23] Presbyterianism comprises the governance of a church through a hierarchical system of church courts, ranging from that found in the local congregation, the kirk session or council, regional bodies (sometimes called presbyteries or synods), to national assemblies. Each of these courts has its own jurisdictions, with an ascending scale of authority, final authority in matters of law and practice lying with the national assembly. Each of the courts is made up of an equal number of clergy and elders. However, even here there are significant areas of personal authority. Most pronounced is the authority of the local clergyperson. The presbyterian minister can be entrusted with considerable authority over worship, education and the material assets of a congregation. Moreover, they may have security of tenure, so that, barring a serious misdemeanour, they are practically unassailable.

Who governs: clergy or laity

A second pertinent area is the relationship between clergy and laity in governance. A church's perspective on clerical orders (deacons, priests/ministers, bishops) and the relation between these and the laity will have a bearing on their understanding of church governance. Some Christian communities eschew the distinction between clergy and laity altogether and, as a result, tend towards heavily communitarian forms of governance. Examples here might be the Religious Society of Friends (Quakers) and the Plymouth Brethren. In the case of the Society of Friends, local meetings enjoy considerable autonomy and key decisions are taken by the monthly meeting, which is open to all members of a local meeting house and emphasizes consensus as the means to making a corporate decision.[24] The monthly meeting appoints various functionaries to organize church matters, but there is no suggestion of a distinct theological status or authority.[25]

The Plymouth Brethren stress the complete autonomy of the local church and there is no distinction between laity and clergy. Services, especially the weekly 'breaking of bread', the most distinctive element of Brethren worship, are led spontaneously by members of meetings and the local meeting is governed by appointed elders who have no jurisdiction beyond their local gathering and aim to lead by example rather than dictate. Amongst the Brethren there are people with recognized whole-time ministries, but there is no suggestion that they are in clerical orders.[26]

Others, such as congregationalists, baptists and presbyterians, accept the distinction between clergy and laity, but tend to understand this as a largely functional expedient with an emphasis on church order and the sacramental and teaching role of the ministry. Such a view leads to forms of church governance in which clergy, other church leaders and laity share authority through participating together in church councils and courts. Presbyterianism, for instance, focuses governance in courts, which are constituted by equal numbers of ministers and elders. One pervasive way of viewing the church court in presbyterian circles is that it is made up entirely of ordained elders, some of whom are called to a particular function, that of being ministers. Congregationalism emphasizes the priesthood of all members of a local church – this is implicit in the view that the local congregation is the primary expression of the visible church and that every member has a right, in principle, to participate in the governance of their local congregation. The local church meeting is the place where all members can participate in decisions on matters of policy and practice.

Episcopal churches tend to reflect a clearer sense of the distinction between clergy and laity, dependent on ordination, and this is not unconnected to the idea of apostolic succession. In such churches there is a tendency to locate governing authority with the clergy, though mostly they also provide for lay involvement in decision making. In the Church of England, to take one instance, there is synodical government. This system aims to engage the laity in the governance of the church. The Synodical Government Measure 1969 provided for the setting up of a General Synod comprised of three houses, Bishops, Clergy and Laity, the latter two being elected by corresponding diocesan bodies; the structure of the General Synod is reflected in diocesan synods. Moreover, at the parish level there is the parochial church council, which also includes clergy and laity. Thus the structures of England's national church reflect a concern to see the cooperation of clergy and laity in governance. However, the distinction between clergy and laity is preserved in the structures. At General Synod matters relating to doctrine and worship can only be agreed 'in terms proposed by the House of Bishops'.[27] On this latter point it is of interest to note that, in some respects, the personal authority of Church of England bishops has recently grown.[28]

In the Roman Catholic Church the relationship between clergy and laity is characterized by inequity. Despite the fact that there seems to be evidence from the early Christian centuries (and beyond) of the involvement of laity in the choice of bishops, presbyters and deacons,[29] the role of Catholic laity in the selection of clergy today is minimal, usually limited only to 'humble consent'.[30] Moreover the imbalance of power is reflected in the almost unbridled authority of the parish priest within the local congregation.[31] The concentration of authority is informed by a tendency to think of the clergy as a 'sacred caste' who are distinguished at quite a fundamental level from those not so sacred, the laity.[32] However, this must be set against, first, the powerful impulse in the Second Vatican Council towards the recognition of lay apostolicity,[33] and second, the practical effect that declining vocations will have on the role of the laity.[34]

A challenge for all churches with an ordained ministry is the tendency towards professionalization, in part as a response to the contemporary crises facing ministers. An understanding of ministry as a profession, with the attendant connotations of power and status, may encourage destructive dependencies rather than the ministry of the whole people of God.[35]

Who governs: male or female

Whether women can enter holy orders is a contentious area for most churches. Given the imbalance of authority that hangs on the question of ordination, it is clear that the gender issue has implications for the exercise of power. The history of the church up to the nineteenth century is one in which men dominated the ranks of the clergy, despite the fact that occasionally women did exercise institutional power. That there were influential women in Christ's circle and the apostolic, and post-apostolic ages is undoubted, though their relationship to clerical office is ambiguous. Some early 'heretical' groups, such as the Montanists, employed women clergy, but this was regarded with disapproval by the leaders of the church in general. There may have been a distinct group of women deaconesses operating within the early church, both East and West, but their standing and function is obscure. Again there is the place of women within religious orders to consider, not least those who had leadership responsibilities. Women may also have played a distinct role within the Celtic church. It was only with the Reformation, however, and amongst Anabaptist groups in particular, that women were first given the right to become clergy in mainstream churches, though it was not until the nineteenth and twentieth centuries that the ordination of women became a matter of pressing concern for most churches. An early development in the 1830s in Germany was the setting up of an order of deaconesses, which subsequently spread to other countries. The first woman to be ordained into a recognized denomination was a congregationalist in the USA in 1853. It was not until 1917 that a woman was ordained into an English congregationalist church. English baptists and presbyterians followed suit in recognizing women's ordination and post-1945 many other British and overseas churches have ordained women into the ministry. However, of the denominations claiming historic succession, only some Anglican and Lutheran churches have ordained women to the priesthood and the episcopate. The Roman Catholic and Orthodox churches have an exclusively male clergy and, indeed, the Catholic Congregation for the Doctrine of the Faith has argued that 'the teaching excluding women from priestly ordination has been set forth by the ordinary and infallible magisterium'.[36]

Who governs: church and state

Ever since the decision of Constantine in AD 337 to grant a favoured position to the church in the Roman Empire, the relationship between church and state has been of great importance in understanding the inner development of the church. First, there is the question of the ways in which ecclesial governance has been shaped by the attempt to ward off the influence of the state. Lindberg argues, for instance, that the development of the medieval papacy was, to a large extent, driven by the papal desire to assert autonomy and even supremacy over European states.[37] Second, there is the way in which the establishment of churches – that is, the recognition by states of particular churches as the church of that state – has shaped patterns of ecclesial governance. Relations with the state is, of course, an issue for all churches, since the secular power will nearly always bear ultimate authority, yet it is a particular issue for those churches who are established in law. Patterns of establishment are very varied, as are the implications of establishment for church governance. In the early days, Constantine and those who followed him exercised considerable control over church affairs. It has been argued, for instance, that the Nicene formula was driven through by Constantine as much for political reasons as for theological ones.[38] Christianity spread through Europe largely by the conversion of political leaders, which meant that those leaders had considerable powers of patronage over the church.[39] This set the scene for a pattern of cooperation and tension between church and state that continues in an attenuated form even today. The Middle Ages saw a series of disputes between state rulers and the papacy over jurisdiction. After the Reformation, Catholicism continued to be established in many European countries and there was the development of established Protestant churches in Scandinavia, the Low Countries, parts of Germany, Switzerland and the British Isles. These normally drew on state financial support and the state was involved in appointments and other ecclesial issues.

From the eighteenth century onwards, decolonization and secularization have led to the disestablishment of many European churches, but established churches remain in parts of Europe. Amongst these the pattern of church–state relationships vary. In England, for example, though the involvement of the state in internal church affairs has been moderated during the twentieth century, yet the Crown in parliament still exercises substantial powers of influence and patronage. There are indeed matters, such as the status of *The Book of Common Prayer* (BCP), over which the church has no jurisdiction, since these are part of British law. The quid pro quo is that the Church of England sends 26 bishops to the House of Lords.

Another very different pattern of church–state relations is that found in Scotland. Though the Church of Scotland is established by law, it is almost wholly independent of the direct involvement of the state in its internal affairs. This is expressed in the monarch or their representative being only an observer at the annual General Assembly of the Kirk. This reflects four and half centuries of debate over the relationship between church and state, significantly informed by a belief in the independence of the church of state control, alongside the idea that church and state play complementary roles in sustaining a godly society.[40]

Systems of church governance

Historically and contemporaneously the main form taken by church government is an episcopal one, which is rule by bishops.[41] Indeed for much of the church's history this was the only form of church government. However, amongst contemporary episcopal churches there are many disparities in the actuality of governance, which reflect different understandings of church and church governance.

Contemporary episcopal churches

The Roman Catholic Church is the largest Christian church and it is governed by an episcopate with the Bishop of Rome, the pope, at its head. Historically the claim is that the governing authority of the pope arises from his being the direct heir of St Peter, the first Bishop of Rome and prince of the apostles, who was, it is said, given his authority by Christ himself. In this sense communion with the See of Rome is, for bishops and local churches, an expression of communion with the historical church community and ultimately with Christ and the apostles. The line of authority is maintained by the power of the Holy Spirit and through the laying on of hands, the apostles to bishops, and from bishops to priests and deacons. The pope in communion with the bishops of the church exercises exclusive teaching and juridical rights

What is characteristic of the Eastern Orthodox Church is its stress on conciliarism.[42] The church is divided into sixteen autocephalous churches, which are relatively autonomous parts each with a head bishop who is not responsible to a higher bishop. The unity of the church as a whole is envisioned as constituted by the gathering of the primates (patriarchs) of the autocephalous churches gathered around Christ, with subordinate bishops and archbishops gathered around them. This pattern, understood in terms of Revelation chapter 21, is called 'Conciliar Hierarchy'. Underpinning this pattern of governance is a theological idea: that the authority of Christ is given, not to particular individuals, but to the church as whole. The patriarchs of the different churches and the subordinate clergy serve the church, and their authority comes from their example of service in presiding at the eucharist and as moral exemplars.[43]

The Anglican Communion is, arguably, the most significant church emerging out of the sixteenth-century Reformation which continues to lay claim to governance by an episcopate whose authority is understood in terms commensurate with the Catholic and Orthodox communities.[44] Anglicans have asserted apostolic succession through the Church of England back to the first Archbishop of Canterbury, St Augustine. The fact that Henry VIII left the legal structures intact after he broke with Rome meant that episcopacy has been an Anglican given and the ground of the church's appeal to apostolic authority. Succession has been understood in different ways, but, in general, there has been an emphasis on the episcopate as enjoying apostolic oversight, which includes and derives from ordination. Succession legitimizes the church's ministry and is the linchpin of the catholicity of local churches and the church as a whole. Governance is exercised by bishops in part through delegation of roles to priests and deacons, and partly through the exercise of a teaching role that has the whole church in view. Each Anglican province governs itself through synods that meet under episcopal chairing, giving rise to the claim that it is the bishop-in-synod that is the seat of Anglican authority in the areas of doctrine, worship and discipline. Typically, synods (called variously councils, etc) are representative involving bishops, clergy and laity. Internationally Anglicanism has no juridical authority, though its common experience, liturgical tradition and links with Canterbury provide the basis for a consultative relationship most clearly expressed in the Lambeth Conferences of Anglican Communion Bishops, which has met every ten years since 1867 and which all bishops attend. At these meetings the Archbishop of Canterbury presides, but the gathering has no statutory authority. The same holds true for the more frequent meetings of the Anglican Consultative Council and the Primates' Meeting.

Other Protestant churches also have forms of episcopal governance. Some Methodist churches operate episcopal politys, though they are likely to justify this in pragmatic rather than theological terms. In the United Methodist Church, for instance, bishops are elected for life, can operate for long periods of time in one conference (the regional grouping of Methodist churches), ordain and appoint clergy to local churches, take a presiding role in national and international conferences and perform a wide range of administrative functions.[45] The British Methodist Church, whilst formally non-episcopal, has two primary authorities, one of which, the circuit superintendent, fulfils bishop-like responsibilities.[46] Other Protestant episcopal churches include the Lutheran churches and the Reformed churches of Hungary and France.

Non-episcopal churches

The primary forms of non-episcopal governance have already been discussed. These are presbyterianism, with its system of ascending courts, and congregationalism, with its emphasis on the local congregation and its looser regional and national associations. An interesting contemporary variant of these 'types' is the United Reformed Church in Britain, which is a church that combines in its governance attention to the local church meeting along with a wider concern for scripture, history, tradition and ecumenical insight. In this way the church marries congregationalist and presbyterian elements in a creative ecumenical mix.[47]

Events, documents and people

Apostolic succession

With the death of the apostles, there was an issue about the continuity of belief and practice. The apostles had been the recognized arbiters of the ascended Christ and legitimate teaching. With their passing the issue of continuity was raised. Initially continuity was understood in terms of faithfulness to apostolic teaching and the bishop's role was seen in relation to this task. By the third century, however, a new idea, apostolic succession, had begun to develop through the writings of Cyprian and Tertullian. Now the continuity of the church was to be found in the fact that the apostles had consecrated bishops as their successors and they, in turn, consecrate other bishops.[48] From this perspective 'the apostolate was kept alive in the episcopate, and in this way became a guarantee of truth and grace'.[49] The episcopate was held to be integral to the catholicity of the church in that they, the bishops, realized apostolic functions, were consecrated members of the apostolic line (the line was maintained in a literal, tactile way), were specially endowed with the Spirit for their task, and succeeded each other in sees that were demonstrably in organic communion with the apostles.[50] This theory clearly identifies the episcopate as a necessary constituent part of the church and suggests that they will have a directive role therein. It is of immense importance, especially to non-Catholics who wish to maintain their catholicity. It has been vital to the self-understanding of the Anglican Communion, amongst others. Moreover it is a doctrine with ecumenical significance, especially in inter-church conversations.[51]

The emergence of the papacy

The emergence of the See of Rome from the fifth century to the twelfth century as the 'most significant institution of Western Christianity' is of immense significance for church governance.[52] The continuing pre-eminence of the papacy in world Christianity and its role in the Reformation suggest the importance of this issue. The early pre-eminence of the Roman see was related to its association with Peter and Paul, widely believed to have been the 'chief' apostles, and the political and cultural dominance of the city. The gospels (Matt 16.18ff) were held to justify the leading role of the see in the Christian world and this claim was bolstered in the sixth century with the translation of the *Epistle of Clement*, which claimed that Peter had, in the face of the gathered Roman church, passed on his authority to Clement and, by implication, to the succession of Bishops of Rome.[53] The document thus legitimated the thought that the Bishop of Rome was in direct succession to Peter, and also that he had pre-eminence in the episcopate as a whole, just as Peter had been recognized as the chief of the apostles.[54] This idea was developed by Pope Leo (440–61) in his argument that, just as in a legal act of inheritance the inheritor assumes the assets and rights of the dead person, so the pope, by his office, had inherited the powers and rights of Peter. In Leo's view the church was to be understood as a new society and the pope, in Peter's stead, was the monarchical head. Leo's successor developed this idea in relation to the Roman state. The church and state were, for Gelasius I (492–6), separate jurisdictions, but the ecclesial jurisdiction was superior to the secular. This was a radical idea that bore fruit in many and various ways over the following centuries. The missionary zeal of Gregory I (590–604), which aimed at forming a Christian commonwealth in the West; the founding of the papal state in 756; Leo's crowning of Charlemagne as Roman Emperor in 800, under protest or not, which cemented Rome as the heart of the empire and church; and the articulation by Nicholas I (858–67) of the idea that the pope was Christ's vicegerent on earth, speaking with the authority of God, whose decisions had the force of law: all of these developments can be seen as elaborations of the vision of Leo the Great of a monarchical papacy. This process was significantly buttressed by the *Donation of Constantine*. This document, generally thought to be a forgery dating from around 750, purports to be the work of Constantine and grants Pope Sylvester I and his successors dominion over the entire Western Roman Empire. The precise reason and context of the forging of this document is unclear, but there is no doubt that it was an attempt to give ideological support to papal ambitions and that is how it was used. This model of governance is part of the on-going experience of Catholicism. In this regard mention must be made of the nineteenth-century Ultramontane movement,[55] which encouraged a centralization of power around the sovereign pontiff and a corresponding standardization of discipline, liturgy and piety. The Vatican Council, called in 1869, and its formal definition of papal infallibility are expressions of the victory of Ultramontanism, as was Pius IX's proclamation of the doctrine of the Immaculate Conception.[56] Hence a distinctive understanding of the magisterium (and indeed the first ecclesial usage of the term itself) came to pass in the nineteenth century.

Luther's To the Christian Nobility of the German Nation[57]

There is a consensus that this document, dated 1520, is one of the most significant ecclesiological statements of the Protestant Reformation. In it Luther attacks the idea, developed from the time of Leo the Great onwards, that the church was a separate estate, governed by the clergy and headed by the Roman pontiff, superior in authority to the secular power. Luther's concern was to provide the theological basis that would allow lay Christians to be involved in the reform of the church. He argued that there was no essential distinction to be drawn between the clergy and the laity; Christians shared in one baptism, one justifying faith and one gospel and so there was no difference amongst them as regards their spiritual status. The only distinction of the clergy was that they had been chosen by the community to exercise particular functions on behalf of the whole. Moreover, Luther held that the authenticity of a priestly vocation was not dependent on episcopal consecration and that a priest need not be celibate.

An implication of Luther's argument was that all Christians were priests and, as such shared a common vocation. Through their work, whether that be labouring as a clergyman or a cobbler, they serve the physical and spiritual needs of the community. This principle led Luther to argue that lay rulers, who are called to discharge justice, are entitled to judge, punish and reform the church.

Luther argued, then, that there was no substantial difference between lay and clergy, that there was only one spiritual estate that embraces all Christians, and that lay people had a role in the governance and reform of the church. He extended this argument by suggesting that the church, and the papal establishment in particular, did not have a monopoly on the interpretation of doctrine or practice. Indeed, for Luther, the interpretation of the scriptures was a function of the whole community.

It is difficult to overstate the significance of Luther's writing. In rejecting apostolic succession and the notion of the two estates, Luther lays down resources for subsequent communitarian approaches to ecclesial governance, as well as a sacralization of the lay life.[58] A weakness is his inability to explain how disputes between Christians of good standing might be resolved.[59] There is also the question of the consistency of his own practice with the principles that he outlined.

Vatican II

The Second Vatican Council (1962–5) was called by Pope John XXIII with the task of 'renewing the life of the Church and bringing up to date its teaching, discipline, and organization, with the unity of all Christians as its ultimate goal'.[60] The Council had a great deal to say about the ministry of the church, a particularly important document in this regard is *Lumen Gentium* (of the church).[61]

Lumen Gentium defines the church's ministry as participation in the three-fold ministry of Christ, as prophet, priest and king: the church is understood as the continuing incarnation of Christ, which acts as an 'instrumental sign' of the union between God and humankind in Christ, on behalf of all humanity. In this sense all Christians are said to participate in Christ's ministry – the document, with its emphasis on the whole people of God, reflects a new awareness on the part of Catholicism of the laity's role in the mission and service of the church. Yet the term 'ministerium' is reserved for bishops, priests and deacons, which suggests a continuing affirmation of an important distinction between clergy and laity, though what this means in detail is ill-defined in the documents.[62] For all that, the rediscovery of the ministry of the whole people of God based on participation in one baptism, confirmation and eucharist, an idea reminiscent of Luther's thinking, has had important ramifications in the growth, since the 1960s, of recognized forms of lay ministry in the church, such as parish sisters, female canon lawyers and female chaplains in educational institutions.

Another important aspect of *Lumen Gentium* was the attempt to modify the relationship between the papacy and local bishops. The model suggested was that of the church as primarily a local entity, whose unity was expressed in its communion with its bishop. The world-wide church was understood as a network of local churches, diverse in practice and culture, yet united in communion.[63] This was an attempt to define the church as the local gathering of Christians around their bishop, rather than an international body gathered around the pope. The bishop is recognized as the highest form of ministry, and his role is envisaged as that of the preserver of faithfulness of practice and belief in the local church. The unity of the church universal is seen as maintained through the shared responsibility of the college of bishops acting in concert with the pope. Each bishop has responsibility for the unity of their local church, and together with the pope they share responsibility for the unity, in faithfulness, of the universal church. The pope has responsibility for unity *within* the college of bishops, not over it. Added to this is the insistence that bishops receive their power directly from Christ, not as substitutes for the pope. All this adds up to a new collegial emphasis and a model of church order rooted in the cooperative relations between local churches, priests and bishops, all of whom receive their ministries from and on behalf of Christ, not from an ecclesial hierarchy.

McLoughlin argues that the Second Vatican Council articulated a model of ministry that is collegial, in the sense that it arises from a perception of the common call to ministry – priestly, royal and prophetic – of all the baptized. Within this overall theology of mission and ministry, the particular ministries of bishop and priest are seen as being related to the ministries of the whole community of faith.[64] This would imply a very different style of ecclesial governance from before. The actual impact of the Council, however, remains uncertain. Certainly, a regular advisory episcopal synod has been set up, but there are also countervailing forces, not least the continuing commitment of the Vatican Curial offices to a hierarchical culture in which a bishop is responsible to the pope, priest to bishop, and people to priest. Moreover, maintenance of the important theological distinction between clergy and laity, in which clergy alone, by a special sacramental gift, are able to represent Christ, offer penance and forgiveness, and celebrate the eucharist, may be a contributory part of the current tensions. The continued adherence to the 'infallible magisterium', even if this is now articulated in collegial terms, might also militate against new ways of conceiving of order and governance. The issue here is complex, reflecting the emergence of 'restorationist' tendencies since the 1970s aimed at restoring the power of the centre, the curia, with a concomitant trend to interpreting collegiality diachronically rather than synchronically.[65]

Conclusion

In *Baptism, Eucharist and Ministry* and *The Nature and Mission of the Church* the WCC has kindled a renewed interest in governance.[66] These documents see authority as being exercised in three overlapping ways: personally, collegially, and communally, and this raises critical questions for all churches.[67] The current essay has sought to provide elements that frame the debate by mapping out some of the variety amongst churches on the issue of governance. Touching on points of sensitivity, it has highlighted resources that churches draw on to meet the challenges they face.

In commenting on governance Wilson writes: 'The structure of church government will need continually to be kept under review so that it encourages Christian believing that is mature and responsible.'[68] It is debatable to what degree contemporary churches are facing up to this task. To take but one example, the generally negative stance on homosexual practice taken by most traditional churches seems hopelessly out of touch with the modern consensus and might be seen to confirm an ingrained homophobia.[69] The current essay has touched on possible reasons for this failure, including the centralized forms of decision making in many churches, the continuing dominance of the clergy, and the marginalization of women and other historically weak groups. These are consonant with a tendency for decision making, especially on matters of belief and practice, to be heavily conditioned by interpretative traditions rather than present experience and insight. The church has a duty of candour in its teaching and practice and only by exemplifying intellectual and moral integrity can Christianity hope to become the 'vital creed of the present and future generations'.[70] It might be surmised that ecclesial governance, patterned around this challenge, would move quickly down the declericalized and democratic trajectory set out by insightful, critical friends of the church.

Notes

1 Delia Thompson (ed.), *The Concise Oxford Dictionary*, 9th edn, Oxford: OUP, 1995.
2 See, for example, Acts 2.42–47, though compare Acts 15.1–29.
3 See Acts 2.14–41; 3.1–26. Ephesians and Colossians also show little interest in structures of governance.
4 Acts 6.1–6.
5 Claire Drury, 'The Pastoral Epistles', in John Barton and John Muddiman (eds), *The Oxford Bible Commentary*, Oxford: OUP, 2001, pp. 1220–33, p. 1220.
6 David McLoughlin, 'Authority as Service in Communion', in Noel Timms and Kenneth Wilson (eds), *Governance and Authority in the Roman Catholic Church*, London: SPCK, 2000, pp. 123–36, p. 123.
7 See Acts 15.
8 H.H. Gerth and C.W. Mills (eds), *From Max Weber: Essays in Sociology*, London: Routledge, 1948, p. 180.
9 Ibid, pp. 295–301.
10 See Chapter 1 of the present volume.
11 Giovanni Colombo, 'Obedience to the Ordinary Magisterium', in Gerard Mannion *et al.* (eds), *Readings in Church Authority*, Aldershot: Ashgate, 2003, pp. 102–5, pp. 102–3. Cf. the preceding chapter of this volume.
12 See the discussion of the 'Spiritual Franciscans' in Malcolm Lambert, *Medieval Heresy*, London: Arnold, 1977, pp. 182–208.
13 Terry Connor and Sarah Lindsell, 'The Lesson of the Voluntary Sector', in Timms and Wilson, *Governance*, pp. 53–69.
14 Michael P Hornsby-Smith, 'Sociological Reflections on Power and Authority', in Timms and Wilson, *Governance*, pp. 12–31, p. 14.
15 Kenneth Wilson, 'Authority and the Churches', in Timms and Wilson, *Governance*, pp. 32–52, p. 33.
16 Nicola Slee, *Faith and Feminism*, London: DLT, 2003, Ch. 8.
17 Elisabeth Schüssler Fiorenza, 'The Ekklēsia of Women', in Mannion *et al.*, *Readings*, pp. 72–77. Cf. Chapter 25 of the present volume.
18 Leonardo Boff, 'The Reinvention of the Church', ibid, pp. 56–64, p. 64.
19 Duncan B. Forrester, *Truthful Action*, Edinburgh: T&T Clark, 2000, pp. 71–89.
20 At this point I am collapsing the distinction between personal, communal and collegial into two categories.
21 John Bowden and Alan Richardson (eds), *A New Dictionary of Christian Theology*, London: SCM, 1983, p. 109.
22 Though they do exercise autonomous power in matters of clergy appointments and pastoral oversight. Lawrence Wareing, 'Christians in Scotland', *Life and Work* (Nov 2006), 18–19.
23 Cf. Chapters 10 and 12.
24 Rachel Muers, *Keeping God's Silence*, Oxford: Blackwell, 2004.

25 http://quakersfp.live.poptech.coop/qfp/chap4/4.01.html (accessed 10 November, 2006).
26 http://web.singnet.com.sg/%7Esyeec/literature/brethren.html (accessed 10 November, 2006).
27 F.L. Cross and E.A. Livingstone (eds), *The Oxford Dictionary of the Christian Church*, 3rd edn, Oxford: OUP, 2005, p. 1580.
28 Wilson, 'Authority', p. 44.
29 See McLoughlin, 'Authority', p. 125. McLoughlin makes the point that by the Council of Chalcedon (AD 451) bishops were being chosen by fellow bishops.
30 Bernard Hoose, *Authority in Roman Catholicism*, Chelmsford: Matthew James, 2002, pp. 4–5.
31 Ibid, p. 5.
32 Ibid, pp. 6–7.
33 See the discussion of Congar's ideas, which were very influential in the Second Vatican Council. Paul Lakeland, *The Liberation of the Laity*, New York: Continuum, 2004, p. 53.
34 See Forrester, *Truthful*, pp. 70–2.
35 Ibid, pp. 88–9.
36 Cross and Livingstone, *Dictionary*, p. 1774. See *Mulieris Dignitatem* www.vatican.va/holy_father/john_paul_ii/apost_letters/documents/hf_jp-ii_apl_15081988_mulieris-dignitatem_en.html (accessed 2 March, 2007). There is a great deal of debate surrounding the interpretation of this document, not least whether there is a connotation of infallibity attached to its teaching.
37 Carter Lindberg, *A Brief History of Christianity*, Oxford: Blackwell, 2006, Ch. 5.
38 Ibid, p. 25.
39 Ibid, p. 566.
40 Forrester, *Truthful*, p. 169.
41 See http://en.wikipedia.org/wiki/Main_Page for general descriptions of systems of church governance.
42 Cf. Chapter 8.
43 Wilson, 'Authority', p. 42.
44 See Chapter 11.
45 Russell E. Richey and Thomas Edward Frank, *Episcopacy in the Methodist Tradition*, Nashville: Abingdon, 2004.
46 Wilson, 'Authority', p. 47.
47 For an example of how this works in practice, see United Reformed Church, 'Sexuality Report'. www.urc.org.uk/documents/sexuality_report/core_report_sexuality/report_2.htm (accessed 9 November, 2006).
48 For a defence of this doctrine see K.E. Kirk (ed.), *The Apostolic Ministry*, London: Hodder, 1957.
49 J.D. Douglas (ed.), *The New International Dictionary of the Christian Church*, Grand Rapids, MI: Zondervan, 1978, pp. 59–60.
50 Cross and Livingstone, *Dictionary*, p. 92.
51 For instance, the preservation of the historic episcopate has been a major concern in recent Anglican–Methodist conversations.
52 Lindberg, *History*, p. 54.
53 Clement was a bishop of Rome, some claim the first after Peter though this is disputed. The *Epistle* is held to be spurious by recent commentators. Evidence for this is that Clement, in his authenticated writings to the Corinthians, is rather indifferent as to whether to call chief ministers bishops or presbyters.
54 It must be borne in mind that, early on, the terms bishop and presbyter were used somewhat interchangeably.
55 Literally meaning looking 'over the mountains' to Rome.
56 Robert Aubert *et al.*, *The Christian Centuries*, vol. 5, London: DLT, 1978, pp. 56–69.
57 *Luther's Works*, vol. 44. Philadelphia: Fortress, 1966, pp. 123–217. Cf. Chapter 9 of this volume.
58 See Max Weber, *The Protestant Ethic and the Spirit of Capitalism*, London: Allen & Unwin, 1968.
59 Alister E..McGrath, *Reformation Thought*, 3rd edn, Oxford: Blackwell, 1999, p. 204.
60 Cross and Livingstone, *Dictonary*, p. 1694.
61 www.vatican.va/archive/hist_councils/ii_vatican_council/documents/vat-ii_const_19641121_lumen-gentium_en.html (accessed 13 December, 2006).
62 McLoughlin, 'Authority', p. 126.
63 Ibid, 'Authority', p. 127.

64 Ibid, p. 134.

65 For further discussion see Richard Gaillardetz, *Teaching with Authority*, Collegeville: Liturgical Press, 1997.

66 World Council of Churches Commission on Faith and Order, *The Nature and Mission of the Church*, Geneva: WCC, 2005; *Baptism, Eucharist and Ministry*, Geneva: WCC, 1982.

67 Bradford Hinze, 'Are Councils and Synods Decision Making?', in Paul M. Collins and Michael A. Fahey (eds), *The Nature and Mission of the Church*, London, T& T Clark International (forthcoming).

68 Wilson, 'Authority', p. 51.

69 Adrian Thatcher, 'Authority and Sexuality in the Protestant Tradition', in Joseph Selling (ed.), *Embracing Sexuality*, Aldershot: Ashgate, 2001, pp. 127–48, p. 135.

70 A. Seth Pringle-Pattison, *The Duty of Candour in Religious Teaching*, London: Hodder, 1920, p. 4.

Further reading

Andrew Bradstock and Christopher Rowland (eds), *Radical Christian Writings*, Oxford: Blackwell, 2002.

F.L. Cross and E.A. Livingstone (eds), *The Oxford Dictionary of the Christian Church*, 3rd edn, Oxford: OUP, 2005.

Duncan Forrester, *Truthful Action*, Edinburgh: T&T Clark, 2000.

Paul Lakeland, *The Liberation of the Laity*, New York: Continuum, 2004.

Gerard Mannion *et al.* (eds), *Readings in Church Authority*. Aldershot: Ashgate, 2003.

Noel Timms and Kenneth Wilson (eds), *Governance and Authority in the Roman Catholic Church*, London: SPCK, 2000.

31

MINISTRY

Eamonn Conway

Introduction

While in practice ministry in the Christian churches is flourishing, theologically speaking it is in a state of some disarray at this time. Prior to the Second Vatican Council the term 'ministry' was not common in Roman Catholic circles and was considered to have a Protestant 'ring' to it. Since the Second Vatican Council and its intentional empowerment of the laity, there has been an explosion of ministries, and attempts by church authorities to circumscribe usage of the term have been largely unsuccessful. Yet what is, and is not, considered to be ministry is difficult to determine.

There is a particular problem in the Roman Catholic Church. Because the ministry of ordained priesthood is restricted to male celibates, an ageing and diminishing category in many countries, increasingly lay people who are not ordained assume some duties appropriate or at least generally restricted to the ordained. This complicates attempts at clarity and definition since although there are ministries proper to the laity, there are also tasks and duties proper to the ordained priesthood currently being performed by the laity because of a shortage of priests. At the same time there is also disarray within the Reformed churches. The recent ordination of women to the priesthood and the episcopate within the Anglican Communion, as well as the ordination of people living openly in same-sex partnerships, have not only disrupted ecumenical relations but have also undermined Anglican unity around matters such as who may minister and by what authority.

The English word 'ministry' translates the Latin *ministerium*, which in turn renders the Greek *diakonia*. It is used frequently in the New Testament, especially in the letters, and its use ranges from reference to general kinds of services to the ministry of the apostles.

I will take Thomas F O'Meara's six characteristics of ministry as a framework for this discussion of Christian ministry. According to O'Meara, ministry is (1) doing something; (2) for the advent of the kingdom; (3) in public; (4) on behalf of a Christian community; (5) which is a gift received in faith, baptism and ordination; and (6) which is an activity with its own limits and identity within a diversity of ministerial actions.[1]

Ministry as 'doing something'

The first point O'Meara stresses is that ministry is about activity. It is concerned with actions that are for the sake of the reign of God and which seek to realize the in-breaking of God's kingdom in the midst of daily life.

The emphasis on ministry as 'doing something' is important in that in the past the laity, the vast majority of Christians, were considered to be purely passive recipients of the actions of a ministering elite, the ordained. They, the vast majority of church members, were the subjects of ministry rather than its agents. The many 'corporal works of mercy' the laity performed were considered private actions more beneficial to their own individual salvation than part of the public life, service and activity of the church as such.

It is also important to point out that the activity that constitutes the ministry of the 'laity' or the 'non-ordained' (neither term is satisfactory) is activity which is *proper* to these ministers as baptized Christians who have been given particular gifts for the service of the Kingdom of God. That is why a term sometimes still used, 'the apostolate of the laity', is also problematic. The term 'laity' is unsatisfactory in that it inevitably conjures up the sense of 'amateur' as opposed to 'professional'.[2] At the same time, the term 'apostolate' seems to tie the work of the laity into that of being ancillary to the hierarchy. Thus the term 'apostolate of the laity', as Enda Lyons points out, seems to portray the laity as 'amateur apostles'.[3]

Yet at the heart of the recovery of a more authentic understanding of ministry since the Second Vatican Council is, as the New Testament understood it, that there is a variety of gifts given by the one Spirit.[4] Thus 'lay' or 'non-ordained' ministries are given by the Spirit, not bestowed upon the laity by the episcopate, which is itself only one ministry within the church, albeit a very important and in fact essential one. While the episcopate has a key role and responsibility in recognizing and authorizing other ministries, those who exercise such ministries are not like a 'reserve force' for the ordained priesthood. Nor are lay ministries 'cast-offs' from the ordained ministry; they are not 'Santa's little helpers' who step in when Santa is short-handed. Certain members of the laity have roles, tasks and responsibilities that are properly their own as ministers within the church at the service of the kingdom.

One way that we can understand the problem here theologically is outlined by George Tavard. In his view, there is a tension between two elements in terms of the church's self-understanding, namely, the institutional element and the charismatic element. If the charismatic element were dominant, then ministry would be understood primarily as the response of the church to its mission to serve the reign of God under the continuous and ever-present guidance of the Holy Spirit. The present mission of the church and the prompting of the Spirit would take precedence over custom and practice; tradition would be seen as something dynamic and developing in response to the church's present circumstances rather than as something necessarily static in fidelity to the church's memory.

Instead, what we have today, according to Tavard, is a domination of *ministerium* by *magisterium*, whereby the present activity of the Spirit is subordinated to the church's memory of Christ and its preservation of the deposit of faith. The result is a privileging of a static and unchanging understanding of ministry based on certain assumptions with regard to Christ's intentions for the structuring of the church. These assumptions are themselves founded upon particular interpretations of the New Testament which are at least open to question in the light of more recent biblical scholarship.[5]

Yet even a casual reading of the accounts of the early church, as reflected, for example, in Luke-Acts and in St Paul's letters to the Corinthians, shows that the first Christians understood themselves to have greater flexibility and responsibility for ordering and structuring ministry than the churches readily accept and admit today. Clearly, ministry from the very beginning was understood as the activity of a variety of believers fulfilling various roles and duties for the sake of the one and united body of believers in Christ. Ministry was initially characterized by the performance of services in response to felt needs as they emerged in the nascent community, and only subsequently came to be understood as the holding of sacral offices in fidelity to an explicit mandate from Christ during his earthly life.

The emphasis on ministry as a vibrant activity serving the reign of God in response to the circumstances of the present day is important. Yet account must also be taken of the fact that in Western culture today a narrow instrumental rationality has become dominant, which can potentially misinform how we understand and practise ministry. Since the Industrial Revolution there has been, as Paul Tillich argued, a separation between 'techno-logical' and 'ontological' reasoning.[6] Technē, in its original and broadest sense, refers to all kinds of activity whereby humans craft, shape and inhabit their world. Thus, for example, the technē includes the activities of the carpenter and the engineer but also of the poet and the artist. Today, the realms of art and the aesthetic have become separated from technnē, and a pervasive technological reasoning, inevitably narrow because it has become devoid of these aspects, tends to over-value and over-emphasize the kinds of activity which appear tangibly and empirically, if not even purely economically, productive. Yet it is the work, for example, of the artist or the poet that perhaps most readily points us in the direction of issues and questions of ultimate concern. Technological reasoning is essentially reduc-tionist.[7] For this reason, we must be conscious of the privileging today of particular kinds of actions and indeed of activism in general when we seek to understand ministry as 'doing something'. The activity of ministry is essentially one of witnessing to, re-imagining and re-presenting God's gracious and free self-giving presence in the world. It is a technnē only in the broadest sense of crafting and shaping the world so that it conforms to the reign of God.

This is why the Tridentine understanding of ordained ministry as representatio Christi, an understanding that reached its high point in the Counter-Reformation, deserves to receive renewed attention. Ministry understood as representation fits in very well with the church's sacramental self-understanding. Echoing Rahner's theology of symbol we can understand a sacrament as the most primordial manner in which one reality re-presents another; in other words, allows or enables 'the other' to be present. Ministry understood primarily as the activity of representation allows us to get the balance right between 'being' and 'doing'. On the one hand, representation implies a kind of passivity in the sense of a self-emptying that allows an 'other' to be present. On the other hand, it requires active participation in the process of enabling 'the other' to be present. Speaking specifically about priestly ministry in contemporary culture, the German bishops have warned that ministry is not, like so much of contemporary activity, about productivity. Ministers allow or enable the kingdom of God rather than 'produce' it as such.[8]

Ministry understood as representation also brings to the fore the concept of receptivity. The first thing a minister 'does' is to receive, obediently, as suggested by St Paul, 'For I received from the Lord what I also handed on to you'.[9] It is actively receiving the Word of God written down in the scriptures and handed down in the tradition of the believing community, and re-presenting this to contemporary believers in order to confirm and nourish them in their discipleship.

The Council of Trent was defending the concept of priest as representatio Christi over against the Reformers and thus over-identified it with ordained ministry. By virtue of baptism every Christian is a representative of Christ and one cannot apply the concept of ministry as representatio Christi to the ordained alone. The ordained minister, and in the first instance the bishop, represents a particular and distinctive aspect of Christ's real presence in the church, that is, Christ's leadership of the church. Christ never ceases to lead and guide the church on its pilgrim journey through time.[10] That is why traditional Roman Catholic theology refers to the priest as representatio Christi capitis ecclesiae. The ministry of the ordained is characterized by re-presenting the leadership of the church by Christ, and serves the church by providing for the church's co-ordination and unity.

For the advent of the kingdom

One of the key emphases of the Second Vatican Council was the recovery of the understanding that the church was not an end in itself but exists to serve, herald and realize the reign of God.[11] To people who live in democratic societies the idea of living in a kingdom may seem vaguely despotic. But in Jesus' time the rule of the king stood in contrast to that of the tyrant or the despot. To dwell in God's kingdom was literally to have reached the 'promised land' in terms of conditions not only for basic personal security but also for human flourishing. The ministry of Jesus himself showed that there is no separate, idealized reign of God. The Kingdom of God is realized fully only at the end of time but it also has a reality here and now, and therefore in the midst of various kinds of tyrannies and despotic forces. God reigns where communities and individuals, despite the reality of sin and evil, allow God's rule to be written in their hearts and to govern their daily activities. One can take Jesus' response to the disciples of John as a charter for the reign of God.[12] Blind people see, lame people walk, lepers are cleansed; the dead are raised and the poor have good news preached to them. In our terms, this means that the Kingdom of God is present and being realized wherever the various elements that diminish people, that rob them of their dignity, that enslave them, are being overcome and removed. Activity which restores people to communities in which they can flourish, which removes the sources of indignity, which restores people to the fullness of themselves, is work for the Kingdom of God.

Such work goes on in many and various ways, within the visible confines of the church as well as outside it. If God's salvific will for all people[13] is not just an aspiration, but a genuine intention, then God must create the possibility for all people, at each time and in every generation, to experience and to respond to God's grace. God's Word goes forth where it will and does not return empty.[14] But is it useful to designate all activity (our first characteristic of ministry) that somehow helps to realize the reign of God (our second) as Christian ministry as such? This leads us to a present difficulty that we must now discuss.

Is every activity for the kingdom ministry as such?

Up until now we have been broadening the common understanding of ministry. But if a category or definition is to be of any use, such an understanding must also be circumscribed. In order to say what ministry is, we must also be able to say what it is not. If everything that heralds God's reign were to be characterized as ministry, then the category would cease to be of any real use and we would have to construct another one. However, the task of delimiting ministry is difficult in the present context because it tends to be interpreted as the hierarchy seeking to exclude the laity from certain privileged tasks and functions. We are still dealing with the fact that in the past all ecclesial ministry became reduced to one ministry, that of the ordained, experienced at times as a powerful elite within the church. The 'power of the priest' became something to be feared, as having control, as it was at times understood to have, not only over events in this life but in the next life as well.[15] It is telling that for many the ordained ministry became so identified with the church that a seminarian was commonly understood to be 'joining the church', or leaving it, if he chose to leave the seminary.

As a result of the Reformation in the Protestant churches and of the Second Vatican Council in the Roman Catholic Church, there has been an increase of activities which have been designated as ministries.[16] Today, people who are not ordained as priests serve as chaplains and pastoral assistants in parishes, schools, hospitals and prisons. They are also leaders of prayer groups, counsellors, youth workers. These people understand themselves, and are often accepted by the people, as ministers. In addition, there has been discussion as to whether the less obvious and public Christian activity of, say, devout long-term hospital patients who offer up their sufferings for the sake of the kingdom, should be dignified with the description of being ministry. Similarly, what of busy parents who, because of their commitments to their families, have no time to take on more structured ministries in the church? Given the foundational nature of the Christian family in the life of the church, is Christian parenting not also important ministry? Many think so and seek to describe it as such.

However, in the Roman Catholic Church, the Roman Curia is uncomfortable with a wide application of the term, preferring to restrict its usage to describing the service of the ordained and that of a few others, most of whom perform liturgical services as readers or distributors of the eucharist.[17] Church authorities sometimes defend their position by arguing that liberal usage of the term would only lead to a 'clericalization of the laity', that is, a loss of the essentially distinct identity of the service of baptized Christians in the church.[18] However, such arguments are at least as motivated by concern about the loss of the distinctiveness of ordained ministry.

It would seem that attempts to delimit and define ministry today are inevitably made against the backdrop of a lay–cleric dichotomy and concerns about authority, power and decision-making within the church.[19] Therefore, in an effort to draw the line, so to speak, with regard to what may or may not be described as ministry, the first step is to realize and accept that ministry is about service, not status; that, as we have already noted, not everything that is of importance to the proclamation of the kingdom needs to be called ministry; that we need to find other ways of valuing and acknowledging service of the Kingdom of God than simply 'dignifying' all valuable activities at the service of the kingdom with the designation 'ministry'. Engagement in ministry is not the only path to salvation for the Christian; in fact, it may not be a path at all. It is possible to be very publicly doing things for the sake of the kingdom, satisfying the three characteristics of ministry named thus far, and at the same time, personally, to be far from the Kingdom of God because of personal sin.

There is a tension in the Christian tradition regarding whether or not ministers are expected to be a kind of Christian elite. Certainly, the reputation of the church has suffered greatly from the failings of ministers in the recent past. However, Christians whose love is genuine, who bear their daily crosses with quiet fortitude, who rejoice in hope, bear suffering in patience, and persevere in prayer, have to be understood as the real 'heroes' of the church and of the kingdom.[20] They are the ones, as Yoder says, 'working with the grain of the universe'.[21] With this in mind we can begin to delimit what is meant by ministry by addressing the next two characteristics in O'Meara's framework.

A public action

When we reflect on the ministry of Jesus in the New Testament it becomes clear that his ministry was very public. Jesus very deliberately engaged in symbolic action to bring about God's reign. Both his words, especially the parables, and his deeds, especially the miracles and the many experiences of table-fellowship, were kingdom events. Jesus' words and deeds literally embodied the kingdom, they put flesh on it, and those who could accept the vision and the reality presented to them in those moments of communion with him were, as he himself said, not far from the Kingdom of God. According to John's Gospel, Jesus spoke openly to the world, taught in synagogues and in the temple, and said nothing in secret.[22] Jesus' death on the cross was also a public act. It was a public displacement of one kind of power by another; a redefining of power by placing it entirely at the service of and subservient to selfless love. So also the resurrection was a public event; one the early Christians understood that they simply had to proclaim as Good News for all.

On any reading of the New Testament, Jesus, his immediate disciples, and later the early church understood the importance and the power of publicly proclaiming the kingdom, and in so doing, confronting and challenging 'the kingdom of this world'. Ministry, in the early church, was not just about personally leading a good life in fidelity to the gospel. Significantly, an important document on ministry in recent times issued by the Bishops of England and Wales, called *The Sign We Give*, lays emphasis on the public nature of ministry.[23]

In order for an action to be public in the sense intended here it is not sufficient, however, that it be well-known or publicized: it must also be *recognized* as a representative activity on behalf of the Christian community. To take as an example: I visit a friend or relative in hospital, comfort them, perhaps even pray with them. Is that ministry? By this definition, no. If, however, as the presbyter in the local Christian community or as someone designated by the Christian community with a particular ministry to the sick I call to comfort and pray with those who are ill, it would be. To take another example: the activity of contemplative men and women who dedicate their lives to praying and working behind closed doors might seem not to satisfy our criterion here. Yet their ministry is public in the sense that is important here, that is, in the sense of witnessing to a single-minded dedication to God through their vowed commitment to their lives of prayer.

Related to the concept of ministry being public is its recognition by the Christian community as an action to be exercised with that community's mandate, on its behalf and for the service of the body as a whole. This brings us to the fourth characteristic of ministry: its authorization.

On *behalf* of Christ and the Christian community

We noted earlier that ministry is about representation: ministers help to bring about something that they by themselves cannot effect. By definition ministers are servants. They put themselves at the disposal of Christ and the church to whom they bear witness and upon whose behalf they act. The issue of recognition and authorization of ministries inevitably arises: who is authorized to act on behalf of Christ and the church, and who gives the authorization? The concept of vocation has always been central to the understanding of ministry, but just how the 'call' is discerned and authorized is the subject of debate. Generally speaking, it has been understood that the discernment of vocations to ministry and their authorization resides with the bishop, who, as 'overseer', is responsible for ordering the many and diverse gifts given by the Holy Spirit for the service of the church and the kingdom. In the churches, various processes exist to assist in the discernment of vocations, as well as for the public recognition and authorization of people in ministries. Ministers are 'ordained', 'instituted', 'installed', 'commissioned' and so on.

Here an important distinction must be made, to which we have already alluded. Because of a shortage of priests, lay people sometimes exercise ministries that properly speaking belong to the ordained. The exercise of such ministries is in a particular sense done on behalf of the ordained. For example, the ministry of the eucharist is understood as the service of the ordained, and presumably this is why lay people who even distribute communion are referred to as 'extraordinary ministers'. However, ministries that are properly speaking 'lay' are not 'extraordinary' at all. They flow from gifts given by the Holy Spirit for the service of the kingdom and are not at all exercised on behalf of the ordained. Thus, the role of the ordained in regard to ministries that are properly speaking lay, is different. In regard to lay ministries, the ordained assists in discerning and authorizing these ministries. The ordained, especially the bishop, has a leadership role in terms of creating the necessary order within the Christian community so that the ministries, gifted not by him but by the Holy Spirit, can flourish and be exercised for the benefit of all. In deciding what ministries properly belong to the lay state it must also be borne in mind that ordained ministry as it has been exercised up until recent times effectively monopolized ecclesial ministry. Thus, what today may seem like ministries being exercised by lay people on behalf of clergy because of a shortage of priests might well be the returning of ecclesial activities to lay faithful that are properly speaking ministries to be exercised by them.

There is another area of contemporary debate relevant here. So far we have spoken about ministries being exercised on behalf of Christ and the church and have not sought in any way to differentiate between authorization by Christ and authorization by the church. Yet the matter of whether ministers act on behalf of Christ, more or less directly, or on behalf of the church, is a key question, the answer to which determines among other things how accountable ordained ministers should be to the Christian community, and not just to Christ.

In Roman Catholic circles this has been an area of some debate, especially since the Second Vatican Council. Certainly, with regard to ordained ministry, the official understanding has been that bishops, priests and deacons exercise a ministry on behalf of Christ *to* the church and mediate *between* Christ and the church. The bishop, and in collaboration with him, priests and deacons, represent Christ as head of the church *to* the Christian community. The ordained act *in persona Christi capitis* and the emphasis is on the distinction, rather than on the unity between the head and the body of the church. Augustine reflects this understanding in his statement, 'With you, I am a Christian; for you, I am a bishop'.[24]

Proponents of this theology of ordained ministry advocate consultation with lay faithful on leadership matters within the church but reject that in any formal sense ordained ministers 'report' to the lay faithful. Some see in attempts to foster a culture of accountability of ministers to the Christian community the influence of secular democratic models that do not respect the unique nature of the church as a divinely instituted community.[25] At the same time, senior prelates such as Walter Kasper, though aware of the danger of merely paying tribute to the 'democratic *Zeitgeist*', note that the church has, over time, adopted feudal and monarchical elements from secular culture that could well be replaced by democratic structural elements more appropriate to its unique constitution.[26] Kasper sees in the Second Vatican Council's emphasis on the church as 'people of God', and the emphasis on church as communion, the basis for a much more mutually supportive and collaborative understanding of ministry exercised in a complementary way by lay and ordained.

Theologically, the matter depends on how we understand the origins of the church and of ministry. In the understanding that dominated up to the Second Vatican Council, Christ first called the apostles and gave them authority to build up the church. The church results from Christ at work in and through their activity. In a sense, the church originates in them and from the beginning they represent Christ to the church. In this understanding, the risen Christ continues to care for and build up his church through the ordained ministers, but their mandate, so to speak, continues to come from Christ and not from the Christian community as such.

Some theological discussion since the Second Vatican Council, however, seeks to locate the origins of ministry within rather than apart from the faith of the Christian community.[27] It claims that the church springs not so much from the prior activity of the apostles but from the faith that is spontaneously brought forth by the death and resurrection of Jesus. It is this shared faith in the resurrection of Jesus that gathers the church into being and to which the apostles and their successors bear witness. According to this understanding, in the beginning was the church as such, rather than the apostles, although the apostles are unique witnesses to the faith that springs forth from the death and resurrection of Christ.

Whatever way we understand the origins of the church, the tradition has always held that the faith response of the first Christians is foundational and enjoys a privileged status. But to the extent that structures originated within the church under the guidance of the Holy Spirit, rather than in immutable forms imposed by Christ, the church has both the authority and the responsibility to be *semper reformanda* in response to its mission in a particular place and time.[28] Fidelity cannot consist in a lazy repetition of structural solutions to new problems, or in the clinging to forms of ministry that once served the mission of the church but are ill-equipped to do so in a very different cultural context. It is argued that from the very beginning, for example, in the encounter with Hellenism, Christianity was challenged by problems to which Christ had not given an explicit answer.[29] The challenge then was to respond creatively under the guidance of the Holy Spirit through careful discernment by the Christian community. The tradition of responding creatively by ordering ministry to the church's mission in each generation is the one to which the church is obliged to remain faithful.

In this latter understanding, the Christian community has far more discretion, but also must assume greater responsibility, for authorizing and structuring ministries, as those on whose behalf such ministries are exercised.

A gift received

O'Meara's fifth characteristic is that ministries are the exercise of particular charisms with which the Holy Spirit gifts the church.

This emphasis on the role of the Holy Spirit is important. It guards against unnecessary anxiety about the state of the church, as though ultimately it depended on some of its members for 'success' in its mission. In addition, we have already noted that ministries are given by the Holy Spirit and not bestowed by certain members of the church, no matter how apparently central or exalted their own ministries are. It is the Holy Spirit that provides for the church as it makes its pilgrim way through time, witnessing to and proclaiming God's reign.

The emphasis on ministry as a gift received is also important. A gift by definition cannot be earned or merited, just accepted graciously. It has been remarked that in contemporary culture people tend to be generous givers but 'mean' receivers. Our culture understands life to be more about self-invention than self-discovery, or to put it in existentialist terms, existence precedes essence and we are, as Sartre said, abandoned to the intolerable necessity of making ourselves.[30]

The Christian self-understanding is that we are not abandoned. But without God's free, gracious self-giving, we would be lost. We are not, and cannot become, self-made men and women. The very act of ministry depends on understanding ourselves as needing to be ministered to, in order to be saved. Thus, both the exercise of ministry, and the experience of being ministered to, require a disposition of humble acceptance of God's acceptance of us. This is why Downey, for example, stresses that 'If there is one disposition, a single attitude cultivated in our day by ministers in the church, it is *active receptivity*'.[31]

A diversity of ministerial actions

When we speak of a variety of gifts given to the church for the service of the kingdom, St Paul's letter to Corinth immediately springs to mind.[32] The context is one of rivalries and jealousies that had developed within and among the community members. St Paul does not avoid naming specific ministries or charisms and even suggesting that these have special importance in the life of the church there. For example, he singles out apostles, prophets and teachers in that order. But he lists many others, and the emphasis throughout is, as Enda Lyons notes, on service rather than rank, and on action rather than on office.[33] In this passage, according to Lyons, St Paul is calling for acceptance by the community of a diversity of functions for the service of the body as a whole, mutual respect among ministers, self-regard for the gifts one has oneself received, and a commitment to working through difficulties rather than shirking responsibility.

Ministerial structure and ministerial action, just like the church itself, should reflect and re-present the trinitarian God and this not only in its activity but in its very being. Ministry understood as diversity in unity best reflects the triune God in whose name ministers act.

Conclusion

The flourishing of ministries in the churches, even in Western culture where the churches seem to be experiencing decline, is a sign of great hope. At the same time, questions have arisen with regard to who may be ordained; how ordained and 'lay' ministries relate to each other; which ministries should be resourced and supported; these questions touch upon the very identity of the church. The process of addressing these questions is beginning rather than ending.

Notes

1 Thomas F O'Meara, *Theology of Ministry*, New Jersey: Paulist, 1983, p. 136.
2 See Chapter 28 of this volume.
3 Enda Lyons, *Partnership in Parish*, Dublin: Columba Press, 1987, p. 96.
4 1 Cor 12.4.
5 See, for example, Peter Schmidt, 'Ministries in the New Testament and the Early Church', in Jan Kerkhofs (ed.), *Europe Without Priests?* London: SCM Press, 1995, pp. 41–88.
6 Paul Tillich, *Systematische Theologie* Bd I, Stuttgart: Evangelisches Verlagswerk, 1951, p. 89ff.
7 See Eamonn Conway, 'Christian Anthropology in a Technological Culture', in Michael Breen, Eamonn Conway and Barry McMillan, *Technology and Transcendence*, Dublin: Columba, 2003, p. 225.

8 See Walter Kasper, *Leadership in the Church*, New York: Crossroad, 2003, p. 67.

9 1 Cor 11.23.

10 See *Lumen Gentium*.

11 See *Lumen Gentium*, esp. a. 9.

12 Lk 7.22; Matt 11.5.

13 See 1 Tim 2.4.

14 Isaiah 55.10–12.

15 See James Joyce's *Portrait of the Artist as a Young Man*: 'No king or emperor on earth has the power of the priest of God. No angel or archangel in Heaven, no saint, not even the Blessed Virgin herself, has the power of the priest of God, has the power of the keys, the power to bind and loose from sin, the power of exorcism . . . the power, the authority, to make the great God of Heaven come down upon the altar and take the form of bread and wine. What an awful power Stephen?'

16 See Thomas F. O'Meara, *New Dictionary of Theology*, p. 657.

17 See, for example, 'On Certain Questions Regarding the Collaboration of the Non-Ordained Faithful in the Sacred Ministry of the Priest' (1997). Available at www.vatican.va/roman_curia/pontifical_councils/laity/documents/rc_con_interdic_doc_15081997_en.html. Accessed Feb 10, 2007.

18 See Cardinal Joseph Ratzinger, *L'Osservatore Romano*, March 11, 1998: 'The doctrine on the nature of priestly ministry and on the unity and diversity of ministerial tasks at the service of the edification of the Body of Christ must be underlined with clarity, in order to avoid devaluing the priesthood, clericalisation of the laity', and 'falling into a "Protestantisation" of the concepts of ministry and of the Church'.

19 See Francis Oakley and Bruce Russett (eds), *Governance, Accountability and the Future of the Catholic Church*, New York: Continuum, 2004.

20 See Rom 12. 8–12.

21 John Howard Yoder, 'Armaments and Eschatology', *Studies in Christian Ethics* 1/1, Edinburgh: T&T Clark, 1988, p. 58.

22 John 18.20.

23 See *The Sign We Give: Report of the Working Party on Collaborative Ministry*, Bishops' Conference of England and Wales, Essex: Matthew James Publishing, 1995.

24 Sermo 340, 1.

25 See the important debate between Donald Wuerls and Peter Steinfels in Oakley and Russett (eds), *Governance, Accountability and the Future of the Catholic Church*, pp. 13–32.

26 Walter Kasper, *Leadership in the Church*, New York: Crossroad, 2003, p. 63.

27 See Peter Hünermann, 'Mit dem Volk Gottes unterwegs. Eine geistliche Besinnung zur Theologie und Praxis des kirchlichen Amtes', in *Geist und Leben* 54 (1981), 179–180.

28 See Peter Schmidt, *Europe Without Priests?*, p. 62.

29 See Peter Neuner, 'Ministry in the Church: Changing Identity', in *Europe Without Priests?*, p. 129.

30 Jean-Paul Sartre, *Being and Nothingness*, trans. Barnes, London: Methuen, 1958, pp. 440–1, cited in Nicholas Lash, *The Beginning and the End of Religion*, Cambridge: Cambridge University Press, 1996, p. 239.

31 Michael Downey, 'Ministerial Identity – A Question of Common Foundations', in Susan K. Wood (ed.), *Ordering the Baptismal Priesthood: Theologies of Lay and Ordained*, Minnesota: Liturgical Press, 2003, p. 16.

32 1 Cor 12. 4–30.

33 Enda Lyons, *Partnership in Parish*, pp. 85–88.

32

THE *SENSUS FIDELIUM*

John J. Burkhard

This chapter explores its subject with particular reference to its development at Vatican II and in postconciliar theology. The theme of the *sensus fidelium* must surely be included among the lively issues discussed in the churches after Vatican II. Yet it is a conciliar teaching that remains largely unknown to the faithful and seems to be a well-guarded secret among those who lead and serve the faithful. Is there a meaningful role for the faithful in expressing the faith and in evangelizing the world, when, in the Roman Catholic Church at least, the pope and the bishops are generally regarded as bearing exclusive responsibility for the proclamation and definition of the faith? Is the teaching of the council a gift that has been buried for the moment, but will be unearthed at some future time in the church's life? Or is the moment now ripe for accepting and living the gift of the *sensus fidelium*?

Although I write primarily from the perspective of the Roman Catholic Church and its ecclesiology, I do not do so exclusively. The theme of the *sensus fidelium* also continues to exercise an influence over the other Christian churches, as witnessed by its inclusion in documents emerging from the modern ecumenical movement. A cursory glance over the ecumenical literature shows that the *sensus fidelium* has found its way into documents emerging from the Anglican–Roman Catholic International Commission's *Authority in the Church I* (1976) and *Elucidation* (1981), the Evangelical–Roman Catholic Dialogue on Mission's *Report 1977–84*, the Christian Church/Disciples of Christ–Roman Catholic International Dialogue's *The Church as Communion in Christ* (1992), the Lutheran–Roman Catholic International Dialogue's *Church and Justification* (1993), the Methodist–Roman Catholic International Dialogue's *The Word of Life: A Statement on Revelation and Faith* (1995), the Lutheran–Catholic Dialogue in the United States' *Scripture and Tradition* (1995), and the Anglican–Roman Catholic International Commission's recent *The Gift of Authority* (1999), which will be examined below. The context is always the issue of how teaching authority is understood and exercised in the communities in dialogue with one another, and the role of the faithful in witnessing to and elaborating the church's faith. For the purposes of the present chapter, perhaps the most helpful reference to the *sensus fidelium* in an ecumenical document comes from the World Council of Churches' *The Nature and Purpose of the Church*, where we read:

> The unity and communion of the Church require a ministry of discernment by the faithful. Discernment is served by the presence of the *sensus fidei* in every member of the community. The *sensus* – a kind of spiritual perception, sense of discernment (flair) – is the fruit of the indwelling of the Holy Spirit by which baptized believers are enabled to recognize what is, or is not, an authentic echo of the voice of Christ

in the teaching of the community; what is, or is not, in harmony with the truth of the Gospel. The *sensus fidelium* – the expression of this *sensus fidei* by all the members – is an essential element in the discernment, reception and articulation of Christian faith.[1]

In spite of all this ecumenical interest, the fact remains that it was principally at the Second Vatican Council that the theme of the *sensus fidelium* was developed, although in the years since the Council it has found its way into the broader theological literature. It is to that Council that we must now turn our attention.

A theme of Vatican II

Many students of theology would be surprised to learn that from the very beginning the documents of Vatican II contained the idea of the *sensus fidelium*. The text from the Preparatory Committee contained a reference to it in the eighth chapter of its 1962 text *De ecclesia*. This chapter dealt with the authority of the hierarchy and the obedience due it by the laity – hardly what today we would consider an auspicious context for the teaching. In subsequent revisions, especially when the new text entitled *Lumen gentium* was put forward as the basis of the future teaching of the council, the *sensus fidelium* would find a more congenial context for its teaching. In this first part of my essay I am not interested in the vagaries of the text but in the question, where did this teaching come from? It can hardly be assumed that teaching about the *sensus fidelium* played an important role in Roman Catholic ecclesiology up to the time of Vatican II.

Several recent studies of the notion have shown how the teaching regarding the *sensus fidelium* began to appear with regularity in the nineteenth century.[2] Before then, the teaching played only a modest role in the theology of the patristic and medieval periods. At the Council of Trent, in its decree on the Roman Catholic doctrine of the real presence of the Lord in the eucharist, the council used the phrase *universum ecclesiae sensum* to point to the faith of believers as representing a 'pillar and bulwark of the truth' (1 Tim 3.15) of the faith.[3] After the challenge of the Reformation, however, a number of Roman Catholic theologians began to incorporate into their treatises a reference to the understanding of the faith by believers as a source of the fuller teaching of the church and a criterion for expressing the infallible character of the Roman Catholic faith. In the post-tridentine period, in addition to the phrase *sensus fidelium*, which had already been employed earlier by Cardinal Cajetan (d.1534), various other phrases began to appear: *universus ecclesiae sensus* (D. Petavius (d.1652)) and *ecclesia infallibilis in credendo* (R. Bellarmine (d.1621) and F. Suarez (d.1617)). But while such phrases played only a minor role in the seventeenth and eighteenth centuries, among the major Catholic theologians of the nineteenth century the phrase began to appear with greater regularity and served to point to the common witness of all the faithful, together with their bishops, to the truth of the Christian faith. These theologians included Johann Adam Möhler (d.1838), representing the famous Roman Catholic School of Tübingen; the advocates of Roman scholasticism who taught at the Collegium Romanum (G. Perrone (d.1876), C. Passaglia (d.1887), C. Schrader (d.1875), and J.B. Franzelin (d.1886)); M.J. Scheeben (d.1888) in Cologne; and in England, Cardinal John Henry Newman (d.1890). Newman, for instance, was famous for his claim that during the second phase of the Arian crisis, when many of the bishops accepted Arian compromise formulas for expressing the faith in Christ, the faithful rose to the task of witnessing to Christ's full divinity by refusing to have anything to do with such compromises.[4] Increasingly, then, a doctrine of the role of the faithful as a true source of the church's faith became a part of the Roman Catholic theology of faith.

One of the occasions in the nineteenth century when the *sensus fidelium* was invoked was in the definition of Mary's Immaculate Conception by Pius IX in 1854. In his instruction to the bishops of the church before issuing a definition, Pius asked them to report back to him on the belief and practices of the faithful in regard to Mary's freedom from sin.[5] The low point of the *sensus fidelium* in the nineteenth century was, perhaps, the interpretation given to the phrase by the Roman theologian, Cardinal J.B. Franzelin, who interpreted it in terms of what he called 'passive infallibility'. Whereas the pope and bishops exercised infallibility in an active way by formally teaching the truth to the faithful, the faithful indeed exercised the infallibility of the church by listening to their leaders and by obeying them.[6] This insight led to the formulation of the church as *ecclesia docens* ('the teaching church'), i.e. the pope and bishops, and the *ecclesia discens* ('the learning church'), i.e. the faithful or the remainder of the church. This fateful distinction by Franzelin considerably weakened the contribution of the faithful by placing them in the ranks of those who only follow their leaders. According to Franzelin, the hierarchy mediates the *sensus fidei* to the believer, even though it is the Holy Spirit who works the operation as an act of faith. The faithful have nothing positive to contribute to the formulation of the faith or to witnessing to the faith. The theology of Franzelin had the unfortunate result of confirming the tendency by the hierarchy to restrict any contributions by the faithful to the formulation of the faith. Franzelin's narrowing of the understanding of the *infallibilitas in credendo* by the faithful eventually became the common opinion of theologians and would manifest itself in the minority's opposition to a more positive understanding of the *sensus fidelium* at Vatican II.

In the meantime, other factors were at work that would move the bishops and theologians to retrieve the positive meaning of the terms *sensus fidelium* and *infallibilitas in credendo*. The following factors led the papacy in particular to look for ways of engaging the laity in the work of evangelization: the growing decline in the church's influence over society due to the anticlericalism of the nineteenth and early twentieth centuries; the spread of militant atheism; the widespread disregard for the church's social teachings aimed at helping workers oppressed by rampant industrialization; and in general a growing secularization of society. A passive laity could not be an ally of the hierarchy in evangelizing the world, which meant, concretely, communicating to the faithful a sense of their dignity as baptized Christians. The movement known as Catholic Action proved to be an effective way of mobilizing the laity to aid the clergy in their apostolic tasks. Catholic Action had the advantage of giving the faithful a sense of worth, while restricting their cooperation to subsidiary help that was always under the direct guidance of the hierarchy and the clergy. The heyday of Catholic Action was the period between the two world wars. But in the light of the devastating effects of World War II and its aftermath, questions were posed regarding the effectiveness of the pastoral approach of 'Catholic Action'. Could the faithful be engaged in a more effective way? In the wake of the positive teaching of Pius XII regarding the 'priesthood of the faithful' and the 'active participation of the faithful' in the liturgy, especially in his encyclical *Mediator Dei* (1947), on the eve of Vatican II the bishops were predisposed to examine anew the issue of the faithful and their apostolic role.

The churches of the Reformation had always maintained a lively appreciation of the faithful and the dignity of each believer. From the start, Martin Luther (d.1546) had insisted on the doctrine of the priesthood of the faithful, even though he sometimes did so as part of his anti-Roman polemic. John Calvin (d.1564) also insisted on the priesthood of the faithful and Calvin emphasized especially the christological dimensions of Jesus' ministry as prophet, priest, and king. In the nineteenth century, Protestant theologians gave this christological teaching of Calvin's even greater emphasis by reason of the participation of the faithful in the threefold ministry of Jesus as prophet, priest, and king.[7]

Christoph Ohly has studied the evolution of Vatican II's principal text on the *sensus fidelium*, article 12 from the *Dogmatic Constitution on the Church*.[8] By studying the changes introduced into the text and listening to the interventions of various bishops at the council, we can gain a better understanding of the council's teaching. The text reads:

> The holy people of God has a share, too, in the prophetic role of Christ, when it renders him a living witness, especially through a life of faith and charity, and when it offers to God a sacrifice of praise, the tribute of lips that honour his name (see Heb. 13:15). The universal body of the faithful (*Universitas fidelium*) who have received the anointing of the holy one (see 1 Jn. 2:20, 27), cannot be mistaken in belief (*in credendo falli nequit*). It displays this particular quality through a supernatural sense of the faith in the whole people (*atque hanc suam peculiarem proprietatem mediante supernaturali sensu fidei totius populi manifestat*), when 'from the bishops to the last of the faithful laity', it expresses the consent of all in matters of faith and morals (*universalem suum consensum de rebus fidei et morum exhibit*). Through this sense of faith (*Illo enim sensu fidei*) which is aroused and sustained by the Spirit of truth, the people of God, under the guidance of the sacred magisterium to which it is faithfully obedient, receives no longer the words of human beings but truly the word of God (see 1 Th. 2:13); it adheres indefectibly to 'the faith which was once for all delivered to the saints' (see Jude 3); it penetrates more deeply into that same faith through right judgement and applies it more fully to life (*recto iudicio in eam profundius penetrat eamque in vita plenius applicat*).[9]

First, we see how the minority voices of the bishops continued to insist on the limited meaning of the faithful's contribution to the church's infallibility. Cardinals A. Ottaviani, G. Siri and E. Ruffini could accept the term *sensus fidelium* only on condition that it was understood as 'passive infallibility', i.e. the laity's simple obedience to the active teaching by the bishops and thus as a secondary/indirect witness to the primary/direct witness of the bishops. Cardinals F. König (Vienna), P.-E. Léger (Montreal) and R. Silva Henriquez (Santiago, Chile) argued for a more positive and direct influence by all the faithful in formulating and witnessing to the church's belief. Their view eventually carried the day. Second, Ohly has shown how article 12 was originally a paragraph in the chapter on the laity. In this context, of course, the claim of the *sensus fidelium* as applying to the lay faithful continued to give the impression that it was less than the authoritative teaching of the bishops and that the laity followed their teaching without really contributing anything to the church's faith. However, once the bishops decided to scrap the schema *De ecclesia* in eleven chapters and to substitute a new schema entitled *Lumen gentium*, the statement on the *sensus fidelium* was eventually incorporated into Chapter Two, 'On the People of God', with the effect that *Lumen gentium* first made general statements that could be claimed of all the faithful, before any discussion of the distinctions in the church between the laity and the hierarchy. Chapter Two of *Lumen gentium* effectively did what Catholic Action had not been able to accomplish – it communicated unambiguously the fundamental dignity and value of each member of the church. This dignity was rooted in the sacramental identity of baptism, before the distinction of tasks, ministry, authority and sacramental ordination in the church was introduced. However important these distinctions are, they can never be used to limit the real dignity and value of all the faithful. This change of location in the document meant that the claim of the *sensus fidelium* was directed at everyone in the church. It was no longer to be thought of as the exclusive possession of the laity, while the clergy and the hierarchy possessed a higher gift of sacred teaching authority.[10] As the text itself clearly said, quoting St Augustine, the *sensus fidelium* pertained to everyone 'from the bishops to the last of the faithful laity (*ab episcopis usque ad extremos laicos fideles*)'. These debates, interventions and rewritings of the text demanded three years of intensive work by bishops and conciliar theologians or *periti*, but clearly were worth the effort.

Sensus fidelium in theology after Vatican II

According to my reckoning, in the period from 1965 to 2005 there have been approximately 150 monographs and articles written on the topic of the *sensus fidelium*.[11] In this section, I propose to examine three of the most influential authors who have treated the topic and so advanced our understanding of the *sensus fidelium* in the postconciliar period. I intend to review the treatments of Jean-Marie Roger Tillard, OP, Wolfgang Beinert and Christoph Böttigheimer. Other authors will be mentioned in passing.

Jean-Marie Roger Tillard, OP (1927–2000)

J.M.R. Tillard is of interest because he had written extensively on the topic over a period of some twenty-five years. In the course of his output on the *sensus fidelium*, Tillard employed a variety of notions in order to understand better the teaching of Vatican II. In his first article, 'Le "Sensus Fidelium". Réflexion théologique', Tillard worked with the understanding that the *sensus fidelium* is best understood as a *conspiratio* between the hierarchical magisterium and the faith of the believers in the church.[12] Tillard showed how important the role of the witness to the faith by the ordinary laity had been to the Marian definitions of Popes Pius IX and Pius XII. The papal definitions represent the *conspiratio* of the faithful and the hierarchy in determining the faith of the church, especially since many influential theologians had expressed reservations about the content and the opportuneness of the definitions. In the wake of the reactions by ordinary believers to Paul VI's teaching in *Humanae vitae* (1968), regarding the morality of the use of artificial means in limiting conception, Tillard called for greater attention to be paid to the voice of the faithful on what had become a divisive issue in the church. In the instance of the Marian definitions, the *conspiratio* between popes and the faithful was seen as something positive. Why should the situation not be similar with regard to Pope Paul VI's teaching and the reaction of the faithful? How, then, is one to understand the role of the faithful? Tillard pointed to the role of the Holy Spirit in this conspiration theory. It is the same Spirit who is the source of the authoritative teaching of the hierarchy and the source of the faith of the laity in what is taught. The faithful do not play a passive role here – mere obedience – but are actively engaged in bringing the faith to expression. When Tillard proceeds to explain the *sensus fidelium* as a fundamental notion of Christian faith, he maintains that it is more than 'an instinct' for the truth. It is genuine knowledge of the truth. Based on deeper 'experience' in some matters of faith, it might not possess the conceptual clarity or logical persuasiveness of the theologians' treatment of the same matter, and it might not possess the authoritative weight of the hierarchy's magisterial teaching, but it is still not less than the truth of the faith, and so must be considered in the church. At this stage in his treatment of the *sensus fidelium*, Tillard sees a twofold 'conspiring' – that of the hierarchy, theologians and the ordinary faithful in witnessing to the faith, and that of the Holy Spirit as the source of saving truth and the whole church as the recipient of the faith. Tillard's first presentation was criticized for two reasons: its lack of sufficient epistemological clarity and its tendency to accept rather naively the role and the witness of the lay faithful. The laity have not always been such staunch confessors and defenders of the faith.[13]

In his writings throughout the 1970s and 1980s, Tillard increasingly considered the notion of *communio/koinonia*. In his major work on ecclesiology, *Église d'églises: l'écclésiologie de communion*,[14] Tillard used the notion of 'communion' as the central and underlying notion of the ecclesiology of Vatican II and so of his own ecclesiology. The *sensus fidelium*, then, had to be rethought on a firmer basis than he had done earlier. Without abandoning his theory of *conspiratio*, Tillard was able to place it in a broader and more satisfying context. He shows how an ecclesiology of communion and a theory of mutuality of roles in the church are compatible with one another. Greater attention to the role of the Holy Spirit in the church is the key. Out of a diversity of roles and responsibilities, the Spirit produces a more profound unity. Just as the church can be understood as a 'communion of churches', so the common witness to the truth of the Christian faith can be understood as a 'communion of roles and tasks'. The roles of the bishops, the theologians and the believing laity constitute a unified, though differentiated, expression of the faith. This expression is more adequate because the different ecclesial roles have been respected and have been able to make their contribution to the framing of the faith. Throughout the process, the rule of communion is that of mutuality, complementarity and common service to the truth of the faith. It is necessary to recognize, however, that such differentiation and mutuality of roles does not preclude situations when there will be conflict among the roles. Tensions are inevitable. They are not a sign of compromise of the truth of the Christian message but the ordinary way in which the Spirit of truth brings about unity in diversity. According to Tillard, Vatican II represented a genuine communion of tasks and roles in the church: communion among the bishops, communion of perceptions at the level of scholarly theological research, a communion of efforts to listen to one another, and a communion of tensions felt at various levels of the church.

On the heels of his book on the ecclesiology of communion, Tillard began to break new ground regarding the *sensus fidelium*.[15] He introduced two new ideas to express the *sensus fidelium* better: symbiosis and 'memory'. By symbiosis, Tillard intended to express forcefully the bond of communion between the bishops and the faithful who, by any understanding of the scientific notion of symbiosis, are both dissimilar yet intimately and beneficially connected with each other. Thus, the hierarchy ordinarily acts 'symbiotically' with the *sensus fidei* of the laity and vice versa. But to fully understand the nature of the symbiosis, Tillard turns to the biblical and liturgical notion of *anamnesis* or *memoria*. The church lives from the *memoria Jesu*, not in the ordinary sense of memory as a mere 'bringing to mind what has been absent up until now', but in the deeper sense of a reality actually being present in its fullness, being 're-lived' or 'becoming actual again'. In the liturgico-sacramental understanding of *anamnesis/memoria*, Tillard points to the eucharist as the moment par excellence of such 'memory' or 'remembering'. Every eucharist is the gathering of the faithful in the *memoria Jesu* and in the power of the Spirit, while from another point of view the liturgical gathering can take place only under the presiding ministry of the bishop or the presbyter as his representative. At the heart of the Christian faith, then, is not a body of doctrinal or historical statements (however important they truly are), but the living presence of the Lord Jesus and his Spirit. That presence as *memoria* accounts for the principle of identity-in-change for Tillard. He uses the Latin expressions that the church is *semper ipsa* but *nunquam idem* in order to claim that, in the midst of inevitable historical change, the church's *memoria Jesu* guides it throughout history, thus rendering it both 'the same subject' (*semper ipsa*) of faith, but not some 'identical reality' (*nunquam idem*) beyond all change. The true dignity of the bishop then lies not in some power he has that others in the church do not possess, but in the indispensable 'ministry of memory' he exercises in the eucharist as the one who calls the community to the 'memory of Jesus'. Basically, this effort calls for communion of both the *sensus fidelium* and the episcopal ministry of *anamnesis*, since communion is the principle of the Spirit's guidance of the church. By a process of 'reception', the bishops attend to what is being said in the church and test it against the 'memory' of the people of God. The bishops must constantly be engaged in the process of rethinking, weighing, testing and clarifying what the faithful are saying against their own sense of the *memoria Jesu*.

Tillard has introduced certain changes in his conspiration theory of the *sensus fidelium* without rejecting it out of hand. To the earlier image of a *conspiratio* he has added the stronger notion of a symbiosis. At the same time, he is careful to add that the ministry of *memoria* occurs primarily in the bishop's presiding at the eucharist, because the eucharist preserves the church in the *memoria Jesu*. He expresses this tension forcefully in his formulation of the law of 'continuity in change'.

This was the last in-depth presentation on the *sensus fidelium* that the great French Dominican made, unless we see his hand active in the formulation of the Anglican–Roman Catholic International Commission's *The Gift of Authority*. In this document, issued one year before Tillard's death in 2000, we can detect the role of *memoria* in the whole area of authority in the church, together with other themes typical of Tillard's thought regarding the *sensus fidelium*.[16] In the Christian understanding, authority does not exist for itself but as a service to the living 'memory of the Lord Jesus'. This is how *The Gift of Authority* expresses it:

> (28) The people of God as a whole is the bearer of the living Tradition. In changing situations producing fresh challenges to the Gospel, the discernment, actualization and communication of the word of God is the responsibility of the whole people of God. The Holy Spirit works through all members of the community, using the gifts he gives to each for the good of all. Theologians in particular serve the communion of the whole church by exploring whether and how new insights should be integrated into the ongoing stream of Tradition. In each community there is an exchange, a mutual give and take, in which bishops, clergy and lay people receive from as well as give to others within the whole body.
>
> (29) In every Christian who is seeking to be faithful to Christ and is fully incorporated into the life of the church, there is a *sensus fidei*. This *sensus fidei* may be described as an active capacity for spiritual discernment, an intuition that is formed by worshiping and living in communion as a faithful member of the church. When this capacity is exercised in concert by the body of the faithful, we may speak of the exercise of the *sensus fidelium* (cf. 'Authority in the Church: Elucidation', 3–4).

The exercise of the *sensus fidei* by each member of the church contributes to the formation of the *sensus fidelium* through which the church as a whole remains faithful to Christ. By the *sensus fidelium*, the whole body contributes to, receives from and treasures the ministry of those within the community who exercise *episcope*, watching over the living memory of the church (cf. 'Authority in the Church I', 5–6). In diverse ways the amen of the individual believer is thus incorporated within the amen of the whole church.

(30) Those who exercise *episcope* in the body of Christ must not be separated from the 'symphony' of the whole people of God in which they have their part to play. They need to be alert to the *sensus fidelium*, in which they share, if they are to be made aware when something is needed for the well-being and mission of the community or when some element of the Tradition needs to be received in a fresh way. The charism and function of *episcope* are specifically connected to the *ministry of memory*, which constantly renews the church in hope. Through such ministry the Holy Spirit keeps alive in the church the memory of what God did and revealed and the hope of what God will do to bring all things into unity in Christ.

In this way, not only from generation to generation, but also from place to place, the one faith is communicated and lived out. This is the ministry exercised by the bishop and by ordained persons under the bishop's care as they proclaim the word, minister the sacraments and take their part in administering discipline for the common good. The bishops, the clergy and the other faithful must all recognize and receive what is mediated from God through each other. Thus the *sensus fidelium* of the people of God and the ministry of memory exist together in reciprocal relationship.[17]

Wolfgang Beinert (b. 1933)

Another scholar who has contributed immensely to the understanding and the growing acceptance of Vatican II's teaching on the *sensus fidelium* is Wolfgang Beinert, who was Professor of Dogmatics at the Catholic University of Regensburg, Germany. Beinert has written about the *sensus fidelium* for over thirty-five years. I have counted eight articles by the German professor since 1971. In general, Beinert's interest in the *sensus fidelium* is directed toward issues of the criteriology of faith statements and the various roles of the hierarchical magisterium, theologians, and the faithful as the sources for Christian faith claims. How are these claims and these voices related to the primary sources of faith enunciated in scripture and tradition?

In his first treatment of the subject, Beinert distinguishes the *sensus fidelium* from *scientia* and places it instead in the realm of *sapientia*.[18] The Middle Ages were correct in seeing theology as 'wisdom' rather than as 'science', where wisdom is founded on a certain experience of the faith and not primarily on an intellectual grasp of the content of faith. From the point of view of mental reflection, faith as *scientia* is higher, while as a global grasp of reality, faith as *sapientia* has the advantage. This does not mean that the *sensus fidelium* as *sapientia* is without knowledge, but that it operates less in a discursive and reflexive way (the way of *scientia*) and more in an experiential and practical manner. In their own way, experience and praxis, too, include knowledge. Now faith requires both conceptual thought and a more-than-conceptual grasp of the truth. Given their relative strengths as independent activities and their mutuality, how do *scientia* and *sapientia* – and therefore the *sensus fidelium* – function when the faith becomes conscious of its content, limits, sources, degree of explicitness, relative degrees of authority, and realms of activity – in other words, in terms of a certain theological criteriology of the faith?[19] The answer to this question is not simple, because the witnesses to the truth of Christian faith are many – pope, bishops and presbyters, theologians, saints, prophets, mystics, and the ordinary lay faithful. Beinert's key to an answer is found in the notion of representation. In the Bible and the fathers of the church, a representative was the personification of the entire community, i.e. the incorporation in his/her person of the community. As qualified witnesses, then, the hierarchy meets this function of representation of Christian truth in a particularly concentrated way ('in besonderer Dichte') by fulfilling those functions that pertain to the membership as a whole, yet without excluding the others. All believers are the recipients of faith and witness to its truth claims, but only the pope and the bishops do so 'representatively' with a clarity, a directness, and an authority that theologians, saints and the ordinary faithful in the church fail to do. Ultimately, the faith claims of the magisterium and the totality of believers are the same, while their criteriological functions differ. The difference is found in how they are exercised and not in the content of their witness. The result is a mutuality of functions and not isolation from one another.

As a criterion of Christian truth, the episcopal and theological magisteria have a certain priority because they interpret this truth critically and are supposed to employ a higher degree of reflection.[20] The representative function of the episcopal magisterium also involves the 'authoritative' formulation of Christian truth. On the other hand, the *sensus fidei* of the laity enjoys the privilege of greater completeness and immediacy in its witness to the faith. Since this truth is expressed in a way that includes the whole person's existence, the laity's *sensus fidei* often expresses this truth better in existential and practical terms rather than in logical, rational and speculative ones. Both functions are necessary in the church and cannot be reduced to each other or transcended by a higher function.

In his next contribution, Beinert returns to the demands of a theological criteriology in the church.[21] He distinguishes between the diachronic and the synchronic community of witnesses. Scripture and tradition belong to the diachronic community; the bishops, theologians and the laity's *sensus fidei* belong to the synchronic community. Beinert employs a communicative model to show how all five expressions of Christian faith exist in relationship to one another. Restricting ourselves to the three synchronic witnesses, how do they interact with each other? The pope and the bishops have the responsibility of guarding the faith of the community, mediating its content in terms of the praxis of Christian life, excluding error by exercising supervision over the church's faith statements, and promoting authentic Christian living. They may not add anything new to the content of revelation, but must help to interpret it for our day. As for theologians, they must strive for a critical, reflexive, methodical, systematic, ecclesial and integrative understanding of the faith. Finally, the *sensus fidelium* is founded on the originating and immediate experience of the faith by believers ('*die originäre und unmittelbare Glaubenserfahrung der Kirchenglieder*') who receive the objectifications of the faith in scripture, tradition, the magisterium and theology. Because the faith must be inculturated in the sense that its existential meaningfulness for contemporary society demands expression, the role of the faithful as synchronic witnesses has special importance.

With respect to the *sensus fidelium* in particular, several conclusions can be drawn. First, the *sensus fidelium* is an independent criterion of the faith that imposes on the faithful the need to 'receive' the faith statements expressed in scripture, tradition, the magisterium and the body of theologians. Second, given each believer's historical context, everyone is called to realize the faith in a unique way. 'Since the church becomes an active and receptive community of believers only in the act of believing of each member, it is the witness of each Christian that makes the church's belief fruitful at all.'[22] Third, in contemporary Western societies at least, only the 'adult faith' of committed and mature Christians can hand on the faith effectively. The formal authority of the church's office-holders and its official teachings are no longer adequate to the task. The *sensus fidelium* involves the task of inculturating the faith as experienced and lived, and this is the special contribution of the faithful who are mature in their faith. Finally, given the complexity and the novelty of the problems faced in society today, the lay faithful's familiarity with the issues must be respected and integrated into the whole church's response to these matters.

In two articles written in the mid-1990s, Beinert extended his thought on the *sensus fidelium* by emphasizing its appropriateness to the church understood as *communio*. Vatican II's ecclesiology of communion means that the highly 'vertical' way of understanding truth (from pope and bishops downward) needs to give way to a more 'horizontal' understanding in which the role of each group of believers – his synchronic witnesses to the faith – is respected. Beinert then develops four rules for determining the *sensus fidelium*. First, there must be a proportionality between the commitment of the believer to Christian faith and praxis and that person's degree of credibility in expressing the *sensus fidei*. Second, the *sensus fidelium* must be shown to benefit the whole church or to foster the true Christian life among the members of a group of believers. Third, a statement of the *sensus fidelium* must be in conformity with the content of the gospel as understood by generally accepted hermeneutical theory. And fourth, the rule of dialogue must always be respected, since the magisterium, theologians and the faithful can arrive at an appropriate statement of the faith and lived praxis only by showing mutual respect and communicating with each other.

The *sensus fidelium* is a true 'theological source' (*locus theologicus*) and it possesses its own intrinsic authority, which is not derived from others. The *sensus fidei* of the laity stands together with the hierarchical magisterium and the magisterium of theologians as a testimony to revelation communicated in the Bible and tradition, but also communicated in a living way in the richness of human experience, both personal and social. Beinert adds the following warning to his treatment:

> If the church is understood primarily as an institution, then the main issues will be those of power and the division of power – that is, hierarchy. The result will be that there is little room for understanding the *sensus fidei* as a true theological source (*locus theologicus*). But if the church is understood to result from God's saving act through Christ in human history – that is, as a sacramental reality – then the day-to-day life of the Christian, including the active witness of Jesus Christ as the very ground for Christian existence, must be an essential dimension of the church. In the logic of the faith, the *sensus fidei* ('Glaubenssinn') and the *consensus fidelium* ('Glaubensübereinstimmung') have great theological meaning.[23]

Christoph Böttigheimer (b. 1960)

In concluding this part of my treatment, I want to refer briefly to some of the more recent currents of thought and impetuses that have influenced the discussion of the *sensus fidelium* in the church. Christoph Böttigheimer, who is Professor of Fundamental Theology at the Catholic University of Eichstätt-Ingolstadt, Germany, is a good example of the recent turn towards the more practical dimensions of the *sensus fidelium*. By the mid-1990s the teaching of Vatican II regarding the *sensus fidelium* was well established and the general contours of the teaching were well known and widely accepted by theologians.[24] But then theologians like Hermann J. Pottmeyer, Franz-Xaver Kaufmann, and C. Böttigheimer began to question why the conciliar teaching had so little effect on the life of the church. Was the conciliar teaching only theory? Where were the results of the teaching in the church's life? To many commentators, it seemed as though the teaching was given little more than lip service in the church. Movements like the Petition of the People of the Church (*Kirchenvolksbegehren*) in Germany and Austria clamoured for changes that never seemed to be discussed or implemented. There was growing frustration at the slow pace of change, even though the council had called for *aggiornamento*, and a sense of disillusionment was beginning to set in. Böttigheimer addressed this phenomenon in two articles on the *sensus fidelium*.

In the first, Böttigheimer used Vatican II's *Dogmatic Constitution on Divine Revelation* as his point of departure.[25] There, we read how the word of God has been entrusted to the whole church – to both bishops and the ordinary faithful – and that the church has the duty to listen attentively to and serve the word of God (art. 10). On the one hand the bishops, in exercising their teaching authority, are admonished: 'This teaching function is not above the word of God but stands at its service', while on the other, they are admonished: 'Thus, as they hold, practise and witness to the heritage of the faith, bishops and faithful display a unique harmony.'[26] The conciliar documents point first to the word of God and only then to the response by the whole church, before any distinctions of office or responsibility are pointed out. Because the responsibility to listen to, receive, grow in understanding and transmit the word of God pertains to all in the church, all need to participate in the process. This means that the hierarchy is not free to ignore the *sensus fidelium*, which represents a true 'theological source' (*locus theologicus*), and that concretely it must create the appropriate institutional means for the laity to express themselves.

In his second article, Böttigheimer concentrates on the need for and the nature of these institutional means.[27] First he examines the relationship of the pope and bishops to theologians in the church, and maintains that the conciliar and postconciliar practice represents a retrieval of earlier practice when theologians exercised a true magisterium of their own in the church, one based on the principles of learning (*scientia*) and interpreting the word of God, yet one that also contributed to the church's pursuit of understanding God's word. Necessarily, there will be moments of tension between the dimensions of independence and mutuality that characterize the relationship of bishops and theologians in the church. Furthermore, both forms of teaching, the hierarchical and the theological, must advert to and indeed encourage the insights and questions of the ordinary faithful in the church. This is the real issue of the *sensus fidelium* in the church today – the lack of any real ecclesiastical means for the faithful to share their perception of divine revelation. Bishops and theologians share the responsibility of encouraging believers to speak out and they must listen to them and validate their experience. The historically tested form this process has taken in the church in the past has been some form of synod which brings all parties together. This does not reduce all to the same function but rather highlights the uniqueness of each one's contribution to the common witness to the faith. The hierarchical magisterium has a greater regulative role to play in formulating and teaching the faith. Theologians must exercise their rationally critical function in order to assure the credibility of the message within and beyond the confines of the church. Finally, the faithful have their contribution to make as an indispensable criteriological principle of Christian revelation, since without their witness the faith would soon lose its vitality and its ability to attract believers. In Böttigheimer's view, the church desperately needs structures of dialogue and communication that conform to its nature as communion.

Sensus fidelium: some unresolved issues

In the most recent phase of the postconciliar discussion of the *sensus fidelium*, more and more commentators point to the need in the church to address the absence of really meaningful structures that are available to the ordinary faithful for sharing their insights and their questions regarding how the faith should be understood, expressed and lived in today's world. Many theologians point to the church's use of synods in the past as an appropriate means for engaging the faithful in the reception of the faith.[28] Not all the Christian churches have the same experience of synodality or conciliarity. In the Orthodox Church and in many of the churches that issued from the Reformation, synodality is a cherished principle of their ecclesiologies. For years, ecumenical documents have pointed to the need for church structures to respect the three dimensions of leadership: the personal, the collegial and the communal.[29] In the Roman Catholic Church, however, the issue is particularly urgent, since the postconciliar church is engaged in finding an equilibrium in its structures that respects the more collegial forms of the first millennium and the more monarchical form of the church since Gregory VII (d.1085). The papacy did not seem to be unduly restricted in the first Christian millennium when it operated out of a communion ecclesiology that gave wider scope to episcopal collegiality. However, it must be admitted that the Roman Catholic Church is far from having resolved the tensions between the synodal forms it knew in the first millennium and the increasing dependence on the papacy as that office was exercised in the second millennium.

In the final section of his article 'Reception, *Sensus fidelium*, and Synodal Life: An Effort at Articulation', Hervé Legrand comments: 'At the level of principle, it is necessary then to revitalize synodal life as the place for the expression of the faith and Christian life.'[30] Legrand points to the use of consultative means in the ecumenical movement and the fruits that consultation has produced. The same is true for the institution of the Synod of Bishops in the postconciliar Roman Catholic Church. Next, he points to the need for such consultation in the life of parishes and in diocesan life. He adds, 'It is not after one or two synods in a diocese that synodality becomes a dimension of diocesan life. Several are necessary before such experimentation is a success.'[31] In his response to Legrand, the late James H. Provost pointed to the importance of both particular councils and provincial councils in the church's life, and then added:

> As Professor Legrand mentioned toward the conclusion of his paper, the new code provides for a limited number of consultative bodies. A presbyteral council, college of consultors, and finance council are all mandatory bodies within a diocese today; diocesan pastoral councils are a possibility even within the law. It was probably not appropriate to legislate in more detail about these new diocesan structures; they need time to mature and to develop in keeping with the possibilities and needs of local churches. Yet it is increasingly difficult to conceive of a diocese in the Catholic Church today without such consultative bodies, some of which must give their consent for the diocesan bishop to act in various matters.

There is a process here of building a new way of interaction within the local church. We are still learning how to do this, but the process can eventually produce that richer synodality which Professor Legrand desires.[32]

The second point I want to mention as a future concern for understanding the *sensus fidelium* regards the whole area of one's underlying ecclesiology. It is true that much progress has been made in understanding and appropriating the Council's ecclesiology, especially the ecclesiology of communion, but much remains to be done. In particular, I want to point to the areas of pneumatology and the question of the relationship between the local and the universal church. The practical mentality in the West, which tries to resolve issues by proceeding immediately to structural solutions, urgently needs to ponder the role of the Holy Spirit in the founding, the continued existence in history and the daily life of the church. The growing interest in trinitarian theology in all the churches, Eastern and Western, is surely a sign of hope, but much still needs to be done. The same is true – and in fact is even more urgent – regarding the local church and the universal church, as the recent controversy between Cardinal Walter Kasper and then Cardinal Joseph Ratzinger, amply demonstrates.[33] Though the controversy focused on the Roman Catholic Church, the tension between local and universal is also found in the other churches. This can be seen in the weak central authority in Orthodoxy, in the continued decline in the appeal of the mainline churches of the Reformation, in the precariousness of unity in the churches of the Anglican Communion, and in the continuing fragmentation among evangelical, fundamentalist, pentecostal communities and the rest of Christianity. Without giving greater attention to these fundamental ecclesiological issues, it is hard to imagine how matters such as the *sensus fidelium* and reception will be able to find the proper ecclesiological soil in which to grow in our churches.

Finally – although many other matters could be mentioned – I want to point to the phenomenon of postmodernism as a worldview, especially in the West. Is its critique of both modernity's excesses and its underlying principles for understanding the world valid? Isn't it possible to distinguish legitimate pluralism from destructive relativism in postmodernism? Does not postmodernism's call for conversation and dialogue conform to a genuine impetus in the Christian understanding of faith? Isn't the rediscovery of the fundamental Christian category of conversion providential for the church that lives in this new postmodern culture and must deal with its deleterious effects?[34] Is postmodernism inevitably hostile to the Christian faith and to the church?[35] I do not mean to be naive about the genuinely destructive aspects of postmodernism, but I am cognizant of the fact that history teaches that the church has generally been successful in navigating the treacherous shoals of the cultural, social and philosophical contexts in which it has been forced to live. If it is inevitable that the church will have to learn to coexist with a new postmodern world, it is hard to imagine how the church will do so without coming to terms with the role of the *sensus fidelium* in its life. The *sensus fidelium* will have to be given its rightful place in the church as a true 'theological source' (*locus theologicus*) of its faith and as a source of the tradition that exists and interacts with the hierarchical magisterium and with the authority of theologians and scholars in the church.

Notes

1 See the World Council of Churches' *The Nature and Purpose of the Church: A Stage on the Way to a Common Statement*, Faith and Order Paper No. 181, Geneva: WCC Publications, 1998, §99.

2 See Marko Mišerda, *Subjektivität im Glauben. Eine theologisch-methodologische Untersuchung zur Diskussion über den 'Glaubens-Sinn' in der katholischen Theologie des 19. Jahrhunderts*, Frankfurt: Verlag Peter Lang, 1996; and Christoph Ohly, *Sensus fidei fidelium. Zur Einordnung des Glaubenssinnes aller Gläubigen in die Communio-Struktur der Kirche im geschichtlichen Spiegel dogmatisch-kanonistischer Ernenntnisse und der Aussagen des II. Vaticanum*, St Ottilien: EOS Verlag, 1999, pp. 33–121. See the earlier article by Wolfgang Beinert, 'Bedeutung und Begründung des Glaubenssinnes (Sensus fidei) als eines dogmatischen Erkenntniskriteriums', *Catholica*, vol. 25 (1971), 271–303.

3 Denzinger-Schönmetzer, *Enchiridion symbolorum, definitionum et declarationum de rebus fidei et morum*, 33rd edition, Rome: Herder, 1965, §1637.

4 Newman dealt with the role of the ordinary faithful in the history of Arianism principally in his *The Arians of the Fourth Century*, 3rd edn, London and New York: Longmans, Green and Co., 1895; but he also treated it in his famous *Rambler* essay from July 1859, 'On Consulting the Faithful in Matters of Doctrine'. See the edition by John Coulson, *On Consulting the Faithful in Matters of Doctrine*, New York: Sheed & Ward, 1961, pp. 53–106. But see the critical remarks of Michael Slusser on Newman's reading of the Arian controversy in his 'Does Newman's "On Consulting the Faithful in Matters of Doctrine" rest upon a mistake?' *Horizons*, vol. 20 (1993), 234–40.

5 See the discussion by J. Robert Dionne, *The Papacy and the Church: A Study of Praxis and Reception in Ecumenical Perspective*, New York: Philosophical Library, 1987, pp. 303–19. The process of consulting the faithful by way of the bishops of the church was also followed by Pius XII in preparation for the definition of Mary's Assumption in 1950. Dionne also examines this process on pp. 319–36.

6 J.B. Franzelin, *Tractatus de divina traditione et scriptura*, Rome, 1870 and 1896. See C. Ohly, *Sensus fidei fidelium*, pp. 98–100 for a summary of Franzelin's theology.

7 See Ludwig Schick, 'Die Drei-Ämter-Lehren nach Tradition und Zweitem Vatikanischen Konzil', *Internationale katholische Zeitschrift: Communio*, vol. 10 (1981), 57–66; Yves Congar, 'Sur la trilogie: prophète-roi-prêtre', *Revue des sciences philosophiques et théologiques*, vol. 67 (1983), 97–115; Peter J. Drilling, 'The Priest, Prophet and King Trilogy: Elements of its Meaning in *Lumen Gentium* and for Today', *Église et théologie*, vol. 19 (1988), 179–206; and Ormond Rush, 'The Offices of Christ, *Lumen Gentium* and the People's Sense of the Faith', *Pacifica*, vol. 16 (2003), 137–52.

8 See 'Das II. Vatikanische Konzil: Der Weg zur Aussage über den Glaubenssinn aller Gläubigen in Lumen Gentium 12', *Sensus fidei fidelium*, pp. 173–272.

9 Norman P. Tanner (ed.), *Decrees of the Ecumenical Councils*, vol. 2: *Trent to Vatican II*, Washington, DC: Georgetown University Press, 1990, p. 858. The other pertinent passages from the documents of Vatican II are *Lumen gentium* 35, *Presbyterorum ordinis* 9, and *Gaudium et spes* 52.

10 One postconciliar commentator put it this way: 'Tradition is obviously not transmitted exclusively by the Magisterium, but also by the faithful, so that the distinction between active functioning of the teaching office and passive reception on the part of the faithful is not appropriate', Leo Scheffczyk, 'Sensus fidelium – Witness on the Part of the Community', *Communio*, vol. 15 (1988), 184.

11 I have reviewed much of this literature in my articles 'Sensus Fidei: theological reflection since Vatican II (1965–89)', *The Heythrop Journal*, vol. 34 (1993), 41–59 and 123–36; and 'Sensus Fidei: recent theological reflection (1990–2001)', *The Heythrop Journal*, vol. 46 (2005), 450–75 and vol. 47 (2006), 38–54. See also idem, 'Sensus fidelium' in *New Catholic Encyclopedia*, 2nd edn, Detroit: Gale Group and Catholic University of America, 2003, vol. 12, pp. 916–18.

12 See the English translation 'Sensus Fidelium', *One in Christ*, vol. 11 (1975), 2–29.

13 See the remarks by Fernand Dumont, 'Remarques critiques pour une théologie de "consensus fidelium"' and Emilien Lamirande, 'La théologie du "sensus fidelium" et la collaboration de l'historien', in *Foi populaire, foi savante*, Paris: Cerf, 1976, pp. 49–60 and 67–72 respectively. Tillard addressed some of these criticisms in his later treatment of the *sensus fidelium* and the roles of the hierarchy, theologians and the faithful in his contribution 'Théologie et vie ecclésiale' in *Initiation à la pratique de la théologie*, 5 vols, eds Bernard Lauret and François Refoulé, Paris: Cerf, 1982, vol. 1, pp. 161–82.

14 Paris: Cerf, 1987. ET by R.C. De Peaux, *Church of Churches: The Ecclesiology of Communion*, Collegeville, MN: Liturgical Press, 1992.

15 'Autorité et mémoire dans l'Église', *Irénikon*, vol. 61 (1988), 336–46 and 481–4. Tillard later

incorporated these ideas in his treatment of the *sensus fidelium* in his last major work on the church, *L'Église locale: ecclésiologie de communion et catholicité*, Paris: Cerf, 1995, pp. 314–24.

16 Tillard was a member of ARCIC-I and ARCIC-II. The latter produced the document *The Gift of Authority*.

17 *Origins*, vol. 29, no. 2 (27 May 1999), 24.

18 'Bedeutung und Begründung des Glaubenssinnes (Sensus fidei) als eines dogmatischen Erkenntniskriteriums', *Catholica*, vol. 25 (1971), 271–303.

19 I have searched largely in vain for recent treatments in theology of the criteriology of faith statements. Though criteriology is in fact practised in contemporary theology, it is almost never the object of explicit reflection. In this regard, Beinert is the exception insofar as he speaks of an 'Erkenntniskriterium' (which I understand and translate as 'criteriology') and examines the *loci theologici* from this perspective in almost all his writings on the *sensus fidelium*. This preoccupation imparts a definite quality of epistemological explicitness to his works that is generally lacking in other theologians' writings. We saw how F. Dumont accused Tillard of a lack of attention in this regard – a lack that Tillard never really addressed in all his subsequent writings. I don't think Tillard ever really saw the problem. Beinert does. See also Beinert's 'Theologische Erkenntnislehre', in *Glaubenszugänge. Lehrbuch der katholischen Dogmatik*, 3 vols, ed. W. Beinert, Paderborn: F. Schöningh, 1995, vol. 1, pp. 45–197, where Beinert treats the theme of the *sensus fidelium* on pp. 167–87. An exception to my claim can be found in Hermann Josef Pottmeyer, 'Normen, Kriterien und Struktur der Überlieferung', *Handbuch der Fundamentaltheologie*, vol. 4: *Traktat theologische Erkenntnislehre*, Freiburg: Herder, 1988, pp. 124–52.

20 On the distinction of the magisterium into two magisteria, the *magisterium cathedrae pastoralis* and the *magisterium cathedrae magistralis*, see Yves Congar, 'A Semantic History of the Term "Magisterium"', in *Readings in Moral Theology, No. 3: The Magisterium and Moral Theology*, eds Charles E. Curran and Richard A. McCormick, New York: Paulist, 1982, pp. 297–313; and Avery Dulles, 'The Magisterium in History: Theological Considerations', *A Church to Believe In: Discipleship and the Dynamics of Freedom*, New York: Crossroad, 1982, pp. 103–17.

21 The article 'Das Finden und Verkünden der Wahrheit in der Gemeinschaft der Kirche', *Catholica*, vol. 43 (1989), 1–30 is a veritable short treatise on a theological criteriology that Beinert began in his article from 1971 and one that has benefited from the progress made in hermeneutical theory in the 1970s and 1980s. Beinert has developed these ideas further in his recent 'Was gilt in der Kirche und wer sagt uns das? Im Spannungsfeld von Lehramt, Theologie und Glaubenssinn', in *Theologie im Dialog. Festschrift für Harald Wagner*, eds Peter Neuner and Peter Lüning, Münster: Aschendorff Verlag, 2004, pp. 159–79.

22 Ibid., p. 23.

23 'Der Glaubenssinn der Gläubigen in Theologie-und Dogmengeschichte. Ein Überblick', in *Der Glaubenssinn des Gottesvolkes – Konkurrent oder Partner des Lehramts?* Quaestiones Disputatae, vol. 151, ed. Dietrich Wiederkehr, Freiburg: Herder, 1994, p. 122.

24 E.g. see the *Catechism of the Catholic Church*, 2nd edn; Vatican City: Libreria Editrice Vaticana, 1997, §§ 91–3, 785 and 889.

25 'Mitspracherecht der Gläubigen in Glaubensfragen', *Stimmen der Zeit*, vol. 214 (1996), 547–54.

26 Norman Tanner (ed.), *Decrees of the Ecumenical Councils*, vol. 2, p. 975.

27 'Lehramt, Theologie und Glaubenssinn,' *Stimmen der Zeit*, vol. 215 (1997), 603–14.

28 See Hervé Legrand, 'Synodes et conseils de l'après-concile. Quelques enjeux ecclésiologiques,' *Nouvelle revue théologique*, vol. 98 (1976), 193–216; James H. Provost, 'The Ecclesiological Nature and Function of the Diocesan Synod in the Real Life of the Church,' in *La synodalité. La participation au gouvernement dans l'Eglise. Actes du VIIe congrès international de Droit canonique*, Paris, 1990, vol. 2, pp. 537–8; and Gilles Routhier, 'La synodalité de l'Église locale,' *Studia Canonica*, vol. 26 (1992), 111–61.

29 See Faith and Order, *Baptism, Eucharist and Ministry*, Faith and Order Paper No. 111, Geneva: WCC Publications, 1982, in the 'Ministry' section §26. The other references with respect to these three dimensions are too numerous to list here.

30 *The Jurist*, vol. 51 (1997), 427. Reprinted in *Reception and Communion Among Churches*, eds Hervé Legrand, Julio Manzanares and Antonio García y García, Washington, DC: Canon Law Department, Catholic University of America, 1997.

31 Ibid., p. 430.

32 'Response to Hervé Legrand', ibid., pp. 433–4.
33 See Kilian McDonnell, 'The Ratzinger/Kasper Debate: The Universal Church and Local Churches', *Theological Studies*, vol. 63 (2002), 227–50.
34 On conversion, see Bernard J. F. Lonergan, 'Theology in its New Context', *A Second Collection*, eds William F. J. Ryan and Bernard Tyrrell, Philadelphia: Westminster, 1974, pp. 65–7; or see the entry 'Conversion' in the index to his *Method in Theology*, New York: Herder and Herder, 1972, pp. 375–6. John Paul II again and again stressed the necessity of conversion in the life of the church. See *Ut Unum Sint* (1995), §§15–17 ('Renewal and Conversion') as but one example from many in his voluminous writings.
35 For more positive assessments of postmodernism, see John J. Burkhard, 'Apostolicity in a Postmodern World', *Apostolicity Then and Now: An Ecumenical Church in a Postmodern World*, Collegeville, MN.: Liturgical Press, 2004, pp. 127–63; Gerard Mannion, 'Ecclesiology and Postmodernity: A New Paradigm for the Roman Catholic Church?' *New Blackfriars*, vol. 85 (2004), 304–28; T. Howland Sanks, 'Postmodernism and the Church,' *New Theology Review*, vol. 11, no. 3 (August 1998), 51–9; and Paul Lakeland, *Postmodernity: Christian Identity in a Fragmented World*, Minneapolis: Fortress, 1997.

Further reading

John J. Burkhard, '*Sensus fidei*: Meaning, Role and Future of a Teaching of Vatican II', *Louvain Studies*, vol. 17 (1992), 18–34.
Patrick J. Hartin, '*Sensus fidelium*: A Roman Catholic Reflection on Its Significance for Ecumenical Thought', *Journal of Ecumenical Studies*, vol. 28 (1991), 74–87.
James L. Heft, '"Sensus fidelium" and the Marian Dogmas', *One in Christ*, vol. 28 (1992), 106–25.
Johannes-Baptist Metz and Edward Schillebeeckx (eds), *The Teaching Authority of the Believers*, Concilium, vol. 180. Edinburgh: T&T Clark, 1985. Contains noteworthy articles by Herbert Vorgrimler, Christian Duquoc and Heinrich Fries.
Hermann Josef Pottmeyer, 'Die Mitsprache der Gläubigen in Glaubenssachen. Eine alte Praxis und ihre Wiederentdeckung', *Internationale katholische Zeitschrift: Communio*, vol. 25 (1996), 134–47.
Karl Rahner, 'What the Church Officially Teaches and What the People Actually Believe', *Theological Investigations*. 23 vols, New York: Crossroad, 1991. Vol. 22, pp. 165–75.
Ormond Rush, 'The Offices of Christ, *Lumen Gentium* and the People's Sense of the Faith', *Pacifica*, vol. 16 (2003), 137–52.
Dietrich Wiederkehr (ed.), *Der Glaubenssinn des Gottesvolkes – Konkurrent oder Partner des Lehramtes?* Quaestiones Disputatae, vol. 151, Freiburg: Herder, 1994. Contains noteworthy articles by Wolfgang Beinert, Franz-Xaver Kaufmann, Sabine Pemsel-Maier and Dietrich Wiederkehr.

33

HERMENEUTICS AND
ECCLESIOLOGY

Simone Sinn

Introduction

The hermeneutical field is marked by two focal points, the theoretical reflection on the *process of interpretation* and the analysis of the *phenomenon of understanding*. As both interpretation as well as understanding are processes that are fundamental to human life, hermeneutical reflection is an issue dealt with in many different disciplines. Philosophers, theologians, literary critics, historians, artists and many more are concerned with hermeneutics. Hermeneutical thinking is a reflective enterprise that crosses disciplinary boundaries. Nevertheless, theology has had a considerable impact on the development of hermeneutics: the interpretation of the biblical scriptures has always been one of the prime points of reference for hermeneutical reflection. In modern times, then, when a general hermeneutics was established, philosophy took a leading role in the development of hermeneutical thinking. The insights from the philosophical inquiry, in turn, stimulated theological reflection.

In order to give a first idea of the scope of hermeneutics today, three questions will point out basic themes in the hermeneutical field. First, there is a methodological question: What are the principles and rules for interpreting texts and other artefacts? This is followed by an epistemological question: How does understanding take place and how is meaning achieved? Finally, this leads to an ontological question: What significance does the process of understanding have for human nature? Whereas the first question, in principle, can be traced back to ancient Greek philosophy,[1] the latter two came to the fore in the modern era. They mark the philosophical turn in hermeneutical thinking. In the nineteenth century, hermeneutics developed from methodology as an auxiliary means to a philosophical approach at its own right.

Whereas up until then the attention was mainly focused on the text, or more generally speaking, on the *interpretandum*, the attention was now directed towards the reader, the *interpreter*. His or her impact on interpretation has been investigated and the process of understanding as a whole examined. One of the highly debated issues since then has been the question whether the text constitutes the reader or vice versa – in other words, if meaning is produced by the text or by the interpreter.

For theology, these and other related hermeneutical questions are of great importance because the central task of the theological endeavour is to interpret the biblical scriptures. Therefore theology itself can be called a hermeneutical discipline. Likewise, church itself can be called a hermeneutical community because the understanding of the scriptural message is at the centre of the life of the church. More precisely, we can say that church is hermeneutical with regard to her *origin*, her *nature* and her *mission*. At the heart of all three aspects is a process of communication and reception of the gospel: First, church comes into being through a hermeneutical process; she is *creatura verbi Divini* (the creation of the divine word). Second, church is a community of the faithful constantly formed and transformed by a hermeneutical process, namely by preaching and listening to the Word and by sharing bread and wine. Third, the church's mission is to give witness to the gospel through word and deed and thereby enable the world to understand God's will and action.

Ecclesial traditions that speak of church as sign and mediator of God's gracious self-communication to the world thereby also conceive of church as a hermeneutical community. In this context, some ascribe sacramentality to the church itself, others confine this term to the actual communication processes of the gospel. Yet, irrespective of specific ecclesial traditions, one can generally say that the pivotal hermeneutical task for the church is to interpret the biblical scriptures in the context of and in relation to the world and to interpret the world in light of the biblical scriptures.

In a theological perspective, the hermeneutical processes related to the biblical scriptures entail a certain complexity. These scriptures are credited with having revelatory character because they bear witness to God's will and action. Yet, at the same time, for Christians they point to a specific event, the coming of Jesus Christ, as *the* revelation of God's will and action. Thus the biblical scriptures themselves are not the ultimate point of reference, but Jesus Christ as the incarnation of the *logos* (cf. John 1). Therefore, the Bible never is to be understood as a self-contained entity but is to be perceived in its referential function. Yet another hermeneutical challenge already entailed in the biblical scriptures is the tension between the letter and the Spirit as referred to in 2 Corinthians 3.

These challenges and complexities have instigated hermeneutical reflections and brought forward distinct hermeneutical approaches in the history of interpreting of the biblical scriptures. The most significant developments in scriptural interpretation will be outlined in the following section. Then the attention is shifted towards hermeneutics in modern philosophical thinking. This section will briefly sketch the most important thinkers in the hermeneutical field, including references to some critical questions that were raised towards hermeneutical thinking in the twentieth century. In this section the idea comes to the fore that existential participation of the individual is key to the interpretation process, as it is in the dialogue between interpretandum and the interpreter that meaning arises. The two historical sections are followed by a systematic section that gives an outline of the fundamental constituents of the hermeneutical process, based on the approach of Paul Ricoeur. Its central idea is that by being existentially involved in the hermeneutical process, the interpretation process becomes a transformative event for the interpreter. Then, looking on ecumenical developments, the Faith and Order document on hermeneutics, *A Treasure in Earthen Vessels*, comes into focus next and is critically analysed. Finally, the findings of these sections are summarized in some concluding remarks on the interrelationship of transformative hermeneutics and participatory ecclesiology.

Significant developments in scriptural interpretation

One of the first ecclesiologically as well as hermeneutically significant processes in the history of the church was the formation of the canon of biblical scriptures. This was a crucial process as the relation between the text on the one hand and the community of interpreters on the other was at stake. The highly debated question at this point is whether the church formed the canon or the canon formed the church.[2] This is not just a historical inquiry, but also implies the systematic question: which is prior to the other, church or canon? Looking at the historical development, we realize that, in the first place, there was not a decision of church authorities, but a reception process in many Christian communities. Christian communities recognized the texts, read in the liturgical framework of a religious service, as texts that authentically speak of the gospel of Jesus Christ. The texts convinced those listening through their content, and therefore were recognized as being original and authentic. The need to define the canon officially became urgent when Marcion presented his canon of scriptures (AD 140/150).[3] He rejected the Hebrew scriptures and recognized only Luke's among the gospels. This was not acceptable to the Christian community and by AD 200 there was a consensus that Christian scriptures include the Hebrew scriptures (the Septuagint) and four gospels together with epistles. For some scriptures it took until the fourth century before it was clear whether they would be regarded part of the canon or not. This quite long process of canonization indicates that canon and church were mutually involved in the formation of one another.

Origen of Alexandria (c. AD 185–c. 253) took the interpretation of scriptures as starting and culminating point for his theology. He was familiar with the scriptural interpretation of the Jewish philosopher Philo of Alexandria (c. 20/10 BC–c. AD 45), who took up the allegorical interpretation from ancient Greek philosophy[4] and applied it to the interpretation of the Torah. The basic distinction was that between the literal and the allegorical sense. The literal sense was sought through the grammatical interpretation, looking at the structure of the text; the allegorical sense was sought by using an external symbolic key in order to decipher the meaning of the text. This twofold differentiation was developed further by Origen to a threefold distinction corresponding to the triangle of body, soul and spirit: the somatic (historical-literal), the psychic (moral), the spiritual (mystical) meaning, each of which reflects a progressively more advanced stage of religious understanding. Finally, Cassian (c. AD 360–c. 432) brought forward the fourfold distinction of meaning that prevailed in scriptural interpretation until the Middle Ages.[5] A famous mnemonic rhyme of the thirteenth century gives an outline of these four meanings: *Littera gesta docet, quid credas allegoria, moralis, quid agas, quo tendas anagogia*.[6] It is important to note that, in essence, all more elaborate distinctions trace back to the duality between the literal and the allegorical meaning. The other meanings can be regarded as distinctions within the allegorical meaning.

Whereas the interpretation tradition of Alexandria put the emphasis on the allegorical meaning, Augustine of Hippo (354–430) increasingly paid attention to the literal meaning. He expounded the semiotic structure of a text and depicted the relation between sign (*signum*) and subject matter (*res*). The most prominent of the medieval thinkers, Thomas Aquinas (1225/6–74) also put emphasis on the literal meaning as the fundamental meaning. Theology on the whole, however, now strongly influenced by Aristotelian philosophy, tended to become more speculative. Biblical texts were not always the starting point for theology, but were used *ex post facto* to proof theological theses. The Renaissance movement, then, made its impact on the hermeneutical development by calling the academic world *ad fontes* (to the sources) and by cultivating a growing interest in the ancient texts and the classical languages.

In the Reformation period, biblical interpretation gained momentum as Martin Luther (1483–1546) established the principle 'scripture alone' (*sola scriptura*) as a key principle for theology, faith and practice. He argued that scripture interprets itself (*sui ipsius interpres*).[7] This hermeneutical principle meant that the literal meaning of the word is primary and that obscure passages are to be understood in the light of the centre of the Bible, Jesus Christ. Luther was convinced that the biblical message was sufficiently clear to be understood. Consequently, he and his fellow Reformers Ulrich Zwingli (1484–1531) and John Calvin (1509–64) rejected the claims of the Roman Catholic Church to be the final authority for the interpretation of the Bible. In contrast, they claimed that church should be reformed in accordance with scripture. All the faithful should have the chance to read the Bible for himself or herself. This required the translation of the Bible into the vernacular and the education of the people so that everybody became literate. Thus the hermeneutical insight of the Reformers triggered not only a new approach to biblical interpretation but also a new conceptualization of ecclesiology. The authority of the Bible was strengthened over against the authority of the magisterium. Furthermore, the maturity of the individual believer was strengthened over against the authority of the church.

The emphasis on the Bible and the literal meaning in the interpretation process, however, was never meant in a literalistic sense. Luther opposed literalistic interpretation of biblical texts by saying: 'If the opponents take scripture over against Christ, we take Christ over against scripture.'[8] Understanding the meaning of the biblical scriptures is geared towards understanding the meaning of Jesus Christ, its subject matter. In order that this might take place, the Holy Spirit is needed, who brings the meaning to our heart and thereby makes it evident to us. Calvin called this the internal witness of the Holy Spirit (*testimonium spiritus Sancti internum*). Whereas the Reformers focused on the work of the Holy Spirit in the *reception process*, some theologians of the following generation directed their attention towards inspiration in the *writing process* of the texts. The Lutheran theologian Matthias Flacius (1520–75) established the idea of the verbal inspiration of the biblical texts. He used this idea in order to back up the principle *sola scriptura* and tried to substantiate the 'objective' authority of the Bible. This 'objectivism', however, was beset with difficulties in the Enlightenment period when through the pioneering work of Johann Salomo Semler (1725–91) the historical interpretation of the Bible was developed. His work laid the foundations for modern biblical exegesis.

Hermeneutical thinking during the Reformation period not only triggered off a new and interesting development of biblical interpretation within the Protestant movement but also, in large part, gave rise to the definition of the Roman Catholic position. In consequence, the first dogmatic decree of the Council of Trent (1545–63) was dedicated to the issue of biblical scriptures and their relation to the tradition of the church. The *Decree Concerning the Canonical Scriptures*, promulgated in 1546 at the fourth session of the Council, says that 'this truth and discipline are contained in the written books, and the unwritten traditions'.[9] At the time of the Council, the unwritten ecclesial tradition was regarded as complementary to the biblical scriptures, and the authoritative interpretation of the scriptures clearly belonged to the church. The *Decree Concerning the Edition and the Use of the Sacred Books* – 'in order to restrain petulant spirits' – leaves no doubt about the hermeneutical prerogative of the church 'to judge of the true sense and interpretation of the holy scriptures'.[10]

Whereas the Council of Trent marked the opposition to the Reformation movement, the Second Vatican Council in the twentieth century opened up new possibilities for ecumenical dialogue. Its dogmatic constitution *Dei Verbum* holds that: 'This teaching office is not above the word of God, but serves it.'[11] Yet, in relation to other interpretations, the teaching office still holds the 'authentic interpretation'. Furthermore, the constitution acknowledges the work of biblical exegesis, but puts it under the authority of ecclesial interpretation.[12] *Dei Verbum* further emphasizes the close connection between the sacred tradition and sacred scripture and argues: 'For both of them, flowing from the same divine wellspring, in a certain way merge into a unity and tend toward the same end.'[13]

In the twentieth century, yet another strand in biblical interpretation emerged. As an alternative to mainstream academic historical-critical exegesis on the one hand and ecclesial interpretation by church authorities on the other, the so-called committed hermeneutical approaches developed. They expressly argue from a specific perspective and against a background of specific experiences; for example, in liberation theologies the experience of oppression and exploitation of the materially poor, or in feminist theologies the experience of patriarchal structures. One basic conviction of these approaches is that there is no such thing as a neutral position for the reader in the hermeneutical process. Therefore, one step in the process of these approaches is the hermeneutics of suspicion, where it is critically asked who benefits from a certain interpretation. Academic biblical interpretation also generally recognizes the existence of different perspectives, but on the whole it tries to control or eliminate their implications for interpretation; the committed hermeneutical approaches, on the other hand, want to make productive use of a specific perspective. This hermeneutical position immediately gives rise to a conceptualization of church according to the specific perspective. The feminist theologian Elisabeth Schüssler Fiorenza, for example, developed the concept of the 'ekklēsia of wo/men', which for her is the moral space and hermeneutical centre of feminist interpretation. In opposition to 'the kyriarchal over-determination of Western forms of ekklēsia', this 'ekklēsia of wo/men' is 'the radical democratic vision of a citizenry of equals'.[14]

This historical outline has indicated some of the main issues in biblical interpretation. One site of struggle is the debate on literal and allegorical meaning. Another crucial theme is the question of who has the legitimate authority to interpret the Bible, the individual faithful or a magisterium. Even more fundamental than this debate on legitimate authority, however, is the question of authority between the reader and the text. Who is the subject of interpretation? The formation of the canon itself gave an important hint. In order to enable an authentic encounter between text and reader, the idea of one dominating the other does not lead very far. The relation between text and reader is not a vertical line, the text being either above or under the reader, but a horizontal plane, where text and reader are understood as interlocutors who enter into dialogue. In this dialogue, the subject matter of the text may come to the fore and enable the experience of understanding and meaning.

Significant developments in modern hermeneutics

The rise of modern hermeneutics is generally traced back to the Protestant theologian Friedrich Daniel Ernst Schleiermacher (1768–1834). He opened up new horizons for the hermeneutical field because he did not conceive of hermeneutics merely as rules and methods for interpreting texts, but reflected more fundamentally on the process of understanding. In the wake of Schleiermacher, hermeneutics turned philosophical. Thinkers who have made significant contributions to hermeneutical thinking in philosophy were Wilhelm Dilthey, Martin Heidegger and Hans-Georg Gadamer. We shall look briefly at the characteristics of their approaches to hermeneutics and then point out some of the challenging questions about hermeneutical thinking that they raised.

Schleiermacher defined hermeneutics as 'the art of understanding' (Kunstlehre des Verstehens).[15] He thought of 'art' in terms of the Greek technē, which involves skill as well as creativity. According to Schleiermacher these two aspects are reflected in the two dimensions implied by hermeneutics: grammatical interpretation, which takes place in relation to what is common to the culture that forms the author; and psychological interpretation, which perceives what is peculiar to the author. Thus the processes involved are comparison – asking what is common, and divination – grasping what is singular. The interpretation is oriented towards grasping the authorial intention. Schleiermacher goes even further by saying that the goal of the hermeneutical process is to understand the author better than he did himself, by raising to consciousness what has been unconscious to the author. This focus on the authorial intention in the hermeneutical process unites Schleiermacher with Romantic thinkers, but he remains critical in his awareness of the possibility of misunderstanding. One of his basic assumptions is that 'misunderstanding occurs as a matter of course, and so understanding must be willed and sought at every point'.[16] Therefore, Schleiermacher's point of departure for hermeneutical reflection is not just to find a method of interpreting obscure passages of text, but to reflect on the nature of the process of understanding itself.

Wilhelm Dilthey (1833–1911) further developed this idea of hermeneutics. His point of reference, however, was no longer confined to texts, but any kind of 'life-expressions' (Lebensäußerungen). For Dilthey, understanding life-expressions in their interrelatedness meant understanding history. In consequence, he wanted to establish 'understanding (Verstehen) of history' as the scientific approach of the Geisteswissenschaften ('human or cultural sciences') as equivalent – in the literal sense of being of equal scientific value – to the 'explanation (Erklären) of nature' in the natural sciences. Thus, he regarded hermeneutics as the foundational discipline for the Geisteswissenschaften and gave hermeneutics epistemological status. In contrast to the precondition of the natural sciences, where objects are observed from an external perspective and the act of observation remains separate from the phenomena observed, Dilthey emphasized shared universal nature as the basis of understanding in the Geisteswissenschaften. There the object of inquiry is not the outside world that has to be explained, but lived experience, in which the observer and the object are internally related. Dilthey's distinction between understanding and explanation as two fundamentally different modes of knowing has been acknowledged as an important contribution to hermeneutics; however, his conceptualization of understanding has been criticized as being too vague, because the difference between interpretandum and interpreter seems to be blurred and the concept of 'life-expressions' overgeneralizes the interpretandum.[17]

Martin Heidegger (1889–1976) carried out the next step, from hermeneutics as epistemology (concerned with the mode of knowing) to hermeneutics as ontology (describing the way of being in the world). In his main work Sein und Zeit (Being and Time), he developed the 'hermeneutics of facticity' in which he examined the fundamental conditions of being in the world. His account is marked by the assumption that Dasein ('being there') essentially co-originates with understanding.[18] Understanding, in Heidegger's view, is not a carefully conducted procedure of critical reflection, a volitional act that we consciously do, but something we are. Understanding is first of all pre-reflective, a mode of being, and as such it is characteristic of human being, of Dasein. Heidegger argues that the world is only intelligible to us by this Vorstruktur des Verstehens ('anticipatory structure of understanding or preunderstanding'). Hence, the hermeneutical situation of Dasein implies that every understanding is shaped by presuppositions and assumptions about the whole of existence. An important consequence is that the hermeneutical circle is no longer regarded as being vicious but is perceived as having an ontologically positive significance.[19] This circle refers to the interplay between our self-understanding and our understanding of the world. Hence the crucial point is not, as traditionally seen, the moment when we are able to leave the hermeneutical circle, when our interpretative endeavours culminate in a lucid and indubitable grasp of the meaning of the text. What matters, according to Heidegger, is the attempt to enter the circle in the right way, with a willingness to realize that investigation into the ontological conditions of my life ought to influence the way in which my life is led. Heidegger's reflections on hermeneutics and understanding became very influential, not only in philosophy, where thinkers like Hans-Georg Gadamer and Paul Ricoeur took up his insights, but also in theology, where Heidegger's ideas influenced Rudolf Bultmann, among others.

Hans-Georg Gadamer (1900–2002) is credited with having achieved a remarkable integration of reflection on hermeneutics in modern times. He developed his philosophical hermeneutics as a supposedly universal philosophical concept. His monumental work *Wahrheit und Methode* (Truth and Method) shows that he owed much to Heidegger and was also in dialogue with Romantic and Diltheyan hermeneutics.[20] His central concept was that of the *wirkungsgeschichtliches Bewußtsein* ('consciousness exposed to the effects of history'). The axiomatic assumption in his hermeneutical approach is that there is a primordial relation of belonging.[21] Gadamer argued that misunderstanding or alienating distancing is secondary, it already takes place on the basis of a more fundamental level of agreement, given by the unity of tradition. In this primordial relation of belonging, history does not belong to us, but we belong to history.[22] Following from this, Gadamer challenged the discrediting of prejudice, authority and tradition by the Enlightenment and rehabilitated them as conditions of understanding by referring to Heidegger's *Vorstruktur des Verstehens*.[23] Legitimate prejudice, true authority and constitutive tradition are re-established not against reason, but against the reign of subjectivity and interiority that mark Dilthey's perspective. Belonging does not mean immediacy but a productive relatedness through historical distance. This implies that we cannot look at history as object; we are still situated in it. As a consequence, we have no overview; we cannot grasp the totality of effects.[24] Yet we are not absolutely restricted by our situation, and this is recognized in the idea of horizon.[25] Within this concept, understanding is described as a 'fusion of horizons', in which the horizon of the interpreter merges with that of the text. Hence, understanding is not to be seen as the action of a subject but as a moving into a process in which past and present are constantly interrelated.[26]

Gadamer's concept has been questioned on several counts, the two most prominent challenges being the debates between Gadamer's hermeneutical approach and critical theory, represented by Jürgen Habermas; and the struggle with Jacques Derrida and the deconstructionist perspective. Whereas the latter debate did not get very far, because the two positions remained worlds apart, the debate between hermeneutics and critical theory is quite instructive.

What alarms representatives of critical theory is the way in which hermeneutical thinking, especially that of Gadamer, deals with tradition. According to Habermas, Gadamer puts too much emphasis on the authority of tradition, leaving no space for critical judgement and reflection aimed at the critique of ideology and structures of domination and violence. Because tradition has the potential to serve ideology and oppressive and violent structures, one has to be suspicious of it. Hence, critical thinking which is sensitive to power structures unveils the ethical problematic that is inherent in classical hermeneutical thinking. From an ethical point of view, understanding cannot easily be conceived as consent within a primordial relationship of belonging. Ethical awareness often requires a dissociation from what is regarded as *the* tradition. Moreover, it radically questions Gadamer's assumption of the unity of tradition. In summary, we can say that the debate between the hermeneutics of tradition and critical theory produced two insights: first, it led to an awareness of the intrinsically ethical nature of hermeneutics. As the hermeneutical process is not ethically neutral, ethical reflection has to be an integral part of the hermeneutical endeavour. Secondly, the debate made obvious the hermeneutical nature of ethics in so far as ethics is linked – either positively or negatively – to 'the effects of history'. Consciously taking this into account advances the cause of ethics.

Gadamer's theory was in a certain sense the 'ultimate' attempt to present a universal concept of hermeneutics and it provoked many debates and further developments, either in continuation or in opposition to Gadamer. But other hermeneutical discourses also evolved apart from philosophical realm. Therefore there is today no common reference point for the many different disciplines that deal with hermeneutical issues. In consequence, the hermeneutical field is very complex and there is no general theory to hermeneutics as a whole. In my view, the centre of gravity of hermeneutical thinking in modern times has shifted from consideration of methods of interpretation to reflection on the process of understanding. It has been shown that understanding is a fundamental element of the human condition itself.

Systematic aspects of the hermeneutical process

What exactly happens when we understand and how can meaning be grasped? In order to look more closely at the process of understanding, the task of this section is to give an outline of the fundamental constituents of the hermeneutical process. This will be done with reference to the hermeneutical thinking of the French philosopher Paul Ricoeur (1913–2005), who took up the insights of the debate between hermeneutics and critical theory and also took into account aspects of semiotics for his hermeneutical theory. Furthermore, he not only built a bridge between different philosophical strands of the Continental and Anglo-American academic worlds, but also linked philosophical and theological hermeneutics by expressly reflecting on biblical interpretation.[27]

The point of departure for Ricoeur's hermeneutical reflections was symbols,[28] metaphors[29] and texts.[30] In his approach, Ricoeur followed Heidegger in the view that ontology constitutes the horizon of hermeneutics. He unfolded the ontological dimension of his hermeneutics by relating it to the insights he had gained from phenomenology and reflective philosophy. Because of these influences, his hermeneutical approach was described as 'hermeneutical phenomenology'. Ricoeur states: 'The ruling idea of this hermeneutical phenomenology is that if self-reflection is the goal, interpretation is the means. In other words, there is no direct way from myself to myself except through the roundabout way of the appropriation of the signs, works of art, and culture.'[31]

For Ricoeur the first locus of interpretation is the polysemy of words, i.e. the multitude of their potential meanings.[32] Because words have more than one potential meaning, they require a context in order to yield an actual meaning. The discernment of the meaning of words within their context is the task of interpretation. Whereas an immediate clarification of meaning is possible in a situation of dialogue through question and answer, this is not possible when confronted with a text. Ricoeur held that the interpretation of a text is the paradigm of interpretation because it epitomizes the problems and possibilities of understanding:

In my view, the text is much more than a particular case of intersubjective communication: it is the paradigm of distanciation in communication. As such, it displays a fundamental characteristic of the very historicity of human experience, namely that it is communication in and through distance.[33]

Two ideas mark Ricoeur's concept of texts as written discourse: the *semantic autonomy* of a text and the text as *work*, i.e. a structured composition. Through writing as intentional exteriorization, the discourse gains a triple autonomy. Being fixed in writing renders the text autonomous from the author, the original addressees and the original context. The first autonomy is towards the author: whereas in spoken discourse the meaning of the discourse and the intention of the speaker coincide, this is no longer the case in written discourse. Its meaning is to be found in what the text actually says, not in what the author meant to say.[34] Here Ricoeur marks a break with Romantic hermeneutics. The second autonomy is towards the original situation of the discourse. Written discourse is not addressed to a specific interlocutor face-to-face, but effectively to everyone who can read. Thirdly, the autonomy from the original context has important implications for the reference of the text.[35] Whereas in spoken discourse the reference is ostensible and ultimately to the situation common to the interlocutors, in written discourse the reference is non-ostensible. To describe the point of reference of written discourse, Ricoeur uses the term *world*: 'Only writing, in freeing itself, not only from its author, but from the narrowness of the dialogical situation, reveals this destination of discourse as projecting a world.'[36] This referential function of a text plays a key role in Ricoeur's interpretation theory. What is to be understood is the 'world *in front of* the text'.

This triple autonomy creates the hermeneutical situation, leads to the focus of meaning, and makes the opening-up of a world possible. 'In short, the work *decontextualizes itself*, from the sociological as well as the psychological point of view, and is able to *recontextualize* itself differently in the act of reading.'[37] With this explication of written discourse, Ricoeur rejects Gadamer's negative perception of distanciation. Distanciation is regarded as genuine and is acknowledged for enabling understanding by opening a world in front of the text. 'Interpretation, philosophically understood, is nothing else than an attempt to make estrangement and distanciation productive.'[38]

Thus Ricoeur's hermeneutics directs the interpreter's attention towards the reference of a text, i.e. the 'about what' of a text. As already mentioned, Ricoeur argued that it is 'the world *in front of* the text' to which the text refers. With this concept he opposed structuralism in its restriction on 'the world *of* the text' and historicism, which tries to get through the text to 'the world *behind* the text'. Ricoeur's notion of 'the world *in front of* the text' reveals the influence of Heidegger's concept of understanding as *being-in-the-world*. Because this reference is ultimately directed towards a new way of existence in the world, Ricoeur also calls the text's projection of a new world its poetic or revelatory function.

> But why call it revelatory? Because through all the traits that it recapitulates and by what it adds, the poetic function incarnates a concept of truth that escapes the definition by adequation as well as the criteria of falsification and verification. Here truth no longer means verification, but manifestation, i.e. letting what shows itself be. What shows itself is in each instance a proposed world, a world I may inhabit and wherein I can project my ownmost possibilities.[39]

Ricoeur has examined the poetic function of discourse paradigmatically in his studies on *metaphors*. Here he emphasizes that *semantic innovation* is brought forward by metaphorical language. Ricoeur points to the relevance of these insights for understanding biblical language. Biblical language is fundamentally poetic language because it is geared towards opening up a new reality in front of the text: 'The proposed world that in biblical language is called a new creation, a new Covenant, the Kingdom of God, is the "issue" of the biblical text unfolded in front of this text.'[40] Like a metaphor, parables are also not fully translatable into moral and theological statements. Hence, poetic language does not primarily address its readers on the volitional and intellectual level, but aims at the transformation of the reader on a non-volitional level of existence.

Thus *metanoia* (transformation) takes place first of all as a *metanoia of imagination* and calls for a reorientation of one's whole existence.[41] The 'world *in front of* the text' addresses the reader in such a way that he or she cannot stay neutral *vis-à-vis* the text. Ricoeur has called this final stage of the interpretation process *appropriation*. This means 'to make one's own' what was initially 'alien' by being existentially involved in the interpretation. This demands a willingness from the reader to let the text speak, to expose himself or herself to the world in front of the text. The term 'appropriation' confronts us with a certain paradox. On the one hand, it seems as if the reader has to play a very active role in integrating the projection of the new reality into his or her existence. On the other hand '[a]ppropriation is also and primarily a "letting-go" . . . It is in allowing itself to be carried off towards the reference of the text that the *ego* divests itself of itself'.[42] In order to illustrate the paradox of appropriation, Ricoeur takes up the image of play that Gadamer developed in his reflection on the work of art. In play there is more than the activity of the subject, there is a peculiar dynamic which means that '[w]hoever plays is also played'.[43] To express that there is no one who holds all the reins, Ricoeur also compares appropriation to dance, where the dancer is carried away by the movement. Play and dance do not work within the framework of utilitarian calculation about what has to be done next, but '[p]lay is an experience which transforms those who participate in it'.[44] What takes place is a *metamorphosis*. In this at the same time active and receptive process, transformation takes place.

This concept of appropriation in the interpretation process shows the ontological horizon of Ricoeur's hermeneutics. To understand means not simply to grasp the meaning of the text, but to grasp the meaning of one's own existence. Understanding is intrinsically related to the self-understanding of the reader.[45] This leads to the important insight that understanding is not something that is 'made' by the subject: 'Understanding then is the complete opposite of a constitution for which the subject would have the key. It would be better in this regard to say that the self is constituted by the issue of the text.'[46]

When relating Ricoeur's insights to the ecclesial practice of hermeneutics, it becomes clear that Ricoeur strongly challenges all who hold that the 'right' authority and the 'right' methodological tools are the key 'to crack the code' of the text. He unambiguously states that '[b]etween absolute knowledge and hermeneutics, it is necessary to choose'.[47] Hermeneutics touches and challenges the self-understanding of those who interpret, be it the individual faithful or the church community. Moreover, the hermeneutical processes initiated by the biblical texts are not confined to church boundaries. Lewis S. Mudge stresses: 'The narrative or narratives which impel ecclesial social reality dynamically forward in time are not contained *within* the church alone, or solely *about* the church. They are narratives about a larger world in which the Christian community articulates in a catalytic and expressive way.'[48]

As regards Ricoeur's concept of appropriation, theologians like Werner G. Jeanrond and Sandra M. Schneiders have taken up his emphasis on transformation as being the culmination point of interpretation. They argue, however, that this transformation process must also include an ethical dimension. According to Jeanrond, *ethical assessment* has to be an intrinsic component of the hermeneutical process because it is necessary to assess whether a possible transformative experience is truly liberating or oppressive.[49] Similarly, Schneiders maintains that existential interpretation significantly involves the interpreter's person, but this involvement still remains a critical one.[50] 'Transformative interpretation, in other words, is not blind submission to the text as answer but an in-depth engagement of the text's subject matter, of its truth claims, in terms of the developed Christian consciousness of the contemporary believer within the contemporary community of faith.'[51] Schneiders ultimately pleads for a genuine dialogue between text and reader, in which the otherness and strangeness of the text is also to be respected. Meaning arises only in this ongoing dialogue between text and reader about its subject matter. Eventually, the transformation of the reader, and possibly also of the text, takes place.[52]

Reflections on hermeneutics in the ecumenical movement

In the ecumenical movement, hermeneutical reflections have again and again become an important issue. One could say that they are a constant undercurrent in the ecumenical endeavour, mostly staying beneath the surface but arising when dialogue begins to flag. The study process on hermeneutics carried out by Faith and Order after the Fifth World Conference in Santiago de Compostela in 1993 can serve as an example for this observation. Until then, Faith and Order had mainly been involved in dialogues striving to reach propositional agreement on theological themes, the most important one being the dialogue on *Baptism, Eucharist and Ministry* (BEM). However, as the responses to this convergence text on BEM were considerably divergent,[53] the atmosphere within Faith and Order at the beginning of the 1990s was marked by disillusionment. Analysing the responses, it became obvious that they rested on unexamined hermeneutical assumptions which underlay denominational as well as ecumenical theologies. These hermeneutical issues concerned the relationship of scripture, tradition and the church. As a result, a study process on hermeneutics was initiated in 1993 which after three consultations led to the report *A Treasure in Earthen Vessels. An instrument for an ecumenical reflection on hermeneutics*, published in 1998.

In the history of Faith and Order, this was the second time that a major document on hermeneutical issues had been published. The first one was produced in 1963 following the Fourth World Conference in Montreal and was called *Scripture, Tradition and Traditions*.[54] This document particularly raised awareness of the distinction between the one Tradition and the many traditions and tried to clarify the relationship between both. In the following years, several reports on the authority of the Bible were put together.[55]

A Treasure in Earthen Vessels takes up these issues in section A, entitled 'Common understanding of the one Tradition'. In section B, called 'One Gospel in many contexts', the relation between contextuality and catholicity is discussed. Finally, in section C the concept of 'Church as a hermeneutical community' is explored. In principle, these reflections on hermeneutics can be credited with advancing the ecumenical movement because they take the step from debating theological propositions to methodologically reflecting the dialogue process itself.

Nevertheless, from a hermeneutical point of view, there are shortcomings in *A Treasure in Earthen Vessels*. The most serious is the definition of ecumenical hermeneutics as 'a hermeneutics for the unity of the Church',[56] because this idea risks reducing hermeneutics to a means for reaching unity. On this account, *A Treasure in Earthen Vessels* misses the chance of looking at hermeneutics in its own right as a reflective endeavour that asks how meaning and understanding come into being. Though contemporary definitions of hermeneutics are quoted at the beginning,[57] insights from modern hermeneutics are not explored further in the reflections that follow.

Instead, the central idea proposed in *A Treasure in Earthen Vessels* is to structure ecumenical hermeneutics around the concept of 'coherence'.[58] Affirming the necessary distinction of the one Tradition and the many traditions, the attempt of section A to come to a 'common understanding' of the one Tradition seems like trying to square the circle. The difficulty or even inconsistency in the report is that in some parts it searches for a common understanding, whereas in other parts it seeks to affirm that there are legitimate different understandings of the gospel.[59] As the notion of coherence is used in both directions it cannot really contribute to clarification. From a hermeneutical perspective, it has to be said that the goal of reaching a common understanding is necessarily deceptive.

In his critical account of *A Treasure in Earthen Vessels*, Ingolf U. Dalferth insists that hermeneutics is an art aimed at enabling understanding.[60] It therefore demands and fosters freedom and cannot serve as an instrument for arriving at a specific understanding or overcoming the divisions between the churches. The concluding paragraph of section A, at least, seems to point to this insight that understanding cannot be intentionally produced, but has to be openly received:

> Yet ultimately, amid the many ecclesial traditions, the one Tradition is revealed in the living presence of Christ in the world, but is not something to be captured and controlled by human discourse. It is a living eschatological reality, eluding all attempts at a final linguistic definition and conceptual disclosure. One way of describing the one Tradition is by speaking about the ecclesial capacity of *receiving* revelation.[61]

The exploration of 'One Gospel in Many Contexts'[62] in section B is considerably shorter than A. The main thrust is to affirm the call for respect and openness in dialogue with Christian communities of different confessions and contexts. This must ultimately be an openness for *metanoia*, when we are willing to see the limitations of our own perspectives.[63] This leads to a valuable discussion on catholicity and contextuality, both of which, in their nurturing and criticizing functions, are vital for an adequate and relevant interpretation of the gospel.

The concept of 'The Church as a Hermeneutical Community'[64] is developed in section C. This chapter promotes two interrelated concerns. The idea of the church as a hermeneutical community implies, on the one hand, participatory structures within churches and, on the other hand, conciliar structures between churches. Ecumenical hermeneutics is a genuinely participatory and communal process: 'Hermeneutics, perhaps especially ecumenical hermeneutics, is not the work of specialists. Ecumenical hermeneutics, in the pursuit of visible church unity, is first and foremost the work of the whole people gathered in believing communities in diverse contexts.'[65] Affirming the participation of all, the report immediately points to the need for formation. The way in which formation is described here is to my mind ambivalent. On the one hand it is argued that the whole church is called to participate and thus the maturity of the faithful in matters of faith is attested, but on the other hand it is maintained that there is a need for the 'churches' to educate 'their members' as 'faithful' hearers and interpreters.[66] The question to be raised at this point is: who is the 'church' when it is separated from 'its members'? The concept of formation here is obviously in danger of remaining a top-down model. Yet, in another paragraph the idea of the indispensability of direct participation is demonstrated much more clearly and consistently: 'All believers, because of their unity with Jesus Christ and the indwelling of the Holy Spirit, have the potential to receive God's word, to discern God's will, and to proclaim the Gospel.'[67]

Speaking then about relations between the churches, the report stresses the need for *collegiality*, which means working within structures that enable coming together in order to speak, discern and act.[68] These structures need to be increased and strengthened by being directed towards the implementation of mutual accountability.[69] A *Treasure in Earthen Vessels* emphasizes that reception of ecumenical agreements also involves the recognition of the other person and the transformative implication that this can have.[70] Finally, the ecclesiological consequence of being a hermeneutical community is pointed out: 'The Church is a communion of persons in relation; thus active participation and dialogue between communities, and within each community at all levels, is one expression of the Church's nature.'[71] This again shows that a participatory hermeneutical approach gives rise to the notion of the church as a participatory community and that a participatory ecclesiology has to be based on a participatory hermeneutics.

Concluding remarks on hermeneutics and ecclesiology

By investigating the process of understanding, hermeneutics can make a significant contribution to ecclesiological reflections. In a hermeneutical perspective it becomes obvious that the interpretation process is ultimately a transformative event. What happens in interpretation is not an actualization of meaning in the sense of a reproduction, but a *creation* of meaning for the interpreter. In the process of understanding, the innovative potential of the *interpretandum* takes effect. This, in turn, implies that the *interpretandum* is not self-contained, but is ultimately geared towards projecting a world and offering a new way of being to the interpreter. This has been set forth by Ricoeur.

In a hermeneutical perspective the *interpretandum* is credited with a dialogical authority. In this dialogue opened up by the *interpretandum*, the interpreter is called to an active and receptive participation. Meaning can arise only through this participatory involvement of the individual. Ingolf U. Dalferth[72] emphasizes that understanding is always 'one's own understanding', as no one can understand for somebody else. Understanding does not simply grasp something, but the meaning of that something *for me*. What this meaning is for me can be seen from how my life is influenced by what I understand. Hence, the process of understanding (*Verstehen*) individualizes in a radical sense. Nevertheless, common ground in what has been grasped as meaning (understanding in the sense of *Verständnis*) is possible, yet never entirely. Dalferth holds that because meaning is a result of the individual process of understanding there can be no completely identical common understanding. At the same time, he stresses that understanding is not a private matter, it does not take place in isolated space but in relation to other processes of understanding, within preceding and following attempts to understand. Understanding appears in time and is always in transition to further understanding. Therefore one important consequence of philosophical reflection on hermeneutics is a twofold observation: in the constant human process of understanding we are, on the one hand, not free to choose whether we want to understand at all. Understanding is necessarily part of our human nature. On the other hand, however, it is essentially necessary that we are free within each single process of understanding. Understanding cannot be determined and prescribed from outside. The freedom to go through one's own process of understanding is a fundamental prerequisite for understanding. In short, participation of the individual is the *conditio sine qua non* for understanding. Furthermore, being aware of the transformational character of the hermeneutical process, it becomes obvious that understanding is not just a cognitive process influencing what we think but an existential process influencing how we live.

From a hermeneutical perspective, the basic ecclesiological question therefore is not who holds the authority to decide on the 'right' meaning, but whether individuals are given space to be directly involved in the interpretation process and experience meaning themselves. Conceiving interpretation as a participatory event reminds us that the church's nature and mission is to open up space for transformative encounters with the biblical scriptures.

The question is how, within such an approach, an ecclesial communion –or moreover a communion of communions – deals with the plurality of meanings emerging from individual understandings. The issue is whether the transformation process that is envisaged in a participatory hermeneutics strengthens relations between the individuals or endangers the community. At this point, we must recall a basic ecclesiological insight, namely that the ecclesial community is a community that is not created and sustained by human beings, but by God himself. Moreover, it is not an identical understanding of the Bible that holds individuals together in this community, but the fact that they all relate to the Bible as their primary source for life. Because we all participate – each in our own way – in the transformative process of understanding the same basic *interpretandum*, we are related to one another. The Bible is this 'third' which, in the midst of differing understandings, sustains our relations.[73] Furthermore, the differing understandings are not to be perceived as a static plurality, each standing self-contained in isolation, but as a dynamic plurality that is constantly moving and interacting because each understanding challenges the other. Interpretation is a site of struggle geared towards creating further, deeper understanding – but never final understanding. The awareness of this ongoing process of understanding allows us to see our own understanding in relation to other understandings and also encourages us to acknowledge that there is legitimate space for other meaningful interpretations.

In conclusion I shall highlight three insights that hermeneutical reflection can offer to ecclesiology. First, a hermeneutical process is a *transformative process*. Where understanding occurs, there transformation takes place and something new takes shape. Basically and essentially, the church as a hermeneutical community is not a static organization but a space where the *viva vox evangelii* enables transformation. Second, at the heart of the life of the church is a *personal process*, the individual person grasping the meaning of biblical texts for his or her own life. Third, it is a deeply *relational process* because it enables the person to relate to the subject matter of the texts, God, and invites the person to relate to all the faithful who share the same texts as the source of life.

Notes

1 The term hermeneutics originates from the Greek verb *hermeneuein* which means to interpret, to explain, to translate. Reference to Hermes, the messenger of the gods, has been made since late

antiquity. 'Hermeneutics' as a distinct term has been used since modern times. As a book title it first appeared in Johann Conrad Dannhauer's *Hermeneutica Sacra Sive Methodus exponendarum S. Literarum proposita & vindicata* (Straßburg 1654). Cf. Hendrik Birus, 'Einleitung', in Hendrik Birus (ed.), *Hermeneutische Positionen: Schleiermacher – Dilthey – Heidegger – Gadamer*, Göttingen: Vandenhoeck und Ruprecht, 1982, p. 7.

2 See, from a hermeneutical perspective, Paul Ricoeur, 'The Canon between the Text and the Community', in Petr Pokorný and Jan Roskovec (eds), *Philosophical Hermeneutics and Biblical Exegesis*, Tübingen: Mohr Siebeck, 2002, pp. 7–26.

3 See Alfred Schindler, 'Kanon II. Kirchengeschichtlich', in *Religion in Geschichte und Gegenwart: Handwörterbuch für Theologie und Religionswissenschaft*, 4th edn, vol. 4, Tübingen: Mohr Siebeck, 2001, col. 767–70.

4 See the account of the Greek origins of hermeneutics in Claus v. Bormann, 'Hermeneutik I. Philosophisch-theologisch', in *Theologische Realenzyklopädie*, vol. 15, Berlin/New York: Walter de Gruyter, 1986, pp. 108–12.

5 Cf. Gerhard Ebeling, 'Hermeneutik', in *Religion in Geschichte und Gegenwart*, 3rd edn, vol. 3, Tübingen: Mohr Siebeck, 1959, col. 249f.

6 'The letter tells us what happened, what should be believed the allegory, the moral meaning what should be done, the anagogy where one should be oriented to.'

7 Cf. Martin Luther, 'Assertio omnium articulorum M. Lutheri per bullam Leonis X. novissimam damnatorum' (1520), in *D. Martin Luthers Werke*, Kritische Gesamtausgabe, vol. 7, Weimar: Hermann Böhlaus Nachfolger, 1897, p. 97 (WA 7, 97).

8 '*Quod si adversarii scripturam urserint contra Christum, urgemus Christum contra Scripturam*'; cf. Martin Luther, 'Propositiones disputatae', No. 49 (1535), in *D. Martin Luthers Werke*, WA 39 I, 47.

9 '[H]*anc veritatem et disciplinam contineri in libris scriptis et sine scripto traditionibus*'; Decretum de Canonicis Scripturis, in Heinrich Denzinger and Peter Hünermann (eds), *Enchiridion symbolorum, definitionum et declarationum de rebus fidei et moru: Kompendium der Glaubensbekenntnisse und kirchlichen Lehrentscheidungen*, 39th edition, Freiburg: Herder, 2001, p. 496 (DH 1501).

10 '[A]*d coercenda petulantia ingenia . . . iudicare de vero sensu et interpretatione Scripturarum Sanctarum*'; Decretum de Editione et Usu Sacrorum Librorum, in DH 1507, p. 498.

11 '*Quod quidem Magisterium non supra verbum Dei est, sed eidem ministrat*'; Dei Verbum, chap. 2, no. 10, in DH 4214, p. 1255.

12 Cf. Dei Verbum, chap. 3, no. 12, in DH 4219, p. 1258.

13 '*Nam ambae, ex eadem divina scaturigine promanantes, in unum quodammodo coalescunt et in eundem finem tendunt*'; Dei Verbum, chap. 2, no. 9, in DH 4212, p. 1255.

14 Elisabeth Schüssler Fiorenza, *Sharing Her Word. Feminist Biblical Interpretation in Context*, Edinburgh: T&T Clark, 1998, p. 132. See the chapters on Black Ecclesiologies, Liberation Ecclesiology, Feminist Ecclesiology and Postmodern Ecclesiologies in this volume.

15 Cf. F.D.E. Schleiermacher, *Hermeneutics: The Handwritten Manuscripts*, ed. Heinz Kimmerle, trans. James Duke and Jack Forstman, Missoula, MT: Scholars Press, 1977, p. 95.

16 Ibid., p. 110.

17 Cf. Hendrik Birus, 'Einleitung', in Hendrik Birus (ed.), *Hermeneutische Positionen: Schleiermacher – Dilthey – Heidegger – Gadamer*, Göttingen: Vandenhoeck und Ruprecht, 1982, p. 10.

18 Cf. Martin Heidegger, *Being and Time*, Oxford: Blackwell, 2005, § 31.

19 'The point of Heidegger's hermeneutical reflection is not so much to prove that there is a circle as to show that this circle possesses an ontologically positive significance', Hans-Georg Gadamer, *Truth and Method*, 2nd edn, translation revised by Joel Weinsheimer and Donald G. Marshall, London: Continuum, 2004, p. 269.

20 'Gadamer's text is like a palimpsest, in which it is always possible to distinguish, as in the thickness of overlaid transparencies, a Romantic layer, a Diltheyan layer and a Heideggerian layer', Paul Ricoeur, 'Hermeneutics and the Critique of Ideology', in John B. Thompson (ed.), *Paul Ricoeur: Hermeneutics and the Human Sciences: Essays on Language, Action and Interpretation*, Cambridge: Cambridge University Press, 1981, p. 70.

21 'Hermeneutics must start from the position that a person seeking to understand something has a bond to the subject matter that comes into language through the traditionary text and has, or acquires, a connection with the tradition from which the text speaks', Gadamer, *Truth and Method*,

p. 295. It is interesting to notice that this belonging is to the *matter* which is handed down in tradition, not to the author.

22 Cf. ibid., p. 278.

23 Cf. ibid., pp. 268–91.

24 Cf. ibid., p. 301.

25 'We define the concept of "situation" by saying that it represents a standpoint that limits the possibility of vision. Hence essential to the concept of situation is the concept of "*horizon*". The horizon is the range of vision that includes everything that can be seen from a particular vantage point', ibid., p. 301.

26 '*Understanding is to be thought of less as a subjective act than as participating in an event of tradition*, a process of transmission in which past and present are constantly mediated', ibid., p. 291.

27 Cf. Paul Ricoeur, 'Philosophische und theologische Hermeneutik', in Paul Ricoeur and Eberhard Jüngel, *Metapher: Zur Hermeneutik religiöser Sprache*, München: Chr. Kaiser Verlag, 1974, pp. 24–45; and the collected essays in Lewis S. Mudge (ed.), *Paul Ricoeur: Essays on Biblical Interpretation*, London: SPCK, 1981.

28 In the concluding chapter of *The Symbolism of Evil*, Boston: Beacon Press, 1969, pp. 347ff., he coins the famous statement: 'The symbol gives rise to thought.'

29 His studies on the function of metaphors were published in 1975 under the meaningful title *La Métaphore Vive*, which has been translated into English as *The Rule of Metaphor*; cf. Paul Ricoeur, *The Rule of Metaphor: Multi-disciplinary studies of the creation of meaning in language*, Toronto: University of Toronto Press, 1979.

30 Cf. Paul Ricoeur, *Interpretation Theory: Discourse and the Surplus of Meaning*, Fort Worth: Texas Christian University Press, 1976; and the collected essays: John B. Thompson (ed.), *Paul Ricoeur: Hermeneutics and the Human Sciences: Essays on Language, Action and Interpretation*, Cambridge: Cambridge University Press, 1981.

31 Paul Ricoeur, 'Reply to Lewis S. Mudge', in Mudge (ed.), *Essays*, p. 43.

32 Cf. Paul Ricoeur, 'The Task of Hermeneutics', in Thompson (ed.), *Paul Ricoeur*, p. 44.

33 Paul Ricoeur, 'The Hermeneutical Function of Distanciation', in Thompson (ed.), *Paul Ricoeur*, p. 131.

34 Cf. Paul Ricoeur, 'The Model of the Text: Meaningful Action Considered as a Text', *Social Research* vol. 38 no. 3 (1971), 534.

35 In hermeneutics the distinction is made between *sense*, the 'what' of discourse, and *reference*, the 'about what' of discourse, the 'world' which it describes in one way or another, cf. Ricoeur, *Interpretation Theory*, p. 19.

36 Ricoeur, 'The Model of the Text', p. 536.

37 Ricoeur, 'Hermeneutics and the Critique of Ideology', p. 91.

38 Ricoeur, *Interpretation Theory*, p. 44.

39 Paul Ricoeur, 'Toward a Hermeneutic of the Idea of Revelation', in Mudge (ed.), *Essays*, p. 102.

40 Ibid., p. 103.

41 Cf. Paul Ricoeur, 'Stellung und Funktion der Metapher in der biblischen Sprache', in Ricoeur and Jüngel, *Metapher*, p. 70.

42 Paul Ricoeur, 'Appropriation', in Thompson (ed.), *Paul Ricoeur*, p. 191.

43 Ibid., p. 186.

44 Ibid., p. 186.

45 Cf. ibid., p. 193.

46 Paul Ricoeur, 'Toward a Hermeneutic of the Idea of Revelation', in Mudge (ed.), p. 108.

47 Paul Ricoeur, 'Appropriation', in Thompson (ed.), *Paul Ricoeur*, p. 193.

48 Lewis S. Mudge, *Rethinking the Beloved Community: Ecclesiology, Hermeneutics, Social Theory*, Geneva: WCC Publications, 2001, pp. 11f.

49 Cf. Werner G. Jeanrond, *Theological Hermeneutics: Development and Significance*, London: Macmillan, 1991, pp. 114ff.

50 'Consequently, any adequate criticism of the biblical text requires not only traditional historical and literary criticism that interrogate the text as witness and as work, not only a sensitive and critical treatment of the worldview that the text incorporates, but especially a thoroughgoing criticism of its ideology, especially in respect to the oppressive distortions of reality for the prosecution of the power agenda of the elements in society that enjoy hegemony', Sandra M. Schneiders, *The*

Revelatory Text: Interpreting the New Testament as Sacred Scripture, 2nd edn, Collegeville, MN: The Liturgical Press, 1999, p. 171.
51 Ibid., p. 177.
52 Cf. ibid., pp. 175f. Schneiders takes the American Declaration of Independence as an example of the development of meaning. She shows how the statement 'all men are created equal' expanded in its meaning.
53 Cf. *A Treasure in Earthen Vessels. An Instrument for an Ecumenical Reflection on Hermeneutics*, Faith and Order Paper No. 182, Geneva: WCC / Faith and Order, 1998, p. 3.
54 Cf. 'Scripture, Tradition and Traditions', in P.C. Rodger and L. Vischer (ed.), *The Fourth World Conference on Faith and Order, Montreal 1963*, Faith and Order Paper No. 42, London: SCM Press, 1964.
55 Cf. the summary in *A Treasure in Earthen Vessels*, ¶19, pp. 16f.
56 Cf. ibid., ¶5, p. 9.
57 Ibid., ¶5, p. 8.
58 Cf. ibid., ¶6, p. 9. The aim to establish a hermeneutics of coherence probably reflects first of all the lack of coherence which was felt painfully at the Faith and Order Conference in Santiago.
59 Ibid., ¶28, p. 21, stresses 'the positive complementarity of traditions'.
60 Cf. Ingolf U. Dalferth, 'Spielraum zum Mißverständnis: Anmerkungen zum Projekt einer ökumenischen Hermeneutik', in Dalferth, *Auf dem Weg der Ökumene: Die Gemeinschaft evangelischer und anglikanischer Kirchen nach der Meissener Erklärung*, Leipzig: Evang. Verlags-Anstalt, 2002, p. 265.
61 *A Treasure in Earthen Vessels*, ¶37, p. 26.
62 Cf. ibid., ¶¶38ff., pp. 27ff.
63 Cf. ibid., ¶39, p. 28.
64 Cf. ibid., ¶¶49ff., pp. 33ff.
65 Ibid., ¶50, p. 33.
66 Cf. ibid., ¶51, p. 33.
67 Ibid., ¶55, p. 35.
68 Cf. ibid., ¶57, p. 36.
69 Cf. ibid., ¶59, p. 37.
70 Cf. ibid., ¶63, p. 39.
71 Ibid., ¶64, p. 39.
72 Cf. Dalferth, 'Spielraum zum Mißverständnis', pp. 245–58.
73 Cf. ibid., pp. 276–8.

Further reading

Hendrik Birus (ed.), *Hermeneutische Positionen: Schleiermacher – Dilthey – Heidegger – Gadamer*, Göttingen: Vandenhoeck und Ruprecht, 1982.
Ingolf U. Dalferth, 'Spielraum zum Mißverständnis: Anmerkungen zum Projekt einer ökumenischen Hermeneutik', in Ingolf U. Dalferth, *Auf dem Weg der Ökumene: Die Gemeinschaft evangelischer und anglikanischer Kirchen nach der Meissener Erklärung*, Leipzig: Evang. Verlags-Anstalt, 2002, pp. 245–78.
Gerhard Ebeling, 'Hermeneutik', in *Religion in Geschichte und Gegenwart: Handwörterbuch für Theologie und Religionswissenschaft*, 3rd edn, vol. 3, Tübingen: Mohr Siebeck, 1959, col. 242–62.
Hans-Georg Gadamer, *Truth and Method*, 2nd edn, translation revised by Joel Weinsheimer and Donald G. Marshall, London: Continuum, 2004.
Martin Heidegger, *Being and Time*. Oxford: Blackwell, 2005.
Werner G. Jeanrond, *Theological Hermeneutics: Development and Significance*, London: Macmillan, 1991.
Lewis S. Mudge, *Rethinking the Beloved Community: Ecclesiology, Hermeneutics, Social Theory*, Geneva: WCC Publications, 2001.
Paul Ricoeur, *Interpretation Theory: Discourse and the Surplus of Meaning*, Fort Worth: Texas Christian University Press, 1976.

Paul Ricoeur and Eberhard Jüngel, *Metapher: Zur Hermeneutik religiöser Sprache*, München: Chr. Kaiser Verlag, 1974.

Friedrich Daniel Ernst Schleiermacher, *Hermeneutics: The Handwritten Manuscripts*, ed. Heinz Kimmerle, trans. James Duke and Jack Forstman, Missoula, MT: Scholars Press, 1977.

Sandra M. Schneiders, *The Revelatory Text: Interpreting the New Testament as Sacred Scripture*, 2nd edn, Collegeville, MN: The Liturgical Press, 1999.

Elisabeth Schüssler Fiorenza, *Sharing Her Word. Feminist Biblical Interpretation in Context*, Edinburgh: T&T Clark, 1998.

John B. Thompson (ed.), *Paul Ricoeur: Hermeneutics and the Human Sciences: Essays on Language, Action and Interpretation*, Cambridge: Cambridge University Press, 1981.

A Treasure in Earthen Vessels: An Instrument for an Ecumenical Reflection on Hermeneutics, Faith and Order Paper No. 182, Geneva: WCC/Faith and Order, 1998.

34

DOCTRINE AND ECCLESIOLOGY

Gemma Simmonds, C.J.

The word doctrine derives from the Latin and Greek for that which is taught, as well as the activity of teaching itself. The Christian community does not see doctrine in exclusively juridical or instrumental terms. The way in which a particular dogma is framed and explained can be subject to difference in nuance and expression according to the era and culture in which it is articulated. Doctrine is as much contained in the liturgical life of the church, the struggle of theologians to understand and explicate God's unfolding self-revelation, and in the example of those striving to live according to the way of Christ, as it is in any body of propositions. The New Testament uses the word from which doctrine derives to mean oral religious instruction and stresses 'doctrine' as one of the primary duties of a bishop (1 Tim 4.13, 16; 2 Tim 4.2). The response hoped for by the apostles to their preaching was not an increase of knowledge or intellectual assent to their propositions, however, but a true change of heart and life (Acts 2:37–41).

The way in which Christian doctrine has developed and been formulated down the ages touches also on the way in which the church has understood its constitution as a church, that is, on the development of ecclesiology. Any discussion of doctrine within the church becomes, inevitably, a discussion of the developing doctrine of the church, since it is in its reflection on the content of doctrine and its development that the church becomes conscious of itself as church and of the challenges posed to it by the question of authenticity and authority.

Doctrine and revelation

The Christian church believes that God's self-revelation, made gradually 'in many and various ways', was made fully and definitively through the life, teaching, death and resurrection of the incarnate Word, Jesus Christ (Heb 1.1–2). No further revelation is expected after Jesus Christ until all creation is reconciled to God by the power of the Holy Spirit, when Christ returns in glory. If revelation is complete, it has nevertheless yet to be explicated and understood in any complete sense. The two pillars on which doctrine is based are the Hebrew and Greek scriptures and the living transmission of Christian truth through the apostles and the leaders and communities that succeeded them, termed tradition. The idea of a faith transmitted from apostolic times to our own has given rise to the notion of a 'deposit of faith', contained in scripture and tradition. For those churches who maintain an episcopal tradition, bishops, perceived as successors to the apostles, have the task of nurturing this faith, but the wider community are not passive recipients of doctrine. The faithful have an equal duty and calling to be collaborators in the task of living and articulating doctrine in their faith, life and worship. The Holy Spirit, who leads all the faithful to the truth, guarantees the inerrancy of Christian belief through the supernatural sense of faith (*sensus fidei*) within the whole body of believers when all the faithful are united in their consent in matters of faith and morals. How this consent is achieved, expressed and understood remains problematic.

Each generation brings to the understanding and articulation of apostolic teaching its own hermeneutic, perceptions and context. The question arises of how Christian doctrine, as it develops in time, remains coherent within itself. There also arises the parallel question of how later teaching relates to revelation and the witness to God's saving work found in the Bible. These issues became crucial at the Reformation. Protestants challenged the way in which current doctrine appeared to them contrary to the beliefs of the Bible. The Catholic counter-argument allowed that developments in the interpretation of doctrine since the apostolic era could be equally authoritative, since they were a response to the inspiration of the same Spirit. Thus claims over the rival authority of scripture and the unfolding interpretation of doctrine provoked differing understandings of the church itself, its governance and its place in the proclamation of revealed truth.[1]

Some theologians have framed doctrine within a dialogue with prevailing modes of thought. The use of Platonic or Aristotelian philosophy by Augustine and Thomas Aquinas is one example, the use of Marxist analysis by twentieth-century liberation theologians is another.[2] Whether theologians make the Christian community the proper *locus* of the emergence and development of doctrine, seeing other disciplines as subordinate to its own internal self-understanding and sources, or whether they adopt a particular method or a concern of their era as an equal and comparable instrument in reflecting on God's saving work, the doctrine that emerges must balance fidelity to original sources with expression in the idiom of its time. This tension is expressed in the terms *ressourcement* and *aggiornamento*. The first refers to a return to primitive sources as the fount of doctrine and the mirror through which it must reflect on its present expression. The other insists rather on the need for theology to consider itself and its articulation in the light of the world's current context and self-understanding.

Confidence in the inerrancy of Christian teaching stems from the belief that the truth of God's intentional self-revelation in Jesus Christ can be received, understood and taught, within the limitations of human understanding, under the power of the Holy Spirit. This truth is self-authenticating and not subject to empirical verification. The power of the Spirit prevents error and does not reside exclusively in any one part of the church, but is present in the mutual dynamic of faith between teachers and taught.

Doctrine and hermeneutics

Present-day historical consciousness leads us to see that there is no such thing as a neutral stance with regard to the past. Each generation is conditioned by its own context and influences both conscious and unconscious, in its attempt to interpret the truth. This 'hermeneutical circle' requires us to adopt a 'hermeneutic of suspicion' in pursuit of some measure of neutrality. Such a stance would be typical of modern-day feminist and liberationist theologies in their desire to extract original truth from the inevitable ideological contamination of doctrine. Other theologies believe that this is an admission of the defeat of theology by alien modes of modern thought, and the mere replacing of one form of myth by another.[3]

The very first reference to the Christian community in the New Testament describes it as being 'faithful to the teaching of the apostles, to the brotherhood, to the breaking of bread and to the prayers' (Acts 2.42). The primitive doctrine (*kerygma*) of the Jesus movement was its proclamation that Jesus died and rose again according to scripture and lives now as Lord and glorified Messiah (1 Cor 15.3–4; Acts 2.36). The gospels reflect different emphases in interpretation of the person and work of Jesus between the communities from which they emerged, which gave rise to different christologies. The New Testament considers Jesus Christ in his life, death, resurrection and teaching to be the fullness of God's gradual and progressive self-revelation (Heb 1.1–2). The apostles as witnesses to the life and ministry of Jesus receive this revelation in an authoritative way through the power of the Holy Spirit and are bound to proclaim it faithfully (Jn 14.25–26; Mt 28.19–20; 1 Cor 9.16).

As its membership among pagans increased, the question arose of the extent to which the emerging Christian community should conform itself to the requirements of the Jewish Law. At the council of Jerusalem (Acts 15.1–35) 'the apostles and elders' gathered to debate this, sending Paul, Luke and other evangelizers from one community to another, instructing them on the decisions reached by the elders and urging obedience to these authoritative statements (Acts 16.4). New Testament reflection on teaching and pastoral structures, the emergence of leadership, the Holy Spirit's work within individuals and communities and the disputed relation between the Law and new life in Christ point already to ways in which the doctrine of the church would develop in the future.

The realization that the *parousia* was not imminent and the extension of the church throughout the Roman Empire threw up challenges of how different communities related to one another and to the original mission of Christ. The first generations of Christian apologists did not offer a notably different explanation of the faith from that of the apostles themselves, but were principally concerned to refute popular prejudices against Christianity and to make its doctrines and practices understandable and appealing to interested pagans. They did this by locating all the wisdom of Greek philosophy in inspiration by the *Logos*, and claiming harmony between the natural and supernatural orders of truth.

The Christian community was compelled by the event of the Incarnation to develop and extend its understanding of God's action in human history. Its reflection on the person and saving work of Jesus led to further doctrinal exploration and definition of what can be said about God. In the first instance the writers of the New Testament drew from their exegesis of the Jewish scriptures and understanding of Jesus as their fulfilment and realization. Further developments in christological thinking led to the formulation of trinitarian doctrine, since increasingly 'high' christology could only be developed within the understanding of the fundamental oneness of God. Christian thought and doctrine thus balances fidelity to its original source and inspiration and a constant dialogue with forms of discourse prevalent within a given society, through which it frames its formulations.

Doctrine and history

The responsibility of those having oversight of communities in the post-apostolic generations would include preserving the teaching of the first apostles from innovations and false interpretations such as Gnosticism (2 Tim 1.11–14; 2 Pet 1.16–21; 1 Jn 2.24). Against those who claimed secret, esoteric knowledge about God's self-revelation and who saw such knowledge as the path to salvation, orthodox Christians claimed inerrancy through the handing on unchanged of the truth proclaimed by the apostles. One of the earliest examples of collective authority over doctrinal matters is the fixing of the Canon of the New Testament against Marcion towards the end of the second century.

Doctrine is not simply the repetition down the centuries of the primitive apostolic *kerygma*. John Henry Newman's *Essay on the Development of Christian Doctrine* sees the Incarnation as the central truth, generating doctrines ruled by principles which allow differences and developments in formulation and content, but never depart from their source and origin. The teaching and deeds of Jesus must be faithfully interpreted in each generation, but with shifts in language and cultural setting this interpretation and articulation changes. A formidably detailed account of how this happens, and the effect on doctrine of such shifts, can be found in Henri de Lubac's exploration of the two words 'mystical' and 'body' in *Corpus Mysticum*.

Revelation *per se* was considered to have come to an end with the death of the last apostle. No one generation or cultural context can lay exclusive or exhaustive claim to the whole truth, however, since the mystery of God is beyond human expression. Since earliest times the church has seen as part of its own task the laying down of the parameters of authentic teaching. Vincent of Lérins' *Commonitorium* set as the characterizing norm 'what has been believed always, everywhere and by all'. This idea remained for later generations the touchstone by which they accepted or rejected doctrinal interpretations. There is irony in the fact that Vincent's original work was written to refute what it saw as the excesses and exaggerations of Augustinian doctrine, while this definition was cited as clinching all arguments during the early modern quarrels about the normative status of Augustine as a doctrinal authority. The patristic era in the West offered very limited access to important and authoritative writings, such as those of the Greek Fathers, or even to exact accounts of the content and significance of councils. In a period of major doctrinal development in the church it proved very difficult for 'what has been believed always, everywhere and by all' to be authenticated.

The study of the history of doctrine offers numerous examples of times when the community's teaching office has exerted itself in response to shifts in circumstance, ideology or articulation. As Christianity spread it came into contact with pagan philosophies and began to express its essential truths in language and concepts derived from sources other than the scriptures. Since the language and thought patterns of the Graeco-Roman world were not always identical to those of the Bible's origins, this gave rise to changes in emphasis that sometimes came to be considered heretical in parts of the community foreign to the context from which they derived. The encounter of Christianity with Platonism and neo-Platonism, Manichaeism and, later, Aristotelianism necessitated the adoption within the Christian community of language and frameworks not native to it.

Doctrine, authority and the great councils

The formulations that articulate the major foundational tenets of Christian doctrine emerged triumphant from the great Ecumenical Councils gathered to settle the controversies of the early centuries. There is no direct historical line from the council of Jerusalem to the later synods and councils of the church, but as awareness of the apostolic succession of the episcopate grew within the church, and as local problems and theological controversies gained wider significance, gatherings of bishops from different communities according to geographical location became more common. Matters for discussion were not always strictly doctrinal, and at the end of the second century the first major debate between different groups of synods was over the date of Easter. It was Constantine, following his unification and Christianization of the Roman Empire, who called and led the Council of Nicaea in 325. His motive in gathering leaders of the churches in both East and West was more about the security of his empire than the doctrinal purity of the church, and doctrine became politically instrumental, endorsed by and, to some extent, subordinate to civil power. Nevertheless, it was at this council that one of the great milestones in the history of the church was initiated, namely the Nicene Creed.

The complexity behind how doctrinal formulations were arrived at can be seen in the case of one of the great formative conflicts of the ancient church, Arianism. Not one single movement deriving from a clearly-recognized leader, it nevertheless takes its name and found its momentum from the conservative theologian of the Alexandrian school, Arius. Arianism offers a powerful example of the interplay of political and social as well as philosophical and theological influences in the development of doctrine.

In theological terms it was an argument about the relationship of Jesus to the Father, whether he is co-eternal and of one substance (*ousia*) with the Godhead. In historical and political terms it underlines the difficulty in formulating doctrine that arose in a community that had spread widely beyond its ethnic origins in a world where communication was slow and uncertain. Before Christianity became the official religion of the Roman Empire it developed independently as a pluralistic community within different commercial and political centres such as Antioch, Alexandria and Rome, whose interpretations and expressions of central teaching differed. The framework of Christian leadership was slow to emerge and by no means clearly and universally recognized. Successive emperors recognized the social and political importance of religious cohesion within the empire, and had a vested interest in the peaceful co-existence of different Christian communities and in the internal unity of the faith itself. They were not beyond forcing the point by dominating the workings of the great councils and promoting their own favoured theological viewpoint. There emerges within Christian writing of the time a need for a generally recognized arbitrator in settling points of doctrine.

The christological and trinitarian understanding of current Western Christianity derives from the doctrinal definitions hammered out in the Councils of Nicaea, Constantinople (381) Ephesus (431) and Chalcedon (451). Not all episcopal sees were represented at them, and participation by the West was always weaker than the East, though as time went on, Rome came to be seen as representing the Western church. The Ecumenical Councils of antiquity came to be seen as embodying the whole church, making clear its faith in the light of apostolic tradition and carrying an authority binding on all churches, whether represented or not.

The addition by the ninth century, in the Latin-speaking Western churches, of the clause *filioque* ('and the Son') to the Nicene-Constantinopolitan Creed's affirmation of belief in the Spirit 'who proceeds from the Father' was a cause of major difficulty to the Greek-speaking churches. Not only did it raise theological problems but in changing a text agreed upon in an ecumenical council it also raised ecclesiological issues. Expressing the idea of a 'double procession' of the Holy Spirit, it reflects the teaching of Augustine, whereas the original agreed text coincides with the expression of doctrine found in the Cappadocian Fathers, for whom there is only one source of being within the Trinity, the Father, from whom both the Son and Spirit derive. Tensions between East and West had other foundations, but were so exacerbated by this controversy that they resulted in permanent schism in 1054. Subsequent doctrinal and ecclesiological roads have crossed little until the twentieth-century revival of interest, in the Western church, in the doctrinal sources and traditions of the East.

While in the Eastern church ultimate authority lay in the five patriarchates, papal representatives to the Council acquired increasing importance and after Leo I successive popes emphasized their authority and juridical primacy with reference to the Petrine succession. From the fifth century onwards the bishop of Rome claimed supreme authority even over the emperor in doctrinal matters. The *pactum Ottonianum* of 962 cemented the relationship between the pope and the German 'Holy Roman Emperors', stipulating that new pontiffs, before their consecration, must take an oath of loyalty to the emperor. This made the papacy dependent on a secular political power, but also had an effect on subsequent councils by joining together the national council and the old Roman synod in a way that foretold the papal general councils of the medieval and modern periods. Gregory VII's *Dictatus Papae* of 1075 first claimed papal power to promulgate laws for the whole church independent of a council and also made naming a council as universal subject to papal approval. In preparing for the fourth Lateran Council of 1215, Innocent III made a considerable point of comparing it with the great councils of the past, seeing the importance of linking doctrine, authority and governance of the church.[4]

The scholastic period – development of the summas

The medieval period saw a shift in gravity from the councils as the *locus* of doctrinal formulation to the schools, where Christian doctrine came to be taught as a body of knowledge. With the expansion of schools in cathedrals and cities into autonomous educational institutions, teaching became a profession governed by official qualifications and the great universities of the thirteenth century were born. Here philosophy, theology and jurisprudence were taught, with theology, the 'queen of sciences', transformed by rational methods of speculation and enquiry. From the end of the patristic era until the early medieval period theological scholarship resided mainly in the monastic schools, consisting principally in faithful transmission of the authentic heritage of the past and the organization of anthologies of original material and commentaries for use by scholars. The sources considered authoritative were the Bible and the fathers, particularly, in the Western church, Augustine, with great emphasis being laid (precariously, in an era of hand copying of texts and often poor linguistic scholarship) on the authenticity of textual tradition. Anselm of Canterbury stands as a pivotal figure in the move towards an emphasis on the rational basis of faith rather than on proof from authority. Combining Christian doctrine, Aristotelian logic and neo-Platonic metaphysics in a dialectical methodology of question and answer, he presupposed that faith could and should seek its roots in reason, thus laying the foundations for Scholasticism.

The rise of urban populations, with an educated ruling and mercantile class, the spread of the mendicant orders and reforms within the church all led towards a major shift in the historical situation which found expression in a new way of dealing with doctrine. The fall of Constantinople in 1204 gave new access to the works of Arabic, Jewish and Greek thinkers, notably Aristotle, in reliable translations, which lent a new logical framework to the previous reliance on neo-Platonism. The theological tradition of the monasteries was intuitional and mystical. That of the schools was fundamentally scientific and rationalistic. Despite many protests within the Christian community Aristotle's philosophy and metaphysics became widely adopted as the key to framing and understanding doctrinal questions. If the Bible was the foundation of all theology and all Christian life, it was argued, it posed the problem of how exactly the word of God is to be construed and understood within its given context. This began as an exercise in linguistic and grammatical interpretation, but the dialectical method of the scholastics led them to question the texts further and organize their questions and answers into a systematic exposition of sacred doctrine.

This system consisted in setting a question, offering a possible answer, posing an objection and then summing up with the definitive answer. This was not a matter of learning by rote, since teachers were required to pose closely-argued *quaestiones* for their students to discuss before they offered an answer, often in the face of the alternative reasons of another teacher in a public *disputatio*.

Arguments and extrapolations from texts were collected as 'sentences' (see Peter Lombard) in collected *Commentaries*, and *quaestiones* came to stand alone in logically-ordered collections called a *summa quaestionum*, the *Summa* of Thomas Aquinas being the most famous. Scholasticism, like any other term (Renaissance, Middle Ages, Dark Ages), which seems to turn a period of history into a neat, self-conscious entity with clearly-defined boundaries, is an identification imposed from without, and does little justice to the disparate realities it attempts to describe. Nevertheless, as a process of doctrinal organization, its strength lies in having provided the first scientific basis for the study and formulation of doctrine. It sought to reconcile reason with revelation, science with faith, and philosophy with theology. Thomas Aquinas solved the setting of any false tension between faith and reason by demonstrating that philosophy and theology, while separate sciences, complement one another. Truths in the natural order cannot contradict those in the supernatural order, since they find their source in the same God, who is truth. Scholasticism carried within it, however, the seeds of its own degeneration. An increasing trend towards those philosophical schools of thought and method known as nominalism and empiricism led to an exacerbation rather than a solution to theological tensions and revealed weaknesses in the hermeneutical and speculative methods of scholastic theology that could only be resolved by the methods and knowledge of later periods, notably the study of historiography and the historicity of revelation.

The Protestant Reformation: scripture and tradition

The voice of mysticism, represented by the likes of Anselm and Bernard, had already been raised in protest against excessive rationalism in the development of doctrine. Arising at the same time as access to literature through the advent of the printing press and at a particularly acute crisis in the church's structures of authority, the *Devotio Moderna* of the fourteenth and fifteenth centuries represented a further counter-movement to the futile subtleties and speculations into which it felt theology had fallen. Appealing to a supposed simplicity of original Christian faith and doctrine, it called above all for the holiness of the interior life, renewal and reform among the church's leaders, and an insistence that knowledge of God lay open to learned and unlearned alike. 'Humanism' describes another highly disparate movement whose principal thrust in Northern Europe was reliance on authentic classical sources for developing the written and spoken word. The 'new learning' associated with it gave fresh access to the languages of the Bible and the fathers, exploring the philological sources of the Greek New Testament without reliance on glosses and interpretations. This led to increasing dissatisfaction with the Latin Vulgate and its theological revision, which inspired many doctrinal debates once new translations, and therefore the meanings of key texts, came into the common sphere. Together with this came an impetus towards the revival and renewal of the Christian church, based on a return *ad fontes*, to the original foundational texts on which the church's beliefs and life are based. This had a particular impact on the understanding of Augustine's theological writings. The return to sources was particularly the thrust of humanist learning in France, where John Calvin learned to apply the philological principles of historical and linguistic contextualization to the study of the Bible.

In the person of Erasmus the 'new learning' led to serious questioning of the church's doctrinal and institutional sources of authority. His *Enchiridion* (1503) proved the fulcrum for one of the major paradigm shifts in ecclesiological thinking. In it he urged church reform through a return to biblical and patristic sources by all the faithful so that their faith, lived through interior conversion, could be transformative at individual and collective levels. This emphasis on 'inner religion' was understood by educated lay people as releasing them from reliance on priests and priestly ministry, and laid the foundations for Protestant lay-centred theologies and spiritualities, although Erasmus remained a Catholic all his life.

While the background to the rise of Protestantism is as socially, politically and ideologically conditioned as that of the early church councils, its doctrinal roots, represented by the theologies of Luther, Calvin and Zwingli and their successors and interpreters, lie in a desire to return to a pure and primitive faith governed by the tenets:

solus Christus: Christ is the only mediator between God and humanity. With this comes the notion of the priesthood of all believers, and thus a departure (in varying degrees) from the Catholic understanding of sacraments and ministerial priesthood and emphasis on the role of the Virgin Mary and the saints.

sola scriptura: this places the Bible as the sole source of Christian doctrine, the inspired and authoritative Word of God, accessible to all without need for interpretation outside itself. This does away with the Catholic understanding of the need for authoritative interpretation through the apostolic tradition mediated through the church's teaching *magisterium* and the Councils.

sola gratia: salvation comes from the unearned gift of God's grace, and through no human merit or co-operation. While Luther held that this in no way contradicted the notion of universal grace, by which God wills the salvation of all, later Protestant theologies moved towards more radical positions.

soli Deo Gloria: since it is only by God's will and action that human salvation is brought about, and both Christ's saving work on the cross and the faith to believe in it are free gifts, then glory belongs to God alone and to no other person.

sola fide: sees justification, or being made righteous with God, as being received by grace through faith alone. This imputes the merits of Christ's sinlessness to sinners.

Protestant Reformation doctrine included a rejection of much of Scholasticism. If salvation is through God's free, gratuitous act alone, and God is wholly other, then attempts by human reasoning to fathom the mystery of God's saving plan are vain. The theological renaissance of the Middle Ages saw an increasingly strong understanding of the role and importance of the church in the economy of salvation. It was in the scholastic period that sacramental theology developed into a much more sharply-defined and theoretically fluent science, reaching agreement on the nature, number and identity of the sacraments. This accompanied a higher profile for the clergy and an increased church presence in society, which in its turn provoked (not always successfully) a call for higher educational standards among the clergy. A renewed understanding of the role of a more educated laity and widespread lay access to biblical and patristic texts led to questions about the role and function of priestly and sacramental structures. Written over a prolonged period of struggle with Donatists and Pelagians, Augustine's doctrines of grace and justification are not without their internal contradictions.[5] The flowering of Augustinian scholarship also opened up new debates in this area.

There is no one, homogenous Protestant Reformation, since the churches that emerged under the influence of Luther, Zwingli, Calvin and the Anabaptists differ markedly.[6] The second generation of Protestant reformers found themselves having to develop a coherent doctrine of the church which would justify the break with Rome. Luther spoke of justification by faith as the 'doctrine by which the church stands or falls'. For him the authentic preaching of the word in the tradition of the apostles, not an episcopally ordained ministry derived from them, is what constitutes the visible church. His insistence on the need for a visible, institutional church led to some confusion in the face of Catholic claims on the one hand and radical Protestant abandonment of the outer forms of church structure on the other.

The Colloquy of Regensburg (Ratisbon) of 1541 failed in its attempt to bring Catholics and Protestants to a compromise that would accomplish reunion. If the identifying 'marks' of the church are that it should be one, holy, catholic and apostolic, then, ran the Protestant argument, the Catholic church had forfeited that identification through its departure from apostolic doctrines, discipline, holiness and forms of governance. The Protestants could lay no such claim, ran Catholic arguments, because they were schismatics, cut off from the main body of the church in a way that Augustine himself had condemned in his own day. Calvin claimed scriptural origin for a divinely ordained ministerial government within the church and conceived of the church as being simultaneously visible, in the community of believers, including within it both good and evil, and invisible, in the fellowship of the elect, known only to God, which will be made manifest at the final judgement. Calvin affirmed that salvation takes place within human history through the Incarnation, in the context of an institution ordained by God, whose marks are pure preaching of the Word and right sacramental administration. In this he aligned himself with the patristic notion, promulgated by the Fourth Lateran Council, that outside the church there is no salvation. This distances him from the radical reformed (Anabaptist) view that the apostolic church, in all its structures, was itself corrupted by its links with the state, so that total separation from secular society was the only possible remedy. This is articulated in the Schleitheim Confession (1527), which justifies a stance of isolation from secular affairs that lies at the heart of Christian pacifism and the origin of such groups and movements as Quakerism and the Amish and Mennonite communities.

The Catholic Reformation: authority, governance and integrity of doctrine

Too late to prevent the dissolving of the church into separate communions, the Catholic Reformation came principally through the Council of Trent, called as a response to the challenge posed by Protestantism for the Catholic Church to reform itself radically from within. The only other book on the altar during the council, apart from the Bible, was

Thomas Aquinas's *Summa*. The council sought to answer some of Protestantism's doctrinal foundations, especially that of justification, defending from Augustine the notion that justification bestows sanctifying grace on human beings, renewing and transforming sinful nature so that it becomes capable of sharing the life of God. The council failed to settle debates between Catholic and Protestant positions on grace and salvation, but stands as a major turning-point in Catholicism's internal organization, having a huge impact on the liturgical and spiritual life of the church, the formation of the clergy, the pastoral role of bishops, sacramental practice, missionary activity and ecclesiastical discipline. The reform of religious life and the establishment of new orders, especially the Jesuits, and (much more slowly) apostolic congregations of women, led to spiritualities of greater active engagement in the church's life and mission by lay people.

Trent also systematized the structures of doctrinal discipline within the church. In 1542 a final and universal court of appeal in heresy trials was set up in Rome whose purpose was to 'maintain and defend the integrity of the faith' and to condemn all false doctrines. Among its many tasks was the keeping and publicizing of an Index of Forbidden Books, whose contents were deemed a danger to the faith and morals of the church. Renamed the Congregation for the Doctrine of the Faith in 1983, this body, under the leadership of Cardinal Joseph Ratzinger, subsequently Pope Benedict XVI, has monitored the writing and teaching of prominent Catholics and played a controversial role in recent decades in the censoring, among others, of Leonardo Boff (liberation theology), Tissa Balasuriya (Mary and the saving work of Christ), Jacques Dupuis (Christian theology and religious pluralism), Sister Jeanine Grammick (pastoral care of the homosexual community) and Charles Curran (moral theology) among others.[7]

The early modern period saw the flowering of systematic study of scripture, patristics and the history of theology extend within the Catholic Church, especially in what came to be known as Jansenist circles in Louvain and the monastery of Port-Royal outside Paris. Similar in scope and purpose to what became known in the twentieth century as *ressourcement*, which led the church to open itself out to currents of thought and practice in the modern world through the Second Vatican Council, in the Jansenist era it led to one of the gravest crises in authority experienced within Catholicism, and to a measure of closure to 'external' sources of thought which was to last for some three hundred years, reaching a peak in the Modernist crisis of the early twentieth century.

The quarrel about interpretation of historical sources revealed a deeper crisis about governance and jurisdiction and how succeeding generations find a balance between fidelity to Christian origins and a response to the conditions of contemporary society. It highlighted the role of history in doctrinal and ecclesiological development, and who within the church has the authority to pronounce definitively on doctrinal matters. Championing Augustine and the pastoral practices of the early church as bindingly normative, the Jansenists argued that the church as a body founded by Christ 'is the same today as it was sixteen hundred years ago . . . and will be the same at the end of the world' (Arnauld). It became clear that what was in fact at stake was the relationship between tradition and the *magisterium*.[8]

During the Protestant Reformation the rulers of those countries which adopted the Reformed religion claimed governorship over the church within their dominion. From this derived various theories about the proper governance of the church and the balance of power between church and state. In France the Four Gallican Articles of 1682 confronted papal claims to ultimate authority with a 'tradition of the church' established by historical criticism and the example of the African church under Cyprian and Augustine, in which bishops and councils decided on matters of faith on an equal footing with Rome. This notion of episcopal autonomy and conciliar governance finds echoes in the Vatican II Dogmatic Constitution *Lumen Gentium*.

The twentieth century and beyond

If the First Vatican Council is chiefly remembered for its promulgation of the doctrine of the infallibility of the pope, the Second Vatican Council stands out as a watershed in the understanding of what it means to be the church. The *ressourcement* movement of French *nouvelle théologie* of the 1940s and 50s and the work of theologians such as Yves Congar and Henri de Lubac drew attention back to the biblical and patristic sources of Christian doctrine but, unlike the earlier similar impetus in Jansenism, this led to a more radical engagement with the social, political and philosophical issues of contemporary society. The constitutions *Lumen Gentium* and *Gaudium et Spes* offer a new look at the character and mission of the church in modern times. In *Lumen Gentium* a sacramental ecclesiology is posited, whereby the church exists primarily in order to make God's saving will and Christ's abiding presence manifest to the world in a concrete form in space and time.[9]

The German theologian Karl Rahner emphasized this dynamic, sacramental mission over the claims of historical structures. Unlike the beleaguered tone of Vatican I, held at a time of political crisis for the church, *Gaudium et Spes* emphasizes the dignity of the human person and the worth of human endeavours and culture. It sets high store by the proper role of the laity within their own social, economic, political and personal tasks, encouraging the people of God to embrace the world and engage with all that promotes the wellbeing of humanity and within which the saving plan of God can be seen at work. The post-Tridentine church thought of itself primarily in institutionalist terms, as a society run along hierarchical lines with clear distinction between clergy and laity. The Second Vatican Council looked to the Bible to find an imagery that would counter the marginalization of the laity, describing the church as communion, the biblical theme of *koinonia*, in which the charismatic gifts of the Spirit are manifest, and as people of God, an extension of the kingdom of God continuous with Israel, not in rejection of it. Of major importance also is the Declaration on Non-Christian Religions, *Nostra Aetate*, which opened the church out to ecumenical and interfaith dialogue. The wording of *Lumen Gentium*'s claim that the one, holy, catholic and apostolic church 'subsists in' the Catholic Church is followed by a declaration that 'many elements of sanctification and of truth are found outside its visible confines', thus allowing for greater recognition of the authentic Christian provenance of other communities. *Nostra Aetate* constitutes a still bolder step, stressing particularly the bonds that unite the Abrahamic peoples and the unity among all people of faith in seeking the truth and understanding of God. The twentieth century saw the establishment of the ecumenical movement which, through initiatives such as the World Council of Churches, has made considerable steps towards the reconciliation of entrenched sectarian positions and produced levels of doctrinal consensus (see the Lima Document on *Baptism, Eucharist and Ministry*) previously unthinkable.

Modern forms of Protestant ecclesiology have a more strongly kerygmatic theme, laying emphasis on the church as event rather than institution. This is found principally in the theology of Karl Barth, who taught that in the church the work of the Holy Spirit takes place, uniting it with Christ's saving work and authorizing its proclamation of Christ to the world. A major shift in twentieth-century doctrine and ecclesiology has seen the renewal of interest in Orthodox theology in the West, principally through its emphasis on pneumatology found in the work of John Zizioulas. For him the church is constituted by the Spirit, who is its very essence. This emphasis on the role of the Spirit is also found in liberation theology.[10] The Brazilian Leonardo Boff criticizes the traditional institutional understanding of the church in *Ecclesiogenesis* and *Church, Charism and Power*. He presents it rather as primarily a 'sacrament of the Holy Spirit' with 'charism as the organizing principle', beyond any specific structure. Its function is to proclaim eschatological liberation from all that enslaves human beings within unjust social, political and economic structures.[11] This emphasis on the centrality of the Spirit's role led to fears that Boff was weakening the validity of ecclesial structures and to his 'silencing' by his former doctoral co-supervisor, Joseph Ratzinger.

As a development of liberation theology, feminist theology also critiques the structures of the church and the fundamentally androcentric orientation of its doctrinal expressions. Post-Christian feminists like Mary Daly and Daphne Hampson consider the situation irredeemable, so far back in the concept of God does mysogyny go, while others urge the recovery of 'Goddess' traditions or of Mary Magdalen as the paradigm for ecclesial leadership rather than Peter. Elizabeth Schussler-Fiorenza (*Discipleship of Equals: a Critical Feminist Ekklesialogy of Liberation*) opposes the theological silencing and exclusion of women in the church. She argues that foundational to the church is Jesus's establishment of a discipleship of equals, which should be reflected in the church's present structures and in its acknowledgment of the 'dangerous memory' of 'women's religious agency as prophets, teachers and wise women'. Rosemary Radford Ruether (*Sexism and God-Talk*) suggests that much of Christianity's sexism is rooted in its christology, making Christ's maleness the theological foundation for the belief that only a male person may image God or represent Christ in the ministerial priesthood. Twentieth-century feminist theologies argue that, while any attribution of gender to God is a reversion to pagan categories, the maleness of Jesus is a contingent, not an essential, aspect of his identity and thus cannot dominate our understanding of the criteria for priesthood.[12] This understanding has underpinned the ordination of women to the priesthood and episcopacy in a number of Christian churches, though the Orthodox and Catholic churches persist in their arguments and practice to the contrary.

Like the epochal shift of medieval Scholasticism, in its incorporation into theological language of the categories and methods of pagan philosophy, liberation theologies have made use of the social sciences as tools for analysis, with much the same reaction to it in more theologically traditional quarters. In its turn postmodernism has taken earlier stress on the need for contextualization in the interpretation of a given text or idea and sharpened it into an understanding of the overarching 'situatedness' of any human mode of expression. The signifying, not the signified, is the dominant element in seeking the value of any given communication, so that notions of an overarching metanarrative, or of a definitive meaning of a text are unacceptable. Truth and meaning are polyvalent, and all interpretations are equally valid or invalid. Thus no sense of a system of theology, or of an ecclesial structure authoritatively built on such a system, can have coherence. What it might mean, from such a perspective, for the church to identify itself as one, holy, catholic and apostolic remains to be explored.

Notes

1 See Chapters 4, 5, 9, 10, 11 and 13 of this volume for the various different perspectives on these developments and debates.
2 Cf. Chapters 38 and 23 of this volume, respectively (and also Chapter 17 with regard to the latter).
3 Cf. also the preceding Chapter 33 of this volume.
4 On authority, see also Chapter 27 of this volume.
5 Cf. Chapter 2 of this volume.
6 Again, cf. Chapters 4, 5, 9, 10, 11 and 12 for discussion of the Protestant and Anglican traditions in greater detail.
7 Cf. Chapter 29 of this volume.
8 On the Jansenists, see also Chapter 5 of this volume.
9 Cf. also Chapters 7 and 13.
10 Cf. Chapter 8.
11 Cf. Chapter 23.
12 Cf. Chapter 25.

35

ECCLESIOLOGY AND ETHICS IN THE WESTERN CHURCH

Lewis S. Mudge

When, how, and with what consequences have moral formation and ethical reflection been considered as intrinsic to the church's being and identity? This question, however expressed, is very much a product of the modern and postmodern worlds of the West. Moral and ethical pluralism reign today in public space. Seldom before has the human question 'How shall we live?' been subject to so many conflicting, and possibly incommensurable, answers. Seldom before has the community of faith felt so clearly called upon to generate an ethic peculiar to itself. This is the case whether one looks to the right (evangelical campaigns against abortion, gay marriage and other issues) or to the left (liberation theology and its successor movements in the interests of global justice and peace).

An adequate analysis must begin with the notion of church as a morally formative community perduring through the ages. Moral formation occurs in the family, in the congregation, in pastoral teaching and preaching, in the shaping power of the liturgy, in magisterial pronouncements of whatever form or authority. Such formation gives context and vocabulary to each believer's struggle for confidence before God. It undergirds the church's efforts to stand for something meaningful to humanity. *Ecclesia* and moral nurture have belonged together from the beginning.

Yet the moral integrity of the faith community through time has constantly been subject to internal controversies and external challenges. Such debates and encounters naturally give rise to reflection, some of which eventually generates fields of academic inquiry such as 'ecclesiology' and 'ethics'. Such inquiries often tend to go their own separate ways and to spawn diverse, competing methods and points of view. We then have different sorts of ecclesiology, different schools of ethical inquiry.

What, then, *is* the appropriate relationship between morality (i.e. mores, lived values, embedded virtues) and the church's fundamental self-understanding? What sorts of ethical reflection (i.e. analyses of the persuasiveness of moral arguments) belong intrinsically to the *ecclesia* of God? These relationships, as the history of this subject shows, may be expressed in many ways and in diverse terminologies. But we can discern that the single, deeply embedded, root question of moral integrity before God in relation to the church's fundamental being has led to different developments in different circumstances, recognizable as precursors to elements in today's ecclesiological and ethical debates.

There seem historically to have been four broad ways of wrestling with such issues: (1) in terms of theological categories and formulas (e.g. Augustine's distinction between the 'invisible' and 'visible' church); (2) in juridical or magisterial terms (e.g. bishops teach certain moral precepts or ethical perspectives); (3) in polemic terms that try to simplify and draw distinctions (e.g. talk about the 'marks' or 'notes' of the true, as opposed to the false, church); and (4) in pragmatic terms (e.g. faith communities find their identity in what they stand for and what they do).

But it will not do to see such categories as having analytic power (like Troeltsch's 'church type,' 'sect type' and 'mystical type') or as constituting a spectrum of ingeniously labelled interlocking possibilities (like H. Richard Niebuhr's notion of five possible relationships between 'Christ and culture'). Each of the modes mentioned above has its own practical and intellectual history. They often come mixed with one another in particular ways in specific situations. It is best in each case to describe each situation for what it is, in the language of its leading figure, without assuming that such instances taken together can be neatly conceptualized in univocal terms. These different modes of action and thought do, of course, participate in what Alasdair MacIntyre calls the 'extended argument'[1] of Christian tradition down the centuries. The terminologies concerned are recognizable to us across chasms of cultural and conceptual difference – and would likewise have been to the historical actors concerned – as arising in the same broad problematic of the ongoing life of the church as morally formative community.

Probing the extended argument: the first nineteen centuries

For practical purposes, this essay must be confined to terminologies and arguments belonging to the history of the Western church. Developments in the East were different and would require another essay entirely. Moreover, for reasons of limited space, much must be treated too briefly or left out altogether. The following touches only on the principal figures, episodes and circumstances.

The pre-Augustinian world

Ethics often relates to ecclesiology in the New Testament with regard to the new community's relation to Jewish practice. Whether Jesus the moral teacher, fulfiller of Torah and non-violent revolutionary, saw something like a 'church' as continuation of his ministry is moot. Luke in the Acts describes a community marked by communal practices, with qualities that serve as primitive marks: apostolic teaching and fellowship, the breaking of bread and the prayers (Acts 2.42). The community also demands a rigorous economic ethic. Ananias and Sapphira deviate from communal norms, are confronted and drop dead at the Apostles' feet (Acts 4.32–5.11). Paul offers an account of *ecclesia* as 'body of Christ' and clearly sees certain virtues as characteristic of it: love, joy, peace and the like (Eph 4.17ff). Challenged over his inclusion of Gentiles in the *ecclesia*, he agrees in Acts 15 to minimal behavioural standards: to 'abstain from what has been sacrificed to idols and from blood an from what has been strangled and from fornication.' (Acts 15.29). The Pastoral Epistles are preoccupied with issues of moral formation in the early congregations. Ephesians (5.21ff), Colossians (3.18ff) and 1 Peter (3.1ff) give the congregations similar sets of 'house rules'. It would seem that the New Testament church is predominantly an *ecclesia* of distinctive moral practices, accompanied by theological commentary on justification (Paul) and on Christ's sufferings as example (Hebrews). The early church is seen by others as an unusual, stubborn, and sometimes admirable, religio-moral community.

Tertullian (c. 160–220) bears witness to this perception by quoting pagans as saying 'See how they love one another.' Indeed, after New Testament times the ethics of *ecclesia* relates less to Jewish and more in contrast to Roman behavioural expectations. In Tertullian one finds what would today be termed a thoroughly sectarian ecclesiology, combined with an absolutist, pacifist, millennarian communal ethic that commands separation from the ways of the world. Over against Roman political society, the church stands for an alternative way of ordering life. Here a certain ethic is already close to being a mark of the church's being, even if not articulated as such. By contrast, in the work of Eusebius of Caesarea (c. 264–340) one finds an ecclesiology, with ethic to match, suitable for the then-new relationship between church and empire. Christianity is already taking over the role of a civil religion, sacralizing power, legitimating the existing order of things and inculcating reverence for authorities. Christianity and the Roman Empire are God's two greatest blessings to humankind. The ethics that goes with this ecclesiology is an ethic of public citizenship.

Still, there has not as yet emerged any authoritative ecclesiology, any doctrinal definition of the church's nature as such. 'The church' was not yet what was later called a theological *locus*, a topic of doctrinal reflection. Cyprian's creed (c. 250) named the church, not as an object of belief in itself, but only as the community 'through' which we believe in the forgiveness of sins and eternal life. The earliest versions of the Nicene and Apostles' creeds made no mention of the 'holy catholic church' as such at all. That reference is added in the Constantinopolitan supplement of 381 to the Creed of the Council of Nicaea of 325, which had been produced under Constantine's auspices. Now the church was not only to be 'believed' as a reliable witness to the truth, but 'believed in', a significant further step. 'We believe in one holy, catholic and apostolic church': with these words there emerged for the first time what came to be called the four 'marks' of the church, later prominent in Catholic attempts to counter Orthodox and Protestant claims. One, holy, catholic, apostolic: these words imply ethics as well as the church's intrinsic nature. We believe the church, i.e. we believe the church's teaching including moral teaching. We believe *in* the church: that gives rise to ecclesiology.

It is plain by now that the Christian community's emerging structure rested substantially upon the theory and practice of episcopacy. The ecclesial-ethical significance of episcopacy had already been clearly expressed in the letters of Cyprian, third-century Bishop of Carthage, who held that the bishop was necessary to the very being (*esse*) of the church, not merely to its well-being (*bene esse*): 'The church is in the bishop, and the bishop in the church.' Bishops were successors to the apostles and so to the *teaching* function of apostles. Hence the beginnings of the juridical, magisterial connection between *ecclesia* and its moral/ ethical being.

Augustine

A full theological-ethical reflection on the church's nature was to come only in the work of Augustine of Hippo (353–430). This bishop and saint came to believe deeply in the Catholic church as a visible, world-wide institution continuous with the church of the apostles. Augustine could say that he believed in the gospel only on the authority of this church, this ongoing, life-forming, sin-forgiving communion.[2]

This, after all, is the community that finally addresses the moral agonies of Augustine's youth. He comes to the gospel after a long struggle for inner moral integrity that had led him, to no avail, through several dualist and rigorist cults. He would not be a Christian were the church as community of moral formation not for him an answer to his quest, precisely by being sensitive to moral dialectics of the sort he knew so well. Interpreting scripture in the light of this experience, he does much to formulate the doctrine of original sin in which fallen human beings are 'unable not to sin' (*non posse non peccare*). The gospel frees us from this dilemma, and hence from moral rigorism and self-flagellation, to a deeper ethic founded in forgiveness and grace. This conviction carries over to Augustine's voluminous writings and to his ministry as bishop.

When, for example, the Donatists press for an unforgiving church of moral rigour and purity, declaring such standards necessary for ecclesial authenticity, Augustine has an answer: the sinner, even the apostate, may ask forgiveness and be restored to communion. The validity of sacrament and preaching is not dependent on the moral purity of the one who performs these offices. Ordination, baptism, absolution and other acts of the church depend not on moral considerations but on the church's objective being and authority as expressed in these sacramental acts. (Here was an anticipation of Council of Trent's declaration that, in the sacraments, grace is conferred *ex opere operato*, 'by the act performed'.)

When the Pelagians assert that salvation is to be earned by doing good works, Augustine replies with his doctrine of grace. It follows that the church's morally formative function is a consequence of grace, not a purely human, or even a divinely aided, effort to make church members (and hence the Body itself) worthy of salvation.

Augustine sums up the world-historical consequences of these convictions with other striking insights in his treatise *The City of God*. Here the church on earth makes present the promise of the fulfilled holy city to come. The true membership of that city, the bishop taught, consists of God's chosen and predestined ones, and is in principle invisible. The church on earth visibly represents the heavenly city, although not all church members are actually citizens of the holy commonwealth, for not all belong to the company of the elect. The earthly church is therefore a *corpus permixtum*, a mixed body of the elect and the non-elect, and likewise of sinners and saints. Elect persons may belong in either of the latter categories. This is a further reason for receiving back the lapsed, for only God knows whom God has chosen. The earthly church's sacraments are nevertheless necessary for salvation. In principle, Augustine agreed with Origen, Cyprian and the very similar language of the Athanasian Creed: *extra ecclesiam nulla salus*, 'no salvation [occurs] outside the church'.

Ethics and ecclesiology thus meet not only in Augustine's thought but in his episcopal role. He is a teacher of moral precepts and also a giver of absolution to those who confess their sins. But in his person he is an embodiment of the historic continuity of the Catholic church, which does not owe its being to the virtues exhibited by its pastors and members, but rather to the gospel taught by the apostles and their successors. Yet in no way does Augustine see either moral formation or ethical interpretation as in themselves foundations for, or 'marks' of, the church's being. Rather, such formation and interpretation properly go on within the church, where the gospel becomes the context for both and the bishop brings the gospel to bear on challenges such as those of Donatism and Pelagianism. For Augustine, the relations between ecclesiology and ethics include elements of all four categories mentioned above: theological, juridical, polemic and practical.

This is one of the many reasons why Augustine's work is so foundational for all that follows in the Western church. Further developments can often be analysed in terms of the relation they bear to his life, work and thought. The version of Augustinianism that dominated the church virtually unchallenged until the Reformation was drafted by the Synod of Orange (529 CE) This gathering affirmed original sin in the sense that humanity has lost all intrinsic power to turn to God. It is not that some are predestined to evil ways; Adam's sin has not left us totally depraved. But free will is weakened by sin, so that no one can love God as he/she ought apart from the effective presence of divine mercy. Turning to God is made possible by grace alone. Our wills cannot experience even a desire to believe or a beginning of faith apart from grace actually at work in us. Yet this grace is not irresistible. Human sinfulness can frustrate God's intent.

God's power to enable us to do the good thus functions only through the sacraments, and therefore through the priestly authority of the church. Baptism is essential for the remission of sins. Baptism enables those who receive it, by the aid and support of Christ, to perform 'those things which belong to the salvation of the soul'. Here is the ecclesially founded semi-Augustinianism that pervaded Latin Christianity for a thousand years and more. In this scheme, ecclesiology and ethics are linked both theologically and juridically, with practical consequences for the laity.

Monasticism

Some believers soon felt that they needed a sterner, more explicit moral-sacramental formation. Holding the semi-Augustinian assumptions of their time, they yearned for a more robustly formational community. The result was the notion of monastic 'rule' for life and conduct, mostly lived within a new kind of ecclesial institution: the monastery. Common life, work and devotion, shaped by the 'rule', provided a rigorous, sometimes ascetic, formation containing many elements, among them certainly an expectation of growth in the virtues, natural and theological. The monastery, in short, provided an intensive context for each member's project of invoking God's promised help in Jesus Christ toward overcoming original sin and living out 'those things which belong to the salvation of the soul'. Here was the chance to 'work out [one's] salvation with fear and trembling'.

No particular monastic venture, of course, exactly matched this generic description. Each of them – from the Benedictines to the Franciscans, Dominicans, Augustinians, Jesuits and onward – had its own objectives and characteristics. But in every case we see a disciplined ethic, a life of carefully considered and elaborated principle, a shared devotional and practical existence that came close to being the lived substance of this expression of *ecclesia*. The theological, juridical and practical elements of this kind of churchly community within the larger church are plain to see.

These Roman Catholic orders also became home to the efforts of cloistered intellectuals to think ethically about moral questions. With the rediscovery of classical philosophy, in particular the use of Aristotle by St Thomas Aquinas, came developments subsequently called 'natural law' theories, elaborations of the notion of the law written on our hearts as human beings, the hierarchy of virtues from natural to theological corresponding to the 'great chain of being'. This work joined similar efforts by Catholics in the newly founded universities: Bologna, Salamanca, Paris and others among them. Moral reasoning, or ethics, here began to distance itself from immediate churchly supervision. Yet it is still theory arising out of the experience of primordial Christian formation. The tradition of Catholic moral teaching continues to the present day, a prolonged or extended field of argument in itself.

Luther

Martin Luther (1483–1546) was an Augustinian twice over: first as an Augustinian monk and then as a theologian reflecting Augustine's thought outside the cloister. Luther's personal struggle also resembled Augustine's, with the difference that he underwent it inside an ecclesial community of intense moral-devotional-liturgical formation. The challenge was that this ecclesial-monastic formation was not giving him what he needed in order to stand before God with integrity and inner assurance. His moral turmoil was resolved by Paul's word, 'the just shall life by faith', in short the foundation for a new sort of ethic for which Luther must next discover or help fashion the appropriate *ecclesia*.

The morals of church leaders beyond the monastery appalled him: indulgences, simony, graft. The church as moral community was subject to a 'Babylonian Captivity'. Moral teaching within the body was nearly reduced to a matter of accumulating merit. Indulgences sold on the basis of this understanding produced major profits. Could this situation be reformed within the existing church structure, or did Luther eventually have to think out an alternative ecclesiology in whose terms moral formation can take place in accord with the gospel of justification? Political events greatly complicated Luther's project, but he came to the conclusion that the church could make do with any polity – these things are *adiaphora*: they make no difference – so long as the gospel was rightly (*recte*) preached and the sacraments rightly administered. Thus it was permissible for the secular nobility in the German Länder to control the appointment of bishops, and so forth.

Luther spoke of the 'two kingdoms', symbolized by the two 'hands' of God, right and left. The right hand of God has to do with the grace in which, by faith, we have our salvation. Salvation takes place for people in the realm of the church. Bringing human beings to God's throne of grace is the church's business. God's left hand, by contrast, represents God's providential care for the public realm, where law is an instrument of God's judgement. Here the conditions of salvation do not operate. The work of grace has nothing directly to do with those public matters reserved to the state. Rather, expertise in matters of government is the criterion of service. Luther is noted for having spoken to the effect that he would rather be ruled by an intelligent Turk (i.e. Muslim) than by an incompetent Christian. It is not that public matters are outside God's concern. It is just that God deals with these matters differently from the way God brings human beings to saving grace. Luther's justification-based ethic does not permit him to devise an adequate gospel-based ethic for the public world.

It appears that there was a conflict in the Reformer's ecclesiological and ethical reflections between what his place in history made possible and what he really would have wanted. Luther's doctrine of the 'two kingdoms' permitted him to propose a morally evangelical, but not perfectionist, ecclesiology in contrast to a morally realistic view of the world. This would logically have led to a 'gathered church' ecclesiology in some form, a voluntary community with an ethic based on justification by faith alone, not one prone to the moral rigorism and occasionally violent politics of the sects on the Reformation's 'left wing'. There is indeed evidence that if he had had his way, Luther would have preferred an *ecclesia* consisting of linked communities of forgiven sinners to a church, however *adiaphora* the question of its structures, lodged within the administrative organs of the German Länder.

Calvin

A generation later, John Calvin (1509–64), already the author of the first, comparatively brief, edition of the *Institutes,* found himself summoned to the newly independent city-state of Geneva as a theological mentor in that community's effort to become an independent Christian community on Reformation principles. Calvin was therefore preoccupied with the organization of a community that gathered at one moment as church and at another as civic commonwealth. Calvin's ecclesiology and his statecraft therefore interpenetrate. He demanded a high degree of moral rectitude both among office-holders and citizens. The state was to uphold pure doctrine and the church's temporal interests. Yet church and state were not to be confused or to interfere with one another. Moral order was to be important in both settings. What sort of ecclesiology and what sort of ethics would emerge in response to this complex challenge?

Although the church was to lead in this holy commonwealth by teaching and example, it is not defined by Calvin as a moral community. Rather it subsists wherever the Word is duly preached and the sacraments duly administered. These are Calvin's 'marks' or 'notes' of ecclesial authenticity. They have a partially polemic intent: to argue against Rome and various secular authorities for the authenticity of his ecclesial experiment in Geneva. Yet how, in organizational terms, Word and Sacrament are guaranteed to be 'rightly administered' is less important to Calvin. He is, furthermore, unwilling to lay upon others the specific ecclesial and moral provisions that Geneva has found suitable for regulating its own Christian life. The element of church discipline, however important, does not appear in Calvin as a 'mark' or 'note', as it does later in the Scots Confession and, by implication, in the Second Helvetic Confession and Heidelberg Catechism.

In all this Calvin follows Augustine. The church on earth is not constituted by the virtue of its members and ministers. Rather, it is a *corpus permixtum* that points through word and sacrament to the saving work of God in Jesus Christ and to the invisible community of the elected saints. There is no hint of either Pelagian or Donatist heresy that would make moral rectitude constitutive as such of the church's being.

While he extends, even radicalizes, Augustine's doctrine that the saints of God are elected before the foundations of the world, Calvin does not see the visible and invisible churches as two different realms. Visibility and invisibility are better seen as two ways of speaking about the one church. It is both a mixed, flawed, gathering of human beings on earth *and* a community characterized by the presence in it of God's elect saints. One cannot in principle know who belongs to which category, even though the church's teaching and worship have elements in them that foster the kinds of assurance and 'confidence' in the gospel that Calvin himself claimed.

How, then, are Calvin's ethics related to this ecclesiology? It is common to contrast Calvin's position with Luther's doctrine of the 'two kingdoms'. Calvin's vision is subtly yet importantly different. The life of the community as civic commonwealth is not simply a matter of secular expertise overseen by God's providence. Grace is present and at work in the community understood as 'world', not merely in the same community understood as 'church'. It is at work particularly in the worldly vocations of believers. The foundations of this conviction are everywhere, in many different forms, in the *Institutes*. Two formulations deserve mention: the so-called 'third use of the law', and the priority Calvin gives to sanctification, even before expounding the doctrine of justification.

One of Calvin's innovations (although he may have been following a similar, though differently stated, formulation in Aquinas) was to understand the Law (or Torah) as having three, rather than Luther's two, 'uses'. Law regulates not only private conduct. It is also the basis of public order, and hence an indispensable element in a Christian social ethic. By 'law', Calvin undoubtedly meant first the Torah, but also the whole medieval tradition of civil law, thought to be compatible with Torah but also based on 'natural law' principles, in which he was trained at the University of Paris. Not only does the law serve as the foundation for public order, restraining the potential sinner, and convict us of our inadequacy, thus rendering us open to grace, but it also serves as a guide to conduct for the redeemed sinner. The redeemed person finds a new relationship to the law. By grace he or she is rendered more able to keep the law because the law no longer stands over against him or her as an impossible demand. This means, quite simply, that the gospel is relevant to the standards that regulate the public world. The gospel, as Luther also believed but with a different emphasis, becomes directly relevant to the practice of public virtue.

A similar dynamic is at work in the sometimes overlooked fact that in the *Institutes*, Book III, the exposition of the Spirit's work in calling us to faith, regeneration and the Christian life – all that falls under the heading of 'sanctification' – precedes the treatment of 'justification'. Luther, of course, has it the other way around. Calvin believes that the work of Christ's death and resurrection, applied to our lives by the power of the Holy Spirit, is such to start us on the road to becoming better persons up to the point at which we gain the gift of realization that we could not be better persons if God had not already accepted us through justification by grace alone.[3] This is the 'mode of becoming which true piety induces'. It includes 'love of righteousness' and other public virtues. 'We are not our own' but our way of life makes a difference to the world.[4]

The upshot is that, for Calvin, grace is indirectly at work in making possible good conduct, even citizenship. It has to do with how we live. And since our living is inevitably social, it has to do with citizenship, and with the lives of public magistrates whose responsibility it is to maintain a body politic in which our citizenship is worked out. Calvin says that 'Civil authority is a calling, not only holy and lawful before God, but also the most sacred and by far the most honourable of all callings in the life of moral men.' Magistrates are 'ordained ministers of divine justice'. They are 'vicars of God'. In administering punishment the magistrate 'does nothing by himself, but carries out the very judgements of God'. And again, magistracy is a 'jurisdiction bestowed by God and on that account to esteem and reverence them as ministers and representatives of God'.

Ecclesial community and civil community are the same people in different yet interacting modes. What produces salvation also produces civic righteousness. Righteousness before God – the result of gracious sanctification – leads to righteousness in the performance of public duties. The ideal church, we may say, is the transformed, sanctified, justified *polis* at prayer.

The Council of Trent

Calvin's later life and work overlapped with the first sessions of the Council of Trent (1545–63), but this council focused largely on the challenges raised by Luther. After all, with Luther most of northern Europe was at stake. Up to then, Calvin only had to do with a small Swiss town.

The Council cleaned up many of the abuses and immoral behaviour attacked by Luther. But many at the Council feared that discussions of ecclesiastical reform could move into debate on the doctrinal issues that Luther had raised, putting fundamental ecclesiastical assumptions in question. In the end, the Council adopted the modified Augustinianism set out by the synod of Orange: God's power to enable us to do the good functioned only through the sacraments, and therefore through the priestly authority of the church. Baptism is essential for the remission of sins. Baptism enables those who receive it, by the aid and support of Christ, to perform 'those things which belong to the salvation of the soul'. There was to be no common ground with Protestants on the question of justification by faith. The distinctive convictions of Protestantism were no longer to be debated but declared to be heresies. The division of the Western church was now a *fait accompli*.

The 'radical reformation'

Within Europe, the church structures built on the work of Luther and Calvin remained territorial: intended, that is, to embrace the *corpus permixtum* represented by whole populations. But the European continent also saw a proliferation of separatist, 'free church', or 'believers' church' communities with corresponding ecclesiologies. The 'radical reformers' behind these movements – Anabaptists, Mennonites, Hutterites and many others – in effect collapsed the classical distinction between the visible, imperfect church on earth, composed of people who needed the forgiveness of sins, and the invisible church of the true saints; instead they demanded visible conformity with Christ's moral teachings as a central tenet of the earthly Christian community. This meant a separation from the territorially conceived Lutheran and Reformed bodies, a rejection of infant baptism, and a policy of withdrawal from the affairs of the state and the practices of warfare and judicial violence.

This radical reformation ecclesiology existed in many forms, most known as varieties of Anabaptists or re-baptizers, and all placing a premium on moral conduct. The objective was to emulate the early church. Scripture, and especially the New Testament, was the final authority. All practices not seen as in accord with it were discarded. Members were expected to live up fully to the ethical demands of Sermon on the Mount. The resulting 'gathered' churches consisted of those who had experienced a new birth and been baptized as conscious believers. If one's new birth was genuine it would issue in good works. Hence Anabaptists and others often practised the custom of expelling those who fell short. Members of these bodies tended to austerity in morals and to simplicity in food, dress and speech. They were often known to outsiders for their honesty and reliability.

The result was a rejection of far more of the traditional ecclesial substance than either Luther or Calvin recommended. Ecclesiology, lived out at the congregational level, became theologically and juridically related to ethics. But above all, this relationship turned on communal formation and practice.

Denominational denouement

The 'denomination' is a distinctive form of *ecclesia* in which differing church traditions with European, and sometimes territorial, roots become transplanted to new lands where they live side-by-side in the same communities and compete with one another for members in a world for which the older controversies are largely meaningless.[5] Traditional ecclesiological distinctions stemming from former circumstances remain, but their meanings become obscure. In some cases, different sorts of moral formation and different ethics emerge to create the distinctions that people can most easily grasp.

These denominational syntheses of ecclesiology and ethics tend to reflect the situations in which their underlying ecclesiologies are now called upon to live. What in Germany had been an Anabaptist, 'radical Reformation' ecclesiology becomes the dominant church in the American South and adjusts its self-understanding accordingly. What had been the majority church in Germany or Scandinavia becomes one denomination among others in, say, Pennsylvania, but a new majority church in Minnesota. The so-called 'historic peace churches' – Mennonites, Brethren, Quakers – were radical minorities in the old country, and remain so in the new. Here ethics and ecclesiology come close to practical merger. Roman Catholicism in some places becomes one denomination among many. In other places, such as Irish Boston or Polish Chicago, it retains its dominant position.[6]

Whatever the situation, the roles of moral formation and ethical reflection in relation to ecclesiology are not what they were in Europe. The tendency in denominationalism is for churches to define themselves in relation to the specific social locations they come to occupy. This means that for practical purposes ecclesiology is increasingly articulated in moral–ethical terms.

The twentieth century

The twentieth century saw issues of ecclesiology and ethics following well-worn paths, but being foregrounded more explicitly by events. Catholic ethical and social teaching sought new directions. Protestant denominations pursued these issues ecumenically with one another and with Roman Catholics.

Modern Catholic ethical and social teaching: Vatican II, Veritatis Splendor *and academic scholarship*

The rich and vigorous tradition of Catholic moral teaching and ethical reasoning grew still more significant in the twentieth century. The long list of papal encyclicals on moral questions, together with the moral and ethical implications of Vatican II, make clear the close connection of moral formation and reflection – however world-oriented – with ecclesiastical authority. *Gaudium et Spes* in particular develops the themes of solidarity with the whole human family and the dignity of the human person, the community of humankind, the common good, and the role of the church in the modern world. The documents of the Council themselves are intended for morally formative purposes. It is taken for granted that such formation and reflection is intrinsic to the church's life without being of its essence.

Simultaneously this period saw a flowering of academic Catholic scholarship in these fields. 'Natural law' principles, originally derived from Aristotle, offered Catholicism the possibility of joining 'the conversation of humankind' (Michael Oakeshott) and reasoning about the 'common good'. Liberation theology consisting of social-ethical reasoning – owing much to scripture and not a little to Karl Marx – emerged in developing nations and spread into the northern hemisphere.[7]

Thinkers in both traditional and liberationist arenas often found themselves at odds with magisterial positions, to the point that certain scholars in Catholic faculties found themselves forbidden to teach candidates for the priesthood. In the South, the challenge of liberation theologies to magisterial positions rose to the point of founding alternative morally formative and ecclesially intentional 'base communities'. Ethics began to challenge traditional ecclesiology. Leonardo Boff argued that moral solidarity with the poor, based on economic interpretations of scripture, led to a literal remaking of the church, hence *ecclesiogenesis*.

An attempt to reaffirm the magisterial authority of Catholic ethics, as well as to clarify its ideational basis, led to the encyclical *Veritatis Splendor*. Previous encyclicals dealing with particular issues had not always sufficiently clarified their underlying assumptions. This document takes the time to do so. It contains a treatment of 'natural law' which better than its predecessors guards against the charge that mere physical and biological constants are being presented as having definitive moral significance. We cannot dissociate the moral act from its bodily dimensions. But there is more than the body involved. The Christian understanding of natural law is here defined (in terms updating Augustine and Thomas) as a 'participated theonomy', or 'a participation of eternal law in the rational creature'. Moral norms rest on a divine indicative imparted to human beings in and through the act of creation itself. Such norms can therefore be found in the structures of human reason, both contemplative and practical. John Paul II improves on scholastic theology by giving 'natural law' a clearer biblical and christological ground without diminishing its ambition to speak to human beings generally.

John Paul also addresses critically the work of academic ethicists, especially those who practice 'consequentialism', 'proportionalism' and the use of social science data in moral reasoning. Such methods enable Catholic thinkers to engage the human conversation but they correspondingly diminish the effective presence of ecclesiastical authority in the resulting arguments. They lead to discussion in which other norms take pride of place. Much academic ethical reasoning, in effect, is held to be not ecclesial enough.

With the subsequent release of the new *Catechism of the Catholic Church*, it becomes clear that the curia wants to keep Catholic ethics strictly within the boundaries of ecclesiastically interpreted tradition. When a politician can be threatened with excommunication for taking a position contrary to magisterial teaching, when bishops are encouraged in the encyclical *Dominus Iesus* to purge Roman Catholic universities under their jurisdiction of faculty members not obedient to the papal instruction, curial moral teaching edges closer and closer to being treated as intrinsic to the church's being.

Encounters of ecclesiology with ethics in the modern ecumenical movement

With the coming of ecumenism, Protestant denominations not only encountered one another but gradually brought Roman Catholics into the conversation. Concerns for ecclesiology and ethics began to flow into the 'Faith and Order' and 'Life and Work' movements respectively. In the earlier years of ecumenical effort these concerns were indeed seen as interrelated, but were pursued by different groups of people with different constituencies. Little effort was expended in exploring the relations between them. But by the early 1970s a need for greater insight concerning the ethical meanings of *ecclesia* and the ecclesial meanings of ethics became apparent. The resulting studies were extremely complex. We must be content with a few representative soundings.

Faith and Order at Louvain, 1971

One approach to the ecclesiology and ethics question was taken by the Faith and Order Commission meeting at Louvain in 1971.[8] On this occasion an attempt was made to frame the historic theme of church unity in a new context, specifically that of human, not simply denominational, divisions. Section themes deliberately moved discussion into territories unfamiliar to many long-time Faith and Order participants: justice, encounters with living faiths, the struggle against racism, inclusion of the handicapped, differences in culture. Preoccupation with the nature of the church gave way to discussion of its social and ethical significance.

Louvain proclaimed that the church *is* the unity of humankind in the form in which this

617

is realizable in this penultimate age. Studying the role of the church in the survival of humankind *is* seeking church unity, only by a new method. This new method included working out the preconditions for a future ecumenical council and trying to lay the groundwork for an ecumenical confession of faith and corresponding ecclesiology with strong moral–ethical content.

A fundamental question arising from this effort was whether the ecclesio-sacramental and the socio-ethical dimensions implied in this question could be held together. Could one speak of the consequences of the church's moral/ethical presence in the world and at the same time do justice to the church's being as a community of Word and Sacrament?

Moves by confessional groups

Moves to link social righteousness to the integrity of church and faith as such were made by two Protestant world communions with reference to apartheid in South Africa. The Lutheran World Federation (LWF) in 1977 and the World Alliance of Reformed Churches (WARC) in 1982 both declared that support by their South African member churches for, or complicity in, the social policy of apartheid raised a *status confessionis*: meaning that such attitudes and practices constituted a fundamental denial of the Christian faith which, if persisted in, would place the ecclesial bodies concerned beyond the limits of the confessional fellowship, if not of the Una Sancta. The WARC suspended two white South African churches from its membership on this account, declaring that the theological defence of apartheid (which had been affirmed by interpreting Calvinism as justifying the South African whites' self-image as a divinely-chosen people) is a heresy and that the systematic exclusion of non-whites from the eucharist is a sin.

The Seoul Convocation

The World Council of Churches' (WCC) 1990 Seoul Convocation on 'Justice, Peace, and the Integrity of Creation' was intended by its organizers to help build a stronger conciliar fellowship in the ecumenical community around shared moral/ethical principles. Some sought a universal council to declare these as 'marks' of the church itself. But in the preparatory process some saw such a 'conciliar process' as implying an ecclesiological commitment they were unprepared to make. It was apparently largely, if not entirely, for this reason that the Roman Catholic Church withdrew its agreement to co-sponsor the event and scaled back its participation. The nature of 'conciliarity' with reference to global social issues was not sufficiently clarified.[9]

But some thought that the moral/ethical content of catholicity could be discerned by reasoning from the local to the universal. An attempt was therefore made to use the Seoul principles to stimulate responses from local communities across the globe. Hope was expressed that hermeneutical criteria could be developed for grasping 'areas of convergence' among the different communities of faith to be involved in the study.[10]

Each contextual study confronted one Seoul affirmation with the experience of people in a particular context. The values expected of participants were a willingness to listen, an openness to being surprised, a readiness to receive and remember. The underlying assumption was that theological commonalities and differences, raised up in local, regional, and world-wide struggles, all of them interconnected, could deepen understanding in each place and for all involved. The 'theology of life' effort thus sought in each place to create and maintain an open space, a theatre for the presentation of the gifts and contributions of others. Acceptance, understanding and affirmation were necessary preconditions to dialogue. The effort was to see connections and build bridges between different symbols of life.

The culmination of this programme prior to the 1998 Harare Assembly was the sponsorship of an event modelled on the *sokoni* (the Swahili word for the traditional African marketplace): a space for exchanges of all kinds – goods, information, ideas, plans, stories, music, gossip, deliberation[11] – in Nairobi, Kenya (January, 1997), at which concerns related to resisting the forces of death and promoting the cause of life were shared among persons of widely differing ideologies and cultural backgrounds. This sort of gathering could enact a new way of understanding the church morally and ethically. As Larry Rasmussen of Union Theological Seminary (New York) memorably put it:

> the most promising way forward is not that of finding the language of normative common ground as that might be offered by theologians and agreed to by heads of communions. This understanding of ecumenical formation is essentially doctrinal and jurisdictional. The most promising way is by arranging a common table, open to participation by the whole people of God, to see what emerges as living church when faith is freely shared on the burning issues we face.[12]

On the Faith and Order side, and for many others, this view seemed to involve potential costs to the integrity and ascertainability of the tradition of faith itself. In the enactment of the *sokoni* the church quite literally became a space in which economic, political and other questions – issues of human well-being as such – were brought into the transforming context of the gospel. Ecclesiology and social thought were close to becoming one. But what criteria of authenticity in the faith could be derived from this sort of enterprise?

Ecclesiology and ethics

The obvious interactions between ecclesiology and ethics in such studies dramatized the necessity of facing the issue explicitly. The middle of the 1990s saw a series of consultations concerning the historic tensions separating the movements for Faith and Order and Life and Work, between concern for what the church *is* and what the church *does*.[13]

Early in the process note was taken of a statement by the American ethicist Stanley Hauerwas that 'the church not only has, but *is*, a social ethic'.[14] Was it then appropriate, as some were doing, to describe the church as a 'moral community'? Acceptance of the latter formula was far from unanimous. The nature of the resistance depended on what the claim was thought to mean.[15] But, in general, disquiet was found among those whose concern was that the church must *be* the church, and would do more for humankind by being so than by risking defining itself in terms of particular present-day moral issues. Some also feared that seeing the church as moral community could open the door to a new Pelagianism, undercutting confidence in salvation by grace alone. Others said that connecting moral interests too closely to ecclesiology could supplant the centrality of the eucharist, diluting the church's essential sacramental being. Still other voices insisted that for the church to become involved in seeking the well-being of society (what is implied by 'ethics' in this discussion) is to be taken in by the surrounding culture, to accede to whatever role that culture gives to 'religion'. The unity thrust of Faith and Order, it was thought by some, could be diluted by questions of social ethics; the moral proposals could be stalled in the seemingly endless unity debate.

But it also began to be seen that ecumenism itself had become morally formative. It had already produced a 'moral deposit' of convictions such as reverence for the dignity of all people as creatures of God, affirmation of the fundamental equality of women and men, the option for the poor, the rejection of all racial barriers, a strong 'no' to nuclear armament, pursuit of non-violent strategies of conflict resolution, the responsible stewardship of the environment. But it was also true that such convictions had been drawn out by moral struggles in society in which the church had had to learn at least as much as it had taught.

In this way the efforts of moral formation in society were seen to have carried their own ecclesial significance: the church had often learned how better to *be* church through these efforts. It followed that the cooperation of people of goodwill around such specific struggles for a peaceful, just, and sustainable world might not be ecclesial *per se*, but it had ecclesial consequences in that it, too, was part of the spiritual and moral formation of the church itself, as mediated by others in God's world.[16]

For some it seemed to follow from such insights that there could be such a thing as 'moral communion' among different Christian communities interacting with the forces around them. The close relationship, as well as distinctions, between such 'moral communion' and the more traditional 'sacramental communion' were explored, not always to everyone's satisfaction. Could one detect a 'resonance' across time and space among communities that interpreted the meaning of 'moral communion' in different situations and in different ways? Could it be said that the Holy Spirit instigates an energy-field of resonance among different perspectives?

The most notable words to come out of these ecumenical discussions take the form of a series of questions:

Is it enough to say . . . that ethical engagement is intrinsic to the church *as* church? Is it enough to say that, if a church is not engaging responsibly with the ethical issues of its day, it is not being fully church? Must we not also say: if the churches are not engaging these ethical issues *together*, then *none of them individually is being fully church?*[17]

Some tentative conclusions

The upshot of such language, if taken seriously, would be to link the church's ecclesiological identity with the causes it stands for in the world, hence an ecclesiology largely couched in social–ethical terms. But the churches to date have shown little inclination to allow such thought-experiments to influence their traditional positions. Ecclesiology and ethics continue to hold the relationships they have had in the different confessional histories described in this essay.

But the churches, by discussing these issues together, have set out a new context of thought and action – a kind of ecumenical 'space' – in which these histories can continue to meet under the pressure of a common calling. The idea has been planted that catholicity calls for participation in an ethic of global resistance to forces that make for death. An ecumenical council that could grapple with these issues in the light of their complex histories still lies – perhaps distantly – in the future.

Notes

1 See Alasdair MacIntyre, *After Virtue: A Study in Moral Theory*, Notre Dame, IN: University of Notre Dame Press, 1981, p. 207: 'A living tradition . . . is an historically extended, socially embodied, argument.'

2 See also Chapter 2 of this volume, 'The Church in the early Christian centuries: ecclesiological consolidation' for a discussion of Augustine.

3 This, by the way, is the logic by which Calvin, in the 1559 edition, places the doctrine of election toward the end of Book III instead of within the exposition of the doctrine of God in earlier editions. Election now arises as a theological reflection on the already established fact of my justification and sanctification. In short, salvation as well as evil prompts the question, Why me? Weal as well as woe prompts this question.

4 The 'Declaration of Debrecen' voted by the World Alliance of Reformed Churches in 1997 reads these 'we are not our own' sayings in a decidedly public context.

5 On 'denomination' see also Chapter18, 'The Church in a North-American perspective'.

6 See also Chapter 9, 'Lutheran ecclesiology'.

7 See also Chapter 23, 'Liberation ecclesiology'.

8 See Ernst Lange, *And Yet It Moves: Dream and Reality of the Ecumenical Movement*, Grand Rapids, MI: Eerdmans, 1979, abridged by Konrad Raiser and Lukas Vischer, and trans. Edwin Robertson from *Die ökumenische Utopie oder Was bewegt die ökumenische Bewegung?* Stuttgart: Kreuz Verlag, ND.

9 It may also be that a classic linguistic confusion added to the difficulties, in that the single English word 'council' can have different sets of distinguishable meanings in Latin, French and German. Clearly the WCC itself is a 'council' in the sense of the Latin *consilium*, the French *conseil* and the German *Rat*, i.e. a consultative body making no claims to conciliarity in the Nicene or Constantinopolitan sense. But a 'conciliar commitment' could also imply the larger, more portentous meaning, as in the Latin *concilium*, French *concile*, or German *Konzil*. Did the Seoul planners mean 'conciliar commitment' as a step on the way to an 'ecumenical council' of the whole church? If so, the claim went much too far – especially, but not only, for Roman Catholics and Orthodox.

10 These methodological expectations for the 'theology of life' programme are recorded from a 1994 memorandum from Julio de Santa Ana to Martin Robra and Sam Kobia. The writer is indebted to Daniel McFee for this document.

11 Larry Rasmussen, 'The right direction, but a longer journey', in Thomas F. Best and Martin Robra (eds), *Ecclesiology and Ethics: Ecumenical Ethical Engagement, Moral Formation, and the Nature of the Church*, Geneva: WCC Publications, 1997, p. 107f.

12 Rasmussen, 'The Right Direction', p. 107.

13 Best and Robra (eds), *Ecclesiology and Ethics*, p. vii.

14 Ibid., p. x.

15 'Costly commitment', ¶55 (in Thomas F. Best and Martin Robra, eds, *Ecclesiology and Ethics: Ecumenical Ethical Engagement, Moral Formation and the Nature of the Church*, Geneva: WCC Publications, 1997, pp. 24–49) comments on misunderstandings of the intent of this term. 'We recognize that the term "moral community" has engendered considerable debate, not least at Tantur. Difficulties have arisen through the term being *misheard* as a full description of the ethical character of the ekklesia. Certainly Ronde did not intend any reductionism of the church, leading to moralism or a self-righteous triumphalism. For Ronde the identity of the church as a "moral community" is a gift of God, a part, though not the whole, of the fullness of the church. The term "moral" has also been *misheard* as "moralistic", thus confusing our understanding of the ekklesia with such movements as Moral Rearmament or with the "moral majority", or as representing the ethical character of the ekklesia as an individual or "ghetto" morality.'

16 Faith and Order Paper 170: Minutes of the Faith and Order Standing Commission, Aleppo, Syria, January 5–12, 1995, ¶¶97–8. The corresponding paragraphs in the 'Costly Commitment' report are 72 and 73, which have essentially the same content but have been edited to include cross-references within the latter document. I use the Aleppo text for clarity in the context of this study paper.

17 'Costly Commitment,' ¶17, in Best and Robra (eds), *Ecclesiology and Ethics*, p. 29.

Further reading

Thomas F. Best and Martin Robra (eds), *Ecclesiology and Ethics: Ecumenical Ethical Engagement, Moral Formation and the Nature of the Church*, Geneva: WCC Publications, 1997.

Gerald Darring, *A Catechism of Catholic Social Teaching*, New York: Sheed and Ward, 1987.

Reinhard Hütter and Theodore Dieter (eds), *Ecumenical Ventures in Ethics: Protestants Engage Pope John Paul's Moral Encyclicals*, Grand Rapids, MI: Eerdmans, 1998.

Ernst Lange, *And Yet It Moves: Dream and Reality in the Ecumenical Movement*, Grand Rapids, MI: Eerdmans, 1979.

George A.Lindbeck, *The Nature of Doctrine: Religion and Theology in a Postliberal Age*, Philadelphia: Westminster, 1984.

Alasdair MacIntyre, *After Virtue: A Study in Moral Theory*, Notre Dame, IN: University of Notre Dame Press, 1981.

Lewis S. Mudge, *The Sense of a People: Toward a Church for the Human Future*, Philadelphia: Trinity, 1992.

——, *The Church as Moral Community: Ecclesiology and Ethics in Ecumenical Debate*, New York: Continuum, 1998.

——, *Rethinking the Beloved Community: Ecclesiology, Hermeneutics, Social Theory*, Lanham, MD: University Press of America, 2001.

H. Richard Niebuhr, *Christ and Culture*, London: Faber and Faber, 1952.

Ronald H. Preston, *Confusions in Christian Ethics: Problems for Geneva and Rome*, London: SCM Press, 1994.

Larry L. Rasmussen, *Moral Fragments and Moral Community: A Proposal for Church in Society*, Minneapolis: Fortress Press, 1993.

Ans Joachim Van der Bent, *Commitment to God's World: A Concise Critical Survey of Ecumenical Social Thought*, Geneva: WCC, 1995.

J. Philip Wogaman, *Christian Ethics: A Historical Introduction*, Louisville, KY: Westminster John Knox, 1993.

John Howard Yoder, *The Politics of Jesus*, Grand Rapids, MI: Eerdmans, 1972.

36

ECCLESIOLOGY AND
WORLD MISSION/*MISSIO DEI*

Paul M. Collins

Introduction: mission: conversion and witness

Church and 'mission' are understood today by many if not all Christians as virtually synonymous. The exploration of the interplay between church and mission in this essay will seek to
bring out how this understanding has become current and what its implications are in relation to the history of the churches as well as current practice. This understanding of the
world church today is rooted in the experiences of the colonial and post-colonial periods of
the nineteenth and twentieth centuries, as it particularly relates to the theory and practice
of 'mission'. The close association of European churches with colonial economics and
politics from the early sixteenth century onwards in the form of missionary endeavours in
the newly discovered lands helped to form those churches' self-understanding as well as
their understanding of mission. With the collapse of European colonialism following World
War II that self-understanding was gradually revised in the light of reflection on what it
meant to live in a post-colonial world.[1] The experience of the churches of the East through
the same periods was very different, as most of them, with the exception of Imperial Russia,
were minority churches generally excluded from political influence. However, as a result
of ecumenical discourse the expression of the self-understanding of the churches of the East
is often formed in the light of the colonial/post-colonial experience and reflection of
the West.

   Another important influence upon the churches' self-understanding was the dissolution
of the medieval vision of Europe as Christendom. This vision was being eroded from
the period of the Renaissance onwards and was further affected by the Reformation
and Enlightenment. The dissolution of the Holy Roman Empire by Napoleon in 1806
marked the end of the last political vestige of Christendom in the West. The conquest of
Constantinople in 1453 and the overthrow of the Romanovs in the Russian Revolution of
1917 mark a similar process in the East. However, despite these significant political events
the churches' self-understanding has taken a long time to catch up with these realities. The
ongoing practice of a parochial system in many churches is evidence of a remnant of feudal
Christendom. The work of such as Grace Davie and Callum Brown[2] has highlighted the
tensions between the expectations of modern Western society and such ancient institutional expression and practice. Reports such as *Mission Shaped Church* (2004)[3] are evidence
of the churches reflecting upon the need to change. Thus the self-understanding of church
and mission in the churches continues to be formed through the continuing after-effects of
Christendom; either in the form of remnants of Christendom as in the Roman Catholic

Church, the Anglican Communion or the Lutheran churches of Europe; or in reaction to and rejection of Christendom as in the tradition of Free churches and house churches.

Understandings of mission and church have also been mutually formed and conditioned for many centuries in terms of the 'Great Commission':

> Go ... and make disciples of all nations, baptizing them ..., and teaching them ...
>
> (Matthew 28. 19–20)

This 'commission' has generally been understood in terms of conversion. Once those in one's locality had been evangelized and converted to Christianity, then mission, understood in terms of evangelization with the aim of conversion, was a task to be performed elsewhere: i.e. it entailed sending others (missionaries) to another place. Mission has been understood in terms of such proselytizing practice at least since late antiquity. The 'mission' of Augustine to Kent, sponsored by Pope Gregory the Great, is a good example of this concept of mission.[4] Others might argue that the so-called 'missionary journeys' of St Paul as recounted in the Acts of the Apostles[5] are evidence of this kind of understanding. However, for many centuries the churches of the East have on the whole understood mission much more in terms of witness (*martyria*) than in terms of proselytization. One explanation of this difference relates to the different status of the churches of the East as minority communities, in contexts where the majority were of another faith or faiths. The context for the Greek Orthodox community for centuries was the Ottoman Empire, ruled by Islamic dynasties, while the St Thomas Christians of India have lived among Buddhists, Hindus and Jains and later Muslims for two millennia. In such contexts the theory and practice of mission are very different from that which accompanied European colonialism.

The context of the Eastern churches brings to the fore another significant feature which shapes understandings of church and mission, and that is the relationship between Christian churches and those of other faith communities. The minority status of Eastern Christians was entirely different from the majority status of the Western churches, and the churches' attitude towards the 'other', as might be expected, was also very different. In the East *martyria* to the 'other' was and is mission; whereas in the West mission was understood as conversion of the 'other'. Thus the two communities which churches in Europe encountered, Jews and Muslims, were often seen as targets for evangelization and conversion, exile or annihilation.[6] The motivation behind the Crusades may have been defensive at their outset, but the destruction of the Infidel became an ambition of the crusaders. An element of the motivation behind this practice may be traced to the particular teaching that 'outside the church there is no salvation' (*extra ecclesia nulla salus*).

On the basis of this teaching, conversion and salvation, church and mission became inextricably bound up together. The imperative behind mission becomes more than witness and the desire to 'disciple the nations'. The imperative for mission is focused on truth claims, on understandings of revelation. Thus self-understanding of church and mission are rooted in particular epistemological and hermeneutical understandings of the reception and dissemination of truth claims. On the basis of 'outside the church there is no salvation', claims about church, salvation and mission become absolute claims. Mission is understood to entail a cognitive process whereby certain claims are transmitted, received and accepted. This is a very different model from understanding church and mission in relational terms. Church understood in terms of the divine *koinonia*, in which faith, hope and love are communicated by the grace of God to bring in God's kingdom of justice and peace, through interpersonal relations and fellowship, is less likely to be concerned with absolute and cognitive claims.

The model of mission with which a church works profoundly influences that church's self-understanding and its praxis both to those within its fellowship and to the 'other'. This has clearly been the case in the past, and it continues to be the case in the contemporary experience of the churches. Often overseas missionary activity has been undertaken by para-church agencies such as the missionary orders (e.g. Jesuits) or the missionary societies (e.g. Society for the Propagation of the Gospel, 1701), and often it has been undertaken on an ad hoc basis, without in-depth reflection about the relation of church and mission to the divine purposes in creating and redeeming the cosmos. It is a feature particularly of the latter half of the twentieth century that such reflection took place in the councils of the churches against the background of post-colonial experience. A significant component of this reflection in the West was consideration of the effects of secularism, and this continues to be a feature of such reflection as churches begin to come to terms with the ongoing effects of secularization and globalization. The landmark events of the twentieth century during which these reflections were conducted, were meetings of the world mission conferences, the Second Vatican Council (1962–5) and the Partners in Mission movement.

Themes, councils and thinkers

In this section six interconnected themes will be explored in relation to the search by the churches in the twentieth century for understandings of mission and church in the post-colonial context. The six themes: salvation, partnership, *missio Dei*, relationality, inculturation and pluralism, will be traced against the background of the churches' struggles to relate initially to one another and latterly also to those of other faith communities. The exploration of each theme will draw upon conciliar and ecclesial sources as well as the thought of major theologians.

Salvation (extra ecclesia nulla salus)

'Salvation' is a major imperative behind the activity of mission understood in terms of evangelization and conversion. In the early church period the understanding that salvation was only to be found within the church was taught by Irenaeus (d. 200), Origen (d. 254) and Cyprian (d. 258) against the background of the church's minority status, which was often accompanied by violent persecution. By the time that Fulgentius of Ruspe (d. 532) reiterated that *extra ecclesia nulla salus*, it was in a context where Christianity was becoming the main religion of the Roman Empire.

> Of this you can be certain and convinced beyond any doubt: not only all pagans but also all Jews, heretics, and schismatics, who die outside the present Catholic Church, will go into the everlasting fire which has been prepared for the devil and his angels.[7]

This became a dominant understanding in the high Middle Ages. It was taught by the fourth Lateran Council in 1215 and the Council of Florence in 1442, while Pope Boniface VIII in the bull *Unam Sanctam* (1302) had also defended this teaching. It continued to be the mainstream understanding in the Roman Catholic Church into the nineteenth century, with Pope Pius IX reiterating the teaching in his allocution *Singulari Quadam* (1854).[8] In this he argues that eternal salvation is only assured for those within the fold of the Roman Catholic Church, and while acknowledging that it would be a mistake to claim to know the mind of God and set limits to the divine mercy, nonetheless he clearly rejects any notion that 'the way of eternal salvation can be found in any religion whatever'.[9]

A change of tone towards the nations of the world in their differences and by implication understandings of where salvation may be found, is to be seen in the encyclical of Pope Benedict XV, *Pacem, Dei Munus Pulcherrimum* (1920). In *Rerum Ecclesiae* (1926) Pope Pius XI drew parallels between the spirituality of certain eastern religions and the contemplative orders of Catholicism, and suggested such cultural overlap could be used to promote conversions.[10] A clearer affirmation of other cultures is a feature of the teaching of Pope Pius XII. In *Summi Pontificatus* (1939) he sets out a theology of human culture and the relationship of the missionary activity of the church to this. In his encyclical, *Evangelii Praecones* (1951), also on mission, Pope Pius XII moved closer still to a modern and explicit statement of the Catholic Church's understanding of mission. Thus by the early 1950s the teaching of the Roman Catholic Church had developed considerably in its explicit affirmation of the place of 'indigenous' cultures in relation to missionary activity. The rise of communism in China and Eastern Europe, and the perceived growth of secularism and secularization, also contributed to these developments. The *ressourcement* or *nouvelle théologie* movement in Europe also prepared the way for change in the Roman Catholic Church; those such as M.D. Chenu, Henri de Lubac and in particular Yves Congar discerned the need to address the secular context of twentieth-century Europe and helped to formulate the teachings of Vatican II.[11]

The Second Vatican Council addressed understanding of church and mission in many of its documents and in doing so embraced a much more inclusive understanding of salvation, thus changing the imperatives in relation to mission. The decree on Missionary Activity, *Ad Gentes* (1965), clearly sets out the universal and inclusive purposes of God in which the church is called to participate. The decree explicitly acknowledges that salvation is not only available within the church:

> This universal design of God for the salvation of the human race is carried out not only, as it were, secretly in the soul of a man, or by the attempts (even religious ones by which in diverse ways it seeks after God) if perchance it may contact Him or find Him, though He be not far from anyone of us (cf. Acts 17:27). For these attempts need to be enlightened and healed; even though, through the kindly workings of Divine Providence, they may sometimes serve as leading strings (*paedagogia*) toward God, or as a preparation for the Gospel. (§3)

The Pastoral Constitution on the Church, *Gaudium et Spes*, reiterates these understandings, clearly valuing human difference and diversity and encouraging an imperative to dialogue related to the church's mission in the world.[12] Reflection on the process and theology of mission are set within a broad and rich context in the documents of the Second Vatican Council and in the papal encyclicals of both Pope Paul VI and Pope John Paul II.[13] While the focus in this section has been on developments in the Roman Catholic Church, a parallel process may be discerned within Protestant and Evangelical churches too. The issue of salvation in these traditions is focused on the name of Jesus,[14] but the effects in relation to the 'other' are much the same. A more inclusive understanding has been fostered among churches of these traditions through the work of the World Council of Churches (WCC).[15]

Partnership: world mission conferences

From the sixteenth century onwards mission was understood as an overseas activity undertaken by particular persons – 'missionaries' – usually sponsored by mission agencies.[16] However, it is from reflection upon the experience and practicalities of this kind of mission that a major development in the understanding of mission emerged through the gathering of representatives from Protestant missionary societies in Edinburgh in 1910.[17] The conference sought to address the problems which faced the missionaries in the mission field as well as the more domestic issues of the sending missionary agencies. From this conference there emerged imperatives towards the Ecumenical Movement as well as co-operation and partnership in mission. As a result of Edinburgh 1910 a succession of Mission Councils or Conferences has been ongoing to the present day.[18] The first two meetings of the International Missionary Council in Jerusalem (1928) and in Tambaram (1938) dealt with significant issues which continue to shape understandings today. At the meeting in Jerusalem the divergence between two main schools of thought regarding mission surfaced and confronted each other for the first time in an international arena. The understanding of mission of the 'old school' was firmly rooted in a conceptuality of the uniqueness of Christianity, while the 'new school' sought to learn from the conceptualities developed by the comparative study of religion.[19] From the perspective of the 'old school' the ideas of the new looked far too syncretistic. Thus the Jerusalem meeting is perhaps the first instance of the churches seeking to grapple with issues surrounding inter-religious relations and the various theological understandings of what would come to be known as pluralism. The meeting of the Council in 1938 in Tambaram has also continued to shape understandings of mission. In particular this relates to the work of the Dutch missiologist Hendrik Kraemer, *The Christian Message in a Non-Christian World*, and its ongoing influence.[20] Kraemer was schooled in Neo-Orthodoxy, but took a more positive stance about world religions. However, in the final analysis he argued for an unambiguous understanding of the utter discontinuity of the Christian gospel in relation to other world faiths.[21] Nonetheless, in the view of Lesslie Newbigin (who himself attended the Council) the outcome of Tambaram was 'a crucial turning point' in that it clearly affirmed that the aim of missionary activity was not the creation of

> 'outposts of Western Christianity scattered throughout the world'. Tambaram marked the emergence of a 'new Christendom', living in cultures different from those of the old Christendom.[22]

Thus in these two early Mission Councils features of the landscape of 'partnership' begin to emerge in terms of partnership between those who had been 'receiving' and those who had been 'sending'.

The language of 'partnership' was adopted explicitly at the IMC conference held in Whitby, Canada, in 1947. A feature of this espousal of partnership was the deliberate abandonment of the language of 'Christian' and 'non Christian' countries, which opened up new understandings in mission theology. The Conference was also very clear about the need for a good relationship with the World Council of Churches, which held its first assembly in

1948. Thus the language of partnership demonstrates not only a new vision of mission but also of the crucial relationship between mission and church. This was taken further at the conferences held in Delhi in 1961 and Mexico City in 1963. The effects of 'partnership' may be seen in the challenge to more traditional models of mission as evangelization in the WCC document *Mission and Evangelism – An Ecumenical Affirmation* (1982), which drew not only on Protestant theologies of mission but also on Roman Catholic and Orthodox theologies. The emphasis on 'partnership' also led to reflection on the effects of political and economic power and the consequent need to change mission strategies and church self-understanding. This echoes the concerns and imperatives of Liberation Theology as well as papal teaching on God's 'preferential option for the poor'.[23]

The initial step towards a language of 'partnership' in 1947 bore fruit in particular in the 'Partners in Mission' movement. This can be seen, for example, in the resolutions of the 1978 Lambeth Conference commending the initiative to the Anglican Communion; §4 of Resolution 15 states,

> 4. Churches should not be content with inviting partners only from those areas which share a natural or racial affinity with them. The insights of other cultures, and of various understandings of mission are vital to growth in a true and balanced theology of mission, and to ensuring the possibility of a creative exchange of resources both personal and material.

Another expression of this movement can be witnessed in churches from across the world creating instruments for gathering together to share common concerns and for mutual support and enrichment. An example of such an initiative is to be seen in the union of a number of Free Church mission agencies in the United Kingdom, in partnership with churches in the developing world, in 1977 in the Council for World Mission. In its foundation document, *Sharing in One World Mission*, a vision of mission and church is set out:

> 2.5 It is precisely this present context of churches in every land that makes it necessary for us to reexamine our missionary method and structure. Today we cannot think of mission in any land apart from the churches that are there. Since we ourselves share in the life of the churches, we know that our weaknesses as well as our gifts make them what they are. Sometimes our fellowships are slow to respond to new challenges. Sometimes purposes are distorted as we seek to maintain status or cling to property. We are well aware of the 'clay' out of which every church is made (2 Corinthians 4:7); holiness is our hope, not our claim. Nor would we claim for any church, local or national, exclusive rights to be God's means for action in the world, as though it had a monopoly of mission in that place. Yet these 'clay pots' hold a treasure. We have come to know and love Jesus Christ through the life of the church. We believe that churches everywhere are the primary bearers of the good news to each community. As the churches celebrate the living Lord so they remain the visible focus for that witness and service which the Holy Spirit inspires and makes fruitful.

In this movement toward partnership not only is a new vision of mission to be discerned, but also a new vision of being church, one might even argue that a new vision of catholicity emerges rooted in the collectivity of local churches bound together in Jesus Christ as equal partners in his Body.

Missio Dei

The understanding that mission is God's (*missio Dei*) rather than the church's is something which became a dominant view in the twentieth century, but its pedigree is much older, and may be traced at least to the writings of Thomas Aquinas. He understood the 'divine missions' as one of the distinguishing marks of the divine persons of the Trinity.[24] His understanding relates closely to Eastern Orthodox teachings concerning the processions of the persons, which can be found in the writings of the Cappadocian Fathers, for example. The two features of twentieth-century reflection on mission already explored, salvation and partnership, are part of a wider re-evaluation of missionary endeavour in terms of divine purposefulness rather than ecclesial strategies.

The (re-)discovery of *missio Dei* is part of this re-visioning. The beginnings of the focus on *missio Dei* may be traced to Karl Barth and his rooting of his theological endeavour in God's self-revelation as Trinity.[25] In his paper *Theology and Mission in the Present Situation*[26] delivered at the Brandenburg Mission Conference in 1932, Barth argued that the imperative for mission is to be seen in the will of the 'Lord of the Church'. Barth argues that the divine will is rooted in God's 'being-in-act'. Thus the mission of the church is rooted in the trinitarian missions of the Son and Spirit from the Father: i.e. *missio Dei*. It was through the contribution of Karl Hartenstein at the IMC at Willingen (1952), that the conceptuality of *missio Dei* was introduced into ecumenical debate. In the 1990s David Bosch[27] interpreted the emergence of *missio Dei* as a fundamental 'paradigm shift' in the understandings of both mission and church in the post-colonial context. In his view mission is to be understood primarily as the initiative and action of God, the Holy Trinity, rather than as a task initiated by the church. Thus the sending agent in mission is God, and the church participates in this divine sending, rather than taking on the role of 'sending agency'. The divine mission so understood is therefore not conceived in relation to church and recruitment; but is conceived in relation to the divine purposes in creating and redeeming the cosmos. A parallel view was embraced in the Vatican II document *Ad Gentes* (1965):

> 2. The pilgrim church is missionary by her very nature, since it is from the mission of the Son and the mission of the Holy Spirit that she draws her origin, in accordance with the decree of God the Father.

The conceptuality of *missio Dei* formed the basis of discussion at the CWME Conference in Mexico City in 1963. While some would argue that during the 1970s and 1980s the coming of God's reign became the focus of mission theology, the work of Bosch has certainly put the conceptuality of *missio Dei* back on the agenda of both churches and theologians.[28]

Relationality: mission and koinonia

The shift to the rooting of mission in the understanding of God as Trinity may be seen as a dimension of the growing ecumenical consensus concerning church understood as *koinonia*,[29] which is also witnessed in the emergence of 'communion ecclesiology' across a variety of Christian traditions.[30] Thus reflection on mission and church has been drawn into what may be called a 'hermeneutic of relationality', which emerges from work on the Trinity, for example by Barth, Rahner, and Moltmann,[31] and on church, by de Lubac, Boff and Staniloae,[32] and has been further developed in the thought of Zizioulas, Gunton, Hardy and Schwöbel.[33] A particular exponent of a trinitarian understanding of mission is Ion Bria, who, as a Romanian Orthodox theologian, brought to the WCC an Eastern perspective on mission as *martyria*, rather than geographical extension and proselytization. Bria is also known for the now famous phrase 'Liturgy after the Liturgy',[34] which points to a missionary understanding of the eucharist as that which empowers the People of God. As regards the trinitarian rooted-ness of mission he clearly expounds a relational hermeneutic:

> Trinitarian theology points to the fact that God is in God's own self a life of communion and that God's involvement in history aims at drawing humanity and creation in general into this communion with God's very life. The implications of this assertion for understanding mission are very important: mission does not aim primarily at the propagation or transmission of intellectual convictions, doctrines, moral commands, etc., but at the transmission of the life of communion, that exists in God.[35]

Michael Amaladoss SJ echoes this understanding, while also focusing on the cosmic dimensions of the divine purposes into which the church is drawn by participating in the *missio Dei*.

> To contemplate the Trinity, our mission in the world is a freeing experience, so that we can carry on our mission without aggression and anxiety, conscious that we are making a real contribution to the realization of God's plan for the world. We learn to be sensitive to what God is doing in the world and to coordinate our mission with God's mission. . . . We begin to see salvation as a cosmic project in which all will be reconciled and transformed, fulfilling God's aim in creation.[36]

Thus the reality of the church's fellowship and the dynamics of mission are interpreted in terms of the relationality of the divine being, understood as *koinonia*. This application of the ontological significance of *koinonia* has not only been made in this kind of theorization but has also become the well-spring for a more practice-based application in terms of models of mission and evangelization. Relational evangelism became a dominant model for practice on both sides of the Atlantic during the latter half of the twentieth century, manifesting itself in such movements as 'church growth', 'cell church' and more recently 'virtual church'.[37] One effect of this emphasis on relationality has undoubtedly been a focus on the local or congregational aspects of church as the core from which evangelization takes place.[38]

Culture: inculturation or contextualization and mission[39]

As well as the interpersonal aspect of the focus on church in its local manifestation, the cultural and contextual aspect has also become a central feature of debate and praxis amongst churches in the twentieth century. However, interest in the cultural aspect of mission and proselytization is much older. A well-known example is Gregory the Great's advice to Augustine of Canterbury concerning the continuing use of pagan places of worship.[40] The practice of 'baptizing' indigenous cultures and beliefs was also a significant feature of the work of Jesuits in the sixteenth and seventeenth centuries.[41] A particular example of 'adaptation' for missiological purposes is to be seen in the work of Roberto de Nobili in the city of Madurai in South India in the first half of the seventeenth century. There he lived as a *sannyasi* (monk or guru), built a church in an Indian style,[42] and began the process of expressing the gospel in terms of Indian philosophy and local traditions and languages. Such inculturation or contextualization as a means of mission evoked much opposition at the time; as such practices continue to do today.

The Lambeth Conference of bishops of the Anglican Communion has discussed issues of cultural adaptation in the mission field from its inception, beginning with issues of worship and marriage discipline, and turning more recently to examine how local world views can be used to express Christian teachings.[43] A parallel process is also to be traced in the Faith and Order movement, where the relationship of faith and mission to culture has been reflected on extensively.[44] The Roman Catholic Church also developed guidelines on 'inculturation' in terms of worship and mission. Decisions at Vatican II encouraged reflection on ways in which Christian faith and practice could be expressed in terms of indigenous practice and culture. *Sacrosanctum Concilium* (1963), the Constitution on the Liturgy, has a section dedicated to 'Norms for adapting the Liturgy to the culture and traditions of peoples':

> 37. Even in the liturgy, the church has no wish to impose a rigid uniformity in matters which do not implicate the faith or the good of the whole community; rather does she respect and foster the genius and talents of the various races and peoples.
>
> 39. Within the limits set by the typical editions of the liturgical books, it shall be for the competent territorial ecclesiastical authority mentioned in Art. 22, 2, to specify adaptations, especially in the case of the administration of the sacraments, the sacramentals, processions, liturgical language, sacred music, and the arts . . .
>
> 40. In some places and circumstances, however, an even more radical adaptation of the liturgy is needed, and this entails greater difficulties.

Alongside liturgical adaptation the Council also sought to value non-Christian religions in *Nostra Aetate* (1965), and in the decree on Missionary Activity, *Ad Gentes* (1965), which, as we have seen already, taught that other religions may be seen as a preparation for the gospel. In the Pastoral Constitution on the Church, *Gaudium et Spes*, Chapter II is devoted to 'The Proper Development of Culture'. This acknowledges the pivotal role of culture in the development of the human race,[45] and is reiterated in *Towards a Pastoral Approach to Culture* (1999),[46] where a particular emphasis is placed upon inculturation as transformation.

> The evangelization of cultures and the inculturation of the Gospel go hand in hand, in a reciprocal relationship which presupposes constant discernment in the light of the Gospel, to facilitate the identification of values and counter-values in a given culture, so as to build on the former and vigorously combat the latter.[47]

For both Roman Catholics and Protestants the relationship between faith, culture, mission and church remains a matter of ongoing debate and discernment, which the processes of globalization and questions of local identity make more complex and urgent.[48]

Pluralism: mission as dialogue[49]

Recognition of the global and local context of the churches as diverse and plural in terms of faith and culture has been a determining feature of twentieth-century reflection on church and mission. Debate in and among the churches continues concerning whether or not non-Christian religions are to be seen 'primarily as "mission fields" [or] . . . as somehow within the salvific purposes of God'.[50] This division was shaped in particular by the contribution of Kraemer[51] at the Tambaram Conference in 1938. The tension between these alternative visions is witnessed in disputes between John Hick and Gavin D'Costa[52] and more recently in the WCC papers for the 2005 Athens conference, *Come, Holy Spirit – Heal and Reconcile: Called in Christ to be reconciling and healing communities.*

> 76 (c) Christian mission involves a holistic response through evangelistic and diaconal work to reach out to people in their experience of exclusion, brokenness and meaninglessness. . . . 77 (a) Impelled by the love of Christ, we commit ourselves to work to ensure that all our neighbours in every place, near and far, have the opportunity to hear and respond to the gospel of Jesus Christ.[53]

One way of responding to the reality of pluralism has been an endeavour to explore inter-religious dialogue as a form of mission.[54] Stanley Samartha sets out three theological reasons for dialogue:[55] (a) God in Christ entered into relationship with people of all faiths and times; (b) the gospel is the offer of true community, which through forgiveness and reconciliation leads to the emergence of a new creation; and (c) Christ promised that the Holy Spirit would lead into all truth, a truth which is relational rather than propositional. Thus dialogue is seen as an expression of a relational understanding of mission, based upon the possibility of a shared search for God.

While there is a general consensus that dialogue is necessary, there is no agreement on its status. Thus Jürgen Moltmann[56] argues that dialogue is not a means to an end, but is an end in itself, in which God's vulnerability is manifest. Chester Gillis,[57] meanwhile, is clear that dialogue is not an end in itself, for him dialogue is not just an exchange of information, it is a learning experience: an encounter in which one is open to change one's notions and views; i.e. it is to be a truth-seeking dialogue. For this to occur one must approach dialogue from the perspective that one does not know truth in its entirety already.[58] Panikkar echoes Gillis, arguing that dialogue is not apologetics.

> Dialogue, however, does imply that the convictions and beliefs one brings to dialogue are subject to a new hermeneutic, which the exchange itself unlocks for the participants.[59]

Thus dialogue itself is being seen as transformational, and this in turn interprets the shared quest for God as also being transformational, not simply the reiteration of received doctrines and traditions. As Israel Selvanayagam[60] argues, evangelism and interfaith dialogue need not be contradictory but complementary.[61] Bevans and Schroeder also argue that dialogue is a fundamental element of the *missio Dei*, appealing to the concept of *Prophetic Dialogue*.[62]

> Christian mission, then, is participation in the dialogical life and mission of the Trinity. But that dialogue is one that is *prophetic*. As the Roman Catholic bishops

of Asia have expressed it, mission (in Asia, but from our perspective, in the whole world) needs to be done in a threefold dialogue: with the poor, with culture and with other religions.[63]

In other words interfaith dialogue and the shared quest for God may be seen as fundamental aspects of Christian understandings of the *missio Dei*.[64]

Conclusion: mission deconstructed

The context in which the reassessment of 'mission' is taking place is one in which pluralism is a central feature, in which at least the 'old' colonialism is gone, and in which the insights of philosophers such as the post-modernists and post-structuralists cannot, indeed should not, be avoided. The deconstruction of 'mission' as recruitment is overdue. Such a perception is not new, Bosch in claiming a paradigm shift made this claim over a decade ago.[65] However, the overcoming of such a deep-seated conceptuality may take several more decades to become generally accepted. Bosch argued that the churches needed to understand that they were not sending agencies, but were sent, participating in God's mission in God's world, and he offered a number of different ways in which this might be understood. Churches have sought to respond to the challenge Bosch laid before them, but it remains to be seen how far they have escaped from the conceptuality of 'recruitment'. It becomes necessary not only to deconstruct the current concept of 'mission', but also to reconsider and re-appropriate what may be understood as the 'mission of God'.

Mission derives from the Latin word *missio*, 'I send'. Before the sixteenth century, as seen already, it was customary to think in terms of the *missio Dei*: the mission of the persons of the Trinity. The mission of God was understood to refer to the divine initiative and purposefulness in creating and redeeming the cosmos. God in overflowing love bestowed existence on everything seen and unseen. Very much in parallel with modern mythology of the big bang, God is understood to have sent matter and existence tumbling out across the vast expanse of the universe, one day to return to God; again in terms of modern cosmology, it will coalesce through entropy. It is fascinating how closely modern cosmology expressed in the Laws of Thermodynamics parallels the insights of theologians of the church in the East and West, Maximus the Confessor and Thomas Aquinas. They envisage the divine purposes in creating and redeeming the cosmos in terms of an *exitus* and a *reditus*: a going out and a returning of all things to the Creator God, the Holy Trinity.[66] In the *missio Dei* the whole of creation has gone out from God, and will return to God.

In one sense each life lived is an *exitus* and *reditus*, a journey from and to God, and it might be argued that the life of the church in the world is parallel to this. Underlying this paradigm of 'mission', God, Father, Son and Holy Spirit whose very life is fellowship, is also a journeying in the created cosmos. The cosmos is created through the Son, the Word (Jn 1.3), and is brooded over by the Holy Spirit from the beginning (Gen 1.1). In the fullness of time the Father sent the Son (Gal 4.4) to bring back the world, and Christ in turn prays the Father to send the Spirit, the Comforter, to complete this mission and this return of all things (e.g. Jn 14.16). God the Holy Trinity is always the primary sending agent, and the church itself is sent. Ideas of 'mission' in terms of conversion and recruitment to church membership need to be re-evaluated in the light of the ultimate goal of God's cosmic mission: 'that God may be all in all'.[67]

Notes

1 'Post-colonial' needs also to take into account the neo-colonialism of the USA.

2 Grace Davie, *Religion in Britain since 1945: believing without belonging*, Oxford: Blackwell, 1994; Grace Davie, *Religion in modern Europe: a memory mutates*, Oxford: OUP, 2000; Callum Brown, *The Death of Christian Britain: understanding secularisation 1800–2000*, London: Routledge, 2001.

3 *Mission Shaped Church: church-planting and fresh expressions of church in a changing context*, London: Church House Publishing, 2004; *Called to Love and Praise: The Nature of the Christian Church in Methodist Experience and Practice*, Peterborough: Methodist Publishing House, 1999.

4 Venerable Bede, *Ecclesiastical History of the English People*, London: Penguin, 1955, 1968, Book I, Chapters 23–32.

5 Acts of the Apostles, see Chs 13 – 28.

6 Jews were expelled from England in 1290 by edict of Edward I.

7 Fulgentius, *De Fide, ad Petrum* 38, 79; MPL 65, 704.

8 J. Neuner and J. Dupuis (eds), *The Christian Faith in the Doctrinal Documents of the Catholic Church*, London and Sydney: Collins, 1983, pp. 281–2.

9 Neuner and Dupuis, *The Christian Faith*, p. 282.

10 *Rerum Ecclesiae* §28.

11 See Gabriel Flynn, *Yves Congar's Vision of the Church in a World of Unbelief*, Aldershot, and Burlington, VT: Ashgate, 2004.

12 E.g. *Gaudium et Spes* (1965), §92.

13 E.g. Pope John Paul II, *Redemptoris missio*, On the permanent validity of the Church's missionary mandate (1990).

14 The understanding that salvation is only to be found within the fellowship of the church is parallel with the Johannine text: 'Jesus said to him, "I am the way, and the truth, and the life. No one comes to the Father except through me"' (John 14.6). See also Acts 4.12 (referring to the name of Jesus), 'There is salvation in no one else, for there is no other name under heaven given among mortals by which we must be saved.'

15 E.g. the Commission on World Mission and Evangelism (CWME) in San Antonio (1989).

16 Here cf., also Chapter 22, on 'Ecclesiology and ecumenism' in this volume.

17 The 1910 Conference at Edinburgh was not the first international missionary conference, such gatherings had been held in Liverpool in 1860, London in 1885 and in New York in 1900. William Carey had argued as early as 1810 that there should be conferences at ten-year intervals for those engaged in the mission field (D.F. Wright, 'World Missionary Conference', in *Dictionary of Scottish Church History and Theology*, ed. Nigel M. de S. Cameron, Edinburgh: T& Clark, 1993, p. 893).

18 World mission conferences: Edinburgh 1910, Jerusalem 1928, Tambaram 1938, Whitby 1947, Willingen 1952, Achimota 1958, New Delhi 1961, Mexico City 1963, Bangkok 1972–3, Melbourne 1980, San Antonio 1989, Salvador de Bahia 1996. The *International Missionary Council* (IMC) was formed in 1921. The mission councils affiliated to the IMC became affiliated to the Commission on World Mission and Evangelism of the WCC (CWME) in 1961 following the meeting in Delhi. The Division on World Mission and Evangelism (DWME) and its Divisional Committee took over the programmatic work and responsibility of the IMC, which ceased to exist.

19 See Olive Chase Quick, 'The Jerusalem Meeting and the Christian Message', *International Review of Mission* 17 (1928), 445–54.

20 Hendrik Kraemer, *The Christian Message in a Non-Christian World*, London: Edinburgh House Press, 1938, 1947.

21 See Thomas J.J. Altizer, 'Mission and Dialogue: 50 Years After Tambaram', *Christian Century*, April (1988), 340.

22 Altizer, 'Mission and Dialogue'.

23 E.g. John Paul II, *Redemptoris Mater* (1987), §37. Cf. also Ch. 23, on 'Liberation ecclesiologies' in this volume.

24 Thomas Aquinas, *Summa theologiae* Ia 42. 5.

25 Karl Barth, *Church Dogmatics*, vol. I.1, 2nd edn, Edinburgh: T&T Clark, 1975.

26 Karl Barth, 'Die Theologie und die Mission in der Gegenwart', *Theologische Fragen und Antworten*, Zollikon, 1957.

27 David J. Bosch, *Transforming Mission: paradigm shifts in theology of mission*, Maryknoll: Orbis, 1991; *Believing in the Future: toward a missiology of Western culture*, Valley Forge, PA: Trinity Press International, 1995.

28 E.g. Lambeth Conference 1998, II.1.a. 'believing that all our mission springs from the action and self-revelation of God in Jesus Christ and that without this foundation, we can give no form or content to our proclamation and can expect no transforming effect from it'.

29 Thomas Best and Gunther Gassmann, *On the Way to Fuller Koinonia. Official Report of the Fifth World Conference on Faith and Order*, Faith and Order Paper 166, Geneva: WCC, 1994; *The Nature and Purpose of the Church*, Faith and Order Paper 181, Geneva: WCC, 1998; *The Nature and Mission of the Church*, Faith and Order Paper 98, Geneva: WCC, 2006.

30 E.g. Leonardo Boff, *Holy Trinity, Perfect Community*, Maryknoll, NY: Orbis, 2000; Miroslav Volf, *After Our Likeness: The Church as the Image of the Trinity*, Grand Rapids, MI: Eerdmans, 1998; John D. Zizioulas, *Eucharist, Bishop, Church*, Brookline, MA: Holy Cross Orthodox Press, 2001.

31 Karl Barth, *Church Dogmatics* Vol.1.1 (2nd edn), Edinburgh: T&T Clark, 1975; Karl Rahner, *The Trinity*, London: Burns & Oates, 1970; Jürgen Moltmann, *The Trinity and the Kingdom of God*, London: SCM, 1981.

32 Henri de Lubac, *The Splendour of the Church*, San Francisco, 1986; Leonardo Boff, *Trinity and Society*, London: Burns and Oates, 1992; Dimitru Staniloae, *Theology and the Church*, New York: St Vladimir's Seminary Press, 1980.

33 John D. Zizioulas, *Being as Communion: Studies in Personhood and the Church*, New York: St Vladimir's Seminary Press, 1985; Colin E. Gunton, *The One, the Three and the Many*, Cambridge: CUP, 1993; Dan Hardy, 'Redeemed Sociality' in Colin E. Gunton and Daniel W. Hardy (eds), *On Being The Church: Essays on the Christian Community*, Edinburgh: T&T Clark, 1989; Christoph Schwöbel, ed., *Trinitarian Theology Today*, Edinburgh: T&T Clark, 1995.

34 Ion Bria, *Liturgy after the Liturgy; Mission and Witness from an Orthodox Perspective*, Geneva: WCC, 1996.

35 Ion Bria (ed.), *Go Forth in Peace*, WCC Mission Series, Geneva, 1986, p. 3.

36 Michael Amaladoss, 'The Trinity on Mission', *Church and Theology in Context*, 40/1 (2002): 106.

37 See Eddie Gibbs, *I Believe in Church Growth*, London: Hodder and Stoughton, 1981; Michael Wooderson, *Good News Down Your Street*, Nottingham: Grove Books, 1982–94; Jim Hollis, *Beyond the Walls: A Congregational Guide for Lifestyle Relational Evangelism*, Discipleship resources, 1995; www.virtualchurch.org

38 Cf. also Ch. 7, 'Postmodern ecclesiologies' in this volume.

39 Cf. also Ch. 26, 'Ecclesiology and religious pluralism' in this volume.

40 Bede, *Ecclesiastical History*, Ch. 30, A copy of the letter which Pope Gregory sent to the Abbot Mellitus (601 CE).

41 E.g. Matteo Ricci adopted and adapted practices in China and translated the Mass into Mandarin; while in South America Jesuits undertook similar work among the Guarani people.

42 See Vincent Cronin, *A Pearl to India: The Life of Roberto de Nobili*, New York: E.P. Dutton & Co., 1959; Roberto de Nobili, *Adaptation (Narratio Fundamentorum quibus Madurensis Missionis Institutum caeptum est et hucusque consisit*, 1619), trans. J. Pujo; Palayamkottai: De Nobili Research Institute, 1971.

43 See Randall T. Davidson (ed.), *The Lambeth Conferences of 1867, 1878, and 1888. With the Official Reports and Resolutions, together with the Sermons preached at the Conferences*, London: SPCK, 1889; Lambeth 1988 resolution 22.

44 E.g. P.C. Rodger and L. Vischer (eds), *The Fourth World Conference on Faith and Order: The Report from Montreal 1963*, London: SCM, 1964, 4th Section Report, pp. 69–80; WCC, *Towards Koinonia in Worship*, Ditchingham, 1994.

45 *Gaudium et Spes*, §58.

46 Pontifical Council for Culture, *Towards a Pastoral Approach to Culture*, 1999.

47 *Towards a Pastoral Approach to Culture*, §5.

48 E.g. a different perspective within the Roman Catholic tradition is witnessed in the declaration from the Congregation of the Doctrine of the Faith, *Dominus Iesus: On the Unicity and Salvific Universality of Jesus Christ and the Church*, Rome, 2000.

49 Again, cf. the chapters on 'Postmodern ecclesiologies' and on 'Ecclesiology and religious pluralism' in this volume.

50 S. Wesley Ariarajah, *Hindus and Christians: A Century of Protestant Ecumenical Thought*, Amsterdam: Editions Rodopi and Grand Rapids, MI: Eerdmans, 1991, p. 138.

51 Kraemer, *The Christian Message*.

52 John Hick and Paul Knitter (eds), *The Myth of Christian Uniqueness*, London: SCM, 1988; Gavin D'Costa (ed.), *Christian Uniqueness Reconsidered: the myth of a pluralistic theology of religions*, Maryknoll, NY: Orbis, 1990.

53 WCC, Athens 2005, Preparatory paper No 1, *Mission and Evangelism in Unity Today*, §§76 (c) and 77 (a).

54 E.g. Gregory Baum, *Compassion and Solidarity: The Church for others*, Paulist Press, 1990; Peter C. Phan, *In Our Own Tongues: Asian perspectives on mission and inculturation*, Maryknoll NY: Orbis, 2003.

55 Stanley Samartha, 'Dialogue as a Continuing Christian Concern', in John Hick and Brian Hebblethwaite (eds), *Christianity and Other Religions: selected readings*, London: Collins, 1980, p. 164.

56 Jürgen Moltmann, 'Christianity and World Religions', in Hick and Hebblethwaite, *Christianity and Other Religions*.

57 Chester Gillis, *Pluralism: A new paradigm for theology*, Louvain: Peeters & W.B. Eerdmans, 1998, p. 40.

58 Here, cf. Chapter 21, 'Comparative Ecclesiology'.

59 Gillis, *Pluralism* p. 44; referring to Raimundo Panikkar, *The Intrareligious Dialogue*, New York, Paulist, 1978, pp. 26–7.

60 Israel Selvanayagam, *A Second Call: Ministry and Mission in a Multifaith Milieu*, Chennai: CLS, 2000.

61 E.g. Lewis S. Mudge, *One Church: Catholic and Reformed – Toward a theology for ecumenical decision*, London: Lutterworth, 1963; Robert J. Schreiter (ed.), *Missions in the Third Millennium*, Maryknoll, NY: Orbis, 2001.

62 Stephen B. Bevans and Roger P. Schroeder, *Constants in Context: A Theology of Mission for Today*, Maryknoll, NY: Orbis, 2004, Ch. 12.

63 Bevans and Schroeder, *Constants in Context*, p. 349.

64 See Amaladoss, 'The Trinity on Mission', pp. 99–106.

65 Bosch, *Transforming Mission*, passim.

66 See Maximus the Confessor, Ambigua PG 91, 1385BC and St Thomas Aquinas, the *Summa Theologiae*, whose overall structure may be interpreted as a moving out from and return to God, through the revelation in Christ.

67 E.g. 1 Cor 15.28.

Further reading

Stephen B. Bevans and Roger P. Schroeder, *Constants in Context: A theology of mission for today*, Maryknoll, NY: Orbis, 2004.

David Jacobus Bosch, *Transforming Mission: paradigm shifts in theology of mission*, Maryknoll, NY: Orbis Books, 1991.

Ion Bria, *Go Forth in Peace: Orthodox Perspectives on Mission*: Geneva: WCC, 1986.

Aasuly Lande and Werner Ustorf (eds), *Mission in a Pluralist World*, Frankfurt am Main: Peter Lang, 1996.

Stephen Neill, *Colonialism and Christian Missions*, London: Lutterworth, 1966.

Israel Selvanayagam, *A Second Call: ministry and mission in a multifaith milieu*, Chennai: CLS, 2000.

World Council of Churches, *Nature and Mission of the Church*, Geneva: WCC, 2006.

Part VI

THE CHURCH IN A TRANS-DISCIPLINARY CONTEXT

37

ECCLESIOLOGY AND
THE SOCIAL SCIENCES

Neil Ormerod

I shall begin with a simple question: What is the goal of ecclesiology? If theology is faith seeking understanding, and ecclesiology is the theology of the church, it would seem that the goal of ecclesiology is an understanding of the church. But what does the word 'church' evoke for us in this setting? If one were to read many current books on ecclesiology the word would probably evoke a highly idealized vision of church, one which relates not to any particular historical period or even denominational community but to a sort of timeless 'universal' church to which we would all like to belong if we could find it, but which sadly does not exist in this earthly realm. However, there are a growing number of books which turn away from this idealistic approach and view the church not in its idealized form but as concrete historical communities, whose existence spans space and time, whose members live and die, and make decisions which shape the operations and structures of those communities for better or worse. Perhaps the first major contribution in this regard was the work of Edward Schillebeeckx, *The Church with a Human Face*,[1] while the most recent is the two-volume work of Roger Haight, *Christian Community in History*.[2] I would like to suggest that this is the first major methodological divide in ecclesiology, between those who study ecclesiology as an idealist Platonic form in some noetic heaven, and those who study it more as a realist Aristotelian form, grounded in the empirical data of historical ecclesial communities.[3]

Idealist accounts of the church tend to take as their basis some major religious category or root metaphor, and attempt to build around it a synthetic account of the church in terms of that category or metaphor. There is the classical 'body of Christ' metaphor of the encyclical, *Mysticii Corporis*; the 'people of God' metaphor of many post-Vatican II ecclesiologies; and more recently the *communio* ecclesiologies which currently dominate the theological horizon. These approaches tend not to be interested in the social sciences, which are rather viewed with suspicion. Warnings are issued about the 'sociological reduction' of the church, which it is feared reduces the church to a merely human institution. As an institution of divine origin the use of sociological categories is considered inappropriate: only religious, theological language is suitable for understanding the church.

On the other hand, realist accounts which seek to understand the church as a developing historical process are faced with a number of significant difficulties. Firstly, how does the task of ecclesiology differ from that of church history? Inevitably this raises questions about the role of the social sciences in both ecclesiology and church history, a debate with strong parallels in the study of secular history. Secondly, accepting the need for the social sciences and given the methodological divisions in them, which do we choose? Indeed there are diverse approaches within the social science which appear irreconcilable. Thirdly and most importantly, how do we relate theology to the social sciences? Again there are diverse suggestions as to how this can be achieved, and even debate over whether it should be!

Ecclesiology or church history?

If the task of ecclesiology is an understanding of the church, and the church is to be understood as a historical developing community, how is ecclesiology to be distinguished from the discipline of church history? Church history provides us with a basic historical narrative of the church. What more can an ecclesiology add to such a narrative?

Of course a parallel question arises simply in the discipline of history itself. What do the social sciences add to the discipline of history? This question has become more pressing with the collapse of the major meta-narrative of Marxism as a 'scientific' reading of history. A postmodern suspicion of 'grand narratives' can leave us with nothing but the particular narratives of concrete communities, lacking any overarching intelligibility to structure our accounts. To adopt such a position is to turn away from any contribution from the social sciences at all.[4]

What then can and do the social sciences provide over and above a historical narrative? Here an image drawn from the writings of Bernard Lonergan might help. Lonergan speaks of upper and lower blades in any empirical study.[5] The lower blade is the collection of relevant empirical data. The upper blade provides a set of heuristic anticipations for the patterns into which the data will fit. In physics such an anticipation is provided by a general form of differential equation, in chemistry by the periodic table. The task of the social sciences is to provide a comprehensive set of patterns which anticipate (all) possible patterns for human social and historical existence. The more systematic and coherent social science becomes, the more such patterns are systematically interrelated and comprehensive in relation to the data. The goal of a science is to bring the upper blade into conjunction with the lower blade, to provide a fit between data and the anticipated patterns.[6]

Hence as a first approximation we may suggest that ecclesiology stands to church history as the social sciences stand to history in general. As the goal of understanding history involves the bringing together of the lower blade of historical narrative with the upper blade of the social sciences, so the goal of ecclesiology is the bringing together of an upper blade which incorporates the social sciences with the lower blade of a narrative of the history of the church. However, such an account of the role of the social sciences in relation to ecclesiology immediately gives rise to two major objections.

Which social sciences? Whose methodology?

Firstly, such substantial achievement is far from the present reality of the social sciences. The social sciences are methodologically and ideologically divided disciplines, with a variety of approaches claiming to be their proper form. There is a *physicalist, positivist* approach which is strong on gathering empirical data, but weak in terms of their upper blade. For such approaches it is enough that 'the data speak for itself'. This approach models itself most closely on the physical sciences, without attending to the key differentiating factors between the physical and the social sciences, and is of little theological value. There is a *functionalist, idealist* approach whose upper blade is an anticipation of patterns of harmony and integration. There are *conflictualist* approaches drawing on a hermeneutic of suspicion whose upper blade involves an anticipation of power plays and conflict. Finally there are *symbolic interactionist* approaches whose methodology is far from settled, particularly in terms of its upper blade. These view the human world as constituted by meaning and value, together with institutional forms which are relatively independent from these meanings and values.[7]

At this stage it might be apposite to give an ecclesiological example to illustrate some ways in which sociology might impact on ecclesiology. Consider then the classical theme of the church as the Body of Christ.

- *Functionalist perspective*: the organic imagery of the 'body' is a classical functionalist account of a social 'body'. It stresses the values of interrelatedness, interdependence and social harmony. This is exactly how Paul uses the imagery of the body in 1 Corinthians 12 – Paul speaks of how the different parts of the body, ears, eyes etc, need the other members for the whole to function. This interdependence means 'there may be no dissension within the body' (v. 25). A functionalist will value this theological metaphor highly.

- *Conflictualist perspective*: a conflictualist perspective on 1 Corinthians 12 would look very different from the above. For a conflictualist would ask, 'In whose interest does this harmony operate?' It would raise the possibility that Paul uses the symbol of the body of Christ to suppress legitimate dissent from his authority. Paul thus evokes a powerful religious symbol, the body of Christ, to reassert his own apostolic authority – 'God has appointed in the church *first apostles*' (v. 27) – in the face of widespread dissent and division. A conflictualist may view this symbol with deep suspicion.

- *Symbolic interactionist*: this is more difficult to specify, but might look something like the following: the Corinthian community was experiencing serious division over a variety of matters (see the earlier chapters of 1 Corinthians) and was on the point of dissolution, perhaps. In this context Paul evokes a powerful religious symbol, the body of Christ, in order to achieve a level of social cohesion and integration to ensure the survival of the group. The value of the symbol is relative to the context Paul and the community are facing. A community that is already stable might require a different symbol to meet its needs. A symbolic interactionist will relativize the symbol to the present needs of the social group.[8]

This diversity of methodologies with a corresponding diversity of ecclesiological implications arises because the social sciences differ from the physical sciences in important ways. Because in fact our human world is constituted by meaning and value, our systematic study of that world will be affected by our philosophical stances towards a variety of epistemological and moral questions. While historically the promise of the social sciences was that they would replace the endless bickering of the philosophers and theologians, in fact they have simply reproduced them in a different forum.

This leaves ecclesiologists in a difficult position. Does one opt for an existing approach in the social sciences or does one wait until the social sciences has 'got its act together' with a generally accepted methodology? One might be waiting a very long time, because the root problems are exactly the same as those facing philosophy and these show no sign of being resolved in the near future. At the very least an ecclesiologist must be aware that the adoption of a particular social scientific approach involves a commitment to particular philosophical positions which will directly impinge on the form one's ecclesiology will take.

641

Social sciences and theology

However, there is a second and more substantial objection to the problem of the relationship between social sciences and ecclesiology. If the task of the social sciences is to provide a systematic, coherent and comprehensive set of patterns into which the data of human communities will fit, that is, to provide a comprehensive upper blade, then what room is there for theology? Surely this would amount to the ultimate reduction of ecclesiology to sociology? Alternatively what does theology add to the understanding of the church if the social sciences already provide a comprehensive understanding?

This is a much more difficult question to deal with because it gets to the heart of the interrelationship of theology to the social sciences. It raises questions not only about how to relate these two disciplines, but also about the very autonomy of the social sciences themselves. Indeed the question of the relationship between the social sciences and theology touches on one of the most difficult of all theological problems, that of the relationship between grace and nature. In fact, if theology is not to be totally excluded from any contribution, then there must be some sense in which the social sciences of necessity are already theological. The argument at its simplest is that the data of the social sciences, that is the data of human communities and history, already includes data pertinent to theological realities of grace and sin. If so, the social sciences can only be comprehensive if they relate in some fashion to these data. Or as Lonergan has argued, 'the only correct general form of [the] understanding [of the human sciences] is theological'.[9] The realization of such a position within the academy is so far from the present reality of both the social sciences and theology that it is worth considering other attempts to resolve the issue to gain a deeper appreciation of the problem.[10]

Clodovis Boff and the method of correlation

We shall begin with a consideration of the work of Clodovis Boff in his book *Theology and Praxis*.[11] Boff has identified five different strategies for dealing with the question of the relationship between theology and the social sciences:[12]

1 *Empiricism, or absence of mediation:* this approach assumes some direct access to social reality unmediated by social theory. It simply lets the social facts 'speak for themselves'. In place of a critical reading that social theory might provide, it substitutes its own naïve, uncritical stance which is adopted as normative.

2 *Methodological purism, or exclusion of mediation:* this position holds to the self-sufficiency of faith and revelation for all theorizing. It has no need to use other disciplines. Boff notes that such purism does not work in classical areas such as christology and the Trinity. One adopts either critical philosophical assumptions or uncritical ones. The same is true in theologies which engage social and historical realities. Perhaps the clearest exponent of methodological purism is Karl Barth.[13]

3 *Theologism, or substitution for mediation:* this pushes purism further by arguing that theology is itself a mediation, so that 'theology pretends to find everything it needs to express the political in its own walls'.[14] The outcome from this is a 'religio-political rhetoric'. Boff refers to it as 'supernaturalism', and it is present in the ideologies of 'Christendom', apoliticism and 'faith without ideology'. We shall later present an understanding of the work of Milbank in these terms.

4   *Semantic mix, or faulty articulation of mediation:* this position makes use of the language of the social sciences, but results in a mixed discourse, drawing on the resources of two distinct realms of knowledge. The social mediation is generally uncritical and not properly assimilated. Boff argues that one side of the mix tends to dominate – 'the mixture is always organized under the domination of the logic of one of the languages in question'.[15] Boff claims that church social teaching documents tend to this mix.

5   *Bilingualism, or unarticulated mediation:* this consists of 'practicing two readings of the real', juxtaposing 'socio-analytic discourse and theological discourse'.[16] This type is perhaps exemplified in the work of Haight on systematic ecclesiology which we consider below.

Yet each of these Boff finds inadequate and so he develops his own proposals for such an engagement.

Boff wants to argue that the social sciences enter into theology of the political as a constitutive part, at the level of its material object, i.e. the social and political. This object is knowable only through the social sciences. He summarizes his position thus:

> The text of a theological reading with respect to the political is prepared and furnished by the sciences of the social. Theology receives its text from these sciences, and practices upon it a reading in conformity with its own proper code, in such a way as to extract from it a characteristically, properly theological meaning.[17]

It is not that the 'political *turns* theological, *becomes* theological by absorption, but by enrichment'.[18] One might say the theological sublates the political.

Problems arise, however, when Boff seeks to become more concrete in terms of the socio-analytic mediation. Boff appeals to the relative autonomy of earthly values, of the social order, to claim an autonomy of the social sciences – 'theology would be incompetent to pronounce upon the internal regime of the sciences' – which is guided by an 'ethic of objectivity . . . Theology possesses no supplementary illumination of a scientific order that might qualify it to invalidate scientific hypothesis'.[19] However, if, as we have suggested, the data encompassed by the social sciences includes data on the theological realities of sin and grace, then this is simply not the case and theology may feel impelled to pronounce upon the internal regime of those sciences.

Boff then raises the question of which approach the theologian should adopt. His position is that theology is 'forced to make a choice among the socio-analytic systems that are de facto at its disposal in the current phase of cultural development'.[20] And in the current phase, he could identify only two basic choices, functionalism and those of a 'dialectic tendency', that is, conflictualism. How does one choose? Boff offers two criteria, one scientific, and the other ethical. The scientific criteria is, which best explains society? On this level, functionalism is best for explaining societies that one 'judges good and to be maintained', whereas Marxism 'take into account the problems of a people that suffers as a result of conflicts and seeks to resolve them, even at the price of revolution'.[21] Boff then expands:

> At this point then we must move on to the second type of criteria – ethical criteria. The question of 'scientificness' raises an antecedent question, one concerned with ideological options and determinate political undertakings, and finally leading to ethics. Before a judgment can be made on the explicative value of a theory, one

must determine the concrete problems this theory claims to explain. The actual determination of these problems implies a decision of an ethical sort.[22]

The choice of social mediation is then determined by a prior ethical option, which for liberation theology will be identified in terms of the preferential option for the poor.

The major flaw in Boff's analysis lies in his understanding of the scientific character of the social sciences. Their 'objectivity' and 'autonomy' imply that theology is left simply to adopt one of the prevailing options in the 'current phase of cultural development'. Here the analogy Boff draws with Aristotle and Aquinas is illuminating. Boff argues that just as Aquinas adopted Aristotle, so theology may adopt Marxism. But Aquinas made significant contributions to and transformation of Aristotle's realist philosophy. So too, theologians may need to take a more active role in the transformation of the social sciences, not simply accept the options which happen to be available.

This criticism of liberation theology goes beyond the question of their adoption of a conflictualist approach, and whether they identify conflict as intrinsic (and normative), or as empirical. It is more fundamental and methodological, dealing with the ways in which we understand the relationship between theology and the social sciences in general. In the end, Boff's position is just another variant on the commonly used correlationist method in theology. Such methods, which seek to correlate situation (as mediated by the social sciences) with tradition (as theologically mediated), must always break down because, as Robert Doran emphasizes, 'the situation is already theological'.[23]

The substitution of mediation: John Milbank

It may seem that the direction in which we are heading is that of a substitution of mediation, wherein theology displaces the social sciences. In order to distinguish it from this we should compare it with the approach of John Milbank. Milbank's writing is complex, dense and controversial. Nonetheless he makes some serious theological points similar to those we have proposed. His position comes out of a postmodern idiom, which rejects master-narratives and rejoices in the concrete particularity of multiple histories. Reason is held in suspicion and persuasive rhetoric is the favoured form of argumentation. Claims to the use of reason are treated as a display of the 'will to power' and are subjected to a genealogical analysis. The strategy that unfolds is roughly as follows.

Firstly, the historical origins of the social sciences during the Enlightenment were an attempt to curtail and contain religion within the private sphere, a process which he refers to as 'policing the sublime' (a reference to Peter Berger's work). This policing ensured the separation of the secular and the sacred each into their own sphere, leading to the eventual irrelevance of religion to the public sphere. This is in essence a genealogical critique. By tracing the origins of the social sciences to these tainted sources he seeks to discredit them as useful tools in theological work. They are from their very origins interested in the elimination of religion.

Secondly, Milbank considers only two of the major approaches, viz., functionalist and conflictualist schools of thought. The first is dismissed as 'metaphysical': 'functionalist sociology adds nothing that is not metaphysical to historiography'.[24] And the metaphysical is simply a master-narrative, cloaked in reason, but really an instance of the will to power. The latter, conflictualism, he condemns as promoting an ontology of primordial violence. Such a conflictual view is basically pagan, not Christian, which promotes the ontological priority of peace. Milbank is suspicious of any 'dialectic method' since it represents the constant temptation to violence in the name of dialectic 'benefits' which only encourage further violence.[25]

Thirdly, Milbank raises an explicitly theological argument against the social sciences. His opening claim of the book is 'once there was no secular'.[26] For Milbank the very existence of the 'secular sphere' is a social construction which would not have been recognized, for example, during Christendom. Within Christendom the whole of society was subsumed within the sacred. According to Milbank, what allows for the creation of the secular is the grace-nature distinction introduced by the scholastics and exemplified in Aquinas. Prior to this an Augustinian theology operated on the basis of the grace-sin dialectic which allowed for no clear 'middle ground' such as the category of nature. By creating the grace-nature distinction Aquinas opened up the possibility of a (relatively) autonomous realm of activity distinct from the sacred. This autonomous realm becomes the secular.

The social model of an Augustinian theology of grace is Christendom, whereas Aquinas paves the way for the modern secular state. Further, in relation to modern theology and its present flirtations with the social sciences, Milbank identifies two options – 'naturalizing the supernatural' or 'supernaturalizing the natural'.[27] The first of these charges he lays at the feet of Rahner and in particular liberation theology. Their supposed levelling out of the supernatural concedes too much autonomy to the secular and social sciences, basically eliminating grace from human history. Milbank prefers the latter option, supernaturalizing the natural, leaving no space for the secular or the social sciences.[28]

Does this mean that Christian theology has nothing to say about societies? From Milbank's postmodern perspective, there are no 'societies' in general, only concrete communities and their histories, so there can be no general 'theory' of society. On the other hand Christianity is itself an embodied social reality with its own history, the history of the church, not as a hypostatized idea, but in the concrete lives of Christian communities. Milbank contends that Christianity is a distinctive ethical practice which requires its own distinctive social theory.

> The theory [i.e. the Christian theory of society], therefore, is first and foremost an *ecclesiology*, and only an account of other human societies to the extent that the Church defines itself, in its practice, as in continuity and discontinuity with these societies. As the Church is *already*, necessarily, by virtue of its institution, a 'reading' of other human societies, it becomes possible to consider ecclesiology as also a 'sociology'.[29]

Talk of a 'Christian sociology' makes sense precisely because there is no universal sociology, only the narratives of particular societies such as the church. It should not be that theology adds to itself a new competence to make 'social pronouncements', rather, 'all theology has to reconceive itself as a kind of "Christian sociology"'.[30]

There are two main advances that come from Milbank's analysis of the relationship between theology and the social sciences. The first is that it focuses our attention on the key theological issue underlying the relationship, that is, the question of the grace-nature debate. Milbank's work makes it clear that the 'solution' to the grace-nature issue impinges directly on the outcome of our studies. Milbank opts for a grace-sin dialectic, as with Augustine, rather than the grace-nature distinction adopted by Aquinas. The consequence is what Boff calls 'theologism', with the political consequence of Christendom.

The second advance is the way Milbank's discussion focuses our attention onto ecclesiology. Milbank conceives ecclesiology concretely and historically. His position is (perhaps paradoxically) opposed to an ecclesial idealism. What we see here is a close connection between the social sciences and ecclesiology, even in Milbank's rejection of the connection. We might compare his position with that of Lonergan. Lonergan maintains the relative autonomy of the social sciences on the basis of the grace-nature distinction. This then has implications for ecclesiology. For the church must become

> not only a process of self-constitution but also a fully conscious process of self-constitution. But to do so it will have to recognize that theology is not the full science of man, that theology illuminates only certain aspects of human reality, that the church can become a fully conscious process of self-constitution only when theology unites itself with all other relevant branches of human studies.[31]

For Lonergan,

> Grace perfects nature, both in the sense that it adds a perfection beyond nature and in the sense that it confers on nature the effective freedom to attain its own perfection. But grace is not a substitute for nature, and theology is not a substitute for empirical human science.[32]

These general observations, however, leave us somewhat short of finding a precise solution to the problem of the relationship between theology and the social sciences. What is required is a theological gestalt, the construction of a framework which is at once theological and social scientific, built from the ground up. It requires nothing less than the development of a theology of history itself, incorporating a massive transposition of the classical grace-nature distinction into social, cultural and historical categories. To my mind the only successful position which achieves this, at least as a starting point, is the work of Robert Doran in *Theology and the Dialectics of History*. Building on Lonergan's notion of the scale of values, of healing and creating in history, and of the analogy of dialectic, Doran has developed a theological construct which can incorporate a reoriented social science into its very heart.

The irony in all this is that Milbank's own position can be identified as a form of functionalism, as suits his own idealistic tendencies.[33] Though Milbank is critical of the social sciences in general, and of functionalism in particular, there is a precise sense in which his own stance can be understood as functionalist. In general Milbank considers ecclesiology to be a Christian 'alternative' or 'substitute' for sociology, so if we want to understand his 'sociological' approach we should consider the details of his ecclesiology. For Milbank the church is a sphere of 'socially aesthetic harmony', a society of friends 'sharing goals, where each new product and social role as it emerges is nonetheless given its "position" and relative weight in the community'.[34] This approach is captured in Milbank's fascinating discussion of the symbols of the circle and the arrow. 'Peace is circular, like a ritual dance or else the laurel crown adorning the brow of the victor.'[35] Justice 'secures the circular repetition of harmony'[36] whereas the arrow represents the constant temptation to violence in the name of dialectic 'benefits' which only encourage further violence.[37] Again we see that the values of functionalism are in the ascendant.

Examples from ecclesiology

I should now like to consider some contributions to the applications of the social sciences to ecclesiology in particular. I have already mentioned in the introductory paragraphs the works of Schillebeeckx and Haight. To these I will add some comments on the foundational contribution of Joseph Komonchak.

Schillebeeckx: The Church with a Human Face

Though primarily a work on the theology of ministry rather than ecclesiology as a whole, Schillebeeckx's book signalled a major engagement with the social sciences to produce a historical theology of ministry within the church. Moreover he engaged with the social sciences with at least some awareness of the problems we have been discussing above. He attacks a dualism which would attempt to separate sociological and historical insights from theological considerations. While he concurs that it would be wrong to reduce ministry to its sociological and historical analysis, he argues that 'there is also such a thing as theological reductionism, which puts the character of ministry as grace alongside and above its socio-historical reality'.[38] One cannot develop an ecclesiology simply using religious categories. To fail to introduce social and historical analysis is to fail to understand the one reality which is church. It is this socio-historical approach which brings a freshness to Schillebeeckx's analysis of ministry throughout the church's history.

Moreover he is aware of some of the diversity of approaches within the social sciences. At the beginning of his investigation, when speaking of the need for social theory, Schillebeeckx asks 'Which theory?' The two major models he mentions are 'models of conflict or integration [i.e. functionalist]'.[39] His own preference seems to be for the conflictualist stance – note he writes of 'liberating systems of communication' which is a reference to Habermas and critical theory – but no clear criteria is given why one should adopt this position rather than the other. Also there is no indication that other approaches might be of value. Indeed the question he poses as foundational, 'What interest do you seek to serve with a particular socio-historical investigation?',[40] presupposes a conflictualist stance. It views history in terms of conflicting interests, which may be part of the picture, but is rarely the whole picture.

Such a methodological option is significant because there is a sense in which it determines the outcomes of his subsequent investigations. For example, Schillebeeckx wants to examine the distinction between episcopal and presbyteral ministry, at least as it arose in the first two centuries of the church. The importance of this example is hard to underestimate, given its impact on subsequent church history, church order and modern ecumenical discussions. Rather than a theological distinction leading to different offices, he uncovers 'a gradually increasing theological legitimation of relationships of subjection and power which are essentially contrary to the gospel'.[41] The theological legitimation of the distinction comes after a process of the centralizing of power, and designates a ranking of that power, which is increasingly focused in the monarchical bishop. For Schillebeeckx, the distinction is little more that an ideological superstructure to support the institutional power relations. I would argue that given the option Schillebeeckx has adopted in relation to the social sciences, such an outcome is inevitable. This is precisely what the upper blade of a conflictualist approach expects and will find, if only as a suspicion.

Schillebeeckx's work on ministry is a significant attempt to integrate social sciences into an ecclesiology, but we can immediately identify its shortcomings in terms of the analysis above. While he engages with the social sciences at one level there is no serious coming to grips with the depth of the problem such engagement involves. Firstly, he limits his considerations to two approaches, the conflictualist and functionalist approaches. Secondly, there is no realization that the social sciences themselves will involve theological notions, and so one's option for a particular approach is never theologically neutral. A more serious engagement with the social sciences is required for the type of project Schillebeeckx envisages.

Haight: Christian Community in History

Though twenty years separate the work of Schillebeeckx and Haight it is not clear that any major advance has occurred in the discipline of ecclesiology, at least in relation to the use of the social sciences. Like Schillebeeckx, Haight envisages a historical form of ecclesiology, one which takes the historical data of the church into the heart of his theological method. Moreover Haight's work is significantly more comprehensive than that of Schillebeeckx, seeking to develop an account of the whole of the Christian church from its origins to the present day. In this his work represents a major achievement. And as with the work of Schillebeeckx, Haight recognizes the need to engage with the social sciences in order to write his historical ecclesiology. However, Haight's methodology is also dominated by a correlationist approach to theology, which I argue below fails to do justice to the reality of the church.[42]

From the outset Haight is clear that 'the primary object of the study of ecclesiology is the empirical church',[43] and that the church is 'not only an empirical and human reality, it is also a historical reality'.[44] He eschews any attempted 'theological reductionism' which would neglect or deny this and turn ecclesiology into some idealized form. Haight then sets up his ecclesiological problematic in the following terms: 'The church is simultaneously a human, historical, social reality on the one hand and a theological reality on the other hand. These two dimensions of the church are quite distinct.'[45] Drawing on the work of Schillebeeckx he argues that 'the church is a single reality in history, but one that must be understood in two irreducible languages',[46] a theological language relating the church to God and a critical, historical sociological language to deal with the human dimension of the church. Nonetheless he insists that 'these are two dimensions of one reality; there are not two churches. We need a theological method that respects these two dimensions of the one church, that does not hold them in balance over and against each other but integrates them into a single understanding.'[47]

It is easy to identify the confusion in Haight's approach. Initially he speaks of a human, historical, social reality and a theological reality. So already we are speaking of two realities. The language then shifts to 'two dimensions' of the one reality. Nonetheless these two dimensions require 'two irreducible languages' to give expression to them, which again gives the impression of two distinct realities.[48] Further, if one of these languages is already theological, why do we need a further theological method to bring these two dimensions into some further integration? If we already have a theological language to describe the relationship of the church to God, then what does the critical historical sociological language add to that? Is not the church that is in relationship to God the same historical church? Certainly we need a single understanding of the church, but it will not be achieved in the fashion Haight spells out.

Similarly Haight's discussion of sociology is disappointingly general and superficial. He appeals to a general 'sociological imagination' which allows space for a variety of disciplines. His use of sociological sources is eclectic and sporadic throughout his text. Indeed, most explicit references to sociological works occur in Chapter 2, 'The Genesis of the Church', with scant explicit reference in other chapters. There is no apparent awareness of the major methodological divisions with the field of sociology, nor of the greater problem we have identified above, that 'the only correct general form of [the] understanding [of the human sciences] is theological'.[49] Once the social sciences are accepted as self-enclosed and completely autonomous from theology then the problem Haight is dealing with is insoluble. We will always end up with two irreducible languages which we then struggle to bring into conjunction.

This difficulty leads to a methodological instability in Haight's approach which becomes evident in the second volume of his work. In that second volume Haight shifts his focus from a historical ecclesiology to a comparative ecclesiology. Acknowledging the divisions that occurred within Western Christianity consequent to the Reformations, his method in the second volume is to compare and contrast the competing ecclesiologies of the different 'branches' of Christianity. The reason given is purely pragmatic, 'the only way to understand the whole church when it is divided into a plurality of churches is by a comparative ecclesiology'.[50] While this may seem reasonable it means a subtle shift from the consideration of the church as historical community per se, to documents and authors writing about the church, usually from their confessional basis. This process amounts to a comparison of ecclesiologies rather than comparison of churches; and ecclesiologies do not stand in a one-to-one relationship with actual church communities. One church community might have a number of competing ecclesiologies at work shaping its life. And any particular ecclesiology serves not simply to present the church as it is, but as the author thinks the church should be.[51] So we can be back into the problem of idealism that Haight's original historical methodology was seeking to overcome.

Overall then, Haight's work does not succeed in the goal it sets itself. Because the methodological issues involved in bringing the social sciences into the heart of ecclesiology are far greater than he realizes, the end result is more a historical narrative of the Christian church, with theological and sociological interests. In the second volume in particular the references to sociology and sociological sources fall away to next to nothing. The problem of bringing the social sciences into the heart of ecclesiology is far more radical than any method of correlation allows for. It requires more than the adoption of a 'sociological imagination' by the ecclesiologist; it requires a fundamental reorientation of the social sciences themselves.

Komonchak: Foundations in Ecclesiology

Though he has not written a work of historical ecclesiology in the manner of Schillebeeckx or Haight, the work of Joseph Komonchak has been foundational for the considerations of this present essay. In a collection of essays published under the title, *Foundations in Ecclesiology*, Komonchak spells out a programme for the re-visioning of ecclesiology as concretely history and as requiring a thorough engagement with the social sciences.[52] Drawing heavily on the writings of Bernard Lonergan, Komonchak's work is foundational and programmatic, and its implementation would of necessity be one of collaboration, for no single scholar could hope to master all aspects that are required. Of the many riches to be found in this work I will focus on three.

Firstly, ecclesiology is concerned with the concrete history of the church, or what Komonchak often refers to as the 'concrete self-realizations of the Church'.[53] The object of ecclesiological study 'is not only *what is said* about the Church in the New Testament, in the apostolic Symbol, in the liturgy, in descriptions of ministry, but also *what was coming to be* as the Church in the formation and reception of all four elements'.[54] Ecclesiology must resist the temptation to focus on texts and documents which speak about the church, in order to focus on the church itself. This is a much richer field of data which incorporates persons, their actions and decisions, the emergence of movements and institutions, the shifts in ecclesial cultures which texts and documents may signify, as well as the realization (and failures) of the redemptive mission of the church throughout history.

Secondly, ecclesiology must engage with the social sciences. He argues that, 'just as one cannot construct a theology without an at least implicit philosophy, so one cannot construct an ecclesiology within an implicit social theory; and without making the implicit explicit and securing its foundations neither constructions can be considered critical'.[55] Coming to grips with social theory is necessary if theology is to move beyond description and move into explanation, to move beyond common sense and into a realm of theory. The church is a social and historical reality so it is essential to a systematic understanding of the church to employ tools developed for a systematic understanding of social and historical realities. 'How can one work out a systematic ecclesiology without working out first such terms as "individual", "community", "society", "meaning", "change", "structure", "institution", "relationship", and so on, and the various relationships, or at least types of relationships, that can obtain among these those terms?'[56] Komonchak is aware of the difficulties involved, in particular 'the ecclesiologist who attempts it will not find himself before a unified body of social theory',[57] though he is less explicit on the theological dimension of social theory itself.[58]

Thirdly, Komonchak places ecclesiology within a larger field of a theology of history. The church as a redemptive process of self-constitution is a historical realization of the twin missions of the Word and Spirit.[59] These divine missions are constitutive of the redemptive intent of God in human history. The history of the church is a moment in the larger history of humanity and so ecclesiology finds its natural home in a larger theology of history itself:

> Where minds have been clarified by the revelation of God, where spirits have been fortified by his promise, and where hearts have been liberated by his love, there exists in and among human societies people who can be agents or subjects of historical action which breaks the reign of sin and permits the recovery of the native powers of the human soul. The doctrine of redemption is the articulation of this possibility in human history. In its full range, soteriology is a theology of history. And as concretely articulated, soteriology requires a theology of the church as an event within the endless struggle of the three historic principles of progress, decline, and redemptive recovery.[60]

Conclusion

The hope of bringing the social sciences into the heart of ecclesiology as envisaged in this present essay and in the work of Komonchak remains largely unfulfilled. Strikingly the methodological article written by Pedro Rodriguez in the collection of essays edited by Peter Phan, *The Gift of the Church*, makes no mention of the role of the social sciences in ecclesiology, despite the appearance of the seminal work by Komonchak in his bibliography.[61] Dennis Doyle may agree with Komonchak that 'social theory can be fruitfully applied to the Church without being reductionist',[62] but one will search his book *Communion Ecclesiology* in vain for any evidence reflecting such agreement. And a recent work in historical ecclesiology by Bernard Prusak, *The Church Unfinished*, demonstrates no awareness at all that social theory may have a contribution to make to ecclesiology.[63]

There is perhaps a natural reluctance on the part of theologians and ecclesiologists in particular to accept the need to engage with yet another body of theory. It may help to realize that the social sciences themselves have an implicitly theological dimension, though this is not something those sciences themselves are near to accepting. However, unless ecclesiology does so engage it will remain a largely descriptive study and fail to become truly systematic. To draw from an analogy in the physical sciences, imagine if chemistry attempted to classify the elements by reference to their colour, hardness and melting points. It might provide an interesting classification scheme, but it would be nothing as compared to a classification by their atomic number. Chemistry only became truly scientific with the discovery of the periodic table. How many of our problems in ecclesiology, for example the relationship and priorities of 'local' and 'universal' church, arise because our categories are descriptive and not explanatory? Unless we can make the shift, we shall never know.

Notes

1 Edward Schillebeeckx, *The Church with a Human Face*, London: SCM, 1985.
2 Roger Haight, *Christian Community in History*, 2 vols, New York: Continuum, 2004–5. The choice of these two works is based on their 'iconic' significance, particularly within Roman Catholic theology. They both represent a major engagement with the issue under consideration.
3 Cardinal Kasper introduced this distinction in his debate with then Cardinal Ratzinger in their discussions on the role and significance of the local versus the universal church. 'The conflict is between theological opinions and underlying philosophical assumptions. One side [Ratzinger] proceeds by Plato's method; its starting point is the primacy of an ideal that is a universal concept. The other side [Kasper] follows Aristotle's approach and sees the universal as existing in a concrete reality', Walter Kasper, 'A Friendly Reply to Cardinal Ratzinger on the Church', *America* (2001), 13.
4 This is basically the position of John Milbank, *Theology and Social Theory: Beyond Secular Reason*, Cambridge, MA: Blackwell, 1991.
5 Bernard J.F. Lonergan, *Insight: A Study of Human Understanding*, Frederick E. Crowe and Robert M. Doran (eds), *Collected Works of Bernard Lonergan*, vol. 3, Toronto: University of Toronto Press, 1992.
6 This connection between upper and lower blades in relation to sociology and history was captured in the quip, 'Sociology is history with the hard work left out; history is sociology with the brains left out', W.J. Cahnman and A. Boskoff, 'Sociology and History: Reunion and Rapprochement', in W. J. Cahnman and A. Boskoff (eds), *Sociology and History*, Glencoe: Free Press, 1964, p. 1.
7 These are standard types discussed in introductory text books in sociology, for example, E. C. Cuff, W. W. Sharrock, and D. W. Francis, *Perspectives in Sociology*, 3rd edn, Boston: Unwin Hyman, 1990.
8 One could provide a similar analysis of the more contemporary ecclesiological symbol, *communio*. This too has functionalist overtones. The question that needs to be asked is 'Why has this symbol arisen now?' For a solid account of the parallels between 'body of Christ' ecclesiology and communion ecclesiology see Edward Hahnenberg, 'The Mystical Body of Christ and Communion Ecclesiology: Historical Parallels', *Irish Theological Quarterly* 70 (2005), 3–30. For a critique of communion approaches see Neil Ormerod, 'The Structure of a Systematic Ecclesiology', *Theological Studies* 63 (2002), 27–9.
9 Bernard J.F. Lonergan, 'Theology and Understanding', in *Collection*, Frederick E. Crowe and

Robert M. Doran (eds), *Collected Works of Bernard Lonergan*, vol. 4, Toronto: University of Toronto Press, 1993, p. 130.

10 This position is argued more fully in Neil Ormerod, 'A Dialectic Engagement with the Social Sciences in an Ecclesiological Context', *Theological Studies* 66 (2005), 815–40. The strategy of that article is to analyse the ways in which social sciences deal with the problem of sin and evil. This present essay draws on my earlier article in various sections, particularly in the analyses of the work of Boff and Milbank.

11 Clodovis Boff, *Theology and Praxis: Epistemological Foundations*, Maryknoll, NY: Orbis, 1987.

12 Ibid., pp. 20–34.

13 For example, Barth refuses to allow 'any general or special anthropology to intervene with its supposedly normative suggestions. We cannot be helped to our goal by any definition of man projected from the sphere occupied by a biological, sociological, psychological or ethical conception. Common to all such anthropologies is the fact that their pictures of man are all products of the same human self-understanding . . . no help is to be found even in the most penetrating analyses of what in any given age . . . is called "modern" man.' Karl Barth, *Church Dogmatics*, ed. Geoffrey William Bromiley and Thomas Forsyth Torrance, trans. G. T. Thomson, Edinburgh: T&T Clark, 1936, IV/3–2, p. 803.

14 Boff, *Theology and Praxis*, p. 26.

15 Ibid., p. 28.

16 Ibid., p. 29.

17 Ibid., p. 31.

18 Ibid., p. 33.

19 Ibid., pp. 51–2.

20 Ibid., p. 56.

21 Ibid., p. 58.

22 Ibid., p. 58.

23 Robert M. Doran, *Theology and the Dialectics of History*, Toronto: University of Toronto Press, 1990, p. 456. For a more detailed analysis and critique of the correlationist approach see Neil Ormerod, 'Quarrels with the Method of Correlation', *Theological Studies* 57 (1996), 707–19.

24 Milbank, *Theology and Social Theory*, p. 111.

25 Ibid., p. 422.

26 Ibid., p. 9.

27 Ibid., p. 207.

28 Ibid., p. 211.

29 Ibid., p. 380.

30 Ibid., p. 381.

31 Bernard J.F. Lonergan, *Method in Theology*, London: DLT, 1972, p. 364.

32 Lonergan, *Insight*, p. 767.

33 Milbank describes his own position as one of 'linguistic idealism', Milbank, *Theology and Social Theory*, p. 343.

34 Ibid., p. 422.

35 Ibid., p. 332.

36 Ibid., p. 334.

37 Ibid., p. 422.

38 Schillebeeckx, *Church with a Human Face*, p. 5.

39 Ibid., p. 41.

40 Ibid.

41 Ibid., p. 69.

42 Haight spells out his understanding of the method of correlation in Roger Haight, *Dynamics of Theology*, New York: Paulist Press, 1990, pp.191–212. See also Roger Haight, 'Historical Ecclesiology: An Essay on Method in the Study of the Church', *Science et Esprit* 39 (1987), 345–74.

43 Haight, *Christian Community in History*, vol. 1, p. 35.

44 Ibid., p. 37.

45 Ibid., p. 38.

46 Ibid., p. 39. He references Schillebeeckx, *Church with a Human Face*, pp. 210–13, which to my mind does not support Haight's assertion of 'two irreducible languages'.
47 Haight, *Christian Community in History*, vol. 1, p. 39.
48 Haight further confuses the matter by referring to Lonergan's distinction between general and special categories. Lonergan never speaks of these as irreducible languages. For Lonergan theology always involves both general and special categories even if it is just speaking about God, as in matters of natural theology.
49 Lonergan, 'Theology and Understanding', p. 130.
50 Haight, *Christian Community in History*, vol. 2, p. 3.
51 Joseph Komonchak makes the point that ecclesiology 'cannot be restricted to the interpretation of statements about the Church, whether these be biblical, traditional, liturgical, magisterial, theology of other . . . Statements about the Church, although a part and at times a determining part, are not the whole of the Church's self-realization in any generation.' Joseph A. Komonchak, *Foundations in Ecclesiology*, ed. Fred Lawrence, vol. 11, *Lonergan Workshop Journal, Supplementary Issue*, Boston, MA: Boston College, 1995, p. 67.
52 Also of value is Joseph A. Komonchak, 'The Significance of Vatican Council II for Ecclesiology', in *Gift of the Church*, Collegeville, MN: Liturgical Press, 2000, 69–92.
53 For example Komonchak, *Foundations in Ecclesiology*, p. 53.
54 Ibid., p. 49. Also pp. 50, 67, 68.
55 Ibid., p. 64.
56 Ibid., pp. 69–70.
57 Ibid., p. 73.
58 This is reflected in Komonchak's actual engagement with social sciences in particular ecclesiological themes. His tendency is to draw on highly reputable authors and theorists rather than engage with social science as a whole requiring reorientation.
59 Komonchak, *Foundations in Ecclesiology*, p. 48.
60 Ibid., p. 81. On the principles of progress, decline and redemption see the whole of Ch. 6, 'Authenticity in history', pp. 121–40.
61 Pedro Rodriguez, 'Theological Method for Ecclesiology', in Peter Phan (ed.), *Gift of the Church*, Collegeville, MN: Liturgical Press, 2000, pp. 129–56.
62 Dennis M. Doyle, *Communion Ecclesiology: Vision and Versions*, Maryknoll, NY: Orbis, 2000, p. 14.
63 Bernard Prusak, *The Church Unfinished: Ecclesiology through the Centuries*, Mahwah, NY: Paulist Press, 2004.

Further reading

Clodovis Boff, *Theology and Praxis: Epistemological Foundations*, Maryknoll, NY: Orbis, 1987.
W. J. Cahnman and A. Boskoff, 'Sociology and History: Reunion and Rapprochement', in W. J. Cahnman and A. Boskoff (eds), *Sociology and History*, Glencoe: Free Press, 1964, pp. 1–18.
C. Cuff, W. W. Sharrock and D. W. Francis, *Perspectives in Sociology*, 3rd edn, Boston: Unwin Hyman, 1990.
Robert M. Doran, *Theology and the Dialectics of History*, Toronto: University of Toronto Press, 1990.
Dennis M. Doyle, *Communion Ecclesiology: Vision and Versions*, Maryknoll, NY: Orbis, 2000.
Edward Hahnenberg, 'The Mystical Body of Christ and Communion Ecclesiology: Historical Parallels', *Irish Theological Quarterly* 70 (2005), 3–30.
Roger Haight, *Christian Community in History*, 2 vols, New York: Continuum, 2004–5.
——, *Dynamics of Theology*, New York: Paulist Press, 1990.
——, 'Historical Ecclesiology: An Essay on Method in the Study of the Church', *Science et Esprit* 39 (1987), 345–74.
Walter Kasper, 'A Friendly Reply to Cardinal Ratzinger on the Church', *America* (2001), 8–14.
Joseph A. Komonchak, *Foundations in Ecclesiology*, ed. Fred Lawrence, Vol. 11, *Lonergan Workshop Journal, Supplementary Issue*, Boston, MA: Boston College, 1995.
——, 'The Significance of Vatican Council II for Ecclesiology', in *Gift of the Church*, Collegeville, MN: Liturgical Press, 2000, pp. 69–92.

Bernard J.F. Lonergan, *Insight: A Study of Human Understanding*, Frederick E. Crowe and Robert M. Doran (eds), *Collected Works of Bernard Lonergan*, Vol. 3, Toronto: University of Toronto Press, 1992.

——, *Method in Theology*, London: DLT, 1972.

——, 'Theology and Understanding', in *Collection*, Frederick E. Crowe and Robert M. Doran, *Collected Works of Bernard Lonergan*, Vol. 4, Toronto: University of Toronto Press, 1993, pp. 114–32.

John Milbank, *Theology and Social Theory: Beyond Secular Reason*, Cambridge, MA: Blackwell, 1991.

Neil Ormerod, 'Quarrels with the Method of Correlation', *Theological Studies* 57 (1996), 707–19.

——, 'The Structure of a Systematic Ecclesiology', *Theological Studies* 63 (2002), 3–30.

——, 'A Dialectic Engagement with the Social Sciences in an Ecclesiological Context', *Theological Studies* 66 (2005), 815–40.

Bernard Prusak, *The Church Unfinished: Ecclesiology through the Centuries*, Mahwah, NY: Paulist Press, 2004.

Pedro Rodriguez, 'Theological Method for Ecclesiology', in Peter Phan (ed.), *Gift of the Church*, Collegeville, MN: Liturgical Press, 2000, pp. 129–56.

Edward Schillebeeckx, *The Church with a Human Face*, London: SCM, 1985.

38

ECCLESIOLOGY
AND PHILOSOPHY

Steven Shakespeare

'What has Jerusalem to do with Athens, the Church with the Academy?' Tertullian's rhetorical question haunts the history of the church's engagements with philosophy.[1] It implies a fundamental separation between the truth that can only be revealed by God, and that which human reason can discover for itself. Philosophy is not simply a method of organizing human thinking. It is an alternative worldview. It is a worldview which has no openness to the gift of grace. It therefore remains a prisoner of human pride.

Tertullian's dismissal of secular wisdom, on the cusp of the second and third centuries, is echoed by the work of a twentieth-century giant of theology, Karl Barth. Barth believed that Christian theology had sinfully abandoned its one and only starting point: the gracious address of God to humankind in the Word of God, Jesus Christ. Only God could initiate us into a relationship with saving truth, for God himself is the truth. All human philosophical attempts to secure a foundation for truth are at best striving after wind. At worst, it is idolatry, replacing God's gift of himself with the work of human hands and minds.

Barth can therefore declare: 'there never has been a *philosophia christiana*, for if it was *philosophia* it was not *christiana*, and if it was *christiana* it was not *philosophia*'.[2] There can be no meeting point between these two fundamentally different approaches to exploring and receiving the truth about how things are with us, the world and God.

In the Christian centuries between Tertullian and Barth, however, there has been a long relationship between the church and philosophy. It has seen evolution and rupture, it has been contested and conflicted, but the relationship between them has never gone away. Even the nay-sayers still use philosophy as a counterfoil, a way of clarifying what the positive nature of pure theology might be. Theology is haunted by philosophy's shades.

This chapter will explore why this is a question that seems to *matter* so much. I will argue that this is indeed a question of *material* practices and bodies as much as it is about something purely theoretical and intellectual. Perhaps this should not surprise us. After all, philosophers since Plato have agonized about the relationship between the ideal and the real, spirit and body, eternity and time, appearance and reality. And Christian philosophy has always been driven by an experience of the divine become human, God made matter in the incarnation of the Word and the eucharist.

Negotiating these border crossings is a serious, risky matter. Small wonder that the borders between philosophy and theology have been blurred and fought over in the process. One issue we need to acknowledge immediately. Tertullian's use of the cities of Athens and Jerusalem to stand for philosophy and theology is significant. He is not simply speaking of different theoretical approaches or beliefs (let alone the relatively modern idea of different academic disciplines), but of different *societies* – incompatible ways of living and being in community.

This essay will take its cue from this. It will explore the historical relationship between philosophy and theology whilst keeping in mind underlying debates about community, relationship and communication – debates which go to the heart of the church's understanding and imagination of its own nature.

In the marketplace of Athens: the early church and Greek philosophy

It is worth dwelling upon Tertullian's remark a little longer. Understanding it in context helps to shed light on what was at stake for him.

It occurs in his work *The Prescriptions against the Heretics*, written around the start of the third century as a general dismissal of all those beliefs which are characterized as false innovations. It is a short book, and does not deal with the details of the various 'heretical' belief systems Tertullian had in view. Instead, it focuses on the processes and personalities through which those teachings had come into existence and spread.

The argument is that the true doctrine of the church has been passed down from the earliest apostles who were with Jesus. The church has been kept faithful to that doctrine by the Holy Spirit. There is therefore no reason to suppose that new teachings are waiting to be discovered, and Tertullian delights in exposing various teachers of these things as lacking any real pedigree or authority (or, indeed, personal morality).

In a key passage, Tertullian mocks the idea that only recently has the full Christian truth been revealed. The church has been getting along very well without these novelties – witness the baptism, the miracles, the ministries and so on. The novelty of heresy is associated with the philosophical schools which have licensed an arbitrary (and ultimately disobedient) speculation:

> Where was Marcion then, the ship-owner of Pontus, the student of Stoicism? Where was Valentinus then, the disciple of Plato? It is well known that they lived not so long ago, about the reign of Antoninus, and at first accepted the doctrine of the catholic Church at Rome under Bishop Eleutherus of blessed memory, until, on account of the ever-restless speculation with which they were infecting the brethren also, they were expelled. [3]

This is important because it shows Tertullian contrasting the church as an established community – bound by an inherited tradition – with alternative philosophical communities, unregulated by such boundaries. Philosophy is more than a set of beliefs. It is a way of life, a school, a community. For Tertullian, it is an unbridled way of life, and leads directly to immorality and corruption.

Two points need to be made here. First, the idea of philosophy as a way of life is not at all unique to Tertullian. Philosophies flourished in the Roman world, not as merely 'academic' pursuits, but as practical paths of salvation. Platonism, Cynicism, Stoicism all fed into quasireligious communities, with their rituals, ethical systems, preachers and symbols. The Jewish historian Josephus, when describing for his pagan audience the various groupings active in Israel before the Jewish Revolt of AD 66, talks of them as philosophical 'schools'. The fact that the Pharisees, Sadducees, Essenes and Zealots were also religious and political movements would not have struck Josephus as a contradiction of his choice of terminology. Philosophy could encompass all these aspects.

So we should not be surprised that one of the most dramatic stories of early Christian missions found in the book of Acts takes place when Paul visits the agora – the marketplace-cum-civic centre – in Athens. Here, in the midst of the quintessential Greek polis, he debates with Stoics and Epicureans. This is where purveyors of philosophical goods must go.

This leads into the second point arising out of Tertullian's characterization of philosophy as an alternative community. The author of Acts remarks somewhat scathingly that 'all the Athenians and foreigners living there would spend their time in nothing but telling or learning something new' (Acts 17.21). One might think that this would lead to the kind of rejection of Athens of which Tertullian would approve. However, this is not how the story turns out. In fact, Paul acknowledges the religious striving of the Athenians, presents Christ as the fulfilment of their worship of an 'unknown god' and even quotes pagan philosopher-poets to support his case. His converts include Dionysius the Areopagite, whose name is pseudonymously attached centuries later in Christian tradition to a mystical philosophical treatise.

Tertullian's response is therefore not the only possible one. From the earliest days of the church, a different kind of rapprochement with philosophy was possible. One of its best-known early exponents is Justin Martyr, who was killed for his faith in AD 165. Justin argues that Christians should not be persecuted by the Roman Empire. In the course of this, he develops the claim that Christianity perfects what is dimly perceived in pagan philosophy. There is fulfilment, rather than contradiction.

A key theme which brings philosophy and theology together is that of the Logos. Usually translated as 'word', it has in fact a richer meaning, encompassing discourse, wisdom and order. It is already used in the gospel of John, which refers to the Logos which was in the beginning with God (and which was God), now made flesh in Jesus. Athens meets Jerusalem at the very source of Christian reflection on Jesus' identity.

Logos theology thus provides a significant link with non-Christian thought. In the 'middle Platonism' exemplified by the Hellenistic first-century Jew Philo of Alexandria, the Logos mediates between God and humankind (Philo claimed the Logos was expressed in the Jewish Law). God is seen as transcending the world of space and time to such a degree that it becomes difficult to conceive how God directly relates to the human world. The Logos becomes the point of contact, expressing God's ordering will and truth in the world we know.

The Logos appeared in a different but related form in Stoic philosophy, as the *logos spermatikos* – the principle of order inherent in the workings of the cosmos. Living in tune with this natural law was a philosophical path of fulfilment and salvation.

Justin draws out some of the implications of this theological approach in relating the church to philosophy – and thereby to a wider *human* community:

> We have been taught that Christ is the firstborn of God, and we have proclaimed that he is the Logos, in whom every race of people have shared. And those who live according to the Logos are Christians, even though they may have been counted as atheists – such as Socrates and Heracleitus and others like them, among the Greeks . . . Whatever either lawyers or philosophers have said well, was articulated by finding and reflecting upon some aspect of the Logos.[4]

The Logos is a principle of mediation, not only between God and humanity but also between the church and its other, the pagan world. Logos theology does not thereby abandon the finality or superiority of Christian claims, but philosophy is nevertheless given a role in relation to the church analogous to that of Israel. As Clement of Alexandria puts it,

> philosophy acted as a schoolmaster to bring the Greeks to Christ, just as the law brought the Hebrews. This philosophy was by way of a preparation, which prepared the way for its perfection in Christ.[5]

The church did not grow and spread in a vacuum. It was part of a wider cultural world which was deeply Hellenistic (i.e. influenced by Greek culture). Inevitably, Christian thinkers had to define themselves (whether through or against) Hellenistic modes of thinking and social organization. Tertullian, for all his anti-philosophical fervour, was himself influenced by Stoicism, from which he derived the belief that the soul is material. And in the very same passage from which we quoted earlier, he uses this argument against the heretics: 'The real thing always comes before the representation of it; the copy comes later.'[6] This is an argument rooted in Platonic thought, for which the eternal forms or essences of things are the 'real thing', whereas the particular realities we experience around us in space or time are only imperfect copies or reflections. Plato's philosophy is not only a theory of how we can know the truth, it is also a path towards that truth, a call to move away from shifting earthly appearances closer to the unchanging eternal truth behind them.

The point here is not that Tertullian was a closet Platonist. It is that Christian theologians lived and breathed in an atmosphere drenched in Greek philosophy. The sharpness of some negative reactions to philosophy is perhaps due to its pervasive and inescapable influence.

For Clement, it was not *necessary* for a Christian to know philosophy, but philosophy could undoubtedly be a contributory factor in bolstering Christian belief. He even spoke of the 'true' gnostic, using a term derived from the Greek word for knowledge. A Gnostic is one who knows the esoteric secrets necessary to understand their place in the world and navigate their way out of it to a spiritual salvation. Here Clement shows himself willing to take risks to affirm the value of philosophical knowledge. 'Gnostic' was a term ordinarily reserved for groups eventually condemned as heretical sects, some of whom (like the Valentinians) were targeted by Tertullian.

With hindsight it is easy to over-simplify the Gnostic movements. At the time they flourished, they represented powerful alternative worldviews and forms of community *within* the Christian churches. Gnostics combined philosophical speculation with the powerful salvific edge of the mystery religions. They tended to believe that human beings were divine sparks, their true eternal souls trapped in this material world. For some, the physical creation was the act of an evil or lesser deity. Gnostics sought enlightenment from Christ, a spiritual guide who had only appeared to share human flesh. Armed with this knowledge, they could find liberation from the world of decay and suffering.

Gnosticism owes much to the devaluation of the material world found in variants of Plato's philosophy. The eternal truth must be free from all taint of change and corruption. However, emphasizing this aspect can distract us from the radical *social* challenge which these groups represented. Appealing to esoteric knowledge, they could break apart from authorized lineages of apostolic authority and church structures. Emphasizing the secondariness of bodies, they could challenge the hierarchical ways in which bodies were defined and organized (not least the subordination of women and their exclusion from positions of leadership which became ever more evident in the mainstream tradition). The otherworldliness and potential elitism of Gnostic groups tells only one part of the story.[7]

Later condemnations make things seem much more cut and dried. However, it is striking that Clement was confident enough to use some of the language of 'gnosticism'. Another Alexandrian theologian, Origen (c. 185–254), went even further in incorporating elements of a Platonic worldview into his defence of Christian faith. Unlike Tertullian, Origen *encouraged* the kind of speculation that would lead the Christian reader of scripture or observer of the world beyond mere surface appearances. He posits a first creation of pure minds which only sink into material forms as they fall away from God. God himself is changeless and impassible. Origen even envisaged a procession of worlds through which souls could be purified and returned to God – a cyclical worldview which allowed even the devil the chance to be redeemed.[8]

Origen's precise views (some of which were later condemned by the church) should not distract us from his significance in integrating Greek cosmic speculation into the church's view of God and salvation. Nowhere was this to be more important than in his approach to the interpretation of scripture. Origen distinguished several levels at which scripture could be read, the lowest of which was the merely literal and historical. The highest was spiritual, concerning deeper mysteries beyond time and space. Again, the dualism and otherworldliness of this approach is only one aspect of its importance. Equally significant is that the act of reading scripture was to become a *philosophical* act of discernment – relying on enlightenment from God, to be sure, but potentially disrupting the authorized traditions and channels of interpretation in the church.

Origen was a contemporary and fellow student of Plotinus, a key figure in the growth of a more mystically inclined 'Neo-Platonism' which was hugely influential on Christian theology and devotion. Plotinus saw the world as a series of emanations from the eternal One, with matter being at the lowest level of the chain of being. It was possible to climb this chain and so conform more closely to the perfection of the deity.[9]

Origen and Plotinus use philosophy to construct a world that makes sense and is an ordered whole, a cosmos. Origen shows how ambiguous this effort can be for Christian identity. If the outer, historical reality is merely a stepping stone towards divine truth, at what point is physical creation entirely abandoned, and Christ himself becomes a wholly spiritual saviour? And what authority can the church claim in regulating the interpretation of scripture or devotion, if they are driven by mystical realities that escape and transcend earthly structures? Is the church itself something that needs to be set aside (as there is no temple in the vision of the redeemed city at the end of the book of Revelation)?

Dwelling on this earliest period of the church's interaction with philosophy is necessary because it continues to set the agenda for so much of what follows. The following points are particularly important to bear in mind. First, the 'philosophy' we have been dealing with here is not simply a method of thinking. It is a specific family of thought, often uniting cosmological speculations with ethical, religious and devotional paths. Secondly, this means that the relationship between the church and philosophy is never merely intellectual. It is also about the way bodies and communities are organized, authority asserted or challenged, and dialogue conducted or refused. It is therefore an ecclesiological issue – in a sense *the* ecclesiological issue par excellence.

The two cities: Augustine's compromise

The potential and difficulties surrounding philosophy's place in the church are well articulated in the seminal work of Augustine of Hippo (354–430). In his *Confessions*, he relates how a reading of Cicero's *Hortensius* awakened in him a love of wisdom (the literal meaning of 'philosophy'). Cicero's advice was 'not simply to admire one or another of the schools of philosophy, but to love wisdom itself, whatever it might be'.[10]

Augustine's journey takes him to the Manichees, a Christian group which bore a close relation to previous Gnostic sects, and whose founder Mani claimed to receive new revelations of wisdom which surpassed the New Testament. Manicheism prevented Augustine accepting the doctrine of the incarnation, as it was impossible for him to think of the divine being so intimately connected with matter, which was itself associated so closely with change and evil. Augustine's scruples are partially overcome by three factors: first, the inability of the Manichees to integrate the latest scientific discoveries into their thought – discoveries made thanks to God's universal gift of reason; secondly, the realization that scripture (especially the doctrine that human beings are made in God's image and likeness) can be interpreted figuratively, freeing the divine from some of the cruder elements of anthropomorphism; and finally, a reading of Neo-Platonist philosophy, which helped him to see that evil was not a material substance, but a moral deficiency and lack.

Given Augustine's reputation as the great advocate of merciless predestination and the utter corruption of the human will before grace, it is striking that his own account of his conversion places so much weight on the 'graced' nature of human reason. In other words, Augustine is able to perceive the presence of God to some extent already at work and being disclosed in human thinking, before any specific Christian revelation comes along. The Neo-Platonists in particular echo many Christian themes, including the mediating role of the Logos in uniting our wisdom to that of God. What is lacking is the specific, bodily incarnation of the Logos in Jesus Christ.[11]

Augustine's position is worked out more fully in *The City of God*. Here he deals with the moral and philosophical confusion – the violent anarchy – he perceives at the heart of Roman polytheism. But he also acknowledges the partial validity of Platonism as the highest kind of philosophy and 'the closest approximation to our Christian position',[12] because it is able to recognize the truth that God is not to be identified with any material thing, that God is One, unchanging, underived and the source of everything else that is.

Thus, when Augustine claims that 'God is without doubt a substance, or better, an essence, which the Greeks call *ousia*'[13] he makes no attempt to hide the philosophical roots of this doctrine. Significantly, it is the human intellect which is seen as being the mundane analogy to God: 'if our mind is not a material object, how can God, the creator of the mind, be himself a material thing?'[14] Augustine, who affirms the goodness of material creation, nevertheless values the immaterial mind above all else.

It is striking that Augustine's meditations on the nature of human thought are seen by many interpreters to anticipate the radical departure of Descartes, over a thousand years later, who attempted to strip away all that could be doubted, to found knowledge on a certainty internal to the thinking process. Augustine's thought seems to lead in a similar direction, as he persistently poses the question 'Who am I?' and finds in the mind the image of truth, of God.

However, simply to assimilate Augustine to this kind of philosophical position misses some important dimensions. First, what is lacking in Platonism for Augustine is precisely the saving truth of the incarnation, and the mystery of God's Trinity – a mystery which underscores human dissimilarity from God. The source of all wisdom and insight remains Christ. Human discovery responds to divine revelation. Secondly, Augustine's questioning proceeds not from radical doubt, but from an experience of grace. It is carried out in the context of prayer and worship, a communal act of the church, even when it is individually expressed. As *The City of God* makes plain, the earthly and heavenly cities co-exist until the final judgement. There is both tension and solidarity between them. Philosophy and the church are in touch with one another, because the church is not a community separate from the world.

Augustine's major controversies as a theologian were with 'Pelagians', a term embracing a variety of views but taken to refer to those who believed Christians must use their moral effort to grow closer to God, and Donatists,[15] who proclaimed a pure church and refused to readmit those who had fallen away in times of persecution. Both therefore offered a vision of the ideal church as a community of the morally blameless. Augustine's seemingly more pessimistic beliefs about human moral perfection actually enable him to reject the idea of a 'pure' church. One consequence of this ecclesiology is that it opens the door for a rich, critical and complex dialogue with philosophy. It is not the church's business to close its ears to the other (despite Augustine's own lapses into justifying the use of coercion against schismatics).

It can easily be seen that this turning away from the wider world did not happen during the formation of the church's creeds. Bitter disputes over the definition of the Trinity or of the divine–human union in Christ were resolved and inflamed by arguments over the use of (mainly Greek) terms with a philosophical heritage. Ideas of being, essence, substance, nature and person were all brought into play. Indeed, controversy over philosophical terminology, and the cultural contexts in which such ideas were deployed, played a major part in the split between the Eastern and Western churches. The East suspected the Latin church of collapsing the distinctions between the different persons of the Trinity, whilst the East in turn was suspected by Westerners of corroding God's unity. Debates over words – sometimes even over the insertion of a single letter in a word – carried enormous doctrinal freight.

One controversy which was to have a lasting effect on the Eastern Orthodox churches in particular was that over icons. The eighth and ninth centuries saw attacks on the use of images in worship by those seeking a purer form of non-idolatrous Christianity (perhaps influenced by the rise of Islam). The eventual acceptance of icons in worship again owed much to a subtle negotiation between ideas of God's transcendent otherness and incarnate nearness. According to the leading theological defender of icons, John of Damascus, the incarnation of Christ hallows matter and licenses the use of statues and pictures of Christ and the saints for the purposes of veneration. This chimes in with the Orthodox stress on deification – that our human salvation lies in being intimately united (though never confused) with God. And this again was made possible by the philosophical distinction between God's essence and God's energies. We can never be identified with God's being-in-himself, but can be united with God's actions and operations (which are full and true *expressions* of God's essence).

Here we see another good example of how theologians seek to make sense of the revealed faith – the nature of God as Trinity, the incarnation, and union with God – in dialogue with earlier philosophical ways of salvation. Neo-Platonism, with its claim that God is unknowable, and yet that all things by degrees participate in the life of God, was an ever-present partner in the formation of Christian self-identity.

Arguments and questions

The situation we have outlined so far began to shift as the church moved out of its earlier period of self-definition, and into life in the turbulent times following the collapse of the Roman Empire. This led to increasing separation and eventual schism between Western and Eastern churches. Whilst the East was preoccupied with survival in the face of Muslim invasion and rule, the monastic orders of the West prepared the way for a different kind of philosophical engagement. Among the most crucial figures to influence this new discourse were Anselm, Abelard, Aquinas – and Aristotle.[16]

A significant text in this period was Boethius' *The Consolation of Philosophy*, dating from the first part of the sixth century, but read and commented upon by many later figures.[17] Written in prison, it takes the form of a dialogue with Philosophia, who comforts Boethius with the knowledge that, despite appearances, there is order and purpose in his fate. What is striking is that, although Boethius is a Christian, there is little or nothing in this text that seems to depend on revealed truth as opposed to that accessible to purely human reason.

Of course to speak of 'pure' human reason in this context is anachronistic. As we have seen, classical philosophers often saw in reason a point of contact or sharing with divine or ultimate reality. This was why theologians such as Augustine felt able to use the 'best' philosophy to support their case. However, such a compromise is always unstable, and raises ambiguities and questions about the nature of theology and its place in the church, as we can see from the work of Anselm (1033/4–1109).

Like John Scotus Eriugena a century before him, Anselm believed that faith in the mysteries of salvation came before rational comprehension of them, but placed a new emphasis on the dynamic quality of faith seeking understanding. Scotus and Anselm used free-standing philosophical arguments to articulate what Christian faith was about.

Reason became a source of authority in itself. Amidst the chaos and anarchy of post-Roman times, these new thinkers revitalized faith in reason as a link between humanity and the divine order, the hierarchy of being itself. Again, it is worth noting that Anselm's philosophical meditations are placed in the context of prayer and the life of his monastic order. However, they leave a lingering question: is philosophy changed by prayer, or is prayer changed by philosophy?

Anselm is best known for his 'ontological argument' for the existence of God and for his theory of the atonement.[18] The ontological argument seeks to demonstrate the existence of God solely from an analysis of the *concept* of God. In Anselm's version, he claims that if God is defined as a being 'than which nothing greater can be thought', then God must necessarily exist, for a God who can be imagined not to exist is evidently a lesser being than a God who exists.

Philosophers have wrestled with this argument ever since, and have been inclined to dismiss it as a logical fallacy. Anselm himself retreats from claiming that it proves God's existence. However, he does maintain that it shows the intellectual coherence of belief in God. Philosophy works within faith to give it an inner necessity – but what does this show us about the self-sufficiency of Christian theology, and its vulnerability to intellectual attack?

Anselm's theory of the atonement also uses rational argument, this time to show how and why Christ's death on the cross effects human salvation. His theory relies on the idea of our sinfulness offending the honour of God, and thus in need of an offering of restitution (which only Christ can fully pay, hence the cross). Ironically, his rationality thus shows itself deeply rooted in the feudal culture of his day, in which ideas of honour and restitution were commonplace.

It is arguable that Anselm's approach begins to reveal more clearly the dangers of taking Christianity's dialogue with philosophy too far. It lays Christianity open to independent logical and dialectical scrutiny, undermining supernatural authority and relativizing its claims. And yet, if Anselm is right that reason itself is God-given, why should the church fear it? In his context, the need to reclaim an ordered, rational picture of the cosmos was more pressing than scruples about theological purity.

As in Anselm's case, monastic orders were ideal locations for new thinking about theology and philosophy. Many became communities of learning, at the heart of a growing university culture. Their crucial role in preserving the church through the ages of confusion gave a particular stamp to their ecclesiology. Once more, philosophy was to be the key dancing partner.

However, the scope of reasoning was disputed. Peter Abelard (1079–1142) is a key source for later scholastic Christian thinking. His work *Sic et Non* juxtaposes contradictory texts from scripture and patristic writing.[19] The text leaves undecided whether these contradictions can be overcome, and invites rational, critical interpretation to bridge the differences.

In this new atmosphere, philosophical questions began to gain greater significance. What could be known and how could we know it? What kind of things are there, and what makes them what they are? Whilst others maintained a more Platonic view that particular things depend for their nature and existence upon actually existing universal essences or forms, Abelard advocated a nominalist line, which denied the existence of universal essences. Individual, particular things come first, and universals are abstractions created by us for convenience. This debate was to resonate for centuries. Far from being merely academic, it lies at the root of the development of the modern world. Was nominalism the basis for future atheism and the secularization of the world? Or did it free the church and the world from captivity to a hierarchical worldview?[20]

These questions were underlined when the twelfth century saw the reinvigoration of an alternative philosophical discourse, that of Aristotle, the pupil and critic of Plato. Plato tended to locate reality in the unchanging world of timeless essences, the forms or ideas which gave stability and definition to the shifting world of appearances in which we normally live. Aristotle eschewed Plato's more idealistic leanings, denying that the forms or ideas of things had any independent existence. His approach was more naturalistic, beginning with the evidence of the senses and the analysis of concepts.

It is worth noting that the rediscovery of Aristotle's work in Western Christianity was largely thanks to Islamic and Jewish scholars. It is remarkable to see the convergences between the thought of the Jew Maimonides, the Muslims Averroes and Avicenna and Christian scholastics like Aquinas. Christian theology, explicitly and implicitly, was being carried out in a religiously pluralistic world, in which philosophy provided a potential universality exceeding the boundaries of the 'universal' church. We might note the works that began to be produced at this time purporting to be dialogues – between Christians and Jews, but also Christians and philosophers. Biased as these were, they show a continuing need to confront the other within and outside the church.

Nervousness over his naturalism made Aristotle controversial for the university theologians, and his works on natural science and metaphysics were indeed banned by the synod of Sens at the instigation of the Faculty of Theology in Paris. In the background was a growing rift between the faculties of arts and theology, a harbinger of theology's demise from its position as 'queen of the sciences'.

The ban failed to work, and Aristotle became a major influence in university education. For Aquinas (1225–74), Aristotle (dubbed by Aquinas simply 'The Philosopher') is clearly the major dialogue partner. Nevertheless, he wishes to make it clear that revealed theology still takes precedence over other means of investigating the truth:

> Holy teaching can borrow from the other sciences, not from any need to beg from them, but for the greater clarification of the things it conveys. For it takes its principles directly from God through revelation, not from the other sciences.[21]

At the same time, he accepts the legitimacy of diverse approaches to the same subject matter:

> The diversification of the sciences is brought about by the diversity of aspects under which things can be known ... Accordingly there is nothing to stop the same things from being treated by the philosophical sciences when they can be looked at in the light of natural reason and by another science when they are looked at in the light of divine revelation. Consequently the theology of holy teaching differs in kind from that theology which is ranked as part of philosophy.[22]

It is worth noting that for Aquinas, the term 'science' does not have the limited scope it has for moderns, but refers to any organized body of knowledge. Even so, he is prepared to grant the relative legitimacy of natural or deductive philosophies (which would include what we would call natural sciences as well as mathematics, logic and metaphysics).

Revelation is thus given a qualitative distinctiveness, but philosophy's (Aristotelian) scope is broad. Aquinas allows natural reason to provide arguments for the existence of God (the 'five ways'), all of which are some variant on observing aspects of the world which are contingent and arguing from them to a necessary source, origin or goal, which is called God.

Aquinas holds theology and philosophy together because he understands nature as *already* participating in the grace of God. It is therefore possible to find analogies within nature for supernatural realities. Aquinas seeks to avoid the extremes of being equivocal (when our words simply cannot connect with God at all, rendering us utterly ignorant) and being univocal (when our words about God apply in a straightforward and direct way, reducing God to the level of a being like any other). His doctrine of analogy licenses us to use words such as 'love' and 'goodness' of God, but preserves the proper mystery by arguing that we cannot know *how* these words are predicated of God.

Aquinas therefore seeks a balance between naturalism and revelation, soul and body – even between the disembodied gaze and earthbound senses: 'Touch is the foundation of all the other senses,' he writes.[23] In a curious way, Aquinas uses natural philosophy to recall Christian theology to its incarnational roots. He also affirms a Christianized version of Aristotle's ethics, in which it is the cultivation of lived virtues – dispositions to goodness – which takes precedence over laws and rules taken out of context. In his way, Aquinas reaffirms Augustine's recognition that Greek moral philosophy also had much to offer.

Recovery, reform and reaction: the birth of the modern period

Scholastic theology continued to debate the finer points of knowledge, language and reality for centuries after Aquinas. At the same time, movements of monastic renewal (like the Franciscans), popular devotion and mysticism offered a very different emphasis. The groundwork for the later Renaissance and Reformation were thus being laid. Though each movement, particularly the latter, brought huge upheaval, it is also important to recognize the lines of continuity.

The Renaissance was essentially a movement of revival, a rediscovery of ancient Hellenistic learning and culture. It gave birth to a Christian humanism, whose foremost representative was Erasmus (1469–1536). The tensions within Erasmus' approach are made plain in his *On The Freedom of the Will.*[24] On the one hand, he wanted to rescue a sense of human freedom and dignity from the pessimistic doctrines he attributed to Luther (1483–1546). On the other, he denied Luther's claim that scripture could be read and understood by ordinary lay people. Following a long tradition in which the interpretation of the Bible demanded a great deal of philosophical and allegorical subtlety, Erasmus wanted to preserve it from baser hands and minds.

Renaissance humanism was driven by a scholarly reading of texts. As with Erasmus, this opened up a renewed appreciation of the human capacity for art, reasoning and virtue, whilst giving enormous power into the hands of the scholarly elite. A loosely Platonic tradition of the philosopher-elite, destined to rule the sensual and ignorant masses, lay behind the more hierarchical elements of this approach.

However, for all their radical differences, Erasmus and Luther still shared a belief in the power of textual interpretation. Whether scholars or ordinary believers, the Word was being delivered into human hands – and the possibility of *critical* reading was born. A broader 'humanism', in which the humanity of the suffering Christ took centre stage in devotion, provided a compelling framework for a deeper philosophical shift.

To describe the Reformation in these terms might appear far-fetched. Surely Protestantism was firmly opposed to scholastic philosophy, and proclaimed the utter corruption of reason itself? Luther did reportedly speak of the 'whore reason' and Calvin's view of human depravity underscored the point. However, Calvin (1509–64) was himself influenced by humanism (as was Zwingli), and wrote of the capacity of the light of reason to guide human endeavours successfully in many areas of life. More telling, it is arguable that what Luther and his allies in fact bequeath the church is an alternative philosophy, a philosophy of passion – and reading.

The Protestant Reformers needed to justify their attacks on, and eventual break with, the Roman Catholic Church. Scripture was their primary authority. However, they needed an account of how scripture was to be read if they were to wrest it from the church's grip. The two elements of this account were the primacy of individual faith, and the primacy of the literal sense of the scriptural text. These emphases set the scene for consequences very far from the Reformers' intentions.

First, making the passionate life of faith central (in common, it has to be said, with earlier medieval tendencies) implied a different account of human nature, in which intellect or reason was no longer the primary attribute which connected us to God. Later philosophies of existence and the person would reaffirm this theme.

Secondly, the freeing of the Bible from scholastic, ecclesially based interpretation represented the victory of a nominalist philosophy. Texts were no longer symbolic allegories referring to universal essences, but had to be taken seriously in their historical and temporal dimensions.

The unintended effects of these movers were particularly ironic. The Reformation's high doctrine of the Bible opened the door for historical critical readings further down the line. And the breaking of the substantial link between human reason and the divine order helped to secularize the world, making it available for the empirical sciences to explore free of ecclesiastical control. Faith became a matter of the heart, an inward drama separated from the world out there – a world increasingly disenchanted, domesticated and subjected to human technological interventions.

From this point on, the radical separation of Christian theology from alternative philosophies became an increasingly live possibility. Rationalism made the inner laws of reasoning independent of divine illumination. Empiricism looked to the evidence of the senses rather than ecclesial authority, developing hypotheses which could be tested by experiment. And these intellectual ideas were rooted in social changes which shook the churches' monopoly on education and its claim to place and deploy all competing philosophies. The chains of being, the links of analogy, which were the glue of a Christian cosmos, were being severed.[25]

We have already noted how Descartes (1596–1650) sought to found philosophy on purely rational grounds (though he reintroduced God to save appearances). Later rationalists and empiricists sought to prune away the supernatural excrescences of Christian belief and recover a 'perennial philosophy' of natural law. Apologists for Christianity sought to work within the new framework. In 1695, John Locke offered a case for *The Reasonableness of Christianity*, in which he argued that nothing in Christian belief was contrary to reason, though accepting there could be truths above reason.[26] Deists went further, rejecting Christian doctrines which claimed to be above reason (such as the resurrection or the Trinity). A more conservative vein was represented by Joseph Butler's 1736 *Analogy of Religion*, which presented arguments for the existence of God based on empirical evidence of design in the world.[27]

Immanuel Kant offered a different version of this tendency in his *Religion Within the Boundaries of Mere Reason* (1794), in which it became clear that the structures and laws of reason had priority over the substantial beliefs of religion.[28] At the same time, Kant's philosophy emphasized the degree to which our structures of knowing shape the world we experience. Reality beyond appearances – the 'thing-in-itself' – was a blank unknown. God became a postulate of our intellectual and moral striving, rather than one with whom we had a substantive or personal relationship.

The death of God – and beyond

These moves were, however, vulnerable to a more radical critique. David Hume, in his *Dialogues Concerning Natural Religion* (posthumously published in 1779), seeks to demolish arguments for the existence of God derived from observation of the world. Elsewhere, he develops a naturalistic account of how religion came into existence, based on a fear of the unknown.[29] This genealogy of religion connected with a developing consciousness of history. Reading texts as historical documents relativized them, and accentuated awareness of historical genesis and change of ideas and institutions. It became possible to imagine different orderings of society driven by human agency, to imagine a world freed from its anchoring in a transcendent reality. The social imagination of the church could no longer dominate the scene, incorporating or anathematizing its rivals.

This new situation is reflected by Schleiermacher's 1799 apologetic work, *On Religion*, whose subtitle – 'Speeches to its Cultured Despisers' – reveals much about its context.[30] Schleiermacher sought to ground religious faith in a holistic response to reality, an 'intuition' of the universe. This stress on elements of feeling and immediacy of relationship accorded well with the Romantic tendency to downplay abstract thought and dogmatic theology. However, it also paved the way for philosophical arguments which claimed that religion was *nothing more* than this or that aspect of human, subjective feeling or social organization.

This tendency reached its culmination in the nineteenth- and early twentieth-century work of the 'masters of suspicion' – most notably Marx, Nietzsche and Freud – each of whom offered reductive accounts of the origin and power of Christian faith. For Marx, religion was the suppressed and spiritualized longing of the people for material liberation. For Nietzsche, Christianity was a slave religion, a self-deluding desire of the weak for vengeance upon their superiors. Nietzsche dramatically popularized the metaphor of the 'death of God', which for him was linked to the loss of all stable frameworks of meaning and value. God and the Platonic, ordered cosmos died together. For Freud, religion was a neurosis, a symptom of our inability psychologically to cope with the world.[31]

This militant materialism and nihilism did not, however, represent the only possible philosophical response to Christianity in the modern era. Idealists sought to overcome the split between lived reality and reason which they believed the rationalists and Kantians had set up. Hegel (1770–1831) worked out a philosophy which embraced history as a dynamic element, in which Christian doctrines were the symbolic expressions of the ultimate reconciliation of the real and the rational, the divine and the human, the finite and the infinite – a reconciliation that was still being worked out in time.[32]

Hegel's philosophy was itself attacked by those who claimed it subordinated Christianity to philosophy, and made the latter the final conceptual expression of ultimate reality. Søren Kierkegaard (1813–55) satirized the grand speculative world-historical sweep of Hegel's thought, which he argued had forgotten what it means to be an individual, existing human being.[33] However, Kierkegaard did not seek a return to older styles of philosophizing. He radicalized the Lutheran emphasis on the drama and decision of faith, rejecting dependence on 'proofs' or external authorities for faith. The believer was like one suspended above 70,000 fathoms, a person of decision and risk. And he developed a complex, teasing, indirect literature to lure his archly reflective contemporaries into a new engagement with faith.

The thinkers we have referred to represent only some of the most important philosophical options and challenges which faced the church as the nineteenth century wore on. Running through all of them, however, issues of community and identity continued to be crucial, in ways which called the churches' own sense of themselves into question.

The growing power of secular analysis of religion reflected the reality of decreasing ecclesial power in Europe. Was the church a provisional body, a parochial community destined to give way to something more truly 'catholic'? Was the kingdom of God to be realized as a community of universal reason and ethics, as Kant dreamed? Or was it, as Hegel believed, to be forged in the labour of history, as modern nation states became the framework in which religion, art, culture and values were reconciled? Is the particularity of the Christian community and its revelation a stepping stone to a more generalized unity of reason and spirit? For Hegel, 'Spirit is most essentially itself in the religious community where the Divine Man or Human God is transformed into the members' universal, inward, chastening self-consciousness.'[34]

Kierkegaard was one of those who rebelled against these grand narratives of universal harmony. Christianity should not be subsumed into speculative philosophy, but must remain a paradox and an offence to reason. At the same time, he did not advocate a return to the ecclesial dominance of old, coming to believe that complacent notions of 'congregation' threatened to water down the strenuous demands of the gospel upon individuals.

The communal landscape was also being increasingly shaken by other voices and movements. Extended contact with non-Christian religions and cultures, movements for social liberation and gender equality, rapid technological change – all threatened to transform the largely elite, Eurocentric, celibate male character of much preceding Christian theology and philosophy.

Material changes in social relationships were therefore interwoven with challenges to the way the churches understood themselves, their practices, their forms of knowledge, language, ritual and witness. As Nietzsche understood, the question of the reality or death of God was not merely about the existence of a supreme being. It was the linchpin of a whole series of related questions about the nature and source of identity, coherence, value and meaning in the universe. For Nietzsche, a new era, a new definition of humanity, could only be born by embracing the collapse of the Christian cosmos. How could the church respond to this new and more menacing philosophical other?

Language, identity, otherness: postmodern philosophy and the church[35]

These traumas continued to dominate the twentieth-century theological landscape. They were intensified by the experience of world wars and genocide, by the collapse of empires and the formation of new forms of global hegemony, experiences which also dented secular optimism about progress and civilization.

In this context, Barth's furious reaction to the liberalism and rationalism of his peers becomes understandable. Barth believed that Christian theology lost its identity if it based itself on anything other than the freely given grace of God in Jesus Christ. Significantly, he called his major work the *Church Dogmatics*, because it was only from *within* the community of faith that theology can be done. Trying to find common ground with other philosophical viewpoints is tantamount to abandoning Christ. The God of the philosophers *deserved* to die, so that the God of revelation could be encountered afresh.

Barth has continued to influence those who have sought a distinctively Christian voice over against secular philosophy and its theological allies. Some have advocated a return to biblical, Hebraic forms of thought as opposed to the ahistorical idealism of Greek philosophy. More recently, theologians such as George Lindbeck, Stanley Hauerwas and the Radical Orthodox school have emphasized the communal framework of the church and its liturgy as the only valid location for Christian speech and witness to God.[36]

This fits with an intensely communitarian aspect of some contemporary philosophy, notably that of Alasdair MacIntyre.[37] This rejects the idea that there can be any neutral, universal foundation for truth and values. Only within communities and the stories they tell can faith and virtue be nurtured. For the theologians we mentioned, this translates into the claim that only within the church can *true* faith and virtue come to expression. Outside, 'the secular' is empty, a mask for the unconstrained will to power. Beyond the church, all is violence and nihilism. Philosophy must once more be overcome and swallowed up by theology – though, ironically, Radical Orthodoxy seeks to do this through rehabilitating a basically Platonic view of the world. Whether this is a fair interpretation or a misreading of MacIntyre is open to debate.

This ecclesiological response to the dilemmas of modernity and its fragmentation has recently gained centre stage, obscuring the other powerful traditions running through contemporary Christian thought. The twentieth century has also witnessed a revival of Thomistic theology, led by thinkers such as Jacques Maritain and Etienne Gilson. E.L. Mascall and Austin Farrer were significant representatives of the broadly 'catholic' approach in Anglican theology.[38]

Also important in Roman Catholic theology has been the 'transcendental' thought of Karl Rahner, who argued that human beings were by nature open to a transcendent dimension. This opened the possibility of dialogue with non-Christian ideologies and faiths, a possibility also envisaged in the Protestant theology of Paul Tillich. Tillich advocated a method of correlation, seeking connections between the yearnings and questions present in contemporary culture and the answers given by Christian revelation.[39]

A further rich area for the interface between theology and philosophy has been the religious existentialism, influenced by Kierkegaard, which emphasized dimensions of passion and decision in the human response to God. Nicolas Berdyaev was a good example of the flowering of this strain of thought in the Orthodox church.[40] John Zizioulas's *Being as Communion* is another example of an Orthodox theologian seeking reconciliation between the insights of existential philosophy and the church's tradition.[41] The Anglican John Macquarrie also sought to integrate insights from Heidegger in particular with the classical theological tradition.[42]

More recently, feminist and liberation theologies have drawn on non-Christian theorists of gender and society to draw attention to structures of domination, in which they claim previous modes of philosophical theology were complicit.[43] These initiatives are linked by a stress on relationality as a key starting point for understanding both humanity in general and the church in particular. Human beings are not considered as isolated nomads, but in their interdependence with others – an interdependence which, for theologians like Zizioulas, reflects the nature of the trinitarian God. We are who we are through our relationships, not despite them. These approaches draw on earlier initiatives which sought to integrate Christian theology with a wider human and evolutionary story, such as the 'process' philosophy of Alfred Whitehead. This continues to influence theologians seeking to break with classical philosophical ideas about God's timelessness, omnipotence and changelessness. God is seen as intertwined with a historical process of development, a co-sufferer and co-creator alongside humanity, rather than an absolute other.[44]

A related area for discussion has been the nature of theology's relationship to science. On the one hand, Hume's natural history of religion opened the way for further attempts to analyse and evaluate religious phenomena scientifically (William James' psychological interpretation of religious experience is a particularly influential example of this[45]). On the other hand, theologians have often sought to make connections with scientific theory, arguing that the world interpreted by science and theology is one world, viewed in different aspects. The world is seen as basically rational and intelligible. The underlying claim is that the scientific and religious communities are not separate worlds, but share a unified horizon of meaning and truth.[46] It is a claim which is placed under strain, not only by the attacks of some atheistic scientists, but also by the institutional contexts which have severed sciences and the humanities. The situation is further complicated by the claims of some more fundamentalist Christian groups to exercise control or influence over educational institutions, so that evolutionary science is challenged or even displaced by literal accounts of the world's creation drawn from the book of Genesis. Questions about communal identity, location and power are never far from the surface in such debates.

Broadly speaking, then, two strategies – communitarian assertiveness, or critical dialogue – continue to shape the church's response to philosophy as it has emerged from a largely European lineage. It is only really beginning to engage with alternative forms of philosophy (e.g. from China, India or Africa), and the dynamic of globalization inevitably means that these encounters are never carried out in isolation from the Western tradition.

Running through all these strands is an insistence on themes of historical locatedness, cultural context, relationship, identity-in-relationship, otherness and witness. In considering the key philosophical issues facing ecclesiology in the wake of the seismic shifts of modernity and its aftermath, I will end by suggesting that one area will remain of key importance as it weaves through and links the others: language.

Across the divides between analytic philosophy (which traces its roots to empiricism) and continental philosophy (which emerges from idealism, existentialism and Marxism), language has emerged as a major focus for debate. This reflects an increasing awareness that the linguistic mediation of thought cannot be ignored. Language and its structures of meaning and reference condition the modes and limits of our thinking.

Analytic philosophy has tended to break language down into its basic units of meaning, and seek the empirical grounds on which language is able to refer and make sense. Some versions of this tendency have been intensely hostile to theology. A.J. Ayer was famous for dismissing theological claims as meaningless, because they did not lend themselves to empirical verification.[47] Ayer's assertions have themselves been criticized for lack of coherence, and philosophers of religion working in this tradition continue to explore arguments for the existence of God, theodicy and other rational defences of Christian belief. This kind of philosophy occupies a more modest role than that of its Hellenistic forebears. It provides a critical reflection on Christian language and practice, a way of stepping back and asking whether Christian belief is coherent.

'Continental' philosophy, with its more historical and cultural perspective, has tended to emphasize the ambiguity attending all linguistic utterances. Jacques Derrida has argued that the difference and temporality inherent to communication with signs make impossible any attempt to state absolute truth, or ground meaning on something purely given and present. This is not an abolition of truth and reference, but an acknowledgement that they cannot be secured on an apparently neutral foundation. There is no 'view from nowhere' – our communication always happens in a context, using signs that are never pure containers or channels of timeless truth.[48] Martin Heidegger (influential on many 'existentialist' Christian theologians) offered a more mystical and poetic account of language as 'the shepherd of Being'. His critique of Western society's reductive faith in technology led him to look beyond a merely instrumental account of how language works. Rather than seeing language simply as a tool, for Heidegger language (especially poetry) clears a space, makes an encounter with being possible.[49]

Straddling both camps, Ludwig Wittgenstein put forward the view that linguistic signs have no meaning as discrete and isolated elements, but only through the rules of grammar and performance which govern their use. And these rules do not float free of material realities, they are embedded in forms of life. Signs wrenched out of their context and deployed in alien forms of life will have a different meaning and role.[50]

Theologians influenced by these views take various tacks. Some accept the end of grand narratives and absolute claims, advocating a form of Christian belief that is nomadic rather than dogmatic, whose language is always fragmentary. Others, as we have seen, believe that Christian language, embedded in the church, is able to offer an alternative overarching narrative to those proposed by secular ideologies.[51]

These issues have a strong relevance for ecclesiology. What is the nature of the church's language? Is it translatable without loss into philosophical or other non-religious terms? How does it refer to realities which transcend empirical verification without lapsing into nonsense, or becoming an ideological cloak for other power interests? Is it only possible to speak and understand the church's language as an insider, from within the community of faith? Or is language inherently open and dialogical, impossible to contain or police within one set of rules?

As the church faces a situation which is post-colonial, global and plural, these questions become ever more insistent. Derrida writes that 'My own presence to myself has been preceded by a language', implying that identity is always forged out of difference and dialogue.[52] The encounter with the other – sexual, religious, cultural, divine – is both distorted and mediated by signs and symbols, which no individual entity (perhaps especially an internally plural and multilingual entity such as the church) can control.

These issues may seem strange and new. And yet in surprising ways, they reconnect us with the church's original engagement with philosophy. In a sense, the church's way of talking about its own identity was always preceded and crossed by other languages, among which the Greek language of philosophy was crucially important. That presence was never merely one of ideas, but of material practices, visions of community, ways of relating body and soul. In its continuing struggles to define itself in relation to that other within and without, the church has been constantly engaged with what it means to believe in a Word made flesh: to communicate in ways that cross boundaries of the material and the spiritual, time and eternity. Perhaps the future for the church lies in seeing itself not just as a partner in dialogue with philosophy, but as *constituted* by this dialogue from the very first.

Notes

1 S.L. Greensdale (ed.), *Early Latin Theology*, The Library of Christian Classics, Vol. V, London: SCM, 1956, p. 36.
2 Karl Barth, *Church Dogmatics*, Edinburgh: T&T Clark, 3/1.6.
3 Greensdale, *Early Latin Theology*, p. 50.
4 Alister McGrath, *The Christian Theology Reader*, Oxford: Blackwell, 1995, p. 4.
5 McGrath, *The Christian Theology Reader*, p. 5.
6 Greensdale, *Early Latin Theology*, p. 50.
7 See Kurt Rudolph, *Gnosis. The Nature and History of Gnosticism*, San Francisco: HarperSanFrancisco, 2000; and Elaine Pagels, *The Gnostic Gospels*, London: Vintage, 1979.
8 See Origen, *On First Principles*, Magnolia: Peter Smith, 2002.
9 See Plotinus, *The Enneads*, Harmondsworth: Penguin, 1991; and the classic study by Arthur Lovejoy, *The Great Chain of Being*, Cambridge MA: Harvard,1972.
10 Augustine, *Confessions*, Harmondsworth: Penguin, 1961, p. 59.
11 Augustine, *Confessions*, pp. 144–6.
12 Augustine, *The City of God*, Harmondsworth: Penguin, 1972, p. 311.
13 Henry Bettenson (ed.), *The Later Christian Fathers*, Oxford: Oxford University Press, 1970, p. 191.
14 Augustine, *The City of God*, p. 307.
15 On these controversies cf. also Chapter 2 of this volume, 'The Church in the early Christian centuries: ecclesiological consolidation'.

16 See David Burrell, *Knowing the Unknowable God*, Notre Dame: University of Notre Dame Press, 1992, for an excellent account of this cross-fertilization.

17 Boethius, *The Consolation of Philosophy*, Harmondsworth: Penguin, 1991.

18 Found respectively in his works *Proslogion* and *Cur Deus Homo* – see *Anselm of Canterbury. The Major Works*, Oxford: Oxford University Press, 1998.

19 Peter Abelard, *Sic et Non*, Chicago: University of Chicago Press, 1977.

20 See G.R. Evans, *Philosophy and Theology in the Middle Ages*, London: Routledge, 1993.

21 Aquinas, *Summa Theologiae Volume 1 (1a 1) Christian Theology*, London: Blackfriars 1964, 1a 1, 5.

22 Aquinas, *Summa* 1a 1, 1.

23 Quoted in Margaret Miles, *The Word Made Flesh. A History of Christian Thought*, Oxford: Blackwell, 2005, p. 171.

24 Desiderius Erasmus and Martin Luther, *Discourse on Free Will*, London: Continuum, 2005.

25 See Michael J. Buckley, *At the Origins of Modern Atheism*, New Haven: Yale University Press, 1990.

26 John Locke, *The Reasonableness of Christianity*, Oxford: Clarendon Press, 2000.

27 Joseph Butler, *The Analogy of Religion*, Adamant: Adamant Media Corporation, 2000.

28 Immanual Kant, *Religion Within the Boundaries of Mere Reason and Other Writings*, Cambridge: Cambridge University Press, 1998.

29 David Hume, *Dialogues Concerning Natural Religion, and the Natural History of Religion*, Oxford: Oxford University Press, 1998.

30 Friedrich Schleiermacher, *On Religion: Speeches to its Cultured Despisers*, Cambridge: Cambridge University Press, 1996.

31 See Karl Marx, *The German Ideology*, New York: Prometheus, 1998; Friedrich Nietzsche, *The Gay Science*, London: Random House, 1974; Sigmund Freud, 'Future of an Illusion', in *Civilization, Society and Religion*, Harmondsworth: Penguin, 1991.

32 G.W.F. Hegel, *Lectures on the Philosophy of Religion*, London: Thoemmes, 1999.

33 Søren Kierkegaard, *Concluding Unscientific Postscript*, Princeton: Princeton University Press, 1992.

34 G.W.F. Hegel, *Hegel's Phenomenology of Spirit*, Oxford: Oxford University Press, 1977, §780, p. 588.

35 See also Chapter 7 of this volume, on 'Postmodern ecclesiologies'.

36 George Lindbeck, *The Nature of Doctrine: Religion and Theology in a Postliberal Age*, London: Westminster John Knox, 1984; Stanley Hauerwas, *The Peaceable Kingdom: A Primer in Christian Ethics*, London: SCM, 2003; John Milbank, Catherine Pickstock and Graham Ward (eds), *Radical Orthodoxy*, London: Routledge, 1999.

37 Alasdair MacIntyre, *After Virtue*, London: Gerald Duckworth, 1997.

38 Jacques Maritain, *True Humanism*, London: Geoffrey Bles, 1938; E.l. Mascall, *He Who Is. A Study in Traditional Theism*, London: Longmans, Green & Co., 1943. Austin Farrer, *Finite and Infinite: A Philosophical Essay*, London: Dacre Press, 1959.

39 Declan Marmion and Mary Hines (eds), *The Cambridge Companion to Karl Rahner*, Cambridge: Cambridge University Press, 2005; Paul Tillich, *Systematic Theology Volume 1*, Chicago: University of Chicago Press, 1973.

40 For example, Nicolas Berdyaev, *Freedom and the Spirit*, Manchester, NH: Ayer, 1972.

41 John Zizioulas, *Being as Communion*, London: Darton, Longman and Todd, 2004.

42 John Macquarrie, *Principles of Christian Theology*, London: SCM, 1977 (revised edition).

43 See, for example, Pamela Sue Anderson, and Beverley Clack (eds), *Feminist Philosophy of Religion: Critical Readings*, Oxford: Blackwell, 2003; and Grace Jantzen, *Becoming Divine: Towards a Feminist Philosophy of Religion*, Manchester: Manchester University Press, 1998.

44 Alfred North Whitehead, *Process and Reality*, New York: Free Press, 1979.

45 William James, *The Varieties of Religious Experience*, Harmondsworth: Penguin, 1983.

46 See F.R. Tennant, *Philosophical Theology*, Cambridge: Cambridge University Press, 1968 (2 vols); Tennant provides an influential, updated version of the design argument which takes evolution into account. See also John Polkinghorne, *One World: The Interaction of Science and Theology*, London: SPCK, 1986.

47 A.J. Ayer, *Language, Truth and Logic*, Harmondsworth: Penguin, 1971.

48 Jacques Derrida, *Writing and Difference*, London: Routledge, 2001.

49 Martin Heidegger, *Poetry, Language, Thought*, New York: HarperCollins, 2001.

50 Ludwig Wittgenstein, *Philosophical Investigations*, Oxford: Blackwell, 1973.
51 For a survey, see Gavin Hyman, *The Predicament of Postmodern Theology: Radical Orthodoxy or Nihilist Textualism?* London: Westminster John Knox, 2002.
52 Jacques Derrida, *Dissemination*, London: Athlone, 1981, p. 340.

Further reading

Diogenes Allen, *Philosophy for Understanding Theology*, Philadelphia: Westminster John Knox, 1985.
Michael J. Buckley, *At the Origins of Modern Atheism*, New Haven, CT: Yale University Press, 1990.
Edward Craig, *The Mind of God and the Works of Man*, Oxford: Clarendon Press, 1987.
G.R. Evans, *Philosophy and Theology in the Middle Ages*, London: Routledge, 1993.
Fergus Kerr, *Theology After Wittgenstein*, London: SPCK, 1997.
Margaret Miles, *The Word Made Flesh. A History of Christian Thought*, Oxford: Blackwell, 2005.
James K.A. Smith, *Who's Afraid of Postmodernism? Taking Derrida, Lyotard and Foucault to Church*, Grand Rapids, MI: Baker, 2007.
Christopher Stead, *Philosophy in Christian Antiquity*, Cambridge: Cambridge University Press, 1994.
John Zizioulas, *Being as Communion*, London: Darton, Longman and Todd, 2004.

INDEX